Scott Foresman/Silver Burdett supports the

# National Standards for Music Education Grades K-4

Developed by the Music Educators National Conference

| Content Standard | ✔ | Achievement Standard |
|---|---|---|
| **1** Singing, alone and with others, a varied repertoire of music | ☐ 1a | Students sing independently, on pitch and in rhythm, with appropriate timbre, diction, and posture, and maintain a steady tempo |
| | ☐ 1b | Students sing expressively, with appropriate dynamics, phrasing, and interpretation |
| | ☐ 1c | Students sing from memory a varied repertoire of songs representing genres and styles from diverse cultures |
| | ☐ 1d | Students sing ostinatos, partner songs and rounds |
| | ☐ 1e | Students sing in groups, blending vocal timbres, matching dynamic levels, and responding to the cues of a conductor |
| | | *Notes* |
| **2** Performing on instruments, alone and with others, a varied repertoire of music | ☐ 2a | Students perform on pitch, in rhythm, with appropriate dynamics and timbre, and maintain a steady tempo |
| | ☐ 2b | Students perform easy rhythmic, melodic, and chordal patterns accurately and independently on rhythmic, melodic, and harmonic classroom instruments |
| | ☐ 2c | Students perform expressively a varied repertoire of music representing diverse genres and styles |
| | ☐ 2d | Students echo short rhythms and melodic patterns |
| | ☐ 2e | Students perform in groups, blending instrumental timbres, matching dynamic levels, and responding to the cues of a conductor |
| | ☐ 2f | Students perform independent instrumental parts[1] while other students sing or play contrasting parts |
| | | *Notes* |

SILVER•BURDETT Making Music

1. E.g., simple rhythmic or melodic ostinatos, contrasting rhythmic lines, harmonic progressions, and chords

# Teacher's Edition

## Part One

### Grade 4

**Editorial Offices:** Glenview, Illinois • Parsippany, New Jersey • New York, New York
**Sales Offices:** Needham, Massachusetts • Duluth, Georgia • Glenview, Illinois
Coppell, Texas • Sacramento, California • Mesa, Arizona

ISBN: 0-382-36594-1



6 7 8 9 10 V064 13 12 11 10 09 08 07 06

# Authors


## PROGRAM AUTHORS

**Jane Beethoven**
Music Author/Consultant
*Westport, Connecticut*

**Susan Brumfield**
Texas Tech University
*Lubbock, Texas*

**Patricia Shehan Campbell**
University of Washington
*Seattle, Washington*

**David N. Connors**
California State University at Los Angeles
*Los Angeles, California*

**Robert A. Duke**
University of Texas at Austin
*Austin, Texas*

**Judith A. Jellison**
University of Texas at Austin
*Austin, Texas*

**Rita Klinger**
Cleveland State University
*Cleveland, Ohio*

**Rochelle Mann**
Fort Lewis College
*Durango, Colorado*

**Hunter C. March**
University of Texas at Austin
*Austin, Texas*

**Nan L. McDonald**
San Diego State University
*San Diego, California*

**Marvelene C. Moore**
University of Tennessee
*Knoxville, Tennessee*

**Mary Palmer**
University of Central Florida
*Orlando, Florida*

**Konnie Saliba**
University of Memphis
*Memphis, Tennessee*

**Will Schmid**
Professor Emeritus
University of Wisconsin—Milwaukee
*Milwaukee, Wisconsin*

**Carol Scott-Kassner**
Music Author/Consultant
*Seattle, Washington*

**Mary E. Shamrock**
Professor Emeritus, California State University at Northridge
*Minneapolis, Minnesota*

**Sandra L. Stauffer**
Arizona State University
*Tempe, Arizona*

**Judith Thomas**
Music Education Consultant
*West Nyack, New York*

**Jill Trinka**
University of St. Thomas
*St. Paul, Minnesota*

## CONTRIBUTING AUTHORS

**Audrey A. Berger**
University of Rhode Island
*Kingston, Rhode Island*

**Roslyn Burrough**
Clinician/Consultant
*Brooklyn, New York*

**J. Bryan Burton**
West Chester University
*West Chester, Pennsylvania*

**Jeffrey E. Bush**
Arizona State University
*Tempe, Arizona*

**John M. Cooksey**
University of Utah
*Salt Lake City, Utah*

**Shelly C. Cooper**
University of Arizona
*Tucson, Arizona*

**Alice-Ann Darrow**
Florida State University
*Tallahassee, Florida*

**Scott Emmons**
University of Wisconsin—Milwaukee
*Milwaukee, Wisconsin*

**Debra Erck**
Austin Independent School District
*Austin, Texas*

**Anne M. Fennell**
Vista Unified School District
*Vista, California*

**Doug Fisher**
San Diego State University
*San Diego, California*

**Carroll Gonzo**
University of St. Thomas
*St. Paul, Minnesota*

**Larry Harms**
University of Southern California
*Los Angeles, California*

**Martha F. Hilley**
University of Texas at Austin
*Austin, Texas*

**Debbie Burgoon Hines**
Consultant
*DeSoto, Texas*

**Mary Ellen Junda**
University of Connecticut
*Storrs, Connecticut*

**Donald Kalbach**
Consultant
*Bound Brook, New Jersey*

**Shirley E. Lacroix**
Rhode Island College
*Providence, Rhode Island*

**Henry Leck**
Butler University
*Indianapolis, Indiana*

**Sanna Longden**
Clinician/Consultant
*Evanston, Illinois*

**Glenn A. Richter**
University of Texas at Austin
*Austin, Texas*

**Carlos Xavier Rodriguez**
University of Iowa
*Iowa City, Iowa*

**Kathleen D. Sanz**
District School Board of Pasco County
*Tampa, Florida*

**Julie K. Scott**
Southern Methodist University
*Dallas, Texas*

**Gwyn Spell**
Clinician/Consultant
*Marietta, Georgia*

**Barb Stevanson**
Austin Independent School District
*Austin, Texas*

**Kimberly C. Walls**
Auburn University
*Auburn, Alabama*

**Jackie Wiggins**
Oakland University
*Rochester, Michigan*

**Maribeth Yoder-White**
Appalachian State University
*Boone, North Carolina*

# Program Contributors

## LISTENING MAP CONTRIBUTING AUTHORS

Patricia Shehan Campbell
*Seattle, Washington*

Jackie Chooi-Theng Lew
*Salisbury, Maryland*

Ann Clements
*Federal Way, Washington*

Kay Edwards
*Oxford, Ohio*

Scott Emmons
*Milwaukee, Wisconsin*

Sheila Feay-Shaw
*Shoreline, Washington*

Kay Greenhaw
*Austin, Texas*

David Hebert
*Seattle, Washington*

Hunter C. March
*Austin, Texas*

Will Schmid
*Milwaukee, Wisconsin*

Carol Scott-Kassner
*Seattle, Washington*

Mary E. Shamrock
*Minneapolis, Minnesota*

Sandra L. Stauffer
*Tempe, Arizona*

## MOVEMENT CONTRIBUTING AUTHORS

Judy Lasko
*New York, New York*

Marvelene C. Moore
*Knoxville, Tennessee*

Dixie Piver
*New York, New York*

Wendy Taucher
*New York, New York*

Susan Thomasson
*Demarest, New Jersey*

Judith Thompson-Barthwell
*Detroit, Michigan*

## TEACHER ADVISORY PANEL

Kathryn Amshoff
*Humble, Texas*

Bevra L. Carruth
*Midland, Texas*

Rebekah Dykhuis
*Austin, Texas*

Gwendolyn J. Farris
*DeSoto, Texas*

Richard Gabrillo
*Georgetown, Texas*

Maria Yolanda Garza
*San Antonio, Texas*

Mary Lee Gilliland
*Memphis, Tennessee*

Jacque Hall
*Arlington, Texas*

Shari Hazell
*Canton, Michigan*

Lynette Hubler
*Bondurant, Iowa*

Tracy Walsh Juarez
*El Paso, Texas*

Barbara Keaton
*Arlington, Texas*

Jim Lovell
*Plano,Texas*

Scott Mahaffey
*San Antonio, Texas*

Laura L. McGregor
*Sugar Land, Texas*

Carol Moeller
*Carmel, Indiana*

Sue Niemi
*Downingtown, Pennsylvania*

Kathy Lee Peinado
*El Paso, Texas*

Domingo Porras
*Edinburg, Texas*

Joseph Puzzo
*Washington, D.C.*

Pam Ramirez
*Brownsville, Texas*

Emily Roden
*Denton, Texas*

Beth Russell
*Noblesville, Indiana*

Chrissie Horany Seligson
*Arlington, Texas*

Tanya Seslar
*Denver, Colorado*

Donna Shortal
*Winter Park, Florida*

Barb Stevanson
*Austin, Texas*

Roseanne Stuetz
*Maywood, New Jersey*

Cathy Warnock
*Mesquite, Texas*

Wendy Weeks
*Abilene, Texas*

Barbara White
*Williamsville, New York*

## CRITIC READERS

Leon Adams
*Little Rock, Arkansas*

Barbara Alvarez
*Muncie, Indiana*

Elaine Bartee
*Jonesboro, Arkansas*

Patsy Biedenfield
*Houston, Texas*

Patricia A. Bourne
*Bothell, Washington*

Shaunda B. Butler
*Pine Bluff, Arkansas*

Kip Caton
*Apex, North Carolina*

Mary Cawley
*Manasquan, New Jersey*

Brenda Chapman
*Jacksonville, Florida*

Scott Chappell
*North Augusta, South Carolina*

Craig Combs
*New York, New York*

Joyce W. Culwell
*Aurora, Colorado*

Shannon M. Daniels
*Wichita Falls, Texas*

Gloria Day
*Tucson, Arizona*

Don Doyle
*Pasadena, California*

Roger Dutcher
*Plainfield, Indiana*

Lana Dye
*Sioux City, Iowa*

Kay Edwards
*Oxford, Ohio*

Sue A. Fordtran
*Corpus Christi, Texas*

Elaine B. Gabriel
*Houston, Texas*

Lona George
*Madison, Wisconsin*

Laura R. Hancock
*Tampa, Florida*

Ann H. Hastings
*Spring, Texas*

Noreen Hofmann
*Charlotte, North Carolina*

Marianne Holland
*Pickens, South Carolina*

Ramona Holmes
*Seattle, Washington*

Mary Jeanette Howle
*Jacksonville, Florida*

Christine Jordanoff
*Pittsburgh, Pennsylvania*

Brenda Kimble
*Champaign, Illinois*

Janice R. Lancaster
*Brandon, Florida*

Anne M. Lanier
*Columbia, South Carolina*

Beverly M. Naumann
*Chesterfield, Missouri*

Marcus L. Neiman
*Medina, Ohio*

Shirley Neugebauer-Luebke
*Sioux City, Iowa*

Carol Nicolucci
*Newton, Massachusetts*

Sandra Nicolucci
*Wellesley, Massachusetts*

Dan Norris
*Foley, Alabama*

Leora Osborn
*Wichita, Kansas*

Johnnie R. M. Patton
*Tyler, Texas*

Teresa Pearl
*Gastonia, North Carolina*

Josephine Y. Poelinitz
*Chicago, Illinois*

Karen M. Renton
*Topsham, Maine*

Cecilia Riddell
*Pasadena, California*

Colleen Riddle
*Spring, Texas*

Cynthia A. Ripley
*Hamburg, New York*

Marc Schneider
*Stamford, Connecticut*

Lynn Schroeder
*Apopka, Florida*

Constance Shelengian
*Scarsdale, New York*

Pattie Simbulan
*Burke, Virginia*

Lisa Stern
*Maitland, Florida*

Lonnie W. Tanner
*Houston, Texas*

Nancy Ash Vondra
*Omaha, Nebraska*

Vanja Y. Watkins
*Salt Lake City, Utah*

Alejandro Ybarra
*Mission, Texas*

Penny E. Zaugg
*Des Moines, Iowa*

## CULTURAL ADVISORS

**CP Language Institute**
*New York, New York*

Doreen Ackom, Zohar Azolay, Iris Bar-Ziv, Kveta Bendl, Yvonne Bernardo, Marco Bertellini, Vadim Besprozranny, Charlotte Cohen, Adrienne Cooper, Janna Deikan, Rajesh Dhameliya, Victor Douger, Christine Dunoyer, Sudkamol Ekkul, Joe Elias, Naomi Finkelstein, Judy Fixler, Mel Gionson, Michal Guterman, Solange Habib, Trina Hedegaard, Dr. Kim Huichin, Chang Huichin Wang, Marija Jaramoxovic, Jacek Jarkowsky, Rebecca Johnson, Mikaela Kull, Edwin Lugo, Yana Manovschi, Herand Markariann, Zahra Meigani, Claudia Mejia, Iveta Mozsnyakova, Deborah Mullens, Fidelma Murphy, Kazuha Okuchi, Gloria Ospina, Andrea Philogene, Thierry Pomies, Virginia Rambal, Wladyslaw Roczniak, Rackelle Roden, Martha Ruiz, Yuki Saito, Esperanza Salazar, Sarah Smith, Eleonore Speckents, Carime Triana, Ilian Troya, Huichin Wang, Cathi Witkowski-Changanaqui, Dieter Wolthoff, Wendy Wu, Bing Yang

# Recordings

## RECORDING PERSONNEL

### Executive Producer

Buryl Red, BR Productions

### Associate Producers for Vocals

Bill and Charlene James, Tom Moore, J. Douglas Pummill, Michael Rafter, Robert Spivak, Jeanine Tesori, Linda Twine

### Associate Producers for Instrumentals

Rick Baitz, Rick Bassett, Joseph Joubert, Bryan Louiselle, Michael Rafter, Buddy Skipper, Jeanine Tesori

### Arrangers/Orchestrators

Rick Baitz, Rick Bassett, Jack Cortner, Bruce Coughlin, Cathy Elliott, Ned Ginsberg, Joseph Joubert, Dick Lieb, Bryan Louiselle, Chris McDonald, Gustavo Moretta, Valerie Naranjo, Janet Pummill, William Pursell, Buryl Red, Mick Rossi, Steve Shapiro, Buddy Skipper, Jeff Steinberg, Jeff Talman, Jeanine Tesori, David Thomas, Linda Twine, Dale Wilson, Ovid Young

### Technical Engineering Staff

Jonathan Duckett, *supervisor*, Dave Darlington, Chris Miller, Tim Polashek, Amy Pummill, Patrick Pummill, Mick Rossi, Dan Rudin, William Santamaria, Bob Schaper, Ted Spencer, Jeff Talman, Tony Zimmerman

### Instrumental Conductors

Bryan Louiselle, Michael Rafter, Buryl Red, Jeanine Tesori, Linda Twine

## CHOIRS

### Children's Choir Conductors and Choirs

Debbie Beinhorn
*Beinhorn Singers*

D. Shawn Berry
*Bak Middle School of the Arts Boys Choir, Bak Middle School of the Arts Mixed Choir*

Darrell Bledsoe
*Darrell Bledsoe Children's Voices, Darrell Bledsoe Men's Chorus, Darrell Bledsoe Singers, Houston Vocal Edition, Richland Singers, Singing Boys of Houston, Spring Singers, Varsity Girls, Varsity Singers*

Linda Bradberry
*The Augusta Children's Choir*

Madeline Bridges
*The Nashville Children's Choir*

Gregg Bunn
*Lone Star Kids*

Lori Casteel
*Kidstyle Singers*

Wayne Causey
*The Cumberland Singers*

Victor Cook
*Victor Cook Singers*

Debra Crowe
*Debra Crowe Singers*

David Czervinske
*David Czervinske Children's Choir, David Czervinske Singers*

Jerri Davidson
*The Daggett Choir*

Connie Drosakis
*Bak Middle School of the Arts 6th Grade Treble Choir*

Lynne Gackle
*Miami Girls Choir*

Ned Ginsburg
*The Broadway Kids*

Charlotte Greeson
*Richland Singers*

Joan Gregoryk
*Chevy Chase Elementary Singers*

Cathy Guajardo
*Cathy Guajardo Singers*

Jacque Hall
*The Mary Moore Singers*

Moses Hogan
*The Moses Hogan Singers Youth Ensemble*

Sandy Holland
*The Charlotte Children's Choir*

Eugenia Huanca
*Eugenia Huanca Group*

Laurie Jenschke
*Eastman Children's Choir, Voices of Fredericksburg, Texas Children's Chorale*

Brenda Jewell
*The Nashville Children's Choir*

Doug Jewett
*The Smokey Mountain Children's Choir*

Rebecca Johnson
*The Sunshine Singers*

Joseph Joubert
*Joseph Joubert Singers*

Mary Ellen Junda
*The Treblemakers Children's Choir of the University of Connecticut*

Jan Juneau
*Woodland Singers*

Henry Leck
*The Indianapolis Children's Choir*

Jeanine Tesori
*Jeanine Tesori Singers*

Carol Lockhart
*The Carol Lockhart Singers*

Chester Mahooty
*American Indian Dance Theater*

Albert McNeil
*Albert McNeil Jubilee Singers*

Jo Morris
*Jo Morris Singers*

Cynthia Nott
*The Children's Chorus of Greater Dallas*

Celia Ong
*Asian American Youth Chorale*

Rosalyn Payne
*Step Chillin'*

Ted Polk
*Carrollton Singers*

Douglas Pummill
*Booker T. Washington Singers, Cantamos!, Children of the Heartland, The Dulcet Singers, Fiesta Americana, Heartland Youth, Heritage Children's Choir, Heritage Youth Choir, The New Horizons Show Choir, The North Texas Hispanic Choir, The Pan American Children's Choir, The Pan American Youth Choir, The Pan Asian Children's Choir, The Rainbow Children's Choir, The Rainbow Youth Choir, United in Youth*

Eddie Quaid
*Cypress Singers*

Lynn Redmond
*The Gwinnette Young Singers*

Steve Roddy
*The Houston Children's Choir, Steve Roddy Boys' Choir*

Kenny Rodgers
*Kenny Rodgers Singers*

Betty Roe
*McCullough Singers, Betty Roe Children's Choir*

Reggie Royal
*Calypso Royals*

Sally Schott
*South Houston Singers*

Marilyn Shadinger
*The Nashville Children's Choir*

Martha Shaw
*The Spivey Hall Children's Choir Chamber Ensemble*

Kay Sherrill
*Judson High School Chorale*

Mark Slaughter
*The Owensboro Children's Choir*

Steve Stevens
*The Seattle Boys Choir, The Seattle Children's Choir*

Cameron Sullenburger
*Wilson Middle School Varsity Boys Choir, Wilson Middle School Varsity Girls Choir, Wilson Middle School Varsity Mixed Choir*

Sheryl Tallant
*Kidstyle Singers*

Barry Talley
*Barry Talley Singers, Deer Park Singers*

Julia Thorn
*DeKalb County Children's Choir*

Judy Tisch
*Bammell Singers*

Marie Tomlinson
*Clitheroe Young Singers*

Darryl Tookes
*The Darryl Tookes Singers*

Walter Turnbill
*The Boys Choir of Harlem*

Linda Twine
*55th Street Jazz Singers, Linda Twine Singers*

Tim Vaughn
*La Porte Singers*

Walt Whitman
*The Soul Children of Chicago, The Walt Whitman Atlanta Singers, Walt Whitman's Soul Children*

Linda Williams
*Sundance Academy Singers, Westwind Singers*

Judith Willoughby
*The Temple University Children's Choir*

Cheryl Wilson
*Garland High School A cappella Choir, Garland High School A cappella Men, Garland High School A cappella Women*

Janet Wilson
*Janet Wilson Singers, Kid Connection*

Karen Wolff
*Cincinnati Children's Choir*

Patrinell Wright
*Total Experience Gospel Choir*

## Key Components

# Welcome music educators!

**Silver Burdett MAKING MUSIC is an active, balanced, and comprehensive music program. It provides both sequential teaching of music elements and skills as well as theme-based instruction for music educators and students.**

*Kindergarten Big Book*

*Student Editions, Grades 1–6*

- **Active music making** develops musical knowledge and skills.
- **Exceptional song literature and recordings** provide a strong foundation for instruction.
- **Balanced organization** presents a comprehensive music curriculum.
- **Proven content** reflects the National Standards for Music Education.

# Active music making that supports your teaching

**Student Editions**

- Dynamic repertoire of song literature
- Opportunities to sing, listen to music, play instruments, read music, move to music, and connect to other disciplines

Grades 1 and 2

**Big Books**

- Big, bold, colorfully illustrated lessons
- Great for small-group and classroom instruction
- Many different musical experiences
- Sturdy easel for easy display
- One volume, Grades K–1; two volumes, Grade 2

**Teacher's Editions**

- Sequential instruction in Units 1–6
- Theme-based instruction in Units 7–12
- National Standards integrated throughout
- Consistent, three-step lesson plan

# Recordings you'll want to carry everywhere

### Ultraportable CD Cases

- Innovative design keeps you organized
- Lightweight and small so you can carry anywhere
- Removable pages for greater flexibility

### Audio CD Booklets

- Quick, easy guide for each grade-level Audio CD package
- Comprehensive list of recorded tracks; includes information on performing groups, instrumentation, track length, page references, and special recorded features

### Professional Recordings

- Superb sound quality—a higher standard in educational recordings
- Artists that people know and recognize
- Variety of children, youth, and adult vocal performers
- Varied and rich repertoire of listening selections
- Widest range of music genres, styles, and cultures—recorded with authenticity
- Tracks for stereo vocals, stereo performance, teach-a-part, sung pronunciation practice, dance practice and performance, interviews, and assessments

# Resources that enhance your music teaching

### Keyboard Accompaniments

- Keyboard accompaniments for classroom use and performances
- Easy-to-use, spiral-bound book—hard-back cover stays upright on any keyboard stand

Grade 5 Grade 1

Grade 3

### Listening Map Transparency Package

- Visual guides for listening selections
- Easy-to-follow graphics that build skills in listening and understanding music
- Reproducible masters to support instruction

### Resource Books

Reproducible masters are available to support the following:

- Pronunciation Practice Guides
- Graphic Organizers
- Assessments and Rubrics
- Music Reading Worksheets
- Music Reading Practice (1–6)
- Orff Arrangements
- Signing Activities
- Keyboard (2–6)
- Recorder (3–6)
- Activity Masters

Grade 2

# More resources for music instruction

### Step into Music, Pre-Kindergarten

- Complete fine arts program that builds early music literacy and language skills
- Effective support for children's physical, emotional, social, and cognitive development

### Silver Burdett MAKING MUSIC, Grades 7–8

- Modular organization for maximum teaching flexibility
- Active music-making experiences
- Comprehensive music instruction
- National Standards integrated throughout

### MAKING MUSIC with Movement and Dance

- Easy-to-follow guide for movement and dance activities
- Folk dances, ethnic dances, and creative movement
- One volume—all grade levels

### *¡A cantar!*

- Traditional and contemporary songs in Spanish
- Theme and element connections
- Recorded pronunciation practice
- Two CDs with all songs and literature
- Primary and Intermediate Levels

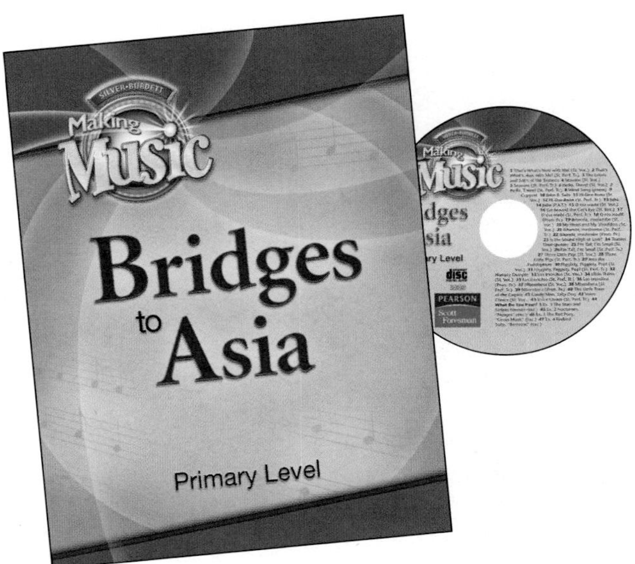


### Bridges to Asia

- Additional lessons to explore the rich musical heritage of Asia
- Pronunciation practice for each song
- Four CDs with all songs and literature
- Primary and Intermediate Levels

### New Activities for the Substitute Teacher

- Songs and activities for substitute teachers
- Song lyrics, teaching strategies, reproducible activity masters, and audio CD
- Integrated activities for all grade levels

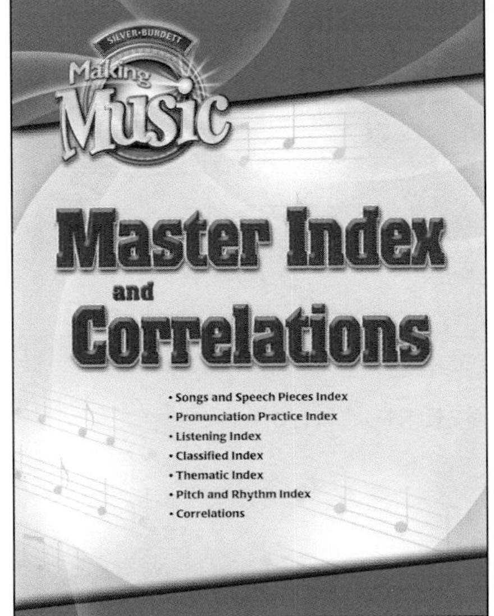


### Master Index and Correlations

- Comprehensive reference to simplify planning
- Grades K–8 index of all songs, speech pieces, listening selections, and more
- Pitch and Rhythm Index
- Thematic Index
- Reading and Phonics Correlations

# Steps to MAKING MUSIC for sequential instruction

**Silver Burdett MAKING MUSIC has a balanced, two-part organization. Part 1 is Steps to MAKING MUSIC, which comprises Units 1–6. Steps to MAKING MUSIC provides sequential instruction using elements, skills, and connections. These systematically progress from unit to unit and grade to grade.**

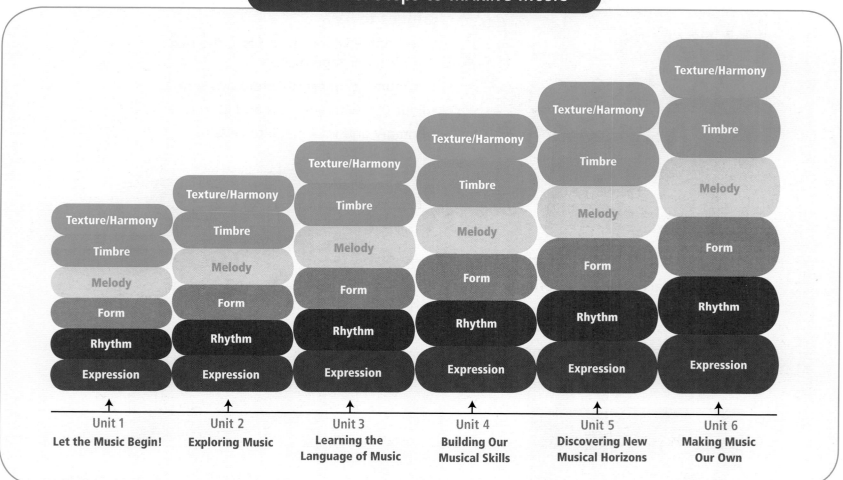

| Unit 1<br>Let the Music Begin! | Unit 2<br>Exploring Music | Unit 3<br>Learning the Language of Music | Unit 4<br>Building Our Musical Skills | Unit 5<br>Discovering New Musical Horizons | Unit 6<br>Making Music Our Own |
|---|---|---|---|---|---|
| Texture/Harmony | Texture/Harmony | Texture/Harmony | Texture/Harmony | Texture/Harmony | Texture/Harmony |
| Timbre | Timbre | Timbre | Timbre | Timbre | Timbre |
| Melody | Melody | Melody | Melody | Melody | Melody |
| Form | Form | Form | Form | Form | Form |
| Rhythm | Rhythm | Rhythm | Rhythm | Rhythm | Rhythm |
| Expression | Expression | Expression | Expression | Expression | Expression |

### Units 1–6: Steps to MAKING MUSIC

- Sequenced instruction to help students learn music elements and skills
- Gradual increase in skill levels that allows students to assimilate and apply learning
- 72 total music lessons—36 weekly core lessons plus 36 lessons to expand instruction

# Paths to MAKING MUSIC for theme explorations

**Paths to MAKING MUSIC is Part 2 of the program and includes Units 7–12. This section increases your students' music knowledge and skills through theme-based activities and lessons. The themes are coordinated from grade to grade so that all students can share related instruction.**

**Units 7–12: Paths to MAKING MUSIC**

| Grade | Unit 7 America Makes Music | Unit 8 From Home to the World | Unit 9 Expanding the Boundaries | Unit 10 Garden of the Earth | Unit 11 The Power of Performance | Unit 12 The Joy of Celebration |
|---|---|---|---|---|---|---|
| 6 | Exploring America's Music | Say It with Drums | Be a Star! | Sound Waves | Strike Up the Chorus | Celebrate the Day |
| 5 | Building America in Song | Music Around the World | In the Pop Style | Keepers of the Earth | We Sing! | Holidays in Song |
| 4 | Going Places U.S.A. | Bring Your Passport | Chasing a Dream | Earth, Sea, and Sky | Sing Out! | Sing and Celebrate |
| 3 | Singing America | Our World of Music | Fun and Games | This Beautiful Planet | Tuneful Tales | Holidays to Share |
| 2 | Music–U.S.A. | Home and Away | Creature Feature | Our Planet Earth | Perform a Story | Celebrate the Season |
| 1 | Making Music at School | My Family and Me | Adventures with Friends | The Great Outdoors | Imagination Station! | Days to Celebrate |
| K | All About Me | My Neighbors and Me | Imagine That! | Nature Walk | Look What I Can Do! | Celebrate with Me! |

### Units 7–12: Paths to MAKING MUSIC

- Thematic units aligned with themes commonly found in social studies, reading, science, and other curricular areas
- Terrific opportunities to make connections and present performances

# Lesson Organization

## Easy-to-teach, flexible, and inspiring lessons

**Objective Bar** focuses your students' learning. The yellow burst highlights the assessed item.

**Lesson at a Glance** lists critical information to streamline planning.

**CD References** make it easy to access your audio collection.

**More Music Choices** provide options for further practice.

**Footnotes** support your instruction and help you make connections.

**Building Skills Through Music** connects music learning to other curricular areas.

LESSON Core 4

**LESSON AT A GLANCE**

**Element Focus** RHYTHM and

**Skill Objective** PLAYING Play sixteenth-note patterns

**Connection Activity** SOCIAL STUDIES Investigate the historical context of a railroad song

**MATERIALS**

- "Drill, Ye Tarriers" CD 3-16
  **Recording Routine:** Intro (4 m.); v. 1; refrain; interlude (4 m.); v. 2; refrain; interlude (4 m.); v. 3, refrain; coda
- **Music Reading Practice, Sequence 6** CD 3-18
- **Dance Directions** for "Drill, Ye Tarriers" p. 554
- *Symphony No. 9,* Movement 1 (excerpt) CD 3-22
- **Resource Book** p. E-7, F-6, I-6
- selected classroom percussion instruments

**VOCABULARY**

symphony movement

**National Standards**

1b Sing easy pieces with technical accuracy
2b Perform easy instrumental pieces with technical accuracy
5a Read quarter, eighth, sixteenth notes in duple meter
5d Use standard notation to record musical ideas
6a Listen and describe events in music using appropriate terms
8b Identify ways music relates to social studies

**MORE MUSIC CHOICES**

For more experience with sixteenth-note patterns: "Camptown Races," p. 270

## 1 Introduce

Have students listen to "Drill Ye Tarriers" **CD 3-16** and discuss the lyrics. Use the suggestions in Across the Curriculum below to engage students in a discussion of railroads.

LESSON 4 Element: RHYTHM Skill: PLAYING Connection: SOCIAL STUD

## Work to the Rhythm

In the 1880s, many different groups of immigrants helped to build American railroads. One of these groups was the Irish. **Sing** "Drill, Ye Tarriers," a song that tells of the hardships and injustices the railroad workers faced.

**Listen** for some clues in the text about what tarriers do.

CD 3-16

### Drill, Ye Tarriers

l, t, d r m s l t
Words and Music by Thomas Ca

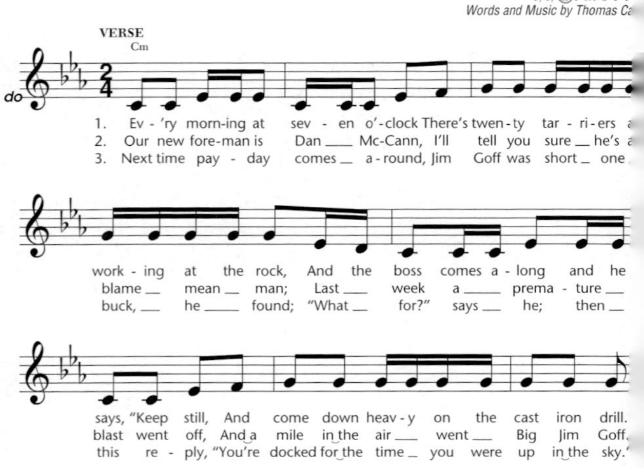

VERSE
Cm

1. Ev - 'ry morn-ing at sev - en o'-clock There's twen-ty tar - ri-ers a work - ing at the rock, And the boss comes a - long and he says, "Keep still, And come down heav - y on the cast iron drill.
2. Our new fore-man is Dan Mc-Cann, I'll tell you sure he's a blame mean man; Last week a prema - ture blast went off, And a mile in the air went Big Jim Goff.
3. Next time pay - day comes a - round, Jim Goff was short one buck, he found; "What for?" says he; then this re - ply, "You're docked for the time you were up in the sky."

54 Reading Sequence 6

## Footnotes

### Movement

▶ **Patterned Dance** Dancing is a natural part of Irish culture. It is said that when two Irishmen meet at a crossroad, they do a little jig. When the Irishmen who worked on the railroad had time to relax, they sang and danced. There were not many women at the railroad camps, so the men danced with each other, just as American cowboys and Argentine sailors did. See p. 554 for a movement pattern to accompany "Drill, Ye Tarriers."

### Building Skills Through Music

▶ **Math** Divide the class into two groups, with one group clapping the rhythm of the verse, the second group clapping a steady beat. Ask students to identify beats with one or more notes. Each beat will equal one [whole]. Review the fractions for 1/2 and 1/4. Have students identify fractions for each note. For example, an eighth note would equal 1/2; a sixteenth note would equal 1/4. Add the fractions for each beat, then for each measure.

### Across the Curriculum

8b ▶ **Social Studies** Students may enjoy reading and then creating a short historical-fact introduction to "Drill, Ye Tarriers" for performances. For interesting facts about the building of railroads across the United States, suggest they read *Ten Mile Day: And the Building of the Transcontinental Railroad* by Mary Ann Fraser (Henry Holt, 1996). This fascinating account of the building of the Transcontinental Railroad in 1869 explores the historical highlights and engineering feats, lives of the many ethnic groups who served as railroad workers, and the effects of the railroads on Native Americans.

54 Reading Sequence 6, p. 492

*Grade 5*

REFRAIN
Cm G7 Cm Gm
So drill, ye tar - ri - ers, drill, And drill, ye tar - ri - ers,
Cm Cm
drill! Oh, it's work all day for sug - ar in your tay,
Cm Gm Cm G7 Cm
Down be-yond the rail - way, And drill, ye tar - ri - ers, drill!

**Railroad Rhythms**

Find the ♩♫ and ♫♩ patterns in the song.

**Sing** the song again, and when one of these patterns comes along, sing the rhythm syllables instead of the words. Good luck!

**Play** the rhythm parts below with the refrain of "Drill, Ye Tarriers."

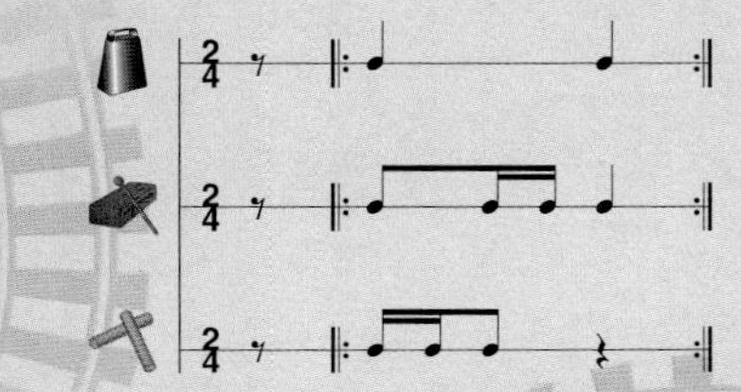

**Listen** to the ♫♩ pattern in this excerpt.

CD 3-22

**Symphony No. 9 ("From the New World")**

**Movement 1**
**by Antonín Dvořák**

The name of this symphony, "From the New World," refers to the United States. Czech composer Antonín Dvořák [an-toh-NEEN d'VOHR-zhahk] wrote it at about the same time railroad workers were singing "Drill, Ye Tarriers."

# 2 Develop

### Reading

Ask volunteers to write three rhythms on the board:

Set a steady beat and then have students

5a
- Read each rhythm with rhythm syllables.
- Look at the notation for "Drill, Ye Tarriers" and count how many times each sixteenth-note rhythm appears in the song. Then read the verse of the song with rhythm syllables.

For more practice performing sixteenth-note rhythms, see Music Reading Practice, Sequence 6 on p. 492 and Resource Book p. E-6.

### Creating

5d Add two beamed eighth notes, a quarter note, and a quarter rest to the rhythms on the board. Draw four blanks (two measures) on the board. Have students

- Decide how to fill in the blanks, using the patterns on the board. (The quarter note and quarter rest can be used only once.)
- Use standard symbols to notate rhythm in simple patterns and perform them using rhythm syllables. Then say their patterns one after another without silent beats in between.

### Playing

Invite students to perform the instrumental parts on p. 55 with the refrain "Drill, Ye Tarriers."

### Listening

6a Play the excerpt from *Symphony No. 9* **CD 3-22** and ask students to listen for the *tiri-ti* rhythm.

# 3 Close

**Element: RHYTHM** ASSESSMENT

1b 2b **Performance/Observation** Have students play their rhythm patterns, or those on p. 55, on selected percussion instruments as ostinatos, while singing "Drill, Ye Tarriers." Observe for rhythmic accuracy.

**Systematic Instruction** follows a consistent, three-step plan.

**Song Notation** on a white background improves readability.

**National Standards** at point of use identify your instructional goals.

**Assessment** allows you to monitor students' understanding.

## Skills Reinforcement

2b ▶ **Recorder** To give students additional experience with rhythm patterns that use eighth and sixteenth notes, have them compose a rhythmic piece to play on their recorders. Invite students to create and notate four, two-beat measures using quarter, eighth, and sixteenth notes. Using their recorders, have them play their compositions on the note G. Some students may want to accompany the verse of "Drill, Ye Tarriers" by playing their composition on G. They will need to repeat their four-measure pieces or have a friend play the second set of four measures.

Another time, have students play the rhythm of the words on the note G during the verse of the song. Make sure they say *daah* on each note so the rhythm is articulated clearly.

A countermelody for "Drill, Ye Tarriers" can be found on Resource Book p. I-6.

## Character Education

▶ **Collaboration** To promote students' understanding of the skills necessary to collaborate with others, discuss singing and professional partnerships. Singing in a group requires vocal control and careful listening to achieve appropriate balance and blend. Individuals often must adjust their performance to benefit the group. Ask students what other situations require that individuals sacrifice control to help the group. (Accept various answers including team sports and medical teams.)

## Technology/Media Link

5d **Notation Software** Have students notate their rhythm patterns from this lesson and print them before playing them.

# The best music, the widest selection

**Favorite songs, award-winning songs, exciting originals! Silver Burdett MAKING MUSIC provides quality song literature of lasting value. An exciting mix of songs and recordings supports every type of music-making experience—singing, playing instruments, moving, listening, creating, reading, and notating.**

## Music that models and instructs

Children's voices provide vocal modeling and adult voices demonstrate style, expression, and cultural authenticity.

- Student soloists
- Student vocal ensembles
- Student choirs
- Adult soloists
- Adult choirs
- Adult vocal ensembles

## Music that represents diverse genres and styles

Your students experience, perform, and evaluate the most diverse range of music.

- Folk
- Traditional
- Multicultural
- Popular
- Contemporary
- Patriotic
- Seasonal
- Holiday

LESSON 6 Element: MELODY Skill: SINGING Connection: CULTURE

Singing Ecuador

**Sing** this song that children in Ecuador enjoy. Look for pitch patterns with *so, mi,* and *la.*

CD 2-27

El juego chirimbolo

(The *Chirimbolo* Game)

*English Words by Alice Firgau* *Singing Game from Ecuador*

*El jue-go chi-rim-bo-lo, ¡qué bo-ni-to es!*

This game is *chi-rim-bo-lo;* Play and you'll have fun.

*Con un pie, o-tro pie, u-na ma-no, o-tra ma-no,*

First one foot, oth-er foot; Then one hand, oth-er hand;

*un co-do, o-tro co-do. El co-do,*

One el-bow, oth-er el-bow. This el-bow.

*El jue-go chi-rim-bo-lo, ¡qué bo-ni-to es! ¡Hey!*

We're play-ing *chi-rim-bo-lo.* Now the game is done. Hey!

54

Grade 2

## Recordings that support music learning

- Listening selections
- Dances
- Instrumental sound banks
- Montages
- Recorded poems and stories
- Recorded interviews
- Recorded assessments

LESSON 1 Element: EXPRESSION Skill: MOVING Connection: RELATED ARTS

Speed Up, Slow Down

**Sing** "Miss Mary Mack" at different speeds, or **tempos.**

**Tempo** is the speed of the beat in music.

CD 2-4 MIDI 5

Miss Mary Mack

*African American Clapping Game Song*

1. Miss Ma-ry Mack, Mack, Mack, All dressed in black, black, black, With sil-ver but-tons, but-tons, but-tons, All down her back, back, back.

2. She asked her mother, mother, mother, For fifteen cents, cents, cents, To see the elephants, elephants, elephants Jump over the fence, fence, fence.

3. They jumped so high, high, high, They touched the sky, sky, sky, And never came down, down, down, 'Til the fourth of July, 'ly, 'ly.

Grade 2

...dings. The Shona are Bantu-...le who live in southeastern Africa, ...babwe.

...has three layers of sound and each ...wn melody. **Sing** "Wai bamba," adding one layer at a time. As each new layer is added, the **texture** of the music will become thicker and **harmony** will be created.

**Harmony** is created when two or more different tones sound at the same time.

**Texture** is the layering of sounds to create a thick or thin quality in music.

▲ Shona mask

CD 2-19

WAI BAMBA

*Shona Wedding Song*

*Wai bam-ba wai, Bam-ba wai, Wi wi wi wi.*

26

Grade 6

## Recordings that express musical artistry

World-class performers, composers, and conductors inspire creative expression and performance.

- Ella Fitzgerald
- Ziggy Marley
- Gloria Estefan
- Yo-Yo Ma
- Itzhak Perlman
- Ludwig van Beethoven
- Leontyne Price
- Carlos Santana
- George Gershwin
- Wynton Marsalis
- The Boys Choir of Harlem
- Seiji Ozawa
- Tito Puente
- John Philip Sousa
- Johann Sebastian Bach
- Whitney Houston
- Duke Ellington, and hundreds more!

# Reading and writing music notation

**A goal of Silver Burdett MAKING MUSIC is to help you develop your students' music literacy. Systematic instruction and practice opportunities permit all your students to become accomplished at reading and writing music notation.**

**Music Reading Lessons** are clearly identified in both the Student Editions and Teacher's Editions.

LESSON 7

LESSON AT A GLANCE

**Element Focus** **MELODY** *So, mi,* and *la*

**Skill Objective** **READING** Sing a song with *so, mi,* and *la,* using hand signs

**Connection Activity** **LANGUAGE ARTS** Read an autumn poem

**MATERIALS**

- "Clouds of Gray" **CD 2-32**
  **Recording Routine:** Intro (2 m.); v. 1; interlude (2 m.); v. 2; coda
  **Music Reading Practice, Sequence 7** **CD 2-34**
- "Wind Has Shaken Autumn Down" (poem)
- "Four Seasons" (poem)
- **Resource Book** pp. D-7, D-26, E-8, F-8

**VOCABULARY**

hand sign *so, mi,* and *la*

◆◆◆◆ National Standards ◆◆◆◆

**1a** Sing independently in rhythm
**1e** Sing in groups, blending vocal timbres, matching dynamic levels, and following a conductor
**4b** Compose instrumental pieces within specific guidelines
**5b** Read notes in treble clef using syllables
**5d** Notate pitch, using standard symbols

**MORE MUSIC CHOICES**

For more experiences reading *so, mi,* and *la:*
"A-Tisket, A-Tasket," p. 238
For another autumn season song:
"The Owl and the Pumpkin," p. 377

**1 INTRODUCE**

Ask the children to look at the falling leaves on p. 56. Have them point to the pitches they know. *(la, so, mi)* Inform the children that the song they will hear starts on *so.*

LESSON 7 Element: MELODY Skill: READING Connection: LANGUAGE ARTS

**Find a New Pitch**

**Sing** this song using *so, mi,* and *la.* **Listen** for a new pitch at the end. Is the new pitch higher or lower than *so, mi,* and *la?*

CD 2-32 *Clouds of Gray*

*Words and Music by Katinka S. Daniel*

1. Clouds of gray are in the sky, Flocks of birds are pass-ing by, Trees now dress in fad-ed brown, Send their leaves all rust-ling down.
2. Lit-tle flow-ers down-ward creep, Nod their drow-sy heads and sleep, All the world must say "good night," Till spring comes with sun-shine bright.

la mi ?

56 Reading Sequence 7

la so mi ?

**New Pitch—New Sign**

As you **sing** the song, show hand signs for *la, so, mi,* and the new pitch. Hum the new pitch.

**Sing an Autumn Poem**

Sing this poem, using the melody from "Clouds of Gray."

**Wind Has Shaken Autumn Down**
*by Tony Johnston*

Wind has shaken autumn down,
left it sprawling on the ground,
shawling all in gold below,
waiting for the hush of snow.

Unit 2 57

**2 DEVELOP**

**Listening**

Ask children to listen for a new pitch as you play the recording of "Clouds of Gray" **CD 2-32**.

ASK **Where in the song was the new pitch?** (at the end)

**Was it higher or lower than *so, mi,* and *la?*** (lower)

**Singing**

1e Have the children sing the song with the words. Then ask them to find *so, mi,* and *la* on the staff in the song. Next, have them sing the first three phrases of the song with pitch syllables and hand signs.

**Reading**

5b Ask the children to look on p. 57 and find the hand sign for the new pitch. Then have them sing the song with pitch syllables and hand signs, humming the new pitch. Use Music Reading Worksheet on p. D-7 in the Resource Book to provide practice notating pitches.

For additional practice with reading *do,* see Reading Sequence 7 on p. 409 and Resource Book p. E-8.

**3 CLOSE**

**Singing**

1a Read aloud the poem "Wind Has Shaken Autumn Down" to the class. Ask the children to say and clap the words with you and notice that the rhythm is the same as "Clouds of Gray." Then have the children sing the poem, using the melody of "Clouds of Gray."

Skill: READING ASSESSMENT

5b **Performance/Observation** Have the children sing the first three lines of "Clouds of Gray," using hand signs and syllables. Observe whether or not the children are performing the hand signs and syllables accurately. Then have them sing the song again with the words.

**Footnotes**

ACROSS THE CURRICULUM

▶ **Language Arts/Poetry** Read aloud the poem "Four Seasons." Invite children to improvise sound effects on percussion instruments as you read.

Spring is showery, flowery, bowery.
Summer: hoppy, choppy, poppy.
Autumn: wheezy, sneezy, freezy.
Winter: slippy, drippy, nippy.

BUILDING SKILLS THROUGH MUSIC

▶ **Writing** Write words from the song on picture icons using singular form and ask children to match the singular form word with its correct plural on another icon. Remind children of the *-s* and *-es* endings and of the special changes in leaf-leaves and sky-skies. Sing the song again and have children hold up the correct icon when each word is sung.

56 Reading Sequence 7, p. 409

SKILLS REINFORCEMENT

5d ▶ **Notating** To reinforce the concept of movable *do*, have children write the music notation of the first line of the song using the system of two or more different staff placements for *so*, *mi*, and *la*.

**Reinforcement** Have the children do this activity as a group at the board.

**On Target** Have the children do this activity as an individual writing assignment on staff paper. See Resource Book p. D-26 for staff paper.

**Challenge** Have children add stems and beams to the pitches to reflect the rhythmic notation.

▶ **Mallets** An Orff arrangement for "Clouds of Gray" can be found on p. F-8 of the Resource Book.

SPOTLIGHT ON

▶ **Autumn** Autumn happens at different times in different parts of the world. The United States is in the northern hemisphere of the earth, where autumn occurs from September 22 or 23 to December 21 or 22. South of the equator, in the southern hemisphere, the seasons are reversed. In the southern hemisphere autumn occurs from March to June. Not only does autumn happen at different times, but it doesn't always bring the same changes. Autumn is sometimes called "fall" because in many places it is the time when all the leaves fall off the trees. This doesn't happen everywhere. In tropical places where the temperature change is not significant, most trees keep all of their leaves. Some places in the world don't even have autumn. At the North and South Poles the only seasons are winter and summer.

TECHNOLOGY/MEDIA LINK

4b **Notation Software** Open the note palette and set up a blank 8-measure template in $\frac{2}{4}$ meter.

- Show children how to select note durations (use quarter notes and rests) and drag notes onto the musical staff.
- Ask children to compose their own 8-measure piece using *so, mi,* and *la* (G, E, and A). Instruct them to use *do* for the last pitch (C).

Children are often highly motivated by seeing their compositions in print! Print children's songs and display them in the classroom.

Unit 2 *Exploring Music* 57

*Grade 2*

**Built-in Reading Sequences** are referenced for access to more practice.

**Instructional Strategies for Reading Music** align with National Standards to meet your specific curricular goals.

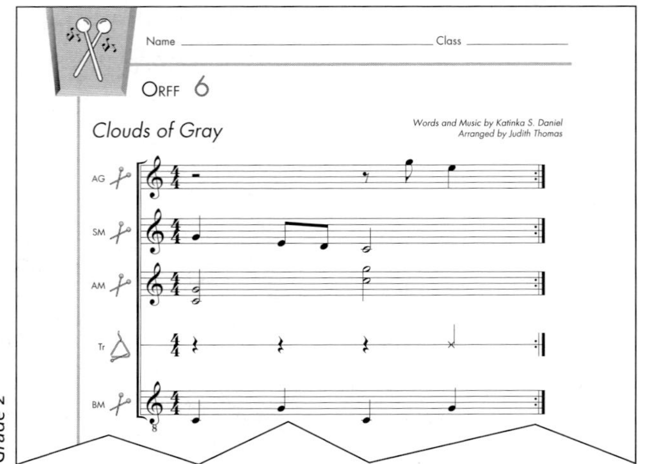


**Orff Accompaniments** add enrichment to many reading lessons.

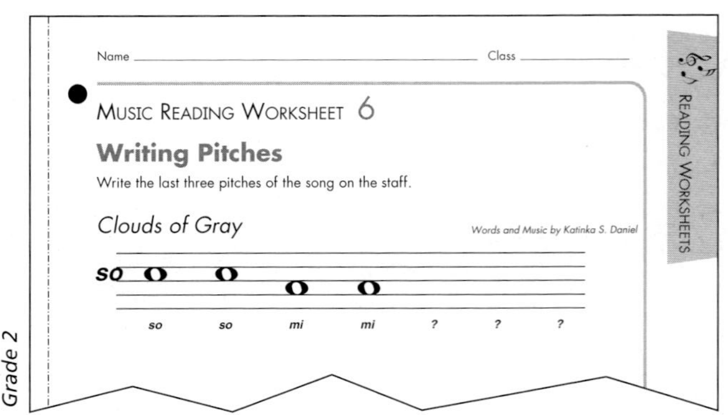


**Music Reading Worksheets** accompany every lesson to reinforce and extend music literacy.

**Music Reading Practice Section** reinforces melodic and rhythmic literacy. The section contains 24 Reading Sequences at each grade level for ample practice.

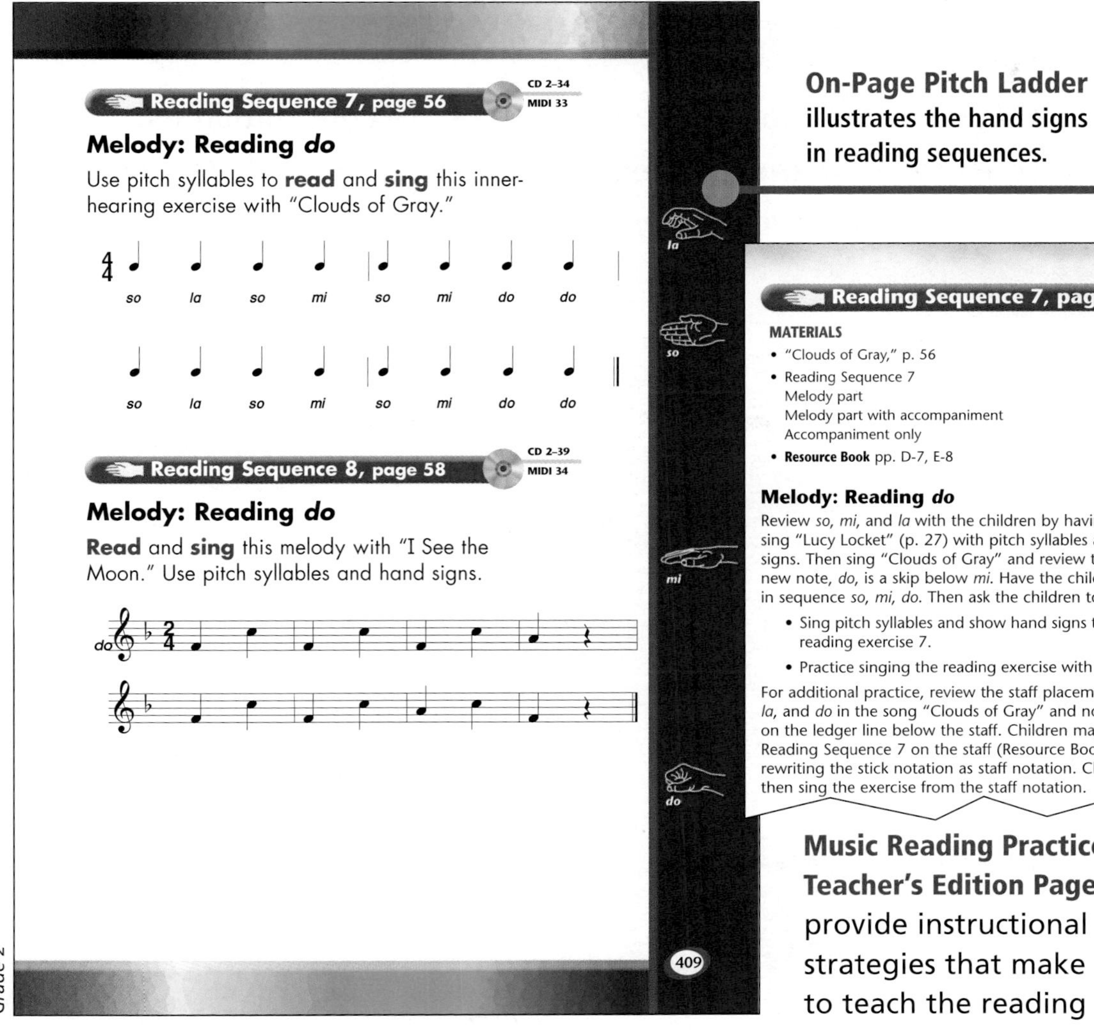
CD 2-34
MIDI 33

**Reading Sequence 7, page 56**

**Melody: Reading *do***

Use pitch syllables to **read** and **sing** this inner-hearing exercise with "Clouds of Gray."

so la so mi | so mi do do |

so la so mi | so mi do do ||

CD 2-39
MIDI 34

**Reading Sequence 8, page 58**

**Melody: Reading *do***

**Read** and **sing** this melody with "I See the Moon." Use pitch syllables and hand signs.



**On-Page Pitch Ladder** illustrates the hand signs used in reading sequences.

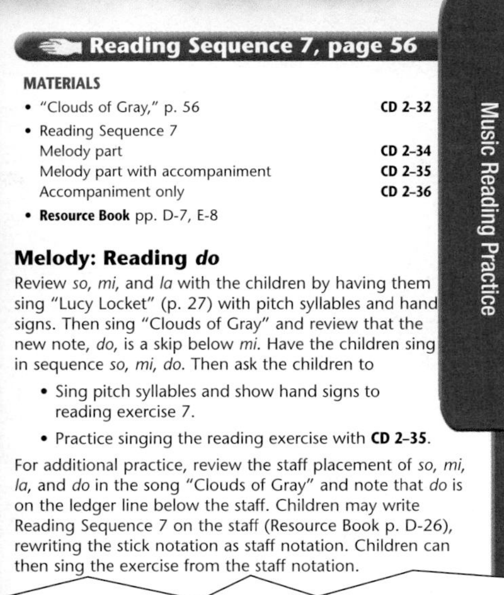
**Reading Sequence 7, page 56**

**MATERIALS**

- "Clouds of Gray," p. 56 — CD 2-32
- Reading Sequence 7
  - Melody part — CD 2-34
  - Melody part with accompaniment — CD 2-35
  - Accompaniment only — CD 2-36
- **Resource Book** pp. D-7, E-8

**Melody: Reading *do***

Review *so, mi,* and *la* with the children by having them sing "Lucy Locket" (p. 27) with pitch syllables and hand signs. Then sing "Clouds of Gray" and review that the new note, *do,* is a skip below *mi.* Have the children sing in sequence *so, mi, do.* Then ask the children to

- Sing pitch syllables and show hand signs to reading exercise 7.
- Practice singing the reading exercise with **CD 2-35**.

For additional practice, review the staff placement of *so, mi, la,* and *do* in the song "Clouds of Gray" and note that *do* is on the ledger line below the staff. Children may write Reading Sequence 7 on the staff (Resource Book p. D-26), rewriting the stick notation as staff notation. Children can then sing the exercise from the staff notation.



**Music Reading Practice Teacher's Edition Pages** provide instructional strategies that make it easy to teach the reading lessons.

**MIDI Tracks** are provided for every Reading Sequence, allowing your students to practice individual parts at various tempos and keys.

**Audio CDs** include both individual vocal and instrumental parts, as well as accompaniment tracks for each Reading Sequence.

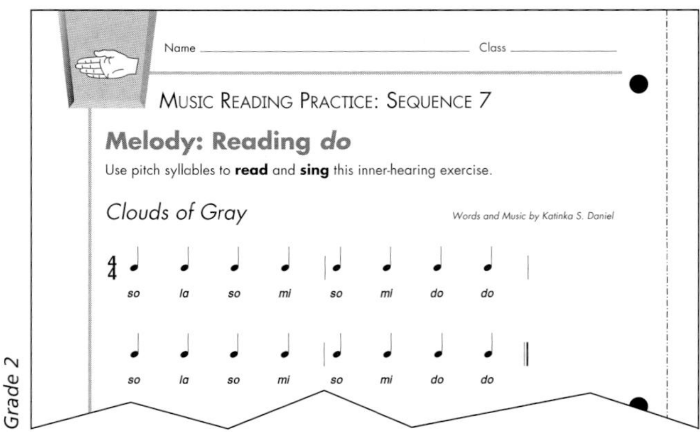
Name ______ Class ______

MUSIC READING PRACTICE: SEQUENCE 7

**Melody: Reading *do***

Use pitch syllables to **read** and **sing** this inner-hearing exercise.

*Clouds of Gray* — *Words and Music by Katinka S. Daniel*

so la so mi | so mi do do |

so la so mi | so mi do do ||

Grade 2

**Music Reading Practice Worksheets** support each Reading Sequence. Use the worksheets to create overhead transparencies for group instruction.

# Activities for creative student performances

**Developmentally appropriate vocal, instrumental, and movement experiences are core throughout Silver Burdett MAKING MUSIC. These varied musical experiences help you teach students critical aspects of expression, rhythm, form, melody, timbre, and texture/harmony.**

LESSON 2 Element: TIMBRE Skill: PLAYING Connection: SCIENCE

## Jug Band S…

Playing in a jug band is a fun way to make … instruments that are easy to play. Gather t… instruments and learn to play them. Decid… instrument you will play in this jug band s…

Sing "Mama Don't 'Low." Imagine how … accompaniment will sound.

Grade 6

LESSON 1 Element: TEXTURE/HARMONY Skill: PLAYING Connection: LANGUAGE ARTS

## A New Day

Each day gives us a new opportunity to care for and enjoy our planet. Music is a great way to start each day.

**Sing** this good morning song!

Grade 2

**Play** these ostinatos to accompany "Every Morning When I Wake Up."

Glockenspiel

Xylophone

Bass Metallophone

## a Sentiment

"Over My Head" is a song strongly tied to the American Civil Rights movement.

**Sing** the song and make an arc in the air with one arm to help hold the long notes for four counts. During the long note held in each phrase, a second group of singers repeats the phrase. This is known as echo singing. Next, **sing** the song with a friend echoing the melody.

### Over My Head

African American Spiritual

Grade 4

**Play F and $C_7$ Piano Chords**

Follow the song notation and play these chords as you **sing**.

**Joyful Form**

Find the words *verse* and *refrain* in this song. Most songs that have a verse and refrain are A B form. **Sing** "Joy to the World." The verse can be sung as a solo. Everyone can join in on the refrain.

### Joy to the World

Words and Music by Hoyt Axton

Grade 3

**Play Joyfully**

**Play** this part on your recorder when you hear the B section.

### Playing instruments

Frequent opportunities encourage your students to make music using instruments.

- Classroom percussion instruments
- Keyboard instruments
- Mallet instruments
- World drumming
- Recorder (3–6)
- Guitar (4–6)

**Sing Together in Harmony**

Welcome to another year of choral music. This year, you will take a journey on a musical landscape composed of rhythm, melody, harmony, and form. With each new song, your awareness of how these musical elements relate to each other will help you understand the composer's technique for creating a song. At the end of this journey, you will no longer be just a visitor to the musical score. It will be a place where you will feel right at home.

Come, let's **sing** "Sail Away" and begin our musical tour.

CD 18-20 MIDI 27

Sail Away

Words and Music by Malcolm Dalgish (adapted)

Dark clouds hide the sun,

Rain comes down and the rivers run. Rivers run down to the sea,

and when you've got

*Don't you want to sail

* "Don't you" is pronounced "donchiew"

404

Grade 5

UNIT 11

We Sing!

Choral singing brings people together in harmony. Groups of people all over the world sing songs together. There are choral songs about every subject imaginable. As long as people keep singing, the tradition of choral music continues!

Back to tempo, lively

Don't you want to sail a-way, don't you want to sail a-way? Don't

you want to sail a-way, don't

## Singing

Instruction on good singing techniques through a variety of songs and choral literature allows your students to perform successfully.

LESSON 2 Element: EXPRESSION Skill: MOVING Connection: SOCIAL S

Games Americans Pl

Folk songs and games are passed down by families and friends. One person teaches another how to sing the song or play the game. Then that person teaches someone else. "Bob-a-Needle" is an African American singing game played in a circle.

CD 8-19

Bob-a-Needle

African American Ring

Bob - a - need - le, bob - a - need - le is a - run - ning.

Bob - a - need - le, bob - a - need - le is a run - ni

**Play the Bob-a-Needle Game**

Play the game as you **sing** the song. Each time you repeat the game, sing and **move** at a faster tempo.

Music—USA

Grade 2

## Moving

A wide variety of movement activities helps you teach rhythmic patterns and develop students' creative expression.

- Body percussion
- Conducting
- Creative and interpretive movement
- Dramatizing/pantomimes
- Finger plays
- Folk and patterned dances
- Game songs (singing and rhythm games)
- Hand jives
- Locomotor movements
- Nonlocomotor movements
- Play-parties
- Popular dance
- Signing

LESSON 11 Element: TEXTURE/HARMONY Skill: LISTENING Connection: STYLE

Alone or Together?

Sometimes you sing alone. Sometimes a musical instrument plays along with your singing.

**Listen** to two recordings of "Make New Friends." In one, the singers sing alone. In the other, you will hear an **accompaniment.** A string quartet, four string instruments, plays along. The lowest sounding instrument is the cello [CHEHL-oh].

An **accompaniment** is a part that supports a main melody. It is usually played by one or more instruments.

CD 2-1

Make New Friends

Traditional Round

Make new friends, but keep the old,

One is sil - ver and the oth - er gold.

36

Grade 3

**Sing and Sign Together**

Now **sing** the song yourself. Practice signing it as you sing.

make

▲ Place right fist over left fist and twist, then repeat.

new

▲ Right hand sweeps up in an arc.

friends

▲ Lock index fingers together, then repeat.

Unit 1 37

# Assessment to monitor learning and growth

**Silver Burdett MAKING MUSIC provides a variety of tools to help you assess your students' music knowledge and skills. Choose from performance, written, and oral assessments according to your specific teaching style and instructional needs.**

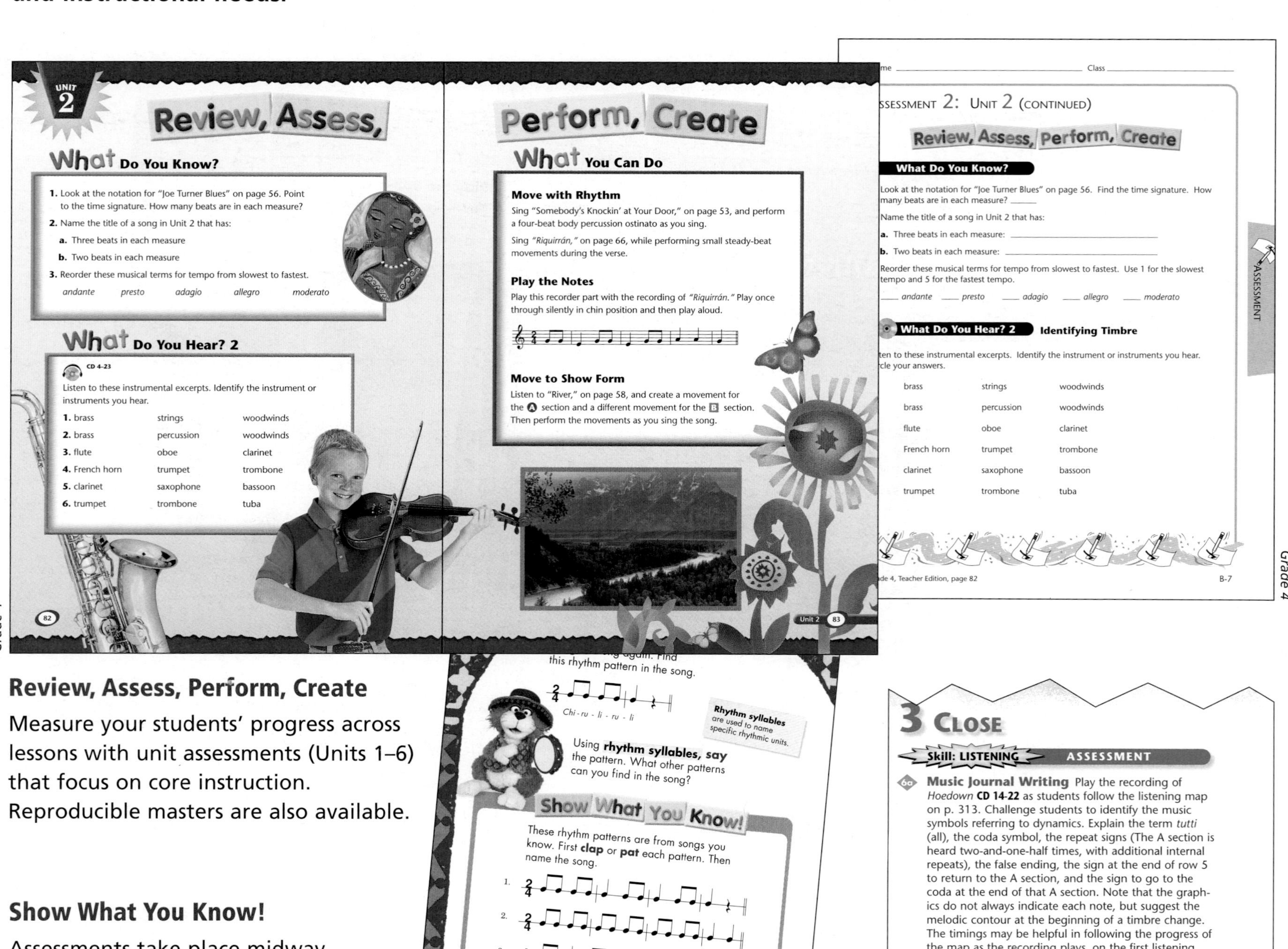

UNIT 2

Review, Assess, Perform, Create

What Do You Know?

1. Look at the notation for "Joe Turner Blues" on page 56. Point to the time signature. How many beats are in each measure?
2. Name the title of a song in Unit 2 that has:
   a. Three beats in each measure
   b. Two beats in each measure
3. Reorder these musical terms for tempo from slowest to fastest.

*andante* *presto* *adagio* *allegro* *moderato*

What Do You Hear? 2

CD 4-23

Listen to these instrumental excerpts. Identify the instrument or instruments you hear.

| | | |
|---|---|---|
| 1. brass | strings | woodwinds |
| 2. brass | percussion | woodwinds |
| 3. flute | oboe | clarinet |
| 4. French horn | trumpet | trombone |
| 5. clarinet | saxophone | bassoon |
| 6. trumpet | trombone | tuba |

What You Can Do

**Move with Rhythm**

Sing "Somebody's Knockin' at Your Door," on page 53, and perform a four-beat body percussion ostinato as you sing.

Sing *"Riquirrán,"* on page 66, while performing small steady-beat movements during the verse.

**Play the Notes**

Play this recorder part with the recording of *"Riquirrán."* Play once through silently in chin position and then play aloud.

**Move to Show Form**

Listen to "River," on page 58, and create a movement for the A section and a different movement for the B section. Then perform the movements as you sing the song.

82 · Unit 2 83

Grade 4

me ______ Class ______

SSESSMENT 2: UNIT 2 (CONTINUED)

Review, Assess, Perform, Create

What Do You Know?

Look at the notation for "Joe Turner Blues" on page 56. Find the time signature. How many beats are in each measure? ______

Name the title of a song in Unit 2 that has:

a. Three beats in each measure: ______

b. Two beats in each measure: ______

Reorder these musical terms for tempo from slowest to fastest. Use 1 for the slowest tempo and 5 for the fastest tempo.

___ *andante* ___ *presto* ___ *adagio* ___ *allegro* ___ *moderato*

What Do You Hear? 2 Identifying Timbre

ten to these instrumental excerpts. Identify the instrument or instruments you hear. cle your answers.

| | | |
|---|---|---|
| brass | strings | woodwinds |
| brass | percussion | woodwinds |
| flute | oboe | clarinet |
| French horn | trumpet | trombone |
| clarinet | saxophone | bassoon |
| trumpet | trombone | tuba |

de 4, Teacher Edition, page 82 · B-7

ASSESSMENT

Grade 4

## Review, Assess, Perform, Create

Measure your students' progress across lessons with unit assessments (Units 1–6) that focus on core instruction. Reproducible masters are also available.

this rhythm pattern in the song.

Chi - ru - li - ru - li

Rhythm syllables are used to name specific rhythmic units.

Using **rhythm syllables, say** the pattern. What other patterns can you find in the song?

Show What You Know!

These rhythm patterns are from songs you know. First **clap** or **pat** each pattern. Then name the song.

**Create** your own rhythm pattern using ♩, ♫, and 𝄽.

**Clap** or **pat** your pattern. **Play** it on an instrument.

Unit 1 17

Grade 2

**3 CLOSE**

Skill: LISTENING · ASSESSMENT

**Music Journal Writing** Play the recording of *Hoedown* **CD 14-22** as students follow the listening map on p. 313. Challenge students to identify the music symbols referring to dynamics. Explain the term *tutti* (all), the coda symbol, the repeat signs (The A section is heard two-and-one-half times, with additional internal repeats), the false ending, the sign at the end of row 5 to return to the A section, and the sign to go to the coda at the end of that A section. Note that the graphics do not always indicate each note, but suggest the melodic contour at the beginning of a timbre change. The timings may be helpful in following the progress of the map as the recording plays, on the first listening.

## Show What You Know!

Assessments take place midway through each unit (Units 1–6) to gauge your students' melodic and rhythmic skills. Reproducible masters are also available.

## End-of-Lesson Assessment

Every lesson is designed to assess your students' understanding of a critical music element, skill, or connection.

# National Standards Correlation for easy planning

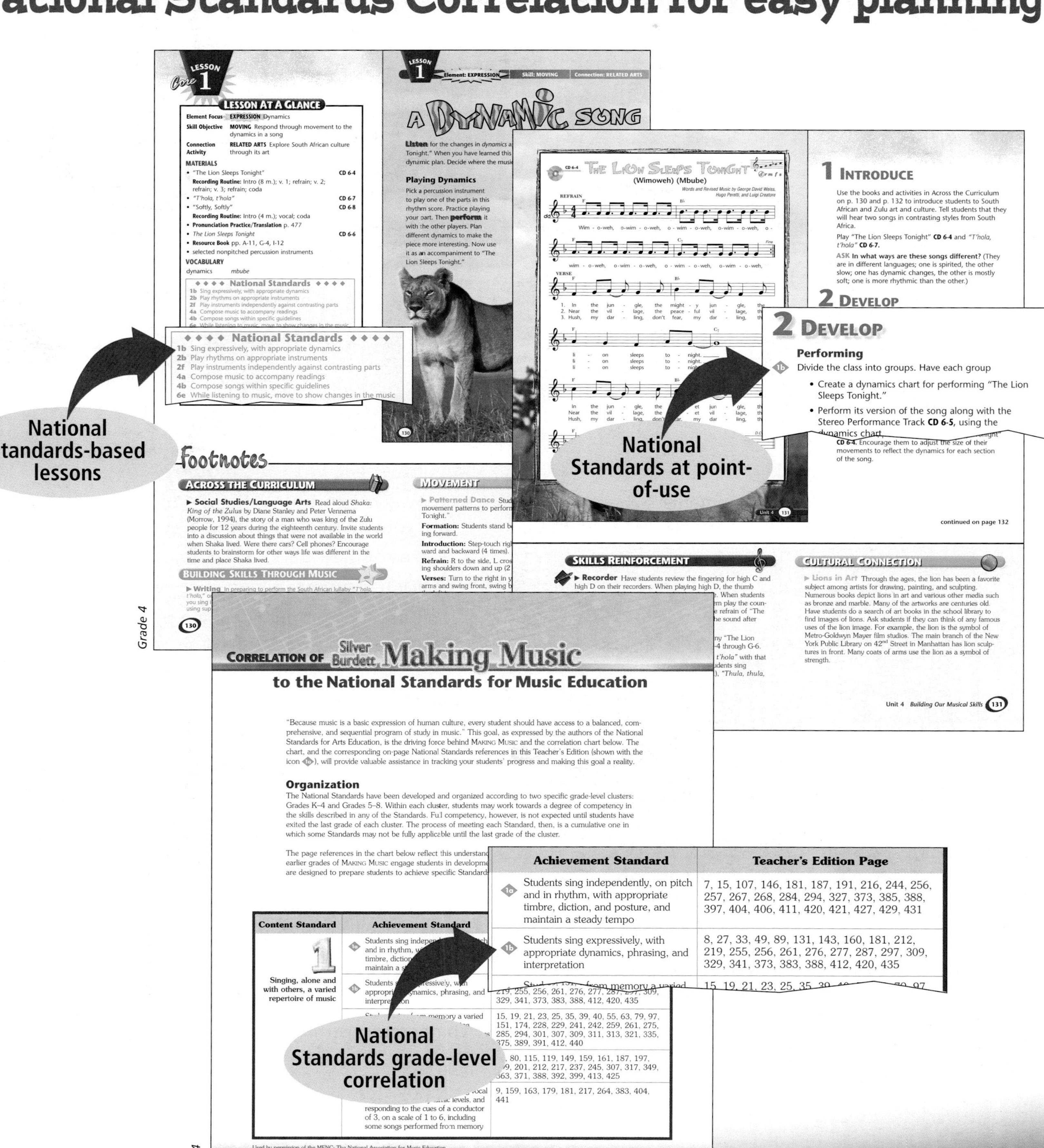

# Media and Technology

## Dynamic tools to motivate and engage students

**MAKING MUSIC DVD**

- Instructional video segments
- Signing activities
- Dances

**MAKING MUSIC with Technology**

- Innovative lessons to integrate technology into your music curriculum
- Dozens of MIDI tracks at each grade level

  MIDI tracks for teaching music elements

  MIDI tracks for music reading practice

  MIDI tracks for choral units (4–6)

**Music Magic Video Library**

- Versatile collection of 25 videos on topics ranging from melody and rhythm to keyboards, dancing, and music for special occasions
- Interviews with world-leading musicians, composers, instrument makers, and dancers

# An online work center that revolutionizes teaching

### Online Lesson Planner and Teacher's Edition

Scott Foresman SuccessNet is a next-generation work center for Silver Burdett MAKING MUSIC teachers. It's a place where teachers can go to plan their lessons, streamline their work, and access standards-based instruction.

- Access instructional notes
- Create custom lesson plans
- Schedule lessons
- Organize resources
- Block out holidays
- Assign dates and times
- Save/edit lessons from year to year
- Print day, week, or monthly views

### Online Resources for Teachers and Students

**Take It to the NET** at *www.sfsuccessnet.com* provides access to an entire collection of music resources.

- Theme musicals
- Grades K–8 index of all songs, listening selections, and more
- Standards-based practice
- Music reference articles
- Adaptations for meeting individual needs
- Rubrics—plus more!

## Register Today!

**To access Take It to the NET, follow three simple steps.**

1 Go to *www.sfsuccessnet.com*

2 Click on the link to register

3 Enter the code **MakingMusic** (no spaces)

**Note:** You must register your students for **Take It to the NET** to access music reference articles.

T27a

Contents

Contents

T27b

## Contents

# Steps to Making Music



= Core Lesson
= Music Reading Lesson

## Unit 3 Learning the Language of Music



## Unit 4 Building Our Musical Skills



= **Core Lesson**

= **Musc Reading Lesson**

## Unit 5 Discovering New Musical Horizons



## Unit 6 Making Music Our Own



= Core Lesson
= Music Reading Lesson

# Paths to Making Music

## Unit 7 Going Places U.S.A.



## Unit 8 Bring Your Passport

## Unit 9 Chasing a Dream



## Unit 10 Earth, Sea, and Sky



## Unit 11 Sing Out!

## Unit 12 Sing and Celebrate



# Music Resources and Indexes

### Student Resources



### Teacher Resources



**Helps for the Teacher**



### Planning and Reference Tools



### Indexes

T33a

Steps to Making Music

Elements and Skills

STEPS TO
Making
Music
1

| Lesson | Elements | Skills |
|---|---|---|

## LESSON 1

CORE
**Expression in Your Music**
pp. 6–9

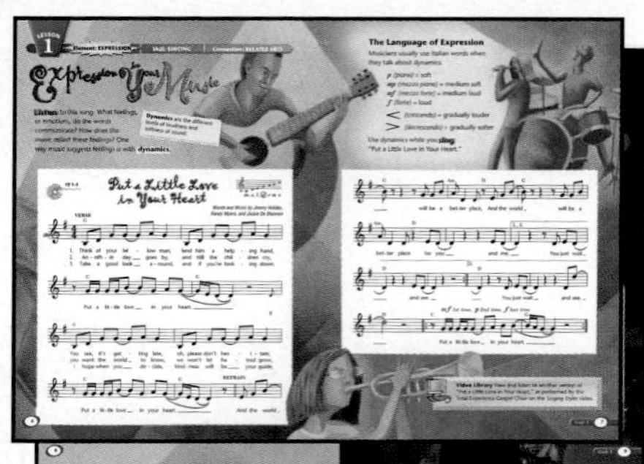

**Element:** Expression
**Concept:** Dynamics
**Focus:** Dynamics

**Secondary Element**
Texture: echo singing

**National Standards:** 1a 1b 1e 6c

**Skill:** Singing
**Objective:** Sing using dynamics

**Secondary Skills**
- **Listening** Identify dynamic levels and changes
- **Reading** Identify various dynamic levels while following the text
- **Listening** Identify differences between songs
- **Creating** Create dynamic plans for a song

**SKILLS REINFORCEMENT**
- **Vocal Development** Practice good posture by focusing on different parts of the body
- **Performing** Perform dynamics using ostinatos
- **Keyboard** Work through keyboard reading exercises

## LESSON 2

**On the Road to Rhythm**
pp. 10–11

Reading Sequence 1, p. 442

**Element:** Rhythm
**Concept:** Duration
**Focus:** 

**Secondary Element**
Form: A B

**National Standards:** 5a 6b 6e 9a

**Skill:** Reading
**Objective:** Read 

**Secondary Skills**
- **Listening** Identify steady beat by ear
- **Performing** Conduct a four-beat pattern

**SKILLS REINFORCEMENT**
- **Listening/Creating** Compare two songs and create new verses
- **Mallets** Play an Orff accompaniment

## LESSON 3

CORE
**Working with Rhythm**
pp. 12–13

**Element:** Rhythm
**Concept:** Beat
**Focus:** Strong and weak beats

**Secondary Element**
Form: call and response

**National Standards:** 2a 6b 6e

**Skill:** Moving
**Objective:** Move to show strong and weak beats

**Secondary Skills**
- **Singing** Sing a song and pat the steady beat

**SKILLS REINFORCEMENT**
- **Performing** Perform STRONG-weak and STRONG-weak-weak patterns
- **Keyboard** Practice a five-line reading and fingering activity

## Connections

## Music and Other Literature



**Connection:** Related Arts
**Activity:** Create a cooperative quilt

**ACROSS THE CURRICULUM** **Art** Read a book and create quilt squares reflecting interests

**SPOTLIGHT ON**
**Mahalia Jackson** Facts about the gospel singer
**Tony Bennett** Facts about the popular singer

**TEACHER TO TEACHER** **Teaching Values** Reinforce positive human values

**MEETING INDIVIDUAL NEEDS**
**Gifted and Talented** Create new verses for a song
**Including Everyone** Perform acts of kindness

**BUILDING SKILLS THROUGH MUSIC** **Language** Determine the use of the word "dynamic"

**Song** "Put a Little Love in Your Heart"

**Listening Selections**
*Put a Little Love in Your Heart*
*The Beat of My Heart*

**M*U*S*I*C M*A*K*E*R*S**
Tony Bennett

**More Music Choices**
"Love Can Build a Bridge," p. 324
*"La copa de la vida,"* p. 414
"The Lion Sleeps Tonight," p. 131

**ASSESSMENT**
**Performance/Observation**
Sing using the dynamic inflection to express meaning of the words

**TECHNOLOGY/MEDIA LINK**
**Video Library** Watch a video featuring a variety of singing styles

---

**Connection:** Social Studies
**Activity:** Compare an Appalachian and a British folk song

**SPOTLIGHT ON** **Jean Ritchie** Facts about the folk song colllector and writer

**TEACHER TO TEACHER** **Program Performance** Create a staged presentation of songs

**SCHOOL TO HOME CONNECTION** **Memories** Ask students to find someone who has personal stories about a soldier

**BUILDING SKILLS THROUGH MUSIC** **Writing** Write paragraphs explaining a story and classroom discussion

**Song** "Soldier, Soldier"

**Listening Selection** *Lazy John*

**More Music Choices**
"Cotton Eye-Joe," p. 288

**ASSESSMENT**
**Performance/Observation**
Read rhythms in a song and perform a counterrhythm

**TECHNOLOGY/MEDIA LINK**
**Notation Software**
Compose rhythm patterns

---

**Connection:** Social Studies
**Activity:** Discuss the origins of work songs

**ACROSS THE CURRICULUM** **Language Arts** Read and discuss a poem

**SPOTLIGHT ON** **Haul Away, Joe** Facts about the song

**CHARACTER EDUCATION** **Responsibility** Discuss students' various responsibilities

**BUILDING SKILLS THROUGH MUSIC** **Language** Summarize lyrics of a song in as few words as possible

**Song** "Haul Away, Joe"

**Poem** "Until I Saw the Sea"

**More Music Choices**
"Old House, Tear It Down!," p. 178
"Blow, Ye Winds," p. 255
"Big Rock Candy Mountain" p. 330

**ASSESSMENT**
**Performance/Observation**
Sing while showing strong and weak beat movements

**TECHNOLOGY/MEDIA LINK**
**Web Site** Research shanties and other work songs

| Lesson | Elements | Skills |
|---|---|---|

## Dancing in Duple Meter

pp. 14–17

Reading Sequence 2, p. 442

**Element:** **Rhythm**
**Concept:** Meter
**Focus:** Duple Meter $\frac{2}{4}$

**Secondary Element**
Timbre: orchestral instruments

**National Standards:**

**Skill:** **Moving**
**Objective:** Move to show strong and weak beats in duple meter

**Secondary Skills**
- **Playing** Play percussion instruments to show strong and weak beats
- **Listening** Identify tempo, mood, instruments, themes, and melody, and create duple meter movements

**SKILLS REINFORCEMENT**
- **Singing** Demonstrate elements of good singing posture while sitting
- **Listening** Create movements for a listening selection

---

LESSON 5

CORE

## I Sing, You Sing

pp. 18–19

**Element:** **Form**
**Concept:** Form
**Focus:** Call and response

**Secondary Element**
Texture/Harmony: layers of sounds

**National Standards:**

**Skill:** **Singing**
**Objective:** Sing a call-and-response song

**Secondary Skills**
- **Improvising** Improvise two-bar calls while others perform responses

**SKILLS REINFORCEMENT**
- **Keyboard** Learn to play the chorus parts
- **Recorder** Play a one-note accompaniment

---

## Making a Melody

pp. 20–23

Reading Sequence 3, p. 443

**Element:** **Melody**
**Concept:** Pitch and direction
**Focus:** Skips, steps, and repeated pitches

**Secondary Element**
Form: A B

**National Standards:**

**Skill:** **Reading**
**Objective:** Identify skips, steps, and repeated pitches in melodic notation

**Secondary Skills**
- **Singing** Sing a song as a dialogue

**SKILLS REINFORCEMENT**
- **Creating** Create and sing new words to a song
- **Recorder** Play along with a song in the Resource Book
- **Singing** Sing a pentatonic scale to practice vocal development

| Connections | Music and Other Literature | |
|---|---|---|
| **Connection:** Social Studies<br>**Activity:** Discuss the geography of Armenia<br>ACROSS THE CURRICULUM<br>**Social Studies** Learn a brief history of Armenia<br>**Social Studies** Discuss with students the boundaries of countries<br>TEACHER TO TEACHER<br>**Teaching Non-English Language Songs** Listen to an Armenian sing a song<br>**Listening Maps** Follow listening maps to enhance listening skills<br>MEETING INDIVIDUAL NEEDS **Pairing Students** Strategies for including students with disabilities<br>BUILDING SKILLS THROUGH MUSIC **Math** Use division to determine the number of measures in a song | **Song** *"Gakavik"* ("The Partridge")<br>**Listening Selection** "Galop" from *Masquerade Suite* (excerpt)<br>M*U*S*I*C M*A*K*E*R*S<br>Aram Khachaturian<br>**Listening Map** *Galop*<br>**More Music Choices**<br>"The Glendy Burke," p. 262<br>*"Beriozka,"* p. 294<br>*"Ai Dunaii moy,"* p. 293<br>*"Minka,"* p. 222 | ASSESSMENT<br>**Performance/Self Assesement** Perform alternating movements to show strong and weak beats in duple meter<br>**Show What You Know!** Mid-unit assessment<br>TECHNOLOGY/MEDIA LINK<br>**Sequencing Software** Create phrases with the C-pentatonic scale<br>**Transparency** Use a transparency to aid tracking |
| **Connection:** Related Arts<br>**Activity:** Learn the "limbo"<br>TEACHER TO TEACHER **Reluctant Singers** Develop strategies for encouraging reluctant singers<br>MOVEMENT **Patterned Dance** Learn the "limbo"<br>BUILDING SKILLS THROUGH MUSIC **Reading** Look up "limber" in the dictionary and connect its meaning to "limbo" | **Song** "Limbo Like Me"<br>**Listening Selection** *Brisad del Zulia* (excerpt)<br>**More Music Choices**<br>"Wings of a Dove," p. 318<br>"All Night, All Day, " p. 180 | ASSESSMENT<br>**Performance/Observation** Sing responses while teachers sings the calls<br>TECHNOLOGY/MEDIA LINK<br>**CD-ROM** Use *Band-in-a-Box* to change instrument combination in the song |
| **Connection:** Social Studies<br>**Activity:** Discuss the meaning of spirituals<br>ACROSS THE CURRICULUM<br>**Social Studies** Read a book about freedom<br>**Social Studies** Relate the lyrics of a song to information on prairie land<br>CULTURAL CONNECTION **Spirituals** African Americans and the Underground Railroad<br>TEACHER TO TEACHER **Comparison Chart** Use a chart to practice developing thinking skills<br>MEETING INDIVIDUAL NEEDS **Body/Kinesthetic** Create movements to illustrate melodic contour<br>BUILDING SKILLS THROUGH MUSIC **Language** Identify examples of dialect, slang, and contractions and discuss how formal grammar changes the character of the words | **Songs**<br>"Gonna Ride Up in the Chariot"<br>"Deep in the Heart of Texas"<br>**Listening Selection** *"Air" in D*<br>**Listening Map** *"Air" in D*<br>**More Music Choices**<br>"Little David, Play on Your Harp," p. 394<br>"Pastures of Plenty," p. 280<br>*"Tengo, tengo, tengo,"* p. 228 | ASSESSMENT<br>**Performance/Observation** Sing a song and point to repeated pitches, steps, and skips<br>TECHNOLOGY/MEDIA LINK<br>**MIDI/Sequencing Software** Change pitch intervals in a song and hear the changes<br>**Transparency** Use a transparency to aid tracking melodic contour |

| Lesson | Elements | Skills | |
|---|---|---|---|
| LESSON 7 CORE **Pentatonic Patterns** pp. 24–25 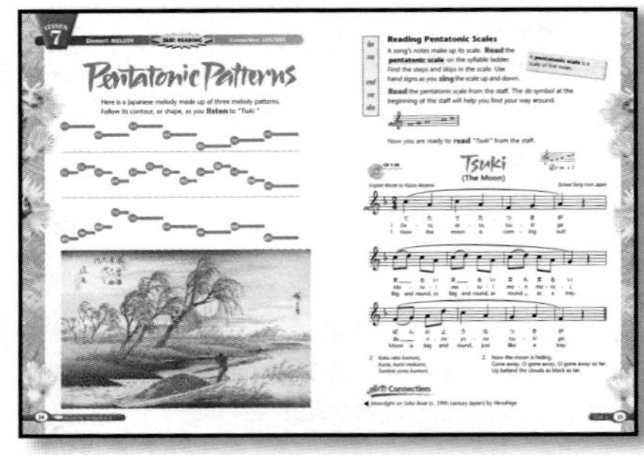 Reading Sequence 4, p. 443 | **Element: Melody**<br>**Concept:** Pattern<br>**Focus:** Pentatonic scale<br><br>**Secondary Element**<br>Rhythm: ♩ ♫ ♩ 𝄽<br><br>**National Standards:** 1c 3b 4b 5b | **Skill: Reading**<br>**Objective:** Read a *do-re-mi-so-la* melody from notation<br><br>**Secondary Skills**<br>• **Listening** Identify pitch syllables and hand signs while singing along with accompaniment<br>• **Analyzing** Place pitch syllables on the staff | **SKILLS REINFORCEMENT**<br>• **Reading** Review pitch syllables and hand signs |
| LESSON 8 **Tonal Center** pp. 26–29 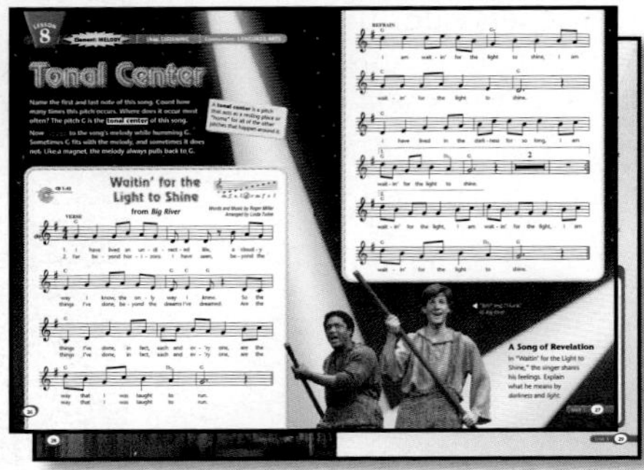 | **Element: Melody**<br>**Concept:** Tonality<br>**Focus:** Tonal center<br><br>**Secondary Element**<br>Form: A B<br><br>**National Standards:**  1b 2b 6b 6e | **Skill: Listening**<br>**Objective:** Identify the tonal center in listening examples<br><br>**Secondary Skills**<br>• **Singing** Sing and maintain the tonal center | **SKILLS REINFORCEMENT**<br>• **Listening** Identify tonal center with on the spot checks<br>• **Recorder** Play during the verse of the song |
| LESSON 9 CORE **Many Voices** pp. 30–33  | **Element: Timbre**<br>**Concept:** Vocal<br>**Focus:** Vocal timbres<br><br>**Secondary Element**<br>Rhythm: upbeat<br><br>**National Standards:** 1b 6b 6c 6d 9a | **Skill: Listening**<br>**Objective:** Identify and describe different vocal timbres<br><br>**Secondary Skills**<br>• **Singing** Sing with a vocal timbre appropriate to a young singer | **SKILLS REINFORCEMENT**<br>• **Keyboard** Identify tonal center with on the spot checks<br>• **Recorder** Play a two-note accompaniment |

## Connections

## Music and Other Literature



**Connection:** Culture
**Activity:** Discuss and create Japanese style art

CULTURAL CONNECTION **Art** Make Japanese lacquerware plates
SPOTLIGHT ON **Japanese Language** New words in Japanese
BUILDING SKILLS THROUGH MUSIC **Writing** Write new lyrics that describe a rising sun

**Song** *"Tsuki"* ("The Moon")

**Arts Connection**
*Moonlight on Sebu River*

**More Music Choices**
"Weevily Wheat," p. 105

ASSESSMENT
**Performance/Observation** Sing using hand signs, pitch syllables, and song text

TECHNOLOGY/MEDIA LINK
**Notation Software** Create a song using rhythms and notes from *"Tsuki"*

---

**Connection:** Language Arts
**Activity**: Relate a musical with the book on which it was based

ACROSS THE CURRICULUM
**Language Arts** History of the novel *The Adventures of Huckleberry Finn*
**Language Arts** Discuss hopes and dreams; make construction paper cut-outs of items that create light

SPOTLIGHT ON **Broadway Musicals** Historical and cultural facts
TEACHER TO TEACHER **Guest Performers** Invite guest performers to the class
MEETING INDIVIDUAL NEEDS **Gifted and Talented** Students produce their own Broadway musical
BUILDING SKILLS THROUGH MUSIC **Writing** Write a paragraph and summarize the narrative of a song

**Song** "Waitin' for the Light to Shine"

M*U*S*I*C M*A*K*E*R*S
Roger Miller
Linda Twine

**More Music Choices**
*"Einini,"* p. 391
"Love Will Guide Us," p. 328

ASSESSMENT
**Observation** Identify the tonal center in various recordings
**Show What You Know!** Mid-unit assessment

TECHNOLOGY/MEDIA LINK
**Web Site** Go to Web site for information on *Big River*
**Multimedia** Use a slide show program to develop scenery and lighting

---

**Connection:** Culture
**Activity:** Discuss differences in culture that contribute to different vocal styles

ACROSS THE CURRICULUM **Language Arts** Modify vocal quality while reading a poem
CULTURAL CONNECTION **Zulu** Geographical and cultural facts of the Zulu people
SPOTLIGHT ON **Throat Singers of Tuva** Description of throat singing and the country of Tuva
TEACHER TO TEACHER
**Practice Listening** Identify timbres of instruments
**Developing Interest in Singing** Make a list of styles of vocal music
BUILDING SKILLS THROUGH MUSIC **Social Studies** Locate countries on a map

**Song** "I'm Gonna Sing"

**Listening Selections**
*Ghel moma* (excerpt)
*Sigit "Alash"* (excerpt)
*I Don't Want to Feel Like That* (excerpt)
*Powwow Song* (excerpt)
"Nahandove" from *Chansons madecasses* (excerpt)
*Rain, Rain, Beautiful Rain* (excerpt)

**Poem** "Hurt No Living Thing"

**More Music Choices**
"Love Can Build a Bridge," p. 324
*Route 66,* p. 279
*Dúlamán,* p. 299

ASSESSMENT
**Observation/Music Journal Writing** Listen to and identify examples of vocal styles

TECHNOLOGY/MEDIA LINK
**Video Library** Describe singing style of performers

| Lesson | Elements | Skills | |
|---|---|---|---|
|  LESSON 10<br>**Layered Sounds ...Cha Cha Cha**<br>pp. 34–35<br> | **Element: Texture/Harmony**<br>**Concept:** Texture<br>**Focus:** Multi-layered ostinatos<br><br>**Secondary Element**<br>Rhythm: ♩, ♫ ♩, 𝄽<br><br>**National Standards:**<br>1c 2b 2f 9b | **Skill: Playing**<br>**Objective:** Play an ostinato accompaniment with a recorded song<br><br>**Secondary Skills**<br>• **Listening** Listen to Latin American percussion instruments | **SKILLS REINFORCEMENT**<br>• **Creating** Create simple ostinato patterns to play with the song<br>• **Moving** Learn a patterned dance |
| LESSON 11<br>CORE<br>**How's the Texture?**<br>pp. 36–37<br> | **Element: Texture/Harmony**<br>**Concept:** Texture<br>**Focus:** Multi-layered ostinato accompaniment<br><br>**Secondary Element**<br>Rhythm: ♪ ♩ ♪<br><br>**National Standards:**<br>2b 2f 5a 6d | **Skill: Playing**<br>**Objective:** Play an ostinato accompaniment<br><br>**Secondary Skills**<br>• **Listening** Listen to aboriginal musicians play the *didgeridoo* | **SKILLS REINFORCEMENT**<br>• **Guitar** Create simple ostinato patterns to play with the song<br>• **Recorder** Play two-note ostinatos |
| LESSON 12<br>**Power in Numbers—Layers of Sound**<br>pp. 38–41<br> | **Element: Texture/Harmony**<br>**Concept:** Texture<br>**Focus:** Layers of sounds<br><br>**Secondary Element**<br>Form: call and response<br><br>**National Standards:**<br>1c 3b 3d 6e | **Skill: Singing**<br>**Objective:** Sing a call-and-response song with layers of voices<br><br>**Secondary Skills**<br>• **Listening** Develop motions to a song and identify form<br>• **Moving** Create stepping and arm motions<br>• **Playing/Singing** Play the rhythm of the words on D or A<br>• **Listening** Describe steel drum recordings | **SKILLS REINFORCEMENT**<br>• **Creating** Create ostinatos on nonpitched percussion instruments |

| Connections | Music and Other Literature | |
|---|---|---|
| **Connection: Style**<br>**Activity:** Discuss Afro-Cuban musical style<br>CULTURAL CONNECTION *Son Montuno Style* Background information on the style<br>SPOTLIGHT ON **The Performer** Poncho Sanchez<br>BUILDING SKILLS THROUGH MUSIC **Writing** Write a paragraph describing timbre of instruments | **Song** *"Sonando"*<br>**Listening Selection** *A Night in Tunisia*<br>**More Music Choices**<br>"Streets of Laredo," p. 272 | ASSESSMENT<br>**Performance/Observation** Perform ostinato rhythms using body percussion and percussion instruments<br>TECHNOLOGY/MEDIA LINK<br>**MIDI/Sequencing Software** Perform rhythms with percussion track on sequencer |
| **Connection: Culture**<br>**Activity:** Discuss the sound and construction of an Australian musical instrument<br>CULTURAL CONNECTION **Didgeridoo** Facts about the instrument<br>MEETING INDIVIDUAL NEEDS **Including Everyone** Peform ostinatos in groups<br>BUILDING SKILLS THROUGH MUSIC **Social Studies** Discuss animals and musical instruments native to Australia | **Song** "Tie Me Kangaroo Down, Sport"<br>**Listening Selection** *Brolga One*<br>**More Music Choices**<br>"Canoe Song," p. 76 | ASSESSMENT<br>**Performance/Observation** Perform ostinato rhythm accompaniments<br>TECHNOLOGY/MEDIA LINK<br>**MIDI/Sequencing Software** Create rhythmic texture using sequencer and the percussion track |
| **Connection: Social Studies**<br>**Activity:** Discuss the origins of steel drums<br>ACROSS THE CURRICULUM<br>**Social Studies** Explore the geography of the Caribbean Sea<br>**Social Studies** Discuss working for pay and slavery<br>**Math** Discuss the math-based story of Rani<br>CULTURAL CONNECTION **The Georgia Sea Islands** Cultural background during time of slavery<br>MOVEMENT **Nonlocomotor Movement** Use body percussion to demonstrate thicker and thinner textures<br>SPOTLIGHT ON **Work Songs**<br>MEETING INDIVIDUAL NEEDS **Solo and Group Singing** improvise calls and responses<br>CHARACTER EDUCATION **Respect** Develop respect for differences among people<br>BUILDING SKILLS THROUGH MUSIC **Reading** Read the feature on the steel drum band | **Song** "Pay Me My Money Down"<br>**Listening Selections**<br>*Pay Me My Money Down* (excerpt)<br>*Eine kleine Nachtmusik* (excerpt)<br>*Somebody* (excerpt)<br>M*U*S*I*C M*A*K*E*R*S<br>Amoco Renegades<br>**More Music Choices**<br>"Love Will Guide Us," p. 328<br>"Pastures of Plenty," p. 280 | ASSESSMENT<br>**Performance/Observation** Sing the cal and responses in the song to create layers of voices<br>TECHNOLOGY/MEDIA LINK<br>**Electronic Keyboard** Create percussion ensembles using electronic keyboards |

# Introducing the Unit

Unit 1 presents the first step in a sequenced approach to understanding music elements. Music skills—Reading, Performing, Creating, Listening, Moving—are the means by which students gain an understanding of these concepts. Presented on p. 3 is a brief overview of the skills that are assessed in this unit. (See below and pp. 4–5 for unit highlights of related curricular experiences.)

For a more detailed unit overview, see Unit at a Glance, pp. 1a–1h.

# Unit Project

Ask students to think about situations in which the phrase "Let the music begin!" might be used—perhaps a processional or ceremony for which music is the official beginning. But in what other situations do we expect music to begin in order for the event to be "right" or "successful"? Allow for sharing of responses (dances, sports events, sometimes the beginning of the school day, background music for special occasions, and so on). Help students realize that on many occasions in our lives, both special and everyday, we expect music to begin and to be part of the event.

Invite students in small groups to look briefly at the lessons in this unit (one lesson to a group); they should ask themselves the question, "What is the situation here in which music plays a part?" Allow time for them to report their findings. These discussions could serve as background for developing a bulletin board display of events/situations in which music plays an important part. Encourage students to bring photos from home—graduations, weddings, recitals, and so on—that connect the topic more closely with themselves as individuals.

**Sounds Surround**

Your journey with music is like a circle—it has no end. Step into the circle and **sing** "Turn the Beat Around."

As you sing, pass the beat around. **Clap** one beat, in turn, around the circle. **Create** different ways to pass the beat around.

CD 1-1
Turn the Beat Around
r, m, s, l t, d r m a m
Words and Music by
Peter Jackson, Jr. and Gerald Jackson
3 times
do
B7 sus4
Turn it up, turn it up, turn it up-side down.
Em D C D Em
Turn the beat _ a - round. _ Love to hear _ per - cus - sion.
Em D C D Em
Turn it up - side down. _ Love to hear _ per - cus - sion.
2

## Across the Curriculum

**Unit Highlights** The following interdisciplinary activities in this unit are related to the music elements presented in the lessons. See Unit at a Glance, pp. 1a–1h, for topical descriptions presented according to lesson sequence.

▶ **ART/RELATED ARTS**

- Create a "quilt" display to illustrate the message of a song (p. 7)

▶ **LANGUAGE ARTS**

- Read and discuss a poem about the sea (p. 13)
- Discuss the social impact of *The Adventures of Huckleberry Finn* (p. 27)
- Articulate and illustrate individual hopes and dreams (p. 28)
- Use a poem to illustrate vocal timbre (p. 32)

▶ **MATHEMATICS**

- Use a math-based story to illustrate monetary compensation (p. 40)

▶ **SOCIAL STUDIES**

- Discuss the location and history of Armenia (p. 14)
- Discuss the current and changing boundaries of various countries of the world (p. 17)
- Read about and discuss historical concepts of freedom (p. 21)
- Identify the characteristics and importance of prairie land (p. 22)
- Discuss the geography and culture of the Caribbean (p. 39)
- Discuss the concept of work-for-pay (p. 40)

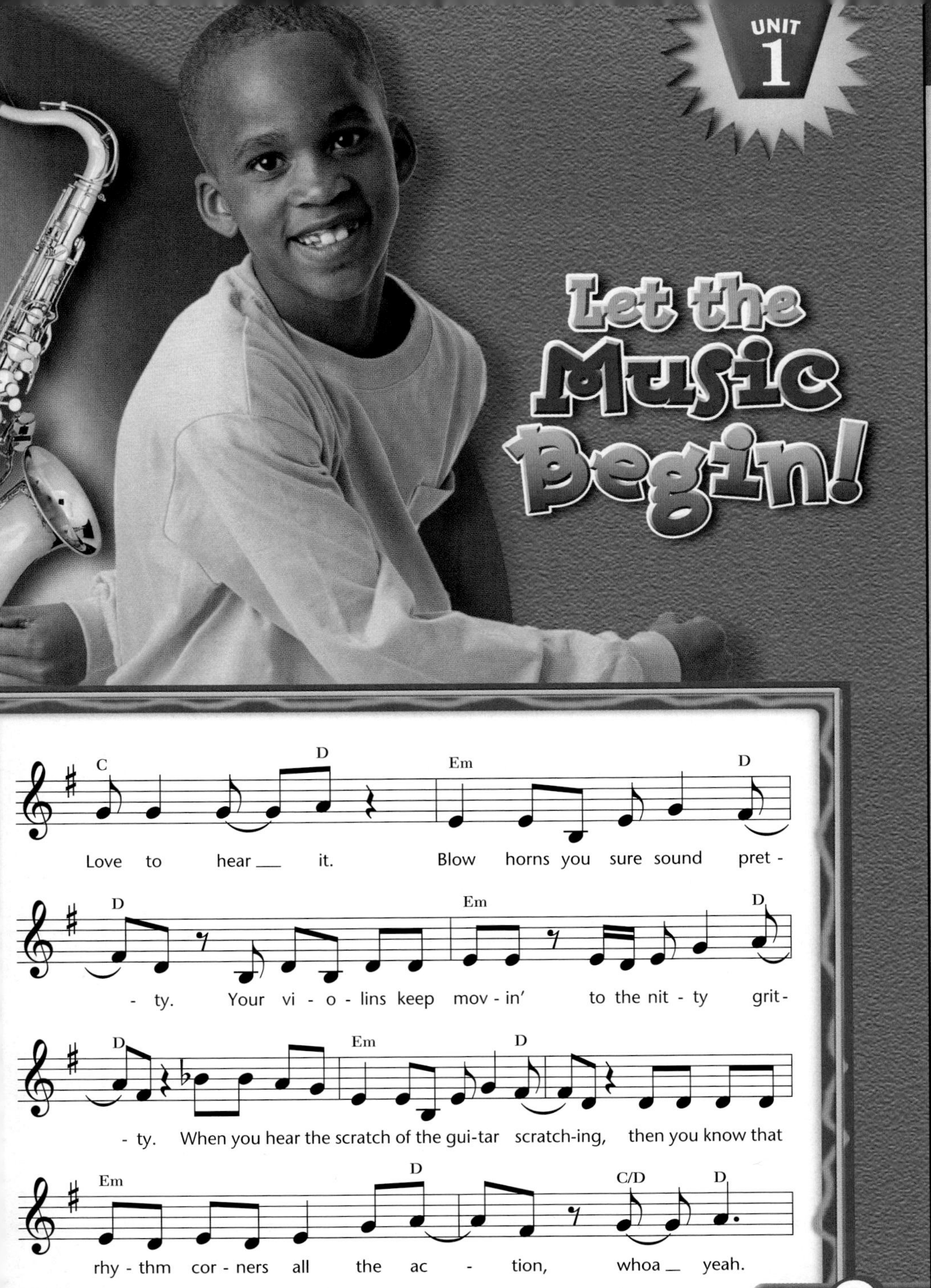
UNIT 1
Let the Music Begin!
C D Em D
Love to hear__ it. Blow horns you sure sound pret -
D Em D
- ty. Your vi - o - lins keep mov - in' to the nit - ty grit-
D Em D
- ty. When you hear the scratch of the gui-tar scratch-ing, then you know that
Em D C/D D
rhy - thm cor - ners all the ac - tion, whoa__ yeah.
Unit 1 3

# MUSIC SKILLS ASSESSED IN THIS UNIT

**Reading Music: Rhythm**

- Read patterns containing quarter, eighth, half, dotted-half, and whole notes (p. 11)
- Read rhythm ostinatos in meter in 4 (pp. 35, 37)

**Reading Music: Pitch**

- Identify skips, steps, and repeated pitches in a melody (p. 23)
- Read a pentatonic melody (p. 25)

**Performing Music: Singing**

- Sing "Put a Little Love in Your Heart" using dynamics (p. 9)
- Sing "Haul Away, Joe," accompanied by steady beat movements (p. 13)
- Sing "Limbo Like Me" (p. 19) and "Pay Me My Money Down" (p. 41) in call-and-response style
- Sing *"Tsuki"* using hand signs and pitch syllables (p. 25)

**Moving to Music**

- Move to show strong and weak beats (pp. 13, 17)

**Performing Music: Playing**

- Play ostinatos on rhythm instruments to accompany *"Sonando"* (p. 35) and "Tie Me Kangaroo Down, Sport" (p. 37)

**Creating Music**

- Create ostinatos to accompany *"Sonando"* (p. 35)

**Listening to Music**

- Identify the tonal center in selected listening examples (p. 27)
- Identify and describe different vocal timbres (p. 33)

## CULTURAL CONNECTION

**Unit Highlights** The musical literature in this unit provides many opportunities for students to explore a variety of world cultures. See Unit at a Glance, pp. 1a–1h, for topical descriptions presented according to lesson sequence.

▶ AFRICAN/AFRICAN AMERICAN

- "Gonna Ride Up in the Chariot": Discuss the connection of spirituals to slavery and the Underground Railroad (p. 20)
- Discuss Zulu customs and singing traditions (p. 30)
- "I'm Gonna Sing" (p. 33)
- Explore the history of the Georgia Sea Islands (p. 38)

▶ AMERICAN

- "Deep in the Heart of Texas" (p. 22)

▶ ASIAN; AUSTRALIAN

- *"Tsuki"*: Explore lacquerware, an ancient Japanese art (p. 25)
- *"Gakavik"* (p. 14)
- Discuss vocal techniques of Tuva singers (p. 31)
- Discuss construction and tone production of the *didgeridoo* (p. 37)

▶ CARIBBEAN

- "Limbo Like Me"; *Brisad del Zulia* (p. 18)
- *"Sonando"*: Discuss Cuban *son montuno* style (p. 34)
- *A Night in Tunisia* (p. 35)
- *Somebody* (steel drum band) (p. 41)

▶ EUROPEAN

- "Haul Away, Joe" (England) (p. 13)
- *Ghel moma* (Bulgaria) (p. 31)

# Opening Activities

**MATERIALS**

- "Turn the Beat Around" **CD 1-1**

  **Recording Routine:**
  Intro (9 m.); vocal; coda
- recorders, keyboard or mallet instruments

## Moving

Play the opening of "Turn the Beat Around" **CD 1-1** and ask students to

- Join you in clapping the beat to establish the tempo and flavor.
- Create an eight-beat body percussion pattern that can easily be reversed. (For example: Snap-snap-clap-clap-pat-pat-stamp-stamp)

Once everyone has a pattern, have students

- Look through the song lyrics to see where the words *turn the beat around* occur. (This is where the patterns will be reversed.)
- Notice where the text concerns instruments (horns, violins, guitar).
- Bounce in place and mime the instrument to the beat. (*Note:* Students are already performing body percussion on *love to hear percussion.*)

Have students perform the routine above while listening to **CD 1-1.** Since there are some quick changes, they will likely need to do this several times in order to develop the needed coordination.

## Playing

Invite students to play phrases using G, A, and B on their recorders. Write these letters on the board. Point to them as they pass by in the recording while students finger them on their recorders. After practicing, invite students to play along.

## Assessment

**Unit Highlights** This unit includes a variety of strategies and methods, described below, to track students' progress and assess their understanding of lesson objectives. Reproducible masters for Show What You Know! and Review, Assess, Perform, Create can be found in the Resource Book.

### ▶ FORMAL ASSESSMENTS

The following assessments, using written language, cognitive, and performance skills, help teachers and students conceptualize the learning that is taking place.

- **Show What You Know!** Element-specific assessments, on the student page, for Rhythm (p. 17) and Melody (p. 29).
- **Review, Assess, Perform, Create** This end-of-unit activity (pp. 42–43) can be used for review and to assess students' learning of the core lessons in this unit.

### ▶ INFORMAL ASSESSMENTS

At the close of each Teacher's Edition lesson in this unit, one of the following types of assessments is used to evaluate the learning of the key element focus or skill objective.

- Observation (p. 29)
- Observation/Music Journal Writing (p. 33)
- Performance/Observation (pp. 9, 11, 13, 19, 23, 25, 35, 37)
- Performance/Interviews (p. 41)
- Performance/Self-Assessment (p. 17)

### ▶ RUBRICS

Visit *www.sfsuccessnet.com* for rubrics to assess students' achievement in music skills.

Coda
Sing 4 times
ⓓ r m
Love to hear it, love to hear it,
Turn the beat a - round. Love to hear per - cus - sion.
Turn it up - side down,
Love to hear per - cus - sion.
Turn the beat a - round. Love to hear per - cus - sion.
Turn it up - side down,
Love to hear per - cus - sion.
Love to hear it. Love to hear it.
Unit 1 5

When the key changes to A in the *coda*, the phrases require A, B, and C♯. Invite students who can play C♯ to do this, plus other students on a keyboard.

## Singing

Along with listening and moving, have students sing the G-A-B and A-B-C♯ phrases that were practiced on the recorder. (This portion serves as a refrain in the song.)

## Reading

Have students

- Find the G-A-B and A-B-C♯ measures in the song notation.
- Sing the letter names along with the recording, from m. 4 through m. 12. (Explain that they won't be singing every note written because the ties join many notes to others; this is a sure sign of syncopation.)

UNIT 1 INTRODUCTION

### Innovative Teacher Support for This Unit

- **Making Music DVD, Grade 4** contains video segments that support lessons, including signing and movement.
- **Making Music with Movement and Dance** provides more opportunities for large group activities in music or physical education classes.
- **Making Music with Technology** provides lesson plans for many technology applications; includes MIDI files.
- ***¡A cantar!*** features recorded songs and lessons from around the Spanish-speaking world; includes strategies for bilingual classes and for English-speaking teachers working with Spanish-speaking students.
- **Bridges to Asia** features recorded songs and lessons from Asian and Pacific region cultures.
- ***www.sfsuccessnet.com*** provides an online lesson planner to conveniently create lesson plans at school or at home. Includes rubrics for assessment, lesson modifications to meet the needs of all students, performance musicals based on program content, and more.

## Technology/Media Link

**Unit Highlights** The following components are used in this unit to reinforce and expand students' understanding of music elements and related themes. See Unit at a Glance, pp. 1a–1h, for a descriptive listing according to lesson sequence.

▶ **CD-ROM**

- Use *Band-in-a-Box* to create an accompaniment (p. 19)

▶ **ELECTRONIC KEYBOARD**

- Use instrument timbres to supplement an ensemble (p. 41)

▶ **MIDI/SEQUENCING SOFTWARE**

- Create sequences that display strong and weak beat (p. 17)
- Alter melodic intervals in a given melody (p. 23)
- Display percussion tracks to perform rhythm patterns (p. 35)
- Use percussion sounds to create layers of texture (p. 37)

▶ **MULTIMEDIA**

- Create a slide show for use as background "scenery" (p. 29)

▶ **NOTATION SOFTWARE**

- Compose, notate, and perform rhythm patterns (p. 11)
- Create an eight-measure pentatonic song (p. 25)

▶ **TRANSPARENCY**

- Display listening maps to analyze form and melodic contour (pp. 17, 23)

▶ **VIDEO LIBRARY/DVD**

- Use video features to explore vocal techniques (pp. 9, 33)

▶ **WEB SITE**

- Go to *www.sfsuccessnet.com* for more information on shanties and work songs (p. 13); *Big River* (p. 29)

LESSON Core 1

## LESSON AT A GLANCE

**Element Focus** **EXPRESSION** Dynamics

**Skill Objective** **SINGING** Sing using dynamics

**Connection Activity** **RELATED ARTS** Create a cooperative quilt

### MATERIALS

1. Think of your fel - low man, lend him a help - ing hand,
2. An - oth - er day goes by, and still the chil - dren cry,
3. Take a good look a - round, and if you're look - ing down,

You see, it's get - ting late, oh, please don't hes - i - tate,
you want the world to know, we won't let ha - tred grow,
I hope when you de - cide, kind - ness will be your guide,

- "Put a Little Love in Your Heart" **CD 1-3**

  **Recording Routine:** Intro (4 m.); v. 1; refrain; v. 2; refrain; v. 3; refrain; coda
- *Put a Little Love in Your Heart* **CD 1-5**
- *The Beat of My Heart* **CD 1-6**
- **Resource Book** pp. G-2, H-2 through H-4

### VOCABULARY

dynamics *piano* *mezzo piano* *mezzo forte*
*forte* *crescendo* *decrescendo*

### ◆◆◆◆ National Standards ◆◆◆◆

**1a** Sing with appropriate posture
**1b** Sing expressively with appropriate dynamics
**1e** Sing in groups, matching dynamic levels
**6c** Use appropriate terms to explain music

### MORE MUSIC CHOICES

Other American popular songs:
"Love Can Build a Bridge," p. 324
*"La copa de la vida,"* p. 414
For more practice with dynamics:
"The Lion Sleeps Tonight," p. 131

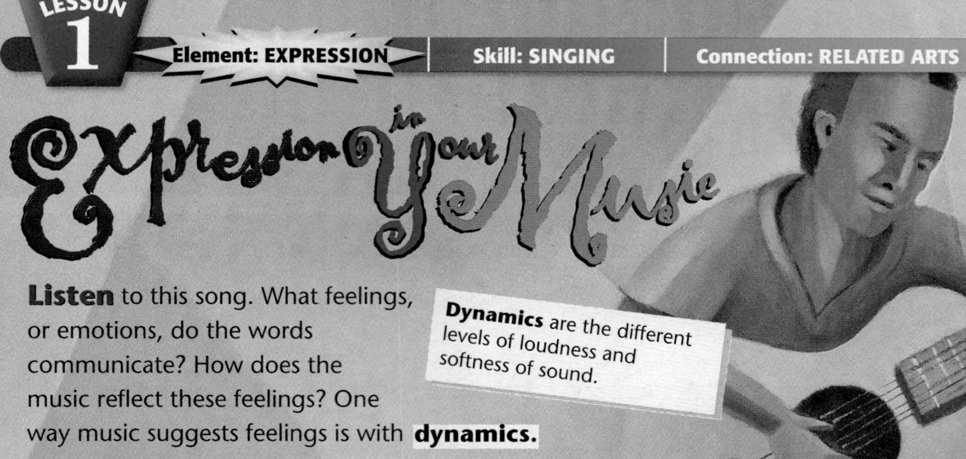

LESSON 1
Element: EXPRESSION
Skill: SINGING
Connection: RELATED ARTS
Expression in Your Music
Listen to this song. What feelings, or emotions, do the words communicate? How does the music reflect these feelings? One way music suggests feelings is with dynamics.
Dynamics are the different levels of loudness and softness of sound.

# Footnotes

## TEACHER TO TEACHER

▶ **Teaching Values** Many contemporary songs, such as "Put a Little Love in Your Heart," may be used as resources to teach values. Sometimes it is too easy to focus totally on musical characteristics, with only passing attention to the lyrics, but that may be the first element to grab students' attention. Don't miss the opportunities songs like this present for reinforcing positive human values.

## BUILDING SKILLS THROUGH MUSIC

▶ **Language** On p. 9, singer Tony Bennett is described as a "dynamic musician." Help students draw on experience and context to determine the meaning of this usage of the word *dynamic*. How is it the same as in music? How is it different?

## MEETING INDIVIDUAL NEEDS

▶ **Including Everyone** Students with and without disabilities benefit from positive interactions early in the school year. The text of "Put a Little Love in Your Heart" provides a good opportunity to discuss kindness and helping others. After students listen to and sing the song, have them share one thing they could do to help others or show kindness. Challenge students to perform an act of kindness before the next music class and report back to the class on what they did. Ask volunteers to share the words they could say to other students. Observe students' participation. Use your observations to group students with disabilities for this and other lessons with students who are particularly empathic.

## The Language of Expression

Musicians usually use Italian words when they talk about dynamics.

*p* *(piano)* = soft
*mp* *(mezzo piano)* = medium soft
*mf* *(mezzo forte)* = medium loud
*f* *(forte)* = loud
< *(crescendo)* = gradually louder
> *(decrescendo)* = gradually softer

Use dynamics while you **sing** "Put a Little Love in Your Heart."

G Am D G
___ will be a bet-ter place, And the world ___ will be a

Am D 1., 2.
bet-ter place for you ___ and me. ___ You just wait ___

D 3. D
___ and see. ___ ___ You just wait ___ and see. ___

*mf* *1st time,* *p* *2nd time,* *f* *last time*

D C G
___ Put a lit-tle love ___ in your heart. ___

**Video Library** View and listen to another version of "Put a Little Love in Your Heart," as performed by the Total Experience Gospel Choir on the *Singing Styles* video.



# 1 Introduce

6c Write the seven vocabulary words *(dynamics, piano, mezzo piano, mezzo forte, forte, crescendo, decrescendo)* and their corresponding symbols on the board or on cards. Discuss the meaning of each term with students, and introduce the word *dynamics* as the term that describes all loud or soft qualities of music. Then have students clap a steady beat. Ask them to identify and interpret the dynamics symbols and terms by changing the volume of their steady beat as you point to each different dynamic level. Have them clap a *crescendo* and *decrescendo* for the appropriate cards as well.

# 2 Develop

### Listening

6c Ask a volunteer to read the text of "Put a Little Love in Your Heart" aloud while the class follows along. (You may also wish to have students take turns reading.) Then have students listen to the recording **CD 1-3,** specifically for dynamic levels and dynamic changes.

ASK **What dynamics do you hear in the recording?** (Answers may vary.)

Encourage students to share findings with the class. Discuss the meaning of the song text and how dynamics help present the message of people taking care of each other. Help students understand why certain dynamics were used in specific parts of the song.

Share with students the activity described in Across the Curriculum below. Explain to students that a quilt is composed of smaller individual pieces that connect to make a whole. Our society functions in very much the same way.

continued on page 8

## Skills Reinforcement

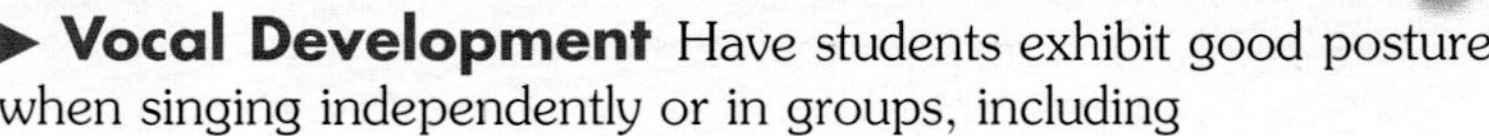

1a ▶ **Vocal Development** Have students exhibit good posture when singing independently or in groups, including

- feet — shoulder width apart, one foot slightly ahead
- knees — relaxed, not locked
- hips — straight, not jutting to the side
- chest — lifted, not caved in
- shoulders — back and down
- head — straight, jaw down
- arms — relaxed and by the sides

Discuss the points listed above and how they can affect singing. Agree on an appropriate gesture that will remind students to check their posture. *Examples*: point to knees, chest, and head, or pull string up from head.

## Across the Curriculum

▶ **Art** Have students read the book *Stand for Children* by Marian Wright Edelman (Hyperion, 1998). Point out to them the quilt illustrations used throughout the book. Invite students to make a quilt square from construction paper. The square should feature symbols that reflect the student's interests. Students can mount photographs of themselves, or self-portraits, on their quilt square. When completed, assemble all the squares to make a giant "quilt" for bulletin board or hallway display.

### Singing

1b Play "Put a Little Love in Your Heart" **CD 1-3** for students. Invite them to listen and then sing when ready. Encourage them to sing with the dynamics of the recording.

### Reading

Play "Put a Little Love in Your Heart" once again while students follow the notation on pp. 6–7 and identify the various dynamic levels.

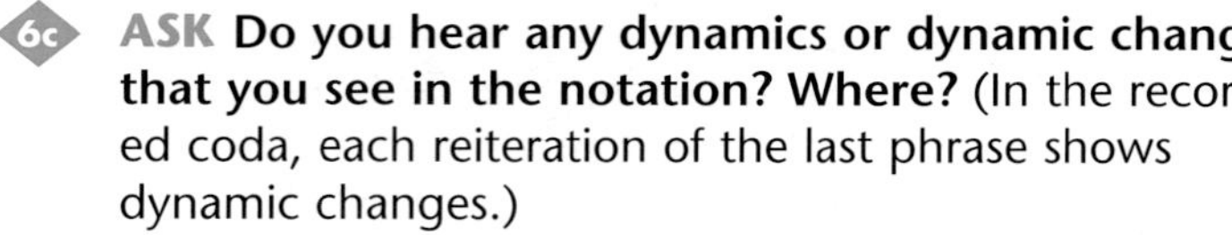

6c **ASK Do you hear any dynamics or dynamic changes that you see in the notation? Where?** (In the recorded coda, each reiteration of the last phrase shows dynamic changes.)

### Listening

Play *Put a Little Love in Your Heart* **CD 1-5** for students. Discuss how Mahalia Jackson's version is different from the song recording of "Put a Little Love in Your Heart." Share with students the information about Mahalia Jackson in Spotlight On, p. 9.

### Creating

1b Divide students into small groups and ask them to create their own dynamic plans for "Put a Little Love in Your Heart." Be sure students are aware of the "road map" for the song, where sections end, where repeats occur, and so on. You may wish to outline the song on the board for students to follow. Encourage students to experiment with dynamic levels, including *crescendos,* and *decrescendos*, until they find those that best express the meaning of the song.

Have students practice in their groups and then perform their work for other students, interpreting the dynamics as planned. The students listening can try to identify the dynamics used by the students performing.

### Moving

For a signing activity to accompany "Put a Little Love in Your Heart," refer to Resource Book p. G-2.

## Expressive Music

"Put a Little Love in Your Heart" has been recorded by many singers. **Listen** for dynamic contrast in this version by the gospel singer Mahalia Jackson.

CD 1-5

**Put a Little Love in Your Heart**

**by Jimmy Holiday, Randy Myers, and Jackie De Shannon as performed by Mahalia Jackson**

Mahalia Jackson (1912–1972) recorded this version of the song in 1969.

Mahalia Jackson ▶

## Moving with Expression

As you **sing** "Put a Little Love in Your Heart," perform these signs each time this phrase is sung.

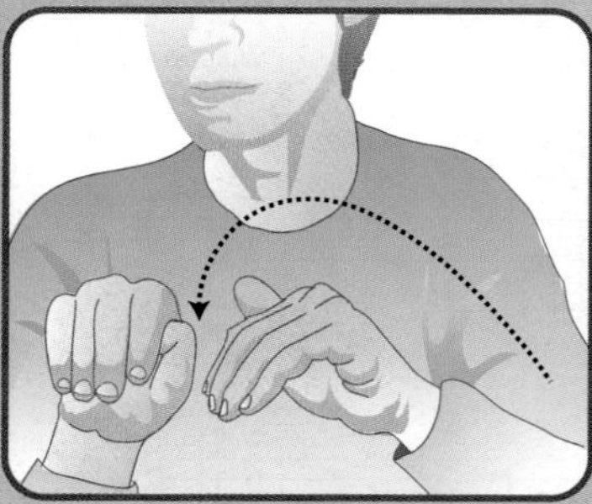

*Put a little*

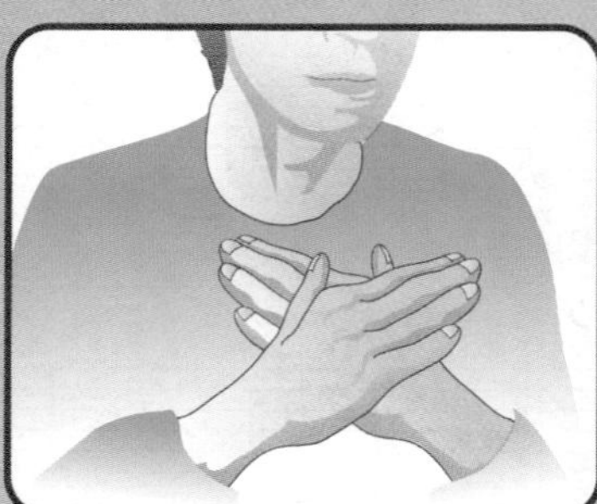

*love*

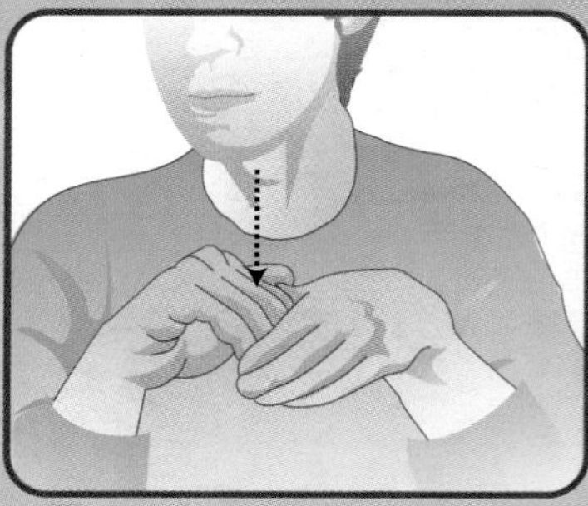

*in your*

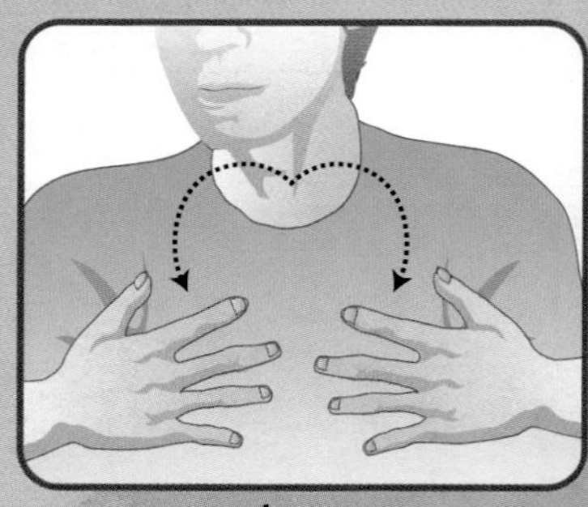

*heart*

8

# Footnotes

## Meeting Individual Needs

▶ **Gifted and Talented** Invite students who need an extra challenge to create and sing new verses for "Put a Little Love in Your Heart." Only two original lines are needed. Each line is two phrases long, with six syllables each and a rhyming final syllable. The topic can be anything that would make the world a better place. For example:

If you see someone sad, gloomy and feeling bad,
(Put a little love in your heart.)
Offer to be a friend, help find a happy end,
(Put a little love in your heart.)
Refrain: And the world...*and so on.*

## Skills Reinforcement

6c ▶ **Performing** Reinforce the meaning of terms and symbols for musical dynamics as follows.

- List dynamic terms on the board or put them on flashcards.
- Create a rhythm ostinato from the first measure of "Put a Little Love in Your Heart."
- Ask students to perform with nonpitched percussion the indicated dynamic as a group by modifying the loudness of the ostinato.
- Ask students to perform indicated dynamics individually.

▶ **Keyboard** Have students work through the keyboard reading exercises on Resource Book pp. H-2 through H-4. These activities will prepare students for additional playing activities throughout the book.

## A Dynamic Musician

Tony Bennett is famous for his smooth voice and singing style. **Listen** for his use of dynamic contrast as he sings *The Beat of My Heart.* When and where does he change the dynamics?

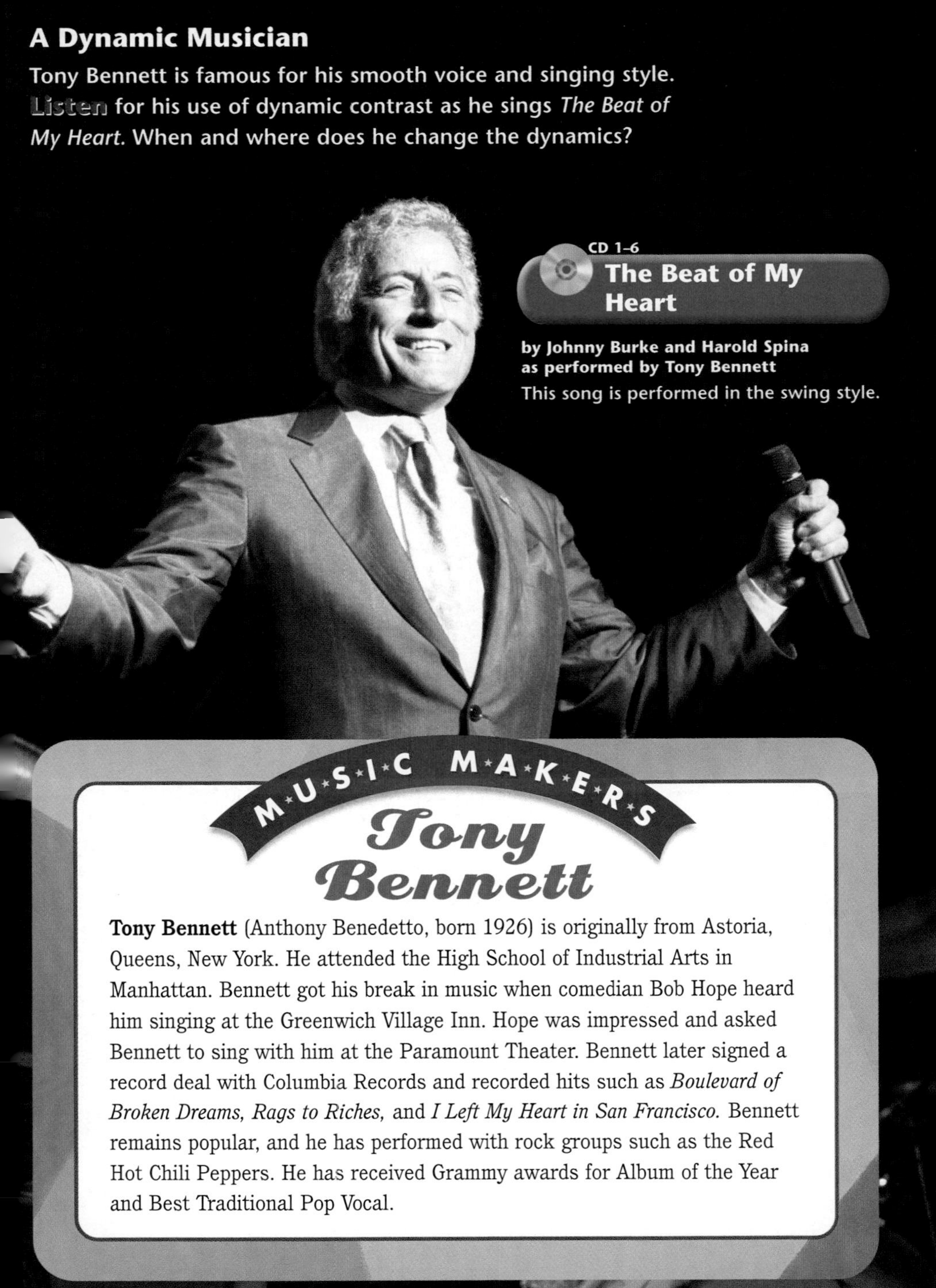

CD 1-6

**The Beat of My Heart**

**by Johnny Burke and Harold Spina as performed by Tony Bennett**

This song is performed in the swing style.

M·U·S·I·C M·A·K·E·R·S

### Tony Bennett

**Tony Bennett** (Anthony Benedetto, born 1926) is originally from Astoria, Queens, New York. He attended the High School of Industrial Arts in Manhattan. Bennett got his break in music when comedian Bob Hope heard him singing at the Greenwich Village Inn. Hope was impressed and asked Bennett to sing with him at the Paramount Theater. Bennett later signed a record deal with Columbia Records and recorded hits such as *Boulevard of Broken Dreams, Rags to Riches,* and *I Left My Heart in San Francisco.* Bennett remains popular, and he has performed with rock groups such as the Red Hot Chili Peppers. He has received Grammy awards for Album of the Year and Best Traditional Pop Vocal.



### Listening

Have students listen to Tony Bennett's *The Beat of My Heart* **CD 1-6.** Direct their attention to the *decrescendo* at the end of the selection. Then have students read the information about the performer on student p. 9.

## 3 Close

**Element: EXPRESSION** — **ASSESSMENT**

1e **Performance/Observation** In small groups, have students sing "Put a Little Love in Your Heart" **CD 1-3** once with the recording, then again without the recording. Encourage students to use appropriate dynamic inflection to express the meaning of the words. Observe students' understanding of and ability to perform dynamics.

### Spotlight On

▶ **Mahalia Jackson** Mahalia Jackson (1911–1972) was a gospel singer and recording artist who recorded about 30 albums and about a dozen gold records. During the 1964 Civil Rights March in Washington, D.C., Jackson sang "I Been 'Buked and I Been Scorned" just before Martin Luther King Jr.'s famous "I Have a Dream" speech. Jackson performed for four American presidents.

▶ **Tony Bennett** Tony Bennett trained as both an artist and a musician. He sang with the Army during World War II. He has performed with Bob Hope and Ray Charles as well as contemporary artists k. d. lang and Elvis Costello. In the 1990s he won additional Grammy Awards. His music continues to reach new audiences.

### Technology/Media Link

**Video Library** Invite students to view a performance of "Put a Little Love in Your Heart" by the Total Experience Gospel Choir. After the performance, ask students

- How does the soloist sing with expression?
- What dynamic is she singing?
- What do soloists and accompaniment singers do to balance their sounds? (soloist sings louder, accompaniment sings softer)

LESSON 2

## LESSON AT A GLANCE

**Element Focus** RHYTHM ♩, 𝄽, ♫, 𝅗𝅥, 𝅗𝅥., 𝅝

**Skill Objective** READING Read ♩, 𝄽, ♫, 𝅗𝅥, 𝅗𝅥., 𝅝

**Connection Activity** SOCIAL STUDIES Compare an Appalachian and a British folk song

**MATERIALS**
- "Soldier, Soldier" **CD 1-7**
  **Recording Routine:** Intro (4 m.); refrain; v. 1; refrain; v. 2; refrain; v. 3; refrain
- **Music Reading Practice, Sequence 1** **CD 1-9**
- *Lazy John* **CD 1-14**
- **Resource Book** pp. D-2, E-2, F-2

**VOCABULARY**

eighth notes, quarter rest, half note, dotted half note, whole note, quarter note

**◆ ◆ ◆ ◆ National Standards ◆ ◆ ◆ ◆**

**5a** Read rhythms in $\frac{4}{4}$ meter
**6b** Describe music by moving to it
**6e** While listening to music, move to show a prominent feature of the music
**9a** Listen to identify music from different historical periods

**MORE MUSIC CHOICES**

For more review of known rhythm patterns:
"Cotton-Eye Joe," p. 288

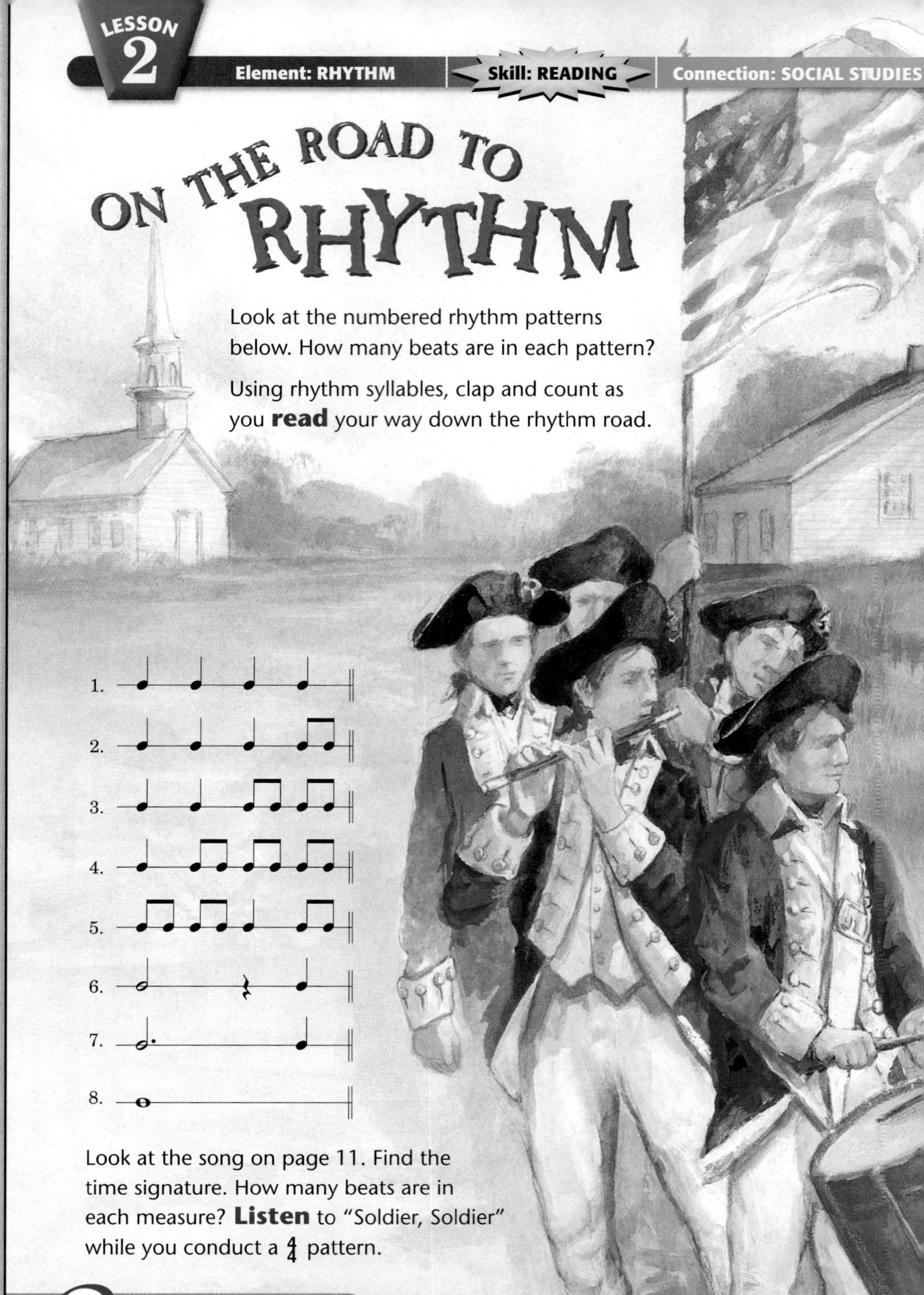
LESSON 2 Element: RHYTHM | Skill: READING | Connection: SOCIAL STUDIES

ON THE ROAD TO RHYTHM

Look at the numbered rhythm patterns below. How many beats are in each pattern?

Using rhythm syllables, clap and count as you **read** your way down the rhythm road.

1. 2. 3. 4. 5. 6. 7. 8.

Look at the song on page 11. Find the time signature. How many beats are in each measure? **Listen** to "Soldier, Soldier" while you conduct a $\frac{4}{4}$ pattern.

10 Reading Sequence 1

## 1 INTRODUCE

Invite students to read the words of "Soldier, Soldier" and discuss how the words would be different in modern times. Share the information from Spotlight On, p. 11, about Jean Ritchie and the folk song process.

# Footnotes

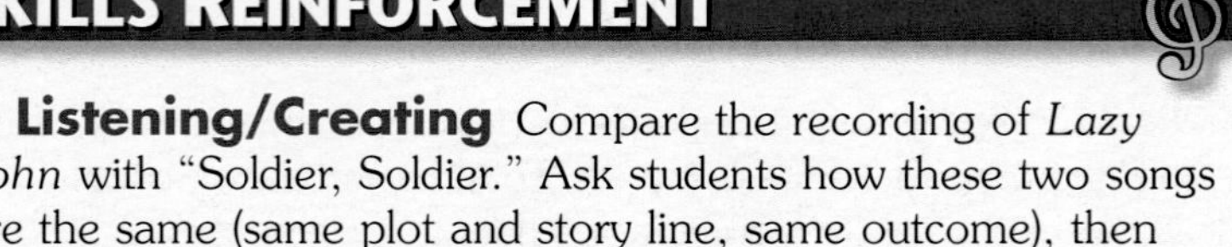
## SKILLS REINFORCEMENT

▶ **Listening/Creating** Compare the recording of *Lazy John* with "Soldier, Soldier." Ask students how these two songs are the same (same plot and story line, same outcome), then how they are different (different characters, rhythm, and melody). Invite students to create new verses for the song.

▶ **Mallets** For an Orff accompaniment to "Soldier, Soldier," refer to Resource Book p. F-2.

## BUILDING SKILLS THROUGH MUSIC

▶ **Writing** Invite students to write a paragraph explaining the original story told in "Soldier, Soldier." Then, as a companion activity, have them write another paragraph, based on the classroom discussion presented above under Introduce.

## TEACHER TO TEACHER

6b ▶ **Program Performance** Both *Lazy John* and "Soldier, Soldier" can be staged and presented in a humorous light in your next PTA program or concert. You might try to

- Cast individual students as Lazy John, the soldier, or the maiden. Or for fun, ask a favorite teacher or principal to come onstage as a surprise character.
- Fill a trunk with oversized items of clothing and props with which to act out the story.
- Have the chorus or class sing the song's narrative parts.

- 9a Program an "Across the Sea" concert of songs and games from the British Isles and their American variations. You can find a number of these songs in this and other grade levels of the MAKING MUSIC textbook.

## A Girl and Her Soldier

**Listen** to this recording of *Lazy John*, a variation of "Soldier, Soldier." Then **compare** the two versions.

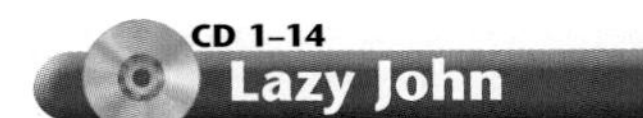
CD 1–14
Lazy John

**arranged and performed by Jean Ritchie**

Jean Ritchie is a folk singer from Kentucky. See page 349 for more information, including a recorded interview with this American legend.

CD 1–7
Soldier, Soldier
s, l, d r m s l
Traditional Song from the United States and England
REFRAIN
do
"Now, sol - dier, sol - dier, will you mar - ry me, with your
mus - ket, fife, and drum?" "Oh, how can I mar - ry such a
rit. last time
accel. last time
Fine
pret - ty girl as you, when I've got no shoes to put on?"
when I've got no hat to put on?"
when I've got no coat to put on?"
when I've got a wife at ___ home?"
VERSE
Then off to the cob - bler ___ she did go, as
hat - ter ___
tai - lor ___
fast as she could run. She bought him a pair of the
hat
coat
D. C. al Fine
fin - est that there were, and the sol - dier put them ___ on.
it ___
it ___

# 2 Develop

### Reading

5a Have students read, clap, and say each rhythm pattern on the "rhythm road," p. 10. Ask a volunteer to perform a pattern individually. Then select another student to choose and perform the next pattern. Refer to Resource Book p. D-2 and have students fill in the incomplete measures in the activity. For an additional reading activity, see p. 442 and Resource Book p. E-2.

### Listening

6e Play "Soldier, Soldier" **CD 1-7** for students as they pat the steady beat. Draw attention to the time signature in the song notation and remind students that in $\frac{4}{4}$ time, there are four beats in each measure. Demonstrate the conducting pattern for four beats per measure.

### Performing

Have students conduct a four-beat pattern while they listen to "Soldier, Soldier" and then sing the song as a group.

### Analyzing

Ask students to match four-beat rhythm patterns in "Soldier, Soldier" on student p. 11 with four-beat patterns from the "rhythm road." Have them identify the words and the measure number in which the pattern occurs.

# 3 Close

**Skill: READING** ASSESSMENT

5a **Performance/Observation** Have students read, clap, and say the rhythm of "Soldier, Soldier" **CD 1-7.** Invite them to perform the patterns from the "rhythm road," p. 10, as a counter-rhythm while singing the song. Have students conduct in a $\frac{4}{4}$ pattern and say each of the patterns as you call out its number. Then you say the patterns at random, having students call the correct number.

## Spotlight On

▶ **Jean Ritchie** Jean Ritchie was born in 1922, the youngest of 14 children of a musical family. Her ancestors came from England, settled in Virginia, and eventually migrated to the Southern Appalachian region of Kentucky. They brought a legacy of "Ritchie family songs," which were passed down through generations. Along the way, some of the songs changed. New ones were written and passed along, too. Jean Ritchie made up "Lazy John" to entertain her children.

9a

Some American folk songs came from those of England, Scotland, and Ireland. Over time, songs sometimes evolve and change until they bear little resemblance to their "parent" versions. Discuss with students why they think this happens.

## School to Home Connection

▶ **Memories** Ask students to find out if anyone they know has stories about the life of a soldier. If so, invite some of these people to speak to the class.

## Technology/Media Link

**Notation Software** Set up a music notation software program for four measures in $\frac{4}{4}$ meter with a repeat sign at the end. Organize students into small groups. Ask them to compose and notate a rhythm pattern using half notes, quarter notes, eighth notes, and quarter rests. Have each group rehearse its pattern on nonpitched percussion instruments as the computer plays the notation. Invite the groups to perform for the class.

## LESSON AT A GLANCE

**Element Focus** **RHYTHM** Strong and weak beats

**Skill Objective** **MOVING** Move to show strong and weak beats

**Connection Activity** **SOCIAL STUDIES** Discuss the origins of work songs

**MATERIALS**

- "Haul Away, Joe" **CD 1-15**

  **Recording Routine:** Intro (8 m.); v. 1; refrain; interlude (4 m.); v. 2; refrain; interlude (4 m.); v. 3; refrain; coda
- "Until I Saw the Sea" (poem)
- **Resource Book** p. H-5
- hand drum

**VOCABULARY**

sea shanty strong beat weak beat

**National Standards**

**2a** Play instruments in rhythm
**6b** Describe music by moving to it
**6e** While listening to music, move to show a prominent feature of the music

**MORE MUSIC CHOICES**

For more work songs:
"Old House, Tear It Down!" p. 178
"Blow, Ye Winds," p. 255
For more practice with strong and weak beat:
"Big Rock Candy Mountain," p. 330

# 1 INTRODUCE

2a Using a hand drum, demonstrate the meter of "Haul Away, Joe" for students. (The $\frac{6}{8}$ time is counted in two beats per measure, the first strong and the second weak.) Allow volunteers to perform the meter on hand drum.



# WORKING WITH RHYTHM

Have you ever rowed a boat or raked leaves? What is similar about these motions? Sea shanties like "Haul Away, Joe" were sung on large sailing ships in the 1700s and 1800s. They often accompanied repetitive motion. This song has a **strong and weak beat** in each measure to fit with the work being done. What kind of work on a ship would use this type of motion?

The **strong beat** is usually the first beat in a measure. The **weak beat** is usually the second or last beat in a measure.

# Footnotes

## SKILLS REINFORCEMENT

6e ▶ **Performing** Assist students in developing variations on the "work motion" theme that will reinforce their skill in keeping a steady beat in duple or triple meter.

▶ **Keyboard** For a five-line reading and fingering activity to prepare students for playing keyboards, refer to Resource Book p. H-5.

## BUILDING SKILLS THROUGH MUSIC

▶ **Language** Review the information from Spotlight On that focuses on the lyrics of the song "Haul Away, Joe." Then have students summarize each verse in as few words as possible. Transfer these summary words to the board and then ask students to sing from memory, using the board for cues.

## SPOTLIGHT ON

▶ **"Haul Away, Joe"** This song has some interesting references in the lyrics. In verse 2, *turf* refers to peat, a heating fuel used in Ireland; *'Taties* are potatoes, a traditional Irish food. *Lime juice ship* speaks of the need for sailors to have citrus fruit on board ship to avoid getting scurvy from lack of vitamin C. Because of this, sailors were sometimes referred to as "limeys."

In verse 3, *King Louie* refers to Louis XVI, the king of France, who reigned from 1774–1792. In 1792 he was convicted of treason, because of his opposition to the revolution and the new constitution, and executed early in 1793.

Moving with a Sea Shanty
With a partner, create work movements to do while you sing "Haul Away, Joe."
CD 1-15
Haul Away, Joe
d m f s l ta d'
Sea Shanty from England
VERSE
C
B♭
do
1. Oh, when I was a lit - tle lad, or so my moth - er
2. Oh, once I was in Ire - land___ dig - gin' turf and
3. King Lou - ie was the King of France be - fore the re - vo -
told___ me, That
'ta - ties, 'Way haul a - way, we'll haul a-way, Joe. But
lu - tion, King
if I did not kiss a gal my lips would grow all
now I'm on a lime - juice ship___ haul - ing on the
Lou - ie got his head cut off which spoiled his con - sti -
mould - y,
brac - es, 'Way haul a - way, we'll haul a-way, Joe.
tu - tion,
REFRAIN
'Way haul a - way, we'll haul a - way for bet - ter weath - er,
'Way haul a - way, we'll haul a - way, Joe.
Unit 1 13

# 2 Develop

### Moving

6b 6e Play "Haul Away, Joe" **CD 1-15.** Ask students to choose a rhythmic "working" motion they can perform that demonstrates the strong and weak beats in the song. Have them perform the motion as they listen to the song.

### Singing

Have students pat the steady beat with you and speak the words of the song on p. 13. Then have them sing along with the recording.

### Moving

Draw students' attention to the photographs on p. 12. Group students in pairs and have them discuss what kinds of work they see in the photos and think of other types of work that use repetitive motion. Talk about why songs to accompany work may have developed. Then come back together as a class and allow each pair of students to share their ideas. Then share the information about the song. Refer to Spotlight On, p. 12, and discuss the origins of work songs.

Have class members, individually or in groups, create movements representing different types of work that demonstrate strong beat–weak beat. Have the class select three of these movements for performance. Divide the class into three groups and have each group perform one of the movements with a verse of "Haul Away, Joe."

# 3 Close

**Skill: MOVING** **ASSESSMENT**

6e **Performance/Observation** Invite students to sing "Haul Away, Joe" **CD 1-15,** using larger and smaller steady beat movements to demonstrate stronger and weaker beats. Observe students' ability to successfully perform this task.

## Across the Curriculum

▶ **Language Arts** Have students read and discuss the poem "Until I Saw the Sea" by Lilian Moore (*Sing a Song of Popcorn*, Scholastic, 1988). Ask how many students have seen the sea, and what did they feel when they first saw it?

Until I saw the sea
I did not know
that wind
could wrinkle water so.
I never knew
that sun
could splinter the whole sea of blue.
Nor did I know before,
a sea breathes in and out
upon a shore.

## Character Education

▶ **Responsibility** In small groups, have students list work responsibilities they have at home, at school, and in the community. Note the similarities and differences. Discuss the importance of hard work, responsibility, and keeping one's commitments. Why is it important for you to do these jobs? How does hard work help you? How does it help others? What impact does singing while working have on the job you're doing?

## Technology/Media Link

**Web Site** Students may be interested in learning more about shanties and other work songs. Have them research these topics at *www.sfsuccessnet.com.*

## LESSON AT A GLANCE

**Element Focus** **RHYTHM** Duple meter $\frac{2}{4}$

**Skill Objective** **MOVING** Move to show strong and weak beats in duple meter

**Connection Activity** **SOCIAL STUDIES** Discuss the geography of Armenia

**MATERIALS**

- *"Gakavik"* **CD 1-17**
- "The Partridge" **CD 1-18**
  **Recording Routine:** Intro (8 m.); vocal; coda
- **Music Reading Practice, Sequence 2** **CD 1-21**
- "Galop" (excerpt) from *Masquerade Suite* **CD 1-24**
- **Pronunciation Practice/Translation** p. 473
- **Resource Book** pp. A-2, B-2, E-3
- world map or globe
- nonpitched percussion instruments

**VOCABULARY**

duple meter

**National Standards**

**1a** Sing independently with appropriate posture
**1c** Sing from memory songs from diverse cultures
**2a** Play instruments in rhythm
**6b** Describe music by moving to it and by explaining how it sounds

**MORE MUSIC CHOICES**

Other songs in duple meter:
"The Glendy Burke," p. 262
*"Beriozka,"* p. 294
Other European folk songs:
*"Ai Dunaii moy,"* p. 293
*"Minka,"* p. 222

# Dancing in DUPLE METER

*"Gakavik"* is a folk song from the Republic of Armenia, a country that became independent in 1991 after being part of the Soviet Union for seventy years.

This song is based on a strong and weak beat pattern known as **duple meter.** Clap the steady beat while you **sing** or **listen** to *"Gakavik."*

**Duple meter** is a basic pattern in which a measure has one strong and one weak beat.

CD 1-17
Gakavik
(The Partridge)
s, l, t, d r m s l
English Words by Mary Shamrock
Folk Song from Armenia
F Gm7 F
do
Ա - րեվ բաց - վեց թուխ ամ պե - րեն,
A - rev pats - vedz tugh am be - ren,
Threat-'ning clouds hide the sky, Soon the sun breaks the gloom;
B♭ Gm7 F
կա - քավ թռ - ավ կա - նաչ սա - րեն.
ga - kav te - rav ga - nach sa - ren.
Moun-tains high, moun-tains green, Ev - 'ry - where bright flow - ers bloom.
Dm F C F
կա - նաչ սա - րեն՝ սա - րի ծե - րեն,
Ga - nach sa - ren sa - ri dze - ren,
Pret - ty par - tridge through the air, Feath-ers shin - ing in the sun;
14 Reading Sequence 2

# Footnotes

## ACROSS THE CURRICULUM

▶ **Social Studies** An independent republic since 1991, Armenia is located in the westernmost part of Asia, bordering on eastern Turkey. It is a little larger than the state of Maryland. The capital city is Yerevan. Armenia was under Russian control from 1922 until 1990. When the Soviet Union dissolved, Armenia became independent. The Armenian language is derived from both Persian and Greek and has its own alphabet.

## BUILDING SKILLS THROUGH MUSIC

▶**Math** Ask students to determine the number of measures needed for

- A 32-beat song in $\frac{2}{4}$ duple meter ($32 \div 2 = 16$)
- A 64-beat song in $\frac{2}{4}$ duple meter ($64 \div 2 = 32$)

Ask students to identify which equation applies to *"Gakavik."* (the second)

## TEACHER TO TEACHER

▶ **Teaching Non-English Language Songs** Students become more sensitive to other cultures by singing songs in languages other than their own. To give students an opportunity to hear a native speaker sing in the original language, play the Pronunciation Practice Track **CD 1-20.** Then use the Pronunciation Practice/Translation section, which begins on p. 472, to teach the non-English version. Students may refer to Resource Book p. A-2.

Gm7 F

բա րեվ ___ բե րավ ծա ղիկ նե ___ րեն:
*pa - rev ___ pe - rav dza - ghik - ne - ren:*
Moun-tains green and flow - ers bright send their joy to ev - 'ry - one.

F

Սի - րու նիկ, սի րու նիկ,
*Si - rov - nig, ___ si - rov - nig,*
Soar ___ and ___ sail, she's fly - ing far ___ and free.

Gm7 Dm7 F

սի - րու -նիկ, ___ նախ - շուն կա - քա - վիկ.
*si - rov - nig, ___ nakh - shoun ga - ka - vik.*
Pret - ty par - tridge, love - ly bird, greet - ing you and me.

### Duple Meter in Movement

Follow these steps to **create** a dance for *"Gakavik."*

- Step right, together, step right, easy kick
- Step left, together, step left, easy kick

-rmenian dancers ▶



# 1 Introduce

Using a large world map or globe, ask volunteers to locate Armenia. Give clues, such as "southwestern Asia" or "east of Turkey." When they find it, ask each volunteer to name one of the countries that borders or is very near Armenia. (Georgia, Azerbaijan, Turkey, and Iran) Share the information about Armenia in Across the Curriculum, on p. 14.

# 2 Develop

### Moving

1c Play *"Gakavik"* **CD 1-17.** Have students demonstrate the strong beat by

- Clapping on the first beat of each measure.
- Listening to the song, clapping on each strong beat.
- Creating a softer sound between each clap, on the weak beat. (beat 2 of each measure)

Identify this pattern of one strong plus one weak beat as duple meter. Discuss the meaning of duple (in twos). Then ask students to check song notation on pp. 14–15 for any signs that might confirm that *"Gakavik"* is in duple meter. (the $\frac{2}{4}$ time signature) Have students perform their duple movements as they sing the song.

Discuss the text of *"Gakavik."*

ASK **Is this song appropriate for a happy or sad occasion?** (happy)

In Armenian tradition, dancing is often part of happy occasions. Teach students the simple dance that goes with this song.

Have students

- Form a line, with each person facing diagonally forward, hands joined, and held up at shoulder height.

**continued on page 16**

## Meeting Individual Needs

▶ **Pairing Students** If students are not mobile enough to perform the *"Gakavik"* dance, encourage them to follow it as well as they can. You might partner a student in a manual wheelchair with a student who walks. The walking student can move the chair left and right, while the wheelchair student improvises arm motions. Students in power wheelchairs can move their chairs on their own with the dance. Students on crutches might be able to stand still and move with the beat. If you have questions about students' abilities, take your cues from them. They can let you know at what level they are comfortable participating.

## Skills Reinforcement

1a ▶ **Singing** Sitting posture is as important as standing posture when singing. Review the points for standing posture that apply to sitting posture (feet, hips, chest, shoulders, head). Students should sit on the front half of their chairs when singing. Agree on a gesture to direct students to use proper singing posture and one to indicate an at-rest position, when they can sit back on their chairs. Practice using the two gestures. (See Skills Reinforcement on p. 7 for specific suggestions to maintain good singing posture.)

- Make three walking steps to the right (r-l-r), then swing left foot slightly over right in a light kick.
- Turn and repeat the pattern in the other direction (l-r-l kick).

The steps taken to the right should be larger than those to the left. This will cause the line to gradually move forward. Each pattern fits two bars of the song.

### Playing

2a Add instruments to *"Gakavik"* to reinforce the strong-weak duple pattern. Choose two nonpitched percussion instruments to alternate in playing the beat. One should have a strong sound, the other weaker. One student can play the steady beat softly on a woodblock, while two others alternate strong and weak beats on different instruments. Invite other students to sing with the recording **CD 1-17** (See Skills Reinforcement on p. 15.)

### Listening

6b Ask volunteers to read aloud the information on Aram Khachaturian, p. 17. Draw students' attention to the listening map for "Galop" from *Masquerade Suite,* p. 16. Discuss the meaning of the word *masquerade.*

**ASK Do you ever masquerade?** (Many students may do this at Halloween.)

**What do you think the tempo and mood of a piece called *Galop* would be?** (fast and lively)

Play *Galop* **CD 1-24** once without the listening map. Ask students to create a duple meter movement to use with *Galop.*

**ASK What type of music group do you hear?** (orchestra)

Invite students to look at section A of the listening map, on lines 1 and 3.

**ASK How often is this section going to be heard?** (three times)

**In which direction will the first melody go?** (up)

## Listening for Form

Follow the listening map as you **listen** to "Galop" from *Masquerade Suite.* Make up a story that involves a masquerade and fits with the music.

CD 1–24
**Galop**

**from *Masquerade Suite***
**by Aram Khachaturian**

"Galop" is one section of music intended to be played at different points during a play titled *Masquerade.*

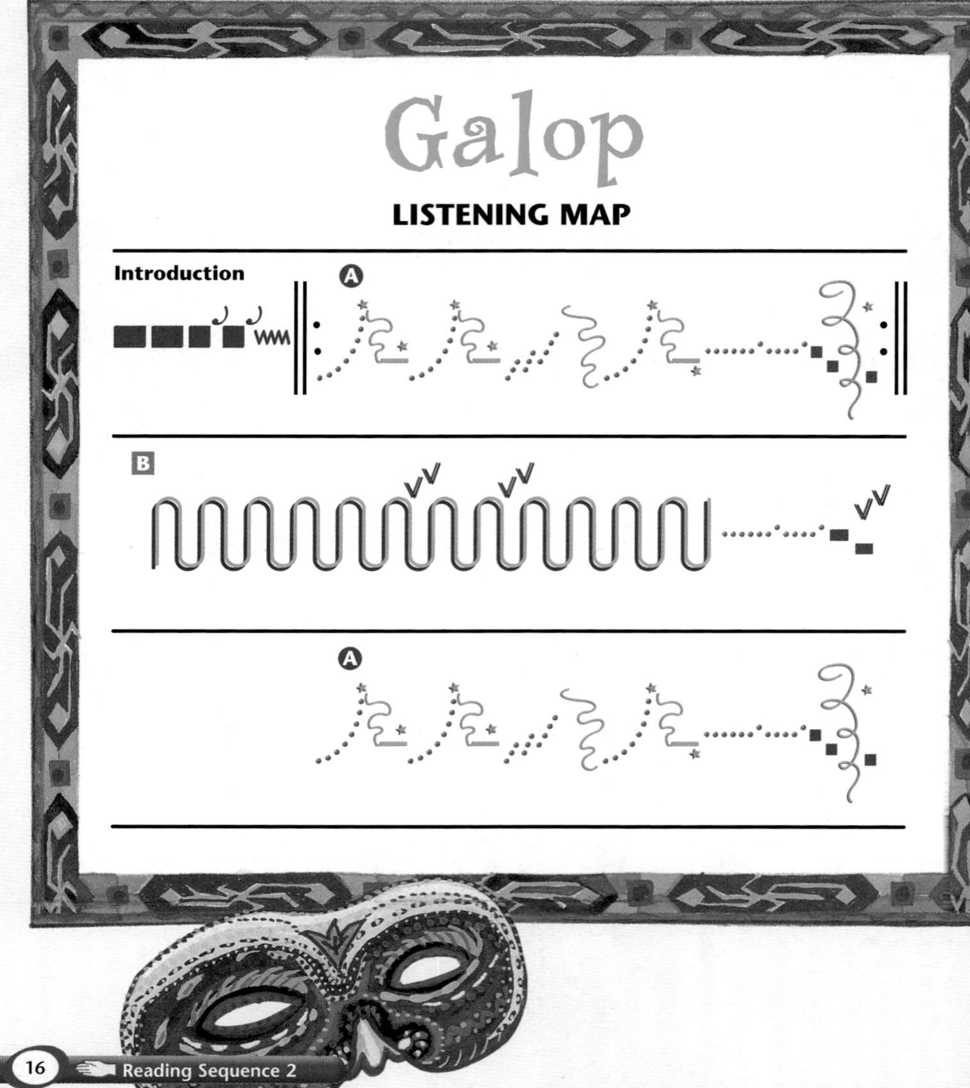




# Footnotes

## Teacher to Teacher

**▶ Listening Maps** Listening skills are as difficult to evaluate as language comprehension. As you watch students follow a listening map, observe whether they are connecting the aural with the visual and are in the right place in the music.

**Reinforcement** To assist students who have trouble following the listening map on p. 16, add numbers to the map as needed to help them keep their place.

**On Target** Most students will be able to accomplish this listening activity by following the steps outlined under Listening in the column above. Allow time for follow-up listening experiences and discussion.

**Challenge** Those students who master this activity easily may be invited to design and add new symbols to the map to illustrate additional details in the music.

## Skills Reinforcement

6b **▶ Listening** Use movement to observe listening skills visually. Convert the listening map for "Galop" into a movement exercise; however, do not use galloping. It is needlessly exhausting and does not fit the basic rhythm of this song. Have students create a movement to represent the A sections and another movement for the B section. Have them plan a movement to indicate the end of each section. Encourage students to create movements that reflect the feeling of the music.

## MUSIC MAKERS

# Aram Khachaturian

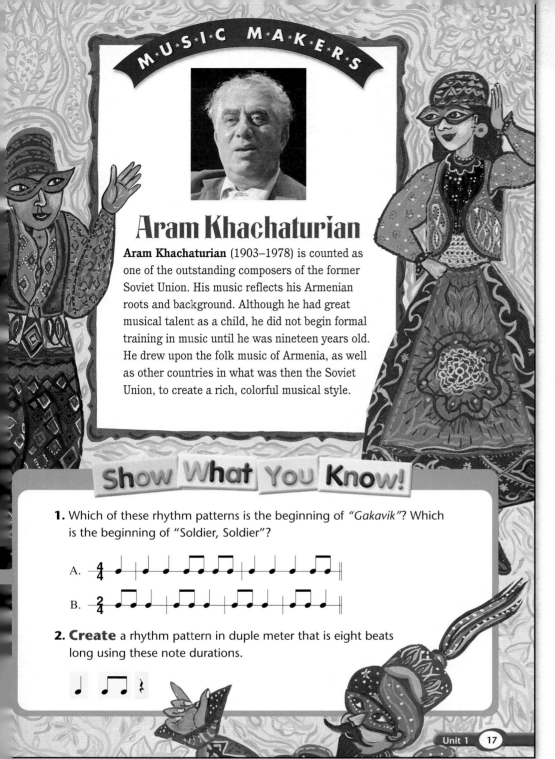

**Aram Khachaturian** (1903–1978) is counted as one of the outstanding composers of the former Soviet Union. His music reflects his Armenian roots and background. Although he had great musical talent as a child, he did not begin formal training in music until he was nineteen years old. He drew upon the folk music of Armenia, as well as other countries in what was then the Soviet Union, to create a rich, colorful musical style.

## Show What You Know!

**1.** Which of these rhythm patterns is the beginning of *"Gakavik"*? Which is the beginning of "Soldier, Soldier"?

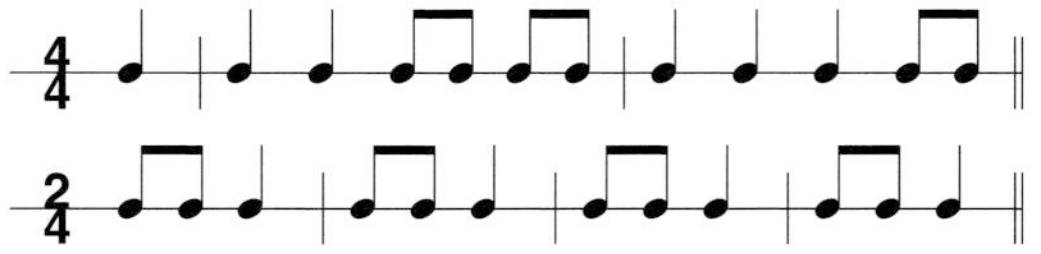

A. 4/4

B. 2/4

**2. Create** a rhythm pattern in duple meter that is eight beats long using these note durations.

Have students listen to the introduction plus the first two melodic up sweeps only to place it in memory. Then have them listen to the entire piece and follow the listening map.

6b When students are ready to focus on the whole piece, establish two duple meter motions: one for each section (both should be easy to perform). Project the listening map on the overhead, if possible. Then have students try performing the motions without the listening map.

### Reading

For more practice with meter and rhythm, see p. 442 and Resource Book p. E-3. Then have students complete the Show What You Know! activity on p. 17. Refer to Resource Book p. B-2.

## 3 CLOSE

**ASSESSMENT**

6b **Performance/Self-Assessment** Divide the class into small groups. Have students

- Listen to the recording of *Galop* **CD 1-24** again.
- Keep the steady beat using alternating movements to show the stronger and weaker beats.
- Use a different set of movements for each section, as in the Develop activity.
- Perform their movements for the class. (If permitted by school policy, you may wish to videotape the performance and allow each group to assess its own work.)

## ACROSS THE CURRICULUM

▶ **Social Studies** Discuss with students the boundaries of countries. Use a map or globe to find the border of the United States and Canada and of the United States and Mexico. Then talk about the boundaries of other countries around the world. Contrast a current map with a map from the past. Draw students' attention to changes in the boundaries of countries from the former Soviet Union. Have them locate Armenia.

For more information on the country of Armenia and its people, students may enjoy *Armenia* by Sakina Dhilawala (Marshall Cavendish, 1997).

## TECHNOLOGY/MEDIA LINK

**Sequencing Software** Set up a sequencing program with four measures in $\frac{2}{4}$ time. Have students work in small groups and record one track using a bass instrument playing half note Cs. Have them record another track using quarter and eighth notes on C, D, E, G, A. Invite students to play their sequences for the class and explain how they created a sense of stronger and weaker beats.

**Transparency** For students who have difficulty tracking the listening map on p. 16, use the transparency on an overhead projector.

LESSON Core 5

## LESSON AT A GLANCE

**Element Focus** **FORM** Call and response

**Skill Objective** **SINGING** Sing a call-and-response song

**Connection Activity** **RELATED ARTS** Learn the limbo

**MATERIALS**

- "Limbo Like Me" **CD 1-25**
  **Recording Routine:** Intro (4 m.); vocal; interlude (4 m.); vocal; coda
- *Brisad del Zulia* (excerpt) **CD 1-27**
- **Resource Book** pp. H-6, I-2
- limbo stick
- small percussion instruments (optional)
- recorders, keyboard

**VOCABULARY**

call and response limbo calypso

**National Standards**

1c Sing songs from diverse cultures
3c Improvise rhythmic variations on familiar melodies
6a Listen to identify form

**MORE MUSIC CHOICES**

Another song from the Caribbean:
"Wings of a Dove," p. 318
For more practice with call and response:
"All Night, All Day," p. 180

# 1 INTRODUCE

Play "Limbo Like Me" **CD 1-25** for students. Encourage students to sing along with the words *limbo like me* when they are ready. Then invite students to learn the limbo, using dance instructions in Movement on p. 19.

LESSON 5
Element: FORM
Skill: SINGING
Connection: RELATED ARTS
I Sing, You Sing
Some songs have parts for a solo and parts for a group to sing. This is known as **call and response,** and it is very similar to a conversation. The solo parts need to be completed by a response from the group.
**Sing** "Limbo Like Me" and take turns being the soloist.
**Call and response** is a musical device in which a portion of a melody (call) is followed by an answering portion (response).
CD 1-25
Limbo Like Me
t, d r m f s l t d'm
Words and Music Adapted by Massie Patterson and Sammy Heyward
Solo
Chorus
I want a girl to lim - bo like me; Lim - bo, lim-bo like me.
Lim - bo, lim - bo, lim - bo like me;
Ev - 'ry - bod - y lim - bo like me; Lim - bo, lim-bo like me.
My lit-tle goat can lim - bo like me;
Mon-key try to lim - bo like me; Lim - bo, lim-bo like me.
Mon-key no can lim - bo like me;
One an' all come lim - bo like me; Lim - bo, lim-bo like me.
Lim - bo, lim-bo like me; Lim - bo, lim-bo like me.
"Limbo Like Me" New words and new music adapted by Massie Patterson and Sammy Heyward. (Based on a traditional song) TRO-© 1963 (Renewed) Ludlow Music Inc., New York, N.Y. Used by permission.
18


## Footnotes

### SKILLS REINFORCEMENT

▶ **Keyboard** Students can learn to play the chorus parts to "Limbo Like Me." Use p. H-6 in the Resource Book.

▶ **Recorder** Have students use Resource Book p. I-2 to learn how to play a two-note accompaniment on the recorder.

### BUILDING SKILLS THROUGH MUSIC

▶ **Reading** Explain to students that people who can easily bend backwards, as shown in the movement photo on p. 19, are said to be "limber." Ask students to find the word used throughout the song on p. 18 that is similar to *limber*. Then have students look up *limber* in the dictionary and connect the meaning to that of *limbo*.

### TEACHER TO TEACHER

▶ **Reluctant Singers** If some students are reluctant to improvise and sing alone, help them find ways that seem less threatening. Try having them speak instead of singing, creating the words and having a friend sing along, standing behind a barrier so no one can see them, writing the words down and reading them, or having you suggest the words. Be clear that the goal is for each student to create and sing his or her own call. Then use some of the alternatives above to help each student work toward this goal.

## Do the Limbo

This song and movement game come from the Caribbean calypso tradition. To play the game, two people hold a stick. The other players take turns bending backwards to go under the stick. The stick is lowered until the last player able to pass under the stick wins.

**Move** as you **listen** to Samaroo Jets perform *Brisad del Zulia.*

CD 1-27
**Brisad del Zulia**

**Traditional Caribbean Calypso as performed by Samaroo Jets**
This performance features steel drums made from oil barrels.

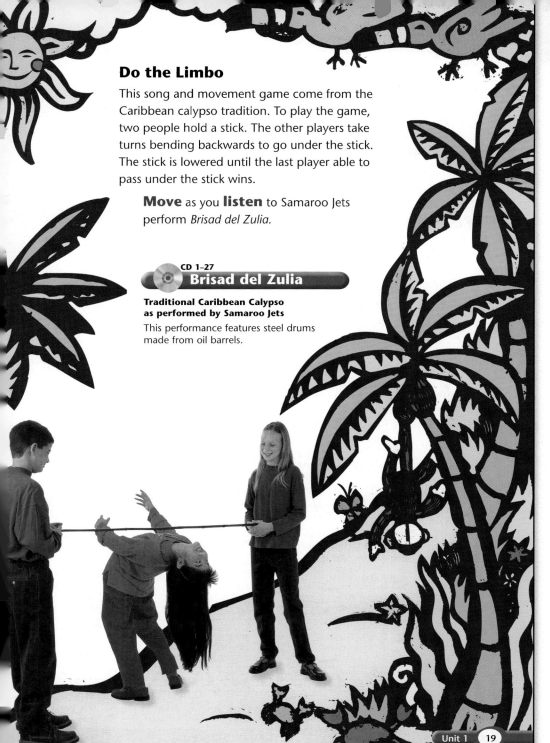

Unit 1 19

# 2 Develop

### Singing

1c Play "Limbo Like Me" again. Ask students to sing along with the repeated part. Have them count how many times it happens in exactly the same way (six), and notice when it changes (at the end).

ASK **How would you describe the parts of the song before the words *limbo like me?*** (sometimes the same, but not always)

6a Help students identify this form as call-and-response.

ASK **Which parts are sung by a soloist?** (the calls)

**Which parts are sung by a group?** (the responses)

In "Limbo Like Me," the calls are written down. Often in call-and-response songs, however, calls are improvised. Improvised calls can vary with each repetition.

### Improvising

3c Have students clap the rhythm of the response, *Limbo, limbo like me.* Then ask everyone to create and clap their own two-bar rhythmic phrase for the call. Count two bars aloud to help them feel the length. As students gain confidence, ask them to include other body percussion.

### Listening

Invite students to listen to *Brisad del Zulia* **CD 1-27.** Ask them to identify and describe the timbre. (steel band)

# 3 Close

**ASSESSMENT**

**Performance/Observation** Have students

- Sing the responses in "Limbo Like Me" **CD 1-25.**
- Sing the song once again without the recording, with the teacher singing the calls and the class singing the responses.

Observe students' performances to assess their understanding of call-and-response form.

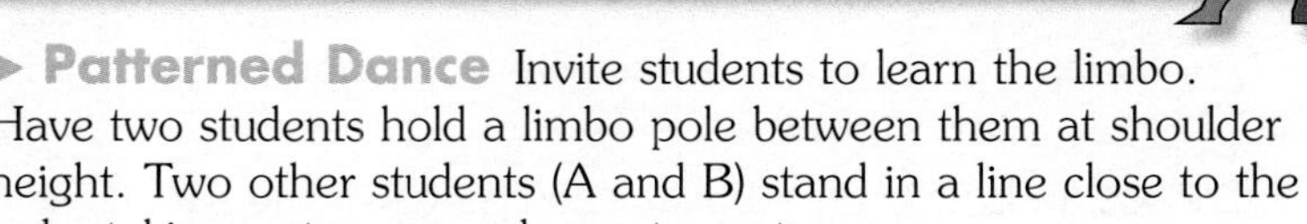


**▶ Patterned Dance** Invite students to learn the limbo. Have two students hold a limbo pole between them at shoulder height. Two other students (A and B) stand in a line close to the pole, taking a step on each quarter note.

- Call: Student A performs a stretch, shake, or twist movement, and bends backward to step under the pole.
- Response: Student B imitates student A.

Student B imitates student A throughout the song. Then they reverse roles. Encourage students to create an echo dance. Ask them to stand side by side and perform movements without the pole.

## Technology/Media Link

**CD-ROM** Set up the computer, keyboard, and *Band-in-a-Box* software. Type in the chord changes of "Limbo Like Me" and choose a Caribbean style to generate an accompaniment. Encourage students to listen to the CD of "Limbo Like Me." Have them observe which instruments are used in the background of the song. Have them change the instrument combination in the file to be similar to that on the CD.

## LESSON AT A GLANCE

**Element Focus** **MELODY** Skips, steps, and repeated pitches

**Skill Objective** **READING** Identify skips, steps, and repeated pitches in melodic notation

**Connection Activity** **SOCIAL STUDIES** Discuss the meaning of spirituals

### MATERIALS

- "Gonna Ride Up in the Chariot" **CD 1-28**

  **Recording Routine:** Intro (4 m.); v. 1; refrain; interlude (4 m.); v. 2; refrain; interlude (4 m.); v. 3; refrain; coda
- **Music Reading Practice, Sequence 3** **CD 1-30**
- "Deep in the Heart of Texas" **CD 1-33**

  **Recording Routine:** Intro (8 m.); vocal; interlude; refrain; (16 m.); vocal; coda
- *"Air" in D* **CD 1-35**
- **Resource Book** pp. C-2, E-4, I-3
- selected melody instruments

### VOCABULARY

step skip interval spiritual

### ◆◆◆◆ National Standards ◆◆◆◆

**1c** Sing songs from diverse cultures
**3c** Improvise rhythmic variations on familiar melodies
**5a** Read half, quarter, and eighth notes in duple meter
**8b** Identify ways music relates to social studies
**9c** Identify uses of music in everyday life

### MORE MUSIC CHOICES

Another African American spiritual:

"Little David, Play on Your Harp," p. 394

For more practice with steps, skips, and repeated pitches:

"Pastures of Plenty," p. 280

*"Tengo, tengo, tengo,"* p. 228



# MAKING A MELODY

Some songs express hope. "Gonna Ride Up in the Chariot" originated with African Americans during slavery when life was very harsh. It is a song of hope for freedom. **Sing** the song and then discuss the words.

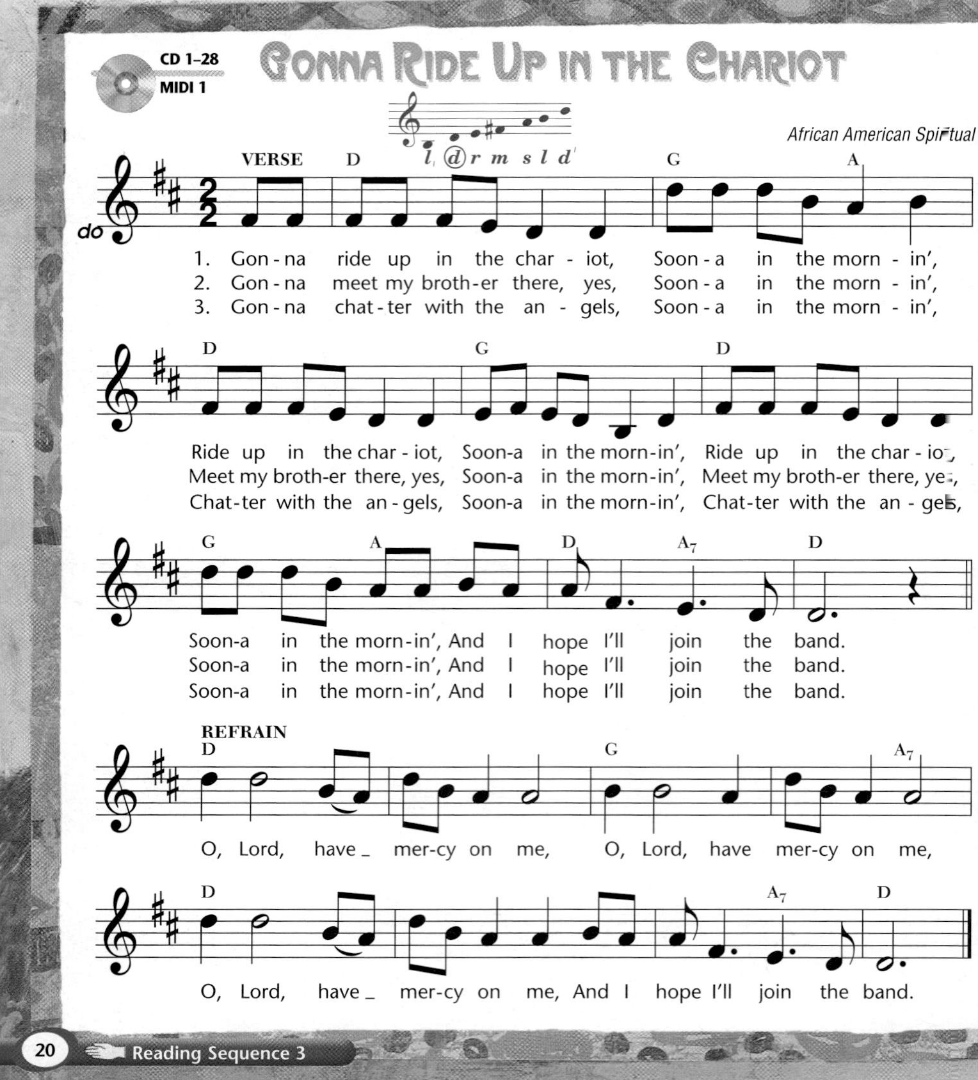

CD 1–28
MIDI 1
GONNA RIDE UP IN THE CHARIOT
African American Spiritual
l, d r m s l d'
VERSE
do
1. Gon-na ride up in the char - iot, Soon-a in the morn - in',
2. Gon-na meet my broth-er there, yes, Soon-a in the morn - in',
3. Gon-na chat-ter with the an - gels, Soon-a in the morn - in',
Ride up in the char - iot, Soon-a in the morn-in', Ride up in the char - iot,
Meet my broth-er there, yes, Soon-a in the morn-in', Meet my broth-er there, yes,
Chat-ter with the an - gels, Soon-a in the morn-in', Chat-ter with the an - gels,
Soon-a in the morn-in', And I hope I'll join the band.
Soon-a in the morn-in', And I hope I'll join the band.
Soon-a in the morn-in', And I hope I'll join the band.
REFRAIN
O, Lord, have mer-cy on me, O, Lord, have mer-cy on me,
O, Lord, have mer-cy on me, And I hope I'll join the band.
20 Reading Sequence 3


# Footnotes

## CULTURAL CONNECTION

8b 9c ▸ **Spirituals** For African Americans in slavery, songs such as "Gonna Ride Up in the Chariot" expressed the hope for a better life after death. These songs also expressed the desire or intent to use the Underground Railroad to escape from the condition of slavery. The lyrics make sense in both contexts.

## BUILDING SKILLS THROUGH MUSIC

▸**Language** Help students identify examples of dialect, slang, and contractions in the lyrics of "Gonna Ride Up in the Chariot." (*gonna, soona, mornin', I'll*) Ask students to then describe how these words would be written using formal grammar. Have students sing a "formal grammar" version of "Gonna Ride Up in the Chariot" and then discuss how this changes the character of the song.

## SKILLS REINFORCEMENT

3c ▸ **Creating** For an expanded activity with "Gonna Ride Up in the Chariot," have students

- Choose an instrument to play when they join the band.
- Create phrases, such as *So I think I'll play the trumpet*, to replace the *Gonna ride up in the chariot* phrases.
- Sing the song with the new words.

▸ **Recorder** Suggestions for playing recorders with "Gonna Ride Up in the Chariot" can be found on Resource Book p. I-3.

## Interval Practice

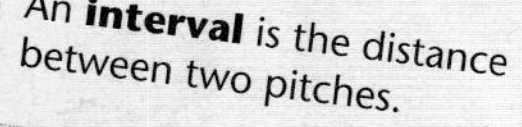

An **interval** is the distance between two pitches.

The melody of this song is composed of notes that either repeat, move by step, or move by skip. **Listen** to "Gonna Ride Up in the Chariot" and look for the **intervals** below in the melody.

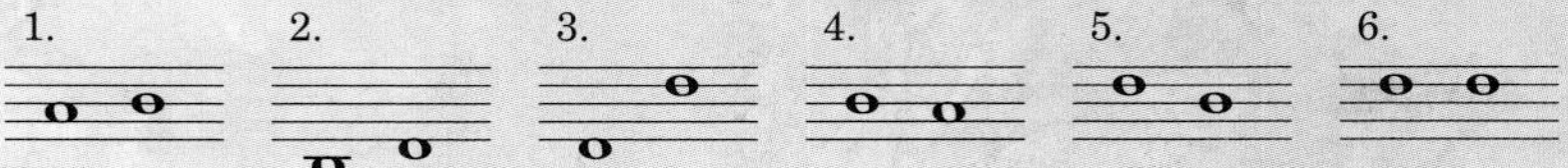


What are the intervals shown above? To determine the interval, count the bottom tone as 1. Then count all lines and spaces up to the next pitch.

**Sing** "Gonna Ride Up in the Chariot" again and **read** the steps, repeats, and skips.

## Compose Using Intervals

**Compose** an introduction for "Gonna Ride Up in the Chariot" to play on a melody instrument. Choose the notes from these pitches. Make sure you use a step, a skip, and a repeated tone in the melody.

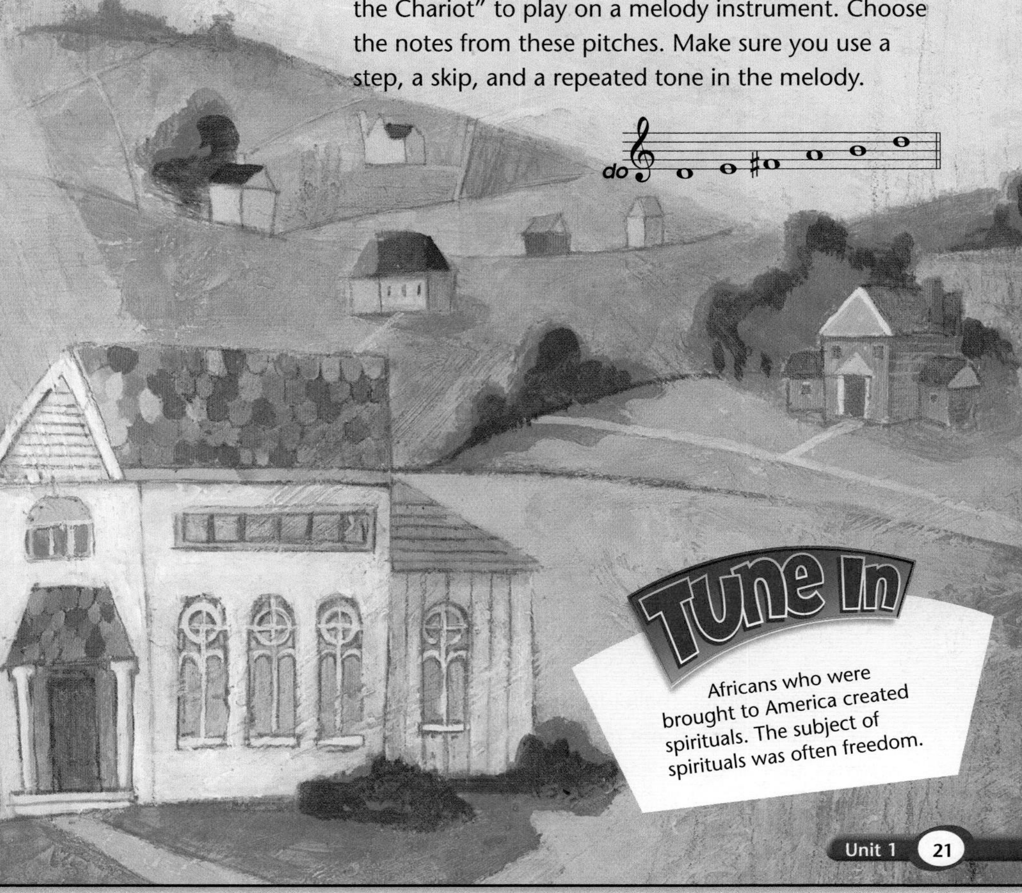


**Tune In**

Africans who were brought to America created spirituals. The subject of spirituals was often freedom.



# 1 Introduce

8b Play "Gonna Ride Up in the Chariot" **CD 1-28** as students follow the lyrics on p. 20. Discuss the origins of this song and what the lyrics meant to those who first sang it. (It represented hope for a better future.) Ask students to sing the song in that spirit. Share with students the information about spirituals. Refer to the Cultural Connection on p. 20.

# 2 Develop

### Reading

Play the song again. Ask students to follow the notation on p. 20, counting the spots where a tone repeats. Then ask students to count the spots where the melody moves to the nearest neighbor tone. This is called a step. Play the song once more. Ask students how many times the melody moves by more than a step. This is called a skip.

### Singing

1c Have students sing the song as a dialogue. Group 1 sings *ride up in the chariot.* Group 2 sings *soon-a in the mornin'*. Both groups sing the last two measures. Have students clap their parts or play them on nonpitched percussion instruments.

### Reading

For a related melody reading activity, see p. 443 and Resource Book p. E-4

continued on page 22

## Across the Curriculum

▶ **Social Studies** Invite students to discuss freedom. What makes people free? Do some people have to fight for their freedom? Why? Was our country always free for all citizens?

Share the book *Amistad Rising: The Story of Freedom* by Veronica Chambers (Harcourt Brace, 1998) an account of the freedom fight aboard the Spanish slave ship *Amistad*.

## Teacher to Teacher

▶ **Comparison Chart** For additional practice developing thinking skills in a musical context, distribute copies of the Comparison chart from Resource Book p. C-2. Have students use the chart to explain, compare, and contrast specific elements in "Gonna Ride Up in the Chariot," using standard terminology. For example, referring to the verse, ask students to list similarities and differences among the four phrases, focusing on such elements as melodic movement, rhythm, and lyrics.

## Creating

Allow students to work individually or in small groups to create and perform melodic phrases, using the "Compose Using Intervals" activity on p. 21.

## Reading

Ask students to follow the notation on p. 22 as they listen to "Deep in the Heart of Texas" **CD 1-33**. After repeated listenings, ask students to identify those places in the melody where the pitches repeat, skip, and move by step. Invite volunteers to play the repeated-note figure, shown at the bottom of p. 22, with the recording.

## Singing

Invite students to sing the song and then answer the questions on p. 22. (Some of the intervals used in this song, and not in "Gonna Ride Up in the Chariot," occur on the words *The stars, night are* (line 1) and *sky is* (line 2).

▲ State capitol, Austin, Texas

### Lone Star Intervals

From the time it was written, in 1941, "Deep in the Heart of Texas" has been an "unofficial" state song of Texas. Which songs represent your home state?

**Listen** to the song as you follow the notes on the staff. Now **sing** the song. Find the steps, skips, and repeated notes in the melody. Then answer these questions:

- How many different intervals can you **identify** in the melody? Which is the smallest? Which is the largest?
- Which intervals in this song were *not* used in "Gonna Ride Up in the Chariot," on page 20?

s, t, d r m s l
CD 1-33

### Deep in the Heart of Texas

Words by June Hershey
Music by Don Swander
do
F C7
The stars at night are big and bright, Deep in the heart of Tex-as;
The prai-rie sky is wide and high, Deep in the heart of Tex-as.
The sage in bloom is like per-fume, Deep in the heart of Tex-as;
Re-minds me of the one I love, Deep in the heart of Tex-as.

Using a recorder, mallet instrument, or keyboard, **play** these repeated notes every time they appear in the song.

C

# Footnotes

## Skills Reinforcement

▶ **Singing** For good vocal development and intonation, have students

- Sing the *do*-pentatonic scale in D.
- Hold *do*' while some students sing *la* and *so* and other students sing *mi* to tune the descending minor thirds. (This is a preparatory step for singing half-steps in tune.)
- Sing the pentatonic scale individually. Record each student's performance.

## Across the Curriculum

▶ **Social Studies** The image of the prairie plays a prominent role in the lyrics of "Deep in the Heart of Texas." Invite interested students to

- Identify for the class where this type of terrain can be found in Texas and other regions of the country.
- Research and share with the class the characteristics and ecological importance of prairie land.

## Baroque Melody

As you follow the listening map, **listen** for steps, skips, and repeated notes in the long, flowing melody, played by the first violins.

CD 1-35
**"Air" in D**

**from *Orchestral Suite No. 3* by Johann Sebastian Bach**

In opera, an *aria* is an extended song for solo voice. Baroque composers used the term *air* to describe melodies modeled on Italian *arias*.

**LISTENING MAP**

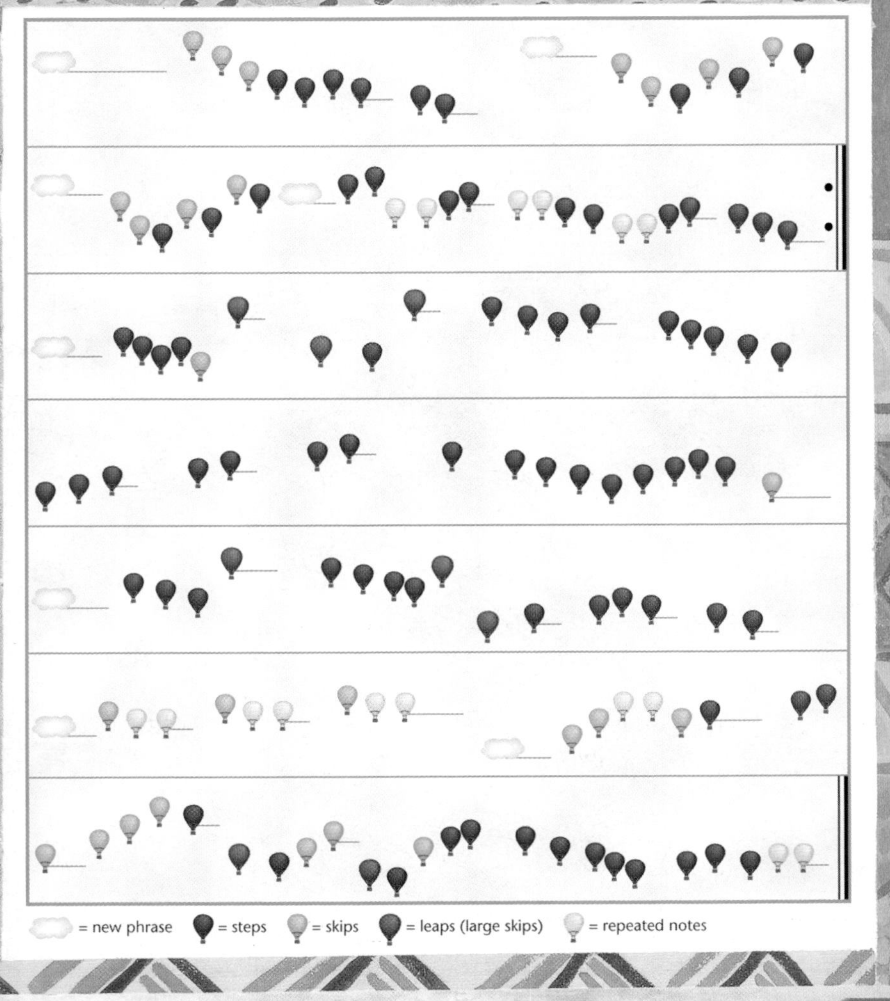




### Listening

Explain to students that melodic steps, skips, and repeated notes can be heard in almost every type of music. In the example illustrated in the listening map on p. 23, the composer assigned the melody to the first violin section of the orchestra. Refer students to p. 233 for a feature on Bach. Additional information can be found on p. 112 in the Teacher's Edition.

Play *"Air" in D* **CD 1-35** and ask students to focus on the contour of the line in the listening map that represents the melody. Ask volunteers to identify and point to segments of the line where steps, skips, and repeated (or sustained) notes occur.

## 3 Close

**Skill: READING** ASSESSMENT

1c **Performance/Observation** Encourage students to sing "Gonna Ride Up in the Chariot" **CD 1-28** and "Deep in the Heart of Texas" **CD 1-33** with good vocal tone. Have them point to (or write) words that are sung on repeated pitches, words where three notes move up or down by step, and words where the melody moves by skip. Observe students' abilities to read skips, steps, and repeated pitches in melody notation.

## Meeting Individual Needs

▶ **Body/Kinesthetic** When students are familiar with the entire melody of *"Air" in D*, divide the class into two groups, representing sections A and B in the music. Invite each group to create a set of movements to illustrate the melodic contour of its section.

**Reinforcement** Have students with limited coordination use in-place movements and repetition. Focus on selected phrases within the section.

**On Target** Once students have performed the entire routine with the recording, guide the class in critiquing the performance.

**Challenge** Encourage interested students to expand their involvement by diagramming their movement routine for future reference, including teaching it to others.

## Technology/Media Link

**MIDI/Sequencing Software** Invite students to

- Use a sequencing program to display in piano roll view the melody track of the MIDI song file "Gonna Ride Up in the Chariot."
- Mute the other tracks.
- Drag pitches up and down to change some intervals.
- Play the file again to show how the melody changed.

**Transparency** Use the transparency for *"Air" in D* to help students follow the contour of the melody.

## LESSON AT A GLANCE

**Element Focus** **MELODY** Pentatonic scale

**Skill Objective** **READING** Read a *do-re-mi-so-la* melody from notation

**Connection Activity** **CULTURE** Discuss and create Japanese style art

**MATERIALS**

- *"Tsuki"* **CD 1-36**
- "The Moon" **CD 1-37**

  **Recording Routine:** Intro (4 m.); v. 1; interlude (4 m.); v. 2; coda
- **Music Reading Practice, Sequence 4** **CD 1-40**
- **Pronunciation Practice/Translation** p. 473
- **Resource Book** pp. A-3, D-3, E-5

**VOCABULARY**

pentatonic scale

**◆◆◆◆ National Standards ◆◆◆◆**

**1c** Sing songs from diverse cultures
**3b** Improvise melodic ostinato accompaniments
**4b** Compose songs within specific guidelines
**5b** Read notes in treble clef using syllables

**MORE MUSIC CHOICES**

Another song with pentatonic patterns:
"Weevily Wheat," p. 105

# 1 INTRODUCE

Invite students to look at the painting on p. 24. Tell students that art is an important part of many cultures, and share information about Japanese-style art from the Cultural Connection on p. 25.



# Pentatonic Patterns

Here is a Japanese melody made up of three melody patterns. Follow its contour, or shape, as you **listen** to *"Tsuki."*

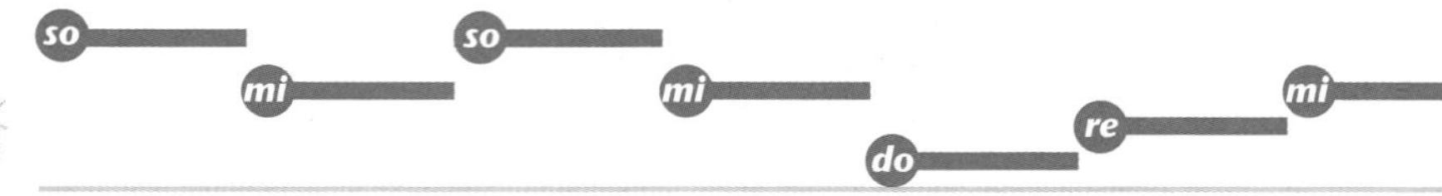


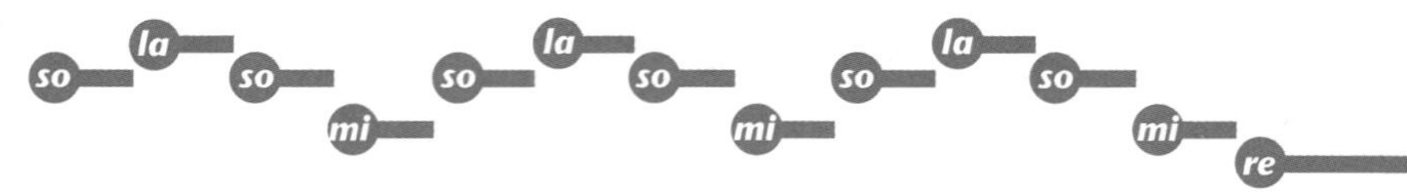

# Footnotes

## SKILLS REINFORCEMENT

▶ **Reading** Students may need to review the pitch syllables and hand signs for *do, re, mi, so,* and *la.* Have students sing simple *so* and *mi* patterns. Next add *la, do,* and *re,* one at a time. Continue to echo sing until students regain confidence.

## BUILDING SKILLS THROUGH MUSIC

▶**Writing** After students are familiar with the lyrics of *"Tsuki,"* have them work in small groups or as a class to write new words that describe a rising sun instead of the moon.

## SPOTLIGHT ON

▶ **Japanese Language** Encourage students to learn some new words in Japanese.

| | | |
|---|---|---|
| *konnichiwa* | means | good day, hello |
| *sayonara* | means | goodbye |
| *dozo* | means | please |
| *domo arigato* | means | thank-you |
| *do itashimashite* | means | you're welcome |
| *tomodachi* | means | friend |
| *sensei* | means | teacher |

la
so
mi
re
do

## Reading Pentatonic Scales

A song's notes make up its scale. **Read** the **pentatonic scale** on the syllable ladder. Find the steps and skips in the scale. Use hand signs as you **sing** the scale up and down.

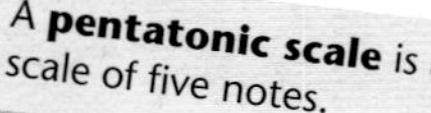

A **pentatonic scale** is a scale of five notes.

**Read** the pentatonic scale from the staff. The *do* symbol at the beginning of the staff will help you find your way around.

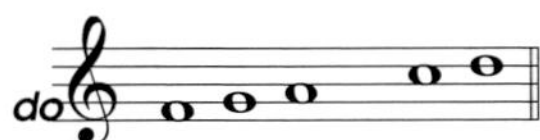


Now you are ready to **read** *"Tsuki"* from the staff.

で た で た つ き が
1. De - ta, de - ta, tsu - ki ga
1. Now the moon is com - ing out!
ま る い ま る い ま ん ま る い
Ma - ru - i ma - ru - i ma - n ma - ru - i,
Big and round, so big and round, as round as a tray.
ぼ ん の よ う な つ き が
Bo n - no yo - na tsu - ki ga.
Moon is big and round, just like a tray.

2. *Kaku reta kumoni,*
*Kuroi, kuroi makuroi,*
*Sumino yona kumoni.*

2. Now the moon is hiding.
Gone away, O gone away, O gone away so far.
Up behind the clouds as black as tar.

**Arts Connection**

◀ *Moonlight on Sebu River* (c. 19th century Japan) by Hiroshige



# 2 Develop

### Reading

5b Divide the class into three groups. Assign each group one pattern on p. 24. Have the groups sing their pattern using the system of pitch syllables and hand signs as you point to the music notation. Switch parts until each group has performed every pattern. For more practice, refer to Resource Book p. D-3. For a related pentatonic reading activity, see p. 443 and Resource Book p. E-5.

### Listening/Singing

Have students listen to *"Tsuki"* **CD 1-36** while following the contour of each pattern on p. 24. Invite students to sing with the accompaniment track, using pitch syllables and hand signs. Have students listen to the Pronunciation Practice Track for *"Tsuki"* **CD 1-39** and sing with the students on the recording. Refer to Resource Book p. A-3. Then have the class sing the song in English and Japanese.

### Analyzing

Draw attention to *do* on the staff at the top of p. 25. Then review the staff placement of each note.

**SAY** When *do* is in a space, *mi* is in the space above it, and *so* is in the space above *mi.* When *do* is in a space, *re* is on the line above it. *La* is on the line above *so.*

### Improvising

Have students create and improvise pentatonic ostinatos to accompany *"Tsuki,"* singing them with pitch syllables and hand signs.

# 3 Close

**Skill: READING** ASSESSMENT

1c **Performance/Observation** Have students sing *"Tsuki"* **CD 1-36**, first using hand signs and pitch syllables, then using the song text. As you point to each pattern on p. 24, have students sing it, using hand signs and pitch syllables. Observe to assess their understanding of and ability to read pentatonic scale.

## Cultural Connection

▶ **Art** Lacquerware is an ancient art in Japan. Lacquer is painted over wood or other materials, often with flower designs.

Invite students to make their own lacquerware plate. You will need paper plates, gesso (canvas primer) and brush for applying it, fine sandpaper, tempera paint (black for the base coat, white, shades of red and gold for floral decoration), brushes (fine), and plastic spray sealer. First, apply the gesso to the plate as a base coat. (Two coats may be needed.) Then paint the plate black, as a background coat. Be sure to let each coat dry thoroughly. Next, paint the design, using fine brush strokes. Look at flowers or plants for design ideas. After the plate is finished, spray it with two coats of spray sealer and let it dry.

## Technology/Media Link

d r m s l
English Words by Kazuo Akiyama
School Song from Japan

4b **Notation Software** Help students set up notation software in the key of F (one flat). Have them create an eight-measure song, using rhythms and notes from "*Tsuki,*" starting and ending their songs on F. Have students play back their work often and make corrections as needed. Be sure to allow them to print their work.

LESSON 8

## LESSON AT A GLANCE

**Element Focus** **MELODY** Tonal center

**Skill Objective** **LISTENING** Identify the tonal center in listening examples

**Connection Objective** **LANGUAGE ARTS** Relate a musical with the book on which it is based

**MATERIALS**

- "Waitin' for the Light to Shine" **CD 1-43**
  **Recording Routine:** Intro (4 m.); v. 1; refrain; interlude (4 m.); v. 2; refrain; coda
- **Resource Book** p. B-2

**VOCABULARY**

tonal center Broadway musical

### ◆◆◆◆ National Standards ◆◆◆◆

**1b** Sing expressively with appropriate dynamics, phrasing, and interpretation
**2b** Perform melodies on appropriate instruments
**6b** Describe music by answering questions about it
**6e** While listening to music, move to show a prominent feature of the music

**MORE MUSIC CHOICES**

For more practice with tonal center:
*"Einini,"* p. 391
"Love Will Guide Us," p. 328

LESSON 8 Element: MELODY | Skill: LISTENING | Connection: LANGUAGE ARTS

# Tonal Center

Name the first and last note of this song. Count how many times this pitch occurs. Where does it occur most often? The pitch G is the **tonal center** of this song.

Now **listen** to the song's melody while humming G. Sometimes G fits with the melody, and sometimes it does not. Like a magnet, the melody always pulls back to G.

A **tonal center** is a pitch that acts as a resting place or "home" for all of the other pitches that happen around it.

CD 1-43
Waitin' for the Light to Shine
from Big River
Words and Music by Roger Miller
Arranged by Linda Twine
VERSE
do
G
1. I have lived an un - di - rect - ed life, a cloud - y
2. Far be - yond hor - i - zons I have seen, be - yond the

C G C G
way I know, the on - ly way I knew. So the
things I've done, be - yond the dreams I've dreamed. Are the

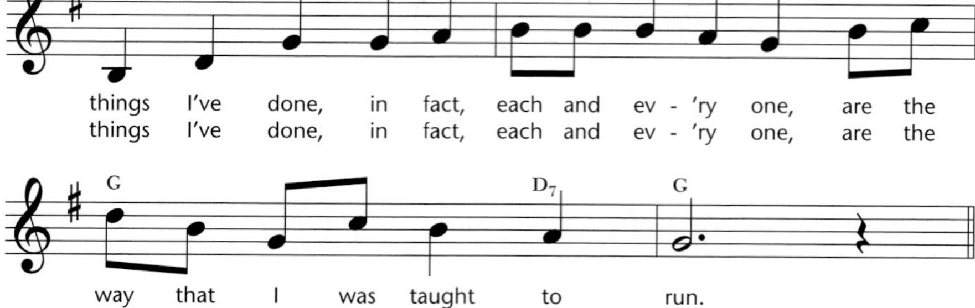
G
things I've done, in fact, each and ev - 'ry one, are the
things I've done, in fact, each and ev - 'ry one, are the
G D7 G
way that I was taught to run.
way that I was taught to run.

26

## Footnotes

### MEETING INDIVIDUAL NEEDS

▶ **Gifted and Talented** There may be a few students in the class who have the skills and would like the opportunity to produce a scene (one short, unified section) of their own "Broadway musical." They can choose songs from this book or elsewhere, modify lyrics or make new ones, create their own dances, invent spoken dialogue, and plan simple staging. It can be presented to the class or other audience group, subject to your approval.

### BUILDING SKILLS THROUGH MUSIC

▶**Writing** Have students write a paragraph to paraphrase and summarize the narrative of "Waitin' for the Light to Shine." Encourage students to use what they have written to help them sing the song expressively.

### SPOTLIGHT ON

▶ **Broadway Musicals** Also known as American musical theater, this genre began to develop after the American Civil War. It came mostly from elements of minstrel shows and vaudeville. Early musicals had songs, dances, comedy sketches, and other acts strung together without a cohesive theme, or with only a loose and insubstantial plot. Important figures in the change to a unified story with strategically inserted music and dance were George M. Cohan, George Gershwin, and Jerome Kern. The 1920s–1950s were the Golden Age of musicals. They were produced in New York City, but reflected many features of the broader American culture. Musicals are still popular today. There are fewer new productions, but some shows that make it to Broadway can be outstanding.

REFRAIN
G G7
I am wait - in' for the light to shine, I am
C G
wait - in' for the light to shine.
G
I have lived in the dark - ness for so long, I am
1. G D7 G 2
wait - in' for the light to shine.
2. G
wait - in' for the light, I am wait - in' for the light, I am
G D7 G
wait - in' for the light to shine.
"Jim" and "Huck" in *Big River*
A Song of Revelation
In "Waitin' for the Light to Shine," the singer shares his feelings. Explain what he means by *darkness* and *light.*
Unit 1 27

# 1 Introduce

Discuss the idea of tonal center or "home tone" with students. Play parts of "Waitin' for the Light to Shine" **CD 1-43.** Explain to students that you will play only part of the recording, and when the music stops, you will ask them to hum the tone that feels like "home." (Stop at the end of verse 1, then try some other spots.) If students have difficulty finding the tonal center, sing it for them. Then leave the activity for a while and try it again later.

# 2 Develop

### Listening

6b **ASK What do you think the phrase *waitin' for the light to shine* means?** (Accept various answers.)

Invite volunteers to share thoughts with the class. Have students listen to "Waitin' for the Light to Shine" and read the text of the song on pp. 26–27. Then share ideas again.

1b Ask volunteers to read aloud the second paragraph on p. 28 that gives the setting for the song and for the show. With this as background, have students sing "Waitin' for the Light to Shine" along with the recording, paying attention to dynamics, phrasing, and interpretation.

Broaden the topic from *Big River* to Broadway musicals. Have students read the first paragraph on p. 28 about Broadway musicals.

**ASK What different kinds of musicians are in a Broadway musical?** (solo singers, chorus, orchestra)

**Where does the orchestra sit?** (in the "pit")

**Do Broadway shows use movement?** (yes, dance)

**Where does the term "Broadway" come from?** (the name of a street in New York City)

**continued on page 28**

## Skills Reinforcement

▶ **Listening** Hearing the tonal center of a song takes practice and leads to increased "in-tune" singing. Regular "quick check" activities will help. Students can

- Play a short portion of a song recording.
- Hum the tonal center.
- Check it with a resonator bell that is the tonal center of the song.

Skip to the end of the recorded example, if possible. That is where the tonal center is likely to be strongest. Also, a good time to have students hum the tonal center is when they are first introduced to a new song with a recording.

## Across the Curriculum

▶ **Language Arts** It is not often that a novel is so powerful that it provokes a firestorm of controversy. Samuel Clemens, better known as Mark Twain, managed to write such a novel in 1885, with *The Adventures of Huckleberry Finn.* Battle lines were quickly drawn. Detractors screamed that the book had no plot, no motive, and no moral. The novel's supporters were quick to present the other side. They pointed to the humor, the accurate portrayal of life, the fine use of dialects, the cohesiveness of the story, and the inherent goodness of Huck. Eventually, the supporters won in the court of public opinion, and the book was canonized into the realm of the "classics" in the late 1940s.

Have students name all the Broadway musicals they can think of. Ask students if anyone has ever seen a Broadway musical. If so, allow them to share the experience with the class.

Have students read p. 29 and discuss the roles of Roger Miller (composer) and Linda Twine (musical director) in developing *Big River*. On the board or on a chart, make a list of the many people needed to produce a musical and their tasks:

- Author—writes the story
- Composer—writes the music
- Lyricist—writes the song words (the lyrics)
- Choreographer—plans and directs the dances
- Director—plans and directs on-stage action
- Musical Director—directs the music and leads the orchestra
- The Cast—the actors, singers, and dancers
- Producers—provide the money and services that get the show ready to present

ASK **Can you think of other people who would be involved in a musical production?** (instrumental musicians, set designers, costume designers, lighting designers, stagehands)

### Singing

Invite students to sing "Waitin' for the Light to Shine" **CD 1-43.** Encourage them to listen carefully to the recording and to each other to maintain good intonation. Focus attention on the tonal center of the song. (G)

For more practice identifying tonal centers, have students complete the Show What You Know activity on p. 29. Refer to Resource Book p. B-2.

## A Light on Broadway

The American Broadway musical has been going strong for more than seventy years. The name *Broadway* comes from the famous New York City street where many of the musical theaters are located. Musicals are plays with speaking, singing, and dancing. The music is usually played by an orchestra in a pit in front of the stage. *West Side Story, The Sound of Music,* and *The Lion King* are famous Broadway musicals. Can you name others?

"Waitin' for the Light to Shine" is from the Broadway musical *Big River*. This show is based on Mark Twain's book *The Adventures of Huckleberry Finn*. In this book, set in the mid-1800s, the main characters, Huck and Jim, travel together on a raft down the mighty Mississippi River.

**Tune In**

Rene Auberjonois (Odo in *Deep Space 9*) and Brent Spiner (Data in *Star Trek—The Next Generation*) have both played the character Duke in *Big River* on Broadway.

28

# Footnotes

## Across the Curriculum

▶ **Language Arts** Ask students to talk with a partner about hopes and dreams they have for their future, what the song calls "light." What is their light? What will it take to get to that light?

Make several different construction paper cutouts of items that create light (such as candles, flashlights, and street lights). Ask students to select a cutout on which to write their hopes for the future. Display these on bulletin boards.

## Teacher to Teacher

▶ **Guest Performers** Nothing has more impact in a music class than guest performers. Contact your local high school choral director to find out if students could perform "show tunes" for the class. (You might also try a local light opera or theater group.) Before the performance, you or the guests can give the class a brief synopsis of the story for the musical. Afterward, give class members an opportunity to ask questions.

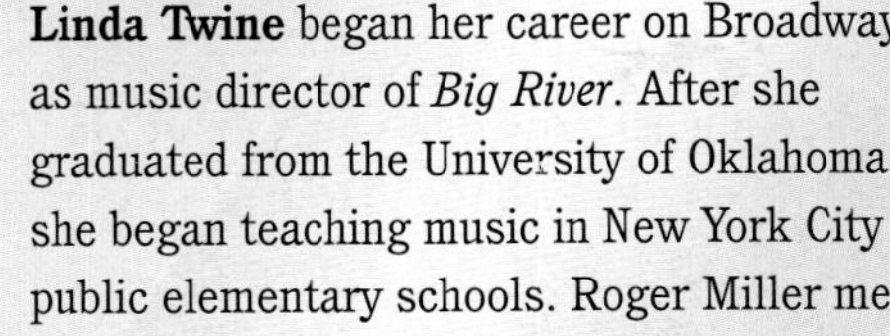


# ROGER MILLER AND LINDA TWINE

**Roger Miller** (1936–1992) wrote the music for *Big River*. He was famous as a country music singer and songwriter. *Big River* was his first attempt at writing a show for the stage, and the show was a big success. It had more than 1,000 performances in New York from 1985 to 1988, and it won seven Tony Awards. Roger Miller was made a member of the Country Music Hall of Fame in 1995.

**Linda Twine** began her career on Broadway as music director of *Big River*. After she graduated from the University of Oklahoma, she began teaching music in New York City public elementary schools. Roger Miller met her and discovered that she understood the style of music he wanted for *Big River*, so he asked her to be music director for the Broadway show.

## Show What You Know!

**Read** the following melodies using pitch syllables.

Look at the phrases above. How would you **identify** the tonal center of these phrases if the beginning were not marked with *do?*



# 3 CLOSE

### Moving

Drawing on student suggestions, develop choreography for "Waitin' for the Light to Shine," to perform while singing. Adapt the arrangement for the available space in the classroom. Designate soloists, chorus, and dancers (chorus and dancers can be the same).

**Element: MELODY** **ASSESSMENT**

6e **Observation** Review the idea of tonal center, or "home tone," with students. Then ask them to listen carefully for the tonal center as you play several brief recordings. (You may wish to use some of the songs learned previously in Unit 1.) After each recording stops, sing two different pitches for students. One will be the tonal center, one will not. Have students listen with eyes closed and raise their hands when they hear the correct tonal center.

## SKILLS REINFORCEMENT

2b ▶ **Recorder** Students can play the recorder during the verse of "Waitin' for the Light to Shine." Remind them to shape the syllable *daah* on each note. Check student hand postion: left hand on top and right hand below with right thumb behind the fourth and fifth holes and right hand fingers curved over the holes.

## TECHNOLOGY/MEDIA LINK

**Web Site** Have students go to *www.sfsuccessnet.com* for links to more information on *Big River* and *The Adventures of Huckleberry Finn*, the book on which the musical is based.

**Multimedia** Use a slide show program to develop "scenery" and lighting for the choreography above. Assigned students can create and operate a slide show to be projected as chorus and dancers perform.

## LESSON AT A GLANCE

**Element Focus** **TIMBRE** Vocal timbres

**Skill Objective** **LISTENING** Identify and describe different vocal timbres

**Connection Objective** **CULTURE** Discuss differences in culture that contribute to different vocal styles

**MATERIALS**

- "I'm Gonna Sing" **CD 2-7**
  **Recording Routine:** Intro (4 m.); v. 1; interlude (4 m.); v. 2; interlude (4 m.); v. 3; interlude (4 m.); v. 4; coda
- *Ghel moma* (excerpt) **CD 2-1**
- *Sigit "Alash"* (excerpt) **CD 2-2**
- *I Don't Want to Feel Like That* (excerpt) **CD 2-3**
- *Powwow Song* (excerpt) **CD 2-4**
- *"Nahandove"* from *Chansons madecasses* (excerpt) **CD 2-5**
- *Rain, Rain, Beautiful Rain* (excerpt) **CD 2-6**
- **Resource Book** pp. H-7, J-4
- world map or globe

**VOCABULARY**

vocal timbre

**National Standards**

**1b** Sing expressively with appropriate dynamics, phrasing, and interpretation
**6b** Describe music by explaining how it sounds
**6c** Use appropriate terms to explain voices
**6d** Identify the sounds of male and female adult voices
**9a** Listen to identify music from different cultures

**MORE MUSIC CHOICES**

Other examples of vocal timbre:
*Route 66*, p. 279
*Dúlamán*, p. 299
"Love Can Build a Bridge," p. 324

# MANY Voices

There are as many different "colors" in the sounds we hear as in the world we see. **Timbre** [TAM-ber] means "the color of a sound." Musicians use words such as *bright, dull, dark, mellow, clear, light, open,* and *shrill* to describe sound colors.

**Timbre** is the unique quality or tone color of sounds.

Every musical instrument has its own timbre, and each instrument can produce different shades of its own color. For example, just as you are able to see differences in shades of yellow or blue, musicians are able to hear differences in sounds.

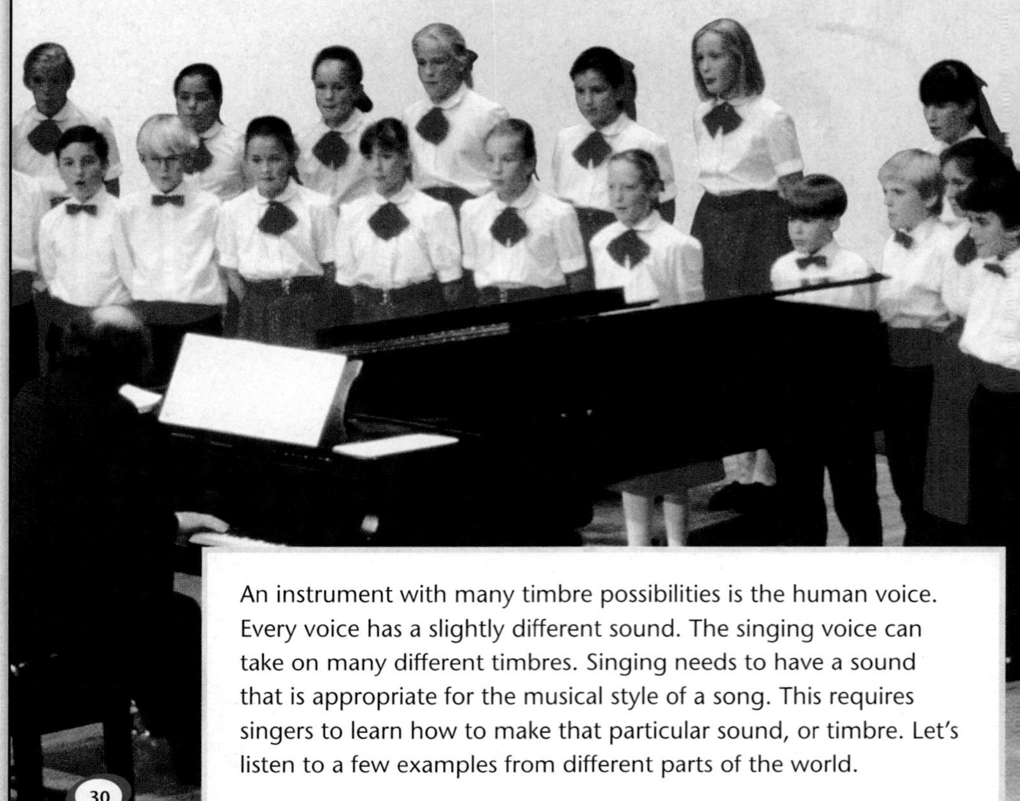

An instrument with many timbre possibilities is the human voice. Every voice has a slightly different sound. The singing voice can take on many different timbres. Singing needs to have a sound that is appropriate for the musical style of a song. This requires singers to learn how to make that particular sound, or timbre. Let's listen to a few examples from different parts of the world.

30

## Footnotes

### CULTURAL CONNECTION

▶ **Zulu** The Zulu people are the largest ethnic group in South Africa. Their home nation is in the KwaZulu/Natal province. They have a highly organized clan life. (A clan consists of several extended households under the authority of the senior man of the group.) Many Zulu, especially men, leave their homes to seek employment in the cities. The *mbube* (mm-BOO-beh) singing tradition (see p. 32) developed in the townships where they lived, dormitory style, on the edges of the cities.

### BUILDING SKILLS THROUGH MUSIC

▶ **Social Studies** Have students locate on a map the countries represented in each of the listening selections on pp. 31–32.

### SKILLS REINFORCEMENT

▶ **Keyboard** Students can accompany "I'm Gonna Sing," p. 33, on keyboard instruments. Use the notation on p. 33. Have students follow the words to the song, as well as the chord symbols above the words, and change chords as indicated in the notation. There are only two chords in the song, A and $E_7$. Have students play an E chord rather than an $E_7$. Have students play the A chord in root position (A on the bottom, C♯, and E), and the E chord in first inversion (G♯ on the bottom, B, and E). In this manner, students may keep the E throughout, and shift only the two bottom notes when the chord changes. Refer to Resource Book p. H-7 for rhythm patterns to accompany this song.

## Voices Around the World

These people learn to sing with the sound typical of their culture. **Listen** to the timbre of the voices of these singers.

▶ Bulgarian singers

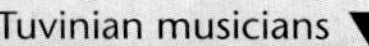

Tuvinian musicians ▼

▲ CD 2-1 **Ghel moma**

**by S. Moutaftshiev**
**as performed by Le Mystère des Voix Bulgares**

One quality of Bulgarian vocal music is harmony created by singing notes very close together, producing a special ringing sound.

◀ CD 2-2 **Sigit "Alash"**

**as performed by Tuvinian singers and musicians**

This man from Tuva is singing *choomej* (singing technique). He changes the inside shape of his mouth to make the higher and lower pitched sounds.

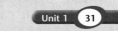

CD 2-3 **I Don't Want to Feel Like That** ▶

**by Teresa Radigan and Donald Schlitz, Jr.**
**as performed by Patty Loveless**

Loveless, a native of Kentucky, is known in country music for her soulful singing.

▲ Patty Loveless

# 1 Introduce

6c Have five students go to the back of the classroom. Ask each student to say the same short statement aloud: "time for pizza," or some other phrase. The remaining students close their eyes, listen to the voices, and identify each student by name. Also give the class a set of words they can use to categorize and describe each voice—smooth, rough, high, low, bright, clear, and so on. Do not include words that express an opinion about the voice (such as *beautiful* or *ugly*).

**SAY** Each voice has a quality that makes it recognizable. This is called *timbre.*

# 2 Develop

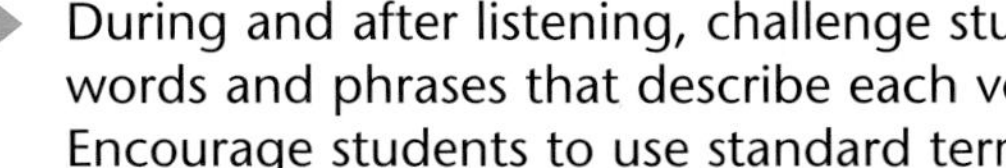

### Listening

Each of the listening examples on pp. 31 and 32 illustrates a highly individual type of singing. Before introducing them, discuss the idea that each type of singing is respected and considered totally acceptable in the culture or cultures in which it is practiced. Listening to and talking about these examples from diverse cultures will help students expand their awareness of world cultures.

9a During and after listening, challenge students to find words and phrases that describe each vocal timbre. Encourage students to use standard terminology in explaining their responses.

The Bulgarian women who sing *Ghel moma* **CD 2-1** have a style of group singing that also makes use of overtones. The vocal sound is straight and direct. The intervals between voice parts tend to be small. The dissonance of the combined upper overtones causes a special ringing quality in the sound. The style reflects the togetherness and bonding of women in this culture. This type of singing has long been part of Bulgarian folk heritage.

**continued on page 32**

## Spotlight On

▶ **Throat Singers of Tuva** Tuva is a country at the crossroads between the old Soviet Union and Outer Mongolia. It is a natural world of mountains, forest, steppes, horses, reindeer, yaks, and sheep. It is home to a very ancient sound on the edges of music, the sound of a "throat singer." The singer is actually doing "overtone singing"—singing the main frequency (the fundamental) and one or two harmonics (overtones) at the same time! The overtones going up intervals are an octave, a fifth, a major third, and so on. Normally these harmonics sound softer than the fundamental, but the throat singers can actually make the overtones louder.

## Teacher to Teacher

▶ **Practicing Listening** Like visual colors, tone colors are much easier to identify than to describe. They must be identified at the moment of hearing until students can identify them easily. Seeing pictures of instruments may assist students in recalling the timbre of the instrument. Brief, informal timbre quizzes can be very helpful. Play 10-second excerpts of five different examples. Students can work in pairs or threes to record their answers. Reveal correct answers immediately. Any examples missed by a sizable number of students should be played again. You may wish to have capable students develop such quizzes for the class using the Sound Bank starting on p. 466, and recordings from the book.

Assign a small group to find Tuva on the map of Asia and show the location to the class. Play the recording of *Sigit "Alash"* **CD 2-2.** Explain that Tuvans use the word *choomej* (KHOO-may) to identify this type of singing. People in Central Asia have been throat singing for centuries, but Tuva has produced the most varied and complex types. "Throat singing" uses the overtone principle. Every sounding tone is accompanied by a series of overtones. Normally these just contribute to the timbre of voices. Throat singers develop the ability to strengthen overtones, making them audible by themselves. Using certain vowel sounds, the singer creates overtones by changing the shape of the mouth cavity and the position of the tongue and lips.

Have students listen to *I Don't Want to Feel Like That* **CD 2-3.** Help them discover that country-and-western singing is full, clear, and open, often with a somewhat nasal quality. Words are not adapted for singing, but pronounced as they are in speech. Individual singers may use special ornaments in their singing. There is little improvisation in this style.

Invite students to listen to *Powwow Song* **CD 2-4.** A powwow is a Native American social and cultural event that affirms identity and preserves tradition. A powwow includes many kinds of songs and dances. Music is provided by one or more large drums, heads facing up, with a circle of people sitting around. Each person beats the drum with a padded beater. One person is the song leader responsible for knowing and starting each song. The other singers follow the leader and join in shortly after the song has begun. Everyone at the powwow can do the dance. The voices sound more relaxed than in many other types of Native American singing. You can hear both men's and women's voices. Notice that it does not seem very important to stay exactly together. Also notice some nasality and pulsation in the vocal sound.

CD 2-4
**Powwow Song**

**Southern Plains Indians**

This music accompanies a ceremonial social dance. Notice the quality of the performers' voices.

**from *Chansons madecasses***
**by Maurice Ravel**
**as performed by Jessye Norman**

Jessye Norman is a well-known soprano who has performed all over the world.

**by Joseph Shabalala**
**as performed by Ladysmith Black Mambazo**

This South African group sings in simple harmony, with open and natural voices.

Jessye Norman

Ladysmith Black Mambazo

Tune In
"Singing cleanses the soul; when the soul is clean, everything is open."
*Joseph Shabalala*
32


# Footnotes

## Across the Curriculum

**▶ Language Arts** Have students read "Hurt No Living Thing" by Christina Rossetti. Assign one student to read each animal's line, changing the voice to imitate the sound the animal might make—chirping, leaping, and so forth. Have them discuss how to use the voice to convey concepts like "fat" or "crawling."

Hurt no living thing:
Ladybird, nor butterfly,
Nor moth with dusty wing,
No cricket chirping cheerily,
Nor grasshopper so light of leap,
Nor dancing gnat, no beetle fat,
Nor harmless worms that creep.

## Skills Reinforcement

**▶ Recorder** Students can play a recorder part to accompany "I'm Gonna Sing." Check that holes are covered securely.

## Your Voice—Your Song

Children's voices have a wonderful sound of their own—often clear and somewhat light. As you grow into your teenage years, you will develop the power and flexibility needed for adult singing. Here's a song about singing. As you **sing**, mix your own special vocal timbre with all the other timbres of your classmates to make a vocal rainbow.

CD 2-7
MIDI 2
I'm Gonna Sing
s, l, d r m
African American Spiritual
do
A
1. I'm gon - na sing when the spir - it says "Sing,"
2. I'm gon - na shout when the spir - it says "Shout,"
3. I'm gon - na pray when the spir - it says "Pray,"
4. I'm gon - na sing when the spir - it says "Sing,"
A E7
I'm gon - na sing when the spir - it says "Sing,"
I'm gon - na shout when the spir - it says "Shout,"
I'm gon - na pray when the spir - it says "Pray,"
I'm gon - na sing when the spir - it says "Sing,"
A
I'm gon - na sing when the spir - it says "Sing,"
I'm gon - na shout when the spir - it says "Shout,"
I'm gon - na pray when the spir - it says "Pray,"
I'm gon - na sing when the spir - it says "Sing,"
A E7 A
And o - bey the spir - it of the Lord.
Unit 1 33

Have students listen to *"Nahandove"* from *Chansons madecasses* **CD 2-5.** Explain that art songs are Western classical songs composed for solo singers who have studied and developed skill in this style. It requires the ability to sing with a full, open tone that includes *vibrato* with dynamics from very soft to very loud, and an even tone quality over a wide range of pitches. The singer adapts pronunciation to make best use of vowels. The singing sound needs to be smooth and continuous. Art songs are sung as the composer sets them down on paper. Very rarely is there any improvisation. A supporting accompaniment is provided for these songs on a piano and sometimes on another instrument or a group. In some instances, the accompaniment also requires considerable skill. Art songs are sung at concerts and recitals.

Explain that *mbube* (mm-BOO-beh) is a style of male group singing developed in recent decades in South Africa. There are mbube competitions in which groups compete for prizes. Singers in a group are very sensitive to each other and sing as one voice, even when they sing harmony. There is often a part for a soloist, who acts as leader of the other singers. The group Ladysmith Black Mambazo has made this kind of singing known around the world. Then play the recording of *Rain, Rain, Beautiful Rain* **CD 2-6.**

### Singing

1b These examples demonstrate that the whole world sings, though not in the same way. Ask students to blend together as they sing "I'm Gonna Sing" **CD 2-7.**

## 3 CLOSE

Element: TIMBRE
ASSESSMENT

6b 9a **Observation/Music Journal Writing** Have students listen as you play brief examples from each of the diverse vocal styles heard in the lesson. Have students point to the picture in the book (or write a brief description) that identifies and categorizes the adult singers in each example.

### TEACHER TO TEACHER

6c 6d ▶ **Developing Interest in Singing** Ask students to think of all the places they hear singing throughout the week. What are the different styles of singing they hear at school, home, on television, the Internet, CDs and recordings, radios, at sporting events, clubs and organizations, church, and concerts? Make a class list of the various styles of vocal music that students name.

To check for understanding of vocal timbres, have students answer the questions in Activity Master 3. Refer to Resource Book p. J-4.

### TECHNOLOGY/MEDIA LINK

**Video Library** Have students view segments featuring different singing styles. Ask them to

- Describe the singing style of each performer. (use of vibrato, voice quality, drama, expression)
- Describe how tone quality relates to the style of the music.

## LESSON AT A GLANCE

**Element Focus** **TEXTURE/HARMONY** Multi-layered ostinatos

**Skill Objective** **PLAYING** Play an ostinato accompaniment with a recorded song

**Connection Activity** **STYLE** Discuss Afro-Cuban musical style

**MATERIALS**

- *"Sonando"* (Spanish) **CD 2-9**
- *"Sonando"* (English) **CD 2-10**
  **Recording Routine:** Intro (10 m.); vocal; interlude (16 m.) vocal; coda
- **Pronunciation Practice/Translation** p. 474
- *A Night in Tunisia* **CD 2-14**
- **Dance Directions** for *"Sonando"* p. 506
- **Resource Book** p. A-4
- nonpitched percussion instruments

**VOCABULARY**

texture ostinato

**National Standards**

- **1c** Sing from memory songs from diverse cultures
- **2b** Perform rhythms on appropriate instruments
- **2f** Play instruments independently against contrasting parts
- **9b** Describe how elements of music are used in various cultures

**MORE MUSIC CHOICES**

Another song with ostinatos:
"Streets of Laredo," p. 272

LESSON 10 Element: TEXTURE/HARMONY Skill: PLAYING Connection: STYLE

LAYERED SOUNDS... CHA CHA CHA

Music has **texture.** It can be thick or thin, depending on the number of layers. The first two measures of *"Sonando"* are rhythm ostinatos you can **play** while you **sing** the song. Practice clapping each ostinato, then **perform** *"Sonando."*

**Texture** is the layering of sounds to create a thick or thin quality in music.

CD 2-9 MIDI 3

SONANDO

English Words by Alice D. Firgau

Words and Music by Peter Terrace
Arranged by Ted Solis, Adapted and Arranged by Kay Edwards

r f s l t
do
G
F
So - nan - do (clap) pa - ra bai - lar,
They're play - ing a cha - cha - cha.
Go - za (clap) mi cha - cha - cha.
Come on, let's have some fun.
34

# 1 INTRODUCE

Play *"Sonando"* **CD 2-9** and have students

- Keep the beat by clapping.
- Create movements.
- Share information from Cultural Connection below.

# Footnotes

## CULTURAL CONNECTION

9b ▶ **Son Montuno Style** *"Sonando"* was composed in *son montuno* style. *Son* is probably the most important musical style of Cuba. It developed by combining African-derived percussion instruments and Spanish-derived plucked strings. S*on montuno* is one of the oldest forms, dating from the mid-1700s.

## BUILDING SKILLS THROUGH MUSIC

▶**Writing** Once students have performed on or listened to the four rhythm instruments featured in the arrangement of *"Sonando"* on p. 34, have them write a short paragraph describing the timbre of each instrument.

## SPOTLIGHT ON

▶ **The Performer** Poncho Sanchez (b. 1951) is well known for his conga playing in Latin jazz and salsa music. He is a Mexican American. Sanchez was born in Laredo, Texas, but he grew up in Los Angeles. At an early age he developed a passion for Afro-Cuban and jazz styles and started playing both as a teenager. Sanchez is an active performer and has recorded several CDs.

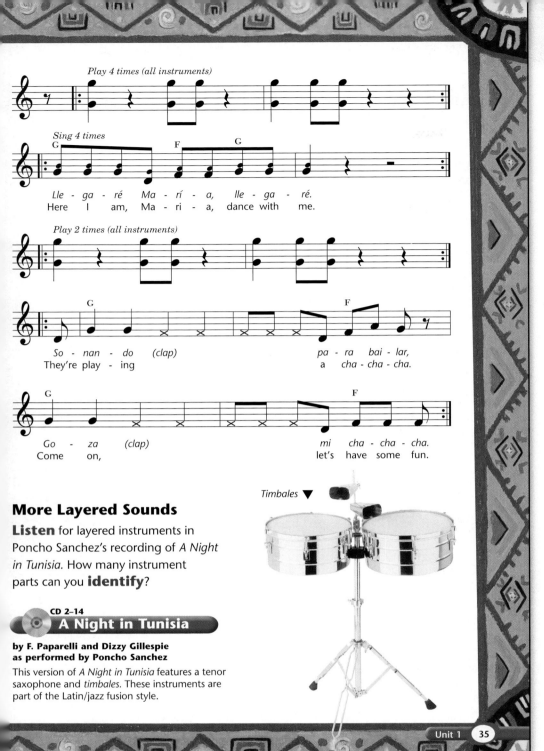

Play 4 times (all instruments)

Sing 4 times

G F G

Lle - ga - ré Ma - rí - a, lle - ga - ré.
Here I am, Ma - ri - a, dance with me.

Play 2 times (all instruments)

G F

So - nan - do (clap) pa - ra bai - lar,
They're play - ing a cha - cha - cha.

G F

Go - za (clap) mi cha - cha - cha.
Come on, let's have some fun.

Timbales ▼

## More Layered Sounds

**Listen** for layered instruments in Poncho Sanchez's recording of *A Night in Tunisia.* How many instrument parts can you **identify**?

CD 2-14
**A Night in Tunisia**

**by F. Paparelli and Dizzy Gillespie**
**as performed by Poncho Sanchez**

This version of *A Night in Tunisia* features a tenor saxophone and *timbales*. These instruments are part of the Latin/jazz fusion style.

Unit 1 35

# 2 Develop

### Singing

Invite students to sing the English version of *"Sonando"* **CD 2-10**. Then have them listen to the Pronunciation Practice Track for the song in Spanish **CD 2-12** and sing with the students on the recording. Refer to Resource Book p. A-4.

### Playing

1c Play *"Sonando"* **CD 2-9** for students. Have them sing the melody. Introduce the percussion ostinatos shown on p. 34.

2b **Conga/maracas pattern:** Use student names in conjunction with a phrase to establish the rhythm (e.g., *Play-the-con-ga, Mich-ael, Kar-en*). To practice, have students pat six hand strokes on the desktop and two on the legs.

**Guiro:** Use the words *play gui-ro.* On *play,* use a longer, two-part stroke on the guiro; on *gui-ro,* use two short, tapped strokes.

2f **Claves:** Use the words *play cla-ve* (rest) *to-day* (rest). Count the pattern carefully, then put all parts together.

### Listening

Have students listen to the combination of Latin American percussion instruments in *A Night in Tunisia* **CD 2-14.** See the Sound Bank entry for *timbales* on p. 470.

# 3 Close

**Element: TEXTURE/HARMONY** ASSESSMENT

**Performance/Observation** Have students perform *"Sonando"* with **CD 2-9.** Assign small groups to tap each of the ostinato rhythms on p. 34, using body percussion. (Students may also create their own ostinatos.) Have them perform the song again with several students playing the ostinatos on small percussion instruments. Observe that students are able to independently perform the ostinatos.

## Skills Reinforcement

▶ **Creating** Invite students to experiment with Latin percussion instruments. Have them create their own rhythmic phrases and ostinatos and perform them with *"Sonando."*

▶ **Moving** For a patterned dance activity to accompany *"Sonando,"* refer to the dance directions on p. 506.

## Technology/Media Link

**MIDI/Sequencing Software** Use a sequencing program to display the percussion tracks of the MIDI song file *"Sonando"* in piano roll view. Mute the other tracks. As the file plays back, have the class watch the display of repeated rhythm patterns. Display one percussion track at a time and have students clap or play the rhythms on instruments. After students practice three tracks, divide the class into three groups to perform the rhythms along with the song.

LESSON
Core 11

## LESSON AT A GLANCE

**Element Focus** **TEXTURE/HARMONY** Multi-layered ostinato accompaniment

**Skill Objective** **PLAYING** Play an ostinato accompaniment

**Connection Activity** **CULTURE** Discuss the sound and construction of an Australian musical instrument

**MATERIALS**

- "Tie Me Kangaroo Down, Sport" **CD 2-15**

  **Recording Routine** Intro (6 m.); v. 1; refrain; interlude (2 m.); v. 2; refrain; interlude (2 m.); v. 3; refrain; interlude (2 m.); v. 4; refrain; interlude (2 m.); v. 5; refrain; interlude (2 m.); v. 6; refrain; interlude (2 m.); coda
- *Brolga One* **CD 2-17**
- **Resource Book** p. I-4
- nonpitched percussion instruments

**VOCABULARY**

didgeridoo ostinato

**◆◆◆◆ National Standards ◆◆◆◆**

**2b** Perform rhythms on appropriate instruments
**2f** Play instruments independently against contrasting parts
**5a** Read half, quarter, and eighth notes and rests in duple meter
**6d** Identify the sounds of instruments from various cultures

**MORE MUSIC CHOICES**

Another song with ostinatos:
"Canoe Song," p. 76

# 1 INTRODUCE

Read the lyrics of "Tie Me Kangaroo Down, Sport" with students. Ask them to describe the animals mentioned in the song.

LESSON
11

Element: TEXTURE/HARMONY

Skill: PLAYING

Connection: CULTURE

# How's the Texture?

When is a country a continent? When it's Australia. Australians have their own names for things found only in their country. "Tie Me Kangaroo Down, Sport" is an Australian song that plays with names.

**Perform** these ostinatos. Then **play** them as a layered accompaniment while you **sing** the song.

Aboriginal Austra[lian] playing the *didge[ridoo]*

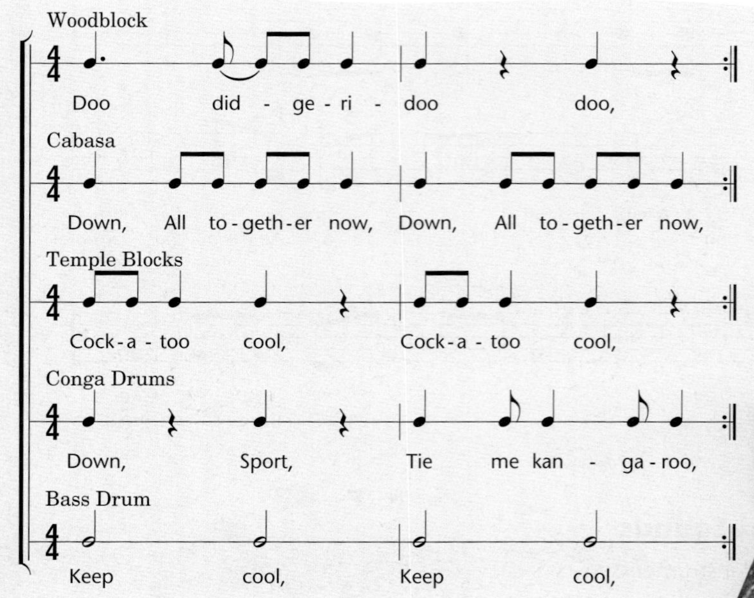
Woodblock
Doo did - ge - ri - doo doo,
Cabasa
Down, All to - geth - er now, Down, All to - geth - er now,
Temple Blocks
Cock - a - too cool, Cock - a - too cool,
Conga Drums
Down, Sport, Tie me kan - ga - roo,
Bass Drum
Keep cool, Keep cool,

**Listen** to *Brolga One* and notice the sound of the *didgeridoo* [DID-jeh-ree-doo]. The *didgeridoo* was invented and played by the aboriginal people of Australia. Now, everyone wants to play the *didgeridoo!* Wouldn't you?

CD 2-17
**Brolga One**

**created and performed by aboriginal musicians with *didgeridoo***

This recording includes singing along with the *didgeridoo*.

36

# Footnotes

## SKILLS REINFORCEMENT

▶ **Guitar** Design a guitar accompaniment for the song "Tie Me Kangaroo Down, Sport." Raise the key one step to "G" and play the chords G, C, and $D_7$. Divide the class into three groups. Assign one chord to each group to play during the song.

▶ **Recorder** For a recorder part to play with "Tie Me Kangaroo Down, Sport," see Resource Book p. I-4.

## BUILDING SKILLS THROUGH MUSIC

▶ **Social Studies** Have students locate Australia on the map. Have them list the animals in the song "Tie Me Kangaroo Down, Sport." Discuss the characteristics of animals and musical instruments indigenous to Australia.

## MEETING INDIVIDUAL NEEDS

▶ **Including Everyone** Give students many opportunities for silent practice before assigning instruments and ostinatos. Assign section leaders (students who have performed the ostinato successfully) to groups (vary ability levels in each group). Group members perform silently, showing good technique and rhythmic accuracy that is modeled by section leaders. Some students, who may be more successful performing only on the word *down* in the song, could be leaders for new rhythm groups. Give students many opportunities to be leaders and to perform different ostinatos on various instruments with different children as this song is sung throughout the school year.

CD 2-15
MIDI 4
Tie Me Kangaroo Down, Sport
s, t, d r m f s
Words and Music by Rolf and Bruce Harris
VERSE
F F7 B♭ Gm7
do
1. Watch me wal - la - bys feed, mate.
2. Keep me cock - a - too cool, Curl.
3. Take me ko - a - - - la back, Jack.
4. Mind me plat - y - pus duck, Bill.
Refrain Tie me kan - ga - roo down, sport.
C F
Watch me wal - la - bys feed.
Keep me cock - a - too cool.
Take me ko - a - - - la back. He
Mind me plat - y - pus duck. Don't
Tie me kan - ga - roo down.
F F7 B♭ Gm7
They're a dan - ger - ous breed, mate. So
Don't go act - ing the fool, Curl. Just
lives some - where on the track, Mac. So
let him go run - ning a - mok, Bill. So
Tie me kan - ga - roo down, sport.
C7 F
watch me wal - la - bys feed. All to - geth- er now! (to Refrain)
keep me cock - a - too cool.
take me ko - a - - la back.
mind me plat - y - pus duck.
Tie me kan - ga - roo down. (to Verses)
5. Play your didgeridoo, Blue.
Play your didgeridoo.
Keep playing 'til I shoot thro', Blue.
Play your didgeridoo.
All together now! Refrain
6. Tan me hide when I'm dead, Fred.
Tan me hide when I'm dead.
So we tanned his hide when he died, Clyde.
And that's it hanging on the shed.
All together now! Refrain
Unit 1 37

# 2 Develop

### Playing

5a Play the song **CD 2-15** and have the class join in on the refrain by the second verse. Help students learn the ostinatos. At least two of them (*cockatoo cool* and *doo, didgeree doo* [rest] *doo*) are simple enough to read from notation. Assist by modeling word patterns if students have problems reading accurately.

Convert patterns to body percussion ostinatos. Ask students to use body percussion that is comfortable enough to repeat many times. Divide the class into four groups. While one group sings, the other three play ostinatos. Try having one ostinato only with each verse. Combine all ostinatos on the refrain.

2b 2f Transfer the body percussion patterns to nonpitched percussion instruments. Ask students to select instruments that allow the pattern to be played clearly and accurately. Combine with the song.

### Listening

6d Invite students to look at the picture of the musician playing the didgeridoo and then share the information about the instrument from Cultural Connection below. Play the recording of *Brolga One* **CD 2-17,** and discuss the layering of sounds in the recording. See the Sound Bank entry for the *didgeridoo* on p. 467.

# 3 Close

**Skill: PLAYING** ASSESSMENT

**Performance/Observation** Invite students to perform "Tie Me Kangaroo Down, Sport" with **CD 2-15,** assigning different groups to tap each of the ostinato rhythms on p. 36, using body percussion. Have them perform the song again on nonpitched percussion instruments and observe their ability to play a multi-layered ostinato accompaniment.

## Cultural Connection

6d ▶ **Didgeridoo** This instrument is unique to the aboriginal peoples of northern Australia. It consists of a length of eucalyptus branch about 3–4 inches in diameter that has had the center hollowed out by termites. Beeswax is layered onto one end as a mouthpiece. Producing a sound on the *didgeridoo* is much like playing a tuba. It plays a fundamental drone plus the overtone two octaves and a third higher. Rhythms and other pitch partials are added by bursts and pulsations of breath. The player can also sing into it while playing. Students can create their own didgeridoos from PVC pipes or other cylindrical materials.

## Technology/Media Link

**MIDI/Sequencing Software** Have students use sequencing software and the MIDI song file for "Tie Me Kangaroo Down, Sport" to create additional layers of texture. Students can choose percussion sounds from those available in the classroom software. Then they can save and play back their new arrangements for each other.

# LESSON 12

## LESSON AT A GLANCE

**Element Focus** **TEXTURE/HARMONY** Layers of sounds

**Skill Objective** **SINGING** Sing a call-and-response song with layers of voices

**Connection Activity** **SOCIAL STUDIES** Discuss the origins of steel drums

**MATERIALS**

- "Pay Me My Money Down" **CD 2-18**
  **Recording Routine:** Intro (4 m.); v. 1, refrain; v. 2, refrain; v. 3, refrain; coda
- *Pay Me My Money Down* (excerpt) **CD 2-20**
- *Eine kleine Nachtmusik* (excerpt) **CD 2-21**
- *Somebody* (excerpt) **CD 2-22**
- **Resource Book** p. J-5
- xylophones, metallophones, glockenspiel

**VOCABULARY**

call and response verse refrain

**National Standards**

**1c** Sing from memory songs from diverse cultures
**3b** Improvise rhythmic and melodic ostinato accompaniments
**3d** Improvise instrumental pieces, using body percussion
**6e** While listening to music, move to show a prominent feature of the music

**MORE MUSIC CHOICES**

Other songs with layered sounds:
"Love Will Guide Us," p. 328
"Pastures of Plenty," p. 280

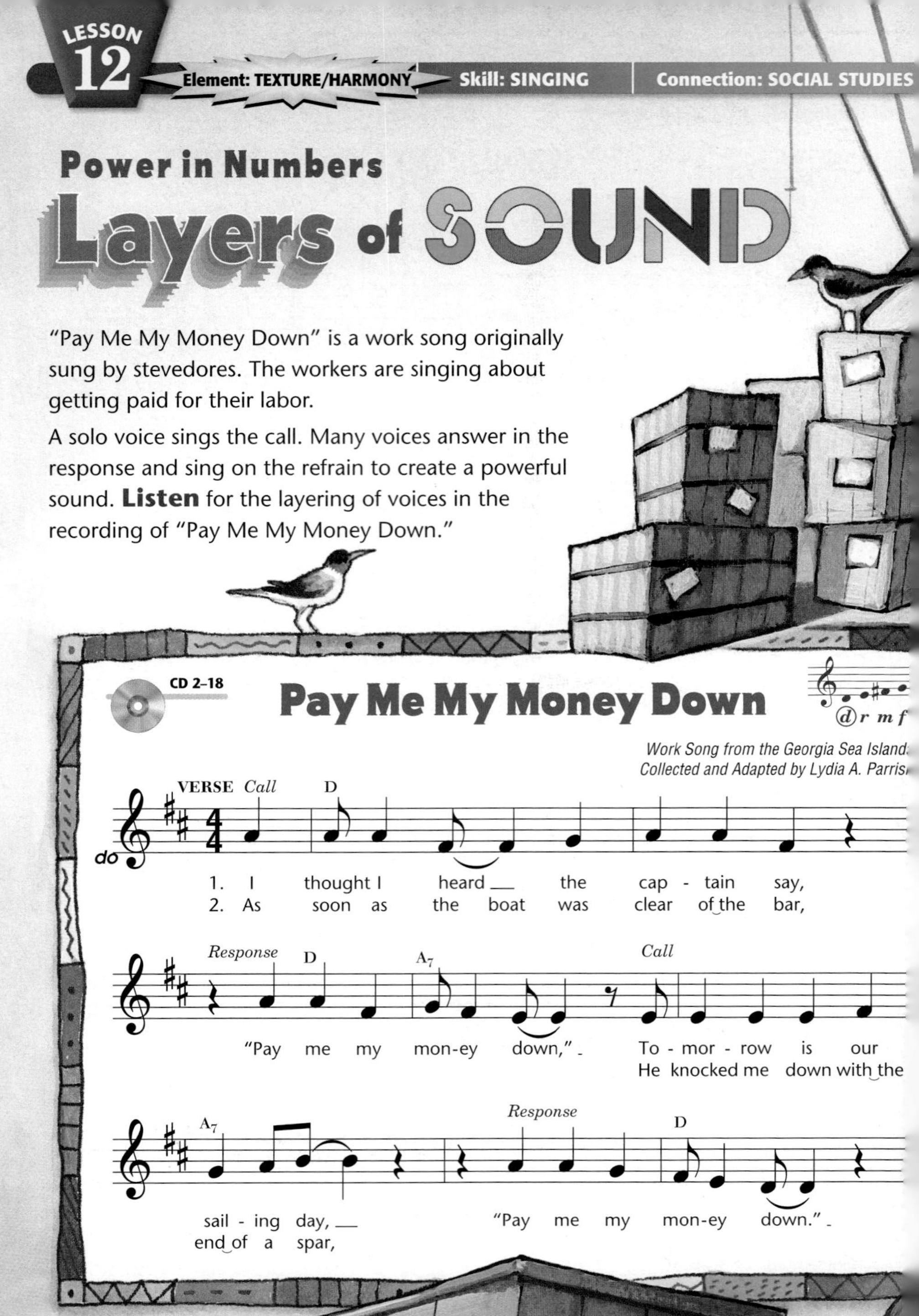
LESSON 12 Element: TEXTURE/HARMONY Skill: SINGING Connection: SOCIAL STUDIES

Power in Numbers

Layers of SOUND

"Pay Me My Money Down" is a work song originally sung by stevedores. The workers are singing about getting paid for their labor.

A solo voice sings the call. Many voices answer in the response and sing on the refrain to create a powerful sound. **Listen** for the layering of voices in the recording of "Pay Me My Money Down."

CD 2-18

Pay Me My Money Down

Work Song from the Georgia Sea Island
Collected and Adapted by Lydia A. Parris

d r m f
VERSE Call
D
do
1. I thought I heard the captain say,
2. As soon as the boat was clear of the bar,
Response
D
A7
"Pay me my money down,"
Call
To-morrow is our
He knocked me down with the
A7
sailing day,
end of a spar,
Response
D
"Pay me my money down."

38

# Footnotes

## CULTURAL CONNECTION

▶ **The Georgia Sea Islands** The Georgia Sea Islands are a group of islands off the coast of Georgia. They developed a unique culture during the time of slavery in the United States because of their isolation from the mainland. The presence of European Americans was minimal on the islands. In many cases, slaves were left to run plantations and other operations rather independently. Inhabitants developed a unique language called Gullah, a mix of English and West African dialects.

## BUILDING SKILLS THROUGH MUSIC

▶ **Reading** Have students read the feature on the steel drum band Amoco Renegades, on p. 41. Then ask students to draw an inference, such as a conclusion or a generalization, based on the information in the text.

## MOVEMENT

3d ▶ **Nonlocomotor Movement** Try this simple body percussion exercise to demonstrate thicker and thinner textures. Divide the class into five groups. Give each group an ostinato to perform that was developed from the name of one or more countries in the Caribbean area. Let each group demonstrate and solidify its ostinato. (It must maintain a steady tempo.) Then have one student act as conductor for all groups, starting and stopping the ostinatos to create contrasts in texture. If only one is sounding, the texture is thin. If all five are sounding, the texture is thick. There should be no attempt to make the patterns louder or softer, only to change the texture.

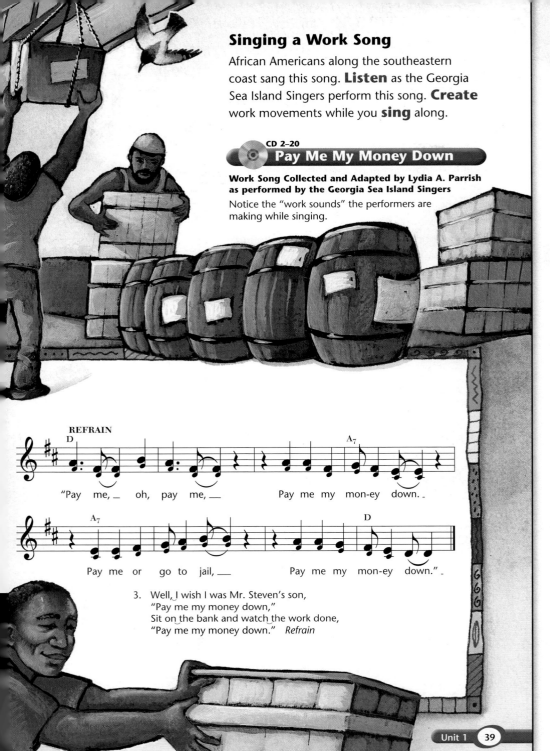

## Singing a Work Song

African Americans along the southeastern coast sang this song. **Listen** as the Georgia Sea Island Singers perform this song. **Create** work movements while you **sing** along.

CD 2–20

### Pay Me My Money Down

**Work Song Collected and Adapted by Lydia A. Parrish as performed by the Georgia Sea Island Singers**

Notice the "work sounds" the performers are making while singing.

REFRAIN

D A7

"Pay me, _ oh, pay me, _ Pay me my mon-ey down. _

A7 D

Pay me or go to jail, _ Pay me my mon-ey down." _

3. Well, I wish I was Mr. Steven's son,
"Pay me my money down,"
Sit on the bank and watch the work done,
"Pay me my money down." *Refrain*



# 1 Introduce

Talk with students about dock workers—what they do, and the advantages and disadvantages of the job. Introduce the word *stevedore.* Invite students to read the text of "Pay Me My Money Down," pp. 38–39. Discuss any other words or phrases students may not be familiar with, such as *clear of the bar* and *spar.* See the Spotlight On, p. 41.

# 2 Develop

### Listening

Play the Georgia Sea Island Singers' version of *Pay Me My Money Down* **CD 2-20.** Invite students to determine places in the song where a motion should happen. Divide the students into small groups. Ask them to

- Develop a motion that illustrates shipboard work to perform in the selected spots.
- Listen again, adding the motions.

Discuss the alternation of solo and group voice parts, and identify call-and-response style. Identify the section of the song that is the same each time (the refrain) and the section that changes (the verse).

### Singing

Invite the class to learn the song. Have them sing call-and-response (solo and group) style during the verse section. Have volunteers sing the solo parts.

ASK **How does the texture of the song change when more voices are added?** (Answers will vary.)

### Moving

Have students develop a stepping motion to go along with the phrases of "Pay Me My Money Down."

For example,

- side-close-side-close
- then side-close-side-close in the other direction

**continued on page 40**

## Across the Curriculum

▶ **Social Studies** The Caribbean Sea is part of the Atlantic Ocean. It is bounded to the south by the northern coast of South America, to the west by the eastern coasts of Central America and some of Mexico, to the north by the Greater Antillean Islands of Cuba, Santo Domingo, Jamaica, and Puerto Rico, and to the east by an island arc reaching from the Virgin Islands on the north to Trinidad at the south. Though there are many individual variations, the island cultures of the Caribbean share some common characteristics because they were all settled by European explorers of various nationalities and African slave groups.

## Meeting Individual Needs

▶ **Solo and Group Singing** Call-and-response songs offer ideal opportunities for students of varying abilities to perform together. Those who need the security of repetition and group support can join in on the responses, while those who need the challenge of performing individually and creating new lyrics can take responsibility for the calls. Security and support derived from group participation are considered very positive qualities in the cultures from which these songs come. It should not be perceived as a limitation if a person cannot handle or does not want an individual part.

Ask pairs or small groups of students to develop an arm motion to go along with this step. They can share their ideas and then perform the movements along with the song with everyone singing and moving together.

## Singing

Invite students to

- Sing the words *pay me my money down* on D.
- Change from D to A on the word *money.*
- Sing the same phrase on A (2 lines below the staff).
- Start on the A and change to D on the word *money.*
- Sing the phrases in sequence.
- Perform them with the song **CD 2-18**.

Have some students sing this part while the rest of the class sings the song. (This Singing activity and the Playing activity below can be combined with the Moving activity on p. 39.)

## Playing

Have students go to mallet instruments. Ask them to play the rhythm of the words *pay me my money down* on a D or an A. Make sure they all play it together. (Speaking the words together first will help.) Once they have mastered this, ask them to

- Start on D, then change to A on the word *money.*
- Start on A, then change to D on *money.*
- Perform the phrase both ways, in sequence—first starting on D, the next time on A.
- Perform with the song **CD 2-18,** using the same phrase routine outlined in the singing activity above.

For an additional playing activity, see Activity Master 4 on Resource Book p. J-5.

## The Power of Layers of Percussion

Caribbean music is filled with layers of instruments. This includes the music of steel drums, made by layering many parts to create an exciting sound. About sixty years ago, musicians in Trinidad discovered how to make drums out of 55-gallon oil storage barrels. Steel drums can be tuned to specific pitches.

Many steel drum bands have fifty players or more! No matter what the size, every band has an "engine room" of instruments such as congas, drum sets, maracas, and claves. The engine room supplies a rhythmic background for the music.

Here is how steel drums are made.

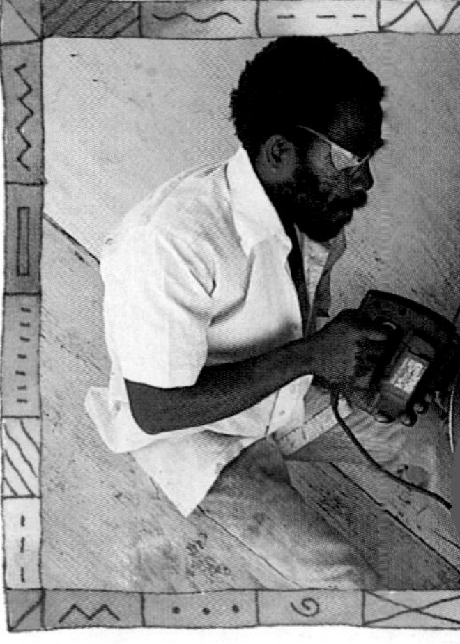

▲ **1.** One end of the barrel is removed. The "skirt" of the barrel is cut to make a high-, medium-, or low-sounding drum.

◀ **2.** The top is hammered into a bowl shape with flat areas that produce definite pitches.

**3.** The entire drum is heated red-hot in a fire to cure the steel. ▶

**Video Library** Watch *Percussion Instruments: Tuned* to learn more about steel drum bands.



# Footnotes

## ACROSS THE CURRICULUM

▶ **Social Studies** Talk with students about getting paid for work. Do people usually get paid before or after their work is finished? Do the students get an allowance? Is it based on work they do at home? Remind students that some people are not paid fairly for their work, and, at some times in history, some were not paid at all. Discuss enslaved people who were taken unwillingly from their homes and made to work for no money. For further information, students may wish to read *From Slave Ship to Freedom Road* by Julius Lester (Dial Books, 1998).

▶ **Math** Discuss the math-based story of Rani, who asks only for one grain of rice, doubled each day for 30 days. How much rice will Rani get? If students got a penny each day and it doubled each day for 30 days, how much money would they have? ($5,368,709.12)

## CHARACTER EDUCATION

▶ **Respect** To help students develop respect for differences among people, instruct them to raise their hand when they agree and lower their hand when they disagree with statements you read. Read statements about various beliefs, such as "My favorite food is hamburgers" and "I like to play video games." Encourage students to pay attention to their classmates' responses. Following the activity, ask students what they noticed about their responses and those of their classmates.

## SKILLS REINFORCEMENT

▶ **Creating** Encourage students to use the word rhythms of "Pay Me My Money Down" to create additional layers of ostinatos using nonpitched percussion instruments. These new ostinatos can be combined with the mallet instrument activity above.

## Classical Music with a Caribbean Flavor

Although steel drum bands are known for playing original calypso music, they also perform arrangements of many other musical styles. **Listen** to the calypso rhythms and layers in this version of *Eine kleine Nachtmusik (A Little Night Music).*

CD 2-21 **Eine kleine Nachtmusik (A Little Night Music)**

**by Wolfgang Amadeus Mozart**

Steel drum bands often play Caribbean versions of European classical orchestral works.

**Amoco Renegades** is one of Trinidad's oldest steel drum bands. Jit Samaroo, director of the band, commented that the name of their group goes back to when "panmen" were considered ruffians more than musicians. The group had over 100 members when it was named champion in 1989 at the steel band competition called "Panorama." For the competition, Amoco Renegades performed *Somebody.*

**Listen** for layers of sound in this recording of *Somebody*.

CD 2-22 **Somebody**

**by Winsford deVine**
**as performed by Amoco Renegades**

This recording was made three days before Amoco Renegades was named champion.



### Listening

Have students

- Read the information about steel drums on p. 40 and the Music Makers feature on Amoco Renegades on p. 41.
- Listen to the recording of *Somebody* **CD 2-22.**
- Describe the types of sounds they heard in the listening selection.

For an additional listening experience with steel drums, have students listen to *Eine kleine Nachtmusik* **CD 2-21.** See the Sound Bank entry for the steel drum on p. 470.

## 3 Close

**Element: TEXTURE/HARMONY — ASSESSMENT**

**Performance/Interviews** Encourage students to sing the responses in "Pay Me My Money Down" **CD 2-18.** Have them sing independently (refrain from prompting them). Lead the class in singing the song again. This time, you sing the calls, and invite students to sing the responses. Encourage some students to sing the call as a solo or in small groups while the rest of the class sings the responses.

As an added layer of texture, you may wish to perform the harmony part in cue notes while students perform the melody.

Invite students to discuss how layering voices and instruments affects timbre. Check for understanding.

### Spotlight On

▶ **Work Songs** Works songs help workers keep their work going smoothly and to keep their spirits up while they do it. Some work songs have special places in them for strong movement, like the Georgia Sea Island Singers' recording in this lesson. With other work songs, workers just move to the strong beat. Then there are songs *about* work that do not necessarily have the rhythm that supports that kind of work, such as "I've Been Working on the Railroad."

▶ **"Pay Me My Money Down"** Students may be unfamiliar with some words in the song. For instance, a "bar" is a long ridge of sand, gravel, or other material near or slightly above the surface of a body of water. A "spar" is a stout pole forming a mast, yard, boom, or gaff.

### Technology/Media Link

**Electronic Keyboard** Introduce students to the wide variety of timbres available on many electronic keyboards. Discuss why such instruments are categorized as electronic. For this lesson, students may use GM steel drum sounds (program number 114 on a MIDI keyboard) to supplement mallet instruments. Claves, guiro, and other percussion kit timbres may also be used for this ensemble.

## Review and Assessment

### What Do You Know?

**MATERIALS**
- *"Tsuki,"* p. 25 — **CD 1-36**
- **Resource Book** p. B-3

Have students read and answer the questions independently and then check their answers with a partner before sharing answers with the rest of the class or with you.

For a more formal assessment, you may wish to duplicate the Unit 1 assessment worksheet and have students work independently or in small groups to complete it. The worksheet is found on Resource Book p. B-3.

### What Do You Hear?

**MATERIALS**
- *What Do You Hear? 1* — **CD 2-23**
- **Resource Book** p. B-4

Review the concept of timbre with the class. Emphasize the fact that timbres refer to the unique "voice" of an instrument or a person.

Divide the class into groups. Then play each of the selections listed. Invite students to make a list of adjectives that describe the timbre of each song. Ask the group captains to read the adjectives. The team with the most (or best) adjectives wins.

UNIT 1

# Review, Assess,

## What Do You Know?

1. Look at the notation for *"Tsuki"* on page 25. Then answer these questions.
   - **a.** Where is *do* located in the music?
   - **b.** Point to all the notes named *so*. How many did you find?
   - **c.** Do the same activity for the notes named *mi*, *re*, *la*, and *do*.
2. Name each dynamic symbol and point to the correct definition.

| | |
|---|---|
| **a.** *mf* | loud |
| **b.** *p* | gradually louder |
| **c.** *mp* | medium loud |
| **d.** (decrescendo) | soft |
| **e.** *f* | medium soft |
| **f.** (crescendo) | gradually softer |

## What Do You Hear? 1

CD 2-23

Listen to these examples of vocal timbre. Briefly describe the timbre of each example using at least three adjectives in each description.

1. *Rain, Rain, Beautiful Rain*
2. *I Don't Want to Feel Like That*
3. *Nahandove*
4. *Sigit "Alash"*

## Footnotes

### Answer Key

**What Do You Know?**

1. **a.** *do* = F
   **b.** *so* = C (9)
   **c.** *mi* = A (9); *re* = G (4); *la* = D (4); *do* = 3

2. **a.** *mf* — medium loud
   **b.** *p* — soft
   **c.** *mp* — medium soft
   **d.** < — gradually louder
   **e.** *f* — loud
   **f.** > — gradually softer

**What Do You Hear?**

Answers will vary and are open to interpretation. Here are some possibilities.

1. smooth, masculine, strong
2. strong, feminine, country
3. feminine, lyrical, floating
4. rough, masculine, low

# Perform, Create

## What You Can Do

### Create Dynamics

Create a dynamics roadmap to follow while you sing "Waitin' for the Light to Shine" on page 26. Remember that dynamics should express the feelings and mood of the song.

### Move to the Beat

Use movement to show strong and weak beats while you sing "*Gakavik*" on page 14. With a partner, create work movements to perform as you sing "Haul Away, Joe" on page 13.

### Read a Melody

Read the notation for *"Tsuki"* on page 25, using pitch syllables and hand signs. Then perform the song again with the words.

### Create Textures

Divide into two groups and perform "Pay Me My Money Down," on page 38, in call-and-response style. Sing the song again with only a few students singing the call and the rest of the class singing the response. Create additional verses to the song and perform them as a solo caller while the rest of the class sings the responses.

## What You Can Do

**MATERIALS**

- "Waitin' for the Light to Shine," p. 26 **CD 1-43**
- *"Gakavik,"* p. 14 **CD 1-17**
- "Haul Away, Joe," p. 13 **CD 1-15**
- *"Tsuki,"* p. 25 **CD 1-36**
- "Pay Me My Money Down," p. 38 **CD 2-18**
- **Resource Book** p. B-5

### Create Dynamics

Review the concept that dynamics can express moods and feelings by changing volume. Ask students to draw a dynamics roadmap as they sing "Waitin' for the Light to Shine."

### Move to the Beat

Use "*Gakavik*" and "Haul Away, Joe" to teach strong and weak beats. Have students listen to the recording and tap the strong beat. Then have them determine with a partner how they would show these through creative movement.

### Read a Melody

Invite students to look at the notation for *"Tsuki."* Have students

- Identify *do, re, mi, so,* and *la* in the song.
- Sing the song with pitch syllables.
- Sing the song with the words.

### Create Textures

Discuss with students that the number of people singing affects texture. Emphasize that texture is different between the call and the response. Have students create additional call-and-response verses to sing with "Pay Me My Money Down." Ask the class to vote on the best new call.

### Technology/Media Link

**Rubrics** Visit *www.sfsuccessnet.com* for rubrics to assess students' achievement in music skills.

| Lesson | Elements | Skills | |
|---|---|---|---|
| LESSON 1<br>CORE<br>**Tempo Time**<br>pp. 48-51<br> | **Element: Expression**<br>**Concept:** Tempo<br>**Focus:** Tempo<br><br>**Secondary Element**<br>Timbre: wind instruments<br><br>**National Standards**<br>1b 3b 5c 6b | **Skill: Moving**<br>**Objective:** Move to show tempo<br><br>**Secondary Skills**<br>• **Singing** Sing a song at an appropriate tempo<br>• **Listening** Identify various tempos in music<br>• **Analyzing** Compare melodies with a Venn diagram<br>• **Improvising** Improvise body percussion at various tempos | **SKILLS REINFORCEMENT**<br>• **Improvising** Improvise and play eight-beat ostinatos |
| LESSON 2<br>**The Score Is Tied**<br>pp. 52-53<br><br>Reading Sequence 5, p. 444 | **Element: Rhythm**<br>**Concept:** Duration<br>**Focus:** Syncopation<br><br>**Secondary Element**<br>Melody: *do*-pentatonic<br><br>**National Standards**<br><br>2b 5a 6e 9c | **Skill: Reading**<br>**Objective:** Read ♪ ♩ ♪ syncopated rhythms in meter in $\frac{4}{4}$ time<br><br>**Secondary Skills**<br>• **Moving** Sing a song and conduct a $\frac{4}{4}$ pattern | **SKILLS REINFORCEMENT**<br>• **Performing** Perform syncopated rhythms<br>• **Mallets** Play an Orff arrangement of a song |
| LESSON 3<br>**Rhythms of the Railroad**<br>pp. 54-55<br><br>Reading Sequence 6, p. 444 | **Element: Rhythm**<br>**Concept:** Pattern<br>**Focus:** ♪ ♩ ♪<br><br>**Secondary Element**<br>Form: verse and refrain<br><br>**National Standards**<br>1c 2d 5a 6e | **Skill: Reading**<br>**Objective:** Read rhythmic patterns consisting of ♪ ♩ ♪ and ♩, ♫, 𝄽 in $\frac{4}{4}$ time<br><br>**Secondary Skills**<br>• **Listening** Listen for long and short sounds, and learn a song by rote | **SKILLS REINFORCEMENT**<br>• **Playing** Read, clap, and play ♪ ♩ ♩ patterns<br>• **Recorder** Play a syncopated accompaniment<br>• **Mallets** Play an Orff arrangement of a song |

| Connections | Music and Other Literature | |
|---|---|---|
| **Connection:** Culture<br>**Activity:** Discover similarities in two Irish selections<br>ACROSS THE CURRICULUM **Language Arts** Read various Irish tales<br>MOVEMENT<br>Nonlocomotor Movement Move in relation to the phrasing of a melody<br>Nonlocomotor Movement Use in-place movements to reinforce the concept of tempo<br>Popular Dance Learn *The Chicken Dance*<br>TEACHER TO TEACHER **Venn Diagram** Compare versions of a song<br>MEETING INDIVIDUAL NEEDS<br>**Thinking Skills** Develop musical thinking skills<br>**Encouraging Participation** Encourage active participation regardless of ability<br>BUILDING SKILLS THROUGH MUSIC **Reading** Read lyrics of a song and focus on the chronology of the events | **Song** "Oh, Danny Boy"<br>**Listening Selections**<br>*Irish Tune from County Derry*<br>*Hungarian Dance No. 6*<br>*The Chicken Dance*<br>**Listening Map** *Hungarian Dance No. 6*<br>**More Music Choices**<br>"Cotton-Eye Joe," p. 288<br>"The Bard of Armagh," p. 296 | ASSESSMENT<br>**Performance/Observation** Perform *The Chicken Dance* and have students listen to a selection and indicate tempos on a listening map<br>TECHNOLOGY/MEDIA LINK<br>**Notation Software** Create a composition and experiment with tempo<br>**Transparency** Indicate tempo on a listening map |
| **Connection:** Mathematics<br>**Activity:** Practice addition skills by tying together note values<br>ACROSS THE CURRICULUM **Language Arts** Read a book about friendship and write in journals<br>CULTURAL CONNECTION **Symbolism in Spirituals** Discuss hidden meanings in songs and spirituals<br>BUILDING SKILLS THROUGH MUSIC **Language** Write a short paragraph explaining the use of the tie in music | **Song** "Somebody's Knockin' at Your Door"<br>**More Music Choices**<br>"Canoe Song," p. 76<br>"Weevily Wheat," p. 105 | ASSESSMENT<br>**Performance/Observation** Read syncopated rhythms in a song<br>TECHNOLOGY/MEDIA LINK<br>**Electronic Keyboard** Select sounds to perform on beats 2, 3, and 4<br>**Sequencing Software** Create ostinatos using limited pitches |
| **Connection:** Social Studies<br>**Activity:** Learn the history of a railroad song<br>SPOTLIGHT ON **Rock Island Line** Background of the song<br>TEACHER TO TEACHER **Hidden Rhythms** Discuss syncopation in tied rhythms<br>BUILDING SKILLS THROUGH MUSIC **Math** Describe as a fraction the number of beats in a pick-up measure | **Song** "Rock Island Line"<br>**More Music Choices**<br>"*Bogando a la luz del sol*," p. 306 | ASSESSMENT<br>**Performance/Observation** Read, clap, and say the rhythms of a song in $\frac{4}{4}$<br>TECHNOLOGY/MEDIA LINK<br>**Notation Software** Create syncopated rhythm patterns |

| Lesson | Elements | Skills | |
|---|---|---|---|
| LESSON 4<br>CORE<br>**Time for the Blues**<br>pp. 56-57<br> | **Element: Rhythm**<br>**Concept:** Meter<br>**Focus:** Meter in 4<br><br>**Secondary Element**<br>Form: blues form<br><br>**National Standards**<br>3b 6b 6c | **Skill: Moving**<br>**Objective:** Perform a four-beat body percussion ostinato<br><br>**Secondary Skills**<br>• **Singing** Sing a song and discuss mood | **SKILLS REINFORCEMENT**<br>• **Improvising** Improvise rhythm ostinatos in $\frac{4}{4}$ time<br>• **Keyboard** Create a walking bass line and a tritone duet accompaniment for a song<br>• **Recorder** Play four-beat patterns with B, A, and G |
| LESSON 5<br>CORE<br>**One Song – Two Sections**<br>pp. 58–61<br> | **Element: Form**<br>**Concept:** Form<br>**Focus:** Verse and refrain<br><br>**Secondary Element**<br>Rhythm: meter in 3<br><br>**National Standards**<br><br>4a 6a 6b 6c 8b | **Skill: Moving**<br>**Objective:** Perform contrasting movements to show verse-and-refrain form<br><br>**Secondary Skills**<br>• **Singing** Sing a song and study verse and refrain<br>• **Signing** Sing and sign specific words in a song | **SKILLS REINFORCEMENT**<br>• **Reading** Prepare reading rhythms in $\frac{3}{4}$ time by performing three-beat movements<br>• **Recorder** Play a recorder accompaniment<br>• **Creating** Create music and movement to accompany a poem |
| LESSON 6<br>**Melody Goes 'Round**<br>pp. 62-63<br><br> Reading Sequence 7, p. 445 | **Element: Melody**<br>**Concept:** Pattern<br>**Focus:** Extended pentatonic patterns<br><br>**Secondary Element**<br>Form: call and response<br><br>**National Standards**<br>1c 3b 5b 6b 6c | **Skill: Reading**<br>**Objective:** Read extended pentatonic patterns<br><br>**Secondary Skills**<br>• **Analyzing** Study intervals in the pentatonic scale<br>• **Performing** Perform hand signs for pitches and introduce *la* | **SKILLS REINFORCEMENT**<br>• **Creating** Improvise and create in D-pentatonic<br>• **Singing** Sing an African song, using the Pronunciation Practice Track |

| Connections | Music and Other Literature | |
|---|---|---|
| **Connection: Social Studies**<br>**Activity:** Discuss jazz history<br>ACROSS THE CURRICULUM **Social Studies** Share books about jazz musicians to discover facts about the history of jazz<br>SPOTLIGHT ON **W.C. Handy** Background information on the musician<br>CHARACTER EDUCATION **Expression of Emotions** Create lyrics for a blues song, drawing from students' discussion of emotions<br>BUILDING SKILLS THROUGH MUSIC **Visual Arts** Illustrate a song | **Song** "Joe Turner Blues"<br>**Listening Selection** *St. Louis Blues* (excerpt)<br>**More Music Choices**<br>"Over the Rainbow," p. 140<br>"Peace Round," p. 348 | ASSESSMENT<br>**Performance/Observation** Sing a song and perform four-beat body percussion ostinatos<br>**Show What You Know!** Mid-unit assessment<br>TECHNOLOGY/MEDIA LINK<br>**CD-ROM** Explore the 12-bar blues section of *Alfred's Essentials of Music Theory*, Vol. 3 |
| **Connection: Social Studies**<br>**Activity:** Locate several North American rivers on a map<br>ACROSS THE CURRICULUM<br>**Social Studies** Discuss rivers and related vocabulary<br>**Language Arts** Discuss the meaning of a phrase and encourage students to write poems on this theme<br>MOVEMENT **Nonlocomotor Movement** Explore various levels in space while moving to music<br>SPOTLIGHT ON **Aaron Copland** Background information on the composer<br>MEETING INDIVIDUAL NEEDS **English Language Learners** Students retell information to each other<br>BUILDING SKILLS THROUGH MUSIC **Math** Develop a problem-solving strategy for questions on meter | **Song** "River"<br>**Listening Selection** "The Boatman's Dance" from *Old American Songs*<br>**Poem** "River"<br>**More Music Choices**<br>"Sweet Betsy from Pike," p. 244<br>"Clementine," p. 341<br>"My Bonnie Lies Over the Ocean," p. 338 | ASSESSMENT<br>**Performance/Observation** Create contrasting movements to perform during the verse and refrain of a song<br>TECHNOLOGY/MEDIA LINK<br>**CD-ROM** Enter chords in *Band-in-a-Box*, and explore playback options |
| **Connection: Culture**<br>**Activity:** Discuss the country of Eritrea<br>CULTURAL CONNECTION **Eritrea** Discuss politics, sociology, and geography<br>SPOTLIGHT ON **The Lyricist** Background information on Hidaat Ephrem<br>BUILDING SKILLS THROUGH MUSIC **Math** Relate geometric figures to the pentatonic scale | **Song** *"Hashewie"* ("Going 'Round)<br>**More Music Choices**<br>"See the Children Playin'," p. 107<br>"Cotton-Eye Joe," p. 288 | ASSESSMENT<br>**Performance/Observation** Read and sing a pentatonic phrase using pitch syllables and hand signs<br>TECHNOLOGY/MEDIA LINK<br>**Video Library** Watch a video featuring call-and-response singing |

| Lesson | Elements | Skills |
|---|---|---|

## LESSON 7

**Scale the Mountain**

pp. 64-65

Reading Sequence 8, p. 445

**Element: Melody**
**Concept:** Pattern
**Focus:** Extended pentatonic patterns

**Secondary Element**
Form: phrase form (aabb)

**National Standards**
3b 5b 6b 6c

**Skill: Reading**
**Objective:** Read extended pentatonic patterns

**Secondary Skills**
- **Performing** Study intervals in the pentatonic scale
- **Listening** Follow warm-up notation

**SKILLS REINFORCEMENT**
- **Creating** Improvise and create in D-pentatonic
- **Notating** Notate ostinatos in stick notation or on the staff

## LESSON 8

CORE

**Melody Rhymes in Time**

pp. 66-67

**Element: Melody**
**Concept:** Pitch direction
**Focus:** Notes in treble clef

**Secondary Element**
Rhythm: ♩, ♫

**National Standards**
2b 2f 5b 8b

**Skill: Playing**
**Objective:** Play a melody on recorder

**Secondary Skills**
- **Singing** Speak rhyming words in a song and then sing them

**SKILLS REINFORCEMENT**
- **Playing** Perform ostinatos on percussion instruments
- **Recorder** Play a five-note countermelody

## LESSON 9

**I Spy an Instrument**

pp. 68-71

**Element: Timbre**
**Concept:** Instrumental
**Focus:** Wind instrument timbres

**Secondary Element**
Form: cumulative song

**National Standards**
4b 6b 6c 6d 8b 9d

**Skill: Listening**
**Objective:** Listen to and identify wind instrument ensembles

**Secondary Skills**
- **Moving** Invent playing motions for instruments
- **Listening** Identify classroom instruments by sound
- **Creating** Compose a duet

**SKILLS REINFORCEMENT**
- **Reading** Follow the roadmap of a song with multiple endings

| Connections | Music and Other Literature | |
|---|---|---|
| **Connection:** Social Studies<br>**Activity:** Discuss life in Appalachia<br>ACROSS THE CURRICULUM **Social Studies** Compare life in Appalachia with life in their own community<br>SPOTLIGHT ON **Musical Spoons** Create accompaniments for a song with spoons<br>BUILDING SKILLS THROUGH MUSIC **Reading** Summarize the text of a song and sing the song from memory | **Song** "Sourwood Mountain"<br>**More Music Choices**<br>"*Feng yang hua gu,*" p. 313<br>"How Can I Keep from Singing?" p. 261 | ASSESSMENT<br>**Performance/Observation** Read and sing pentatonic melody from stick notation<br>TECHNOLOGY/MEDIA LINK<br>**Web Site** Explore string instruments at *www.sfsuccessnet.com* |
| **Connection:** Language Arts<br>**Activity:** Discuss the use of rhyming words in poetry and songs<br>ACROSS THE CURRICULUM **Language Arts** Discuss rhyming words in a song<br>MEETING INDIVIDUAL NEEDS **Recorder Tips** Students check each other's progress and offer constructive feedback<br>BUILDING SKILLS THROUGH MUSIC **Social Studies** Locate Latin America on a map and discuss Latin American culture | **Song** "*Riqui rán*"<br>**More Music Choices**<br>"Ode to Joy," p. 152<br>"*Somos el barco,*" p. 352<br>"*La raspa,*" p. 302 | ASSESSMENT<br>**Performance/Observation** Play the melody of "*Riqui rán*" on recorder using a good tone<br>**Show What You Know!** Mid-unit assessment<br>TECHNOLOGY/MEDIA LINK<br>**MIDI/Sequencing Software** Play recorder with the MIDI song file |
| **Connection:** Science<br>**Activity:** Discuss how sounds are produced by brass and woodwind instruments<br>ACROSS THE CURRICULUM<br>**Science** Discuss how instruments produce sound<br>**Science** Explore and create homemade wind instruments<br>CULTURAL CONNECTION **Italian: The Language of Music** Discuss Italian terms in music<br>SPOTLIGHT ON **Instrument Demonstrations** Have musicians play instruments for students<br>TEACHER TO TEACHER **Managing the Creating Activity** Discuss timbres of different instruments<br>MEETING INDIVIDUAL NEEDS **Role-Playing Musicians** Have students role-play being musicians<br>SCHOOL TO HOME CONNECTION **Instruments at Home** Share photos or drawings of instruments that students have at home<br>BUILDING SKILLS THROUGH MUSIC **Science** Follow the scientific method to prove or disprove a hypothesis | **Song** "*Eh, cumpari!*" ("Hey, Buddy!")<br>**Listening Selections**<br>*One-Minute Brass Mysteries*<br>*One-Minute Woodwind Mysteries*<br>*"Allegro molto"* from *Quartet*<br>"Fanfare" from *La Peri*<br>**More Music Choices**<br>*Symphony No. 6 in F,* Mvt. 4, p. 365<br>*1812 Overture*, p. 293 | ASSESSMENT<br>**Performance/Observation** Listen to wind music and identify instruments using pictorial references<br>TECHNOLOGY/MEDIA LINK<br>**MIDI/Sequencing Software** Change the instrument playing the melody in a song file |

| Lesson | Elements | Skills | |
|---|---|---|---|
| LESSON 10<br>CORE<br>**Listening to Wind Instruments**<br>pp. 72-75<br> | **Element: Timbre**<br>**Concept:** Instrumental<br>**Focus:** Wind instruments<br><br>**Secondary Element**<br>Expression: articulation<br><br>**National Standards**<br>6b 6d 6e 9c 9d 9e | **Skill: Listening**<br>**Objective:** Listen to and identify wind instrument ensembles<br><br>**Secondary Skills**<br>• **Moving** Perform mirror motions to differing sections | **SKILLS REINFORCEMENT**<br>• **Singing** Experiment with *staccato* and *legato* articulations<br>• **Listening** Discuss instrumental timbres in home recordings |
| LESSON 11<br>**Paddle Along, Singing a Song**<br>pp. 76-77<br> | **Element: Texture/Harmony**<br>**Concept:** Texture<br>**Focus:** Multi-layered melodic ostinato accompaniment<br><br>**Secondary Element**<br>Rhythm: ♪ ♩ ♪<br><br>**National Standards**<br>1d 2b 2f 8a | **Skill: Playing**<br>**Objective:** Play melody ostinatos<br><br>**Secondary Skills**<br>• **Singing** Identify and sing repeated melody ostinatos | **SKILLS REINFORCEMENT**<br>• **Creating/Playing** Create original nonpitched percussion recordings |
| LESSON 12<br>CORE<br>**Ostinatos Everywhere**<br>pp. 78-81<br> | **Element: Texture/Harmony**<br>**Concept:** Texture<br>**Focus:** Melody ostinatos<br><br>**Secondary Element**<br>Rhythm: meter in 3<br><br>**National Standards**<br>1c 1d 2f 3b 4a | **Skill: Playing**<br>**Objective:** Play melody ostinato<br><br>**Secondary Skills**<br>• **Singing** Learn a song in the Setswana language<br>• **Moving/Playing** Transfer body percussion ostinatos to instruments<br>• **Listening** Listen to melody ostinatos<br>• **Creating** Create melody ostinatos to accompany poems | **SKILLS REINFORCEMENT**<br>• **Singing** Practice breath control exercises<br>• **Playing/Creating** Play ostinatos on pitched percussion instruments |

| Connections | Music and Other Literature | |
|---|---|---|
| **Connection: Language Arts**<br>**Activity:** Read about and compare lives of musicians<br>**ACROSS THE CURRICULUM** **Language Arts** Explore the instruments that play in an orchestra<br>**SPOTLIGHT ON**<br>**Percy Grainger** Background information on the composer<br>**Wynton Marsalis** Background information on the musician<br>**TEACHER TO TEACHER** **Live Demonstrations** Teachers of instrumental music play instruments for the class<br>**AUDIENCE ETIQUETTE** **Specific Genres** Describe and model appropriate concert behavior for a variety of musical genres<br>**CHARACTER EDUCATION** **Responsibility** Discuss the roles of band, orchestra, and ensemble members to help students understand the importance of assuming responsibility<br>**BUILDING SKILLS THROUGH MUSIC** **Language** Write a paragraph describing similarities and differences in a symphony orchestra and concert band | **Listening Selections**<br>"Presentation of Pairs" from *Concerto for Orchestra*<br>"Lord Melbourne" from *Lincolnshire Posy*<br>*Knozz-Moe-King* (excerpt)<br>*Little Birdie*<br>*"Allegro"* from *Concerto for Two Trumpets* (excerpt)<br>**MUSIC MAKERS**<br>Béla Bartók<br>Marsalis Family<br>**More Music Choices**<br>"Fossils" from *Carnival of the Animals,* p. 220<br>"Mars, the Bringer of War" from *The Planets*, p. 377 | **ASSESSMENT**<br>**Observation/Written Assessment** Identify types of musical groups and write facts about them<br>**TECHNOLOGY/MEDIA LINK**<br>**Web Site** Visit *www.sfsuccessnet.com* for information on Bartók and Grainger. |
| **Connection: Related Arts**<br>**Activity:** Identify and describe repeated patterns in music and visual art<br>**ACROSS THE CURRICULUM** **Language Arts** Read and write about imaginary canoe rides<br>**CULTURAL CONNECTION** **Canoes** Research the use of canoes in cultures<br>**BUILDING SKILLS THROUGH MUSIC** **Science** Demonstrate sound waves with a tuning fork and a tray of water | **Song** "Canoe Song"<br>**Arts Connection**<br>*Watercolor Ripple*<br>**More Music Choices**<br>"Little David, Play on Your Harp," p. 394<br>*Twist and Shout*, p. 238 | **ASSESSMENT**<br>**Performance/Observation** Perform melody ostinatos and sing a song<br>**TECHNOLOGY/MEDIA LINK**<br>**Sequencing Software** Create an ostinato on D and A |
| **Connection: Culture**<br>**Activity:** Explore African culture through poems and proverbs<br>**ACROSS THE CURRICULUM** **Art** Create visual art that uses repeated patterns<br>**SPOTLIGHT ON** **Bobby McFerrin** Background information on the musician<br>**TEACHER TO TEACHER**<br>**Plan a Performance** Prepare a student performance of the song<br>**Managing Improvised Ostinatos** Perform body percussion ostinatos<br>**MEETING INDIVIDUAL NEEDS** **Peer Tutoring** Have students help each other and model activities<br>**BUILDING SKILLS THROUGH MUSIC** **Writing** Create a short poem using a repeated phrase | **Song** *"Hey, m'tswala"*<br>**Listening Selection** *Circlesong 7*<br>**Poems**<br>"The Night"<br>"Enjoy the Earth"<br>**MUSIC MAKERS**<br>Bobby McFerrin<br>**More Music Choices**<br>*"Ochimbo,"* p. 134<br>*"Tina singu,"* p. 300 | **ASSESSMENT**<br>**Performance/Self-Assessment** Perform a song with melody ostinatos keeping in mind the three goals set by the students for performing the song<br>**TECHNOLOGY/MEDIA LINK**<br>**Notation Software** Create ostinatos and experiment with the copy and paste |

# INTRODUCTION

UNIT 2

## INTRODUCING THE UNIT

Unit 2 presents the next step in a sequenced approach to understanding music elements. Presented on p. 45 is a brief overview of the skills that are assessed in this unit. (See below and pp. 46–47 for unit highlights of related curricular experiences.)

For a more detailed unit overview, see Unit at a Glance, pp. 43a–43h.

## UNIT PROJECT

Engage students in a conversation about what explorers do. Point out that explorers often record their discoveries and learning in a diary or journal. Then, tell students that they are *music* explorers. Help them begin a music journal or diary that they will use to record the new information they discover and the new things they learn to do throughout this unit.

As students progress through the unit, have them record what they are discovering about music in their "Music Explorer" journals. Encourage students to write about the musical things they can do, as well as the new information they are learning about music. At the end of the unit, have students review their own journals and write a letter to a friend or family member about what they have learned. Encourage them to write from the perspective of an explorer reporting his or her findings to someone else.

As an extension of the "Music Explorer" journal project, make a class video that documents what the explorers are learning. Record students' performances of songs and dances in the unit. On different days, have three or four students speak about what they learned, rather than writing in their journals on that day. Have students view the tape at the end of the unit to assist in summarizing what they have learned.

### Sing and Swing

In the late 1950s and early 1960s, some songs with nonsense words were called doo-wop.

**Sing** "We Go Together," a song written in the style of 1950s rock 'n' roll. Then **identify** the nonsense words.

## We Go Together

from *Grease*

CD 2–27

m, f, s, l, t, d r m

Lyrics and Music by Warren Casey and Jim Jacobs

do

B♭ Gm E♭

1. We go to - geth - er, ___ like ra - ma la - ma la - ma ka
2. We're one of a kind ___ like dip da dip da dip

F B♭

ding - a da ding ___ a - dong, Re - mem - bered for -
doo - wop ___ da doo - bee doo. Our names ___ are

Gm E♭

ev - er ___ as shoo - bop sha wad - da wad - da
signed ___ boog-e - dy boog-e - dy boog-e - dy boog-e - dy

F B♭

yip - pi - ty boom - de boom. Chang chang
shoo - by - doo - wop ___ she - bop Chang chang





## ACROSS THE CURRICULUM

**Unit Highlights** The following interdisciplinary activities in this unit are related to the music elements presented in the lessons. See Unit at a Glance, pp. 43a–43h, for topical descriptions presented according to lesson sequence.

▶ **ART/RELATED ARTS**

- Explore relationships between music, movement, and poetry (p. 61)
- Create visual artwork that uses repeated patterns (p. 78)

▶ **LANGUAGE ARTS**

- Read novels based on Irish stories and tales (p. 49)
- Read a novel and write expressively about sharing and friendship (p. 53)
- Discuss the meaning of a figurative phrase and read a related poem (p. 60)
- Explore rhyming words in songs and poems (p. 66)
- Read a book describing instruments of the orchestra (p. 72)
- Read a novel and write expressively about canoeing (p. 76)

▶ **SCIENCE**

- Explore the construction and sound production of musical instruments (p. 69)
- Create homemade wind instruments (p. 71)

▶ **SOCIAL STUDIES**

- Read short biographies that provide a historical overview of jazz (p. 56)
- Use a map to find, name, and describe rivers (p. 58)
- Read a book about Appalachia and discuss regional characteristics (p. 64)

UNIT 2
EXPLORING MUSIC
Gm E♭ F7
chang-it - ty chang - shoo-bop, that's the way it ___ should
chang-it - ty chang - shoo-bop, we'll al - ways be ________ like
1. B♭ Gm E♭ F 2. B♭
be. ______ wha - oooh, yeah! one, ______
E♭ B♭ E♭
wa wa ___ wa waah. ______ When we go
E♭
out at night, - and stars are shin - in' bright -
B♭ Gm7 B♭7 E♭
up in the skies a - bove, ______ or at the
E♭
high school dance, - where you can find ro - mance, -
Unit 2 45

# MUSIC SKILLS ASSESSED IN THIS UNIT

### Reading Music: Rhythm

- Read syncopated rhythm patterns (p. 53)
- Read and conduct rhythm patterns in meter in 4 (p. 55)

### Reading Music: Pitch

- Read extended pentatonic patterns, using pitch syllables and hand signs (p. 63)
- Read and sign a song from notation (p. 65)

### Performing Music: Singing

- Sing "Joe Turner Blues," accompanied by body percussion ostinatos (p. 57)
- Sing melodies based on the extended pentatonic scale (p. 63)
- Sing "Canoe Song," accompanied by ostinatos (p. 77)

### Moving to Music

- Move to show tempo (p. 51)
- Perform contrasting movements to show AB form (p. 61)

### Performing Music: Playing

- Play a recorder melody with *"Riqui rán"* (p. 67)
- Play melody ostinatos to accompany a song (p. 77)
- Play rhythm and melody ostinatos to accompany a song (p. 81)

### Creating Music

- Create pentatonic ostinatos to accompany "Sourwood Mountain" (p. 64)

### Listening to Music

- Identify wind instruments by sound (p. 71)
- Aurally identify wind instrument ensembles (p. 75)

## CULTURAL CONNECTION

**Unit Highlights** The musical literature in this unit provides many opportunities for students to explore a variety of world cultures. See Unit at a Glance, pp. 43a–43h, for topical descriptions presented according to lesson sequence.

**▶ AFRICAN/AFRICAN AMERICAN**

- "Somebody's Knockin' at Your Door": Discuss symbolism used in spirituals (p. 52)
- "Joe Turner Blues" (p. 56)
- *"Hashewie"*: Explore the history and customs of Eritrea (p. 62)
- *"Hey, m'tswala"* (p. 79)

**▶ AMERICAN**

- "The Boatman's Dance" from *Old American Songs* (p. 61)
- "Sourwood Mountain" (Appalachia) (p. 65)
- Discuss the practical and cultural significance of canoes in Native American life (p. 77)

**▶ EUROPEAN**

- "Oh, Danny Boy" (Ireland) (p. 48)
- *"Eh, cumpari!"* (Italy): Discuss Italian musical terms (p. 68)

**▶ LATIN AMERICAN**

- *"Riqui rán"* (p. 66)

# Opening Activities

**MATERIALS**

- "We Go Together" **CD 2-27**
  **Recording Routine:**
  Intro (8 m.); vocal
- *In the Still of the Night* **CD 2-29**
- keyboards or mallet instruments

## Moving

Play "We Go Together" **CD 2-27** and have students tap the beat as they listen. (Tap the half-note beat, then the quarter-note beat.) Then play the recording again and have students copy you as you model different movement patterns to the quarter-note beat. Use patterns such as *pat-pat-clap-clap* or *wave-wave-snap-snap.* Extend four-beat patterns to eight beats and encourage students, working in groups, to create simple hand-jive motions to accompany the music. Play the recording again and have each group demonstrate its hand jive for the class. Have class members join in on each one.

## Singing

Have students

- Find the scat syllables in the lyrics of "We Go Together."
- Listen to the scat syllables and sing the rest of the words as you play the recording again.
- Read the text at the beginning of the song to learn the term "doo-wop."
- Sing all of the lyrics with the recording.

## Playing

Help students find the chord symbols in the music on pp. 44–46. Have them identify the pattern B♭-Gm-E♭-F and find how many times it occurs. Help them recognize that this pattern does not occur in the middle section of the music. Then, have students play the pitches B♭-Gm-E♭-F, using

## ASSESSMENT

**Unit Highlights** This unit includes a variety of strategies and methods, described below, to track students' progress and assess their understanding of lesson objectives. Reproducible masters for Show What You Know! and Review, Assess, Perform, Create can be found in the Resource Book.

### ▶ FORMAL ASSESSMENTS

The following assessments, using written language, cognitive, and performance skills, help teachers and students conceptualize the learning that is taking place.

- **Show What You Know!** Element-specific assessments, on the student page, for Rhythm (p. 57) and Melody (p. 67).
- **Review, Assess, Perform, Create** This end-of-unit activity (pp. 82–83) can be used for review and to assess students' learning of the core lessons in this unit.

### ▶ INFORMAL ASSESSMENTS

At the close of each Teacher's Edition lesson in this unit, one of the following types of assessments is used to evaluate the learning of the key element focus or skill objective.

- Observation/Written Assessment (p. 75)
- Performance/Observation (pp. 51, 53, 55, 57, 61, 63, 65, 67, 71, 77)
- Performance/Self-Assessment (p. 81)

### ▶ RUBRICS

Visit *www.sfsuccessnet.com* for rubrics to assess students' achievement in music skills.

## Doo-Wop Singing

Doo-wop groups usually had four or five vocalists and a rhythm section, which included guitar, bass, drums, and piano. The Four Tops, the Platters, and the Five Satins are three famous doo-wop groups. Can you name any others?

**Listen** to *In the Still of the Night,* the Five Satins' biggest hit.

CD 2-29

**In the Still of the Night**

**by Fred Parris**
**as performed by the Five Satins**

Forty years after this song's initial release, the group Boyz II Men recorded their own version of this doo-wop classic.

### MUSIC MAKERS

### The Five Satins

Fred Parris formed **The Five Satins,** a doo-wop singing group, in 1954 while he was still in high school. Parris wrote the song *In the Still of the Night* two years later. The song made the Five Satins famous.

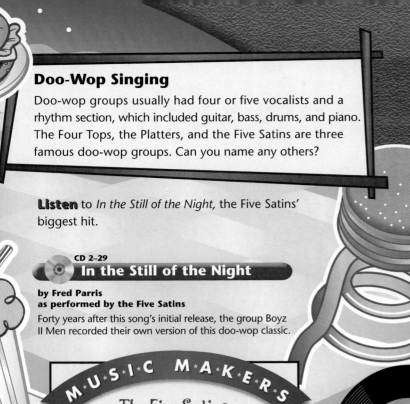

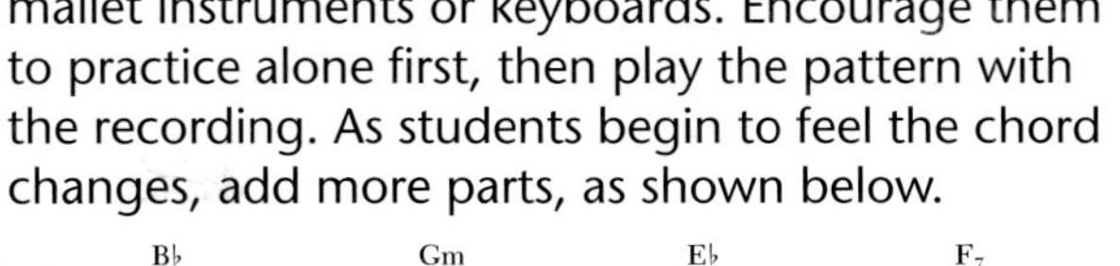

mallet instruments or keyboards. Encourage them to practice alone first, then play the pattern with the recording. As students begin to feel the chord changes, add more parts, as shown below.

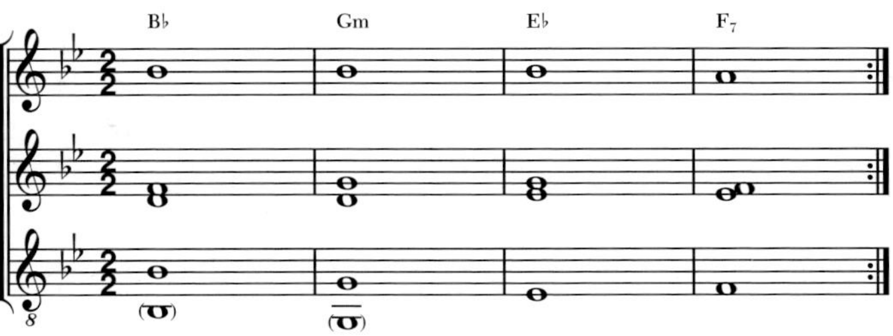


## Listening

Tell students that they are going to hear a popular doo-wop song from the 1950s. Invite students to listen to *In the Still of the Night* **CD 2-29** and then describe ways in which it is similar to and different from "We Go Together."

### Innovative Teacher Support for This Unit

- **Making Music DVD, Grade 4** contains video segments that support lessons, including signing and movement.
- **Making Music with Movement and Dance** provides more opportunities for large group activities in music or physical education classes.
- **Making Music with Technology** provides lesson plans for many technology applications; includes MIDI files.
- ***¡A cantar!*** features recorded songs and lessons from around the Spanish-speaking world; includes strategies for bilingual classes and for English-speaking teachers working with Spanish-speaking students.
- **Bridges to Asia** features recorded songs and lessons from Asian and Pacific region cultures.
- ***www.sfsuccessnet.com*** provides an online lesson planner to conveniently create lesson plans at school or at home. Includes rubrics for assessment, lesson modifications to meet the needs of all students, performance musicals based on program content, and more.

## Technology/Media Link

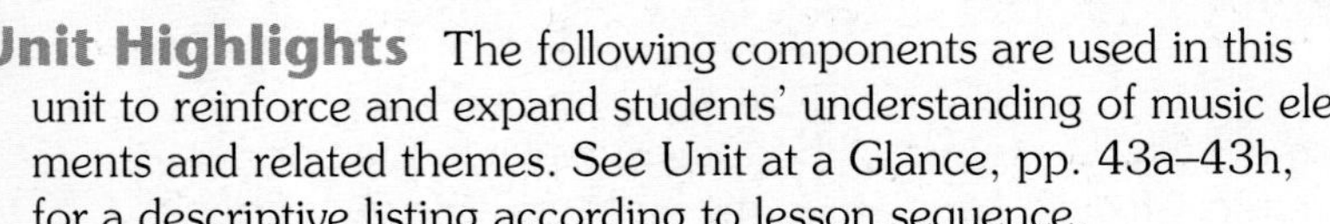

**Unit Highlights** The following components are used in this unit to reinforce and expand students' understanding of music elements and related themes. See Unit at a Glance, pp. 43a–43h, for a descriptive listing according to lesson sequence.

▶ **CD-ROM**

- Use *Essentials of Music Theory* to create accompaniments (p. 57)
- Use *Band-in-a-Box* to perform a song in different styles (p. 61)

▶ **ELECTRONIC KEYBOARD**

- Use different timbres to perform as "fills" (p. 53)

▶ **MIDI/SEQUENCING SOFTWARE**

- Sequence melodic patterns to create layered ostinatos (p. 53)
- Use the MIDI song file *"Riquirrán"* to alter tempo, mute tracks, and accompany a recorder part (p. 67)
- Create new timbre arrangements for *"Eh, cumpari!"* (p. 71)
- Sequence an ostinato pattern to accompany a song (p. 77)

▶ **NOTATION SOFTWARE**

- Create short compositions to demonstrate different tempos (p. 51)
- Create rhythms using a syncopated pattern (p. 55)
- Create ostinato compositions (p. 81)

▶ **TRANSPARENCY**

- Display a listening map to analyze tempo (p. 51)

▶ **VIDEO LIBRARY/DVD**

- Explore call-and-response singing (p. 63)

▶ **WEB SITE**

- Go to *www.sfsuccessnet.com* for more information on string instruments (p. 65); Bartók, Grainger, Marsalis family (p. 75)

Core LESSON 1

## LESSON AT A GLANCE

**Element Focus** **EXPRESSION** Tempo

**Skill Objective** **MOVING** Move to show tempo

**Connection Activity** **CULTURE** Discover similarities in two Irish selections

**MATERIALS**

- "Oh, Danny Boy" **CD 2-30**

  **Recording Routine:** Intro (6 m.); v. 1; interlude (4 m.); v. 2; coda
- *Irish Tune from County Derry* **CD 2-32**
- *Hungarian Dance No. 6* **CD 2-33**
- *The Chicken Dance* **CD 3-1**
- **Resource Book** p. C-8
- **Dance Directions** for *The Chicken Dance* p. 507
- nonpitched percussion instruments

**VOCABULARY**

| | | |
|---|---|---|
| tempo | *adagio* | *andante* |
| *moderato* | *allegro* | *presto* |

**◆◆◆◆ National Standards ◆◆◆◆**

**1b** Sing expressively with appropriate interpretation
**3b** Improvise rhythmic ostinato accompaniments
**5c** Identify and use terms for tempo
**6b** Describe music by moving to it

**MORE MUSIC CHOICES**

For more practice with tempo:
*Cotton-Eye Joe,* p. 288
For another song from Ireland:
"The Bard of Armagh," p. 296

# Tempo Time

"Walk! Don't run!" When someone says that to you, what do you do? You change the speed of your movement. In music, **tempo** can help communicate the feeling of a song.

**Tempo** is the speed of the beat.

Read the words of "Oh, Danny Boy." Before you **sing** the song, decide what tempo would be best.

CD 2-30
Oh, Danny Boy
l, t, d r m f s l t d' r' m'
Words by Thomas Moore
Folk Melody from Ireland
do
1. Oh, Dan - ny Boy, the pipes, the pipes are call - ing,
2. But when you come and all the flow'rs are dy - ing,
From glen to glen, and down the moun - tain side;
If I am dead, as dead I well may be;
The sum - mer's gone, and all the ros - es fall - ing,
You'll come and find the place where I am ly - ing,
'Tis you, 'tis you must go, and I must bide.
And kneel and say an A - ve there for me.

## Footnotes

### MEETING INDIVIDUAL NEEDS

▶ **Thinking Skills** Help students develop thinking skills by asking questions that extend or challenge their musical thinking. For example, encourage students to explain why they think the tempo they suggest for "Oh, Danny Boy" is the best. When students compare the Grainger version of the song later in the lesson, encourage them to explain why they made the choices they did.

### BUILDING SKILLS THROUGH MUSIC

▶**Reading** Ask students to read the lyrics of "Oh, Danny Boy" and focus on the chronology of the events the character is describing. Which parts of the lyrics refer to the present? (Verse 1, lines 1–4, 8) To the future? (Verse 2)

### MOVEMENT

▶ **Nonlocomotor Movement** To help students feel the phrasing of "Oh, Danny Boy," have them move to the phrases of the music. Model a large arc in the air by moving your arm in slow motion. As you face the students, move your arm from right to left so that your arm travels in the same direction that students would read a phrase marking in music. Have students copy your motion as they listen to "Oh, Danny Boy." Then have them use their fingers to trace phrase lines on the song notation as they listen again. Use the same movements while listening to *Irish Tune from County Derry.*

## What's the Best Tempo?

"Oh, Danny Boy" is based upon a famous Irish melody. Composers and musicians from many different cultures have created their own arrangements of this tune. **Listen** to this version by the Australian composer Percy Grainger (1882–1961). Here are some words you can use to describe the tempo.

*adagio*—slow *andante*—walking speed *presto*—very fast
*moderato*—moderate *allegro*—fast

CD 2-32

### Irish Tune from County Derry

**Folk Melody from Ireland**
**arranged by Percy Grainger**

This version of the "Oh, Danny Boy" melody is performed by a wind ensemble.

G7 Am F C Am
But come ye back when sum-mer's in the mead - ow,
And I shall hear, tho' soft you tread a - bove me,
G7 Am F C D7 G
Or when the val - ley's hushed and white with snow,
And all my grave will warm - er, sweet - er be,
G7 C F C Am
'Tis I'll be here in sun-shine or in shad - ow,
For you will bend and tell me that you love me,
D7 C F G7 C
Oh, Dan - ny Boy, oh, Dan - ny Boy, I love you so.
And I shall sleep in peace un - til you come to me.

# 1 Introduce

Invite students to wave their hands as though waving goodbye, only in slow motion. Have them wave as they normally would. Then ask them to wave very quickly.

ASK **What did you change in your wave?** (the speed)

**SAY** In music, the speed of the beat is called *tempo.*

# 2 Develop

### Singing

1b Invite students to read the information about the tempo symbols and terms on p. 49. Then have them read the lyrics for the first verse of "Oh, Danny Boy."

ASK **What tempo do you think would be best for this song? Be ready to give a reason for your answer.** (Answers will vary. Ask students to give the reason for their answers.)

Play "Oh, Danny Boy" **CD 2-30.** Have students

- Listen, following the song notation.
- Describe the tempo, including any changes.
- Sing the song, interpreting the tempo appropriately when performing.

### Listening

5c Draw students' attention to the tempo terms on p. 49. Encourage them to practice saying each word.

ASK **Which word means "walking speed"?** *(andante)*

**Which tempo is the fastest?** *(presto)*

**Which is the slowest?** *(adagio)*

**SAY** Listen to another version of "Oh, Danny Boy." This version is called *Irish Tune from County Derry.* Be ready to describe the tempo.

continued on page 50

## Across the Curriculum

▶ **Language Arts** Students may enjoy reading the following Irish stories and tales.

*The Last Snake in Ireland: A Story About St. Patrick,* by Sheila MacGill-Callahan (Holiday House, 1999).

*Finn MacCoul and His Fearless Wife: A Giant of a Tale from Ireland,* by Robert Byrd (Penguin Putnam Books, 1998).

*Brave Margaret: An Irish Adventure,* by Robert D. San Souci (Simon and Schuster, 1999).

*O'Sullivan Stew: A Tale Cooked Up in Ireland,* by Hudson Talbott (Penguin Putnam Books, 1998).

## Teacher to Teacher

▶ **Venn Diagram** Divide students into pairs. Give each pair a copy of the Venn diagram chart on Resource Book p. C-8. While students listen to *Irish Tune from County Derry,* have them discuss the characteristics of the music with their partners. One student writes in the left circle, and the other, in the right circle. Then repeat this activity for "Oh, Danny Boy." Have the other student write in the right circle. After listening to both pieces, have students write their common characteristics in the space where the circles overlap. Invite students to share their findings with the class.

Play *Irish Tune from County Derry* **CD 2-32.** Have students

- Listen to the recording.
- Discuss the tempo with a partner.
- Share findings with the class.

### Analyzing

Have students compare *Irish Tune from County Derry* **CD 2-32** with "Oh, Danny Boy" **CD 2-30** using a Venn diagram. Refer to Teacher to Teacher on p. 49.

### Improvising

Establish a steady beat using a hand drum.

 Invite students to

- Improvise eight-beat rhythm ostinatos using body percussion.
- Transfer their ostinatos to nonpitched percussion instruments.
- Play their ostinatos at fast and slow tempos, then choose one ostinato for everyone to play.

Draw an arch on the board. Label the left end *slow* and the right end *fast,* as on a speedometer. Have one student use a mallet or stick as the needle on the speedometer to control the tempo, while the rest of the class plays the ostinato. Repeat with a different ostinato and different student leader.

### Listening

Have students turn to p. 50 and preview the listening map at the bottom of the page. Ask them to read and define the tempo terms. Play *Hungarian Dance No. 6* **CD 2-33.** As students listen, have them

- Point to the tempos on the listening map.
- Tap the beat lightly to show changes in tempo.

Ask students to describe the tempo changes they heard in the music.

### Listening for Tempo

**Listen** to *Hungarian Dance No. 6*, a composition for orchestra. There are many tempo changes in this music. As you listen, point to the appropriate word in the tempo meter below.

CD 2-33
**Hungarian Dance No. 6**

**by Johannes Brahms**

The *Hungarian Dances* were inspired by folk melodies of Eastern Europe.

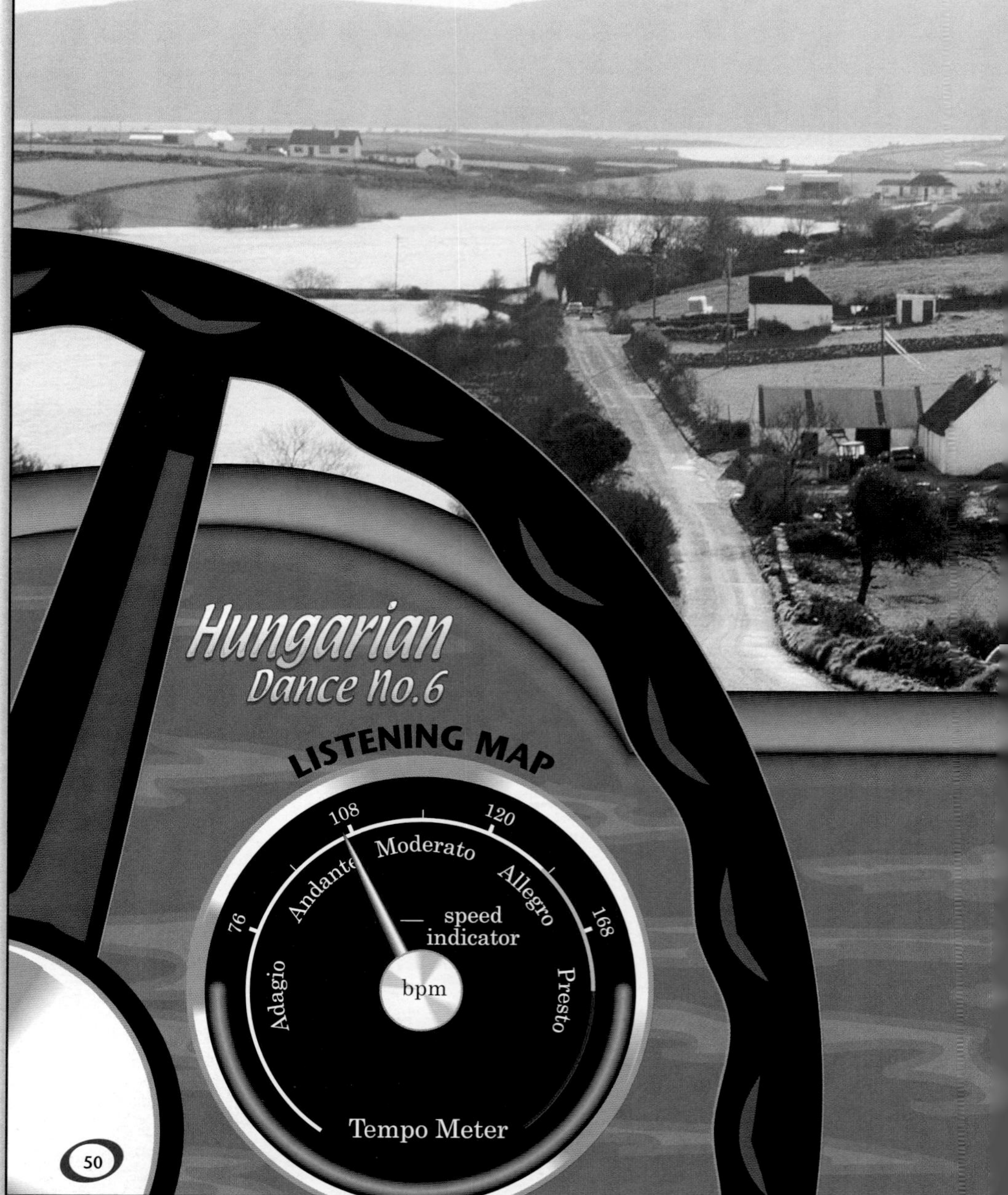


## Footnotes

### Skills Reinforcement

▶ **Improvising** Guide students in improvising and playing ostinatos, using the following process.

- Echo clap eight-beat rhythms to establish the length of the ostinato they will create.
- Invite students to use body percussion to create an eight-beat ostinato.
- Encourage them to create a pattern that can be repeated several times.
- When they are comfortable performing the ostinato, have them transfer the rhythm from body percussion to an instrument of their choice.

### Movement

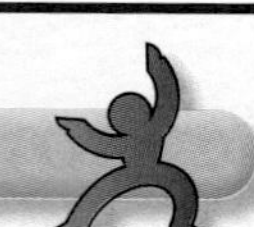

▶ **Nonlocomotor Movement** Use in-place movements to extend students' experiences with *Hungarian Dance No. 6.* Ask students to stand in a circle and practice passing a beach ball or gym ball to a drumbeat. Then have them pass the ball to the beat of *Hungarian Dance No. 6.* The movement and visual reinforcement of the traveling ball will reinforce the concept of tempo for some students.

▶ **Popular Dance** For specific instructions for *The Chicken Dance,* turn to Dance Directions on p. 507 in Teacher's Edition.

## Do the Chicken Dance!

**Listen** to *The Chicken Dance* and **move** with the music. Do your movements match the tempo of the music?

CD 3-1

**The Chicken Dance**

**by Werner Thomas**

*The Chicken Dance* is a favorite activity at celebrations and dances.

▲ **1.** Chirp with your hands.

▲ **2.** Flap your wings.

▲ **3.** Waddle downward.

▲ **4.** Clap four times.

### Moving

6b Invite the class to look at the photographs of students moving on p. 51.

**SAY** These are movements for *The Chicken Dance.* Be ready to discuss how your movements change by the end of the music.

Play *The Chicken Dance* **CD 3-1.** Model the movements for the students. Then have them perform the dance.

**ASK How did the tempo change in *The Chicken Dance?*** (The tempo varied from slow to fast, or *adagio* to *presto.*)

# 3 Close

**Element: EXPRESSION** ASSESSMENT

**Performance/Observation** Invite students to do *The Chicken Dance* **CD 3-1** on their own. Watch to see if students are appropriately interpreting the tempo and if their movements match the tempo of the music.

Divide the class in half. Play a recording from the lesson. While one group moves, have the other group point to the appropriate tempo symbols and terms on p. 50 to indicate the tempo of the music. Then have the groups switch roles and repeat. Observe both groups during the music to assess students' understanding of tempo.

## Meeting Individual Needs

▶ **Encouraging Participation** Use the following suggestions to help all students participate in *The Chicken Dance* movement activity.

**Reinforcement** Students with disabilities may have difficulty with some of the movements in this dance. You may wish to invite students in wheelchairs to be in the center of the circle and wheel right and left as other students step right and left.

**On Target** Students who are confident in their movements may be paired with students in wheelchairs. Have the walker follow the dance movements while pushing the chair, as the wheelchair user performs the hand and arm movements.

**Challenge** Encourage interested students to create a new movement routine for *The Chicken Dance.*

## Technology/Media Link

**Notation Software** Have students experiment with tempo, using the *Making Music* software. Invite them to create a short composition, then try playing it back at different tempos. (The tempo icon is located on the left side of the screen in the icon column.) Tempo is controlled with a red dot that slides to the left and right on a yellow line.

**Transparency** The *Hungarian Dance No. 6* listening map shows various tempos from slowest to fastest in a display like an old speedometer. Use the transparency to help students indicate the tempo heard on the recording.

LESSON 2

## LESSON AT A GLANCE

**Element Focus** **RHYTHM** Syncopation

**Skill Objective** **READING** Read ♪ ♩ ♪ syncopated rhythms in $\frac{4}{4}$ time

**Connection Activity** **MATHEMATICS** Practice addition skills by tying together note values

**MATERIALS**

- "Somebody's Knockin' at Your Door" **CD 3-3**
  **Recording Routine:** Vocal; interlude (2 m.); vocal
- **Music Reading Practice, Sequence 5** **CD 3-4**
- **Resource Book** pp. D-5, E-6, F-3, H-30

**VOCABULARY**

tie rhythm syncopation

**◆ ◆ ◆ ◆ National Standards ◆ ◆ ◆ ◆**

**2b** Perform melodies on appropriate instruments
**5a** Read quarter notes and eighth notes in duple meter
**6e** While listening to music, move to show a prominent feature of the music
**9c** Identify uses of music in everyday life

**MORE MUSIC CHOICES**

Other songs with syncopated patterns:
"Canoe Song," p. 76
"Weevily Wheat," p. 105

# 1 INTRODUCE

6e Play "Somebody's Knockin' at Your Door" **CD 3-3.** Have students keep a steady beat as they listen for long and short sounds in the song. Encourage them to sing with the recording when ready.

LESSON 2 

Skill: READING | Connection: MATHEMATICS

# The Score Is Tied

Rhythm is created by patterns arranged in many ways. What makes rhythm interesting is the way long and short sounds are arranged over the steady beat.

**Listen** to the rhythms in "Somebody's Knockin' at Your Door."

Using rhythm syllables, **read** the following rhythms. Then clap the rhythms as you **sing** the song. Are these rhythms the same as the rhythms in the song?

# Footnotes

## CULTURAL CONNECTION

9c ▶ **Symbolism in Spirituals** Many African American songs and spirituals had words that seemed to express religious faith, but also contained symbols of their struggle for freedom and even secret messages that helped them plan for escape. "Follow the Drinkin' Gourd," on p. 266, is one example of a song that helped people escape. Discuss with students what hidden messages could be communicated through "Somebody's Knockin' at Your Door."

## BUILDING SKILLS THROUGH MUSIC

▶ **Language** Have students write to inform by producing a short paragraph explaining the use of the tie in music. Have them bring poems into class that use syncopated rhythms when spoken.

## SKILLS REINFORCEMENT

▶ **Performing** Clap four-beat rhythm patterns using combinations of ♩, ♫, 𝄽, and ♪ ♩ ♪. Have students echo clap each pattern as a group and individually. Then have them determine how many beats are in each pattern.

▶ **Mallets** Encourage students to play the patterns on melody instruments. They may also wish to orchestrate the pattern
2b on nonpitched percussion instruments or play the arrangement of "Somebody's Knockin' at Your Door" on p. F-3 of the Resource Book.

## Tie It All Together

We can notate the rhythm of the song words using the **tie.**

A **tie** connects two notes of the same pitch.

Did you know tied notes can be written another way? For instance, these two rhythms sound the same: ♪ ♪♪ ♪ = ♪ ♩ ♪

For practice, let's add ties to the rhythms on page 52 to make them match the rhythm of the words. Be careful, the third line is tricky!



# 2 Develop

### Reading

 Have students clap and say the rhythms on p. 52.

ASK **Are these rhythms the same as or different from the rhythms in "Somebody's Knockin' at Your Door"?** (They are different, but similar.)

Remind students that eighth notes can be written with single stems as well as beamed together. Draw ♫ = ♪ ♪ on the board. Have students find the words in the song that fit the rhythm pattern of *short-long-short* (*somebody's* and *why don't you*). Tell students that the tie is used to connect notes together. Have students refer to the rhythm notation on p. 52 and explain, using standard terminology, where ties should be added so that the rhythms match the song. Tell students that the ♪ ♩ ♪ pattern is an example of syncopation. Refer to p. 444 and to Resource Book pp. D-5 and E-6 for related reading activities.

### Moving

 Have students read aloud and clap the rhythm of "Somebody's Knockin' at Your Door." Review a four-beat conducting pattern and invite students to conduct while listening to and singing "Somebody's Knockin' at Your Door" **CD 3-3.**

# 3 Close

**Element: RHYTHM** ASSESSMENT

**Performance/Observation** Invite students to read the syncopated patterns in "Somebody's Knockin' at Your Door" with rhythm syllables. Observe each student's ability to perform the ♪ ♩ ♪ pattern accurately.

## Across the Curriculum

▶ **Language Arts** Students may enjoy reading *Who's That Knocking at My Door?* by Tilde Michels (Barrons, 1992). It is the story of a group of individuals (a fox, a hunter, and so on) who have to share a shelter during a terrible blizzard. Talk about how sharing during difficult times made this group better friends.

Invite students to write in their journals about sharing and the friendships they have developed through sharing. You may wish to give students the sentence frame, "When I share, I feel ___________ because ___________."

## Technology/Media Link

**Electronic Keyboard** Have students select drum sounds or sound effects to play on beats 2, 3, and 4 at the end of the first, second, and last phrases of "Somebody's Knockin' at Your Door."

**Sequencing Software** Set up a sequencing program to play a click while recording and to loop for two measures of $\frac{4}{4}$. Prepare handouts showing a diagram of a keyboard with the names of the notes written on the keys. Refer to Resource Book p. H-30. Let several students come to the computer, one at a time. Each one should choose a sound with which to sequence an ostinato on one of the tracks, using D, E, F♯, A, or B. Play the sequence as a layered ostinato while the class plays the song "Somebody's Knockin' at Your Door."

LESSON 3

## LESSON AT A GLANCE

**Element Focus** **RHYTHM** ♪ ♩ ♪

**Skill Objective** **READING** Read rhythm patterns consisting of ♪ ♩ ♪ and ♩, ♫, 𝄽 in $\frac{4}{4}$ time

**Connection Activity** **SOCIAL STUDIES** Learn the history of a railroad song

**MATERIALS**

- "Rock Island Line" **CD 3-9**

  **Recording Routine:** Intro (4 m.); refrain; verse; refrain; interlude (4 m.); refrain; verse; refrain; coda
- **Music Reading Practice, Sequence 6** **CD 3-11**
- **Resource Book** pp. D-6, E-7, F-4, I-5
- pencils

**VOCABULARY**

rhythm syncopation

**National Standards**

- **1c** Sing from memory songs from diverse cultures
- **2d** Play instruments, echoing rhythms
- **5a** Read quarter and eighth notes and rests, including the *syncopa* pattern, in duple meter
- **6e** While listening to music, move to show a prominent feature of the music

**MORE MUSIC CHOICES**

Another song with syncopated patterns:

*"Bogando a la luz del sol,"* p. 306

## 1 INTRODUCE

Share the information in Spotlight On, p. 55, about the Rock Island Line railroad and the song.

2d Clap four-beat rhythm patterns consisting of ♩, ♫, 𝄽, and ♪ ♩ ♪. Have students echo clap or play each pattern while saying the rhythm syllables as a group or individually.

LESSON 3 Element: RHYTHM | Skill: READING | Connection: SOCIAL STUDIES

# Rhythms of the Railroad

Rhythm has a powerful effect on people. Some rhythms make work easier and smoother. "Rock Island Line" is a railroad work song that uses rhythm to help everyone work together. ♪ ♩ ♪ is one important rhythm in the song. **Sing** "Rock Island Line" and **identify** this rhythm. How many times does it occur?

CD 3-9
Rock Island Line
s, l, t, d r m f s l

Edited with New Additional Material by Alan Lomax

Railroad Song
New Words and New Arrangement by Huddie Ledbetter

REFRAIN
F
do
I say the Rock Is - land Line is a might - y good road,
F
C7
I say the Rock Is - land Line is the road to ride.

F
I say the Rock Is - land Line is a might - y good road,
F Bb F Bb
If you want to ride it, got to ride it like you find it,

F Bb C7 F Fine

Get your tick - et at the sta - tion for the Rock Is - land line.

# Footnotes

## TEACHER TO TEACHER

▶ **Hidden Rhythms** Once students have learned the pattern ♪ ♩ ♪ and are comfortable with reading, writing, playing, composing, and improvising with it, they should be led to discover the "hidden" syncopated patterns that often occur as a result of tied eighth-note rhythms. The overall concept of syncopated rhythms (accented sounds occurring between the beats in a measure) can then be discussed.

## BUILDING SKILLS THROUGH MUSIC

▶ **Math** Have students describe as a fraction the number of beats in the pick-up measure of "Rock Island Line." (3/8)

## SKILLS REINFORCEMENT

▶ **Mallets** For a mallet accompaniment to "Rock Island Line," see Resource Book p. F-4.

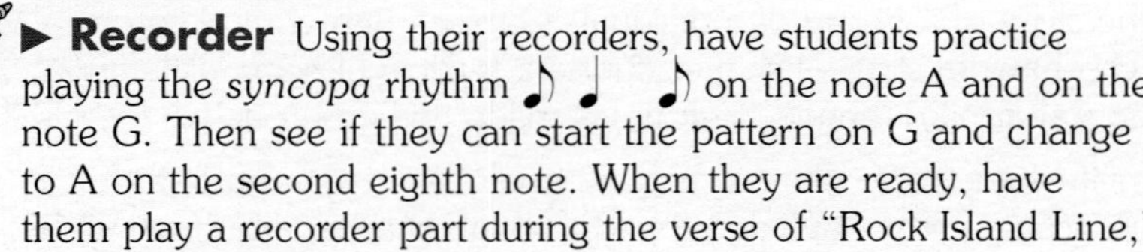

▶ **Recorder** Using their recorders, have students practice playing the *syncopa* rhythm ♪ ♩ ♪ on the note A and on the note G. Then see if they can start the pattern on G and change to A on the second eighth note. When they are ready, have them play a recorder part during the verse of "Rock Island Line," as notated below.

For a recorder accompaniment to "Rock Island Line," see Resource Book p. I-5.

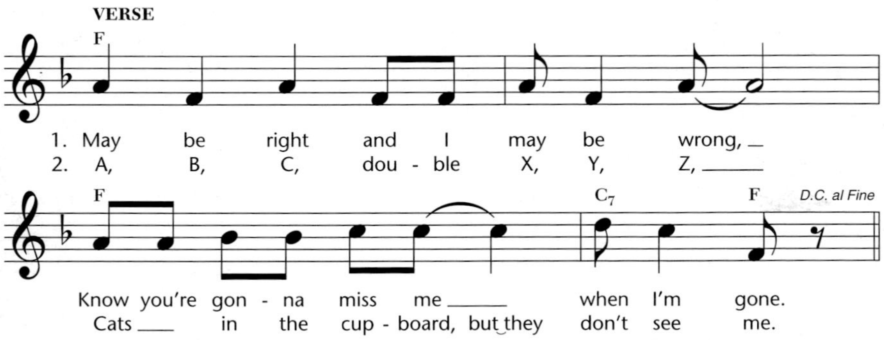

VERSE

F

1. May be right and I may be wrong, ___
2. A, B, C, dou - ble X, Y, Z, ___

F C7 F D.C. al Fine

Know you're gon - na miss me ___ when I'm gone.
Cats ___ in the cup - board, but they don't see me.

**Syncopation** is an arrangement of rhythm in which important notes begin on weak beats or weak parts of beats, giving an off-balance movement to the music.

### All Aboard for Rhythm!

♪♩♪ is called **syncopation.**

**Play** these syncopated ostinatos on percussion instruments.

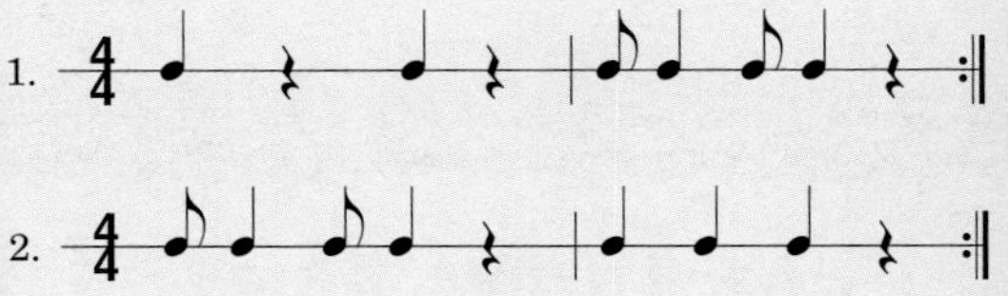

1. 4/4 ♩ 𝄽 ♩ 𝄽 | ♪♩♪♩ 𝄽 :‖

2. 4/4 ♪♩♪♩ 𝄽 | ♩ ♩ ♩ 𝄽 :‖

Form two groups. As everyone **sings** the song, group 1 **performs** the first ostinato, and group 2 performs the second.

Unit 2 55

# 2 Develop

## Listening

6e 1c Sing or play the recording of "Rock Island Line" **CD 3-9** for the class. Have students

- Keep a steady beat while listening to the song.
- Listen for long and short sounds in the song.
- Learn the song by rote, then sing along.

## Reading

Draw students' attention to the rhythms on Resource Book p. D-6. Have students

- Clap and read the rhythms aloud.
- Clap the rhythm as they sing "Rock Island Line" or listen to the recording.
- Compare the rhythm on the worksheet to the rhythm of the words. (Rhythms are different.)

Have students draw in ties so that the rhythms on the worksheet match the rhythms in "Rock Island Line."

For a related reading activity, see p. 444 and Resource Book p. E-7.

# 3 Close

**Element: RHYTHM** ASSESSMENT

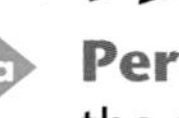

5a **Performance/Observation** Have students refer to the notation of "Rock Island Line" and read, clap, and say the rhythm of the song. Draw attention to the time signature and remind students that in $\frac{4}{4}$ time, there are four beats in each measure. Review the conducting pattern for $\frac{4}{4}$ time. Have students

- Conduct a four-beat pattern while listening to the recording of "Rock Island Line" **CD 3-9.**
- Sing "Rock Island Line" in a group.
- Take turns conducting the class.

Observe that students are able to conduct the four-beat pattern accurately.

## Spotlight On

▶ **Rock Island Line** "Rock Island Line" was made famous by the legendary blues singer Huddie "Leadbelly" Ledbetter. He learned the song from a work gang at an Arkansas prison while he was touring the South in the 1930s with Library of Congress collector John Lomax. Lomax recorded the men singing as they were chopping stacks of wood, keeping time swinging their axes as they sang. Leadbelly learned that the song originated in the early 1900s when the Rock Island Railroad Company had purchased rights to cut across Arkansas, through Little Rock and across West Memphis, dividing the state in half. Over the years, as the song grew popular, the references to work were dropped, and "Rock Island Line" became known purely as a railroad song.

## Technology/Media Link

**Notation Software** Invite students to experiment with the pattern ♪♩♪ using music notation software. Encourage them to create rhythms, placing the pattern ♪♩♪ in various places within the measure. Then have students play their rhythm patterns back to hear the syncopation.

LESSON Core 4

## LESSON AT A GLANCE

**Element Focus** **RHYTHM** Meter in 4

**Skill Objective** **MOVING** Perform a four-beat body percussion ostinato

**Connection Activity** **SOCIAL STUDIES** Discuss jazz history

**MATERIALS**

- "Joe Turner Blues" **CD 3-14**
  
  **Recording Routine:** Intro (4 m.); v. 1; v. 2; v. 3; coda
- *St. Louis Blues* (excerpt) **CD 3-17**
- **Resource Book** p. B-6, H-8, I-6
- **Dance Directions** for "Joe Turner Blues" p. 508

**VOCABULARY**

time signature blues

**National Standards**

**3b** Improvise rhythmic ostinato accompaniments
**6b** Describe music by answering questions about it
**6c** Use appropriate terms to explain music notation

**MORE MUSIC CHOICES**

Other songs in $\frac{4}{4}$ time:
"Over the Rainbow," p. 140
"Peace Round," p. 348

# 1 INTRODUCE

Write the words *happy* and *sad* on the board.

**SAY** When people are sad, sometimes they say they have the blues. People sing the blues, too.

Discuss the importance of jazz history with students and share the information on W. C. Handy and other jazz musicians from Spotlight On, p. 57, and Across the Curriculum below.

LESSON 4 Element: RHYTHM | Skill: MOVING | Connection: SOCIAL STUDIES

# Time for the Blues

If you say, "I feel blue," it usually means you feel sad about something. If you sing the blues, you are singing about your feelings.

A **time signature** is found at the beginning of most written music. Find the time signature in "Joe Turner Blues."

**Perform** this four-beat pattern while you **sing** "Joe Turner Blues."

| 1 | 2 | 3 | 4 |
|---|---|---|---|
| *pat* | *clap* | *snap* | *clap* |

The **time signature** tells how many beats are in each measure (top number) and the kind of note that gets one beat (bottom number).

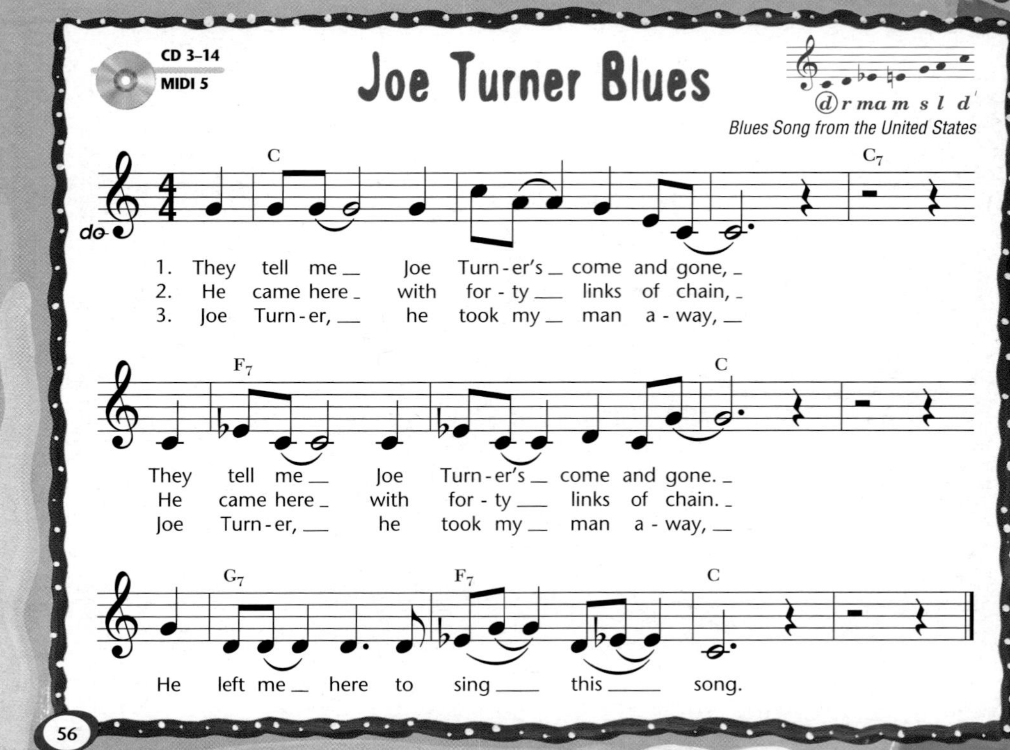

CD 3-14
MIDI 5
Joe Turner Blues
d r m a m s l d'
Blues Song from the United States
C C7 F7 G7
do
1. They tell me Joe Turn-er's come and gone,
2. He came here with for-ty links of chain,
3. Joe Turn-er, he took my man a-way,
They tell me Joe Turn-er's come and gone.
He came here with for-ty links of chain.
Joe Turn-er, he took my man a-way,
He left me here to sing this song.
56


# Footnotes

## ACROSS THE CURRICULUM

▶ **Social Studies** Encourage students to read about W. C. Handy and other jazz musicians in *Jazz: My Music, My People* by Morgan Monceaux (Knopf, 1994). The book includes short biographies of "Jelly Roll" Morton, Louis Armstrong, Duke Ellington, Ella Fitzgerald, Charlie Parker, and others, with a colorful painting of each. The biographies are arranged in chronological order, providing a historical overview of jazz.

## BUILDING SKILLS THROUGH MUSIC

▶ **Visual Arts** After students have listened to "Joe Turner Blues" and *St. Louis Blues*, have them illustrate one of the songs.

## SKILLS REINFORCEMENT

3b ▶ **Improvising** Set up mallet instruments with the C blues scale (C, D, E♭, F, G, A, B♭, C). Invite students to take turns improvising during measures 3–4, 7–8, and 11–12 while singing "Joe Turner Blues."

▶ **Keyboard** For an activity with a walking bass line and tritone duet accompaniment for "Joe Turner Blues," refer to Resource Book p. H-8.

▶ **Recorder** For practice playing four-beat patterns with the notes B, A, and G, refer to Resource Book p. I-6.

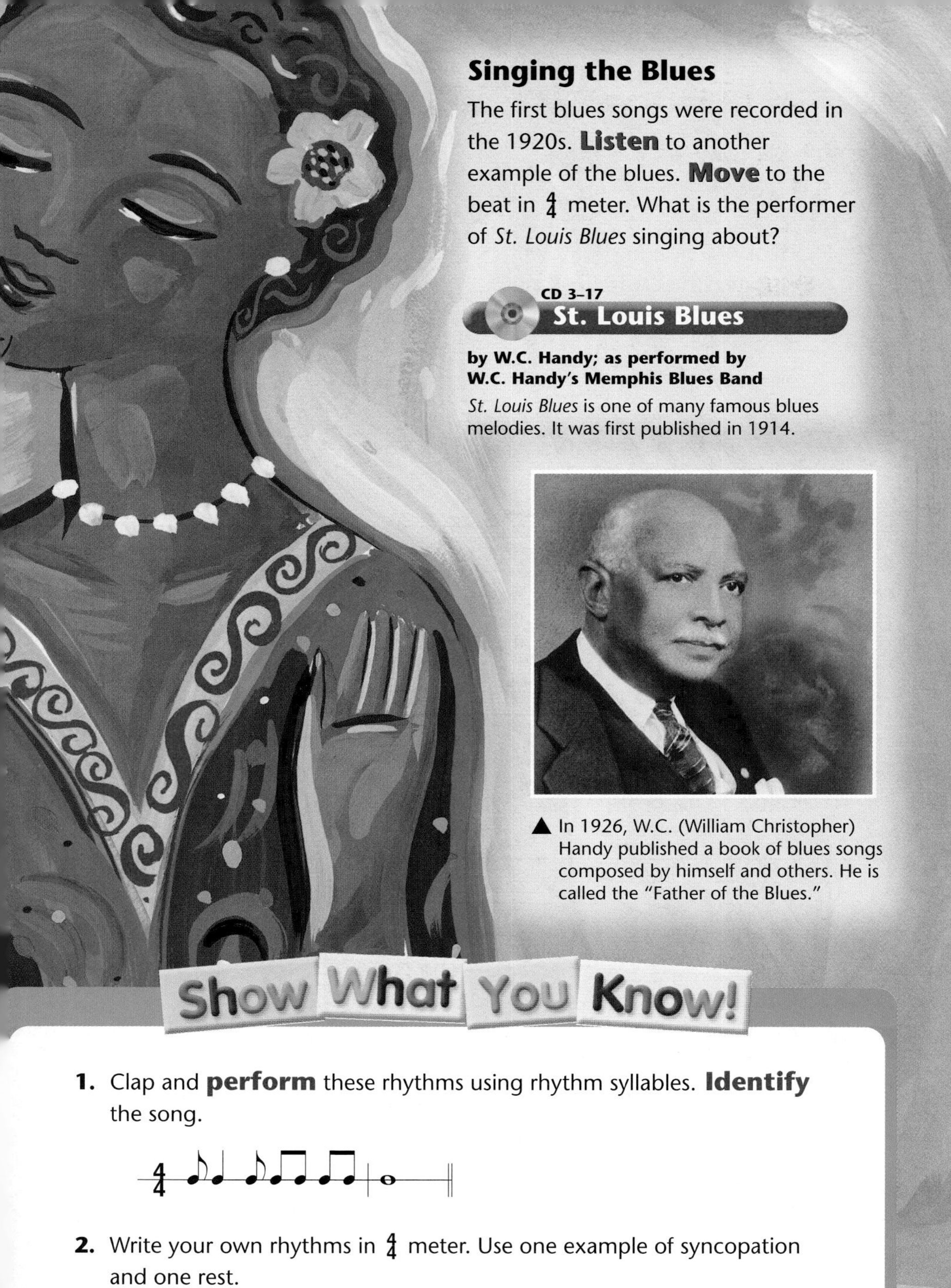

### Singing the Blues

The first blues songs were recorded in the 1920s. **Listen** to another example of the blues. **Move** to the beat in $\frac{4}{4}$ meter. What is the performer of *St. Louis Blues* singing about?

CD 3-17
**St. Louis Blues**

**by W.C. Handy; as performed by W.C. Handy's Memphis Blues Band**

*St. Louis Blues* is one of many famous blues melodies. It was first published in 1914.

▲ In 1926, W.C. (William Christopher) Handy published a book of blues songs composed by himself and others. He is called the "Father of the Blues."

### Show What You Know!

1. Clap and **perform** these rhythms using rhythm syllables. **Identify** the song.

$\frac{4}{4}$

2. Write your own rhythms in $\frac{4}{4}$ meter. Use one example of syncopation and one rest.



# 2 Develop

### Singing

6b Invite students to read the information on p. 56. Then play "Joe Turner Blues" **CD 3-14** as students listen.

ASK **How does the singer feel?** (sad)

Play the recording again. Have students sing along.

### Listening/Moving

6c Model the body percussion ostinato on p. 56 (pat-clap-snap-clap), and invite students to join you.

ASK **How many beats are in this pattern?** (four)

**Which beat is the strongest?** (the first beat)

**What symbol tells you that the beats are grouped in patterns of four?** (the time signature)

3b Play "Joe Turner Blues" again. Invite students to invent and perform their own four-beat ostinatos with the song.

6b **SAY** Listen to this music and decide if it is also in $\frac{4}{4}$ time.

Play *St. Louis Blues* **CD 3-17.** Invite students to move with the music.

ASK **Is this music in $\frac{4}{4}$ time?** (yes)

**How do you know?** (Have students explain.)

Have students do the Show What You Know activity on p. 57. Refer to Resource Book p. B-6.

For a dance that reinforces meter in 4 and 12-bar blues, refer to the Dance Directions for "Joe Turner Blues" on p. 508.

# 3 Close

**Element: RHYTHM** ASSESSMENT

**Performance/Observation** Have students sing "Joe Turner Blues" while performing their four-beat body percussion ostinatos. Observe that students are able to sequence the four-beat pattern without making mistakes.

## Spotlight On

▶ **W.C. Handy** William Christopher Handy (1873–1958) was born in Florence, Alabama. Handy, who played the cornet, learned to read music and studied classical music as a young man. Handy recognized that blues songs (songs that told the stories of everyday African Americans in the South) had popular appeal. He collected, arranged, and composed blues songs and organized his own bands to perform them. Eventually, he became co-owner of a music publishing firm in Memphis, Tennessee. The songs "The Memphis Blues" (1912) and "St. Louis Blues" (1914), which were published there, soon became popular throughout the country. In the 1920s and 1930s, Handy spent much of his time in New York recording blues songs and promoting the welfare of African American musicians and composers.

## Character Education

▶ **Expression of Emotions** Explore various ways people react to situations and how they express their feelings. Have students identify situations that evoke certain emotions and write the emotion on the board (for example, sadness, disappointment, anger). Divide students into small groups, assigning one situation and emotion to each group. Invite each group to create lyrics for a 12-bar-blues song, drawing ideas from the list of situations and emotions.

## Technology/Media Link

**CD-ROM** Invite students to explore the 12-bar blues section of *Alfred's Essentials of Music Theory,* Vol. 3. Have them create their own compositions. Then encourage students to move to the music, using various four-beat patterns of their own invention.

LESSON Core 5

## LESSON AT A GLANCE

**Element Focus** **FORM** Verse and refrain

**Skill Objective** **MOVING** Perform contrasting movements to show verse and refrain form

**Connection Activity** **SOCIAL STUDIES** Locate several North American rivers on a map

**MATERIALS**

- "River" **CD 3-18**

  **Recording Routine:** Intro (7 m.); v. 1; refrain; interlude (2 m.); v. 2; refrain; interlude (2 m.); v. 3; refrain; coda
- *The Boatman's Dance* **CD 3-20**
- "River" (poem)
- **Resource Book** p. I-7
- map of the United States

**VOCABULARY**

| | | |
|---|---|---|
| verse | refrain | AB form |
| interlude | coda | introduction |

**National Standards**

**4a** Compose music to accompany readings
**6a** Listen to identify form
**6b** Describe music by moving to it
**6c** Use appropriate terms to explain music
**8b** Identify ways music relates to language arts

**MORE MUSIC CHOICES**

Other verse and refrain songs:

"Sweet Betsy from Pike," p. 244

"Clementine," p. 341

"My Bonnie Lies Over the Ocean," p. 338

# Footnotes

## MEETING INDIVIDUAL NEEDS

▶ **English Language Learners** Comprehension can be challenging for students learning English. Oral retellings are one effective way to monitor comprehension. Divide students into pairs and invite them to tell their partner the meaning of the text of "River". Ask students about specific words or phrases, such as *raised, younger days,* and *seasons.*

## BUILDING SKILLS THROUGH MUSIC

▶ **Math** Once students have experienced the rhythm-reading activity in Skills Reinforcement, p. 59, have them develop a problem-solving strategy to answer the following questions:

"Which single note will fill half a measure in $\frac{3}{4}$ time?" (dotted quarter note)

"Which two notes can be combined to fill half a measure?" (quarter note and eighth note)

## ACROSS THE CURRICULUM

▶ **Social Studies** Use a large map to help students find and name rivers near where you live. Trace the flow of the rivers and develop river-related vocabulary such as the following.

- Source—the starting point of a river
- Mouth—the ending point of a river
- Delta—the land built up around a river's mouth
- Tributary—a stream, creek, or smaller river that flows into a larger river

Discuss with students how to find geographical directions on the map. Help them develop sentences that tell the direction in which specific rivers flow. For example, "The Mississippi River flows from north to south."

### Different Ways to Move

**Move** to show the different sections of "River." **Improvise** one motion for the A section **(verse)** and one for the B section **(refrain)**. Move as you **listen** to the song.

A **verse** is a section of a song where the melody stays the same when it repeats, but the words change.
A **refrain** is a section of a song that is sung the same way every time it repeats.

F C7 F
fad - ed on by. But all of the mem - o - ries
love's mel - o - dies, I've felt my own mus - ic with -
friends that I know, And here's to the song that's with -
B♭ F C7 F
lin - ger still, Like the light in a fad - ing sky.
in me rise Like the wind in the au - tumn trees.
in me now; I will sing it where' - er I go.
B REFRAIN
F C7 F C7
Riv - er, take me a - long, In your sun - shine sing me your
C7 B♭ F
song. Ev - er mov - ing and wind - ing and free, You
B♭ F B♭ F
roll - ing old riv - er, you chang - ing old riv - er, Let's
B♭ C7 F
you and me, riv - er, Run down to the sea.
Unit 2 59

# 1 Introduce

Ask students to name rivers they know in their community or state or rivers they have heard about in other parts of the United States. Write the names of the rivers on the board and help students locate them on a map. Encourage students to talk about rivers they have seen or any river experiences they may have had, such as swimming, boating, or fishing.

# 2 Develop

## Singing

6c Have students look at the notation for "River" and discover where the words *verse* and *refrain* and the letters A and B are found in the song. Play "River" **CD 3-18** and have students

- Listen and follow the words during the verses.
- Sing along with the refrain.

Continue to guide students to identify aurally this example of verse-refrain (AB) form.

6a **ASK How many verses are in the song?** (three)

**Other than having different words, how are the verse and refrain different?** (melody, rhythm)

**How many sections are there in "River"?** (two)

**What are they called?** (verse and refrain, or A and B)

## Moving

Invite students to move as they listen to "River."

**SAY** Think of a motion you can perform with the verse, or A section. Think of a different motion for the refrain, or B section.

6b Play "River," encouraging students to move with the song. Repeat the activity and ask students to sing as they move to the refrain.

continued on page 60

## Skills Reinforcement

▶ **Reading** Prepare students to read rhythms in $\frac{3}{4}$ time by having them perform a three-beat movement, such as pat-clap-snap, as they listen to "River." Then have students clap and say the rhythms for the first 12 measures of the refrain (through the word *free*). Prepare or practice the pitch *fa*, using the verse of "River." Sing the verse with pitch syllables and hand signs, except for *fa*, which can be hummed. *Fa* is easily identified as the pitch on the line above *mi*. Sing the verse with pitch syllables and hand signs for all pitches.

▶ **Recorder** For more practice in feeling meter in 3, have students play the recorder accompaniment to "River," on Resource Book p. I-7.

## Movement

▶ **Nonlocomotor Movement** Encourage students to explore various levels in space (low, middle, and high) as they move to the music in this lesson. Have them move at one level during the A sections of the songs "River" and *The Boatman's Dance* and the poem "River," and then at a different level for the B sections.

### Moving

Help students learn signs for the refrain of "River." Model the signs for the words *river, sunshine,* and *rolling.* Have students

- Practice the signs.
- Sing the refrain only, signing *river, sunshine,* and *rolling* when they occur in the song.
- Sing the entire song, signing with the B section.

Invite students to read the "Flowing Along" section at the top of p. 61.

Write these words on the board: *introduction, interlude, verse, refrain, coda.*

Ask volunteers to read the "Movement Clues" section on p. 61 aloud. Point to the appropriate word on the board as they read each clue.

Play *The Boatman's Dance* **CD 3-20.** Invite students to move to the music, changing movements each time a new section begins. Point to the appropriate word on the board to help students change movements at the right time. The form of *The Boatman's Dance* is introduction, verse, refrain, interlude, verse, refrain, and coda.

### Sing It with Signing

Practice the signs below, then **sing** and sign the refrain of "River."

▲ *river*

▲ *sunshine*

▲ *rolling*

60

## Footnotes

### Across the Curriculum

▶ **Language Arts** Discuss with students the meaning of the phrase "you can't step in the same river twice." Invite students to discuss this saying with a partner, and encourage them to write poems on this theme.

Read aloud the poem "River Winding" by Charlotte Zolotow (*The Random House Book of Poetry for Children,* by Jack Prelutsky, Random House, 1983).

Rain falling, what things do you grow?
Snow melting, where do you go?
Wind blowing, what trees do you know?
River winding, where do you flow?

### Spotlight On

▶ **The Composer** Aaron Copland (1900–1990), born in Brooklyn, NY, was one of the best-known American composers of the twentieth century. His music frequently reflects themes of American life and culture, and he often used folk melodies in his orchestral music. Most of Copland's music is very accessible to listeners. Copland wanted everyone to enjoy music, and he wrote several books, including *What to Listen for in Music,* to encourage listeners. Copland's suite *Old American Songs* features several folk melodies, such as "The Boatman's Dance" and "I Bought Me a Cat." In addition to the orchestral version with soloist, the suite has been arranged for piano and soloist, as well as for piano and chorus.

## Flowing Along

**Listen** to *The Boatman's Dance*. This song has a verse and a refrain, as well as an introduction, **interludes,** and a *coda*. **Move** to show the different sections of the music. Here are some clues to help you.

An **interlude** is a short musical connection between sections of a piece of music.

### Movement Clues

- The music for the introduction, interludes, and *coda* is slow.
- The music for the verse, section A, is fast.
- The music for the refrain, section B, has the word *boat* in it.

CD 3-20
**The Boatman's Dance**

**from *Old American Songs***
**by Aaron Copland**

This piece was written for solo baritone voice, orchestra, and choir.

Read the poem "River." Think about how a river moves and how the poem is divided into sections (like the song in this lesson). Then **create** expressive movements while a friend reads the poem aloud.

### River

*by Lawrence Locke*

The river moans.
The river sings.

Listen to the Fox, the Menominee,
The Susquehanna, Colorado, Platte,
The Ottowa, Snake, Bear,
And the Delaware.

Listen to the river.
The river moans.
The river sings.

The river is always going home.



### Creating

8b Invite students to read the poem "River" on p. 61.

ASK **Which lines of the poem are repeated?** *(The river moans. The river sings.)*

**If we call the first two lines of the poem an A section, where is another A section?** (repeated lines near the end)

**What is different about the second A section?** (It has an extra line, *Listen to the river.*)

**If we call the repeated parts A sections, what is the middle part called?** (B)

**What label can we use for the last line?** (coda)

**What is the difference between the form of the song "River" and the form of the poem "River"?** (The song is AB, and the poem is ABA coda.)

4a Divide students into groups of four or five. Have students

- Read the poem "River" expressively.
- Create movements to accompany the poem.
- Create music to accompany the poem.

See Skills Reinforcement below for additional creative activity suggestions.

## 3 Close

**Element: FORM** ASSESSMENT

**Performance/Observation** Invite students to sing and move to "River" **CD 3-18.** Have students use movements of their choice for the A (verse) and B (refrain) sections. Observe that students change motions when sections change.

### Skills Reinforcement

▶ **Creating** Encourage students to explore relationships between music and movement as they create an accompaniment to the poem "River." Divide students into groups of four or five. Have them read and discuss the poem and then create movements to perform, as one student reads the poem aloud. Encourage students to explore various levels of movement. Then have students improvise sounds to go along with the movements performed by another group. Encourage players to watch movers and respond to them. Have movers and players switch roles. Invite groups to perform the poem, movements, and music for the rest of the class.

### Technology/Media Link

**CD-ROM** Set up the computer, keyboard, and *Band-in-a-Box* software. Have students

- Point out the chord symbols found above the staff of "River."
- Take turns entering the chord symbols into *Band-in-a-Box*. (Remind them to enter a small "b" for the flat sign on B♭ chords.)
- Explore the waltz and jazz-waltz playback styles, using the styles menu. Determine which is the best choice for "River."
- Sing "River" along with the *Band-in-a-Box* accompaniment.

LESSON 6

## LESSON AT A GLANCE

**Element Focus** **MELODY** Extended pentatonic patterns

**Skill Objective** **READING** Read extended pentatonic patterns

**Connection Activity** **CULTURE** Discuss the country of Eritrea

**MATERIALS**

- *"Hashewie"* **CD 3-21**
- "Going 'Round" **CD 3-22**
  **Recording Routine:** Intro (6 m.); vocal; coda
- **Music Reading Practice, Sequence 7** **CD 3-25**
- **Pronunciation Practice/Translation** p. 474
- **Resource Book** pp. A-5, D-8, E-8

**VOCABULARY**

pentatonic scale call and response ledger lines

**◆ ◆ ◆ ◆ National Standards ◆ ◆ ◆ ◆**

- **1c** Sing from memory songs from diverse cultures
- **3b** Improvise melodic ostinato accompaniments
- **5b** Read notes in treble clef using letters and syllables
- **6b** Describe music by answering questions about it
- **6c** Use appropriate terms to explain music notation

**MORE MUSIC CHOICES**

Other songs with extended pentatonic patterns:
"See the Children Playin'," p. 107
"Cotton-Eye Joe," p. 288

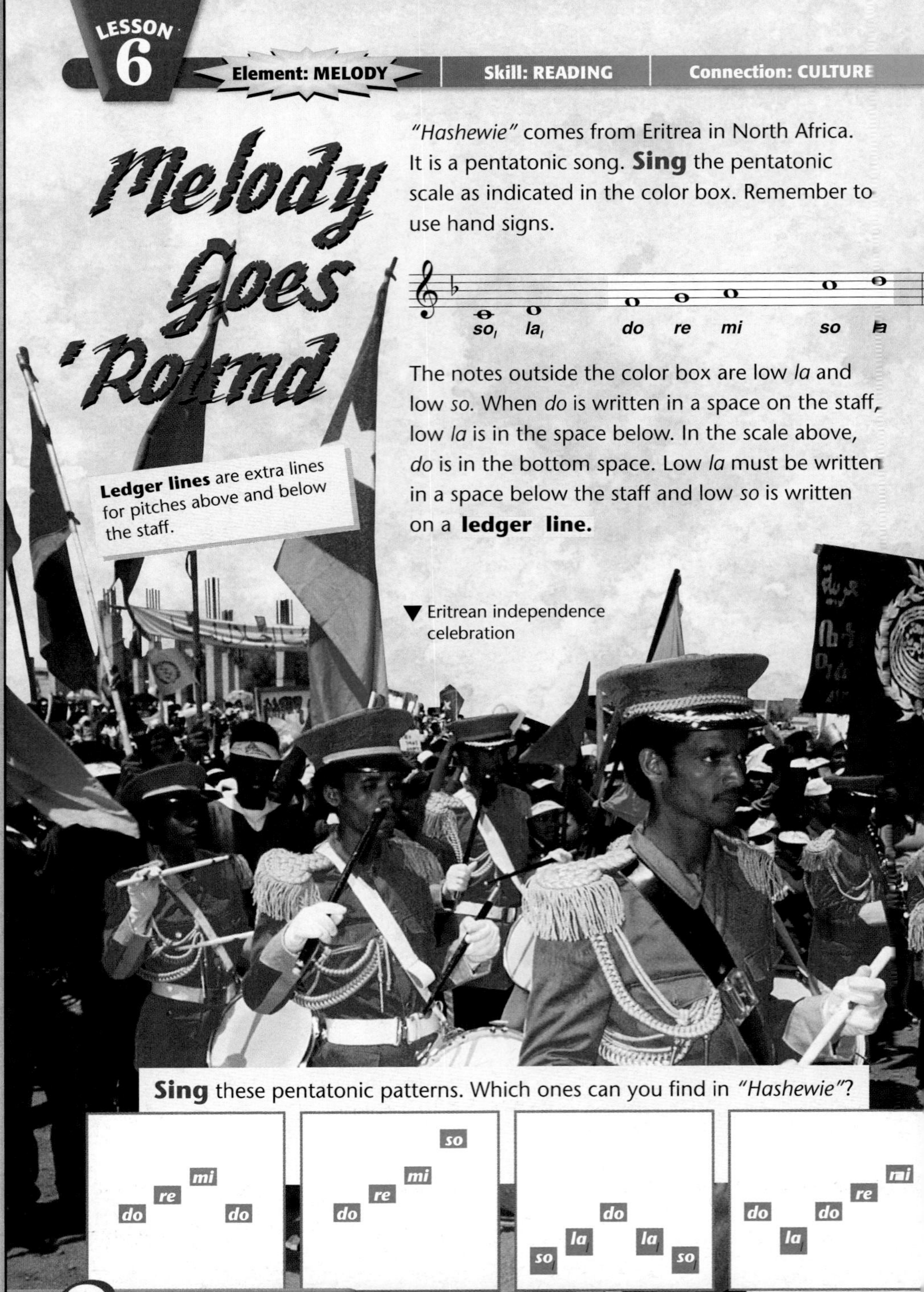
LESSON 6 Element: MELODY | Skill: READING | Connection: CULTURE

# Melody Goes 'Round

*"Hashewie"* comes from Eritrea in North Africa. It is a pentatonic song. **Sing** the pentatonic scale as indicated in the color box. Remember to use hand signs.



The notes outside the color box are low *la* and low *so*. When *do* is written in a space on the staff, low *la* is in the space below. In the scale above, *do* is in the bottom space. Low *la* must be written in a space below the staff and low *so* is written on a **ledger line.**

**Ledger lines** are extra lines for pitches above and below the staff.

▼ Eritrean independence celebration

**Sing** these pentatonic patterns. Which ones can you find in *"Hashewie"*?



62 Reading Sequence 7

# 1 INTRODUCE

Have students echo sing pentatonic patterns on *loo* as a group and individually. Share the information about Eritrea and the lyricist from Cultural Connection below and Spotlight On, p. 63. Then have the class sing the song *"Hashewie"* **CD 3-21.**

# Footnotes

## CULTURAL CONNECTION

▶ **Eritrea** Eritrea lies along the coast of the Red Sea and once was a region of Ethiopia. Since May of 1993, the Eritrean People's Liberation Front has maintained Eritrea's independence, but the country has been engaged in numerous border disputes with Ethiopia and Yemen. Eritrea is comprised of nine ethnic groups with Tigrinya and Tigre making up the largest percentage of the population. Tigrinya and Arabic are the predominant languages.

## BUILDING SKILLS THROUGH MUSIC

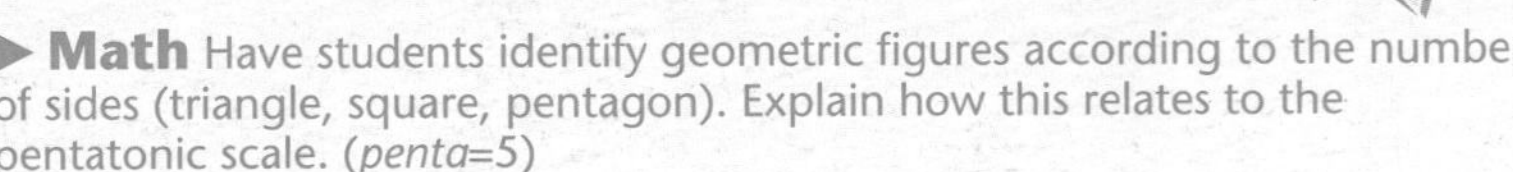

▶ **Math** Have students identify geometric figures according to the number of sides (triangle, square, pentagon). Explain how this relates to the pentatonic scale. (*penta*=5)

## SKILLS REINFORCEMENT

3b ▶ **Creating** Encourage students to create pentatonic patterns on pitched percussion instruments or by using only the black keys on a piano.

▶ **Singing** Invite students to listen to the Pronunciation Practice Track for *"Hashewie"* **CD 3-24** and sing with the students on the recording. Refer to Resource Book p. A-5.

To compare the use of pentatonic patterns in songs from diverse cultures, invite students to sing "Sourwood Mountain" on p. 65.

## Reading low *la* and low *so*

**Read** *"Hashewie"* using pitch syllables and hand signs. Then **sing** the leader's part while your friends sing the response *Shewie.*

CD 3-21
Hashewie
(Going 'Round)
s, l, (d) r m
Tigrinya Words by Hidaat Ephrem
Folk Song from Eritrea, Africa
do
Call
Response
Call
Ha - shew - i - e ___ Shew - i - e Ha - shew - i - e ___
I will go 'round, _ Shew - i - e You will go 'round, _
Response
Call
Response
Fine
___ Shew - i - e Ha - shew - i - e ___ Shew - i - e.
___ Shew - i - e We all go 'round, _ Shew - i - e.
Call (Tigrinya)
Response
D. C. al Fine
Bi - ha - de ha - bir - na Shew - i - e.
Ha-shew - ie e - na - bel - na
A - lem kit - fel - to
Ku - lu - me - nin - et - na
Ha-shew - i - e ni - bel
Nef' - lit - a - di - na
Bi - ha - de ha - bir - na
Call (English)
Response
D.C. al Fine
All to - geth - er 'round, Shew - i - e.
Say - ing 'round and 'round,
So the world would know,
Who ___ we ___ are,
Let's ___ say ___ 'round,
All to - geth - er 'round,
Go - ing 'round and 'round,
Tune In
"In Eritrea, you sing wherever you are. I'm used to singing when I'm walking, and learned many Eritrean values through song."
Hidaat Ephrem
Unit 2 63

# 2 Develop

### Analyzing

6b Draw attention to the shaded area of the pentatonic scale on p. 62.

6c **ASK Where are the steps in the pentatonic scale?** (between *do* and *re, re* and *mi,* and *so* and *la*)

**Where are the skips?** (between *so* and *mi*)

### Performing

5b Have students identify each notated pitch on the staff on p. 62, using its pitch syllable and hand sign. Then ask them to sing each pitch as you point to it (in F-*do*). Point out the missing notes by singing the interval from *do* to $la_|$. (Sing $la_|$ as *loo.*) Encourage students to use standard terminology in explaining and comparing these intervals.

**ASK Was the second sound higher or lower than *do?*** (lower) **Is it a step or a skip away from *do?*** (skip)

Repeat the process for $so_|$ by singing *do* $la_|$ $so_|$. (Sing $so_|$ as *loo.*)

### Reading

Draw students' attention again to the pentatonic scale on p. 62. Point out that the notes outside the box are part of the pentatonic scale, too. Review the staff placement of each note with students. Then have them sing the patterns at the bottom of p. 62. For practice writing the melody using standard notation, ask students to complete the worksheet on Resource Book p. D-8. For a related reading activity, see p. 445 and Resource Book p. E-8.

# 3 Close

**Element: MELODY** — **ASSESSMENT**

1c **Performance/Observation** Have students sing *"Hashewie"* **CD 3-21.** Use Resource Book p. D-8 to have students read and sing a pentatonic phrase, using pitch syllables and hand signs. Observe that students use proper hand signs and syllables.

## Spotlight On

▶ **The Lyricist** As a native of Asmara, Eritrea, Hidaat Ephrem's early years included a rich oral tradition in languages, songs, chants, and stories. During her childhood in her native land, she learned to express herself through singing. In 1972, Ephrem left Asmara and moved to the United States to study at the University of Minnesota. She lived in the United States during the war between Eritrea and Ethiopia. Ephrem now resides in Seattle, where she writes poetry and teaches songs to Eritrean young people in the area. This keeps her beloved music alive in her new homeland.

## Technology/Media Link

**Video Library** Have students watch the video for a performance of call-and-response singing.

LESSON 7

## LESSON AT A GLANCE

**Element Focus** **MELODY** Extended pentatonic patterns

**Skill Objective** **READING** Read extended pentatonic patterns

**Connection Activity** **SOCIAL STUDIES** Discuss life in Appalachia

**MATERIALS**

- "Sourwood Mountain" **CD 3-28**

  **Recording Routine:** Intro (4 m.); v. 1; interlude (2 m.); v. 2; interlude (2 m.); v. 3; coda
- **Music Reading Practice, Sequence 8** **CD 3-30**
- **Resource Book** pp. C-8, D-9, E-9

**VOCABULARY**

pentatonic *do*ˡ

**National Standards**

**3b** Improvise melodic ostinato accompaniments
**5b** Read notes in treble clef using letters and syllables
**6b** Respond to music by answering questions about it
**6c** Use appropriate terms to explain music notation

**MORE MUSIC CHOICES**

Other songs with extended pentatonic patterns:
*"Feng yang hua gu,"* p. 313
"How Can I Keep from Singing?" p. 261

# 1 INTRODUCE

Share information about life and culture in the Appalachian Mountains from Across the Curriculum below and Spotlight On, p. 65. Invite students to listen to "Sourwood Mountain" **CD 3-28.**



# Scale the Mountain

Have you ever climbed a mountain or been to the top of a tall building? You probably saw things from the top that you could never see from the bottom. Let's climb the pentatonic mountain below and discover what's at the top.

You already know some notes below *do*. Now **identify** the mystery note at the top of the pentatonic scale.

**Sing** the notes up and down the pentatonic scale. Then try skipping around from *do* to all the other notes.

**Read** this melody using pitch syllables and hand signs.

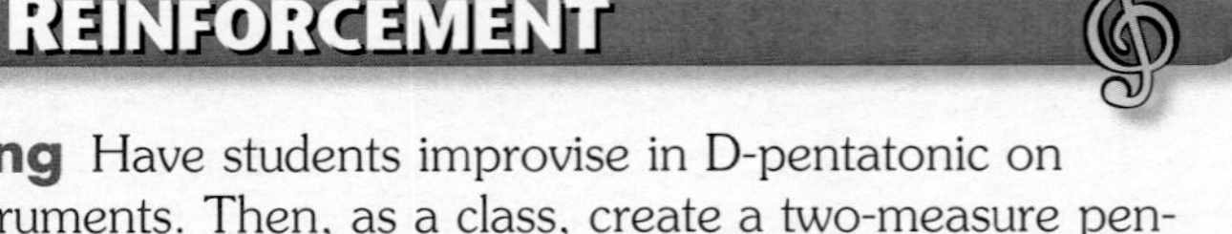


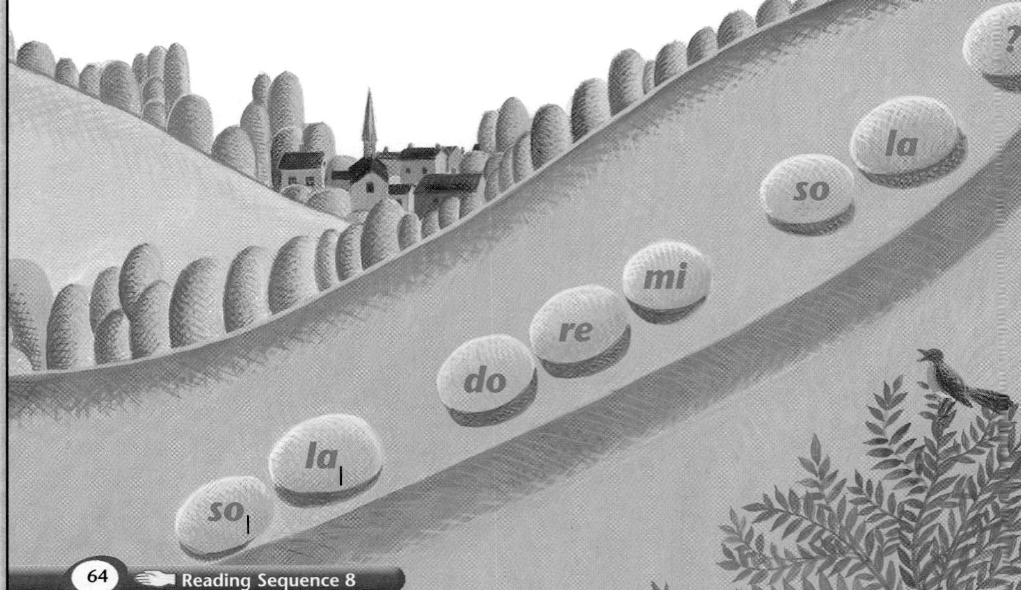




# Footnotes

## ACROSS THE CURRICULUM

▶ **Social Studies** Read aloud the book *Appalachia: The Voices of Sleeping Birds* by Cynthia Rylant (Harcourt, 1998). The author was raised in Appalachia and shares the beauty of this part of the United States with poetic text that projects emotion as well as content. After reading, create a Venn diagram on the board or use Resource Book p. C-8. Encourage students to compare life in Appalachia as described in the book with life in their community.

## BUILDING SKILLS THROUGH MUSIC

▶ **Reading** Have students paraphrase and summarize the text of "Sourwood Mountain" to recall and organize the ideas of the song. Then have them sing the song from memory, using the summary as clues.

## SKILLS REINFORCEMENT

3b ▶ **Creating** Have students improvise in D-pentatonic on barred instruments. Then, as a class, create a two-measure pentatonic ostinato. Have some students perform the ostinato as others sing "Sourwood Mountain" without the recording. (The recording of "Sourwood Mountain" is in a different key.)

5b ▶ **Notating** Encourage students to write the ostinato in stick notation or on staff paper in their manuscript books. You may wish to use the melody later for melodic dictation.

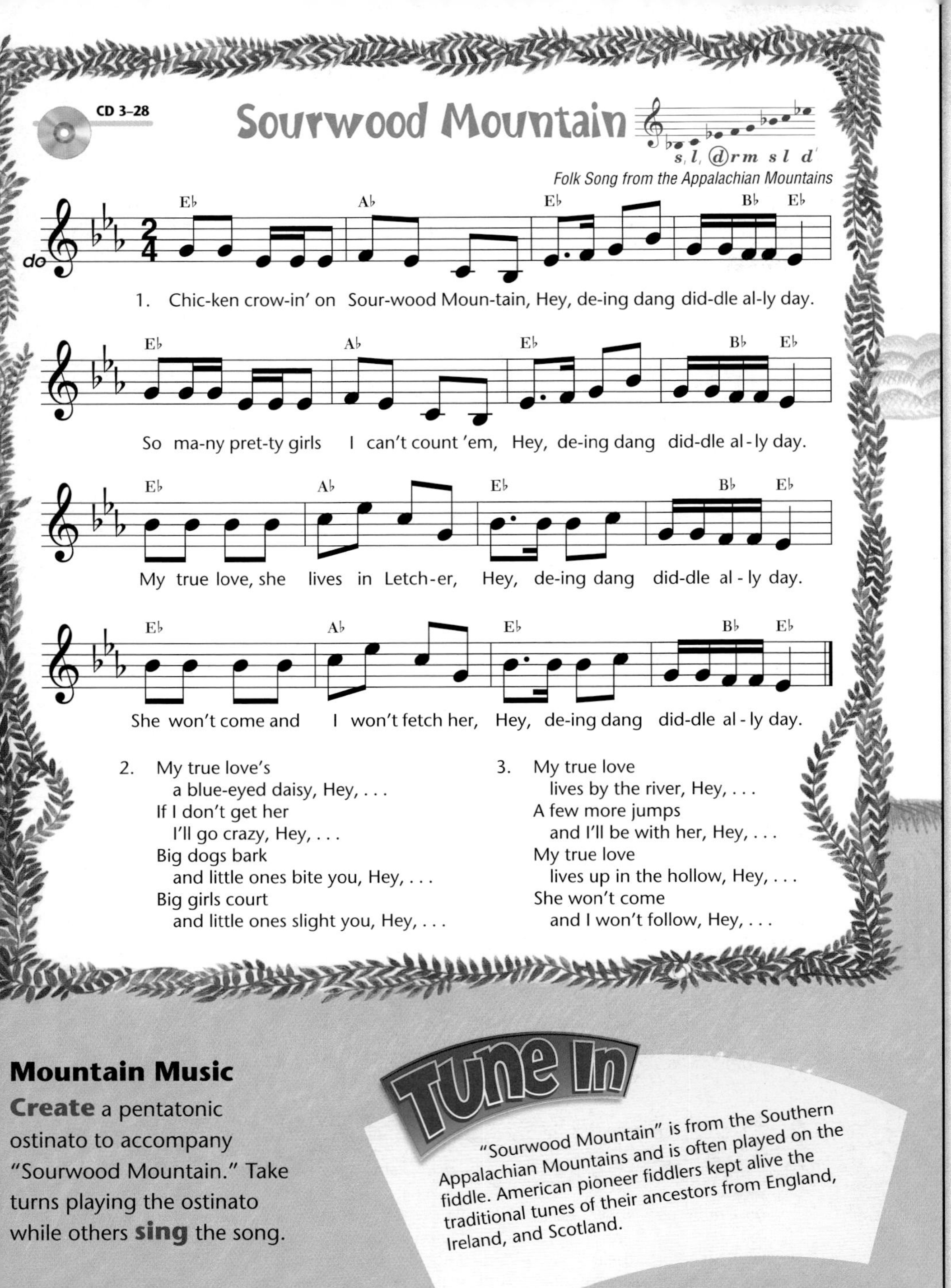

CD 3-28

# Sourwood Mountain

s, l, do r m s l d'

*Folk Song from the Appalachian Mountains*

do
E♭ A♭ E♭ B♭ E♭
1. Chic-ken crow-in' on Sour-wood Moun-tain, Hey, de-ing dang did-dle al-ly day.
So ma-ny pret-ty girls I can't count 'em, Hey, de-ing dang did-dle al-ly day.
My true love, she lives in Letch-er, Hey, de-ing dang did-dle al-ly day.
She won't come and I won't fetch her, Hey, de-ing dang did-dle al-ly day.

2. My true love's
   a blue-eyed daisy, Hey, . . .
   If I don't get her
   I'll go crazy, Hey, . . .
   Big dogs bark
   and little ones bite you, Hey, . . .
   Big girls court
   and little ones slight you, Hey, . . .

3. My true love
   lives by the river, Hey, . . .
   A few more jumps
   and I'll be with her, Hey, . . .
   My true love
   lives up in the hollow, Hey, . . .
   She won't come
   and I won't follow, Hey, . . .

**Mountain Music**

**Create** a pentatonic ostinato to accompany "Sourwood Mountain." Take turns playing the ostinato while others **sing** the song.

**Tune In**

"Sourwood Mountain" is from the Southern Appalachian Mountains and is often played on the fiddle. American pioneer fiddlers kept alive the traditional tunes of their ancestors from England, Ireland, and Scotland.

Unit 2 65

# 2 Develop

### Reading

Use Resource Book p. D-9 to review the notes of the pentatonic scale. Have students sing the known notes of the extended pentatonic scale (in E♭-*do*) using pitch syllables and hand signs. Draw attention to the missing note by singing the interval from *la* to *do*'. (Sing *do*' on *loo*.)

6b **ASK Is *do*' higher or lower than *la?*** (higher)

**Is it a step or a skip?** (skip)

Introduce the note as *do*'. Then have students sing the exercise on p. 64. See p. 445 and Resource Book p. E-9 for a related reading activity.

### Listening

6c Play "Sourwood Mountain" **CD 3-28.** Have students

- Listen to the song and follow the warm-up notation on p. 64.
- Listen again while singing the exercise softly, then compare the notated exercise with the song, using standard terminology.

Explain that the exercise is the "skeleton" of the song. The rhythm of the song varies a little because of the words of each verse.

### Singing

5b Play the Stereo Performance Track of "Sourwood Mountain" **CD 3-29** and have students sing the song with pitch syllables and hand signs. Then have them sing again with the text.

# 3 Close

**Skill: READING** ASSESSMENT

**Performance/Observation** Have students sing and sign the "skeleton" on p. 64 or perform the song from the notation on p. 65. Observe each student's ability to sing and sign the extended pentatonic scale.

## Spotlight On

▶ **Musical Spoons** Spoons are traditionally used to add improvised rhythmic accompaniment to Appalachian music. Ask students to bring two large metal spoons from home or borrow them from the cafeteria. With practice, spoons can be played by placing them back-to-back, holding the end of the handles together with one hand, and lightly tapping them on the thigh. Use the other hand to tap spoons from above so that they have a tapping, bouncing action. Have students use spoons to create a simple rhythm accompaniment to "Sourwood Mountain."

## Technology/Media Link

**Web Site** Have students explore string instruments at *www.sfsuccessnet.com.*

# Core LESSON 8

## LESSON AT A GLANCE

**Element Focus** MELODY Notes in treble clef

**Skill Objective** PLAYING Play a melody on recorder

**Connection Activity** LANGUAGE ARTS Discuss the use of rhyming words in poetry and songs

**MATERIALS**

- *"Riqui rán"* (Spanish) **CD 3-33**
- *"Riqui rán"* (English) **CD 3-34**

  **Recording Routine:** Intro (8 m.); v. 1; interlude (8 m.); v. 2; interlude (16 m.); v. 3; coda
- **Pronunciation Practice/Translation** p. 475
- **Resource Book** pp. A-6, B-6, I-8
- recorders
- pitched percussion instruments or keyboards

**VOCABULARY**

letter names

**◆ ◆ ◆ ◆ National Standards ◆ ◆ ◆ ◆**

**2b** Perform melodies on appropriate instruments
**2f** Play instruments independently against contrasting parts
**5b** Read notes in treble clef using letters
**8b** Identify ways music relates to language arts

**MORE MUSIC CHOICES**

For more practice playing recorder:
"Ode to Joy," p. 152
*"Somos el barco,"* p. 352
Another song in Spanish:
*"La raspa,"* p. 302

## 1 INTRODUCE

Invite students to think of words that rhyme with names of instruments or other items in the room. To explore rhyming words further, see Across the Curriculum below.



# Melody Rhymes in Time

Humor can be expressed in any language. **Listen** for the humorous Spanish rhymes in this song.

CD 3-33
MIDI 6

## Riqui rán

r m f s l t d

*Translated by J. Olcutt Sanders* *Folk Song from Latin America*

do

C F C F C G7 C

1. A - se - rrín, a - se - rrán. Los ma - de - ros de San Juan co - men que - so, co - men pan. Los de Ri - que, al - fe - ñi - que; los de
1. A - se - rrín, a - se - rrán. All the woods-men of San Juan eat their cheese and eat their pan. Those from Ri - que, al - fe - ñi - que; Those from

G7 C G7 C

Ro - que, al - fon - do - que, Ri - qui, ri - que, ri - qui rán. 2. A - se -
Ro - que, al - fon - do - que, Ri - qui, ri - que, ri - qui rán. 2. A - se -

C F C F C F

rrín, a - se - rrán. Las a - be - jas vie - nen, van; Miel la - bo - ran pa - ra el pan. Li - ban flor - es las de Ri - que cual al -
rrín, a - se - rrán. Los chi - qui - llos ¿dón - de es - tán? To - dos a dor - mir se van. So - ña - rán con al - fe - ñi - que co - mo
rrín, a - se - rrán. All the bees fly hith - er, yon; Gath - er nec - tar for their pan. Sip - ping from the flowers of Ri - que nec - tar
rrín, a - se - rrán. Where have all the chil - dren gone? They have put their night-gowns on. They will dream of al - fe - ñi - que as the



# Footnotes

## ACROSS THE CURRICULUM

▶ **Language Arts** Explore rhyming words in *"Riqui rán"* and other songs or poems students know. Have students

- Sing the song as a class.
- Find and list rhyming words in the song.
- Think of additional words that rhyme with those on their lists.

## BUILDING SKILLS THROUGH MUSIC

▶ **Social Studies** Have students locate Latin America on the map. Then discuss Latin American culture.

## SKILLS REINFORCEMENT

▶ **Playing** Have students move and speak the rhythm of these ostinatos and then transfer to percussion instruments. Encourage students to play expressively to convey the mood of a lullaby.

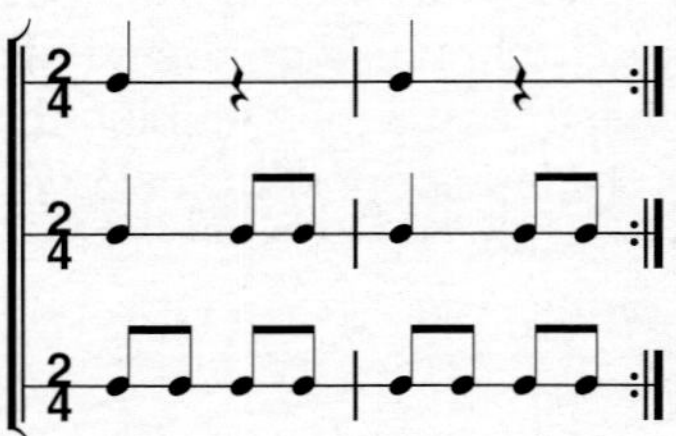

▶ **Recorder** For a recorder challenge, have students extend the recorder melody on p. 67, using the recorder part on Resource Book p. I-8.

### Name It and Play It

Name the notes in this melody for recorder. **Play** the melody with the first four measures of each verse of *"Riqui rán."*

Name the notes below and find these measures in *"Riqui rán."*

## Show What You Know!

1. **Sing** this melody using pitch syllables.
2. Now **identify** the letter names for the pitches above. **Play** the melody on a xylophone or keyboard.
3. **Sing** this melody using pitch syllables. Then sing the notes using letter names and **play** the melody on recorder.



# 2 Develop

### Singing

8b Have students read the text above *"Riqui rán"* on p. 66. Then play *"Riqui rán"* **CD 3-33.**

ASK **What rhyming words did you hear?** (Accept a variety of answers.)

Use the Pronunciation Practice Track **CD 3-36** and refer to Resource Book p. A-6. Then have students sing the song with the recording.

### Playing

Invite students to look at the recorder melody on p. 67. Have them

- Tap and say the rhythm with syllables, then identify the notes, using letter names.
- 2b Play and compare the recorder melody to the first four measures of *"Riqui rán."*
- 2f Play along with the song.

### Reading

5b Help students identify other pitches in *"Riqui rán"* by letter name. Have them

- Find parts of *"Riqui rán"* that are similar to the recorder melody and name the pitches by letter.
- Choose one line of the song and, with a partner, identify the pitches by letter names.

Have students do the Show What You Know activities on p. 67. Refer to Resource Book p. B-6 for a worksheet that provides additional practice with reading notation, using rhythm and pitch syllables.

# 3 Close

**Skill: PLAYING** ASSESSMENT

**Performance/Observation** Have students play the recorder melody with *"Riqui rán,"* first "playing silently" in chin position, then playing aloud. Remind them to think about producing a good tone.

## Meeting Individual Needs

▶ **Recorder Tips** Each student's level of physical development, growth, and coordination will vary, and may pose some challenges for recorder playing. To help students produce the best possible sound, be sure that

- Students' fingers cover the holes completely, particularly the thumb hole on the back of the recorder.
- The tip of the recorder mouthpiece is inserted between the lips, resting lightly on the lower lip. The upper teeth should not bite the mouthpiece.

Encourage students to check each other and offer constructive comments. Students may use a small mirror to check their own lip position, also called *embouchure* [AHM buh shur].

## Technology/Media Link

**MIDI/Sequencing Software** Play the MIDI song file *"Riqui rán"* as students play recorder parts. Use a slower tempo and mute some accompaniment tracks if students are having difficulty. When students are secure in their performance, mute the melody track, play the accompaniment tracks, and increase the tempo.

LESSON 9

## LESSON AT A GLANCE

**Element Focus** **TIMBRE** Wind instrument timbres

**Skill Objective** **LISTENING** Identify wind instruments by sound

**Connection Activity** **SCIENCE** Discuss how sounds are produced by brass and woodwind instruments

### MATERIALS

- *"Eh, cumpari!"* **CD 3-37**
- "Hey, Buddy!" **CD 3-38**

  **Recording Routine** Intro (8 m.); v. 1; interlude (4 m.); v. 2; interlude (4 m.); v. 3; interlude (4 m.); v. 4; interlude (4 m.); v. 5; interlude (4 m.); v. 6; coda
- **Pronunciation Practice/Translation** p. 476
- *One-Minute Woodwind Mysteries* **CD 4-1**
- *"Allegro molto"* from *Quartet* **CD 4-6**
- *One-Minute Brass Mysteries* **CD 4-7**
- "Fanfare" from *La Peri* **CD 4-11**
- **Resource Book** p. A-8
- selected classroom instruments

### VOCABULARY

| | | | |
|---|---|---|---|
| timbre | flute | clarinet | oboe |
| bassoon | saxophone | trumpet | French horn |
| trombone | tuba | | |

### ◆◆◆◆ National Standards ◆◆◆◆

**4b** Compose instrumental pieces within specific guidelines
**6b** Describe music by answering questions about it or explaining how it sounds
**6c** Use appropriate terms to explain musical instruments
**6d** Identify the sounds of orchestral and band instruments
**8b** Identify ways music relates to science and foreign languages
**9d** Describe roles of musicians in various settings

### MORE MUSIC CHOICES

For more practice with wind timbres:
*Symphony No. 6 in F*, Mvt. 4, p. 365
*1812 Overture*, p. 293

LESSON 9 Element: TIMBRE | Skill: LISTENING | Connection: SCIENCE

# I Spy an Instrument

Each instrument has its own special sound, or timbre. To make a sound on most wind instruments, the player blows air into the instrument, causing the air to vibrate. The string instrument's sound is made by vibrating strings. **Sing** this Italian song about six instruments.

CD 3-37 MIDI 7

## Eh, cumpari! (Hey, Buddy!)

Words and Music by Julius La Rosa and Archie Bleyer

d r m f s
do
D A7
Eh, cum - pa - ri! Ci vo' su - na - ri.
Hey, good bud - dy! It's time to play!
Chi si so - na 1. 'U fris - ca - let - tu? 2. 'U sax - o - fo - na? 3. 'U man - du - li - nu?
Who will play on 1. the pic - co - lo? 2. the sax - o - phone? 3. the man - do - lin?
E co - mu si so - na 'u fris - ca - let - tu? 'u sax - o - fo - na? 'u man - du - li - nu?
And how do you play on the pic - co - lo? the sax - o - phone? the man - do - lin?
68

# Footnotes

## CULTURAL CONNECTION 

8b ▶ **Italian: The Language of Music** As students learn the Italian lyrics of *"Eh, cumpari!"* point out other Italian musical terms they already know. Terms for dynamics, such as *forte, piano,* and so on, are Italian words. Tempo words like *adagio, moderato,* and *presto* are also from the Italian language. Students can learn other Italian words by reading *Count Your Way Through Italy* by Jim Haskins (Carolrhoda Books, 1991).

## BUILDING SKILLS THROUGH MUSIC

▶ **Science** Have students plan and implement a simple experiment to prove or disprove this hypothesis: A bottle full of water will make a higher sound than an empty bottle. Use follow-up discussion to help students relate the results to the sound production of selected instruments in this lesson. Be sure to follow the scientific method.

## SKILLS REINFORCEMENT 

▶ **Reading** Help students follow the multiple endings and verses of *"Eh, cumpari!"* Have them find the "1" (for verse 1) in the second line of the music. Then have them find the words *'U friscalettu* each time they occur in the song (lines 2, 3, and first ending). Then direct students to the first ending, on the next-to-last line, where they will see *'u friscalett'e.* Tell students that for the first verse, they skip all other endings and go to the first ending. For the second verse, they skip endings 6, 5, 4, 3 and go to the second ending, then the first. The same pattern continues throughout the song.

CD-ROM Using Making Music software, compose a piece of music with two different timbres. Think about how you can use timbre to organize your composition.
A7
6. continue on
5. continue on
A - fu - mm'a - fu - mm'a la trom - bon', pa - pa pa - pa a la trum -
A-foom - a - foom on the trom-bone, pa - pa - pa - pa on the trum -
4. continue on
3. continue on
be - tt', a-zing - a - zing 'u vi - u - lin, a-pling - a - pling 'u man - du -
pet, a - dzing - a - dzing the vi - o - lin, a-pling - a - pling the man - do -
2. continue on
1. continue on
lin, tu - tu tu - tu 'u sax - o - fon, (whistle) 'u fris - ca -
lin, too-too - too - too the sax - o - phone, the pic - co -
D
le - tt'e ti - pi - ti ti - pi - ti - ta.
lo and ti - pi - ti ti - pi - ti - ta.
4. . . . 'U viulinu? . . .
5. . . . A la trumbetta? . . .
6. . . . A la trombona? . . .
4. . . . the violin? . . .
5. . . . the brassy trumpet? . . .
6. . . . the slide trombone? . . .
Unit 2 69

# 1 Introduce

6b Before students enter the classroom, place two contrasting percussion instruments out of sight. (Some possibilities are triangle, woodblock, jingle bells, or *guiro*.) When students are ready, play one of the instruments without showing it to the class.

**ASK What instrument am I playing?** (Identify it by name.)

**How do you know?** (Accept a variety of descriptions of the sounds, encouraging students to use standard terminology in explaining their responses.)

Repeat the procedure for the second instrument.

**SAY** The sound of an instrument is its *timbre.*

Share the information about how instruments work from Across the Curriculum below.

# 2 Develop

## Singing

6c Invite students to

- Read the information about timbre on p. 68.
- Name the instruments pictured on pp. 69–71.

Invite students to listen to the Pronunciation Practice Track for *"Eh, cumpari"* **CD 3-40** and sing with the students on the recording. Refer to Resource Book p. A-8.

Play *"Eh, cumpari!"* **CD 3-37.** Invite students to listen for the instruments as they sing along with the recording.

**ASK Which instruments in the song are string instruments?** (mandolin, violin)

**Which instruments in the song are wind instruments?** (piccolo, saxophone, trumpet, trombone)

Play the recording again and have students sing the entire song.

**continued on page 70**

## Across the Curriculum

8b ▶ **Science** Help students explore how instruments work. Sound begins when vibration sets air in motion. For string instruments, the vibration begins when someone plucks or strums a string or when a bow is drawn across it. For most woodwind instruments, a reed vibrates. For brass instruments, the player's lips vibrate. Flutes and whistles work when the player blows air across or into the mouthpiece of the instrument, which splits the air column, causing the air to vibrate. For most percussion instruments, a mallet or hand strikes the instrument, causing the material, such as the skin of a drumhead, to vibrate. Encourage students to explore how various classroom instruments produce vibrations.

## Meeting Individual Needs

9d ▶ **Role-Playing Musicians** All students can be successful and have fun performing *"Eh, cumpari!"* by playing the roles of various professional musicians (singers, members of the orchestra, conductor, and so on). Consider the movements required for different instruments, and assign students to appropriate roles. Invite instrumentalists to sit in string, woodwind, and brass "sections" (as they would in an actual orchestra), with singers behind the players. Players will pantomime the appropriate instrument as it is mentioned. Singers will sing the entire song. The conductor will cue both groups. Give students with disabilities opportunities for leadership roles (for example, chorus or instrumental section leaders, conductor).

### Moving

Invite students to

- Invent a "playing" motion for each of the instruments in *"Eh, cumpari!"* and perform their motion as they sing about that instrument.
- Keep the beat, using a motion of their choice during the rest of the song.

### Listening

Students may enjoy this timbre game.

- Ask three students to choose an instrument (while others are not looking) and place it out of view.
- Have each "player" improvise a short pattern on the instrument.
- Invite the rest of the class to identify the instrument.

Encourage students to use standard terminology in describing and explaining the sound of each musical instrument.

**SAY** When you name an instrument by its sound, you are identifying it by its timbre. (Write *timbre* on the board.)

**ASK** **What does the word *timbre* mean?** (the sound or tone color of an instrument)

### Creating

**SAY** Think about how you can use the sounds of two different instruments to organize a composition.

Working in pairs, ask students to

- Compose a piece for two instruments.
- Rehearse their composition.
- Notate or graph their composition.
- Perform their composition for the class.
- Write about how they used timbre in their compositions.

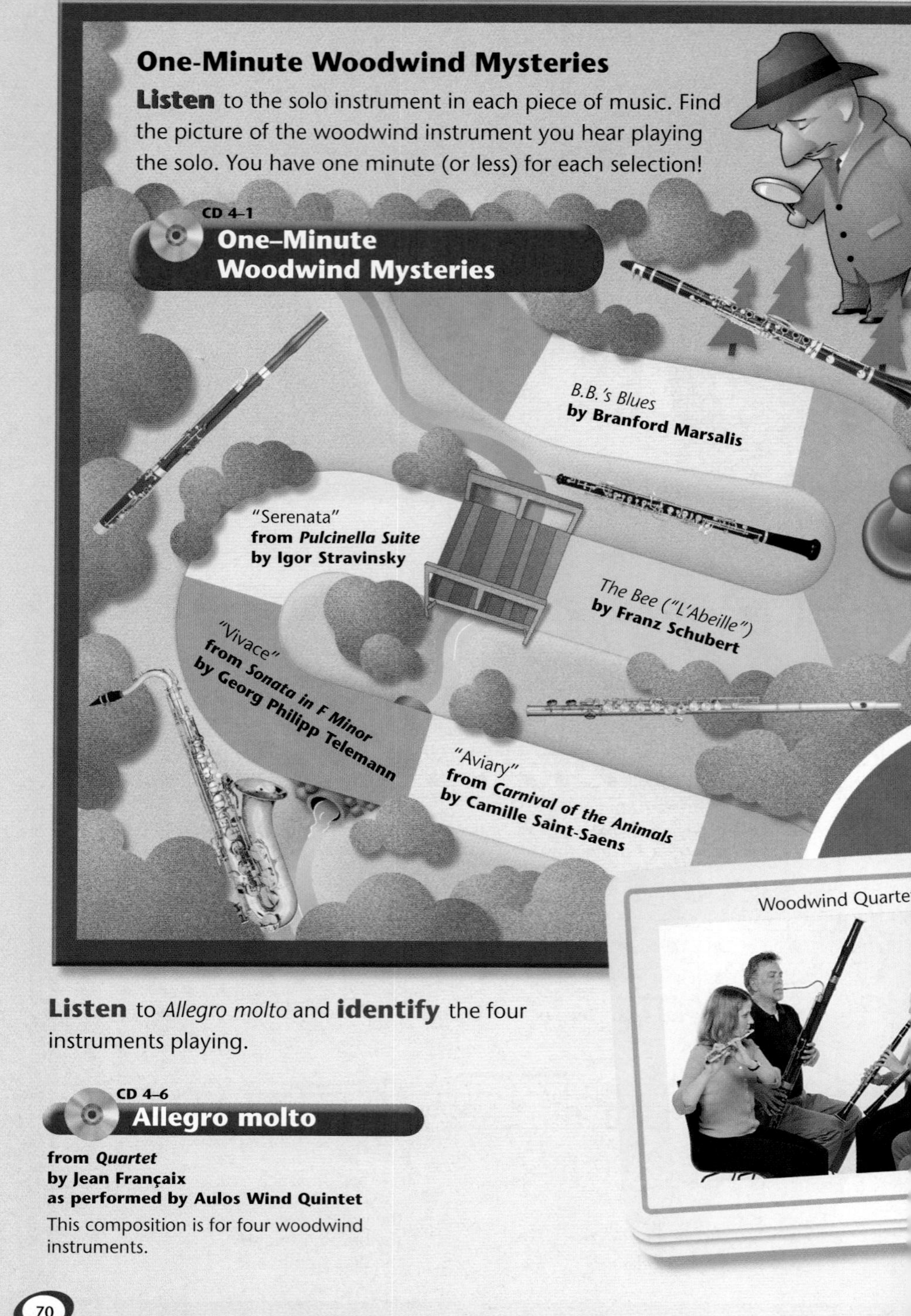

**One-Minute Woodwind Mysteries**

**Listen** to the solo instrument in each piece of music. Find the picture of the woodwind instrument you hear playing the solo. You have one minute (or less) for each selection!

CD 4-1
**One–Minute Woodwind Mysteries**

*B.B.'s Blues*
**by Branford Marsalis**

"Serenata"
**from *Pulcinella Suite***
**by Igor Stravinsky**

*The Bee ("L'Abeille")*
**by Franz Schubert**

"Vivace"
**from *Sonata in F Minor***
**by Georg Philipp Telemann**

"Aviary"
**from *Carnival of the Animals***
**by Camille Saint-Saens**

Woodwind Quartet

**Listen** to *Allegro molto* and **identify** the four instruments playing.

CD 4-6
**Allegro molto**

**from *Quartet***
**by Jean Françaix**
**as performed by Aulos Wind Quintet**

This composition is for four woodwind instruments.

70

## Footnotes

### Teacher to Teacher

▶ **Managing the Creating Activity** Ask questions about timbre before beginning the Creating activity above to help students focus. You might ask students to name classroom instruments with contrasting timbres, and have them explain their answers. Encourage students to think about whether their composition will feature only one timbre at a time or both together.

### Spotlight On

▶ **Instrument Demonstrations** Explore resources in the community for providing instrument demonstrations in your school. Members of folk music groups, community ensembles, or independent musicians may be willing to share their music with the students.

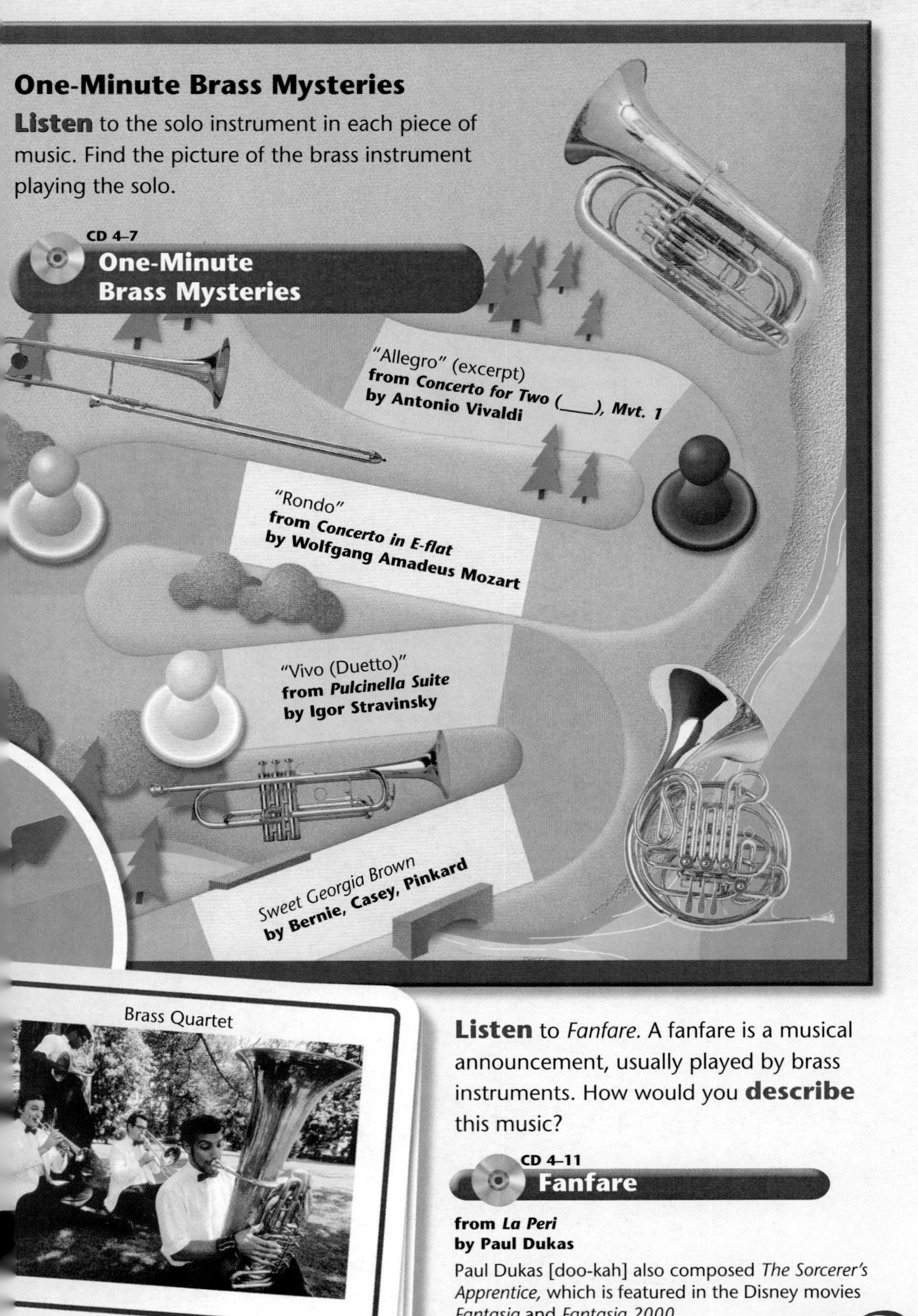

## One-Minute Brass Mysteries

**Listen** to the solo instrument in each piece of music. Find the picture of the brass instrument playing the solo.

CD 4-7 **One-Minute Brass Mysteries**



Brass Quartet

**Listen** to *Fanfare.* A fanfare is a musical announcement, usually played by brass instruments. How would you **describe** this music?

CD 4-11 **Fanfare**

**from *La Peri***
**by Paul Dukas**

Paul Dukas [doo-kah] also composed *The Sorcerer's Apprentice,* which is featured in the Disney movies *Fantasia* and *Fantasia 2000.*

Unit 2 71

### Listening

6d Ask students to name and categorize the instruments on p. 70.

6c **SAY** These instruments are from the woodwind family. All of them except the flute have a reed that vibrates to make sound.

Play *One-Minute Woodwind Mysteries* **CD 4-1** through **CD 4-5.** Have students point to each instrument as they hear it. Then play Françaix's *Quartet* **CD 4-6.**

**ASK Which woodwind instruments do you hear?** (flute, oboe, clarinet, bassoon)

**Which woodwind instrument shown on p. 70 is missing?** (saxophone)

### Listening

6d Ask students to name and categorize the brass instruments on p. 71.

**ASK What vibrates to make sound on brass instruments?** (the players' lips)

Play *One-Minute Brass Mysteries* **CD 4-7** through **CD 4-10.** Have students point to each instrument as they hear it. Then play "Fanfare" from *La Peri* **CD 4-11.**

**ASK When is a fanfare played?** (before special events, as a musical announcement)

**What words would you use to describe this music?** (Accept a variety of answers.)

For more information about these instruments, see the Sound Bank on p. 466.

## 3 Close

**ASSESSMENT**

**Performance/Observation** Have students listen to *One-Minute Woodwind Mysteries* while looking at the pictures of instruments on p. 70. Ask them to point to the picture (or write the name) of the woodwind instrument heard in each excerpt. Repeat the assessment with *One-Minute Brass Mysteries.* Check students' answers.

### Across the Curriculum

8b ▶ **Science** Encourage students to explore and experiment with homemade wind instruments. They might use bottles of various shapes and sizes or different kinds of whistles. Garden hoses of different lengths with funnels attached make great "brass" instruments. Have students work in pairs or groups to describe differences in the size, shape, and sound of the instruments.

### School to Home Connection

6d ▶ **Instruments at Home** Invite students to list the instruments found in their homes and in homes of their relatives and neighbors. Encourage them to find photos or draw the instruments to share this information with their classmates.

### Technology/Media Link

**MIDI/Sequencing Software** Invite students to work in small groups to create their own timbre arrangements for *"Eh, cumpari!"* Have students use the MIDI song file to play back the song, explore various MIDI sounds for the melody, and assign different MIDI sounds to the melody and the accompaniment tracks.

LESSON Core 10

## LESSON AT A GLANCE

**Element Focus** **TIMBRE** Wind instruments

**Skill Objective** **LISTENING** Listen to and identify wind instrument ensembles

**Connection Activity** **LANGUAGE ARTS** Read about and compare lives of musicians

**MATERIALS**

- "Presentation of Pairs" from *Concerto for Orchestra* **CD 4-12**
- "Lord Melbourne" from *Lincolnshire Posy* **CD 4-13**
- *Knozz-Moe-King* (excerpt) **CD 4-14**
- *Little Birdie* **CD 4-15**
- *"Allegro"* from *Concerto for Two Trumpets* (excerpt) **CD 4-16**
- index cards, paper, and pencils

**VOCABULARY**

band orchestra jazz combo

**National Standards**

- **6b** Describe music by moving to it, answering questions about it, and explaining how it sounds
- **6d** Identify the sounds of orchestral and band instruments
- **6e** While listening to music, move to show a prominent feature of the music
- **9c** Identify uses of music in everyday life
- **9d** Describe roles of musicians in various settings
- **9e** Demonstrate appropriate audience behavior

**MORE MUSIC CHOICES**

For more practice in identifying instrumental timbres:

"Fossils" from *Carnival of the Animals,* p. 220

"Mars, the Bringer of War" from *The Planets,* p. 377

LESSON 10 Element: TIMBRE Skill: LISTENING Connection: LANGUAGE ARTS

# Listening to Wind Instruments

Orchestras contain string, woodwind, brass, and percussion instruments. Look at this picture of an orchestra. How many woodwind and brass instruments can you **identify**?

**Listen** to this music for orchestra. After an introduction played by a snare drum, you will hear woodwind and brass instruments accompanied by string instruments. **Identify** the woodwind and brass instruments in the order you hear them played.

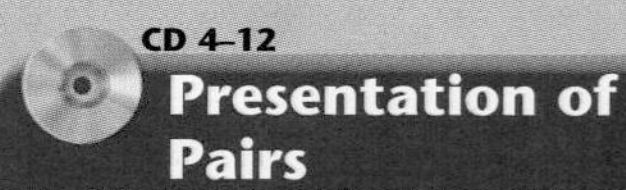

CD 4-12 **Presentation of Pairs**

**from *Concerto for Orchestra* by Béla Bartók**

*Concerto for Orchestra* was Béla Bartók's last complete work for orchestra.

72

# Footnotes

## ACROSS THE CURRICULUM

▶ **Language Arts** Use the book *Meet the Orchestra* by Ann Hayes (Harcourt Brace, 1995) to introduce descriptions of the musical instruments that make up an orchestra. The text is accompanied by watercolor illustrations of animals playing the various instruments.

## BUILDING SKILLS THROUGH MUSIC

▶ **Language** Using the Venn Diagram on Resource Book p. C-8, have students list similarities and differences in a symphony orchestra and a concert band. Have them write a paragraph describing the similarities and differences.

## SPOTLIGHT ON

▶ **The Composer** Percy Grainger (1882–1961) (see p. 74) was born in Australia and educated in Germany and England. As a young man, he performed as a concert pianist. Grainger also spent time collecting folk songs on wax cylinders, a precursor to the vinyl record disc. Part of his collection is now in the United States Library of Congress. In 1914, Grainger moved to the United States, where he continued to compose and teach. He also helped create the Grainger Museum in Melbourne, Australia.

Grainger used folk melodies in many of his compositions, and he often made several versions of the same piece. His compositions for wind ensemble are some of his most popular works in the high school and college band repertoire today.

**Béla Bartók** (1881–1945) was a composer, folk song collector, and pianist. He traveled through Hungary, Romania, Slovakia, Turkey, and North Africa recording on a phonograph and collecting thousands of songs. In his own compositions, Bartók often used the folk music he had collected—especially that of his native country, Hungary.

▼ The San Francisco Symphony Youth Orchestra, performing in Davies Symphony Hall under the direction of Resident Conductor, Edwin Outwater

Unit 2 73

# 1 Introduce

Invite students to explore pp. 72–75 and name the instruments pictured.

ASK **Which instruments are wind instruments?** (trombone, trumpet, French horn, bassoon, oboe, clarinet, flute)

**Which are woodwinds and which are brasses?** (woodwinds—bassoon, clarinet, oboe, flute; brasses—trombone, trumpet, French horn)

**Which instruments are not woodwinds or brasses?** (bass, cello, viola, violin, percussion)

Help students identify various instruments by name.

# 2 Develop

## Listening

6b Ask students to look at the orchestra photo on pp. 72–73.

For more information about these instruments, see the Sound Bank on p. 466.

ASK **What instrument families are in the orchestra?** (strings, woodwinds, brass, percussion)

Play *Presentation of Pairs* **CD 4-12.** Challenge students to identify and categorize the instruments they hear by name and by family.

9d Invite students to read and discuss the information about Béla Bartók on p. 73.

## Moving

6e Play *Presentation of Pairs* again. Invite students to move with the music.

A section (instrument duets): Walk with a partner to the steady beat.

B section (brass *legato* chorale): Face a partner and mirror each other's motions, moving freely.

continued on page 74

## Teacher to Teacher

▶ **Live Demonstrations** If there is an instrumental music program in your school or district, invite teachers and older students to present live demonstrations of various wind instruments for the students in your classes. Provide performers with a list of songs familiar to your students and ask whether they could play one or more of the melodies as part of the demonstration. Prepare your students by asking them to think of questions they might want to ask the guest musicians. After the demonstration, follow up by having your students write letters to thank the musicians and to ask any additional questions they may have.

## Skills Reinforcement

▶ **Singing** Select a familiar song from this unit or another section of the book. Have students sing the melody *legato* (smoothly) and then *staccato* (with shortened, detached notes). Create icons that show *legato* and *staccato,* such as

and ask students to point to the icon for each articulation as they hear it in *Lord Melbourne* and *Presentation of Pairs*.

## Listening

Direct students to the concert band photo on pp. 74–75. Have students point out which instruments are woodwinds and which are brass.

ASK **Which family of instruments is missing from the band—brass, woodwind, percussion, or string?** (string)

 Play *Lord Melbourne* **CD 4-13.** Encourage students to listen carefully to determine which instruments play when, categorize those instruments by family, and identify which sections are the same and which are different.

ASK **Which instruments do you hear first?** (brasses)

**Which instruments play in the middle section?** (woodwinds)

**How are the first and last sections the same?** (Both feature brass instruments; both are loud.)

**How is the middle section different?** (Woodwinds play the melody; dynamics are soft.)

Share information about Percy Grainger from Spotlight On, p. 72.

 Invite students to discuss family members or friends who play instruments. Have them read and discuss the information about the Marsalis family on p. 74. Have students compare the Marsalis family's musical activities with those of Béla Bartók and other musicians they may know.

Play *Little Birdie* **CD 4-15,** performed by the Ellis Marsalis Trio and additional musicians. As students listen, have them

- Look at the Marsalis family photos.
- Point to the player performing the melody.

 ASK **What instruments do you hear in the jazz ensemble?** (trumpet, trombone, saxophones, piano, bass, drums)

**Which instruments are wind instruments?** (trumpet, trombone, saxophone)

### Winds in the Band

Almost all of the instruments in a band are members of either the wind or percussion families. Look at this photo of a band and **identify** the various woodwind and brass instruments.

Now **listen** to this performance. Which instruments play first—woodwinds or brass?

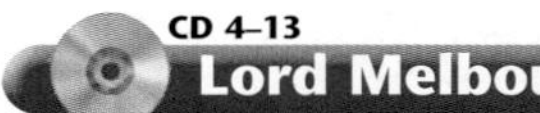
CD 4–13
**Lord Melbourne**

**from *Lincolnshire Posy***
**by Percy Grainger**

The selections in *Lincolnshire Posy* are based on folk melodies collected by Percy Grainger. Lincolnshire is a county in the eastern part of England.

## Marsalis Family

Ellis Marsalis ▶

◀ Wynton Marsalis

**Branford, Wynton, Delfeayo, and Ellis Marsalis** are members of a very musical family. Branford plays saxophone, Wynton plays trumpet, Delfeayo plays trombone, and Ellis (the father of the three brothers) plays the piano. When playing together, they make a jazz combo. As solo performers, Branford and Wynton have won several awards. They have performed on television shows such as Jay Leno's *Tonight Show*. Wynton also serves as the artistic director of "Jazz at Lincoln Center."

74

## Footnotes

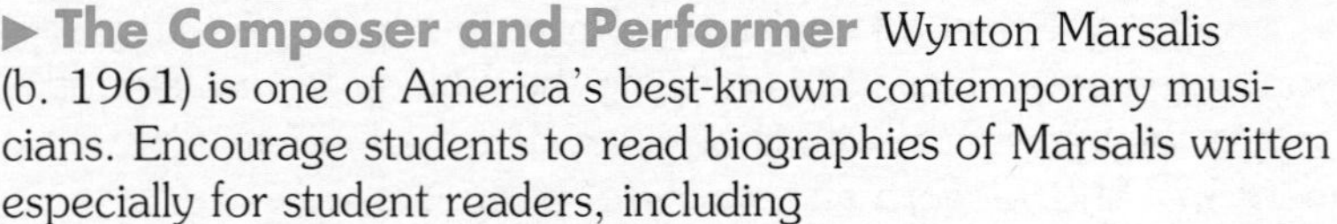

### Spotlight On

▶ **The Composer and Performer** Wynton Marsalis (b. 1961) is one of America's best-known contemporary musicians. Encourage students to read biographies of Marsalis written especially for student readers, including

*Wynton Marsalis* by Veronica Freeman Ellis (Raintree/Steck-Vaughn, 1998)

*Wynton Marsalis: Gifted Trumpet Player* by Craig Awmiller (Children's Press, 1996)

*Wynton Marsalis: Trumpet Genius* by Leslie Gourse (Franklin Watts, 1999)

### Audience Etiquette

 ▶ **Specific Genres** Discuss the variety of musical genres and styles presented in this lesson. Then invite students to describe or practice appropriate audience behavior for these situations.

- A rock concert held outdoors. (It is appropriate to move, dance, clap, and sing along with the music.)
- A chorus, band, or orchestra concert in an auditorium. (Quiet and stillness are expected. Applaud only at the end of pieces.)
- A jazz concert. (Audiences tend to nod or tap feet to the music. It is okay to applaud after a solo, even if the piece is not over.)
- An opera performance. (It is appropriate to call out *"Bravo!"* [for a male performer] or *"Brava!"* [for a female performer] after a singer has sung an exceptional rendition of an *aria.*)

CD 4-14
**Knozz-Moe-King**

**written and performed by Wynton Marsalis**

Wynton Marsalis is best-known as a jazz musician. In *Knozz-Moe-King*, he is playing a trumpet in a quartet.

◀ Branford Marsalis

▲ Delfeayo Marsalis

CD 4-15
**Little Birdie**

**by Vince Guaraldi**
**as performed by the Ellis Marsalis Trio**

*Little Birdie* is a reference to Woodstock, the bird character in the "Peanuts" cartoon strip.

CD 4-16
**Allegro**

**from *Concerto for Two Trumpets***
**by Antonio Vivaldi**
**as performed by Wynton Marsalis**

Marsalis also performs classical music. Here, he is playing with an orchestra.

Unit 2 75

Discuss the information about Wynton Marsalis on p. 74. To help students compare the two different styles performed by the trumpeter, have them

- Listen to *Knozz-Moe-King* **CD 4-14.**
- Write words describing the music on an index card.
- Listen to Vivaldi's *"Allegro"* from *Concerto for Two Trumpets* **CD 4-16.**
- Write words describing the music on a different index card.

ASK **What instruments did you hear besides the trumpet?** (The instruments of an orchestra are heard.)

**What words did you use to describe the music?** (Accept a variety of answers.)

**Which recording is jazz, and which is classical?** (*Knozz-Moe-King* is jazz; *Allegro* is classical.)

Have students use their index cards to compare the musical styles of the two compositions. Encourage them to express and justify, using proper music terminology, their personal preferences.

## 3 Close

**Skill: LISTENING** ASSESSMENT

**Observation/Written Assessment** Play short examples from the listening selections in this lesson and have students

- Listen to the examples and identify the ensembles as a band, an orchestra, or a jazz combo.
- Write two facts about each ensemble on a sheet of paper.

**SAY** Think about what you have learned about bands, orchestras, and jazz ensembles. What instruments are in each? What kinds of music do they play?

Give students time to write two facts on each card. Then encourage them to compare answers.

Invite students to vote for their favorite listening example from this lesson and give reasons to justify their personal preference. Close by playing that example.

## Skills Reinforcement

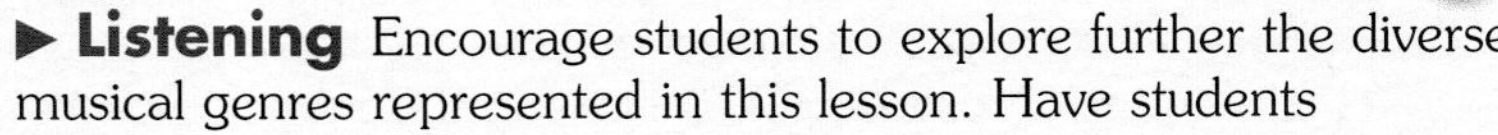

9c ▶ **Listening** Encourage students to explore further the diverse musical genres represented in this lesson. Have students

- Find two recordings at home and listen to the instrumentation of each.
- Write a paragraph in which they compare and contrast the instrumentation and style of the two recordings.
- Identify the genre of each recording.
- Share their findings with the class.

As a follow-up activity, invite students to justify, using proper music terminology, their personal preference for one of the works and the style it represents.

## Character Education

▶ **Responsibility** To help students understand the importance of assuming responsibility, discuss the roles of band, orchestra, and jazz ensemble members. List the responsibilities they must assume (for example, being on time, being prepared, being courteous, and following directions). Lead students to an understanding that each group member must assume a certain role as well as the responsibility that accompanies that role. Help students understand the behaviors that typify responsible behavior and challenge them to demonstrate these consistently.

## Technology/Media Link

**Web Site** Invite students to go to *www.sfsuccessnet.com* for more information on Bartók, Grainger, and the Marsalis family.

LESSON 11

## LESSON AT A GLANCE

**Element Focus** **TEXTURE/HARMONY** Multilayered melody ostinato accompaniment

**Skill Objective** **PLAYING** Play melody ostinatos

**Connection Activity** **RELATED ARTS** Identify and describe repeated patterns in music and visual art

**MATERIALS**

- "Canoe Song" **CD 4-17**

  **Recording Routine:** Intro (4 m.); v. 1; instrumental with ostinato; v. 1; v. 2 (with ostinato); coda
- recorders and selected pitched percussion instruments

**VOCABULARY**

ostinato

**◆ ◆ ◆ ◆ National Standards ◆ ◆ ◆ ◆**

**1d** Sing ostinatos
**2b** Perform melodies on appropriate instruments
**2f** Play instruments independently against contrasting parts
**8a** Define common terms used with different meanings in the various arts

**MORE MUSIC CHOICES**

Other songs with melody ostinatos:

*Twist and Shout,* p. 238

"Little David, Play on Your Harp," p. 394

# 1 INTRODUCE

**ASK If you were traveling on a river, what kind of transportation would you use?**

Invite students to show the motion they would use to paddle a canoe.

**SAY** The motion you are using is a repeated pattern. Listen for a repeated pattern in this song.

LESSON 11 Element: TEXTURE/HARMONY | Skill: PLAYING | Connection: RELATED ARTS

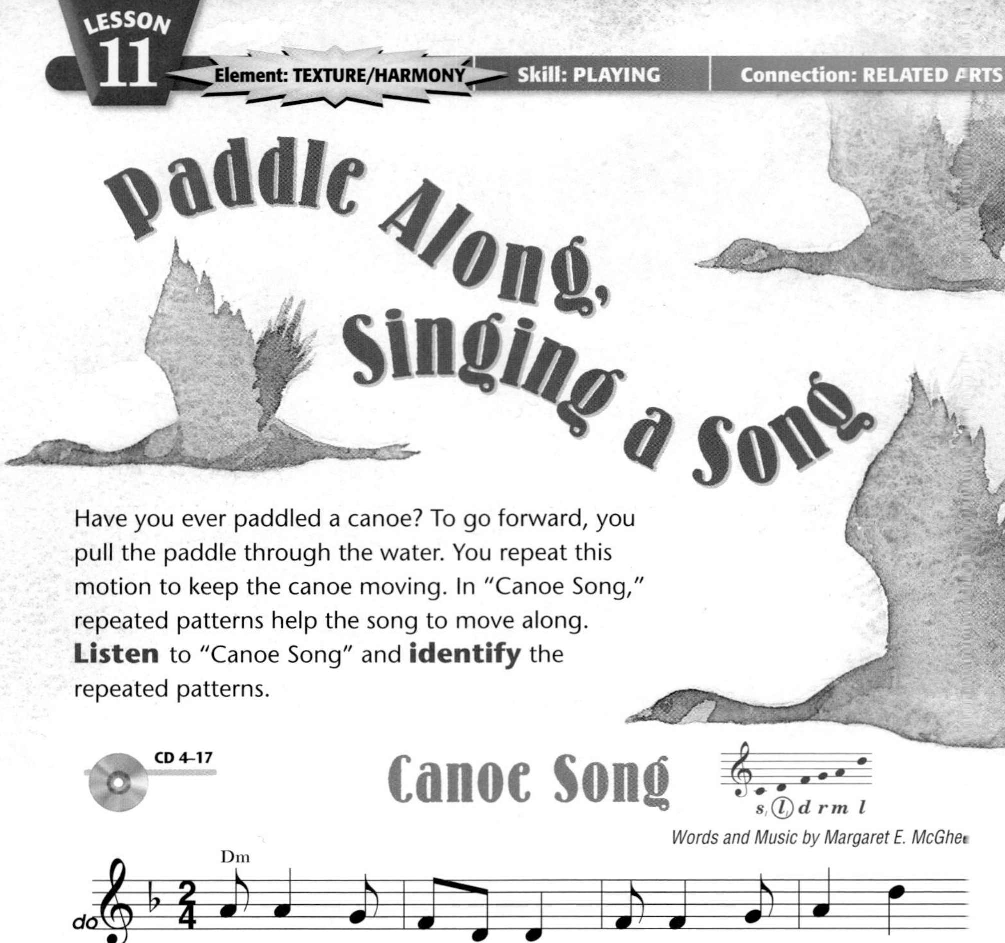

# Paddle Along, Singing a Song

Have you ever paddled a canoe? To go forward, you pull the paddle through the water. You repeat this motion to keep the canoe moving. In "Canoe Song," repeated patterns help the song to move along. **Listen** to "Canoe Song" and **identify** the repeated patterns.

CD 4-17

## Canoe Song

s, l, d r m l

*Words and Music by Margaret E. McGhee*

Dm

1. My pad - dle's keen and bright, Flash - ing with sil - ver,
2. Dip, dip and swing her back, Flash - ing with sil - ver,

Fol - low the wild goose flight, Dip, dip and swing.
Fol - low the wild goose track, Dip, dip and swing.

**Sing** this **ostinato** to accompany "Canoe Song."

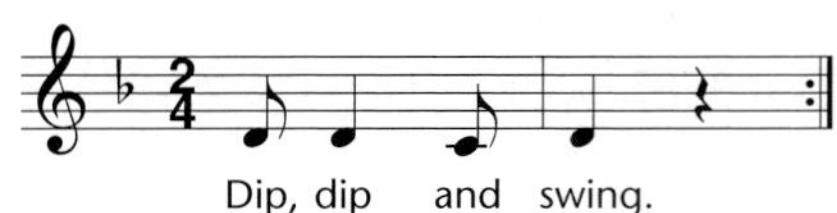


An **ostinato** is a repeated rhythm or melody pattern played throughout a piece or a section of a piece.

## Footnotes

### ACROSS THE CURRICULUM

▶ **Language Arts** Invite students to share the feeling of riding along in a canoe by reading the book *Canoe Days* by Gary Paulsen (Doubleday, 1999). In this book, the narrator paddles around a lake in a canoe while the wildlife continues its daily routines—insects fly overhead, fish feed underwater, and animals hunt. Then ask students to write in their journals about an imaginary canoe ride. Would it be on a lake? a river?

### BUILDING SKILLS THROUGH MUSIC

▶ **Science** Have students demonstrate the generation of sound waves by striking a tuning fork and touching it to a tray of water. Have them then describe and compare the resulting ripples with those depicted in the painting on p. 77.

### SKILLS REINFORCEMENT

▶ **Creating/Playing** Encourage students to create their own nonpitched percussion ostinatos to include in the musical texture of "Canoe Song." Have students clap or pat to show how they would play a rhythm ostinato. Then ask them to transfer their movement to a nonpitched percussion instrument. Ask students to notate their ostinatos so others can play them.

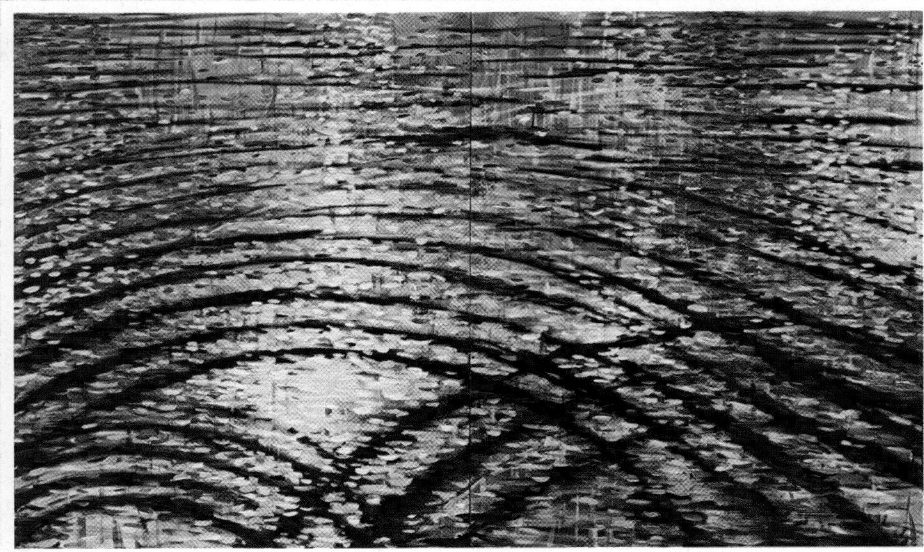

▲ *Watercolor Ripple* (1995) by the modern American artist Gerrit Greve. What repeated patterns do you see in this painting?

### Play an Ostinato

Adding melody ostinatos to a song changes the musical texture. As more ostinatos are added, the texture becomes thicker.

Practice these ostinatos for "Canoe Song." Then **perform** them with the song to make the texture thicker.

## 2 Develop

### Singing

1d Play "Canoe Song" **CD 4-17.** Have students

- Identify the repeated pattern in the accompaniment. *(dip, dip, and swing)*
- Sing the repeated pattern with the recording.

**SAY** In music, a repeated pattern is called an *ostinato.*

Have students sing the melody of "Canoe Song." Then divide the class in half. Have one group sing the melody while the other sings the ostinato. Then have the groups reverse roles.

8a Have students look for repeated patterns in *Watercolor Ripple* on p. 77.

### Playing

2b Invite students to read the information about ostinatos on p. 77. Then help groups of students learn to play the ostinatos to accompany the song. Have them

- Tap the rhythm of the ostinatos as they sing.
- Find the pitches on the appropriate instrument.
- Transfer the rhythm to the instrument.

Encourage students to continue singing as they play.

**ASK** **When we add ostinatos, how does the musical texture change?** (More parts equal thicker texture.)

## 3 Close

**Element: TEXTURE/HARMONY** ASSESSMENT

2f **Performance/Observation** Have students sing "Canoe Song" **CD 4-17.** Assign small groups to perform the ostinatos using voices and body percussion. Then ask students to sing the song again with some playing the ostinato parts on recorder and pitched percussion instruments.

### Cultural Connection

▶ **Canoes** For many centuries, canoes were used for transportation and hunting. Today they are used for camping, adventure trips, fishing, and hunting. Encourage students to find out all they can about how canoes were made by Native Americans and European settlers in America. Various styles of canoes can also be found in many other world cultures. What do canoes from other cultures look like and how are they made? Where and for what are they used today?

### Technology/Media Link

**Sequencing Software** As a class, have students select a keyboard voice and record an ostinato pattern, using the notes D and A for "Canoe Song." Play this track individually as you circulate around the room helping students create ostinato patterns on their classroom instruments. When students can play with confidence, have them layer their patterns with the sequenced track.

LESSON Core 12

## LESSON AT A GLANCE

**Element Focus** **TEXTURE/HARMONY** Melody ostinatos

**Skill Objective** **PLAYING** Play melody ostinatos

**Connection Activity** **CULTURE** Explore African culture through poems

**MATERIALS**

- *"Hey, m'tswala"* **CD 4-19**
  **Recording Routine:** Intro (10 m.); vocal; interlude (4 m.); vocal; coda
- **Pronunciation Practice/Translation** p. 477
- *Circlesong 7* **CD 4-22**
- "The Night" (poem)
- "Enjoy the Earth" (poem)
- **Resource Book** p. A-9
- selected pitched and nonpitched percussion instruments

**VOCABULARY**

ostinato

**◆ ◆ ◆ ◆ National Standards ◆ ◆ ◆ ◆**

**1c** Sing songs from diverse cultures
**1d** Sing ostinatos
**2f** Play instruments independently against contrasting parts
**3b** Improvise rhythmic and melodic ostinato accompaniments
**4a** Compose music to accompany readings

**MORE MUSIC CHOICES**

Other songs from Africa:
*"Ochimbo,"* p. 134
*"Tina singu,"* p. 300

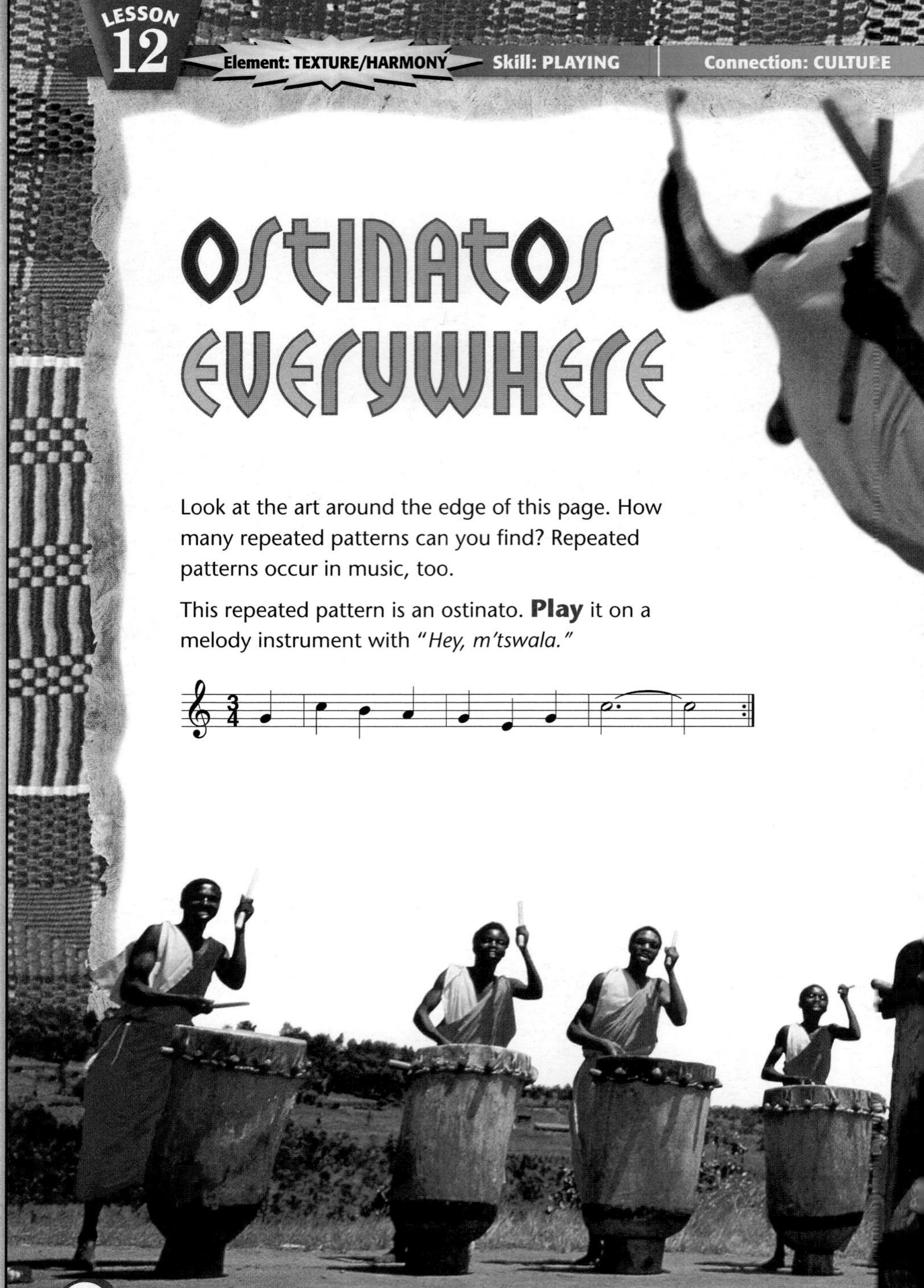
LESSON 12 Element: TEXTURE/HARMONY Skill: PLAYING Connection: CULTURE

# Ostinatos Everywhere

Look at the art around the edge of this page. How many repeated patterns can you find? Repeated patterns occur in music, too.

This repeated pattern is an ostinato. **Play** it on a melody instrument with *"Hey, m'tswala."*

78

# Footnotes

## ACROSS THE CURRICULUM

▶ **Art** As a correlation to musical ostinatos, have students create a visual artwork that uses repeated patterns. Before beginning the project, explore the use of repeated patterns in clothing, posters, various objects in the environment, and in the structure of rooms or buildings. Ask students to describe their created patterns verbally or in writing.

## BUILDING SKILLS THROUGH MUSIC

▶ **Writing** Guide students to create a short poem similar to those on p. 81. Require that a phrase be repeated. Read selected examples to the class and invite students to create instrumental ostinatos to accompany the readings.

## MEETING INDIVIDUAL NEEDS

▶ **Peer Tutoring** Peer tutoring helps both the student who is tutoring and the student being tutored to strengthen and improve their skills and knowledge. As you group students for singing, playing, improvising, and creating ostinatos, pair strong students with those who need support or additional help. For example, have a peer tutor move to show a fellow student how to play an ostinato. The tutor can tap or move as the peer watches, listens, and plays. The tutor must decide how best to show the peer how the pattern should be played.

CD 4-19
Hey, m'tswala
d r m s
Folk Song from Africa
Hey, m'tswa - la, ne - ye ti - pa ya - me tswa - la.
Create a Texture
To create a thicker texture, play these ostinatos as you sing "Hey, m'tswala."
Unit 2 79


# 1 Introduce

Invite students to look for patterns in their clothing and in objects around the room. Remind them that patterns can include color, shape, and design. Then have students

- Look for patterns in the art on pp. 78–81.
- Describe the patterns to a partner.

**ASK What is the word for a repeated pattern in music?** (ostinato)

**SAY** Today we will be singing and playing ostinatos.

# 2 Develop

## Reading

Help students sight-read the melody of *"Hey, m'tswala."* Have them tap and say the rhythm. Then have students

- Sing the pitches *do, re, mi,* and *so* with hand signs (in C-*do*).
- Identify the first pitch of the song as *so.*
- Identify the remaining pitches, using pitch syllables.
- Sing the melody, using pitch syllables.

After sight-reading, have students listen to *"Hey, m'tswala"* **CD 4-19** to check their work.

## Singing

Have students listen and sing along with the Pronunciation Practice Track for *"Hey, m'tswala"* **CD 4-21.** Refer to Resource Book p. A-9. Then invite students to sing the entire song. Encourage them to sway from side to side with the 𝅗𝅥. as they sing in $\frac{3}{4}$ time.

continued on page 80

## Teacher to Teacher

▶ **Plan a Performance** Help students plan a performance of *"Hey, m'tswala,"* with ostinatos. Have students

- Try different beginnings (for example, an ostinato with movement) and decide on one.
- Determine the order for adding parts to the texture.
- Decide how many repetitions of an ostinato should be performed before adding the next one.
- Explore changes in dynamics to create variety.
- Experiment with different endings.

Keep track of students' decisions on the board. After practicing, have students perform for another class. Videotape the performance and allow students to assess their own work.

## Skills Reinforcement

▶ **Singing** Breath control is the ability to release air slowly over a number of beats. Breath control is even more important to good singing than the amount of air a singer can inhale. To develop breath control, have students

- Hold an index finger up about six inches from the mouth and pretend it is a candle. Exhale on a silent *oo,* like blowing out a candle. (Make sure students aim the flow of air at the finger [candle]. You may also use a pinwheel for this exercise, making it spin evenly.)
- Sizzle *(sss)* to help learn breath control: Exhale fully, inhale, and then exhale on *sss* for eight counts. Gradually extend the counts to 16. (Conduct the release of air to help students exhale slowly.)

1d Have students sight-read the melody ostinatos on pp. 78–79. Follow the procedure on p. 79 for sight-reading the melody.

Invite students to sing *"Hey, m'tswala"*

- In unison.
- With one ostinato.
- With two ostinatos.

ASK **Which of these is harmony—when we sing the song by itself or when we sing with ostinatos?** (The song plus one or more ostinatos creates harmony.)

**When is the musical texture thinnest?** (when the song is sung by itself)

**When is the musical texture thickest?** (when the song is sung with two ostinatos)

### Moving/Playing

3b Invite students to play the two nonpitched percussion ostinatos on p. 79. Then have them create movement ostinatos for *"Hey, m'tswala."*

2f Have students transfer their body percussion ostinatos to nonpitched instruments, then to pitched percussion. Allow students time to explore creating ostinatos using C-pentatonic pitches (C, D, E, G, A). Add the pitched ostinatos to *"Hey, m'tswala."*

### Listening

Play *Circlesong 7* **CD 4-22.**

**SAY** When you hear an ostinato, sing quietly or move with the music to show the pattern.

After listening, have students demonstrate the ostinatos they discovered or created.

Ask students to read the information about Bobby McFerrin on p. 80. Share additional information from Spotlight On below.

**Circlesong Ostinatos**

**Listen** to *Circlesong 7*. The melody and ostinatos are by Bobby McFerrin and other musicians.

CD 4-22
**Circlesong 7**
**by Bobby McFerrin**

Bobby McFerrin says, "I've always felt that singing a song without words makes one song a thousand songs, because the people who hear it can bring their own stories to it."

MUSIC MAKERS

BOBBY MCFERRIN

**Bobby McFerrin** (born 1950) began piano and music theory lessons as a child. He turned to singing in his twenties and soon became a leading vocal recording artist. Many of his recordings are *a cappella*—singing with no accompaniment. McFerrin performs in many styles, such as jazz, classical, and free improvisation. He has won many Grammy awards and is often a guest conductor of symphony orchestras.

80

## Footnotes

### Spotlight On

**▶ The Composer and Performer** Bobby McFerrin (b. 1950) has been praised for his explorations of the human voice in his recordings and in concerts throughout the world. On some of his recordings, McFerrin sings all the parts. On others, the music is performed by his group, Voicestra. His CD *Circlesongs* was created with a group of 12 singers who improvised the music on the spot in the recording studio. The lyrics for the songs have no specific meaning. The *a cappella* vocal sound of *Circlesong 7* is similar to that of the Zulu people and the group Ladysmith Black Mambazo.

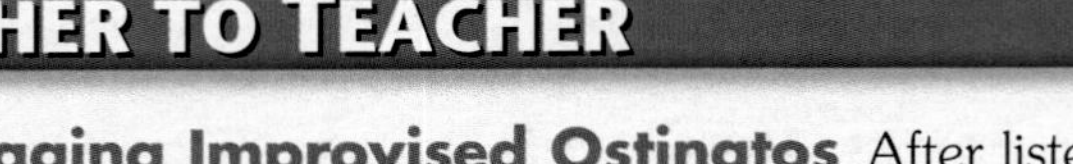

### Teacher to Teacher

3b **▶ Managing Improvised Ostinatos** After listening to *Circlesong 7,* invite students to improvise their own composition using only ostinatos. Divide students into groups of two or three, and have each group create a voice or body percussion ostinato.

Choose one group to begin their ostinato. Add other groups to the texture one at a time. Groups may have to adjust their ostinatos or improvise on the spot to fit into the texture. Allow the improvisation to evolve and then conclude. Try again, beginning with a different small group. As students gain confidence, add percussion instruments.

**Layers of Movement**

How good are you at doing several movements at once? **Create** a movement ostinato while you **listen** to *Circlesong 7*. Be ready to **improvise** a movement solo while your classmates **perform** the ostinato.

▲ Half the class improvises movements.

▲ Half the class performs the ostinato.

**Patterns in Poetry**

Read each of these poems from Africa. Which poem uses a repeated pattern?

**The Night**

*Poem of the Fipa, Africa*

The night is over
before one has finished
counting the stars.

**Enjoy the Earth**

*Poem of the Yoruba, Africa*

Enjoy the earth gently
Enjoy the earth gently
For if the earth is spoiled
It cannot be repaired
Enjoy the earth gently

### Creating

Divide students into small groups. Invite them to read the poems on p. 81.

**SAY** African music often includes ostinatos, like the ones you heard in *"Hey, m'tswala"* and *Circlesong 7.*

4a Have each group

- Choose one poem.
- Work together, creating ostinatos to accompany the poem.
- Notate (using standard notation or icons) the ostinatos used in their compositions.
- Perform their compositions for the class.

## 3 CLOSE

**Element: TEXTURE/HARMONY** ASSESSMENT

**Performance/Self-Assessment** Review *"Hey, m'tswala"* **CD 4-19** and its ostinatos. Then, working in groups, have students

- Practice the song with ostinatos.
- Write down three goals for performing.
- Perform for the class.
- Assess whether they met their goals.

Observe students' ability to sing ostinatos as groups perform. Have students switch parts until everyone has performed an ostinato.

### SKILLS REINFORCEMENT

▶ **Playing/Creating** Use the following suggestions to help all students participate in performing ostinatos.

**Reinforcement** Students with disabilities may play on just the downbeat of each rhythm ostinato. For melody ostinatos, encourage students to use a simple bordun pattern; for example, C and G.

**On Target** Most students will be able to move from body percussion to nonpitched percussion to pitched percussion, as directed in this lesson. With each progression, have students first practice the performance in a slow tempo.

**Challenge** Encourage interested students to play their ostinatos on more than one instrument and describe how the difference in timbre affects the performance.

### TECHNOLOGY/MEDIA LINK

**Notation Software** Have students use various software programs to create ostinatos on their own. Show students how to use the "copy" and "paste" functions to repeat an ostinato as many times as needed. Provide students with options for creating a composition with one or more ostinatos.

Option 1: Compose a melody, then add at least one ostinato as an accompaniment.

Option 2: Compose the ostinato first, then compose a melody to go with it.

Option 3: Compose a piece from ostinatos only. Use at least two ostinatos, either together or separately.

UNIT 2 Review and Assessment

## What Do You Know?

**MATERIALS**
- "Joe Turner Blues," p. 56 — **CD 3-14**
- **Resource Book** p. B-7

Have students read and answer the questions independently and then check their answers with a partner before sharing answers with the rest of the class or with you.

For a more formal assessment, you may wish to duplicate the Unit 2 assessment worksheet and have students work independently or in small groups to complete it. The worksheet is found on Resource Book p. B-7.

## What Do You Hear?

**MATERIALS**
- *What Do You Hear? 2* — **CD 4-23**
- **Resource Book** p. B-7

Review the concept of *timbre*. Reference the Sound Bank beginning on p. 466, and play recordings of various instruments. Have students identify the instruments by ear.

Have students listen to What Do You Hear? 2 and answer the questions either independently or in small groups.

For a more formal assessment, you may wish to duplicate the Unit 2 assessment worksheet found on Resource Book p. B-7.

UNIT 2

# Review, Assess,

## What Do You Know?

**1.** Look at the notation for "Joe Turner Blues" on page 56. Point to the time signature. How many beats are in each measure?

**2.** Name the title of a song in Unit 2 that has:

**a.** Three beats in each measure

**b.** Two beats in each measure

**3.** Reorder these musical terms for tempo from slowest to fastest.

*andante* *presto* *adagio* *allegro* *moderato*

## What Do You Hear? 2

**CD 4-23**

Listen to these instrumental excerpts. Identify the instrument or instruments you hear.

| | | |
|---|---|---|
| **1.** brass | strings | woodwinds |
| **2.** brass | percussion | woodwinds |
| **3.** flute | oboe | clarinet |
| **4.** French horn | trumpet | trombone |
| **5.** clarinet | saxophone | bassoon |
| **6.** trumpet | trombone | tuba |

# Footnotes

## Answer Key

### ▶ What Do You Know?

**1.** four

**2. a.** "River," *"Hey, m'tswala"*

**b.** *"Hashewie,"* "Sourwood Mountain," *"Riquirrán," "Eh, cumpari!,"* "Canoe Song"

**3.** *adagio, andante, moderato, allegro, presto*

### ▶ What Do You Hear?

**1.** woodwinds—*"Allegro molto"* from *Quartet for Oboe, Clarinet, Flute, and Bassoon*

**2.** brass—"Fanfare" from *La Péri*

**3.** oboe—*"Serenata"* from *Pulcinella Suite*

**4.** French horn—*Concerto in E-flat for Horn and Orchestra, K. 417, Rondo*

**5.** bassoon—*"Vivace"* from *Sonata in F Minor for Bassoon*

**6.** tuba—*Sweet Georgia Brown*

# Perform, Create

## What You Can Do

### Move with Rhythm

Sing "Somebody's Knockin' at Your Door," on page 53, and perform a four-beat body percussion ostinato as you sing.

Sing *"Riquirrán,"* on page 66, while performing small steady-beat movements during the verse.

### Play the Notes

Play this recorder part with the recording of *"Riquirrán."* Play once through silently in chin position and then play aloud.

### Move to Show Form

Listen to "River," on page 58, and create a movement for the **A** section and a different movement for the **B** section. Then perform the movements as you sing the song.

Unit 2 83

## WHAT YOU CAN DO

**MATERIALS**

- "Somebody's Knockin' at Your Door," p. 53 **CD 3-3**
- *"Riquirrán,"* p. 66 **CD 3-33**
- "River," p. 58 **CD 3-18**
- recorders
- **Resource Book** p. B-8

### Move with Rhythm

Invite students to create four-beat body percussion ostinatos to perform with "Somebody's Knockin' at Your Door." Encourage them to emphasize beats 1 (strongest) and 3 in their body percussion parts. (for example, pat-snap-clap-snap)

Ask students to demonstrate their rhythmic awareness by performing a single movement (such as clapping) on the steady beat to *"Riquirrán."* They might also vary their movements, using those for "Somebody's Knockin' at Your Door." (See Moving on p. 53 or Performing under Skills Reinforcement on p. 52.)

### Play the Notes

Review soprano recorder fingerings for G, A, and E. Make sure students play the notes with a gentle "doo," keeping their faces and hands relaxed and close to their instruments. First, ask students to finger the notes without playing them. Then, invite them to play the recorder part for *"Riquirrán."*

### Move to Show Form

Have students sing "River" and vary the movements to bring out the feeling of the sections.

Encourage students to use the words to create their movements. For example, ask how they would move to express *moving, winding, and free.* Ask how they would show *winter wind.*

*Note:* The What You Can Do on this page is available as a blackline master, using Resource Book p. B-8.

### TECHNOLOGY/MEDIA LINK

**Rubrics** Visit *www.sfsuccessnet.com* for rubrics to assess students' achievement in music skills.

| Lesson | Elements | Skills | |
|---|---|---|---|
| **LESSON 1** CORE **Walking Along, Singing a Song** pp. 88-91   | **Element: Expression**<br>**Concept:** Articulation<br>**Focus:** *Legato* and *staccato* articulation<br><br>**Secondary Element**<br>Timbre: string instruments<br><br>**National Standards**<br>1b 4b 4c 5c | **Skill: Listening**<br>**Objective:** While listening to music, move to indicate *legato* and *staccato* articulation<br><br>**Secondary Skills**<br>• **Singing** Sing the *legato* and *staccato* phrases and perform arm movements to match<br>• **Creating** Create found sounds piece that shows *legato* and *staccato* | **SKILLS REINFORCEMENT**<br>• **Singing** Sing while walking or hiking and learn a harmony part |
| **LESSON 2** **Rhythm and Dance** pp. 92-95   Reading Sequence 9, p. 446 | **Element: Rhythm**<br>**Concept:** Pattern<br>**Focus:** ♩, ♫, and ♬♬<br><br>**Secondary Element**:<br>Texture/Harmony: two-chord song<br><br>**National Standards**<br>2f 5a 5b 5d 6c 8b | **Skill: Reading**<br>**Objective:** Read rhythms from notation, including ♩, ♫ and ♬♬<br><br>**Secondary Skills**<br>• **Performing** Echo clap at rhythm patterns<br>• **Conducting** Conduct a two-beat pattern while singing<br>• **Analyzing** Read rhythm patterns in a song and determine a new pattern<br>• **Listening** Follow a listening map | **SKILLS REINFORCEMENT**<br>• **Recorder** Play a countermelody<br>• **Singing** Sing chord roots on *loo*<br>• **Mallets** Play an Orff arrangement |
| **LESSON 3** CORE **Rhythm in the Wind** pp. 96-97   | **Element: Rhythm**<br>**Concept:** Pattern<br>**Focus:** ♬♬<br><br>**Secondary Element**<br>Texture/Harmony: two-part singing<br><br>**National Standards**<br>1c 2b 2f 5a | **Skill: Playing**<br>**Objective:** Play an accompaniment that includes ♬♬<br><br>**Secondary Skills**<br>• **Reading** Speak and clap sixteenth note rhythms | **SKILLS REINFORCEMENT**<br>• **Recorder** Chin practice, and then play the part |

## Connections

## Music and Other Literature



**Connection: Social Studies**

**Activity:** Discuss historical events during the time in which Franz Joseph Haydn lived

**ACROSS THE CURRICULUM**
- **Language Arts** Write a story about hiking in mountains; read a book about Mount Everest climbers
- **Related Arts** Create a drawing to illustrate a *legato* theme and *staccato* accompaniment
- **Language Arts** Write about Franz Joseph Haydn

**SPOTLIGHT ON**
- **Joseph Haydn** Background information on the composer
- **In Haydn's Time** Discuss events in Haydn's time

**TEACHER TO TEACHER** **Giving Directions** Suggestions for giving directions

**MEETING INDIVIDUAL NEEDS** **Including Everyone** Create visual reminders of verse

**BUILDING SKILLS THROUGH MUSIC** **Social Studies** Discuss historical events and place them in chronological order

**Song** "The Happy Wanderer"

**Listening Selections**
"Serenade" from *String Quartet in F, Op. 3, No. 5, Mvt. 2*
"*Allegretto pizzicato*" from *String Quartet No. 4*

**M*U*S*I*C M*A*K*E*R*S**
Franz Joseph Haydn

**More Music Choices**
"Love Will Guide Us," p. 328
*Thunder and Lightning Polka*, p. 213

**ASSESSMENT**
**Performance/Observation** Listen to a selection and conduct *legato* and *staccato* passages in a correct manner

**TECHNOLOGY/MEDIA LINK**
**Electronic Keyboard** Explore various *staccato* and *legato* timbres and play chord roots

---

**Connection: Culture**

**Activity:** Explore historical, social, and musical activities of the Ozark Mountain region

**ACROSS THE CURRICULUM**
- **Social Studies** Locate Ozark Mountain states on a map
- **Social Studies** Have students research the southern United States

**SPOTLIGHT ON** **Paw-Paw Tree** Information about the tree and its fruit

**CHARACTER EDUCATION** **Respect** Help students understand personal space

**TEACHER TO TEACHER** **Play-Party Instructions** Dealing with uneven numbers of boys and girls in dance activities

**BUILDING SKILLS THROUGH MUSIC** **Writing** Ask students to write movement instructions for others

**Song** "Paw-Paw Patch"

**Listening Selection** *College Hornpipe*
**Listening Map** *College Hornpipe*
**Arts Connection** Ozark carving

**More Music Choices**
"Sourwood Mountain," p. 65
"Cumberland Gap," p. 138

**ASSESSMENT**
**Performance/Observation** Read ♬♬ patterns in a song

**TECHNOLOGY/MEDIA LINK**
**Notation Software** Notate the rhythm of sentences
**Transparency** Follow the ♬♬ patterns on a listening map

---

**Connection: Culture**

**Activity:** Discuss Japanese art forms

**ACROSS THE CURRICULUM** **Science/Art** Read a book about how artists portray the weather

**CULTURAL CONNECTION** **Japanese *Noh* Theater** Discuss Japanese art forms

**BUILDING SKILLS THROUGH MUSIC** **Theater** Invite students to give a dramatic reading of Japanese song lyrics

**Song** "*Ōsamu kosamu*" ("Biting Wind")

**More Music Choices**
"*Sakura*," p. 308
"*Feng yang hua gu*," p. 313

**ASSESSMENT**
**Performance/Observation** Play an accompaniment for a song that contains ♬♬ patterns

**TECHNOLOGY/MEDIA LINK**
**Electronic Keyboard** Record each part of a song on a separate track

| Lesson | Elements | Skills | |
|---|---|---|---|
| LESSON 4<br>**Shining with Meter**<br>pp. 98–99<br><br>Reading Sequence 10, p. 446 | **Element: Rhythm**<br>**Concept:** Meter<br>**Focus:** Meter in 4<br><br>**Secondary Element**<br>Melody: prepare *ti*<br><br>**National Standards**<br>2f 5a 5d 6e | **Skill: Moving**<br>**Objective:** Perform a body percussion ostinato in $\frac{4}{4}$ time<br><br>**Secondary Skills**<br>• **Reading** Echo clap and say eight-beat rhythm patterns<br>• **Performing** Create and perform contrasting movements | **SKILLS REINFORCEMENT**<br>• **Playing** Play an Orff accompaniment<br>• **Recorder** Play a two-part accompaniment on four notes |
| LESSON 5<br>CORE<br>**Back to the Beginning**<br>pp. 100-103<br> | **Element: Form**<br>**Concept:** Form<br>**Focus:** ABA sectional form<br><br>**Secondary Element**<br>Rhythm: ♪ ♩ ♪<br><br>**National Standards**<br>3a 5d 6a 6c 6e | **Skill: Moving**<br>**Objective:** Use contrasting movements to show ABA sectional form<br><br>**Secondary Skills**<br>• **Singing** Determine the form of a song<br>• **Performing** Create and perform contasting movements | **SKILLS REINFORCEMENT**<br>• **Reading** Analyze the melody and crate transferable body percussion parts |
| LESSON 6<br>CORE<br>**A Multiplication Melody**<br>pp. 104–105<br><br>Reading Sequence 11, p. 447 | **Element: Melody**<br>**Concept:** Tonality<br>**Focus:** Extended pentatonic patterns<br><br>**Secondary Element**<br>Rhythm: <br><br>**National Standards**<br>3b 5b 6c | **Skill: Reading**<br>**Objective:** Sing an extended pentatonic song from notation<br><br>**Secondary Skills**<br>• **Singing** Sing a song with pitch syllables and the words | **SKILLS REINFORCEMENT**<br>• **Creating** Create a pentatonic countermelody<br>• **Recorder** Play a four-note accompaniment<br>• **Keyboard** Play a pentatonic ostinato pattern<br>• **Mallets** Play an Orff accompaniment |

| Connections | Music and Other Literature | |
|---|---|---|
| **Connection:** Culture<br>**Activity:** Discuss the function of motivational songs in our culture<br>ACROSS THE CURRICULUM **Language Arts** Read books about Noah's ark<br>CULTURAL CONNECTION **Motivational Songs** Discuss motivational songs<br>BUILDING SKILLS THROUGH MUSIC **Writing** Rewrite song verses in small groups | **Song** "Rise and Shine"<br><br>**More Music Choices**<br>"Sailing Down My Golden River," p. 332<br>"This Pretty Planet," p. 355 | ASSESSMENT<br>**Performance/Observation** Sing a song and create and perform a body percussion ostinato in $\frac{4}{4}$ time<br>**Show What You Know!** Mid-unit assessment<br><br>TECHNOLOGY/MEDIA LINK<br>**Notation Software** Notate rhythm patterns and create body percussion ostinatos |
| **Connection:** Social Studies<br>**Activity:** Discuss why important places and times are remembered through music<br>ACROSS THE CURRICULUM<br>**Social Studies** Discover historical signifigance of Jerusalem and other cities<br>**Science** Demonstrate an exothermic reaction<br>SPOTLIGHT ON<br>**The Arranger** Biographical information about Linda Twine<br>**The Composer** Biographical information about Modest Mussorgsky<br>**The Music** Information about what inspired Mussorgsky's music<br>MOVEMENT **Patterned Dance** Create a patterned dance for two sections<br>TEACHER TO TEACHER **Improvising** Give students ideas for improvising body percussion<br>BUILDING SKILLS THROUGH MUSIC **Math** Calculate the total number of beats in a song | **Songs**<br>"Walk in Jerusalem"<br>"Cement Mixer"<br><br>**Listening Selection** "The Hut of Baba Yaga" from *Pictures at an Exhibition*<br><br>**More Music Choices**<br>"All Night, All Day," p. 180 | ASSESSMENT<br>**Performance/Observation** Create and perform contrasting steady-beat movements for the A and B sections of a song<br><br>TECHNOLOGY/MEDIA LINK<br>**Notation Software** Create AB form with short melodies |
| **Connection:** Mathematics<br>**Activity:** Create a song lyric to help remember multiplication tables<br>ACROSS THE CURRICULUM **Math** Create lyrics from multiplication tables<br>MOVEMENT **Game Song** Introduce the "Weevily Wheat" game to class<br>BUILDING SKILLS THROUGH MUSIC **Math** Replace lyrics of a song with numbers for multiplication | **Song** "Weevily Wheat"<br><br>**More Music Choices**<br>"Somebody's Knockin' at Your Door," p. 53<br>"Cotton-Eye Joe," p. 288<br>"Sourwood Mountain," p. 65 | ASSESSMENT<br>**Performance/Observation** Read a song using pitch syllables and hand signs in which the scale is extended *do*-pentatonic<br><br>TECHNOLOGY/MEDIA LINK<br>**Electronic Keyboard** Improvise ostinatos |

| Lesson | Elements | Skills | |
|---|---|---|---|
| LESSON 7<br>**A New Home Tone**<br>pp. 106–107<br><br>Reading Sequence 12, p. 447 | **Element: Melody**<br>**Concept:** Tonality<br>**Focus:** *La*-pentatonic melodic patterns<br><br>**Secondary Element**<br>Rhythm: tie<br><br>**National Standards**<br>1a 2f 3b 5d 6c | **Skill: Reading**<br>**Objective:** Read *la*-pentatonic melodic patterns<br><br>**Secondary Skills**<br>• **Analyzing** Discuss the pitch set in the song and determine the tonal center (*la*) | **SKILLS REINFORCEMENT**<br>• **Creating** Create *la*-pentatonic patterns<br>• **Mallets** Play an Orff accompaniment |
| LESSON 8<br>**Follow that Melody!**<br>pp. 108–109<br> | **Element: Melody**<br>**Concept:** Pattern<br>**Focus:** Prepare *fa*<br><br>**Secondary Element**<br>Rhythm: ♩ ♫<br><br>**National Standards**<br>2f 3b 5b | **Skill: Reading**<br>**Objective:** Read melodies including *fa* in staff notation<br><br>**Secondary Skills**<br>• **Listening/Singing** Learn a song by rote<br>• **Moving** Learn a movement game | **SKILLS REINFORCEMENT**<br>• **Creating** Create melodic patterns that include *fa*<br>• **Reading** Review pentatonic melody patterns |
| LESSON 9<br>CORE<br>**Strings and Things**<br>pp. 110–113<br> | **Element: Timbre**<br>**Concept:** Instruments<br>**Focus:** String instrument timbres<br><br>**Secondary Element**<br>Expression: articulation<br><br>**National Standards**<br>6c 6d 9a 9e | **Skill: Listening**<br>**Objective:** Identify string instruments by sound<br><br>**Secondary Skills**<br>• **Analyzing** Discuss shape, sound, and range of string instruments | **SKILLS REINFORCEMENT**<br>• **Listening** Listen to instruments in the Sound Bank |

## Connections

## Music and Other Literature



**Connection: Culture**
**Activity:** Discuss folk songs, how they are collected, and what they tell us about a culture

**ACROSS THE CURRICULUM** **Social Studies** Create a facts treasure hunt about Mississippi

**CULTURAL CONNECTION** **Song Background** Discuss the Lomax family

**SCHOOL TO HOME CONNECTION** **Field Recordings** Make a "field recording" of an adult singing and talking about a song he or she learned as a child

**BUILDING SKILLS THROUGH MUSIC** **Language** Invite students to make a list of chores they might perform

**Song** "See the Children Playin'"

**Arts Connection** *Children Dancing*

**More Music Choices**
"The Canoe Song," p. 76
"Pastures of Plenty," p. 280

**ASSESSMENT**

**Performance/Observation** Read a song using pitch syllables and hand signs in which the scale is *la*-pentatonic

**TECHNOLOGY/MEDIA LINK**
**Web Site** Learn about John Lomax at *www.sfsuccessnet.com*

---

**Connection: Culture**
**Activity:** Discuss same or similar games played across cultures

**CULTURAL CONNECTION** **Game Songs** Discuss game songs that have similar movements

**TEACHER TO TEACHER** **Preparing for *Fa*** Aurally prepare students to learn *fa*

**BUILDING SKILLS THROUGH MUSIC** **Math** Write new words for four counting measures at the end of a song

**Song** "*Son macaron*"

**More Music Choices**
"Chairs to Mend," p. 149
"*Canción de cuna*," p. 144
"Pay Me My Money Down," p. 38

**ASSESSMENT**

**Performance/Observation** Read a song using pitch syllables and hum a mystery note (*fa*)

**Show What You Know!** Mid-unit assessment

**TECHNOLOGY/MEDIA LINK**
**Notation Software** Determine the pitch set for a song

---

**Connection: Culture**
**Activity:** Discuss the design and construction of string instruments from different cultures

**ACROSS THE CURRICULUM**
**Social Studies** Compare Bach, Mozart, the Baroque, and the Classical periods
**Language Arts** Read books about Wolfgang Amadeus Mozart

**CULTURAL CONNECTION** **String Instruments** Discuss various string instruments and cultures

**SPOTLIGHT ON**
**The String Quartet** Discussion of the ensemble and the type of music
**The Composer** Biographical information on the Johann Sebastian Bach
**Child Prodigies** Discuss prodigies in modern times

**AUDIENCE ETIQUETTE** **Attending a Live Concert** Discuss appropriate behavior at concerts

**BUILDING SKILLS THROUGH MUSIC** **Language** Read about Mozart and state the main idea of the text

**Listening Selections**
*String Instrument Montage*
*Eine kleine Nachtmusik*
"Gigue" from *Partita in E Major*

**M*U*S*I*C M*A*K*E*R*S**
Wolfgang Amadeus Mozart
Hilary Hahn

**Arts Connection** *Danse dans un Pavillion*

**More Music Choices**
"Presentation of Pairs" from *Concerto for Orchestra*, p. 72
"Spring" from *The Four Seasons*, p. 371

**ASSESSMENT**

**Observation** Listen to and identify string instruments in the Sound Bank

**TECHNOLOGY/MEDIA LINK**
**Web Site** Visit *www.sfsuccessnet.com* to learn about composers
**Video Library** Watch video featuring bowed and plucked string instruments

| Lesson | Elements | Skills | |
|---|---|---|---|
| LESSON 10 **Partners in Song** pp. 114–117  | **Element: Texture/Harmony**<br>**Concept:** Layers<br>**Focus:** Partner songs<br><br>**Secondary Element**<br>Rhythm: $\frac{5}{4}$ meter and syncopation<br><br>**National Standards**<br>1d 2b 2f 6b | **Skill: Singing**<br>**Objective:** Sing a three-part partner song<br><br>**Secondary Skills**<br>• **Playing** Play a melody in unison and echo | **SKILLS REINFORCEMENT**<br>• **Recorder** Play an ostinato |
| LESSON 11 **Echo a Sentiment** pp. 118–119  | **Element: Texture/Harmony**<br>**Concept:** Layers<br>**Focus:** Echo Singing<br><br>**Secondary Element**<br>Rhythm: upbeat<br><br>**National Standards**<br>1d 2b 2d 8b | **Skill: Singing**<br>**Objective:** Sing a song in two parts by echo singing<br><br>**Secondary Skills**<br>• **Playing** Play a melody in unison and echo | **SKILLS REINFORCEMENT**<br>• **Keyboard** Play a keyboard duet with an echo part |
| LESSON 12 CORE **Music, Music...Everywhere** pp. 120–123  | **Element: Texture/Harmony**<br>**Concept:** Layers<br>**Focus:** Layers of sound<br><br>**Secondary Element**<br>Expression: accents<br><br>**National Standards**<br>2b 4b 5a 6e | **Skill: Playing**<br>**Objective:** Perform a speech piece while playing a six-part layered percussion accompaniment<br><br>**Secondary Skills**<br>• **Performing** Echo speak phrases and perform voice modifications<br>• **Listening** Listen and discuss textures and layers<br>• **Performing** Create a found sound piece from classroom materials | **SKILLS REINFORCEMENT**<br>• **Creating** Create a found sound piece |

## Connections

## Music and Other Literature

**Connection:** Culture
**Activity:** Learn about the Caribbean islands

ACROSS THE CURRICULUM
**Social Studies** Learn about Harry Belafonte and his connection to Caribbean islands
**Art** Create illustrations that reflect personal interpretations of a song

SPOTLIGHT ON "Turn the World Around"

MEETING INDIVIDUAL NEEDS
**Including Everyone** Give students a choice of melodies when they perform with the recording
**English Language Learners** Ensure that students know the vocabulary by matching words with illustrations

CHARACTER EDUCATION **Social Responsibility** Discuss ways students can make the world a better place

BUILDING SKILLS THROUGH MUSIC **Language** Re-write verses using formal grammar and discuss how this changes the rhythm and character of the lyrics

**Song** "Turn the World Around"

**More Music Choices**
"Wings of a Dove," p. 318
"Shake the Papaya Down," p. 378

ASSESSMENT
**Performance/Observation** Echo sing a song twice through and alternate parts on the repeat

TECHNOLOGY/MEDIA LINK
**Web Site** Visit *www.sfsuccessnet.com* for more information on Harry Belafonte

---

**Connection:** Social Studies
**Activity:** Discuss the role of African American spirituals in the development of American music

ACROSS THE CURRICULUM
**Social Studies** Discuss the history of African American spirituals
**Language Arts** Read and write about civil rights marches

MOVEMENT **Creative Movement** Create movements that will be echoed by a partner

BUILDING SKILLS THROUGH MUSIC **Social Studies** Discuss the relevancy of a song in American history

**Song** "Over My Head"

**More Music Choices**
"Lullaby and Dance," p. 386
"Follow the Drinkin' Gourd," p. 266

ASSESSMENT
**Performance/Observation** Echo sing a song twice through and alternate parts on the repeat

TECHNOLOGY/MEDIA LINK
**MIDI/Sequencing Software** Change General MIDI voices for parts of the song

---

**Connection:** Science
**Activity:** Discuss the types of materials used to create musical instruments

ACROSS THE CURRICULUM **Science** Discuss the materials of early and modern instruments

SPOTLIGHT ON **The Poet** Biographical information about Dennis Lee

TEACHER TO TEACHER **Body Percussion** Use a variety of sounds when teaching rhythms

MOVEMENT
**Creative Movement** Create movements to perform with "Bundle-Buggy Boogie Woogie"
**Creative Movement** Create a dancing dinner scene

MEETING INDIVIDUAL NEEDS
**English Language Learners** Create visual aids to help students learn the meaning of words
**Review** Review terms learned in Unit 1 through Unit 3

BUILDING SKILLS THROUGH MUSIC **Science** Describe what makes certain objects more suitable as instruments than others

**Song** "Bundle-Buggy Boogie Woogie"

**Listening Selection** *Kitchen Stomp* (excerpt)

M*U*S*I*C M*A*K*E*R*S
Luke Cresswell
Steve McNicholas

**More Music Choices**
"Can You Canoe?," p. 170
"The Continents," p. 357
"The Planets Chant," p. 377
"Straighten Up and Fly Right," p. 128
"Route 66," p. 276

ASSESSMENT
**Performance/Observation** Perform a speech piece with a layered rhythmic ostinato accompaniment

TECHNOLOGY/MEDIA LINK
**Sequencing Software** Use digital audio to record student performances

# Introducing the Unit

Unit 3 presents the next step in a sequenced approach to understanding music elements. Presented on p. 85 is a brief overview of the skills that are assessed in this unit. (See below and pp. 86–87 for unit highlights of related curricular experiences.)

For a more detailed unit overview, see Unit at a Glance, pp. 83a–83h.

# Unit Project

Explain to students that learning the proper language and terms is necessary in order to understand and talk about music. The "language of music" can be used to describe a world of customs, traditions, and feelings. It can communicate the familiar comfort of "home," or the experience of visiting previously unknown people and places.

Invite students to read the text on p. 84 and then the lyrics of "My Home's Across the Blue Ridge Mountains." Point out that this region of the United States has an interesting and colorful past. To explore this further, divide the class into groups. Have each group research the region, using one of the following topics: Location, Geography, History, Legends and Myths, Food, Music, Musical Instruments, Native Peoples. Have each group present its information to the class.

As a culminating activity, students could hold a "Blue Ridge Mountain Day" to share their knowledge with the rest of the school. Participants could prepare traditional recipes of the region, play home-made instruments, and listen to the type of music popular in the region.

**Song of Home**

People often sing about places that are dear to them. In the United States, we sing our national anthem, or we sing a state song to express pride and love for our home.

"My Home's Across the Blue Ridge Mountains" is about fond memories of home. **Sing** the song and think of a place that is special to you.



## Across the Curriculum

**Unit Highlights** The following interdisciplinary activities in this unit are related to the music elements presented in the lessons. See Unit at a Glance, pp. 83a–83h, for topical descriptions presented according to lesson sequence.

▶ **ART/RELATED ARTS**

- Depict *legato* and *staccato* or *pizzicato* expression (p. 90)
- Create artistic interpretations of a song about the weather (p. 96)
- Create artworks to express song text meanings (p. 116)

▶ **LANGUAGE ARTS**

- Discuss mountain climbing and write a story (p. 88)
- Research and write about Haydn (p. 90)
- Read about Noah's Ark (p. 98)
- Read accounts of the life of Mozart (p. 110)
- Explore and write about civil rights marches (p. 119)

▶ **MATH**

- Sing a song using a new multiplication series (p. 104)

▶ **SCIENCE**

- Conduct an experiment illustrating a chemical reaction (p. 102)
- Explore the development of instrument construction (p. 122)

▶ **SOCIAL STUDIES**

- Research and discuss the Ozark Mountain region (p. 92)
- Research information about the southern United States (p. 95)
- Locate on a map historically important cities (p. 101)
- Create a fact treasure hunt (p. 106)
- Compare the Baroque and Classical periods (p. 110)
- Explore the customs of the Caribbean (p. 115)
- Explore the social significance of spirituals (p. 119)

UNIT 3

# Learning the Language of Music

A7 D

I'm go - in' back to North Caro - li - - na.
I'm gon - na leave here Mon - day morn - - in'.
One ______ more kiss be - fore I leave ______ you.

D

I'm go - in' back to North Caro - li - - na.
I'm gon - na leave here Mon - day morn - - in'.
One ______ more kiss be - fore I leave ______ you.

A7 D D. C. al Fine

I may nev - er see you an - y - more.

Unit 3 85

UNIT 3 INTRODUCTION

## MUSIC SKILLS ASSESSED IN THIS UNIT

### Reading Music: Rhythm

- Read a song using rhythm syllables (p. 95)
- Read and perform a rhythm ostinato to accompany a song (p. 99)

### Reading Music: Pitch

- Read an extended pentatonic song, using pitch syllables and hand signs (p. 105)
- Read a *la*-pentatonic song, using pitch syllables and hand signs (p. 107)
- Read a song to prepare *fa* (p. 109)

### Performing Music: Singing

- Sing a spiritual in ABA form (p. 103)
- Perform a three-part partner song (p. 117)
- Sing an echo song (p. 119)

### Moving to Music

- Perform a body percussion ostinato to accompany a song (p. 99)
- Move to illustrate ABA form (p. 103)

### Performing Music: Playing

- Play mallet instruments to accompany a song (p. 97)
- Play melodic ostinatos to accompany a song (p. 77)
- Play a keyboard to accompany a song (p. 119)
- Perform layered percussion ostinatos (p. 123)

### Creating Music

- Improvise and combine pentatonic patterns (p. 107)
- Move to illustrate echo singing (p. 118)

### Listening to Music

- Identify *legato* and *staccato* passages (p. 91)
- Aurally identify string instruments (p. 113)

## CULTURAL CONNECTION

**Unit Highlights** The musical literature in this unit provides many opportunities for students to explore a variety of world cultures. See Unit at a Glance, pp. 83a–83h, for topical descriptions presented according to lesson sequence.

▶ AFRICAN AMERICAN

- "Walk in Jerusalem": Move to a spiritual (p. 100)
- "See the Children Playin'": Discuss a song's origin (p. 106)
- "Over My Head": Perform a song associated with the American Civil Rights movement (p. 118)

▶ AMERICAN

- "Paw-Paw Patch" (p. 93)
- "Rise and Shine": Discuss motivational songs (p. 98)
- "Weevily Wheat": Sing a traditional game song (p. 105)

▶ ASIAN

- Explore features of Japanese *Noh* theater (p. 96)
- *String Instrument Montage:* Listen to examples of instruments from India, Indonesia, and Japan (p. 111)

▶ CARIBBEAN

- "Turn the World Around": Discuss cultural influences on Caribbean countries (p. 114)

▶ EUROPEAN

- *Serenade:* Read about Austrian composer Joseph Haydn (p. 91)

▶ LATIN AMERICAN

- *"Son macaron":* Explore the similarities of game songs from around the world (p. 109)

# Opening Activities

**MATERIALS**
- "My Home's Across the Blue Ridge Mountains" **CD 4-29**
  **Recording Routine:** Intro (4 m.); refrain; v. 1; refrain; v. 2; refrain; v. 3; refrain; coda
- *Ozark Mountain Jubilee* **CD 4-31**
- xylophones, Autoharps

## Listening

Invite students to find a partner. As they listen to "My Home's Across the Blue Ridge Mountains" **CD 4-29,** have students add a pat/clap/clap partner's hands/clap on every quarter-note pulse. Repeat the activity, this time asking students to sing with the recording.

## Moving

Invite students to perform the following routine with the song.

Formation: Stand in a circle, with hands held.

*Refrain*

Mm. 1–6: Using quarter-note steps, walk counterclockwise.

Mm. 7–8: Stand, facing center, and clap hands/clap partner's hands on either side in a quarter-note pulse.

*Verse*

Mm 9–14: Walk into the circle four counts, and out four counts; repeat twice more.

Mm 15–16: Repeat measures 7–8.

## Reading

Have students clap and speak the rhythm in measure 2 (*Mountains*).

ASK **In what other measures does that same, or a similar, rhythm occur?** (mm. 4, 6, 10, 12, 14)

**Which measures use identical rhythms?** (mm. 1, 3, 5 and mm. 9, 11, 13)

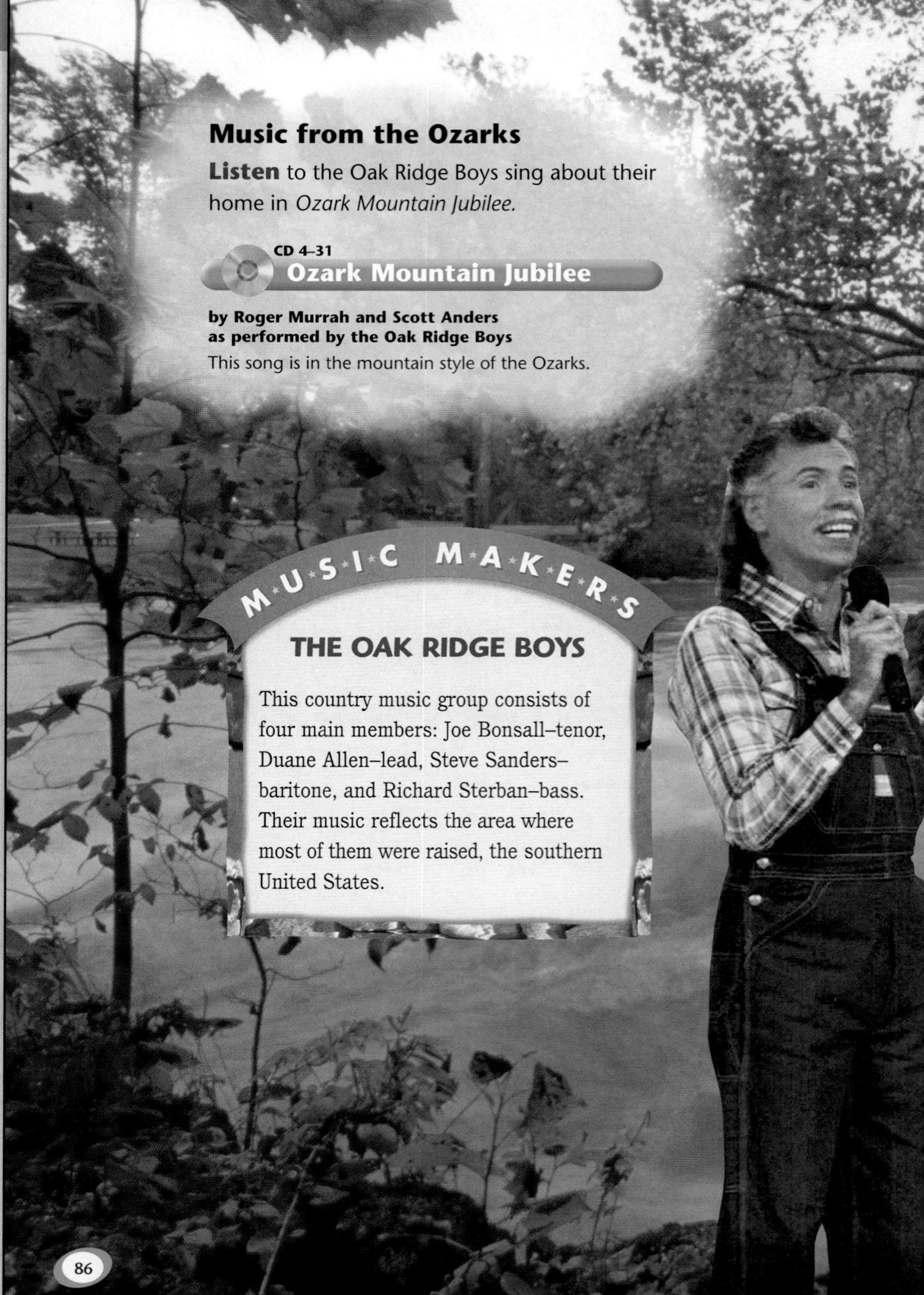

### Music from the Ozarks

**Listen** to the Oak Ridge Boys sing about their home in *Ozark Mountain Jubilee.*

CD 4-31
**Ozark Mountain Jubilee**

**by Roger Murrah and Scott Anders**
**as performed by the Oak Ridge Boys**
This song is in the mountain style of the Ozarks.

MUSIC MAKERS

**THE OAK RIDGE BOYS**

This country music group consists of four main members: Joe Bonsall–tenor, Duane Allen–lead, Steve Sanders–baritone, and Richard Sterban–bass. Their music reflects the area where most of them were raised, the southern United States.

86

## Assessment

**Unit Highlights** This unit includes a variety of strategies and methods, described below, to track students' progress and assess their understanding of lesson objectives. Reproducible masters for Show What You Know! and Review, Assess, Perform, Create can be found in the Resource Book.

**▶ FORMAL ASSESSMENTS**

The following assessments, using written language, cognitive, and performance skills, help teachers and students conceptualize the learning that is taking place.

- **Show What You Know!** Element-specific assessments, on the student page, for Rhythm (p. 99) and Melody (p. 109).
- **Review, Assess, Perform, Create** This end-of-unit activity (pp. 124–125) can be used for review and to assess students' learning of the core lessons in this unit.

**▶ INFORMAL ASSESSMENTS**

At the close of each Teacher's Edition lesson in this unit, one of the following types of assessments is used to evaluate the learning of the key element focus or skill objective.

- Observation (p. 113)
- Performance/Observation (pp. 91, 95, 97, 99, 103, 105, 107, 109, 117, 119, 123)

**▶ RUBRICS**

Visit *www.sfsuccessnet.com* for rubrics to assess students' achievement in music skills.

Have students clap the rhythm of the words while following the notation and then sing the song again.

## Playing

Invite students to play the following mallet instrument arrangement to accompany the song. Students may also follow the chord symbols above the music and accompany the song on Autoharp.

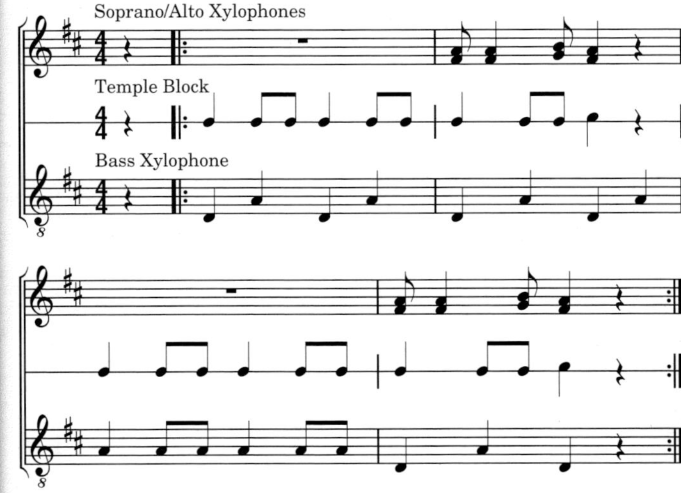


### Innovative Teacher Support for This Unit

- **Making Music DVD, Grade 4** contains video segments that support lessons, including signing and movement.
- **Making Music with Movement and Dance** provides more opportunities for large group activities in music or physical education classes.
- **Making Music with Technology** provides lesson plans for many technology applications; includes MIDI files.
- ***¡A cantar!*** features recorded songs and lessons from around the Spanish-speaking world; includes strategies for bilingual classes and for English-speaking teachers working with Spanish-speaking students.
- **Bridges to Asia** features recorded songs and lessons from Asian and Pacific region cultures.
- ***www.sfsuccessnet.com*** provides an online lesson planner to conveniently create lesson plans at school or at home. Includes rubrics for assessment, lesson modifications to meet the needs of all students, performance musicals based on program content, and more.

## Technology/Media Link

**Unit Highlights** The following components are used in this unit to reinforce and expand students' understanding of music elements and related themes. See Unit at a Glance, pp. 83a–83h, for a descriptive listing according to lesson sequence.

**▶ ELECTRONIC KEYBOARD**

- Use different timbres to illustrate *staccato* and *legato* (p. 91)
- Explore keyboard percussion sounds to create a duet (p. 97)
- Improvise ostinatos in G-pentatonic (p. 105)

**▶ MIDI/SEQUENCING SOFTWARE**

- Select voices for each part of a song (p. 119)
- Create and record a canon (p. 123)

**▶ NOTATION SOFTWARE**

- Assign rhythm values to a written sentence (p. 95)
- Notate and create body percussion ostinatos (p. 99)
- Create melodies using the C-pentatonic scale (p. 103)
- Create a *do*-pentatonic song (p. 109)

**▶ TRANSPARENCY**

- Use a listening map to discern rhythm patterns (p. 95)

**▶ VIDEO LIBRARY/DVD**

- Use the video to explore the string family of instruments (p. 113)

**▶ WEB SITE**

- Go to *www.sfsuccessnet.com* for more information on John Lomax (p. 107), Bach and Mozart (p. 113), and Harry Belafonte (p. 117)

Core LESSON 1

## LESSON AT A GLANCE

**Element Focus** **EXPRESSION** *Legato* and *staccato* articulation

**Skill Objective** **LISTENING** While listening to music, move to indicate *legato* and *staccato* articulation

**Connection Activity** **SOCIAL STUDIES** Discuss historical events during the time in which Franz Joseph Haydn lived

**MATERIALS**

- "The Happy Wanderer" **CD 4-32**

  **Recording Routine:** Intro (4 m.); v. 1; interlude (2 m.); v. 2; interlude (2 m.); v. 3; interlude (2 m.); v. 4; coda
- "Serenade" from *String Quartet in F, Op. 3, No. 5, Mvt. 2* **CD 4-34**
- *"Allegretto pizzicato"* from *String Quartet No. 4* **CD 4-35**
- visual of words *legato, staccato*
- nonpitched percussion instruments, keyboards

**VOCABULARY**

*legato* *staccato* *pizzicato* slur

**◆◆◆◆ National Standards ◆◆◆◆**

**1b** Sing expressively with appropriate interpretation
**4b** Compose pieces within specific guidelines
**4c** Compose music using a variety of sound sources
**5c** Identify and use terms for articulation

**MORE MUSIC CHOICES**

Other examples of *legato* and *staccato:*

"Love Will Guide Us," p. 328

*Thunder and Lightning Polka,* p. 213

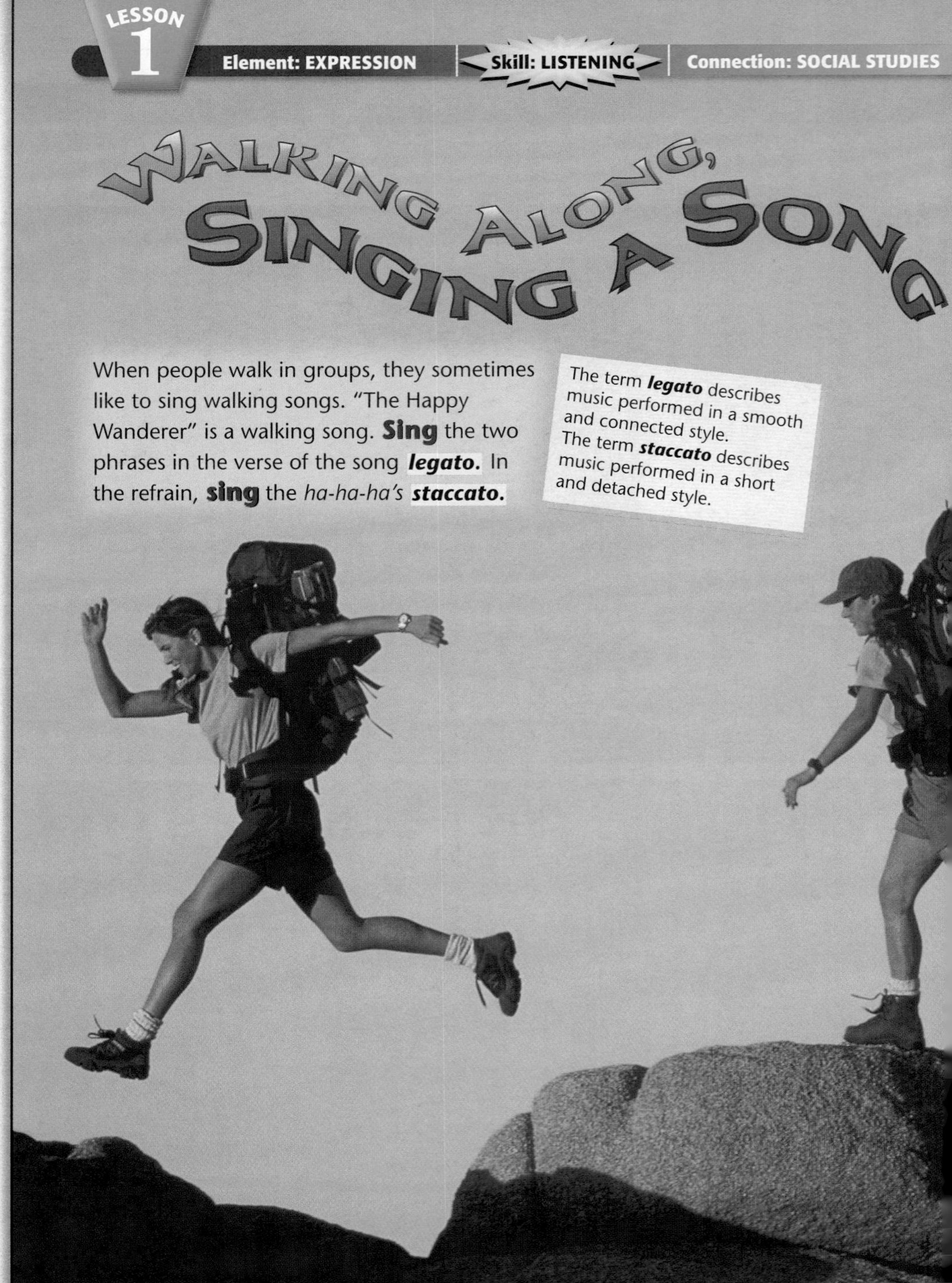



# Walking Along, Singing a Song

When people walk in groups, they sometimes like to sing walking songs. "The Happy Wanderer" is a walking song. **Sing** the two phrases in the verse of the song ***legato.*** In the refrain, **sing** the *ha-ha-ha's* ***staccato.***

The term ***legato*** describes music performed in a smooth and connected style. The term ***staccato*** describes music performed in a short and detached style.

88

# Footnotes

## MEETING INDIVIDUAL NEEDS

▶ **Including Everyone** Invite students to create visual reminders for each of the verses of "The Happy Wanderer." For example, they may want to illustrate key words like *mountain, stream, hat,* and *skylark* to help them remember the order of verses.

## BUILDING SKILLS THROUGH MUSIC

▶ **Social Studies** Write the events mentioned in Spotlight On, p. 90, on the board in random order. Discuss, in general terms, the importance and context of each event. Then have students place the events in the correct chronological order.

## ACROSS THE CURRICULUM

▶ **Language Arts** Invite interested students to read *To the Top!: Climbing the World's Highest Mountain* by S. A. Kramer (Random House, 1993). It is the story of Edmund Hillary and Tenzing Norgay, the first two people to climb to the top of Mount Everest.

Discuss mountain climbing and hiking with students. Ask them to brainstorm things they might see on the way up a mountain and write a story about it.

## Move with Expression

To help you **sing** the phrases in the verses smoothly, draw an arc in the air with your hand.

THE HAPPY WANDERER
CD 4-32
d r m f s l t d' r' m'
Words by Antonia Ridge
Music by Friedrich W. Möller
VERSE
do
1. I love to go a - wan-der - ing, A - long the moun-tain track,
2. I love to wan - der by the stream That danc - es in the sun.
3. I wave my hat to all I meet, And they wave back to me.
4. High o - ver-head, the sky-larks wing, They nev - er rest at home,
And as I go I love to sing, My knap-sack on my back.
So joy - ous - ly it calls to me, "Come! Join my hap - py song!"
And black-birds call so loud and sweet From ev - 'ry green-wood tree.
But just like me, they love to sing, As o'er the world we roam.
REFRAIN
Val - de ri (val - de ri) val - de ra, (val - de ra) val - de ri, (val - de ri) val - de
ra, ha, ha, ha, ha, ha, Val - de ri, (val - de ri) val - de ra, (val - de ra)
My knap - sack on my back.
"Come! Join my hap - py song!"
From ev - 'ry green - wood tree.
As o'er the world we roam.
Unit 3 89

# 1 INTRODUCE

Play "The Happy Wanderer" **CD 4-32** for students. After listening,

**ASK Where are the singers in the song walking?** (along a mountain track, by a stream)

**What birds are mentioned in the song?** (skylarks, blackbirds)

Tell students that "The Happy Wanderer" is a hiking song. Refer to the Across the Curriculum on p. 88 and discuss places one might go hiking and how one might move while doing so.

# 2 DEVELOP

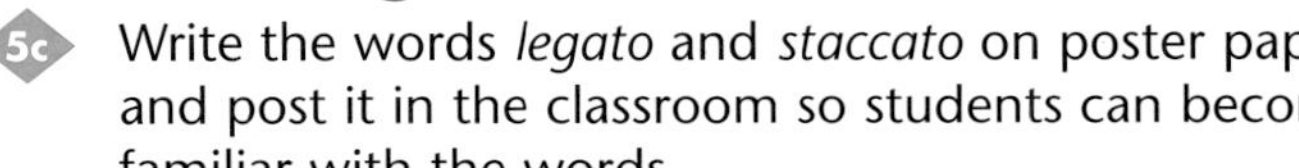

### Listening

5c Write the words *legato* and *staccato* on poster paper and post it in the classroom so students can become familiar with the words.

Discuss the meaning of the words with students. Then play "The Happy Wanderer" **CD 4-32** again**,** asking students to listen for *legato* and *staccato* singing. After listening, encourage students to use standard terminology in describing the articulation used and explaining their responses.

**ASK Which words in the song are sung *staccato?*** (the "ha-ha's" in the refrain)

### Singing

1b Have students sing "The Happy Wanderer" **CD 4-32.** Encourage them to show the *legato* phrases by making an arc in the air with their arms. Invite students to show the *staccato* phrases by bouncing as they sing. For more information about teaching the harmony part in the refrain, refer to Skills Reinforcement below.

**continued on page 90**

## SKILLS REINFORCEMENT

▶ **Singing** Invite students to sing "The Happy Wanderer" when they go hiking or walking around the room.

**Reinforcement** Have students with limited coordination participate by using in-place movements.

**On Target** Most students will be able to keep a steady beat as they walk and sing this song with others.

**Challenge** As an additional activity, invite interested students to form two groups. Focusing on the refrain, teach group 1 the melody part and group 2, the harmony part. Once students have mastered the two parts, have the two groups sing the entire refrain in harmony.

## SPOTLIGHT ON

▶ **The Composer** Franz Joseph Haydn (1732–1809) was born in Rohrau, Austria. As a child, he often heard folk music, which inspired him to compose some of his most beautiful music. For many years, he was a musician at the court of a wealthy nobleman named Esterhazy. The Esterhazy orchestra performed almost every day. Haydn was largely responsible for standardizing the string quartet. In his late symphonies he used a larger orchestra with more emphasis on brass, clarinets, and percussion. He influenced other composers, primarily Mozart and Beethoven.

### Creating

4b Divide the class into groups of four to six students. Ask each group to create a four-phrase movement composition that shows *legato* and *staccato* movements. *Legato* could be shown by flowing arm movements; contracting the body and expanding it slowly; stretching in place, and so on. *Staccato* could be shown by bouncing, shrugging the shoulders, punching, or dabbing.

4c Invite students to accompany their movement composition with nonpitched percussion, "found" sounds in the classroom, or body percussion. Sustained sounds for *legato* could include suspended cymbal, gong, finger cymbals, humming, or a sustained vocal "oo." Short sounds for *staccato* might include woodblock, *claves, maracas,* or mouth clicks.

Encourage each group to perform its composition for the rest of the class. Allow students to make constructive evaluations of the performances.

### Listening

Share with students the information from Spotlight On, p. 89 and below, about Franz Joseph Haydn and have them read about his life in Music Makers, p. 91.

Discuss with students the instruments in a string quartet (two violins, viola, cello) and why these instruments are categorized as strings.

Explain that in Haydn's *Serenade*, the violins always play *legato* and sometimes play *slurs* (two or more pitches played on one bowstroke).

Point out that when the lower instruments play *staccato,* the players are plucking the strings. This technique is called *pizzicato.*

### Hear the Difference

**Listen** to a *legato* theme while you follow the notation. The curved lines in the score are called **slurs.**

A **slur** is a curved line connecting two or more notes of different pitch that tells the performer to play or sing the notes *legato.*

Joseph Haydn

CD 4-34
**Serenade, Op. 3, No. 5**
**by Joseph Haydn**
*Serenade* was written for string quartet.

In this piece, the violins always play *legato*. Sometimes they play two-note slurs, which connect the notes. Slurs above or below the noteheads look like this: 

Now **listen** to the viola and cello. They are playing ***pizzicato*** [pit-see-KAH-toh].

The term ***pizzicato*** refers to plucking the strings instead of bowing.

**Listen** to the entire *Serenade.*
**Create** movements to show the difference between *legato* and *pizzicato.*

**Listen** to a string quartet movement that is played only *pizzicato.* How do the performers make the notes sound more expressive?

CD 4-35
**Allegretto pizzicato**
**from *String Quartet No. 4***
**by Béla Bartók**
See page 73 for a Music Makers feature on this composer.

90

## Footnotes

### Across the Curriculum

▶ **Related Arts** Invite students to listen to "Serenade" from *String Quartet in F* **CD 4-34** again. Have them use a large piece of paper and colored pencils or marking pens to create a drawing of the *legato* theme and the *staccato* or *pizzicato* accompaniment.

▶ **Language Arts** Encourage students to find readings about Franz Joseph Haydn in the library and to write a biography about the composer.

### Spotlight On

▶ **In Haydn's Time** Franz Joseph Haydn was composing music in Austria when Thomas Jefferson was born (1743), when Benjamin Franklin flew his famous kite (1752), when the American Revolution began (1775), and when the Declaration of Independence was signed (1776). Also during Haydn's lifetime, the steam engine was invented by James Watts (1769), and Eli Whitney made the first cotton gin (1793).

# Franz Joseph Haydn

**Joseph Haydn** (1732–1809) was born in a small town in Austria, near the Hungarian border. He had a beautiful singing voice. At the age of eight, he was asked to go to Vienna and join the choir of St. Stephen's Cathedral. As an adult, he supported his family by serving as a royal court musician for a noble family named Esterházy. In this job, he wrote music to please the royal family. He had his own maid and footman, as well as a good salary. Haydn wrote more than 100 symphonies. He lived a long life and died a world-famous figure.

Unit 3 91

Play the opening theme from *Serenade* **CD 4-34.** Invite students to listen to the theme while following the notation in their books.

ASK **Which instruments are playing *legato?*** (violins)

**Which instruments are playing *pizzicato?*** (viola, cello)

As an additional listening experience, play *Allegro pizzicato* **CD 4-35** and have students compare the two string quartet performances.

ASK **In *Allegro pizzicato,* which instruments are playing *legato?*** (None; all instruments are playing *pizzicato.*)

**How do the performers make the notes sound more expressive?** (by using changes in dynamics and accenting some notes more than others)

## 3 Close

### Moving

Invite students to listen to the entire *Serenade* and add creative movement in their individual space.

**Skill: LISTENING** — ASSESSMENT

**Performance/Observation** Have students listen to Haydn's "Serenade" from *String Quartet in F, Op. 3, No. 5*. During the first section of the piece, ask them to conduct with the recording, using crisp, precise movements to indicate *staccato* playing in the viola and cello accompaniment. In the second section, invite students to conduct using smooth, flowing movements to indicate the *legato* passages.

Observe that each student is able to conduct in both a *legato* and *staccato* style in response to the music.

## Teacher to Teacher

▶ **Giving Directions** When presenting a lesson to students, give the directions in the form of questions rather than commands. For example, you might begin instructions with the words "What would happen if..." or "Can you think of another way to..." or "How can we improve..." In this way the lesson is not what the teacher "wants" but what the student is willing to try because he or she is part of the group responding to a challenge.

## Technology/Media Link

**Electronic Keyboard** Have students explore the various timbres on electronic keyboards to discover *staccato* (such as xylophone or marimba) and *legato* (strings or organ). Students may play the chord roots (F and B♭) on keyboard as the class sings "The Happy Wanderer" **CD 4-32.**

LESSON 2

## LESSON AT A GLANCE

**Element Focus** **RHYTHM** ♩, ♫, and ♬♬

**Skill Objective** **READING** Read rhythms from notation, including ♩, ♫, and ♬♬

**Connection Activity** **CULTURE** Explore historical, social, and musical activities of the Ozark Mountain region

**MATERIALS**

- "Paw-Paw Patch" **CD 4-36**

  **Recording Routine:** Intro (8 m.); v. 1; interlude (4 m.); v. 2; interlude (4 m.); v. 3; coda
- **Music Reading Practice, Sequence 9** **CD 4-38**
- *College Hornpipe* **CD 5-1**
- **Resource Book** pp. D-10, E-10, F-7
- **Dance Directions** for "Paw-Paw Patch" p. 508

**VOCABULARY**

sixteenth notes

**National Standards**

**2f** Play instruments independently against contrasting parts
**5a** Read rhythms in duple meter
**5b** Read notes in treble clef using syllables
**5d** Notate rhythm, using standard syllables
**6c** Use appropriate terms to explain music notation
**8b** Identify ways music relates to social studies

**MORE MUSIC CHOICES**

Other songs with ♬♬ patterns:
"Sourwood Mountain," p. 65
"Cumberland Gap," p. 138

# Rhythm and Dance

**Listen** to "Paw-Paw Patch," a popular game song. This version comes from the Ozark Mountains in Missouri, Arkansas, and Oklahoma. A paw-paw is a wild fruit that grows throughout the South.

**Sing** the words of "Paw-Paw Patch" as you tap a steady beat. Then **sing** them again as you clap the rhythm. How many sounds did you clap on the beats in the color boxes?

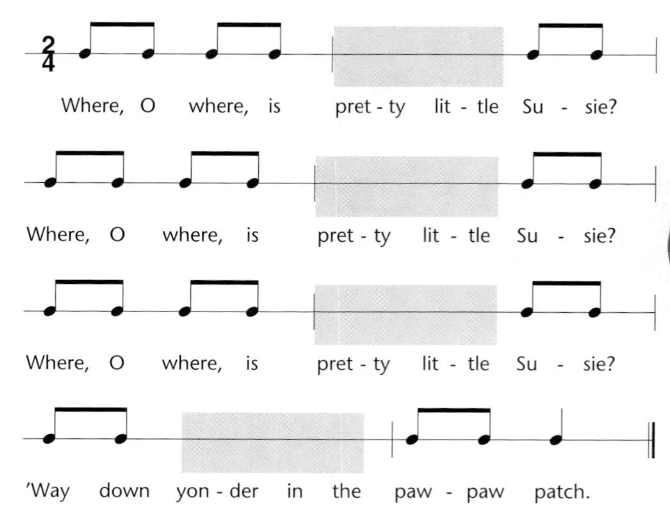

2/4
Where, O where, is pret - ty lit - tle Su - sie?
Where, O where, is pret - ty lit - tle Su - sie?
Where, O where, is pret - ty lit - tle Su - sie?
'Way down yon - der in the paw - paw patch.

**Arts Connection**

This wooden folk art carving of a fiddle player is from the Ozark Mountain region. ▶

# Footnotes

## ACROSS THE CURRICULUM

8b ▶ **Social Studies** Invite students to locate Missouri, Arkansas, and Oklahoma on a map of the United States. Ask them to locate the Ozark Mountains on the map. Help them find other information about the Ozarks. How high are they? How many states do they cross?

## BUILDING SKILLS THROUGH MUSIC

▶ **Writing** After they have learned the play-party movements to "Paw-Paw Patch," have students write the instructions for other students. Ask a group of dancers to follow another student's directions, pretending they are unfamiliar with the dance. Invite students to revise their directions as needed.

## SKILLS REINFORCEMENT

▶ **Recorder** Students can play a recorder countermelody to accompany "Paw-Paw Patch" **CD 4-36.** Remind students to
2f create a space between each repeated pitch by making a *dah* sound. For practice in ensemble playing, some students can play the recorder, while others sing and perform rhythm syllables with body percussion.

## Paw-Paw Patterns

When there are four even sounds on a beat, they can be notated like this.

**Read** the song again using rhythm syllables. **Perform** it with body percussion.

stamp
clap
pat

CD 4-36
Paw-Paw Patch
s, t, d r m f s l
Play–Party Song from the United States
do
F
1. Where, O where, is pret - ty lit - tle Su - sie?
2. Come on, boys, let's go find her,
3. Pickin' up paw - paws, put 'em in her pock - ets,
C7
Where, O where, is pret - ty lit - tle Su - sie?
Come on, boys, let's go find her,
Pickin' up paw - paws, put 'em in her pock - ets,
F
Where, O where, is pret - ty lit - tle Su - sie?
Come on, boys, let's go find her,
Pickin' up paw - paws, put 'em in her pock - ets,
C7
F
'Way down yon - der in the paw - paw patch.

# 1 Introduce

Share information about the Ozark Mountain region (Across the Curriculum, p. 92), the paw-paw tree (Spotlight On, p. 94), and the play-party (Teacher to Teacher, below) with students. Invite them to read the information on p. 94 about play-parties.

# 2 Develop

### Performing

Clap four-beat rhythm patterns using ♩, ♫, and ♬♬.

Have students

- Echo clap each pattern as a group and individually.
- Determine the number of beats in each pattern. (four)

6c Have students keep a steady beat, as they listen to "Paw-Paw Patch" **CD 4-36.**

Draw attention to the time signature and remind students that in $\frac{2}{4}$ time, there are two beats in each measure. Demonstrate the conducting pattern for $\frac{2}{4}$ time.

Have students conduct a two-beat pattern while

- Listening to "Paw-Paw Patch" **CD 4-36.**
- Singing "Paw-Paw Patch" as a group.

Have students take turns conducting the class.

### Analyzing

5a Have students

- Keep a steady beat as they sing the words of "Paw-Paw Patch" **CD 4-36.**
- Find the known rhythms, using the notation on p. 93, and have them write the notation on the overhead or the worksheet on Resource Book p. D-10.

**continued on page 94**

## Character Education

▶ **Respect** Play-parties and movement games involve being aware and considerate of others' needs for personal space. To help students understand personal space, divide them into pairs. Have them stand about six feet apart, facing their partner and making eye contact. While one partner remains stationary, have the other partner slowly move toward him or her, getting as close as possible without touching. Reverse roles. Have students discuss their feelings as their partner moved closer to them. Ask: Was there a time when you wanted to tell your partner to stop or back up? Did you and your partner differ in the amount of personal space each wanted? Why is it important to be considerate of others' needs? How do you recognize when you have invaded someone's personal space? How can you tell someone kindly that he or she has gotten too close? How can you honor another person's need for personal space?

## Teacher to Teacher

▶ **Play-Party Instructions** Instructions for play-parties are traditionally given in terms of actions for "boys" and "girls," using terms such as "head couple" and "new couple." Often teachers are faced with adapting these instructions for class settings in which there are unequal numbers of boys and girls. One way to assign parts is to divide the class into "reds" and "blues," rather than grouping them by gender. Make chains of red and blue yarn, and have students wear them around their necks. This way, they can easily spot which students are in one group or the other.

Read, clap, and say the song, using rhythm syllables.

**SAY** Clap the rhythms you know, and I will clap the ones you are not familiar with.

Ask students to keep a steady beat and listen as you clap the rhythm of the words *pretty little.*

Have students describe the pattern you clapped.

**ASK How many beats did you pat during my clapped pattern?** (one)

**How many sounds did I clap?** (four)

**How many times does this exact pattern occur in the song?** (three)

**Is there another place where there are four sounds on the beat?** (Yes, on the words *yonder in the.*)

**SAY** When there are four even sounds on a beat, you can write them using sixteenth notes.

Show students the symbol for four sixteenth notes and give them the rhythm syllables.

### Reading/Notating

Have students

- Volunteer to write the ♬♬ music notation pattern in the empty beats on the overhead or worksheet.
- Write the appropriate rhythm syllable under each note.
- Read, clap, and say the rhythm, using the system of rhythm syllables.
- Perform the song again, using the body percussion suggestions on p. 93.

For a related reading activity, see p. 446 and Resource Book p. E-10.

### Party Time

In the frontier days, before television and stereos were in most homes, the "play-party" was a popular singing and dancing game. Young people made up motions to familiar songs and accompanied their plays with singing. The fiddle and banjo were often used in play-parties.

**Sing** and **move** to "Paw-Paw Patch," and you'll see why it was one of the favorites.

▲ Lead girl walks around the lines.

▲ Lead girl walks around the lines and boys follow.

▲ Partners join hands and walk the same pathway.

▲ Partners take turns joining both hands and forming an arch while others pass under.

## Footnotes

### Spotlight On

▶ **The Paw-Paw Tree** The paw-paw tree is well known throughout the United States. It can attain heights of 30 feet or more. The leaves are about a foot long and shaped like a beagle's ear. The fruit of the paw-paw was a major food source for Native Americans. It is like many tropical fruits, with a thick skin covering a creamy, custardlike interior with lots of large seeds, like a watermelon. The taste is somewhat like a combination of banana and mango and is very nutritious. Paw-paws drop seeds that grow in the shade of the trees' wide canopy. Since the seedlings get little sunlight, they grow slowly, only becoming sturdy when the parent tree dies, allowing the sun to nourish the smaller plant.

### Skills Reinforcement

▶ **Singing** "Paw-Paw Patch" **CD 4-36** is a song that can be sung on only two chords, F and C (or $C_7$). Explain that a chord root is the lowest note of a triad—a chord of three tones, each the interval of a third from its nearest neighbor. Play the song and ask students to sing the chord roots F and C on *loo,* changing the tones at the proper time in the song. Students may also enjoy playing the chord roots on a mallet instrument. They may also take turns playing the chord roots on a keyboard.

▶ **Mallets** See Resource Book p. F-7 for an Orff arrangment of "Paw-Paw Patch."

**Listen** to *College Hornpipe* and follow the pattern throughout the music.

CD 5-1
**College Hornpipe**

**Traditional**

*College Hornpipe* features Yo-Yo Ma, cello; Edgar Meyer, bass; and Mark O' Connor, fiddle.

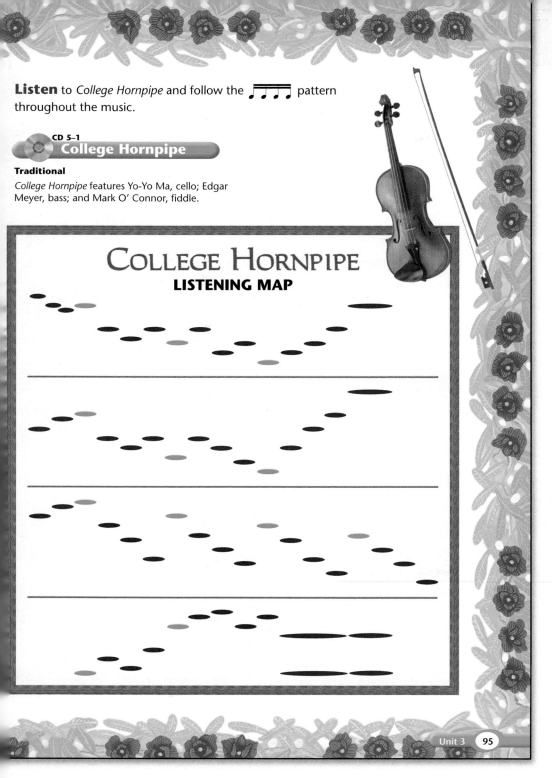

## College Hornpipe
**LISTENING MAP**



### Listening

Tell students that the pattern is present in both songs and instrumental music. Invite students to listen to *College Hornpipe* **CD 5-1** and identify the instruments they hear. For more information on the cello, refer to the Sound Bank on p. 466.

Have students look at the listening map on p. 95. Explain that each icon represents one note. (The melody goes by fast!) The first three (purple) icons are pickups. Every green icon represents the first of four sixteenths. Have students listen again and follow the contour of the map of the first verse of the selection.

ASK **Where do you hear the pattern in this piece?** (Every green icon represents the beginning of a pattern.)

Have students listen to the recording again and point to each green icon as they hear it in the recording.

## 3 Close

### Moving

Invite students to perform the play-party while singing "Paw-Paw Patch" **CD 4-36.** Students may refer to the illustrations on p. 94.

5b **Performance/Observation** Have students sing "Paw-Paw Patch" **CD 4-36** while moving to the steady beat and while following the notation on p. 93. First, they should use rhythm syllables and then the song lyrics.

Observe that students are accurately reading the notation on the student page.

## Across the Curriculum

▶ **Social Studies** Plan an event with the social studies teachers in your school. Encourage students to research information about traditions, music, food, literature (folktales), arts, and dances from the southern United States. Plan an afternoon activity in which students share their findings with other students. This could include period dress, food, dances, crafts, and retelling of stories.

## Technology/Media Link

5d **Notation Software** Have students

- Write a short sentence and assign rhythm values to each syllable of the sentence.
- Go in pairs to a computer center, notate the rhythm values, and type the words underneath.
- Type their names on the score and print their work to be posted in the room.

**Transparency** Use the transparency to help students follow the pattern as it is played in the *College Hornpipe* listening map. The green icons represent the beginning of each pattern.

## Lesson At A Glance

**Element Focus:** **RHYTHM**

**Skill Objective** **PLAYING** Play an accompaniment that includes

**Connection Activity** **CULTURE** Discuss Japanese art forms

### MATERIALS

- *"Ōsamu kosamu"* **CD 5-2**
- "Biting Wind" **CD 5-3**

  **Recording Routine:** Intro (4 m.); vocal; coda
- **Pronunciation Practice/Translation** p. 477
- **Resource Book** pp. A-10, I-9
- bass metallophone, metallophone, xylophone, suspended cymbal, finger cymbals

### VOCABULARY

sixteenth notes *koto*

**◆ ◆ ◆ ◆ National Standards ◆ ◆ ◆ ◆**

**1c** Sing songs from diverse cultures
**2b** Perform rhythms and melodies on appropriate instruments
**2f** Play instruments independently against contrasting parts
**5a** Read rhythms in duple meter

### MORE MUSIC CHOICES

Other melodies from Asia:
*"Sakura,"* p. 308
*"Feng yang hua gu,"* p. 313

# 1 Introduce

Share and discuss with students the information about Japanese *Noh* theater found in the Cultural Connection below.

LESSON 3
Element: RHYTHM
Skill: PLAYING
Connection: CULTURE
Rhythm in the Wind
The song "Ōsamu kosamu" is about children facing the bitter cold wind.
Look at the music for "Ōsamu kosamu." How many groups of can you find?
Listen for the pattern in the song "Ōsamu kosamu."
m, s, l
CD 5-2
Ōsamu kosamu (Biting Wind)
English Words by Gloria J. Kiester
Folk Song from Japan
Ō - sa - mu, ko-sa-mu,
Bit-ing wind, bit-ing cold;
Ya - ma-ka-ra ko - zoo ga na - i - te - ki - ta
Child-ren of the moun-tains are cry-ing from the cold;
na - n to it - te na - i - te - ki - ta?
Why are they cry-ing, cry-ing from the cold?
"Sa-mu-i to it - te na - i - te - ki - ta!"
"We are in the wind; it's bit-ter, bit-ter cold!"
96


# Footnotes

## Across the Curriculum

▶ **Art/Science** Invite students to read *How Artists See the Weather: Sun Wind Snow Rain* by Colleen Carroll (Abbeville, 1996). This book provides some scientific aspects of weather and demonstrates how various artists have used their art to portray the weather. Invite students to create their own artistic interpretations of the song "*Ōsamu kosamu*" and place them on display.

## Building Skills Through Music

▶ **Theater** Invite students to give a dramatic reading of the lyrics of "*Ōsamu kosamu.*" Ask, "Why are the children of the mountain crying?" Then have the class sing the song expressively, with the preceding discussion in mind.

## Cultural Connection

▶ **Japanese *Noh* Theater** The Japanese culture is renowned in the areas of architecture, sculpture, painting, calligraphy, print making, and the performing arts. The oldest dramatic art form in Japan is *Noh* theater. It began in the fourteenth century and is still performed today. A *Noh* play begins with recitation and dancing by a principal and secondary figure. The chorus, which is seated, chants a story accompanied by flute and three drums. The drama has symbolic movement (similar to mime) with brilliant-colored costumes, chant-like singing, masks on an empty stage, and a symbolic pine tree backdrop.

### Practicing Rhythms

**Play** this percussion accompaniment while others **sing** *"Ōsamu kosamu"* in two parts.

Xylophone
Metallophone
Finger Cymbal
Cymbal
Bass Metallophone
Tune In
The *koto*, featured in the recording of *Ōsamu kosamu*, is the national instrument of Japan. It generally has 13 strings. The sound is produced by plucking the silk strings.
Unit 3 97

# 2 Develop

### Reading

5a Clap rhythm patterns and have the class echo. Include some patterns with [four sixteenth notes]. Ask students to look at *"Ōsamu kosamu,"* p. 96, and identify the words on which the sixteenth-note patterns occur.

### Singing

Sing *"Ōsamu kosamu"* **CD 5-2** Part 1 for students.

ASK **What happens in measures 3 and 4?** (The note is held.)

1c Have students listen to and then sing with the Pronunciation Practice for *"Ōsamu kosamu"* **CD 5-5.** Repeat with Part 2 **CD 5-6.** Refer to Resource Book p. A-10 for phonetics. Then have students sing *"Ōsamu kosamu"* **CD 5-2** in Japanese.

### Playing

2f Prepare mallet instruments in C-*do* pentatonic. Refer students to the score on p. 97 and have them

- Speak and clap the rhythm of the xylophone part.
- Speak and clap all parts together.

Add instruments to *"Ōsamu kosamu"* one by one, beginning with the bass metallophone tremolo. Have students independently practice the metallophone and xylophone parts by patting them before playing them. Divide the xylophone part so some play the top note, others the bottom. Finally, add the nonpitched percussion.

# 3 Close

**Element: RHYTHM** ASSESSMENT

2b **Performance/Observation** Have students sing *"Ōsamu kosamu"* while performing the accompaniment on p. 97. Observe students' ability to play the sixteenth-note and other rhythms accurately while others sing.

## Skills Reinforcement

▶ **Recorder** Part 1 of "*Ōsamu kosamu*" can be played on soprano recorder. Invite students to "chin practice" the melody 2f (balance recorder on chin and sing letter names of the notes while the fingers move). Divide the class into two groups. Invite one group to play Part 1 on recorders as the other group sings Part 2. Refer to Resource Book p. I-9 for a two-part accompaniment.

## Technology/Media Link

**Electronic Keyboard** After students are able to say the rhythm of "*Ōsamu kosamu,*" invite them to explore the keyboard's percussion sounds and select a sound for each line of the song. Help students create a percussion duet by recording each part on a separate track.

LESSON 4

## LESSON AT A GLANCE

**Element Focus** **RHYTHM** Meter in 4

**Skill Objective** **MOVING** Perform a body percussion ostinato in $\frac{4}{4}$ time

**Connection Activity** **CULTURE** Discuss the function of motivational songs in our culture

**MATERIALS**

- "Rise and Shine" **CD 5-7**

  **Recording Routine:** Intro (4 m.); v. 1; interlude (1 m.); v. 2; interlude (1 m.); v. 3; interlude (1 m.); v. 4; interlude (1 m.); v. 5; interlude (1 m.); v. 6; interlude (1 m.); v. 7; interlude (1 m.); v. 8; coda
- **Music Reading Practice, Sequence 10** **CD 5-9**
- **Resource Book** pp. B-9, E-11, I-10

**VOCABULARY**

meter bar line

**◆ ◆ ◆ ◆ National Standards ◆ ◆ ◆ ◆**

**2f** Play instruments independently against contrasting parts
**5a** Read rhythms in $\frac{4}{4}$ meter
**5d** Notate rhythm, using standard symbols
**6e** While listening to music, move to show a prominent feature of the music

**MORE MUSIC CHOICES**

Other songs in $\frac{4}{4}$ time:

"Sailing Down My Golden River," p. 332
"This Pretty Planet," p. 355

# 1 INTRODUCE

Share with students the information about motivational songs with in Cultural Connection below.

**SAY** "Rise and Shine" is a motivational song that is fun to sing. It makes people feel good!



# Shining with Meter

The song "Rise and Shine" can make you want to sing and dance. The time signature is $\frac{4}{4}$. This tells you there are four beats in every measure. **Bar lines** divide the song into measures. Look at the rhythm below. Notice where the bar lines are placed.

A **bar line** is the verti[cal line] drawn through a staff [to] separate measures.

Clap the rhythm above. **Create** new measures in $\frac{4}{4}$ time by saying first names of classmates in rhythm.

**Sing** "Rise and Shine."

Folk Song from the United States

1. Rise ___ and shine ___ and give God the glo - ry, glo - ry.
2. God said to No - ah, "There's gonna be a flood - y, flood - y."
3. No - ah, he built him, he built him an ark - y ark - y.
4. Ani - mals, they came on, they came on by two - sies, two - sies.

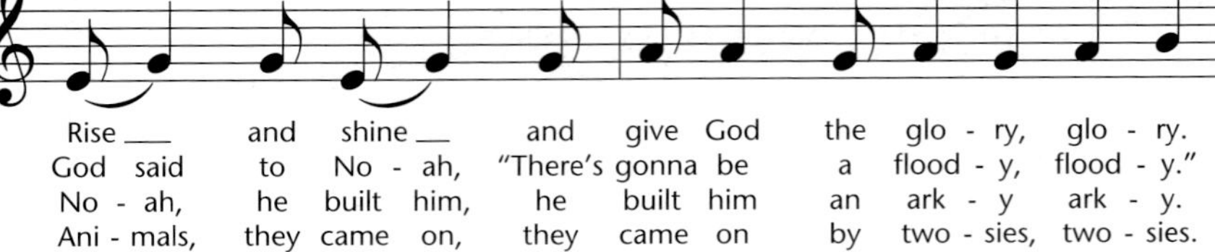


Rise ___ and shine ___ and give God the glo - ry, glo - ry.
God said to No - ah, "There's gonna be a flood - y, flood - y."
No - ah, he built him, he built him an ark - y ark - y.
Ani - mals, they came on, they came on by two - sies, two - sies.



# Footnotes

## ACROSS THE CURRICULUM

▶ **Language Arts** Students may have questions about the information in "Rise and Shine," such as: How big was Noah's ark? What animals were there? How long did the flood last? The following book provides answers to many of these questions: *Noah's Ark* by Selina Hastings (Thomas Nelson, 1997).

## BUILDING SKILLS THROUGH MUSIC

▶ **Writing** Assign a verse of "Rise and Shine" to each of eight small groups of students. Have each group rewrite its verse as two complete sentences, removing the repeated phrases. Discuss how this changes the character of the song.

## CULTURAL CONNECTION

▶ **Motivational Songs** Motivational songs are used all over the world to develop a "team spirit" within groups. National anthems are an example of motivational songs. Other kinds of motivational songs or cheers are found today throughout the business world as well. Many sports teams also encourage crowd participation through the use of songs and cheers. Invite students to share with the class stories and descriptions of places where they have participated in motivational songs or cheers.

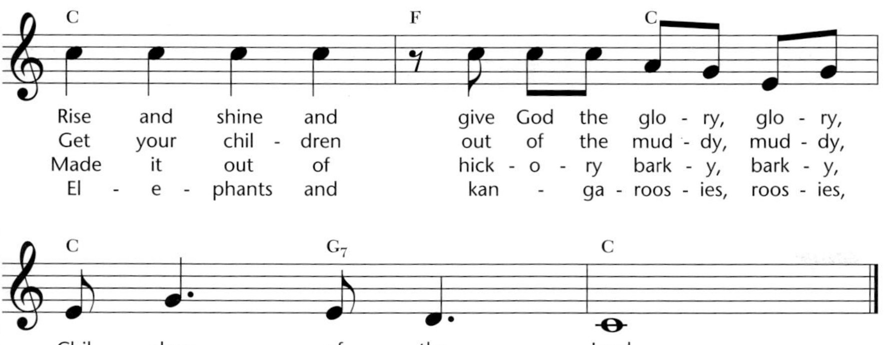
C
F
C
Rise and shine and give God the glo - ry, glo - ry,
Get your chil - dren out of the mud - dy, mud - dy,
Made it out of hick - o - ry bark - y, bark - y,
El - e - phants and kan - ga - roos - ies, roos - ies,
C
G7
C
Chil - dren of the Lord.

5. Rained and rained
   for forty daysies, daysies.
   Rained and rained
   for forty daysies, daysies.
   Nearly drove those animals crazy, crazy, . . .

6. Noah, he sent out,
   he sent out a dovey, dovey.
   Noah, he sent out,
   he sent out a dovey, dovey.
   Sent him to the heavens abovey, bovey, . . .

7. Sun came out
   and dried off the landy, landy.
   Sun came out
   and dried off the landy, landy.
   Ev'rything was fine and dandy, dandy, . . .

8. This is the end,
   the end of my story, story.
   This is the end,
   the end of my story, story.
   Ev'rything is hunky-dory, dory, . . .

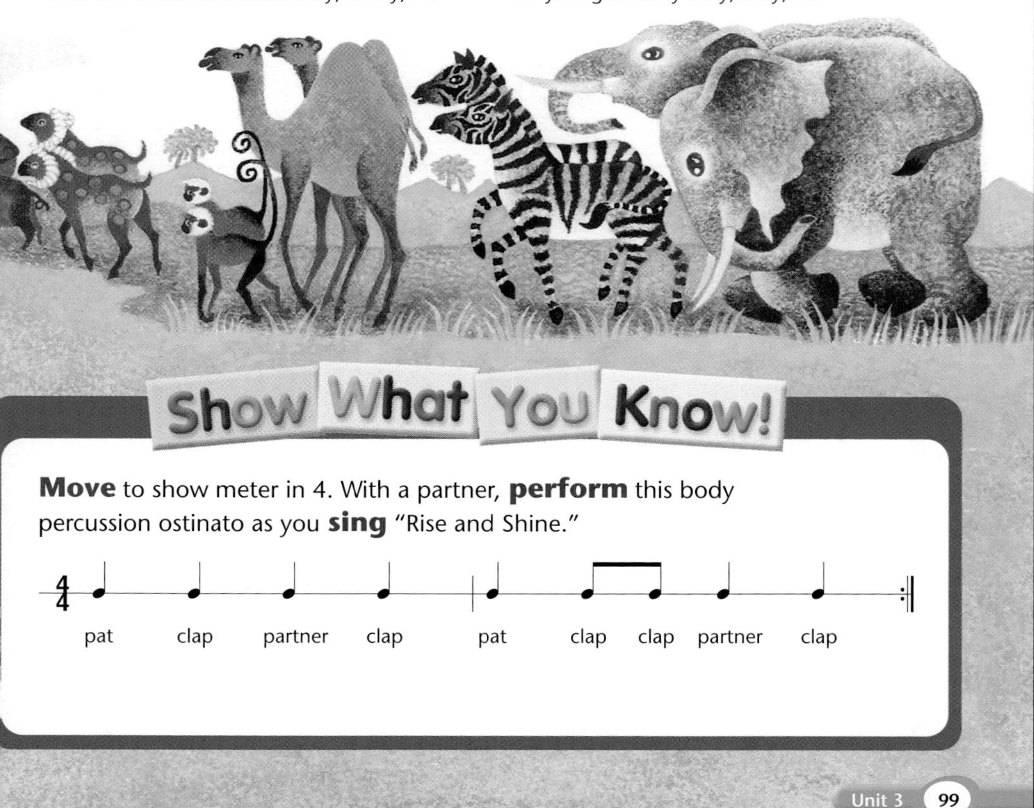

## Show What You Know!

**Move** to show meter in 4. With a partner, **perform** this body percussion ostinato as you **sing** "Rise and Shine."

4/4 pat clap partner clap | pat clap clap partner clap :||

# 2 Develop

### Reading

5a Ask students to echo you as you clap eight-beat rhythm patterns in 4/4 time. Invite students to identify and explain the time signature of "Rise and Shine." Have them clap and say the rhythm at the top of p. 98. Then encourage students to create their own rhythm patterns.

See p. 446 and Resource Book p. E-11 for a related reading activity.

### Singing/Moving

6e Have students listen to the first verse of "Rise and Shine" **CD 5-7**, patting their knees on beat 1 and using body percussion of their choice on beats 2, 3, and 4. Encourage students to sing the entire song while performing their body percussion ostinato.

Organize students into partners and invite them to create a hand-clap game to accompany the song.

### Performing

Have students perform their hand-clap games for the rest of the class. Invite them to try varying their patterns for different verses. Students may also enjoy dramatizing some of the verses.

# 3 Close

**Element: RHYTHM** ASSESSMENT

**Performance/Observation** Have students sing "Rise and Shine" **CD 5-7** and perform a rhythm pattern using body percussion as an ostinato in 4/4 time. Observe that students are able to maintain the body percussion ostinato throughout the duration of the song.

Refer students to the Show What You Know! assessment on p. 99 and use Resource Book p. B-9.

## Skills Reinforcement

2f ▶ **Playing** After students are comfortable singing "Rise and Shine," have them add this accompaniment to the song.

Alto Xylophone/Metallophone
(Play 3 times)
Bass Xylophone/Metallophone

▶ **Recorder** For an accompaniment to "Rise and Shine" using the notes D, E, G, and A, refer to Resource Book p. I-10.

## Technology/Media Link

5d **Notation Software** Have small groups of students notate a four-beat rhythm pattern and print it. After each group has printed its pattern, have groups trade printed rhythms and create body percussion ostinatos that use the printed rhythms.

LESSON 5 Core

## LESSON AT A GLANCE

**Element Focus** **FORM** ABA sectional form

**Skill Objective** **MOVING** Use contrasting movements to show ABA sectional form

**Connection Objective** **SOCIAL STUDIES** Discuss why important places and times are remembered through music

**MATERIALS**

- "Walk in Jerusalem" **CD 5-12**

  **Recording Routine:** Intro (4 m.); refrain; v. 1; refrain; v. 2; refrain; coda

- "Cement Mixer" **CD 5-14**

  **Recording Routine:** Intro (4 m.); vocal; coda

- "The Hut of Baba Yaga" from *Pictures at an Exhibition* **CD 5-16**

**VOCABULARY**

*D.C. al Fine* ABA

**◆ ◆ ◆ ◆ National Standards ◆ ◆ ◆ ◆**

**3a** Improvise "answers" to given melodic phrases
**5d** Notate rhythm and pitch, using standard syllables
**6a** Listen to identify form
**6c** Use appropriate terms to describe music
**6e** While listening to music, move to show changes in the music

**MORE MUSIC CHOICES**

Another song in ABA sectional form:

"All Night, All Day," p. 180

LESSON 5 | Element: FORM | Skill: MOVING | Connection: SOCIAL STUDIES

# Back to the Beginning

The song "Walk in Jerusalem" is an African American spiritual. Look at the song. Notice that the **A** section is repeated after the **B** section. **Sing** "Walk in Jerusalem."

# Footnotes

## SPOTLIGHT ON

▶ **The Arranger** Linda Twine, a native of Oklahoma, remembers spirituals from her childhood. She learned to play blues piano by listening to performers like Nat "King" Cole, but her mother insisted that she take formal piano lessons, too. Ms. Twine continued her music training at Oklahoma City University and the Manhattan School of Music. After teaching music for three years, she began a career of conducting, composing, and arranging.

## BUILDING SKILLS THROUGH MUSIC

▶ **Math** Ask students to determine the number of beats in each section of "Walk in Jerusalem." (16) Then have them calculate the total number of beats in the song, keeping in mind the *D.C. al Fine*. (16 X 3 = 48)

## SKILLS REINFORCEMENT

▶ **Reading** Help students discover how the rhythm patterns in "Walk in Jerusalem" reinforce the song's ABA form.

**Reinforcement** Have students identify and compare the lines in the song that contain similar rhythm patterns. (1, 2, 3) (4, 5, 6)

**On Target** Invite students to

- Speak and clap each set of patterns.
- Choose a different level of body percussion to perform each set.

**Challenge** Those students who master this activity easily may be invited to

- Transfer the body percussion to different nonpitched percussion instruments.
- Perform the rhythm of the song without singing.

## Form in Movement

Show the four phrases of the Ⓐ section by making an arc in the air. Then **create** your own movement for the B section.

A

B

VERSE B

E♭ A♭ E♭
1. John said the cit - y was just four square, _
2. John, oh, _ John, _ what do you say? _

E♭ A♭ E♭
Walk in Je - ru - sa - lem just like John, And
Walk in Je - ru - sa - lem just like John, That

E♭ A♭ E♭
he de - clared he'd meet me there! _
I'll be there in the com - ing day, _

E♭ A♭ E♭ *D.C. al Fine*
Walk in Je - ru - sa - lem just like John.
Walk in Je - ru - sa - lem just like John.

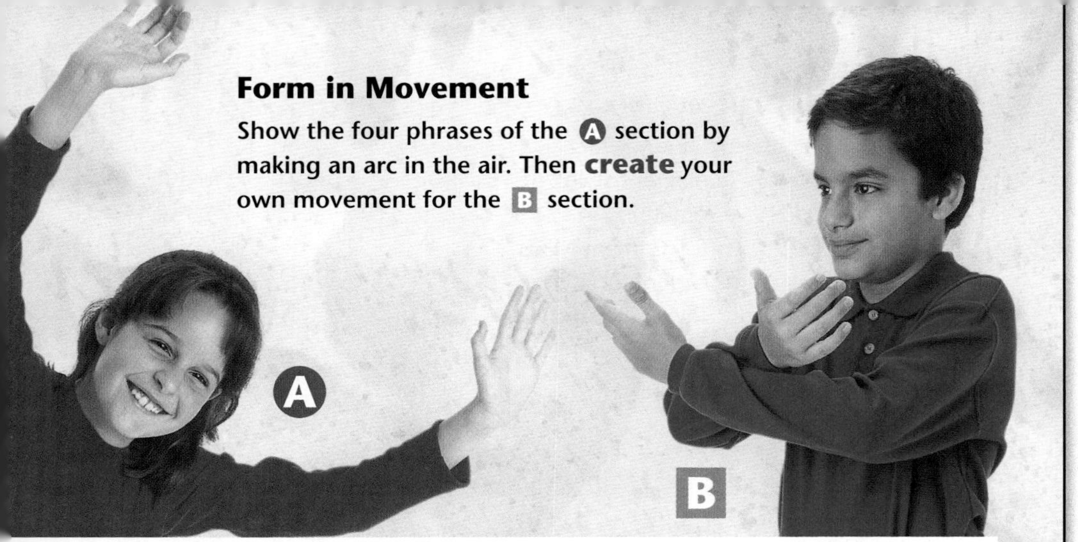

# 1 Introduce

Ask students to read the text of "Walk in Jerusalem." Ask them why this music refers to the city of Jerusalem. Share information with students about important cities from Across the Curriculum below. Lead them to understand why important places and times are remembered through music.

# 2 Develop

### Singing

6c Ask students to look at the notation for "Walk in Jerusalem" and find the words *D.C. al Fine.* Discuss with students the meaning of *D.C. al Fine* (return to the beginning). Help them find the word *Fine,* which indicates the end of the song.

Have students sing "Walk in Jerusalem" **CD 5-12.**

**ASK Which parts of the song were alike?** (the beginning and the end)

**SAY** When songs have a similar beginning and end, with a contrasting middle section, they are in ABA sectional form.

### Moving

6e Ask students to sing "Walk in Jerusalem" **CD 5-12,** showing the four phrases of the A section by making an arc from shoulder to shoulder. Have them create another "in place" movement for the B section.

**continued on page 102**

## Across the Curriculum

▶ **Social Studies** Jerusalem holds a place of importance for many religious faiths. For this reason, "Walk in Jerusalem" appears in the musical tradition of many faiths. Jerusalem is not the only holy city. Encourage students to name other cities that are historically and religiously significant, such as Rome and Mecca.

Holy cities are frequently mentioned in news broadcasts. Although students may be familiar with cities in their state or country, they may not know the location of cities such as Jerusalem. Encourage students to use a globe or map to find the location of historically important cities.

## Movement

▶ **Patterned Dance** Invite students to create a patterned dance routine for "Cement Mixer," on p. 102. Have them work in groups of four students, with each student suggesting a distinct move for a portion of the song as follows:

A Section

- First move performed three times (six measures)
- Second move performed once (two measures)

B Section

- Third move performed twice (four measures)
- Fourth move performed twice (four measures)

Encourage each group to perform their version of the dance for the class.

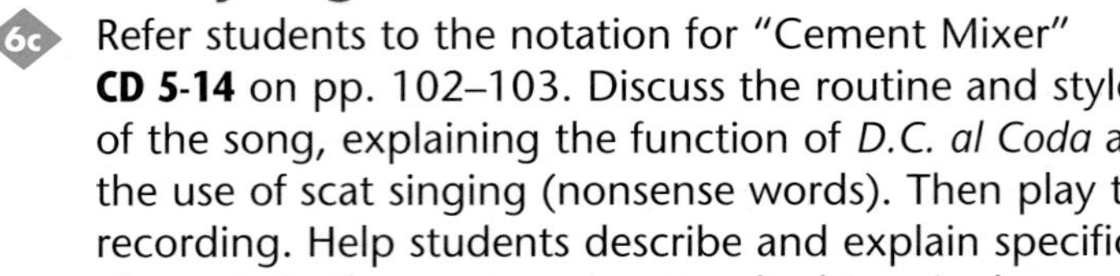

## Analyzing

6c Refer students to the notation for "Cement Mixer" **CD 5-14** on pp. 102–103. Discuss the routine and style of the song, explaining the function of *D.C. al Coda* and the use of scat singing (nonsense words). Then play the recording. Help students describe and explain specific elements in the music, using standard terminology.

ASK **In which order do the A and B sections occur?** (AABA)

**How does this compare to the form of "Walk in Jerusalem"?** (In "Cement Mixer," the A section is repeated and there is a *coda*.)

**How is the B section different from the A section?** (Discuss such features as different rhythm and melody patterns, and different lyrics.)

## Singing

Have students sing the A sections with the recording. Then divide the class and have one group sing the A sections and the other group, the B section. Allow groups to switch parts.

## Creating

3a Point out that there are rests at the end of all but one phrase in the A section (lines 1–3). Invite students to create improvised body percussion rhythms to perform during the rests. See Teacher to Teacher below for specific suggestions.

## Moving

6e See Movement, p. 101, and invite students to perform a patterned dance routine to accompany "Cement Mixer."

Add a Section and Mix
"Walk in Jerusalem" and the jazz song below are in different styles. But they do have something in common. Listen to "Cement Mixer" and identify the order of the A and B sections. How is this form similar to that of "Walk in Jerusalem"? How is it different?
CD 5-14
Cement Mixer
Words and Music by Slim Gaillard and Lee Ricks
Swing
F A Dm7 Gm7 C7
do
Ce - ment mix - er! put - ti, put - ti,
Ce - ment mix - er! put - ti, put - ti,
Last Time to Coda
Ce - ment mix - er! put - ti, put - ti,
1.
A pud-dle o' voot - y, pud-dle o' goot - y, pud-dle o' scoot - y.
102

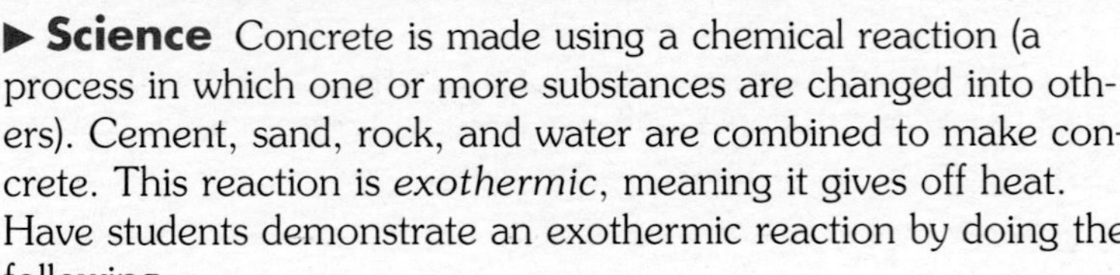

# Footnotes

## Across the Curriculum

▶ **Science** Concrete is made using a chemical reaction (a process in which one or more substances are changed into others). Cement, sand, rock, and water are combined to make concrete. This reaction is *exothermic*, meaning it gives off heat. Have students demonstrate an exothermic reaction by doing the following:

- Record the temperature.
- Soak steel wool in vinegar for one minute.
- Squeeze out the vinegar and wrap the steel wool around the end of a thermometer.
- Place the wool/thermometer in the jar, sealing the lid.
- Allow five minutes, then read the temperature and compare it with the first reading.

## Teacher to Teacher

▶ **Improvising** Improvisation is a skill that needs time to develop. In "Cement Mixer," there are many places at the end of measures that have rests. Give students ideas for improvising in these places by demonstrating finger snaps, clapping, patting knees, brushing hands, stamping feet, shrugging shoulders, or other single body movements. Encourage all students to participate, but suggest they do each improvisation in a single place rather than several levels of body percussion. This will help assure that the rhythm will stay constant. Hand-held nonpitched instruments could be included.

### Picture This

Russian composer Modest Mussorgsky [moo-SORG-skee] (1839–1881) was inspired to write musical descriptions of a series of paintings. **Listen** to one example. It illustrates another variation of ABA form.

CD 5–16

**The Hut of Baba Yaga**

**from *Pictures at an Exhibition***
**by Modest Mussorgsky (orchestrated by Maurice Ravel)**

Baba Yaga is a fiendish, terrifying figure from Russian folklore. How does Mussorgsky's music "paint" this image?

2.
F
A pud-dle o' veet, Con - crete.
B
F7 F dim F7 B♭ F7 B♭
First you get some grav - el, Pour it in a vout;
F
To mix a mess o' mor - tar, you add ce - ment and wa - ter.
C7
D. C. al Coda
See the mel - low roon - y come out, slurp, slurp, slurp.
Coda
N.C.
F6
Who wants a buck - et of ce - ment?

### Listening

Explain to students that ABA form, in one variation or another, is used in almost every type of music. Share with students the information in Spotlight On below.

Play *The Hut of Baba Yaga* **CD 5-16** and have students listen to the entire piece. Play the recording again to help students aurally identify the following variant of ABA form. (The indicated timings are approximate).

Section
A (0–1:10)
B (1:10–1:40)
B (1:40–2:22)
A (2:22–3:20)

## 3 Close

### Performing

Divide the class into small groups. Ask each group to choose one of the songs in this lesson and create a new movement that shows ABA form. Have each group perform its movement for the class as it sings the song.

**Element: FORM** — ASSESSMENT

**Performance/Observation** Review with students the two songs in diverse styles presented in this lesson. Have students sing or listen to "Walk in Jerusalem" **CD 5-12** or "Cement Mixer" **CD 5-14**, performing small steady-beat movements during the A sections and different movements during the B section.

Observe that students understand form by their performance of different movements in the two sections.

### Spotlight On

**The Composer** Modest Mussorgsky (1839–1881) is considered by many to be the most original talent of the Russian nationalist composers. He is known mainly for his opera *Boris Godounov*, the tone poem *Night on Bald Mountain*, and his massive piano composition, *Pictures at an Exhibition*, which is perhaps best known in the orchestration by Maurice Ravel. Despite Mussorgsky's short life, strict commitment to Russian music, and limited formal musical training, his music influenced many composers beyond the borders of his native country.

**The Music** Mussorgsky had been a close friend of the Russian architect and painter Victor Hartmann. Shortly after Hartmann's death at an early age, another friend helped to arrange an exhibition of paintings by Hartmann. Mussorgsky, deeply moved by the exhibit, decided to use ten pictures as the subjects for a suite for piano; he composed *Pictures at an Exhibition* as a memorial tribute to his friend.

### Technology/Media Link

**Notation Software** Pass out blank sheets of staff paper and ask students to write two eight-measure melodies using notes from the C-pentatonic scale. (Write the names of the notes on the board.) Have students use eighths, quarters, half notes, and their corresponding rests in their melodies. When students have completed their melodies, ask them to choose one melody as an A section and the other as a B section. Have them take turns entering their notes into the computer. When students are finished entering their compositions into the computer, have them experiment with different timbres as they play back their melodies.

## LESSON AT A GLANCE

**Element Focus** **MELODY** Extended pentatonic patterns

**Skill Objective** **READING** Sing an extended pentatonic song from notation

**Connection Activity** **MATHEMATICS** Create a song lyric to help remember multiplication tables

**MATERIALS**

- "Weevily Wheat" **CD 5-17**
  **Recording Routine:** Intro (4 m.); vocal; instrumental; vocal-recording in F major
- **Music Reading Practice, Sequence 11** **CD 5-19**
- **Resource Book** pp. D-12, E-12, F-8, H-10, I-11

**VOCABULARY**

scale pentatonic pitch ladder

◆◆◆◆ **National Standards** ◆◆◆◆

**3b** Improvise melodic ostinato accompaniments
**5b** Read notes in treble clef using syllables and letter names
**6c** Use appropriate terms to explain music and music notation

**MORE MUSIC CHOICES**

Other songs using the *do*-pentatonic scale:
"Somebody's Knockin' at Your Door," p. 53
"Cotton-Eye Joe," p. 288
"Sourwood Mountain," p. 65

# 1 INTRODUCE

Begin the lesson by discussing what a weevil is and why you might not want any in your wheat. (Weevils are insects that infest grains.) Then sing short extended pentatonic patterns for the students, using a neutral syllable (such as *loo*). Have students echo sing each pattern, using pitch syllables and hand signs, as a group and individually.



# A Multiplication Melody

la
so
mi
re
do
la,
so,

This American play-party song is based on an old song from Scotland. "Charlie" is really Bonnie Prince Charles Stuart. Many songs have been written about his valiant, but unsuccessful, attempts to restore his family to the Scottish throne in the 1700s.

Do you recognize the scale shown on this pitch ladder? What kind of scale is it?

First, notice where *do* is placed on the staff. In this song, *do* is written on line two. **Identify** the other notes of the scale from the lines and spaces on the staff. **Read** the scale using pitch syllables and hand signs.

do

## Footnotes

### ACROSS THE CURRICULUM

▶ **Math** Challenge students to sing the last two lines of "Weevily Wheat" by substituting all the numbers 1–10 in multiples of 5, 6, 7, and 8, following the song's rhythm, but at a much slower tempo. Ask students to write out all the words that fit the new multiplication series. Try singing the song with these numbers.

### BUILDING SKILLS THROUGH MUSIC

▶ **Math** Have students rewrite the last two lines of "Weevily Wheat," using the numbers 6, 7, 8, and 9 for multiplication. Allow the class to sing the song with the new words.

### MOVEMENT

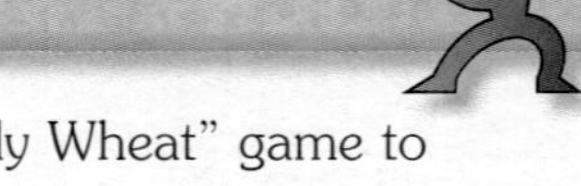

▶ **Game Song** Introduce the "Weevily Wheat" game to the class.

*Formation:* Have students stand in groups of four, in a circle, and number off.

All join hands and step clockwise during the first phrase (*Don't want your weevily wheat, don't want your barley...*). The circle reverses on the next phrase (*Take some flour in half an hour and bake a cake for Charlie...*). On the last phrase (*Five times five...*), all stand in place and layer hands in the center to the beat (#1 puts left hand in, #2 puts left hand on top, followed by 3 and 4). All then layer right hands, then left hands again (by pulling out from the bottom), and so on, until the end of the verse.

**Twistification Hand Game**

**Sing** "Weevily Wheat." The multiplication game mentioned in the last two lines of "Weevily Wheat" is known as "Twistification." **Create** your own verses using other multiplication tables.

CD 5-17
Weevily Wheat
s, l, (d) r m s l
Traditional
Don't want your wee-vi-ly wheat, Don't want your bar-ley.
Take some flour in half an hour and bake a cake for Char-lie.
Five times five is twen-ty-five, Five times six is thir-ty.
Five times sev'n is thir-ty-five, Five times eight is for-ty.
Twistification Hand Game
Unit 3 105

# 2 Develop

### Reading

Point out the staff notation of the extended pentatonic scale, p. 104. Have students identify the staff placement of *do* (line 2) and then review the staff placement of the other notes in G–*do*. Use Reading Music Worksheet, Resource Book p. D-12, and ask students to sing pitches, using pitch syllables and hand signs, as you point to them.

See p. 447 and Resource Book p. E-12 for a related pentatonic reading activity.

### Singing/Analyzing

Have students

- Listen to "Weevily Wheat" **CD 5-17** while following the staff notation.
- Read and sing "Weevily Wheat" from staff notation, using pitch syllables and hand signs.
- Sing the song with lyrics and play the game described in Movement, p. 104.

- Determine how many different pitches are used in the song. (seven, because *so* and *la* appear in two different octaves)

For an additional singing activity, have students create lyrics based on the multiplication tables of 6, 7, 8, and so on. See Across the Curriculum, p. 104.

# 3 Close

**Element: MELODY** ASSESSMENT

**Performance/Observation** Have students sing "Weevily Wheat" **CD 5-17** while following the notation, using hand signs and pitch syllables.

Observe that students sing the correct pitch syllables and perform the correct hand signs.

## Skills Reinforcement

▶ **Creating** Invited students to improvise their own pentatonic patterns and perform them by singing them with pitch syllables and hand signs. Have them play the patterns as an ostinato with "Weevily Wheat" and then combine them to make a countermelody.

▶ **Recorder** Turn to p. I-11 in the Resource Book for a four-note steady-beat accompaniment to "Weevily Wheat."

▶ **Keyboard** For a pentatonic ostinato pattern to play with "Weevily Wheat," refer to Resource Book p. H-10.

▶ **Mallets** For an Orff accompaniment to "Weevily Wheat" and practice playing ascending and descending pentatonic scales, refer to p. F-8 in the Resource Book.

## Technology/Media Link

**Electronic Keyboard** Have students choose a General MIDI voice for "Weevily Wheat," such as guitar or banjo, to improvise ostinatos in G-pentatonic.

## LESSON AT A GLANCE

**Element Focus** **MELODY** *La*-pentatonic melody patterns

**Skill Objective** **READING** Read *la*-pentatonic melody patterns

**Connection Activity** **CULTURE** Discuss folk songs, how they are collected, and what they tell us about a culture

**MATERIALS**
- "See the Children Playin'" **CD 5-22**
  **Recording Routine:** Intro (4 m.); v. 1; interlude (4 m.); v. 2; coda
- **Music Reading Practice, Sequence 12** **CD 5-24**
- **Resource Book** pp. D-13, E-13, F-9
- xylophone, hand drum, woodblock

**VOCABULARY**
*la*-pentatonic scale

**National Standards**
- **1a** Sing independently on pitch
- **2f** Play instruments independently against contrasting parts
- **3b** Improvise rhythmic or melodic ostinatos
- **5d** Notate pitch using standard symbols
- **6c** Use appropriate terms to explain music

**MORE MUSIC CHOICES**
Other songs in *la*-pentatonic:
"The Canoe Song," p. 76
"Pastures of Plenty," p. 280

# 1 INTRODUCE

Share and discuss information about folk songs and John Lomax with the students. See Cultural Connection below. Then sing short *la*-pentatonic patterns for students, using a neutral syllable (such as loo). Help students perform the patterns independently by having them echo sing each pattern with pitch syllables, as a group and individually.



# A New Home Tone

mi
re
do

la,
so,

Even though "See the Children Playin'" uses the same notes as "Weevily Wheat" in its scale, it sounds very different. Can you figure out why?

"See the Children Playin'" uses the notes of the pentatonic scale, and its **tonic** note is low *la*. Its scale is called the *la*-pentatonic scale.

The **tonic** is the key, or home, tone in a scale.

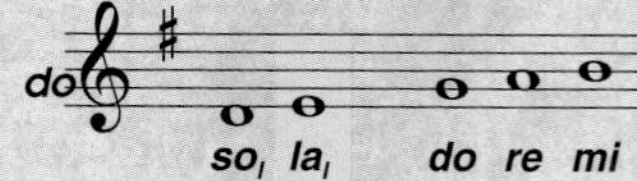


## Arts Connection

▼ *Children Dancing* (1948) is by Robert Gwathmey. He is famous for painting scenes from African American life.

# Footnotes

## ACROSS THE CURRICULUM

▶ **Social Studies** Invite students to learn more about Mississippi by reading the book *Mississippi* by Kathleen Thompson (Raintree/Steck-Vaughn, 1996) or *Mississippi* by Anna Ready (Lerner Publications, 1993). Use the books to create a fact treasure hunt. Write questions in advance to which students can find answers in the books. When they have found the answers, have them create their own questions and trade with another student or group of students.

## BUILDING SKILLS THROUGH MUSIC

▶ **Language** Invite students to make a list of chores they might perform. Have them make another list of chores that the children in "See the Children Playin'" might perform. Then lead a discussion to compare and contrast the two lists. Have students perform the song, substituting specific chores for the phrase *"Do your chores now."*

## CULTURAL CONNECTION

▶ **Song Background** "See the Children Playin'" is based on the folk song "Sea Lion Woman," collected by Library of Congress archivist John Lomax. During his long career, Lomax and his son Alan traveled throughout the United States recording folk songs in cotton fields, prisons, and anywhere else they could find people to sing for them. They preserved more than 6000 songs for the Library of Congress Archive of Folk Songs. Now, many of their recordings are on CD, and some can be heard on the Library of Congress Web site.

CD 5-22
See the Children Playin'
s, l d r m
Words by Reginald Royal
Folk Melody from Mississippi
do
Em
1. See ___ the chil-dren play - in', two - by - two play - in',
2. Ma - ma calls the chil-dren, "Do ___ your chores now, chil-dren."
Am7
Em
In ___ the fields play - in', and the work ain't done play - in'.
In ___ the fields chil-dren, dad-dy's com - in' home chil-dren.
Em
Ma - ma she's watch-in', chil - dren play - in' watch-in',
See ___ the chil-dren play - in', with ___ their dad - dy play - in',
Am7
Em
And it's get - tin' late watch-in' still the work ain't done watch-in'.
And their ma - ma too play - in', 'cause the work's all done play - in'.

**Read** the song using pitch syllables and hand signs. Use *do* to find your starting pitch.

### Hear the Children Playin'

**Perform** these ostinatos with the song.

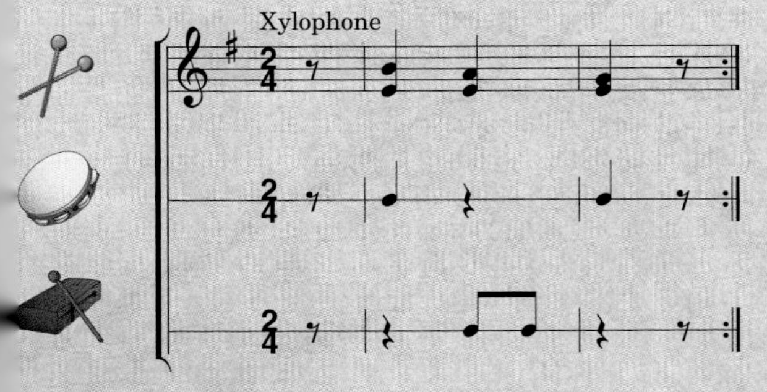
Xylophone

Unit 3 107

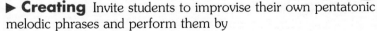

# 2 Develop

## Reading

6c Use the Reading Music Worksheet on Resource Book p. D-13 to review the notes of the pentatonic scale.

Have students listen to "See the Children Playin'" **CD 5-22** while following the notation.

ASK **Where is *do* on the staff?** (line 2)

**What is its letter name?** (G)

**What is the starting pitch of the song?** (*mi*)

**What is its letter name?** (B)

1a Have students sing "See the Children Playin'" using pitch syllables and hand signs. Invite a group of students to accompany the song with the ostinatos on p. 107.

See p. 447 and Resource Book p. E-13 for a related pentatonic reading activity.

## Analyzing

ASK **How many different pitches are used in the song?** (five)

Tell students that the song uses a pentatonic scale.

**On what pitch does the song end?** (*la*,)

Remind students that the song's final note is its tonic. Draw attention to the *do* indicator, and point out that the treble clef shows us where G is written on the staff, while the *do* indicator shows us which note is *do*. We can find the tonic (low *la*) from there.

# 3 Close

**Element: MELODY** ASSESSMENT

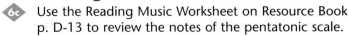

**Performance/Observation** Have students sing the *la*-pentatonic scale and then sing "See the Children Playin'" **CD 5-22** with pitch syllables and hand signs, reading from the notation.

Observe that students accurately sing pitch syllables and perform hand signs in *la*-pentatonic.

## Skills Reinforcement

▶ **Creating** Invite students to improvise their own pentatonic melodic phrases and perform them by

- 3b Playing them as an ostinato.
- 2f Combining them to make a countermelody.
- 5d Singing them with pitch syllables and hand signs.

Have students notate their pentatonic patterns on staff paper and save in a portfolio.

▶ **Mallets** For a mallet and nonpitched percussion accompaniment to "See the Children Playin'," refer to Resource Book p. F-9.

## School to Home Connection

▶ **Field Recordings** Invite students to tape their own "field recordings." Have them ask an older person to sing a song he or she learned as a child. Have students ask questions such as "What is the name of the song?" "How old were you when you learned it?" "Who taught it to you?" "What other songs do you remember?" "Where did you live?" Have students bring tapes to school and share with the class.

## Technology/Media Link

**Web Site** For more information about John Lomax, have students visit *www.sfsuccessnet.com.*

## LESSON AT A GLANCE

**Element Focus** **MELODY** Prepare *fa*

**Skill Objective** **READING** Read melodies including *fa* in staff notation

**Connection Activity** **CULTURE** Discuss same or similar games played across cultures

**MATERIALS**

- *"Son macaron"* **CD 5-27**
  **Recording Routine:** Intro (4 m.); vocal; interlude (4 m.); vocal; coda
- **Resource Book** pp. B-9, D-15

**VOCABULARY**

melodic contour

**◆ ◆ ◆ ◆ National Standards ◆ ◆ ◆ ◆**

**2f** Play instruments independently against contrasting parts
**3b** Improvise rhythmic and melodic ostinato accompaniments
**5b** Read notes in treble clef using letters or syllables

**MORE MUSIC CHOICES**

For more preparation of *fa*:
"Chairs to Mend," p. 149
*"Canción de cuna,"* p. 144
"Pay Me My Money Down," p. 38

# 1 INTRODUCE

Share information with students about game songs. Refer to Cultural Connection on p. 109. Ask students to share with the class any game songs they know. Then play the recording of *"Son macaron"* **CD 5-27.**

# Follow that Melody!

*"Son macaron"* is believed to be a nonsense song. **Listen** to the song and follow the graph of the melody on the right.

Look at the song notation and use *do* to find your way around the staff. What is the starting pitch?

You may notice a note on the staff that you do not yet know. **Read** the song with pitch syllables and hum the mystery note. How many times does it occur in this song?

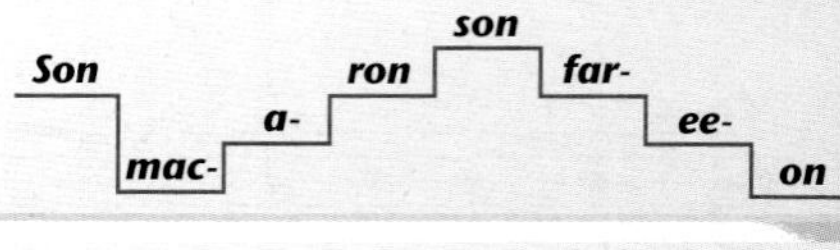

Son
mac-
a-
ron
son
far-
ee-
on

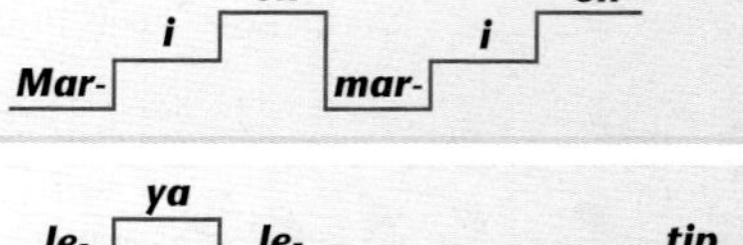

Mar-
i
-on
mar-
i
-on

le- ya le- ya tip tip tip

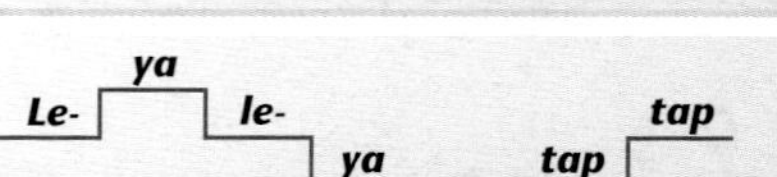

Le-
ya
le-
ya
tap
tap
tap

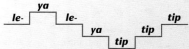

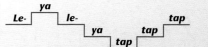

***One beat, two beats, three beats. Catch!***

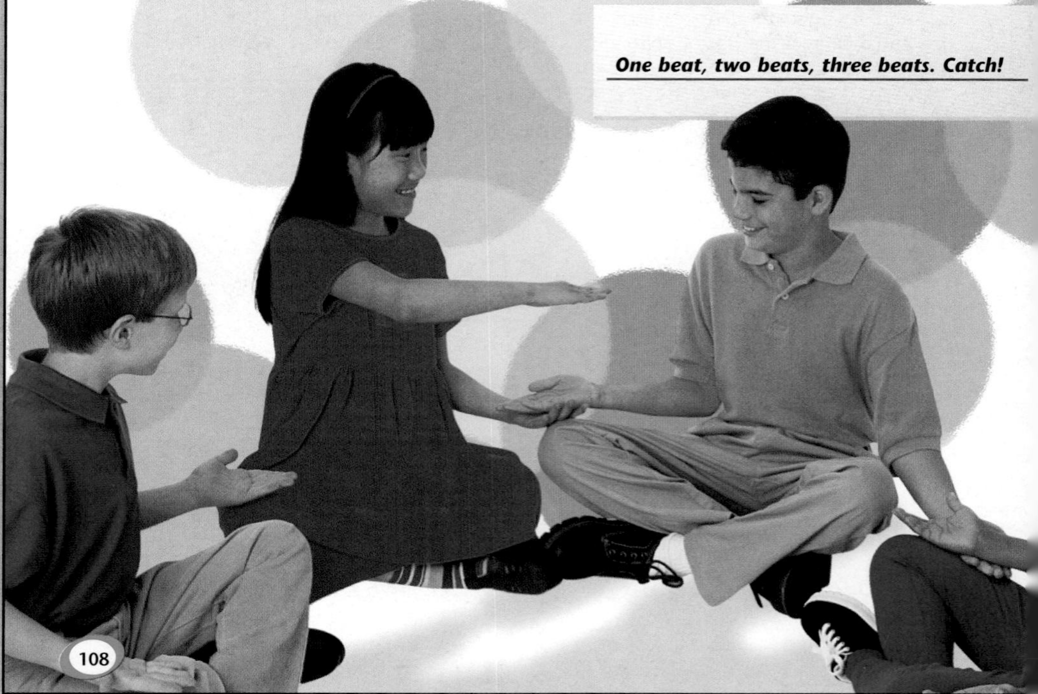

## Footnotes

### TEACHER TO TEACHER

▶ **Preparing for *fa*** You will notice that the staff notation in this lesson contains the new note *fa*. This note will be "presented" in the next unit. However, attention can and should be drawn to the melodic contour without actually naming the new note. Students should be able to hear that the new note falls between *mi* and *so*. Tell students that until the "new note" is named, they should "hum" on that note rather than use a pitch syllable.

### BUILDING SKILLS THROUGH MUSIC

▶ **Math** Invite students to write new words for the four counting measures at the end of *"Son macaron."* Have them count by 2s, 3s, or other chosen methods and then sing the song with the new words.

### SKILLS REINFORCEMENT

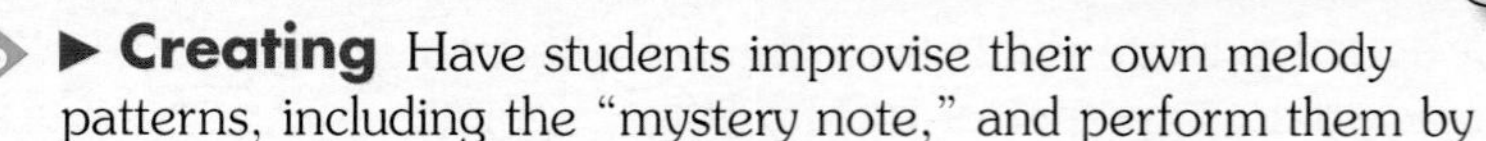

3b ▶ **Creating** Have students improvise their own melody patterns, including the "mystery note," and perform them by

- Playing them as an ostinato.
- 2f Playing patterns one after another.

▶ **Reading** Have students review pentatonic melody patterns and do the Show What You Know! on p. 109. Refer to Resource Book p. B-9.

## Stay in the Game

**Sing** *"Son macaron."* After you learn the song, play the game.

## Show What You Know!

**Identify** whether these melodies are *do*- or *la*-pentatonic.

**Compose** a melody using the G-pentatonic scale. Choose either *do* or *la* as your tonic.



# 2 Develop

### Listening/Singing

Have students

- Listen to *"Son macaron"* **CD 5-27** while following the melodic contour of the graph on p. 108.
- Learn the song by rote, phrase by phrase.

### Reading

Have students

- Read, clap, and say the rhythm of *"Son macaron"* using rhythm syllables.
- Sing the song with pitch syllables and hum the mystery note *(fa).*

For more practice with pitch syllables and melodic contour, refer to Resource Book p. D-15.

### Moving

Have students play this game with *"Son macaron."* Players sit in a circle with left hand (palm up) on the left neighbor's right knee and right hand (palm up) on the right neighbor's left hand. Starting player passes the beat left by tapping right hand of person beside him/her, using his/her right hand, then placing it back on his/her other neighbor's palm. This continues to the left until *1 beat, 2 beats, 3 beats, catch!* On *catch!* the person getting tapped must quickly pull away. If he/she can avoid getting tapped, the "tapper" is out. If he/she is tapped, then he/she is out!

# 3 Close

**Element: MELODY** ASSESSMENT

**Performance/Observation** Have students sing *"Son macaron"* **CD 5-27.**

Invite them to read all the notes they know and hum the mystery note. Observe and assess each student's ability to identify the mystery note *(fa)* according to its relative position to *mi* and *so.*

## Cultural Connection

▶ **Game Songs** The moving activity of the lesson describes a game that is played while singing the nonsense song *"Son macaron."* This same game (or a slight variation) is also played with other songs from around the United States and other countries. For example, *"Aquaqua"* from Israel, "Quack Diddledeoso" from the western United States, "Freddy Oka" from the eastern United States, and "Stella Ella" from Canada all use the same game movements. Ask students how they think this might happen. (Children from different cultures teach each other songs when they move or meet. Songs are passed down through folk traditions and change slightly.)

## Technology/Media Link

**Notation Software** Help students determine the pitch set for "*Son macaron.*" (C-E-F-G-A) Divide the class into three groups. Ask each group to

- Use the pitch set and familiar note values to compose a four-measure phrase in $\frac{2}{4}$.
- Enter its phrase into the computer and experiment with different timbres.
- Combine its phrase with that of the other groups.

Have the class perform and compare the different versions of the complete 12-measure song.

## LESSON AT A GLANCE

**Element Focus** **TIMBRE** String instrument timbres

**Skill Objective** **LISTENING** Identify string instruments by sound

**Connection Activity** **CULTURE** Discuss the design and construction of string instruments from different cultures

**MATERIALS**

- *String Instrument Montage* **CD 5-29**
- *Eine kleine Nachtmusik* **CD 5-30**
- "Gigue" from *Partita in E Major* **CD 5-31**

**VOCABULARY**

string bass *rebab* lute *sitar*
*koto* violin

**◆◆◆◆ National Standards ◆◆◆◆**

**6c** Use appropriate terms to explain musical instruments
**6d** Identify the sounds of instruments from various cultures
**9a** Listen to identify music from different cultures
**9e** Demonstrate appropriate audience behavior

**MORE MUSIC CHOICES**

Other selections featuring strings:

"Presentation of Pairs" from *Concerto for Orchestra,* p. 72
"Spring" from *The Four Seasons,* p. 371

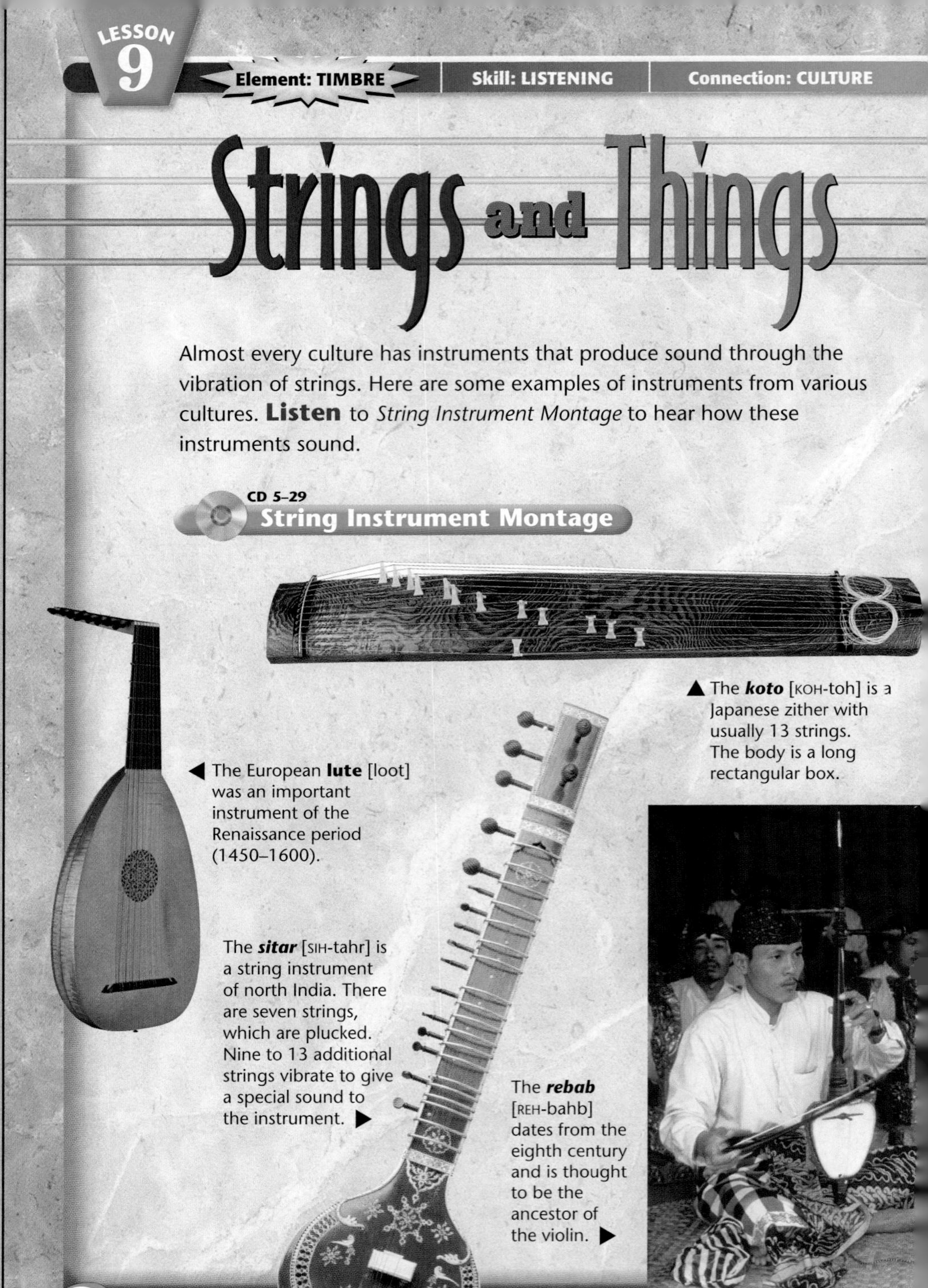


# Strings and Things

Almost every culture has instruments that produce sound through the vibration of strings. Here are some examples of instruments from various cultures. **Listen** to *String Instrument Montage* to hear how these instruments sound.

CD 5–29 **String Instrument Montage**

▲ The ***koto*** [KOH-toh] is a Japanese zither with usually 13 strings. The body is a long rectangular box.

◀ The European **lute** [loot] was an important instrument of the Renaissance period (1450–1600).

The ***sitar*** [SIH-tahr] is a string instrument of north India. There are seven strings, which are plucked. Nine to 13 additional strings vibrate to give a special sound to the instrument. ▶

The ***rebab*** [REH-bahb] dates from the eighth century and is thought to be the ancestor of the violin. ▶

110

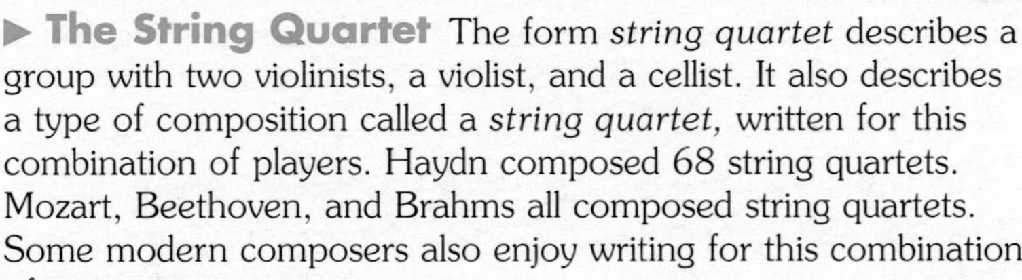

## Footnotes

### SPOTLIGHT ON

▶ **The String Quartet** The form *string quartet* describes a group with two violinists, a violist, and a cellist. It also describes a type of composition called a *string quartet,* written for this combination of players. Haydn composed 68 string quartets. Mozart, Beethoven, and Brahms all composed string quartets. Some modern composers also enjoy writing for this combination of instruments.

### BUILDING SKILLS THROUGH MUSIC

▶ **Language** After students have read about Mozart on p. 111, have them state the main idea. (Mozart was a child prodigy.) Share information from Spotlight On above. Lead students to define the term prodigy from the context of the paragraph.

### ACROSS THE CURRICULUM

▶ **Language Arts** Encourage students to read more about Mozart by reading aloud *Wolfgang Amadeus Mozart* by Mike Venezia (Children's Press, 1995). Students may also be interested in Mozart's childhood, which is detailed in *Mozart* by Ann Rachlin (Barron, 1992).

▶ **Social Studies** Bach and Mozart lived and wrote in two different periods of European history—Bach in the Baroque period and Mozart in the Classical period. The styles of these two periods contrasted greatly. Have students find references to these periods in the library and find out what some of the differences were—differences in clothing styles, the way the artwork looked, differences in architecture, and so on.

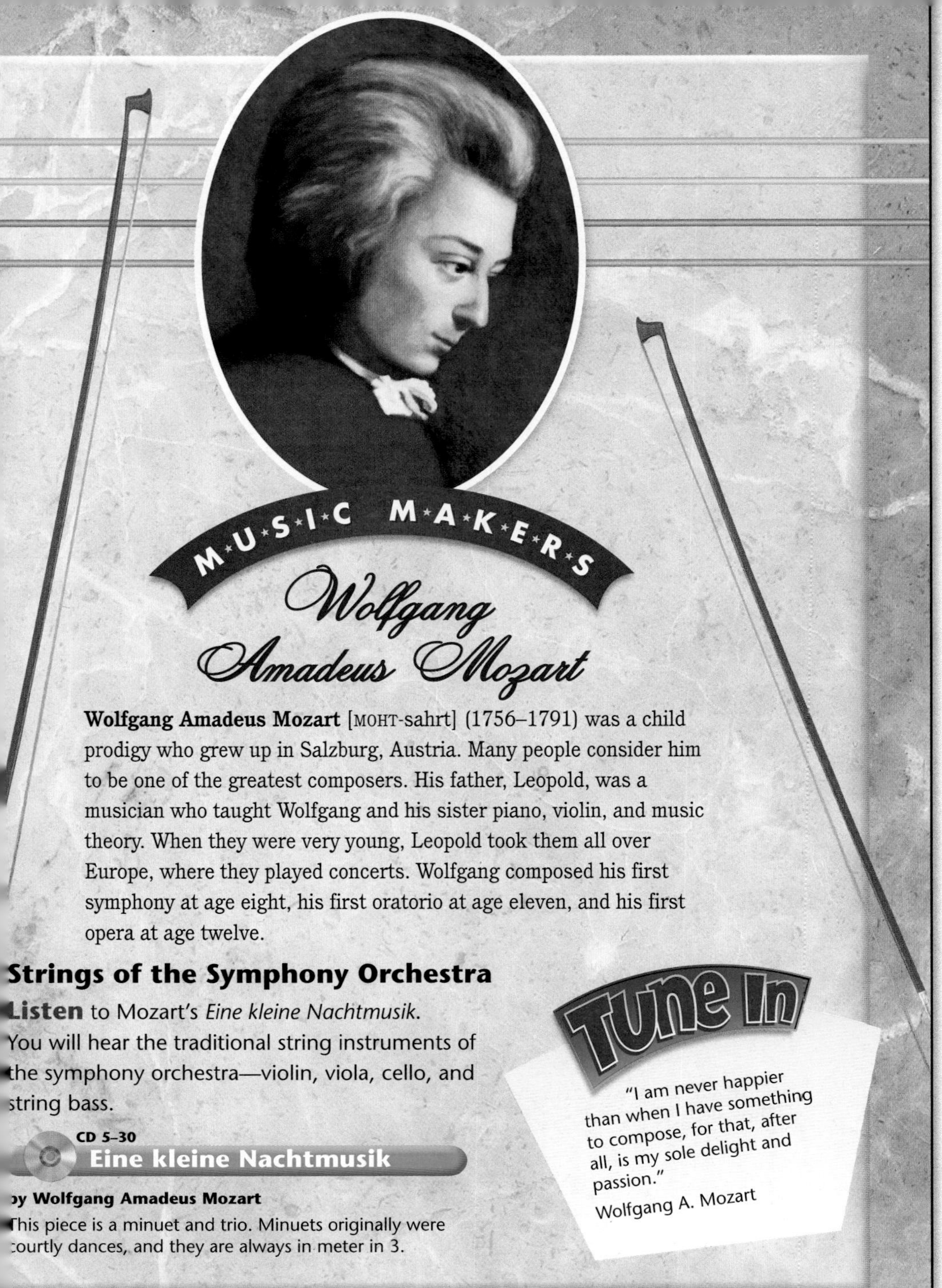

M·U·S·I·C M·A·K·E·R·S

*Wolfgang Amadeus Mozart*

**Wolfgang Amadeus Mozart** [MOHT-sahrt] (1756–1791) was a child prodigy who grew up in Salzburg, Austria. Many people consider him to be one of the greatest composers. His father, Leopold, was a musician who taught Wolfgang and his sister piano, violin, and music theory. When they were very young, Leopold took them all over Europe, where they played concerts. Wolfgang composed his first symphony at age eight, his first oratorio at age eleven, and his first opera at age twelve.

**Strings of the Symphony Orchestra**

**Listen** to Mozart's *Eine kleine Nachtmusik.* You will hear the traditional string instruments of the symphony orchestra—violin, viola, cello, and string bass.

CD 5-30

**Eine kleine Nachtmusik**

by Wolfgang Amadeus Mozart

This piece is a minuet and trio. Minuets originally were courtly dances, and they are always in meter in 3.

TUNE IN

"I am never happier than when I have something to compose, for that, after all, is my sole delight and passion."
Wolfgang A. Mozart

Unit 3 111

# 1 Introduce

**SAY** String instruments are found in almost every culture. Some are used as folk instruments, some are used as a part of an orchestra or chamber group.

Some string instruments may be familiar to students, but others may be new to them. Invite students to share names and descriptions of string instruments they have seen or heard.

# 2 Develop

### Analyzing

Invite students to look at the pictures of early European and non-European string instruments on p. 110.

Share the information from the Cultural Connection below about string instruments.

6c **ASK How would you describe each instrument?** (*Rebab* has a pear-shaped body; lute has a pear-shaped body; *sitar* has a long neck, seven strings, and moveable metal frets; *koto* has a long rectangular box, which sits on the floor.)

9a Ask students to listen to and categorize each of the string instruments in *String Instrument Montage* **CD 5-29.**

**ASK What do these instruments have in common?** (strings)

**How are they different?** (in size, number of strings, sound)

**Which one plays the lowest tones?** (*koto* and *sitar*)

**Which one plays the highest?** (lute and *rebab*)

**How do you know?** (The size of the instruments and the thickness of the strings determine higher and lower pitches.)

**continued on page 112**

## Cultural Connection

▶ **String Instruments** Almost every culture has some kind of string instruments. For example, the *oud,* used in Arabic and Islamic communities, is an instrument dating from as early as the sixth century. The *lute* was an important instrument in Europe during the Renaissance. The *sitar* is a classical instrument of India. The *koto* is considered the national instrument of Japan. South American cultures often use single-string instruments. The *erhu* is a Chinese string instrument. The *rebab* exists in various forms in North Africa, the Middle East, Iran, Central Asia, India, China, Zaire, Indonesia, and Spain. The *rebab,* pictured on p. 110, is from Central Java.

## Audience Etiquette

9e ▶ **Attending a Live Concert** Talk with students about appropriate behavior at concerts where *Eine kleine Nachtmusik* might be performed. Discuss these ideas.

- Plan to arrive at least 15 minutes ahead of time.
- Read about the composer and the music you will hear before going to the concert to help understand what you are going to hear.
- Be silent during a performance. Noise disturbs the people around you.
- Listen actively during the performance.
- Stay in your seat until the work being performed is completed and you hear applause.

## Listening

Invite students to listen to *Eine kleine Nachtmusik* **CD 5-30.** Ask them to count the measures of the trio aloud while showing each phrase by making an arc in the air from shoulder to shoulder.

Encourage students to hum the melody as they listen once again. Then, invite them to perform the movement on p. 112 with the recording.

Have students listen to *Partita in E Major,* "Gigue" **CD 5-31** and follow the contour of the first phrase with their hands.

ASK **Does the melody go in a downward direction or an upward direction at the very beginning?** (downward)

**After the melody moves downward, what happens then?** (It moves upward in a scale passage.)

Share with the students the information about J. S. Bach in the Spotlight On below.

ASK **How is the timbre of the violin the same or different from the timbre of the other string instruments in this lesson?** (The *rebab* also has a smooth connected sound since it too, is played by bowing, but the sound is much thinner and more nasal. The *koto* is plucked and has much more resonance due to the large soundboard. It also has lower tones. The *sitar* is plucked but has a thinner sound; the vibration of the sympathetic strings under the main strings create a ringing quality.)

**Moving to the Music**

Hum this melody from *Eine kleine Nachtmusik.* Choose a partner and walk gracefully toward each other for two measures and away for two measures.

**Arts Connection**

▲ *Danse dans un Pavillion* by Jean Antoine Watteau (1684–1721). The dancers in this painting are performing a courtly dance, similar to the minuet.



112

# Footnotes

## Spotlight On

▶ **The Composer** There is no doubt that Johann Sebastian Bach is one of a handful of composers whose achievements count as among the greatest in musical history. Born in 1685 into a long line of musicians, he held many prominent positions in various musical institutions of the time—organist at New Church in Arnstadt, Germany; Kapellmeister for the Prince of Anhalt-Kothen and the Duke of Sachsen-Weimar; and cantor of St. Thomas Church in Leipzig, where he had the responsibility for directing the music programs of four churches. He wrote a great deal of sacred music, but also wrote fugues, dance suites, concertos, and pieces for solo instruments. His compositions for violin and cello alone are among his most striking works. The only musical form he never attempted was opera. Bach died in 1750.

## Skills Reinforcement

▶ **Listening** Students may need more experience listening to string instruments. Refer to the Sound Bank on pp. 466 through 471 and have students read the information about various string instruments. (All are color coded with a key at the bottom of the page.) Then play the examples for each selection. At the end of the activity, play several selections and have the students identify by ear the instrument being played.

When Mozart was a child, he enjoyed stunts such as playing piano with his hands hidden under a cloth so that he couldn't see the keys.

## Classical Music—Here and Now

Many great classical composers are so widely respected that musicians today continue to perform their works. **Listen** to Bach's *Gigue* for solo violin, performed by Hilary Hahn.

**CD 5-31**
**Gigue**
**from *Partita in E Major* by Johann Sebastian Bach as performed by Hilary Hahn**

The *gigue,* or jig, is a dance originally from Ireland and England.

### MUSIC MAKERS
### Hilary Hahn

**Hilary Hahn** (born 1979) began playing violin at age four. Amazingly, she was playing the Bach Partitas by age eight. Two years later, she was admitted to the world-renowned Curtis Institute of Music in Philadelphia. Hahn enjoys taking time in her busy concert schedule to visit classrooms to play for students and to encourage them in their musical studies. While on tour, she keeps in touch with her fans through her Web site journal, where she also sends "postcards" from cities around the world.



Invite students to read Music Makers feature on Wolfgang Amadeus Mozart (p. 111) and Hilary Hahn (p. 113). Have them discuss any similarities and differences between the two musicians. Encourage them to discuss the lives of other talented musicians with whom they are familiar. Refer to the Spotlight On below for more examples of child prodigies.

## 3 CLOSE

**Element: TIMBRE** **ASSESSMENT**

6d **Observation** Have students listen to *String Instrument Montage* **CD 5-29** or the Sound Bank recordings of string instruments. Ask them to point to the picture of each instrument on p. 110 as they hear that instrument.

Here are the string instruments listed in the Sound Bank on pp. 466–471.

- *balalaika* **CD 19-11**
- cello **CD 19-13**
- dulcimer **CD 19-18**
- *erhu* **CD 19-20**
- guitar **CD 19-24**
- *koto* **CD 19-26**
- lute **CD 19-27**
- *sitar* **CD 19-34**
- string bass **CD 19-37**
- viola **CD 19-44**
- violin **CD 19-45**

Observe and assess each student's ability to identify and categorize string instruments by sound.

### SPOTLIGHT ON

▶ **Child Prodigies** Introduce students to three other former child prodigies.

**Herbie Hancock** Born in 1940 in Chicago, Illinois, Hancock was a major influence in the development of fusion jazz. He began playing piano at the age of seven and debuted with the Chicago Symphony at 11.

**Itzhak Perlman** Born in 1945 in Tel Aviv, Israel, he showed early promise even though handicapped by polio. He came to the United States to play on television when he was only 13.

**Sarah Chang** Born in Philadelphia in 1980 of Korean parents, this gifted young woman began studying violin at the age of four. At five she performed with major symphony orchestras and performed as a surprise guest with the New York Philharmonic.

### TECHNOLOGY/MEDIA LINK

**Web Site** Students may be interested in learning more about Mozart, Bach, and other composers who wrote for string instruments. Have them visit *www.sfsuccessnet.com.*

**Video Library** Students may also enjoy viewing the string instrument segments on the video.

LESSON 10

## LESSON AT A GLANCE

**Element Focus** **TEXTURE/HARMONY** Partner songs

**Skill Objective** **SINGING** Sing a three-part partner song

**Connection Activity** **CULTURE** Learn about the Caribbean islands and the cultures that influence them

### MATERIALS

- "Turn the World Around" **CD 5-32**

  **Recording Routine:** Intro (8 m.); "Turn the World Around" v. 1 (2x); v. 2 (2x); v. 3 (2x); "So Is Life" (2x); "Do You Know Who I Am?" (2x); interlude (4 m.); vocal improv. interlude (6 m.); interlude (2 m.); "Turn the World Around" v. 4 (2x) with "So Is Life"; "Turn the World Around" v. 5 (2x) with "Do You Know Who I Am?"; "Turn the World Around" v. 6 (2x) with "So Is Life" and "Do You Know Who I Am?"; coda
- *Jump in the Line* (excerpt) **CD 5-34**
- maracas, claves, bongos, conga

### VOCABULARY

partner songs calypso

### National Standards

**1d** Sing partner songs
**2b** Perform rhythms and melodies on appropriate instruments
**2f** Play instruments independently against contrasting parts
**6b** Describe music by moving to it

### MORE MUSIC CHOICES

Another Caribbean folk song:
"Wings of a Dove," p. 318
Other partner songs:
"Shake the Papaya Down," p. 378

LESSON 10
Element: TEXTURE/HARMONY
Skill: SINGING
Connection: CULTURE
Partners in Song
*Calypso* is a lively style of music from the Caribbean. This style has African roots, but it was developed in Trinidad. "Turn the World Around" is a calypso song with three melodies that are sung at the same time. Melodies that fit together in this way are known as **partner songs.**
**Sing** "Turn the World Around."
**Partner songs** are two or more different songs that can be sung at the same time to create a thicker texture.
CD 5-32
Turn the World Around
l, t, d r m
Words by Harry Belafonte
Music by Robert Freedman
1. We come from the fire, living in the fire,
2. We come from the water, living in the water,
3. We come from the mountain, living on the mountain,
Go back to the fire, turn the world around.
Go back to the water, turn the world around.
Go back to the mountain, turn the world around.
4. Water make the river, river wash the mountain, Fire make the sunlight, turn the world around.
5. Heart is of the river, body is the mountain, Spirit is the sunlight, turn the world around.
6. We are of the spirit, truly can the spirit, Only can the spirit, turn the world around.
114

# Footnotes

## SPOTLIGHT ON

▶ **"Turn the World Around"** Harry Belafonte says that he has always liked $\frac{5}{4}$ time. When he found Bob Freedman's "very singable music," he welcomed the opportunity to write the lyrics. Belafonte based "Turn the World Around" on African mythology.

## BUILDING SKILLS THROUGH MUSIC

▶ **Language** Have students, working in small groups, re-write the verses of "Turn the World Around" using formal grammar. Discuss how this changes the rhythm and character of the lyrics.

## CULTURAL CONNECTION

▶ **Caribbean Islands** Harry Belafonte popularized folk music from his native country, Trinidad. Trinidad is one of the larger islands of the Caribbean. Other islands include the Bahamas, Cuba, the Dominican Republic, Haiti, and Puerto Rico. The music of each island was influenced by "African culture" or "the people of Africa." However, each has its own distinctive style due to influences from people of other countries, including the French in Haiti, Spanish in the Dominican Republic, British in Trinidad, and Spanish in Cuba and Puerto Rico.

## More Songs—More Texture

**Sing** "So Is Life" alone and then with "Turn the World Around."

### So Is Life



**Listen** to the recording of "Turn the World Around." You will hear a third melody being sung to create a thicker texture. **Sing** "Do You Know Who I Am?" alone and then with "Turn the World Around" and "So Is Life."

### Do You Know Who I Am?





# 1 Introduce

Have the class read about *calypso* on p. 114. Also, share the information about the Caribbean Islands and the many cultures that influence them. Refer to Cultural Connection on p. 114. One of the most important and beloved calypso artists of the Caribbean is Harry Belafonte, the lyricist of this song. The songs in this lesson are in $\frac{5}{4}$ meter. Clap some five-beat patterns with a 3 + 2 feeling and have students echo you. As a challenge, add some syncopation. See the songs on pp. 114–115 for rhythm ideas.

# 2 Develop

### Listening

Have students listen to "Turn the World Around" **CD 5-32.**

ASK **What happens when more than one melody is being performed?** (The texture is thicker and harmony is produced.)

### Singing

Invite students to sing "Turn the World Around" **CD 5-32** and to learn all six verses.

Have students sing "So Is Life." When they are comfortable, divide the class into two groups and combine the two songs.

1d Ask students to sing "Do You Know Who I Am?" When they feel confident, divide the class into three groups and have them perform all three songs together with the Stereo Performance Track **CD 5-33.**

### Playing

2f Encourage students to practice each of the percussion ostinatos on p. 116 by clapping them. Practice clapping each rhythm while singing the song.

**continued on page 116**

## Across the Curriculum

▶ **Social Studies** Harry Belafonte loves islands, especially Caribbean islands. He wrote a lyrical tribute to Jamaica in the book *Island in the Sun* (Dial Books for Young Readers, 1999) that students will enjoy.

Harry Belafonte wrote the Foreword of the book *Children Just Like Me* by Barnabas and Anabel Kindersley (Dorling Kindersley, 1995). This book focuses on the lives of children from around the world. Students will enjoy this collection of dreams, beliefs, hopes, fears, and day-to-day activities in the lives of children.

For more about calypso, invite students to read *Caribbean Carnival: Songs of the West Indies* by Irving Burgie (Morrow, 1992). It is a collection of calypso songs by Burgie and others.

## Meeting Individual Needs

▶ **Including Everyone** Give students a choice of melodies when they perform with the recording, but encourage them to try different melodies they may not know as well. Some students with disabilities may "volunteer" to play a rhythm but may not be successful in front of their peers. Increase the success for all eager students by observing how they "silently" perform or move to the rhythms, using patterns that can be transferred to instruments. Create new and "important" rhythms (for example, steady beat) to be performed on highly desirable instruments—drums, for example, for students who may not be successful with more complex rhythms.

When students are confident with each rhythm, divide the class into four groups. Assign each group one of the percussion parts. Layer the rhythms, beginning with the conga, and add one part at a time.

Ask volunteers to perform the rhythms individually on instruments as the rest of the class sings the song.

### Moving

Use movement to reinforce and extend the idea of harmony as students perform two or more melodies together. These movement patterns for the partner songs should be learned separately. Then have students perform them together with the three songs.

Divide the class into three groups and assign a song to each group. Have the students refer to the pictures in the book when necessary.

**"Turn the World Around"**
Formation: Students stand in a small circle with arms at sides.
Measures 1–2: All walk backward, expanding the circle. Arms come out to sides.
Measure 3: All walk quickly forward, drawing the circle inward.
Measure 4: All turn (or spin) in place to complete their own circle.
Return to the starting position to repeat the pattern for all additional verses.

**"So Is Life"**
Formation: Students stand in a line about three feet apart, shoulder to shoulder.
Measure 1: Touch your hands to your chest and look to your right.
Measure 2: Step out to the right and look forward.
Measure 3: Touch your hands to your chest and look to the left.
Measure 4: Step out to the left and look forward.
Repeat this pattern for measures 5–8.
Repeat entire sequence for additional verses.

### Playing Partners

Now that you can sing the partner songs, let's add some instruments. Practice each percussion part by clapping the rhythm. Now **play** an instrument.

**Perform** a different movement for each partner song.

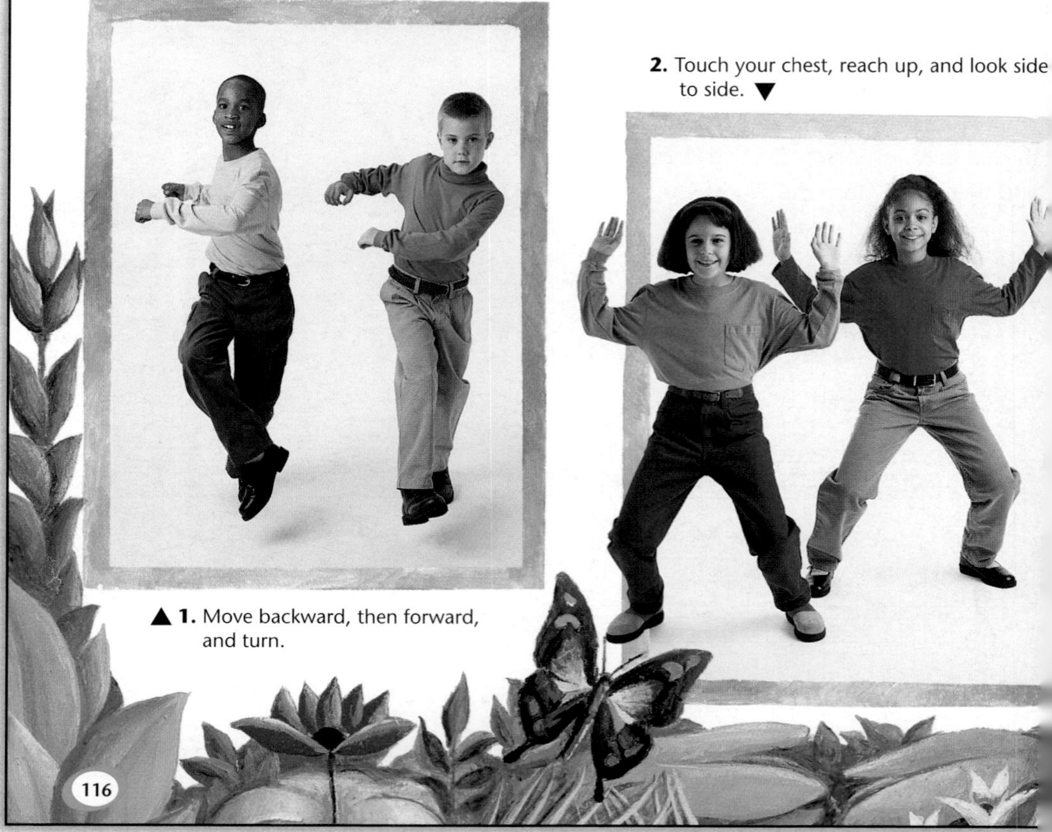

**2.** Touch your chest, reach up, and look side to side. ▼

▲ **1.** Move backward, then forward, and turn.

116

## Footnotes

### Across the Curriculum

▶ **Art** Ask students to create an illustration that shows what the verses mean to them. Combine students' ideas into a class book illustrating the song text meanings. Display the artwork at performances of "Turn the World Around."

### Skills Reinforcement

▶ **Recorder** In addition to the percussion instruments suggested on p. 116, a recorder ostinato can be added to a performance of any or all of the partner songs found in this lesson. Before they play the recorder, have students clap the rhythm.

For an extra challenge, students may try playing the melodies of the three partner songs on recorder as well.

## The Man and His Music

Harry Belafonte is known for his performances of calypso music.

**Listen** to him perform *Jump in the Line*.

CD 5-34

### Jump in the Line

**by Harry Belafonte, Ralph DeLeon, Gabriel Oller, Steve Samuel**

In this selection, Belafonte refers to getting up and dancing.

Harry Belafonte ▼

▲ **3.** Step out, raise your hands, and then step back.



**"Do You Know Who I Am?"**

Formation: Students stand apart in a random spatial pattern.

Measures 1–2: Step out with the left foot, raise your hands up and slide the left foot back next to the right foot.

Measures 3–4: Step out with the right foot, raise your hands up and slide the right foot back next to the left foot.

Repeat this pattern for measures 5–8.

Repeat entire sequence for additional verses.

### Listening

Invite students to listen to Harry Belafonte perform *Jump in the Line* **CD 5-34.** Encourage students to identify those instruments and rhythms in the selection that sound Caribbean. Then invite students to move to the beat of the music.

## 3 Close

**Skill: SINGING** ASSESSMENT

**Performance/Observation** Invite students to sing "Turn the World Around," "So Is Life," and "Do You Know Who I Am?" **CD 5-32** together as partner songs, with approximately one-third of the class singing each song. Have students sing these songs with and without the recording.

Invite students to plan a classroom performance of the song with singers, instrumentalists, and movers. Have them change groups on repeated performances.

Assess the ability of the class to perform independent melodies simultaneously.

### Meeting Individual Needs

▶ **English Language Learners** To ensure that students know the vocabulary in "Turn the World Around," write out *fire, water, mountain, river, sunlight,* and *spirit* on sentence strips. Ask students to hold up the correct sentence strip while singing the words. After singing, ask students to match the sentence strips to illustrations of the terms.

### Character Education

▶ **Social Responsibility** To help students understand how they can help "turn the world around," make a list of problems they see in today's world (for example, the environment, homelessness). Have students brainstorm specific ways they could contribute to lessening one problem in particular. Over the following weeks, have students note the specific ways they have contributed to alleviating this problem and keep a record of class efforts. Question students about how they feel after making these efforts and what they learned.

### Technology/Media Link

**Web Site** Invite students to visit *www.sfsuccessnet.com* for more information on Harry Belafonte.

LESSON 11

## LESSON AT A GLANCE

**Element Focus** **TEXTURE/HARMONY** Echo singing

**Skill Objective** **SINGING** Sing a song in two parts by echo singing

**Connection Activity** **SOCIAL STUDIES** Discuss the role of African American spirituals in the development of American music

**MATERIALS**

- "Over My Head" **CD 5-35**
- **Recording Routine:** Intro (4 m.); v. 1; v. 2; v. 3; interlude (4 m.); v. 4; coda
- **Resource Book** p. H-11
- mallet instruments, recorders, keyboard

**VOCABULARY**

echo singing harmony spiritual

**National Standards**

**1d** Sing part songs
**2b** Perform rhythms and melodies on appropriate instruments
**2d** Play instruments, echoing melodic patterns
**8b** Identify ways music relates to social studies

**MORE MUSIC CHOICES**

Another song with two-part harmony:
"Lullaby and Dance," p. 386
Another African American song:
"Follow the Drinkin' Gourd," p. 266

## 1 INTRODUCE

Share information about spirituals found in Across the Curriculum on p. 119. Discuss with students why spirituals are an important part of America's musical heritage and how these songs have been preserved for us. (oral tradition, church, performing groups, and so on)

LESSON 11 Element: TEXTURE/HARMONY | Skills: SINGING | Connection: SOCIAL STUDIES

# Echo a Sentiment

"Over My Head" is a song strongly tied to the American Civil Rights movement.

**Sing** the song and make an arc in the air with one arm to help hold the long notes for four counts. During the long note held in each phrase, a second group of singers repeats the phrase. This is known as echo singing. Next, **sing** the song with a friend echoing the melody.

CD 5-35
MIDI 8
Over My Head
drm
African American Spiritual
do
F
C7
1. O - ver my head, (O - ver my head,) I hear mu - sic in the air. (I hear mu - sic in the air.) Yes, o - ver my head, (Yes, o - ver my head,) I hear mu - sic in the air. (I hear mu - sic in the air.) O - ver my
2. O - ver my head, (O - ver my head,) I hear sing-ing in the air. (I hear sing-ing in the air.) Yes, o - ver my head, (Yes, o - ver my head,) I hear sing-ing in the air. (I hear sing-ing in the air.) O - ver my

118

# Footnotes

## MOVEMENT

▶ **Creative Movement** Invite students to create echo movements to perform while singing "Over My Head" **CD 5-35.** Divide students into groups of two. Have one person create a movement that will be echoed by the partner at the appropriate time in the music. For a variation on this activity, encourage students to use their bodies to convey a mood or a facial expression such as happiness, sadness, wonder, awe, or anger. At the appropriate time, the partner echoes the sentiment.

## BUILDING SKILLS THROUGH MUSIC

▶ **Social Studies** Ask students to suggest at least two important periods in American history when songs such as "Over My Head" might have been particularly relevant. (civil war and civil rights) Discuss the meaning of the word *civil*.

## SKILLS REINFORCEMENT

▶ **Keyboard** Students can also use keyboards to play a duet version of "Over My Head." Have them use the notation on page 118. Ask the student playing the melody to play in the written octave and the student playing the echo to play one octave lower or higher than written. Students may play right-handed using the thumb on F, index finger on G, and middle finger on A. Refer to Resource Book p. H-11 for a broken-chord accompaniment.

2d

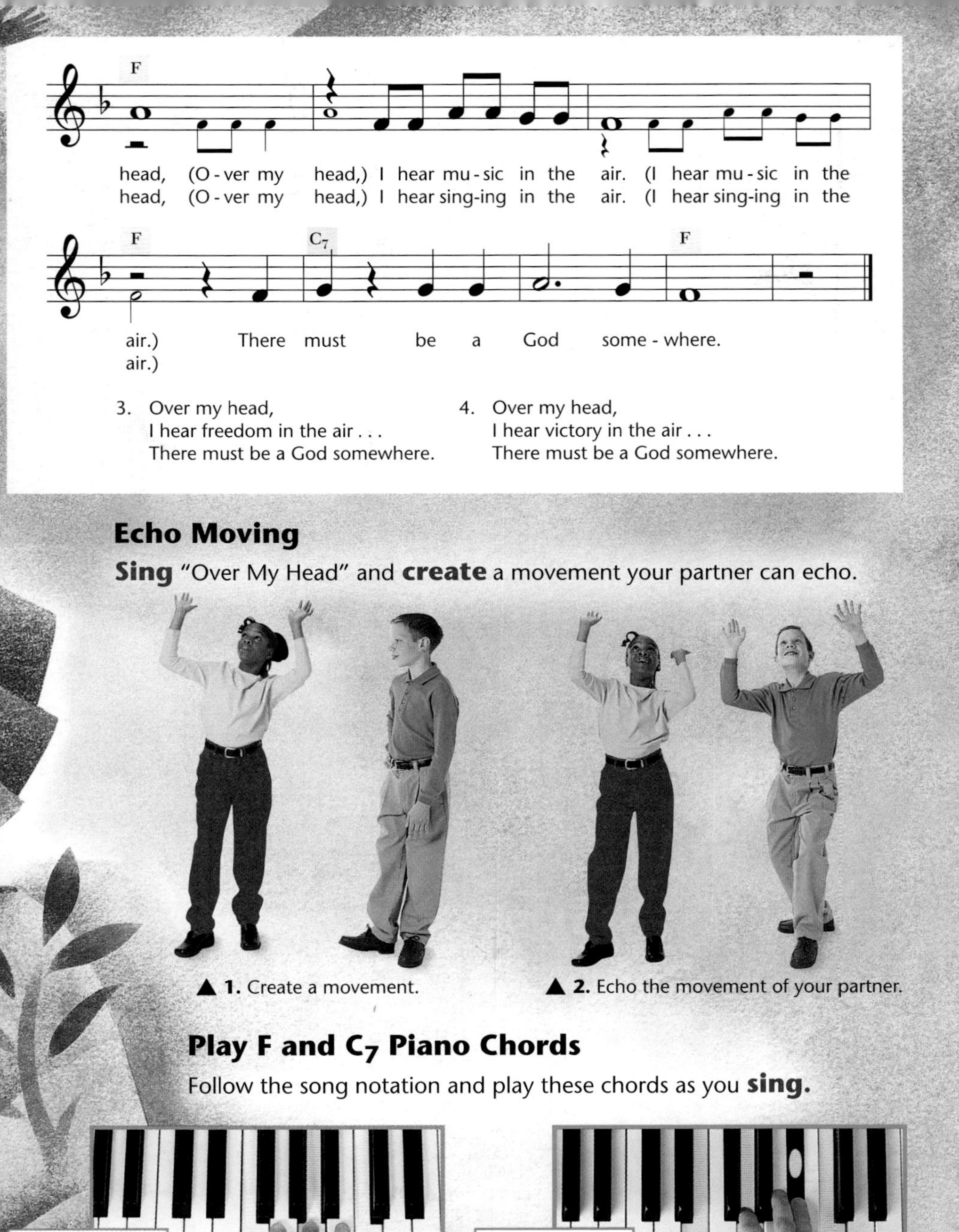
F
head, (O - ver my head,) I hear mu - sic in the air. (I hear mu - sic in the
head, (O - ver my head,) I hear sing-ing in the air. (I hear sing-ing in the
F C7 F
air.) There must be a God some - where.
air.)

3. Over my head,
I hear freedom in the air . . .
There must be a God somewhere.

4. Over my head,
I hear victory in the air . . .
There must be a God somewhere.

**Echo Moving**

**Sing** "Over My Head" and **create** a movement your partner can echo.

▲ **1.** Create a movement.

▲ **2.** Echo the movement of your partner.

**Play F and $C_7$ Piano Chords**

Follow the song notation and play these chords as you **sing.**

F
C7
Unit 3 119

# 2 Develop

### Singing

Sing *do-re-mi* patterns and ask students to echo sing.

Sing "Over My Head" again and encourage students to use a movement gesture to help them hold the whole notes for four counts. Point out that holding the long notes while another part is being sung creates harmony.

1d Divide students into two groups and have them sing both parts of "Over My Head" **CD 5-35.**

### Playing

2b Encourage students to play the melody of "Over My Head" on mallet instruments or recorders.

When students are confident that they can play the song in unison, divide them into two groups and have them play both parts. Then divide them into pairs. Encourage them to practice the song in pairs and perform it for the rest of the class. Challenge the class by dividing it into four groups, with two groups singing and two groups playing "Over My Head."

"Over My Head" is a two-chord song. Invite students to follow the chord symbols in the music and play F and $C_7$ chords on a keyboard instrument as they sing the song.

# 3 Close

**Element: TEXTURE/HARMONY** — **ASSESSMENT**

**Performance/Observation** In small groups, have students echo sing "Over My Head" **CD 5-35.** Ask students to sing the song twice, to give everyone a chance to sing the echo part.

Observe and assess both groups in their ability to echo the melody.

## Across the Curriculum

8b ▶ **Social Studies** Spirituals are a type of religious folk song. Many spirituals talk about "the Promised Land," referring to life in a better place after death. However, for many enslaved African Americans, these songs had double meanings. They talked about going to Heaven, but they were also talking about reaching the North and freedom. More recently, spirituals and freedom songs became associated with the African American Civil Rights Movement.

▶ **Language Arts** Share the book *Civil Rights Marches* by Linda and Charles George (Children's Press, 1999). Invite students to examine the various reasons that explain why people have marched to express their rights. Invite students to write in their journals about something for which they would march.

## Technology/Media Link

**MIDI/Sequencing Software** Have students sing along with the MIDI song file for "Over My Head." Ask volunteers to take turns selecting complementary General MIDI voices for each part of the song.

LESSON Core 12

## LESSON AT A GLANCE

**Element Focus** **TEXTURE/HARMONY** Layers of sound

**Skill Objective** **PLAYING** Perform a speech piece while playing a six-part layered percussion accompaniment

**Connection Activity** **SCIENCE** Discuss the types of materials used to create musical instruments

**MATERIALS**

- "Bundle-Buggy Boogie Woogie" **CD 5-37**
  **Recording Routine:** Intro (4 m.); vocal; interlude (4 m.); vocal; coda
- *Kitchen Stomp* (excerpt) **CD 5-39**
- **Resource Book** pp. J-6, J-7
- nonpitched percussion instruments
- visual of chant words

**VOCABULARY**

unison texture ostinato

**◆ ◆ ◆ ◆ National Standards ◆ ◆ ◆ ◆**

**2b** Perform rhythms on appropriate instruments
**4b** Arrange instrumental pieces within specific guidelines
**5a** Read rhythms in $\frac{4}{4}$ meter
**6e** While listening to music, move to show a prominent feature of the music

**MORE MUSIC CHOICES**

Other speech pieces:
"Can You Canoe?" p. 170
"The Continents," p. 357
"The Planets Chant," p. 377
Other songs in "swing" style:
"Straighten Up and Fly Right," p. 128
"Route 66," p. 276

LESSON 12 Element: TEXTURE/HARMONY Skill: PLAYING Connection: SCIENCE

# MUSIC, MUSIC... EVERYWHERE

Music can be found in almost any place. Think about the sounds you hear at a construction site. The machinery creates sounds. These sounds can have a steady beat, or other rhythm pattern, and even pitch. When layered together, they create a unique texture that has a musical character. Many musicians are fascinated with these types of sounds and use them in their own compositions.

**Listen** to the recording of "Bundle-Buggy Boogie Woogie." Notice the layering of sounds to create texture.

CD 5-37
Bundle-Buggy Boogie Woogie
Poem by Dennis Lee
Arranged by Konnie Saliba
Swing Style
Well way up north on a fine bright day, a
bun - dle bug - gy boo - gied at the break of day. It did the
boo - gie woo - gie here, it did the boo - gie woo - gie there. It did the
bun - dle bug - gy boo - gie woo - gie ev - er - y - where.


120

## Footnotes

### TEACHER TO TEACHER

▶ **Body Percussion** When teaching rhythm patterns to students, explore different levels of body percussion for more interesting sounds. For example, have students identify and interpret symbols and terms referring to dynamics when performing the following clapping activity. Clap with fingers against a flat palm (***mp***), with hands cupped to create a more hollow sound (***f***), or with fingers against the back of the hand (***p***). Try some patterns using finger snaps, patting knees, or stamping.

### BUILDING SKILLS THROUGH MUSIC

▶ **Science** Share with students the information in Across the Curriculum, p. 122. Then, after they have performed their stomp compositions (see Performing, p. 123), ask students to describe the timbre of their chosen "found sounds."

### MOVEMENT

▶ **Creative Movement** Have students create movements that can be performed to "Bundle-Buggy Boogie Woogie" **CD 5-37.** Help students analyze the structure of the song by finding repeated rhyming words.

- *day, day*
- *here, there, everywhere*
- *hop, bop*
- *low, go*

Movements should shake and vibrate but still permit the students to pronounce the words clearly. For each group of rhyming words, have students create a jump that students do on the rhymed word. Help students stay together by practicing landing (not beginning) the jump on the rhymed word.

TEXTURE

SOUNDS

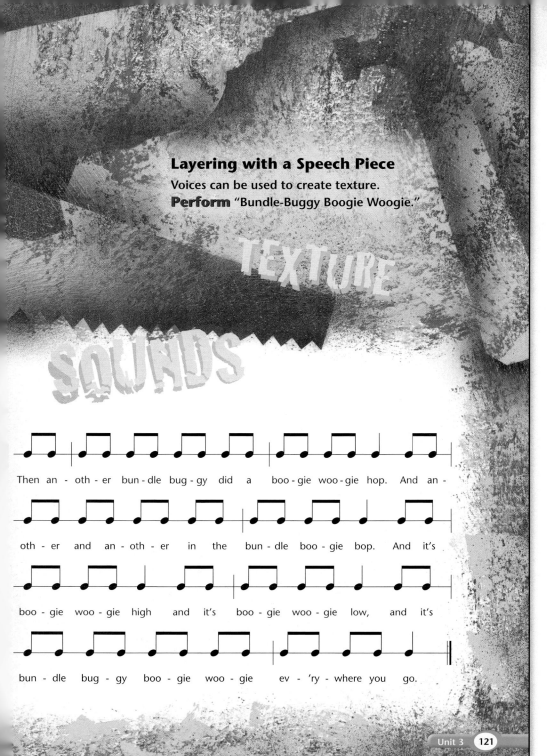

**Layering with a Speech Piece**
Voices can be used to create texture.
**Perform** "Bundle-Buggy Boogie Woogie."

Then an - oth - er bun - dle bug - gy did a boo - gie woo - gie hop. And an -
oth - er and an - oth - er in the bun - dle boo - gie bop. And it's
boo - gie woo - gie high and it's boo - gie woo - gie low, and it's
bun - dle bug - gy boo - gie woo - gie ev - 'ry - where you go.



# 1 Introduce

When performing a speech piece, it is important to emphasize good diction, expressive speech, and varied dynamics. Invite students to listen to "Bundle-Buggy Boogie Woogie" **CD 5-37** and notice the diction and expression used by the performers.

# 2 Develop

### Performing

Have students echo speak "Bundle-Buggy Boogie Woogie" after you, phrase by phrase. Prepare a word visual on the board for students to read.

4b Ask students to choose places in the chant where they would like to add dynamics or a change in voice level. (whisper, high voice, low voice, funny voice, and so on)

Try students' ideas and then choose an arrangement the majority of students likes best.

Have students speak "Bundle-Buggy Boogie Woogie."

6e Add movement by having students sway and snap fingers on beats 2 and 4.

### Moving

For a creative movement activity for "Bundle-Buggy Boogie Woogie," refer to Movement on p. 120.

continued on page 122

## Skills Reinforcement

2b ▶ **Creating** As an extension of the performing activity on p. 123, have students do some research for interesting sound sources at home. For the next class, have students bring in their found sounds to share with the class. Based on what is brought in, invite students to create a layered found-sound piece. Create several ostinatos that students can play. Plan an introduction, body, and *coda*.

## Meeting Individual Needs

▶ **English Language Learners** If some students in your class are not fluent in English, you may wish to ask the class to create visual aids to help all students have success in learning the text of "Bundle-Buggy Boogie Woogie." The visuals could be used while students perform the speech piece; these visuals will provide some information about students' comprehension of the text.

▶ **Review** To review terms learned in Unit 1 through Unit 3, invite students to complete the crossword puzzle on Activity Master 6. See Resource Book p. J-7.

## Playing

Ask students to read and clap each of the rhythms on p. 122.

Divide the class into six groups. Assign one ostinato to each group. Have groups perform each ostinato twice, using body percussion. To help them remember, have students create a special pattern that matches the rhythm. Then practice layering ostinatos using body percussion and whispered speech. Have one group begin, then add another after two measures, and so on.

Transfer each ostinato to nonpitched percussion instruments and invite students to perform ostinatos beginning with one part (unison) and adding ostinatos one by one to create a thicker texture until all parts are playing.

Then have students perform "Bundle-Buggy Boogie Woogie" with the accompaniment. Discuss with students the effect of layering sounds. Explain that each time a new instrument or voice is added to the arrangement, the texture gradually becomes thicker.

## Listening

Invite students to listen to *Kitchen Stomp* **CD 5-39** after they read the Music Makers information about Luke Cresswell and Steve McNicholas.

**ASK What sounds do you hear in the recording?** (pots and pans, rolling trash cans, waitress calling orders, knives chopping)

**How do musicians achieve different textures?** (varying the number of instruments [sound sources], playing at different dynamic levels)

## Moving

Have students create a *Kitchen Stomp* diner scene. Students can improvise different activities that occur in a kitchen or restaurant while listening to *Kitchen Stomp* **CD 5-39.** Refer to Movement on p. 123.

## Playing the Part

**Create** a thicker texture by adding these percussion parts to "Bundle-Buggy Boogie Woogie."

**Listen** for layers of sound and texture in this recording.

CD 5-39
**Kitchen Stomp**

**from *Stomp Out Loud***
**created by Luke Cresswell and Steve McNicholas**

*Stomp Out Loud* uses sounds found on the streets of New York in creative ways.

122

# Footnotes

## ACROSS THE CURRICULUM

▶ **Science** From the earliest times, humans have attempted to produce musical sounds from the materials they have available to them in their environment. The earliest musical instruments were produced from wood, stone, animal bones, and skins. Many musical instruments today are still produced using those same materials. In modern times, musical instruments have been produced with some success from artificial materials such as plastic and rubber. The key to finding a good quality sound source is determined by the temper of the material. It must have the ability to vibrate when struck. For this reason, some materials are more suitable than others.

## SPOTLIGHT ON

▶ **The Poet** Poet Dennis Lee (b. 1939) wrote the poem "Bundle-Buggy Boogie Woogie" as part of his book *Jelly Belly*, published in 1983. Lee was born in Toronto, Canada. He writes poetry for both adults and children. Lee is married, has two grown-up daughters, one son, and one grandson. His children inspired him to begin writing children's poetry. Lee is probably best known for his work as the lyricist for the 1980's Jim Henson TV series *Fraggle Rock*. In his spare time, Lee enjoys crossword puzzles, jazz and blues music, and anything played on the cello.

### Your Turn to Stomp

As the creators of *Stomp* know, sounds can be organized, and music can be made without traditional instruments. Let's create an indoor storm by performing these actions in sequence.

Action 1: Rub your palms together.

Action 2: Snap your fingers.

Action 3: Pat your legs lightly, getting faster.

Action 4: Stand and stamp your feet.

The storm can fade away if you reverse the order and end with rubbing your palms together.

**Create** another kind of composition by layering the sounds of things found in the room. Organize your composition with a beginning, a middle, and an end. Then teach the parts to your "stomp" group.

**Perform** your composition for your class.

MUSIC MAKERS

## LUKE CRESSWELL and STEVE McNICHOLAS

In 1991, **Luke Cresswell and Steve McNicholas** created the percussion dance troupe known as *Stomp.* What is it that makes attending *Stomp* so special for people of any age? It is probably because the performers create their music from everyday items such as brooms, hubcaps, lids, and signs. They even make percussion instruments out of aluminum sinks tied around their shoulders! Both Cresswell and McNicholas believe that anyone can make music with common household items.

**Take It to the Net** For more information about *Stomp,* visit *www.sfsuccessnet.com.*



### Performing

Invite students to create their own stomp composition. Have students create a "storm" with body percussion. Refer to the activity on p. 123. Encourage students to find other sound sources around the room to add to the composition. Remind students that some materials are better than others for producing musical sounds. Refer to Across the Curriculum on p. 122 for more details.

For an additional creating activity, see Activity Master 5 on Resource Book p. J-6.

## 3 CLOSE

**Skill: PLAYING** ASSESSMENT

**Performance/Observation** Invite students to perform "Bundle-Buggy Boogie Woogie" **CD 5-37** with selected students playing the percussion ostinatos on p. 122.

Observe and assess each student's ability to independently play a percussion part in the layered accompaniment.

## MOVEMENT

▶ **Creative Movement** Invite students to create a dancing diner scene. Have them listen to *Kitchen Stomp* **CD 5-39** and create a section movement map on the board. Here are some suggested movements. Have students

- Carry a book or a cafeteria tray like a waiter and travel around the room. Have them switch the tray from hand to hand, spin, and move it over and under the legs.
- Mimic the waitress saying "ordering" on the track. Create various ways a waiter or waitress may place an order at the kitchen counter in a restaurant.
- Use the top of their desk like a kitchen counter working surface. Have them chop with one hand, flip pancakes, toss a pizza, and shake spices.

## TECHNOLOGY/MEDIA LINK

**Sequencing Software** Use a digital audio recording program to record students performing "Bundle-Buggy Boogie Woogie." Post recordings on the school Web site.

Instead of recording all parts on one track, record each entrance of the canon on a separate track, as follows. Conduct the steady beat as group one records a track. Select another track, start recording, conduct the steady beat, and cue the second group to start at the proper time. Continue until all groups are recorded, and then play the entire canon for the class.

## UNIT 3 Review and Assessment

## WHAT DO YOU KNOW?

**MATERIALS**
- "Weevily Wheat," p. 105 **CD 5-17**
- **Resource Book** p. B-10

Have students read and answer the questions independently and then check their answers with a partner before sharing answers with the rest of the class or with you.

For a more formal assessment, you may wish to duplicate the Unit 3 assessment worksheet and have students work independently or in small groups to complete it. The worksheet is found on Resource Book p. B-10.

## WHAT DO YOU HEAR?

**MATERIALS**
- *What Do You Hear? 3* **CD 5-40**
- **Resource Book** p. B-10

Invite students to listen to string instruments in the Sound Bank on pp. 466–471. Have them identify the instruments by sound alone.

Have students listen to What Do You Hear? 3 and answer the questions independently or in small groups. For a more independent assessment, you may wish to duplicate the Unit 3 assessment worksheet found on Resource Book p. B-10.

UNIT 3

# Review, Assess,

## What Do You Know?

1. Look at the notation for "Weevily Wheat," on page 105, and answer these questions.
   - **a.** Where is *do* located in the music?
   - **b.** What are the letter names for *do, re, mi, so,* and *la* in this song?
   - **c.** Point to all the notes that are named *so*ˌ and *la*ˌ. How many did you identify?
2. Perform these examples using rhythm syllables and patting.

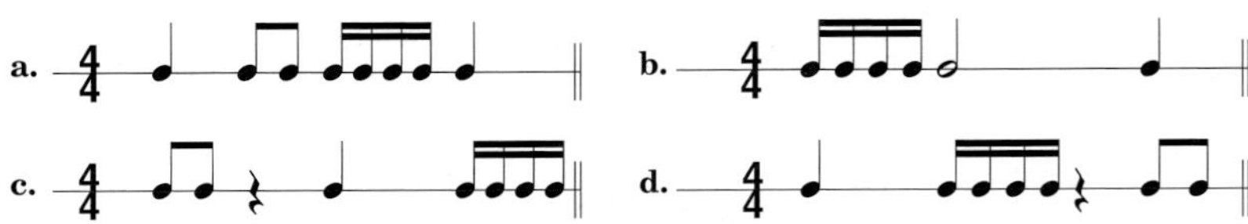


## What Do You Hear? 3

CD 5-40

Identify which string instrument is being played in each example.

| | |
|---|---|
| **1.** *koto* | cello |
| **2.** violin | banjo |
| **3.** viola | *sitar* |

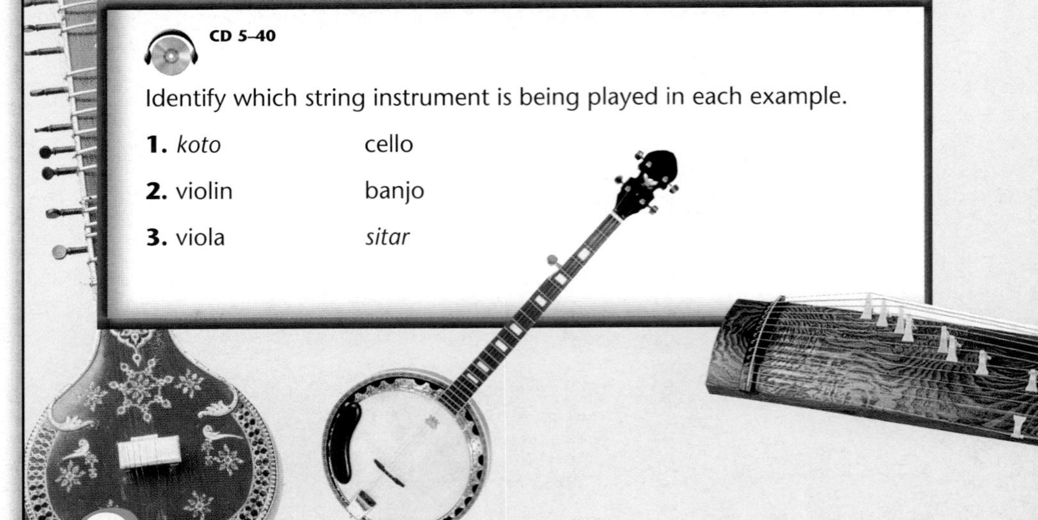



# Footnotes

## ANSWER KEY

### ▶ What Do You Know?

**1.** **a.** *do* = G
**b.** *do* = G, *re* = A, *mi* = B, *so* = D, *la* = E
**c.** *so*ˌ = 8, *la*ˌ = 7

**2.** **1.** *ta ti-ti ti-ri-ti-ri ta*
**2.** *ti-ri-ti-ri ta-a ta*
**3.** *ti-ti [rest] ta ti-ri-ti-ri*
**4.** *ta ti-ri-ti-ri [rest] ti-ti*

### ▶ What Do You Hear?

**1.** *koto*

**2.** violin

**3.** *sitar*

# Perform, Create

## What You Can Do

### Read Melody

Read the notation for "See the Children Playin'," on page 107, and identify whether the song is *do-* or *la*-pentatonic. Sing the song using pitch syllables and hand signs. Sing the song again using the words.

### Play Rhythms

Sing *"Ōsamu kosamu,"* on page 96. Perform the ostinato accompaniment on page 97 by patting the rhythms on your thighs. Then sing the song and play the accompaniment on the percussion instruments.

### Find Sounds

Perform the speech piece "Bundle-Buggy Boogie Woogie," on page 120. Practice the rhythm ostinatos on page 122 and then perform them with the speech piece. Look around your classroom and home for materials that produce musical sounds when struck by a mallet. Create other ostinatos in $\frac{4}{4}$ time and play them using those sounds. Be sure to use the ♬♬ pattern. Perform these patterns with "Bundle-Buggy Boogie Woogie."

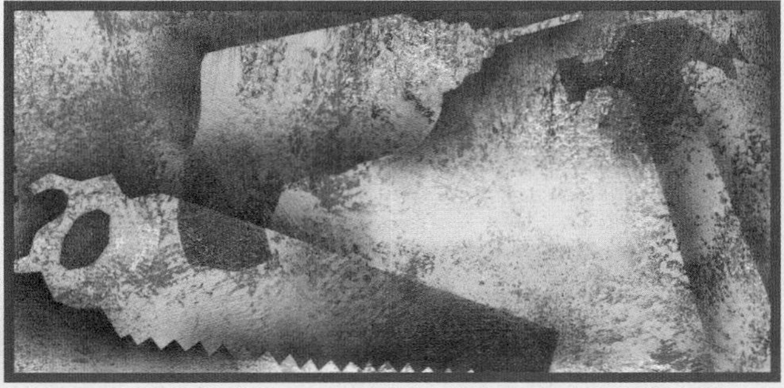



## WHAT YOU CAN DO

**MATERIALS**
- "See the Children Playin'," p. 107 — **CD 5-22**
- *"Ōsamu kosamu,"* p. 96 — **CD 5-2**
- "Bundle-Buggy Boogie Woogie," p. 120 — **CD 5-37**
- **Resource Book** p. B-11

### Read Melody

Have students look at the melody of "See the Children Playin'." Have them identify *do* and determine whether the song is *do* or *la*-pentatonic by looking at the melody. Then invite them to sing the song using pitch syllables and then the words.

### Play Rhythms

Invite students to listen to *"Ōsamu kosamu."* Ask students to choose a line and create movement that shows the rhythm of the melody.

Invite students to play the ostinato accompaniment on p. 97 as the rest of the class sings the song. Rotate players and singers several times.

### Find Sounds

Invite students to perform the speech piece "Bundle-Buggy Boogie Woogie." Assign students to each of the percussion groups on p. 122. Ask students to play "Bundle-Buggy Boogie Woogie" by tapping the rhythm and performing the ostinato parts. Have students find sounds from everyday objects and create additional ostinatos to perform with the speech piece.

### TECHNOLOGY/MEDIA LINK

**Rubrics** Visit *www.sfsuccessnet.com* for rubrics to assess students' achievement in music skills.

| Lesson | Elements | Skills | |
|---|---|---|---|
|  LESSON 1 CORE **A Dynamic Song** pp. 130–133  | **Element: Expression**<br>**Concept:** Dynamics<br>**Focus:** Dynamics<br><br>**Secondary Element**<br>Texture/Harmony: I-IV-$V_7$ chords<br><br>**National Standards**<br>1b 2b 2f 4a 4b 6e | **Skill: Moving**<br>**Objective:** Respond through movement to the dynamics in a song<br><br>**Secondary Skills**<br>• **Performing** Create a dynamics chart<br>• **Creating** Write a poem and speak it with dynamics<br>• **Playing** Play a rhythm accompaniment; add a two-chord accompaniment<br>• **Reading** Interpret graphic notation<br>• **Creating** Create a vocal sound piece | **SKILLS REINFORCEMENT**<br>• **Recorder** Play a countermelody<br>• **Signing** Sign the words to a song<br>• **Singing** Compare lullabies from diverse cultures |
| LESSON 2 **Feeling Upbeat** pp. 134–135  Reading Sequence 13, p. 448 | **Element: Rhythm**<br>**Concept:** Beat<br>**Focus:** Upbeats<br><br>**Secondary Element**<br>Timbre: percussion<br><br>**National Standards**<br>2b 2f 4b 6c | **Skill: Playing**<br>**Objective:** Play rhythm ostinatos with upbeats to accompany a song<br><br>**Secondary Skills**<br>• **Singing** Sing and perform a movement pattern<br>• **Reading** Read patterns with upbeats | **SKILLS REINFORCEMENT**<br>• **Creating** Create and perform ostinatos |
| LESSON 3 CORE **Discover a New Rhythm** pp. 136–137  | **Element: Rhythm**<br>**Concept:** Pattern<br>**Focus:** ♩, ♪♩♪, and ♪♪♬<br><br>**Secondary Element**<br>Timbre: string instruments<br><br>**National Standards**<br>2b 5a 6d | **Skill: Singing**<br>**Objective:** Sing a song from notation that includes ♩, ♪♩♪, and ♪♪♬<br><br>**Secondary Skills**<br>• **Reading** Read ♪♪♬ rhythm patterns<br>• **Playing** Perform ostinatos on nonpitched instruments | **SKILLS REINFORCEMENT**<br>• **Keyboard** Play a chordal accompaniment<br>• **Reading** Reinforce notation abilities |

## Connections

## Music and Other Literature

### Connection: Related Arts
**Activity:** Explore South African culture though art

**ACROSS THE CURRICULUM**
**Drama/Arts** Create masks and perform a drama
**Social Studies/Language Arts** Read the book Shaka, King of the Zulus

**MOVEMENT** **Patterned Dance** Learn movement patterns to a song

**CULTURAL CONNECTION**
**Lions in Art** Discuss the lion's image in art
**African Lullabies** Discuss performance practices

**MEETING INDIVIDUAL NEEDS** **Including Everyone** Suggestions for modifying playing patterns

**CHARACTER EDUCATION** **Respect and Courtesy** Discuss the importance of encouraging other people's ideas

**BUILDING SKILLS THROUGH MUSIC** **Writing** Ask students whether they will sing a lullaby loudly or softly

**Songs**
"The Lion Sleeps Tonight"
*"T'hola, t'hola"* ("Softly, Softly")

**Listening Selection** *The Lion Sleeps Tonight*

**M·U·S·I·C M·A·K·E·R·S**
Lebo M.

**More Music Choices**
*"Tina Singu,"* p. 300
"Singin' in the Rain," p. 360
"Circle 'Round the Moon," p. 403

**ASSESSMENT**
**Performance/Observation**
Sing "The Lion Sleeps Tonight" with dynamic contrast

**TECHNOLOGY/MEDIA LINK**
**CD-ROM** Use *Alfred's Essentials of Music Theory* to explore dynamics

### Connection: Social Studies
**Activity:** Discuss the people, foliage, and fauna of Kenya

**ACROSS THE CURRICULUM** **Social Studies/Science** Read books about Africa and create a collage

**MOVEMENT**
**Patterned Dance** Movements based on African dances
**Game Song** Learn a follow-the-leader dance game

**BUILDING SKILLS THROUGH MUSIC** **Language** Discuss possible messsages of song lyrics

**Song** *"Ochimbo"*

**Listening Selection** *Jin-go-lo-ba*

**More Music Choices**
"My Bonnie Lies Over the Ocean," p. 338

**ASSESSMENT**
**Performance/Observation**
Play rhythm ostinatos that contain upbeats as an accompaniment for *"Ochimbo"*

**TECHNOLOGY/MEDIA LINK**
**Web Site** Learn about African drumming and music ensembles

### Connection: Culture
**Activity:** Discover Middle Eastern musical instruments presentation

**CULTURAL CONNECTION** **Instruments of the Middle East** Discuss instruments of the area

**MEETING INDIVIDUAL NEEDS** **Developing Interest** Developing interest in Middle Eastern instruments

**CHARACTER EDUCATION** **Respect for Differences** Encourage respect for different cultures, people, and music

**BUILDING SKILLS THROUGH MUSIC** **Math** Count the number of measures in the notation of a song and calculate the number of rhythm patterns

**Song** *"Ala Da'lona"* (Arabic and English)

**More Music Choices**
"The Continents," (speech piece) p. 357
*"Sambalele,"* p. 397

**ASSESSMENT**
**Performance/Observation**
Sing a song, using rhythm syllables, that contains the  pattern

**TECHNOLOGY/MEDIA LINK**
**Video Library** Watch a Turkish line dance

| Lesson | Elements | Skills | |
|---|---|---|---|
|  LESSON 4 **Finding New Rhythm Patterns** pp. 138–139  Reading Sequence 14, p. 448 | **Element: Rhythm**<br>**Concept:** Pattern<br>**Focus:**<br><br>**Secondary Element**<br>Melody: *la* and *do*<br><br>**National Standards**<br>5a 5d 6b 6e | **Skill: Reading**<br>**Objective:** Read rhythm patterns with in $\frac{2}{4}$ time<br><br>**Secondary Skills**<br>• **Performing** Echo clap patterns<br>• **Listening** Tap the steady beat or conduct in duple meter | **SKILLS REINFORCEMENT**<br>• **Creating** Create rhythm patterns to accompany a song<br>• **Reading** Practice notating rhythms |
| LESSON 5 CORE **Finding the Form** pp. 140–143  | **Element: Form**<br>**Concept:** Form<br>**Focus:** AABA sectional form<br><br>**Secondary Element**<br>Melody: steps, leaps, and repeats<br><br>**National Standards**<br>1b 4a 6a 6b 6c 6e 7b | **Skill: Moving**<br>**Objective:** Perform contrasting movements to show contrasting song sections<br><br>**Secondary Skills**<br>• **Listening** Discuss the vocal style on a recording<br>• **Singing** Sing and analyze the form of the song<br>• **Listening** Compare two versions of a song<br>• **Creating** Create an accompaniment for a poem | **SKILLS REINFORCEMENT**<br>• **Recorder** Play a counter melody<br>• **Singing** Develop legato singing style |
| LESSON 6 **In Search of a New Note** pp. 144–147 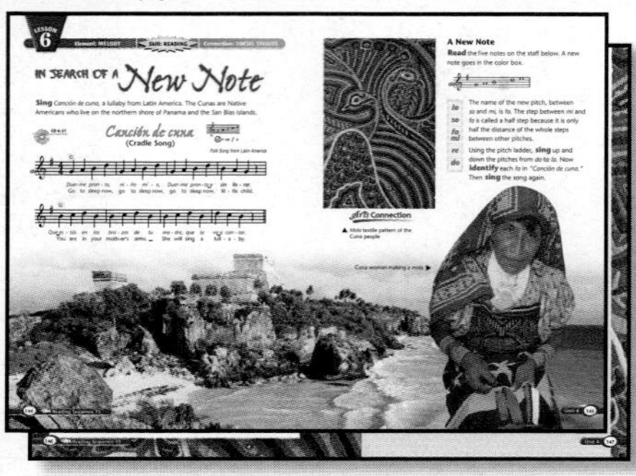 Reading Sequence 15, p. 449 | **Element: Melody**<br>**Concept:** Pattern<br>**Focus:** *Do, re, mi, fa, so* and *la*<br><br>**Secondary Element**<br>Rhythm: $\frac{3}{4}$ time<br><br>**National Standards**<br>1a 2b 5b 5d 6c | **Skill: Reading**<br>**Objective:** Sing a song from notation that includes *do, re, mi, fa, so* and *la*<br><br>**Secondary Skills**<br>• **Singing** Introduce, sing, and discuss *fa* (C)<br>• **Listening** Listen to instrumentation | **SKILLS REINFORCEMENT**<br>• **Reading** Read six-note scales<br>• **Singing** Practice singing Spanish songs<br>• **Mallets** Play an Orff instrument accompaniment<br>• **Vocal Development** Work on correcting intonation |

## Connections

## Music and Other Literature



**Connection: Social Studies**
**Activity:** Discuss the importance of the Cumberland Gap during the Westward Expansion movement

SPOTLIGHT ON **Cumberland Gap** Historical significance of the natural pass

MOVEMENT
**Creative Movement** Create movements to match the rhythms of a song
**Patterned Dance** Follow dance directions to a song

BUILDING SKILLS THROUGH MUSIC **Science** Research geological formations in your region of the country

**Song** "Cumberland Gap"
**Arts Connection** *Daniel Boone Escorting Pioneers*

**More Music Choices**
"My Bonnie Lies Over the Ocean," p. 338
"Clementine," p. 341

ASSESSMENT
**Performance/Observation** Read and clap the rhythm of "Cumberland Gap"
**Show What You Know!** Mid-unit assessment

TECHNOLOGY/MEDIA LINK
**MIDI/Sequencing Software** Isolate tracks and answer questions about the accompaniment

---

**Connection: Language Arts**
**Activity:** Dramatize a poem related to rainbows

ACROSS THE CURRICULUM
**Fine Arts/Science** Read a book about pointillist painter Georges Seurat and learn about the artist's use of color
**Language Arts** Read a collection of poems about rainbows

SPOTLIGHT ON
**"Over the Rainbow"** The composer discusses his inspiration for the song
**Rainbows** Information about how they occur

MEETING INDIVIDUAL NEEDS **Including Everyone** Techniques for helping students to track lines of music

MOVEMENT **Creative Movement/Locomotor Movement** Students move to describe phrases in songs

SCHOOL TO HOME CONNECTION **Collecting Memories** Interview older friends and relatives about "The Wizard of Oz" and "Over the Rainbow"

BUILDING SKILLS THROUGH MUSIC **Language** Compare artists Judy Garland and Patti LaBelle using a Venn diagram

- 

**Song** "Over the Rainbow"

**Listening Selections**
*Over the Rainbow* (Judy Garland)
*Over the Rainbow* (Patti LaBelle)

**Poem** "Prism in the Window"

**M*U*S*I*C M*A*K*E*R*S**
Judy Garland
Patti LaBelle

**More Music Choices**
"Singin' in the Rain," p. 360
"Little Shop of Horrors," p. 422
"Ode to Joy," p. 152

ASSESSMENT
**Performance/Observation** Sing "Over the Rainbow" and perform contrasting movements for A and B sections of the song

TECHNOLOGY/MEDIA LINK
**Video Library** Compare different singing styles

---

**Connection: Social Studies**
**Activity:** Discuss the life and culture of the Cuna people

ACROSS THE CURRICULUM
**Social Studies/Art** Read a book about the Cuna people and their art
**Language Arts/Related Arts** Read books about folktales and create dramatizations

CULTURAL CONNECTION **The Cuna People** Information about the culture of the Cuna people

TEACHER TO TEACHER **Notation Preparation** Suggested sequence for preparing students to write music

MEETING INDIVIDUAL NEEDS **English Language Learners** To check for comprehension, have students illustrate lyrics

BUILDING SKILLS THROUGH MUSIC **Math** Find ways geometric shapes found in artwork are also present in music notation

**Songs**
"*Canción de cuna*" ("Cradle Song")
"*Cantando mentiras*" ("Singing Tall Tales")
**Arts Connection** Mola textile pattern

**More Music Choices**
"Oh, How Lovely Is the Evening," p. 217
"*Cielito lindo,*" p. 270
"*Bogando a la luz del sol,*" p. 306
"*Al quebrar la piñata,*" p. 432

ASSESSMENT
**Performance/Observation** Sing and read a song from notation that contains the new note *fa*

TECHNOLOGY/MEDIA LINK
**CD-ROM** Create and experiment with the *Band-in-a-Box*

| Lesson | Elements | Skills |
|---|---|---|

### Lesson 7 Moving to a New Note

pp. 148–149

Reading Sequence 16, p. 449

**Element:** Melody
**Concept:** Pattern
**Focus:** *Do, re, mi, fa, so* and *la*

**Secondary Element**
Texture/Harmony: rounds

**National Standards**
1d 2f 4b 5b 5d

**Skill:** Singing
**Objective:** Sing and read *do, re, mi, fa, so* and *la* in a new key

**Secondary Skills**
- **Reading** Locate *fa* and sing it in notation
- **Creating** Create and sing melodic patterns
- **Reading** Perform melodies with hand signs

**SKILLS REINFORCEMENT**
- **Recorder** Play a two-note ostinato

### Lesson 8 CORE United by Melody

pp. 150–153

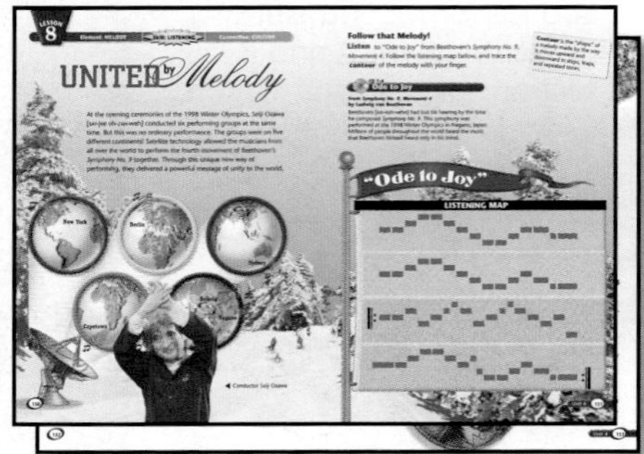


**Element:** Melody
**Concept:** Pitch and direction
**Focus:** Melodic contour

**Secondary Element**
Form: aaba

**National Standards**
1c 2b 6b 6e 9c 9d

**Skill:** Listening
**Objective:** Perform hand movements to show melodic contour

**Secondary Skills**
- **Singing** Learn to sing a song in German
- **Playing** Play the melody on bells or recorder
- **Analyzing/Describing** Research and write about Beethoven

**SKILLS REINFORCEMENT**
- **Keyboard** Play the melody
- **Recorder** Play a harmony

### Lesson 9 CORE Percussion on Parade

pp. 154–157

**Element:** Timbre
**Concept:** Instrumental
**Focus:** Percussion timbre

**Secondary Element**
Rhythm: 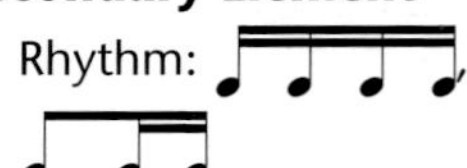 

**National Standards**
2b 2f 4b 6b 6c 6d

**Skill:** Playing
**Objective:** Play a percussion ensemble piece

**Secondary Skills**
- **Listening** Play a percussion identification game
- **Listening** Compare and contrast listening selections
- **Describing** Describe percussion instruments

**SKILLS REINFORCEMENT**
- **Read** Read percussion parts to "Wu long"
- **Playing/Creating** Create body percussion parts

| Connections | Music and Other Literature | |
|---|---|---|
| **Connection: Culture**<br>**Activity:** Discuss advertising, past and present<br>CULTURAL CONNECTION **Advertising** Information about advertising and current trends<br>MEETING INDIVIDUAL NEEDS **Hearing the Diatonic Scale** Exercises for teaching students to hear the diatonic scale<br>BUILDING SKILLS THROUGH MUSIC **Social Studies** Develop a Public Service Announcement on why music is important in the world | **Song** "Chairs to Mend"<br><br>**More Music Choices**<br>"This Pretty Planet," p. 355<br>"For the Beauty of the Earth," p. 356 | ASSESSMENT<br>**Performance/Observation** Sing and read a song that contains the new note fa in a new key<br>**Show What You Know!** Mid-unit assessment<br><br>TECHNOLOGY/MEDIA LINK<br>**MIDI/Sequencing Software** Use the MIDI file to teach round singing |
| **Connection: Culture**<br>**Activity:** Discuss the role of music in special events<br>CULTURAL CONNECTION<br>**1998 Winter Olympics** Information about the satellite-linked performance<br>**A Piece for Many Occasions** Information about "Ode to Joy"<br>SPOTLIGHT ON<br>**Beethoven's Ninth** Information about Beethoven's *Symphony No. 9*<br>**The Conductor** Biographical information about Seiji Ozawa<br>TEACHER TO TEACHER **Instrument Tips** Code words for managing student behaviors<br>MEETING INDIVIDUAL NEEDS **Body/Kinesthetic** Create movements to correspond to phrases<br>BUILDING SKILLS THROUGH MUSIC **Writing** Write a brief paragraph about people around the world singing about joy | **Song** "Ode to Joy" (German and English)<br><br>**Listening Selection** *Symphony No.9*, Movement 4 ("Ode to Joy") (excerpt)<br><br>**M*U*S*I*C M*A*K*E*R*S**<br>Ludwig van Beethoven<br><br>**Listening Map** *"Ode to Joy"*<br><br>**More Music Choices**<br>"Sailing Down My Golden River," p. 332<br>"For the Beauty of the Earth," p. 356<br>"Love Can Build a Bridge," p. 324<br>"*Somos el barco*," p. 352 | ASSESSMENT<br>**Performance/Observation** Listen to a selection and show the melodic contour through hand movements<br><br>TECHNOLOGY/MEDIA LINK<br>**Electronic Keyboard** Play the melody on various keyboard sounds<br>**Transparency** Follow melodic contour on a listening map |
| **Connection: Culture**<br>**Activity:** Discuss similarities and differences between percussion instruments of various cultures<br>ACROSS THE CURRICULUM<br>**Science** Share information about the construction of percussion instruments<br>**Social Studies/Literature** Read books about the Chinese New Year and create a mini-drama<br>CULTURAL CONNECTION ***Luogo* Ensemble** An additional resource for more Chinese music literature<br>SPOTLIGHT ON **The Composer** Biographical information on Carlos Chávez<br>TEACHER TO TEACHER **Focus Help** Focus student attention during movement activities<br>MEETING INDIVIDUAL NEEDS **Including Everyone** Match instrumental parts with students' abilities<br>BUILDING SKILLS THROUGH MUSIC **Language** Share details from this lesson with a partner as he or she consults the book for accuracy | **Listening Selections**<br>*Toccata for Percussion*, Movement 3<br>*Wu long (Dragon Dance)*<br>*Lian xi qu (étude)*<br><br>**More Music Choices**<br>*Mars, the Bringer of War*, p. 377<br>*Rag puria kalyan*, p. 192<br>*The Stars and Stripes Forever*, p. 159<br>"*Feng yang hua gu*," p. 313<br>"*Niu lang zhi-nü*," p. 335 | ASSESSMENT<br>**Performance/Observation** Play a Chinese percussion piece with appropriate instruments<br><br>TECHNOLOGY/MEDIA LINK<br>**Sequencing Software** Create percussion ensemble pieces using MIDI sounds |

| Lesson | Elements | Skills |
|---|---|---|

## LESSON 10

**America in Two Parts – Melody and Countermelody**
pp. 158–159

**Element: Texture/Harmony**
**Concept:** Texture
**Focus:** Countermelody

**Secondary Element**
Melody: steps, leaps, and repeats

**National Standards**
1d 1e 6b 6e 8b

**Skill: Singing**
**Objective:** Sing a song with a countermelody

**Secondary Skills**
- **Listening** Listen for the rhythm of phrases in a song
- **Listening** Listen for countermelodies

**SKILLS REINFORCEMENT**
- **Singing** Develop strategies for singing countermelodies

## LESSON 11

CORE
**One Song, Different Textures**
pp. 160–161

**Element: Texture/Harmony**
**Concept:** Texture
**Focus:** Countermelody

**Secondary Element**
Rhythm: $\frac{3}{4}$ time

**National Standards**
1b 1d 4b 6b 8b

**Skill: Singing**
**Objective:** Sing a song with a countermelody

**Secondary Skills**
- **Listening** Listen to a recording and describe the texture

**SKILLS REINFORCEMENT**
- **Arranging** Create arrangements of a song

## LESSON 12

**Harmony Tones**
pp. 162–163

**Element: Texture/Harmony**
**Concept:** Harmony
**Focus:** I and $V_7$ chords

**Secondary Element**
Form: ABC

**National Standards**
1e 2b 2f 6b 6e

**Skill: Playing**
**Objective:** Play I and $V_7$ chords during the A section of a song

**Secondary Skills**
- **Analyzing/Describing** Describe the timbre of an accompaniment
- **Singing** Sing the melody and discuss its contour

**SKILLS REINFORCEMENT**
- **Guitar** Use a capo, and play I and $V_7$ chords
- **Listening** Do a listening activity in Resource Book

| Connections | Music and Other Literature | |
|---|---|---|
| **Connection: Social Studies**<br>**Activity:** Discuss the history and meaning of a patriotic song<br>**Across the Curriculum** **Language Arts** Write additional verses for a song<br>**Social Studies** Use a map to determine areas referenced in lyrics<br>**Spotlight On** **The National Anthem** Background information on the national anthem<br>**School to Home Connection** **American Visuals** Share family photos and magazine clippings of natural settings and scenes depicting modern life in cities and towns<br>**Building Skills Through Music** **Language** Identify lyrics that are plural or possessive | **Song** "America, the Beautiful"<br>**Listening Selection** *The Stars and Stripes Forever*<br>**More Music Choices**<br>"The Star-Spangled Banner," p. 441 | **Assessment**<br>**Performance/Observation** Sing "America, the Beautiful" with a countermelody<br>**Technology/Media Link**<br>**Web Site** Visit *www.sfsuccessnet.com* to learn more about John Philip Sousa |
| **Connection: Social Studies**<br>**Activity:** Discuss the impact of a song on a culture<br>**Across the Curriculum** **Social Studies** Information about the nineteenth century religious revival and the music<br>**Teacher to Teacher** **Sustaining Phrases** Sustaining long notes and phrases<br>**Building Skills Through Music** **Social Studies** Discuss "Amazing Grace" and the life of John Newton | **Song** "Amazing Grace"<br>**Listening Selection** *Amazing Grace*<br>**More Music Choices**<br>"The Wheel of the Water," p. 362<br>"Cycle Song of Life," p. 370 | **Assessment**<br>**Performance/Observation** Sing "Amazing Grace" with a countermelody<br>**Technology/Media Link**<br>**Sequencing Software** Experiment with melodies and countermelodies |
| **Connection: Culture**<br>**Activity:** Discuss the characteristics of gospel singing<br>**Spotlight On** **Gospel Singing** The history of gospel singing and current practices<br>**Teacher to Teacher** **Chord Roots** Teaching students to hear and sing the roots of chords<br>**Building Skills Through Music** **Science** Investigate characteristics and composition of bone | **Song** "Dry Bones"<br>**More Music Choices**<br>"Wade in the Water," p. 268<br>"Little David, Play on Your Harp," p. 394 | **Assessment**<br>**Performance/Observation** Sing "Dry Bones and perform chord changes (I and $V_7$) on melody classroom instruments at the appropriate time in the music<br>**Technology/Media Link**<br>**Web Site** Go to *www.sfsuccessnet.com* to learn more about spirituals and gospel music |

# Introducing the Unit

Unit 4 presents the next step in a sequenced approach to understanding music elements. Presented on p. 127 is a brief overview of the skills that are assessed in this unit. (See below and pp. 128–129 for unit highlights of related curricular experiences.)

For a more detailed unit overview, see Unit at a Glance, pp. 125a–125h.

# Unit Project

To begin the students' exploration of Unit 4, tell them that many styles of music are represented in this unit. Ask them to look through the unit to find examples of the following and then write down each page number on a piece of paper.

- A folk song
- A song from a movie
- A street call
- An excerpt from a symphony
- An African American spiritual
- A song with a countermelody

Invite volunteers to identify each musical example. Ask if anyone has identified additional examples.

Have students bring to class three different recorded examples of music in different styles. The music can be vocal or instrumental. The recordings may come from their own collections or from a school or public library. Students should present these examples to the class, along with a list of musical skills that they think are necessary for a successful performance.

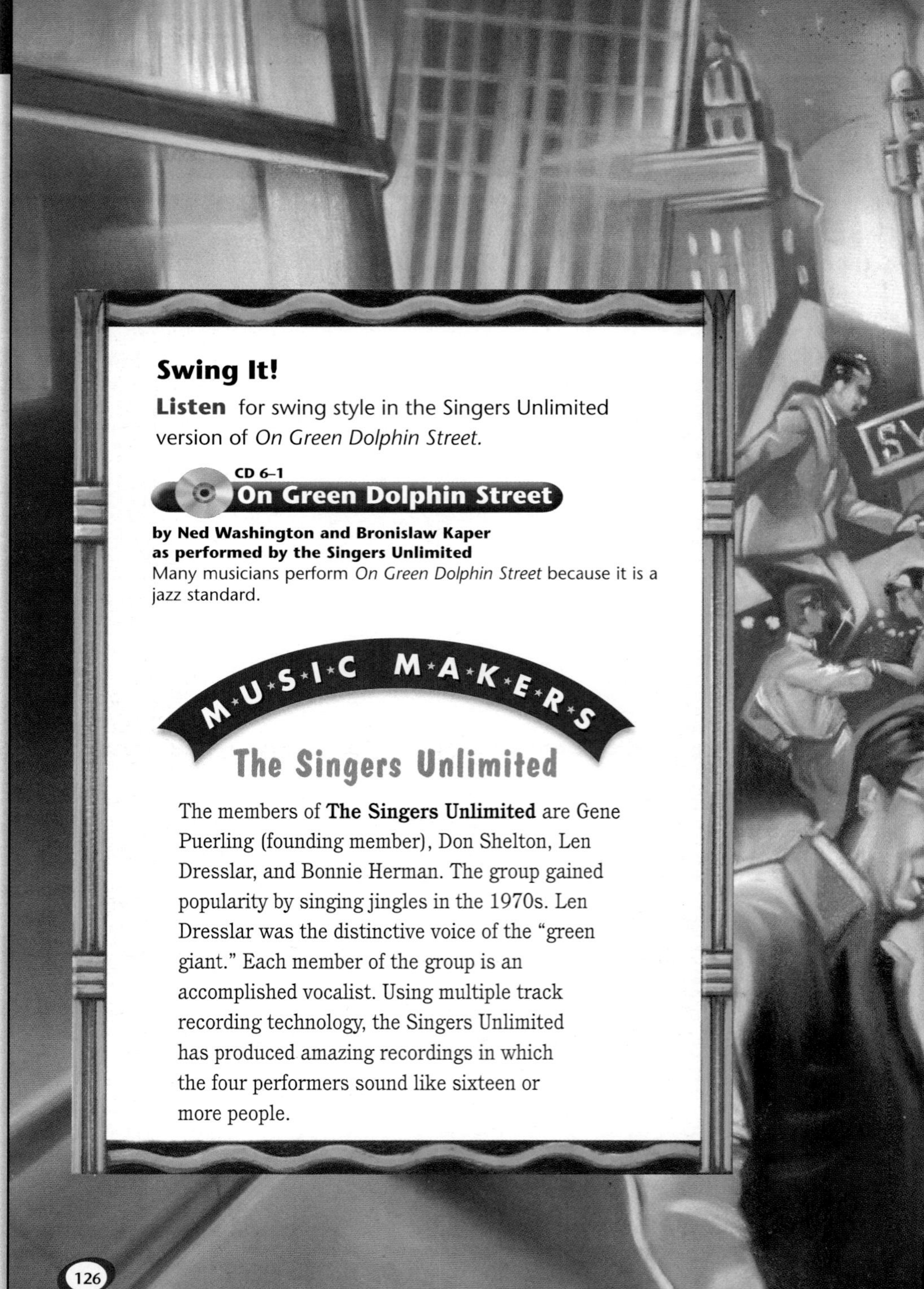

**Swing It!**

**Listen** for swing style in the Singers Unlimited version of *On Green Dolphin Street.*

CD 6–1

**On Green Dolphin Street**

**by Ned Washington and Bronislaw Kaper as performed by the Singers Unlimited**

Many musicians perform *On Green Dolphin Street* because it is a jazz standard.

MUSIC MAKERS

**The Singers Unlimited**

The members of **The Singers Unlimited** are Gene Puerling (founding member), Don Shelton, Len Dresslar, and Bonnie Herman. The group gained popularity by singing jingles in the 1970s. Len Dresslar was the distinctive voice of the "green giant." Each member of the group is an accomplished vocalist. Using multiple track recording technology, the Singers Unlimited has produced amazing recordings in which the four performers sound like sixteen or more people.

126

## Across the Curriculum

**Unit Highlights** The following interdisciplinary activities in this unit are related to the music elements presented in the lessons. See Unit at a Glance, pp. 125a–125h, for topical descriptions presented according to lesson sequence.

**▶ ART/RELATED ARTS**

- Construct lion masks in Zulu style and create a mini-drama (p. 132)
- Read about techniques used by painter Georges Seurat (p. 140)
- Explore *mola* art of the Cuna people (p. 144)
- Construct a "dragon" for the Chinese New Year (p. 156)

**▶ LANGUAGE ARTS**

- Dramatize a poem about rainbows (p. 142)
- Create a performance piece based on folk stories (p. 146)
- Write additional lyrics for "America, the Beautiful" (p. 158)

**▶ SCIENCE**

- Read an account of a scientist's work in Kenya (p. 134)
- Explore science concepts through art activities (p. 140)
- Research the origins of percusssion instruments and demonstrate their acoustical properties (p. 155)

**▶ SOCIAL STUDIES**

- Read and discuss the story of a historical Zulu king (p. 130)
- Design an illustrated map of Africa (p. 134)
- Read about the life of the Cuna people (p. 144)
- Explore the sights and sounds of Chinese New Year (p. 156)
- Locate and describe regions referenced in "America, the Beautiful" (p. 158)
- Explore the historical context of "Amazing Grace" (p. 160)

UNIT 4

# Building Our Musical Skills





## MUSIC SKILLS ASSESSED IN THIS UNIT

**Reading Music: Rhythm**
- Read a song containing ♩ ♪. ♬ (p. 137)
- Read a song in mixed meter (p. 139)

**Reading Music: Pitch**
- Read *do, re, mi, fa, so, la* songs in different keys (pp. 147, 149)

**Performing Music: Singing**
- Sing an Arabic (p. 137) and a Latin American folk song (p. 147)
- Sing a countermelody (pp. 159, 161)
- Sing an African American spiritual (p. 163)

**Moving to Music**
- Perform movements to reflect the dynamics of a song (p. 133) and to show form (p. 143)

**Performing Music: Playing**
- Play ostinatos on nonpitched percussion instruments to accompany a song (p. 135)
- Perform in a percussion ensemble (p. 157)
- Play classroom instruments to accompany a two-chord song (p. 163)

**Creating Music**
- Create a vocal piece (p. 133)
- Create rhythm ostinatos (p. 135)
- Create a musical dramatization (p. 143)

**Listening to Music**
- Compare two performances of a song (p. 142)
- Use hand motions while listening to show melodic contour (p. 153)
- Listen to and describe a variety of orchestral percussion instruments (p. 155)

## CULTURAL CONNECTION

**Unit Highlights** The musical literature in this unit provides many opportunities for students to explore a variety of world cultures.

▶ AFRICAN/AFRICAN AMERICAN
- Explore the cultural background of lion imagery in art (p. 131)
- *"T'hola, t'hola":* Discuss an African lullaby (p. 133)
- *"Ochimbo":* Move to a folk song from Kenya (p. 134)
- "Dry Bones": Explore African American gospel music (p. 162)

▶ AMERICAN
- "Cumberland Gap": Discover a folk song from Kentucky (p. 138)
- "America, the Beautiful": Discuss this song's background (p. 158)
- "Amazing Grace": Explore an American hymn (p. 160)

▶ ASIAN
- Perform and discuss Chinese *luogu* ensembles (p. 156)

▶ EUROPEAN
- "Chairs to Mend": Discuss the connection of a song to the field of advertising (p. 148)
- "Ode to Joy": Discuss the impact of this composition (pp. 151, 152)

▶ LATIN AMERICAN
- *"Canción de cuna":* Explore customs of the Cuna (p. 145)
- *Toccata for Percussion:* Discover a Mexican composer (p. 155)

▶ MIDDLE EASTERN
- *"Ala Da'lona":* Sing an Arabic folk song (p. 136)
- Explore Middle Eastern musical instruments (p. 136)

# Opening Activities

| MATERIALS | |
|---|---|
| • "Straighten Up and Fly Right" | **CD 6-2** |
| **Recording Routine:** Intro (4 m.); vocal; coda | |
| • *On Green Dolphin Street* | **CD 6-1** |
| • selected classroom instruments | |

## Listening

Invite students to listen to *On Green Dolphin Street* **CD 6-1** and tap the beat. Ask students to

- Identify the style. (*a cappella,* jazz fusion)
- Describe the elements of the music that identify it as jazz. (harmony, swing style)

Have students read the information on p. 126 and the Music Makers about the Singers Unlimited. Discuss multiple track recording technology with students.

## Analyzing

Have students look at the music to "Straighten Up and Fly Right" **CD 6-2** as they listen to the recording.

**ASK How would you describe this melody to someone who has not seen or heard the song?** (It has many repeated notes.)

**What keeps all the repeated notes from becoming boring?** (the use of harmony and the rhythmic accompaniment)

## Swinging Music

Although swing **style** has its roots in 1930s-1940s jazz, today it is still a favorite style of music for performing, listening, and dancing.

**Style** is the special sound that is created when music elements such as rhythm and timbre are combined.

CD 6-2
Straighten Up and Fly Right
l, t, d r m
Swing Style
Words and Music by Nat King Cole and Irving Mills
do
A buz-zard took a mon-key for a ride in the air. The
mon-key thought that ev-'ry-thing was on the square. The
buz-zard tried to throw the mon-key off his back, but the
mon-key grabbed his neck and said, "Now lis-ten, Jack!"
Straight-en up and fly right. Straight-en up and fly right.
Ain't no use in div-in'. What's the use in jiv-in'?
Straight-en up and fly right. Cool
128

## Assessment

**Unit Highlights** This unit includes a variety of strategies and methods, described below, to track students' progress and assess their understanding of lesson objectives. Reproducible masters for Show What You Know! and Review, Assess, Perform, Create can be found in the Resource Book.

### ▶ FORMAL ASSESSMENTS

The following assessments, using written language, cognitive, and performance skills, help teachers and students conceptualize the learning that is taking place.

- **Show What You Know!** Element-specific assessments, on the student page, for Rhythm (p. 139) and Melody (p. 149).
- **Review, Assess, Perform, Create** This end-of-unit activity (pp. 164–165) can be used for review and to assess students' learning of the core lessons in this unit.

### ▶ INFORMAL ASSESSMENTS

At the close of each Teacher's Edition lesson in this unit, the following type of assessment is used to evaluate the learning of the key element focus or skill objective.

- Performance/Observation (pp. 133, 135, 137, 139, 143, 147, 149, 153, 157, 159, 161, 163)

### ▶ RUBRICS

Visit *www.sfsuccessnet.com* for rubrics to assess students' achievement in music skills.

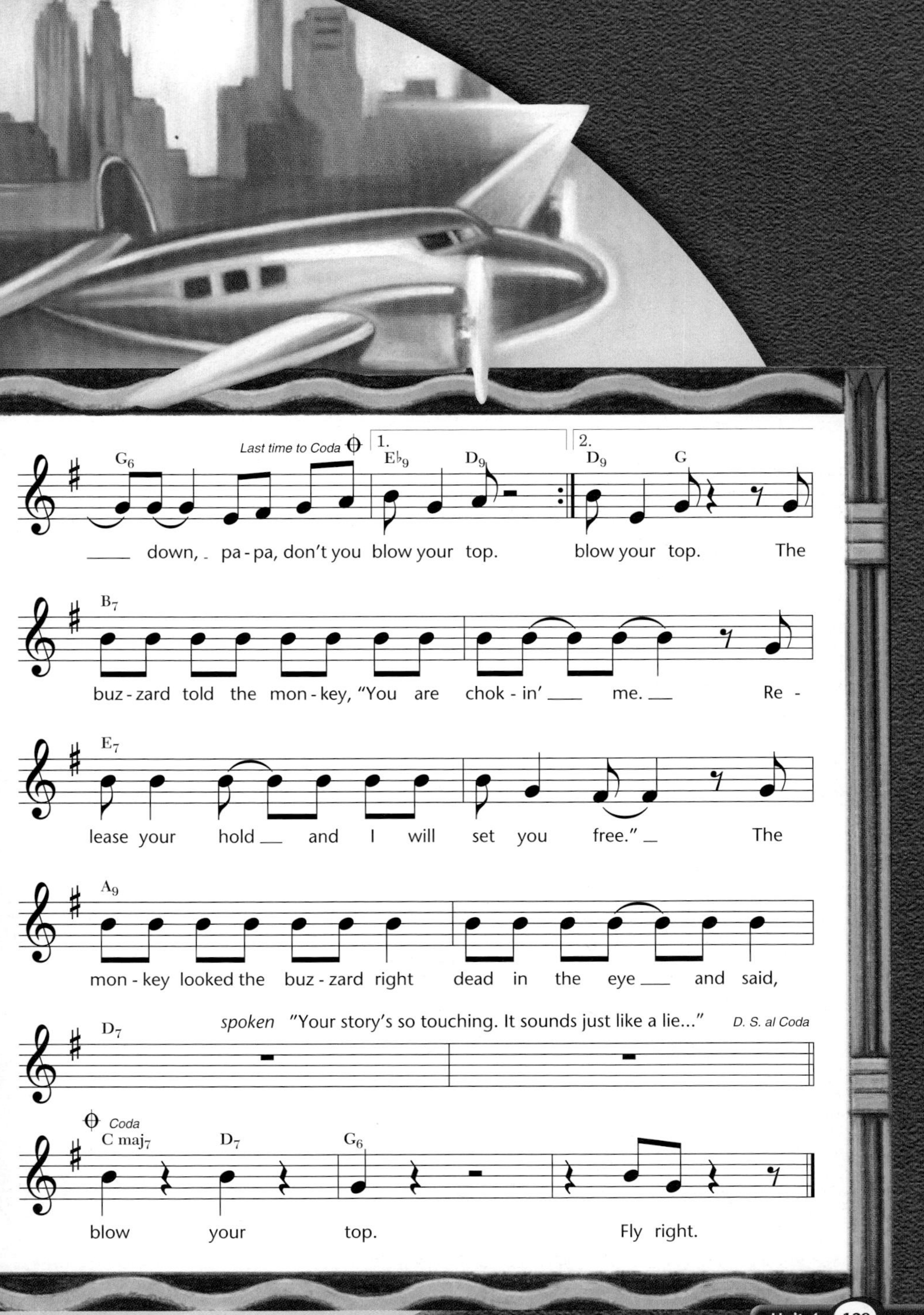
Last time to Coda
1.
2.
G6 Eb9 D9 D9 G
down, pa-pa, don't you blow your top. blow your top. The
B7
buz-zard told the mon-key, "You are chok-in' me. Re-
E7
lease your hold and I will set you free." The
A9
mon-key looked the buz-zard right dead in the eye and said,
D7
spoken "Your story's so touching. It sounds just like a lie..."
D. S. al Coda
Coda
C maj7 D7 G6
blow your top. Fly right.
Unit 4 129

## Singing

Help students navigate through the song notation by first explaining the first and second endings and the *D.S al Coda.* Then play the recording **CD 6-2** and have students follow the music.

Play the song again and invite students to

- Pat the steady beat in their laps.
- Sing mm. 1–2 on a neutral syllable, such as *dah.* (Point out that in swing style, the eighth notes are not sung evenly.)
- Sing the song with the recording.

### Innovative Teacher Support for This Unit

- **Making Music DVD, Grade 4** contains video segments that support lessons, including signing and movement.
- **Making Music with Movement and Dance** provides more opportunities for large group activities in music or physical education classes.
- **Making Music with Technology** provides lesson plans for many technology applications; includes MIDI files.
- ***¡A cantar!*** features recorded songs and lessons from around the Spanish-speaking world; includes strategies for bilingual classes and for English-speaking teachers working with Spanish-speaking students.
- **Bridges to Asia** features recorded songs and lessons from Asian and Pacific region cultures.
- ***www.sfsuccessnet.com*** provides an online lesson planner to conveniently create lesson plans at school or at home. Includes rubrics for assessment, lesson modifications to meet the needs of all students, performance musicals based on program content, and more.

## Technology/Media Link

**Unit Highlights** The following components are used in this unit to reinforce and expand students' understanding of music elements and related themes. See Unit at a Glance, pp. 125a–125h, for a descriptive listing according to lesson sequence.

▶ **CD-ROM**

- Explore dynamics using *Essentials of Music Theory* (p. 133)
- Use *Band-in-a-Box* to create a song accompaniment (p. 147)

▶ **ELECTRONIC KEYBOARD**

- Play a melody with appropriate timbre, style, and dynamics (p. 153)

▶ **MIDI/SEQUENCING SOFTWARE**

- Isolate tracks and analyze note values (p. 139)
- Isolate and layer tracks to help learn a round (p. 149)
- Create and record a percussion piece (p. 157)
- Record and then alter a countermelody (p. 161)

▶ **TRANSPARENCY**

- Display a listening map to illustrate melodic contour (p. 153)

▶ **VIDEO LIBRARY/DVD**

- Explore Turkish line dance (p. 137)
- Compare vocal styles (p. 143)

▶ **WEB SITE**

- Go to *www.sfsuccessnet.com* to learn more about African drumming and music ensembles (p. 135), John Philip Sousa (p. 159), and spirituals and gospel music (p. 163)

LESSON
Core 1

## LESSON AT A GLANCE

**Element Focus** **EXPRESSION** Dynamics

**Skill Objective** **MOVING** Respond through movement to the dynamics in a song

**Connection Activity** **RELATED ARTS** Explore South African culture through its art

**MATERIALS**

- "The Lion Sleeps Tonight" **CD 6-4**
  **Recording Routine:** Intro (8 m.); v. 1; refrain; v. 2; refrain; v. 3; refrain; coda
- *"T'hola, t'hola"* **CD 6-7**
- "Softly, Softly" **CD 6-8**
  **Recording Routine:** Intro (4 m.); vocal; coda
- **Pronunciation Practice/Translation** p. 477
- *The Lion Sleeps Tonight* **CD 6-6**
- **Resource Book** pp. A-11, G-4, I-12
- selected nonpitched percussion instruments

**VOCABULARY**

dynamics *mbube*

**National Standards**

**1b** Sing expressively, with appropriate dynamics
**2b** Play rhythms on appropriate instruments
**2f** Play instruments independently against contrasting parts
**4a** Compose music to accompany readings
**4b** Compose songs within specific guidelines
**6e** While listening to music, move to show changes in the music

**MORE MUSIC CHOICES**

Another selection from Africa:
*"Tina singu,"* p. 300
Examples that feature dynamic activities:
"Singin' in the Rain," p. 360
"Circle 'Round the Moon," p. 403

# A DYNAMIC SONG

**Listen** for the changes in *dynamics* as you **sing** "The Lion Sleeps Tonight." When you have learned this song, **create** your own dynamic plan. Decide where the music should be softer or louder.

### Playing Dynamics

Pick a percussion instrument to play one of the parts in this rhythm score. Practice playing your part. Then **perform** it with the other players. Plan different dynamics to make the piece more interesting. Now use it as an accompaniment to "The Lion Sleeps Tonight."

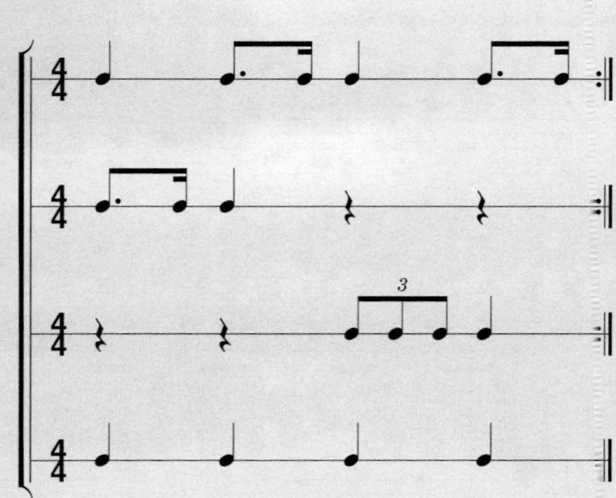

# Footnotes

## ACROSS THE CURRICULUM

▶ **Social Studies/Language Arts** Read aloud *Shaka: King of the Zulus* by Diane Stanley and Peter Vennema (Morrow, 1994), the story of a man who was king of the Zulu people for 12 years during the eighteenth century. Invite students into a discussion about things that were not available in the world when Shaka lived. Were there cars? Cell phones? Encourage students to brainstorm for other ways life was different in the time and place Shaka lived.

## BUILDING SKILLS THROUGH MUSIC

▶ **Writing** In preparing to perform the South African lullaby *"T'hola, t'hola,"* on p. 132, have students write their answers to the questions "Will you sing it loudly or softly? Why?" Invite students to explain their answers, using supporting context material.

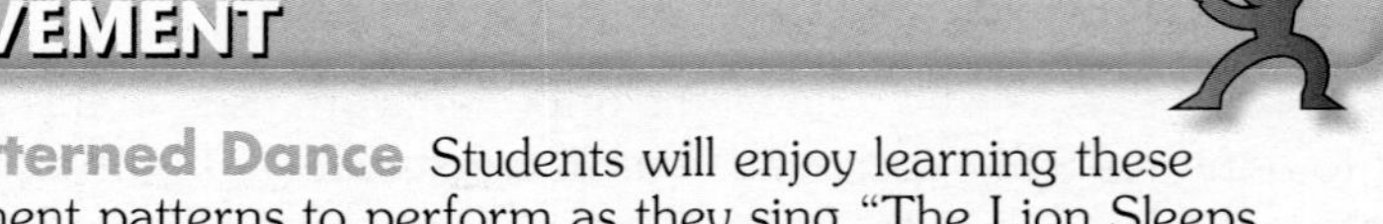


▶ **Patterned Dance** Students will enjoy learning these movement patterns to perform as they sing "The Lion Sleeps Tonight."

**Formation:** Students stand beside or in front of their chairs, facing forward.

**Introduction:** Step-touch right and left (4 times). Step-touch forward and backward (4 times).

**Refrain:** R to the side, L cross behind; R, L together while moving shoulders down and up (2 times). Reverse (2 times).

**Verses:** Turn to the right in your own space, tap L toe. Bend arms and swing front, swing back. Then reverse action: Turn to the left in your own space, tap R toe. Bend arms and swing front, swing back.

**Coda:** Step-touch right and left (8 times).

CD 6-4
The Lion Sleeps Tonight
(Wimoweh) (Mbube)
d r m f s
Words and Revised Music by George David Weiss, Hugo Peretti, and Luigi Creatore
REFRAIN
do
F
B♭
Wim - o-weh, o-wim - o-weh, o - wim - o-weh, o-wim - o-weh, o -
F
C7
Fine
wim - o-weh, o-wim - o-weh, o - wim - o-weh, o-wim - o-weh,
VERSE
F
B♭
1. In the jun - gle, the might - y jun - gle, the
2. Near the vil - lage, the peace - ful vil - lage, the
3. Hush, my dar - ling, don't fear, my dar - ling, the
F
C7
li - on sleeps to - night.
li - on sleeps to - night.
li - on sleeps to - night.
F
B♭
In the jun - gle, the qui - et jun - gle, the
Near the vil - lage, the qui - et vil - lage, the
Hush, my dar - ling, don't fear, my dar - ling, the
F
C7
D.C al Fine
li - on sleeps to - night.
li - on sleeps to - night.
li - on sleeps to - night.
Unit 4 131

# 1 Introduce

Use the books and activities in Across the Curriculum on p. 130 and p. 132 to introduce students to South African and Zulu art and culture. Tell students that they will hear two songs in contrasting styles from South Africa.

Play "The Lion Sleeps Tonight" **CD 6-4** and *"T'hola, t'hola"* **CD 6-7.**

ASK **In what ways are these songs different?** (They are in different languages; one is spirited, the other slow; one has dynamic changes, the other is mostly soft; one is more rhythmic than the other.)

# 2 Develop

### Performing

1b Divide the class into groups. Have each group

- Create a dynamics chart for performing "The Lion Sleeps Tonight."
- Perform its version of the song along with the Stereo Performance Track **CD 6-5**, using the dynamics chart.

Invite students to explain how they chose the dynamics for their version of the song. Students can discuss the success of each version.

### Moving

6e Have students perform the movement pattern described in Movement, p. 130, with "The Lion Sleeps Tonight" **CD 6-4.** Encourage them to adjust the size of their movements to reflect the dynamics for each section of the song.

continued on page 132

## Skills Reinforcement

▶ **Recorder** Have students review the fingering for high C and high D on their recorders. When playing high D, the thumb should move slightly away from the thumb hole. When students are comfortable fingering these notes, have them play the countermelody on Resource Book p. I-12 during the refrain of "The Lion Sleeps Tonight." Remind them to break the sound after each repeated pitch.

▶ **Signing** For a signing activity to accompany "The Lion Sleeps Tonight," refer to Resource Book pp. G-4 through G-6.

▶ **Singing** To compare the style of *"T'hola, t'hola"* with that of other lullabies from diverse cultures, have students sing *"Canción de Cuna"* (p. 144), *"Einini"* (p. 391), *"Thula, thula, ngoana"* (p. 227), and *"Xiao"* (p. 314).

## Cultural Connection

▶ **Lions in Art** Through the ages, the lion has been a favorite subject among artists for drawing, painting, and sculpting. Numerous books depict lions in art and various other media such as bronze and marble. Many of the artworks are centuries old. Have students do a search of art books in the school library to find images of lions. Ask students if they can think of any famous uses of the lion image. For example, the lion is the symbol of Metro-Goldwyn Mayer film studios. The main branch of the New York Public Library on 42nd Street in Manhattan has lion sculptures in front. Many coats of arms use the lion as a symbol of strength.

### Creating

4a Divide the class into small groups. Ask each group to

- Write a four-line poem about a lion.
- Practice saying the poem, varying the dynamics.
- Select nonpitched percussion instruments.
- Accompany the poem using a variety of rhythms in which dynamics figure prominently.
- Perform for the class.

### Playing

2b Have students learn the rhythm parts on p. 130 by rote. Encourage students to practice playing each line of the rhythm score. Repeat each line as many times as needed for students to feel confident. See Meeting Individual Needs below.

Divide the class into four groups. Assign one line of rhythm to each. Have the fourth group start first to establish a basic beat.

2f Invite students to take turns playing the four parts on nonpitched percussion instruments. Have students play the rhythm parts as the rest of the class sings "The Lion Sleeps Tonight" **CD 6-4.**

### Singing

Invite students to listen to the Pronunciation Practice Track for *"T'hola, t'hola"* **CD 6-10** and sing with the students on the recording. Refer to Resource Book p. A-11.

Have students sing *"T'hola, t'hola"* **CD 6-7.** Make sure they use the appropriate vocal sound for this lullaby. Have them try making their voices softer and softer at the end of the song. See how softly they can sing and still be audible. Remind students to hold the last whole note for its full value.

## MUSIC MAKERS

## Lebo M.

**Lebo M.** (Lebo Morake, born 1966) is from South Africa. When he was fifteen, Morake left his home to pursue a music career in the United States. After studying at the Duke Ellington School of Music, he worked with the band Earth, Wind & Fire. One of his most famous projects was providing the authentic African instruments and singing for *The Lion King* Broadway production. He is a well-known musician in South Africa and the United States.

**Listen** for dynamic contrast as Lebo M. performs his version of *The Lion Sleeps Tonight.*

CD 6-6

**The Lion Sleeps Tonight**

**by George David Weiss, Hugo Peretti, and Luigi Creatore as performed by Lebo M.**

This version of the song is performed in the South African style of *a cappella* singing called *mbube.*

### Another Dynamic Song

This lullaby from South Africa is in the Bantu language. Will you sing it loudly or softly? Why?

CD 6-7
T'HOLA, T'HOLA
(Softly, Softly)
l, d r f s l d'
Folk Song from South Africa
do
D Em D Em D Em D Em
T'ho - la, t'ho - la ngoa-na - me; T'ho - la, t'ho - la ngoa-na - me,
Soft - ly, soft - ly, my ba - by; Soft - ly, soft - ly, my ba - by.
D Em D Em D Em D Em
Di pe - re se - ra peng. Ra - peng sa - ma ha - pu.
Hush, it is just the wind Blow - ing through the branch - es.

# Footnotes

## ACROSS THE CURRICULUM

▶ **Drama/Arts** Have students construct lion masks in Zulu style. Then invite them to create a mini-drama based on "The Lion Sleeps Tonight." Help students decide how to present the song with movement, created narration, and simple scenery depicting a Zulu village. Sources for artwork and mini-drama ideas include *Making Masks* by Vivian Frank and Deborah Jaffe (W. Foster, 1977); *Learning About Cultures* by John Gust and J. Meghan McChesney (Teaching and Learning Co., 1995); *Traditional African Designs* by Gregory Mirow (Dover, 1997); *The Kid's Multicultural Art Book: Art and Craft Experiences from Around the World* by Alexandra M. Terzian (Williamson Pub., 1993).

## MEETING INDIVIDUAL NEEDS

▶ **Including Everyone** The following suggestions may be used in organizing the playing activity on p. 130 for "The Lion Sleeps Tonight."

**Reinforcement** Some students may not have the strength or skill to continue their chosen rhythm pattern throughout the entire song. Have these students alternate their patterns with the steady beat. If students "get off" their pattern, suggest that they continue performing a steady beat, watch others playing the same pattern, and rejoin the ensemble when they feel confident.

**On Target** Most rhythmically skilled students will be able to keep a strong steady beat as others practice the other patterns in the rhythm score. Have students first perform the patterns separately and then in different combinations.

**Challenge** Encourage interested students to create new ostinatos, based on the melodic rhythm of the song, to add to the ensemble.

D Em D Em D Em
Ei - tsa li lo tse - la tsa ea-ngoa-na - me, E pu-tsoa ea khao - ha mo
Once on a time was a young li - on ba - by, Took him to the doc - tor to
D Em D Em D Em D Em
ko - ko Hon-goa-na - me E - i, e - i-ngoa-na - me, E - i,
make him mind his man-ners. E - i, soft - ly, my ba - by, E - i,
D Em D Em D Em D Em
E - i-ngoa-na - me. Ha le so bone kon - ko - ti, Ha le so bone kon - ko -
Soft - ly, my ba - by. There was a lit - tle white dove, yes, there was a lit - tle
D Em D Em D Em
ti, T'ho - la, t'ho - la ngoa - na - me,
dove, "T'ho - la, t'ho - la," he sang me,
D Em D Em D
T'ho - la, t'ho - la ngoa - na - me.
"T'ho - la, t'ho - la," he sang me.

### Creating Dynamics

You can make sounds of many different dynamics with your voice. Look at these shapes on the right. First experiment with a vocal sound that each shape seems to suggest. Use a neutral syllable such as "ah." Then see how softly or loudly you can perform the sound. **Compose** a piece by putting the symbols in an order that you like. (Repeat any symbol as many times as you like.) Decide what dynamics will make your performance expressive and interesting.

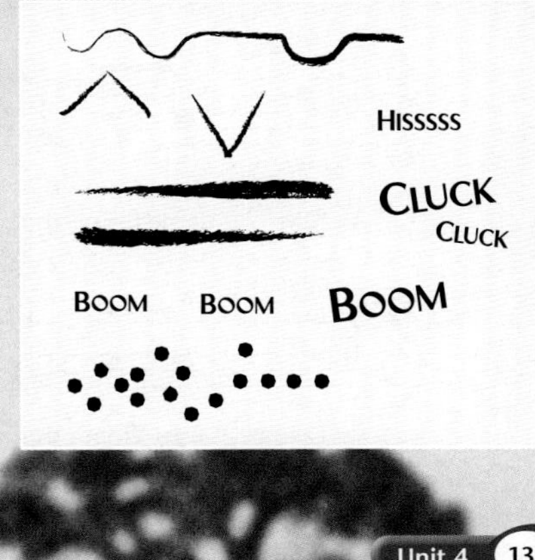
Hisssss
Cluck
Cluck
Boom
Boom
Boom

### Reading

Have students examine the vocal score on the bottom of p. 133. Ask them to experiment with their voices to interpret the graphic notation on the page. For example, a wavy line might indicate a wavering change in pitch.

## 3 Close

### Creating

4b Divide the class into small groups. Ask each group to create a piece using the vocal notation icons at the bottom of p. 133. Encourage them to change the order of the vocal sounds, and add some rhythms from p. 130. Finally, have them add dynamics to their piece to make it more interesting. Invite each group to perform for the class.

**Element: EXPRESSION** ASSESSMENT

**Performance/Observation** Have students sing "The Lion Sleeps Tonight" **CD 6-4** with appropriate dynamics, while making larger and smaller steady beat movements to visually indicate louder and softer portions of the song.

Observe each student's ability to convey dynamic contrast through movement.

## Character Education

**▶ Respect and Courtesy** To help students understand their need to respond with respect and courtesy to the creative efforts of their classmates, discuss the importance of encouraging other people's ideas. Ask: What are some ways you can be supportive of another person? What are some words or phrases you can use to make others feel good about their efforts? Using body language only, what are some ways you show someone that you don't support their ideas? How does it make you feel when you see someone roll their eyes, sigh heavily, or make a face in response to your ideas? Using body language only, what are some ways to show someone you support them? Encourage students to remember that working in a group requires people to share and consider various ideas, perhaps relinquishing some individual control. Remind students that creative collaboration involves both giving and receiving respect and courtesy.

## Cultural Connection

**▶ African Lullabies** After students have completed this lesson, share with them that African lullabies are often anything but soft. Each time the class sings "The Lion Sleeps Tonight" or *"T'hola, t'hola"* again, allow students to choose different dynamic levels for the entire song.

## Technology/Media Link

**CD-ROM** Invite students to explore the dynamics lesson in Vol. 1 of *Alfred's Essentials of Music Theory*.

LESSON 2

## LESSON AT A GLANCE

**Element Focus** **RHYTHM** Upbeats

**Skill Objective** **PLAYING** Play rhythm ostinatos with upbeats to accompany a song

**Connection Activity** **SOCIAL STUDIES** Discuss the people, foliage, and fauna of Kenya

**MATERIALS**

- *"Ochimbo"* **CD 6-11**
  **Recording Routine:** Intro (4 m.); v. 1; interlude (8 m.); v. 2; coda
- **Music Reading Practice, Sequence 13** **CD 6-13**
- *Jin-go-lo-ba* **CD 6-16**
- **Resource Book** pp. D-16, E-14
- **Dance Directions** for "Bongo," p. 509
- nonpitched percussion instruments (drums and rattles)

**VOCABULARY**

upbeat ostinato bar line phrase

**National Standards**

**2b** Perform rhythms on appropriate instruments
**2f** Play instruments independently against contrasting parts
**4b** Compose pieces within specific guidelines
**6c** Use appropriate terms to explain music

**MORE MUSIC CHOICES**

For more practice with upbeats:
"My Bonnie Lies Over the Ocean," p. 338

# 1 INTRODUCE

Use the books and activities in Across the Curriculum below to introduce students to Kenyan culture and wildlife.

Ask students to read the information about the *ochimbo* bird on p. 134. Play *"Ochimbo"* **CD 6-11.** Ask students to sing the phrase *ochimbo bird* with the recording every time it occurs in the song.

LESSON 2
Element: RHYTHM
Skill: PLAYING
Connection: SOCIAL STUDIES
FEELING UPBEAT
This song is about the *ochimbo* bird, which is found in Kenya and other central African countries. What is the message the singers are sending to the bird?
**Sing** *"Ochimbo"* and tap the strong, or first, beat of each measure.
CD 6-11
MIDI 9
OCHIMBO
s d m l
Words by Margaret Marks
Folk Song from Kenya
As Sung by Ruth Nthreketha
Leader
F
do
O take your fair share, good fish - ing good hunt - ing O - chim - bo bird.
Chorus
O take your fair share, good fish - ing good hunt - ing O - chim - bo bird.
Leader
Take fish from the stream, Take game from the plain, good fish - ing good hunt - ing O - chim - bo bird.
Chorus
Take fish from the stream, Take game from the plain, good fish - ing good hunt - ing O - chim - bo bird.
134
Reading Sequence 13

# Footnotes

## SKILLS REINFORCEMENT

4b ▶ **Creating** Students will enjoy creating their own ostinatos and performing them for the class. See the Reading Music Worksheet on creating rhythms on Resource Book p. D-16.

## BUILDING SKILLS THROUGH MUSIC

▶ **Language** Have the class chant the words of "*Ochimbo*" in the Leader/Chorus format. Then, lead a discussion on what possible messages are conveyed through the lyrics. Finally, ask students to write new words to the song from the point of view of the ochimbo bird. Ask, "What message might the bird want to communicate to humans?"

## ACROSS THE CURRICULUM

▶ **Social Studies/Science** Students may enjoy reading *Kenya: Let's All Pull Together* from the *Exploring Cultures of the World* series by David C. King (Benchmark Books, 1997) and *Elephant Woman: Cynthia Moss Explores the World of Elephants* by Laurence Pringle and Cynthia Moss (Atheneum Books, 1997). The latter describes Moss's 25 years in Kenya while studying elephant families at Amboseli National Park.

Help students design a map of Africa, highlighting Kenya. Invite students to create a collage of visual "features" of the country, including the *ochimbo* bird, elephant families, other plants and animals, geography, people, musical instruments, and art. As students learn about music from other African nations, you may wish to add information about those nations to the display.

## Find the Upbeat

Look at the first phrase of "*Ochimbo*." Does the phrase begin on the strong beat? When a phrase begins before a bar line, an **upbeat** occurs.

An **upbeat** is one or more notes that occur before the first bar line of a phrase.

**Play** these ostinatos on drums or other percussion instruments to accompany "*Ochimbo*." Find the upbeat in each ostinato.

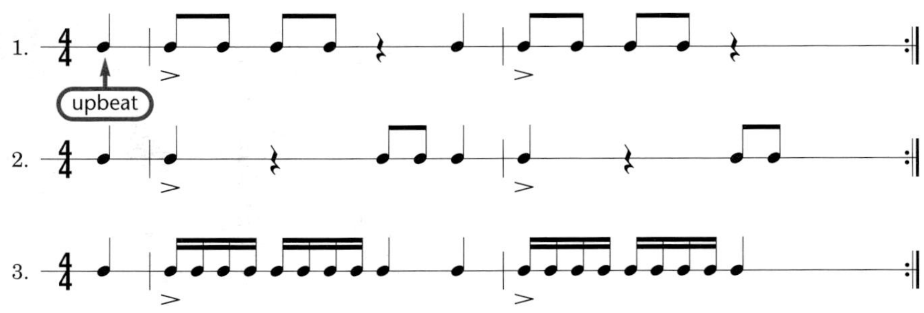


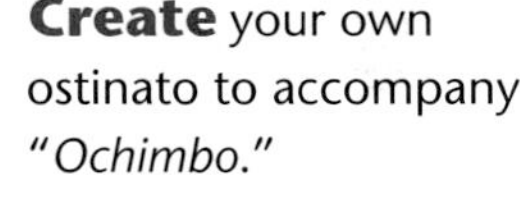


**Create** your own ostinato to accompany "*Ochimbo*."

This drummer belongs to the Kikuyu tribe, a farming group in Kenya. He is performing at a lodge in a game reserve. ▶

Unit 4 135

# 2 Develop

### Singing

Have students create four-beat movement patterns and perform them as they sing *"Ochimbo"* **CD 6-11.**

### Reading

Ask students to sing the song again and tap only on the strong beat.

ASK **Which words did we sing on the strong beats?** (*take, O of Ochimbo, fish, game*)

**Which word did we sing *before* the first strong beat of the song?** (O)

**Is this word before or after the first bar line in the music?** (before)

6c Have students read the information on p. 135 and find the upbeats in the song. Have students sing *"Ochimbo"* again, snapping their fingers on each upbeat. For a related reading activity, see p. 448 and Resource Book E-14.

### 2b Playing

Have students read about the Kenyan drummer on p. 135. Ask them to sing and clap the ostinato patterns on the same page. Invite them to play the patterns on large and small drums and rattles and then perform the ostinatos with *"Ochimbo"* **CD 6-11.**

### Moving

For a movement activity that reinforces upbeat in *"Ochimbo,"* see Movement below.

# 3 Close

**Element: RHYTHM** ASSESSMENT

2f **Performance/Observation** Have students sing *"Ochimbo"* while clapping the ostinato. Have them sing the song again with students performing the ostinato parts on nonpitched percussion instruments. Observe each student's ability to play upbeats accurately.

## Movement

▶ **Patterned Dance** These movements, based on African dances from diverse cultures, can be performed with the song "*Ochimbo.*" Ask students to

- Step in place on each quarter note beat.
- Step in place twice slowly (one step for two quarter notes).
- Step on beats 1 and 3. Raise knee on beats 2 and 4.
- Lower arms on beats 1 and 3. Raise arms on beats 2 and 4.
- Perform knee and arm motions simultaneously.

▶ **Game Song** For a follow-the-leader dance game called "Bongo," use the Dance Performance Track for *Jin-go-lo-ba* **CD 6-16** and refer to the Dance Directions on p. 509.

## Technology/Media Link

**Web Site** To learn more about African drumming and music ensembles, have students visit *www.sfsuccessnet.com.*

Core LESSON 3

## LESSON AT A GLANCE

**Element Focus** **RHYTHM** ♩., ♫, and ♪♬

**Skill Objective** **SINGING** Sing a song from notation that includes ♩., ♫, and ♪♬

**Connection Activity** **CULTURE** Discover Middle Eastern musical instruments

**MATERIALS**

- *"Ala Da'lona"* (Arabic) **CD 6-18**
- *"Ala Da'lona"* (English) **CD 6-19**

  **Recording Routine:** Intro (free improvisation, then 4 m.); instrumental; interlude (4 m.); vocal; coda
- **Pronunciation Practice/Translation** p. 479
- **Resource Book** pp. A-12, D-17, H-12
- nonpitched percussion instruments

**VOCABULARY**

*oud* *tabl* *darabukah* *zurna*

◆◆◆◆ **National Standards** ◆◆◆◆

**2b** Perform rhythms on appropriate instruments

**5a** Read rhythms in $\frac{2}{4}$ meter

**6d** Identify the sounds of instruments from various cultures

**MORE MUSIC CHOICES**

Look for the ♪♬ rhythm in the following songs.

"The Continents" (speech piece), p. 357

*"Sambalele,"* p. 397

# 1 INTRODUCE

Use the Cultural Connection below to introduce students to some Middle Eastern instruments. Encourage them to read the questions above *"Ala Da'lona,"* p. 136. Invite students to listen to *"Ala Da'lona"* **CD 6-18.** Then have them sing the song together.



# Discover a New Rhythm

Read the words of *"Ala Da'lona."* What feelings are expressed? In what way will this affect how you **sing** this song?

## Ala Da'lona

*English Words by Alice Firgau*

*Arabic Folk Song*

*A - la Da' - lo - na, A - la Da' - lo - na,*

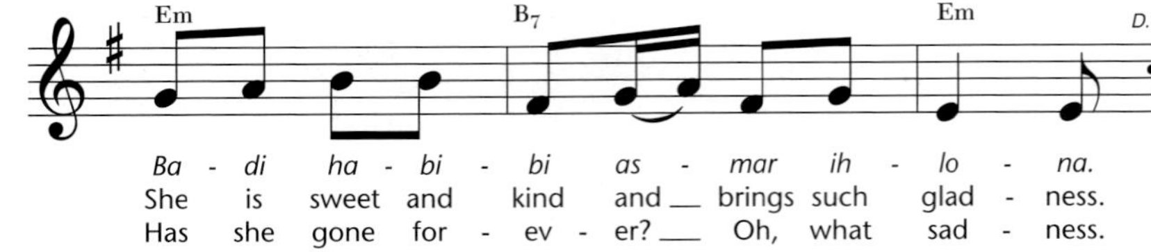


### Find the New Rhythm

Find the  pattern in the song. **Read** this pattern with rhythm syllables.

136

# Footnotes

## CULTURAL CONNECTION

▶ **Instruments of the Middle East** The *oud* is a folk instrument played in eastern Mediterranean countries such as Turkey, Iran, and Syria. Ask students to name other string folk instruments from their cultures.

The body of a *darabukah* is usually fairly small, often made of wood or pottery, with a goblet shape. The *zurna* has a double reed like an oboe. Frame drums are found around the world.

## BUILDING SKILLS THROUGH MUSIC

▶ **Math** Have students count the total number of measures in the notation of *"Ala Da'lona,"* including the repeat and the *D.C. al Fine.* (24) Then ask them to calculate the maximum number of ♪♬ rhythm patterns that could be performed in this number of measures. (48)

## MEETING INDIVIDUAL NEEDS

6d ▶ **Developing Interest** Point out the photographs of Tunisian musicians on p. 137. Then have students listen to the Stereo Performance Track of *"Ala Da'lona"* **CD 6-20.** As students listen, direct them in the following activity.

- Imagine holding the instrument you are hearing now. Is it a string instrument? Percussion? Wind?
- How would it be played?
- Move as if you are playing each of the instruments you are hearing.

Play the recording again and ask students to list all the instrumental sounds they hear. Invite them to identify familiar classroom percussion instruments—tambourine, finger cymbals, and hand drums.

## Instruments of the Middle East

The recording of "*Ala Da´lona*" features an instrument called the *ud* [ood]. How does this instrument produce sound?

**Listen** for the *ud* and drums in the introduction of the recording of "*Ala Da´lona*." The drums are the *tabl* [TAH-buhl] and the *darabukah* [dah-rah-BOO-kuh].

◀ The *ud* has been used in Middle Eastern music for more than 1,000 years.

**Play** these ostinatos on percussion instruments to accompany *"Ala Da´lona."* Which ostinatos contain the new rhythm pattern you learned?

These players from Hammamet, Tunisia, are playing a frame drum, a *zurna*, and a *darabukah*. ▼

# 2 Develop

### Reading

Have students sing *"Ala Da'lona"* **CD 6-19** while tapping the steady beat. Then, clap rhythms that include

 and have students echo.

Have students clap and say the following rhythm.

**ASK How many sounds are on the third beat?** (four)

Have students echo clap the following rhythm.

**ASK How many sounds are on the third beat?** (three)

Invite students to find the rhythm in *"Ala Da'lona,"* p. 136, read the rhythm of the song using rhythm syllables, then sing the song with **CD 6-19.**

### Singing

Invite students to listen to the Pronunciation Practice Track for *"Ala Da'lona"* **CD 6-21.** Have them sing with the students on the recording. Refer to Resource Book p. A-12. Then have students perform the song in Arabic **CD 6-18.**

# 3 Close

### Playing

Have students read about the instruments on p. 137, and in the sound bank on p. 467. Then clap and say the ostinatos on the same page. Ask students to choose classroom instruments on which to play the ostinatos.

**Skill: SINGING** **ASSESSMENT**

**Performance/Observation** Have students sing *"Ala Da'lona"* while following the notation on p. 136, first using rhythm syllables and then the song text. Observe each student's ability to read and sing the rhythm pattern.

## Skills Reinforcement

▶ **Keyboard** Students can try a chordal accompaniment with *"Ala Da'lona."* They will be using Em, Am, and $B_7$ chords. See Resource Book p. H-12 for keyboard diagrams to guide students in finding the correct hand and finger positions.

▶ **Reading** The Reading Music Worksheet, Notating Rhythms, will help students to write the rhythms found in *"Ala Da'lona."* See Resource Book p. D-17.

## Character Education

▶ **Respect for Differences** To encourage respect for different cultures, people, and music, have students write down attributes of his/her experiences, culture, and family that are unique, special, and different. Invite students to share what they have written. Discuss the importance of accepting and being non-judgmental of those who are different.

## Technology/Media Link

**Video Library** Show students the video episode that illustrates a Turkish line dance. Invite them to experiment with movements from the style in the video. Students may use their movements to create a dance for *"Ala Da'lona."*

LESSON 4

## LESSON AT A GLANCE

**Element Focus** RHYTHM ♫♩

**Skill Objective** **READING** Read rhythm patterns with ♫♩ in $\frac{2}{4}$ time

**Connection Activity** **SOCIAL STUDIES** Discuss the importance of the Cumberland Gap during the Westward Expansion Movement

**MATERIALS**

- "Cumberland Gap" **CD 6-22**
  **Recording Routine:** Intro (4 m.); v. 1; interlude; (2 m.); v. 2; interlude (2 m.); v. 3; interlude; v. 4; coda
- **Music Reading Practice, Sequence 14** **CD 6-24**
- **Dance Directions** for "Cumberland Gap" p. 510
- **Resource Book** pp. B-12, D-18, E-15

**VOCABULARY**

rhythm patterns rhythm syllables

**National Standards**

**5a** Read rhythms in duple meter
**5d** Notate rhythm using standard symbols
**6b** Describe music by moving to it
**6e** While listening to music, move to show a prominent feature of the music

**MORE MUSIC CHOICES**

Other American folk songs:
"My Bonnie Lies Over the Ocean," p. 338
"Clementine," p. 341

# 1 INTRODUCE

Invite students to look at the painting of *Daniel Boone Escorting Pioneers* on p. 139. Explain to students that the Cumberland Gap was an opening in the mountains that settlers used when moving west. Share the information from Spotlight On below.

LESSON 4 Element: RHYTHM | Skill: READING | Connection: SOCIAL STUDIES

# Finding New Rhythm Patterns

The Cumberland Gap is a passage through the Appalachian Mountains of Virginia, Kentucky, and Tennessee.

Look at the music for "Cumberland Gap" and find the ♫♩ rhythm pattern. Now **listen** carefully to hear this pattern in the song.

CD 6-22
MIDI 11

## Cumberland Gap

l ⓓ r m s l d'

*Play-Party Song from Kentucky*
*Adapted by Jill Trinka*

VERSE
D G D G D
do
1. Lay down, boys, take a lit-tle nap, lay down, boys, take a lit-tle nap,

D G D G D
Lay down, boys, take a lit-tle nap, for-ty-one miles to Cum-ber-land Gap.

REFRAIN
D G
Cum-ber-land Gap, Cum-ber-land Gap, Ooo,

D G D
Hoo, Way low down in Cum-ber-land Gap.

2. Cumberland Gap is a mighty fine place, . . .
   *(3 times)*
   Three kinds of water to wash your face.
   *Refrain*

3. Cumberland Gap, with its cliffs and rocks, . . .
   *(3 times)*
   Home of the panther, bear, and fox.
   *Refrain*

4. Me and my wife and my wife's grandpap, . . .
   *(3 times)*
   We raise Cain at Cumberland Gap.
   *Refrain*

# Footnotes

## SPOTLIGHT ON

▶ **Cumberland Gap** The Cumberland Gap is a natural pass in the Appalachian Mountains near the point where Tennessee, Kentucky, and Virginia meet. American pioneer Daniel Boone blazed a trail through the Cumberland Gap in 1775, as part of a longer route called the Wilderness Road. Between 1775 and 1810, over 200,000 pioneers used the Cumberland Gap to go west. Today, people can visit Cumberland Gap National Historical Park.

## BUILDING SKILLS THROUGH MUSIC

▶ **Science** Using the Cumberland Gap as a starting point, ask students to research this type of geological formation. Ask, "Are there any such formations in our own region of the country?" (For example, the Grand Canyon, Appalachian Mountains, Delaware Water Gap, and so on)

## SKILLS REINFORCEMENT

5d ▶ **Reading** Use the Reading Music Worksheet for more rhythm notation practice. See Resource Book p. D-18.

▶ **Creating** Have students create rhythm patterns to accompany familiar songs. Students can notate the patterns and play them on instruments. Then combine rhythms to create an interesting texture.

*Arts* Connection

*Daniel Boone Escorting Pioneers (1775)* by George Caleb Bingham (1811–1879). Boone, a legendary American frontiersman, helped blaze a trail through the Cumberland Gap.

### Cumberland Patterns

Find the word *Cumberland* in the song. Ask yourself these questions.

- How many beats are used for the word *Cumberland*?
- How many sounds are on the beat?
- Does *Cumberland* have the same sound as ♩♫?
- What rhythm pattern fits with *Cumberland?*

Now **read** "Cumberland Gap" using rhythm syllables.

## Show What You Know!

Show what you know and **read** the following rhythm patterns.

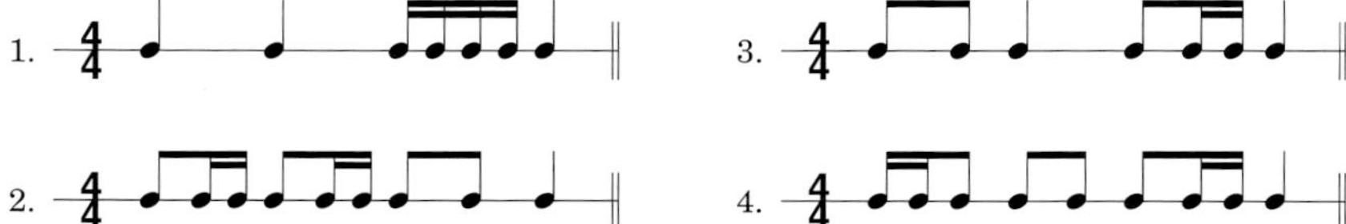


**Create** four rhythm patterns of your own using ♩, ♫, 𝄽, ♬, ♫♫, ♩♫.

**Notate** your patterns. Add words to match the rhythm. Then have a partner clap them with you.



# 2 Develop

### Performing

Clap four-beat rhythm patterns using ♩, 𝄽, ♫, ♩♫, and ♫♩.

Have students echo clap each pattern, as a group and individually, and then determine the number of beats in each pattern. (4)

### Listening

6e Have students keep a steady beat while listening to "Cumberland Gap" **CD 6-22.** Remind students that in $\frac{2}{4}$ time, there are two beats in each measure. Demonstrate a two-beat conducting pattern.

### Reading

Have students do the Show What You Know! activity on p. 139. Refer to Resource Book p. B-12.

5a After students read, clap, and say each rhythm pattern on p. 139, invite a volunteer to perform a pattern individually. Then have that volunteer choose someone else to perform the next pattern. Continue the game as time permits.

See p. 448 and Resource Book p. E-15 for a related reading activity.

# 3 Close

**Skill: READING** — **ASSESSMENT**

**Performance/Observation** Have students read and clap the rhythm of "Cumberland Gap," p. 138. Then ask them to sing "Cumberland Gap" while performing the rhythm patterns on p. 139 as a counter-rhythm. For an extra challenge, try rearranging the patterns. At the $\frac{3}{4}$ measures, stop playing and resume with the next $\frac{2}{4}$ measure. Observe each student's ability to read the ♫♩ pattern.

## Movement

6b ▶ **Creative Movement** Have students show rhythm patterns from "Cumberland Gap" using body percussion. Discuss possibilities for creating sounds (snap, clap, patsch, stamp, slide) and decide which sounds suit each rhythm. Change patterns to fit the meter change. Have students step the beat in a circle, sing, and perform their body percussion.

▶ **Patterned Dance** For a patterned dance to "Cumberland Gap," refer to the Dance Directions on p. 510.

## Technology/Media Link

**MIDI/Sequencing Software** Use a MIDI sequencing program on a computer connected to a projector or large screen to display the MIDI song file of "Cumberland Gap" for the class.

- Isolate the melody track and play it back in either notation or graphic view.
- Isolate the guitar and banjo tracks and play them back.
- Ask students to determine the predominant note value in the accompaniment tracks.

Core LESSON 5

## LESSON AT A GLANCE

**Element Focus** **FORM** AABA sectional form

**Skill Objective** **MOVING** Perform contrasting movements to show contrasting song sections

**Connection Activity** **LANGUAGE ARTS** Dramatize a poem related to rainbows

**MATERIALS**

- "Over the Rainbow" **CD 6-27**
  **Recording Routine:** Intro (4 m.); vocal; coda
- *Over the Rainbow* (Judy Garland) **CD 6-29**
- *Over the Rainbow* (Aretha Franklin) **CD 6-30**
- **Resource Book** p. I-13
- streamers
- xylophone, metallophone, glockenspiels, pitched and nonpitched percussion instruments

**VOCABULARY**

phrases vocal style coda

**National Standards**

- **1b** Sing expressively, with appropriate interpretation
- **4a** Compose music to accompany readings
- **6a** Listen to identify form
- **6b** Describe music by moving to it
- **6c** Use appropriate terms to explain music notation
- **6e** While listening to music, move to show changes in the music
- **7b** Use musical terms to explain style preferences

**MORE MUSIC CHOICES**

Other music from movies or musical theater:

"Singin' in the Rain," p. 360
"Little Shop of Horrors," p. 422

A song in aaba form:

"Ode to Joy," p. 152

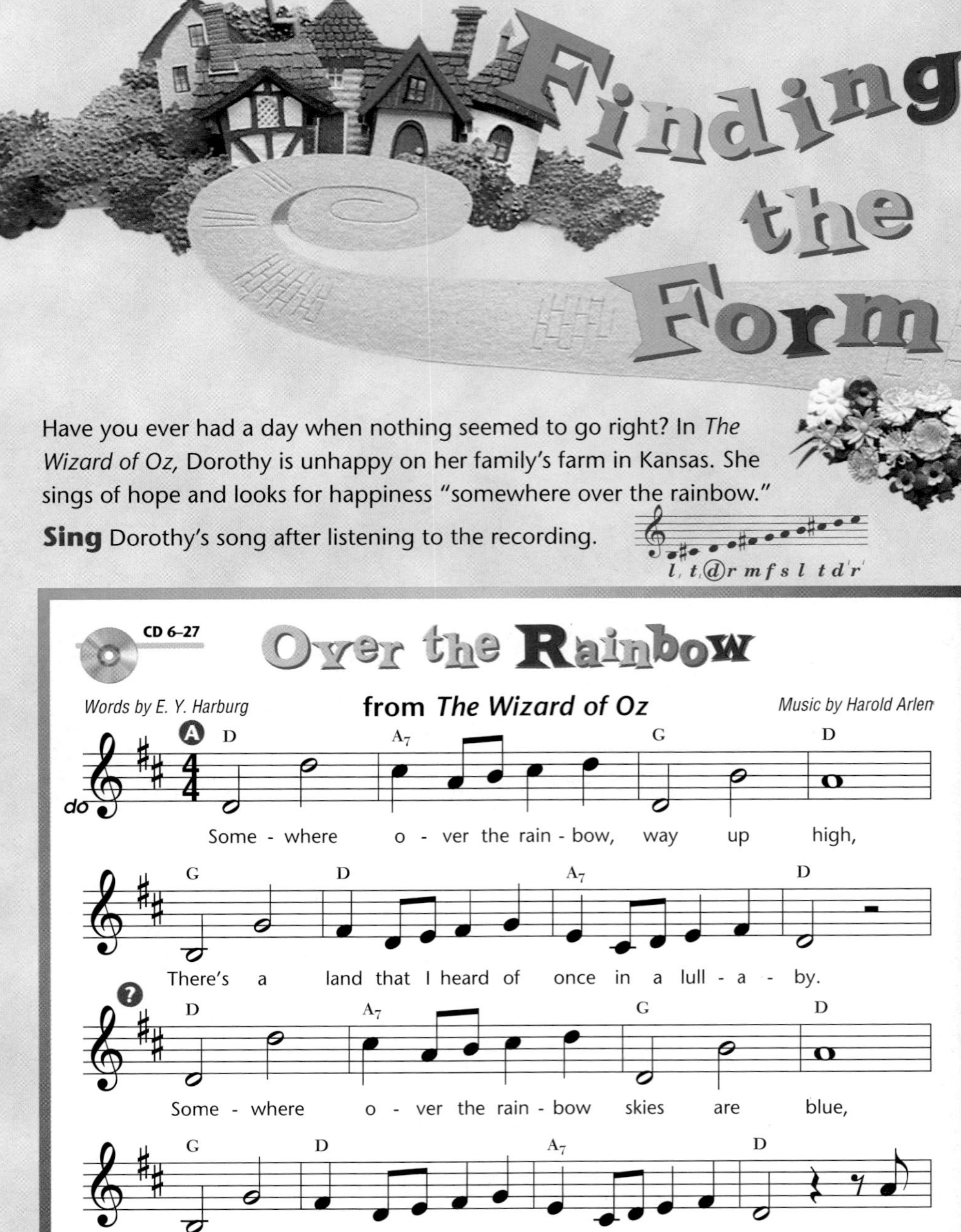
LESSON 5 Element: FORM | Skill: MOVING | Connection: LANGUAGE ARTS

# Finding the Form

Have you ever had a day when nothing seemed to go right? In *The Wizard of Oz,* Dorothy is unhappy on her family's farm in Kansas. She sings of hope and looks for happiness "somewhere over the rainbow."

**Sing** Dorothy's song after listening to the recording.

l, t,(d) r m f s l t d' r'

CD 6-27

## Over the Rainbow

from *The Wizard of Oz*

Words by E. Y. Harburg — Music by Harold Arlen

A
D A7 G D
do
Some - where o - ver the rain - bow, way up high,
G D A7 D
There's a land that I heard of once in a lull - a - by.
?
D A7 G D
Some - where o - ver the rain - bow skies are blue,
G D A7 D
And the dreams that you dare to dream real-ly do come true. Some -

140

# Footnotes

## MEETING INDIVIDUAL NEEDS

▶ **Including Everyone** Help students focus by asking everyone to trace, with their fingers, the first two lines of "Over the Rainbow" and call these lines "A." Do the same for the repeated A sections, the B section, and the *coda*. You may wish to have students work in partners as you discuss the song.

## BUILDING SKILLS THROUGH MUSIC

▶ **Language** Ask students to read the Music Makers features on the singers Judy Garland and Patti LaBelle (pp. 142–143). Then have students compare and contrast the two artists, using a Venn diagram (see Resource Book p. C-8).

## ACROSS THE CURRICULUM

▶ **Fine Arts/Science** Encourage students to read *Paintings* by Claude Delafosse and Gallimard Jeunesse (Scholastic, 1993), which describes the colorful techniques of the famous pointillist painter Georges Seurat. This book allows students to see both up-close and far-away views of the artist's use of color. After reading about his technique, have students use a magnifying glass to closely view a color TV screen, noticing the groupings of primary colors.

For more ideas on this theme, have students explore *Science Art: Projects and Activities That teach Science Concepts and Develop Process Skills* by Deborah Schecter (Scholastic, 1998).

B
D
A7
day I'll wish up - on a star and wake up where the clouds are far be -
D
hind me; ______ Where trou-bles melt like lem - on drops, a -
E7
A
A7
way, a - bove the chim-ney tops, that's where you'll find me.
?
D
G
D
Some - where o - ver the rain - bow blue - birds fly,
G
D
A7
Birds fly o - ver the rain - bow, why, then, oh why, can't
D
Coda 3
D
I? If hap-py lit - tle blue-birds fly be -
A7
rit.
D
yond the rain-bow, why, oh why, can't I? ______

### Find the Phrases

Find the phrases of "Over the Rainbow" that are the same. Look for a melody that repeats, even though the words are different. How many **A** phrases can you find? How many **B** phrases? What is the order of the **A** and **B** phrases in this song?

Tune In

*The Wizard of Oz* was just the first of many adventures for Dorothy. L. Frank Baum wrote 14 books about the "Wonderful World of Oz."

# 1 Introduce

Talk with students about things performers might think about when they want to sing a particular song. (words, mood, tempo, style, and so on) Discuss "Over the Rainbow" as a song that has been performed in different ways by various performers.

# 2 Develop

### Listening

Invite students to listen to *Over the Rainbow* **CD 6-29**, as sung by Judy Garland. Have them

- Follow the words of the song, pp. 140–141.
- Read the words of the song together.

7b **ASK If you were singing this song, would you sing it the way Judy Garland did?** (Answers will vary.)

**If you wanted to sing it differently, what would you do?** (Accept various answers.)

### 6a Singing

Invite students to sing "Over the Rainbow" **CD 6-27** with the recording.

**ASK Which lines have exactly the same pitches and rhythms, but different words?** (lines 1, 3, and 8; and lines 2, 4, and 9)

6c **SAY** We will label these sections with the letter "A."

**ASK Which lines are totally different from the rest?** (5–7, 10–11)

**SAY** Let's label lines 5–7 with the letter "B." The last two lines of the song are called a *coda*. The *coda* lets us know the song is ending. In Italian, the word *coda* means "tail."

**ASK Is the *coda* most like the A section or the B section of the song?** (B)

continued on page 142

## Movement

6e ▶ **Creative Movement/Locomotor Movement** Students can move to describe phrases in "Over the Rainbow" and other songs.

**Reinforcement** One basic approach is to have students walk or use a hand motion in one direction, then change direction on each new phrase.

**On Target** Have students move arms in an arc to show phrases in the air; then change direction for each new phrase.

**Challenge** Encourage interested students to create a different body movement for each phrase. The same pattern should be used for similar phrases.

## Spotlight On

▶ **"Over the Rainbow"** In Stanley Green's *Encyclopedia of the Musical Film,* the lyricist of "Over the Rainbow," E.Y. Harburg, explained how the lyrics evolved: "Kansas is an arid, colorless place without many flowers. In the scene early in the movie, Dorothy was having trouble at home and, naturally, she had an impulse to run away. Since the only colorful thing she had ever seen was a rainbow, I thought it would be fitting for her to want to go to the other end of the rainbow because that would be full of bright colors."

Harburg was a New Yorker and not familiar with the midwestern states. He didn't realize that Kansas has a gentle landscape that includes many beautiful wildflowers. From his misperception, however, came a lyric that many consider one of his most beautiful.

### Moving

Invite students to try these movements with "Over the Rainbow" **CD 6-27.**

**Formation:** Students may stand beside or in front of chairs or find an open spot on the floor.

**Suggested Movements:** Hold a streamer in the right or left hand. For the A phrases, move the arm in large circular motions. During the B phrases, move the arm in small zigzag motions in front of the body. Encourage students to create their own movements for the coda.

### Listening

Invite students to listen to the Aretha Franklin recording of *Over the Rainbow* **CD 6-30.** Have them use standard terminology to explain their comparison of this musical performance to that of the Judy Garland recording. Have students focus on

- **Introduction:** Judy Garland's version uses a spoken introduction to set the mood. Aretha Franklin's version begins with a soft instrumental introduction.
- **Voices:** Franklin has a blues/gospel quality to her voice and uses a wider range of dynamics, resulting in a more emotional interpretation of the song.
- **Instrumental accompaniment:** Garland's accompaniment includes soft orchestral strings and woodwinds. Franklin is accompanied by a jazz combo of piano, guitar, bass, and light percussion.
- **Rhythm and melody:** Although both singers take liberties with the printed song, Franklin makes much more use of improvisation and ornamentation (varying and altering the rhythm and melody).

Allow students to state and then justify, using standard music terminology, their personal preferences for specific and general style elements of each performance.

### Creating

In small groups, have students learn the poem "Prism in the Window." Invite them to prepare their own dramatizations to perform with the poem.

### Move Over the Rainbow

As you **listen** to the recording of "Over the Rainbow" **move** to show the A and B phrases of the song.

A Make large, slow, circular motions by moving your arms through the air.

B Make small, quick, zigzag motions by moving your hand through the air in front of you.

**Create** your own motions to show the A and B phrases of the song. Then **move** as you **listen** to the recording again.

## Judy Garland

**Judy Garland** (1922–1969), born Frances Gumm, was one of the most famous movie stars of the 1930s and 1940s. Her career as an actress began when she was just two years old. It lasted for more than 40 years.

She was fourteen when she recorded her first album and just sixteen when the movie *The Wizard of Oz* was filmed. Her role as Dorothy made her a superstar, and her performance of *Over the Rainbow* made the song a hit. The song became her lifelong theme song.

142

## Footnotes

### Across the Curriculum

▶ **Language Arts** The poem "Prism in the Window," p. 143 in the Teacher Edition, is one of a quartet of poems titled "Four Poems for Roy G Biv" from *Who Shrank My Grandmother's House? Poems of Discovery* by Barbara Esbensen (HarperCollins, 1992). Each poem offers a unique, poetic view of rainbows.

### Spotlight On

▶ **Rainbows** Rainbows have fascinated people throughout history. A rainbow is a colorful arc that sometimes appears in the sky after it rains. The ends of the rainbow sometimes seem to rest on the earth, which has led to many legends about what can be found at the end of the rainbow. Rainbows are formed when the sun's rays hit drops of water. The rays are bent and reflected by the raindrops, which break up the light into its essential colors, and the rainbow is seen in this way by the observer. Rainbows can only be seen when the observer is between the sun and the water drops.

## Listen Over the Rainbow

**Listen** to two versions of "Over the Rainbow." **Describe** to a partner how they are the same, and how they are different.

CD 6–29 **Over the Rainbow**

**by E.Y. Harburg and Harold Arlen**
**as performed by Judy Garland from *The Wizard of Oz***

This song, which was almost cut from the movie, went on to win an Academy Award in 1939 for "Best Song."

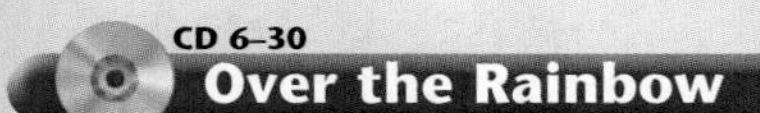
CD 6–30 **Over the Rainbow**

**by E.Y. Harburg and Harold Arlen**
**as performed by Aretha Franklin**

This recording was made in 1960. Accompanying the 18-year-old singer, on piano, bass, and drums, is the Ray Bryant Trio. What other instruments can you hear playing softly in the background?

MUSIC MAKERS

### Aretha Franklin

**Aretha Franklin** (born 1942), the "Queen of Soul," was born in Memphis, Tennessee. As a young girl, she sang at the Detroit church of her father, the Rev. C.L. Franklin. Her first recordings, made when she was 14, reflect her deep gospel roots. In the 1960s, high-energy, soul classics like "Respect" and "Chain of Fools" made her famous. During this period of the Civil Rights Movement, Franklin became a symbol of African Americans' growing confidence and pride.



**Prism in the Window**

I wake to light
falling through glass
colors splintering and clashing
in the air

The noise of morning sunlight
being smashed apart
wakes me

This is my alarm!
Color falls on color
I hear cymbal sound
breaking into rainbow dust
shattering
into seven
rainbow chimes!

PRISM! *Barbara Esbensen*

4a Have students identify words in the poem that suggest sounds and then create an accompaniment for the poem, using pitched and nonpitched instruments. Invite students to improvise a pentatonic accompaniment, using Orff instruments. Students can then perform the poem with the accompaniment.

## 3 Close

### Performing

Divide the class into small groups. Have each group identify ABA form presented aurally by finding another song in their textbook with two contrasting sections and determine if it is in ABA or AABA form. Ask students to listen to and then perform the song, using movement, instruments, streamers, or other props in a way that shows the contrast between the sections.

**Element: FORM** ASSESSMENT

**Performance/Observation** Have students sing "Over the Rainbow" **CD 6-27**, performing creative movements of their choice for the phrases labeled "A" and contrasting movements for the phrases labeled "B."

Observe that students perform contrasting movements for the two sections.

### Skills Reinforcement

1b ▶ **Singing** *Legato* singing is smooth, with no separation between notes. In order to sing a beautiful *legato* line, students need appropriate posture, breath support, and resonance. To develop *legato* singing, try the following.

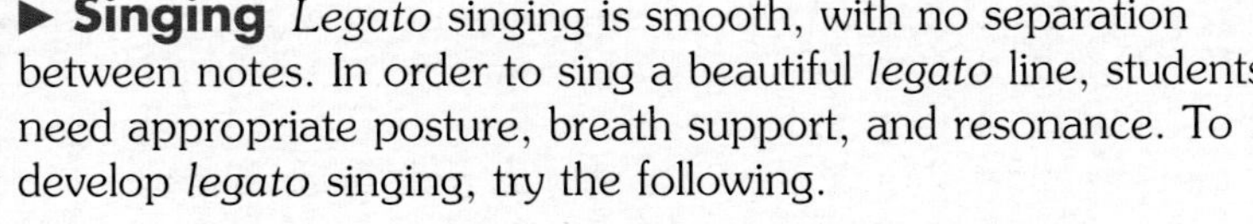

- Select a phrase of a song and have students make an "ss" sound as you sing the phrase.
- Have students sing the phrase on the syllable "noo," which will help develop resonance as well as *legato* singing.
- Have students sing the phrase with words. Listen to make sure students are not sliding on descending intervals or slurring their diction.

▶ **Recorder** For a recorder accompaniment to "Over the Rainbow," see Resource Book p. I-13.

### School to Home Connection

▶ **Collecting Memories** Older friends and relatives may remember *The Wizard of Oz* film, the book by L. Frank Baum, the song "Over the Rainbow," and Judy Garland. Ask students to interview people about their experiences with the film, book, or song. Give students class time to report their findings.

### Technology/Media Link

**Video Library** Use the video to give students the opportunity to compare and contrast different vocal styles.

## LESSON AT A GLANCE

**Element Focus** **MELODY** *Do, re, mi, fa, so,* and *la*

**Skill Objective** **READING** Sing a song from notation that includes *do, re, mi, fa, so,* and *la*

**Connection Activity** **SOCIAL STUDIES** Discuss the life and culture of the Cuna people

**MATERIALS**

- *"Canción de cuna"* **CD 6-31**
- "Cradle Song" **CD 6-32**
  **Recording Routine:** Intro (4 m.); vocal; interlude (4 m.); vocal; coda
- **Music Reading Practice, Sequence 15** **CD 6-35**
- *"Cantando mentiras"* **CD 6-38**
- "Singing Tall Tales" **CD 6-39**
  **Recording Routine:** Intro (6 m.); v. 1; interlude (6 m.); v. 2; coda
- **Pronunciation Practice/Translation**, p. 479
- **Resource Book** pp. A-13, A-14, D-19, E-16, F-10
- selected pitched percussion instruments, guitars

**VOCABULARY**

*fa* pitch ladder

**National Standards**

**1a** Sing independently on pitch.
**2b** Play melodies on appropriate instruments
**5b** Read notes in treble clef using syllables
**5d** Notate pitch and rhythm using standard symbols
**6c** Use appropriate terms to describe music

**MORE MUSIC CHOICES**

Other Spanish-language songs:
*"Cielito lindo,"* p. 270
*"Bogando a la luz del sol,"* p. 306
*"Al quebrar la piñata,"* p. 432
Another song that includes *do, re, mi, fa, so,* and *la*:
"Oh, How Lovely Is the Evening," p. 217



# IN SEARCH OF A New Note

**Sing** *Canción de cuna,* a lullaby from Latin America. The Cunas are Native Americans who live on the northern shore of Panama and the San Blas Islands.

Folk Song from Latin America

G
do
Duer-me pron - to, ni - ño mí - o, Duer-me pron-to y sin llo - rar.
Go to sleep now, go to sleep now, go to sleep now, lit - tle child.

G
Que es - tás en los bra - zos de tu ma - dre, que te va a can - tar.
You are in your moth-er's arms. She will sing a lull - a - by.

# Footnotes

## MEETING INDIVIDUAL NEEDS

▶ **English Language Learners** To ensure that students understand that the verses in *"Cantando mentiras"* (on p. 146) are "tall tales," invite them to illustrate one thing from the song that they think is not really true (for example, rabbits go swimming). After they have illustrated one line from the song and displayed their drawings, encourage students to create new "tall tale" lines for the song, such as *cats that moo.*

## BUILDING SKILLS THROUGH MUSIC

▶ **Math** Invite students to find examples of parallel lines, circles, right angles, rectangles, and perpendicular lines in the photo and artwork on pp. 144 and 145. Then ask students to

- Describe pairs of shapes that are congruent.
- Suggest ways in which geometric shapes are present in music notation.

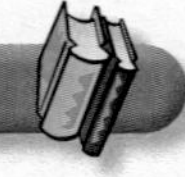

## ACROSS THE CURRICULUM

▶ **Social Studies/Art** Encourage interested students to read *Mola: Cuna Life Stories and Art* by Maricel E. Presilla (Holt, 1996). The book tells about the life of the Cuna people, illustrated with beautiful photos of *molas. Molas* are "wearable artworks" made by Cuna women. They sew together layers of fabric of various colors and textures, then stitch and cut the fabric to make elaborate designs. *Molas* have traditionally shown scenes of Cuna legends, culture, and daily life. As American popular culture has reached the Cunas, *mola* subject matter has expanded to include things like cartoon characters, as well. The Cuna women wear *molas* on special occasions.

## A New Note

**Read** the five notes on the staff below. A new note goes in the color box.

| |
|---|
| *la* |
| *so* |
| *fa* |
| *mi* |
| *re* |
| *do* |

The name of the new pitch, between *so* and *mi*, is *fa*. The step between *mi* and *fa* is called a half step because it is only half the distance of the whole steps between other pitches.

Using the pitch ladder, **sing** up and down the pitches from *do* to *la*. Now **identify** each *fa* in *"Canción de cuna."* Then **sing** the song again.

**Arts Connection**

▲ *Mola* textile pattern of the Cuna people

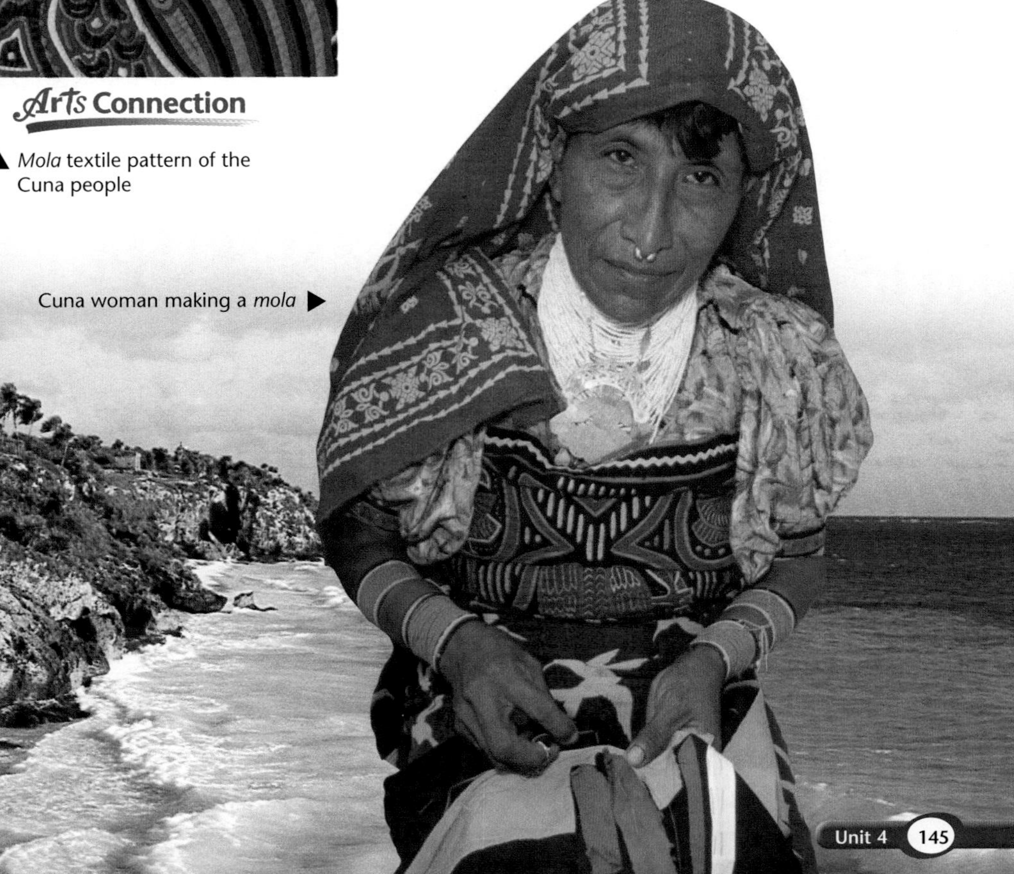

Cuna woman making a *mola* ▶



# 1 Introduce

Use the information and activities in Footnotes below to discuss the life and culture of the Cuna people.

Sing short melodic patterns including *fa*, using a neutral syllable (such as *loo*).

Have students

- Echo sing each pattern (on *loo*), as a group and individually.
- Play patterns on barred instruments (set up in F-*do*).

Play *"Canción de cuna"* **CD 6-31** for students and have students

- Learn the melody by rote.
- Sing along when they are ready.

# 2 Develop

### Reading

Using Resource Book p. D-19, draw attention to the *do* at the beginning of the staff, and review the staff placement of each note.

**SAY** When *do* is on a line, *mi* is on the line above it, and *so* is on the line above *mi*. *Fa* is in the space between *mi* and *so*.

Have students

- Read the melody of *"Canción de cuna"* from the notation on p. 144, using pitch syllables and hand signs.
- Sing *"Canción de cuna"* from notation, using pitch syllables and hand signs.

### Singing

Use Resource Book p. D-19 to review the notes of the G-*do* pentatonic scale.

continued on page 146

## Cultural Connection

▶ **The Cuna People** Although the Cuna people live in what is technically Panama, since 1925 they have largely governed themselves. There are about 40,000 Cunas, who make a living primarily by fishing and farming, harvesting crops such as bananas, plantains, sweet potatoes, and tropical fruits. Almost all of the crops are grown on the mainland, so the Cunas who live on the San Blas de Cuna Islands must travel by boat to the mainland to work. Cuna women are known for their beautiful fabric artworks called *molas* which tell the stories of Cuna culture.

## Skills Reinforcement

▶ **Reading** For more practice reading the six-note scales, see Resource Book p. D-19.

▶ **Singing** Students may be challenged by the Spanish words in the story. Invite students to listen to the Pronunciation Practice Tracks for *"Canción de cuna"* **CD 6-34** and *"Cantando mentiras"* **CD 6-41** and sing with the students on the recordings. Refer to Resource Book pp. A-13 and A-14.

▶ **Mallets** For an Orff instrument accompaniment to *"Canción de cuna,"* see Resource Book p. F-10.

Have students

- Sing the G-*do* pentatonic scale, ascending and descending.
- Sing intervals, starting on *do* and jumping up to each of the other notes and back again *(do–re, do–mi, do–so, do–la).*

Sing a descending *do*-hexachordal pattern for students *(la-so-fa-mi-re-do),* using pitch syllables. Hum *fa* or sing it on a neutral syllable.

**ASK On which note did my pattern end?** *(do)*

**On which note did it begin?** *(la)*

**How did the melody move?** (It started high—on *la*—and moved straight down to *do.)*

**Where does the note I am humming fall in the scale?** (between *mi* and *so*)

**SAY** The note between *mi* and *so* is called *fa.*

Demonstrate the hand sign for *fa,* and write it in its place on the letter ladder. Have students

- Sing the descending pattern, using pitch syllables and hand signs.
- Sing all known notes, from top to bottom, with pitch syllables and hand signs.
- Sing the pattern *so-fa-so,* using hand signs.

Point out that *so* and *fa* are next to each other. Then, have students sing the pattern *mi-fa-mi,* with hand signs.

**ASK Are *mi* and *fa* next to each other?** (yes)

**Does *fa* sound closer to one of these notes than the other?** (Yes, *fa* sounds closer to *mi* than to *so.)*

Explain that the step between *mi* and *fa* is actually a smaller step in sound, called a *half step.* Even though the half step looks like a step on the letter ladder and the staff, it sounds different.

For another reading activity using "*Canción de cuna,*" see p. 449 and Resource Book p. E-16.

## Focus on *Fa*

Find *fa* in the examples below. The *do* finder will help you find your way around the staff.

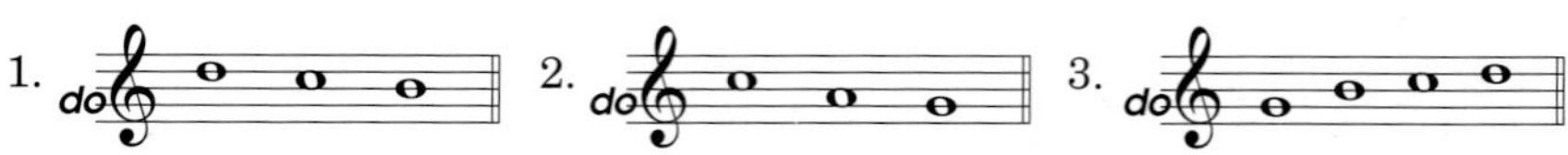
1. do
2. do
3. do

Here is another song with *fa.* The words of this song from Latin America send a silly message. **Listen** to *"Cantando mentiras."* What makes this song funny?

CD 6-38
Cantando mentiras
(Singing Tall Tales)
t,d r m f s
English Words by Alice Firgau
Folk Song from Latin America
G D7
do
1. A ho - ra que es - ta - mos des - pa - cio,
2. Los pe - rru - cos po - nen hue - vos,
1. Let's make up fan - tas - tic sto - ries,
2. Hound dogs lay eggs, we can tell you,
D7 G
Va - mos a can - tar men - ti - ras.
Las ga - lli - nas a la - drar,
Let's sing of tales that are tall;
Chick - ens can bark, it is true;
G D7
Por el rí - o van las lie - bres,
Ya los sa - pos cre - cen co - las,
Rab - bits go swim - ming in riv - ers,
Pond frogs can't swim in the wa - ter,
D7 G
Por el mon - te las an - gui - las.
Por - que no sa - ben na - dar.
Eels through the un - der - brush crawl.
So they grow tails that are new.

# Footnotes

## Across the Curriculum

▶ **Language Arts/Related Arts** Share the book *American Tall Tales* by Mary Pope Osborne (Knopf, 1991). This collection of famous American folk stories will introduce students to this genre of writing.

Divide students into small groups. Invite each group to choose one of the tales and create a performance piece for the rest of the class. Have one group perform this tall tale. During the performance, all students should sing the song *"Cantando mentiras."* After the song, have another group perform their tall tale. Have the class sing the song again, then have the next group perform, and so on.

## Teacher to Teacher

5d ▶ **Notation Preparation** Choose a pattern for students to write and then sing it on a neutral syllable. Have students

- Echo with pitch syllables and hand signs.
- Show the pattern with hand signs only.
- Show hand signs and write pitch syllables.
- Determine the meter and rhythm and then complete the stick notation with pitch syllables.
- Transfer stick notation to a staff.
- Show pattern with hand signs and then write the pitches on a staff.

## Practice *fa*

Now that you know *fa*, find the patterns below in *"Cantando mentiras."* **Sing** the patterns as you **read** them from the staff.

1. so-fa-mi-fa  2. re-mi-fa-so  3. do-re-mi-fa-mi

One of the lines in the song contains a note you do not yet know. Point to the mystery note. You will learn about this note later.

◀ Latin guitarist

### Latin Guitar

The guitar is a popular instrument throughout Latin America. You can accompany the two songs in this lesson, using just one or both chords shown below. Practice the chords first. Then **play** them as others **sing**.



### Playing

Invite students to accompany *"Canción de cuna"* (G chord) and *"Cantando mentiras"* (G and D7 chords) on guitar, following the chord symbols indicated in each song's notation. Have students refer to the photos and diagrams on p. 147 to practice playing the chords individually and in succession.

## 3 Close

### Reading

Have students

- Read the staff notation of the *fa* patterns on p. 146.
- Look at *"Cantando mentiras"* on p. 146.
- Find *do* on the staff.
- Find and identify patterns containing *fa* in the song.
- Look at the patterns on p. 147, and follow the same steps to identifying them.

**Skill: READING** ASSESSMENT

**Performance/Observation** Invite students to sing *"Canción de cuna"* **CD 6-33** or *"Cantando mentiras"* **CD 6-38** while following the notation in their books. Have them sing once using hand signs and syllables and again using the song text.

Observe each student's ability to accurately read and sing *fa* in music notation.

## Skills Reinforcement

▶ **Vocal Development** *So-mi* is often sung with *mi* slightly flat. To correct intonation, try this activity. Use pitch syllables and hand signs. Sing slowly and softly. Have students sing and sustain *so* (C5) while you sing *mi* (A4). Listen for an accurate minor third. Switch parts. Then divide the class in groups and repeat.

Next, have one group sustain *so* while the other group sings *so-fa-mi*. Listen for an accurate half step and minor third. Show students that *so* to *fa* is a whole step and *fa* to *mi* is a half step.

Another exercise is to have one group sustain *so* while the other group sings *mi-fa-so*, Listen for accuracy. Then try the same procedure singing *do-re-mi*.

## Technology/Media Link

**CD-ROM** Set up the computer, keyboard, and *Band-in-a-Box* software. Have students

- Identify the chord symbols found above the staff of *"Cantando mentiras"* and enter them into *Band-in-a-Box*.
- Use the styles menu to choose and generate a Latin-style accompaniment.
- Experiment with changing the instrument combination.
- Sing *"Cantando mentiras"* with the *Band-in-a-Box* accompaniment.

LESSON 7

## LESSON AT A GLANCE

**Element Focus** **MELODY** *Do, re, mi, fa, so,* and *la*

**Skill Objective** **SINGING** Sing and read *do, re, mi, fa, so,* and *la* in a new key

**Connection Activity** **CULTURE** Discuss advertising, past and present

**MATERIALS**

- "Chairs to Mend" **CD 7-1**

  **Recording Routine:** Intro (8 m.); unison vocal; three-part round
- **Music Reading Practice, Sequence 16** **CD 7-3**
- **Resource Book** pp. B-13, D-21, E-17
- recorders

**VOCABULARY**

key signature half-step whole-step

◆ ◆ ◆ ◆ **National Standards** ◆ ◆ ◆ ◆

**1d** Sing rounds
**2f** Play instruments independently against contrasting parts
**4b** Compose music within specified guidelines
**5b** Read notes in treble clef using syllables
**5d** Notate pitches using standard symbols

**MORE MUSIC CHOICES**

For more practice with *fa:*

"This Pretty Planet," p. 355

"For the Beauty of the Earth," p. 356

# 1 INTRODUCE

Ask students to imagine a time before there were computers, or television, or radio, or even billboards. If they wanted to sell a product or service, how would they advertise it? Discuss the information on advertising in Cultural Connection below. Play "Chairs to Mend" **CD 7-1** for students, then discuss how people in earlier times used songs as advertising.



# MOVING A New Note

Let's see what happens to *fa* when a different note becomes *do*. Look at the half-steps and whole-steps on the keyboard below.

*Fa* is always a half-step above *mi*. When *do* is C, *mi* is E and *fa* is F. What happens when *do* is F? Find *fa* on the keyboard. Remember that *fa* is a half-step above *mi.*

To show this note on the staff, we mark it with a flat sign (♭) and call it B-flat.

do re mi fa so

If the flat sign is placed at the beginning of the staff, it is called a **key signature.** It means that all the Bs in this song are really B-flats.

do re mi fa so

key signature

A **key signature** tells which notes are to be performed with a flat or sharp throughout a piece of music.

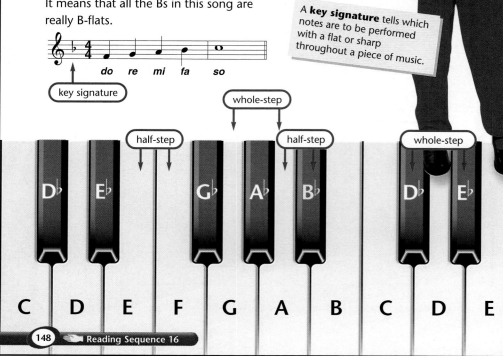

whole-step half-step half-step whole-step

D♭ E♭ G♭ A♭ B♭ D♭ E♭

C D E F G A B C D E



# Footnotes

## SKILLS REINFORCEMENT

**2f** ▶ **Recorder** For additional practice playing high C and D on recorder, have students play the ostinato below with "Chairs to Mend." For ensemble practice, advanced students can play the song melody on recorder while others play the ostinato.

## BUILDING SKILLS THROUGH MUSIC

▶ **Social Studies** Share the information on Advertising from Cultural Connection on p. 148. Explain to the students that Public Service Announcements (PSAs) are used on television and the radio to promote important information or causes. Have the students work in groups to develop a PSA on "Why music is important in the world."

## CULTURAL CONNECTION

▶ **Advertising** Advertising is used to promote products, services, or ideas. It tries to inform, influence, or persuade people. Outdoor signs for shops in Babylon around 3000 B.C. were the first known advertising. Town criers in ancient Egypt called out to people, announcing the arrival of cargo ships. Today in the United States, over $100 billion is spent on advertising each year. Ask students to think of places they notice advertising—television, radio, Internet, billboards, magazines, and so on. Talk about how advertising affects students when they choose things such as clothing, food, and entertainment. Music plays an important part in advertising. Discuss with students why musical ads might be particularly effective.

## What's for Sale?

Before the days of commercials, the street cry was a singing advertisement. You may have heard a similar cry from a vendor at a ball game. **Listen** to this song. What items are being advertised?

Look at the key signature of this song. Can you find *fa?* **Sing** "Chairs to Mend" using pitch syllables. Then you can sing this song as a round.

CD 7-1
MIDI 12
Chairs to Mend
s, d r m f s l
Street Call from England
I
F
do
Chairs to mend, old chairs to mend.
II
Mack - er - el, fresh mack - er - el.
III
Rags? Rags? An - y old rags?

## Show What You Know!

These melodies contain all of the notes you have learned. **Sing** each melody. Do any sound familiar?

1. so so so so fa mi fa fa
2. so mi fa so mi fa so so fa mi fa re
3. mi fa so mi mi fa so mi mi fa so mi so fa mi

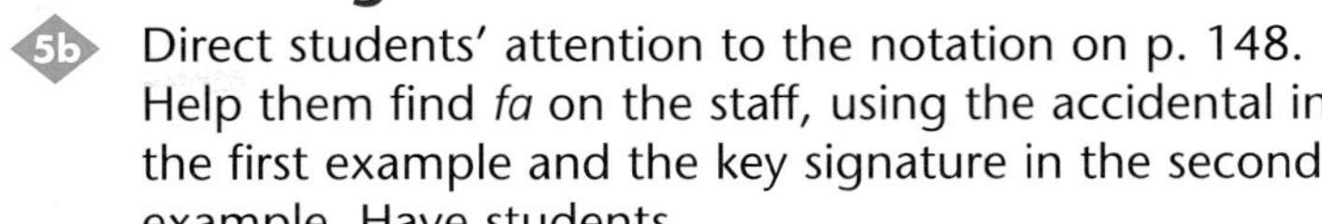

# 2 Develop

### Reading

5b Direct students' attention to the notation on p. 148. Help them find *fa* on the staff, using the accidental in the first example and the key signature in the second example. Have students

- Find each *fa* in the song. (mm. 1, 2, and 3)
- Sing "Chairs to Mend" **CD 7-1** using pitch syllables and hand signs.

See p. 449 and Resource Book p. E-17 for a related reading activity.

### Creating

4b For additional practice, have students create their own melody patterns that include *fa.* Write a measure on the board. Designate a line or space as *do.* Have students add three or four pitches, including one *fa.* Then practice singing the pattern together.

### Singing

1d Divide the class into three groups. Assign each group one line of "Chairs to Mend." Have each group practice its line separately, then put the groups together. Create a layered round by having each group repeat its line a specified number of times.

### Reading

Have students sing the melodies in Show What You Know! Refer to Resource Book p. B-13. Then, for more practice finding half-steps and whole-steps, see Resource Book p. D-21.

# 3 Close

**Skill: SINGING** ASSESSMENT

**Performance/Observation** In small groups, have students sing "Chairs to Mend" **CD 7-1**, first using hand signs and pitch syllables and then again using the song text. Observe each student's ability to read and sing *fa* in a new key (F major).

## Teacher to Teacher

5d ▶ **Hearing the Diatonic Scale** When students understand the principle of key signatures (that in order to maintain the pattern of whole and half steps in the diatonic scale, we must use accidentals in every key except the key of C), divide them into small groups and ask them to compose a short melody in F-*do*. Students may develop their melodies by singing or playing mallet instruments, then notating them. Encourage students to use all notes in the F-major scale. Groups may then play their melodies for the rest of the class, who can determine whether or not the melodies include a B♭. Have them sing their melodies without a B♭, perhaps with a B♮ to hear if it makes any difference.

## Technology/Media Link

**MIDI/Sequencing Software** Use the MIDI song file for "Chairs to Mend" to help students learn to sing the song as a round. When students are confident singing the melody, have them sing it along with the voice 1 and voice 2 tracks. Then have them sing voice 2 with the same tracks. When students are comfortable with this combination, add voice 3 and have students sing voices 2 and 3. Continue until students can sing all three parts independently.

Core LESSON 8

## LESSON AT A GLANCE

**Element Focus** **MELODY** Melodic contour

**Skill Objective** **LISTENING** Perform hand movements to show melodic contour

**Connection Activity** **CULTURE** Discuss the role of music in special events

**MATERIALS**

- Movement 4 ("Ode to Joy") from *Symphony No. 9* (excerpt) **CD 7-6**
- *"Ode to Joy"* (German) **CD 7-7**
- "Ode to Joy" (English) **CD 7-8**

  **Recording Routine:** Intro (4 m.); vocal; interlude (4 m.); vocal; coda
- **Pronunciation Practice/Translation** p. 480
- **Resource Book** pp. A-15, H-14, I-14
- tuned bells or recorders

**VOCABULARY**

choral movement symphony contour

**National Standards**

**1c** Sing songs from diverse cultures
**2b** Play melodies on appropriate instruments
**6b** Describe music by moving to it and explaining how it sounds
**6e** While listening to music, move to show a prominent feature of the music
**9c** Identify uses of music in everyday life
**9d** Describe roles of musicians in various settings

**MORE MUSIC CHOICES**

For more practice following melodic contour:
"Sailing Down My Golden River," p. 332
"For the Beauty of the Earth," p. 356
Other songs about brotherhood:
"Love Can Build a Bridge," p. 324
*"Somos el barco,"* p. 352

# UNITED by Melody

At the opening ceremonies of the 1998 Winter Olympics, Seiji Ozawa [SAY-jee oh-ZAH-wah] conducted six performing groups at the same time. But this was no ordinary performance. The groups were on five different continents! Satellite technology allowed the musicians from all over the world to perform the fourth movement of Beethoven's *Symphony No. 9* together. Through this unique new way of performing, they delivered a powerful message of unity to the world.



◀ Conductor Seiji Ozawa



# Footnotes

## TEACHER TO TEACHER

▶ **Instrument Tips** Develop code words to manage students' physical behavior with instruments.

- Rest—both hands on knees and off of all instruments
- Ready—instrument in hands, silently waiting for cues
- Play—proper technique and posture when playing instrument

## BUILDING SKILLS THROUGH MUSIC

▶ **Writing** Teach students "Ode to Joy." Direct their attention to p. 150. Have them read the information. Share the information presented in the Cultural Connection on p. 151. Ask students to write a brief paragraph using the prompt "People all over the world singing together about joy..."

## MEETING INDIVIDUAL NEEDS

▶ **Body/Kinesthetic** When students have learned the entire melody of "Ode to Joy," divide them into four groups, each of which sits in a circle. Assign each group a different melodic phrase from the song. Then refer students to the "Ode to Joy" listening map on p. 151. Invite each group to create a movement for its melodic phrase. Help group members follow the appropriate contour on the listening map and to hum the melody as the group plans its movement. Encourage the groups to write out their ideas or to draw them. Then let each group perform its movement as you play the recording of *Symphony No. 9* several times. Guide the class in critiquing the performance.

## Follow that Melody!

**Listen** to "Ode to Joy" from Beethoven's *Symphony No. 9, Movement 4.* Follow the listening map below, and trace the **contour** of the melody with your finger.

**Contour** is the "shape" of a melody made by the way it moves upward and downward in steps, leaps, and repeated tones.

CD 7-6

### Ode to Joy

**from *Symphony No. 9, Movement 4***
**by Ludwig van Beethoven**

Beethoven [BAY-toh-vehn] had lost his hearing by the time he composed *Symphony No. 9.* This symphony was performed at the 1998 Winter Olympics in Nagano, Japan. Millions of people throughout the world heard the music that Beethoven himself heard only in his mind.

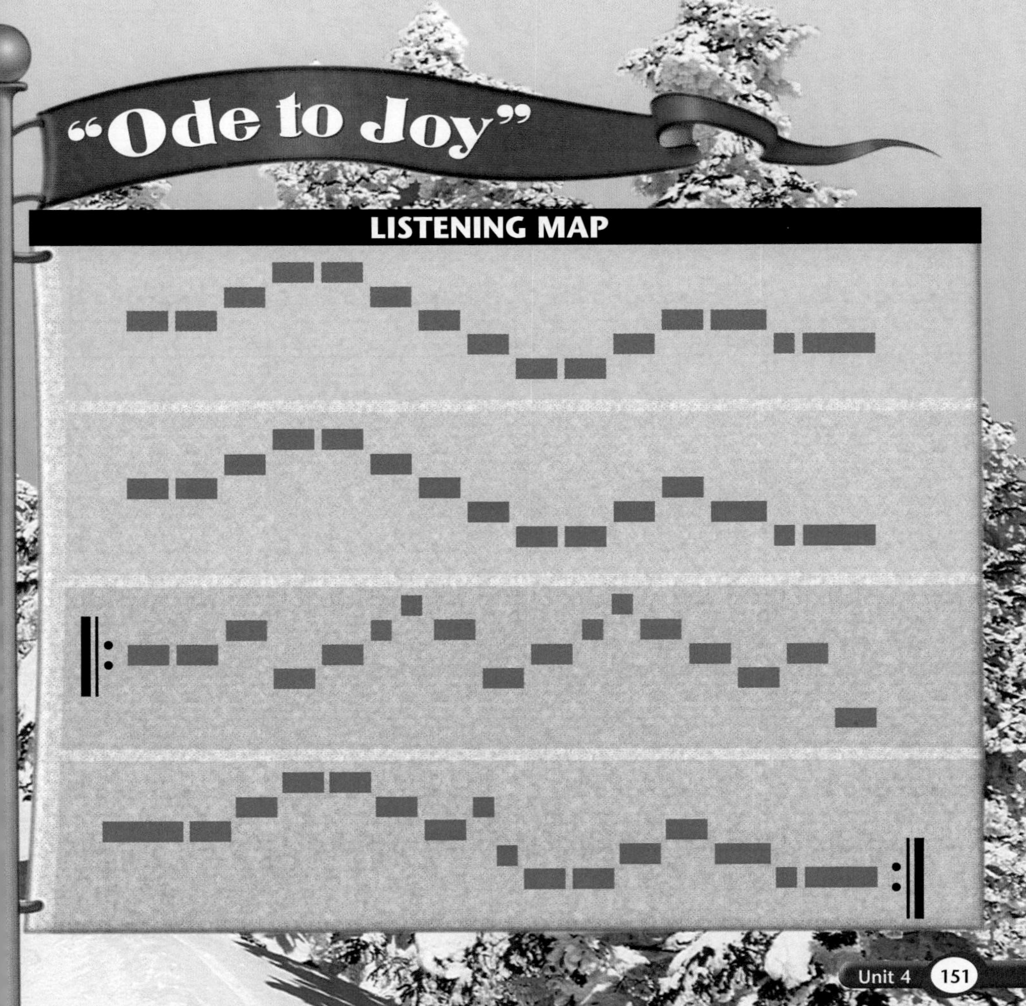




# 1 INTRODUCE

9c Invite students to think of a special occasion at which they might hear music. (a wedding, athletic event, parade, religious celebration, festival, and so on) Discuss with students what purpose music serves in each type of celebration. Talk about the music students may have heard in connection with the Olympics. Share with students the information in Cultural Connection and Spotlight On below.

# 2 DEVELOP

### Listening

6b Have students

- Listen to the "Ode to Joy" section from Movement No. 4 of *Symphony No. 9* **CD 7-6.**
- Follow the listening map on p. 151.
- Listen again, using hand motions to draw in the air the melodic contour.
- Use appropriate words to describe the music. (dramatic, exciting, and so forth)

ASK **Does this music move mostly by steps or mostly by skips?** (mostly by steps)

**SAY** There are only six different notes in this melody.

### Singing

1c Invite students to

- Sing the English version of "Ode to Joy" **CD 7-8,** p. 152, using hand motions to show melodic contour.
- Listen to the German version **CD 7-7.**
- Learn the song in German, using the Pronunciation Practice Track **CD 7-10.** (Refer to Resource Book p. A-15.)
- Sing "Ode to Joy" **CD 7-7** in German.

**continued on page 152**

## CULTURAL CONNECTION

9c ▶ **A Piece for Many Occasions** Introduce students to Beethoven the man by reading the Beethoven passage from *Lives of the Musicians: Good Times, Bad Times (and What the Neighbors Thought)* by Kathleen Krull (Harcourt Brace, 1993). Point out that the "Ode to Joy" has been heard around the world in many different settings. The power of this stirring music is understood the world over. Beethoven's famous melody was played during the Chinese student protest at Tiananmin Square and at the fall of the Berlin Wall, both in 1989.

## SPOTLIGHT ON

▶ **Beethoven's Ninth** A unique aspect of Beethoven's amazing *Symphony No. 9* is the use of solo voices and chorus in the last movement. This had not been done before in a symphony. Beethoven selected the stanzas from Schiller's poem that expressed the ideas of lasting joy and the brotherhood of humankind. The inspirational melody of "Ode to Joy" repeatedly arches upward as the lyrics speak of comradeship and unity. Have students listen for how the melody's contour helps suggest the mood of the lyrics. "Ode to Joy" expresses Beethoven's highest aspirations and his desire to rise above all difficulties. Point out that at the first performance, Beethoven had to be turned toward the audience to see their enthusiastic response, because he was totally deaf.

### Playing

2b Help students learn to play the melody of "Ode to Joy" on bells or recorders. Encourage those who play other instruments to bring them to class and play. You may need to help students who play transposing instruments to transpose the melody so it will sound at the correct pitch.

### Moving

6e Invite students to move with "Ode to Joy."

**Formation:** Students stand in a circle or line.

**Suggested Movements:** Have students pretend they are athletes at the Olympic Games. Divide the class into four groups. Ask each group to choose a country to represent. Have students

- Pretend they are carrying flags from their country and create four different movements (one movement per phrase).
- Alter movements by shifting flags from low to high to represent the contour of the melody. On the last measure the flag should be in front of the student's body.
- Step to the whole note while holding their flag, keeping their arms still.
- As a movement challenge, step to the whole note in one direction in their formation and move the flags to the contour of the melody.

## A Message of Joy

Poet Friedrich Schiller (1759–1805) wrote the original German words to this song. **Sing** the message of "Ode to Joy" in English or in German.

CD 7-7

## Ode to Joy

s, (d) r m f s

Words by Friedrich Schiller
English Words by Georgette LeNorth

Music by Ludwig van Beethoven

G D G D
Freu - de, schön - er Göt - ter - fun - ken, Toch - ter aus E - ly - si - um,
Come and sing a joy - ful cho - rus, Lift your voic - es to the sky.

G C G D G
wir be - tre - ten feu - er - trunk - en, Himm - li - sche, dein Hei - lig-tum!
Help - ing hands now join in friend-ship, Keep - ing hearts and spir - its high.

D G D G D $Bm_7$ Em D
Dei - ne Zau - ber bin - den ___ wied - er, was die ___ Mo - de streng ge - teilt;
Sis - ter, broth-er, care for each oth - er, Care for the world and keep it free.

G C G D G
al - le Men-schen wer - den Brüd - er, wo dein sanf - ter Flü - gel weilt.
Come ___ to - geth - er, sing to - geth - er, As a peace-ful fam - i - ly.

152

# Footnotes

## Cultural Connection

9d ▶ **1998 Winter Olympics** The time? Winter, 1998. The place? Minami Stadium in Nagano, Japan. A stadium full of people watched on big-screen TVs as satellites transmitted the event into the homes of millions of awestruck television viewers. The event? Celebrating the brotherhood of all peoples, Seiji Ozawa conducted six choruses singing from six different countries in a performance of Beethoven's "Ode to Joy." Following a conductor who could not see them, the choristers took their cues from Ozawa via satellite during both the rehearsals and performance. Why try such a challenging way to perform a piece of music? When asked to comment, Ozawa replied, "People all over the world singing together about joy...that's the purpose."

## Skills Reinforcement

2b ▶ **Keyboard** The melody of "Ode to Joy" is relatively easy for students to play on keyboards. Have them position their right hand with the thumb on G. The hand stays in this position during the entire melody, except for the low D in m. 12. Students can reach down with the thumb for this note, then go right back to the original position. See Resource Book p. H-14 for a student worksheet that includes instructions and notation.

▶ **Recorder** Students will enjoy playing a harmony part for "Ode to Joy." See Resource Book p. I-14 for notation and instructions.

Letter Names for Notes
Beethoven's melody has only six different notes. These notes are identified on the flags below. Find these notes in "Ode to Joy."
D
G
A
B
C
D
Review how to play the notes above on the recorder. Then **play** "Ode to Joy" along with the recording.
MUSIC MAKERS
Ludwig van Beethoven
**Ludwig van Beethoven** (1770–1827) is one of the most famous composers of all time. During his lifetime, Beethoven composed a variety of music including works for solo piano, small ensembles, and orchestra. He was born in Germany and began studying piano when he was very young. His first composition was published when he was only twelve years old. In his twenties, Beethoven gradually began to lose his hearing. Even after becoming completely deaf, he continued to write music.
Unit 4 153


# 3 Close

## Analyzing/Describing

Share Footnotes information about Beethoven and Seiji Ozawa. Have students write about why they think some music, like "Ode to Joy," is still popular after hundreds of years, while other pieces are soon forgotten. Encourage them to explain their ideas on how music like Beethoven's has been passed down through the years. (by notating or recording it, through oral tradition, and so on)

Encourage students to

- Research Beethoven and *Symphony No. 9.*
- Pretend to be Beethoven, and write a journal entry about composing this symphony and your reactions to its first performance. Some questions students might think about as they write are: Was Beethoven surprised by how much people liked his symphony? Did he dream that people would still be listening to it almost 200 years later? How would it feel to write a great symphony but be able to hear it only in your mind?
- Exchange journal pages with a friend for helpful comments.
- Make any changes based on these comments.

Students can share their journal pages with the class.

**Performance/Observation** Have students listen to *Ode to Joy* **CD 7-6** once again. As they listen, ask them to use hand motions to show the contour of the melody.

To observe whether they can perform this activity independently, ask them to close their eyes as they move their hands to show melodic contour.

## Spotlight On

▶ **The Conductor** Seiji Ozawa (b. 1935) recently retired as music director of the Boston Symphony Orchestra after more than twenty-five years in the post—longer than anyone else has conducted an American orchestra. In the fall of 2002, Ozawa became music director of the Vienna State Opera Orchestra, one of the most illustrious orchestras in the history of music. Seiji Ozawa was born in Shenyang, China, to Japanese parents. He studied music from an early age and graduated from Tokyo's Toho School of Music with prizes in composition and conducting. Ozawa is best known for conducting the Tanglewood Music Festival, held every summer near Great Barrington, Massachusetts. In 1994, the 1,180-seat Seiji Ozawa Hall was opened at Tanglewood to honor this great conductor.

## Technology/Media Link

**Electronic Keyboard** Show students how to play "Ode to Joy" on a keyboard in a five-finger pattern. Have students

- Choose the GM voice that seems to fit the melody the best. Ask them why it seems best to them.
- Decide whether the melody should be played *staccato* or *legato.*
- Decide how loudly or softly the melody should be played and whether to change the dynamics while playing by using the volume slider.

**Transparency** Use the transparency for *Ode to Joy* to help students follow the contour of the melody.

LESSON Core 9

## LESSON AT A GLANCE

**Element Focus** **TIMBRE** Percussion timbre

**Skill Objective** **PLAYING** Play a percussion ensemble piece

**Connection Activity** **CULTURE** Discuss similarities and differences between percussion instruments of various cultures

**MATERIALS**

- *Toccata for Percussion,* Movement 3 — **CD 7-11**
- *Wu long (Dragon Dance)* — **CD 7-13**
- *Lian xi qu (étude)* — **CD 7-14**
- **Resource Book** pp. J-8 and J-9
- small hand cymbals, small and large gongs, drums

**VOCABULARY**

| | | | |
|---|---|---|---|
| percussion | glockenspiel | maracas | tom-tom |
| snare drum | bass drum | claves | timpani |
| *luogu* | *toccata* | *étude* | |

**◆◆◆◆ National Standards ◆◆◆◆**

**2b** Play rhythms on appropriate instruments
**2f** Play instruments independently against contrasting parts
**4b** Compose instrumental pieces within specific guidelines
**6b** Describe music by explaining how it sounds
**6c** Use appropriate terms to explain music
**6d** Identify the sounds of orchestral instruments

**MORE MUSIC CHOICES**

Other recordings that feature percussion:
*Mars, the Bringer of War,* p. 377
*Rag puria kalyan,* p. 192
*The Stars and Stripes Forever,* p. 159
Other Asian selections:
*"Feng yang hua gu,"* p. 313
*"Niu lang zhi nü,"* p. 335

LESSON 9 — Element: TIMBRE | Skill: PLAYING | Connection: CULTURE

# Percussion on Parade

How do you think the first instruments were created? Long ago, people discovered that they could make sounds on objects they found around them. These objects developed into percussion instruments that we play today. You can also make sounds on objects you find around you.

## Percussion Identification

◀ **Maracas** make a crisp, rattling sound when shaken.

▲ **Tom-toms** produce sharp sounds.

▼ A **glockenspiel** has metal bars that produce a light, ringing sound.

154

# Footnotes

## TEACHER TO TEACHER

▶ **Focus Help** When performing body percussion or instrumental parts, some students have trouble focusing and begin simply making noise. Try this procedure to help students focus. Have a secure student perform a pattern once. Without stopping, add a second person, asking them to sound the same as the first student. Add the student with the focus problem as the third. Praise the student for accomplishing the task.

## BUILDING SKILLS THROUGH MUSIC

▶ **Language** Ask students to count off—1, 2—to form pairs. Have all number "1" students tell their partners as much detail from this lesson about percussion instruments as they can remember. Ask all number "2" students to check the information for accuracy and then hand their books to their partners. All number "1" students move down one partner and repeat the process. Conclude with a class review.

## SPOTLIGHT ON

▶ **The Composer** Carlos Chávez (1899–1978) was born in Mexico City. He traced his paternal ancestry to the early Spanish settlers in Mexico. Chávez made many contributions to the cultural life of his country. For many years, he was the director of the National Conservatory of Mexico. He organized and conducted one of Mexico's finest symphony orchestras and appeared many times as a guest conductor in the United States. Chávez had a deep interest in the people who lived in Mexico before the time of Cortés. He heard the music of Mexican Indians when he was a child. Later he became interested in the music of the Mayas, Aztecs, and Toltecs. Chávez studied instruments that were preserved in museums and included their sounds in his music.

**Listen** to *Toccata for Percussion.* **Identify** the percussion instruments as you hear them.

**by Carlos Chávez**

Chávez [CHAH-vehs] (1899–1978) traveled all over Mexico learning about Mexican-Indian music. Much of the music he composed was influenced by the rhythms of these cultures.

◀ A **snare drum** can make a long, raspy roll or a sharp, short sound.

◀ **Claves** produce a bright, hollow sound when struck together.

A **bass drum** produces a deep boom or a soft "thudding" sound. ▶

▲ **Timpani,** also called kettledrums, can sound like a roll of thunder or a quiet "thump."

These instruments are featured in the Sound Bank on page 466.



# 1 Introduce

6b Ask several students to find an object in the room they may strike, shake, or scrape to make a sound. Have
6c each one demonstrate. Then ask class members to close their eyes while the sounds are demonstrated at random. Have students identify the sounds by ear only, then find words to describe the sounds. Tell the students that timbre is the musical term for describing tone color or the sound of an instrument.

Use the activity in Across the Curriculum below to explore instrument construction and how the construction materials that were available influenced what instruments a culture developed.

# 2 Develop

### Listening

Read, or select students to read, the descriptions of orchestral percussion instruments on pp. 154–155 as students follow in their books.

6d Have students listen to *Toccata for Percussion,* Mvt. 3 **CD 7-11,** by Carlos Chávez. Ask them to listen for different percussion timbres and categorize them by identifying the instruments that are playing.

Play the percussion identification game. Have each student find a partner and share one book. When students hear a specific instrument in *Toccata for Percussion,* have them point to the picture of the instrument. Switch partners and play the game again.

Divide students into groups. Assign an instrument from *Toccata for Percussion* to each group. Play the piece again, asking students to raise their hands or stand up when they hear their instruments. Assist each group in responding at the appropriate time. After the activity, discuss how students can recognize their instrument (by listening for unique qualities in its timbre). Repeat the activity with different instrument assignments.

**continued on page 156**

## Across the Curriculum

▶ **Science** Instruments that are struck, shaken, or scraped to produce sound are known as percussion instruments. Although many percussion instruments today are manufactured from man-made materials, traditionally they were made from natural materials such as wood, clay, leather, gourds, seedpods, or bamboo. Various metals were also discovered to have potential for percussive sound. As an individual or group project, students might find it interesting to research the origins of a particular percussion instrument. They will find that the instruments in particular cultures are influenced by the materials available to people living at that time and in that place. Students can report back to the class on the natural materials involved in their instruments' construction and the changes that have been made over the years.

## Skills Reinforcement

2f ▶ **Reading** The instrumental parts in the *Wu long* ensemble, pp. 156 and 157, are ideal for practicing rhythm syllables learned in previous lessons. Start with the large gong part and then the small gong/cymbal part, followed by the drum part. After reading them as written, invite students to

- Read the large gong line as another group reads the gong/cymbal line and a third reads the drum line.
- Read the large gong line while individuals take turns reading one bar each of the other two parts.

▶ **Playing/Creating** Have students create body percussion for *Wu long*. For example, the large gong part might be *pat-clap.* Have students read the part with rhythm syllables and then improvise body percussion until they find a combination that fits.

## Playing

Have students read the information about *luogu* ensembles and the Dragon Dance on p. 156. Ask whether any students have seen a Dragon Dance on television or in person. If so, let them describe it. Discuss the occasion for dragon dances (Chinese New Year), combining information students can offer with that provided in Footnotes below. Have students listen to the recording of *Wu long* **CD 7-13.**

Explain to students that Chinese musicians use rhythm syllables to learn parts in music. Have them listen to *Wu long* practice syllables **CD 7-12.**

Divide the class into four groups, one for each percussion part in *Wu long.* Have each group

- Use rhythm syllables to learn their part.
- Practice each part individually on instruments.
- Practice their parts in combination, until they can play all parts together.

Students may enjoy creating their own dragons for a dragon dance. See Activity Master 7 on Resource Book pp. J-8 and J-9 for detailed instructions.

## Listening

Invite students to listen to *Lian xi qu* (*étude*) **CD 7-14** and focus on such elements as instrumental timbre and the use of repeated rhythm patterns. Help students apply basic criteria in describing and evaluating this composition.

ASK **How is this piece the same as or different than *Wu long?*** (Accept various answers.)

### Percussion in China

Percussion instruments play an important role in many types of music, including marching bands. Where have you heard a marching band perform? At a parade? At a football game? Children in Chinese communities hear *luogu* [loo-OH-goo] percussion ensembles at parades, festivals, and concerts. The sound of the *luogu* ensemble is as familiar in China as the sound of a marching band is in the United States.

▲ A *luogu* ensemble includes gongs, drums, cymbals, bells, and woodblocks.

As you **listen** to the percussion piece *Wu long,* follow the notation on the next page.

**Traditional Dance from China**

*Wu long* is played for the Dragon Dance, a traditional dance often performed in parades for Chinese New Year. It is performed by a *luogu* ensemble using Chinese instruments.

In the Dragon Dance, many people carry a fabric dragon on sticks. As they move in a spiraling pattern, the dragon's body appears to slither down the street. ▶

# Footnotes

## ACROSS THE CURRICULUM

▶ **Social Studies/Language Arts** Have students read the following books about Chinese New Year sights and sounds and create a mini-drama, complete with narration and Dragon Dance to celebrate this festival.

- *Happy New Year!: Kung-Hsi Fa-Ts'Ai!* by Demi (Crown, 1998)
- *The Dancing Dragon* by Marcia Vaughan (Mondo, 1996)
- *Chin Chiang and the Dragon's Dance* by Ian Wallace, (Grolundwood-Douglas, 1998)
- *Lion Dancer: Ernie Wan's Chinese New Year* by Kate Waters (Demco, 1990).

Students may create a dragon from construction paper, fabric, and dowels as an art project to be used in their event.

▶ ***Luogu* Ensemble** Students may enjoy performing other Chinese *luogu* ensembles. *The Lion's Roar: Chinese Luogu Percussion Ensembles* by Han Kuo-Huang and Patricia Shehan Campbell (World Music Press, 1997), has many ensembles, further cultural facts, musical background, and instruction in playing Chinese percussion ensembles.

## Your Turn to Play

You can play *Wu long* with your class. Practice each part below using rhythm syllables. Then **play** the parts on percussion instruments. The ✕ in the drum part indicates that you play on the rim of the drum.

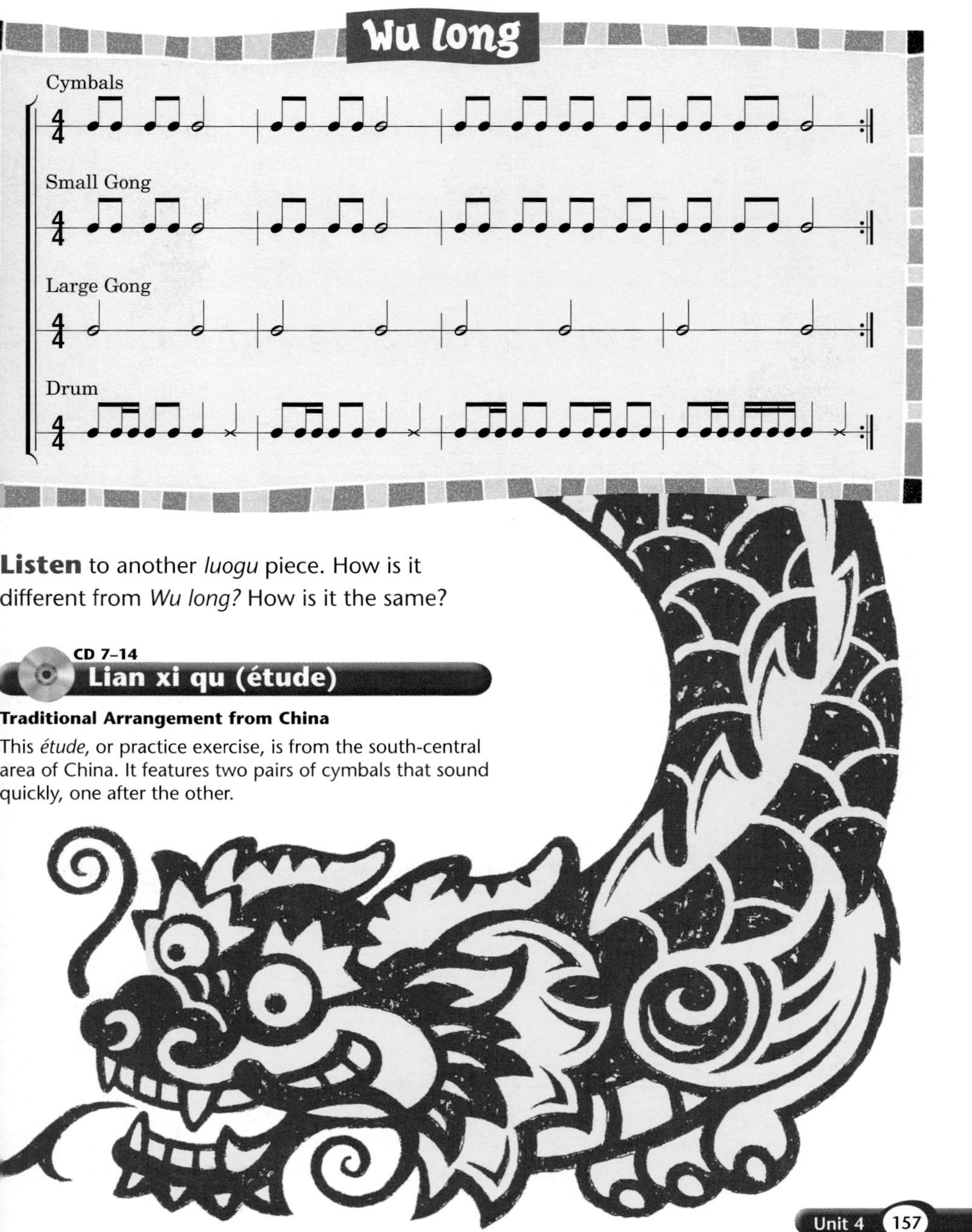


**Listen** to another *luogu* piece. How is it different from *Wu long?* How is it the same?

CD 7–14
**Lian xi qu (étude)**

**Traditional Arrangement from China**

This *étude*, or practice exercise, is from the south-central area of China. It features two pairs of cymbals that sound quickly, one after the other.



# 3 Close

### Describing

List all the percussion instruments from this lesson on the board. Have students describe the look and sound of each instrument and tell whether the instrument belongs to the orchestra or the *luogu* ensemble. For more on categorizing these intruments and others from various cultures, have students visit the Sound Bank, beginning on p. 466.

**Skill: PLAYING** ASSESSMENT

**Performance/Observation** Have students play *Wu long,* first using body percussion and again with selected students playing their parts on percussion instruments.

Observe students' performances, using the following criteria.

- Is each student able to maintain his or her individual part during the performance?
- Are the members of the ensemble staying together?

## Meeting Individual Needs

▶ **Including Everyone** Every individual has a need to fit in and feel successful with the group. Instrumental parts such as those in the *Wu long* ensemble can accommodate individual capabilities. Those who have limited rhythmic facility can stay on the large gong part, while more confident students can play the gong/cymbal part. Those who are most able can perform the drum part. Students can perform the four-bar exercise in groups of three or more. A student can do a part alone if he or she can maintain it successfully. If not, that student should be teamed with one or more students who can. The goal is a performance that "locks in tight," a tribute to the ability of all individuals to work as a team.

## Technology/Media Link

4b **Sequencing Software** Use a computer with sequencing software and a MIDI keyboard to record a percussion ensemble. In small groups, have students

- Compose, then sketch an eight-measure percussion part made up of ♩, ♫, ♩♬, ♬♩, and 𝄽.
- Rehearse their parts, using the MIDI keyboard set to a percussion sound.
- Record each percussion part on a different track.

Students can play back the rhythms, using different General MIDI percussion voices.

LESSON 10

## LESSON AT A GLANCE

**Element Focus** **TEXTURE/HARMONY** Countermelody

**Skill Objective** **SINGING** Sing a song with a countermelody

**Connection Activity** **SOCIAL STUDIES** Discuss the history and meaning of a patriotic song

**MATERIALS**

- "America, the Beautiful" **CD 7-15**

  **Recording Routine:** Intro (4 m.); v. 1; interlude (4 m.); v. 2 (with countermelody); interlude (4. m.); v. 3 (with countermelody); coda
- *The Stars and Stripes Forever* **CD 7-17**

**VOCABULARY**

countermelody texture

**National Standards**

**1d** Sing part songs
**1e** Sing in groups, following a conductor
**6b** Describe music by moving to it
**6e** While listening to music, move to show a prominent feature of the music
**8b** Identify ways music relates to language arts and social studies

**MORE MUSIC CHOICES**

Another patriotic song:
"The Star-Spangled Banner," p. 441

# 1 INTRODUCE

Invite students to read and discuss the information above "America, the Beautiful" on p. 158. Share with them the additional activities and information in Across the Curriculum below.

Play "America, the Beautiful" **CD 7-15.**

LESSON 10
Element: TEXTURE/HARMONY
Skill: SINGING
Connection: SOCIAL STUDIES
America in Two Parts ~ Melody and
Katharine Lee Bates was feeling pride for her country when she wrote the words to "America, the Beautiful" in 1893. She found her inspiration for the song as she stood on the top of Pikes Peak in Colorado.
CD 7-15
MIDI 13
America, the Beautiful
r m f s l t di r' m'
Words by Katharine Lee Bates
Music by Samuel A. Ward
Countermelody by Buryl Red
1. O beau - ti - ful for spa - cious skies, For am - ber waves of grain,
2. O beau - ti - ful for Pil - grim feet, Whose stern im - pas-sioned stress
3. O beau - ti - ful for pa - triot dream That sees be-yond the years
For pur - ple moun-tain maj - es - ties A - bove the fruit - ed plain!
A thor-ough-fare for free - dom beat A - cross the wil - der - ness!
Thine al - a - bas - ter cit - ies gleam, Un - dimmed by hu - man tears!
A - mer - i - ca! A - mer - i - ca! God shed His grace on thee
A - mer - i - ca! A - mer - i - ca! God mend thine ev - 'ry flaw,
A - mer - i - ca! A - mer - i - ca! God shed His grace on thee
And crown thy good with broth - er-hood From sea to shin - ing sea!
Con - firm thy soul in self con-trol, Thy lib - er - ty in law!
And crown thy good with broth - er-hood From sea to shin - ing sea!
158

# Footnotes

## SPOTLIGHT ON

▶ **The National Anthem** In 1916, U.S. leaders searched for a song that would instill national pride. President Woodrow Wilson ordered that "The Star-Spangled Banner" be played at all government gatherings. In 1926, "America, the Beautiful" was also nominated for the honor of becoming our national anthem. "The Star-Spangled Banner" won out, becoming the official U.S. national anthem in 1931.

## BUILDING SKILLS THROUGH MUSIC

▶ **Language** Have students examine the lyrics of "America, the Beautiful" and list the words that are plural or possessive. Then list examples of words in the lyrics that are NOT plural or possessive, but often are mistakenly sung with an added "s" sound.

## ACROSS THE CURRICULUM

8b ▶ **Language Arts** Katharine Lee Bates was vacationing in Colorado when she wrote, "Some of the other teachers and I decided to go on a trip to 14,000 foot Pikes Peak. We hired a prairie wagon. Near the top, we had to leave the wagon and go the rest of the way on mules. I was very tired. But when I saw the view, I felt great joy. All the wonder of America seemed displayed there, with the sea-like expanse." Have students write extra lyrics for "America the Beautiful" that describe the beauty of nature in America.

▶ **Social Studies** Provide a map of the United States. Have students determine the location of the regions described by these lyrics: *amber waves of grain, purple mountains, fruited plains, sea to shining sea.* Encourage students to give reasons for their choices.

# Countermelody

**Sing** the melody of "America, the Beautiful." Then **sing** the **countermelody** below. Adding a countermelody creates a thicker texture than either part sung alone.

A **countermelody** is a contrasting melody that is played or sung at the same time as the main melody.

Countermelody
do
O _______ beau-ti-ful, O _______ beau-ti-ful,
O _______ beau-ti-ful, O _______ beau-ti-ful,
A-mer-i - ca, A-mer-i - ca, A-mer-i - ca, the beau-ti-ful.
We sing A - mer - i - ca. We sing A - mer - i - ca.

### Patriotic Countermelodies

**Listen** for two countermelodies in *The Stars and Stripes Forever.*

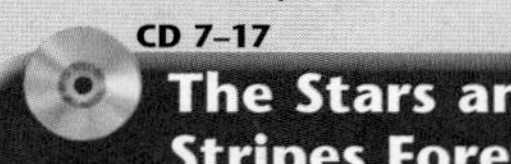

CD 7–17
**The Stars and Stripes Forever**

**by John Philip Sousa**

Sousa [SOO-zah] (1854–1932) composed more than 100 marches in his lifetime. *The Stars and Stripes Forever* was his favorite. It is played today by high school, college, and community bands throughout the United States.

**View from Pikes Peak, Colorado ▲**

## 2 Develop

### Listening

6b Ask students to listen to "America, the Beautiful" **CD 7-15** again and tap the rhythm of each phrase.

ASK **What did you discover about the rhythm?** (All the phrases have the same rhythm.)

### Singing

Have students

- Sing "America, the Beautiful" **CD 7-15** while following the notation on p. 158.
- Sing the countermelody with the recording.

### Listening

6e Play *The Stars and Stripes Forever* **CD 7-17** several times. As students listen, point out each of the three themes. Have students hold up one, two, or three fingers to show each of the three themes. When students can identify the melodies, invite them to listen for countermelodies in the "Trio" section. (one played by piccolos, the other by trombones)

### Singing

1d 1e Divide the class into two groups. Have one group sing the melody of "America, the Beautiful" **CD 7-15,** while the other group sings the countermelody on p. 159. Ask students to describe how this affects the texture of the music. (singing the melody and countermelody together creates harmony, resulting in a thicker texture)

## 3 Close

**Element: TEXTURE/HARMONY** ASSESSMENT

**Performance/Observation** Divide the class into two groups. Have one group sing the melody of "America, the Beautiful" while the other group sings the countermelody. Switch parts. Observe each group's ability to sing the countermelody with "America, the Beautiful" without prompting from the teacher.

## Skills Reinforcement

▶ **Singing** Teach students to sing countermelodies using this sequence.

- Students sing the melody independently.
- Students sing the melody while the teacher sings the countermelody.
- Have students describe differences between the melody and countermelody.
- Teach the countermelody.
- Students sing the countermelody while the teacher sings the melody.
- Students sing the two parts together.

## School to Home Connection

▶ **American Visuals** Invite students to share family photos, magazine illustrations, and so on, of both natural settings and scenes depicting modern life in our nation's cities and towns. Create collages of the incredible diversity of land, people, and unique features of life in America.

## Technology/Media Link

**Web Site** Have students visit *www.sfsuccessnet.com* to learn more about American composer and band leader John Philip Sousa.

## LESSON AT A GLANCE

**Element Focus** **TEXTURE/HARMONY** Countermelody

**Skill Objective** **SINGING** Sing a song with a countermelody

**Connection Activity** **SOCIAL STUDIES** Discuss the impact of a song on a culture

**MATERIALS**

- "Amazing Grace" **CD 7-18**

  **Recording Routine:** Intro (8 m.); v. 1; interlude (8 m.); v. 2; interlude (8 m.); v. 3; interlude (8 m.); v. 1
- *Amazing Grace* **CD 7-20**

**VOCABULARY**

lyrics countermelody texture

**National Standards**

- **1b** Sing with appropriate expression
- **1d** Sing part songs
- **4b** Arrange songs within specific guidelines
- **6b** Describe music by answering questions about it
- **8b** Identify ways music relates to other arts

**MORE MUSIC CHOICES**

For more practice singing in parts:

"The Wheel of the Water," p. 362

"Cycle Song of Life," p. 370

# 1 INTRODUCE

8b Invite students to read and discuss how the lyrics for "Amazing Grace" were written. Ask students to analyze the painting by Michele Wood on p. 161. Lead them to notice that the painting has many layers and that they will be adding a layer to "Amazing Grace."



# One Song, DIFFERENT TEXTURES

John Newton was a slave trader. When he realized slavery was wrong, he expressed his feelings through lyrics. Later, his lyrics were used with this early American hymn. **Listen** to the song and **describe** the texture.

CD 7-18

## Amazing Grace

s, l, d r m s

Words by John Newton — Early American Melody

1. A - maz - ing grace, how sweet the sound, That saved a wretch like me! I once was lost, but now am found, Was blind, but now I see.
2. 'Twas grace that taught my heart to fear, And grace my fears re - lieved; How pre - cious did that grace ap - pear The hour I first be - lieved!

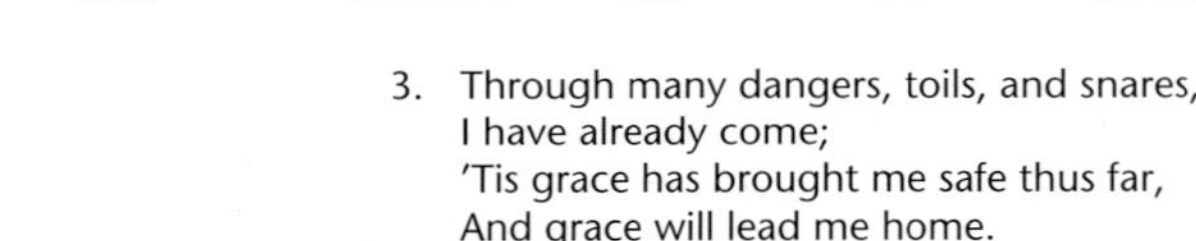
3. Through many dangers, toils, and snares,
I have already come;
'Tis grace has brought me safe thus far,
And grace will lead me home.



# Footnotes

## TEACHER TO TEACHER

1b ▶ **Sustaining Phrases** "Amazing Grace" calls for a sustained, *legato* vocal style. Remind students to take deep breaths to sustain the long notes at the end of each phrase. Have students stand when they sing, and remind them to breathe only where they see a punctuation mark in the words. Conduct the music so that students hold tied notes to full value. Remind students to sing through the vowels, putting the final consonants on at the last moment.

## BUILDING SKILLS THROUGH MUSIC

▶ **Social Studies** Discuss with students the background information on how "Amazing Grace" came to be written on p. 160. Encourage students to research the life of John Newton (1725–1807) and learn when slavery was finally abolished in America.

## ACROSS THE CURRICULUM

▶ **Social Studies** In the early part of the nineteenth century, a great religious revival swept the American frontier. Since few churches were large enough to hold the crowds that attended the meetings, clearings were made in the wilderness, crude benches and pulpits were erected, and services were conducted in the open. Settlers came from miles around and camped for several days to attend services that went on for hours. These camp meetings were characterized by impassioned preaching and energetic singing. That "Amazing Grace" continues to have a powerful impact even today is demonstrated by the number of well-known singers who perform and record it each year.

**Sing** "Amazing Grace." Then sing this countermelody with a small group while the rest of the class sings "Amazing Grace." How does the texture change?

## Comparing Textures

A thicker texture can be created by adding voices to the same melody line.

**Listen** to *Amazing Grace.*
**Compare** the texture of the recording with the texture of the song.

**as performed by Judy Collins**
This recording by Judy Collins has two distinct textures—solo and chorus.

Painting by Michele Wood from *I See Rhythm* by Toyomi Igus ▶

# 2 Develop

### Listening

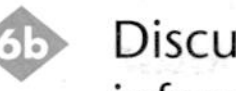


Discuss the impact music has on a culture and share information from Across the Curriculum on p. 160. Play "Amazing Grace" **CD 7-18.** Encourage students to identify the diverse styles heard in the recording. (Verse 1 is sacred harp style. Verse 2 is traditional hymn style. Verse 3 is African American spiritual style. Verse 4 is gospel style.)

ASK **How would you describe the texture in this recording?** (It varies according to the style.)

### Singing

1d Play "Amazing Grace" and invite students to sing.

ASK **Does our singing change the texture?** (Yes, the texture is thicker.)

Sing or play the countermelody on p. 161 for students and ask them to echo it. Then have half the class sing each part together.

ASK **Does adding a countermelody change the texture again?** (Yes, it becomes thicker.)

### Listening/Comparing

Play *Amazing Grace* **CD 7-20,** as sung by Judy Collins. Have students compare this recording to the previous one. (It most closely resembles verse 1 in sacred harp style.)

# 3 Close

**Skill: SINGING** — **ASSESSMENT**

**Performance/Observation** Divide the class into two groups. Have one group sing "Amazing Grace" **CD 7-18** while the other group sings the countermelody. Then switch parts.

Observe each group's ability to sing the countermelody with "Amazing Grace" without any prompting.

## Skills Reinforcement

▶ **Arranging** Divide the class into small groups. Ask each to prepare a performance of "Amazing Grace" that varies the texture for each verse.

- Encourage students to add instruments. A xylophone could help singers with the countermelody; an Autoharp could supply harmony.
- Have each group perform for the rest of the class.
- Discuss the success of the performances. How well did each group fulfill the assignment?

## Technology/Media Link

**Sequencing Software** Have students, working in small groups,

- Record the melody and countermelody of "Amazing Grace" on separate tracks of a digital recording program.
- Experiment with altering the countermelody, both rhythmically and melodically.
- Play the new countermelody with the melody and evaluate the results.

LESSON 12

## LESSON AT A GLANCE

**Element Focus** **TEXTURE/HARMONY** I and $V_7$ chords

**Skill Objective** **PLAYING** Play I and $V_7$ chords during the A section of a song

**Connection Activity** **CULTURE** Discuss the characteristics of gospel singing

**MATERIALS**

- "Dry Bones" **CD 7-21**
  **Recording Routine:** Intro (12 m.); vocal
- selected pitched and nonpitched percussion instruments, guitars, Autoharp, keyboard
- **Resource Book** p. J-10

**VOCABULARY**

*a cappella* chord harmony spiritual

**National Standards**

- **1e** Sing in groups, following a conductor
- **2b** Play melodies and chords on appropriate instruments
- **2f** Play instruments independently against contrasting parts
- **6b** Describe music by answering questions about it
- **6e** While listening to music, move to show a prominent feature of the music

**MORE MUSIC CHOICES**

Other African American spirituals:

"Wade in the Water," p. 268
"Little David, Play on Your Harp," p. 394

# 1 INTRODUCE

Discuss with students that "Dry Bones" is an African American spiritual. Invite students to share any information they might know about spirituals. "Dry Bones" is sung in a gospel style. Share information about gospel singing in Spotlight On below.

LESSON 12 Element: TEXTURE/HARMONY Skill: PLAYING Connection: CULTURE

HARMONY TONES

**Listen** to "Dry Bones." Where does the **harmony** change in the song?

**Harmony** is two or more different tones sound at the same time.

CD 7-21
MIDI 14

DRY BONES

African American Spiritual

A
C G7 C
do
E - ze - kiel cried, "Them dry bones!" E - ze - kiel cried, "Them dry bones!"
C G7 C
E - ze - kiel cried, "Them dry bones!" Now hear the word of the Lord.
B
C
The foot bone con-nect - ed to the leg bone,
C♯
The leg bone con-nect - ed to the knee bone,
D
The knee bone con-nect - ed to the thigh bone,
D♯
The thigh bone con-nect - ed to the hip bone,
E
The hip bone con-nect - ed to the back bone,

162

# Footnotes

## SPOTLIGHT ON

▶ **Gospel Singing** Gospel singing started in African American Pentecostal churches at the end of the nineteenth century, and it developed into its present-day style during the 1920s and 1930s. Two kinds of gospel singing became popular—the all-male quartet and choruses with soloists. Both kinds of gospel singing influenced rock 'n' roll, especially gospel's use of call and response and strong driving rhythms with the emphasis on beats 2 and 4, often called the "backbeat."

## BUILDING SKILLS THROUGH MUSIC

▶ **Science** Encourage students to investigate the characteristics and composition of bone. Ask, "What is the term for the overall structure of bones, as described in the lyrics of "Dry Bones"? (skeleton) Challenge students to sing the lyrics in reverse order, from the "head bone" down.

## SKILLS REINFORCEMENT

2b

▶ **Guitar** Students' awareness of chord changes in "Dry Bones" can be enhanced by encouraging some of them to try playing guitar chords during the A section of the song (before it becomes chromatic). This should be a manageable task because it is a relatively short passage using only two chords. The easiest way to perform these chords on the guitar is to use a capo on the third fret and play an A and $E_7$, which will then sound C and $G_7$.

▶ **Listening** For more practice with listening, have students do Activity Master 8 on Resource Book p. J-10.

F
The back bone con-nect - ed to the shoul - der bone,
F♯
The shoul - der bone con-nect - ed to the neck ___ bone,
G
The neck bone con-nect - ed to the jaw ___ bone,
A♭
The jaw bone con-nect - ed to the head ___ bone, Now
A♭ E♭7 A♭ A♭
hear the word of the Lord.
Them bones, them bones gon - na
Them bones, them bones, them ___
A♭ E♭7
do
walk a - round, Them bones, them bones gon - na
dry ___ bones, Them bones, them bones, them ___
A♭
walk a-round, Them bones, them bones gon - na walk a-round
dry ___ bones, Them bones, them bones, them ___ dry ___ bones.
A♭ E♭7 A♭
Now hear the word of the Lord.
Now hear the word of the Lord.

**Playing Harmony**

**Sing** "Dry Bones." Then **play** C and $G_7$ **chords** in the Ⓐ section of the song on the Autoharp or keyboard.

A **chord** is three or more notes arranged in intervals of a third, sounded at the same time.

Unit 4 163

# 2 Develop

## Analyzing/Describing

6b Play "Dry Bones" **CD 7-21.** Ask students to use standard terminology to explain and describe the musical performance of the accompaniment (vocal; male and female voices; some percussion) and the style of singing. (emotional, liberties taken with rhythm, close harmonies, nonsense syllables)

## Singing

Have students look at the first note of each full measure at the beginning of lines 3 through 11. Show them these pitches on a keyboard as they sing "Dry Bones" **CD 7-21.** Help students discover that these notes move up by half step, and have them practice playing this section of the song on real or imaginary keyboard instruments.

## Playing

2b Have students play a two-chord accompaniment each time they sing the refrain of "Dry Bones." They can play C and $G_7$ on Autoharp, keyboard, or guitar. See Skills Reinforcement on p. 162.

6e Have students create a body percussion routine to add texture to "Dry Bones." Invite them to perform the song with body percussion accompaniment. You may also add nonpitched percussion instruments as accompaniment or to supply sound effects.

# 3 Close

Skill: PLAYING
ASSESSMENT

2f **Performance/Observation** Have students sing "Dry Bones." As they sing, ask groups to play correct chords during the refrain using Autoharp, keyboard, guitar or pitched percussion instruments. Observe that students play accurately and independently.

## Teacher to Teacher

1e

▶ **Chord Roots** A fundamental part-singing skill is the ability to sing *chord roots* with a song. Begin with simple songs that use I and V chords. Establish the key of F major and have students sing the chord roots, *do* and *so*. Then have them

- Sing patterns using *do* and *so* from the teacher's hand signs.
- Sing the A section of "Dry Bones."
- Sing the song as the teacher sings chord roots.
- Describe what the teacher is singing (chord roots).
- Sing chord roots from the teacher's hand signs, while the teacher sings the A section.
- Sing in two parts—melody and chord roots.

## Technology/Media Link

**Web Site** Invite students to visit *www.sfsuccessnet.com* to learn more about spirituals and gospel music.

UNIT 4 Review and Assessment

## WHAT DO YOU KNOW?

**MATERIALS**
- "The Lion Sleeps Tonight," p. 131 **CD 6-4**
- **Resource Book** p. B-14

Invite students to listen to "The Lion Sleeps Tonight" and review the dynamics in the recording.

Have students read and answer the questions in the assessment independently and then check their answers with a partner before sharing answers with the rest of the class or with you.

For a more formal assessment, you may wish to duplicate the Unit 4 assessment worksheet and have students work independently or in small groups to complete it. The worksheet is found on Resource Book p. B-14.

## WHAT DO YOU HEAR?

**MATERIALS**
- *"Ala Da'lona,"* p. 136 **CD 6-18**
- "Cumberland Gap," p. 138 **CD 6-22**
- *What Do You Hear? 4* **CD 7-23**
- **Resource Book** p. B-14

Invite students to listen to *"Ala Da'lona"* and "Cumberland Gap" to review the rhythm patterns in this unit.

Distribute the Unit 4 assessment worksheet found on Resource Book p. B-14. Have students listen to *What Do You Hear? 4* and mark their answers accordingly.

# Review, Assess,

## What Do You Know?

**1.** Which symbol below is called *fortissimo*? What does it mean?

*pp* *p* *mp* *mf* *f* *ff*

**2.** If you saw this symbol (*p*), how would you perform the music?

## What Do You Hear? 4

CD 7-23

Point to the line below that matches the rhythms performed on the recording.

**1.** a.  b. 

**2.** a.  b. 

**3.** a.  b. 

164

# Footnotes

## ANSWER KEY

**▶ What Do You Know?**

**1.** *ff*; very loud

**2.** softly

**▶ What Do You Hear?**

**1.** b

**2.** a

**3.** b

# Perform, Create

## What You Can Do

### Move to Show Contour

Sing "Amazing Grace," on page 160, with eyes closed. Move your hand in an arc to show the contour of the melody.

### Play Rhythms

Perform all four of the percussion lines of "*Wu long,*" on page 157, using rhythm syllables. Perform the piece as a group using body percussion. Have different people play each part. Perform the piece again using percussion instruments.

### Move to Show Form

Sing "Ode to Joy," on page 152. Perform small, steady-beat movements during the a phrases and different movements during the b phrase.

### Sing with Texture

Sing "America, the Beautiful," on page 158. Create a thick texture by singing the melody and the countermelody together.

Unit 4 165

## What You Can Do

**MATERIALS**

- "Amazing Grace," p. 160 **CD 7-18**
- *Wu long,* p. 157 **CD 7-13**
- "Ode to Joy," p.152 **CD 7-7**
- "America, the Beautiful," p. 158 **CD 7-15**
- **Resource Book** p. B-15
- classroom percussion instruments

### Move to Contour

Divide students into four groups. Each group is assigned to a phrase of "Amazing Grace." As all students sing the song, have each group stand up and move according to the melodic contour as their phrase is being sung.

### Play Rhythms

Review rhythm patterns from this unit with the students, and have them perform *Wu long* using rhythm syllables. Then have students use the rhythms of the piece to create body percussion parts.

### Move to Form

Invite students to conduct a four-beat pattern as they sing "Ode to Joy." Then ask students to create differing steady-beat movements to perform while they sing the "a" and "b" phrases. Have them sing and move to "Ode to Joy" and show the form.

### Sing with Texture

Have the entire class study both the melody and the countermelody of "America, the Beautiful." Have them sing both parts in small groups.

Note: The What You Can Do on this page is available as a blackline master, using Resource Book p. B-15.

### Technology/Media Link

**Rubrics** Visit *www.sfsuccessnet.com* for rubrics to assess students' achievement in music skills.

| Lesson | Elements | Skills | |
|---|---|---|---|
| LESSON 1<br>CORE<br>**Row with the Tempo**<br>pp. 170–171<br><br> | **Element: Expression**<br>**Concept:** Tempo<br>**Focus:** Sudden tempo changes<br><br>**Secondary Element**<br>Meter: $\frac{6}{8}$<br><br>**National Standards**<br>2f 5c 6b | **Skill: Listening**<br>**Objective:** Listen to music and create "tempo maps" to show tempo changes<br><br>**Secondary Skills**<br>• **Performing** Speak at various speeds<br>• **Playing** Play accompaniment parts on percussion instruments | **SKILLS REINFORCEMENT**<br>• **Performing** Sing or move to pieces in varying tempos |
| LESSON 2<br>CORE<br>**Doin' Fine in Triple Time**<br>pp. 172–175<br><br> | **Element: Rhythm**<br>**Concept:** Meter<br>**Focus:** Meter in 3<br><br>**Secondary Element**<br>Expression: tempo<br><br>**National Standards**<br>1c 6b 6d 6e 9a | **Skill: Moving**<br>**Objective:** Perform original movements to accompany songs in meter in 3<br><br>**Secondary Skills**<br>• **Singing** Sing a folk song in Tagalog, Korean, and English<br>• **Listening** Describe sounds of traditional instruments performing a Korean folk song | **SKILLS REINFORCEMENT**<br>• **Analyzing** Select and accompany with body percussion parts<br>• **Creating** Improvise triple meter pieces |
| LESSON 3<br>**Sounds of Spain**<br>pp. 176–177<br><br><br>Reading Sequence 17, p. 450 | **Element: Rhythm**<br>**Concept:** Pattern<br>**Focus:** ♩. ♪<br><br>**Secondary Element**<br>Form: verse/refrain<br><br>**National Standards**<br>2b 5a 6c 6d 6e | **Skill: Reading**<br>**Objective:** Read a song from notation that contains ♩. ♪<br><br>**Secondary Skills**<br>• **Listening** Discover patterns of strong and weak beats<br>• **Singing** Listen to Pronunciation Practice and sing in Spanish | **SKILLS REINFORCEMENT**<br>• **Listening** Describe instruments used in recorded accompaniment<br>• **Keyboard** Play accompaniment using ♩. ♪ |

## Connections

### Connection: Language Arts
**Activity:** Experiment with tempo changes when reading poetry

**Across the Curriculum**
**Social Studies** Locate cities on two rivers on a map
**Language Arts** Read a biography

**Meeting Individual Needs** **Including Everyone** Develop leadership skills

**Building Skills Through Music** **Language** Write a short descriptive paragraph of a photograph from the 1800s

## Music and Other Literature

**Speech Piece** "Can You Canoe?"

**Listening Selection** *Hungarian Dance No. 19*

**M*U*S*I*C M*A*K*E*R*S**
Johannes Brahms

**More Music Choices**
"The Continents," p. 357
"The Planets Chant," p. 377

**Assessment**

**Observation/Music Journal Writing** Draw listening maps to indicate heard tempo changes

**Technology/Media Link**
**Web Site** Go to *www.sfsuccessnet.com* for information on Brahms and his music

---

### Connection: Culture
**Activity:** Discuss traditional music from the Philippines and Korea

**Across the Curriculum**
**Language Arts** Read aloud stories about Philippine children's dreams
**Art** Create a sleeping mat model

**Cultural Connection**
**Music in the Philippines** Indigenous, Spanish, and Western pop influences
**Korean Traditional Music** Information on the music of Korea's heritage

**Spotlight On**
**Languages** Facts, about Tagalog, Filipino, and Korean
**Korea** Geographical, cultural, and political facts

**Building Skills Through Music** **Math** Use geometry to determine what figure would best describe a measure in $\frac{3}{4}$

**Songs**
"*Santa Clara*" (Tagalog and English)
"*Doraji*" ("Bluebells")

**Listening Selections**
*Doraji* (excerpt)
*Sanjo*

**M*U*S*I*C M*A*K*E*R*S**
Hi-za Yoo

**More Music Choices**
"*Sakura*," p. 308
"*Xiao*" p. 314
"*Niu lang zhi nü*," p. 335

**Assessment**

**Performance/Observation** Maintain the steady beat in $\frac{3}{4}$ time

**Technology/Media Link**
**Electronic Keyboard** Play to reinforce meter in 3

---

### Connection: Culture
**Activity:** Discuss the influence of Moors on Spanish culture

**Across the Curriculum**
**Language Arts** Read a Spanish folktale
**Social Studies** Locate Spain on a map

**Cultural Connection** **Moors in Spain** Moorish influence on Spanish culture

**Building Skills Through Music** **Art** Describe the elements of art used to highlight a figure in a painting

**Song** "*La Tarara*" (Spanish and English)

**Arts Connection** *Girl with a Guitar*

**More Music Choices**
"America," p. 440
"Circle 'Round the Moon," p. 403

**Assessment**

**Performance/Observation** Read and sing dotted rhythms accurately

**Technology/Media Link**
**CD-ROM** Play a rhythm game to identify same and different phrases

| Lesson | Elements | Skills | |
|---|---|---|---|
|  **Tearing Through Rhythm**<br>pp. 178–181<br><br>Reading Sequence 18, p. 450 | **Element: Rhythm**<br>**Concept:** Pattern<br>**Focus:** ♪ ♩.<br><br>**Secondary Element**<br>Melody: contour<br><br>**National Standards**<br> | **Skill: Reading**<br>**Objective:** Read a song from notation that contains ♪ ♩.<br><br>**Secondary Skills**<br>• **Performing** Say four-beat rhythm patterns<br>• **Listening** Determine the meter<br>• **Analyzing** Recognize rhythm patterns; compare dotted-rhythm patterns in two songs | **SKILLS REINFORCEMENT**<br>• **Listening** Identify dotted rhythms presented aurally<br>• **Guitar** Play a two-chord accompaniment<br>• **Composing** Create and notate rhythm patterns<br>• **Recorder** Play an accompaniment<br>• **Mallets** Play an Orff accompaniment |
| LESSON 5 CORE **Know the Rondo**<br>pp. 182–185<br> | **Element: Form**<br>**Concept:** Form<br>**Focus:** Rondo Form<br><br>**Secondary Element**<br>Meter: $\begin{smallmatrix}6\\8\end{smallmatrix}$<br><br>**National Standards**<br> | **Skill: Moving**<br>**Objective:** Perform a speech rondo accompanied by contrasting movements<br><br>**Secondary Skills**<br>• **Analyzing** Read three poems and link them in rondo form<br>• **Performing** Pat a steady beat and perform rhythm patterns using body percussion<br>• **Playing** Play percussion accompaniments to speech pieces | **SKILLS REINFORCEMENT**<br>• **Improvising** Improvise contrasting body percussion patterns to make a rondo<br>• **Creating** Create class poems and move to them in rondo form |
|  **Laugh and Sing**<br>pp. 186–187<br><br>Reading Sequence 19, p. 451 | **Element: Melody**<br>**Concept:** Pattern<br>**Focus:** Prepare *ti*, major scale<br><br>**Secondary Element**<br>Texture/Harmony: round<br><br>**National Standards**<br>1a 1d 4b 6b | **Skill: Singing**<br>**Objective:** Sing a song that includes *do, re, mi, fa, so, la, ti, do*<br><br>**Secondary Skills**<br>• **Analyzing** Identify a missing note and how it sounds in relation to *do* and *la* | **SKILLS REINFORCEMENT**<br>• **Creating/Playing** Play created rhythm ostinatos<br>• **Mallets** Play an Orff accompaniment |

| Connections | Music and Other Literature | |
|---|---|---|
| **Connection: Culture**<br>**Activity:** Discuss African American spirituals and work songs<br>ACROSS THE CURRICULUM **Language Arts** Read about how buildings are built<br>CULTURAL CONNECTION<br>**Spirituals** Created to instill hope<br>**Work Songs** Purpose and characteristics<br>MEETING INDIVIDUAL NEEDS **English Language Learners** Match pictures with words of the song<br>CHARACTER EDUCATION **Support and Compassion** Discuss situations where people can be "built up" or "torn down"<br>TEACHER TO TEACHER **Intervals** Learn intervals using pitch syllables or numbers<br>BUILDING SKILLS THROUGH MUSIC **Science** Discuss sounds that construction workers produce | **Songs**<br>"Old House, Tear It Down!"<br>"All Night, All Day"<br><br>**Arts Connection**<br>*Mother and Child*<br><br>**More Music Choices**<br>"Gonna Ride Up in the Chariot," p. 20<br>"Wade in the Water" p. 268 | ASSESSMENT<br>**Performance/Observation**<br>Read and sing accurately ♪♩<br>**Show What You Know!**<br>Mid-unit assessment<br><br>TECHNOLOGY/MEDIA LINK<br>**Electronic Keyboard**<br>Play an accompaniment to reinforce dotted-quarter and eighth-note rhythms |
| **Connection: Language Arts**<br>**Activity:** Write poetry to be performed in rondo form<br>ACROSS THE CURRICULUM<br>**Science** Read, talk, and write about preparations for winter<br>**Art** Create colors and shapes to represent rondo form<br>MEETING INDIVIDUAL NEEDS **Cooperation** Develop individual and group cooperation and interaction<br>SPOTLIGHT ON **Rondo** Facts about rondo form<br>CHARACTER EDUCATION **Respect** Work in groups to create a rondo using group members' personal characteristics<br>AUDIENCE ETIQUETTE **At School Assemblies and in the Classroom** Practice and reinforce proper audience behavior<br>BUILDING SKILLS THROUGH MUSIC **Writing** Discuss snow and write a paragraph about local weather | **Speech Piece** "Heave-Ho"/"Going, Going, Gone"/"The Snow"<br><br>**Listening Selections**<br>*ABACA Dabble*<br>*Rondo: Allegro*<br>**Listening Map** *Rondo: Allegro*<br><br>**More Music Choices**<br>*Fossils*, p. 220<br>"*La raspa*," p. 302<br>*Walking Song*, p. 347 | ASSESSMENT<br>**Performance/Observation**<br>Perform movements to indicate understanding of rondo form<br><br>TECHNOLOGY/MEDIA LINK<br>**Notation Software** Use the software to reinforce the concept of rondo form<br>**Transparency** Follow rondo form for *Rondo: Allegro* |
| **Connection: Social Studies**<br>**Activity:** Learn about the geography of Australia<br>MOVEMENT **Patterned Dance** Learn an Australian greeting<br>ACROSS THE CURRICULUM **Social Studies** Read about the geography of Australia; research plan and animal life<br>SCHOOL TO HOME CONNECTION **Bird Research** Find out more about the kookaburra<br>BUILDING SKILLS THROUGH MUSIC **Language** Substitute words in the lyrics of a song from Australia | **Songs** "Kookaburra"<br><br>**More Music Choices**<br>"My Bonnie Lies Over the Ocean," p. 338<br>"*Sambalele*," p. 397 | ASSESSMENT<br>**Performance/Observation**<br>Identify *ti* aurally<br><br>TECHNOLOGY/MEDIA LINK<br>**MIDI/Sequencing Software** Use the song file as an aid to learning to sing in harmony |

| Lesson | Elements | Skills | |
|---|---|---|---|
| LESSON 7 CORE **Where's the New Note?** pp. 188–191  Reading Sequence 20, p. 451 | **Element: Melody**<br>**Concept:** Pattern<br>**Focus:** Prepare *ti*, major scale<br><br>**Secondary Element**<br>Rhythm: syncopation<br><br>**National Standards**<br>1a 2b 5b 6b 6c | **Skill: Reading**<br>**Objective:** Sing a song, read from notation that contains *do, re, mi, fa, so, la, ti, do*<br><br>**Secondary Skills**<br>• **Listening/Singing** Sing and play short melodic patterns with *ti*<br>• **Analyzing** Identify *ti* aurally and where it falls in the scale<br>• **Reading/Singing** Sing a song using pitch syllables<br>• **Listening** Identify instruments; identify *do* and *ti* aurally; perform with hand signs | **SKILLS REINFORCEMENT**<br>• **Recorder** Practice leaps and play countermelodies<br>• **Mallets** Play an Orff accompaniment<br>• **Creating** Accompany a song with Caribbean-style percussion instruments |
| LESSON 8 CORE **Performing Together** pp. 192–195  | **Element: Timbre**<br>**Concept:** Instrumental and vocal<br>**Focus:** Ensemble Timbres<br><br>**Secondary Element**<br>Meter: $\frac{4}{4}$<br><br>**National Standards**<br>2b 2f 6c 6d 9e | **Skill: Listening**<br>**Objective:** Identify the sounds of a variety of instrumental and vocal ensembles<br><br>**Secondary Skills**<br>• **Playing** Practice and play xylophone parts of an Orff piece | **SKILLS REINFORCEMENT**<br>• **Playing** Read parts using rhythm syllables; transfer to instruments<br>• **Listening** Identify instrumental and vocal ensembles |
| LESSON 9 **Sound of a Round** pp. 196–197  | **Element: Texture/Harmony**<br>**Concept:** Texture<br>**Focus:** Round<br><br>**Secondary Element**<br>Expression: tempo<br><br>**National Standards**<br>1d 2f 5a | **Skill: Singing**<br>**Objective:** Sing a round<br><br>**Secondary Skills**<br>• **Playing** Read notes of an accompaniment; layer parts; play as a round<br>• **Analyzing** Visualize layering of parts in a round | **SKILLS REINFORCEMENT**<br>• **Singing** Listen to Pronunciation Practice and sing in Spanish |

| Connections | Music and Other Literature | |
|---|---|---|
| **Connection: Culture**<br>**Activity:** Discuss the musical culture of the Caribbean<br>ACROSS THE CURRICULUM **Language Arts** Read about a lost dog and its family's efforts to find him<br>MEETING INDIVIDUAL NEEDS **English Language Learners** Discuss concepts of lost and founds<br>SPOTLIGHT ON **Trinidad** Facts about its musical styles and cultural roots; origin of steel drum band<br>MOVEMENT **Game Song** Learn a game song to "Missy-La, Massa-La"<br>TEACHER TO TEACHER **Diction-Vowels** Practice in singing pure vowels<br>BUILDING SKILLS THROUGH MUSIC **Science** Discuss how sound is produced in three instrumental families | **Song** "Missy-La, Massa-La"<br><br>**Listening Selection** *A-Cling, A-Cling* (excerpt)<br>**Listening Map** *A-Cling A-Cling*<br>**Arts Connection** Caribbean mural<br><br>**More Music Choices**<br>"For the Beauty of the Earth," p. 356<br>"Cycle Song of Life (refrain)," p. 371 | ASSESSMENT<br>**Performance/Observation** Recognize and sing *ti* at sight<br>**Show What You Know!** Mid-unit assessment<br><br>TECHNOLOGY/MEDIA LINK<br>**CD-ROM** Use a melody game to identify same and different melodic phrases<br>**Transparency** Use the listening map to follow the selection |
| **Connection: Culture**<br>**Activity:** Explore classical music from India<br>ACROSS THE CURRICULUM **Language Arts** Read about Schubert's childhood; write about personal musical learning experiences<br>CULTURAL CONNECTION **Indian Classical Music** Description of Indian music built on ragas and talas<br>SPOTLIGHT ON **Types of Ensembles** Chamber, wind, jazz, string quartet, woodwind quartet<br>MEETING INDIVIDUAL NEEDS<br>**Including Everyone** Create rhythm patterns that are playable by all<br>**Assigning Parts** All participate successfully playing together in an ensemble, according to abilities<br>BUILDING SKILLS THROUGH MUSIC **Math** Find which geometric shapes correspond to the number of members in a musical group | **Orff Parts** "Orfferondo"<br><br>**Listening Selections**<br>*"Scherzo"* from *Piano Trio No. 2* (excerpt)<br>*Rag puria kalyan-gat in tintal* (excerpt)<br>*"Canzoni prima a 5"* from *Canzoni et Sonate* (excerpt)<br>*That's the Way*<br>**MUSIC MAKERS** Rockapella<br><br>**More Music Choices**<br>"Mars, the Bringer of War" from *The Planets*, p. 377<br>Little David, Play on Your Harp (chorus), p. 395 | ASSESSMENT<br>**Music Journal Writing** Listen to and describe instrumentation and style of various vocal and instrumental ensembles accurately<br><br>TECHNOLOGY/MEDIA LINK<br>**Video Library** See and hear small ensembles |
| **Connection: Culture**<br>**Activity:** Discuss the role of rounds in English culture<br>TEACHER TO TEACHER **Singing Rounds** Help students gain confidence in singing rounds<br>CULTURAL CONNECTION **Rounds in English Tradition** Definition of a "catch"<br>BUILDING SKILLS THROUGH MUSIC **Writing** Read the lyrics of a song and write a paragraph summarizing their meaning | **Songs**<br>"Ah, Poor Bird"<br>"*Los niños en España cantan*" ("In Spain, the Children Sing")<br><br>**More Music Choices**<br>"Peace Round," p. 348<br>"This Pretty Planet," p. 355<br>"*Yibane amenu*," p. 316 | ASSESSMENT<br>**Performance/Observation** Sing two rounds, maintaining independence of assigned part<br><br>TECHNOLOGY/MEDIA LINK<br>**Notation Software** Use to notate and play back a round |

| Lesson | Elements | Skills |
|---|---|---|

## LESSON 10 Round and A Round

pp. 198–199

**Element:** **Texture/Harmony**
**Concept:** Texture
**Focus:** Round

**Secondary Element**
Melody: major scale

**National Standards**
1d 2b 5d 7b

**Skill: Singing**
**Objective:** Sing a round

**Secondary Skills**
- **Playing** Play a keyboard accompaniment
- **Listening** Compare computer music with other types of music heard
- **Performing** Speak computer-related words as an introduction

**SKILLS REINFORCEMENT**
- **Keyboard** Develop strategies for playing two-chord keyboard accompaniments

## LESSON 11 CORE Calling all Chords

pp. 200–201

**Element:** **Texture/Harmony**
**Concept:** Harmony
**Focus:** Two-chord accompaniment (I and V)

**Secondary Element**
Melody: contour

**National Standards**
1d 2b 2f

**Skill: Playing**
**Objective:** Play a two-chord accompaniment

**Secondary Skills**
- **Analyzing** Figure out how to play a melody on diagram of resonator bells

**SKILLS REINFORCEMENT**
- **Recorder** Play a countermelody including low D and F♯

## LESSON 12 Chords in a Diddy

pp. 202–203

**Element:** **Texture/Harmony**
**Concept:** Harmony
**Focus:** Two-chord accompaniment (I and IV)

**Secondary Element**
Rhythm: patterns

**National Standards**
2b 2f 4a

**Skill: Playing**
**Objective:** Play a two-chord accompaniment

**Secondary Skills**
- **Singing/Playing** Sing chord roots; play barred instrument accompaniment

**SKILLS REINFORCEMENT**
- **Keyboard** Play exercises with alternate fingering

## Connections

## Music and Other Literature



**Connection:** Related Arts
**Activity:** Discuss the use of computers and other technology in creating visual arts and music

**TEACHER TO TEACHER** **Round Reinforcement** Do exercises that help with singing rounds

**BUILDING SKILLS THROUGH MUSIC** **Math** Discuss the use of symmetry in art and math

**Song** "The Computer"

**Listening Selection** "Orbital View" from *Mars Suite* (excerpt)
**Arts Connection** Computer fractal

**More Music Choices**
"Mars, the Bringer of War" from *The Planets*, p. 377

**ASSESSMENT**
**Performance/Observation**
Sing a round, maintaining an assigned part while hearing other parts simultaneously

**TECHNOLOGY/MEDIA LINK**
**Notation Software** Notate an accompaniment

---

**Connection:** Science
**Activity:** Discuss the food chain

**ACROSS THE CURRICULUM** **Language Arts** Read a poem about advice for a frog

**SPOTLIGHT ON** **Frogs** Facts about frogs

**BUILDING SKILLS THROUGH MUSIC** **Science** Describe the life cycle of the frog

**Song** "Frog Music"

**More Music Choices**
"The Bard of Armagh," p. 296
"*Corrido de Kansas*," p. 274
"The Wheel of the Water," p. 362

**ASSESSMENT**
**Performance/Observation**
Sing a song and play a two-chord accompaniment with accuracy

**TECHNOLOGY/MEDIA LINK**
**CD-ROM** Enter eight-measure chord progressions using I and V chords

---

**Connection:** Related Arts
**Activity:** Create a "movie scene" to go with a song

**ACROSS THE CURRICULUM** **Language Arts** Create movements and lyrics based on a book about "funny walks"

**SPOTLIGHT ON** **"Do Wah Diddy Diddy"** Facts about the song

**BUILDING SKILLS THROUGH MUSIC** **Social Studies** Develop a time line and determine when particular rock 'n' roll groups were popular

**Song** "Do Wah Diddy Diddy"

**More Music Choices**
"*Tengo, tengo, tengo*," p. 228

**ASSESSMENT**
**Performance/Observation**
Sing a song and play a two-chord accompaniment with accuracy

**TECHNOLOGY/MEDIA LINK**
**Electronic Keyboard** Generate arrangements to accompany a song

# INTRODUCING THE UNIT

Unit 5 presents the next step in a sequenced approach to understanding music elements. Presented on p. 167 is a brief overview of the skills that are assessed in this unit. (See below and pp. 168–169 for unit highlights of related curricular experiences.)

For a more detailed unit overview, see Unit at a Glance, pp. 165a–165h.

# UNIT PROJECT

Lead a brief discussion around the term *horizon*. Point out to students that

- The term can refer specifically to the visual line at which the earth (land or water) meets the sky, so it will appear different depending on the viewer's observation point.
- As a broader term, *horizon* can mean the limit or boundary of a person's experience or knowledge.

Knowing this, ask students to describe the meaning of the phrase "discovering new horizons." (to look in new directions; to expand your experience and knowledge in new ways) Reinforce that this is the purpose of this unit—to offer new horizons relating to music.

Assign a small group of students to each lesson in this unit to find out what the "new music horizon" will be and where on the globe it takes place. Allow time for the groups to share their findings.

A bulletin board may be developed on which students post photos or clippings relating to new musical experiences. Invite them to report briefly to the class on the items added. If they are able to bring CDs or other sound material to class, these could also be shared.

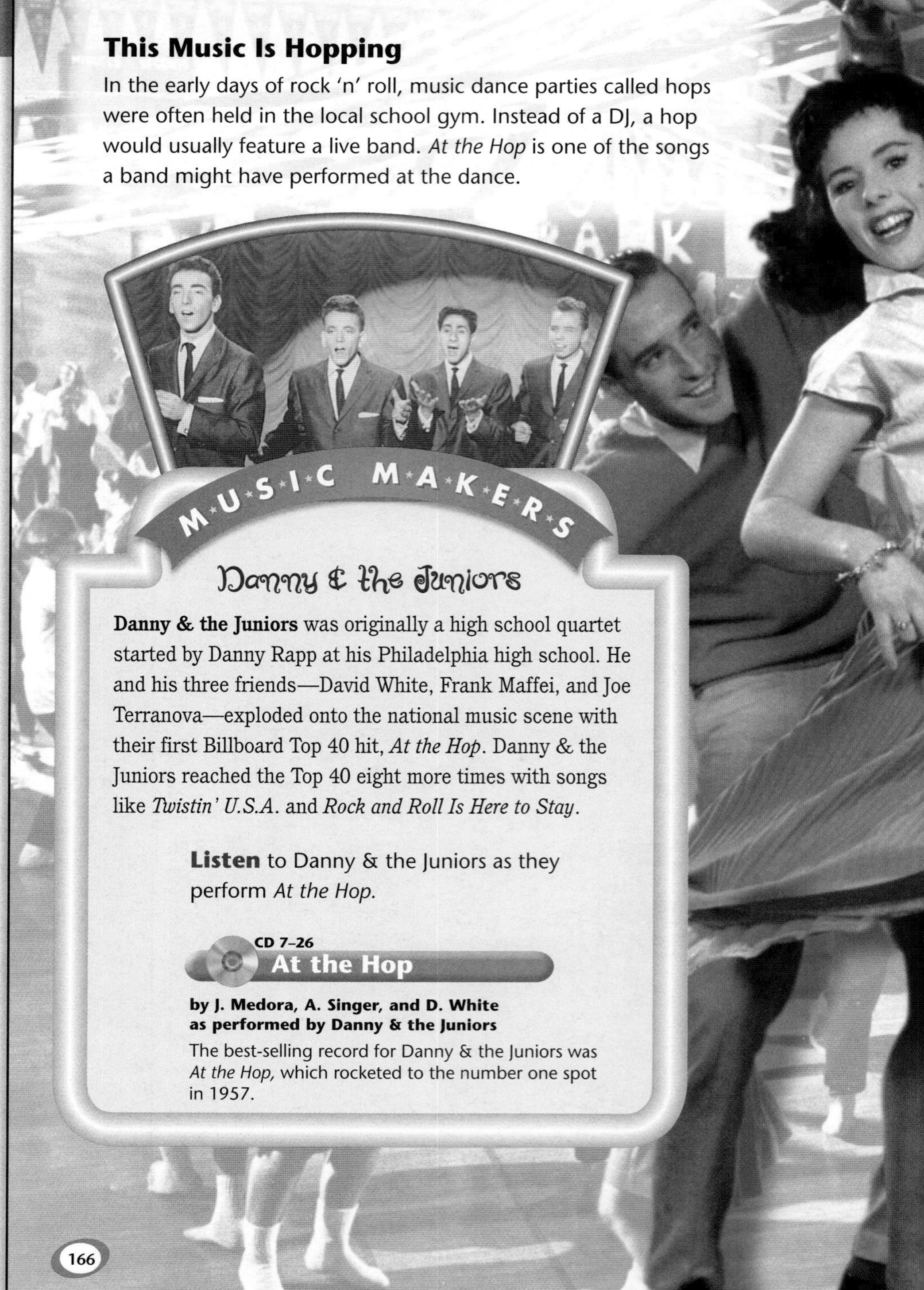

**This Music Is Hopping**

In the early days of rock 'n' roll, music dance parties called hops were often held in the local school gym. Instead of a DJ, a hop would usually feature a live band. *At the Hop* is one of the songs a band might have performed at the dance.

MUSIC MAKERS

Danny & the Juniors

**Danny & the Juniors** was originally a high school quartet started by Danny Rapp at his Philadelphia high school. He and his three friends—David White, Frank Maffei, and Joe Terranova—exploded onto the national music scene with their first Billboard Top 40 hit, *At the Hop*. Danny & the Juniors reached the Top 40 eight more times with songs like *Twistin' U.S.A.* and *Rock and Roll Is Here to Stay*.

**Listen** to Danny & the Juniors as they perform *At the Hop*.

CD 7–26
**At the Hop**

**by J. Medora, A. Singer, and D. White as performed by Danny & the Juniors**

The best-selling record for Danny & the Juniors was *At the Hop*, which rocketed to the number one spot in 1957.

166

## ACROSS THE CURRICULUM

**Unit Highlights** The following interdisciplinary activities in this unit are related to the music elements presented in the lessons. See Unit at a Glance, pp. 165a–165h, for topical descriptions presented according to lesson sequence.

**ART/RELATED ARTS**

- Create a model of a sleeping mat to illustrate a Filipino story (p. 173)
- Create designs to illustrate rondo pattern (p. 184)
- Explore the use of the computer in art and music (p. 198)

**LANGUAGE ARTS**

- Read a biography of Johannes Brahms (p. 171)
- Read a story from the Philippines (p. 173)
- Read a Spanish folktale and write alternate endings (p. 176)
- Read a book about how buildings are built, and share related experiences (p. 179)
- Read a "lost and found" true story (p. 190)
- Read a book about the childhood and early music education of Franz Schubert (p. 192)
- Discuss a song-related poem about frogs (p. 200)
- Create new lyrics for a song (p. 202)

**SCIENCE**

- Read a book about winter and discuss how animals prepare for the season (p. 182)

**SOCIAL STUDIES**

- Identify the location of place names mentioned in a speech piece (p. 171)
- Locate Spain on a map and discuss regional musical influences (p. 176)
- Read a book about Australia and discuss features such as animal life and climate (p. 186)

UNIT 5

# Discovering New Musical Horizons

Unit 5 167



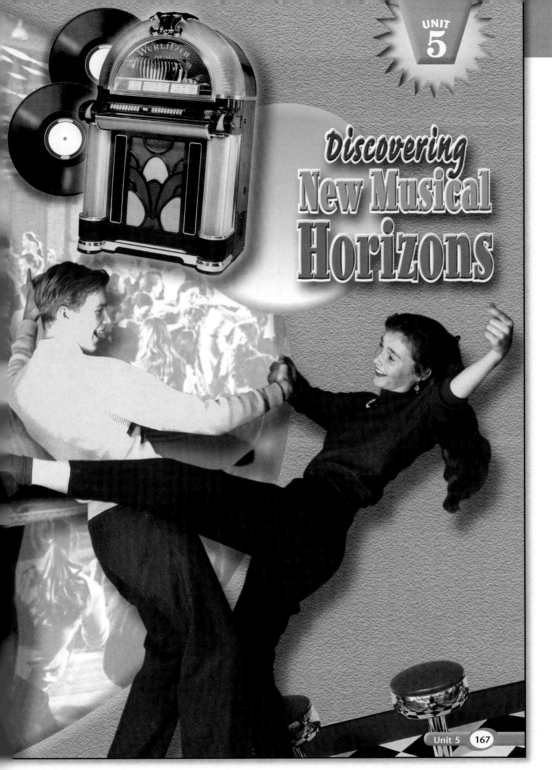

## MUSIC SKILLS ASSESSED IN THIS UNIT

### Reading Music: Rhythm

- Read a song containing ♩. ♪ (p. 177)
- Read a song containing ♪ ♩. (p. 181)

### Reading Music: Pitch

- Read a *do, re, mi, fa, so, la, ti, do'* song (p. 187)
- Read a *do, re, mi, fa, so, la, ti, do'* song, using pitch syllables and hand signs (p. 191)

### Performing Music: Singing

- Sing a round from Australia (p. 187)
- Sing rounds from England and Mexico (p. 197)
- Sing a round about the computer (p. 199)

### Moving to Music

- Perform original movements to accompany songs in meter in 3 (p. 175)
- Perform a speech rondo accompanied by contrasting movements (p. 185)

### Performing Music: Playing

- Play a two-chord accompaniment on keyboard, bells, and Autoharp (p. 201)
- Play a two-chord accompaniment on keyboard (p. 203)

### Creating Music

- Create and perform compositions in triple meter (p. 174)
- Create rhythm ostinatos to accompany a song (187)
- Create a Caribbean-style rhythm accompaniment (p. 190)

### Listening to Music

- Create "tempo maps" to show tempo changes (p. 171)
- Listen to and write descriptions of different ensemble timbres (p. 195)

## CULTURAL CONNECTION

**Unit Highlights** The musical literature in this unit provides many opportunities for students to explore a variety of world cultures. See Unit at a Glance, pp. 165a–165h, for topical descriptions presented according to lesson sequence.

**AFRICAN AMERICAN**

- Explore African American spirituals and work songs (p. 179)

**AMERICAN**

- Listen to and perform an American rock 'n' roll song (p. 166)
- Explore the vocal timbre of a popular American group (p. 193)

**ASIAN; AUSTRALIAN**

- Explore the musical and cultural traditions of the Philippines (p. 173)
- Sing and listen to examples of Korean traditional music (p. 175)
- Sing a song about an Australian bird (p. 186)
- Explore the classical music tradition of India (p. 195)

**CARIBBEAN**

- Explore the musical roots of Trinidad (p. 188)

**EUROPEAN**

- Discuss the cultural and musical influence of the Moors in Spain (p. 176)
- Sing a round from England and explore the origins of this tradition (p. 197)
- Perform an early British rock 'n' roll song (p. 203)

**LATIN AMERICAN**

- Sing a round from Mexico (p. 197)

# Opening Activities

**MATERIALS**

- "At the Hop" **CD 7-27**

  **Recording Routine:** Intro (14 m.); v. 1; refrain; interlude (12 m.); v. 2; refrain; coda
- *At the Hop* **CD 7-26**
- keyboards or other bass instruments

## Listening

Ask students to skim pp. 166–169 to find out what "horizon" they are looking at. Help students identify the time period (the late 1950s) and the musical style (early rock 'n' roll in the U.S.). Then ask for volunteers to read the text on p. 166 and the feature on Danny & the Juniors.

Invite students to listen to Danny and the Juniors' version of *At the Hop* **CD 7-26**. Ask them to keep the beat by

- Bouncing their fists in the air in front of them when there is singing on the recording.
- Clapping in the spaces between the singing.

## Singing

Ask students to look at the text for the refrain of "At the Hop," on p. 169.

**ASK** **How many times does the phrase *Let's go to the hop* occur?** (5)

**What is the only other main text?** (*Come on*)

Play the recording **CD 7-27** and ask students to

- Keep the beat, as before, on the verse.
- Sing the main text on the refrain.
- Perform a body percussion pattern, with the beat, on mm. 2, 4, 6, and 8 of the refrain.
- Add the *Oh, baby* text on the refrain.

Moving and Singing
As you sing "At the Hop" add some dance movements.
At the Hop
CD 7-27
d r m s l d' r' m'
Words and Music by A. Singer, J. Medora, and D. White
VERSE
1. Well, you can rock it, you can roll it, do the stomp and e-ven stroll it at the hop.
swing it, you can groove it, you can real - ly start to move it at the hop.
When the rec-ord starts a spin - nin', you ca - lyp - so when you chick-en at the hop.
Where the jump-in' is the smooth-est and the mu - sic is the cool-est at the hop.
Do the dance sen - sa - tion that is sweep-in' the na - tion at the hop.
All the cats and the chicks can get their kicks at the hop.
168


# Assessment

**Unit Highlights** This unit includes a variety of strategies and methods, described below, to track students' progress and assess their understanding of lesson objectives. Reproducible masters for Show What You Know! and Review, Assess, Perform, Create can be found in the Resource Book.

**▶ FORMAL ASSESSMENTS**

The following assessments, using written language, cognitive, and performance skills, help teachers and students conceptualize the learning that is taking place.

- **Show What You Know!** Element-specific assessments, on the student page, for Rhythm (p. 181) and Melody (p. 191).
- **Review, Assess, Perform, Create** This end-of-unit activity (pp. 204–205) can be used for review and to assess students' learning of the core lessons in this unit.

**▶ INFORMAL ASSESSMENTS**

At the close of each Teacher's Edition lesson in this unit, the following types of assessments are used to evaluate the learning of the key element focus or skill objective.

- Music Journal Writing (p. 195)
- Observation/Music Journal Writing (p. 171)
- Performance/Observation (pp. 175, 177, 181, 185, 187, 191, 197, 199, 201, 203)

**▶ RUBRICS**

Visit *www.sfsuccessnet.com* for rubrics to assess students' achievement in music skills.

REFRAIN
G
Let's go to the hop! Let's go to the hop!
G
C7
(Oh, ba - by!) Let's go to the hop! (Oh, ba - by!)
G
D
C
Let's go to the hop! Come on.
1. G
12
2. G
Let's go to the hop! 2. Well, you can Let's go to the hop!

## Playing

The harmony for this song is a typical 12-bar-blues formula. Using keyboards or other bass instruments, have students accompany the song by playing the chord roots as shown below.

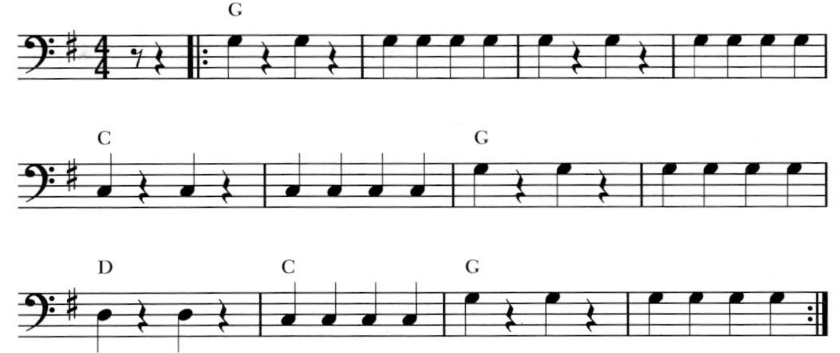
G
C
G
D
C
G

## Performing

Have students combine singing, movement, and instruments with the recording of "At the Hop" **CD 7-27**. During the verse, encourage students to replace the steady-beat motions with dance movements.

### INNOVATIVE TEACHER SUPPORT FOR THIS UNIT

- **MAKING MUSIC DVD, Grade 4** contains video segments that support lessons, including signing and movement.
- **MAKING MUSIC with Movement and Dance** provides more opportunities for large group activities in music or physical education classes.
- **MAKING MUSIC with Technology** provides lesson plans for many technology applications; includes MIDI files.
- ***¡A cantar!*** features recorded songs and lessons from around the Spanish-speaking world; includes strategies for bilingual classes and for English-speaking teachers working with Spanish-speaking students.
- **Bridges to Asia** features recorded songs and lessons from Asian and Pacific region cultures.
- ***www.sfsuccessnet.com*** provides an online lesson planner to conveniently create lesson plans at school or at home. Includes rubrics for assessment, lesson modifications to meet the needs of all students, performance musicals based on program content, and more.

## TECHNOLOGY/MEDIA LINK

**Unit Highlights** The following components in this unit reinforce and expand students' understanding of music elements and related themes. See Unit at a Glance, pp. 165a–165h.

▶ **CD-ROM**

- Play a rhythm game to identify same and different phrases (p. 177) and to identify same and different melodic phrases (p. 191)
- Enter eight-measure chord progressions using I and V chords (p. 201)

▶ **ELECTRONIC KEYBOARD**

- Accompany a song to reinforce meter in 3 (p. 175)
- Play an accompaniment to reinforce eighth-note/dotted-quarter note rhythm (p. 181)
- Generate arrangements to accompany a song (p. 203)

▶ **MIDI/SEQUENCING SOFTWARE**

- Use a MIDI song file to learn to sing in harmony (p. 187)

▶ **NOTATION SOFTWARE**

- Create contrasting sections to reinforce rondo form (p. 185)
- Notate and play back a round (p. 197)
- Notate *arpeggios* as an accompaniment (p. 199)

▶ **TRANSPARENCY**

- Display a listening map to illustrate rondo form (p. 185) and for pitch reading and timbre activities (p. 191)

▶ **VIDEO LIBRARY/DVD**

- Use the video to explore ensemble timbres (p. 195)

▶ **WEB SITE**

- Go to *www.sfsuccessnet.com* to learn more about Brahms (p. 171)

Core LESSON 1

## LESSON AT A GLANCE

**Element Focus** **EXPRESSION** Sudden tempo changes

**Skill Objective** **LISTENING** Listen to music and create "tempo maps" to show tempo changes

**Connection Activity** **LANGUAGE ARTS** Experiment with tempo changes when reading poetry

**MATERIALS**

- "Can You Canoe?" (speech piece) **CD 7-29**

  **Recording Routine:** Intro (4 m.); vocal; interlude (4 m.); vocal; interlude (4 m.); vocal; coda
- *Hungarian Dance No. 19* **CD 7-31**
- hand drums, woodblocks, triangles

**VOCABULARY**

tempo *andante* *moderato* *allegro*

**National Standards**

**2f** Play instruments independently against contrasting parts
**5c** Identify and use terms for tempo
**6b** Describe music by explaining how it sounds

**MORE MUSIC CHOICES**

Other speech pieces:

"The Continents," p. 357

"The Planets Chant," p. 377

# 1 INTRODUCE

Invite students to read "Can You Canoe?" on p. 170 aloud.

**ASK** **Is this a nonsense poem?** (No, but it uses language more for sound than meaning.)

Ask if anyone can identify the location of Kalamazoo or Kamloops. Then share the information from Across the Curriculum: Social Studies on p. 171.

LESSON 1 Element: EXPRESSION | Skill: LISTENING | Connection: LANGUAGE ARTS

# Row with the TEMPO

The tempo, or speed of the beat, plays a big role in giving music mood or feeling. Listen to the following speech piece. Notice the tempo changes. Raise your hand when you hear the tempo change.

CD 7-29

## Can You Canoe?

Words by Dennis Lee

Speech Piece

Can you ca - noe in Kal - a - ma - zoo?
I can ca - noe in Kal - a - ma - zoo;
Can you ca - noe in Kam - loops?
I can ca - noe in Kam - loops; but I
Can you ca - noe at a quar - ter to two in a
can - not ca - noe at a quar - ter to two in a
van when the traf - fic jam loops?
van when the traf - fic jam loops.

170

# Footnotes

## SKILLS REINFORCEMENT

▶ **Performing** For more practice with varying tempos, have students sing or move to the following pieces.

- *The Chicken Dance,* p. 51 **CD 3-1**
- *"Minka,"* p. 222 **CD 9-21**
- *ABACA Dabble,* p. 184 **CD 8-17**

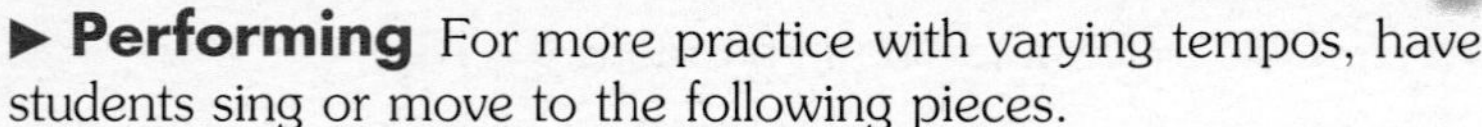

## BUILDING SKILLS THROUGH MUSIC

▶ **Language** Once students have read about Brahms, on p. 171, and listened to *Hungarian Dance No. 19*, ask them to look closely at the accompanying image of the composer. Have them write a short, descriptive paragraph, based on such elements as clothing, posture, and facial expression. Remind students that the approximate time period this photo was originally taken was the mid-1800s.

## MEETING INDIVIDUAL NEEDS

▶ **Including Everyone** For some students, successful public performance experiences may help them overcome poor perceptions of themselves and their capabilities. After observing students perform different activities with tempos, speaking, and playing instruments in smaller groups and with partners, assign students a leadership role (deciding, setting, and maintaining different tempos, cueing different groups). Be sure to assign specific leadership tasks based on your observation of the student's success performing the tasks. If leading a specific group, assign the student to a group of peers who will be supportive and offer sincere praise for his or her leadership skills.

### Continue Canoeing

Use the speech piece for your own experiments with tempo. **Perform** "Can You Canoe?" at an easy flowing tempo, called *andante.* Next **perform** the piece in a medium tempo, *moderato.* Now, repeat the speech piece in a rapid, lively tempo, *allegro.*

**Perform** these rhythm patterns with "Can You Canoe?"

**Listen** to the following piece. Notice the tempo changes and suggest names for these tempos.

CD 7-31
**Hungarian Dance No. 19**
**by Johannes Brahms**
Brahms wrote the *Hungarian Dances* for piano four hands. This orchestral setting of No. 19 was arranged by Antonín Dvořák.

MUSIC MAKERS

**Johannes Brahms**

**Johannes Brahms** (1833–1897) was born in Hamburg, Germany, to a musical family. He began piano lessons at an early age and was admired as a composer and pianist. He composed piano works, four symphonies, four concertos, choral works, and many songs.

Unit 5 171

## 2 Develop

### Performing

Write an objective statement on the board, such as "At 6:33 this morning the sun rose," or "In the daytime it's light, but at night it's dark." Have students speak the statement at a medium tempo, a fast tempo, and a slow tempo. Have students describe how the tempo changes affect the performance of the statement.

5c Have students identify and define the tempo terms and symbols on p. 171. Then have students speak "Can You Canoe?" **CD 7-29** using *andante, moderato,* and *allegro* tempos. Ask for volunteers to play a steady drumbeat at each tempo as students say the speech piece, appropriately interpreting each pre-determined tempo.

### Playing

2f Have students practice the accompaniment parts on p. 171 using body percussion and then percussion instruments. Perform "Can You Canoe?" several times, allowing students to take turns playing percussion parts and reciting the speech piece. Invite students to experiment with different tempos for the piece.

### Listening

6b Play *Hungarian Dance No. 19* **CD 7-31** and ask students to listen for and describe tempo changes in the piece, using the Italian terms on p. 171. Encourage students to think of real-life situations with "tempo" changes. (for example, a person slowing down as he or she walks, or a nervous animal as it begins to run)

## 3 Close

**Element: EXPRESSION** — **ASSESSMENT**

5c **Observation/Music Journal Writing** Have students listen to *Hungarian Dance No. 19* **CD 7-31** and draw listening maps that indicate the tempo changes heard in the recording. Assess students' understanding by having them explain, either through discussion or an entry in their journals, how their maps represent the music.

## Across the Curriculum

▶ **Social Studies** Canoeing would indeed be possible in the two cities mentioned: Kamloops (pop. 80,000), in the Canadian province of British Columbia, lies on the Thompson River; Kalamazoo (pop. 90,000), in western Michigan, is on the Kalamazoo River.

▶ **Language Arts** Interested students will enjoy reading *Brahms* by Ann Rachlin (Barrons Juveniles, 1993). This biography of Johannes Brahms focuses on his childhood and his early musical learning.

## Technology/Media Link

**Web Site** To learn more about Johannes Brahms and his music, have students visit *www.sfsuccessnet.com.*

## LESSON AT A GLANCE

**Element Focus** **RHYTHM** Meter in 3

**Skill Objective** **MOVING** Perform original movements to accompany songs in meter in 3

**Connection Activity** **CULTURE** Discuss traditional music from the Philippines and Korea

**MATERIALS**

- *"Santa Clara"* (Tagalog) **CD 7-32**
- *"Santa Clara"* (English) **CD 7-33**

  **Recording Routine:** Intro (8 m.); vocal; interlude (16 m.); vocal; coda
- *"Doraji"* **CD 7-36**
- "Bluebells" **CD 7-37**

  **Recording Routine:** Intro (4 m.); vocal; instrumental; vocal; coda
- **Pronunciation Practice/Translation** pp. 480, 481
- *Doraji* (excerpt) **CD 7-40**
- *Sanjo* **CD 7-41**
- **Resource Book** pp. A-16, A-17
- globe or world map

**VOCABULARY**

triple meter *kayagum*

**National Standards**

- **1c** Sing songs from diverse cultures
- **6b** Describe music by moving to it
- **6d** Identify the sounds of instruments from various cultures
- **6e** While listening to music, move to show a prominent feature of the music
- **9a** Listen to identify music from different cultures

**MORE MUSIC CHOICES**

Other selections from Asian countries:

*"Sakura,"* p. 308

*"Xiao,"* p. 314

*"Niu lang zhi nü,"* p. 335

LESSON 2 | Element: RHYTHM | Skill: MOVING | Connection: CULTURE

# Doin' Fine in Triple Time

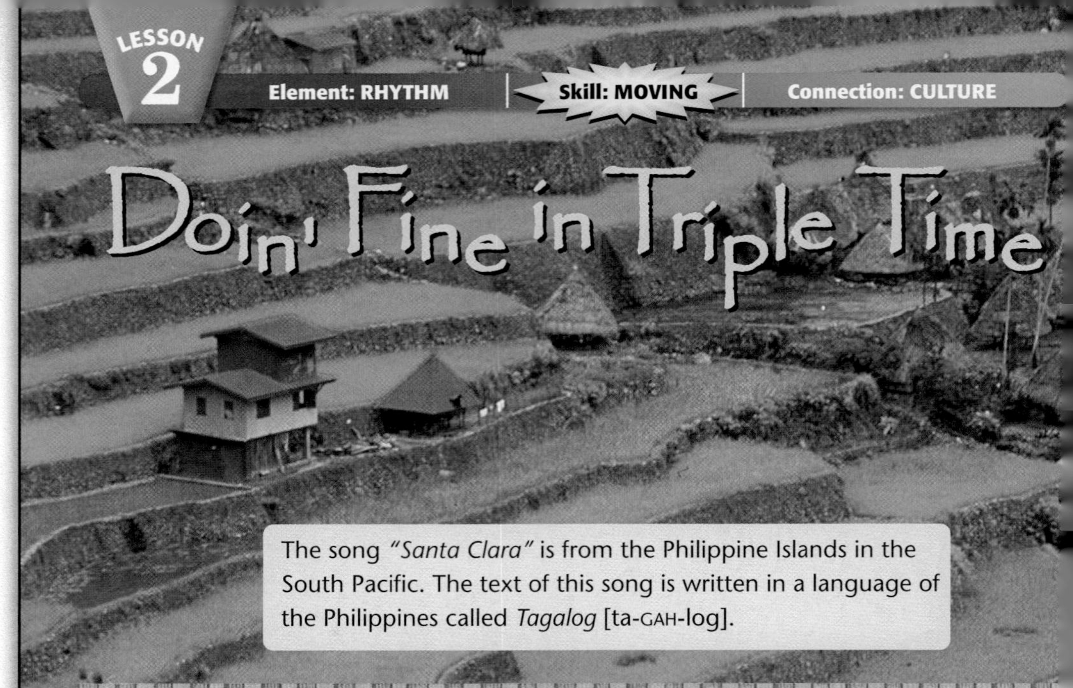

The song *"Santa Clara"* is from the Philippine Islands in the South Pacific. The text of this song is written in a language of the Philippines called *Tagalog* [ta-GAH-log].

CD 7-32

## Santa Clara

m, f, s, l, ta, t, (d) r m

English Words by Alice Firgau

Folk Song from the Philippines
As sung by Sonny Alforque

San - ta Cla - rang, pi - nung pi - no
San - ta Cla - ra, this I will do.

Ang pa - nga - ko ko ay ga - ni - to.
In my heart I vow and prom - ise you,

Pag - da - ting ko po sa U - ban - do. Ay mag -
On the road I'll go to U - ban - do; While I'm

172

# Footnotes

## SKILLS REINFORCEMENT

6b ▶ **Analyzing** Assemble students in small groups and ask them to find three or more songs in their textbooks that are in triple meter; for example, *"Cielito lindo"* (p. 270) or *"Hey m'tswala"* (p. 79). Have each group sing a known song for the class, accompanied by a body percussion pattern that demonstrates triple meter.

## BUILDING SKILLS THROUGH MUSIC

▶ **Math** Review with students the $\frac{3}{4}$ time signature of the songs *"Santa Clara"* (p. 172) and *"Doraji"* (p. 174). Point out that in this meter, there are three equal beats in each measure. Then ask: What geometric figure would best describe a measure in $\frac{3}{4}$? (equilateral triangle) What kind of triangle is traced in the air when conducting meter in 3? (right triangle)

## SPOTLIGHT ON

▶ **Languages** Tagalog is the basis for Filipino, which is the national language of the Philippines. Tagalog is the dominant language of Luzon, the large northern island, and the national capital, Manila. Since early in the Spanish colonial period, it has been written in a Spanish-style alphabet. However, it does not use c, f, j, q, v, x, or z, and it has the consonant combination ng.

The written Korean alphabet has 34 symbols—24 consonants and 10 vowels. This system was developed by Saejong, fourth king of the Josan Era, in about A.D. 1400. The language developed from Chinese roots, but became uniquely Korean at this point.

Both languages are accent based rather than tone based—word meanings are not derived from different inflections of vowel sounds.

### Feeling Strong

**Listen** to the strong triple feeling in this song: ONE-two-three, ONE-two-three. As you listen, **move** to show meter in 3 by performing these repeated motions: PAT-clap-snap.

**Create** hand movements of your own to go with the song. Always use the same movement for the strong beat.

◀ Filipino classical dancers

E7 A
sa - sa - yaw ng pan - dang - go. A - ru -
there I'll dance the fan - dan - go. A - ru -
A D E7 A
ray, a - ra - ru - ray, Ang pa - nga - ko'y tu - tu - pa - rin. A - ru -
ray, a - ra - ru - ray, And may my prom - ise be ful - filled. A - ru -
A D E7 A
ray, a - ra - ru - ray, Ang pa - nga - ko'y tu - tu - pa - rin.
ray, a - ra - ru - ray, And may my prom - ise be ful - filled.

## 1 Introduce

6b Have students locate the Philippine Islands on a globe or world map. Talk about where the Philippines are located and share with students the information about music in the Philippines from Cultural Connection below.

Divide the class into two groups. Ask one group to count aloud at a steady tempo: "ONE-two-three, ONE-two-three." Have the other group perform a PAT-clap-snap body percussion. Have the two groups switch parts. Have each half of the class alternate performing it without counting aloud. Explain that this activity demonstrates triple meter—musical time in sets of three.

Tell students they will be singing and listening to songs in triple meter from two different Asian cultures.

## 2 Develop

### Moving

Play *"Santa Clara"* **CD 7-32** for students. Ask them to listen for the strong beat in the song and create movements to demonstrate triple meter. Encourage students to create movements that emphasize beat 1 of each measure. Play the song again and have volunteers demonstrate their movement patterns. Invite the class to give constructive comments.

**continued on page 174**

### Cultural Connection

▶ **Music in the Philippines** Before the Spanish arrived in the Philippines, a number of indigenous groups populated the islands. They practiced their own musical traditions, but many of those traditions have been lost. Recently there has been renewed interest in reclaiming these native cultures and their musical traditions. Spain dominated the Philippines for several centuries, which caused urban musical life to parallel that of Madrid. Musicians were trained to play European instruments in a European style. Spanish dances were very prominent. *"Santa Clara"* is representative of the Spanish influence in the Philippines. Since the United States' presence in the Philippines, Western pop music has become part of the culture.

### Across the Curriculum

▶ **Language Arts** Read aloud the book *The Mats* by Francisco Arcellana (Kane/Miller, 1999). While their father is away, seven Philippine children dream about the sleeping mats that he will bring them when he returns. The father comes home with special sleeping mats created by an artist for each child. He also brings mats in memory of three other children in the family who have died.

▶ **Art** Invite students to create a model of a sleeping mat for themselves. These can be made from straw placemats or paper bags.

### Singing

1c Identify the language of *"Santa Clara"* as Tagalog (tah-GAH-log). Using the Pronunciation Practice Track for *"Santa Clara"* **CD 7-35,** have students learn the song in Tagalog. Refer to Resource Book p. A-16 for a phonetic guide. Emphasize to students that many languages are spoken in the world today, and we can demonstrate "global awareness" by our willingness to learn them.

Then have students sing *"Santa Clara"* **CD 7-33** in English. Discuss the meaning of the text.

### Moving

Have students locate Korea on a globe or world map, and discuss its location relative to the Philippines. Share the information with students about Korea from Spotlight On below.

6e Play *"Doraji"* **CD 7-36** for students. As they listen, ask them to create movements in triple meter to accompany the song. Discuss how *"Doraji"* has a different feeling than *"Santa Clara"* and how students' movement patterns can reflect the difference.

### Singing

Use the Pronunciation Practice Track to help students learn *"Doraji"* **CD 7-39** in Korean. Refer to Resource Book p. A-17 for a phonetic guide. When students are confident with the Korean version, have them sing the song in English with **CD 7-37.** Discuss the nature images in the text.

## Make Mine $\frac{3}{4}$ Time

**Listen** to the Korean song *"Doraji,"* another song in $\frac{3}{4}$. Unlike most other Asian cultures, Korea has folk songs in $\frac{3}{4}$ time. Is the tempo faster or slower than the tempo of *"Santa Clara"*?

CD 7-36
Doraji (Bluebells)
s, l, d r m s
English Words by Patricia Shehan Campbell
Folk Song from Korea
Do - ra - ji, do - ra - ji, pek do - ra - ji,
Blue - bells, blue - bells, Love - ly blue - bells,
Sim - sim san - chuh neh pek do - ra - ji.
Deep in the moun - tains my blue - bells grow.
Hahn du bu - ri - man keh - yuh - do
Gather - ing blue - bells in wide val - leys.
Teh kwang - chu - ri su - ri - sal sal num - nun - goo - na.
Bas - kets of blue - bells will o - ver - flow.
174

## Footnotes

### SPOTLIGHT ON

▶ **Korea** Korea is divided into two parts, North Korea and South Korea. Both parts of Korea are on the Korean Peninsula, which is south of northeastern China. Until the 1900s, most Korean people were farmers, but today both countries are mostly industrial. The arts in Korea were influenced by those of China and by the teachings of Buddhism and Confucianism. Favorite ideas expressed in traditional Korean art were love of nature, respect for learning, and loyalty to the government. Artistic expression today in democratic South Korea is very much influenced by the West. The North Korean government maintains strict control of its artists.

### SKILLS REINFORCEMENT

▶ **Creating** Encourage students to perform original compositions in triple meter.

**Reinforcement** Some students may be most comfortable participating in this activity by choosing a body percussion to perform on the downbeat of each measure.

**On Target** Invite other students to create a three-beat pattern to be used as an ostinato. The pattern may be performed using body percussion or transferred to nonpitched percussion instruments.

**Challenge** Encourage interested students to improvise pentatonic melodies over the rhythm ostinatos.

## Folk Melody, Folk Instruments

**Listen** for meter in 3 in this version of *Doraji.*

CD 7-40

**Doraji**

**Folk Song from Korea**

This version of *Doraji* is played on traditional Korean instruments and is sung in Korean folk style.

*Sanjo* is a traditional Korean instrumental form that has been used for centuries. **Listen** to this modern interpretation by Hi-za Yoo. She is playing the *kayagum* [ki-AH-gum], a Korean string instrument.

CD 7-41

**Sanjo**

**written and performed by Hi-za Yoo**

This excerpt is one of five sections. In *Sanjo* form, each section becomes faster and more complex.

MUSIC MAKERS
Hi-za Yoo
As a child in Korea, Hi-za Yoo studied traditional dance and instruments, and she became an outstanding performer. She has performed mainly in the Los Angeles area, where she has established an institute for teaching Korean music and dance.
Unit 5 175

### Listening

Introduce the listening version of *Doraji* **CD 7-40**, sung by adult Korean folk-style singers and accompanied by Korean instruments. Share information from Cultural Connection below about Korean traditional music. The timbre of the voices and instruments may be quite different from what students are accustomed to hearing. Ask students to compare the vocal timbre of the adult Korean singers with that of the children's voices on **CD 7-36**. Remind them that different cultures enjoy different types of musical sound.

After playing one verse, have students describe the sounds that they hear. (plucked strings of different ranges, a double-reed instrument, a flute, a drum)

6d Direct students' attention to the information on Hi-za Yoo and the *kayagum* on p. 175. Her story illustrates that when people move from one culture to another, their music goes with them. Point out that Ms. Yoo is fluent in both Korean traditional music and European classical music. Then play *Sanjo* **CD 7-41** to demonstrate the sound of the *kayagum.*

# 3 Close

### Moving

Divide students into groups of three to create three-beat movements for *"Santa Clara"* **CD 7-32.** Remind students that their movements should follow the steady beat throughout the song. Give groups time to practice. Have half the groups perform while the rest of the class watches and then switch. Do the same activity for *"Doraji"* **CD 7-36,** asking students to use movement that illustrates the differences in tempo and feeling between this song and *"Santa Clara."*

**Skill: MOVING** — **ASSESSMENT**

**Performance/Observation** Have students sing *"Santa Clara"* and *"Doraji"* while performing steady-beat movement patterns that reflect the tempo and meter of each song. Assess each student's ability to maintain the steady beat in $\frac{3}{4}$ time.

## Cultural Connection

▶ **Korean Traditional Music** The style of music heard in the traditional recordings of *Doraji* and *Sanjo* is not something known and enjoyed by all Koreans today. In general, the current music of Korea is very Western. Western musical traditions such as choral singing and orchestral music are very strong in Korea. Traditional styles such as that on the recordings are maintained at some universities and in special music institutes. They are valued as part of Korean cultural heritage. The three women heard singing on *Doraji* have been designated as "national living treasures" and are supported by the Korean government.

## Technology/Media Link

**Electronic Keyboard** Use keyboards to reinforce $\frac{3}{4}$ time. Ask students to select appropriate instrument voices to accompany *"Doraji"* on a keyboard. Have half the class play dotted-half note Fs throughout the song. Have the other half of the class play an F-major *arpeggio* in quarter notes throughout the song. Explain that the dotted-half notes (bass part) should equal three of the quarter notes.

## LESSON AT A GLANCE

**Element Focus** RHYTHM ♩. ♪

**Skill Objective** **READING** Read a song from notation that contains ♩. ♪

**Connection Activity** **CULTURE** Discuss the influence of the Moors on Spanish culture

**MATERIALS**

- *"La Tarara"* (Spanish) **CD 8-1**
- *"La Tarara"* (English) **CD 8-2**

  **Recording Routine:** Intro (8 m.); refrain; v. 1; refrain; interlude (8 m.); refrain; v. 2; refrain; coda
- **Music Reading Practice, Sequence 17** **CD 8-5**
- **Pronunciation Practice/Translation** p. 481
- **Resource Book** pp. A-18, D-22, E-18, H-15

**VOCABULARY**

dotted-quarter note    eighth note

**◆ ◆ ◆ ◆ National Standards ◆ ◆ ◆ ◆**

**2b** Play accompaniments on appropriate instruments
**5a** Read rhythms in duple meter
**6c** Use appropriate terms for music notation
**6d** Identify the sounds of instruments from various cultures
**6e** While listening to music, move to show a prominent feature of the music

**MORE MUSIC CHOICES**

For more review of ♩. ♪ patterns:
"America," p. 440
"Circle 'Round the Moon," p. 403

# 1 INTRODUCE

Play the Stereo Performance Track for *"La Tarara"* **CD 8-3** and have students listen to the various timbres. Refer to Cultural Connection below and share the information about Moorish influence in Spain.

# Sounds of Spain

The music of Spain has been influenced by many different cultures. The Moors, an Arabic people, lived in southern Spain for nearly seven centuries. They brought with them the *vihuela* [vee-HWAY-la], an ancestor of the guitar.

**Listen** for the sound of the *vihuela* in *"La Tarara."*

▲ Castanets
CD 8–1
La Tarara
m, si, l, t, d r m
English Words by Alice D. Firgau
Folk Song from Spain
REFRAIN
Em B7
La Ta - ra - ra, sí, la Ta - ra - ra, no,
La Ta - ra - ra, yes, La Ta - ra - ra, no,
Em B7 Em Fine
La Ta - ra - ra, ma - dre, que la bai - lo yo.
La Ta - ra - ra, ma - ma, is a dance I know.
VERSE
Em B7
1. Tie - ne la Ta - ra - ra un jar - dín de flo - res y me
2. Tie - ne la Ta - ra - ra un ces - to de fru - tas y me
1. If I want to wan - der in her gar - den bow - ers, La Ta -
2. If I want a bas - ket of the fruit she'll har - vest, La Ta -
Em B7 D. C. al Fine
da, si quie - ro, siem - pre las me - jor - es.
da, si quie - ro, siem - pre las ma - du - ras.
ra - ra al - ways gives me her best flow - ers.
ra - ra al - ways gives me just the rip - est.

## Footnotes

### CULTURAL CONNECTION

▶ **Moors in Spain** Spain came under Muslim rule in 711 when Tariq ibn-Ziyad and a Muslim army crossed the Strait of Gibraltar. The army defeated Roderick of Spain, and over the next few years it established control in city after city. During their reign of almost 800 years, the Moors imprinted Spain with their architecture, art, and music. As Spanish factions slowly regained control, many Moors were driven out, but their influences still linger. The last Moorish stronghold was defeated in 1492.

### BUILDING SKILLS THROUGH MUSIC

▶ **Art** Have students look at the Arts Connection *Girl with a Guitar* on p. 177. Ask students to describe the elements of art used to highlight the girl in the painting. (Answers may include shading, the picture over her head, and so on.)

### ACROSS THE CURRICULUM

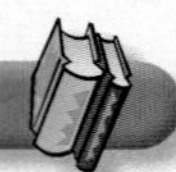

▶ **Social Studies** Have students locate Spain on a map or globe and discuss ways that music of other neighboring countries might have influenced the folk music of Spain.

▶ **Language Arts** Share the story *The Beautiful Butterfly: A Folktale from Spain* by Judy Sierra (Houghton Mifflin, 2000) and invite students to learn about this popular Spanish tale.

Invite students to write alternative endings to the book. What would have happened if the fish didn't spit out the mouse? What if the king didn't care?

## Arts Connection

◀ *Girl with a Guitar* by Jan Vermeer (1632–1675). How is the instrument in this painting similar to the *vihuela* shown below?

### It's All the Same

Say the words to the refrain in rhythm and tap the beat with your foot. Now clap the rhythm pattern below while you say the words.

La Ta - ra - ra sí,

You can use the tie to show the sound that lasts for one and a half beats.

La Ta - ra - ra sí,

There is an easier way to write the same rhythm, using ♩. ♪

La Ta - ra - ra sí,

Vihuela ▶

**Identify** and **read** the new rhythm pattern in *"La Tarara."*

# 2 Develop

### Listening

6e Have students pat the steady beat while listening to *"La Tarara"* **CD 8-1.** Encourage them to determine the meter by discovering the pattern of strong and weak beats. Point out the time signature. Remind students that in $\frac{2}{4}$ time there are two beats in each measure.

### Singing

Invite students to listen to the Pronunciation Practice Track for *"La Tarara"* **CD 8-4** and sing with the students on the recording. Refer to Resource Book p. A-18 for a phonetic guide.

### Reading

Have students keep a steady beat as they say the words to the refrain of *"La Tarara"* in rhythm. Have them say the rhythms on the Music Reading Worksheet found on Resource Book p. D-22.

ASK **Is the rhythm the same or different from the rhythm of the words of the song?** (different)

**Where is it different?** (on the syllable *"-ra"*)

5a 6c Have students draw a tie between the first two notes of the first full measure, which will change the rhythm to fit the words of the song. Have them say the syllables *"-ra-ra"* in rhythm, while patting the steady beat. Show them the ♩. ♪ pattern. Explain that this pattern is how the *"-ra-ra"* rhythm is usually written, and it is called a dotted-quarter and eighth note.

See p. 450 and Resource Book p. E-18 for a related reading activity.

# 3 Close

Element: RHYTHM
ASSESSMENT

5a **Performance/Observation** Have students sing *"La Tarara"* **CD 8-1** while following the notation. Ask them to sing with rhythm syllables, and observe the accuracy with which they read the notation.

## Skills Reinforcement

6d ▶ **Listening** Ask students to describe the instruments used to accompany *"La Tarara."* Discuss the Moorish instrument *vihuela* and have students compare its sound to that of the traditional guitar. For more information on the *vihuela*, have students refer to p. 471 in the Sound Bank.

2b ▶ **Keyboard** Invite students to play an accompaniment for *"La Tarara"* **CD 8-1,** using the dotted-quarter/eighth-note rhythm. The accompaniment is based on two broken-chord positions.

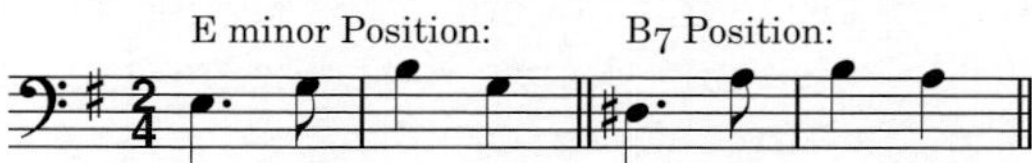

E minor Position:
B7 Position:

For a keyboard accompaniment to *"La Tarara,"* refer to Resource Book p. H-15.

## Technology/Media Link

**CD-ROM** Use *Making More Music's* "Rhythm" game to help students identify same and different phrases. Before class, start the CD-ROM program in the school's computer lab or at the classroom's computer learning center. When students arrive, have them

- Organize themselves into small groups.
- Select the "Games" icon and then choose the "Rhythm" game.
- Click the green arrow to begin playing.

LESSON 4

## LESSON AT A GLANCE

**Element Focus** RHYTHM ♪♩.

**Skill Objective** READING Read songs from notation that include ♪♩.

**Connection Activity** CULTURE Discuss African American spirituals and work songs

**MATERIALS**

- "Old House, Tear It Down!" **CD 8-8**
  **Recording Routine:** Intro (4 m.); v. 1; interlude (4 m.); v. 2; coda
- **Music Reading Practice, Sequence 18** **CD 8-10**
- "All Night, All Day" **CD 8-13**
  **Recording Routine:** Intro (2 m.); v. 1; v. 2; coda
- **Resource Book** pp. B-16, D-23, E-19, F-11, G-8, I-15, J-13

**VOCABULARY**

| | |
|---|---|
| eighth note | dotted-quarter note |
| call and response | *D.C. al Fine* |

**National Standards**

- **1a** Sing independently on pitch
- **1b** Sing expressively with appropriate dynamics
- **1e** Sing in groups, while following a conductor
- **2b** Play accompaniments on appropriate instruments
- **3d** Improvise instrumental pieces, using traditional sounds
- **5a** Read rhythms in quadruple meter
- **5d** Notate rhythm using standard symbols
- **6e** While listening to music, move to show a prominent feature of the music

**MORE MUSIC CHOICES**

Other African American spirituals:

"Gonna Ride Up in the Chariot," p. 20

"Wade in the Water," p. 268

Have you ever tried singing a song to pass the time while you work? Songs have long been used to make work go faster. **Sing** the song "Old House, Tear It Down!" Notice how the rhythms give the song energy.

CD 8-8

### OLD HOUSE, TEAR IT DOWN!

*Collected by John Work* — *African American Work Song*

l d r m

1. Old house, tear it down! Who's gon-na help me tear it down?
2. New house, build it up! Who's gon-na help me build it up?

Bring me a ham-mer, tear it down! Bring me a saw, tear it down!
Bring me a ham-mer, build it up! Bring me a saw, build it up!

Next thing you bring me, tear it down! Is a wreck-ing ma-chine, tear it down.
Next thing you bring me, build it up! Is a car-pen-ter man, build it up.



## Footnotes

### MEETING INDIVIDUAL NEEDS

▶ **English Language Learners** For students learning English, you may wish to provide a series of pictures to illustrate "Old House, Tear It Down!" including house, hammer, saw, wrecking machine, and so on. While singing, invite students to select the picture that matches the words. You may also want to ask students to discuss why an old house might be torn down.

### BUILDING SKILLS THROUGH MUSIC

▶ **Science** Focus students' attention on the illustrations on p. 179. Lead a discussion of the activities taking place. Ask students to describe the sound that each worker might be producing and identify the source and the means by which the sound is produced. Have students suggest rhythm patterns that each worker might use to accompany the song "Old House, Tear It Down!"

### SKILLS REINFORCEMENT

▶ **Listening** Clap four-beat rhythm patterns for students, using known rhythms and the two patterns presented in this lesson. Have individual students indicate whether or not each clapped pattern contains a dotted rhythm figure.

▶ **Guitar** The song "Old House, Tear It Down!" is well suited for easy guitar accompaniment. The single chord change from Em to Am can be fingered more easily if the Em is pressed with the second and third fingers (instead of the often-indicated first and second fingers). Using this fingering, the second and third fingers simply slide down one string. By adding the first finger on the second string, the Am chord is complete.

2b

## Rewriting Rhythms

**Read** the first line of the song. Then clap part 2 of the rhythm pattern below while you say the words.

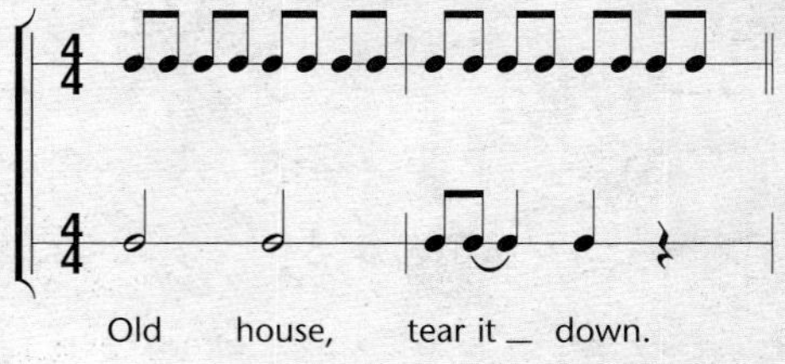

$\frac{4}{4}$ ♫ ♫ ♫ ♫ | ♫ ♫ ♫ ♫ ||

$\frac{4}{4}$ 𝅗𝅥 𝅗𝅥 | ♫ ♩ ♩ 𝄽 |
Old house, tear it _ down.

You can use ♪ ♩. to write the same rhythm.

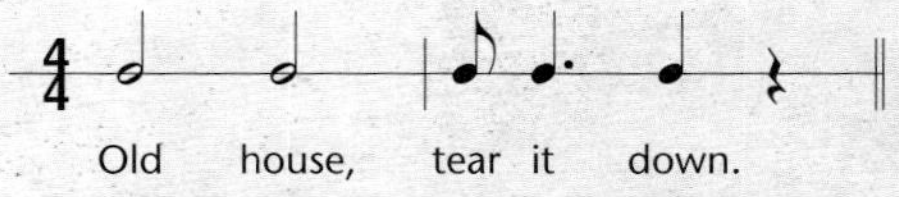

$\frac{4}{4}$ 𝅗𝅥 𝅗𝅥 | ♪ ♩. ♩ 𝄽 ||
Old house, tear it down.

**Read** the entire song using rhythm syllables.



# 1 Introduce

Ask students to think about a time when they had to do some difficult work. Did they do anything to make the work easier? Some people sing to make the work easier and lessen the burden.

Share with students the information about African American spirituals and work songs in Cultural Connection below.

# 2 Develop

### Performing

Using rhythm syllables, lead students in saying four-beat rhythm patterns with 𝅗𝅥, ♫ ♩., ♪ ♩.

Have students

- Echo say the rhythms as a group and individually
- Determine the number of beats in each pattern. (four)

### Listening

Have students

- Listen to the recording of "Old House, Tear It Down!" **CD 8-8** while keeping a steady beat.
- Determine the meter by finding the pattern of strong and weak beats. (strong, weak, weak, weak)

Draw attention to the time signature. Remind students that in $\frac{4}{4}$ time there are four beats in each measure. Demonstrate the conducting pattern for meter in 4.

### Performing

Have students conduct a four-beat pattern while listening to "Old House, Tear It Down!" **CD 8-8.** Invite volunteers to take turns conducting as the rest of the class sings the song.

**continued on page 180**

## Across the Curriculum

▶ **Language Arts** Share the book *Construction Zone* by Tana Hoban (Greenwillow, 1997) and invite students to learn more about how buildings are built. Pay attention to the equipment that might be the "wrecking machine" described in "Old House, Tear It Down!"

Invite students to share their construction stories. Use this time to facilitate oral language skills. Have they ever seen a house being built? Being torn down? How about a skyscraper or a freeway being built?

## Cultural Connection

▶ **Spirituals** Songs known as "spirituals," such as "All Night, All Day," have traditionally been an important part of African American culture. When slavery existed in the United States, enslaved African Americans created these songs to instill hope for a better future. The songs were often sung in call-and-response style, a characteristic from African heritage. Spirituals were normally passed on through oral tradition. Variations in melody and rhythm were part of the process.

▶ **Work Songs** African American work songs share the same history as the spiritual. Both evolved from African rhythms and melodies. The purpose of the work song however was specifically for keeping a steady rhythm and beat for the workers. During the early 1900s, the work song became the source for ragtime, blues, and jazz songs.

## Analyzing

Using the Recognizing Rhythm Patterns Worksheet on Resource Book p. D-23, have students

- Say the rhythmic notation of the first two measures.
- Compare the pattern to the words of "Old House, Tear It Down!" on student p. 178.

**ASK Does the rhythm you performed match the rhythm of the words?** (not exactly)

**Where is the difference?** (in measure 2, on the words *tear it*)

**How can we use a tie to change the rhythm to fit the words?** (tie the second eighth note in m. 2 to the following quarter note)

Have students draw the tie in the correct spot on the Resource Book worksheet and then say the rhythm of the words. Encourage students to keep a steady beat as you say the ♪ ♩. rhythm.

**ASK How many beats did you say during my pattern?** (two)

**How many sounds did I perform?** (two)

**Were both sounds the same length?** (No; the first sound was shorter than the second.)

Show students the ♪ ♩. pattern at the bottom of the Resource Book worksheet.

**SAY** This two-beat rhythm pattern of short and long sounds can be written an easier way using an eighth note and a dotted-quarter note.

Next review note values and tied notes by having the class read and discuss p. 179 in their books.

Invite students to have some fun using ties to match two rows of rhythm patterns. See Resource Book p. J-13.

### Two Patterns Alike and Different

The two patterns below are alike because both patterns are made up of two sounds: one long and the other short.

1.
2.

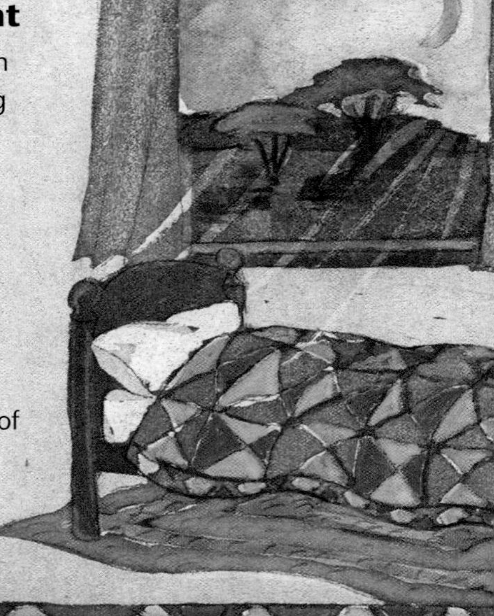

How are they different?

**Sing** "All Night, All Day."

Conduct the song in a four-beat pattern. **Identify** the lines that contain one or both of the rhythm patterns above.

CD 8-13
ALL NIGHT, ALL DAY
s, l, t, d r m s
African American Spiritual
REFRAIN
do
G C G
All night, all ___ day, An - gels watch-ing o - ver me, my Lord. _
G D7 G
Fine
All night, all ___ day, An - gels watch-ing o - ver me.
VERSE Call
G
Response
C G
1. Now I lay me down _ to sleep, An - gels watch-ing o - ver me, my Lord. _
2. If I die be - fore _ I wake,
Call
G
Response
D7 G
D. C. al Fine
Pray the Lord my soul _ to keep, An - gels watch-ing o - ver me.
Pray the Lord my soul _ to take,
180 Reading Sequence 18

## Footnotes

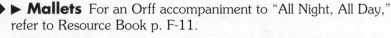

### SKILLS REINFORCEMENT

3d 5d ▶ **Composing** Invite students to create rhythm patterns and notate them on blank cards. Organize students into groups and assign each group a meter of 2, 3, or 4 beats per measure. Each student will compose one measure and notate his or her rhythm on a card. The group can then decide on the best order, creating a rhythm composition. Each group then performs its entire composition by using body percussion or playing on instruments.

▶ **Recorder** For a recorder accompaniment to play with "All Night, All Day," refer to Resource Book p. I-15.

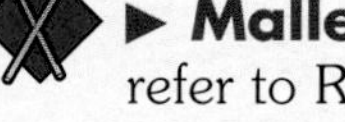
▶ **Mallets** For an Orff accompaniment to "All Night, All Day," refer to Resource Book p. F-11.

▶ **Moving** For a signing activity to accompany "All Night, All Day," refer to Resource Book p. G-8.

### CHARACTER EDUCATION

▶ **Support and Compassion** To encourage students to consider the importance of supportive, compassionate relationships, discuss situations in which they have and have not felt supported and nurtured. Point out to students that the song "Old House, Tear It Down!" describes destroying and building a house. Similarly, people can be "built up" and "torn down." Have students take part in the following activity. Ask them to think of a time when someone "tore them down." Describe what happened, how the other person responded, and how their response made them feel. Then ask them to do the same activity, describing a time when someone "built them up." Invite students to role play responses to various situations (for example, losing a ballgame, singing a solo, making a bad grade on a test, and so on), demonstrating ways to build people up.

*Arts* Connection

▲ *Mother and Child* (1919) by Martha Walter. How would the music change if a mother were to sing "All Night, All Day" as a lullaby to her young child?

## Show What You Know!

**Perform** these rhythms using rhythm syllables.

1. 4/4 ♩. ♪ ♩ ♩ ‖
2. 4/4 ♪ ♩. ♩ ♩ ‖

Using the rhythms above, **compose** your own rhythm pattern. Make it four measures long. Be sure there are four beats in each measure. **Perform** it for the rest of the class.



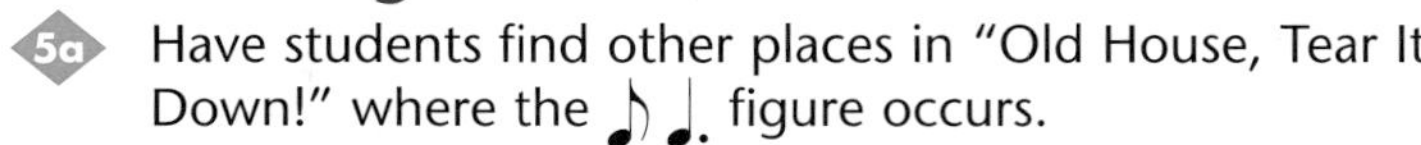

### Reading

5a Have students find other places in "Old House, Tear It Down!" where the ♪ ♩. figure occurs.

For an additional reading activity using "Old House, Tear It Down!" see p. 450 and Resource Book p. E-19.

1a Have students turn to pp. 180–181 in their books. Read and clap with them the two rhythm patterns notated above the song. Then invite students to sing "All Night, All Day" **CD 8-13** with the recording.

1e 1b Have students conduct using a four-beat pattern as they sing again. Remind them to sing with expression appropriate for a lullaby.

### Analyzing

Have students look at the notation for "All Night, All Day" on p. 180. Ask them whether this song has any of the same four-beat rhythm patterns as "Old House, Tear It Down!" Have students find either of the new dotted-quarter note/eighth-note patterns in the song and identify them by the words and measure numbers on which they occur. (♩. ♪ —mm. 2 and 6; ♪ ♩. —mm. 4 and 12)

For more practice with rhythms, have students do the activities in the Show What You Know! on p. 181. Refer to Resource Book p. B-16.

## 3 Close

**Skill: READING** ASSESSMENT

5a **Performance/Observation** Have students sing "Old House, Tear It Down!" **CD 8-8** or "All Night, All Day" **CD 8-13** while following the notation and conducting a four-beat pattern. Ask students to sing the song, first using rhythm syllables and again using the song text. Assess each student's ability to read the ♪ ♩. rhythm pattern in each song.

### Teacher to Teacher

1a ▶ **Intervals** An interval is the relationship between two pitches. Have students learn intervals using pitch syllables or numbers. Use the first interval in familiar songs (such as "Here Comes the Bride" for a perfect 4th) to reinforce a specific interval. To help students learn intervals, have them sing the following pentatonic pattern in various keys: *do re do mi do so do la do do*ˡ You might also ask students to sing the appropriate numbers— 1 2 1 3 1 5 1 6 1 8—to reinforce the pitches of the pattern.

Play interval identification games in which you play and/or sing the interval and students sing back with pitch syllables and/or numbers.

### Technology/Media Link

2b **Electronic Keyboard** Have students play an accompaniment for "All Night, All Day" to reinforce the ♪ ♩. rhythm. Ask students to select appropriate instrument voices on an electronic keyboard for the accompaniment. Have selected students play a ♪ ♩. repeated rhythm on the chord roots of the song.

You may also wish to invite students to select a timbre and play the response *tear it down* as the class sings "Old House, Tear It Down!"

LESSON Core 5

## LESSON AT A GLANCE

**Element Focus** **FORM** Rondo form

**Skill Objective** **MOVING** Perform a speech rondo accompanied by contrasting movements

**Connection Activity** **LANGUAGE ARTS** Write poetry to be performed in rondo form

**MATERIALS**

- "Heave-Ho"/"Going, Going, Gone"/ "The Snow" (speech pieces) **CD 8-15**
- **Recording Routine:** Intro (4 m.); Heave-Ho vocal; Going, Going, Gone vocal; Heave-Ho vocal; The Snow vocal; Heave-Ho vocal; coda
- *ABACA Dabble* **CD 8-17**
- *Rondo: Allegro* **CD 8-18**
- hand drums, woodblocks, maracas

**VOCABULARY**

rondo

### National Standards

**2f** Play instruments independently against contrasting parts
**3d** Improvise instrumental pieces, using body percussion
**4b** Compose songs within specific guidelines
**5d** Notate pitch and rhythm, using standard symbols
**6a** Listen to identify form
**6b** Describe music by moving to it
**6c** Use appropriate terms to explain music
**6e** While listening to music, move to show a prominent feature of the music
**9e** Demonstrate appropriate audience behavior

**MORE MUSIC CHOICES**

Other examples of rondo form:
*Fossils*, p. 220
"*La raspa*," p. 302
*Walking Song*, p. 347

LESSON 5 Element: FORM | Skill: MOVING | Connection: LANGUAGE ARTS

# KNOW the RONDO

"Heave–Ho," "Going, Going, Gone," and "The Snow" are speech pieces. Each has different rhythm patterns. Keep a steady beat as you **perform** these speech pieces.

CD 8-15
A Heave-Ho
Words by Dennis Lee
Speech Piece
Heave - Ho, buck-ets of snow, the gi - ant is comb-ing his beard. The
snow is as high as the top of the sky, and the world has dis - ap - peared.

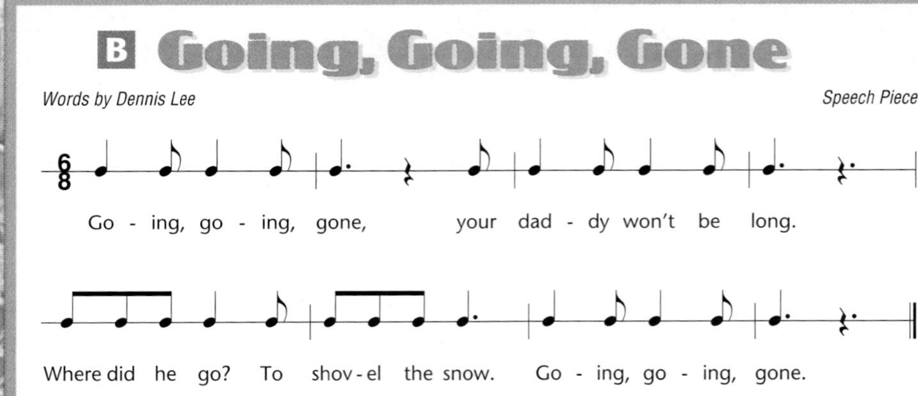

B Going, Going, Gone
Words by Dennis Lee
Speech Piece
Go - ing, go - ing, gone, your dad - dy won't be long.
Where did he go? To shov - el the snow. Go - ing, go - ing, gone.

182

## Footnotes

### ACROSS THE CURRICULUM

▶ **Science** Read aloud the book *Big Snow* by Berta Hader (Simon & Schuster, 1967) and encourage students to talk about preparations for winter. In this book, animals are preparing for the winter.

Invite students to write in their journals about their families' preparations for winter. What special things need to be done?

### BUILDING SKILLS THROUGH MUSIC

▶ **Writing** Invite students to perform the speech pieces "Heave-Ho"/ "Going, Going, Gone"/"The Snow." Discuss that snow is the solid form of rain. Ask students to estimate the number of days it snows in a year where they live. Then have them write a brief paragraph about the weather where they live.

### SKILLS REINFORCEMENT

3d ▶ **Improvising** Have students clap the rhythm of the words to "Heave-Ho" as the A section of their rondo. Ask a small group of students to use a clap-snap pattern to keep the beat for the A section.

The B and C sections should be the same length as the A section (eight measures with two beats each). Count the measures aloud for students as they improvise body percussion patterns. You may wish to vary the piece by asking students to perform patting and snapping for one section and clapping and stamping for the other.

Alternate the sections in an ABACA pattern, and you will have a rondo!

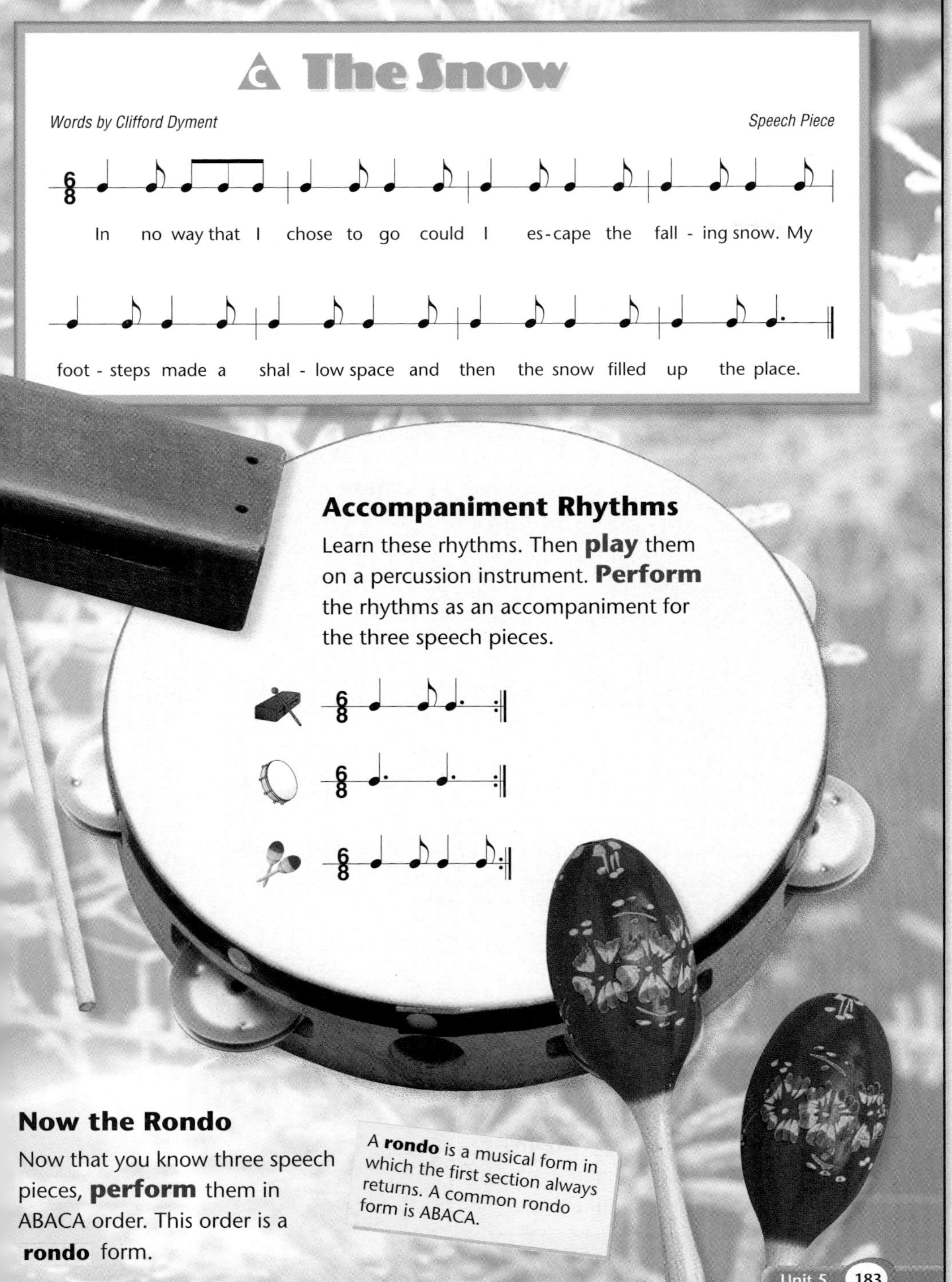

## C The Snow

Words by Clifford Dyment — Speech Piece

In no way that I chose to go could I es-cape the fall - ing snow. My
foot - steps made a shal - low space and then the snow filled up the place.

### Accompaniment Rhythms

Learn these rhythms. Then **play** them on a percussion instrument. **Perform** the rhythms as an accompaniment for the three speech pieces.

### Now the Rondo

Now that you know three speech pieces, **perform** them in ABACA order. This order is a **rondo** form.

A **rondo** is a musical form in which the first section always returns. A common rondo form is ABACA.

Unit 5 183

# 1 Introduce

Draw three circles on the board, leaving equal amounts of space between them. Ask a student to draw in a contrasting shape between circles 1 and 2, and another student to draw in a different contrasting shape between circles 2 and 3. Ask students to identify the pattern (3 "sames" with 2 "differents" between) and the theme that links them all (shapes).

6c Then draw an apple on the board. Ask a student to draw two more apples, and have two other students draw contrasting fruits between that fit with the theme of fruits (banana, orange, lemon, and so on). Tell students that when you build a piece of music this way, it is called a rondo.

# 2 Develop

### Analyzing

Direct students' attention to the three poems on pp. 182–183. Ask them to identify the theme that links the poems. (the topic: winter, or more specifically, snow) Ask how the class might go about making a rondo out of these. (use one poem three times, with the other two poems in between)

### Performing

6e Direct students' attention to "Heave-Ho." Ask them to join you in patting a steady duple beat. Then have students say the poem independently, still patting the steady beat. Ask them to say it one more time, this time doing a pat-clap pattern to prepare the drum part in the second row of rhythms on p. 183.

Have students speak and pat the words in rhythm for "Going, Going, Gone" and "The Snow." Then ask half the class to perform the rhythm patterns on p. 183 using body percussion. Have the other half of the class speak the poem. Then switch parts.

continued on page 184

## Meeting Individual Needs

**▶ Cooperation** This lesson offers an ideal opportunity for developing individual/group cooperation and interaction. Goals for this speech rondo activity should be that everyone, within his or her own ability level, can be successful, and everyone should have the support of the entire group.

**Reinforcement** Allow some students to choose a body percussion to perform a steady beat (the strong beat of each measure of the speech pieces).

**On Target** Arrange for most of the class to perform "Heave-Ho" (the A section). Invite soloists to perform the "Going, Going, Gone" (B) and "The Snow" (C) portions. If a student does not feel ready to do a solo, invite him or her to perform with a partner.

**Challenge** Encourage interested students to create their own accompaniment, using nonpitched percussion instruments.

## Spotlight On

**▶ Rondo** The musical form known as "rondo" descended from the Baroque French *rondeau*. The French *rondeau* was not in rondo form as we know it today. Rondo form was most popular during the Classical period (roughly 1750–1825). Rondos are usually found as one movement of a larger work, such as a symphony, concerto, or a sonata for a solo instrument. Many creative ways are found to vary rondo form, but listeners can always count on hearing the A section return several times, always in the tonic key.

Once students are confident speaking each of the poems, have the class perform them in rondo form with the Stereo Vocal **CD 8-15.** Then have them perform independently with the Stereo Performance Track **CD 8-16.**

### Playing

For instrumental parts to play with the rondo, transfer the body percussion patterns to the percussion parts on p. 183 and select students to play each of these parts. Divide the remainder of the class in half.

- One half will perform "Going, Going, Gone."
- One half will perform "The Snow."
- Everyone performs "Heave-Ho" together.

Establish a moderate-tempo, steady beat. This will unify the poems musically. Keep the tempo steady and go from one poem to the next, with no space in between.

### Analyzing

6a Have students listen to *ABACA Dabble* **CD 8-17.** Ask them to think about what they have learned about rondo form and to listen for that form. Have students identify rondo form in *ABACA Dabble* by

- Verbalizing what they heard.
- Creating hand signals for each section of the rondo.
- Signaling each section as they hear it.

### Moving

Invite students to look at the movement pictures on p. 184. Have students create movements for the three different sections of *ABACA Dabble* **CD 8-17.** For the A section, have students create movements in which they move the entire body (torso, arms, and legs). For the B section, have students create movements in which they use legs only. Hands are on the hips. For the C section, have students move everything but the feet.

Encourage students to move in the style *of ABACA Dabble.* Have them perform the movements at the proper time as they listen to *ABACA Dabble* again.

## A Mondo Rondo

**Listen** to *ABACA Dabble.* Remember the first melody—that's the A section. Raise your hand each time you hear the A section.

**by Bryan Louiselle**
This rondo is in a big band, swing style.

After each A section, you hear a different section. The new sections are labeled B and C.

Now **listen** to *ABACA Dabble* again and **move** to show rondo form.

**Create** a movement for the A section that uses your entire body.

**Move** only your legs for the B section.

**Create** a movement for the C section that uses your torso.



# Footnotes

## Across the Curriculum

▶ **Art** Invite students to create a design that uses three colors or shapes (or both) in the rondo pattern. The designs might also be distinguished by contrasting ornaments or trim. Students will enjoy posting their designs on a bulletin board to see how many variations on ABACA were created.

## Skills Reinforcement

▶ **Creating** Invite students to create class poems or raps about winter where they live. (In southern climates, students might use the idea of how little difference there is between seasons.) Help them to insert some repeated ideas or phrases to create a feeling of unity. Then have students arrange their poems into a rondo and add an accompaniment of their choice.

## Character Education

▶ **Respect** To demonstrate respect, apply the rondo form to personal attributes. Arrange students in groups of five, challenging them to create a rondo using their group members. Rather than considering physical attributes, they should focus on personal characteristics. For example, three people in the group might describe themselves as very honest while the other two see themselves as open-minded and forgiving. Students should identify unifying elements (How are we similar?) and contrasting elements (How are we different?). After each group shares its creation, explore the idea that each individual is different from, yet related to, the others in their group and that each part (individual) contributes to the whole. Encourage students to accept similarities and differences without judging someone as better than or not as good as someone else.

## Follow the Form

**Listen** to this rondo for piano by Ludwig van Beethoven (1770–1827). As you follow the listening map, **identify** each appearance of section Ⓐ.

**from *Piano Sonata in C Minor, Op. 13* ("Pathétique")**
**by Ludwig van Beethoven**
**as performed by Vladimir Horowitz**

*Rondo: Allegro* is the third movement of this piano sonata, originally published in 1799.

### Rondo: Allegro
**LISTENING MAP**

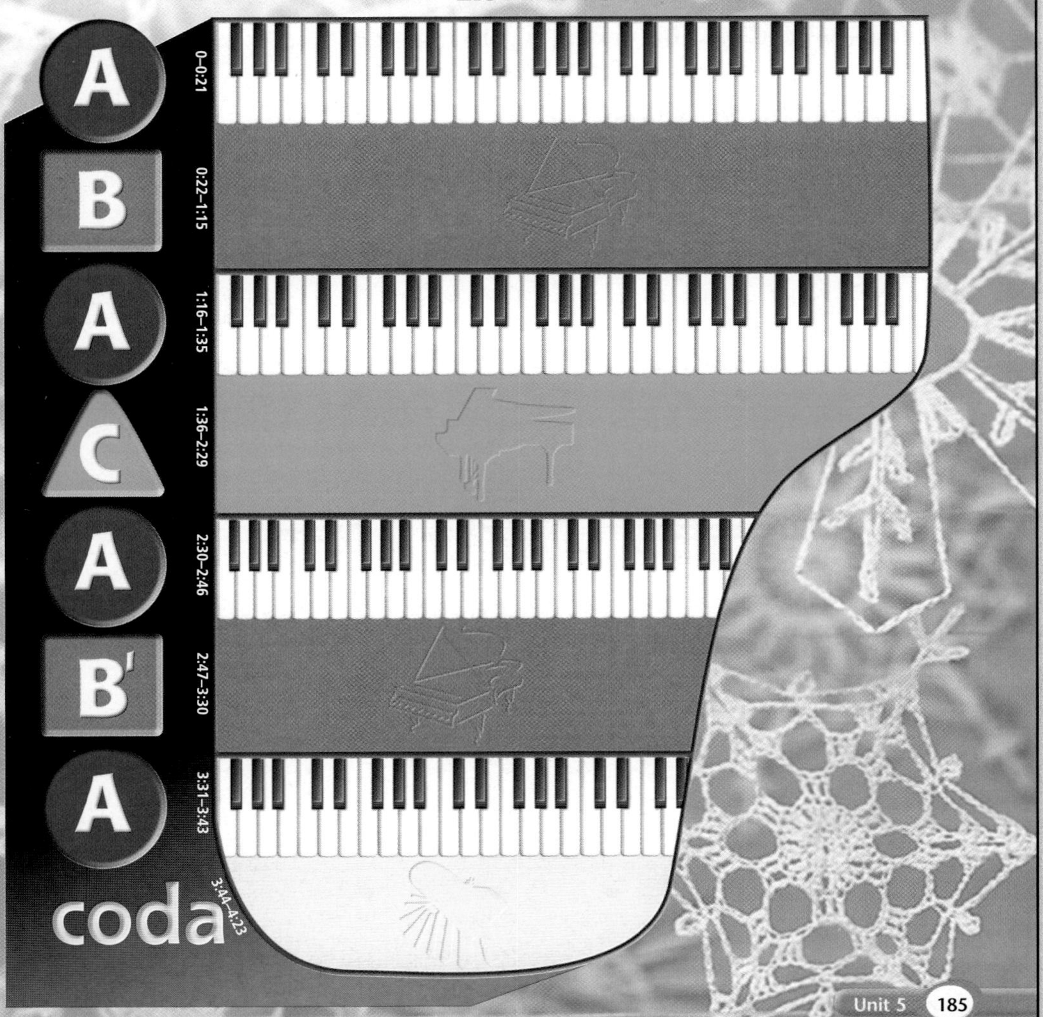




### Listening

Refer students to the listening map for *Rondo: Allegro*. Allow them to revisit the feature on Beethoven, on p. 153. Write the rondo pattern ABACABA (Coda) on the board and ask students to describe how this differs from the pattern they heard in *ABACA Dabble*.

Play *Rondo: Allegro* **CD 8-18** as students follow the map. Ask them to tap lightly on the keyboard art, one white key per beat, each time the A section occurs.

### Creating

Invite students to work in groups of three to create new poems and their own rondos. (See Across the Curriculum and Skills Reinforcement on p. 184.) Ask each group to demonstrate rondo form in whatever way they choose—visual, movement, or sound. Encourage them to keep their rondo fairly simple. Give
6a students a brief preparation time. Then have each group perform its rondo for the rest of the class.
9e Explain to students that, as actively involved listeners, they should practice appropriate concert etiquette during all live musical performances. See Audience Etiquette below.

## 3 Close

**Performance/Observation** Have students perform a rondo speech piece by combining "Heave-Ho," "Going, Going, Gone," and "The Snow" **CD 8-15**, using contrasting steady-beat movements to accompany each section of the piece.

Assess each student's understanding of rondo form by observing correct movements from each student during contrasting sections of the speech piece.

### Audience Etiquette

**▶ At School Assemblies and in the Classroom**
School assemblies and classroom performances provide excellent opportunities for practicing and reinforcing proper audience behaviors. Encourage in students such actions as

- Be attentive to your personal space, and respect the space of others.
- Use good eye contact and look attentively at the speakers or performers.
- Be active listeners. Concentrate and think about what you hear.
- Show appreciation by clapping at appropriate times.

### Technology/Media Link

**Notation Software** To reinforce the concept of rondo form, provide students with a four-measure long, five-note pentatonic musical phrase that they can use as an A section. Divide students into small groups and have them

- 5d Use notation software to compose and notate a B and C section.
- 4b Create their contrasting sections, using the same key signature, time signature, five-note pentatonic scale, and measure length as the A section.
- Print their work and perform these pieces for the others.

**Transparency** Use the transparency for *Rondo: Allegro* to help students follow the rondo form. Refer to the indicated timings for each section to guide students through the piece.

LESSON 6

## LESSON AT A GLANCE

**Element Focus** **MELODY** Prepare *ti;* major scale

**Skill Objective** **SINGING** Sing a song that includes *do, re, mi, fa, so, la, ti, do*'

**Connection Activity** **SOCIAL STUDIES** Learn about the geography of Australia

**MATERIALS**

- "Kookaburra" **CD 8-19**

  **Recording Routine:** Intro (8 m.); vocal; interlude (4 m.); vocal in 4-part round twice; coda
- **Music Reading Practice, Sequence 19** **CD 8-21**
- "How Do You Doo-tee?" (speech piece) **CD 8-24**

  **Recording Routine:** Intro (4 m.); vocal; interlude (2 m.); instrumental 5 times with 2-measure interludes; coda
- **Dance Directions** for "How Do You Doo-tee?" p. 510
- **Resource Book** pp. D-24, E-20, F-12

**VOCABULARY**

round

**National Standards**

**1a** Sing independently on pitch
**1d** Sing rounds
**4b** Compose instrumental pieces within specific guidelines
**6b** Describe music by answering questions about it

**MORE MUSIC CHOICES**

Other songs with *ti* patterns:
"My Bonnie Lies Over the Ocean," p. 338
*"Sambalele,"* p. 397

# 1 INTRODUCE

Invite students to look at the art on pp. 186–187 and discuss what they know about exotic birds. Share information about Australia from Across the Curriculum below.

LESSON 6 Element: MELODY | Skill: SINGING | Connection: SOCIAL STUDIES

# Laugh and Sing

Do you know that the kookaburra is a bird? It's called "the laughing bird" because its song sounds like a hilarious cackle! Of course, you know that a gum tree doesn't really grow bubble gum. It's actually a eucalyptus tree. And the bush in Australia isn't like the bush in your mother's rose garden—it's another name for the forest.

**Sing** this silly song from Australia.

CD 8-19
MIDI 15
Kookaburra
d m f s l t d'
Words and Music by Marion Sinclair
do
Kook - a - bur - ra sits on the old gum tree,
Mer - ry, mer - ry king of the bush is he.
Laugh, kook - a - bur - ra, laugh, kook - a - bur - ra,
Gay your life must be.

# Footnotes

## MOVEMENT

▶ **Patterned Dance** For an Australian greeting activity called "How Do You Doo-tee?" **CD 8-24,** refer to Dance Directions on p. 510.

## BUILDING SKILLS THROUGH MUSIC

▶ **Language** Have students read the paragraph on p. 186 and then answer these questions.

- What is another name for the forest? (bush)
- What is another name for the eucalyptus tree? (gum tree)

Ask students to sing "Kookaburra," substituting the word *forest* for *bush* and *eucalyptus* for *old gum tree.*

## ACROSS THE CURRICULUM

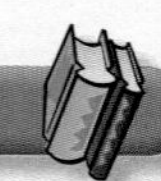

▶ **Social Studies** Share the book *Australia* by David Petersen (Children's Press, 1998) and invite students to learn more about Australia—a continent and a country all in one. What are the climate and landscape like in Australia? What kinds of plants and animals live there? Share the book *Here Is the Coral Reef* by Madeleine Dunphy (Disney Press, 1998) and invite students to learn more about Australia's Great Barrier Reef.

### Kookaburra Rhythm

**Perform** this pattern using rhythm syllables.

Which line of "Kookaburra" matches this rhythm?

### Kookaburra Pitch

**Sing** the melody below, using pitch syllables and hand signs. As you can see, there is a note missing! Hum the missing note. How does the new note sound compared to *la?* Compared to high *do?* How does this melody relate to the rhythm pattern above?





# 2 Develop

### Singing

Play "Kookaburra" **CD 8-19** for students. Have them learn the melody by rote and sing when ready.

Refer students to the rhythm pattern on p. 187. Have them pat the pattern as they say the rhythm syllables. Help students discover that this pattern matches the rhythm of the third line of "Kookaburra."

1a Have students sing the pitch syllable phrase on p. 187, using pitch syllables and hand signs. Ask them to hum the note marked with a question mark. As they sing, have them show the melodic contour with their hands.

### Analyzing

6b Using the Name That Tune! Worksheet on Resource Book p. D-24, draw students' attention to the "missing" note in the melodic contour.

ASK **Between which two notes does the missing note occur?** (between *la* and *do'*)

**How does it sound compared to *la?*** (higher)

**How does it sound compared to *do'?*** (lower)

For a related reading activity with "Kookaburra," see p. 451 and Resource Book p. E-20.

### Singing

1d Sing melody patterns for students, some with *ti* and some without. Encourage students to raise their hands when they hear *ti.* Then have students sing "Kookaburra" **CD 8-19** as a round.

# 3 Close

**Element: MELODY** ASSESSMENT

**Performance/Observation** Have students sing "Kookaburra" **CD 8-19** while following the notation. Have students listen as you sing melody patterns with and without the new note *ti.* Assess students' understanding by having them raise their hands if the pattern contains the new note.

## Skills Reinforcement

4b ▶ **Creating/Playing** In small groups, have students compose rhythm ostinatos to accompany "Kookaburra." Invite them to select rhythm and melody percussion instruments for each ostinato and perform the song for the class.

▶ **Mallets** For an Orff accompaniment to "Kookaburra," refer to Resource Book p. F-12.

## School to Home Connection

▶ **Bird Research** The kookaburra is quite an unusual bird. Ask students to research the behavior of this bird, as well as of other unusual birds. Encourage the students to find out all they can about their state bird, national bird, and wild birds that live in their town or city.

## Technology/Media Link

1d **MIDI/Sequencing Software** Play the MIDI song file of "Kookaburra" to help students learn to sing in harmony. Have all students sing the melody as all tracks play. Mute tracks 3 and 4 as students sing part 2. Have some students sing part 1 and some sing part 2 as tracks 1, 2, and 3 play. Continue adding parts and tracks until students are singing independently.

LESSON Core 7

## LESSON AT A GLANCE

**Element Focus** **MELODY** Present *ti;* major scale

**Skill Objective** **READING** Sing a song, read from notation, that contains *do, re, mi, fa, so, la, ti, do*ˡ

**Connection Activity** **CULTURE** Discuss the musical culture of the Caribbean

**MATERIALS**

- "Missy-La, Massa-La" **CD 8-25**
  **Recording Routine:** Intro (16 m.); vocal; interlude (16 m.); vocal; coda
- **Music Reading Practice, Sequence 20** **CD 8-27**
- *A-Cling, A-Cling* (excerpt) **CD 8-30**
- **Resource Book** pp. B-16, D-25, E-21, F-14, I-16
- barred instruments

**VOCABULARY**

major scale

**National Standards**

**1a** Sing independently, with appropriate diction
**2b** Play rhythms and melodies on appropriate instruments
**5b** Read notes in treble clef using syllables
**6b** Describe music by answering questions about it
**6c** Use appropriate terms to describe music

**MORE MUSIC CHOICES**

Other songs with *ti* patterns:
"Cycle Song of Life" (refrain), p. 370
"For the Beauty of the Earth," p. 356

LESSON 7 | Element: MELODY | Skill: READING | Connection: CULTURE

# WHERE'S THE NEW NOTE?

Have you ever lost something, only to find it right under your nose? Sometimes things seem to turn up where you least expect to find them.

**Listen** to "Missy-La, Massa-La." Learn to **sing** the song and then play the game with your friends.

CD 8-25

## MISSY-LA, MASSA-LA

d r m f s l t d'

*Game Song from the Caribbean*

do
C F C G7
Mis - sy - la, mas - sa - la, Mis - sy lost her gold ring, go 'way.

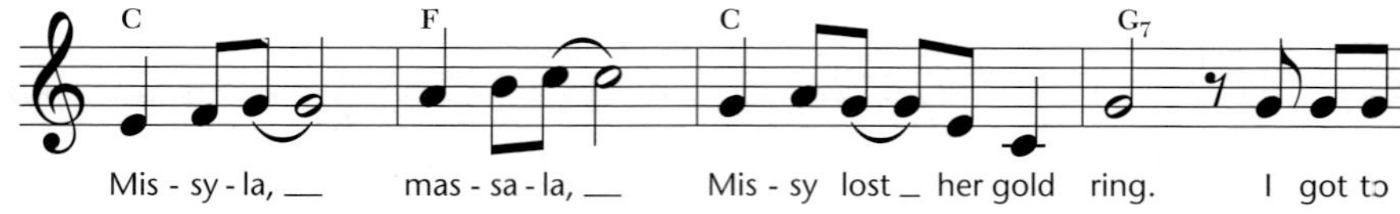
C F C G7
Mis - sy - la, mas - sa - la, Mis - sy lost her gold ring. I got to

F C G7 C
find 'em, find 'em, find 'em, find 'em, Find 'em, let me see la, la, la, la

F C G7 C
find 'em, find 'em, find 'em, find 'em, Find 'em, let me see.

# Footnotes

## MEETING INDIVIDUAL NEEDS

▶ **English Language Learners** Discuss the concepts of "lost" and "found" with students who are learning the English language. What does it mean to find something? Does that mean it was lost by someone else? Share the phrase "nothing is lost until you stop looking" with students. Ask them to consider this phrase. What does it mean to them? Have they ever lost something?

## BUILDING SKILLS THROUGH MUSIC

▶ **Science** Ask students to

- Examine closely the instruments shown on p. 190 (flute, guitar, *ukulele*, banjo) and those depicted in the painting on p. 191. (steel drums, conga)
- Discuss how the sound is produced in the three instrumental families represented. (woodwind, strings, percussion)

## SPOTLIGHT ON

▶ **Trinidad** Trinidad is the largest and southernmost island of the Caribbean. You can recognize it by its shape—it looks like a boot! The people of Trinidad come from many countries, including Africa, India, Lebanon, China, Syria, and Europe. This explains why the songs of Trinidad have so many different musical roots. Along with calypso style, Trinidad is best known for a unique musical invention—the steel drum band. The drums, also known as "pans" were originally made out of fifty-gallon oil barrels that washed up on the Antillean shores. (The Antilles is the main group of islands in the West Indies.) Today, steel drum bands play many different kinds of music, but they are still best known for playing the calypso music of the Caribbean.

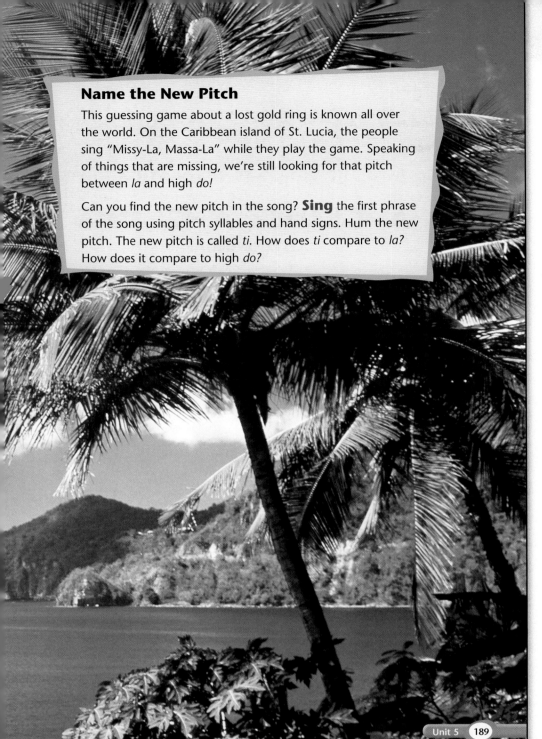

### Name the New Pitch

This guessing game about a lost gold ring is known all over the world. On the Caribbean island of St. Lucia, the people sing "Missy-La, Massa-La" while they play the game. Speaking of things that are missing, we're still looking for that pitch between *la* and high *do!*

Can you find the new pitch in the song? **Sing** the first phrase of the song using pitch syllables and hand signs. Hum the new pitch. The new pitch is called *ti*. How does *ti* compare to *la?* How does it compare to high *do?*



# 1 Introduce

Invite students to look at the pictures and painting on pp. 188–191. Explain that the setting is the Caribbean. Ask students to share what they know about music from the Caribbean (steel drums, African rhythms). Refer students to p. 470 in the Sound Bank for more information on steel drums.

Share information from Spotlight On, on p. 188, and explain that children in the Caribbean play game songs just like children in the United States do. Refer to the Movement activity below.

# 2 Develop

### Singing

Using a neutral syllable (such as *loo*), sing short melody patterns containing *ti* in C-*do* for students.

 Have students

- Echo sing each pattern on a neutral syllable, as a group and individually.
- Play patterns on barred instruments (set up in C-*do*).

### Reading

Play "Missy-La, Massa-La" **CD 8-25** for students.

Have them

- Sing the song with the lyrics.
-  Read and sing lines 3 and 4 using pitch syllables and hand signs.
- Follow the staff notation while listening.
- Find phrases that are similar. (1 and 2, 3 and 4)

**continued on page 190**

## Movement

▶ **Game Song** "Missy-La, Massa-La" is a game song. The players stand in a circle shoulder-to-shoulder and sing the song. A person stands in the center and watches as those in the circle silently pass a ring (or any object) from person to person behind their backs. At any given time, the person in the center tries to find who has the ring in their possession. When the person is found, the players trade places.

## Skills Reinforcement

▶ **Recorder** Have students practice playing leaps from C down to G and from C down to A. Ask them which leap requires two fingers to move at the same time (C down to G). When students play this leap, they need to make sure that no additional notes are accidentally added. For more practice in playing leaps on recorder, have students play two countermelodies for "Missy-La, Massa-La" on Resource Book p. I-16.

▶ **Mallets** For an Orff accompaniment to "Missy-La, Massa-La," refer to Resource Book p. F-14.

### Analyzing

Sing the first two measures of "Missy-La, Massa-La," p. 188, for students. Use pitch syllables for each note except *ti.* Hum *ti.*

**ASK Where does the note I am humming fall in the scale?** (between *la* and *do*ˡ)

**SAY** The note between *la* and *do*ˡ is called *ti.*

Demonstrate the hand sign for *ti.*

Have students sing all the known notes from top to bottom, using pitch syllables and hand signs. Then ask them to sing the pattern *la-ti-do*ˡ using hand signs.

**ASK Does *ti* sound closer to one of these notes than the other?** (Yes, *ti* sounds closer to *do*ˡ than to *la.*)

Explain that the distance between *ti* and *do*ˡ is a half-step. Point out that *la* and *ti* are also next to each other on the staff, but they are a whole-step apart.

### Reading

Invite students to look at measures 1 and 2 of "Missy-La, Massa-La." Give them the starting pitch *(mi)* and have them sing mm. 1–2 using pitch syllables. To reinforce the new note *ti,* have them repeat the activity. Then have students read the entire song with pitch syllables. For more practice, refer to Resource Book p. D-25. See p. 451 and Resource Book p. E-21 for a related singing and reading activity.

### Listening

Invite students to listen to *A-Cling, A-Cling* **CD 8-30** and identify the instruments in the listening map on p. 190. (guitar, *ukulele,* banjo) Have students listen again and direct their attention to the hand signs on the map. Tell them that *do* and *ti* can be heard alternating back and forth in the accompaniment.

Note: The order of *ti-do* changes at about 1:27. Then, for a few measures, the chords change on every quarter note (rather than on every half note). At 1:34, the chord changes settle back onto half notes again.

Invite students to sing *do* and *ti* and perform the hand signs as they listen to the selection.

### Hear the New Note

As you **listen** to *A-Cling, A-Cling,* follow the map and **perform** the hand signs for *ti* and *do.*

**Traditional Melody from Nevis**
This selection is from Nevis, an island in the West Indies.

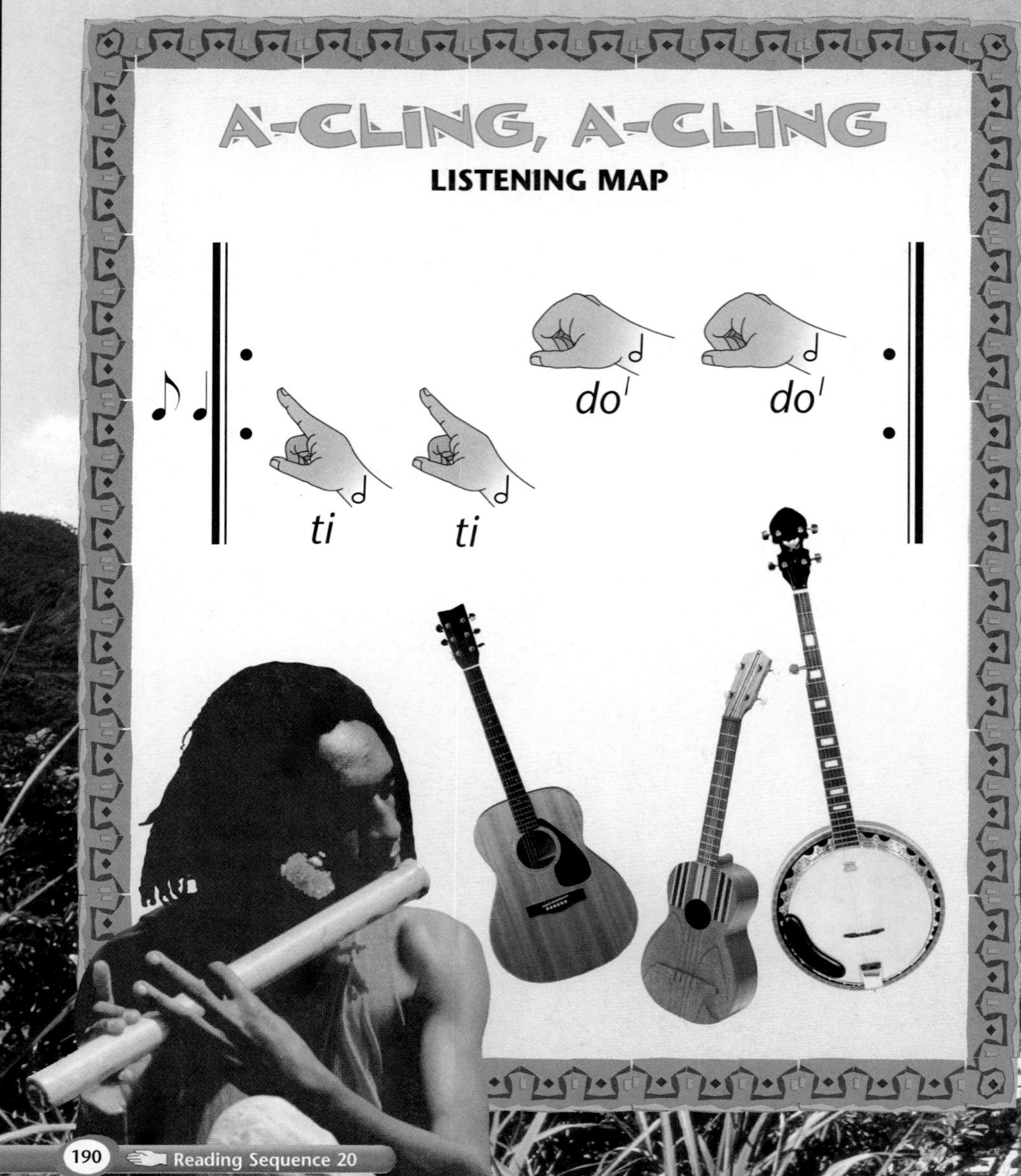


## Footnotes

### Skills Reinforcement

▶ **Creating** Encourage students to use Caribbean-style percussion instruments to accompany the song "Missy-La, Massa-La." They can experiment with using the *guiro, cabasa,* and maracas. They should try to maintain a continuous eighth-note pattern in which certain notes are stressed by either a harder or slightly altered stroke on the instrument. Additional parts can be created for other instruments with simpler rhythms. Allow students time to experiment with these rhythmic arrangements in order to determine the proper "fit" between their created parts. Finally, have students perform these arrangements while singing the song.

### Across the Curriculum

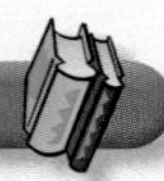

▶ **Language Arts** Explore with students another "lost and found" story by reading aloud the book *Lost* by Paul Brett Johnson and Celeste Lewis (Orchard, 1996). This is a true account of a family who lost their dog in Arizona's Tonto National Forest. The dog and his family are reunited after 29 days. The book is interesting for students because of the artistic layout. On one side of the page are color paintings of the dog and his attempts to stay safe. On the other side are shaded pencil drawings depicting the family's efforts to find the dog.

*Arts* Connection

▲ Mural of musicians playing traditional Caribbean instruments (Anonymous)

## Show What You Know!

1. **Identify** the note *ti* in these examples. Then **sing** each example using pitch syllables.



2. **Identify** the songs or listening selections that have these patterns. Find other songs in the book that use the new note *ti.*



# 3 Close

### Analyzing

Direct students to the Show What You Know! on p. 191. Have students read and sing the examples in exercise 1 and find other songs with *ti* in the melody as described in exercise 2. Refer to Resource Book p. B-16.

**Skill: READING** — ASSESSMENT

**Performance/Observation** Invite students to sing "Missy-La, Massa-La" **CD 8-25** while following the notation on p. 188, first using hand signs and pitch syllables and again using the song text. Assess each student's ability to recognize and sing *ti* at sight.

## Teacher to Teacher

**1a** ▶ **Diction-Vowels** Students need practice in learning to sing with pure vowels. Here are some common one-sound vowels in English.

- a  cat  *cat's* on the *mat*
- ih  king  *king will sit*
- ou  could  she *could* cut *wood*
- au  awesome  *often* she's *awesome*
- uh  hungry  he *must* be *hungry*

Have students compare with these pure vowels.

- Ee
- Eh  ih (kitty)
- Ah  a (cat) au
- ou
- oo  uh

## Technology/Media Link

**CD-ROM** To help students identify same and different melodic phrases, use *Making More Music's* "Melody" game. Before class, start the CD-ROM program in the school's computer lab or in the classroom's computer learning center. Have students

- Organize themselves into small groups.
- Select the "games" icon and then choose the "Melody" game.
- Click the green arrow to begin play.

**Transparency** Invite students to follow the listening map for *A-Cling, A-Cling.* Use the transparency and an overhead projector for large classes.

Lesson Core 8

## Lesson At A Glance

**Element Focus** **TIMBRE** Ensemble timbres

**Skill Objective** **LISTENING** Identify the sounds of a variety of instrumental and vocal ensembles

**Connection Activity** **CULTURE** Explore classical music from India

**MATERIALS**

- "Orfferondo" **CD 8-35**
- *"Scherzo"* from *Piano Trio No. 2* (excerpt) **CD 8-31**
- *Rag puria kalyan-gat in tintal* (excerpt) **CD 8-32**
- *"Canzoni prima a 5"* from *Canzoni et sonate* (excerpt) **CD 8-33**
- *That's the Way* **CD 8-34**
- recorder, glockenspiel, xylophones, metallophone, triangle, woodblock, tambourine, finger cymbals, claves, *guiro,* hand drum

**VOCABULARY**

ensemble trio quintet

**National Standards**

**2b** Perform rhythms on appropriate instruments
**2f** Play instruments independently against contrasting parts
**6c** Use appropriate terms to explain music performances
**6d** Identify the sounds of a variety of instruments and voices
**9e** Demonstrate appropriate audience behavior

**MORE MUSIC CHOICES**

Other ensemble listening examples:

"Mars, the Bringer of War" from *The Planets* (orchestra), p. 377

*Little David, Play on Your Harp* (chorus), p. 395

Lesson 8 — Element: TIMBRE | Skill: LISTENING | Connection: CULTURE

# Performing Together

Performing with others is a fun part of making music. Rock, pop, classical—just about any style of music can be performed by a group. Musicians use the French word **ensemble,** meaning "together," to talk about group performance. Everyone in an ensemble pays special attention to what every member of the group is doing. Everyone in an ensemble must listen to each other to perform well together.

In music, an **ensemble** is a group of musicians who perform together.

**Listen** to these examples of ensembles performing.

CD 8-31
**Scherzo**

**from *Piano Trio No. 2 in E-flat Major, Op. 100* by Franz Schubert**

In Western classical music, a piano trio is not three pianos. It is a piano, cello, and violin.

Piano trio ▲

CD 8-32
**Rag puria kalyan**

**Raga from North India as performed by David Trasoff and Zakir Hussein**

This Indian classical music ensemble plays the *sarod,* a string instrument, and the *tabla* (drums).

▼ Classical Indian musicians

192

## Footnotes

### Across the Curriculum

▶ **Language Arts** Invite students to read the book *Schubert* by Ann Rachlin (Barrons, 1994). Focused on Schubert's childhood and his early music education, this book introduces students to the life of this remarkable composer. Ask students to write in their journals about their own early musical learning. Students should reflect on experiences they have had learning music thus far.

### Building Skills Through Music

▶ **Math** Have students count the number of members in each ensemble pictured on pp. 192–193. Then ask,

- What geometric shape or shapes would correspond to each group? (trio = three sides = triangle; quintet = five sides = pentagon)

### Meeting Individual Needs

▶ **Including Everyone** Tell students that music class is an *ensemble* where everyone belongs, where everyone is valued, where everyone can be successful, and where everyone is happy for the contributions of other classmates. Guide students in doing the activity described under Playing on p. 195, using the score in their student texts. Then have students create some new rhythms that can be learned by ear and played by every member of the class. Also, have them identify nonplaying tasks that are necessary for the final performance. (conducting, deciding additional parts, and order of parts) Give dignity to all parts and help students choose their own part after some rehearsing.

CD 8-33
**Canzoni prima a 5**

**from *Canzoni et Sonate***
**by Giovanni Gabrieli**
**as performed by Canadian Brass**

This brass piece is performed by two groups, one echoing the other. This is called antiphonal style.

CD 8-34
**That's the Way**

**by Greg Clark and Scott Leonard**
**as performed by Rockapella**

This selection features close harmony and vocal percussion.

## Rockapella

Vocalists Scott Leonard (high tenor), Kevin Wright (tenor), Elliott Kerman (baritone), Barry Carl (bass), and Jeff Thacher (vocal percussion) are the group **Rockapella**. The group started out singing barbershop and doo-wop on the streetcorners of Manhattan, a borough of New York City. After some time, they began to sing contemporary music and recorded *Zombie Jamboree.* The group is best-known for recording the soundtrack to *Where in the World Is Carmen Sandiego?*



# 1 Introduce

Ask students to picture themselves on a team of three to eight members (select a game such as basketball that most of them will identify with). Ask them to suggest how each individual can contribute to making sure the team plays the very best that it can. Here are some examples.

- Know the rules of the game.
- Be aware of what other players are doing.
- Be ready to support team members when needed.
- Use your own skills to the best advantage.
- Practice away from the game to improve your skills.

Tell students that the same things apply in small-group music making. Musicians try to make the music sound the very best that they can to satisfy themselves and to please their listeners.

# 2 Develop

### Listening

6d Tell students you would like them to develop a small memory "database" of ensemble sounds. As students listen to the following selections, have them write characteristics of each ensemble on the board. Have them consider ensemble size, expression, timbre, and style.

Invite a volunteer to write the word *trio* on the board. *Trio* means "three." Play *Scherzo* **CD 8-31** and ask students to identify the instruments they hear. (violin, cello, piano) Invite three volunteers to form a "sound sync" ensemble. Have them sit in the front of the class and pretend to play *Scherzo* as students listen to it again. Suggest to students that they choose one of the three instruments to follow carefully throughout the piece.

continued on page 194

## Spotlight On

**▶ Types of Ensembles** Most students will be quite familiar with types of pop ensembles. Here are a few with which the students may not be as familiar.

- Chamber ensemble—a small orchestral ensemble that performs in a small room
- Wind ensemble—a medium sized ensemble (40–60 performers) of woodwinds, brass, and percussion
- Jazz ensemble—a varied group of saxophone, trumpet, trombone, string bass, piano, and percussion players specializing in jazz
- String quartet—an ensemble consisting of two violins, a viola, and a cello
- Woodwind quintet—an ensemble consisting of a flute, an oboe, a clarinet, a bassoon, and a French horn

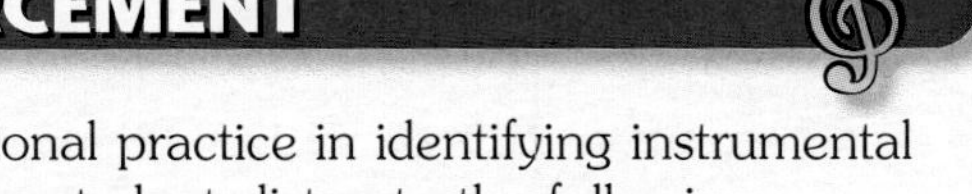

## Skills Reinforcement

6c **▶ Listening** For additional practice in identifying instrumental and vocal ensembles, have students listen to the following examples.

- *Brisad del Zulia* **CD 1-27** (steel band)
- *Irish Tune from County Derry* **CD 2-32** (wind ensemble)
- *Serenade* **CD 4-34** (string quartet)
- *Toccata for Percussion,* Mvt. 3 **CD 7-11** (percussion ensemble)
- *On Green Dolphin Street* **CD 6-1** (jazz vocal quartet)
- *El mariachi* **CD 13-6** *(mariachi)*
- *Bumper Harvest Celebration* **CD 14-19** (traditional Chinese orchestra)

9e Ask students to identify the style of this music. (European classical—early 1800s) Tell them that at that time the term *piano trio* identified a group with these three instruments: piano, violin, and cello. Also tell them that listeners to this music traditionally are seated on chairs. They are quiet and attentive until the piece is over. Then they applaud. If there are several sections, or movements, in a piece, the audience waits until all the sections are over before applauding.

Use a similar format for the other listening examples. For the Northern Indian raga *Rag puria kalyan-gat in tintal* **CD 8-32**, the "sound sync" group should be seated cross-legged on the floor on a rug or mat, playing an imaginary *sarod* (held diagonally across lap), a *tanpura* (held vertically), and *tabla.* Listeners to this type of music pay careful attention and may applaud at especially exciting parts of the music and at the end. Share with students the information about classical Indian music from the Cultural Connection on p. 195.

For *Canzoni prima a 5* **CD 8-33,** played by the Canadian Brass, the "sound sync" group will include two trumpet players, a trombone player, a French horn player, and a tuba player. Listeners and performers should be seated in chairs. This style is performed in concert rooms or halls. Listeners are quiet and attentive and hold their applause until the end of the piece.

For *That's the Way* **CD 8-34**, sung by Rockapella, the "sound sync" group will consist of five students with microphones. Audience behavior will depend on where the group is performing. In a concert performance, the audience sits in chairs, listens quietly, and applauds at the end of each song. Have students read the Music Makers information on Rockapella, on p. 193.

## Playing Together

Here is an instrumental selection for your class to play as an ensemble. **Listen** to all the parts and stay together. **Perform** the three sections in the following order: ABACA. Do you remember the name of this musical form? If not, the title of the piece will give you a clue.

# Footnotes

## Meeting Individual Needs 

▶ **Assigning Parts** With a minimum of preplanning, the concept of *ensemble* can offer an opportunity for everyone to successfully participate together in music making. The ability to keep a steady beat with the group is the minimal necessary skill. Someone who is very beat secure needs to act as leader so that others still gaining security can lock into the steady beat. Those with moderate beat security can play rhythm patterns with quicker durations including rests. For those individuals who cannot maintain a steady beat when playing an instrument, "special effects" can almost always be added as an introduction or a coda, using instruments such as rattles, bells, cymbals, and so on.

## Skills Reinforcement 

2f ▶ **Playing** Ask students to read each line of the "Orfferondo" rhythms on pp. 194–195 with rhythm syllables, then clap it. Divide the class into two groups, and combine two parts. When that is secure, try three parts, and so on, until all parts are read and clapped. Then transfer the rhythms to instruments and practice the ensemble until students are confident. Then divide the class into "quintets." Have each quintet rehearse together, then perform for the other members of the class. Have each group give itself a name (the "Outer Space Quintet," for example). Encourage students to behave as professional performers—enter together for the performance, bow to the audience, then bow again at the end of the piece. Remind class members to applaud as each group enters, listen attentively, then applaud again at the end.

### Playing

Now that students have practiced being various kinds of ensembles as a "sound sync" group, invite them to be a real ensemble by playing classroom intruments in a group. Have students look at "Orfferondo" on pp. 194–195. Place students in a circle and number off 1s and 2s. Have students

- Listen to the recording of "Orfferondo" **CD 8-35** and pat the steady beat.
- Look at the bass xylophone part on p. 194 and pat the pattern starting with the left hand. (Have students pat the knee of their neighbor when the left hand crosses over to "play" the upper octave c.)
- Practice the alto and soprano xylophone parts. (Invite the 1s to play the soprano part, and invite the 2s to play the alto part.)

Once students are patting the parts accurately, have them transfer over to instruments. Use a similar process to teach the other parts in the arrangement. When students are able to read and play all parts, have them observe the form and play "Orfferondo."

See Skills Reinforcement, p. 194, for additional "Orfferando" playing suggestions.

## 3 Close

ASSESSMENT

**Music Journal Writing** Have students

- Listen to each of the recordings in this lesson.
- Write descriptions of the different timbres produced by each ensemble in their journals.

Collect the journals and check their answers for accurate descriptions of instruments, styles, and ensemble sizes.

### Cultural Connection

▶ **Indian Classical Music** India's tradition of "art" or "classical" music traces its roots back to at least 2000 B.C., with strong connections to the spiritual principles of Hinduism. It has its own complex theoretical base, requiring great dedication and much hard work for a performer to become highly skilled. Structurally, it builds on ragas (melodic formulas) and talas (rhythmic cycles) woven together over a drone—there is no harmony as in the Western chordal system. The music has its own system of pitch syllables, used by both vocalists and instrumentalists. Music reading is not a necessary skill, but the ability to improvise is crucial. Improvisations are usually based on composed melodies.

### Technology/Media Link

**Video Library** Invite students to see and hear other small ensembles featured throughout the video.

LESSON 9

## LESSON AT A GLANCE

**Element Focus** **TEXTURE/HARMONY** Round

**Skill Objective** **SINGING** Sing a round

**Connection Activity** **CULTURE** Discuss the role of rounds in English culture

**MATERIALS**

- "Ah, Poor Bird" **CD 8-36**

  **Recording Routine:** Intro (4 m.); vocal; interlude (4 m.); vocal in round 2 times; coda
- *"Los niños en España cantan"* **CD 8-38**
- "In Spain, the Children Sing" **CD 8-39**

  **Recording Routine:** Intro (2 m.); vocal (unison) interlude (2 m.); vocal (2-part canon); coda
- **Pronunciation Practice/Translation** p. 482
- **Resource Book** p. A-19
- Orff instruments

**VOCABULARY**

unison round ostinato

**National Standards**

**1d** Sing rounds
**2f** Play instruments independently against contrasting parts
**5a** Read rhythms in quadruple meter

**MORE MUSIC CHOICES**

Other rounds:
"Peace Round," p. 348
"This Pretty Planet," p. 355
*"Yibane amenu,"* p. 316

# 1 INTRODUCE

Ask students if they have ever watched lasagna being made—pasta, sauce, cheese, pasta, and so on. This layering results in a texture of different flavors. Tell students they are going to layer a song to make a texture of sounds.

LESSON 9 Element: TEXTURE/HARMONY | Skill: SINGING | Connection: CULTURE

# Sound of a Round

"Ah, Poor Bird" is a folk song from England. What do you think the lyrics mean?

**Sing** the song in unison.

CD 8-36

## Ah, Poor Bird

l t, d r m s l

Traditional Round from England

I
Dm
II
do
Ah, poor bird, take your flight.

III
Far a - bove the sor - rows of this sad night!

### Learning to Sing a Round

A **round** is a follow-the-leader process in which all perform the same melody but start at different times.

Let's add layers to the song. First **sing** measure 1 as an ostinato. Do the same with measures 2 and 3. **Perform** the ostinatos, together in groups.

Now that your ear is able to hear the harmony created by the ostinatos, **perform** "Ah, Poor Bird" as a **round.** Each part must wait one measure before beginning.

196

## Footnotes

### SKILLS REINFORCEMENT

► **Singing** Invite students to listen to the Pronunciation Practice for *"Los niños en España cantan"* **CD 8-41** and sing with the students on the recording. Refer to Resource Book p. A-19 for a phonetic guide.

### BUILDING SKILLS THROUGH MUSIC

► **Writing** Have the class read the lyrics of "Ah, Poor Bird." Then use the question posed on p. 196 ("What do you think the lyrics mean?") to lead a discussion. Have students write a paragraph summarizing their response to the question.

### TEACHER TO TEACHER

► **Singing Rounds** To help students gain confidence in singing rounds, first have them learn the song thoroughly in unison. Then make part of the song into an ostinato, which some students can sing to accompany the melody. For example, the last measure of "Ah, Poor Bird" can be performed as an osinato. To begin singing a round, have the class start the song and you sing the second part of the round. Then gradually add a few students to your part until the class is divided.

### Parts to Play

Add more layers to "Ah, Poor Bird" to **create** a thicker texture. **Perform** this accompaniment as you **sing** the song.

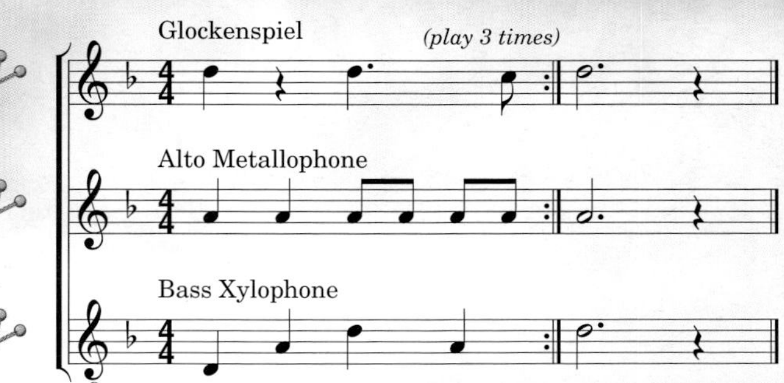
Glockenspiel
(play 3 times)
Alto Metallophone
Bass Xylophone

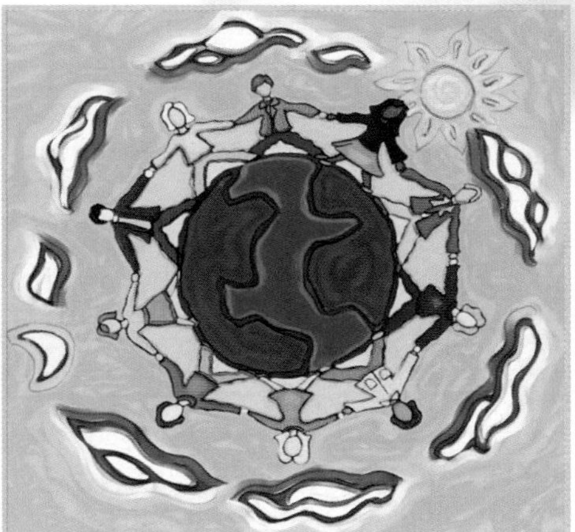

### Another Round

This next round is from Mexico. First **sing** it by layering line 1 and line 2. Then sing the entire song as a round.

s, t, (d) r m f s

CD 8–38

## Los niños en España cantan
### (In Spain, the Children Sing)

*English Words by S. T.*

*Folk Song from Mexico*

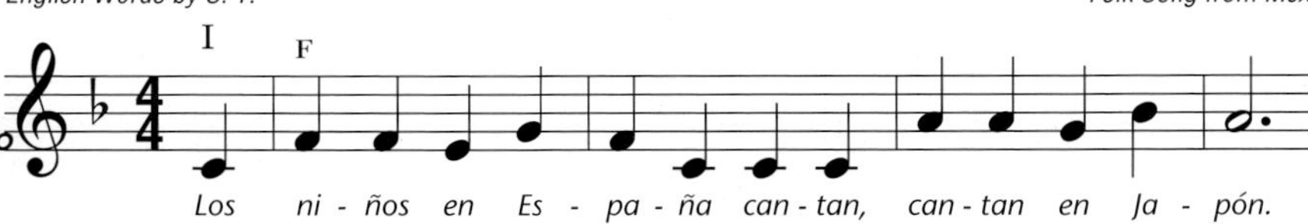
I
F
do
Los ni - ños en Es - pa - ña can - tan, can - tan en Ja - pón.
In Spain, the chil-dren sing all day. Yes, al - so in Ja - pan.

II
Los pa - ja - ri - tos can - tan, can - tan to - dos su can - ción.
Oh, ev - 'ry - where the birds join in with wom - an, child, and man.

Unit 5 197

## 2 Develop

Have students listen to "Ah, Poor Bird" **CD 8-36.** Discuss possible meanings for the text. Ask students to check the song credits to see what country it comes from. (England) Mention the importance of rounds in English musical history as described in Cultural Connection below.

### Singing

1d Have half the class sing "Ah, Poor Bird," m. 1, as an ostinato. Add the other half of the class singing m. 2. When this is comfortable, regroup and add m. 3. Layer all three parts, having them enter as they will in the round. Keep a strong steady beat to hold the song together. See Teacher to Teacher, on p. 196, for general suggestions regarding singing rounds.

### Playing

2f 5a Ask students to read the rhythms and pitches of the accompaniment part on p. 197. When students are confident, have them play the parts on instruments, one layer at a time. Have the class sing in unison with instruments, then try the song as a round with instruments.

### Analyzing

Invite students to learn *"Los niños en España cantan"* **CD 8-38** as a round, using the same procedure as for "Ah, Poor Bird."

## 3 Close

Skill: SINGING
ASSESSMENT

**Performance/Observation** Have students sing "Ah, Poor Bird" and *"Los niños en España cantan"* as rounds. Assign students to specific parts. Assess each group's ability to independently sustain its part during the performance of the round.

### Cultural Connection

**Rounds in English Tradition** A particular type of round, the "catch," was a noteworthy feature of the English musical profile during the seventeenth and eighteenth centuries. A catch was a round in three parts, intended for male voices, usually with lighthearted words. It originated in the Italian Renaissance. The *caccia* was a song in which the singer "catches" the beginning of a line from the previous singer. Singing catches was a popular social pastime, at first among working-class men but later through all social classes. Texts can be constructed so that when two lines (sometimes three) are sung together, a new meaning emerges.

### Technology/Media Link

**Notation Software** Have students, working in a lab or at the classroom computer center, use notation software to notate and play back "Ah, Poor Bird." Have students

- Set up three treble clef staff lines.
- Choose the key of D minor (one flat).
- Notate "Ah, Poor Bird" as a round. Bring in Voice 2 after one measure rest, and Voice 3 after two measures rest. When Voices 1 and 2 end, notate their parts with rests.

LESSON 10

## LESSON AT A GLANCE

**Element Focus** **TEXTURE/HARMONY** Round

**Skill Objective** **SINGING** Sing a round

**Connection Activity** **RELATED ARTS** Discuss the use of computers and other technology in creating visual arts and music

**MATERIALS**

- "The Computer" **CD 8-42**
  **Recording Routine:** Intro; vocal (unison); interlude (2 m.); vocal (round); coda
- "Orbital View" from *Mars Suite* (excerpt) **CD 8-44**
- keyboards

**VOCABULARY**

round unison chord

**National Standards**

- **1d** Sing rounds
- **2b** Play chords on appropriate instruments
- **5d** Notate rhythm, pitch, and meter using standard symbols
- **7b** Use musical terms to explain style preferences

**MORE MUSIC CHOICES**

Another piece about space:

"Mars, the Bringer of War" from *The Planets*, p. 377

# 1 INTRODUCE

Talk with students about computers. What do they use computers for? Point out that computers can be used to create music and art. Share with the class the information in Across the Curriculum below. Tell students that they will learn a song about computers and listen to a piece created with a computer. Have them listen to "The Computer" **CD 8-42.**

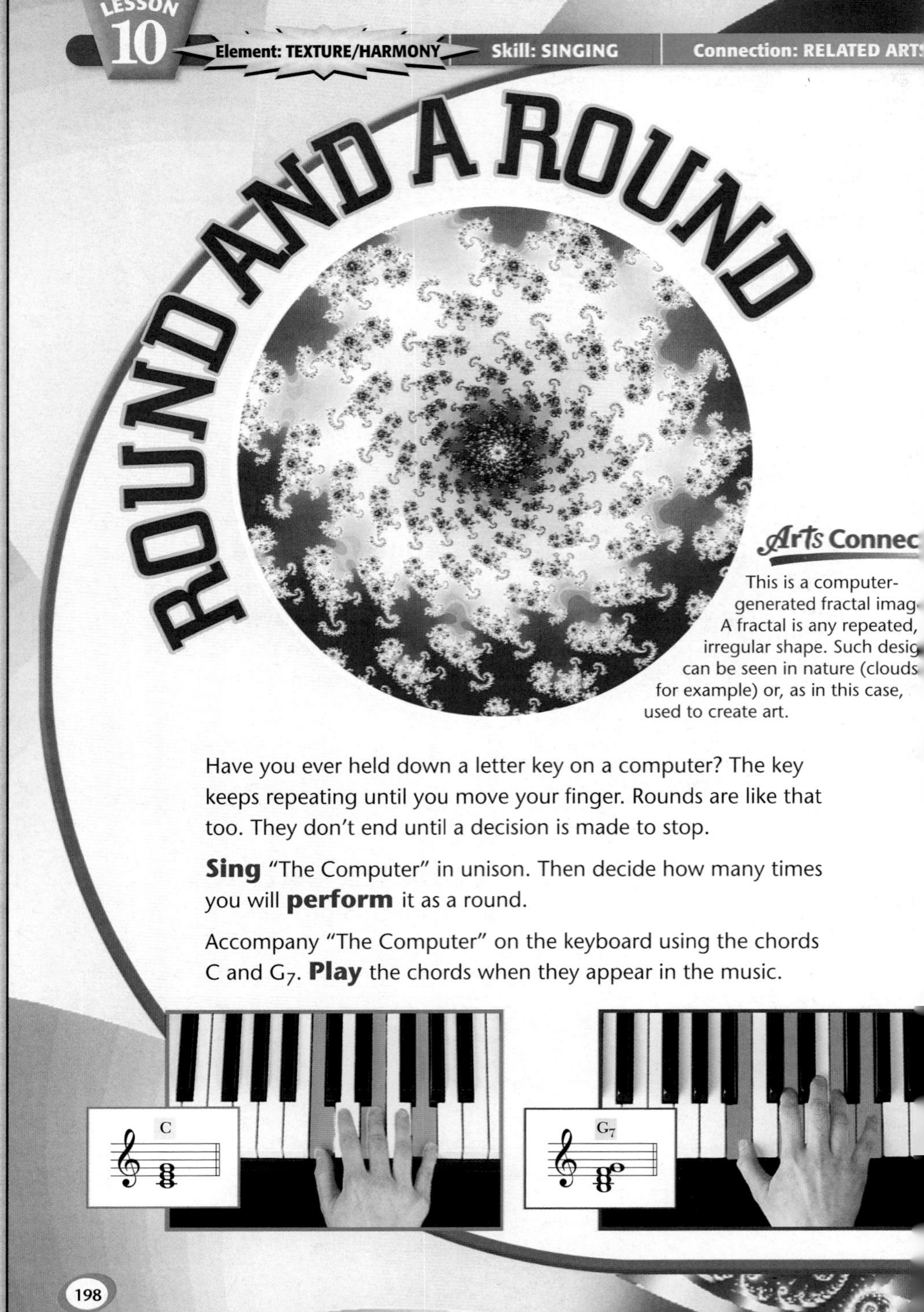

LESSON 10 Element: TEXTURE/HARMONY Skill: SINGING Connection: RELATED ARTS

# ROUND AND A ROUND

**Arts Connec**

This is a computer-generated fractal imag A fractal is any repeated, irregular shape. Such desig can be seen in nature (clouds for example) or, as in this case, used to create art.

Have you ever held down a letter key on a computer? The key keeps repeating until you move your finger. Rounds are like that too. They don't end until a decision is made to stop.

**Sing** "The Computer" in unison. Then decide how many times you will **perform** it as a round.

Accompany "The Computer" on the keyboard using the chords C and $G_7$. **Play** the chords when they appear in the music.



198

## Footnotes

### ACROSS THE CURRICULUM

▶ **Related Arts** Use "The Computer" as a springboard for discussing the role computer technology plays in the music and art of today—for recording, composing, notating, producing, transmitting, downloading, and creating artworks like the example on p. 198. The text of "The Computer" is a comment on the artistic value of all this. No matter how complex the process, the product will be no better than the skills and imaginations of those who worked on it.

### BUILDING SKILLS THROUGH MUSIC

▶ **Math** Discuss the use of symmetry in art and math. Have students look closely at the computer fractal art on p. 198. Ask them to describe specific features of the image in mathematical terms, using such words as *symmetry*, *spiral*, and *circle*.

### SKILLS REINFORCEMENT

2b ▶ **Keyboard** Have students practice both C and $G_7$ chords on keyboard. Then have them practice moving from one chord to the other at a steady tempo. Invite students to play the chords as the class sings "The Computer."

Some students may need more experience at the keyboard before they are able to change chords throughout the song. If so, divide the playing into two parts. One student can play C chords, and another can play $G_7$ chords as they occur in the song.

CD 8-42

# THE COMPUTER

Words by Fitzhugh Dodson

Music by Mary Shamrock

### Describing Texture

**Listen** to "Orbital View" from *Mars Suite*. **Describe** the texture of this computer music.

**from *Mars Suite***
**by Michael McNabb**

*Mars Suite* was composed for the NASA movie *Mars in 3-D*. Images from the film were sent by the Viking lander during its mission to Mars.

Computer music workstation ▼

# 2 Develop

### Singing

1d Ask students to learn "The Computer" **CD 8-42** by imitation: say a line and have them echo. Then have students sing with the recording.

ASK **What is unusual about the ending of the song?** (It ends on *so* and never sounds like a final ending.)

Divide the class into two groups and have students sing the song as a round. Provide a rhythmic steady beat movement to help the groups stay synchronized.

### Playing

2b Encourage students to play the keyboard accompaniment with "The Computer," as shown on p. 198. See Skills Reinforcement on p. 198 if you wish to use an easier version of this keyboard activity.

### Listening

7b To help students categorize an example of electronic instrumental music, play *Orbital View* **CD 8-44**. After listening, ask students to compare this computer music to other types of music they have heard. Allow them to share their views by applying basic criteria in evaluating what they like and dislike, and why.

# 3 Close

### Performing

Have students select a computer-related word and rhythmically speak it as an introduction or coda to "The Computer."

**Element: TEXTURE/HARMONY** ASSESSMENT

**Performance/Observation** Divide the class into two groups and have them sing "The Computer" **CD 8-42** as a round. Observe how well students are able to maintain their parts while hearing other parts at the same time.

## Teacher to Teacher

▶ **Round Reinforcement** In singing rounds, students often have difficulty singing their own line while hearing other lines at the same time. Having students "follow the leader" at a distance of four beats may help. The teacher or leader claps four beats. Students clap these four beats as the leader performs four beats some other way (snapping, stamping, patting, and so on). The students proceed to do the second movement while the leader moves on to yet a third, and so on. When the leader wants to stop, he or she puts both hands in a silent position—behind the back or folded under the chin. Students copy this action four beats later.

## Technology/Media Link

5d **Notation Software** Have students notate an accompaniment for "The Computer." Ask them to

- Set up a notation file with eight measures in duple meter.
- Add a repeat sign at the end.
- Use the note palette to click in quarter-note C-major and $G_7$ *arpeggios* as a song accompaniment.
- Play the files as the class sings the song.

LESSON Core 11

## LESSON AT A GLANCE

**Element Focus** **TEXTURE/HARMONY** Two-chord accompaniment (I and V)

**Skill Objective** **PLAYING** Play a two-chord accompaniment

**Connection Activity** **SCIENCE** Discuss the food chain

**MATERIALS**

- "Frog Music" **CD 8-45**

  **Recording Routine:** Intro (8 m.); vocal (unison); interlude (4 m.); vocal (2-part canon); coda
- **Resource Book** p. I-17
- Orff instruments, resonator bells or keyboard, Autoharp

**VOCABULARY**

chord accompaniment ostinato

**National Standards**

**1d** Sing rounds
**2b** Perform melodies and chords on appropriate instruments
**2f** Play instruments independently against contrasting parts

**MORE MUSIC CHOICES**

Other I-V songs:
"Bard of Armagh, The," p. 296
"*Corrido de Kansas*," p. 274
"Wheel of the Water, The," p. 362

# 1 Introduce

Share the information in Spotlight On below and invite students to share what they know about frogs. Read the poem "Advice for a Frog (Concerning a Crane)" in Across the Curriculum below. Then have students read the words to "Frog Music." Discuss with students how the frog fits into the food chain.

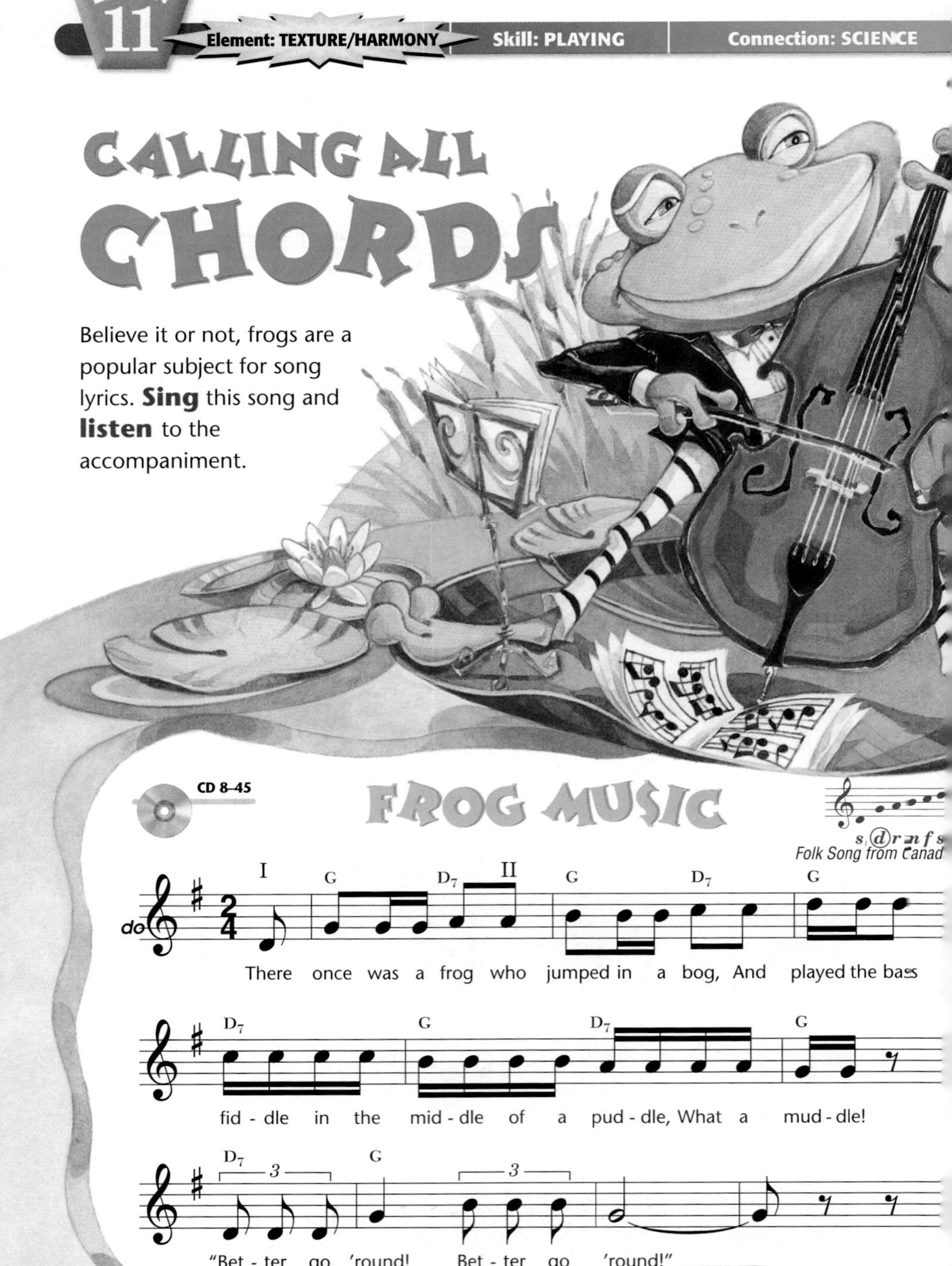
LESSON 11 Element: TEXTURE/HARMONY Skill: PLAYING Connection: SCIENCE

CALLING ALL CHORDS

Believe it or not, frogs are a popular subject for song lyrics. **Sing** this song and **listen** to the accompaniment.

CD 8-45

FROG MUSIC

Folk Song from Canad

I G D7 II G D7 G
There once was a frog who jumped in a bog, And played the bass
D7 G D7 G
fid - dle in the mid - dle of a pud - dle, What a mud - dle!
D7 G
"Bet - ter go 'round! Bet - ter go 'round!"

200

# Footnotes

## Spotlight On

▶ **Frogs** Frogs are amphibians that do not have tails. There are thousands of species of frogs across the world, but the most common one in the U.S. and Canada is the leopard frog. (There are more that 600 species of leopard frogs.) Leopard frogs are usually found in ponds and marshes, but sometimes they are found far from water.

## Building Skills Through Music

▶ **Science** Encourage students to

- Investigate and describe the life cycle of the frog. (egg, tadpole, adult frog)
- Write new words for "Frog Music," based on the tadpole stage.

## Across the Curriculum

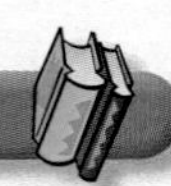

▶ **Language Arts** Share the poem "Advice for a Frog (Concerning a Crane)" by Alice Schertle from *The 20th Century Children's Poetry Treasury,* selected by Jack Prelutsky (Knopf, 1999). Discuss the poem with students.

Watch out, Old Croaker.
Here comes Stick Walker,
Here comes Pond Poker,
Here comes Death.
Take a breath, Slick Skin.
Muck down, sink in.
Don't make bubbles.
Good luck, Grin Chin—
Here comes Trouble.

## The Chord

**Listen** to the song again and raise your hand when you hear the chords change. Then point to the places in the music where the chords change.

**Play** these ostinatos with the song.

Glockenspiel
Alto Metallophone
Alto Xylophone
Bass Xylophone
G D7 G D7 G D7
His mu - sic was short, For soon he was caught, And now in the mid-dle
G D7 G
of a grid - dle he is fry - ing and is cry - ing:
D7 3 G 3
"Rath - er be drown'd! Rath - er be drown'd!"
Unit 5 201

# 2 Develop

### Analyzing

Draw a diagram of D, G, A, B, C, and D′ resonator bells on the board. Invite students to figure out how to play the melody of "Frog Music." Have them look at the contour of the melody and observe steps, skips, and repeats.

### Playing

2b Ask several students to play quarter notes on G and D several times, using bells, keyboard, or Orff instruments. Identify G as *do* and D as *so*. Point out that if G is #1 in the scale, D will be #5. Have the class sing "one-five" several times on the appropriate pitches. Identify these as "chord roots" for the I and V chords of the G scale. Have a volunteer play these chord roots with "Frog Music" **CD 8-45** as the rest of the class sings.

2f Add the other instrumental parts on p. 201. You may wish to use these phrases to help students learn their parts.

| | |
|---|---|
| Alto xylophone | *hurry up, frog-gie* |
| Alto metallophone | *in the pond* |
| Glockenspiel | *drowned (rest) and then he* |

1d Add singers on the I and V chord roots, singing *too bad, froggie.* Then have the class sing the song as a round.

# 3 Close

**Element: TEXTURE/HARMONY** ASSESSMENT

2b **Performance/Observation** Have students sing "Frog Music" **CD 8-45** while following the notation and playing the chord roots on imaginary keyboards. Then have the class sing the song again, with selected students playing the chord roots on keyboard instruments or bells and playing the chords on Autoharp. Observe whether students are able to play the correct chord at the right moments in the song.

## Skills Reinforcement

▶ **Recorder** Teach students the fingering for F♯ on their recorders. Begin by having students finger low D. Then have them raise only the pointer of their right hand. This is the fingering for F♯. Students can practice playing rhythm patterns that use low D and F♯ before playing the countermelody below.

2f

For additional countermelodies that reinforce the five-note scale, refer to Resource Book p. I-17.

## Technology/Media Link

**CD-ROM** After discussing I and V chords with students, reinforce the sound of the chord functions by having them create and enter their own eight-measure chord progressions into *Band-in-a-Box*. Instruct students to begin and end with a I chord. Invite students to sing chord roots as the program plays back the chord progression. Encourage them to play their progressions with several different background styles.

LESSON 12

## LESSON AT A GLANCE

**Element Focus** **TEXTURE/HARMONY** Two-chord accompaniment (I and IV)

**Skill Objective** **PLAYING** Play a two-chord accompaniment

**Connection Activity** **RELATED ARTS** Create a "movie scene" to go with a song

**MATERIALS**

- "Do Wah Diddy Diddy" **CD 8-47**
  **Recording Routine:** Intro (2 m.); two verses; vocal coda
- **Resource Book** p. H-16
- Orff instruments
- resonator bells (A, C♯, D)

**VOCABULARY**

chord accompaniment

**National Standards**

**2b** Perform melodies on appropriate instruments
**2f** Play instruments independently against contrasting parts
**4a** Arrange music to accompany dramatizations

**MORE MUSIC CHOICES**

Another two-chord song:
*"Tengo, tengo, tengo,"* p. 228

# 1 INTRODUCE

Play "Do Wah Diddy Diddy" **CD 8-47.** Ask students to listen with eyes closed and imagine how the music might be used in a movie. Tell them it was an early British rock song that was also used in the movie *Stripes* as a marching song. Point out that words like *do, wah,* and *diddy* are nonsense words. Invite students to plan their own music video to go with the song.

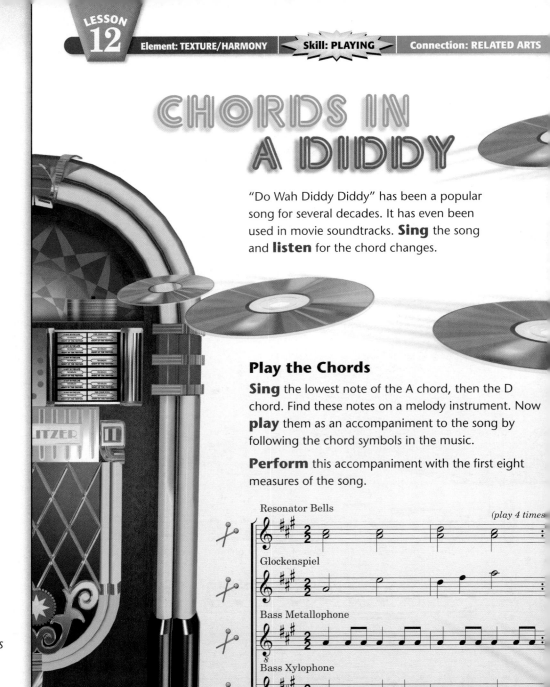

# CHORDS IN A DIDDY

"Do Wah Diddy Diddy" has been a popular song for several decades. It has even been used in movie soundtracks. **Sing** the song and **listen** for the chord changes.

### Play the Chords

**Sing** the lowest note of the A chord, then the D chord. Find these notes on a melody instrument. Now **play** them as an accompaniment to the song by following the chord symbols in the music.

**Perform** this accompaniment with the first eight measures of the song.

## Footnotes

### SPOTLIGHT ON

▶ **"Do Wah Diddy Diddy"** This song was first recorded in 1964 by a British rock group called the Manfreds. Manfred Mann, from South Africa, was the leader and keyboardist. It became a #1 hit in Great Britain. Soon it was introduced in the U.S. and became #1 here as well. The song was used in the British film *Stardust* (1975) and the U.S. film *Stripes* in 1981 (starring Bill Murray).

### BUILDING SKILLS THROUGH MUSIC

▶ **Social Studies** Share the information on the song "Do Wah Diddy Diddy" in Spotlight On. Guide students in developing a time line beginning with the dates from the Spotlight On. Ask students to research other rock 'n' roll groups and when they were popular, then add them to the time line.

### ACROSS THE CURRICULUM

▶ **Language Arts** Share the book *Funny Walks* by Judy Hindley (Bridgewater, 1997) and invite students to create movements based on the book. When they have perfected their movements, invite them to create new lyrics for "Do Wah Diddy Diddy" that are based on their "funny walks."

CD 8-47
DO WAH DIDDY DIDDY
m f s l d
Words and Music by Jeff Barry and Ellie Greenwich
do
A D A
There he was just a - walk - in' down the street,
fore I knew it he was walk - in' next to me,
A D A
Sing-in' Do wah did - dy did-dy down did-dy do, Pop - pin' his fin - gers and a-
Took my hand just as
D A
shuf - fl - in' his feet, Sing - in' Do wah did - dy did - dy
nat - ural as can be,
D A
down did - dy do. He looked good, (yeah, yeah) He looked
We walked on, (yeah, yeah) To my
A
fine, (yeah, yeah) He looked good, he looked fine, and I
door, (yeah, yeah) We walked on to my door, and he
1. 2.
A A
near - ly lost my mind. Be - stayed a lit - tle more, Sing - in'
3 times
A D A
Do wah did - dy did - dy down did - dy do.
Unit 5 203

# 2 Develop

## Singing/Playing

Tell students that "Do Wah Diddy Diddy" **CD 8-47** uses a two-chord accompaniment. The song is in the key of A. The accompanying chords are A and D—A is the I chord root in the key, and D is the IV chord root. Have students sing *one* on the note A and sing *four* on the note D until they are comfortable with the sound. Then have students sing the appropriate chord root number words with the recording.

2f Add the instrumental parts on p. 202 to the song. Use the following phrases to help students learn their parts:

| | |
|---|---|
| Bass xylophone | *one __ one, one, four, four, one* |
| Bass metallophone | *do, diddy do, diddy* |
| Glockenspiel | *do__ wah__ did-dy done* |
| Bells | *yeah__ yeah__ oh__ yeah* |

## Performing

4a Combine "Do Wah Diddy Diddy" with one of the music video possibilities developed earlier in the lesson. The song can be performed in call-and-response style to provide opportunities for solo singing.

# 3 Close

**Skill: PLAYING** — **ASSESSMENT**

**Performance/Observation** Have students sing "Do Wah Diddy Diddy" **CD 8-47** while playing one of the percussion accompaniment parts from p. 202 on an imaginary keyboard instrument. Have the class sing the song again, with selected students playing the I and IV chord accompaniment on real keyboard instruments. Observe students' ability to perform the chords and sing the song.

## Skills Reinforcement

▶ **Keyboard** There are times when the arrangement of black keys and white keys to be played requires the use of an alternate fingering. The melodic phrase *Singin' Do wah diddy diddy down diddy do* is such a time.

2b

For an activity to reinforce good fingering patterns while playing "Do Wah Diddy Diddy," refer to Resource Book p. H-16.

## School to Home Connection

▶ **The Rock 'n' Roll Era** Encourage students to interview friends and family to learn about popular dances and recording artists of the 1950s and 1960s. Invite them to bring in recordings and share songs and dances with the class.

## Technology/Media Link

**Electronic Keyboard** Have students use the auto-accompaniment feature of an electronic keyboard to generate arrangements of "Do Wah Diddy Diddy." Have them set the keyboard to play accompaniments based on the root of a chord. Then select a rock 'n' roll accompaniment pattern, and press the A and D keys to follow the chords of the song.

# Review and Assessment

## WHAT DO YOU KNOW?

**MATERIALS**
- "The Computer," p. 199 **CD 8-42**
- **Resource Book** p. B-17

Have students read and answer the questions independently and then check their answers with a partner before sharing answers with the rest of the class or with you.

For a more formal assessment, you may wish to duplicate the Unit 5 assessment worksheet and have students work independently or in small groups to complete it. The worksheet is found on Resource Book p. B-17.

## WHAT DO YOU HEAR?

**MATERIALS**
- *What Do You Hear? 5* **CD 8-49**
- **Resource Book** p. B-18

Review the types of instruments that belong in each ensemble and their characteristics.

Have students listen to *What Do You Hear? 5* and choose the ensemble they hear in each example. Students can work either independently or in small groups.

For a more formal assessment, you may wish to duplicate the Unit 5 assessment worksheet found on Resource Book p. B-18.

UNIT 5

# Review, Assess,

## What Do You Know?

**1.** Look at the notation for "The Computer," on page 199.

**a.** What pitch is named *do* in this song?

**b.** Point to all the pitches that are called *ti*. How many did you identify?

**c.** Do the same activity for the pitches named *so, fa, mi, la, re,* and *do*.

**2.** Match each of these tempo words with the correct definition.

| | |
|---|---|
| **a.** *andante* | very fast |
| **b.** *moderato* | slow |
| **c.** *allegro* | moderate |
| **d.** *adagio* | walking speed |
| **e.** *presto* | fast |

▲ Brass quintet

## What Do You Hear? 5

**CD 8-49**

Listen to these examples and point to the picture of the ensemble you hear.

▲ Classical music trio

▲ Pop group

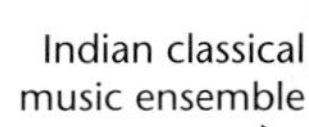

Indian classical music ensemble ▶

204

# Footnotes

## ANSWER KEY

### ▶ What Do You Know?

**1. a.** *do* = C

**b.** There is one pitch named *ti*.

**c.** *so* = G (6), *fa* = F (10), *mi* = E (8), *la* = A (1), *re* = D (8), *do* = C (3)

**2.**

| | |
|---|---|
| **a.** *andante* | walking speed |
| **b.** *moderato* | moderate |
| **c.** *allegro* | fast |
| **d.** *adagio* | slow |
| **e.** *presto* | very fast |

### ▶ What Do You Hear?

**1.** Indian classical music ensemble—*Rag puria kalyan - gat in tintal*

**2.** Pop group—*That's the Way*

**3.** Classical music trio—*"Scherzo"* from *Piano Trio No. 2 in E-flat Major, Op. 100*

**4.** Brass quintet—*"Canzoni prima a 5"* from *Canzoni et Sonate*

# Perform, Create

## What You Can Do

### Sing Rounds and Rhythms

Sing *"Los niños en España cantan,"* on page 197, as a round. Create and perform steady-beat movement patterns that reflect the tempo and meter of the song.

### Read and Sing *ti*

Sing "Missy-La, Massa-La," on page 188, from the notation using hand signs and pitch syllables. Then sing the song again using the words.

### Play Chords

Practice the rhythm patterns for the accompaniment to "Do Wah Diddy Diddy," on page 202. Then sing the song and play the accompaniment on mallet instruments.

### Move to Show Form

Perform a rondo speech piece by combining "Heave-Ho," "Going, Going, Gone," and "The Snow," on pages 182–183. Create a different steady-beat movement to accompany each section of the speech piece.

## What You Can Do

**MATERIALS**

- *"Los niños en España cantan,"* p. 197 **CD 8-38**
- "Missy-La, Massa-La," p. 188 **CD 8-25**
- "Do Wah Diddy Diddy" (excerpt), p. 203 **CD 8-47**
- "Heave-Ho"/"Going, Going, Gone"/ "The Snow" (speech piece), p. 182 **CD 8-15**
- **Resource Book** p. B-19

### Sing Rounds and Rhythms

When teaching *"Los niños en España cantan,"* it is helpful to have the class internalize the steady beat pattern through movement. Invite them to walk the piece, taking a step on the first and third beats of each measure.

### Read and Sing *ti*

Review the pitch syllables of "Missy-La, Massa-La" with the class. Then, invite them to sing the song slowly, using hand signals and pitch syllables together. Practice with the class until the song is up to tempo. Then encourage students to try it with the words.

### Play Chords

Ask the class to look at the accompaniment for "Do Wah Diddy Diddy." Have students use body percussion to represent each rhythm. When they feel comfortable with these rhythms, have students transfer them to instruments and play the song.

### Move to Show Form

Invite students to look at "Heave-Ho"/"Going, Going, Gone"/"The Snow." Have them create movements that reflect the character of each. Invite students to perform the speech piece and use their created movements in rondo form.

### Technology/Media Link

**Rubrics** Visit *www.sfsuccessnet.com* for rubrics to assess students' achievement in music skills.

| Lesson | Elements | Skills | |
|---|---|---|---|
| LESSON 1 CORE **Accent on Freedom** pp. 210–213  | **Element: Expression**<br>**Concept:** Articulation<br>**Focus:** Accents<br><br>**Secondary Element**<br>Rhythm: syncopation<br><br>**National Standards**<br>1b 1d 2b 3b 4a 4b 5a 5c 6c 6d 8a | **Skill: Singing**<br>**Objective:** Sing a song, performing accents where appropriate<br><br>**Secondary Skills**<br>• **Listening** Listen for accented notes and identify in notation<br>• **Creating** Write a poem describing a painting<br>• **Playing** Play rhythms on classroom percussion instruments<br>• **Listening** Follow a listening map and identify accented notes | **SKILLS REINFORCEMENT**<br>• **Reading** Clap and say rhythms in duple meter<br>• **Improvising/Composing** Create and notate a rhythm composition |
| LESSON 2 **Rhythms on the Ranch** pp. 214–215  | **Element: Rhythm**<br>**Concept:** Meter<br>**Focus:** Meter in 2<br><br>**Secondary Element**<br>Melody: contour<br><br>**National Standards**<br>2b 4b 5a 6b 6e | **Skill: Moving**<br>**Objective:** Perform steady beat movements that reflect the meter of a song<br><br>**Secondary Skills**<br>• **Playing** Read and play rhythm ostinatos<br>• **Singing** Echo phrases; sing in Spanish and English | **SKILLS REINFORCEMENT**<br>• **Guitar** Accompany song with two chords |
| LESSON 3 **Ringing Rhythm** pp. 216–217  Reading Sequence 21, p. 452 | **Element: Rhythm**<br>**Concept:** Meter<br>**Focus:** Meter in 3<br><br>**Secondary Element**<br>Texture: rounds<br><br>**National Standards**<br>1a 1d 1e 5b 6e | **Skill: Singing**<br>**Objective:** Sing a song in meter in 3 while conducting a beat pattern in 3<br><br>**Secondary Skills**<br>• **Listening** Pat strong and weak beats while listening<br>• **Analyzing** Practice conducting pattern in 3<br>• **Reading** Sing using pitch syllables and hand signs | **SKILLS REINFORCEMENT**<br>• **Vocal Development** Develop techniques for singing voiced and unvoiced consonants |

## Connections

## Music and Other Literature

### Connection: Related Arts
**Activity:** Discuss ways in which music, the visual arts, and poetry use accent in expression

ACROSS THE CURRICULUM **Language Arts** Use an allegory as a basis for writing a short story; write a poem or paragraph to express what freedom means

SPOTLIGHT ON
**The Strauss Family** Facts about the father and sons as musicians
**The Artist** Facts about Picasso

MEETING INDIVIDUAL NEEDS **English Language Learners** Illustrate what the word "freedom" means

CHARACTER EDUCATION **Ambition/Goal-Setting/Persistence** Create artwork that illustrates goals and plans for achieving them

BUILDING SKILLS THROUGH MUSIC **Social Studies** Identify symbols in America that represent freedom

**Song** "America, the Free"

**Listening Selection** *Thunder and Lightning Polka*
**Listening Map** *Thunder and Lightning Polka*
**Arts Connection** *Three Musicians*

**More Music Choices**
"We Shall Not Be Moved," p. 437
"We Shall Overcome," p. 326

ASSESSMENT
**Performance/Observation** Sing accents expressively

TECHNOLOGY/MEDIA LINK
**Transparency** Use a listening map to aid following a selection
**Notation Software** Practice entering accents and *staccato* marking

### Connection: Culture
**Activity:** Discuss ranch life

ACROSS THE CURRICULUM **Language Arts** Hear a story of amazing, humorous happenings on a ranch

CULTURAL CONNECTION **Ranch Life** Description of ranch life on the Western frontier

BUILDING SKILLS THROUGH MUSIC **Language** Use context clues to discern the meaning of unfamiliar English words

**Song** "*El rancho grande*" ("The Big Ranch")

**More Music Choices**
"*Beriozka*," p. 294
"Oh, Susanna," p. 264

ASSESSMENT
**Performance/Observation** Use two-beat movement patterns to show meter in 2

TECHNOLOGY/MEDIA LINK
**Notation Software** Compose a percussion ensemble piece to accompany song

### Connection: Related Arts
**Activity:** Read and discuss a rhyme about bells

ACROSS THE CURRICULUM **Language Arts** Compare a children's rhyme with lyrics to a song

MEETING INDIVIDUAL NEEDS **Including Everyone** Use movements to show the first beat of each measure

BUILDING SKILLS THROUGH MUSIC **Science** Describe and compare the timbres of different bells

**Song** "Oh, How Lovely Is the Evening"

**More Music Choices**
"The Star-Spangled Banner," p. 441
"*Einini*," p. 391

ASSESSMENT
**Performance/Observation** Sing while conducting in meter in 3

TECHNOLOGY/MEDIA LINK
**Web Site** Read more about bells

| Lesson | Elements | Skills |
|---|---|---|

## LESSON 4 — CORE

### Skipping with Rhythms

pp. 218–221

Reading Sequence 22, p. 452

**Element: Rhythm**
**Concept:** Meter
**Focus:** Meter in 4

**Secondary Element**
Form: ABA

**National Standards**

**Skill: Creating**
**Objective:** Create a composition using familiar rhythm patterns

**Secondary Skills**
- **Reading** Identify score indications; perform body percussion parts
- **Listening** Identify a rhythm aurally; identify rondo form aurally

**SKILLS REINFORCEMENT**
- **Recorder** Play a countermelody
- **Mallets** Play an Orff accompaniment
- **Reading** Review pitch reading skills

## LESSON 5 — CORE

### Theme and Variations

pp. 222–225

**Element: Form**
**Concept:** Form
**Focus:** Theme and variations

**Secondary Element**
Rhythm: syncopation

**National Standards**

**Skill: Listening**
**Objective:** Perform a body percussion pattern to accompany the main melody (theme) of a theme and variations

**Secondary Skills**
- **Singing** Sing after reading the rhythm of a song
- **Playing** Play an accompaniment
- **Creating** Create and perform own version of a song; create a class theme and variations
- **Moving** Move to a rhythm pattern using body percussion

**SKILLS REINFORCEMENT**
- **Playing** Add percussion ostinatos to an accompaniment; play a scale as a countermelody

## LESSON 6 — CORE

### Find the Sequence

pp. 226–229

Reading Sequence 23, p. 453

**Element: Melody**
**Concept:** Pattern
**Focus:** Melodic sequence

**Secondary Element**
Melody: major tonality

**National Standards**

1c 2b 2c 4b 5b 6b 9d

**Skill: Creating**
**Objective:** Create movements to show melodic sequence

**Secondary Skills**
- **Reading** Discover a repeating pattern called a sequence

**SKILLS REINFORCEMENT**
- **Creating** Create and notate a two-measure melody pattern

| Connections | Music and Other Literature | |
|---|---|---|
| **Connection: Science**<br>**Activity:** Explore the origins of fossils and the information that can be learned from them<br>**ACROSS THE CURRICULUM** **Language Arts** Look into the world of myths<br>**Science** Investigate fossils at a museum<br>**SPOTLIGHT ON** **The Listening Selection** Facts about *Carnival of the Animals* and the composer<br>**MEETING INDIVIDUAL NEEDS** **Reluctant Singers** Singing game to encourage and listen to reluctant or self-conscious singers<br>**MOVEMENT** **Game Song** Learn a singing game for the song<br>**BUILDING SKILLS THROUGH MUSIC** **Reading** Answer a multiple choice question after reading a poem | **Song** "Dry Bones Come Skipping"<br><br>**Listening Selection** "Fossils" from *Carnival of the Animals*<br>**Poems**<br>"Bones"<br>"A Poem to Help You Figure Out What Bone the Patella Is"<br>"Gotta Find a Footprint<br>**M*U*S*I*C M*A*K*E*R*S**<br>Camille Saint-Saëns<br><br>**More Music Choices**<br>"*Bogando a la luz del sol*," p. 306<br>"Seagull, Seagull, Sit on the Shore," p. 383 | **ASSESSMENT**<br>**Performance/Observation**<br>Create and perform an ABA speech piece using familiar rhythms and given poems<br>**Show What You Know!**<br>Mid-unit assessment<br><br>**TECHNOLOGY/MEDIA LINK**<br>**Sequencing Software**<br>Compose a four-part ostinato to accompany singing |
| **Connection: Culture**<br>**Activity:** Discuss the significance of the *balalaika* to Russian culture and compare it to other string instruments<br>**ACROSS THE CURRICULUM** **Related Arts** Design and decorate plates in a theme and variations activity<br>**CULTURAL CONNECTION** ***Balalaika*** Description of and facts about the Russian instrument<br>**SPOTLIGHT ON**<br>***The Red Poppy*** Story of the ballet<br>**Russian Nesting Boxes** Facts about origin and manufacturing<br>**MOVEMENT** **Patterned Dance** Learn dance steps to a Ukrainian song<br>**SCHOOL TO HOME CONNECTION** **Art Objects from Other Lands** Ask students to search their homes for art objects from other countries<br>**BUILDING SKILLS THROUGH MUSIC** **Writing** Write a paragraph describing a listening selection | **Song** "*Minka*" (Ukrainian and English)<br><br>**Listening Selection** "Russian Sailors' Dance" from *The Red Poppy*<br>**M*U*S*I*C M*A*K*E*R*S**<br>Reinhold Glière<br><br>**More Music Choices**<br>"*Ai Dunaii moy*," p. 293<br>"*Beriozka*," p. 294 | **ASSESSMENT**<br>**Performance/Observation**<br>Perform body percussion patterns to match mood of theme and variations<br><br>**TECHNOLOGY/MEDIA LINK**<br>**Notation Software**<br>Create variations on the main melody of a song |
| **Connection: Related Arts**<br>**Activity:** Explore textile production as an art form in Africa<br>**ACROSS THE CURRICULUM** **Related Arts** Consult photographs and descriptions in books about African textiles<br>**CULTURAL CONNECTION**<br>**Lullabies and Work Songs** Dual purpose of a song<br>**Czech Culture** Read a story about a Czech girl from Prague<br>**SPOTLIGHT ON** **The Composer** Brief biography of Czech composer Antonín Dvorák<br>**TEACHER TO TEACHER** **Compare Sequences** Discover sequences in other known and new songs<br>**BUILDING SKILLS THROUGH MUSIC** **Math** Devise a pattern of four-digit numerical sequences and explain the pattern | **Songs**<br>"*Thula, thula, ngoana*" ("Sleep, Sleep, Baby")<br>"*Tengo, tengo, tengo*" ("I Have Three Sheep")<br><br>**Listening Selection** *Slavonic Dance, Op. 46, No. 1* (excerpt)<br><br>**More Music Choices**<br>"Wings of a Dove," p. 318 | **ASSESSMENT**<br>**Performance/Observation**<br>Sing and perform movements that indicate recognition of a melodic sequence<br>**Show What You Know!**<br>Mid-unit assessment<br><br>**TECHNOLOGY/MEDIA LINK**<br>**Notation Software**<br>Compose a musical sequence |

| Lesson | Elements | Skills | |
|---|---|---|---|

## Lesson 7

**A Slovak Melody**

pp. 230–231

Reading Sequence 24, p. 453

**Element: Melody**
**Concept:** Pattern
**Focus:** Melodic sequence; practice *fa* and *ti*

**Secondary Element**
Expression: tempo

**National Standards**
5a 5b 6b

**Skill: Moving**
**Objective:** Move to show music with and without melodic sequences

**Secondary Skills**
- **Listening** Follow notation and discover a design, or pattern
- **Reading** Sing using hand signs and pitch syllables to discover a sequence

**SKILLS REINFORCEMENT**
- **Reading** Review rhythms, clap, and say the melodic rhythm
- **Singing** Practice pronunciation of a song text

## Lesson 8

CORE

**Keyboard Classics**

pp. 232–235

**Element: Timbre**
**Concept:** Instrumental timbres
**Focus:** Keyboard instrument timbre

**Secondary Element**
Melody: patterns

**National Standards**
3b 4c 6b 6d 6e 9a

**Skill: Listening**
**Objective:** Identify timbres of different keyboard instruments

**Secondary Skills**
- **Improvising** On mallet instruments, improvise four-beat call-and-response phrases
- **Moving** Improvise movements to organ music in a minor tonality

**SKILLS REINFORCEMENT**
- **Composing/Playing** Create and play compositions for keyboard

## Lesson 9

CORE

**Round and Round**

pp. 236–237

**Element: Texture/Harmony**
**Concept:** Texture
**Focus:** Rounds

**Secondary Element**
Melody: minor tonality

**National Standards**
1d 2b 2f 4b 6b

**Skill: Singing**
**Objective:** Sing the thin and thick texture of rounds

**Secondary Skills**
- **Reading** Speak and tap the rhythm of a round; locate second part entrance in a round
- **Moving** Suggest movements to accompany a round
- **Listening** Identify major and minor tonalities of a familiar melody; identify a round, ostinato, countermelody, and instruments aurally

**SKILLS REINFORCEMENT**
- **Recorder** Play ostinatos to add additional harmony parts

## Connections

## Music and Other Literature



### Connection: Culture

**Activity:** Discuss how national clothing is an expression of national culture

CULTURAL CONNECTION **National Clothing** Relate clothing styles to culture

MOVEMENT

**Patterned Dance** Learn steps to "*Tancovačka*"

**Locomotor Movements** Teach alternative movements for students with difficulty distinguishing right and left

BUILDING SKILLS THROUGH MUSIC **Writing** Write dance instructions for another group to follow

**Song** "*Tancovačka*" ("Dancing")

**More Music Choices**

"We Shall Overcome," p. 326

"Clementine," p. 341

ASSESSMENT

**Performance/Observation** Sing and perform movements that indicate recognition of a melodic sequence

TECHNOLOGY/MEDIA LINK

**CD-ROM** Play a melody game to reinforce listening skills to distinguish same from different

### Connection: Style

**Activity:** Listen to the styles of keyboard pieces from the past 300 years

ACROSS THE CURRICULUM

**Social Studies** Read a book to learn more about Bach; use a Venn diagram to compare students' childhood with that of Bach's

**Science** Explore facts about how a synthesizer produces musical sounds

SPOTLIGHT ON

**The Composer** Facts about the composer Chopin

**The Composer** Facts about John Williams, film composer

TEACHER TO TEACHER **Venn Diagram** Tips for using a Venn diagram to compare and contrast two listening selections

MEETING INDIVIDUAL NEEDS **Including Everyone** Partners with and without disabilities play chords and improvise

BUILDING SKILLS THROUGH MUSIC **Science** Review and summarize how acoustic keyboard instruments produce vibration for sound

**Listening Selections**

"Gigue" from *French Suite No. 5* (excerpt)

*Toccata in D Minor*

*Waltz in D-flat*

*Prelude in A Major*

*Close Encounters of the Third Kind* (excerpt)

**Listening Map** *Close Encounters of the Third Kind* (excerpt)

**M*U*S*I*C M*A*K*E*R*S**

Johann Sebastian Bach

Vladimir Ashkenazy

**More Music Choices**

*Piano Trio No. 2, "Scherzo,"* p. 192

ASSESSMENT

**Observation** Demonstrate knowledge of various keyboard instruments and their timbres

TECHNOLOGY/MEDIA LINK

**Transparency** Use the listening map to trace the progress of the music

### Connection: Genre

**Activity:** Sing and explore rounds

ACROSS THE CURRICULUM **Language Arts** Explore texture in fabrics discuss the meaning of the word "texture"

TEACHER TO TEACHER **Groups in Concentric Circles** Strategies for moving within circles

BUILDING SKILLS THROUGH MUSIC **Writing** Create new words for a round

**Song** "Let Music Surround You"

**Listening Selection** *Symphony No. 1*, Movement 3 (excerpt)

**More Music Choices**

"Peace Round," p. 348

ASSESSMENT

**Performance/Observation** Sing rounds with good vocal quality, demonstrating ability to maintain a part

TECHNOLOGY/MEDIA LINK

**Notation Software** Create a melodic variation of a song

| Lesson | Elements | Skills | |
|---|---|---|---|
| **LESSON 10** **Harmony Moves Me** pp. 238–239   | **Element: Texture/Harmony**<br>**Concept:** Harmony<br>**Focus:** I, IV, $V_7$ chords<br><br>**Secondary Element**<br>Expression: tempo<br><br>**National Standards**<br>2a 3b 6e 9a | **Skill: Playing**<br>**Objective:** Play instruments to accompany a popular song<br><br>**Secondary Skills**<br>• **Moving** Twist to music | **SKILLS REINFORCEMENT**<br>• **Improvising** Improvise non-pitched percussion ostinatos |
| **LESSON 11** **Chords Galore** pp. 240–243 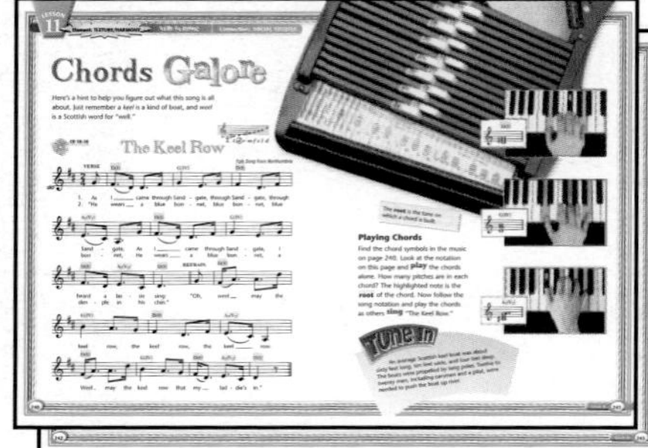  | **Element: Texture/Harmony**<br>**Concept:** Harmony<br>**Focus:** I, IV, $V_7$ chords<br><br>**Secondary Element**<br>Rhythm: dotted rhythm patterns<br><br>**National Standards**<br>1c 2b 2c 2f 4b 6b | **Skill: Playing**<br>**Objective:** Play harmony using I, IV, and $V_7$ chords<br><br>**Secondary Skills**<br>• **Singing** Follow notation, sing along to Autoharp, guitar, or keyboard accompaniment<br>• **Listening/Analyzing** Aurally identify chords as they change | **SKILLS REINFORCEMENT**<br>• **Playing** Play I, IV, $V_7$ chords on Autoharp to accompany familiar songs<br>• **Creating** Compose melodies to fit given chord progressions<br>• **Playing** Play a chord accompaniment to a song |
|  **LESSON 12** **Singing in Parts** pp. 244–245   | **Element: Texture/Harmony**<br>**Concept:** Harmony<br>**Focus:** Two-part harmony<br><br>**Secondary Element**<br>Form: AB<br><br>**National Standards**<br>1a 1d 2b 6b | **Skill: Singing**<br>**Objective:** Sing a song in two-part harmony<br><br>**Secondary Skills**<br>• **Listening** Follow lyrics that tell a story | **SKILLS REINFORCEMENT**<br>• **Vocal Development** Sustain *ti* to feel tension and resolution to *do*; sing major scale ascending and descending<br>• **Keyboard** Play a two-handed accompaniment<br>• **Recorder** Play a countermelody |

## Connections

## Music and Other Literature



**Connection:** Culture
**Activity:** Explore American culture through a popular song and dance

**ACROSS THE CURRICULUM** **Social Studies** Research the 1960s for events, leaders, clothing styles, and cars

**MEETING INDIVIDUAL NEEDS** **Peer Coaching** Appoint peer coaches to help less experienced students play instruments

**CHARACTER EDUCATION** **Respect** Discuss differences in trends and traditions

**SCHOOL TO HOME CONNECTION** **Sharing with Family** Ask older family members to share popular dance moves from their generation

**BUILDING SKILLS THROUGH MUSIC** **Language** Read information under Music Makers and summarize the paragraph for a partner

**Listening Selection** *Twist and Shout*
**MUSIC MAKERS**
The Isley Brothers

**More Music Choices**
"The Bard of Armagh," p. 296
"For the Beauty of the Earth," p. 356
"Love Will Guide Us," p. 328
"*Rio Grande*," p. 256

**ASSESSMENT**
**Performance/Observation** Demonstrate ability to move to a recorded selection and play an ostinato on roots of the I, IV, and $V_7$ chords

**TECHNOLOGY/MEDIA LINK**
**CD-ROM** Practice chord progressions

---

**Connection:** Social Studies
**Activity:** Discuss the role of lighthouses in sailing history

**ACROSS THE CURRICULUM**
**Social Studies** Share a book about lighthouses; locate Northumbria on a map
**Social Studies** Learn about the lives of *Los californios*

**CULTURAL CONNECTION** **The Legacy of *Los Californios*** Learn about the first peoples of California

**TEACHER TO TEACHER**
**Singing Chords** Reinforce students' abilities to sing chord tones in proper range
**Singing the Bass Line** Prepare students for playing chords on instruments

**BUILDING SKILLS THROUGH MUSIC** **Math** Compute the total square footage in an average Scottish keel boat

**Songs**
"The Keel Row"
"*El borrego*" ("The Lamb")"

**More Music Choices**
"Little David, Play on Your Harp," p. 394
"My Bonnie Lies Over the Ocean," p. 338

**ASSESSMENT**
**Performance/Observation** Accompany a song, playing chordal changes at correct time points in music

**TECHNOLOGY/MEDIA LINK**
**Electronic Keyboard** Perform an "oom-pah" accompaniment to a song

---

**Connection:** Social Studies
**Activity:** Read about and discuss the California gold rush and Westward expansion in the United States

**ACROSS THE CURRICULUM**
**Social Studies** Plan a covered wagon trip west
**Language Arts** Read a book about life on the prairie

**SCHOOL TO HOME CONNECTION** **Families on the Move** Discuss with family members any moves the family has made

**BUILDING SKILLS THROUGH MUSIC** **Social Studies** Research dates of chronological events and put them in order

**Song** "Sweet Betsy from Pike

**More Music Choices**
"Lullaby and Dance," p. 387
"*Einini*," p. 391

**ASSESSMENT**
**Performance/Observation** Sing a song in two-part harmony accurately

**TECHNOLOGY/MEDIA LINK**
**Web Site** Go to Web site for information on the California Gold Rush

# Introducing the Unit

Unit 6 presents the next step in a sequenced approach to understanding music elements. Presented on p. 207 is a brief overview of the skills that are assessed in this unit. (See below and pp. 208–209 for unit highlights of related curricular experiences.) For a more detailed unit overview, see Unit at a Glance, pp. 205a–205h.

# Unit Project

Students make music their own by engaging in music through performing, listening, and creating. Help students celebrate their own musicianship and keep track of music that is their own in individual "Unit 6" journals. Have students prepare pages with these headings.

- Music I Can Perform
- Music I Have Heard
- Music I Can Read
- Music I Created
- Music Symbols and Vocabulary
- My Ideas About Music

As students engage in the music in Unit 6, have them record what they learn in the pages of their journals. For example,

- Have them write the title of a song they have learned on the "Music I Can Perform" page, and then add a sentence that describes what they did or how they performed through singing, playing instruments, or moving.
- Use the "My Ideas About Music" page as a space for students to record self-assessments, class assessments, and their thinking about or reactions to music.
- At the end of the unit, encourage students to celebrate their own musicianship by reviewing what they have recorded in their journals and writing about themselves as musicians on the last page.

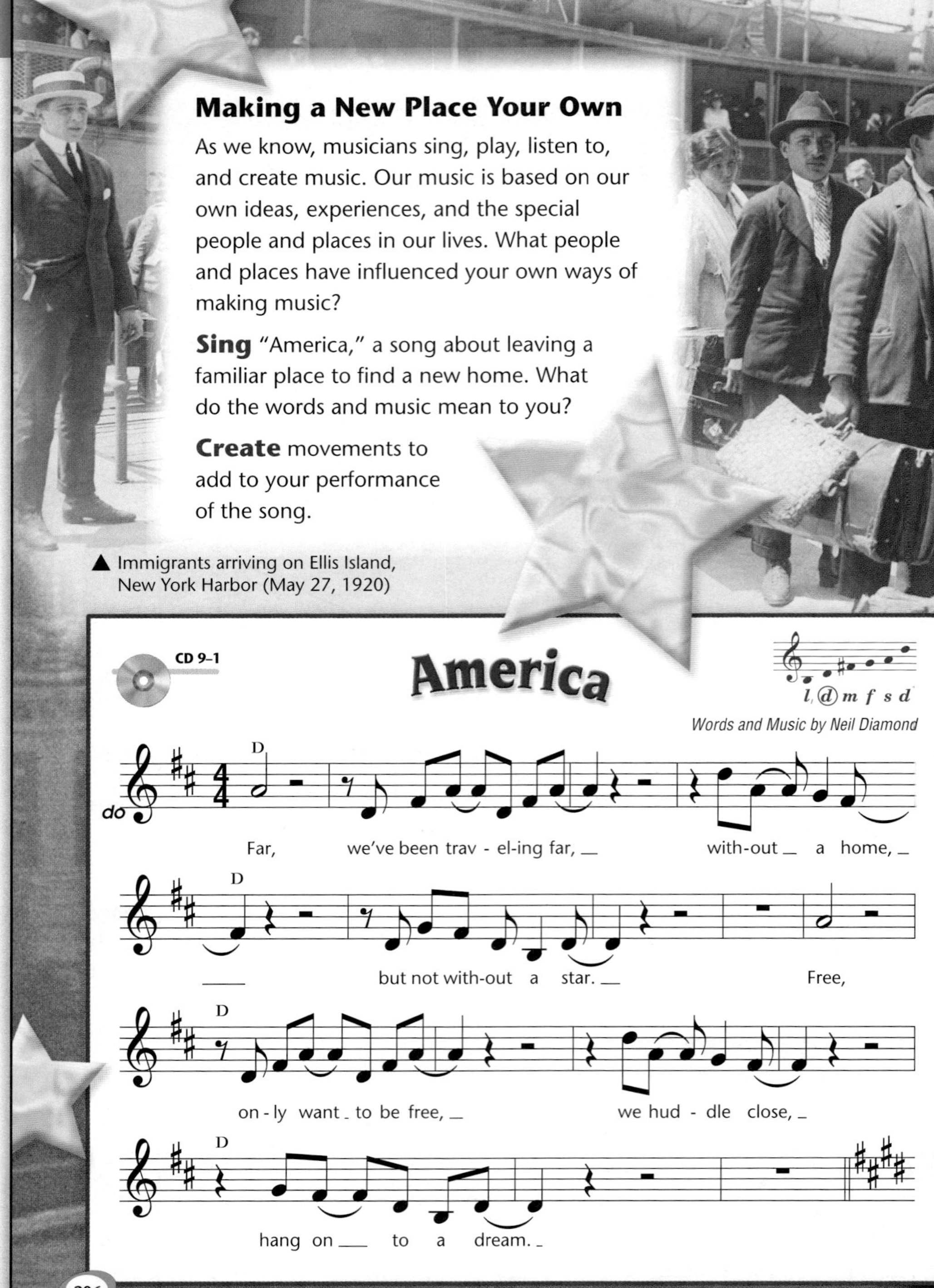

**Making a New Place Your Own**

As we know, musicians sing, play, listen to, and create music. Our music is based on our own ideas, experiences, and the special people and places in our lives. What people and places have influenced your own ways of making music?

**Sing** "America," a song about leaving a familiar place to find a new home. What do the words and music mean to you?

**Create** movements to add to your performance of the song.

▲ Immigrants arriving on Ellis Island, New York Harbor (May 27, 1920)



## Across the Curriculum

**Unit Highlights** The following interdisciplinary activities in this unit are related to the music elements presented in the lessons. See Unit at a Glance, pp. 205a–205h, for topical descriptions presented according to lesson sequence.

▶ **ART/RELATED ARTS**

- Design and decorate plates in a theme-and-variations activity (p. 224)
- Consult photographs and descriptions in books about African textiles (p. 226)

▶ **LANGUAGE ARTS**

- Use an allegory as a basis for writing a short story (p. 210)
- Write a poem to express what freedom means (p. 212)
- Hear a story of humorous happenings on a ranch (p. 214)
- Compare a children's rhyme with lyrics to a song (p. 217)
- Look into the world of myths (p. 218)
- Describe texture in fabrics (p. 236)
- Read a book about life on the prairie (p. 244)

▶ **SCIENCE**

- Investigate fossils at a museum (p. 221)
- Explore how a synthesizer produces musical sounds (p. 235)

▶ **SOCIAL STUDIES**

- Read a book to learn more about Bach; use a Venn diagram to compare students' childhood with that of Bach's (p. 232)
- Research popular culture of the 1960s (p. 238)
- Share a book about lighthouses; locate Northumbria on a map (p. 240)
- Explore the history of Mexican *ranchos* (p. 242)
- Plan an imaginary covered wagon trip west (p. 244)

UNIT 6

# Making Music Our Own

f, s, l, ta, d r m f s d'

do

E — E
On the boats and on ___ the planes, they're com - ing to A -
Nev-er look - ing back ___ a - gain, they're com - ing to A -

E — C♯m — B
mer - i - ca. Home, don't it seem so ___ far ___
mer - i - ca. Home, to a new and ___ shin -

E — B
___ a-way, oh, we're trav - el - ing light ___ to - day,
- y place, make our bed and we'll say ___ our grace,

Unit 6 207



## Music Skills Assessed in This Unit

**Reading Music: Rhythm**

- Read, clap, and count the rhythm of a round (p. 217)
- Read the rhythm of a song to identify similar patterns (p. 221)

**Reading Music: Pitch**

- Sing a song with hand signs and pitch syllables to identify melodic sequence (pp. 229, 231)

**Performing Music: Singing**

- Sing accents expressively (p. 213)
- Sing a round while conducting meter in 3 (p. 217)
- Sing a round with good vocal quality, demonstrating ability to maintain a part (p. 237)
- Sing a song in two-part harmony accurately (p. 245)

**Moving to Music**

- Use two-beat movement patterns to show meter in 2 (p. 215)
- Perform body percussion patterns (p. 225)
- Perform created movements to show a descending sequence (p. 229)
- Perform movements that indicate recognition of a melodic sequence (p. 231)

**Performing Music: Playing**

- Demonstrate ability to play an ostinato on roots of the I, IV, and $V_7$ chords (p. 239)
- Accompany a song, playing chordal changes at correct points in music (p. 243)

**Creating Music**

- Create an ABA speech piece (p. 221)

**Listening to Music**

- Demonstrate knowledge of various keyboard instruments and timbres (p. 235)

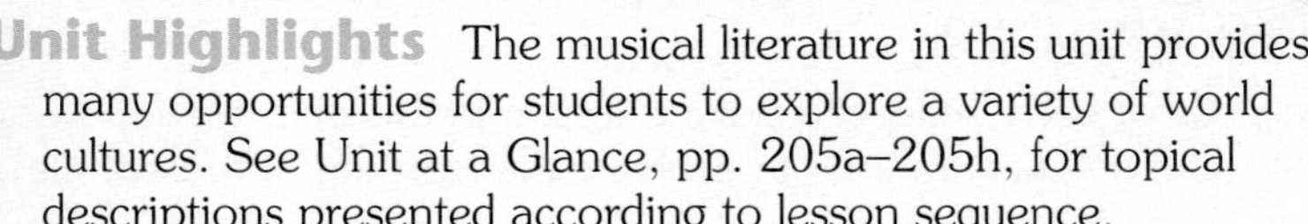

## Cultural Connection

**Unit Highlights** The musical literature in this unit provides many opportunities for students to explore a variety of world cultures. See Unit at a Glance, pp. 205a–205h, for topical descriptions presented according to lesson sequence.

**AFRICAN**

- Explore the cultural background of an African lullaby (p. 226)

**AMERICAN**

- Perform a contemporary American patriotic song (p. 210)
- Explore ranch life on the Western frontier (p. 215)
- Sing a traditional song from the United States (p. 218)
- Sing a Spanish-language folk song from New Mexico (p. 228)
- Discuss the history and musical legacy of *Los californios* (p. 241)
- Sing a popular folk song from the United States (p. 244)

**EUROPEAN**

- Perform a traditional German round (p. 217)
- Sing a folk song from Ukraine (p. 222)
- Discuss the construction and cultural significance of the Russian *balalaika* (p. 222)
- Discuss the Czech folk dance background of a listening selection; read a story about a Czech girl from Prague (p. 228)
- Relate Slovak national clothing styles to its culture (p. 230)

# Opening Activities

**MATERIALS**

- "America" **CD 9-1**

  **Recording Routine:** Intro (8 m.); vocal; coda
- nonpitched percussion instruments

## Listening

Play "America" **CD 9-1** and invite students to tap the beat as they listen. Have them find the $\frac{4}{4}$ time signature at the beginning of the music. Invite them to move, using a four-beat pattern (for example, pat-clap-snap-clap), or to conduct meter in 4 as they listen to "America" again.

## Singing

Invite students to sing "America" with the recording. Encourage them to demonstrate good singing posture and to listen to and blend with the voices around them.

## Reading

Ask students to find the following symbols in the song notation: repeat signs, double bar, a four-measure rest.

As students identify each symbol, have them explain to a partner what that symbol means. Then have them sing the song again, observing the signs in the music.

## Analyzing

Invite students to look at the song notation again and find measures that are the same and measures that are similar. For example, the melody and rhythm for the phrases *they're coming to America* is sometimes the same and sometimes similar (higher by one step).

## Moving

Arrange students into groups of four or five to create their own movements for "America." Assign each group a section of the song. Have each group demonstrate its movement as the class sings the song again.

New U.S. citizens celebrate after taking the oath of citizenship. ▶

## ASSESSMENT

**Unit Highlights** This unit includes a variety of strategies and methods, described below, to track students' progress and assess their understanding of lesson objectives. Reproducible masters for Show What You Know! and Review, Assess, Perform, Create can be found in the Resource Book.

### ▶ FORMAL ASSESSMENTS

The following assessments, using written language, cognitive, and performance skills, help teachers and students conceptualize the learning that is taking place.

- **Show What You Know!** Element-specific assessments, on the student page, for Rhythm (p. 221) and Melody (p. 229).
- **Review, Assess, Perform, Create** This end-of-unit activity (pp. 246–247) can be used for review and to assess students' learning of the core lessons in this unit.

### ▶ INFORMAL ASSESSMENTS

At the close of each Teacher's Edition lesson in this unit, the following types of assessments are used to evaluate the learning of the key element focus or skill objective.

- Performance/Observation (pp. 213, 215, 217, 221, 225, 229, 231, 237, 239, 243, 245)
- Observation (p. 235)

### ▶ RUBRICS

Visit *www.sfsuccessnet.com* for rubrics to assess students' achievement in music skills.

**Arts Connection**

*America* (1985) by Chinese-American artist Diana Ong (born 1940) ▶







## Playing

Play "America" **CD 9-1** and invite students to identify the percussion instruments they hear. Have them identify similar percussion instruments in the classroom. Then invite students to accompany "America" using the ostinatos below.

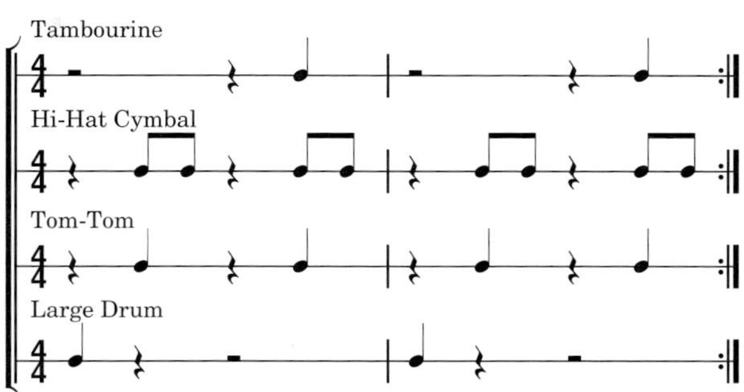



You may wish to write the ostinatos on the board or on a chart, or teach them by rote. Have students tap or clap the rhythm and then transfer to the appropriate percussion instrument.

### Innovative Teacher Support for This Unit

- **Making Music DVD, Grade 4** contains video segments that support lessons, including signing and movement.
- **Making Music with Movement and Dance** provides more opportunities for large group activities in music or physical education classes.
- **Making Music with Technology** provides lesson plans for many technology applications; includes MIDI files.
- ***¡A cantar!*** features recorded songs and lessons from around the Spanish-speaking world; includes strategies for bilingual classes and for English-speaking teachers working with Spanish-speaking students.
- **Bridges to Asia** features recorded songs and lessons from Asian and Pacific region cultures.
- ***www.sfsuccessnet.com*** provides an online lesson planner to conveniently create lesson plans at school or at home. Includes rubrics for assessment, lesson modifications to meet the needs of all students, performance musicals based on program content, and more.

## Technology/Media Link

**Unit Highlights** The following components are used in this unit to reinforce and expand students' understanding of music elements and related themes. See Unit at a Glance, pp. 205a–205h, for a descriptive listing according to lesson sequence.

▶ **CD-ROM**

- Play a melody game to reinforce listening skills to distinguish same from different (p. 231)
- Arrange and perform chord progressions (p. 239)

▶ **ELECTRONIC KEYBOARD**

- Perform an "oom-pah" accompaniment to a song (p. 243)

▶ **NOTATION SOFTWARE**

- Practice entering accents (p. 213)
- Compose a percussion ensemble piece to accompany a song (p. 215)
- Create variations on the main melody of a listening selection (p. 225)
- Compose a musical sequence (p. 229)
- Create a melodic variation of a song (p. 237)

▶ **SEQUENCING SOFTWARE**

- Compose a four-part ostinato to accompany singing (p. 221)

▶ **TRANSPARENCY**

- Use the listening map for visual reinforcement of accents (p. 213)
- Use a listening map to aid in following a selection (p. 235)

▶ **WEB SITE**

- Go to *www.sfsuccessnet.com* to find more information on bells (p. 217) and music of the California Gold Rush (p. 245)

LESSON Core 1

## LESSON AT A GLANCE

**Element Focus** **EXPRESSION** Accents

**Skill Objective** **SINGING** Sing a song, performing accents where appropriate

**Connection Activity** **RELATED ARTS** Discuss ways in which music, the visual arts, and poetry use accent in expression

**MATERIALS**

- "America, the Free" **CD 9-3**
  **Recording Routine:** Intro (4 m.); vocal
- *Thunder and Lightning Polka* **CD 9-5**
- nonpitched percussion instruments

**VOCABULARY**

accent

### National Standards

**1b** Sing expressively with appropriate interpretation
**1d** Sing part songs
**2b** Perform rhythms on appropriate instruments
**3b** Improvise rhythmic ostinato accompaniments
**4a** Compose music to accompany readings
**4b** Compose instrumental pieces within specific guidelines
**5a** Read rhythms in duple meter
**5c** Identify and use symbols and terms for articulation
**6c** Use appropriate terms to explain music notation
**6d** Identify the sounds of orchestral instruments
**8a** Define common terms used with different meanings in the various arts

**MORE MUSIC CHOICES**

Other freedom songs:

"We Shall Not Be Moved," p. 437

"We Shall Overcome," p. 326

LESSON 1 Element: EXPRESSION | Skill: SINGING | Connection: RELATED ARTS

# Accent on Freedom

An **accent** indicates to p… or sing a note with more emphasis than the other notes.

A musical **accent** (>) gives special importance or stress to certain notes. Find the accents in this patriotic song. Then perform them as you sing the song.

CD 9-3

## America, the Free

d r m f s l ta t d' r'

*Words and Music by Phyllis Wolfe-White (adapted)*

I am the voice of A - mer - i - ca, I am free-dom's song.
I am the wings of an ea - gle, I am proud and strong! A -
mer - i - ca, the beau - ti - ful, A - mer - i - ca, the free, A -
mer - i - ca, the hope of all I ev - er dream to be.
ev - 'ry op - por - tu - ni - ty.
Last time to Coda
Solo 1 I can be (a doc - tor,)
Solo 2 I can be (an ar - tist,)
Solo 3 I can be (a bank - er,)
210



# Footnotes

## MEETING INDIVIDUAL NEEDS

▶ **English Language Learners** Ask students to create an illustration of what freedom means to them. This word can be difficult to grasp for students. When students have completed their illustrations, ask them to tell a partner about their picture. Then hang the pictures on the walls and invite students to gallery-walk through the collection.

## BUILDING SKILLS THROUGH MUSIC

▶ **Social Studies** After students have learned the song "America, the Free," have them identify symbols that are used in America to represent freedom. (for example, the eagle, the liberty bell, the Statue of Liberty, the American flag, and so on) Divide students into small groups to develop a speech piece using the American symbols of freedom.

## ACROSS THE CURRICULUM

▶ **Language Arts** Read aloud *When Daffodils Ran Free* by A. Roberta Wiatt (V & M Graphics, 2000). In a mystical land the daffodils run free, but when they fall they cannot get up. Thus, they die. The daffodils decide it would be better to be planted and return each spring.

Invite students to use this book as a model to write a short story about a person who desires freedom but must choose between freedom and something else that is important to him or her.

# 1 INTRODUCE

Write this question on the board: "What does freedom mean to you?" Select three students to read the question aloud, with each student emphasizing one of the following words: *freedom, mean, you.*

ASK **Did changing the emphasized word change the meaning of the question?** (Yes, and it will change the response to the question.)

Explain that the emphasis on a certain word can also be called an accent. Encourage students to think of questions in which changing the word accent would change the meaning of the question. For example: *When* will we sing?—answer: at noon; When will we *sing*?—answer: as soon as we finish *playing*, but before we *listen.*

# 2 DEVELOP

## Listening

**SAY** Accents in music are a way to emphasize specific notes.

Then play "America, the Free" **CD 9-3.** Invite students to listen to the song and find the accented notes in their books. After listening, have students point out the accented notes.

6c ASK **What special symbol shows that a note is accented?** (accent mark, as found on p. 210)

Invite a volunteer to draw an accent mark on the board.

continued on page 210

## SKILLS REINFORCEMENT

5a ▶ **Reading** Have students look at the notation for "America, the Free" and find phrases or lines in which the rhythm is the same or very similar. Invite students to read (clap and say) the rhythm for the entire song.

## CHARACTER EDUCATION

▶ **Ambition/Goal-Setting/Persistence** Encourage students to consider goals they have for themselves and the steps to achieve these by creating original artwork that illustrates their goals and plans for attaining their goals. Explain to students that the text of "America, the Free" encourages them to think about what they want to be. Ask students to include the following items in their artwork: their name (no other words); a drawing (or pictures) of who they want to be; drawings or pictures showing the steps they must take to achieve their goal. (Drawings or magazine cuttings may be used.) Allow students to share their artwork. Discuss the role of ambition and persistence in achieving goals. Ask students the following questions: What other qualities are important in reaching goals? Describe someone you know who has had clear goals and worked to achieve them. How were they able to accomplish this?

### Singing

1b Invite students to sing "America, the Free" **CD 9-3** with the recording. Encourage them to emphasize the accented notes and use a *legato* singing style for the rest of the song.

1d For an independent performance of the song, invite up to six students to sing the solo parts. Part 2, on p. 211, may be sung by the combined soloists. Encourage students to compose their own lyrics, to replace those that appear in parentheses.

### Creating

Invite students to look at the painting *Three Musicians* by Pablo Picasso. Share information about Picasso in Spotlight On, p. 213. Then help students identify the connections between this fine arts example and music.

8a **ASK How did the artist use color to accent shapes and objects in the painting?** (The guitar player is accented by the orange and yellow colors and the sharp angles in the design of the fabric of his clothes; the music notation seems accented because it pops out from the white background; the clarinet player seems accented by his size and the stark contrast of white, black, and blue in his clothing.)

Divide students into small groups. Encourage them to create a poem describing the painting. Have them devise their own accent marks and put them under or over the words that should be emphasized in the poem.

4a Then have students create a nonpitched percussion introduction and coda for the poem. The introduction and coda should also include accented notes.

### Playing

Choose three contrasting rhythm patterns from "America, the Free," pp. 210–211. Write the rhythms on the board or on a chart.

2b Invite students to play the rhythms using various classroom percussion instruments.

**Arts Connection**

▲ *Three Musicians* (1921) by Pablo Picasso. Many of Picasso's works feature musical subjects. *Three Musicians* is in the "cubist" style. Artists who painted in this style used geometric shapes such as circles, squares, and triangles in abstract forms.

### Accents Everywhere

Accents can be found everywhere in music, poetry, art, and dance. Look at the painting by Picasso. How did the artist use such elements as shape and color to give the impression of accents? What instruments are depicted in *Three Musicians*?

212

## Footnotes

### ACROSS THE CURRICULUM

▶ **Language Arts** Return to the opening question of the lesson: "What does freedom mean to you?" Invite students to write a poem or a paragraph to answer that question. Create a "Freedom Seekers" bulletin board or display in which students can share their writing. Allow time for students to read their poetry and prose aloud to the class. Highlight words that are common in students' writing, and use those words to create vocabulary for review. Choose some of these works as an introduction for a performance of "America, the Free."

### SKILLS REINFORCEMENT

4b ▶ **Improvising/Composing** To reinforce students' experience with accents, invite them to create a rhythm composition in a familiar meter of their choice.

**Reinforcement** Some students may be most comfortable participating in this activity by choosing a body percussion to perform a steady beat.

**On Target** Have students work individually, in pairs, or in small groups to create, notate, and perform a composition that

- Is at least 8–16 measures long.
- Includes at least two accents.
- Is written for instruments of their choice.

3b **Challenge** While students perform their compositions, invite others to improvise an appropriate ostinato accompaniment.

## Accents Make the Difference

Listen for accents in this instrumental piece. What instruments play the accents?

CD 9-5

**Thunder and Lightning Polka**

**by Johann Strauss**

Johann Strauss lived in Austria where German is spoken. The words for thunder and lightning in German are *Donner und Blitz.*



To reinforce the concept of accents, write or alter one or two accents in each rhythm and then have students play the pattern with the accents.

Have one student play a pattern without accents. Then have him or her decide where to place accents without writing them in or telling the class, and play it again with those accents. Have classmates tell which notes were accented; ask the student if classmates are correct.

### Listening

**ASK If you were composing a piece called "Thunder and Lightning" for orchestra, what instruments would you use to create the effect of thunder and lightning?** (Accept a variety of answers, and encourage students to provide reasons or explanations for their choices.)

Invite students to look at the listening map for *Thunder and Lightning Polka.* Point out the repeat signs in each row and ask students to find how many times they will hear each section within the repeat signs (given in parentheses). Then ask students to find the accents in the notation. Play *Thunder and Lightning Polka* **CD 9-5.** Encourage students to raise their hands when they hear accented notes as they listen to the piece.

**ASK What instruments created the "thunder and lightning" accents?** (cymbals and drums)

## 3 Close

**Element: EXPRESSION** ASSESSMENT

**Performance/Observation** Invite students to sing "America, the Free" **CD 9-3,** performing accents where appropriate. Observe students' ability to sing the accents expressively.

### Spotlight On

**The Artist** Pablo Picasso (1881–1973) was born in Málaga, Spain. After growing up around people in the arts, he went to Barcelona for formal art training, then to Paris to begin his life as an artist. From 1900 to about 1905, he painted in the Impressionist and Symbolist styles, portraying the hard, darker side of life, since he was often cold, hungry, and penniless in Paris. Starting in 1905 he worked through a neo-classical period, a primitive period, and launched into a style of his own in which rules were broken: a profile of a nose placed on the front of a face, or the front view of an eye put on the side of a head. He distorted the rules of perspective. Picasso was a pioneer, and his revolutionary approaches to painting resulted in Cubism, the style of *Three Musicians.* His style continued to transform until his death, long after Cubism.

### Technology/Media Link

**Transparency** Display the transparency for *Thunder and Lightning Polka.* Invite students to trace the progress of the selection with their finger on the map in their book, as you trace on the overhead projection.

**Notation Software** Help students to insert expression markings using the classroom computer's notation software. Have students

- Set up the program for the key of C and $\frac{4}{4}$ time.
- Notate the first four lines of "America, the Free."
- Use the program's expression tool to practice entering accents.

LESSON 2

## LESSON AT A GLANCE

**Element Focus** **RHYTHM** Meter in 2

**Skill Objective** **MOVING** Perform steady beat movements that reflect the meter of a song

**Connection Activity** **CULTURE** Discuss ranch life

**MATERIALS**
- *"El rancho grande"* **CD 9-6**
- "The Big Ranch" **CD 9-7**

  **Recording Routine:** Intro (8 m.); vocal; interlude (8 m.); vocal; coda
- **Pronunciation Practice/Translation** p. 482
- **Resource Book** p. A-20
- nonpitched percussion, including maracas, claves, and *guiros;* guitars

**VOCABULARY**

meter ostinato

**National Standards**

**2b** Perform chords on appropriate instruments
**4b** Compose instrumental pieces within specific guidelines
**5a** Read rhythms in duple meter
**6b** Describe music by answering questions about it
**6e** While listening to music, move to show a prominent feature of the music

**MORE MUSIC CHOICES**

Other songs in meter in 2:
*"Beriozka,"* p. 294
"Oh, Susanna," p. 264

# 1 INTRODUCE

Invite students to read the lyrics to *"El rancho grande"* and share what they know about life on a ranch. Share with students the information in Cultural Connection, p. 215.

LESSON 2 Element: RHYTHM | Skill: MOVING | Connection: CULTURE

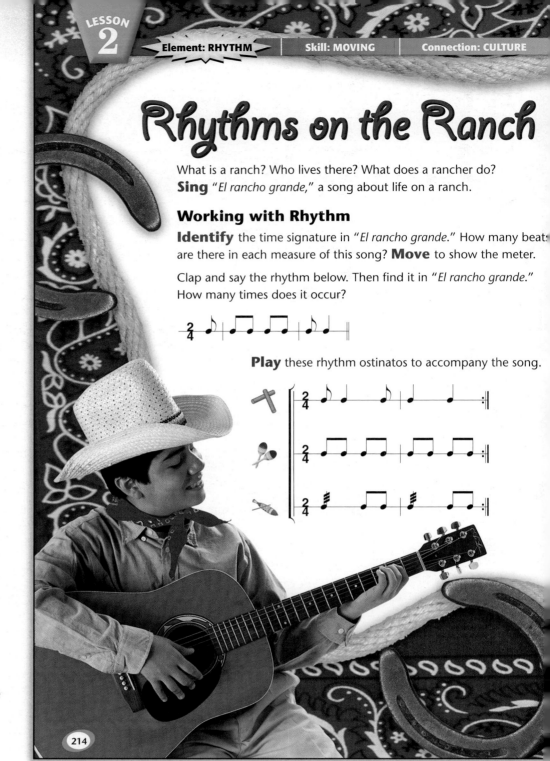

# Rhythms on the Ranch

What is a ranch? Who lives there? What does a rancher do? **Sing** *"El rancho grande,"* a song about life on a ranch.

### Working with Rhythm

**Identify** the time signature in *"El rancho grande."* How many beats are there in each measure of this song? **Move** to show the meter.

Clap and say the rhythm below. Then find it in *"El rancho grande."* How many times does it occur?

**Play** these rhythm ostinatos to accompany the song.



## Footnotes

### ACROSS THE CURRICULUM

▶ **Language Arts** Read aloud the book *Meanwhile Back at the Ranch* by Trinka Hakes Noble (Puffin, 1992). While the rancher is gone, some amazing things are happening on his ranch. Students will love the humor in this book! Invite students to write additional events that could have happened on the ranch while Rancher Hicks was away.

### BUILDING SKILLS THROUGH MUSIC

▶ **Language** Have students draw on experience and context to discern the meaning of unfamiliar English words in *"El rancho grande."* Examples might include *yonder, prairie,* and *chaps.*

### SKILLS REINFORCEMENT

2b ▶ **Guitar** The song *"El rancho grande"* is clearly meant to be accompanied by guitar and with only two chords (G and $D_7$), very suitable for beginning guitarists. Use a simple "thumb-strum" (sweep of the thumb down the chord) rhythm in the right hand. An authentic and effective addition to the right-hand style is alternating the bass note (strings 6 and 5 on the G chord; strings 4 and 5 on the D chord). To make this alternating bass task easier, you can tune the guitar to open G. The G chord is then played with open strings, and the $D_7$ chord is played by barring at the seventh fret. Or, in keeping with a root–fifth alternation of bass strings, use strings 6 and 4 while playing the G chord to have a G–D pattern, not a G–B pattern.

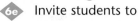

m, fi, s, l, t, d r m f fis

CD 9-6

# El rancho grande

(The Big Ranch)

English Words by Alice D. Firgau

Music by Silvano R. Ramos

VERSE

A - llá en el ran - cho gran - de, A - llá don - de vi - ví - a, Ha - bía u - na ran - che - ri - ta, Que a - le - gre me de - cí - a, Que a - le - gre me de - cí - a:

Out yon - der on a prai - rie, The ranch where I was liv - ing, I heard a pret - ty cow - girl, Who hap - pi - ly was sing - ing, Who hap - pi - ly was sing - ing:

REFRAIN

Te voy ha - cer tus cal - zo - nes, Co - mo los u - sa el ran - che - ro; Te los co - mien - zo de la - na, Te los a - ca - bo de cue - ro.

A pair of chaps I will make you, Just like the ones for a ranch - er; With wool and leath - er I'll make them. Oh, do please give me your an - swer.



# 2 Develop

## Moving

Invite students to

- Tap the beat as they listen to the verse of *"El rancho grande"* **CD 9-6.**
- Use a different motion to show the beat during the refrain.

Then have students find the time signature at the beginning of the song.

ASK **How many beats are in each measure?** (two)

Play the song again. Invite students to move, this time using two-beat motions (for example, pat-clap). Change motions for the refrain.

## Playing

5a Have students

- Find the repeated rhythms in *"El rancho grande."*
- Tap and say the repeated rhythms.

Invite students to read and play the rhythm ostinatos on p. 214. Have them tap and say the rhythms first, then play the ostinatos on *guiros,* maracas, and claves.

## Singing

Using the Pronunciation Practice for *"El rancho grande"* **CD 9-9**, have students echo each phrase. Refer to Resource Book p. A-20. Then have them sing the song **CD 9-6.**

# 3 Close

**Element: RHYTHM**

ASSESSMENT

**Performance/Observation** Have students sing *"El rancho grande,"* performing a two-beat movement pattern during the verse, and a different two-beat pattern during the refrain. Observe students' ability to move to show duple meter.

## Cultural Connection

**Ranch Life** Cowboys were people who took care of cattle for large ranch owners in the days of the Western frontier in the United States. Because cowboys faced much danger and hardship, they were often thought of as heroes. Ranch life could be pretty lonely, and after their daily work was done, cowboys had to find their own entertainment. There weren't any movies, or radio, or television. So often, cowboys sat around a campfire in the evenings and sang songs. Guitars were important instruments to cowboys because they were portable. On ranches near the border of Mexico, like the well-known King Ranch in South Texas, the songs might be in English or Spanish, or both.

## Technology/Media Link

**Notation Software** Use music notation software to help students compose a percussion ensemble piece to accompany *"El rancho grande."*

- Create a file with four staves and eight measures in duple meter, with a repeat bar at the end.
- Show students how to select different percussion sounds for each staff.
- Have students compose a percussion ensemble in pairs, one instrument per staff.
- If time allows, add dynamic markings to the composition.

LESSON 3

## LESSON AT A GLANCE

**Element Focus** **RHYTHM** Meter in 3

**Skill Objective** **SINGING** Sing a song in meter in 3 while conducting a beat pattern in 3

**Connection Activity** **RELATED ARTS** Read and discuss a rhyme about bells

**MATERIALS**

- "Oh, How Lovely Is the Evening" **CD 9-10**
  **Recording Routine:** Intro (4 m.); vocal (unison); interlude (4 m.); vocal (3-part round); coda
- **Music Reading Practice, Sequence 21** **CD 9-12**
- **Resource Book** pp. D-26, E-22

**VOCABULARY**

round dotted-half note

**National Standards**

**1a** Sing independently, with appropriate diction
**1d** Sing rounds
**1e** Sing in groups, following a conductor
**5b** Read notes in treble clef, using syllables
**6e** While listening to music, move to show a prominent feature of the music

**MORE MUSIC CHOICES**

Other songs in meter in 3:
"*Einini*," p. 391
"Star-Spangled Banner, The," p. 441

# 1 INTRODUCE

Invite students to read the lyrics to "Oh, How Lovely Is the Evening." Discuss the calming effect the "sweet ringing" of the bells is having on the singer, making the evening lovely. Share with students the poem in Across the Curriculum, p. 217, and compare and contrast the effect of the bells in each text.

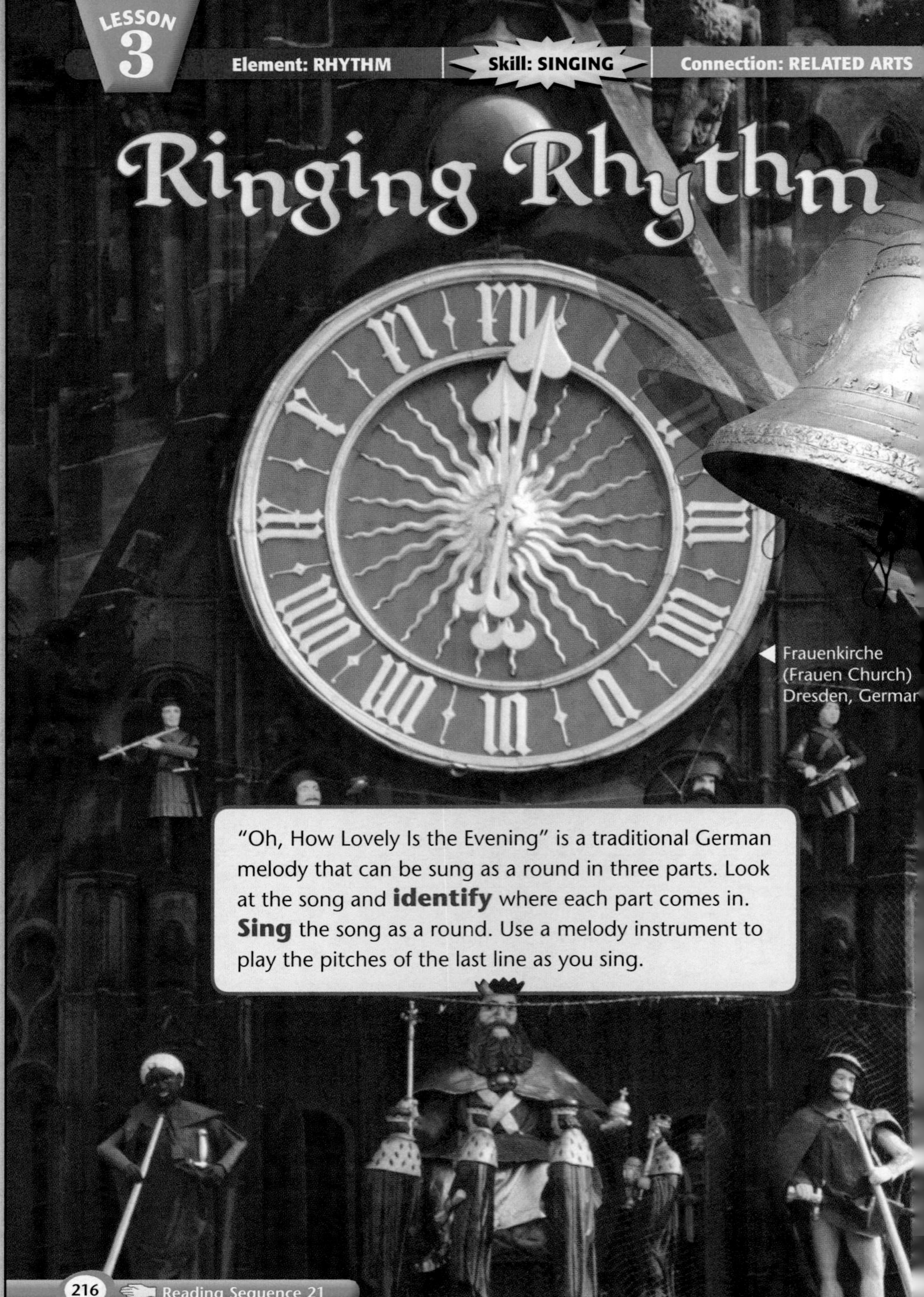


# Ringing Rhythm

Frauenkirche (Frauen Church) Dresden, Germar

"Oh, How Lovely Is the Evening" is a traditional German melody that can be sung as a round in three parts. Look at the song and **identify** where each part comes in. **Sing** the song as a round. Use a melody instrument to play the pitches of the last line as you sing.



## Footnotes

### MEETING INDIVIDUAL NEEDS

▶ **Including Everyone** Students can use a variety of movements to show the first beat of each measure of "Oh, How Lovely Is the Evening," from tapping a finger to moving their head. Have students choose a movement for the strong beats. Include at least one movement that each student can perform successfully. Have students move on the first beat as you sing and tap three beats, alternating tapping and no tapping.

### BUILDING SKILLS THROUGH MUSIC

▶ **Science** Invite students to bring to class different types of bells. After demonstrating each type, ask students to describe the timbre and explain why the timbre varies from bell to bell.

### SKILLS REINFORCEMENT

1a ▶ **Vocal Development** Voiced consonants are those that engage the vocal cords, and unvoiced consonants are those that do not engage the vocal cords. The following voiced consonants are sustained: *m, n, ng, th (these), v, z, zh*. These unvoiced consonants have a hissing quality: *f, s, sh, th (think)*.

Voiced consonants are sung on the same pitch as their accompanying vowel. To avoid sliding on initial consonants, students should think the first vowel sound before singing, and sing short consonants and long vowels.

It is helpful to sing unvoiced consonants at the end of a word *(should, short),* and save the final consonant for the cut-off.

## hythms in Time

- Look at the song again. **Identify** the rhythms you already know.
- Clap a steady beat and say the first two lines of "Oh, How Lovely Is the Evening" using rhythm syllables.

  How many notes are in the last line? How many measures? How many notes are in each measure?
- This song has three beats in each measure. How many beats is each note of the last line?
- Clap a steady beat and say the whole song using rhythm syllables.

### Ringing and Singing

One group can **sing** the last line of the song as an ostinato, while others sing the entire song. Then sing the song as a three part round. **Create** your own instrumental accompaniment.



# 2 Develop

### Listening

6e Play "Oh, How Lovely Is the Evening" **CD 9-10.** Have students pat the strong beat of each measure (beat 1) on their knees, and clap the weaker beats of each measure (beats 2 and 3). See Meeting Individual Needs, p. 216, for more movement suggestions.

### Analyzing

Draw attention to the time signature, and remind students that in meter in 3, there are three beats in each measure. Demonstrate the conducting pattern for meter in 3. Have students practice conducting the song with the recording.

### Reading

5b Have students read, clap, and count the rhythm for "Oh, How Lovely Is the Evening." Encourage them to sing the song, using pitch syllables and hand signs. Use Music Reading Worksheet on Resource Book p. D-26 for more practice with meter in 3. See p. 452 and Resource Book p. E-22 for a related reading activity.

### Singing

1e Have students sing "Oh, How Lovely Is the Evening" **CD 9-10**, as volunteers take turns conducting the class.

# 3 Close

### Singing

1d Invite students to sing "Oh, How Lovely Is the Evening" as a round.

**Skill: SINGING** — **ASSESSMENT**

**Performance/Observation** Have students sing "Oh, How Lovely Is the Evening" **CD 9-10** while conducting a beat pattern in 3. Observe students' ability to sing in meter in 3 while conducting the pattern accurately.

## Across the Curriculum

▶ **Language Arts** "Oranges and Lemons" is a children's rhyme. It uses the names of many famous church bells in London.

> Oranges and lemons, say the bells of St. Clement's.
> You owe me five farthings, say the bells of St. Martin's.
> When will you pay me? say the bells of Old Bailey.
> When I grow rich, say the bells of Shoreditch.
> When will that be? say the bells of St. Stepney.
> I'm sure I don't know, says the Great Bell of Bow.

Have students compare this rhyme with the lyrics to "Oh, How Lovely Is the Evening."

## Technology/Media Link

**Web Site** Invite students to visit *www.sfsuccessnet.com* to read more about bells, including some famous bells.

LESSON Core 4

## LESSON AT A GLANCE

**Element Focus** **RHYTHM** Meter in 4

**Skill Objective** **CREATING** Create a composition using familiar rhythm patterns

**Connection Activity** **SCIENCE** Explore the origins of fossils and the information that can be learned from them

**MATERIALS**

- "Dry Bones Come Skipping" **CD 9-15**
  **Recording Routine:** Intro (2 m.); vocal; interlude (2 m.); vocal; coda
- **Music Reading Practice, Sequence 22** **CD 9-17**
- "Fossils" from *Carnival of the Animals* (excerpt) **CD 9-20**
- "Bones" (poem)
- "A Poem to Help You Figure Out What Bone the Patella Is" (poem)
- "Gotta Find a Footprint" (poem)
- **Resource Book** pp. B-20, E-23, F-16
- nonpitched percussion instruments

**VOCABULARY**

ABA form *Fine* *D.C. al Fine*

**National Standards**

**1b** Sing expressively with appropriate interpretation
**2f** Play instruments independently against contrasting parts
**4b** Compose instrumental pieces within specific guidelines
**5a** Read rhythms in quadruple meter
**5b** Read notes in treble clef using syllables
**6a** Listen to identify form
**6b** Describe music by answering questions about it, or moving to it
**6e** While listening to music, move to show a prominent feature of the music

**MORE MUSIC CHOICES**

Other songs in meter in 4:
"*Bogando a la luz del sol,*" p. 306
"Seagull, Seagull, Sit on the Shore," p. 382

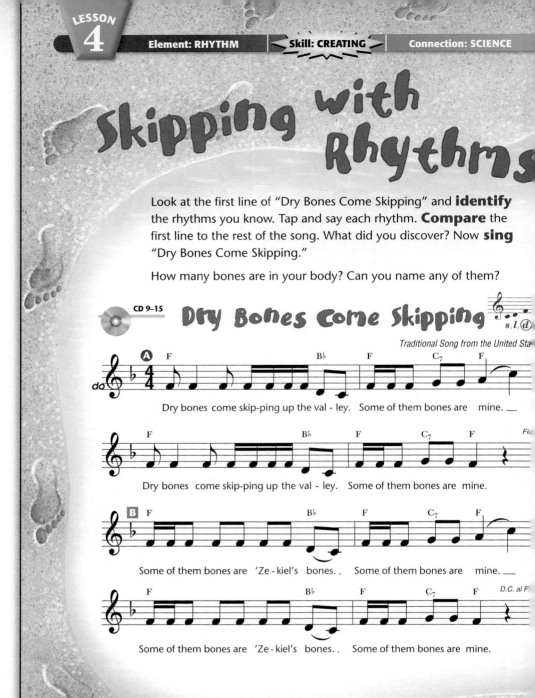

LESSON 4 Element: RHYTHM Skill: CREATING Connection: SCIENCE

# Skipping with Rhythms

Look at the first line of "Dry Bones Come Skipping" and **identify** the rhythms you know. Tap and say each rhythm. **Compare** the first line to the rest of the song. What did you discover? Now **sing** "Dry Bones Come Skipping."

How many bones are in your body? Can you name any of them?

CD 9-15

## Dry Bones Come Skipping

s, l, d

Traditional Song from the United States

A F B♭ F C7 F
do
Dry bones come skip-ping up the val - ley. Some of them bones are mine. __
F B♭ F C7 F Fine
Dry bones come skip-ping up the val - ley. Some of them bones are mine.
B F B♭ F C7 F
Some of them bones are 'Ze - kiel's bones. _ Some of them bones are mine. __
F B♭ F C7 F D.C. al Fine
Some of them bones are 'Ze - kiel's bones. _ Some of them bones are mine.

# Footnotes

## ACROSS THE CURRICULUM

▶ **Language Arts** Read aloud the book *The Bone Keeper* by Megan McDonald (DK Publishing, 1999). This book invites students into the world of myths. For interested readers, share the book *Bones: Our Skeletal System* by Seymour Simon (Morrow Junior, 1998) and invite students to learn more about the systems that hold our bodies together.

## BUILDING SKILLS THROUGH MUSIC

▶ **Reading** Have students read the poem "Gotta Find a Footprint," on p. 221, and then answer the following multiple-choice question. (The answer is "c.")

What would a scientist use to determine how big a dinosaur was?
**a.** footprints **b.** bones **c.** both footprints and bones

## SKILLS REINFORCEMENT

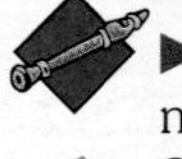

▶ **Recorder** Students may need to practice this counter-melody slowly before playing along with "Dry Bones Come Skipping." Make sure they articulate each eighth note clearly and take a breath at the end of each two-measure phrase.

2f

▶ **Mallets** For an Orff accompaniment to "Dry Bones Come Skipping," refer to Resource Book p. F-16.

## Connect the Bones

**Create** a *bones* composition. Use the same meter and Ⓐ Ⓑ Ⓐ form as "Dry Bones Come Skipping."

Ⓐ **Compose** four measures of rhythm in meter in 4. Use rhythms you know. Look at "Dry Bones Come Skipping" for ideas. Decide how you will perform your rhythm. Will you use an instrument or body percussion?

Ⓑ Choose one of the poems below for the Ⓑ section. Read the poem, then decide how you will **perform** it. Will you speak it or sing it? Will you use movements or instruments to accompany the poem? Will you perform the poem once or more than once?

Ⓐ Repeat your Ⓐ section rhythm!

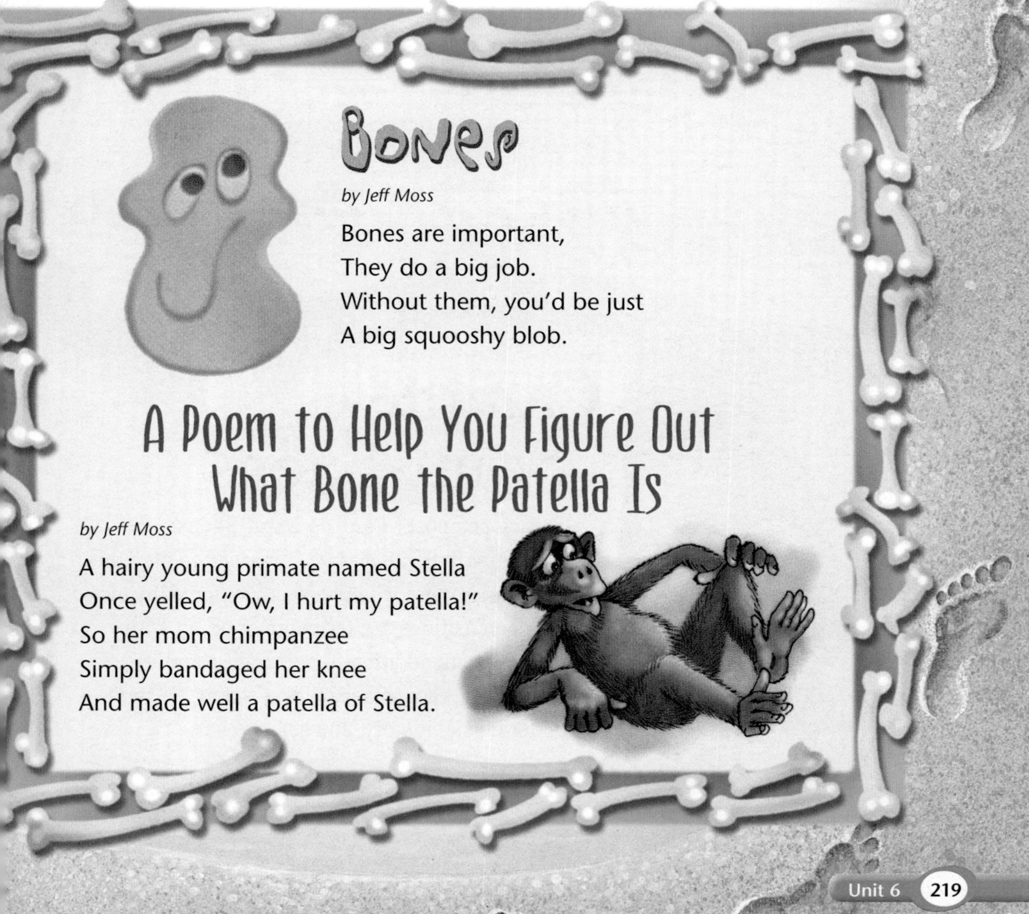

### Bones

*by Jeff Moss*

Bones are important,
They do a big job.
Without them, you'd be just
A big squooshy blob.

### A Poem to Help You Figure Out What Bone the Patella Is

*by Jeff Moss*

A hairy young primate named Stella
Once yelled, "Ow, I hurt my patella!"
So her mom chimpanzee
Simply bandaged her knee
And made well a patella of Stella.

Unit 6 219

# 1 Introduce

Invite students to explore the art on pp. 218–219. Read the poems on p. 219 as a class. Discuss bones, and why we have bones. See how many of the bones of the human body students can name.

# 2 Develop

### Reading

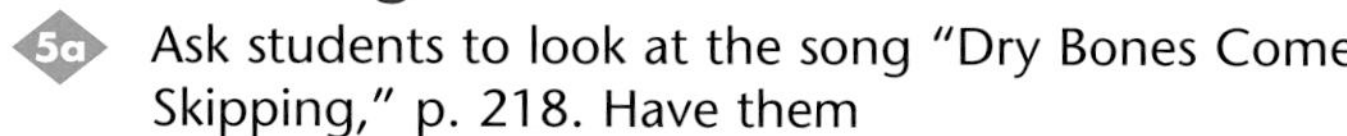

5a Ask students to look at the song "Dry Bones Come Skipping," p. 218. Have them

- Tap and say the rhythm of the first line, then compare it to the second line. (They are similar.)
- Tap and say the rhythm of the third line, then compare it to the fourth line. (They are similar.)
- Tap and say the rhythm of the entire song.

6b ASK **Where does the song end?** (at the end of the second line)

**What symbols in the music tell you that this is the end of the song?** (the double bar line and the word *Fine*)

**Which symbol tells you to go back to the beginning?** (*D.C.*, which is *da capo,* or "the head," in Italian)

### Singing

1b Invite students to sing "Dry Bones Come Skipping" **CD 9-15.** For a related reading and singing activity, see Resource Book p. E-23.

### Creating

6a ASK **Which part of "Dry Bones Come Skipping" do you sing twice?** (the A section)

**What is the form of the song?** (ABA)

continued on page 220

## Movement

6e ▶ **Game Song** Invite students to learn this singing game for "Dry Bones Come Skipping."

Have students sit in a circle. To prepare for passing a bone (for example, a rubber dog bone), have students tap the beat with their right hands, first in front of themselves and then in front of the person to their right as they sing. Say the words *pick* and *pass* to cue students about when to pass.

A section: Pass the bone to right. The student holding the bone at the end of the A section keeps it.

B section: Student with the bone taps it on his or her knee, and his or her name is sung in the song.

A section: Passing the bone resumes. Remind students that the bone should be in front of them on the word *dry*.

## Meeting Individual Needs

▶ **Reluctant Singers** Singing solo within the context of a game provides a safety net for reluctant or self-conscious singers. When "Dry Bones Come Skipping" is familiar, use the singing game as an opportunity to listen to individual singing voices. Have the class sing the first half of each B section phrase as a call, and the student holding the bone sing the second half of the phrase as a solo response. For example:

Class: *Some of them bones are Adam's bones,*

Adam: *Some of them bones are mine.*

Make notes about singing voices and offer supportive feedback during this and other singing activities.

 Invite students to create pieces in ABA form. Following the directions on p. 219, have small groups of students

- Compose an A section using familiar rhythms in quadruple meter, then perform it using body percussion or nonpitched percussion instruments.
- Choose a poem from p. 219 and perform it by speaking or singing. Add movement or instrument accompaniment, and perform the poem and the accompaniment as the B section.
- Practice and perform their ABA compositions for the class.

As groups perform their compositions, have classmates give feedback on whether each composition has met the ABA criterion.

### Reading

**ASK What is a fossil?** (It is the remains of a plant or animal that lived anywhere from thousands to millions of years ago. Most fossils are found in sedimentary rock.)

Share information in Across the Curriculum on p. 221.

**SAY** A composer named Camille Saint-Saëns wrote a piece of music called *Fossils,* but he was thinking of old songs, not old bones. (See Spotlight On, p. 220.)

Have students

- Tap the rhythm of the body percussion pattern on p. 220 or from an overhead transparency.
- Perform the body percussion parts as indicated.

### Listening

Play the first minute of *Fossils* **CD 9-20.** Have students

- Identify the rhythm when they hear it.
- Identify the instrument that plays the rhythm. (xylophone)
- Categorize the instrument by family. (percussion)

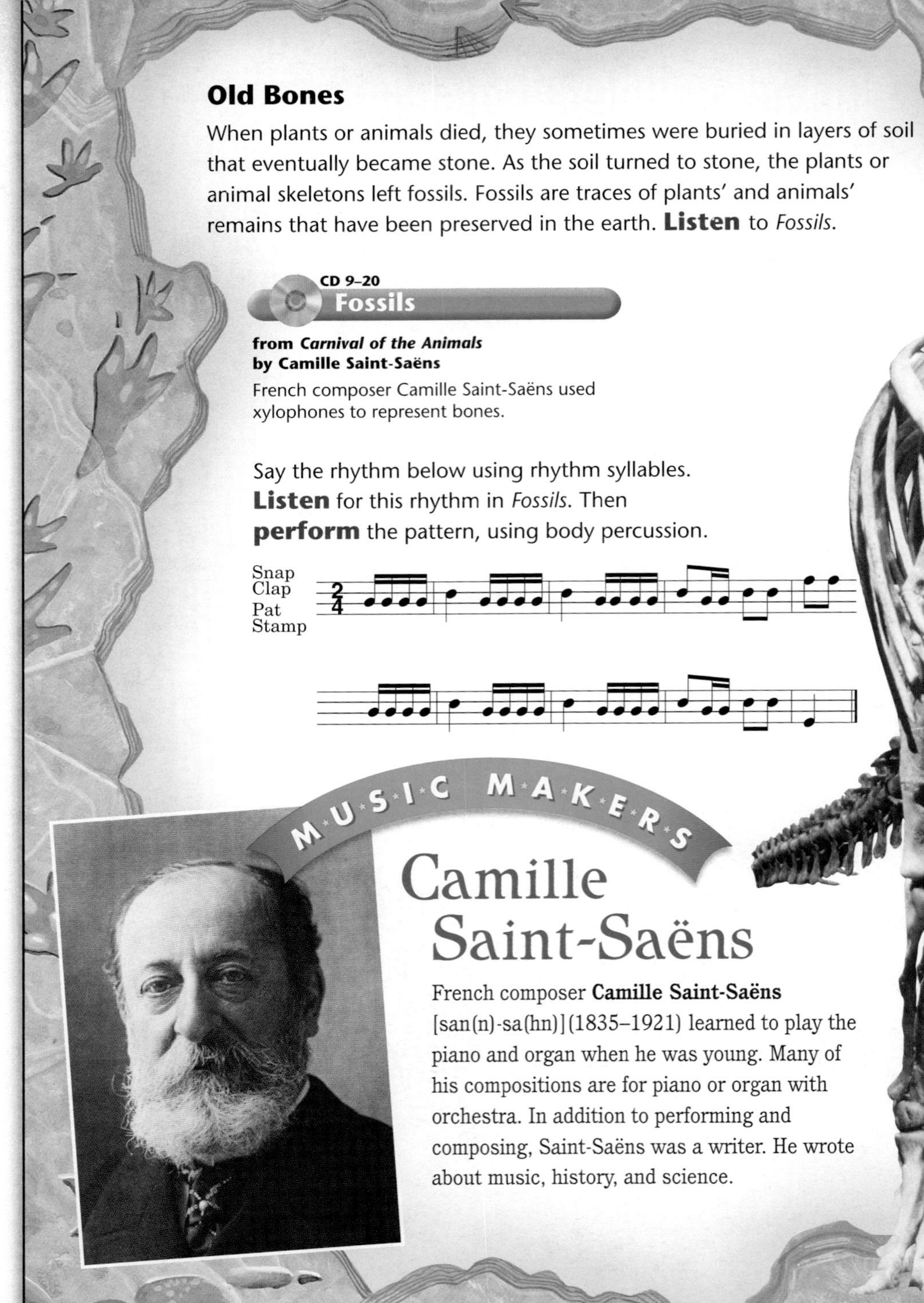

## Old Bones

When plants or animals died, they sometimes were buried in layers of soil that eventually became stone. As the soil turned to stone, the plants or animal skeletons left fossils. Fossils are traces of plants' and animals' remains that have been preserved in the earth. **Listen** to *Fossils.*

CD 9-20
**Fossils**

**from *Carnival of the Animals* by Camille Saint-Saëns**

French composer Camille Saint-Saëns used xylophones to represent bones.

Say the rhythm below using rhythm syllables. **Listen** for this rhythm in *Fossils.* Then **perform** the pattern, using body percussion.



MUSIC MAKERS

## Camille Saint-Saëns

French composer **Camille Saint-Saëns** [san(n)-sa(hn)] (1835–1921) learned to play the piano and organ when he was young. Many of his compositions are for piano or organ with orchestra. In addition to performing and composing, Saint-Saëns was a writer. He wrote about music, history, and science.

220 Reading Sequence 22

# Footnotes

## SKILLS REINFORCEMENT

5b ▶ **Reading** In addition to providing a review of familiar rhythms, "Dry Bones Come Skipping" is a good song for reviewing pitch reading skills. Have students

- Identify the starting and ending pitch as *do.*
- Sing the first measure of the song, using hand signs and pitch syllables and compare them to find the similar melody.
- Sing the second measure of the song using hand signs and pitch syllables and compare them to find the two different phrase endings.
- Sing the entire song using hand signs and pitch syllables.

## SPOTLIGHT ON

▶ **The Listening Selection** *Carnival of the Animals* is a funny musical zoo in which composer Camille Saint-Saëns uses sound to paint a portrait of different animals (and some people, too!). Saint-Saëns wrote the piece just for fun, for his friends and pupils. He didn't consider it good enough to play in public, and he would probably be quite dismayed to know that it is now one of his best-known and most popular pieces. Besides fossils, the piece also includes beautiful swans, majestic lions, bouncy kangaroos, braying mules, and dancing elephants, among others.

### Create a Fossil Rap

Fossils give us clues about plants and animals that lived many years ago. Much of what we know about dinosaurs comes from studying their fossilized bones.

Use "Gotta Find a Footprint" to **create** a rap in A B A C A D A form.

## Gotta Find a Footprint

*by Jeff Moss*

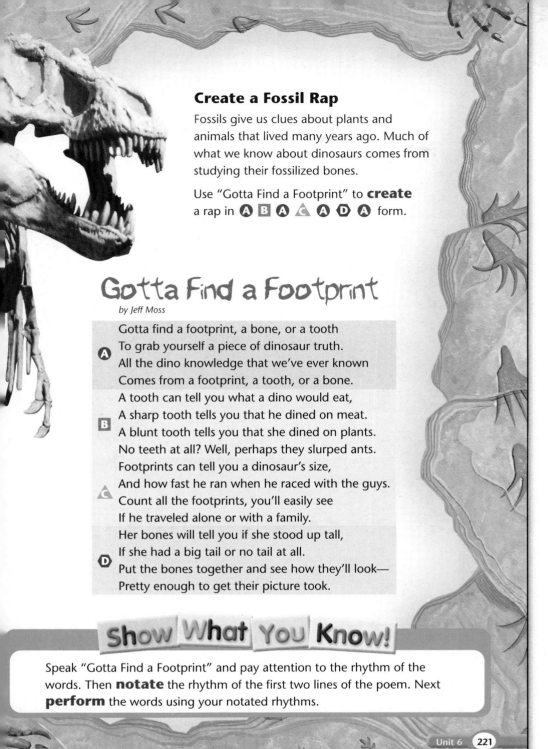

A
Gotta find a footprint, a bone, or a tooth
To grab yourself a piece of dinosaur truth.
All the dino knowledge that we've ever known
Comes from a footprint, a tooth, or a bone.

B
A tooth can tell you what a dino would eat,
A sharp tooth tells you that he dined on meat.
A blunt tooth tells you that she dined on plants.
No teeth at all? Well, perhaps they slurped ants.

C
Footprints can tell you a dinosaur's size,
And how fast he ran when he raced with the guys.
Count all the footprints, you'll easily see
If he traveled alone or with a family.

D
Her bones will tell you if she stood up tall,
If she had a big tail or no tail at all.
Put the bones together and see how they'll look—
Pretty enough to get their picture took.

### Show What You Know!

Speak "Gotta Find a Footprint" and pay attention to the rhythm of the words. Then **notate** the rhythm of the first two lines of the poem. Next **perform** the words using your notated rhythms.



**SAY** This rhythm is in the A section of *Fossils*.

Play the recording again, and have students

- Move to the rhythm each time they hear it.
- Keep track of how many A sections they hear.

**ASK How many A sections did you hear?** (three)

**What is the difference between the first two A sections and the third one?** (The rhythm is repeated in the first two A sections, but only performed once in the last A section.)

**What is the form of *Fossils?*** (rondo, or ABACA)

**What "old" tunes did you hear in the B section?** ("Twinkle, Twinkle" and "At Pierrot's Door")

### Creating

Help students learn the poem "Gotta Find a Footprint" by echo speaking the poem after you. Divide the class into four groups, one group for each section of the poem: A, B, C, or D. Write the letters of the rondo form ABACADA on the board. Point to each lettered section as students read the appropriate part of the poem, to effect a rondo performance.

For additional practice with rhythm, have students do the Show What You Know! on p. 221. Refer to Resource Book p. B-20.

## 3 Close

**Skill: CREATING** | **ASSESSMENT**

**Performance/Observation** Invite students to create four-measure body percussion ostinatos using familiar rhythm patterns. Then have students create an ABA speech piece by performing the four-measure body percussion part for A sections and reciting or singing one of the short poems on p. 219 as the B section. Observe students' ability to perform accurately the rhythm patterns in the piece they created.

### Across the Curriculum

► **Science** Suggest that students visit a local museum and look at fossils. Fossils are bones of animals and traces of plants that have been preserved. Saint-Saëns "preserved" some old tunes by using them in his composition *Fossils*. Encourage students to ask museum staff to share with them how they preserve the fossils in their collection.

Explain to students that fossils are the record books of the history of life on Earth. Fossils can help explain many things, such as why and when a certain kind of organism became extinct, where oil may be found underground and the way that organisms have changed gradually over many years. Fossils also help geologists identify the type of soil in which they are found. Fossils may even help us to understand ancient life on other planets.

### Technology/Media Link

4b

**Sequencing Software** Have students use sequencing software to compose a four-part ostinato.

- Review the pitches of the F-pentatonic scale.
- Have students work in pairs to sequence four measures in four different tracks using the pitches of the F-pentatonic scale.
- Loop the sequence playback and play it as the class sings "Dry Bones Come Skipping."
- During the performance, students may turn tracks on and off to vary the texture of the accompaniment.

LESSON
Core 5

## LESSON AT A GLANCE

**Element Focus** **FORM** Theme and variations

**Skill Objective** **LISTENING** Perform a body percussion pattern to accompany the main melody (theme) of a theme and variations

**Connection Activity** **CULTURE** Discuss the significance of the *balalaika* to Russian culture and compare it to other string instruments

**MATERIALS**

- "*Minka*" (Ukrainian) **CD 9-21**
- "*Minka*" (English) **CD 9-22**

  **Recording Routine:** Intro (4 m.); vocal; instrumental with variations; interlude (1 m.); vocal; instrumental
- **Pronunciation Practice/Translation** p. 482
- "Russian Sailors' Dance" from *The Red Poppy* **CD 9-26**
- **Dance Directions** for *"Minka"* p. 511
- **Resource Book** p. A-21
- xylophones or keyboards

**VOCABULARY**

theme and variations *balalaika*

**National Standards**

- **2f** Play instruments independently against contrasting parts
- **4b** Compose or arrange songs or instrumental pieces within specific guidelines
- **5a** Read rhythms in duple and quadruple meters
- **6b** Describe music by moving to it
- **6d** Identify the sounds of instruments from various cultures
- **6e** While listening to music, move to show a prominent feature of the music
- **8b** Identify ways music relates to other school subjects

**MORE MUSIC CHOICES**

Other songs from Russia:

*"Ai Dunaiĭ moy,"* p. 293

*"Beriozka,"* p. 294

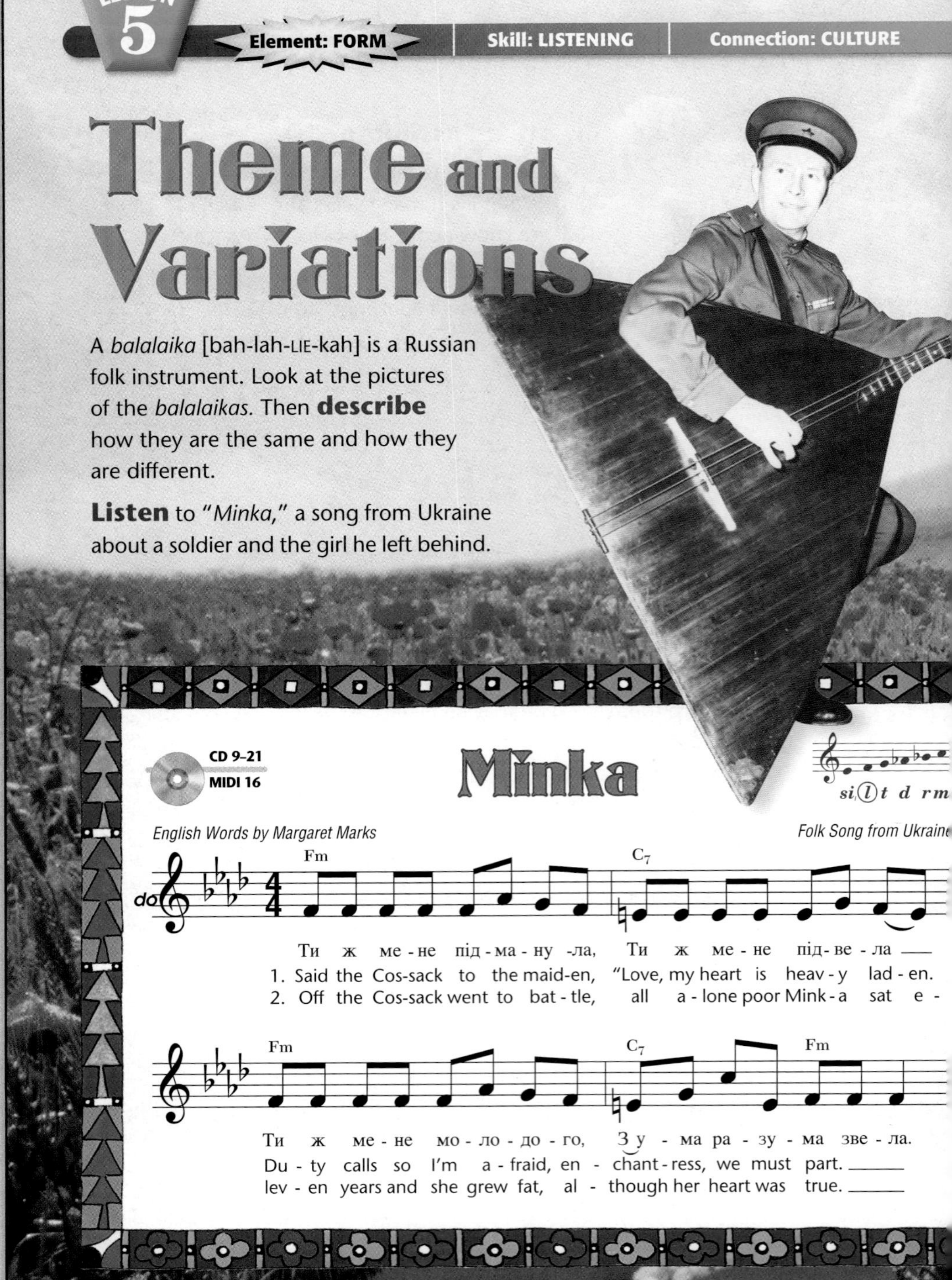
LESSON 5 Element: FORM | Skill: LISTENING | Connection: CULTURE

# Theme and Variations

A *balalaika* [bah-lah-LIE-kah] is a Russian folk instrument. Look at the pictures of the *balalaikas*. Then **describe** how they are the same and how they are different.

**Listen** to "*Minka*," a song from Ukraine about a soldier and the girl he left behind.

CD 9-21
MIDI 16

## Minka

English Words by Margaret Marks

Folk Song from Ukraine

si ⓛ t d r m
do
Fm
C7
Ти ж ме - не під - ма - ну -ла, Ти ж ме - не під - ве - ла
1. Said the Cos-sack to the maid-en, "Love, my heart is heav - y lad - en.
2. Off the Cos-sack went to bat - tle, all a - lone poor Mink - a sat e -
Fm
C7
Fm
Ти ж ме - не мо - ло - до - го, З у - ма ра - зу - ма зве - ла.
Du - ty calls so I'm a - fraid, en - chant - ress, we must part.
lev - en years and she grew fat, al - though her heart was true.

222

# Footnotes

## MOVEMENT

▶ **Patterned Dance** Invite students to learn a patterned dance to perform with the Ukrainian song "*Minka*" **CD 9-21.** Refer to Dance Directions on p. 511. Ask students to also perform the dance steps for the Armenian song *Gakavik*, on p. 14. Then discuss how the two dance patterns from these diverse cultures are similar. (Both use step-kick patterns.)

## BUILDING SKILLS THROUGH MUSIC

▶ **Writing** Have students listen again to *Russian Sailors' Dance* and then write a paragraph describing such elements as the rhythm, the instruments used, and the form.

## CULTURAL CONNECTION

▶ ***Balalaika*** The *balalaika* is one of the most popular folk instruments in Russia. The body of the instrument has a triangular shape with three strings. The neck is long and has frets to guide finger placement. The size of the *balalaika* and its tuning varies according to the region of Russia in which the instrument is made and played. Different sizes of *balalaikas* have different names, such as piccolo, prime, and bass. Most people think of the *balalaika* as an instrument for accompanying folk songs and dances. However, *balalaika* orchestras were also popular in Russia in the late nineteenth and early twentieth centuries. The *balalaika* is a symbol of Russian culture, but it is also enjoyed by neighboring countries.

### Variety Is the Spice of Life

**Sing** *"Minka."* The melody of the song can be called a **theme.** Now think of a way to vary or change *"Minka."* How will you make the theme different? Will you change the dynamics, tempo, melody, rhythm, or timbre of the music? Practice your **variation,** then **perform** it for the class. Be ready to explain how you made your variation.

**Theme** is an important melody that occurs several times in a piece of music. **Variation** is music that is repeated, but changed in some important way.

A♭ E♭
Ти ж ме - не під - ма - ну - ла, Ти ж ме - не під - ве - ла
I be-seech you fair - est Mink - a, wait for me, I hate to think an -
When at last her Cos-sack lov - er came back home and looked her o - ver,
Fm C7 Fm
Ти ж ме - не мо - ло - до - го, З у - ма ра - зу - ма зве - ла.
oth - er man might come and tink - er with your faith - ful heart!"
he be - gan to court an - oth - er. Broke her heart in two!

**MIDI** Use the *"Minka"* song file with sequencing software to create variations of the melody.

# 1 Introduce

Have students compare the shapes and designs of the *balalaikas* pictured in their books to other string instruments they are familiar with. Use students' responses to help them conclude that the *balalaika* is categorized as a string instrument. Then ask students to describe the similarities and differences among the *balalaikas.*

**SAY** The *balalaika* is a string instrument from Russia.

 Play *"Minka"* **CD 9-21** and encourage students to listen for the sound of the *balalaika.*

Share with students the information on the *balalaika* and its Russian cultural significance in Cultural Connection, p. 222.

# 2 Develop

## Singing

5a Have students

- Read (clap and say) the rhythm of *"Minka."*
- Sing the song with **CD 9-21.**
- Describe what happens to the tempo of the song. (tempo gets faster)

Teach the pronunciation of *"Minka"* using the Pronunciation Practice **CD 9-24**. Refer to Resource Book p. A-21 for a Pronunciation Practice Guide.

## Playing

 Invite students to play an accompaniment for *"Minka"* on xylophones.

Have students

- Sing and move to the pattern. Pat right hand on leg for the pitch F and left hand on leg for C.
- Sing *"Minka"* **CD 9-21** and move to the pattern.

**continued on page 224**

## Skills Reinforcement

2f ▶ **Playing** Add the following percussion ostinatos to the accompaniment for *"Minka."* Have students move to show the rhythm of the ostinato while they sing the song. Then guide them in transferring their movements to the instruments.

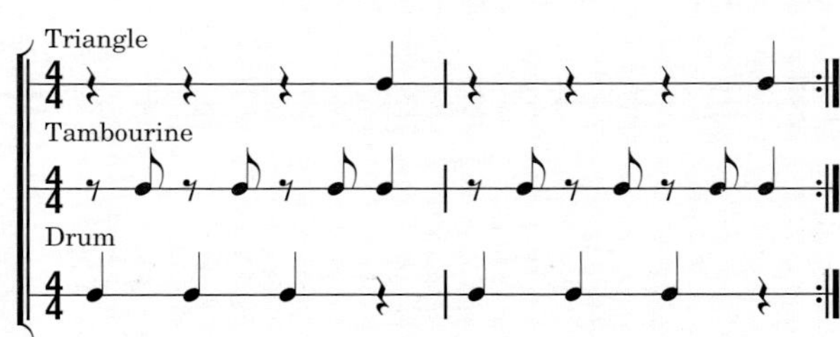

Triangle
Tambourine
Drum

## Spotlight On

▶ ***The Red Poppy*** The listening selection *Russian Sailors' Dance,* on p. 224, is from a ballet called *The Red Poppy,* written by Reinhold Glière (1875–1956) in 1927 and premiered by the Bolshoi Ballet. The story is about a dancer who gives her life for the good of her country. *The Red Poppy* brought Glière international fame. The *Russian Sailors' Dance* is one of Glière's few pieces that is performed outside the former Soviet Union today. Like many of Glière's works, the music is based on Russian folk song themes. Because of Glière's style of writing, he was very popular with the Soviet authorities and did not suffer persecution as some other composers did at the hands of the Soviets.

- Transfer movements to xylophones and play the pattern.
- Play the accompaniment with the song.

See Skills Reinforcement on p. 223 for percussion accompaniments.

### Creating

**SAY** Changing the tempo and adding an accompaniment are two ways to vary a song.

**ASK** **How else could we vary *"Minka"*?** (Accept a variety of answers.)

4b Divide students into groups of four or five. Have each group create and perform its own version of *"Minka."* Encourage the class to listen and describe how each group varied the theme.

### Moving

5a Invite students to read the rhythm of the body percussion pattern at the bottom of p. 224. Have them

- Clap and say the rhythm.
- Move to the rhythm, using the body percussion indicated.

**SAY** This is the rhythm of the main melody of a composition called *Russian Sailors' Dance* by Reinhold Glière.

Share with students information from Spotlight On, p. 223.

### Listening

6e Play the first minute of *Russian Sailors' Dance* **CD 9-26,** and have students

- Signal when they hear the rhythm of the theme.
- Move to the theme, using the body percussion pattern.

**SAY** Listen to the entire piece this time and listen for all the ways that the theme is changed or varied.

Play *Russian Sailors' Dance* and have students write about what they hear happening in each variation as they listen. After listening,

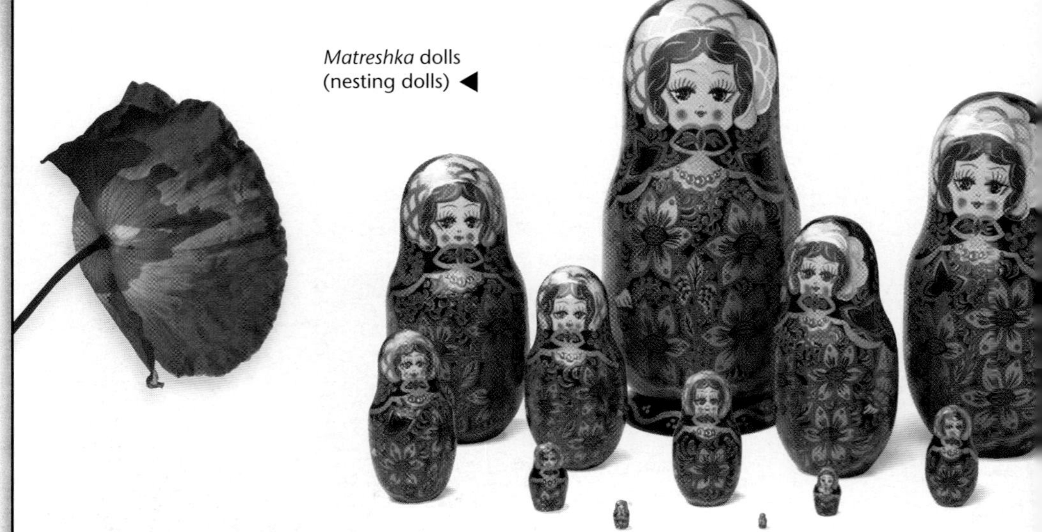

*Matreshka* dolls (nesting dolls) ◀

### Russian Variations

Tap the rhythm of Glière's theme as you **listen** to *Russian Sailors' Dance.*

**from *The Red Poppy***
**by Reinhold Glière**

In this piece, Russian composer Reinhold Glière wrote variations on a theme.

**Theme and variations** is musical form in which each section is a variation of the original theme.

**Move** to the rhythm of the theme using body percussion.

Now **listen** for the **theme and variations.**
How many variations do you hear?



## Footnotes

### ACROSS THE CURRICULUM

8b ▶ **Related Arts** Engage students in a visual arts-based theme-and-variations activity. Collect a variety of plates and photographs of plates—cafeteria plates, everyday plates, china, decorative plates, and so on. Have students describe the similarities and differences among the plates. Look at shape, size, design, color, material, and purpose. Then make a variety of sizes of durable paper plates available to the students. Have them design their own plates by adding decorations using markers, colored pencils, crayons, paper, string, or other objects. Have each student write a card explaining the design and purpose of his or her plate. Create a "Variations on a Plate" display to showcase students' work.

### SKILLS REINFORCEMENT

▶ **Playing** Play the scale shown below on xylophones or keyboards. Note that the last four notes of the scale are repeated. Invite students to play the scale as a countermelody to the theme of *Russian Sailors' Dance*. Tell students that this countermelody makes up the main contour of the melody.

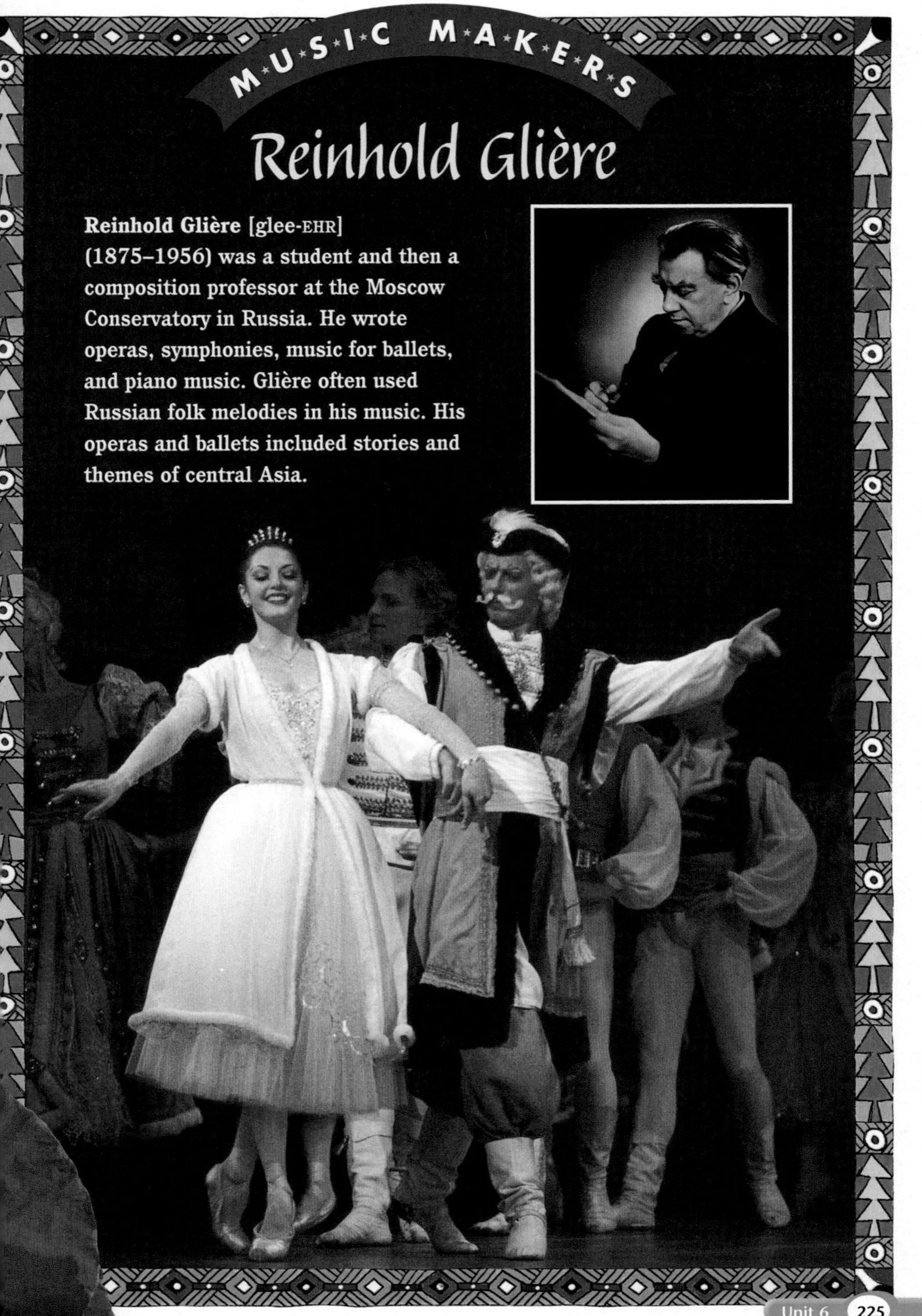

MUSIC MAKERS

## Reinhold Glière

**Reinhold Glière** [glee-EHR] (1875–1956) was a student and then a composition professor at the Moscow Conservatory in Russia. He wrote operas, symphonies, music for ballets, and piano music. Glière often used Russian folk melodies in his music. His operas and ballets included stories and themes of central Asia.

Unit 6 225

**SAY** The form of *Russian Sailors' Dance* is called theme and variations. The main melody is the theme.

**ASK How was the theme varied?** (Accept answers that describe changes in tempo, dynamics, instruments, rhythm, and melody.)

### Creating

 Invite students to create a class theme and variations.

As a class, have students

- Write a rhythm pattern, 8 to 16 measures long, that will serve as a theme.
- Clap the theme together.

Then divide the class into groups of four or five. Have each group

- Create a variation on the class theme, changing dynamics, tempo, and/or instruments, or by adding movement.
- Perform its variation for the rest of the class.

Invite the class to arrange all of the group variations to create a theme and variations. Begin with a class performance of the theme and then the variations in the order the students have determined. Practice the theme and variations, then record the students' performance.

## 3 CLOSE

**Element: FORM** ASSESSMENT

 **Performance/Observation** Have students listen to *Russian Sailors' Dance* and perform the body percussion pattern on p. 224 with the theme each time the theme returns. Have students change some aspect of the way they perform the pattern during each variation to match the mood of that variation; for example, enlarge the movements and change posture if they hear a slow, loud variation. Observe students' ability to listen and respond to changes from section to section and to play with the recording.

### SPOTLIGHT ON

**▶ Russian Nesting Boxes** Nesting boxes, like the dolls pictured at the top of p. 224, have been made in Russia for over a hundred years. The Chinese invented nesting boxes about a thousand years ago. Starting with the largest doll, each doll contains another, which contains another, and so on, until the last one, which contains only a grain of rice. The Russians discovered this Chinese art form in the 1800s and began making the dolls, which they call *Matreshka* (Russian for "mother") dolls. The outer shape of the doll is cut while it turns on a lathe; this shape is cut in half and the inside of each half is carved out to create a thin shell. Then traditional woman's clothing is hand painted on the doll. Russian artists carved and presented 70 dolls for the World's Fair of 1900 in Paris, and since then the dolls' popularity has soared worldwide.

### SCHOOL TO HOME CONNECTION

**▶ Art Objects from Other Lands** Invite students to search their homes for an art object from another country, such as a set of Russian nesting dolls. Students may ask parents or older relatives where the object is from, how it was made, if it is a piece of fine art or folk art, and so on. If permission is granted, students may bring the object to class and tell about it.

### TECHNOLOGY/MEDIA LINK

**Notation Software** Invite students to use notation software to create their own variations on the main melody of *Russian Sailors' Dance*. Have them set up a staff and notate the melody, as shown on p. 224. As students alter rhythmic values and pitches, have them save each version as a separate variation.

## LESSON AT A GLANCE

**Element Focus** **MELODY** Melodic sequence

**Skill Objective** **CREATING** Create movements to show melodic sequence

**Connection Activity** **RELATED ARTS** Explore textile production as an art form in Africa

**MATERIALS**

- *"Thula, thula, ngoana"* **CD 9-27**
- "Sleep, Sleep, Baby" **CD 9-28**
  **Recording Routine:** Intro (4 m.); vocal; instrumental; vocal; coda
- **Music Reading Practice, Sequence 23** **CD 9-31**
- **Pronunciation Practice/Translation** p. 483
- *"Tengo, tengo, tengo"* **CD 9-35**
- "I Have Three Sheep" **CD 9-36**
  **Recording Routine:** Intro (8 m.); v. 1; v. 2; instrumental; v. 1; v. 2; coda
- **Pronunciation Practice/Translation** p. 483
- *Slavonic Dance, Op. 46, No. 1* (excerpt) **CD 9-34**
- **Resource Book** pp. A-22, A-23, B-20, E-24, G-12
- glockenspiels, woodblock, bass xylophone

**VOCABULARY**

melodic sequence

### ◆ ◆ ◆ ◆ National Standards ◆ ◆ ◆ ◆

**1c** Sing from memory songs from diverse cultures
**2b** Perform melodies on appropriate instruments
**2c** Play instruments expressively on a variety of pieces
**4b** Compose pieces within specific guidelines
**5b** Read notes in treble clef using syllables
**6b** Describe music by answering questions about it
**9d** Describe the roles of musicians in various settings and cultures

**MORE MUSIC CHOICES**

Another song with melodic sequences:
"Wings of a Dove," p. 318

LESSON 6 | Element: MELODY | Skill: CREATING | Connection: RELATED ARTS

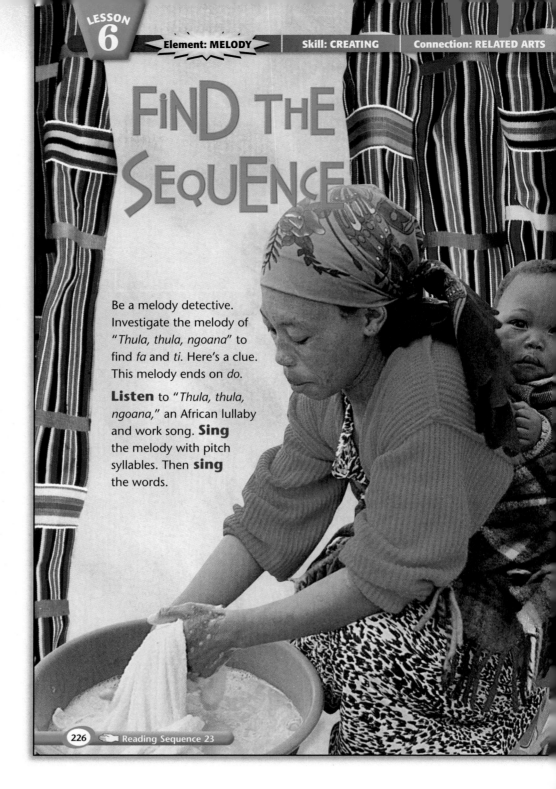

# FIND THE SEQUENCE

Be a melody detective. Investigate the melody of *"Thula, thula, ngoana"* to find *fa* and *ti.* Here's a clue. This melody ends on *do.*

**Listen** to *"Thula, thula, ngoana,"* an African lullaby and work song. **Sing** the melody with pitch syllables. Then **sing** the words.

226 Reading Sequence 23

# Footnotes

## CULTURAL CONNECTION

9d ▶ **Lullabies and Work Songs** *"Thula, thula, ngoana"* ("Sleep, Sleep, Baby") is an example of a song that serves more than one purpose. It is both a lullaby and a song for working. The rhythm of the song and the movements that go with it can both comfort a child and keep a rhythm going for work. Ask students to think of and share lullabies and work songs they know. Who sings these songs? When? Why?

## BUILDING SKILLS THROUGH MUSIC

▶ **Math** Invite students to devise a pair of four-digit numerical sequences, using the numbers 1–7, and then explain the pattern used to create the sequence. Help students choose a key, transfer their numerical sequences to staff notation (the first note of the scale is "1"), and then perform them.

## ACROSS THE CURRICULUM

▶ **Related Arts** To help students explore the art and meaning behind textile production in Africa, share these two colorful and informative books.

*The Art of African Textiles* by Duncan Clarke (Thunder Bay Press, 1997) offers photographs of all the major African national styles, including the raffia style of Zaire, the royal Kente cloth of Ashanti kings, and the ceremonial fabrics of the Yoruba people.

*Technology, Tradition and Lurex: The Art of Textiles in Africa* edited by John Picton (Antique Collector's Club, 1996), was published to go with the Barbican Art Gallery Exhibition for the Africa '95 Season, and covers 150 years of textile making.

CD 9-27
THULA, THULA, NGOANA
(Sleep, Sleep, Baby)
Folk Song from the Lesotho Region of South Africa
t, d r m f s
Thu - la, thu - la, ngoa - na, thu - la, thu - la, ngoa - na,
Sleep my lit - tle ba - by, sleep my lit - tle ba - by,
Thu - la, thu - la, ngoa - na, thu - la, thu - la, ngoa - na.
Sleep my lit - tle ba - by, sleep my lit - tle ba - by.

## Sing and Sequence

**Sing** *"Thula, thula, ngoana"* again. Trace the shape of the melody as you sing. Notice the shape, or contour, of the first two measures. How many times does this contour occur in the rest of the melody?

**Describe** what happens to the starting note each time the contour pattern is repeated. The pattern you have found is a **melodic sequence.**

A **melodic sequence** is a melody pattern that begins on a different pitch each time it is repeated.

**Create** movements to show the melodic sequence of *"Thula, thula, ngoana."*

## Hear a Sequence

**Listen** for melodic sequences in this music. The most obvious sequence starts immediately after the loud opening chord.

CD 9-34

**Slavonic Dance, Op. 46, No. 1**

**by Antonin Dvořák**

The folk dances of Bohemia inspired Dvořák to compose this music. This region is now part of the Czech Republic.

# 1 Introduce

Invite students to study the colorful African textiles used as background art on p. 226. Point out that one of the kinds of work possibly done while singing *"Thula, thula, ngoana"* is producing fabric. To explore the art of African textiles, see Across the Curriculum on p. 226.

# 2 Develop

### Reading

5b Direct students to look at *"Thula, thula, ngoana."* Have them identify the first pitch of the song as *mi*, and read and sing mm. 1–2 using the system of hand signs and pitch syllables. Ask students to read about sequences on p. 227 in their books.

ASK **How many times does the pattern repeat?** (four)

**What happens each time the pattern is repeated?** (It starts one pitch lower.)

Use the Pronunciation Practice **CD 9-30** to teach students how to pronounce the words of *"Thula, thula, ngoana,"* and refer to Resource Book p. A-22 for a Pronunciation Practice Guide.

Have students sing *"Thula, thula, ngoana"* with **CD 9-27.**

For a related *"Thula, thula, ngoana"* reading activity, see p. 453 and Resource Book p. E-24.

### Moving

Have students read the information about *"Thula, thula, ngoana"* on p. 226. Invite them to think of some kind of work that a person might do while singing *"Thula, thula, ngoana."* Have students create a movement that illustrates the work they chose and also reflects the level of the melodic sequence.

See Skills Reinforcement below for practice in creating and performing a melody pattern.

continued on page 228

## Skills Reinforcement

2b ▶ **Creating** For a warm-up activity, have students do the Show What You Know! on p. 229. Refer to Resource Book p. B-20. Then have students create and notate a two-measure melody pattern, then move the whole pattern to three different pitch levels. Invite them to read and play the patterns they created. Have them

- Tap the rhythm.
- Sing the pitches, using hand signs and pitch syllables.
- Find the pitches on a xylophone.
- Play the patterns.
- Play the patterns while singing the song.

## Spotlight On

▶ **The Composer** Antonín Dvořák (1841–1904) was born near Prague, in what is now the Czech Republic. His parents wanted him to become a butcher, like his father, and sent him off to learn the trade. Soon, however, he left his job and went to Prague to study music. After a successful public performance of one of his compositions, Dvořák applied for a government stipend for musicians, and he included a score of one of his symphonies with the application. The judges, including Johannes Brahms, were so impressed by the power of Dvořák's music that they granted him a three-year stipend.

Dvořák came to the United States in 1892 and stayed until 1895. He traveled throughout the country and spent a summer in a Czech community in Spillville, Iowa, where his visit is still celebrated.

### Listening

See Spotlight On, p. 227, and Cultural Connection, below, to share information with students on composer Antonín Dvořák and *Slavonic Dance, Op. 46, No. 1* **CD 9-34.** Familiarize students with the main theme (mm. 1–4 below) and its sequence (mm. 5–8) before playing the recording.

Students may also recognize the appearance of a shorter, two-measure melodic sequence that begins at 0:25.

Ask students to read the opening paragraph on p. 228. Then have them

- Listen to *"Tengo, tengo, tengo"* **CD 9-35**.
- Compare the song to *"Thula, thula, ngoana"* **CD 9-27**.

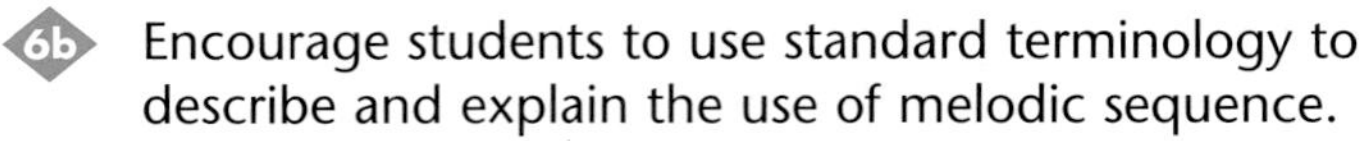

6b Encourage students to use standard terminology to describe and explain the use of melodic sequence.

**ASK How are these songs from two diverse cultures similar?** (They both contain a melodic sequence.)

**How is the sequence in *"Tengo, tengo tengo"* different?** (The repeating pattern is longer; it has two sections.)

### Singing

1c Have students sing *"Tengo, tengo, tengo"* while conducting a two-beat pattern.

**ASK What are the words in the first half of the sequence?** (*Tengo, tengo tengo*)

**What are the words in the second half?** (*y tú no tienes nada*)

## *Tengo una secuencia* (I Have a Sequence)

Sheepherding was a major occupation of the early Spanish settlers in New Mexico. Shepherds probably made up songs like *"Tengo, tengo, tengo"* to pass the time and to entertain one another.

**Listen** for the melodic sequence in this song. **Compare** this sequence to the melody pattern in *"Thula, thula, ngoana,"* on the previous page. How is it different? How is it the same?

Now **sing** or **play** the new sequence. To continue the sequence, **create** an additional two lines for the song. (You can end your melody by making the last note *do*.)

# Footnotes

## CULTURAL CONNECTION

▶ **Slavonic Dances** For centuries, Antonín Dvořák's native region of Bohemia had been under the strong political and cultural influence of Austria. It was this national "identity crisis," perhaps, that led Dvořák, along with Bedrich Smetana, to establish a Czech national school of music. The *Slavonic Dances* were just one result of his passionate interest in Czech folk songs and dances. *Op. 46, No. 1*, presented in this lesson, is labeled a *furiant*, a fast Czech folk dance with a repeated two-beat rhythm in a three-beat measure. Also represented throughout the collection is the *sousedka* (Czech waltz), *skocna* (leap dance), *spacirka* (strutting circle dance), and *kolo* (Serbian round dance).

▶ **Czech Culture** For a taste of Czech culture and traditions, read aloud the book *Eva's Summer Vacation: A Story of the Czech Republic* by Jan MacHalek (Soundprints, 1999).

## TEACHER TO TEACHER

▶ **Compare Sequences** Once students have been introduced to the concept of melodic sequence, they can discover sequences in other songs from diverse cultures. For example, have students sing and then describe and compare the sequences in "*Minka*" (p. 222) and "*Tanckovačka*" (p. 230) with those in "*Thula, thula, ngoana*" and "*Tengo, tengo, tengo*."

## Accompany the Sequence

**Play** the accompaniment below as others **sing** *"Tengo, tengo, tengo."* To help you get ready, follow these steps.

- Sing the bass xylophone part, using pitch syllables and then letter names. Then play it.
- Tap or clap the woodblock part, using rhythm syllables. Then play it.
- Play the glockenspiel part, first by itself and then with the other parts.

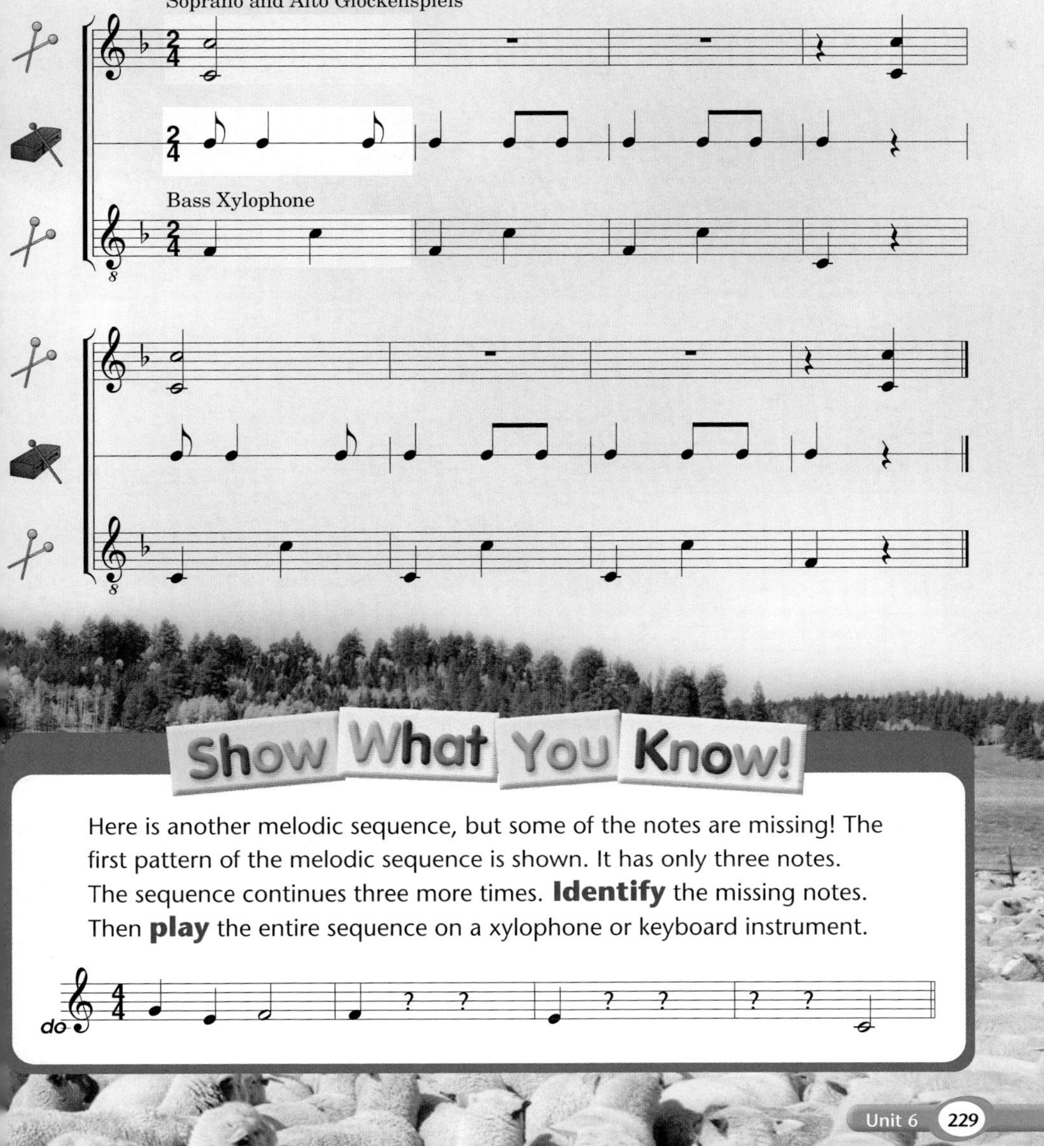


Here is another melodic sequence, but some of the notes are missing! The first pattern of the melodic sequence is shown. It has only three notes. The sequence continues three more times. **Identify** the missing notes. Then **play** the entire sequence on a xylophone or keyboard instrument.

Unit 6 229

Have students

- Sing the first part of the sequence with pitch syllables (*so-so-mi-mi-do-do*) and describe the way it moves. (It moves down by skips.)
- Sing the second part of the sequence with pitch syllables (*mi-do-do-re-mi-fa-re*) and describe the way it moves. (It begins with a skip down, moves up by steps, then ends with a skip down.)

### Playing

 Divide the class into two groups. Have

- Group 1 play line 1 of *"Tengo, tengo, tengo"* on melody instruments.
- Group 2 respond by playing the melodic sequence (line 2).
- Both groups create an interlude by playing the sequence two more times, moving the starting pitch down by a step each time, and ending on *do.*

Have students follow the procedure outlined on p. 229 to perform the mallet accompaniment to *"Tengo, tengo, tengo."*

For additional practice with melodic sequence, have students do the Show What You Know! on p. 229. Refer to Resource Book p. B-20.

## 3 Close

**Element: MELODY** ASSESSMENT

 **Performance/Observation** Have students sing *"Thula, thula, ngoana"* **CD 9-27** with eyes closed and perform their own created movements to show the descending sequence. Observe their ability to show the descending sequence independently.

### Skills Reinforcement

 ▶ **Creating** Many examples of melodic sequence are found in art music of great composers, and this important compositional device can also be used by young composers in the classroom. Begin by writing short melodic motives on cards, from which students can choose at random. Once the motive has been chosen, allow students to determine how the sequence should be repeated (up or down, by skip or step, or by repetition). Once the new melody is determined, invite students to decide on meter and rhythm. The new melody can then be sung or played on instruments, written in stick and staff notation, and text may be created by students. The teacher may help by adding harmony and accompaniment.

### Technology/Media Link

**Notation Software** Work with students to compose a musical sequence and notate it with notation software.

- Set up and display a music notation file.
- Suggest that students use the C-major scale for the composition and that they consider starting the composition on either C, E, or G.
- Have students tell you which pitches and rhythms to use to compose a one- or two-measure melody, then copy and paste the melody twice, at successively higher or lower pitches. Finally, compose an ending (suggest ending on C or E).
- Play back the melody.

LESSON 7

## LESSON AT A GLANCE

**Element Focus** **MELODY** Melodic sequence; practice *fa* and *ti*

**Skill Objective** **MOVING** Move to show music with and without melodic sequences

**Connection Activity** **CULTURE** Discuss how national clothing is an expression of national culture

**MATERIALS**

- "*Tancovačka*" **CD 9-39**
- "Dancing" **CD 9-40**

  **Recording Routine:** Intro (8 m.); vocal; interlude (4 m.); vocal; coda
- **Music Reading Practice, Sequence 24** **CD 9-43**
- **Pronunciation Practice/Translation** p. 483
- **Dance Directions** for *"Tancovačka"* p. 512
- **Resource Book** pp. A-24, E-25

**VOCABULARY**

melodic sequence

**National Standards**

**5a** Read rhythms in duple meter

**5b** Read notes in treble clef, using syllables

**6b** Describe music by answering questions about it, or moving to it

**MORE MUSIC CHOICES**

For more practice singing *fa* and *ti*:

"Clementine," p. 341

"We Shall Overcome," p. 326

# 1 INTRODUCE

Invite students to look at and discuss the clothing they and their classmates are wearing. Discuss the fact that clothes can express personality. In the same way, national clothing can express one side of a nation's cultural personality. See Cultural Connection below for further connection possibilities between clothing and culture.

LESSON 7 | Element: MELODY | Skill: MOVING | Connection: CULTURE

# A Slovak Melody

Slovak culture has a long history of folk songs and dances. Find a sequence in this Slovak melody. Look for lines that have a similar shape. Does the sequence move upward or downward? **Sing** *"Tancovačka"* and point to the sequences.

CD 9-39

## Tancovačka
### (Dancing)

Slovak Folk Song

VERSE s, l, t, (d) r m f s

Tan - cuj, tan - cuj, vy - krú - caj, vy - krú - caj,
Come and dance, turn light - ly, turn light - ly A -

Len mi pie - cku ne - zrú - caj, ne - zrú - caj.
round the camp - fire burn - ing so bright - ly. The

Do - brá pie - cka na zi - mu, na zi - mu,
snow falls fast and cold is the weath - er. Come

Ked' ne - má - me pe - ri - nu, pe - ri - nu.
dance, come dance, we'll ___ all turn to - geth - er.



## Footnotes

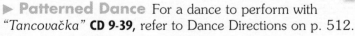

### MOVEMENT

▶ **Patterned Dance** For a dance to perform with *"Tancovačka"* **CD 9-39**, refer to Dance Directions on p. 512.

▶ **Locomotor Movements** Some students may have difficulty distinguishing left from right. This could pose problems in creating dance movements for *"Tancovačka."* If students are challanged by this, suggest dance ideas that do not require movements from left to right, such as moving in and out of the center of a circle.

### BUILDING SKILLS THROUGH MUSIC

▶ **Writing** After they have created their dance (see Moving, p. 231), have students

- Write the directions for another group to follow.
- Exchange papers and perform another group's dance.

### CULTURAL CONNECTION

▶ **National Clothing** Help students think of a way in which the clothes shown on pp. 230 and 231 might reflect the national personality of Slovak culture. For example, the free-flowing blousy skirt and shirts, which allow great freedom of movement, could illustrate the value of political and personal freedom.

Invite students to research other national clothing styles and relate the clothing to the history, traditions, and culture of the people. For example, many Native American cultural and religious values are directly reflected in their clothing.

REFRAIN
Tra la la la, La la la la,
La la la la, La la la la la,
Tra la la la, La la la la,
La la la la, La la la la la la la la la.

**Practice *fa* and *ti***

**Sing** the first four lines of *"Tancovačka"* again, this time using pitch syllables.

**Move** to show the melodic contour of *"Tancovačka."* Use a repeated movement to go with the melodic sequence in the first four lines. Use different movements for the last four lines of the song.

# 2 Develop

## Listening

Play *"Tancovačka"* **CD 9-39** and have students

- Follow the notation in their books.
- Look for a design, or pattern, in the song.

## Reading

5b 6b Identify the last note of the song as *do*. Then, have students identify the first note of the first line *(mi)*, second line *(re)*, and third line *(do)*, and sing the first three lines, using hand signs and pitch syllables.

ASK **How are the first three lines the same?** (The melodic contour is the same; the rhythm is the same.)

**How are the first three lines different?** (Each starts on a different pitch.)

**What is the name for a melodic pattern that moves down by step?** (sequence)

Play *"Tancovačka"* **CD 9-39** and invite students to sing along. See p. 453 and Resource Book p. E-25 for a related reading activity.

## Moving

6b Have students create a dance for *"Tancovačka."* Assign small groups the A section (first four lines) or the B section (last four lines) of the song. Have groups read the directions in their books, create movements for their section, and share their ideas with the class. Use these ideas to create a class dance for the entire song.

# 3 Close

**Element: MELODY** ASSESSMENT

**Performance/Observation** Have students sing *"Tancovačka"* **CD 9-39,** as they perform movements that show when they are singing a melodic sequence and when they are singing something other than a melodic sequence. Observe their ability to show the difference.

## Skills Reinforcement

5a ▶ **Reading** The rhythm of *"Tancovačka"* provides an excellent opportunity for reviewing rhythms. Have students find measures of rhythm that are the same. Then clap and say those measures. After practicing patterns, have them clap and say the entire melody.

To help develop fluency, concentration, and inner hearing, divide the class in half. Have one half of the class clap the even-numbered lines and the other half clap the odd-numbered lines. Students must concentrate and be ready to come in as each group finishes the previous line.

▶ **Singing** Invite students to listen to the Pronunciation Practice for *"Tancovačka"* **CD 9-42** and refer to Resource Book p. A-24 for the Pronunciation Practice Guide.

## Technology/Media Link

**CD-ROM** Reinforce listening skills for same and different melodies by having students play *Making More Music*'s "Melody" game. In small groups, have students

- Start the program in the school's computer lab or at their classroom computer learning center.
- Take turns selecting the "games" icon and playing the "Melody" game.
- Click the green arrow to start the game.
- Describe the differences between the melody patterns before choosing the correct answer.

LESSON Core 8

## LESSON AT A GLANCE

**Element Focus** **TIMBRE** Keyboard instrument timbre

**Skill Objective** **LISTENING** Identify timbres of different keyboard instruments

**Connection Activity** **STYLE** Listen to the styles of keyboard pieces from the past 300 years

**MATERIALS**

- "Gigue" from *French Suite No. 5* (excerpt) **CD 10-1**
- *Toccata in D Minor* **CD 10-2**
- *Waltz in D-flat* **CD 10-3**
- *Prelude in A Major* **CD 10-4**
- *Close Encounters of the Third Kind* (excerpt) **CD 10-5**
- **Resource Book** p. C-8
- xylophones, metallophones, glockenspiels, keyboards

**VOCABULARY**

harpsichord, organ, *pianoforte*, piano, synthesizer

**National Standards**

**3a** Improvise "answers" to given melodic phrases
**4c** Compose music using a variety of sound sources
**6b** Describe music by moving to it
**6d** Identify the sounds of instruments from various cultures
**6e** While listening to music, move to show a prominent feature of the music
**9a** Listen to identify music from different historical periods

**MORE MUSIC CHOICES**

Another example of keyboard timbre:
*Piano Trio No. 2, "Scherzo,"* p. 192



# KEYBOARD CLASSICS

The harpsichord is one of the oldest keyboard instruments. Harpsichords were popular in the 1600s and 1700s.

Although the harpsichord looks similar to a piano, it sounds much different. When you press a key on a harpsichord, the string inside is plucked by a quill. Originally, harpsichord quills were feathers. Today quills are made of leather or plastic.

**Listen** to the harpsichord in *Gigue* by Bach.

CD 10–1 **Gigue**

**from *French Suite No. 5* by Johann Sebastian Bach**

See page 113 for another *gigue* by Bach, played on violin.

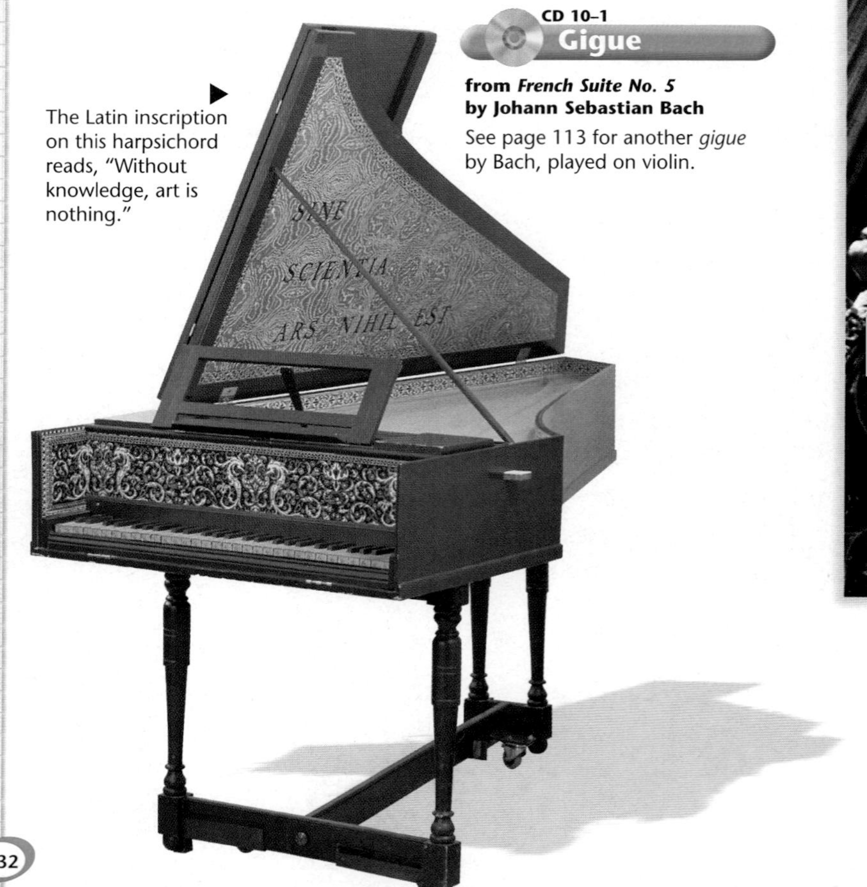


The Latin inscription on this harpsichord reads, "Without knowledge, art is nothing."

# Footnotes

## ACROSS THE CURRICULUM

▶ **Social Studies** Read aloud the book *Sebastian: A Book About Bach* by Jeanette Winter (Harbrace, 1999) and invite students to get to know this composer.

Have students compare their childhood and the things that they have at home to the childhood and things that Bach had. A Venn diagram provides a good way of organizing this information. See Resource Book p. C-8.

## BUILDING SKILLS THROUGH MUSIC

▶ **Science** Have students review and summarize how each acoustic keyboard instrument presented in this lesson produces vibration to make sound. (harpsichord/piano = strings; organ = air column)

## MEETING INDIVIDUAL NEEDS

▶ **Including Everyone** Learning to play chords or improvise melodies at the keyboard can be a pleasurable activity for students who spend time alone after school. Some students will need frequent opportunities at the keyboard to develop independence and some level of skill. The theme of this lesson gives another opportunity for these experiences. Establish playing the keyboard as a privilege and have students with and without disabilities work as partners, taking turns improvising at the keyboard, as others improvise using xylophones or other instruments. Have students who would benefit from having positive attention play a short improvisation for the class.

## Pipes Galore

Organ pipes can be small and thin, or long and thick. They are made of wood or metal. Pipe organs can have hundreds or even thousands of pipes. The different pipe shapes and sizes produce different sounds when air is blown through them.

**Listen** to this famous composition for organ. Notice how the timbre changes as the air moves through the different pipes of the organ.

CD 10–2
**Toccata in D Minor**

**by Johann Sebastian Bach**

This organ selection was written in 1708. It is frequently performed today and is one of Bach's most famous works.

### MUSIC MAKERS
### Johann Sebastian Bach

**Johann Sebastian Bach** (1685–1750) was a German composer of the Baroque era (1600–1750). Among the first instruments he learned to play were the violin and organ. During his lifetime, Bach was famous for his ability to improvise on the organ. He was employed by the nobility of several cities in Germany as an organist, choir director, teacher, and composer. Bach wrote church, orchestra, keyboard, vocal, and choral music.



# 1 Introduce

Invite students to find and name keyboards in the room or in the school, such as piano and electronic keyboards or synthesizers. Talk with them about the differences between various types of keyboards and why all such instruments are categorized as "keyboard intruments." (They use the same arrangement of white and black keys.)

# 2 Develop

### Listening

Play Johann Sebastian Bach's *Gigue* **CD 10-1.** Invite students to tap the beat as they listen. Encourage them to keep the beat in different ways as the music continues.

**ASK How would you describe the timbre of the instrument you heard?** (Accept a variety of answers.)

**SAY** The instrument you heard is a harpsichord.

Then invite students to turn to p. 232 in their books and read the information about the harpsichord.

**ASK Why is the harpsichord categorized as a keyboard instrument?** (It uses a set of keys, similar to that of the piano and organ.)

Have students

- Quiz each other on harpischord facts.
- Listen to the Bach *Gigue* again and move to or tap the beat of the music, with students taking turns leading the class.

### Improvising

Have students set up xylophones, metallophones, and glockenspiels with the following pitches in all octaves: C, D, F, G, and A.

Establish D as the tonal center by having one student play a D-A bordun in alternating half notes on a bass instrument.

**continued on page 234**

## Skills Reinforcement

4c **▶ Composing/Playing** Invite students to create short melodic phrases on acoustic or electronic keyboards available in school or at home. Have them organize their phrases in question-and-answer phrase form. Then invite students to share the compositions they create by playing them for the class. Invite those who take keyboard lessons to play pieces they have learned for their classmates.

## Spotlight On

**▶ The Composer** Frederic Chopin (1810–1849) grew up near Warsaw, Poland. He was performing and composing music for the piano by the time he was eight. When he was 21, he moved from Poland to Paris. There he became a famous pianist, teacher, and composer. The modern piano was a fairly new instrument, and Chopin became famous for his new and original ideas for piano music. Almost all of Chopin's compositions are for solo piano, but he did write several pieces for piano and orchestra and some chamber music for piano and string instruments.

Then improvise four-beat or eight-beat call-and-response phrases. To get started:

- Have one student play a four-beat "question" that begins on D.
- Have the remainder of the class play a four-beat "answer" that ends on D.

Continue, using small groups and eight-beat patterns.

For practice creating keyboard pieces in question-and answer phrases, see Skills Reinforcement, p. 233.

### Moving

Play the opening minute of Bach's *Toccata in D Minor* **CD 10-2.** Have students improvise movements as they listen to the opening minute of the music.

**ASK What instrument is playing?** (organ)

Play the recording again as students turn to p. 233. Have students read the information about the organ. Encourage them to use standard terminology in responding to the following questions.

**ASK How are the harpsichord and organ the same?** (Both have keys, both are categorized as keyboard instruments, and so on.)

**How are they different?** (Accept a variety of answers, including that the organ can play more loudly and has more timbres, and the harpischord has strings while the organ has pipes.)

For more detailed information on the harpsichord and organ, refer students to pp. 468–469 in the Sound Bank.

### Listening

Play a fast three-beat pattern on a drum (for example, strong-weak-weak strokes). Have students create movements that show a three-beat pattern. Then have students conduct a three-beat pattern. Say the words "down, out, up" to help students remember the direction of the movements.

### *Piano and Forte*

The first pianos were called *pianoforte* because the performer could make both soft *(piano)* and loud *(forte)* sounds by touching the keys in different ways. When the player presses a piano key, a hammer inside the instrument strikes one or more strings. Striking harder makes a louder sound.

▲ *Pianoforte Cantata* (1835)

The first *pianofortes* were made around 1700. By 1825, the piano looked and sounded similar to the pianos we know today. **Listen** to these piano pieces.

CD 10-3

**by Frederic Chopin**

This piece has the nickname "Minute" Waltz because it is played in a very fast tempo. However, it usually takes longer than one minute to play.

CD 10-4

**by Frederic Chopin**
**as performed by Vladimir Ashkenazy**

Chopin (1810–1849) was an acclaimed pianist during his lifetime and is considered one of the greatest composers for the instrument.

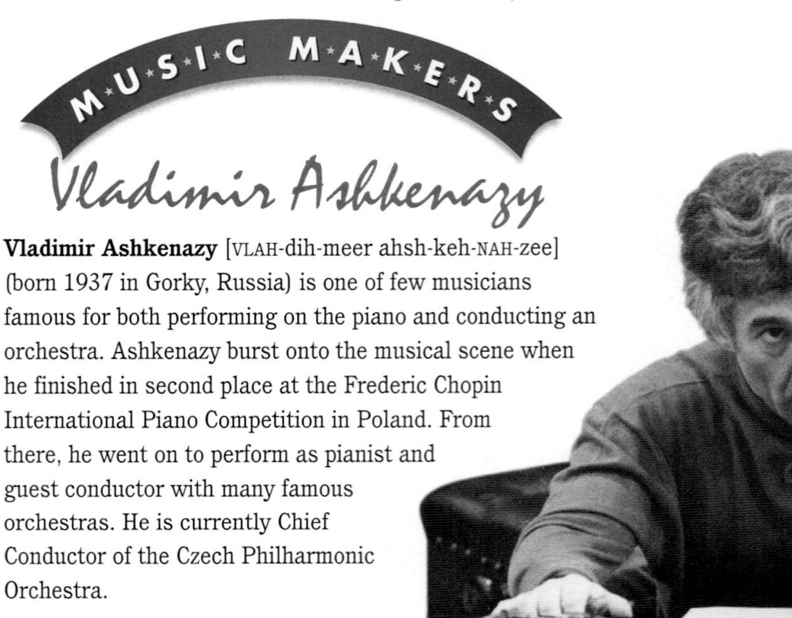


**Vladimir Ashkenazy** [VLAH-dih-meer ahsh-keh-NAH-zee] (born 1937 in Gorky, Russia) is one of few musicians famous for both performing on the piano and conducting an orchestra. Ashkenazy burst onto the musical scene when he finished in second place at the Frederic Chopin International Piano Competition in Poland. From there, he went on to perform as pianist and guest conductor with many famous orchestras. He is currently Chief Conductor of the Czech Philharmonic Orchestra.

234

## Footnotes

### Teacher to Teacher

▶ **Venn Diagram** For additional practice developing thinking skills in a musical context, engage students in the following activity.

Distribute copies of the Venn diagram from Resource Book p. C-8. Use the Venn diagram to compare and contrast the two Chopin listening examples from this lesson. Have students write style characteristics of one composition in the left circle and style characteristics of the other in the right circle. Then list common characteristics in the center space.

### Spotlight On

▶ **The Composer** John Williams was born in New York City in 1932. He studied composition at U.C.L.A. and piano at Juilliard in New York. Williams returned to Los Angeles and studied with some of the great film composers there. Williams has become one of the most successful composers of his time. He has won many awards for his motion picture music (he has composed over 75 film scores) and has written themes for television shows, and even the themes for the 1984, 1988, and 1996 summer Olympic Games. His career as a conductor has included leading the major symphony orchestras of Boston (Pops), London, Cleveland, Chicago, Philadelphia, Pittsburgh, Denver, San Francisco, Dallas, Indianapolis, and Los Angeles.

### The Newest Keyboards

Electronic music was created in the 20th century. The best-known electronic instrument is the synthesizer. It might look like a keyboard, but it can mimic the sounds of all types of instruments, as well as produce completely new sounds. **Listen** to this synthesizer version of *Close Encounters of the Third Kind.*

**CD 10-5**

**Close Encounters of the Third Kind**

**by John Williams**

This music comes from the movie soundtrack. The main theme features the pattern *re, mi, do,* low *do,* and low *so.*

# Close Encounters of the Third Kind

**LISTENING MAP**



**SAY** The next piece we are going to hear is sometimes called the "Minute Waltz."

Play *Waltz in D-flat* **CD 10-3.**

**ASK Why do you think it has that title?** (Because it is so fast, it can be played in about a minute.)

Play *Prelude in A Major* **CD 10-4.** Have students conduct a three-beat pattern as they listen. Start on the downbeat.

**ASK What instrument was playing?** (piano)

Have students read about the piano and Vladimir Ashkenazy, on p. 234. See Spotlight On, p. 233, for additional information on Chopin.

Have students read about synthesizers, and have a student demonstrate all of the sounds possible on the classroom electronic keyboard if one is available.

Play *Close Encounters of the Third Kind* **CD 10-5** and discuss the different kinds of electronic instrumental sounds used in the recording. See Across the Curriculum below for information on the way sound is produced on a synthesizer.

Point out to students that the aurally-presented keyboard selections in this lesson represent three diverse musical periods.

- Baroque (1600–1750): *Gigue; Toccata in D Minor*
- Romantic (1830–1900): *Waltz in D-flat; Prelude in A*
- Modern (1900–present): *Close Encounters of the Third Kind*

## 3 CLOSE

**Element: TIMBRE** ASSESSMENT

6d 9a **Observation** Have students listen to excerpts from *Gigue, Toccata in D Minor, Prelude in A Major,* and *Close Encounters of the Third Kind,* and point to the picture in the book of the instrument they hear in each example. Have them point to the listening map when they hear the excerpt of *Close Encounters of the Third Kind.* Observe students' ability to identify and categorize keyboard timbres by pointing to the appropriate pictures.

## ACROSS THE CURRICULUM

▶ **Science** A relatively new musical instrument that has revolutionized the way music is produced is the synthesizer. Most of us know it in its familiar keyboard form today. Synthesizers produce sound with electricity. When voltage is applied in a controlled way to an oscillator, a signal, or frequency (pitched sound) is the result. Increasing the voltage raises the pitch of the sound, and decreasing the voltage lowers the pitch. Many other aspects of sound are ultimately controlled with voltage, including loudness. The inventions of the transistor and digital technology have made it possible for everyone to own an inexpensive and lightweight synthesizer.

Students may wish to research the following related topics: MIDI (Musical Instrument Digital Interface), sampling, processing, and EWI (Electronic Wind Instrument).

## TECHNOLOGY/MEDIA LINK

**Transparency** Display the transparency for *Close Encounters of the Third Kind.* Invite students to trace the progress of the piece with their finger on the map in their book, as you trace on the overhead projection. Invite students to sing and perform the hand signs for *re, mi, do,* $do_l$, and *so* each time they occur in the piece.

LESSON Core 9

## LESSON AT A GLANCE

**Element Focus** **TEXTURE/HARMONY** Rounds

**Skill Objective** **SINGING** Sing the thin and thicker textures of a round

**Connection Activity** **GENRE** Sing and explore rounds

**MATERIALS**

- "Let Music Surround You" **CD 10-6**

  **Recording Routine:** Intro (4 m.); vocal (unison); interlude (2 m.); vocal (4-part canon, two times); coda
- *Symphony No. 1,* Mvt. 3 (excerpt) **CD 10-8**
- keyboards, xylophones, or bells

**VOCABULARY**

melody harmony unison round texture

**◆ ◆ ◆ ◆ National Standards ◆ ◆ ◆ ◆**

**1d** Sing rounds
**2b** Perform melodies on appropriate instruments
**2f** Play instruments independently against contrasting parts
**4b** Arrange songs within specific guidelines
**6b** Describe music by moving to it, or explaining how it sounds

**MORE MUSIC CHOICES**

For more practice singing a round:
"Peace Round," p. 348

# 1 INTRODUCE

Write the words "unison" and "round" on the board. Encourage students to define each in their own words. Then play "Let Music Surround You" **CD 10-6.** Have students raise one hand when they hear unison singing and two hands when they hear a round.

**ASK How does the texture of a round change?** (It starts thin and gets thicker as parts are added.)

LESSON 9 **Element: TEXTURE/HARMONY** **Skill: SINGING** **Connection: GENRE**

# Round and Round

A melody performed alone has a thin musical texture. A melody performed with an accompaniment has a thicker musical texture.

When a melody is performed as a round, harmony is created and the musical texture changes from thin to thicker.

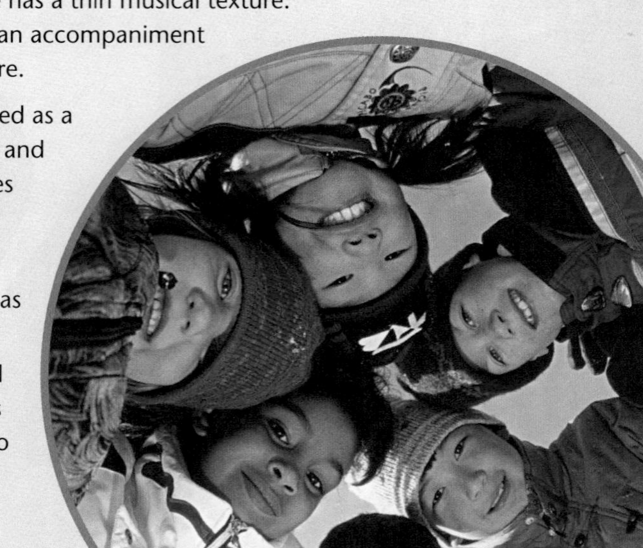

Silently read the words of "Let Music Surround You" as you **listen** to the song.

**Sing** "Let Music Surround You" in unison and then as a round. Stand in a circle to let the music surround you as you sing.

CD 10-6
Let Music Surround You
s, ta (d) r m f s
Words and Music by Fran Smartt Addicott
do
I A G A G II A G A G
Let mus-ic sur-round you, let it warm your heart.
III A G A G IV A G A
Those who sing in har-mo-ny, ne-ver _ grow a - part.

**Create** a motion for each phrase of the song. **Perform** the motions as you **sing** in unison and in harmony.

## Footnotes

### SKILLS REINFORCEMENT

▶ **Recorder** Have students play one of the ostinatos below on recorder to add additional harmony parts to "Let Music Surround You."

2f

Part 1
Part 2

### BUILDING SKILLS THROUGH MUSIC

▶ **Writing** Using the lyric stem *Let music surround you*, invite students to create new words for the round on p. 236.

### ACROSS THE CURRICULUM

▶ **Language Arts** Invite students to explore texture in fabrics. Place four or more pieces of fabric or articles of clothing made of different fabrics in an opaque bag so that students will not see the articles. Have students touch each piece of fabric or clothing, then write a short list of words describing the texture, or feel, of the fabric. Invite them to compare their lists of descriptive words.

Have students discuss the difference in meaning of the word "texture" when applied to the sense of hearing and the sense of touch.

## A Symphony Goes Round

Now **listen** to an orchestra perform the melody below as part of a symphony.

CD 10-8

**Symphony No. 1, Movement 3**

**by Gustav Mahler**

The melody in this movement is a minor-key variation on the familiar round *"Frère Jacques."*

Mahler changed the texture in his symphony by presenting the melody as a round. To make the texture even thicker, he added an ostinato and a countermelody. **Play** the ostinato below.

**Listen** to the countermelody. What instruments play the ostinato and countermelody?

### Creating Textures

With a group of friends, **create** your own arrangement using the melodies above. Will you play in unison, or as a round? How will the texture change? Will you start with ostinatos or the melody?

Unit 6 237

# 2 Develop

### Singing

1d Invite students to sing "Let Music Surround You"

- In unison.
- With one group in unison and another singing the last two measures as an ostinato.
- As a round.

### Moving

6b Invite students to create movements to go with "Let Music Surround You." Divide the class into four groups. Have them stand in concentric circles. Have the center group begin singing the song with movements, and the outer groups begin moving and singing their parts every two measures, as marked, from the inside out. See Teacher to Teacher, below, for suggestions on organizing this activity.

### Listening

2b Invite students to play the melody at the top of p. 237 on keyboards, xylophones, or bells. Then play the excerpt from Mahler's *Symphony No. 1* **CD 10-8.** Have students signal when they hear the melody and again when they hear a round.

Invite students to play the ostinato on p. 237. Then play the recording again and have students signal when they hear it within the symphony.

4b Have students create their own arrangement by following the directions on the bottom of p. 237.

# 3 Close

**ASSESSMENT**

1d **Performance/Observation** Have students sing "Let Music Surround You" **CD 10-6** as a round. Observe each student's ability to maintain a part and create thin and thicker textures while singing rounds.

## Teacher to Teacher

▶ **Groups in Concentric Circles** The song/movement round in four parts for "Let Music Surround You" is best done with a large class of 40 or more students. Divide the class into four groups, starting with about three students for the center circle, then six to eight students for the second circle, then 10 to 11 students for the third circle, and finally about 15 to 20 students for the outer circle. This arrangement will allow for students to perform the movements they have created without colliding with each other as they move. To intensify the surrounding effect, have students in circles 1 and 3 walk in one direction, and those in circles 2 and 4 walk in the opposite direction around their circle as they sing and move to their part. Watch for students in the outer circles who may be tempted to move too soon when they see classmates moving inside the circle.

## Technology/Media Link

4b **Notation Software** Invite students to use notation software to create their own melodic variation for "Let Music Surround You." Have students

- Sing "Let Music Surround You" as a class, both in unison and as a round.
- Set up notation software in the key of A.
- "Scramble" the notes and the rhythms in each measure (simply reorder them within their measure) and notate the scrambled melody.
- Print a copy of their work.
- In small groups, sing the original melody, followed by each individual's variation.

## LESSON AT A GLANCE

**Element Focus** **TEXTURE/HARMONY** I, IV, and $V_7$ chords

**Skill Objective** **PLAYING** Play instruments to accompany a popular song

**Connection Activity** **CULTURE** Explore American culture through a popular song and dance

**MATERIALS**
- *Twist and Shout* **CD 10-9**
- xylophones, bells, keyboards

**VOCABULARY**

ostinato harmony

**National Standards**

**2a** Play instruments on pitch and in rhythm
**3b** Improvise rhythmic ostinato accompaniments
**6e** While listening to music, move to show a prominent feature of the music
**9a** Listen to identify music from different historical periods

**MORE MUSIC CHOICES**

For more practice with I, IV, and $V_7$ chords:
"Bard of Armagh, The," p. 296
"For the Beauty of the Earth," p. 356
"Love Will Guide Us," p. 328
*"Rio Grande,"* p. 256

# 1 INTRODUCE

Invite students to stand and explore all the ways they can twist their own arms, legs, feet, hands, and torsos. Tell them that a dance called the "Twist" was popular in the 1960s. To explore more about American culture during the 1960s, see Across the Curriculum below.

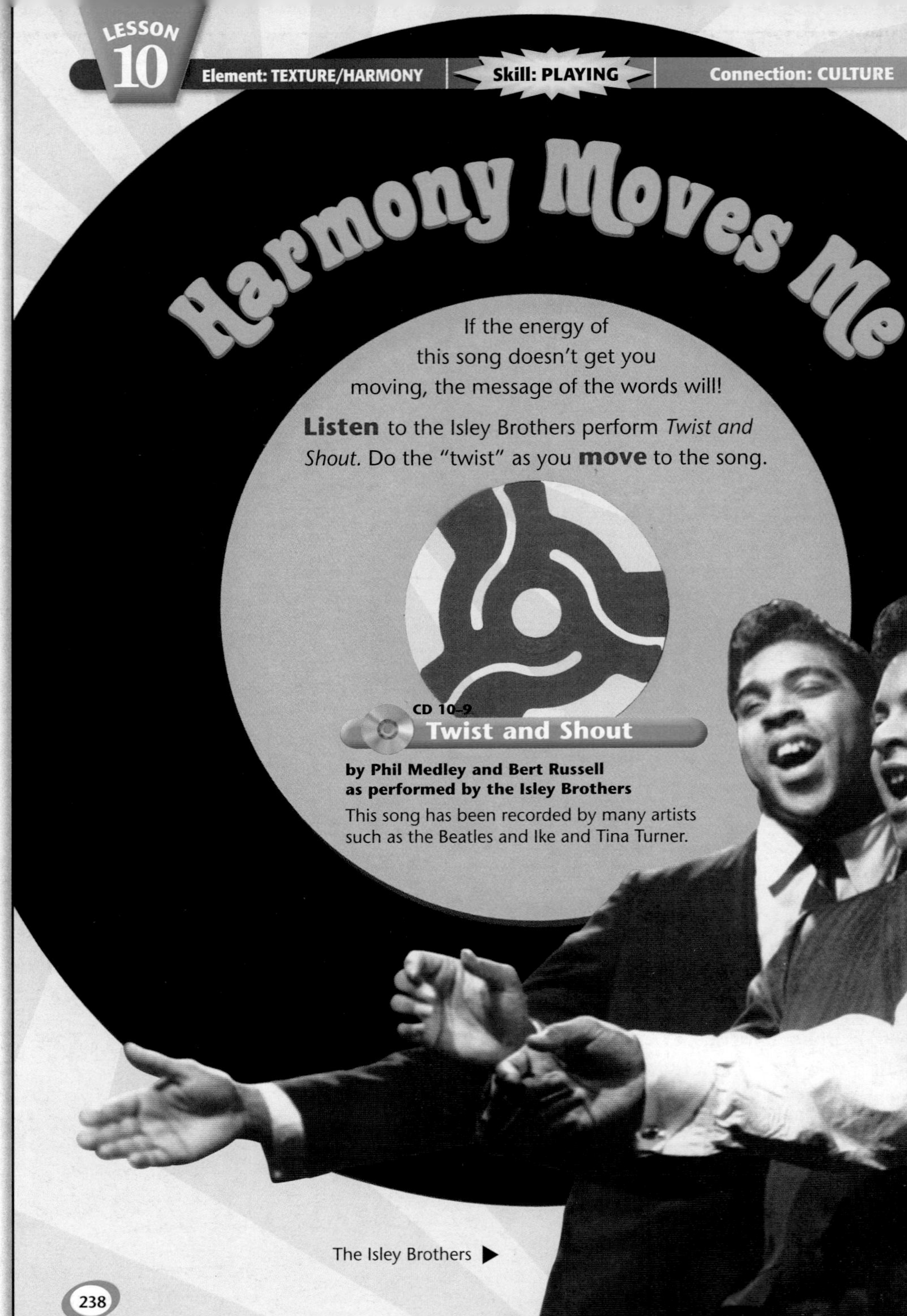

LESSON 10
Element: TEXTURE/HARMONY
Skill: PLAYING
Connection: CULTURE
Harmony Moves Me
If the energy of this song doesn't get you moving, the message of the words will!
**Listen** to the Isley Brothers perform *Twist and Shout.* Do the "twist" as you **move** to the song.
CD 10-9
Twist and Shout
by Phil Medley and Bert Russell
as performed by the Isley Brothers
This song has been recorded by many artists such as the Beatles and Ike and Tina Turner.
The Isley Brothers
238


## Footnotes

### ACROSS THE CURRICULUM

**▶ Social Studies** Help students search the library for pictures of life in the United States during the 1960s. Give them questions to guide their library exploration, such as: What did people wear when they were at a dance party and doing the "Twist"? What United States presidents were in office during the 1960s? Who were other important leaders? What did cars look like during the 1960s? What important events happened in the 1960s?

### BUILDING SKILLS THROUGH MUSIC

**▶ Language** Have students
- Read the information under Music Makers on p. 239.
- Turn to a neighbor and summarize the paragraph.

### SKILLS REINFORCEMENT

3b **▶ Improvising** Invite students to improvise rhythm ostinatos to accompany *Twist and Shout* **CD 10-9**.

**Reinforcement** Some students may be most comfortable participating in this activity by choosing a body percussion to perform a steady beat.

**On Target** Most students will be able to tap or clap a steady beat as they listen to the recording. Continue by having students create four-beat ostinatos, emphasizing beats 2 and 4. Then transfer their ostinatos to such instruments as drums, tambourine, cowbell, and woodblock.

**Challenge** Encourage interested students to transfer their ostinatos to pitched instruments, following the I-IV-$V_7$ chord progression outlined at the top of p. 239.

## Play Your Own Harmony

Practice the ostinato pattern below on any melody instrument.

**Listen** to *Twist and Shout* again. To add harmony, **play** the ostinato shown above. The notes of this ostinato are the lowest notes of the chords used in *Twist and Shout*.

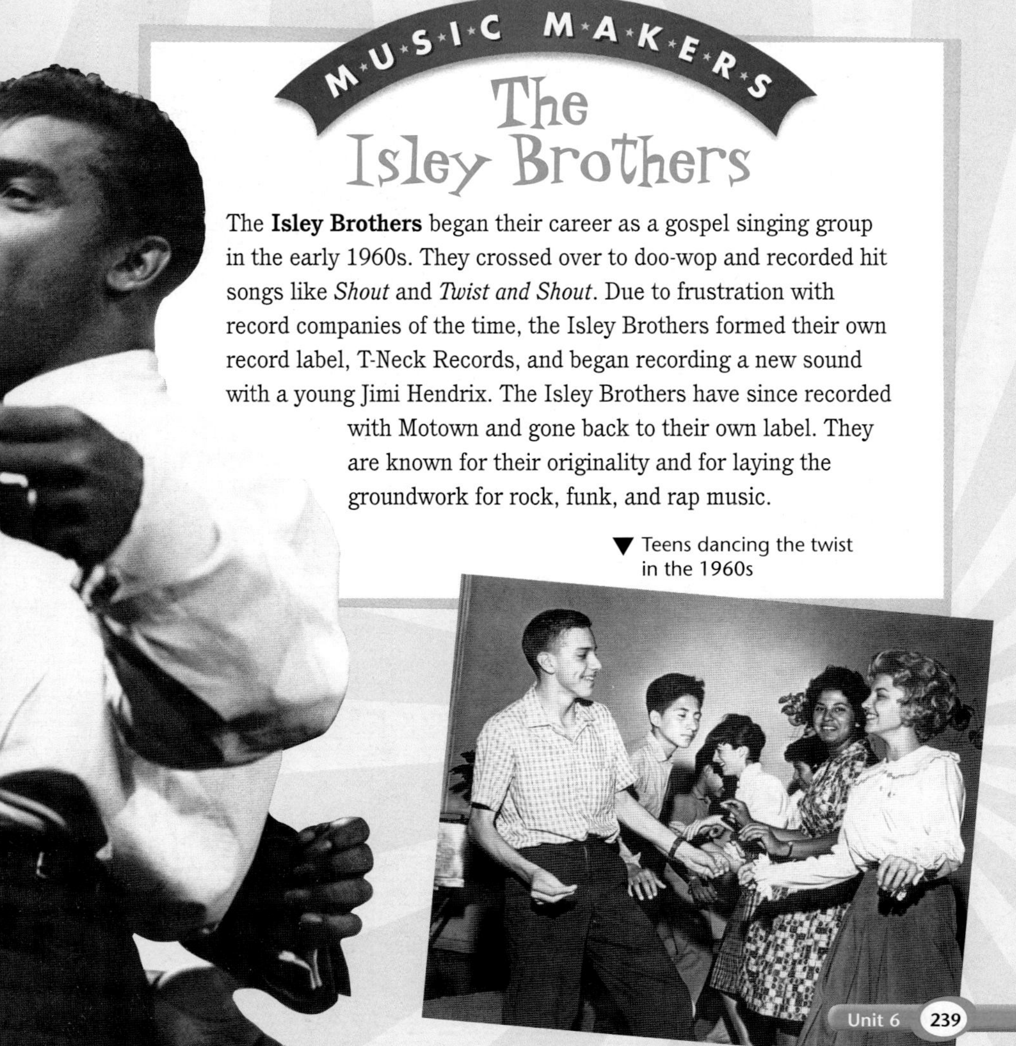

MUSIC MAKERS

### The Isley Brothers

The **Isley Brothers** began their career as a gospel singing group in the early 1960s. They crossed over to doo-wop and recorded hit songs like *Shout* and *Twist and Shout*. Due to frustration with record companies of the time, the Isley Brothers formed their own record label, T-Neck Records, and began recording a new sound with a young Jimi Hendrix. The Isley Brothers have since recorded with Motown and gone back to their own label. They are known for their originality and for laying the groundwork for rock, funk, and rap music.

▼ Teens dancing the twist in the 1960s



# 2 Develop

### Moving

6e Play the recording of *Twist and Shout* **CD 10-9.** Invite students to listen and twist in their own space.

9a After listening and moving, have students read about the history of *Twist and Shout* and about the Isley Brothers in their books.

### Playing

Invite students to play an ostinato to accompany *Twist and Shout* **CD 10-9.** Have them

- Find the ostinato pattern on the top of p. 239 and review the notes using letter names.
- Move to the ostinato pattern by patting their legs as though playing the xylophone ostinato.
- Transfer their movements to an instrument.

Have students play the ostinato without the recording first, then have them play it with the song. They should begin after the four-measure introduction and rest during the interlude.

**SAY** When we play the ostinato with the song, we are playing a harmony part. The notes we are playing are the roots of the I, IV, and $V_7$ chords. These chords are played throughout *Twist and Shout.*

# 3 Close

**ASSESSMENT**

2a **Performance/Observation** Divide the class into "twisters" and "players." Invite the "twisters" to move to *Twist and Shout* **CD 10-9** while the "players" perform the ostinato and play the root of the I, IV, and $V_7$ chords. Observe students' ability to play the ostinato accurately, then switch "twisters" and "players" and assess the next group of students.

## Character Education

▶ **Respect** To encourage respect for differences, discuss the era in which *Twist and Shout* was popular. Explain to students that the Twist was a popular dance in the 1960s; yet, other dances are "in" today. Ask students the following questions: What are some other ways that trends or styles of the 1960s differ from ours today? How are the trends of the 1960s similar to our current trends? Point out to students that although the Twist may seem outdated today, dancing is still valued. Explain to students that because of the diversity of American society and the fleeting nature of popular trends, we have many differences in trends and traditions. Recognizing differences is appropriate; however, we should also notice similarities and value trends for what they meant to people at that time. Ask students, What character traits aren't trendy and never go "out of style"?

## School to Home Connection

▶ **Sharing with Family** Have students ask older family members to share their "twist" moves or other popular dance moves from their younger years.

## Technology/Media Link

**CD-ROM** For more practice with chord progressions, invite students to explore Volume 3 of *Alfred's Essentials of Music Theory*.

LESSON 11

## LESSON AT A GLANCE

**Element Focus** **TEXTURE/HARMONY** I, IV, and $V_7$ chords

**Skill Objective** **PLAYING** Play harmony using I, IV, and $V_7$ chords

**Connection Activity** **SOCIAL STUDIES** Discuss the role of lighthouses in sailing history

**MATERIALS**

- "The Keel Row" **CD 10-10**
  **Recording Routine:** Intro (8 m.); v. 1; refrain; interlude (8 m.); v. 2; refrain; coda
- "*El borrego*" **CD 10-12**
- "The Lamb" **CD 10-13**
  **Recording Routine:** Intro (4 m.); vocal; interlude (4 m.); vocal; coda
- **Pronunciation Practice/Translation** p. 484
- **Resource Book** pp. A-25, D-27, I-18
- Autoharp, keyboard
- metallophones, glockenspiel, maracas

**VOCABULARY**

scale interval chord root

**◆◆◆◆ National Standards ◆◆◆◆**

**1c** Sing from memory songs from diverse cultures
**2b** Play chords on appropriate instruments
**2c** Play instruments expressively on a variety of pieces
**2f** Play instruments independently against contrasting parts
**4b** Compose songs within specific guidelines
**6b** Describe music by answering questions about it

**MORE MUSIC CHOICES**

Other songs with I, IV, and $V_7$ chords:
"Little David, Play on Your Harp," p. 394
"My Bonnie Lies Over the Ocean," p. 338

LESSON 11 Element: TEXTURE/HARMONY | Skill: PLAYING | Connection: SOCIAL STUDIES

# Chords Galore

Here's a hint to help you figure out what this song is all about. Just remember a *keel* is a kind of boat, and *weel* is a Scottish word for "well."

CD 10-10

## The Keel Row

Folk Song from Northumbria

s, t, d r m f s l d
VERSE
D(I) G(IV) D(I) A7(V7) D(I) G(IV) D(I) A7(V7) D(I)
do
1. As I came through Sand - gate, through Sand - gate, through Sand - gate, As I came through Sand - gate, I heard a las - sie sing:
2. "He wears a blue bon - net, blue bon - net, blue bon - net, He wears a blue bon - net, a dim - ple in his chin."
REFRAIN
D(I) G(IV) D(I) A7(V7) D(I) G(IV) D(I) A7(V7) D(I)
"Oh, weel may the keel row, the keel row, the keel row.
Weel may the keel row that my lad - die's in."

# Footnotes

## ACROSS THE CURRICULUM

▶ **Social Studies** Invite students into a conversation about boats coming into harbor. How are ships and boats protected from crashing as they approach the land? Share the book *Beacons of Light: Lighthouses* by Gail Gibbons (William Morrow & Company, 1990), and introduce students to one of the oldest protection mechanisms for ships.

Invite students to locate Northumbria on a map.

## BUILDING SKILLS THROUGH MUSIC

▶ **Math** Given the information presented in the Tune In on p. 241, ask students to compute the total square footage in an average Scottish keel boat. (60 X 10 = 600 square feet)

## SKILLS REINFORCEMENT

▶ **Playing** Have students

- Aurally determine appropriate chords to accompany familiar songs in F-, C-, and G-*do*.
- Play I, IV, or $V_7$ chords on the Autoharp or keyboard to accompany familiar songs.

4b ▶ **Creating** Have students

- Compose melodies to fit given progressions using I, IV, and $V_7$ chords.
- Sing, play, and notate their melodies.
- Create words to fit their melodies.
- Perform their songs with I, IV, and $V_7$ accompaniment.

The **root** is the tone on which a chord is built.

### Playing Chords

Find the chord symbols in the music on page 240. Look at the notation on this page and **play** the chords alone. How many pitches are in each chord? The highlighted note is the **root** of the chord. Now follow the song notation and play the chords as others **sing** "The Keel Row."

**Tune In**

An average Scottish keel boat was about sixty feet long, ten feet wide, and four feet deep. The boats were propelled by long poles. Twelve to twenty men, including oarsmen and a pilot, were needed to push the boat up river.



# 1 Introduce

Engage students in a discussion of what the song "The Keel Row" might be about, once they have read the lyrics and the text at the top of the page. (A woman hopes that the boat her "laddie" is in "rows well" and arrives safely home.) For more about dangers of the seacoast and the importance of lighthouses—topics important to the people of Northumbria—see Across the Curriculum on p. 240.

# 2 Develop

### Singing

1c Play "The Keel Row" **CD 10-10** and have students

- Follow the notation on p. 240 while listening.
- Sing when ready, as you accompany with chords on the Autoharp, guitar, or keyboard at a slow tempo.

### Listening/Analyzing

ASK **Was I playing melody or accompaniment?** (accompaniment)

**SAY** Chords are often used to accompany a melody. Chords are created by playing more than one note at a time. A triad is a chord with three notes.

Ask students to sing the song again, notice the words on which the chords change, and raise their hands when they hear the chords change.

ASK **How many different chords did you hear?** (three)

continued on page 242

## Teacher to Teacher

▶ **Singing Chords** When singing in F- and G-*do*, it is often necessary to have students sing the chords from low *fa* and low *so* because of the extreme upper vocal range. Using instruments, and reminding students that the lower *fa* and *so* are still the fourth and fifth scale degrees, should prevent any confusion. Once students have a firm grasp on chords in their root position, it will be helpful to teach inversions through vocal chording. Explain that when chords are arranged from their lowest to highest notes, they are in their root position. When the notes are arranged in a mixed-up order, however, the chord is in an *inversion*.

## Cultural Connection

▶ **The Legacy of *Los californios*** The Mexican *rancho* song *"El borrego,"* on p. 242, can be traced back to as early as 1807, when it was mentioned in the journal of a visitor from Russia. The term *Los californios* refers not only to Mexican settlers who lived in present-day California from the 1770s until the 1840s, but also to those of Spanish, Native American, and African descent. Although the music of *Los californios* may sound like music from Mexico or Spain, it is really neither. Instead, the music of *Los californios* combined the sounds of its many diverse cultures to produce a unique kind of music. See Across the Curriculum on p. 242 for more information on the history and people of this time and place.

### Playing

**SAY** The note a chord is named after is called its *root*. In a D chord, for instance, the root is D.

Have students follow the instructions on p. 241 and take turns playing the I, IV, and $V_7$ chords in D major on keyboard or Autoharp. When they are ready, have students accompany "The Keel Row" **CD 10-10.**

Refer students to the recorder countermelody for "The Keel Row" on Resource Book p. I-18.

### Analyzing

Select a student to read the text at the top of p. 242. Share the additional information on *Los californios* from Cultural Connection, p. 241, and Across the Curriculum below. Play *"El borrego"* **CD 10-12** to help students aurally identify elements reflecting the diverse cultural background of the song.

6b Ask students to follow the chord symbols in the music of *"El borrego"* as they listen again to the recording. Help students discover that the I, IV, and $V_7$ chords used in this song are the same as those used in *"The* Keel Row." The pattern, or progression, of the chords, however, is different.

**ASK What is the pattern for the chords in the A section of *"El borrego"*?** (IV-I-$V_7$-I)

**What is the pattern for the chords in the first half of the B section?** (the same as the A section)

**What is the pattern for the chords in the second half of the B section?** ($V_7$-I-$V_7$-I)

### Singing

1c Use the Pronunciation Practice **CD 10-15** to teach students the Spanish words of *"El borrego."* Refer to Resource Book p. A-25 for a Pronunciation Practice Guide. Then have students

- Echo sing each phrase.
- Sing the song in Spanish, then in English.
- Sing the entire song again while holding up fingers to indicate the number of the chord being played (I, IV, or V).

## Same Chords, New Song

*"El borrego"* comes from the musical heritage of *Los californios*—Mexican ranchers who lived in California territory in the early 1800s. **Listen** to the song as you follow the chord symbols in the music. Then **compare** the chords to those in "The Keel Row," on page 240.

CD 10-12
El borrego
(The Lamb)
English Words by Julie Scott
Folk Song from Mexico
l, t, d r m f s l
A
do
G(IV) D(I) A7(V7) D(I) G(IV)
Se - ño - ra, su bo - rre - gui - to, me quie -
Se - ño - ra, your lit - tle lamb wants to take
D(I) A7(V7) D(I) G(IV) D(I) A7(V7)
re lle - var al rí - o, y yo le di - go que
me down to the cold riv - er, but I must tell the lamb,
D(I) G(IV) D(I) A7(V7) D(I)
no, por - que me mue - ro de frí - o.
"No!" be - cause the cold wa - ter makes me shiv - er.
B Faster
G(IV) D(I) A7(V7) D(I) G(IV)
Sa - le la lin - da, sa - le la fe - a, y el bo - rre -
Out goes the beau - ty, brim-ming with laugh - ter, Out goes the
D(I) A7(V7) D(I) A7(V7) D(I)
gui - to con su za - le - a. To - pe que to - pe,
lamb, who's frol - ick - ing af - ter. Bump in - to her, then
A7(V7) D(I) A7(V7) D(I) A7(V7) D(I)
to - pe con e - lla. To - pe que to - pe, to - pe con él.
bump in - to him. Then bump in - to her, then bump in - to him.
242

# Footnotes

## ACROSS THE CURRICULUM

▶ **Social Studies** *Los californios* lived on *ranchos* (cattle ranches) that were created when the Mexican governor distributed large tracts of California land to influential people in the community. Each *ranchero* (ranch owner) might hire as many as 100 *vaqueros* (ranch hands and cowboys), many of whom were Native Americans who had been trained at Catholic missions like the one pictured on p. 243.

The *ranchos* were often situated very far apart. On special occasions, people would gather together at a *rancho* for celebrations, where they would sing and dance to songs such as *"El borrego."* Many towns and cities in southern California still celebrate their Mexican *rancho* roots with annual fiestas.

## TEACHER TO TEACHER

▶ **Singing the Bass Line** One way to prepare students for playing chords on instruments is to have them sing the bass note first. After reminding students that *"El borrego"* uses I, IV, and $V_7$ chords, help them discover that the I chord is based on *do*, the IV chord is based on *fa*, and the $V_7$ chord is based on *so*. Have students follow the notation for the bass line on p. 243 as they sing the notes using pitch syllables. Ask them to indicate which chord number they are singing by holding up 1, 4, or 5 fingers.

Divide the class into two groups. Have one group sing the bass notes using pitch syllables, while the other group sings *"El borrego."* Let the groups switch and perform the song again.

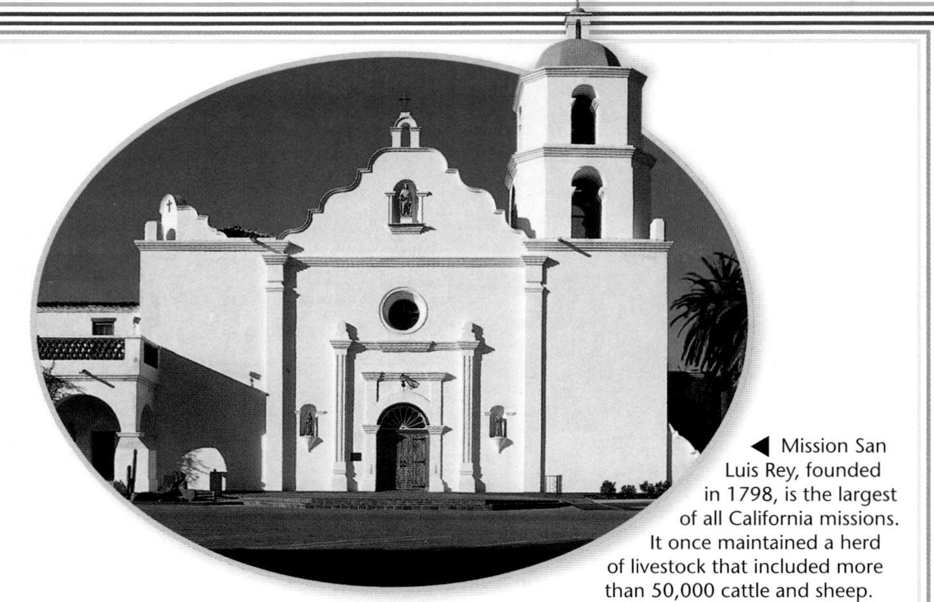

◀ Mission San Luis Rey, founded in 1798, is the largest of all California missions. It once maintained a herd of livestock that included more than 50,000 cattle and sheep.

## Mallets and Maracas

**Play** this accompaniment during the B section of "*El borrego.*"

### Playing

Refer students to the instrumental accompaniment parts on p. 243 for the B section of "*El borrego.*" Have students

- Identify the letter names of the notes used in the two patterns of the bass metallophone part, and then play the entire part.
- Identify the letter names of the notes used in the two patterns of the soprano metallophone/alto glockenspiel part, and then play the part.
- Play both parts while others sing "*El borrego*" **CD 10-12**.
- Read the maraca part using rhythm syllables. (stems down = left hand; stems up = right hand)
- Play all of the accompaniment parts while others sing the song.

For an instrumental accompaniment for the A section of "*El borrego,*" see Skills Reinforcement below.

See Resource Book p. D-27 for more practice with I, IV, and $V_7$ chords.

## 3 Close

**Element: TEXTURE/HARMONY** ASSESSMENT

**Performance/Observation** Review with students the similarities and differences in the I-IV-$V_7$ chord progression used in the two songs from diverse cultures presented in this lesson. Then have groups of students accompany "The Keel Row" **CD 10-10** or "*El borrego*" **CD 10-12** with chords on Autoharp or keyboards. Observe each student's ability to play chord changes at the correct points in the music.

## Skills Reinforcement

▶ **Playing** Once students have identified the chord changes in the A section of "*El borrego,*" they can learn to play the following accompaniment. Lead students to notice that the parts are very similar to the those in the B section. To help students learn the hand coordination of the maraca part, have them say "**Both**, right, right, **both**, right, right."

## Technology/Media Link

**Electronic Keyboards** Invite students to perform an "oom-pah" accompaniment to "The Keel Row."

- Have students play the chord roots on beat one of each measure.
- Show students how to play the D, G, and $A_7$ chords, using their right hands.
- At each keyboard, have one student play D, one play G, and one play $A_7$ on beat two of the appropriate measures.
- Guide students in the correct way to play measures with two chord symbols.
- Have students perform the song with the MIDI accompaniment.

## LESSON AT A GLANCE

**Element Focus** **TEXTURE/HARMONY** Two-part harmony

**Skill Objective** **SINGING** Sing a song in two-part harmony

**Connection Activity** **SOCIAL STUDIES** Read about and discuss the California Gold Rush and westward expansion in the United States

**MATERIALS**

- "Sweet Betsy from Pike" **CD 10-16**
  **Recording Routine:** Intro (4 m.); verses 1–6 with refrains and 4 m. interludes; coda
- **Resource Book** pp. H-17, I-19, J-14

**VOCABULARY**

melody harmony

**◆◆◆◆ National Standards ◆◆◆◆**

**1a** Sing independently on pitch
**1d** Sing part songs
**2b** Play chords on appropriate instruments
**6b** Describe music by answering questions about it

**MORE MUSIC CHOICES**

For more practice singing in harmony:
"*Einini,*" p. 391
"Lullaby and Dance," p. 386

# 1 INTRODUCE

Invite students to read about and discuss the discovery of gold in California in the mid-1800s and the hard trip many people made by covered wagon across the plains and mountains to get to the gold. See Across the Curriculum below for an activity involving an imaginary covered wagon trip and literature about the plains that people crossed in their wagons.

# SINGING IN PARTS

Gold was discovered in California in 1848. By 1849, thousands of Americans rushed to California to seek their fortunes. Some, like "Sweet Betsy from Pike," traveled in covered wagons to get there. The trip was long and hard. **Sing** "Sweet Betsy from Pike" and find out what happened on the way.

CD 10–16
MIDI 17

## SWEET BETSY FROM PIKE

t, d r m f s l t d'

Folk Song from the United States
Adapted and Arranged by Lillian Wiedman

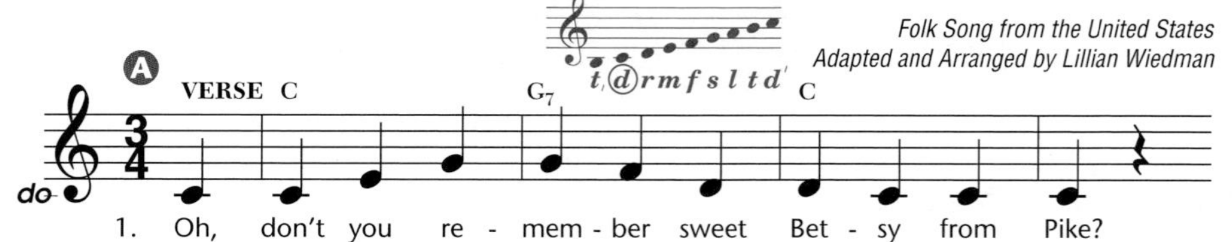
A VERSE C G7 C
do
1. Oh, don't you re - mem - ber sweet Bet - sy from Pike?
2. One ev' - ning quite ear - ly they camped on the Platte,
3. They soon reached the de - sert where Bet - sy gave out.

C D7 G
She crossed the wide prai - ries with her hus - band, Ike,
'Twas near by the road on a green shad - y flat.
And down on the sand she lay roll - ing a - bout.

Am Em F C
With two yoke of ox - en, an old yel - low dog,
Poor Bet - sy, quite tired, lay down for re - pose,
While Ike, in great tears, looked on in sur - prise:

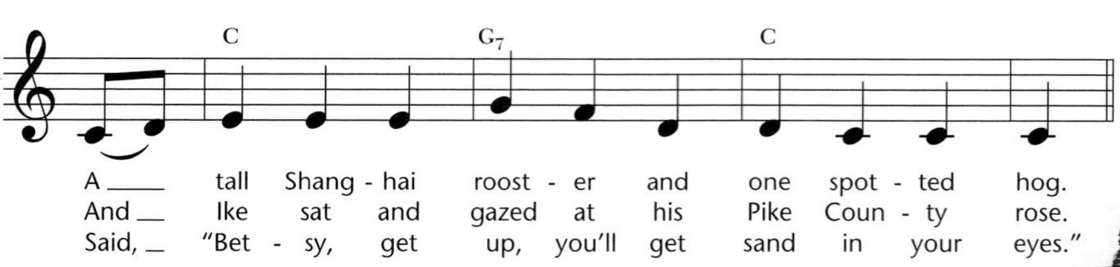
C G7 C
A tall Shang - hai roost - er and one spot - ted hog.
And Ike sat and gazed at his Pike Coun - ty rose.
Said, "Bet - sy, get up, you'll get sand in your eyes."

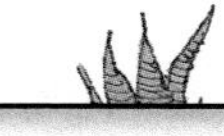
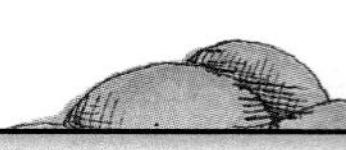

# Footnotes

## SKILLS REINFORCEMENT

1a

▶ **Vocal Development** Have students echo the following patterns in F-major, sustaining *ti* before resolving to *do*:

*so*, *-la*, *-ti*, *-do* *do-re-ti*, *-do* *do-la*, *-ti*, *-do*

Let students express what they feel when *ti* is sustained. (*ti*=tension and *do*=resolution) Define *ti* as the "leading tone" in major keys. Ask students to sing a C-major scale ascending and descending, sustaining *ti* before singing *do*.

## BUILDING SKILLS THROUGH MUSIC

▶ **Social Studies** Have students research the dates of the following historical events and then place them in chronological order: The California Gold Rush (1848); the invention of the first successful steamboat (1807); the American Civil War (1861). Create a time line and have students list songs for each of the historical events.

## ACROSS THE CURRICULUM

▶ **Social Studies** Have students plan a covered wagon trip to Sacramento, California, using these questions: How many miles is the trip, and how long will it take from your town? What important landforms will you encounter on your journey? (desert, prairie, mountains, rivers) What provisions will you need for this challenging trip? What time of year will be best to start your journey from your current location? Why?

▶ **Language Arts** Read aloud the book *If You're Not from the Prairie...* by Dave Bouchard (Atheneum, 1995), and share with students information about the prairie. By the end, readers connect with people who live on the prairie "because we all share the same sun."

REFRAIN

B Too - ra - lee, too - ra - lay,

Too - ra - lee, too - ra - lay,

Sing-ing too - ra - lee, too - ra - lee, too - ra - lee ay.

4. The rooster ran off and the oxen all died,
The last piece of bacon that morning was fried.
Poor Ike got discouraged and Betsy got mad,
The dog wagged his tail and looked awfully sad. *Refrain*

5. The alkali desert was burning and hot,
And Ike, he decided to leave on the spot:
"My dear old Pike County, I'll go back to you."
Said Betsy, "You'll go by yourself if you do." *Refrain*

6. They swam the wide rivers, they crossed the tall peaks,
They camped out on prairies for weeks and for weeks,
Fought hunger and rattlers and big storms of dust,
Determined to reach California or bust. *Refrain*

**Two-Part Harmony**

**Identify** the refrain of "Sweet Betsy from Pike." **Sing** the melody first, and then learn the harmony part. **Perform** both parts together.



# 2 Develop

## Listening

**ASK Do you know any songs that tell a story?** (Accept a variety of answers.)

**SAY** This song tells a story about a part of United States history.

6b Play "Sweet Betsy from Pike" **CD 10-16.** Have students follow the lyrics as they listen.

**ASK Where were Betsy and Ike going?** (California)

**Do you think it was an easy trip or a hard trip?** (Accept a variety of answers.)

## Singing

**ASK Which part of the song is sung in harmony?** (refrain)

1d Invite students to sing the first verse and refrain in unison with the recording. Then have them

- Practice the harmony echoes of the refrain, then sing the echoes while listening to the melody.
- Sing the harmony part only of the last line, then sing the harmony while listening to the melody.

After practicing the refrain, have students sing the entire song, dividing into harmony for the refrain.

# 3 Close

**Skill: SINGING** — **ASSESSMENT**

**Performance/Observation** Have students sing "Sweet Betsy from Pike" **CD 10-16** in two parts. Observe students' ability to sing accurately together in harmony.

To review terms learned in Unit 4 through Unit 6, invite students to complete the crossword puzzle on Activity Master 11. See Resource Book p. J-14.

## Skills Reinforcement

▶ **Keyboard** Encourage students to play a two-hand accompaniment with "Sweet Betsy from Pike." The accompaniment
2b uses C-major, G-major, A-minor, F-major, and E-minor chords in closest position. The minor chords will be the most challenging. For more on this accompaniment, see Resource Book p. H-17.

▶ **Recorder** For more harmony with "Sweet Betsy from Pike," have students learn and play the recorder countermelody on p. I-19 in the Resource Book.

## School to Home Connection

▶ **Families on the Move** Ask students to discuss with family members any moves the family has made. Did they move across town or across the country? Did they hire movers and fly to the new town, or did they put everything in a truck and drive it to the new house themselves? Were pets happy with the move? Have the class discuss what it would be like if they used only a covered wagon and had to limit the number of items taken.

## Technology/Media Link

**Web Site** Invite students to visit *www.sfsuccessnet.com* for information on music of the California Gold Rush.

# Review and Assessment

## What Do You Know?

**MATERIALS**
- **Resource Book** p. B-21

Invite students to review concepts they have studied in this unit. Have students read and answer the questions independently and then check their answers with a partner before sharing answers with the rest of the class or with you.

For a more formal assessment, you may wish to duplicate the Unit 6 assessment worksheet and have students work independently or in small groups to complete it. The worksheet is found in the Resource Book on p. B-21.

## What Do You Hear?

**MATERIALS**
- *What Do You Hear? 6* — **CD 10-18**
- **Resource Book** p. B-21

Invite students to review sound qualities and other characteristics of the four instruments listed: the piano, the harpsichord, the organ, and the synthesizer. Refer to Unit 6, Lesson 8, if necessary.

Have students listen to *What Do You Hear? 6* and choose the instrument they hear in each example. Students can work either independently or in small groups.

For a more formal assessment, you may wish to duplicate the Unit 6 assessment worksheet found on Resource Book p. B-21.

## What Do You Know?

Match the terms below with their definitions.

| | |
|---|---|
| **1.** accent | a melody started at different times |
| **2.** theme and variations | a melody pattern repeated at a higher or lower pitch level |
| **3.** melodic sequence | stress on certain notes |
| **4.** round | a melody repeated with changes |

## What Do You Hear? 6

 **CD 10–18**

Listen to the following examples of keyboard music. Point to the name of the instrument you hear in each example.

| | | | |
|---|---|---|---|
| **1.** piano | harpsichord | organ | synthesizer |
| **2.** piano | harpsichord | organ | synthesizer |
| **3.** piano | harpsichord | organ | synthesizer |
| **4.** piano | harpsichord | organ | synthesizer |

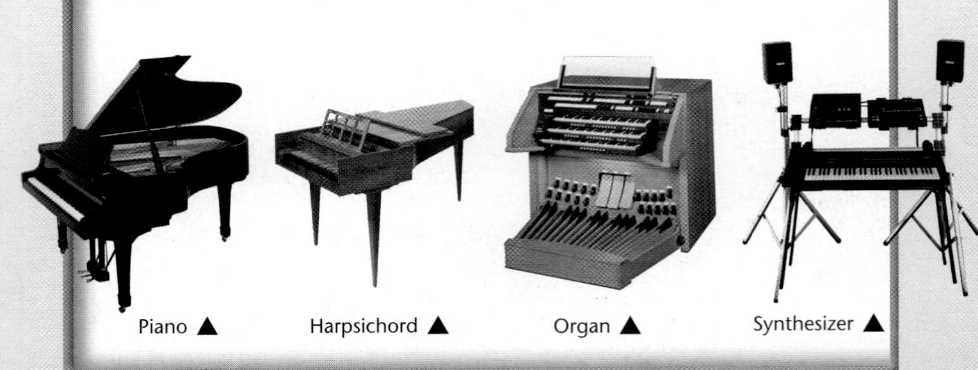

Piano ▲ Harpsichord ▲ Organ ▲ Synthesizer ▲



## Footnotes

### Answer Key

**▶ What Do You Know?**

1. accent—stress on certain notes
2. theme and variations—a melody with changes
3. melodic sequence—a melody pattern repeated at a higher or lower pitch level
4. round—a melody started at different times

**▶ What Do You Hear?**

1. organ—*Toccata in D Minor*
2. synthesizer—*Close Encounters of the Third Kind*
3. piano—*Waltz in D-flat*
4. harpsichord—"Gigue" from *French Suite No. 5*

# Perform, Create

## What You Can Do

### Move to Variations

Listen to *Russian Sailors' Dance,* on page 224, and perform the body percussion pattern. Create your own body percussion part for *Russian Sailors' Dance* and perform it for the class.

### Perform with Accents

Sing "*El rancho grande,*" on page 215. Decide where to add accents and then perform them as you sing.

### Create with Rhythms

Sing "Dry Bones Come Skipping," on page 218. Perform small steady-beat movements to accompany the A sections and different steady-beat movements with the B section. Using the rhythms in the song, create a rhythm ostinato. Perform the ostinato on nonpitched percussion instruments as you sing the song.

### Move with Sequences

Sing "*Tancovačka,*" on page 230. Perform hand movements to show the contour of the melodic sequences in the verse.

### Sing in Rounds

Sing "Let Music Surround You," on page 236, as a round. Always sing with good vocal quality.

## What You Can Do

**MATERIALS**

- *Russian Sailors' Dance,* p. 224 **CD 9-26**
- *"El rancho grande,"* p. 215 **CD 9-6**
- "Dry Bones Come Skipping," p. 218 **CD 9-15**
- *"Tancovačka,"* p. 230 **CD 9-39**
- "Let Music Surround You, " p. 236 **CD 10-6**
- **Resource Book** p. B-22
- nonpitched percussion instruments

### Move to Variations

Look at *Russian Sailors' Dance* and invite students to perform the body percussion part. Divide the class into groups to decide what other body percussion patterns could be used with this piece.

### Perform with Accents

Ask the class to turn to *"El rancho grande."* Encourage students to decide where accents belong. Tell them that word accents generally get the stress.

### Create with Rhythms

Invite the class to listen to "Dry Bones Come Skipping" and create contrasting steady-beat movements for the A and B sections of the song. Then ask students to create ostinatos using combinations of rhythms they know. Have students play and move as they sing the song.

### Move with Sequences

Look at *"Tancovačka"* with the class. Have students clap the first sequence in a high position. Have them clap the second one in front of their chests, and the last sequence at hip level.

### Sing in Rounds

Invite students to sing "Let Music Surround You" as a round. First practice each entrance separately as an ostinato. Then invite students to put the parts together as a round.

For a blackline master of What You Can Do, see Resource Book p. B-22.

### Technology/Media Link

**Rubrics** Visit *www.sfsuccessnet.com* for rubrics to assess students' achievement in music skills.

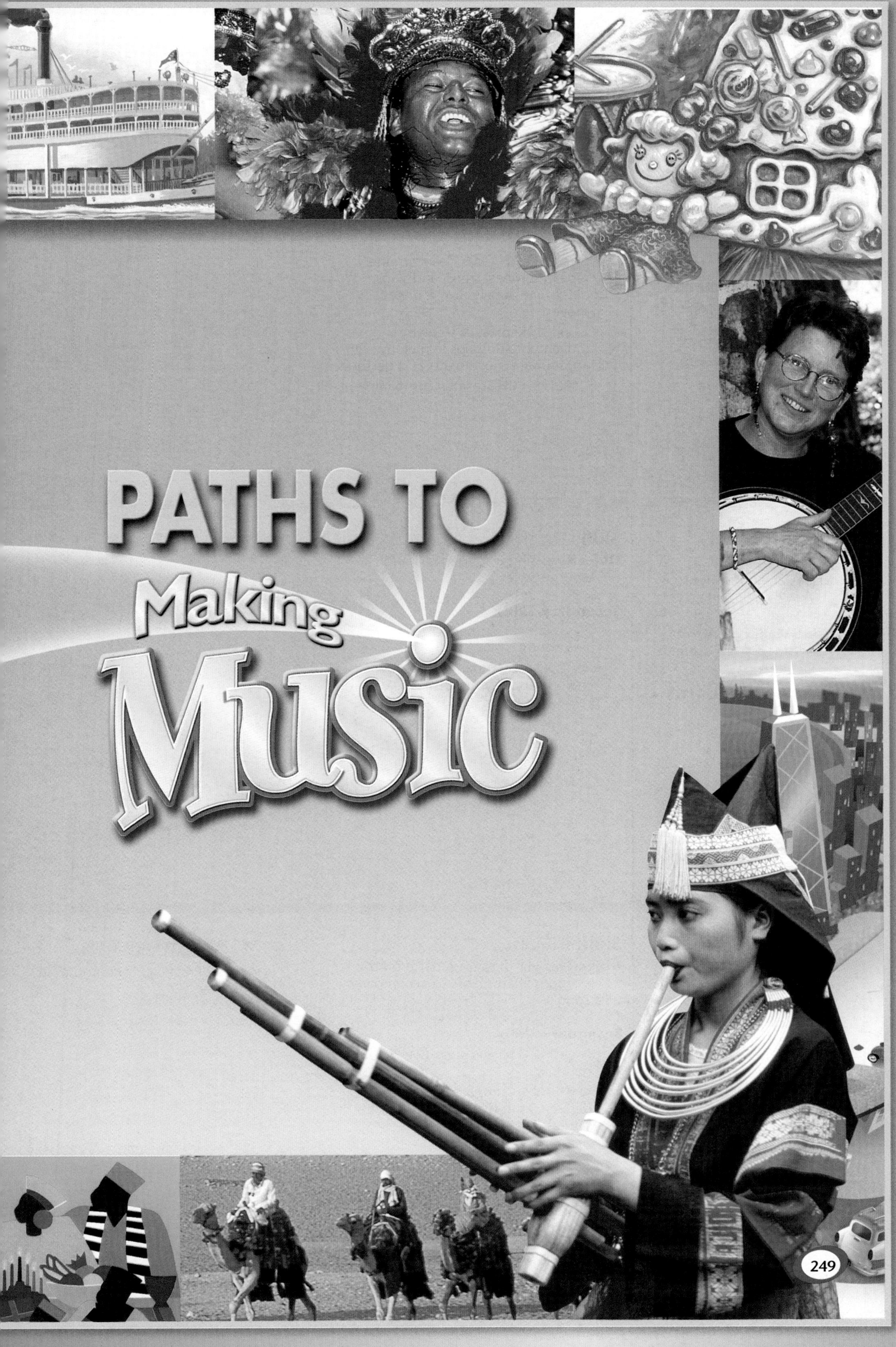
PATHS TO
Making
Music
249

| Lesson | Elements | Skills | |
|---|---|---|---|
| LESSON 1 **Ride the Wave, Sing a Shanty** pp. 254-257  | **Element: Melody**<br>**Concept:** Pitch and direction<br>**Focus:** Steps, leaps, and repeated patterns<br><br>**Secondary Element**<br>Form: verse/refrain<br><br>**National Standards**<br>1a 1b 2a 2b 4b 5b 6e 9c | **Skill: Singing**<br>**Objective:** Sing steps, leaps, and repeated patterns<br><br>**Secondary Skills**<br>• **Listening** Compare two songs after listening<br>• **Singing/Analyzing** Determine repeated tones, steps, and skips; determine aurally how a melody moves<br>• **Moving** Represent stepwise movement and skips in melody with appropriate movements and gestures<br>• **Creating** Create an accompaniment for a poem | **SKILLS REINFORCEMENT**<br>• **Creating** Compose a sound piece using classroom instruments<br>• **Recorder** Practice playing notes in upper register |
| LESSON 2 **Sailing to the Gulf** pp. 258-259  | **Element: Form**<br>**Concept:** Style<br>**Focus:** Call-and-response style<br><br>**Secondary Element**<br>Rhythm: rhythm ostinato<br><br>**National Standards**<br>1c 2f 6a 8b | **Skill: Singing**<br>**Objective:** Sing a song in call-and-response style<br><br>**Secondary Skills**<br>• **Analyzing** Compare the form of two songs<br>• **Playing** Accompany a song on melody and rhythm instruments | |
| LESSON 3 **The Celtic Connection** pp. 260-261 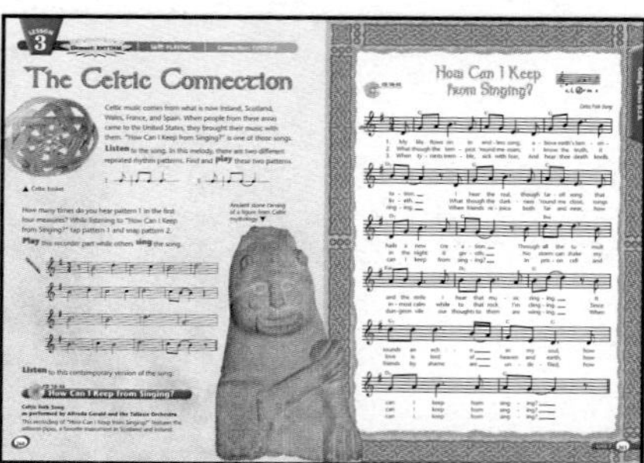 | **Element: Rhythm**<br>**Concept:** Pattern<br>**Focus:** Rhythm patterns<br><br>**Secondary Element**<br>Texture/Harmony: I, IV, and $V_7$ chords<br><br>**National Standards**<br>1b 1c 2b 4b 5a | **Skill: Playing**<br>**Objective:** Play a rhythm pattern on classroom instruments to accompany a song<br><br>**Secondary Skills**<br>• **Reading** Tap and snap two rhythm patterns<br>• **Listening** Compare similarities and differences in two recordings of the same song | **SKILLS REINFORCEMENT**<br>• **Recorder** Practice playing notes in low register |

| Connections | Music and Other Literature | |
|---|---|---|
| **Connection:** Social Studies<br>**Activity:** Examine how sea shanties are linked to American history<br>ACROSS THE CURRICULUM<br>**Language Arts/Social Studies** Read about and discuss the history of whaling<br>**Social Studies** Discuss the song "Rio Grande," as well as trading area<br>SPOTLIGHT ON *Chanty or Shanty?* Origin of shanties; derivation of the word; use of shanties to lighten work<br>TEACHER TO TEACHER **Management Tip** Create aids in settings with limited resources<br>MEETING INDIVIDUAL NEEDS<br>**English Language Learners** Create strategies using visual aids for increased comprehension<br>**Working Together** Create group activity to simulate actual environments<br>BUILDING SKILLS THROUGH MUSIC **Language** Determine the meanings of unfamiliar words in a poem | **Songs**<br>"Blow, Ye Winds"<br>"Rio Grande"<br><br>**Poem** "The Sea Wolf"<br><br>**More Music Choices**<br>"Haul Away, Joe," p. 13 | ASSESSMENT<br>**Performance/Observation** Perform and recognize steps, leaps, and repeated tones<br><br>TECHNOLOGY/MEDIA LINK<br>**Web Site** Research shanties and other work songs |
| **Connection:** Social Studies<br>**Activity:** Sing a sea shanty that was sung in the Gulf of Mexico<br>CULTURAL CONNECTION **Sea Shanties** Learn about the role of sea shanties<br>MOVEMENT **Creative Movement** Imitate movement seen in a painting<br>SPOTLIGHT ON **The Artist** Facts about German artist Julius Stockfleth<br>BUILDING SKILLS THROUGH MUSIC **Math** Solve a division word problem | **Song** "'Round the Bay of Mexico"<br><br>**Arts Connection**<br>*The Port of Galveston*<br><br>**More Music Choices**<br>"Limbo Like Me," p. 18<br>"Pay Me My Money Down," p. 38 | ASSESSMENT<br>**Performance/Observation** **Identify** parts in a call-and-response style song<br><br>TECHNOLOGY/MEDIA LINK<br>**Electronic Keyboard** Select appropriate sounds for an accompaniment |
| **Connection:** Culture<br>**Activity:** Examine the Celtic folk heritage<br>ACROSS THE CURRICULUM<br>**Language Arts** Read about many different Celtic peoples<br>**Social Studies** On a world map, locate countries home to the Celtic people<br>CULTURAL CONNECTION **Celtic Music** Facts about Celtic music, the "oral tradition," and Celtic instruments<br>BUILDING SKILLS THROUGH MUSIC **Language** Discuss the meaning of song lyrics | **Song** "How Can I Keep from Singing?"<br><br>**Listening Selection** *How Can I Keep from Singing?* (excerpt)<br><br>**More Music Choices**<br>"The Bard of Armagh," p. 296<br>*"Einini,"* p. 391 | ASSESSMENT<br>**Performance/Observation** **Create** and perform an introduction and coda using given rhythm patterns<br><br>TECHNOLOGY/MEDIA LINK<br>**Notation Software** Record and play back layered rhythm patterns as accompaniment to song |

| Lesson | Elements | Skills | |
|---|---|---|---|
| LESSON 4 **Get that Pioneer Spirit** pp. 262-265   | **Element: Rhythm**<br>**Concept:** Pattern<br>**Focus:** ♩ ♬♩. , ♬♩ ♩. and ♪ ♩ ♪ rhythm patterns<br><br>**Secondary Element**<br>Melody: pitch patterns<br><br>**National Standards**<br>1e 2b 2d 2f 4b 5a 6a 9a | **Skill: Reading**<br>**Objective:** Read ♩ ♬♩. , ♬♩ ♩. and ♪ ♩ ♪ rhythm patterns<br><br>**Secondary Skills**<br>• **Listening** Determine aurally number of rhythmic phrases and total number of phrases in a song<br>• **Singing** Sing and tap steady beat<br>• **Moving** Perform a patterned dance to two songs<br>• **Playing** Create and accompany a song using appropriate nonpitched percussion instruments | **SKILLS REINFORCEMENT**<br>• **Recorder** Accompany a song with ostinatos on barred instruments<br>• **Creating** Create a rhythm composition using all rhythms experienced<br>• **Keyboard** Play chords of a song on off-beats |
| LESSON 5 **What's in a Song?** pp. 266-269   | **Element: Timbre**<br>**Concept:** Vocal timbres<br>**Focus:** Tone color of adult and child singing voices<br><br>**Secondary Element**<br>Harmony: minor tonality<br><br>**National Standards**<br>1a 2b 6c 6d 8b 9a | **Skill: Singing**<br>**Objective:** Sing a song in a manner appropriate to a child's voice<br><br>**Secondary Skills**<br>• **Listening** Determine difference in sound between children's voices and an adult female soloist<br>• **Playing** Play an Orff accompaniment to a song<br>• **Performing** Experiment with vocal tone color<br>• **Listening/Performing** Recite a poem using changing vocal timbre | **SKILLS REINFORCEMENT**<br>• **Singing** Group self-conscious singers for support in solo parts before asking individuals to sing alone |
|  LESSON 6 **Meter Matters** pp. 270-273   | **Element: Rhythm**<br>**Concept:** Pattern<br>**Focus:** $\frac{3}{4}$ time in slow and fast tempos<br><br>**Secondary Element**<br>Expression: tempo<br><br>**National Standards**<br>2a 2e 4c 6b | **Skill: Creating**<br>**Objective:** Create and perform ostinatos in $\frac{3}{4}$ time in several tempos<br><br>**Secondary Skills**<br>• **Listening** Echo clap patterns; identify meter aurally and compare tempo with two songs<br>• **Singing** Use the Pronunciation Practice before singing in Spanish; sing with the recording<br>• **Analyzing** Analyze two recorded songs; discover effect of tempo on a song<br>• **Reading** Speak and clap given rhythm patterns; create and play an ostinato<br>• **Moving** Perform simple movements to a song | **SKILLS REINFORCEMENT**<br>• **Guitar** Play a "thumb-strum-strum" rhythm to accompany two songs<br>• **Recorder** Play a countermelody<br>• **Keyboard** Perform an ensemble accompaniment |

## Connections

## Music and Other Literature

### Connection: Social Studies

**Activity:** Examine Stephen Foster's legacy to American music

**ACROSS THE CURRICULUM** **Language Arts/Social Studies** Read a book about pioneer figures; write biographical profiles for recitation

**CULTURAL CONNECTION** **The Forty Niners** A favorite song is brought to California by the gold seekers in 1849

**SPOTLIGHT ON** **The Songwriter and Composer** Facts about Stephen Foster and his songs

**MEETING INDIVIDUAL NEEDS** **Aiding Comprehension** Use visual aids to assist in recognition of pitch patterns

**MOVEMENT** **Patterned Dance** Introduce dance movements to "The Glendy Burke" and "Oh, Susanna"

**BUILDING SKILLS THROUGH MUSIC** **Social Studies** Research historical events during Stephen Foster's lifetime

**Songs**
"The Glendy Burke"
"Oh, Susanna"

**More Music Choices**
*"Ala Da'lona,"* p. 136
*"Ai Dunaii moy,"* p. 293
"Somebody's Knockin' at Your Door," p. 53

**ASSESSMENT**

**Performance/Observation**
**Create** and perform a rhythm composition using given patterns

**TECHNOLOGY/MEDIA LINK**

**Web Site**
Read information about Stephen Foster

### Connection: Language Arts

**Activity:** Read a poem about Harriet Tubman

**ACROSS THE CURRICULUM**
**Language Arts/Social Studies** Read a book about the Underground Railroad and runaway slaves
**Social Studies/Art** Read a book about code words in quilt patterns

**CULTURAL CONNECTION** **African American Spirituals** History of origins of spirituals, description of performance style

**SPOTLIGHT ON** **Harriet Tubman** Facts about the escaped slave and her leadership role in the Underground Railroad

**TEACHER TO TEACHER** **The Constellation Connection** Learn how constellations helped slaves find their way

**MOVEMENT** **Creative Movement** Use movement that suggests "wading in the water"

**CHARACTER EDUCATION** **Courage** Discuss the courage and conviction of those who assisted with the Underground Railroad

**BUILDING SKILLS THROUGH MUSIC** **Science/Art** Recreate the Big Dipper

**Songs**
"Follow the Drinkin' Gourd"
"Wade in the Water"

**Poem** "Harriet Tubman"

**More Music Choices**
"All Night, All Day," p. 180
"I'm Gonna Sing," p. 33
*Many Voices,* pp. 30-33

**ASSESSMENT**

**Performance/Observation**
Sing on pitch and with a head tone

**TECHNOLOGY/MEDIA LINK**

**Video Library** Watch the Total Experience Gospel Choir

### Connection: Culture

**Activity:** Compare the music of Mexico with an American cowboy ballad

**ACROSS THE CURRICULUM**
**Language Arts** Read about the life of the cowboy
**Social Studies** Research of Spanish missions in California
**Language Arts** Read and discuss the poem "The Cow"

**CULTURAL CONNECTION** **Spanish Influence In the United States** Visible in American architecture and home furnishing style

**SPOTLIGHT ON**
**Ballads** Historical facts about ballads
**Treaty of Guadalupe Hidalgo** Facts about the Mexican-American war

**BUILDING SKILLS THROUGH MUSIC** **Social Studies** Locate the region of the United States that was annexed as a result of the Treaty of Guadalupe Hidalgo

**Songs**
"*Cielito lindo*" (Spanish and English)
"Streets of Laredo"

**Listening Selection** *El siquisirí*

**More Music Choices**
"River," p. 58
"*Cantando mentíras,*" p. 146
"*El borrego,*" p. 242

**ASSESSMENT**

**Performance/Observation**
Perform accurately created ostinatos in fast and slow tempos, maintaining a steady beat

**TECHNOLOGY/MEDIA LINK**

**MIDI/Sequencing Software** Experiment with playing songs in fast and slow tempos; add percussion or chord root tracks to a song

| Lesson | Elements | Skills |
|---|---|---|

## Lesson 7 "Driving" to Kansas

pp. 274-275

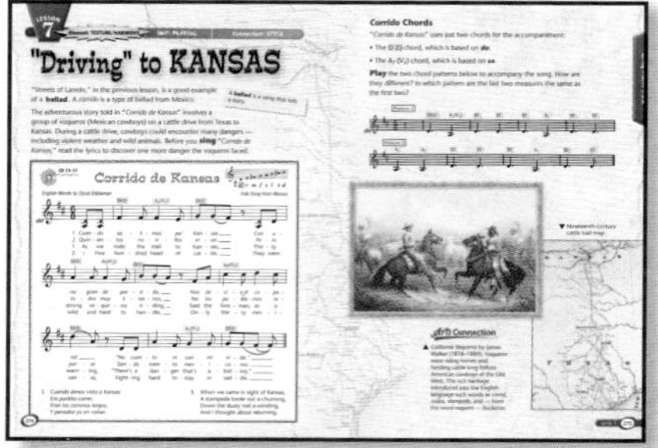


**Element: Texture/Harmony**
**Concept:** Chordal accompaniment
**Focus:** I-$V_7$ accompaniment

**Secondary Element**
Melody: pattern

**National Standards**
1c 2b 6e

**Skill: Playing**
**Objective:** Play bass note patterns from I and $V_7$ chords to accompany a song

**Secondary Skills**
- **Singing** Perform a song in Spanish
- **Analyzing** Identify song key and chord letter names

**SKILLS REINFORCEMENT**
- **Playing** Add another layer to a song

## Lesson 8 Take a Road Trip

pp. 276-279

**Element: Rhythm**
**Concept:** Style
**Focus:** Swing eighth notes

**Secondary Element**
Expression: articulation

**National Standards**

**Skill: Playing**
**Objective:** Play eighth-note rhythm patterns while singing a song in swing style

**Secondary Skills**
- **Listening** Identify ways to interpret a song; compare two singers' vocal styles
- **Singing** Be aware of swing style elements when singing
- **Moving** Interpret a song with movements

**SKILLS REINFORCEMENT**
- **Singing** Sing and listen to two songs in swing style

## Lesson 9 Give Me Five

pp. 280-281

**Element: Melody**
**Concept:** Pattern
**Focus:** Melody patterns in *la*-pentatonic

**Secondary Element**
Rhythm: syncopation in $\frac{4}{4}$ time

**National Standards**
2b 2d 5b

**Skill: Playing**
**Objective:** Create and play parts to accompany a *la*-pentatonic melody

**Secondary Skills**
- **Reading** Sing and read *la*-pentatonic patterns
- **Singing** Echo phrases, then sing
- **Performing** Play an Orff accompaniment with a song

**SKILLS REINFORCEMENT**
- **Creating** Notate *la*-pentatonic scales before notating melodies on given pitches

| Connections | Music and Other Literature | |
|---|---|---|
| **Connection:** Style<br>**Activity:** Sing a Mexican *corrido*<br>SPOTLIGHT ON **Cattle Drives** Learn how cowboys moved cattle from one place to another<br>TEACHER TO TEACHER **Orff Instruments** Play pitches up one octave<br>BUILDING SKILLS THROUGH MUSIC **Technology** Research cattle drives and maps of Texas and Kansas on the classroom computer | **Song** *"Corrido de Kansas* ("Kansas Corrido")<br>**Arts Connection**<br>*California Vaqueros*<br>**More Music Choices**<br>"I'm Gonna Sing," p. 33<br>"Over My Head," p. 118<br>*"El rancho grande,"* p. 215 | ASSESSMENT<br>**Performance/Observation** Show correct chord numbers and play the correct pitches to accompany a song<br>TECHNOLOGY/MEDIA LINK<br>**Notation Software** Notate I and $V_7$ chord changes<br>**Web Site** Visit *www.sfsuccessnet.com* for more information about the music of Mexico |
| **Connection:** Style<br>**Activity:** Explore swing style music<br>ACROSS THE CURRICULUM **Social Studies/Math** Locate states and cities along Route 66 on a map; calculate distances<br>**Language Arts** Read and discuss the poem "Maps"<br>CULTURAL CONNECTION **Road to Opportunity** Immortalization of Route 66, a migration route to California, in a novel and a film<br>SPOTLIGHT ON<br>**Roadside Architecture** Evolution of the model from auto camps and cabins throughout the U.S.A.<br>**The Big Band Era** History of performers of Big Band music and its popularity<br>MEETING INDIVIDUAL NEEDS **English Language Learners** Create strategies using oral retellings for clearer understanding of various phrases<br>BUILDING SKILLS THROUGH MUSIC **Social Studies** On a map, locate cities mentioned in a song | **Song** "Route 66"<br>**Listening Selection**<br>*Route 66*<br>M*U*S*I*C M*A*K*E*R*S<br>Harry James<br>**More Music Choices**<br>*On Green Dolphin Street*, p. 126<br>"Straighten Up and Fly Right," p. 128 | ASSESSMENT<br>**Performance/Observation** Sing the song and swing the eighth notes in the accompaniment part<br>TECHNOLOGY/MEDIA LINK<br>**Web Site** Visit *www.sfsuccessnet.com* for more information about jazz |
| **Connection:** Social Studies<br>**Activity:** Discuss how a folk song reflects social and political issues<br>SPOTLIGHT ON **The Songwriter and Composer** Facts about Woody Guthrie, the popular folk singer<br>MEETING INDIVIDUAL NEEDS **Teaching with Visuals** Make visuals of instruments before actual instruments are played<br>BUILDING SKILLS THROUGH MUSIC **Math** Draw a pentagon and label each side with notes from the la pentatonic scale | **Song** "Pastures of Plenty"<br>M*U*S*I*C M*A*K*E*R*S<br>Woody Guthrie<br>**More Music Choices**<br>"Canoe Song," p. 76<br>"See the Children Playin'," p. 107 | ASSESSMENT<br>**Performance/Observation** Create and perform ostinatos to accompany the song<br>TECHNOLOGY/MEDIA LINK<br>**CD-ROM** Use rhythm tracks to accompany improvised melodies on a melody instrument |

| Lesson | Elements | Skills | |
|---|---|---|---|
| LESSON 10 **The Beat Goes On** pp. 282-285  | **Element: Rhythm**<br>**Concept:** Meter<br>**Focus:** Beat and meter<br><br>**Secondary Element**<br>Melody: phrases<br><br>**National Standards**<br>1a 1c 2a 2b 5a 6a 9b | **Skill: Singing**<br>**Objective:** Sing a song in meter in 4, in various meters, and perform a steady beat<br><br>**Secondary Skills**<br>• **Reading** Speak and clap four different rhythm patterns, discover repeated rhythms, order patterns to match song<br>• **Analyzing** Gain insight into Chippewa music; meet a Native American scholar<br>• **Listening** Follow the music keeping a steady beat | **SKILLS REINFORCEMENT**<br>• **Creating** Create an accompaniment on bells, shakers, and drums |
| LESSON 11 **California, Here We Come!** pp. 286-287  | **Element: Melody**<br>**Concept:** Pattern<br>**Focus:** Melodic sequence<br><br>**Secondary Element**<br>Rhythm: changing meter, steady beat<br><br>**National Standards**<br>1b 6b 6e | **Skill: Singing**<br>**Objective:** Sing melodic sequences<br><br>**Secondary Skills**<br>• **Listening** Determine how phrases are alike or different and discover sequences | **SKILLS REINFORCEMENT**<br>• **Playing** Experiment with playing sequences<br>• **Signing** Sign a song |
| | | | |

UNIT 7 **UNIT AT A GLANCE**

| Connections | Music and Other Literature | |
|---|---|---|
| **Connection:** Culture<br>**Activity:** Discuss how Native American music reflects values and beliefs<br>**ACROSS THE CURRICULUM**<br>**Social Studies** Research various Native American tribes<br>**Art/Language Arts** Appreciate full-color reproductions of Native American Art; recreate art pieces for display<br>**CULTURAL CONNECTION**<br>**Native American Music** Traditional instruments used in celebrations<br>**Chippewa Music** Characteristics of the music of Lakers and Woods Native Americans<br>**SPOTLIGHT ON**<br>**"I Walk in Beauty"** History and meaning of the lyrics of the song<br>**"Farewell to the Warriors"** History behind the story of the song<br>**CHARACTER EDUCATION** **Health** Discuss the importance of maintaining inner balance and peace<br>**BUILDING SKILLS THROUGH MUSIC** **Social Studies** Research the nearest Native American tribes | **Songs**<br>"I Walk in Beauty"<br>"Farewell to the Warriors"<br>**Listening Selection** *Interview with J. Bryan Burton*<br>**M*U*S*I*C M*A*K*E*R*S**<br>J. Bryan Burton<br>**More Music Choices**<br>"And My Heart Soars" (poem). p. 359<br>"The Earth Is Our Mother," p. 358 | **ASSESSMENT**<br>**Performance/Observation** Sing the song while keeping the steady beat<br>**TECHNOLOGY/MEDIA LINK**<br>**Web Site** Visit *www.sfsuccessnet.com* for more information about the music of Native American people |
| **Connection:** Social Studies<br>**Activity:** Explore California's image in music<br>**ACROSS THE CURRICULUM** **Social Studies** Discuss facts about California using a map for reference; and its allure<br>**SPOTLIGHT ON** **Al Jolson** Facts about the popular entertainer in theater, music, and the stage<br>**BUILDING SKILLS THROUGH MUSIC** **Science** Learn about the Golden Gate Bridge and how it is supported | **Song** "California, Here I Come"<br>**M*U*S*I*C M*A*K*E*R*S**<br>Al Jolson<br>**More Music Choices**<br>*"Tancovačka,"* p. 230<br>*"Thula, thula ngoana,"* p. 227 | **ASSESSMENT**<br>**Performance/Observation** Sing the song and clap to identify melodic sequences<br>**TECHNOLOGY/MEDIA LINK**<br>**Sequencing Software** Use the software and a computer to demonstrate the similar phrase shapes in a sequence |
| | | |

# Introducing the Unit

This unit is based on a musical journey across the United States from New York City to California. This provides the opportunity to develop a simulated vacation trip across America.

See below and pp. 252–253 for unit highlights of related curricular experiences. For a more detailed unit overview, see Unit at a Glance, pp. 249a–249h.

# Unit Project

A vast array of integrated activities involving most subject areas can be developed from a simulated vacation trip.

Using a highway map, plot the route driven from New York to a specific city in California.

- What is the length of the trip?
- How long will it take to complete?
- What other cities will be involved in the trip?
- What points of interest are found in each of these cities?

On the trip, students will be visiting many different cities. Have them research the cities and design a postcard they might send home when visiting one of these cities. Display these various postcards using the heading "My Summer Vacation."

Vacations can be very expensive. Having gathered the information concerning distance and length of the trip, calculate the costs, including gasoline, accommodations, and sightseeing.

Food is a necessary part of any vacation. Help students discover any distinctive foods that are associated with the cities on the trip. Have students collect recipes of these special dishes and collectively publish a "Trip Cook Book."

### Song of the City

"Theme from New York, New York" was written for a movie *New York, New York.* Read the words to this song. Create a story about someone from a small town who really wants to live in the big city. What are some reasons a person might want to live in a big city?

CD 10–22

## Theme from New York, New York

*Words by Fred Ebb* *Music by John Kander*

Start spread-in' the news, I'm leav-ing to - day,

I wan - na be a part of it New York, New York.

250

## Across the Curriculum

**Unit Highlights** The following interdisciplinary activities in this unit are related to the music elements or themes presented in the lessons and are intended to enhance student learning. See Unit at a Glance, pp. 249a–249h, for topical descriptions presented according to lesson sequence.

**▶ ART/RELATED ARTS**

- Read a book about code words in quilt patterns (p. 268)
- Appreciate full-color reproductions of Native American art; recreate art pieces for display (p. 285)

**▶ LANGUAGE ARTS**

- Read about the life of the cowboy (p. 271)
- Read and discuss the poems "The Cow" (p. 273) and "Maps" (p. 278)

**▶ MATH**

- Locate on a map states and cities along Route 66; calculate distances (p. 277)

**▶ SOCIAL STUDIES**

- Read about and discuss the history of whaling (p. 254)
- Discuss the song "Rio Grande," as well as trading areas (p. 256)
- Locate on a world map countries that are home to the Celtic people (p. 261)
- Read a book about pioneer figures (p. 263)
- Read a book about the Underground Railroad (p. 266)
- Research Spanish missions in California (p. 271)
- Research various Native American tribes throughout Arizona and New Mexico (p. 283)
- Discuss facts about California, using a map for reference (p. 286)

UNIT 7
NASHVILLE
GOING PLACES U.S.A.
Begin a musical trip around the United States. Start on the east coast with "Theme from New York, New York" and travel to the west coast with "California, Here I Come."
W YORK CITY
B♭7 E♭ Fm7 B♭7
These vag - a - bond shoes are long-ing to stray,
Fm7 B♭7 E♭ E♭7
And step a - round the heart of it New York, New York.
Unit 7 251

UNIT 7 INTRODUCTION

## Music Skills Assessed in This Unit

**Reading Music: Rhythm**

- Read rhythm patterns (p. 261)
- Perform student-created rhythm patterns (p. 265)

**Reading Music: Pitch**

- Recognize steps, leaps, and repeated tones (p. 257)
- Clap to identify melodic sequences (p. 287)

**Performing Music: Singing**

- Perform steps, leaps, and repeated tones (p. 257)
- Sing on pitch and with a head tone (p. 269)
- Sing the song and swing the eighth notes in the accompaniment part (p. 279)

**Moving to Music**

- Raise hands to distinguish between solo and chorus parts in a song (p. 259)
- Sing the song while keeping the steady beat (p. 285)

**Performing Music: Playing**

- Perform an introduction and coda using given rhythm patterns (pp. 261 and 265)
- Perform created ostinatos in fast and slow tempos, maintaining a steady beat (p. 273)
- Perform ostinatos to accompany the song (p. 281)

**Creating Music**

- Create an introduction and coda using given rhythm patterns (pp. 261 and 265)
- Create ostinatos to accompany the song (p. 281)

**Listening to Music**

- Listen and compare song attributes (p. 255)
- Identify solo and chorus parts in a song (p. 259)

## Cultural Connection

**Unit Highlights** The musical literature in this unit provides many opportunities for students to explore a variety of world cultures. See Unit at a Glance, pp. 249a–249h, for topical descriptions presented according to lesson sequence.

**AFRICAN/AFRICAN AMERICAN**

- "Follow the Drinkin' Gourd" (p. 266)
- Learn about the origins and styles of spirituals (p. 267)
- "Wade in the Water" (p. 268)

**AMERICAN**

- "Blow, Ye Winds" (p. 255)
- "Rio Grande" (p. 256)
- "Oh, Susanna" (p. 264)
- "Streets of Laredo" (p. 272)
- Learn about Route 66, a migration route to California, which was immortalized in a novel, a film, and a song (p. 277)
- Learn about traditional Native American instruments used in celebrations (p. 282)
- "Farewell to the Warriors" (p. 284): Learn characteristics of the music of Lakes and Woods Native Americans (p. 284)

**EUROPEAN**

- Discover the origin of sea shanties (p. 258)
- Explore facts about Celtic music (p. 260)
- "How Can I Keep from Singing?" (p. 261)

**LATIN AMERICAN**

- "*Cielito lindo*" (p. 270)
- Discover the influence of the Spanish on American architecture and home furnishing styles (p. 271)
- "*Corrido de Kansas*" (p. 274)

# Opening Activities

**MATERIALS**

"Theme from New York, New York" **CD 10-22**

**Recording Routine:**
Intro (4 m.); vocal; coda

**Dance Directions** for "Theme from New York, New York" p. 513

## Listening

Invite students to listen to the recording of "Theme from New York, New York." Ask students to describe the feeling of the song. (lively, upbeat, excited)

Explain to students that the song was written for a 1977 movie called *New York, New York.* However, it was Frank Sinatra who made the song popular in a 1979 release. Have students listen again, this time showing the phrases by moving their hand from one shoulder to the other.

## Reading

Ask students to look at the song lyrics and discuss what these phrases mean: *king of the hill; cream of the crop at the top of the heap; vagabond shoes; If I can make it there, I'd make it anywhere.*

Next, have students find the *D.S.* and *Coda* signs to determine how to follow the score with the recording.

Tell students that a rhythmic characteristic of the song is the two-beat triplet. Ask them to find the two-beat triplets in the score. (The first example occurs in measure 1. There are 13 altogether.)

Have students echo speak these rhythms after you. Then have them echo sing some of these measures.

**SAY** Whole notes usually appear after each triplet.

**ASK** **How many can you find?** (17)

Then read the words of the song together.

## Assessment

**Unit Highlights** The lessons in this unit were chosen and developed to support the theme "Going Places U.S.A." Each lesson, as always, presents a clear element focus, a skill objective, and an end-of-lesson assessment. The overall sequence of lessons, however, is organized according to this theme, rather than concept or skill development. In this context, formal assessment strategies, such as those presented in Units 1–6, are no longer applicable.

▶ **INFORMAL ASSESSMENTS**

At the close of each Teacher's Edition lesson in this unit, the following type of assessment is used to evaluate the learning of the key element focus or skill objective.

- Performance/Observation (pp. 257, 259, 261, 265, 269, 273, 275, 279, 281, 285, 287)

▶ **RUBRICS**

Visit *www.sfsuccessnet.com* for rubrics to assess students' achievement in music skills.

blues are melt-ing a - way, I'll make a

brand new start of it in old New York.

If I can make it there I'd make it

an - y-where come on, come through New York, New York.



## Singing

Play the recording of "Theme from New York, New York" **CD 10-22** and invite students to sing along, making certain they hold the long notes at the ends of phrases for four beats.

To help students hold the long notes for four beats, have them show each whole note as a movement gesture from one shoulder to the other.

ASK **What makes the ending of the song more exciting?** (It modulates to a higher key.)

Have students sing the song again. This time, ask them to lightly tap the rhythm of each measure that has a triplet figure.

## Moving

Refer to Dance Directions, on p. 513 in the Teacher's Edition, for a patterned movement activity to accompany "Theme from New York, New York." Use the Stereo Vocal/Dance Performance Track **CD 10-22.**

### Innovative Teacher Support for This Unit

- **Making Music DVD, Grade 4** contains video segments that support lessons, including signing and movement.
- **Making Music with Movement and Dance** provides more opportunities for large group activities in music or physical education classes.
- **Making Music with Technology** provides lesson plans for many technology applications; includes MIDI files.
- ***¡A cantar!*** features recorded songs and lessons from around the Spanish-speaking world; includes strategies for bilingual classes and for English-speaking teachers working with Spanish-speaking students.
- **Bridges to Asia** features recorded songs and lessons from Asian and Pacific region cultures.
- ***www.sfsuccessnet.com*** provides an online lesson planner to conveniently create lesson plans at school or at home. Includes rubrics for assessment, lesson modifications to meet the needs of all students, performance musicals based on program content, and more.

## Technology/Media Link

**Unit Highlights** The following components are used in this unit to reinforce and expand students' understanding of music elements and related themes. See Unit at a Glance, pp. 249a–249h for a descriptive listing according to lesson sequence.

**▶ CD-ROM**

- Use rhythm tracks to accompany improvised melodies on a melody instrument (p. 281)

**▶ ELECTRONIC KEYBOARD**

- Experiment and select appropriate sounds for accompaniment parts (p. 259)

**▶ MIDI/SEQUENCING SOFTWARE**

- Experiment with playing songs in fast and slow tempos; add percussion or chord root tracks to a song (p. 273)
- Use the software and a computer to demonstrate the similar phrase shapes in a sequence (p. 287)

**▶ NOTATION SOFTWARE**

- Record and play back layered rhythm patterns as accompaniment to the song (p. 261)
- Notate I and $V_7$ chord changes (p. 275)

**▶ VIDEO LIBRARY/DVD**

- Watch a performance by the Total Experience Gospel Choir (p. 269)

**▶ WEB SITE**

- Research shanties and other work songs (p. 257)
- Read about Stephen Foster (p. 265)
- Learn more about the music of Mexico (p. 275)
- Read about country music and jazz (p. 279)
- Find more information about the music of Native American people (p. 285)

# LESSON 1

## LESSON AT A GLANCE

**Element Focus** **MELODY** Steps, leaps, and repeated patterns

**Skill Objective** **SINGING** Sing steps, leaps, and repeated patterns

**Connection Activity** **SOCIAL STUDIES** Examine how sea shanties are linked to American history

**MATERIALS**

- "Blow, Ye Winds" **CD 10-25**
  **Recording Routine**: Intro (4 m.); v. 1; refrain; v. 2; refrain; interlude (6 m.); v. 3; refrain; v. 4; refrain; v. 5; refrain; interlude (6 m.); v. 6; refrain; v. 7; refrain; coda
- "Rio Grande" **CD 10-28**
  **Recording Routine:** Intro (4 m.); v. 1; refrain; v. 2; refrain; v. 3; refrain; v. 4; refrain; coda
- "The Sea Wolf" (poem) **CD 10-30**
- **Dance Directions** for "Blow, Ye Winds" p. 514
- **Resource Book** pp. H-30, I-20, I-21
- melodic visuals (mm. 1, 2, and 3 on large cards)
- soprano recorders, barred instruments or keyboards

**VOCABULARY**

shanty steps leaps solo/chorus

**National Standards**

- **1a** Sing independently
- **1b** Sing expressively
- **2a** Play instruments maintaining steady tempo
- **2b** Perform melodies on appropriate instruments
- **4b** Compose instrumental pieces within specific guidelines
- **5b** Notate pitch, using symbols
- **6e** While listening to music, move to show a prominent feature of the music
- **9c** Describe what makes certain music suitable for certain uses

**MORE MUSIC CHOICES**

For another shanty:
"Haul Away, Joe," p. 13

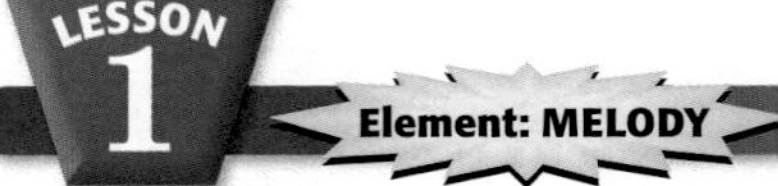


# Ride the Wave
## SING A SHANTY

We'll start our trip with whale watching in the Atlantic. Of course, on board you may have to work a little, and working on a ship can be really hard. Imagine being on board for weeks, or even years! How would you pass the time, raise your spirits, or lighten your work? You might sing a sea shanty. From about 1493 to 1928, this is what most sailors did.

**Sing** "Blow, Ye Winds." How do the tones in the color boxes move? Now sing "Rio Grande" on page 256 and **identify** steps, leaps, and repeated notes in the song.

254

# Footnotes

## MEETING INDIVIDUAL NEEDS

▶ **English Language Learners** The song text for "Blow, Ye Winds" and the poem "The Sea Wolf" contain several references to sailing. This vocabulary will be unfamiliar to some students. You may want to provide visual supports for the sailing references such as "sculling in with the tide." In addition, you may want to ask students familiar with the vocabulary to illustrate the poem or the words of the song for students who are less familiar with these concepts.

## BUILDING SKILLS THROUGH MUSIC

▶ **Language** Have students use context to determine the meaning of the following words from the poem "The Sea Wolf" on p. 257: *sculling, crested, plunging, lair.*

## ACROSS THE CURRICULUM

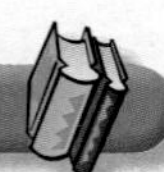

▶ **Language Arts/Social Studies** Provide students with historical information about whaling in the U.S. and many other countries, a once profitable trade. The book *Thar She Blows! Whaling in the 1860s* by Sue Kassirer (Soundprints, 1997) provides readers with background information about this trade and the people who worked aboard whaling ships. For interested readers, recommend *Black Hands, White Sails: The Story of African American Whalers* by Pat and Fredrick McKissack (Scholastic, 1999), the story of whaling and the abolitionist movement. Discuss whaling today with students. Explain that only Native Americans are still permitted to whale off the coast of the United States. *Arctic Whales and Whaling* by Bobbie Kalman (Crabtree, 1988) provides a glimpse into whaling today.

CD 10-25

# Blow, Ye Winds

s, l, t, d r m f s

*Folk Song from the United States*

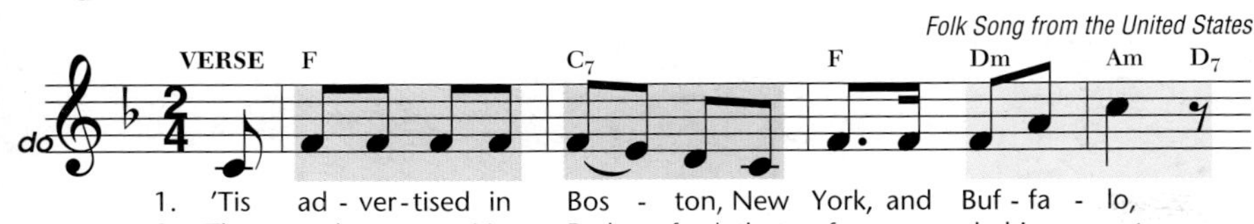


1. 'Tis ad - ver - tised in Bos - ton, New York, and Buf - fa - lo,
2. They send you to New Bed - ford, that fa - mous whal-ing port,
3. It's now we're out to sea, my boys, the wind be - gins to blow,
4. The skip-per's on the quar-ter-deck a - squint-ing at the sails,

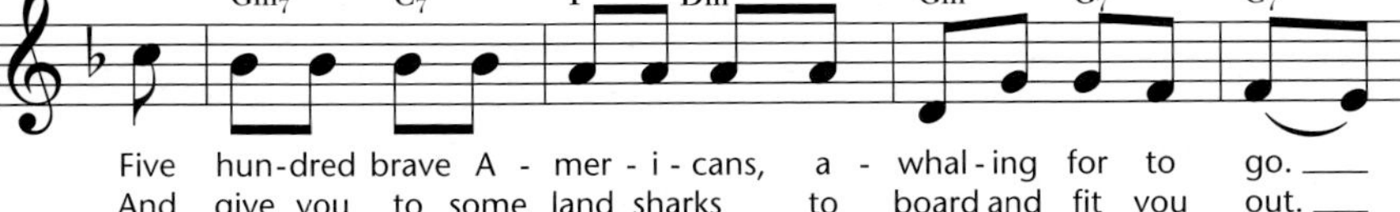

Five hun-dred brave A - mer - i - cans, a - whal - ing for to go. ___
And give you to some land sharks _ to board and fit you out. ___
One half the watch is sick on deck and the oth - er half be - low. ___
When up a - loft the look-out sights a school _ of ___ whales. _

Sing-ing, "Blow, ye winds in the morn - ing, And blow, ye winds, high - O!

Clear a - way your run-ning gear, And blow, ye winds, high - O!"

5. "Now clear away the boats, my boys,
and after him we'll trail,
But if you get too near to him,
he'll kick you with his tail!" *Refrain*

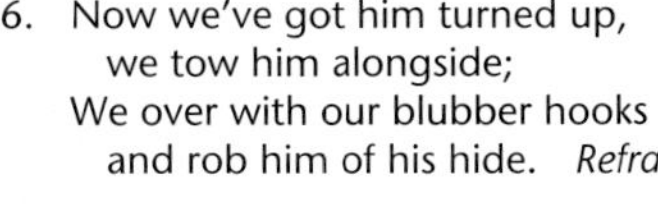

6. Now we've got him turned up,
we tow him alongside;
We over with our blubber hooks
and rob him of his hide. *Refrain*

7. Next comes the stowing down, my boys;
'twill take both night and day,
And you'll all have fifty cents apiece
when you collect your pay. *Refrain*

## 1 Introduce

Have students read p. 254. Share information about shanties from Spotlight On below. Explain that many sea shanties are in a lively tempo and have a solo/chorus structure. The lead singer would sing the solo and the sailors would sing together on the refrain.

## 2 Develop

### Listening

Play the recording of "Blow, Ye Winds" **CD 10-25**.

ASK **Is this a work song or a story song?** (a story song)

Play the recording of "Rio Grande" **CD 10-28**.

ASK **Is this song a work song or does it tell a story?** (a work song)

Have students listen to and compare "Rio Grande" with "Blow, Ye Winds." (similarities include strong, lively tempo; solo/chorus; words about the sea or sailing)

### Singing/Analyzing

1b Have the class echo you as you sing melodic fragments from the song of pitches that stay the same. Then sing an example of pitches that move by steps and end with pitches that skip. (mm. 2–3 and 8–9)

5b Prepare and show the three melodic visuals for "Blow, Ye Winds":

- Measure 1 (four notes on same pitch)
- Measure 2 (melody moves by steps)
- Measure 3 (melody moves by skips)

Have students

- Read and sing the notation, using pitch syllables or letter names.
- Sing "Blow, Ye Winds" **CD 10-25** as they follow the notation.

**continued on page 256**

## Spotlight On

▶ ***Chanty or Shanty?*** Originally developed for use on sailing ships as early as 1498, shanties were adapted and used in many different occupations. Shanties originated in the woods and railway yards, or the docks and ships. From these two backgrounds come the two different spellings: *chanty* or *shanty*. The former stems from the belief that the word *chant* is its origin. Some believe it comes from the French word *chantez*, which means "sing" or "chant." The latter may come from the type of houses that workers lived in around the rail and lumber yards—shanty-towns. In any case, shanties were used to lighten work and ease the boredom of repetitive tasks.

## Meeting Individual Needs

9c ▶ **Working Together** Work on merchant vessels was difficult. Working together in time to the strong rhythm of a sea shanty made it easier for the sailors to pull up the heavy anchor or set the riggings. It also helped them relax after strenuous activity. Have students sing the songs while pretending to pull a heavy rope downward all together. Thus, they may capture the feeling of how singing a shanty helped the sailors do their work.

**ASK How many measures have repeated tones?** (12)

**Which measures include repeated tones?** (1, 3, 4, 5, 6, 7, 9, 10, 11, 13, 14, 15) **include steps?** (2, 7, 8) **include skips?** (3, 7, 10, 11, 13, 14, 15)

Invite the class to sing the song and show the contour of the melody in the air.

### Moving

For a patterned dance for "Blow, Ye Winds," refer to Dance Directions on p. 514. Use the Dance Practice Track **CD 10-27** to teach the dance. This particular activity allows students to change partners on each new verse.

### Analyzing

By rote, teach students to sing phrase 4 of "Rio Grande"— *We are bound for Rio Grande!* Tell students that the solo was the shantyman's part. The chorus was sung by the sailors. Ask students to listen to the recording **CD 10-28** and then join in on the sailors' parts (chorus).

Without the recording, have the class echo the five chorus phrases after you sing each one.

**ASK Does the melody in the measures of the chorus move mostly by steps or skips, or do many pitches stay the same?** (mostly by skips)

Play the first two measures of "Rio Grande."

**ASK Does the melody move mostly by steps and skips, or does it stay on the same pitch?** (mostly by steps)

### Singing

1a Invite a volunteer to sing the solo parts and have the class sing the chorus parts.

1b Point out that the soloist sings mostly in steps and the chorus in skips. Divide the class. One half will sing with the soloist, the other half with the chorus.

### Playing

2a Encourage students to play the step-wise pattern G, F♯, E, and D on soprano recorders over phrase 3 of the verse and phrase 2 of the refrain.

CD 10-28
Rio Grande
d r m f s l t d'
Shanty from the United States
VERSE
Solo
1. Oh say, were you ev - er in Ri - o Grande?
2. A jol - ly good ship and a jol - ly good crew,
3. The an - chor's a - weigh and the sails they are set,
4. Good - bye to Sal - ly and Sar - ah and Sue,
Chorus
A - way for Ri - o!
Solo
It's there that the riv - er runs down gold - en sand,
A jol - ly good mate and a jol - ly good crew,
The gals that we're leav - ing we'll nev - er for - get,
To all who are list'-ning, it's good - bye to you,
Chorus
We are bound for Ri - o Grande!
REFRAIN
Chorus
And a - way for Ri - o! A - way for Ri - o!
Solo
So fare ye well my bon-ny young girl,
Chorus
We are bound for Ri - o Grande!
Tune In
Hunting whales for oil was a main occupation of sailors. Voyages could last up to three years. Many sailors were injured or killed by a whale's tail.
256

# Footnotes

## Across the Curriculum

▶ **Social Studies** The song "Rio Grande" refers to the sea trade among the Brazilian port and province of *Rio Grande do Sul*, the cities of the United States East coast (such as Baltimore), and England. Historically, these areas supported active trading, and the region today still is a center for ocean commerce. The *Rio Grande* of the song is not a river, although it is called a river. It is actually the mouth of the passage connecting the *Lagoa dos Patos* with the open sea.

The song "Rio Grande" was usually sung when sailors were hauling up the anchor and heading out to sea. There are many versions of the song. Some versions have lyrics that more obviously refer to southern Brazil and its Portuguese heritage.

## Skills Reinforcement

4b ▶ **Creating** Invite students to create a simple accompaniment for "Blow, Ye Winds" by composing a sound piece using classroom instruments to represent sounds of the sea. This activity could include such things as

- A quiet sea at sunrise (cymbals, tremolos on barred instruments).
- A ship sailing over the waves (woodblock, ratchet, soprano recorder, slapstick).
- A storm brewing (rain sticks, cymbals, tremolo on timpani, whip).
- A storm subsiding (cymbals, tremolos on barred instruments).

▶ **Recorder** For practice playing notes in the upper register and for solo and chorus playing, refer students to Resource Book pp. I-20 and I-21.

## Tales of the Sea

Sailors also told tales to pass the time. These tales were often about natural disasters they encountered. Many times they used their imagination to make their own tales more enjoyable. Listen to the recording of one such tale.



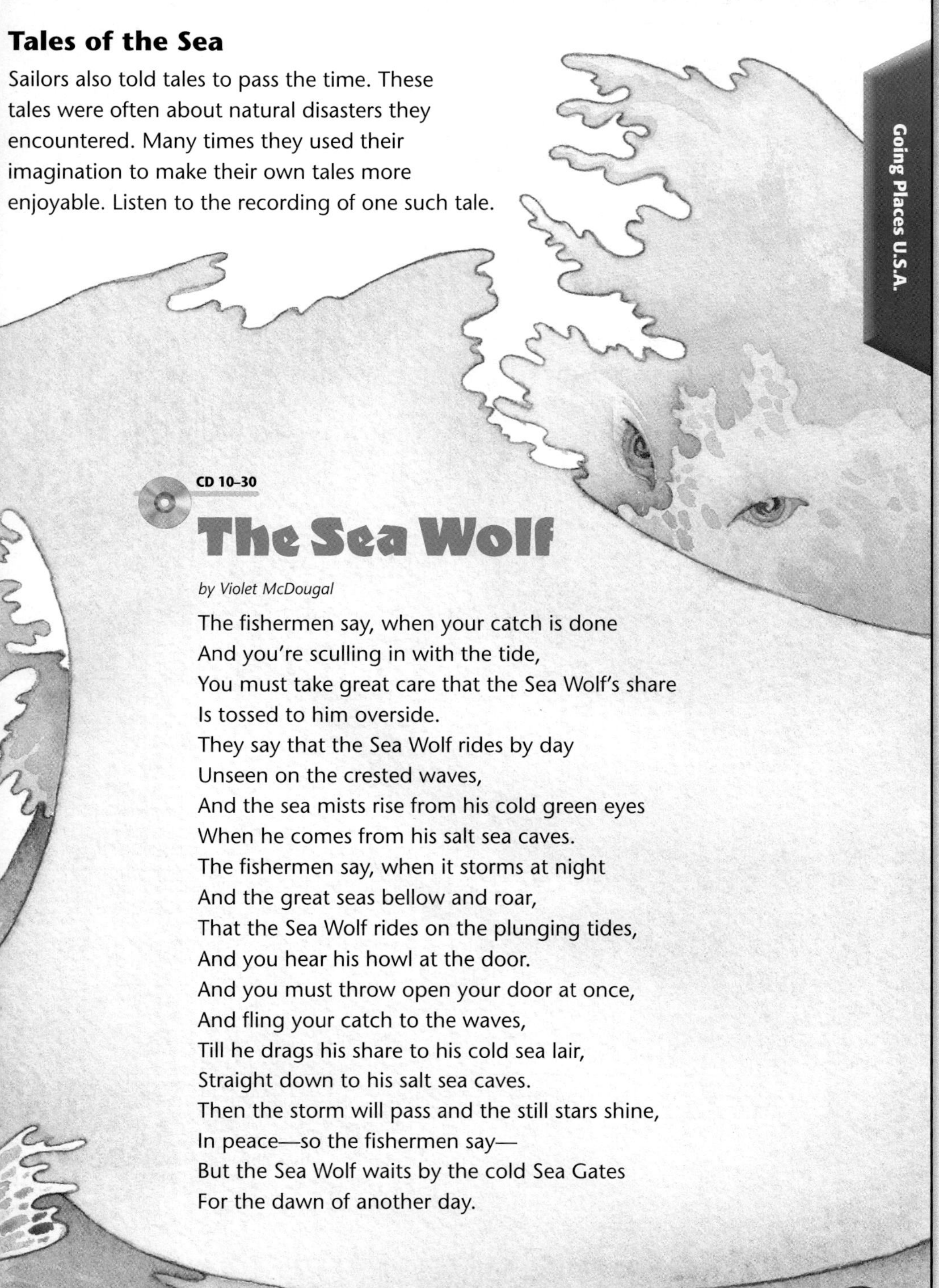

CD 10-30

# The Sea Wolf

*by Violet McDougal*

The fishermen say, when your catch is done
And you're sculling in with the tide,
You must take great care that the Sea Wolf's share
Is tossed to him overside.
They say that the Sea Wolf rides by day
Unseen on the crested waves,
And the sea mists rise from his cold green eyes
When he comes from his salt sea caves.
The fishermen say, when it storms at night
And the great seas bellow and roar,
That the Sea Wolf rides on the plunging tides,
And you hear his howl at the door.
And you must throw open your door at once,
And fling your catch to the waves,
Till he drags his share to his cold sea lair,
Straight down to his salt sea caves.
Then the storm will pass and the still stars shine,
In peace—so the fishermen say—
But the Sea Wolf waits by the cold Sea Gates
For the dawn of another day.



### Moving

1a 6e Have students choose partners ("1's" and "2's"). Then have the 1's sing the solo portions while the 2's sway gently, representing the stepwise melody. Then have the 2's sing the chorus portions while the 1's use arm gestures or stepping motions to represent the skips in the melody. Repeat and switch parts.

### Creating

Have students follow along as they listen to the poem "The Sea Wolf" **CD 10-30.** Discuss the poem with the class.

ASK **Do you think the Sea Wolf is real?** (Answers will vary.)

**What might have made sailors at sea imagine a creature like a Sea Wolf?** (actual events, such as extreme weather conditions; unfamiliar sea creatures; superstition)

Invite students to create a musical accompaniment to the poem, incorporating basic rhythmic patterns from songs in simple meter, such as "Blow, Ye Winds."

## 3 Close

**Element: MELODY** ASSESSMENT

1a 2b **Performance/Observation** Divide the class into small groups and provide each with a barred instrument or a keyboard. Invite a student in each group to play a short melody pattern that moves by steps, skips, or stays on the same pitch.

Have others in each group

- Sing the pattern on *la.*
- Tell if what they sang moved by steps, skips, or stayed on the same pitch.

Evaluate each group's ability to perform and recognize steps, leaps, and repeated tones in the melody patterns.

## Teacher to Teacher

▶ **Management Tip** If the classroom has too few classroom instruments to go around for the step, skip, or same interval assessment, use a single keyboard or classroom instrument as a model. Duplicate the keyboard illustration on Resource Book p. H-30 so that students can work without actual instruments. Students can write their responses on the same sheet of paper.

## Technology/Media Link

**Web Site** Students may be interested in learning more about shanties and other work songs. Have them research these topics at *www.sfsuccessnet.com.*

# LESSON 2

## LESSON AT A GLANCE

**Element Focus** **FORM** Call-and-response style

**Skill Objective** **SINGING** Sing a song in call-and-response style

**Connection Activity** **SOCIAL STUDIES** Sing a sea shanty that was sung in the Gulf of Mexico

**MATERIALS**

- "'Round the Bay of Mexico" **CD 10-31**

  **Recording Routine:** Intro (4 m.); v. 1; interlude (2 m.); v. 2; interlude (2 m.); v. 3; interlude (2 m.); v. 4; coda
- selected classroom instruments, such as bass metallophone, bass xylophone, alto and soprano xylophones, keyboard instruments, or recorder

**VOCABULARY**

shanty    Gulf of Mexico    mains'l

**National Standards**

**1c** Sing from memory songs from diverse cultures
**2f** Play instruments independently against contrasting parts
**6a** Listen to identify form
**8b** Identify ways music relates to social studies

**MORE MUSIC CHOICES**

For more songs that use call and response:

"Limbo Like Me," p. 18
"Pay Me My Money Down," p. 38

## 1 INTRODUCE

Select a student to read the opening text for "'Round the Bay of Mexico." Share with students the information about sea shanties from Cultural Connection below.

LESSON 2 Element: FORM | Skill: SINGING | Connection: SOCIAL STUDIES

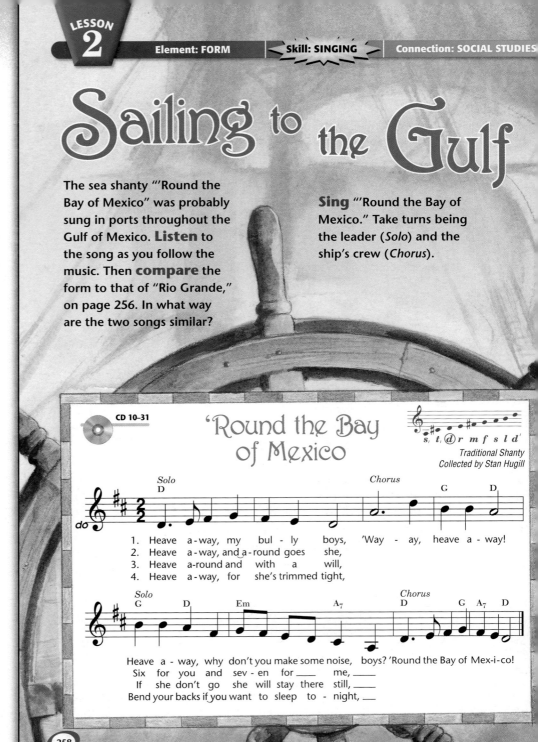

# Sailing to the Gulf

The sea shanty "'Round the Bay of Mexico" was probably sung in ports throughout the Gulf of Mexico. **Listen** to the song as you follow the music. Then **compare** the form to that of "Rio Grande," on page 256. In what way are the two songs similar?

**Sing** "'Round the Bay of Mexico." Take turns being the leader (*Solo*) and the ship's crew (*Chorus*).

CD 10-31
'Round the Bay of Mexico
s, t, d r m f s l d'
Traditional Shanty
Collected by Stan Hugill
Solo
Chorus
1. Heave a-way, my bul-ly boys, 'Way - ay, heave a - way!
2. Heave a-way, and a-round goes she,
3. Heave a-round and with a will,
4. Heave a-way, for she's trimmed tight,
Heave a - way, why don't you make some noise, boys? 'Round the Bay of Mex-i-co!
Six for you and sev - en for ___ me, ___
If she don't go she will stay there still, ___
Bend your backs if you want to sleep to - night, ___




# Footnotes

## CULTURAL CONNECTION

8b ▶ **Sea Shanties** These are songs that originated with sailors who were performing the strenuous tasks of sailing a ship. The rhythmic nature of the shanties helped the sailors work in unison as they raised the sails. The "shantyman" would lead the songs by singing the solos, and the sailors would respond by singing the chorus as they heaved the sails. The subject of the songs usually depicted some aspect of the life of sailors, such as the places they had seen, beloved captains, or even bad food.

## BUILDING SKILLS THROUGH MUSIC

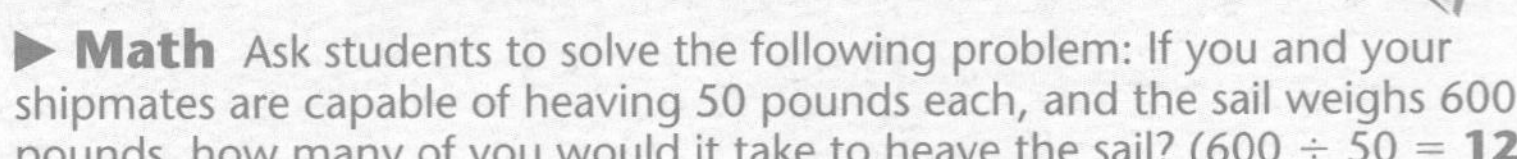

▶ **Math** Ask students to solve the following problem: If you and your shipmates are capable of heaving 50 pounds each, and the sail weighs 600 pounds, how many of you would it take to heave the sail? ($600 \div 50 = \mathbf{12}$)

## MOVEMENT

▶ **Creative Movement** Have students look at the painting on p. 259 and discuss the movements and strength required to heave up the huge sails on such a ship. Let students try sitting on the floor as they pretend to reach forward and grab the rope, then pull it backwards. Ask them to create motions for the words of the "solo" parts that would be sung by the shantyman. Divide the class into two groups, "solo" and "chorus." Have them pantomime the "solo" parts and heave the ropes on the "chorus" parts as they sing "'Round the Bay of Mexico." Let students trade parts and perform the song again.

Courtesy of the Rosenberg Library, Galveston, Texas

**Arts Connection**

▲ *The Port of Galveston* by Julius Stockfleth (1857–1935). Sailing ships and tugboats are shown navigating this busy Texas Gulf Coast seaport in the late 19th century.

**Tune In**

Shanties were sung as crews raised and lowered the ship's sails, which could weigh up to 2,500 pounds. The crew would rest as the leader sang, and then haul the sails during the chorus.

### Form a Chorus

**Perform** these accompaniments during the chorus phrases of "'Round the Bay of Mexico."

# 2 Develop

### Analyzing

Have students listen to "'Round the Bay of Mexico" **CD 10-31** and compare it to "Rio Grande" **CD 10-28**.

ASK **What technique is used in "'Round the Bay of Mexico" that is also used in "Rio Grande"?** (solo, chorus)

**How is the form of "'Round the Bay of Mexico" different from that of "Rio Grande"?** ("'Round the Bay of Mexico" has no refrain.)

### Singing

1c Play the recording of "'Round the Bay of Mexico" again and have students sing the chorus parts each time they occur in the song. Tell them to join in singing the solo parts as soon as they are ready.

Divide students into two groups. One group will sing the solo parts and the other will sing the chorus parts. Have groups trade parts and sing the song again.

### Playing

Have students look at the chorus accompaniment parts on p. 259 and then

- Learn and sing each of the chorus parts.
- Transfer the accompaniment parts to mallet or keyboard instruments, or recorder.
- Create words for the rhythm ostinato, then transfer the rhythm to a nonpitched percussion instrument.
-  2f Play or sing the accompaniment parts with the chorus each time it occurs in the song.

# 3 Close

**ASSESSMENT**

6a **Performance/Observation** To assess students' understanding of call-and-response style, have them raise their hands each time their part occurs as they sing "'Round the Bay of Mexico" in two groups.

## Spotlight On

▶ **The Artist** Originally from Germany, Julius Stockfleth (1857–1935) was a marine and landscape painter. He settled in Galveston, Texas, and remained there for over 20 years. Stockfleth was the first artist to provide a comprehensive collection of paintings depicting Galveston and the shipping industry in the western Gulf Coast. He is also known for his paintings of the Galveston hurricane, which occurred in 1900 and killed more than 6,000 people.

## Technology/Media Link

▶ **Electronic Keyboard** Encourage students to experiment and select appropriate sounds for the three chorus accompaniment parts for "'Round the Bay of Mexico." Tell students that the concertina and the accordion were instruments that were often played by sailors on ships.

LESSON 3

## LESSON AT A GLANCE

**Element Focus** **RHYTHM** Rhythm patterns

**Skill Objective** **PLAYING** Play a rhythm pattern on classroom instruments to accompany a song

**Connection Activity** **CULTURE** Examine the Celtic folk heritage

**MATERIALS**

- "How Can I Keep from Singing?" **CD 10-33**

  **Recording Routine:** Intro (4 m.); v. 1; interlude (2 m.); v. 2; interlude (2 m.); v. 3; coda
- *How Can I Keep from Singing?* (excerpt) **CD 10-35**
- **Resource Book** p. I-22
- recorders
- rhythm sticks, finger cymbals

**VOCABULARY**

Celtic rhythmic phrase

**National Standards**

**1b** Sing expressively with appropriate dynamics
**1c** Sing songs from diverse cultures
**2b** Perform rhythm patterns on appropriate instruments
**4b** Create instrumental pieces within guidelines
**5a** Read notation in $\frac{3}{4}$ meter

**MORE MUSIC CHOICES**

For more songs from Ireland and Scotland:
"Bard of Armagh, The" p. 296
*"Einini,"* p. 391

# 1 INTRODUCE

Have students read the opening text on p. 260. Share the information from Cultural Connection below. Tell students that "How Can I Keep from Singing?" is of Celtic origin.

LESSON 3 Element: RHYTHM | Skill: PLAYING | Connection: CULTURE

# The Celtic Connection

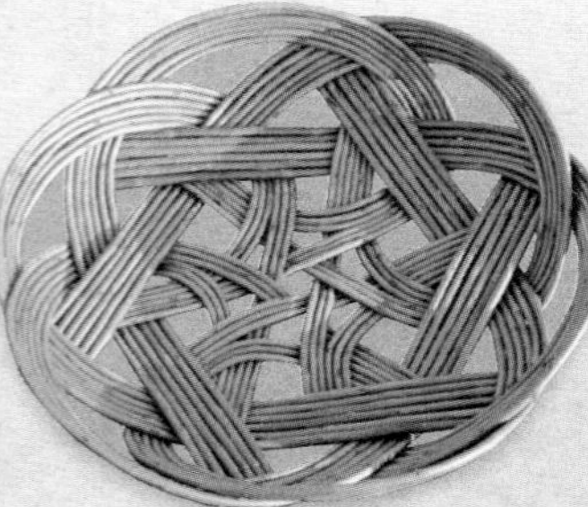

▲ Celtic basket

Celtic music comes from what is now Ireland, Scotland, Wales, France, and Spain. When people from these areas came to the United States, they brought their music with them. "How Can I Keep from Singing?" is one of those songs.

**Listen** to the song. In this melody, there are two different repeated rhythm patterns. Find and **play** these two patterns.

1. 
2. 

How many times do you hear pattern 1 in the first four measures? While listening to "How Can I Keep from Singing?" tap pattern 1 and snap pattern 2.

**Play** this recorder part while others **sing** the song.

Ancient stone carving of a figure from Celtic mythology ▼

**Listen** to this contemporary version of the song.

CD 10-35
**How Can I Keep from Singing?**

**Celtic Folk Song**
**as performed by Alfreda Gerald and the Taliesin Orchestra**

This recording of "How Can I Keep from Singing?" features the *uilleann* pipes, a favorite instrument in Scotland and Ireland.



# Footnotes

## CULTURAL CONNECTION

▶ **Celtic Music** Celtic music was preserved through "oral" tradition, which means it typically was not written down or printed. Musicians learned the music by ear, memorized it, and passed it on to future generations of musicians. For this reason, as in folk tradition, variations on melodies are quite common. Traditional Celtic instruments include accordion, concertina, whistle, fiddle, flute, and *uilleann* pipes.

## BUILDING SKILLS THROUGH MUSIC

▶ **Language** Lead students in a discussion about the meaning of the lyrics in "How Can I Keep from Singing?" Have them write a sentence describing what they do when they are scared, unhappy, or excited. Ask volunteers to share their sentences. Substitute shared answers for the phrase in the song, *How can I keep from singing?*

## SKILLS REINFORCEMENT

▶ **Recorder** For practice playing notes in the low register, refer students to Resource Book p. I-22.

CD 10-33
How Can I Keep From Singing?
s, l, (d) r m s
Celtic Folk Song
do
G C G
1. My life flows on in end - less song, a - bove earth's lam - en -
2. What though the tem - pest 'round me roars, I know the truth, it
3. When ty - rants trem - ble, sick with fear, And hear their death knells
D7 G C
ta - tion. I hear the real, though far - off song that
liv - eth. What though the dark - ness 'round me close, songs
ring - ing. When friends re - joice both far and near, how
D7 G Bm
hails a new cre - a - tion. Through all the tu - mult
in the night it giv - eth. No storm can shake my
can I keep from sing - ing? In pris - on cell and
Em D7 G
and the strife I hear that mu - sic ring - ing. It
in - most calm while to that rock I'm cling - ing. Since
dun - geon vile our thoughts to them are wing - ing. When
G7 C G
sounds an ech - o in my soul, how
love is lord of heaven and earth, how
friends by shame are un - de - filed, how
D7 G
can I keep from sing - ing?
can I keep from sing - ing?
can I keep from sing - ing?
Going Places U.S.A.
Unit 7 261


# 2 Develop

### Reading

2b Ask students to tap rhythm pattern 1 and snap rhythm pattern 2 on p. 260. Then have them put the two examples together by tapping the first example three times and snapping the second once. Have students read aloud the words of the song in rhythm while tapping and snapping the rhythm.

### Listening

5a Invite the class to listen to "How Can I Keep from Singing?" **CD 10-33** and follow the notation.

Then invite students to listen to the recording of *How Can I Keep from Singing?* **CD 10-35**, as performed by Alfreda Gerald and the Taliesin Orchestra.

ASK **How are the two recordings different from and similar to each other?** (Accept various answers.)

### Singing

1b 1c Have students sing "How Can I Keep from Singing?" Discuss proper breathing techniques to achieve the appropriate dynamics and phrasing.

### Playing

Direct students' attention to the recorder part on p. 260. Have recorder players

- Read and tap the rhythm.
- Practice playing the part.
- Play the part while others sing the song.

# 3 Close

**Element: RHYTHM** ASSESSMENT

2b 4b **Performance/Observation** Divide the class into groups. Have each group create an introduction and a *coda* to the song using rhythm patterns 1 and 2 on p. 260. Observe that students accurately perform the rhythm, using body percussion, rhythm sticks, or finger cymbals.

## Across the Curriculum

▶ **Language Arts** Students may enjoy reading *Step into the Celtic World* by Fiona MacDonald (Lorenz Books, 2000) to discover some fascinating facts about the many different Celtic peoples. Use *The Art of the Celts* by David Sandison (Laurel Glen, 1999) to demonstrate the rich artistic legacy of the Celtic people.

▶ **Social Studies** On a map, have students locate Ireland, Scotland, and Wales. These countries are home to most of the Celtic people.

## Technology/Media Link

**Notation Software** Set up a notation program with one measure repeated in $\frac{3}{4}$ time and three staves. Set each staff to percussion instruments. Have groups of three children compose and notate rhythm patterns in each track. Play back the layered rhythms as the class sings "How Can I Keep from Singing?"

LESSON 4

## LESSON AT A GLANCE

**Element Focus** **RHYTHM** ♩ ♫, ♫♩, and ♪♩ ♪ rhythm patterns

**Skill Objective** **READING** Read ♩ ♫, ♫♩, and ♪♩ ♪ rhythm patterns

**Connection Activity** **SOCIAL STUDIES** Examine Stephen Foster's legacy to American music

**MATERIALS**

- "The Glendy Burke" **CD 11-1**
  **Recording Routine:** Intro (4 m.); v. 1; refrain; interlude (4 m.); v. 2; refrain; coda
- "Oh, Susanna" **CD 11-3**
  **Recording Routine:** Intro (7 m.); v. 1; refrain; interlude (7 m.); v. 2; refrain; coda
- **Resource Book** p. H-18
- visuals, each containing a rhythm pattern
- selected nonpitched percussion instruments, drums

**VOCABULARY**

rhythmic phrase ostinato

**◆◆◆◆ National Standards ◆◆◆◆**

**1e** Sing in groups, following a conductor
**2b** Perform on classroom instruments
**2d** Echo short rhythms and melodic patterns
**2f** Play instruments independently against contrasting parts
**4b** Create short instrumental pieces within guidelines
**5a** Read eighth and quarter notes in $\frac{2}{4}$
**6a** Identify simple forms
**9a** Listen to identify music from different historical periods

**MORE MUSIC CHOICES**

For more practice with rhythm patterns:
*"Ala Da'lona,"* p. 136
*"Ai Dunaii moy,"* p. 293
"Somebody's Knockin' at Your Door," p. 53

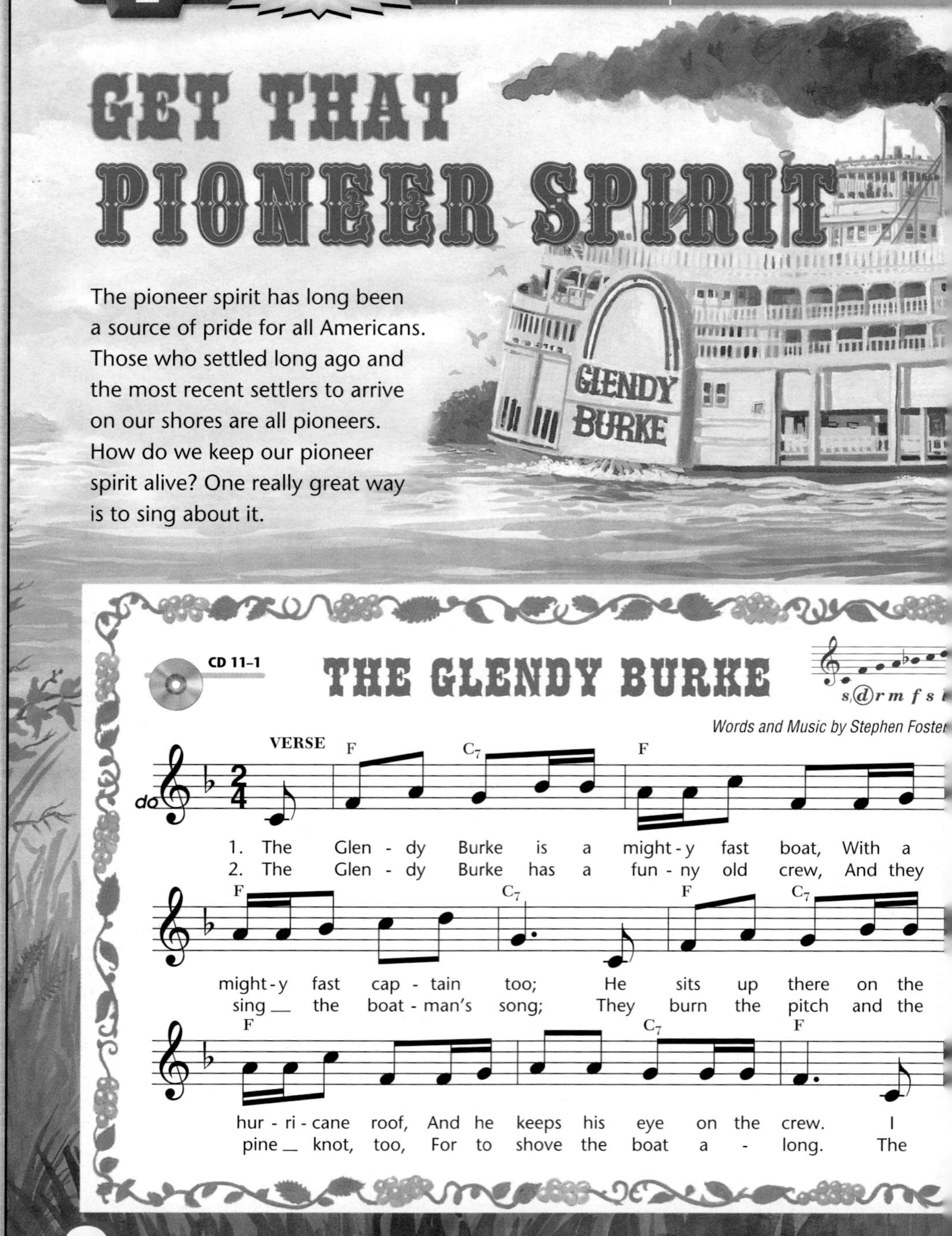

# GET THAT PIONEER SPIRIT

The pioneer spirit has long been a source of pride for all Americans. Those who settled long ago and the most recent settlers to arrive on our shores are all pioneers. How do we keep our pioneer spirit alive? One really great way is to sing about it.

## THE GLENDY BURKE

CD 11-1

*Words and Music by Stephen Foster*

s,(d)r m f s
VERSE
F C7 F
do
1. The Glen - dy Burke is a might - y fast boat, With a
2. The Glen - dy Burke has a fun - ny old crew, And they
F C7 F C7
might - y fast cap - tain too; He sits up there on the
sing the boat - man's song; They burn the pitch and the
F C7 F
hur - ri - cane roof, And he keeps his eye on the crew. I
pine knot, too, For to shove the boat a - long. The
GLENDY BURKE

# Footnotes

## MEETING INDIVIDUAL NEEDS

▶ **Aiding Comprehension** For the Reading activity on p. 264, some students may not be able to discriminate between the pitch patterns well enough to identify the number of *do-re-mi* patterns in "Oh, Susanna." You may want to use a color highlighter to mark the patterns so that students can count them more easily.

## BUILDING SKILLS THROUGH MUSIC

▶ **Social Studies** After sharing the information about Stephen Foster from Spotlight On, have students research events happening in the U.S. during the years of his life. How might these events have affected his music?

## SPOTLIGHT ON

▶ **The Songwriter and Composer** Stephen Foster (1826–1864), an American songwriter and composer, was born in Lawrenceville, Pennsylvania. As a young child he could pick out tunes on the piano, and he taught himself to play many instruments. He composed more than 200 songs and a few instrumental pieces. Many of Foster's songs were written for minstrel shows, a popular source of entertainment for people in the 1840s. He composed songs that captured the pioneer spirit in America. "Oh, Susanna" and "My Old Kentucky Home" are two of them. Although his family discouraged his musical talent by insisting he have a business career, he was always primarily interested in writing music and verses. Many of his songs are still performed today.

## Preparing for Pioneer Singing

**Read** the following examples using rhythm syllables. Then clap the rhythm patterns.

1\.

2\.

**Sing** "The Glendy Burke." Which pattern above can you **identify** in the song?

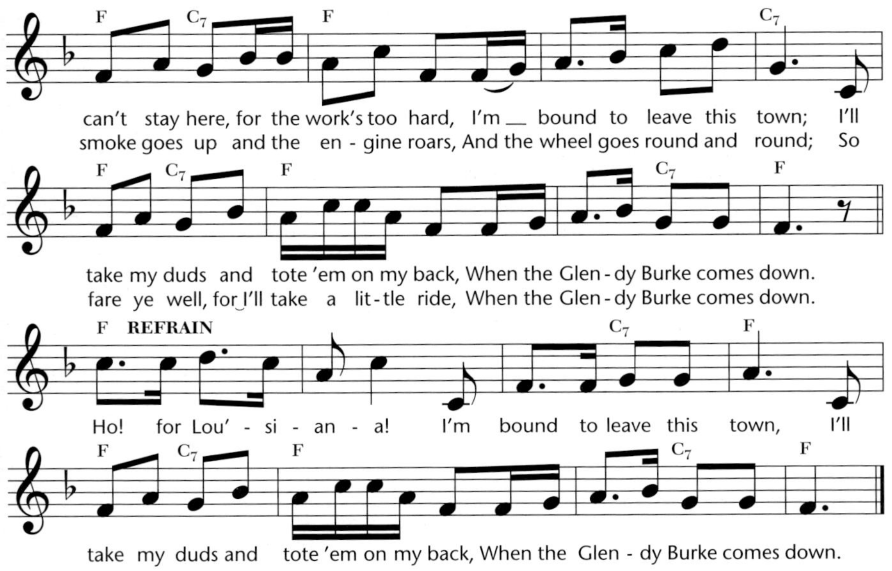

F C7 F C7

can't stay here, for the work's too hard, I'm __ bound to leave this town; I'll
smoke goes up and the en - gine roars, And the wheel goes round and round; So

F C7 F C7 F

take my duds and tote 'em on my back, When the Glen - dy Burke comes down.
fare ye well, for I'll take a lit - tle ride, When the Glen - dy Burke comes down.

F REFRAIN C7 F

Ho! for Lou' - si - an - a! I'm bound to leave this town, I'll

F C7 F C7 F

take my duds and tote 'em on my back, When the Glen - dy Burke comes down.



# 1 Introduce

Share with the class the information in Spotlight On, p. 262. Then, referring to "The Glendy Burke," explain that the crew of a boat sang together to make the work more pleasant and easier—by keeping a common rhythm going.

# 2 Develop

### Reading

5a Make a separate chart for each rhythm pattern from Lesson at a Glance on p. 262, and show each pattern on a different colored background. Have students speak and clap each separate rhythm pattern.

5a Ask students to

- Look at the music for "The Glendy Burke" and decide which phrases have the rhythms  and  . (1 and 2)
- Speak the words to the song and clap only the  and  rhythms.
- Sing the song with the recording **CD 11-1**.

### Listening

6a Have students

- Listen to "The Glendy Burke" **CD 11-1** to determine how many phrases there are in the song. (four in the verse, two in the refrain)
- Mark each phrase by moving a hand from one shoulder to the other.
- Read and clap the two rhythm patterns on p. 263.
- Identify those phrases in the song whose rhythm pattern is the same as, or similar to, one of the patterns on p. 260.

continued on page 264

## Across the Curriculum

▶ **Language Arts/Social Studies** Select several of the biographies from *Great Lives: The American Frontier* by Patricia Calvert (Simon & Schuster's Children's Books, 1997). Invite groups of students to learn more about famous and not-so-famous pioneer figures, such as Daniel Boone, Sacagawea, and Charlotte Darkey Parkhurst. Ask students to create dialogues from these biographical profiles and recite them as short dramatic performances.

For interested readers, recommend the Newbery Award–winning book *Caddie Woodlawn* by Carol Ryrie Brink (Simon & Schuster's Children's Books, 1990). This is the story of an 11-year-old girl raised with pioneer spirit.

## Skills Reinforcement

▶ **Recorder** Students can play this recorder part on the refrain of "The Glendy Burke." To focus on ensemble playing, group students in pairs. During the first refrain, have the "1's" play and the "2's" sing. Switch parts on the second refrain.

Lesson 4 Continued

### Singing

9a 1e Introduce "Oh, Susanna" **CD 11-3** by telling the class that this song is one of the best known of all Stephen Foster's songs. It established his fame as a songwriter and a major figure in our American musical heritage. Ask students to sing the song while tapping the steady beat. Invite volunteers to lead the class by conducting the steady beat.

### Reading

After singing, have the class

- Count the number of times the *do-re-mi* pattern occurs. (ten times).
- Count the number of times the *mi-re-do* pattern occurs. (five times)

2d Have students echo clap rhythms with the ♪ ♩ ♪ pattern from the refrain. Write the rhythm of measures 17–18 of the refrain on the board.

5a Ask students to

- Clap and speak the rhythm.
- Identify the words or syllables of the song with syncopated rhythm. *(-san-na, Oh)*

### Moving

Refer to Movement on p. 265 for movements students can perform with both "The Glendy Burke" **CD 11-1** and "Oh, Susanna" **CD 11-3**.

**Reading Challenges**

Count and **identify** the *do-re-mi* and the *mi-re-do* patterns in "Oh, Susanna." Sing only the *do-re-mi* patterns and "think" the rest of the song.

Take this challenge. **Sing** all of "Oh, Susanna" using pitch syllables.



## Footnotes

### Cultural Connection

▶ **The Forty-Niners** "Oh, Susanna" became the favorite song of the "forty-niners," those who trekked to California in search of gold in 1849. As they traveled from many parts of the country, they brought "Oh, Susanna" with them.

### Skills Reinforcement

4b ▶ **Creating** Notate all the rhythms students have experienced thus far: ♩ ♫ 𝅗𝅥 ♫♬ ♬♫ Provide an opportunity for students to create a rhythm composition, using these rhythms. Ask students to perform their compositions for the class.

2f ▶ **Keyboard** Have students refer to the chord symbols for the song "Oh, Susanna" and play chords on the offbeats. Refer to Resource Book p. H-18.

REFRAIN
B♭ F C7
Oh, Su - san - na, Oh, don't you cry for me,
F C7 F
I've_ come from Al - a - ba - ma With my ban - jo on my knee.
Going Places U.S.A.

## Pioneer Dancing

**Move** to the song "Oh, Susanna" or "The Glendy Burke" by following these dance movements.

**Verse**

**Refrain**

▲ Girls take 8 steps in and 8 steps back while boys clap. Switch the movements.

▲ Partners link right arms and circle to the right. Link left arms and circle to the left.

Visit **Take It to the Net** at *www.sfsuccessnet.com* to learn more about Stephen Foster and his music.

# 3 Close

## Playing

In small groups of four to six, have the class perform "Oh, Susanna" with a rhythm ostinato created by the students. Allow them to choose an appropriate nonpitched percussion instrument to accompany their singing.

**Element: RHYTHM** — **ASSESSMENT**

4b **Performance/Observation** Divide the class into partners. Display the colored visuals, each containing a rhythm pattern. Ask students to

- Clap patterns 1, 2, or 3; then clap phrase 1 of "The Glendy Burke."
- Create a rhythm composition using rhythmic phrases containing ♩ ♬♩, ♬♩, and ♪♩ ♪ rhythm patterns.

2b Have one student clap the rhythm composition while his or her partner keeps a steady beat on a drum. Reverse roles.

When ready, have each set of partners perform for the class. Observe each student's ability to read and perform the composed rhythm patterns.

## Movement

▶ **Patterned Dance** Introduce students to movements for "The Glendy Burke" and "Oh, Susanna."

*Formation:* Divide students into partners and have them stand in a large circle. (Refer to the movement pictures on p. 265.)

Verses: Girls take 8 steps in and 8 steps out as the boys clap. Then the boys take 8 steps in and 8 steps out as the girls clap.

Refrains: Partners link right arms and circle to the right. Link other arms and circle to the left.

Interludes: All stand and clap.

## Technology/Media Link

**Web Site** Encourage students to visit *www.sfsuccessnet.com* for more information on Stephen Foster.

LESSON 5

## LESSON AT A GLANCE

**Element Focus** **TIMBRE** Tone color of adult and child singing voices

**Skill Objective** **SINGING** Sing a song in a manner appropriate to a child's voice

**Connection Activity** **LANGUAGE ARTS** Read a poem about Harriet Tubman

**MATERIALS**

- "Follow the Drinkin' Gourd" **CD 11-5**

  **Recording Routine:** Intro (4 m.); refrain; v. 1; refrain; v. 2; refrain; coda
- "Wade in the Water" **CD 11-7**

  **Recording Routine:** Intro (10 m.); refrain (twice); v. 1; refrain; v. 2; refrain; v. 3; refrain; coda
- "Harriet Tubman" (poem) **CD 11-9**
- bass and alto xylophones, soprano and alto glockenspiels

**VOCABULARY**

vocal timbre tone color solo/chorus

**National Standards**

**1a** Sing independently with appropriate timbre
**2b** Perform rhythms and melodies on appropriate instruments
**6c** Use appropriate terminology in explaining music performances
**6d** Identify children's voices and male and female adult voices
**8b** Identify ways music relates to other subjects
**9a** Listen to identify music from different historical periods and cultures

**MORE MUSIC CHOICES**

For other African American spirituals:
"All Night, All Day," p. 180
"I'm Gonna Sing," p. 33
For more music to explore vocal timbres:
Many Voices, pp. 30–33

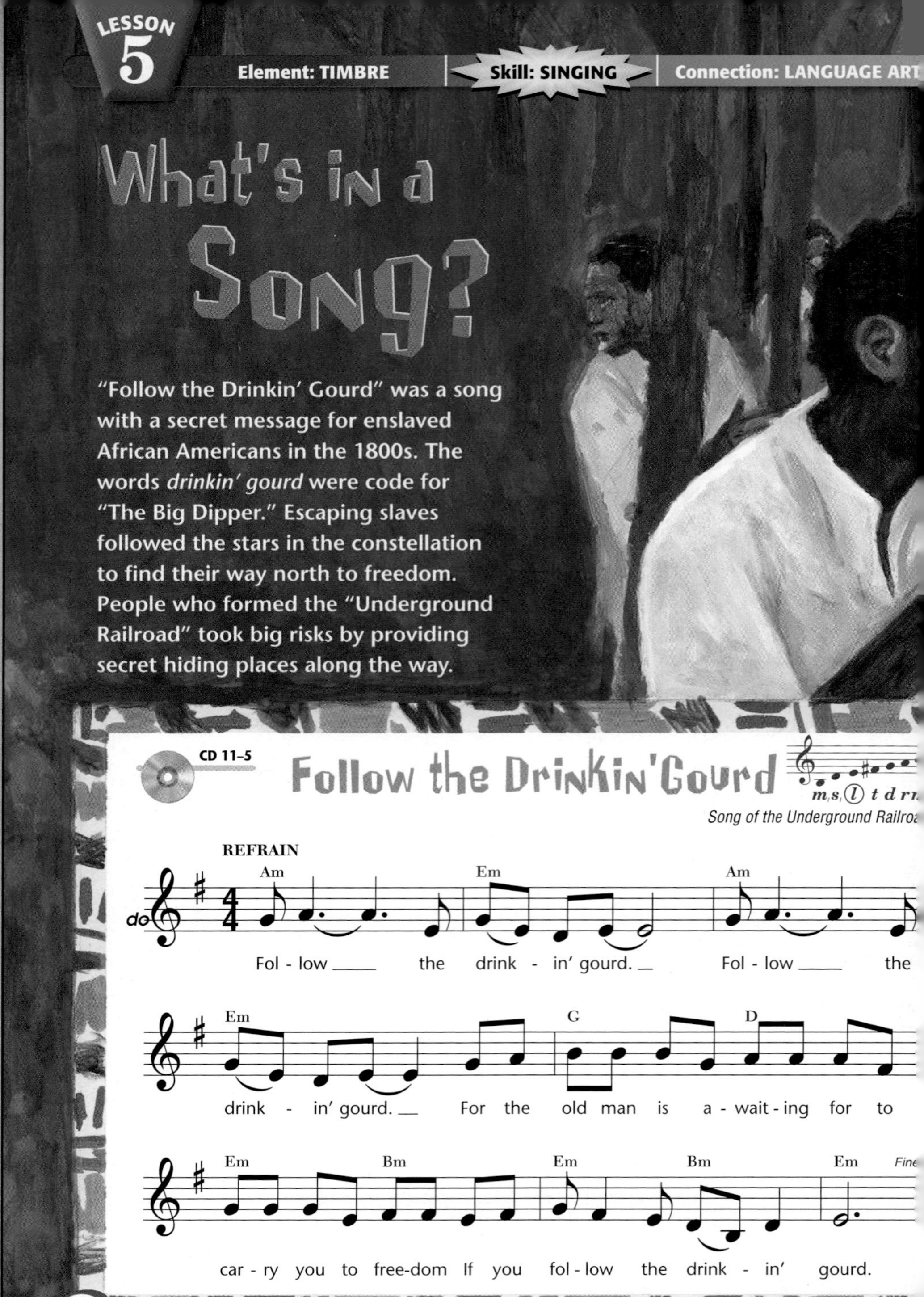
LESSON 5 Element: TIMBRE | Skill: SINGING | Connection: LANGUAGE ART

# What's in a Song?

"Follow the Drinkin' Gourd" was a song with a secret message for enslaved African Americans in the 1800s. The words *drinkin' gourd* were code for "The Big Dipper." Escaping slaves followed the stars in the constellation to find their way north to freedom. People who formed the "Underground Railroad" took big risks by providing secret hiding places along the way.

CD 11-5
Follow the Drinkin' Gourd
Song of the Underground Railroa
REFRAIN
Am Em Am Em G D Em Bm Em Bm Em Fine
Fol - low the drink - in' gourd. Fol - low the drink - in' gourd. For the old man is a - wait - ing for to car - ry you to free - dom If you fol - low the drink - in' gourd.
266

# Footnotes

## ACROSS THE CURRICULUM

▶ **Language Arts/Social Studies** Students may enjoy reading *Follow the Drinking Gourd* by Jeanette Winter (Knopf, 1988). This is a retelling of the folk song, the runaway slaves, and the Underground Railroad story. Students can read a story about a boy and his father helping slaves escape northward in *The Drinking Gourd* by F. N. Monjo (HarperCollins, 1970).

## BUILDING SKILLS THROUGH MUSIC

▶ **Science/Art** Share with students the first paragraph in Teacher to Teacher. Refer students to the art at the top of p. 267 showing the pattern of stars that make up the Big Dipper. Distribute squares of construction paper. Ask students to draw the points of the Big Dipper on their paper and then punch small holes where the stars are. Then have them use flashlights to shine light through the paper, projecting the constellation on the wall.

## TEACHER TO TEACHER

9a ▶ **The Constellation Connection** The *drinkin' gourd* referred to in the song is the Big Dipper. This is a famous constellation because the two stars at the front of the "cup" point to the North Star. By following the *drinkin' gourd*, slaves could find their way northward. Ask students to read the words to the song and find the clues that helped slaves find their way. *(sun comes up, riverbank, dead trees)*

Refer students to *"Niu lang zhi nü"* **CD 14-15**, p. 335, and explore the "constellation connection" between this Chinese folk song and "Follow the Drinkin' Gourd." After students have listened to or sung each song, and identified the culture of each, ask them to suggest reasons why such two diverse cultures might find inspiration from a similar source.

Vocal Timbres
Listen to "Follow the Drinkin' Gourd."
Who is singing—men, women, children?
Do you hear a chorus or a solo voice? Is this song
accompanied? If you hear instruments, identify them.
Musicians refer to differences in sound as timbre.
Going Places U.S.A.
Choose an instrument and play this accompaniment
while others sing "Follow the Drinkin' Gourd."
REFRAIN Soprano and Alto Xylophones
Alto Xylophone
Bass Xylophone
VERSE
Em Am Em G D Em Bm Em Bm Em D.C. al Fine
1. When the sun comes up and the first quail calls, Fol - low the drink - in' gourd. For the old man is a - wait - ing for to car - ry you to free-dom If you fol - low the drink - in' gourd.
2. Now the river-bank will make a mighty good road; Dead trees will show you the way. And the left foot, peg - foot, trav - el - in' on, Just you fol - low the drink - in' gourd.
Unit 7 267

# 1 Introduce

9a Stories of the Underground Railroad are an important part of American history. It was said that both "Follow the Drinkin' Gourd" and "Wade in the Water" were songs that Harriet Tubman sang to help encourage her people to seek freedom. Both songs are spirituals and are an important part of our American musical heritage. Discuss with students the information about African American spirituals in Cultural Connection below.

# 2 Develop

## Listening

6d Ask students to listen to "Follow the Drinkin' Gourd" **CD 11-5**.

ASK **How do the verses sound different?** (The refrain is sung by a children's chorus; the verses are sung by an adult female soloist.)

Point out to students that what distinguishes their voices is called *vocal tone color* or *vocal timbre*. Have students listen to "Wade in the Water" **CD 11-7** with their books closed and categorize the voices heard on the recording.

ASK **Who sang the solo parts?** (a solo adult male voice) **the chorus parts?** (a group of adult male singers)

## Singing

1a 6c Invite students to sing verses 1 and 2 of "Follow the Drinkin' Gourd" **CD 11-5**. Then ask them to

- Follow the music as they listen again. (Invite them to join in the vocal refrain.)
- Use standard terminology to discuss and explain the style of the singing. (gospel, with a bit of swing)
- Sing the song again, snap on the offbeats (beats 2 and 4), and add a gentle sway.
- Experiment with singing the verses in call-and-response (solo-group) style.

**continued on page 268**

## Cultural Connection

8b ▶ **African American Spirituals** Spirituals are a blend of music from two cultures representing diverse musical genres: the melodies and rhythms of West Africa and the church hymns of white colonial settlers. Since instruments were not generally available to most enslaved Africans, early spirituals were sung unaccompanied. Although the improvised harmonies were hymnlike, the rhythmic and melodic elements grew into a unique vocal style—full of syncopated rhythms.

Refer to the Classified Index and have students listen to and identify examples of each genre (West African music and church hymns) that are found in this book.

## Spotlight On

▶ **Harriet Tubman** Harriet Tubman (ca. 1820–1913) was born into slavery in Maryland. When she discovered that the "property" owned by her deceased master was to be sold, she escaped to freedom. She found what it was like to be free and wanted to help others be free, too. Her nineteen trips leading runaway slaves to freedom by way of the Underground Railroad were successful because she was a master in planning escape strategies. Tubman planned for food, clothing, escape routes, and places to stop and rest. She never lost a "passenger" of the more than 300 slaves she led to freedom. Throughout her life, she continued to care about others. She helped the sick and disabled and raised money for schools and destitute children. She died in 1913 in the Harriet Tubman Home for the Aged and Indigent Negroes in Auburn, New York.

### Playing

Invite students to play the Orff accompaniment on p. 267 while they sing "Follow the Drinkin' Gourd." Have students

- Pat the rhythms for each part.
- Play each part independently from the rest.
- Perform the accompaniment as a group.
- Repeat the song several times and trade places with someone who has not yet played an accompaniment part.

### Performing

Tone color can be experienced in speech as well as in the singing voice. To help students identify this connection between music and poetry, have them

- Speak and learn the words to the poem "The Little Black Train" by rote.

  There's a little black train a-comin',
  Get all your business right.
  There's a little black train a-comin',
  And it may be here tonight.

- Experiment in small groups with changing the tone color by speaking the words in various ways
  1. Begin with a solo voice and add voices until there is a group.
  2. Start with a group and take away voices one by one down to a solo voice.
  3. Begin with a whisper and *crescendo* to very loud.
  4. Begin very loud and *decrescendo* to a whisper.

**ASK Can you think of other ways to change vocal color?** (Answers will vary.)

Encourage students to bring vocal recordings to class and discuss the vocal tone used in each, using standard terminology. Ask students to identify such things as male or female voice, adult or child voice, and vocal style used.

**Listen** to "Wade in the Water." How is the timbre in this song different from what you heard in "Follow the Drinkin' Gourd"? **Sing** both songs either with a group or as a soloist. How can you vary the timbre of each song as it is being performed?

## Footnotes

### ACROSS THE CURRICULUM

▶ **Social Studies/Art** Tell students that through code words in the songs, slaves were able to communicate the routes to freedom to one another without the knowledge of slave owners. Another way of communicating routes was through the creation of quilts. The patterns in the quilts were actually maps that showed the way to the freedom train. Read aloud *Sweet Clara and the Freedom Quilt* by Deborah Hopkinson (Knopf, 1993). Invite students to make quilts with construction paper that show them how to get home. Display these quilts during performances of "Follow the Drinkin' Gourd."

### SKILLS REINFORCEMENT

▶ **Singing** Some students may be self-conscious about singing a solo on the verses of "Wade in the Water." Instead of singing a solo, group two or three students together to sing the solo part, and have the rest of the class sing *God's gonna trouble the water.*

The octave leap at the end of the refrain and the beginning of the verse may be difficult for some students to hear. Practice the leap several times with the entire class before asking any one student to perform it. Use movement to show the leap of the octave.

CANADA

▲ Routes of the Underground Railroad.

## An Important Song— An Important Person

**Harriet Tubman** was born a slave around 1820 in Maryland. In 1849, she escaped to freedom in Philadelphia by way of the Underground Railroad. After experiencing freedom, she knew that she must free other slaves. Harriet Tubman made numerous trips south to lead about 300 people to freedom. It is said that she often sang "Wade in the Water" to send a message of hope to the people she helped.

CD 11-9

# Harriet Tubman

*by Eloise Greenfield*

Harriet Tubman didn't take no stuff
Wasn't scared of nothing neither
Didn't come in this world to be no slave
And wasn't going to stay one either.

"Farewell!" she said to her friends one night
She was mighty sad to leave 'em
But she ran away that dark, hot night
Ran looking for her freedom.

She ran to the woods and ran through the woods
With the slave catchers right behind her
And she kept on going till she got to the North
Where mean men couldn't find her.

Nineteen times she went back South
To get three hundred others
She ran for her freedom nineteen times
To save black sisters and brothers.

Harriet Tubman didn't take no stuff
Wasn't scared of nothing neither
Didn't come in this world to be no slave
And didn't stay one either.

And didn't stay one either.



### Listening/Performing

Have students read p. 269 and listen to the recorded poem "Harriet Tubman" **CD 11-9**. Then invite them to apply what they learned about changing vocal timbres and by reciting the poem.

Invite students to

- Write a description about how Harriet Tubman prepared for a journey. Draw a route she might haven taken.
- Create dialogue and a minidrama to perform for a school assembly.

For additional information about Harriet Tubman, share Spotlight On, p. 267.

### Singing

Have students listen to "Wade in the Water" **CD 11-7** and then sing both the verses and the refrain.

## 3 Close

**Skill: SINGING** — **ASSESSMENT**

**Performance/Observation** As part of their performance, encourage students to sing solos on the verses of "Wade in the Water" **CD 11-7** and sing as a group on the refrains. Observe and assess each student's ability to sing in an appropriate manner. Criteria for assessment include singing on pitch and singing with a head tone.

### Movement

▶ **Creative Movement** Use the song "Wade in the Water" to suggest moving through different environments. Name a place for students: a rainforest, quicksand, tall grasses of the African plains, an Antarctic iceberg, all are possibilities. Whisper the place to one student, and ask him or her to move in that environment without words. Let others guess "where" the student is from the movement. Ask the observers to not only guess the place, but verbally describe the movement clues that give information for their answers. Be specific! This may also be done with small groups of students.

### Character Education

▶ **Courage** Discuss the courage and conviction evidenced by Harriett Tubman and others who assisted with the Underground Railroad. Help students realize that being courageous doesn't mean being without fear; instead, it means that fears have been recognized and controlled. Discuss other historical situations that would have required great courage. Challenge students to consider everyday situations that require them to have courage.

### Technology/Media Link

**Video Library** For more experiences with different vocal timbres, have students watch the performance by the Total Experience Gospel Choir.

LESSON 6

## LESSON AT A GLANCE

**Element Focus** **RHYTHM** $\frac{3}{4}$ time in slow and fast tempos

**Skill Objective** **CREATING** Create and perform ostinatos in $\frac{3}{4}$ time in several tempos

**Connection Activity** **CULTURE** Compare the music of Mexico with an American cowboy ballad

**MATERIALS**

- *"Cielito lindo"* (Spanish) **CD 11-10**
- *"Cielito lindo"* (English) **CD 11-11**
  **Recording Routine:** Intro (16 m.); v. 1; refrain; interlude (16 m.); v. 2; refrain; refrain; coda
- "Streets of Laredo" **CD 11-14**
  **Recording Routine:** Intro (8 m.); v. 1; interlude (1 m.); v. 2; interlude (8 m.); v. 3; interlude (1 m.); v. 4; interlude (8 m.); v. 5; coda
- *El siquisirí* **CD 11-16**
- **Pronunciation Practice/Translation** p. 484
- **Resource Book** pp. A-26, H-19
- temple blocks, hand drum

**VOCABULARY**

*mariachi* band    ballad    tempo    ostinato

**National Standards**

**2a** Perform in rhythm in a steady tempo
**2e** Play instruments in groups, blending timbres
**4c** Use a variety of sound sources when composing
**6b** Describe music by answering questions about it

**MORE MUSIC CHOICES**

For another song in $\frac{3}{4}$ time:
"River," p. 58

For more songs in the Spanish language:
*"Cantando mentíras,"* p. 146
*"El borrego,"* p. 242

# Meter Matters

Here's a riddle: What has three to twelve instruments (violins, trumpets, guitars, harps), plays terrific music, and is really popular in Mexico and the southwestern part of the United States?

. . . A *mariachi* band!

**Listen** to *"Cielito lindo"* and "Streets of Laredo." Both songs are in meter in 3. **Compare** and **describe** the tempo of each song.

CD 11–10
MIDI 19
Cielito lindo
m, f, s, l, t, d r m f
English Words by Alice Firgau
Folk Song from Mexico
VERSE
do
B♭ F7 B♭ F7
1. De la sie - rra mo - re - na, Cie - li - to
1. From the dark, dis - tant moun-tain, Cie - li - to
B♭ F7
lin - do, vie - nen ba - jan - do,
lin - do, I see de - scend - ing,
F7
Un par de o - ji - tos ne - gros, Cie - li - to
Your dark eyes flash - ing bright - ly, Cie - li - to
F7 B♭
lin - do, de con - tra - ban - do.
lin - do, love's mes - sage send - ing.
270

## Footnotes

### SKILLS REINFORCEMENT

▶ **Guitar** *"Cielito lindo"* and "Streets of Laredo" have much in common from a guitar-playing perspective. For both, use a relaxed "thumb-strum-strum" rhythm for $\frac{3}{4}$ meter. Play both with the capo on fret 1, so that *"Cielito lindo"* can be fingered using A-D-$E_7$, and "Streets of Laredo" using E-A-$B_7$ while still remaining in their notated keys. Less experienced guitar players can substitute B for the $B_7$ chord.

2a

### BUILDING SKILLS THROUGH MUSIC

▶ **Social Studies** Share the information on the Treaty of Guadalupe Hidalgo from Spotlight On, p. 272. Distribute maps of the U.S. and have students outline and highlight the region that was annexed to the United States.

### SPOTLIGHT ON

▶ **Ballads** A ballad is a folk song that tells a story. Not all ballads were sung. For example, a literary ballad is a narrative poem concerned with things that are marvelous, historical, heroic, or sentimental. Some ballads date as early as the ninth century. By the sixteenth century, the word *ballad* could be used to mean anything singable, if simple and for solo voice. In Shakespeare's time, there were ballad sellers whose wares were collections of ballads. In the twentieth century, Cecil J. Sharp, a collector of folk music, recorded ballads on field trips in the Southern Appalachian region of the United States—and continued the practice of selling them. The cowboy period in America produced an abundance of ballads, and "Streets of Laredo" is one of them.

# 1 INTRODUCE

**SAY** *"Cielito lindo"* is a very well-known folk song from Mexico. It is sung and known throughout the Spanish-speaking world.

Share the information from Spotlight On, p. 270, and Cultural Connection, below, about ballads and Spanish influence in the United States.

# 2 DEVELOP

## Listening

Model clap patterns in meter in 3 for the class to echo. Ask students to perform a PAT-clap-clap pulse in $\frac{3}{4}$ meter. Have half of the class maintain the pulse pattern while the other half echo claps your patterns.

## Creating

Have students

- Listen to the recording of *"Cielito lindo"* **CD 11-11** and keep the beat with a PAT-clap-clap pattern.
- Sing along with the recording and clap the first beat of each measure.

Divide the class into small groups. Ask students to create a body percussion ostinato for *"Cielito lindo,"* using any combination of snap, pat, clap, or stamp. Allow students to choose one ostinato for everyone to learn.

## Singing

Invite students to listen to and sing with the Pronunciation Practice Track of *"Cielito lindo"* **CD 11-13.** As they listen, have them follow the Pronunciation Practice Guide on Resource Book p. A-26. Repeat the activity several times until students are comfortable singing the Spanish words. Then invite students to sing the entire song in Spanish with the recording **CD 11-10.** Encourage students who are fluent in Spanish to sing solos on the verses and have the rest of the class join in on the refrains.

**continued on page 272**

## ACROSS THE CURRICULUM

▶ **Language Arts** Students may enjoy reading *Cowboys of the Wild West* by Russell Freedman (Houghton Mifflin, 1990). True-to-life accounts portray what the life of the cowboy was really like. Students may enjoy reading about and singing some of the songs found in *Songs of the Wild West* (Simon & Schuster, 1991), an informative illustrated songbook.

Use the photo-essay *Charro: The Mexican Cowboy* by George Ancona (Harcourt Brace, 1999) to introduce students to Mexican cowboys. This book provides an overview of their history, traditions, and celebrations.

▶ **Social Studies** California has 21 Spanish missions. Ask students to research and find out where they are located, who built them (Mexican missionaries acting for the government of Spain), and when they were built (1769–1823).

## CULTURAL CONNECTION

▶ **Spanish Influence in the United States** Early Spanish explorers traveled from Mexico into parts of what are now the United States. In the eighteenth century, there were temporary posts as far north as what is now British Columbia. The colonists who occupied these outposts left a lasting Spanish heritage.

Spanish influence is very evident in the western United States. The Spanish Franciscan Friars established a series of missions throughout California. Today, a very popular form of architecture is referred to as "mission." The Spanish influence is also evident in the furnishings of many homes. This type of furniture, prevalent in the west, is known as "mission style."

### Analyzing

6b Have students compare the recordings of *"Cielito lindo"* **CD 11-10** and "Streets of Laredo" **CD 11-14.**

**ASK How are the songs alike?** (Both are in $\frac{3}{4}$ time; both are folk songs.)

**How are they different?** ("Streets of Laredo" is in a slow $\frac{3}{4}$ tempo; *"Cielito lindo"* is in a fast $\frac{3}{4}$ tempo that feels like one beat to the measure instead of three. One song is in English. The other is in Spanish. Also, the instrumentation is different.)

### Listening

Play *El siquisirí* **CD 11-16** and ask students to identify the meter. Have them describe the tempo in relationship to *"Cielito lindo"* and "Streets of Laredo." (See Analyzing above for answers.)

### Singing

**SAY** "Streets of Laredo" is an American cowboy ballad. It tells the story of "the cowboy's lament."

Teach "Streets of Laredo" **CD 11-14** phrase by phrase. Play the recording and ask students to draw an arc line in the air (from left to right) for each four-measure phrase. Have the class sing the song with the recording.

### Reading

Write the rhythm patterns at the top of p. 273 on the board. Have students

- Speak and clap each pattern.
- Create an ostinato using any combination of the four rhythms.

Encourage students to create a pattern that does not duplicate the rhythm of the words of "Streets of Laredo." Play this ostinato on temple blocks. Add a hand drum for the pulse. Invite students to accompany the singing with the temple block ostinato.

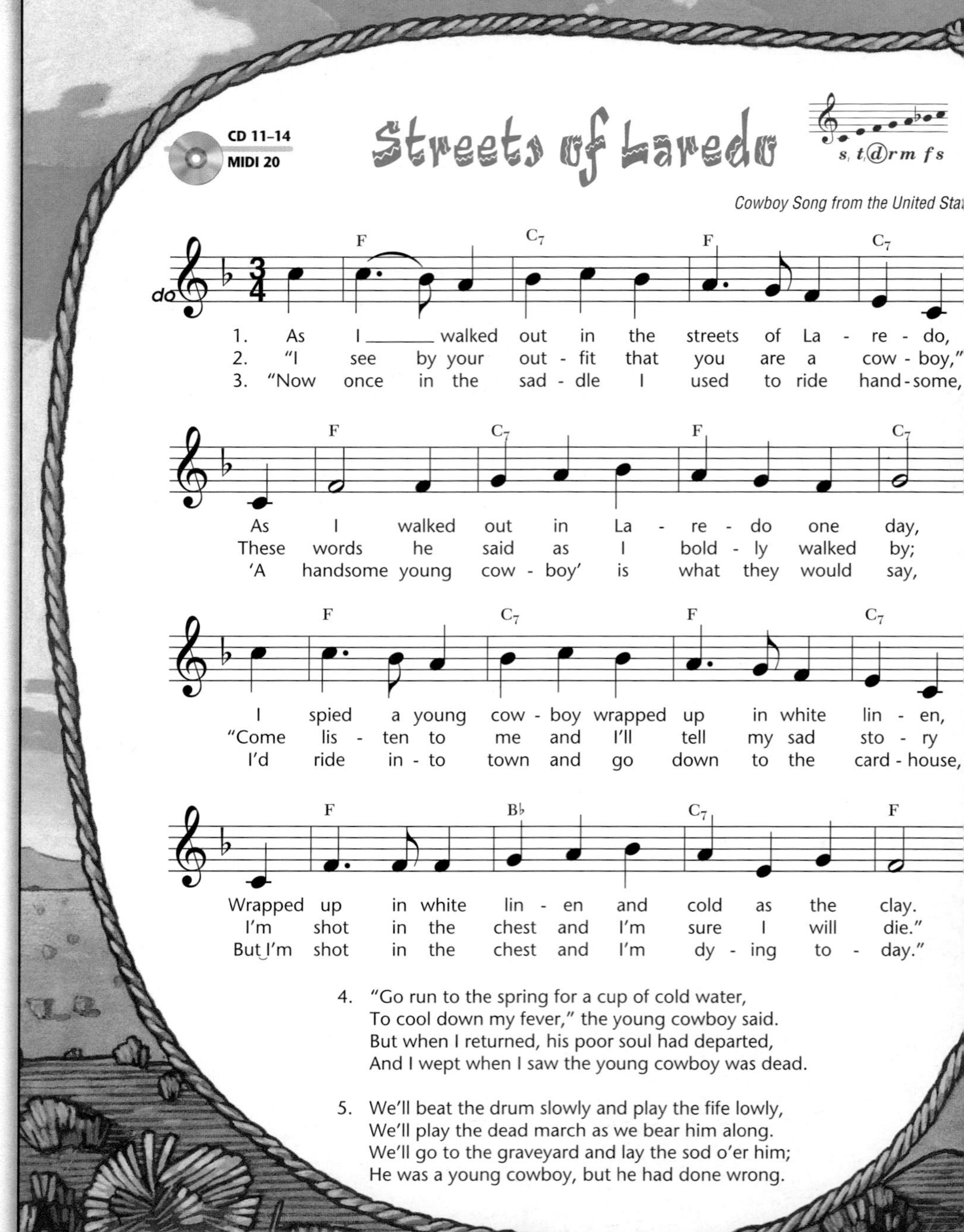


## Footnotes

### Spotlight On

▶ **Treaty of Guadalupe Hidalgo** In 1845, the independent republic of Texas was annexed to the United States. This was the time that gold-seekers were traveling to California in search of wealth. In 1846, after years of fierce border fights, a war broke out between the United States and Mexico. The United States–Mexican War ended in 1848 with the Treaty of Guadalupe Hidalgo. The treaty terms included the annexation of half of Mexico to the United States, for which the United States government paid 15 million dollars. This land includes parts of present-day California, Utah, New Mexico, Arizona, and Nevada. The southwestern border of Texas was established at the Rio Grande.

### Skills Reinforcement

▶ **Recorder** Invite students to play a recorder countermelody during "Streets of Laredo." Remind them to break after each long sound. This part will help students feel the beat moving in sets of three. Play the two phrases and ask students to identify how they are different. 2a 2e

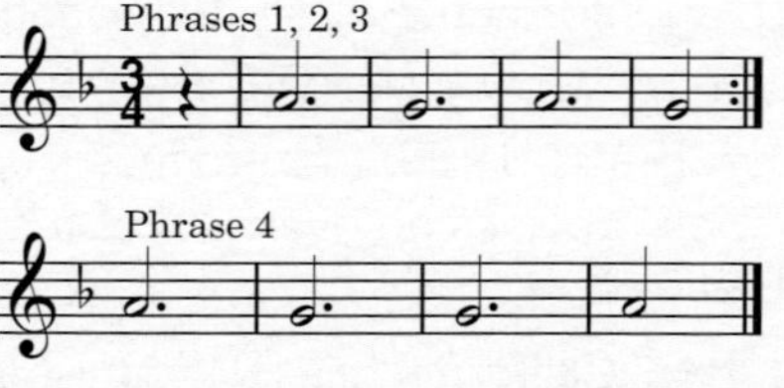


▶ **Keyboard** Use Resource Book p. H-19 to have students perform a keyboard ensemble accompaniment using a countermelody, broken chords, and bass.

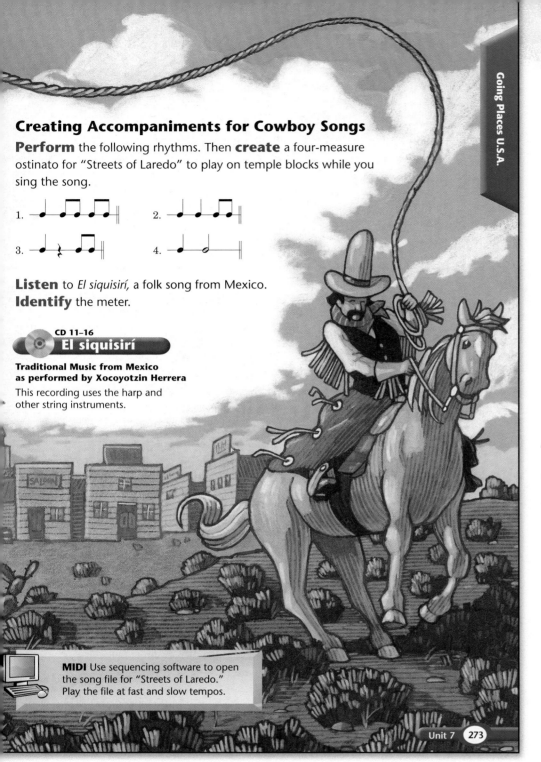

### Creating Accompaniments for Cowboy Songs

**Perform** the following rhythms. Then **create** a four-measure ostinato for "Streets of Laredo" to play on temple blocks while you sing the song.

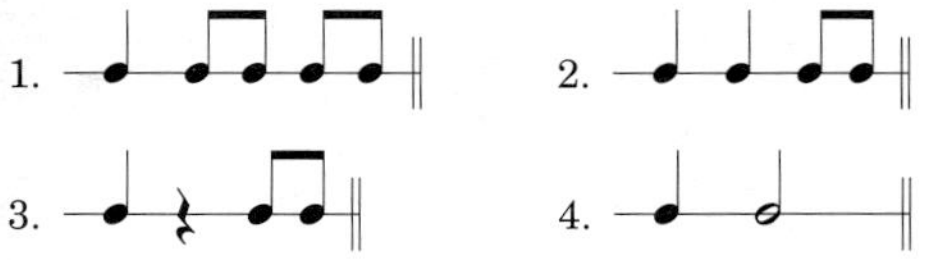

1. 2.

3. 4.

**Listen** to *El siquisirí,* a folk song from Mexico. **Identify** the meter.

CD 11–16
**El siquisirí**

**Traditional Music from Mexico as performed by Xocoyotzin Herrera**

This recording uses the harp and other string instruments.

**MIDI** Use sequencing software to open the song file for "Streets of Laredo." Play the file at fast and slow tempos.



### Moving

Invite small groups to create a simple movement for each verse of "Streets of Laredo." Ask for suggestions, such as

- Form a circle.
- Move to the right on verse 1.
- Move to the left on verse 2.
- Show phrases in the air with smooth arc-like arm movements.

Have students perform their movements while singing the song.

## 3 Close

### Analyzing

Have students sing "Streets of Laredo" **CD 11-14** and *"Cielito lindo"* **CD 11-10.**

ASK **If you reverse the two tempos, what is the effect?** (Students will give various answers, but guide them to see that the character of each song is lost.)

**Skill: CREATING** ASSESSMENT

2a 4c **Performance/Observation** Encourage students to create simple ostinato accompaniments using the rhythms on p. 273. Then have them accompany each song with the ostinato they have created. (Students should determine that simpler rhythms are needed for the faster song.) Help students conclude that tempo greatly affects the character and style of the music, even though the songs may be in the same meter.

Assess each student's ability to create and perform ostinatos in fast and slow tempos. Observe whether or not students maintain a steady beat and accurately perform the rhythms.

## Across the Curriculum

▶ **Language Arts** Share the poem *The Cow* by Jack Prelutsky (*The Random House Book of Poetry,* 1983) with students.

The cow mainly moos as she chooses to moo
and she chooses to moo as she chooses.
She furthermore chews as she chooses to chew
and she chooses to chew as she muses.
If she chooses to moo she may moo to amuse
or may moo just to moo as she chooses.
If she chooses to chew she may moo as she chews
or may chew just to chew as she muses.

Have students speak the poem in rhythm at various tempos. Encourage students to keep a steady beat with a drum and create an ostinato on nonpitched percussion instruments to accompany the reading.

## Technology/Media Link

**MIDI/Sequencing Software** Using the MIDI song file for "Streets of Laredo," have students play the song at a fast tempo (♩. = 180). Discuss what effect this has on the music. What would *"Cielito lindo"* sound like if it were in the tempo of "Streets of Laredo" (♩. = 60)?

For another MIDI activity, have students add a percussion track or a track using the chord roots to "Streets of Laredo."

LESSON 7

## LESSON AT A GLANCE

**Element Focus** **TEXTURE/HARMONY** I-$V_7$ accompaniment

**Skill Objective** **PLAYING** Play bass-note patterns from I and $V_7$ chords to accompany a song

**Connection Activity** **STYLE** Sing a Mexican *corrido*

**MATERIALS**

- "*Corrido de Kansas*" **CD 11-17**
- "Kansas *Corrido*" **CD 11-18**

  **Recording Routine:** Intro (4 m.); v. 1; interlude (4 m.); v. 2; interlude (4 m.); v. 3; coda
- **Pronunciation Practice/Translation** p. 485
- **Resource Book** p. A-27
- keyboard, bass xylophone or metallophone

**VOCABULARY**

*corrido* *vaqueros* I-$V_7$ chords

**National Standards**

**1c** Sing songs from diverse cultures
**2b** Perform chords and melodies on appropriate instruments
**6e** Respond through movement to prominent music characteristics

**MORE MUSIC CHOICES . . .**

For more practice singing songs with I and $V_7$ chords:

"*El rancho grande*," p. 215
"I'm Gonna Sing," p. 33
"Over My Head," p. 118

# 1 INTRODUCE

Select individuals to read the text at the top of p. 274. Invite students to look at and read about the painting on p. 275. Lead students in a discussion of the life of a *vaquero* on a cattle drive. See Spotlight On below. Tell students that they will learn a *corrido* about one *vaquero's* experience.

LESSON 7 Element: TEXTURE/HARMONY Skill: PLAYING Connection: STYLE

# "Driving" to KANSAS

"Streets of Laredo," in the previous lesson, is a good example of a **ballad**. A *corrido* is a type of ballad from Mexico.

A **ballad** is a song that tel[ls] a story.

The adventurous story told in "*Corrido de Kansas*" involves a group of *vaqueros* (Mexican cowboys) on a cattle drive from Texas to Kansas. During a cattle drive, cowboys could encounter many dangers — including violent weather and wild animals. Before you **sing** "*Corrido de Kansas*," read the lyrics to discover one more danger the *vaqueros* faced.

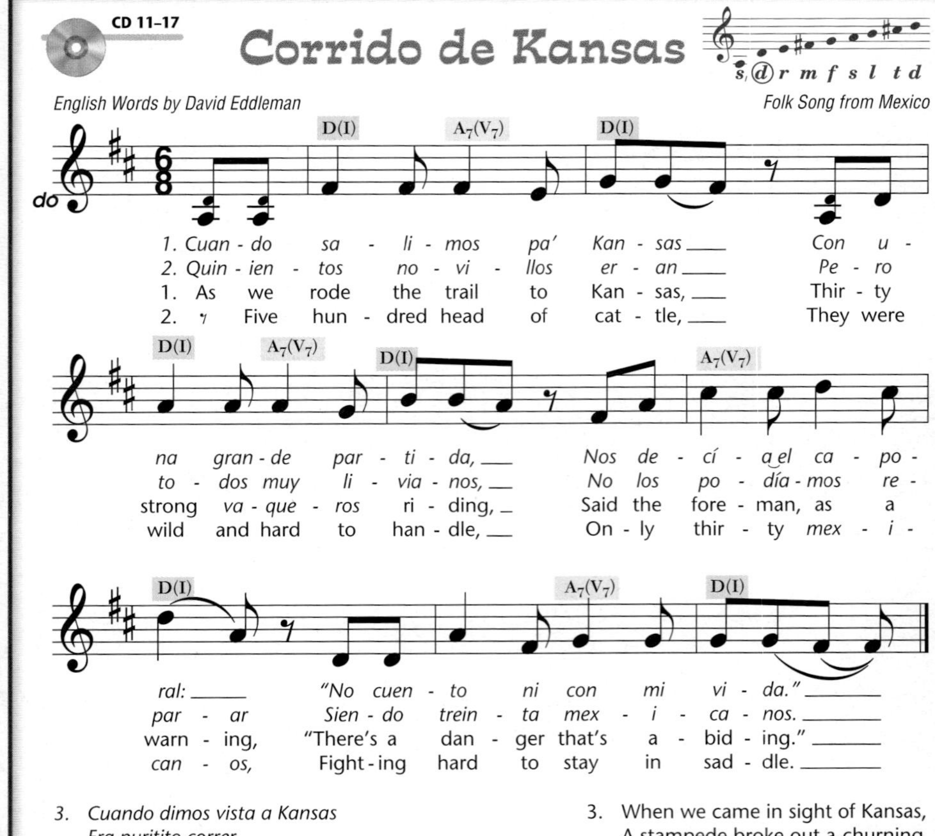

CD 11-17
Corrido de Kansas
s, d r m f s l t d
English Words by David Eddleman
Folk Song from Mexico
do
D(I) A7(V7) D(I)
1. Cuan - do sa - li - mos pa' Kan - sas Con u -
2. Quin - ien - tos no - vi - llos er - an Pe - ro
1. As we rode the trail to Kan - sas, Thir - ty
2. Five hun - dred head of cat - tle, They were
D(I) A7(V7) D(I) A7(V7)
na gran - de par - ti - da, Nos de - cí - a el ca - po -
to - dos muy li - via - nos, No los po - día - mos re -
strong va - que - ros ri - ding, Said the fore - man, as a
wild and hard to han - dle, On - ly thir - ty mex - i -
D(I) A7(V7) D(I)
ral: "No cuen - to ni con mi vi - da."
par - ar Sien - do trein - ta mex - i - ca - nos.
warn - ing, "There's a dan - ger that's a - bid - ing."
can - os, Fight - ing hard to stay in sad - dle.
3. Cuando dimos vista a Kansas
Era puritito correr,
Eran los caminos largos,
Y pensaba yo en volver.
3. When we came in sight of Kansas,
A stampede broke out a-churning,
Down the dusty trail a-winding,
And I thought about returning.

274

# Footnotes

## SPOTLIGHT ON

▶ **Cattle Drives** In the 1870s, Mexicans and Texans began moving longhorn cattle to Abilene, Kansas for sale. After the cattle were branded, they were rounded up and herded to the north. The job of the cowboys was to keep the cattle together as much as possible to prevent them from wandering away from the herd, where they might be lost or become prey to a wild animal. As the cowboys traveled, they told stories and sang songs. Many of these have become the tall tales and cowboy songs that we still know today.

## BUILDING SKILLS THROUGH MUSIC

▶ **Technology** Using the classroom computer, assist students in finding maps encompassing Texas and Kansas. If time permits, have them research cattle drives.

## TEACHER TO TEACHER

2b

▶ **Orff Instruments** When playing the chord patterns on p. 275 on bass Orff instruments, have students play the pitches up an octave. The first two measures are shown below as an example.

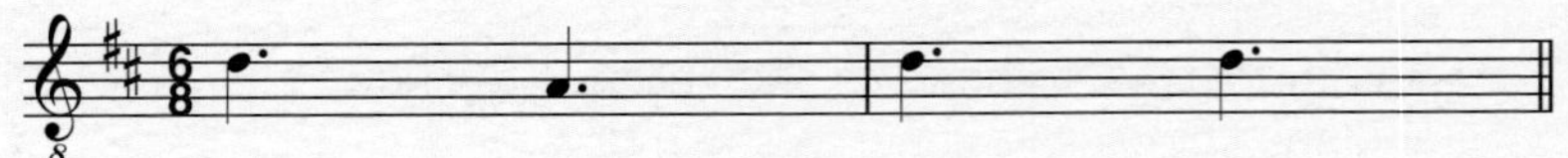

The bass Orff instrument pitches will actually sound in the range written on p. 275.

## *Corrido* Chords

"*Corrido de Kansas*" uses just two chords for the accompaniment:

- The D (I) chord, which is based on ***do***.
- The $A_7$ ($V_7$) chord, which is based on ***so***.

**Play** the two chord patterns below to accompany the song. How are they different? In which pattern are the last two measures the same as the first two?

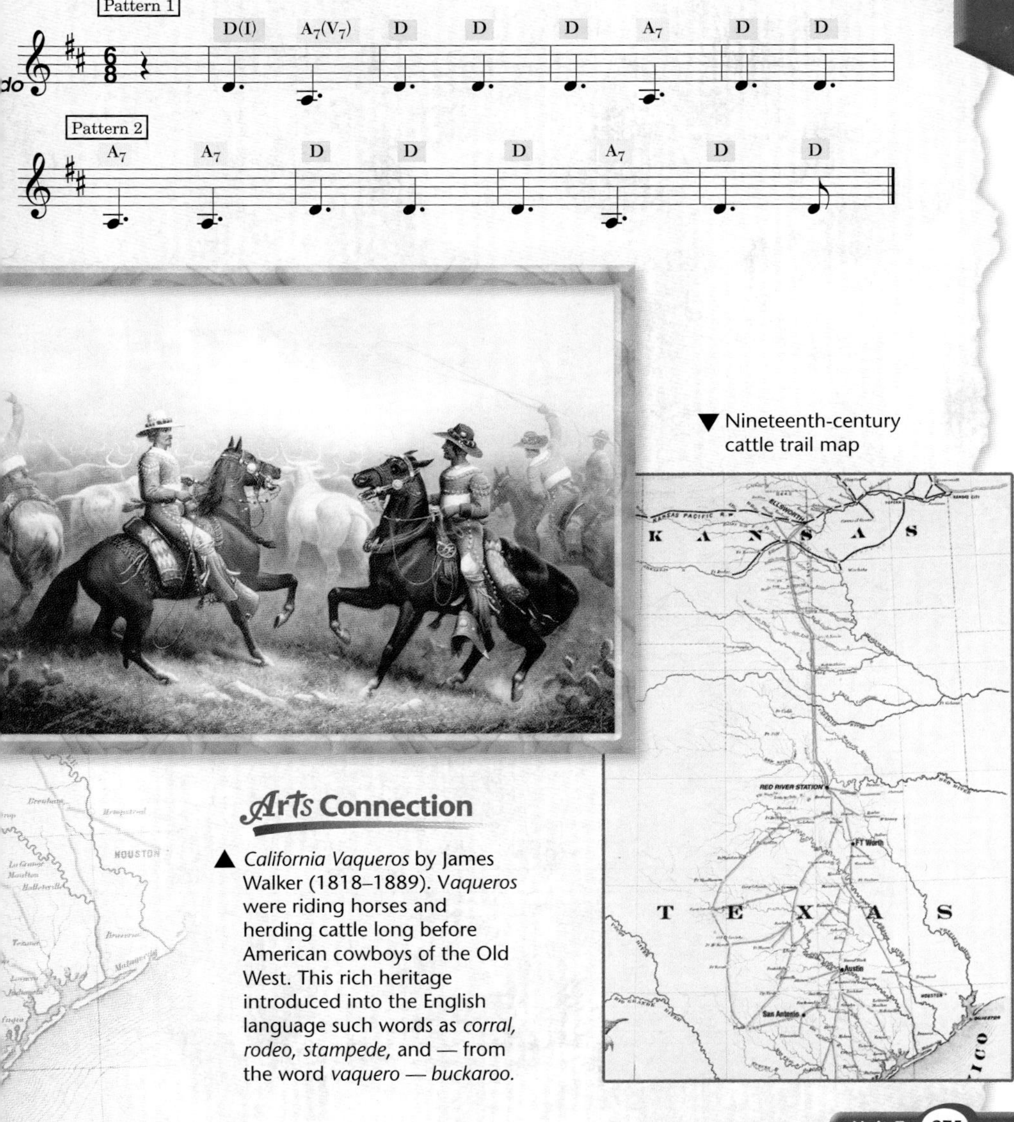


▼ Nineteenth-century cattle trail map

*Arts* Connection

▲ *California Vaqueros* by James Walker (1818–1889). *Vaqueros* were riding horses and herding cattle long before American cowboys of the Old West. This rich heritage introduced into the English language such words as *corral, rodeo, stampede*, and — from the word *vaquero* — *buckaroo.*

Going Places U.S.A.



# 2 Develop

### Singing

1c Play *"Corrido de Kansas"* **CD 11-17** and discuss the story of this Mexican ballad. Have students echo sing each phrase with the Pronunciation Practice **CD 11-20**. Then invite them to sing along with the recording.

### Analyzing

Have students identify the chords that are used in the song by finding them in the score on p. 274.

ASK **In what key is this song written?** (D)

**What chord numbers do you see written in Roman numerals above the notes?** (I, $V_7$)

**What are the letter names of these chords?** (D, $A_7$)

Invite students to read the text at the top of p. 275.

ASK **What is the difference between the two patterns?** (Pattern 1 begins on D; pattern 2 begins on A.) **In which pattern are the last two measures the same as the first two?** (pattern 1)

### Playing

6e Play "*Corrido de Kansas*" again and have students

- Say the letter names of each pattern in rhythm while showing one finger for the I chord (D) and five fingers for the $V_7$ chord ($A_7$).
- Sing "*Corrido de Kansas*" while showing the I and $V_7$ chords at the appropriate times with their fingers.

2b Let students take turns playing D and A on a keyboard or bass Orff instrument to accompany the song. See Teacher to Teacher on p. 274.

# 3 Close

**Element: TEXTURE/HARMONY** **ASSESSMENT**

**Performance/Observation** As students sing "*Corrido de Kansas,*" observe to see that they are showing the correct chord numbers and playing the correct pitches to accompany the song.

## Skills Reinforcement

▶ **Playing** Invite students to add one more layer to "*Corrido de Kansas.*"

**Reinforcement** Encourage students who have difficulty to choose the part they are most comfortable with.

**On Target** Have students learn this recorder part.

**Challenge** Divide the class into three groups. Group 1 will sing the song, group 2 will play the bass part, and group 3 will play the recorder. Allow the groups to switch parts.

## Technology/Media Link

▶ **Notation Software** Help students notate the I and $V_7$ chord changes in "*Corrido de Kansas*" as full chords. Help them to write the chords in the correct sequence and then play them back as they sing along.

▶ **Web Site** To learn more about the music of Mexico, invite students to visit *www.sfsuccessnet.com*.

LESSON 8

## LESSON AT A GLANCE

**Element Focus** **RHYTHM** Swing eighth notes

**Skill Objective** **PLAYING** Play eighth-note rhythm patterns while singing a song in swing style

**Connection Activity** **STYLE** Explore swing style music

**MATERIALS**

- "Route 66" **CD 11-21**
  **Recording Routine:** Intro (4 m.); vocal; coda
- *Route 66* **CD 11-24**
- selected rhythm instruments

**VOCABULARY**

swing style syncopation flatted third

### ◆◆◆◆ National Standards ◆◆◆◆

**1b** Sing expressively
**2b** Perform rhythms on appropriate instruments
**2e** Play instruments in groups, following a conductor
**6c** Use appropriate terms to explain music performances
**6e** Respond through movement to prominent music characteristics
**7b** Explain personal preferences for specific styles
**9a** Listen to identify music from different historical periods

**MORE MUSIC CHOICES**

For more examples of swing style:
*On Green Dolphin Street*, p. 126
"Straighten Up and Fly Right," p. 128

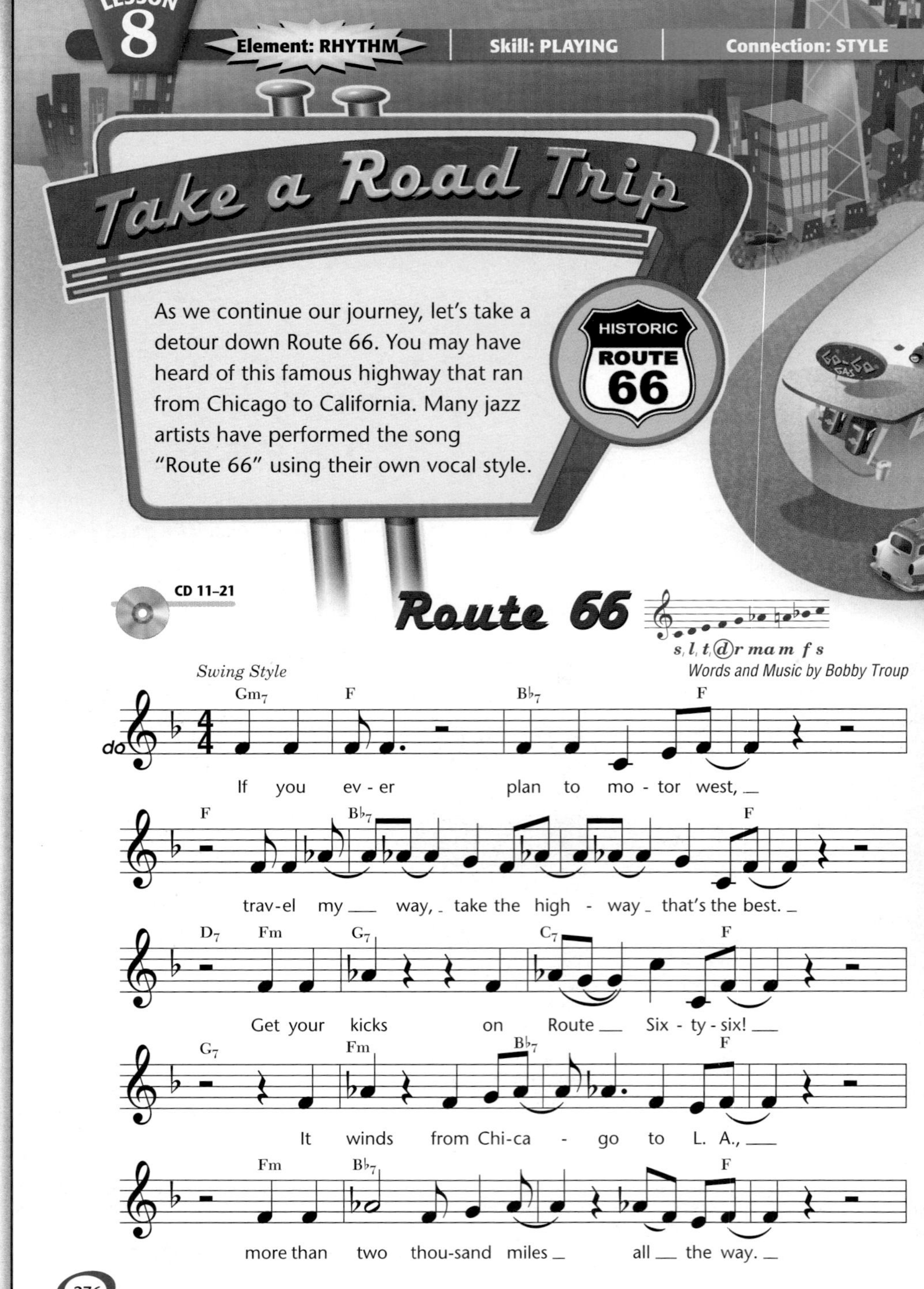
LESSON 8 Element: RHYTHM | Skill: PLAYING | Connection: STYLE

# Take a Road Trip

As we continue our journey, let's take a detour down Route 66. You may have heard of this famous highway that ran from Chicago to California. Many jazz artists have performed the song "Route 66" using their own vocal style.



CD 11-21

## Route 66

*s, l, t, d r ma m f s*

*Swing Style*

Words and Music by Bobby Troup



276

# Footnotes

## SKILLS REINFORCEMENT

1b ▶ **Singing** For additional experience with swing styles, have students sing and listen to "Straighten Up and Fly Right" **CD 6-2**, p. 128, or "Bundle-Buggy Boogie Woogie" **CD 5-38**, p. 120.

## BUILDING SKILLS THROUGH MUSIC

▶ **Social Studies** Bring in a large map of the U.S. Have students locate the many cities mentioned in the song "Route 66." Are any of the cities mentioned in the song state capitals? (Oklahoma City, Oklahoma)

## SPOTLIGHT ON

▶ **Roadside Architecture** The evolution of tourist-targeted facilities is well represented in the roadside architecture along Route 66. For example, most Americans who drove the route did not stay in hotels. They preferred the accommodations that emerged from automobile travel—motels (motor hotels). Motels evolved from earlier features of the American roadside, such as the auto camp and the tourist home. The national outgrowth of the auto camp and tourist home was the cabin camp (sometimes called cottages) that offered minimal comfort at affordable prices. Many of these cottages are still in operation. Eventually, auto camps and cabin camps gave way to motels, in which all of the rooms were under a single roof. Motor courts offered additional amenities, such as adjoining restaurants, souvenir shops, and swimming pools.

Mel's DINER
Going Places U.S.A.
Swing Rhythms
Listen to "Route 66." Are the rhythms of the melody performed exactly as they are notated?
D7 Fm G7 C7 F Fm
Get your kicks on Route __ Six - ty - six! __
Gm7 F F7 B♭7
Now you go thru Saint Loo - ey and Jop - lin, Mis - sour - i and
F F7
O - kla - ho - ma Cit - y is might - y pret - ty; You'll see __
B♭7 F
__ Am - a - ril - lo; __ Gal - lup, New Mex - i - co; __ Flag -
Gm7 C7 F
- staff, Ar - i - zo - na; Don't __ for - get Wi - no - na, King -
A♭ Gm7 F
- man, Bar - stow, San __ Ber - nar - di - no. Won't you __
Unit 7 277

# 1 INTRODUCE

Ask the class if they have heard of a famous highway called Route 66. Direct students' attention to the opening paragraph on p. 276 and share the information about roadside architecture on Route 66 in Spotlight On, p. 276.

# 2 DEVELOP

## Listening

6c Ask students to identify and discuss ways a performer might decide to sing a particular song. (Consider such factors as tempo, lyrics, accompaniment, and style.)

Invite students to listen to *Route 66* as performed by Harry James's big band **CD 11-24**.

ASK **What does *vocal style* mean?** (the manner in which a person sings a song)

7b **If you were singing this song, how would you sing it? What might you do differently and why?** (Recognize various answers.)

**What is meant by *vocal timbre*?** (the particular quality of a voice)

## Singing

1b 9a Invite students to sing "Route 66" **CD 11-21**. Point out that the song is in "swing" style, an American popular song style with a strong jazz influence.

ASK **What musical elements make up this style?** (uneven "swing" eighth notes, syncopated rhythms, flatted notes, rests at the beginning and end of some phrases)

Have students sing "Route 66" again to reinforce the style elements.

**continued on page 278**

## CULTURAL CONNECTION

▶ **Road to Opportunity** Share with students the importance of Route 66 during the time of the Dust Bowl. In his famous social commentary, *The Grapes of Wrath,* John Steinbeck proclaimed United States Highway 66 the "Mother Road." Steinbeck's classic 1939 novel, combined with the 1940 film re-creation of the epic odyssey, served to immortalize Route 66 in the American consciousness. Thousands of families migrated to California to escape the despair of the Dust Bowl. Certainly in the minds of those who endured that particularly painful experience, and in the view of generations of children to whom they recounted their story, Route 66 symbolized the "road to opportunity." See School to Home Connection on p. 281 for resources on the Dust Bowl.

## ACROSS THE CURRICULUM

▶ **Social Studies/Math** Invite students to locate Route 66 on a map of the United States. Encourage them to find the cities named in the lyrics of the song and to chart a road trip that shows the route from Chicago to Los Angeles. Have students determine the number of miles in this trip and then estimate the cost of gasoline to make this trip today. Ask them to name other cities along Route 66 that are not mentioned in the song. Have them list all the states traversed by Route 66.

### Playing

2b 2e To give students a better feeling of swing style, write the following accompaniment on the board and have them play it, using appropriate rhythm instruments. Remind students to swing the eighth notes. Invite volunteers to lead the class by conducting a steady beat.

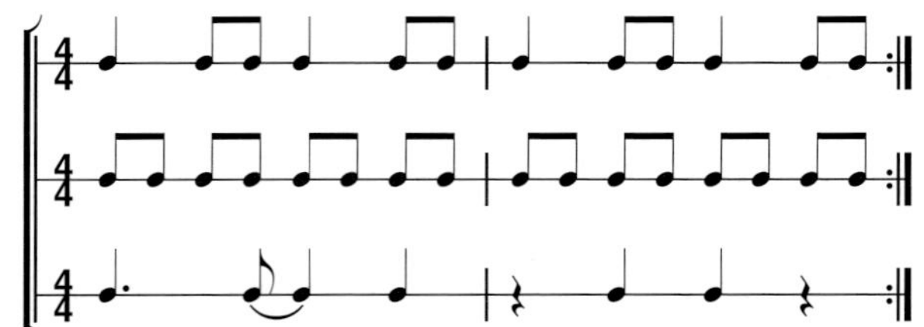

### Moving

6e Teach students the following movements to accompany "Route 66" **CD 11-21**.

*Formation:* Students stand in small groups.

| | |
|---|---|
| Measures 1–4: | Pretend to turn a steering wheel to the left. |
| Measures 5–8: | Turn steering wheel to the right. |
| Measures 9–12: | Alternate step-snap while moving forward in a crouched position. |
| Measures 13–16: | Move both arms across body to the left shaking the index finger. |
| Measures 17–20: | Move both arms to the right. |
| Measures 21–24: | Alternate step-snap while moving forward in a crouched position. |
| Measures 25–36: | Students create gestures in pairs to represent the different places referenced in the song and perform the gestures on the downbeat of the measure. |
| Measures 37–40: | Turn to the right and step forward eight times, shaking the finger. |
| Measures 41–44: | Turn to the left and move as above. |

Welcome to Sunny California

### Let's Swing!

In swing style, eighth notes are performed unevenly. The first eighth note of each beat is a little longer than normal. The second eighth note of each beat is a little shorter.

Imitate the swing style you hear on the recording of "Route 66." **Listen** especially to the way the eighth notes on the words *Oklahoma City is might–* are performed in swing style.

Bb7 F
___ get hip ___ to this time - ly tip, ___

D7 Fm G7 C7 F
When you make _ that Cal - i - for - nia trip, __

D7 Fm G7 C7 F
get your kicks on Route ___ Six - ty - six! ___

D7 *p* Fm G7 C7 F
Get your kicks on Route ___ Six - ty - six! ___

278

## Footnotes

### Across the Curriculum

▶ **Language Arts** The song "Route 66" is a kind of road map in that the lyrics describe cities along the famous road's path. Share with students the poem "Maps" by Dorothy Brown Thompson (*The Random House Book of Poetry for Children,* 1983).

High adventure and bright dream
Maps are mightier than they seem;
Ships that follow learning stars
Red and gold of strange bazaars
Ice floes hid beyond all knowing
Planes that ride where winds are blowing!
Train maps, maps of wind and weather,
Road maps—taken altogether
Maps are really magic wands
For home-staying vagabonds!

### Spotlight On

▶ **The Big Band Era** From the late 1920s to 1940s, Big Band music was very popular. Numerous bands toured across America, bringing live music to their fans. Dance bands played throughout the United States, providing a major form of entertainment to the American public. A musician with Tommy Dorsey's band, Bobby Troup, wrote the song "Route 66." Such famous bands as Woody Herman, Benny Goodman, Harry James, Les Brown, Jack Teagarden, Benny Carter, Ina Ray Hutton, and Tommy Dorsey became household names. Many famous vocalists got their start or received valuable training singing with these bands. The famous popular vocalist Frank Sinatra spent time singing with the Dorsey band. Sinatra has often admitted that listening to Dorsey helped him develop his phrasing, breathing, musical taste, and knowledge.

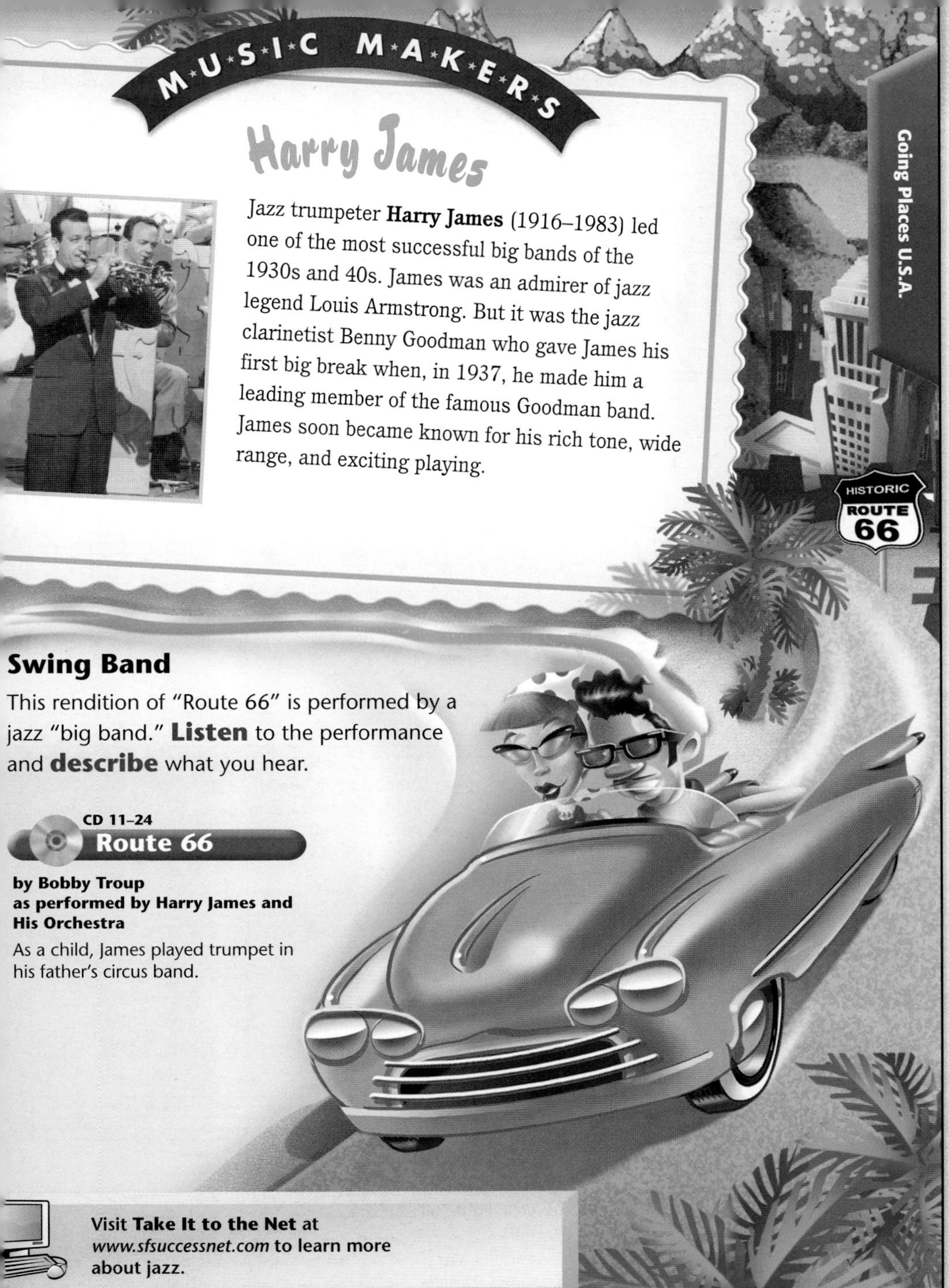

MUSIC MAKERS

## Harry James

Jazz trumpeter **Harry James** (1916–1983) led one of the most successful big bands of the 1930s and 40s. James was an admirer of jazz legend Louis Armstrong. But it was the jazz clarinetist Benny Goodman who gave James his first big break when, in 1937, he made him a leading member of the famous Goodman band. James soon became known for his rich tone, wide range, and exciting playing.



### Swing Band

This rendition of "Route 66" is performed by a jazz "big band." **Listen** to the performance and **describe** what you hear.

CD 11-24
**Route 66**

**by Bobby Troup**
**as performed by Harry James and His Orchestra**

As a child, James played trumpet in his father's circus band.

Visit **Take It to the Net** at *www.sfsuccessnet.com* to learn more about jazz.



Measures 45–48: Alternate step-snap while moving forward in a crouched position.

Measures 49–51: Repeat above, but step backward.

### Listening

Have students listen once again to *Route 66* **CD 11-24**. Point out that it is an example of the swing style of the 1930s and 40s. Have students describe specific elements of the performance, such as vocal timbre, instrumentation, and tempo.

## 3 CLOSE

**Element: RHYTHM** ASSESSMENT

**Performance/Observation** Have students sing "Route 66" **CD 11-21** and play the accompaniment notated from p. 278 in the Teacher's Edition. Observe and assess each student's ability to play the swing eighth notes in the part.

### MEETING INDIVIDUAL NEEDS

▶ **English Language Learners** Sometimes comprehension is challenging for students learning English. Oral retellings are one effective way to monitor comprehension. Ask students to tell a partner what the song lyrics are about. Ask students what it means to "motor west," "get your kicks," or "get hip." Point out that "Saint Looey" is St. Louis, Missouri. A class discussion will help your students understand these idioms.

### TECHNOLOGY/MEDIA LINK

**Web Site** For more information on jazz, have students visit *www.sfsuccessnet.com.*

## LESSON AT A GLANCE

**Element Focus** **MELODY** Melody patterns in *la*-pentatonic

**Skill Objective** **PLAYING** Create and play parts to accompany a *la*-pentatonic melody

**Connection Activity** **SOCIAL STUDIES** Discuss how a folk song reflects social and political issues

**MATERIALS**

- "Pastures of Plenty" **CD 11-25**

  **Recording Routine**: Intro (4 m.); v. 1; interlude (4 m.); v. 2; interlude (4 m.); v. 3; interlude (4 m.); v. 4; coda
- alto glockenspiel, bass xylophone

**VOCABULARY**

*la*-pentatonic ostinato

**◆◆◆◆ National Standards ◆◆◆◆**

**2b** Perform melodic patterns on classroom instruments
**2d** Echo short rhythms and melodic patterns
**5b** Read notes, using standard symbols

**MORE MUSIC CHOICES**

For more practice with *la*-pentatonic:

"Canoe Song," p. 76
"See the Children Playin'," p. 107

# 1 INTRODUCE

Give students a quick overview of Woody Guthrie. Share the information from Spotlight On, p. 281. Then have students read about Woody Guthrie in the Music Makers feature on p. 281. Most of his song lyrics were about social or political issues or love for the land. The song "Pastures of Plenty" speaks of the migrant worker and his or her difficult life on the road.



# Give Me Five

How many notes are in a scale? Eight is a correct answer, but not the only correct one. There are many different scales with various numbers of notes. The pentatonic scale has only five notes.

**Sing** the pentatonic song "Pastures of Plenty."

CD 11-25
Pastures of Plenty
s, l, d r m s
Words and Music by Woody Guthrie
Em G B Am
1. It's a might-y hard row that my poor hands has hoed. My poor feet has trav-eled a hot dust-y road. Out of your Dust Bowl and west-ward we rolled, And your des-erts was hot and your moun-tains was cold.
2. I worked in your or-chards of pea-ches and prunes; Slept on the ground in the light of the moon. On the edge of the ci-ty you'll see us and then, We come with the dust and we're gone with the wind.
3. Green pas-tures of plen-ty from dry de-sert ground, From the Grand Cou-lee Dam where the wa-ters run down. Ev-ery state in the Un-ion us mi-grants has been, We'll work in this fight, and we'll fight 'till we win.
4. It's al-ways we ram-bled, that riv-er and I; All a-long your green val-ley I will work 'till I die. My land I'll de-fend with my life if it be, 'Cause my pas-tures of plen-ty must al-ways be free.




280

# Footnotes

## MEETING INDIVIDUAL NEEDS

**▶ Teaching with Visuals** An important tool in successful teaching is to make visuals that help teach lessons. These visuals can be melodic fragments, pictures to show form, or, as in this lesson, a visual of the xylophone bars. Using a large visual of the xylophone bars made from posterboard, model for the entire class how to play E with the left hand, B with the right and cross the left hand over to play the high E. Have students practice on the cardboard model before playing the instruments.

## BUILDING SKILLS THROUGH MUSIC

**▶ Math** Ask students to recall the mathematical term for a five-sided figure. (pentagon) Have them draw a pentagon and label each side with the notes from the *la*-pentatonic scale.

## SKILLS REINFORCEMENT

**▶ Creating** Review with students the meaning of pentatonic. Have them think of other words that begin with "penta." Have them notate *la*-pentatonic scales starting on D and E. Then ask them to notate melodies, using the pitches *do, re, mi, so,* and *la.* The tonal center, or resting tone, will be *la.*

## Pentatonic Pastures

**Listen** to Woody Guthrie's "Pastures of Plenty." This song uses the pitches *do, re, mi, so,* and *la.* The tonal center (resting place) is *la.*

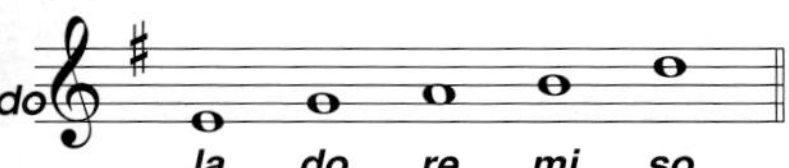


**Play** this accompaniment as others **sing** "Pastures of Plenty."

### Woody Guthrie

**Woody Guthrie** (1912–1967) was named after President Woodrow Wilson. At a very young age, he loved making music. By the end of his life, he had written more than 1,000 songs! Many of his songs are about his love for America and social issues of the times. "Pastures of Plenty" is about the migrant workers and the troubles they faced during the Dust Bowl. Woody Guthrie was a great American folk singer, guitarist, and composer. Many people were influenced by Guthrie—Bruce Springsteen, Joan Baez, Bob Dylan, and Guthrie's son, Arlo Guthrie.





# 2 Develop

### Reading

Remove Fs and Cs from the alto glockenspiel and the bass xylophone and have students play the *la*-pentatonic scale starting on E. Write the following melody patterns in *la*-pentatonic on the board.

5b Ask students to sing and read the melody patterns.

### Singing

2d Ask individuals and small groups of students to echo sing with you each phrase of the melody of "Pastures of Plenty" **CD 11-25**. Then invite the class to sing the song with the recording.

### Performing

Have students refer to the Orff accompaniment on p. 281. Have them pat the patterns on their knees before playing on instruments. Use a visual of the xylophone bars to model how to play. Refer to Meeting Individual Needs on p. 280. (Both patterns are left knee, right knee, cross left hand over to beyond right knee, then right knee again.)

2b Ask students to sing the fragments of the melody in the alto glockenspiel part and then play it.

Have them sing the song with the accompaniment.

# 3 Close

**Skill: PLAYING** — **ASSESSMENT**

**Performance/Observation** Invite students to create ostinato patterns in *la*-pentatonic to accompany "Pastures of Plenty" **CD 11-25**. Observe students' ability to play the ostinato with the song.

## Spotlight On

**▶ The Songwriter and Composer** Woody Guthrie (1912–1967) went from singing about the plight of workers to helping them do something about it. During this period, the differences between the rich and the poor in this country were more pronounced than at any other time. In early 1940, Woody traveled to New York City. There he met Pete Seeger, Lee Hays, Leadbelly, and Cisco Houston. These people became central to his musical and political activities. Guthrie said, "I am out to sing the songs that make you take pride in yourself and in your work. And the songs that I sing are made up for the most part by all sorts of folks just about like you." In 1966, Guthrie was given the Conservation Service Award by the U.S. Department of the Interior because of his love for and kinship with the land that is expressed in so many of his songs and writings.

## School to Home Connection

**▶ Read a Book** For interested readers, recommend *Children of the Dust Bowl: The True Story of the School at Weedpatch Camp* by Jerry Stanley (Random House, 1993). It is the story of homeless farm workers' children and the school they created. Encourage readers to share information from the book with family members and classmates.

## Technology/Media Link

**CD-ROM** Use one of the rhythm tracks in *Band-in-a-Box* as an accompaniment, while students improvise melodies on a melody instrument in E *la*-pentatonic.

LESSON 10

## LESSON AT A GLANCE

**Element Focus** **RHYTHM** Beat and meter

**Skill Objective** **SINGING** Sing a song in meter in 4, in various rhythms, and perform a steady beat

**Connection Activity** **CULTURE** Discuss how Native American music reflects the values and beliefs of the people

### MATERIALS

- "I Walk in Beauty" **CD 12-1**
  **Recording Routine:** Intro (4 m.); vocal; coda
- "Farewell to the Warriors" **CD 12-3**
  **Recording Routine:** Intro (9 m.); vocal; interlude (9 m.); vocal; coda
- *Interview with J. Bryan Burton* **CD 12-6**
- **Pronunciation Practice/Translation** p. 485
- **Resource Book** p. A-28
- drums and rattles
- colored rhythm visuals

### VOCABULARY

steady beat meter drums shakers (rattles)

### ◆◆◆◆ National Standards ◆◆◆◆

**1a** Sing independently in rhythm
**1c** Sing songs from diverse cultures
**2a** Play instruments maintaining a steady tempo
**2b** Perform rhythms on classroom instruments
**5a** Read simple rhythms in $\frac{4}{4}$ meter
**6a** Listen to identify simple forms
**9b** Describe elements in music from various cultures

### MORE MUSIC CHOICES

For more Native American melodies and poetry:
"And My Heart Soars" (poem), p. 359
"The Earth Is Our Mother," p. 358

# THE BEAT GOES ON . . .

How do you know you are alive? One good answer is that you have a pulse. Music has a pulse, called the beat.

The song "I Walk in Beauty" has a very steady pulse, like a heartbeat. It speaks of the Navajo belief of an inner beauty called *hozho*.

**Sing** "I Walk in Beauty" and lightly tap the pulse on your chest.

d r m s l d' r'

CD 12-1

## I WALK IN BEAUTY

Words and Music by Arliene Nofchissey Williams (Navajo)

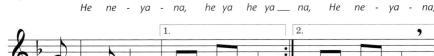

He ne - ya - na, he ya he ya na, He ne - ya - na,

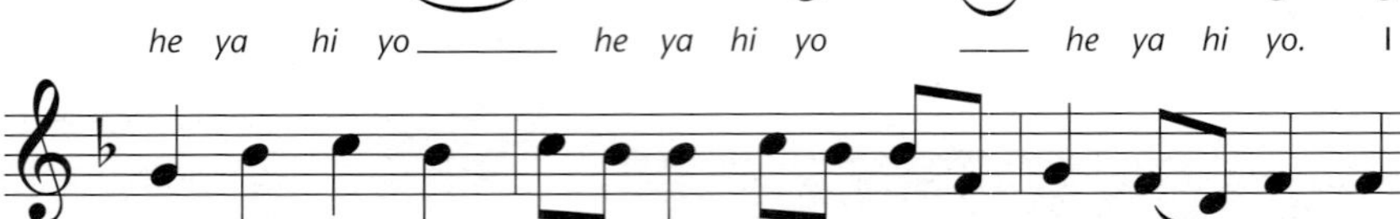
1.
2.
he ya hi yo he ya hi yo he ya hi yo. I

yearn for beau - ty, yes I do, yes I do; I learn of beau - ty,

# Footnotes

## CULTURAL CONNECTION

9b ▶ **Native American Music** Rattles and drums are the major instruments used by Native Americans in their traditional music. Drums frequently represent the heartbeat of Mother Earth. The only melody instrument used is a flute, usually made from wood or cane. It is often decorated. Historically, only the Plains people and some of the Native Americans from the Southwest used flutes, but it is now common to hear a flute in celebrations and powwows anywhere in North America.

## BUILDING SKILLS THROUGH MUSIC

▶ **Social Studies** Share the information from Across the Curriculum, p. 283, on Native American tribes. Have students
- Research the tribes nearest to their community.
- Create a speech piece using the names of the tribes.

## SPOTLIGHT ON

▶ **"I Walk in Beauty"** This song was first recorded at Brigham Young University in Utah, where many Native American students study. "I Walk in Beauty" is now frequently sung at powwows, and it is sung in many languages and versions. The song's message is that if a person maintains inner balance and peace, he or she will walk in beauty. A poetic translation of the original Navajo is

"In Beauty I walk
With Beauty before me, I walk
With Beauty behind me, I walk
With Beauty all around me, I walk
With Beauty within me, I walk
In Beauty, it is finished."

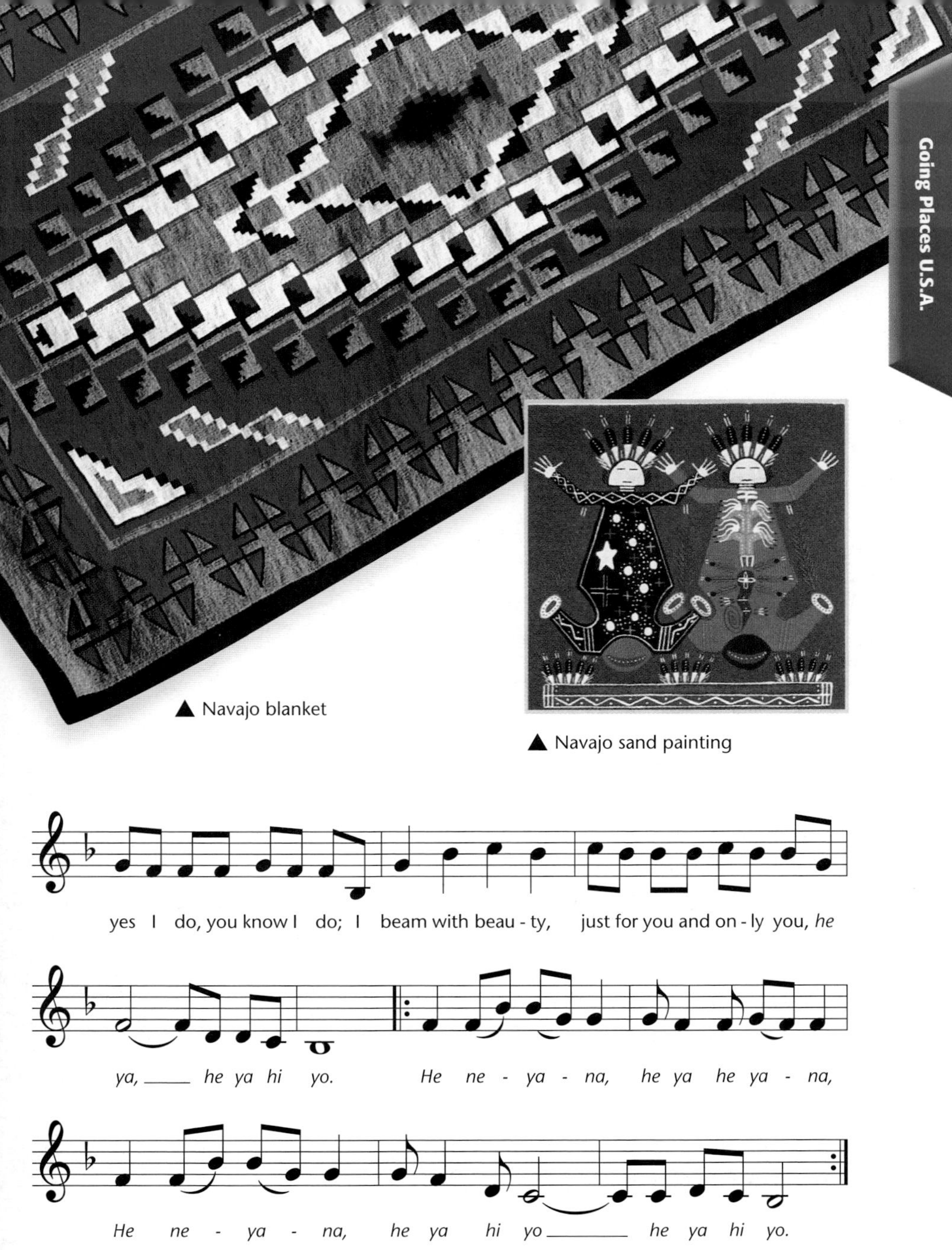

Going Places U.S.A.
yes I do, you know I do; I beam with beau - ty, just for you and on - ly you, he
ya, he ya hi yo. He ne - ya - na, he ya he ya - na,
He ne - ya - na, he ya hi yo he ya hi yo.
Unit 7 283


▲ Navajo blanket

▲ Navajo sand painting

# 1 Introduce

Ask students what instruments they associate with Native American music. When they tell you drums and rattles, point out that in traditional Native American music, and in this composed popular-style song, it is characteristic to have a strong steady beat. The steady beat is provided by a drum beaten steadily or rattles shaken evenly. See Cultural Connection, p. 282.

# 2 Develop

### Reading

Write the following rhythms on the board or create rhythm visuals, each in a different color. Mix the order so that it is not the same as the first five measures of "I Walk in Beauty."

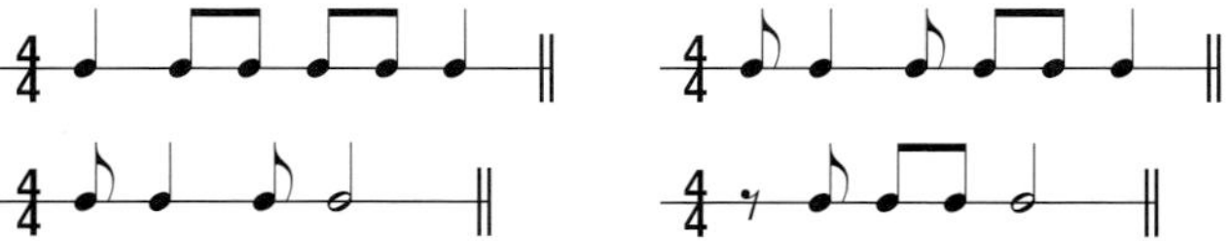

6a Have students

- Listen several times to the first five measures of "I Walk in Beauty" **CD 12-1**.
- 5a Clap the rhythm of these five measures.
- Look at the colored visuals. Speak and clap the rhythms on each visual.
- Listen several times to the first five measures of the melody.

ASK **Are there any notated rhythms that are repeated?** (yes)

Have students listen to the first ten measures of the melody.

ASK **What order should the visuals be in to become the rhythm of the beginning of the song?**

**continued on page 284**

## Across the Curriculum

▶ **Social Studies** The two Native American tribes who were nomadic hunters were the Navajo and the Apache, who live in Arizona and New Mexico. Other Native Americans in these states who are not nomadic hunters fall into two categories: agricultural desert and river tribes, who live at the southern end of the two states, and agricultural pueblo tribes, who live in the mountainous northern regions. Ask some students to research the names of some of the tribes who are agricultural desert and river tribes. (Tohono O'odham, Yaqui, Pima, Yuma, Mojave, Cocopa)

Then have other students research the names of some of the tribes who are agricultural pueblo tribes. (Hopi, Zuni, Acoma, Santo Domingo, San Ildefonso, Isleta, Cochiti, Picuris)

## Skills Reinforcement

▶ **Creating** Native American songs are often sung unaccompanied; if instruments are used, they are usually bells, shakers, and drums. Invite some students to create an accompaniment on these instruments for one of the music selections while the others sing it. Have the players practice the accompaniment so that it complements rather than competes with the melody.

Have students listen to the recording again and follow the notation in their books.

**ASK Are there any parts of the song that are alike?** (yes, the beginning and the end)

Have students

- Sing the song and pat the steady beat.
- Sing the song and transfer the steady beat to drums or shaker instruments.

Share with students the information about "I Walk in Beauty" in Spotlight On, p. 282. Emphasize the song's message of the Navajo belief that to "walk in beauty" means to maintain a sense of peace and inner balance.

## Analyzing

Discuss the information about the characteristics of Chippewa music found in Cultural Connection below. Then play the recording of "Farewell to the Warriors" **CD 12-3** and share the information about the song in Spotlight On below.

**ASK Which of these characteristics are found in this song?** (all but the last one)

Have students

- Look at the music and count how many times the time signature changes. (four times)
- Echo speak the words in rhythmic phrases.
- Repeat and identify the different phrase lengths (phrase 1 = upbeat and 2 measures; phrase 2 = upbeat and 2 measures; phrase 3 = 2 measures; phrase 3 = 3 measures)

Help students discover that although the meter frequently changes in this song, the beat remains constant.

### A Changing Meter—A Steady Beat

Look at the notation for "Farewell to the Warriors" and **sing** the song. Notice that the meter changes, but the beat stays the same.

s, l, d r m s l
CD 12-3

# FAREWELL TO THE WARRIORS

As sung by Mrs. Charles Mee, about 1908

Native American Song of the Chippewa

Um - be a - ni - ma - djag wa - su - gi - di -

zha - min, ya wi a ya wi a
3
ya ya wi a ya wi a

### The People and Their Songs

The song "Farewell to the Warriors" is a Chippewa song. The Chippewas live near the Great Lakes. After the Revolutionary War, some Chippewas (more commonly called Ojibways) moved to land they were given on the Grand River in Ontario, Canada.

"I Walk in Beauty" was composed by Navajo singer/songwriter Arliene Nofchissey Williams. The Navajos are from the southwest region of the United States.

Find the areas of the Chippewa and Navajo Nations on a map.

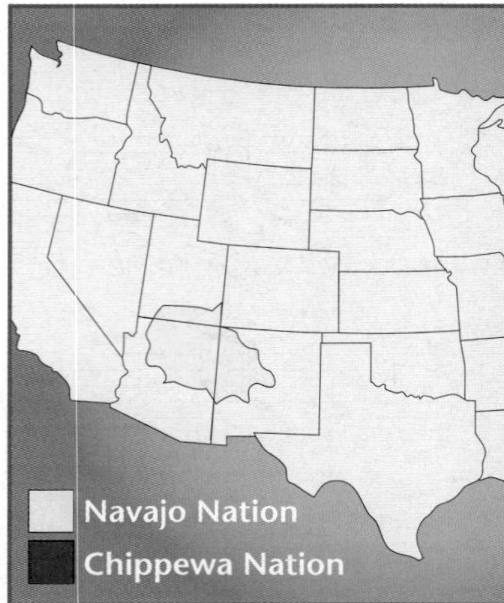
Navajo Nation
Chippewa Nation

# Footnotes

## SPOTLIGHT ON

▶ **"Farewell to the Warriors"** The story of this song is unusual because it is a Chippewa song that tells of the bravery of a woman who defended her people during a surprise attack by Dakota raiders. The story says that the heroine, Bica'ganab, was lighting a fire for breakfast when she heard someone shout, "The Dakota are upon us!" It was thought that Bica'ganab was killed. But when those who had escaped in canoes were out in the water, they saw a woman fighting the Dakota with a club. Although the Dakota followed her, she actually fought them and at the same time tore their canoe with her hands. The Dakota were forced into the water, where she continued to pound them with her paddle. She became a genuine heroine to the Chippewa.

## CULTURAL CONNECTION

▶ **Chippewa Music** Chippewas are Native Americans of the Lakes and Woods tribes. Some of the characteristics of the music of Lakes and Woods Native Americans are found in "Farewell to the Warriors." These characteristics are changing meters, melodies from 6 to 35 measures, generally descending melodic lines, phrases which vary in length, no chromatic alteration, and a number of different tonalities.

MUSIC MAKERS

# J. Bryan Burton

**J. Bryan Burton** (born 1948) is a music educator of Choctaw and European descent. His interest in Native Americans has led him to learn about many Native American singers and dancers and about their history and culture. Dr. Burton teaches at West Chester University in West Chester, Pennsylvania. He is the author of a collection of songs. His book *Moving Within the Circle* is about the history of various Native American people, their customs, and their music.



**Listen** as J. Bryan Burton talks about his work.

CD 12-6
**Interview with J. Bryan Burton**

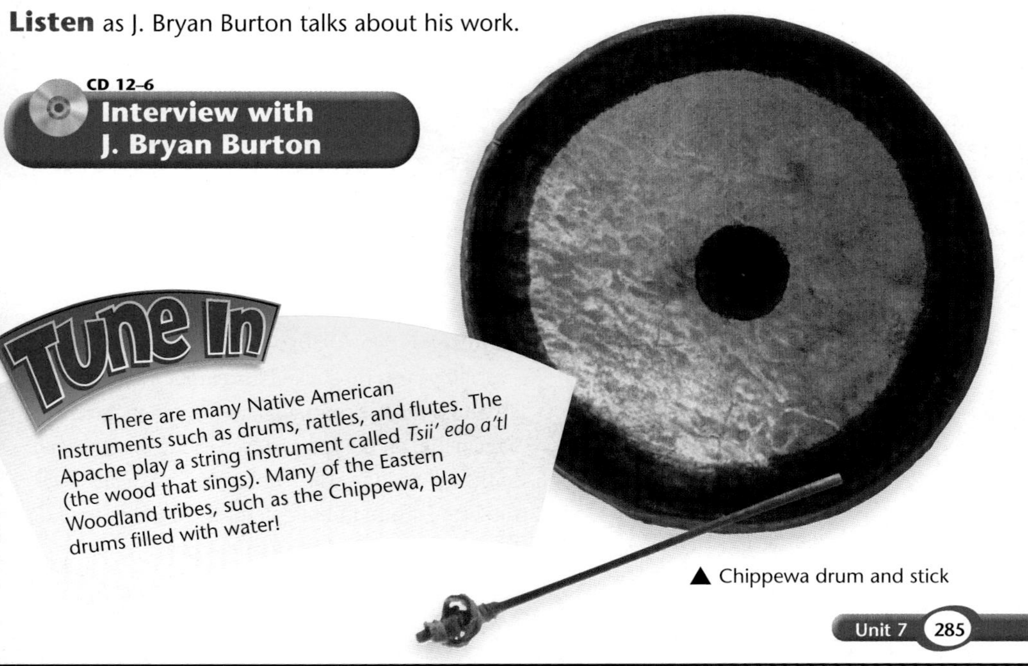

**Tune In**

There are many Native American instruments such as drums, rattles, and flutes. The Apache play a string instrument called *Tsii' edo a'tl* (the wood that sings). Many of the Eastern Woodland tribes, such as the Chippewa, play drums filled with water!

▲ Chippewa drum and stick



### Listening

Have students

- Listen to the recording of "Farewell to the Warriors" **CD 12-3** and follow the music.
- Pat a pulse on their knees.

### Singing

1c To assist students in learning the Chippewa words, have them listen to the Pronunciation Practice for "Farewell to the Warriors" **CD 12-5**. Refer to Resource Book p. A-28 for a Pronunciation Practice Guide. Once they are comfortable singing the words, have students sing the song, keeping a steady pulse on drums or shakers.

Invite students to look at the map on p. 284 and discuss the geographic locations of the Navajo and Chippewa Nations. Remind students that the songs in this lesson represent just two of the many diverse Native American cultures.

Have students read the Music Makers information about J. Bryan Burton and listen to him discuss his life and work as a collector and scholar of Native American music **CD 12-6.**

## 3 Close

**Element: RHYTHM** — ASSESSMENT

**Performance/Observation** Have students sing "I Walk in Beauty" **CD 12-1** and "Farewell to the Warriors" **CD 12-3** while patting their knees with a steady beat. Observe each student's ability to sing the song while keeping a steady beat.

2b For an additional activity, divide the class into teams of four to six. Using the rhythm patterns on the board or the colored rhythm visuals, ask each team to create a different rhythm from the rhythm of the song "I Walk in Beauty." Each team must use one of the rhythms more than once.

## Across the Curriculum

▶ **Art/Language Arts** Display *Native American Art* by David W. Penney and George C. Longfish (Levin Associates, 1994) for students to see the vast array of art, including almost 300 full-color reproductions created by Native Americans. Invite students to recreate art pieces for display during class performances.

Invite students to learn more about this group of people by reading *The Chippewa* by Alice Osinski (Children's Press, 1989).

## Character Education

▶ **Health** "I Walk in Beauty" reminds us of the importance of maintaining inner balance and peace. This is crucial for the continuation of strong physical and emotional health. Discuss the link between physical and emotional health. When you don't feel well physically, how do you feel emotionally? When you feel sadness or some other negative emotion, how do you feel physically? What can you do to keep yourself healthy emotionally and physically? As a class, compile a list of behaviors students can adopt to improve their emotional and physical health.

## Technology/Media Link

**Web Site** For more information on Native American music, have students visit *www.sfsuccessnet.com.*

LESSON 11

## LESSON AT A GLANCE

**Element Focus** **MELODY** Melodic sequence

**Skill Objective** **SINGING** Sing melodic sequences

**Connection Activity** **SOCIAL STUDIES** Explore California's image in music

**MATERIALS**

- "California, Here I Come" **CD 12-7**

  **Recording Routine:** Intro (8 m.); vocal; interlude (16 m.); vocal; coda

- **Resource Book** p. G-13, J-15

**VOCABULARY**

melodic sequence pitch

**◆ ◆ ◆ ◆ National Standards ◆ ◆ ◆ ◆**

**1b** Sing expressively

**6b** Describe music by answering questions about it

**6e** While listening to music, move to show prominent features of the music

**MORE MUSIC CHOICES**

For more songs with melodic sequence:

*"Tancovačka,"* p. 230

*"Thula, thula, ngoana,"* p. 227

LESSON 11 Element: MELODY Skill: SINGING Connection: SOCIAL STUDIES

# CALIFORNIA, HERE WE COME!

Ever since the Gold Rush in 1849, people have come to California. "Go West" became a common phrase among easterners seeking to make their fortunes. The song "California, Here I Come" captures the spirit of California as a land of opportunity. Al Jolson wrote the song in 1923.

**Listen** to and then **sing** "California, Here I Come." When the same melodic phrase repeats but starts on a different pitch level, we call it a melodic sequence. How many melodic sequences can you **identify** in this song?

MUSIC MAKERS

## Al Jolson

**Al Jolson** (1886–1950) was an entertainer for over 40 years. He started his career dancing on street corners. Eventually, he worked in a circus, vaudeville, on the radio, in recording studios, and in the movies (his 1927 film, *The Jazz Singer,* was the first feature talking picture). Al Jolson was known as the "World's Greatest Entertainer."

286



# 1 INTRODUCE

Share with students that the words and music for "California, Here I Come" were composed by Al Jolson, one of the great musical theater personalities of the early 1900s. He was constantly traveling from one city to another, and he could hardly wait to see California again! Have students tell what they know about California. Refer to Spotlight On and Across the Curriculum below.

# Footnotes

## SPOTLIGHT ON

▶ **Al Jolson** Point out that in early musical theater, actors, and singers performed on stage without the help of amplification and without elaborate sets and props. Entertainers like Al Jolson (1886–1950) did everything—he sang, danced, and told jokes. Al Jolson even wrote his own songs and jokes. He was billed as "The World's Greatest Entertainer." He worked in a carnival, circus, burlesque company, vaudeville theater, in radio and recording studios, and movies.

## BUILDING SKILLS THROUGH MUSIC

▶ **Science** Share the information in Across the Curriculum about the Golden Gate Bridge. Display pictures of different bridges for students to examine. For each picture, ask students to suggest explanations of how the bridge is supported.

## ACROSS THE CURRICULUM

▶ **Social Studies** "California, Here I Come" introduces the San Francisco Golden Gate Bridge, the longest suspension bridge of its time. Invite students to learn more about this famous bridge, "the bridge that couldn't be built," by reading *The Golden Gate Bridge* by Craig and Katherine Doherty (Blackbirch Marketing, 1995). Invite students to find California on their map. How big is California? How far away is California from where they live? What is the capital of California? How many people live in California? Discuss with students why songs like "California, Here I Come," "Route 66," and "Sweet Betsy from Pike" feature the state in lyrics. (temperate climates, career opportunities, wealth, hope for a better future, and so on) On another day, let students complete a word puzzle about different places in the U.S.A., using Resource Book p. J-15.

# 2 Develop

## Listening

Invite students to

- Listen to the recording of "California, Here I Come" **CD 12-7.**
- Follow the words of the song in the book and mark the phrases in the air.
- Listen as you sing the first phrase of the song and then the second phrase.

ASK **Do these two phrases sound alike or different?** (alike, but also different)

**How are they alike and different?** (The second phrase was at a lower pitch than the first one.)

**SAY** When a phrase has the same shape, but it is repeated at a different pitch level, we call it a melodic sequence.

Have students listen to the song again.

ASK **How many times did you hear that same melodic sequence?** (twice—lines 1–2 and lines 4–5)

**Was there another place in the song with a shorter sequence?** (yes, measures 9–10; 13–14; 15–16)

## Singing

Invite students to sing "California, Here I Come" **CD 12-7**.

# 3 Close

ASSESSMENT

**Performance/Observation** Have students sing "California, Here I Come" **CD 12-7** and clap once at the beginning of any phrase that is a melodic sequence. Observe students' understanding of the beginning of each melodic sequence by clapping at the appropriate time.

## Skills Reinforcement

▶ **Playing** Some students may find hearing melodic sequence to be quite a challenge. To reinforce what they are hearing, have students play the first four measures of "California, Here I Come" on a xylophone. Then have them learn the next four measures. Demonstrate to students that the melody is exactly the same, but it's just being played at a different place on the instrument. Have them experiment with playing the melody at other starting pitches.

▶ **Signing** For a signing activity for "California, Here I Come," refer to Resource Book p. G-13.

## Technology/Media Link

**Sequencing Software** Before class begins, use sequencing software to record the melody of "California, Here I Come." Connect the classroom computer to a large-screen television or a projection device. Select the sequencing program's "piano-roll" view (graphic editor). Use the graphic view of the song to demonstrate the similar phrase shapes in a sequence.

| Lesson | Elements | Skills | |
|---|---|---|---|
| **LESSON 1** **Russian Music – A Tree with Many Branches**<br>pp. 292-295<br> | **Element: Melody**<br>**Concept:** Pitch and direction<br>**Focus:** Melodic contour<br><br>**Secondary Element**<br>Timbre: instrumental tone color<br><br>**National Standards**<br>1a 1c 2b 2f 5b 6b 9a 9e | **Skill: Listening**<br>**Objective:** Listen and show the melodic contour in a Russian folk melody<br><br>**Secondary Skills**<br>• **Singing** Sing in Russian and English; sing and follow notation<br>• **Playing** Improvise an accompaniment on unpitched percussion<br>• **Listening / Describing** Tell something about the music or culture of Russia | **SKILLS REINFORCEMENT**<br>• **Mallets** Play a mallet accompaniment<br>• **Recorder** Play a simplified version of the song<br>• **Singing** Use ascending and descending vocal patterns to practice singing in tune |
| **LESSON 2** **The Irish Harper**<br>pp. 296-299<br> | **Element: Timbre**<br>**Concept:** Instrumental<br>**Focus:** Instruments of Ireland<br><br>**Secondary Element**<br>Melody: pattern<br><br>**National Standards**<br><br>1b 2c 5b 6a 6b 6c 6d 6e | **Skill: Listening**<br>**Objective:** Identify traditional Irish instruments<br><br>**Secondary Skills**<br>• **Singing** Sing long phrases and smooth octave leaps<br>• **Moving** Create movements to perform to a listening selection<br>• **Reading** Follow notation on a listening map; sing using pitch syllables | **SKILLS REINFORCEMENT**<br>• **Playing** Accompany the song on the Autoharp<br>• **Mallets** Play a mallet accompaniment |
| **LESSON 3** **Song of South Africa**<br>pp. 300-301<br> | **Element: Rhythm**<br>**Concept:** Beat<br>**Focus:** Melodic rhythm and steady beat<br><br>**Secondary Element**<br>Melody: pattern<br><br>**National Standards**<br>1c 2f 5a | **Skill: Playing**<br>**Objective:** Play melodic rhythms and steady beat to accompany a song<br><br>**Secondary Skills**<br>• **Singing** Sing in Zulu and layer in three parts | **SKILLS REINFORCEMENT**<br>• **Mallets** Accompany song with nonpitched instruments |

## Connections

## Music and Other Literature



**Connection:** Culture
**Activity:** Explore Russia through its music and related arts

ACROSS THE CURRICULUM
**Social Studies** Research geographical data related to Russia
**Related Arts** Learn more about Russian nesting dolls

CULTURAL CONNECTION **Fabergé Eggs** The creation of Fabergé eggs and their use as gifts in czarist Russia

SPOTLIGHT ON *1812 Overture* History of the composition

AUDIENCE ETIQUETTE **Preparing to Attend a Performance** Research artists and composers and listen to recorded selections before attending a live performance

CHARACTER EDUCATION **Values** Discuss how character traits, beliefs, and values are transmitted from generation to generation

BUILDING SKILLS THROUGH MUSIC **Art** Draw or paint a scene to depict the Independence Day celebration described in the text

**Songs**
*"Aii Dunaii moy"* ("Oh, My Merry Dunaii")
*"Beriozka"* ("The Birch Tree")

**Listening Selections**
*1812 Overture* (excerpt)
*Symphony No. 4*, Movement 4 (excerpt)
M*U*S*I*C M*A*K*E*R*S
Piotr Ilyich Tchaikovsky

**More Music Choices**
*"Tancovačka"* p. 230
*"Minka,"* p. 222

ASSESSMENT
**Performance/Observation** Trace melodic contour in the air while listening

TECHNOLOGY/MEDIA LINK
**Web Site** Read more about Piotr Tchaikovsky

---

**Connection:** Culture
**Activity:** Discuss characteristics of music and dance from Ireland

ACROSS THE CURRICULUM **Social Studies** Encourage students to locate Ireland on a map

CULTURAL CONNECTION
**Have Song, Will Travel** How songs of Irish immigrants to the United States became transformed in America
**Irish Words** Meaning of Irish words in song lyrics

SPOTLIGHT ON
**The Chieftains** Facts about the band
**Riverdance** Facts about the dance company and influence of other cultures
***Dúlamán*** Facts about the song

BUILDING SKILLS THROUGH MUSIC **Science** Build a harp with a shoe box and rubber bands

**Song** *"The Bard of Armagh"*

**Listening Selections**
*MacAllistrum's March–Mairseail Alasdroim*
*Crowley's Reel*
*Crowley's/Jackson's*
*Dúlamán*
**Listening Map** *Dúlamán*
M*U*S*I*C M*A*K*E*R*S
James Galway

**More Music Choices**
"How Can I Keep from Singing?" p. 261
"Oh, Danny Boy," p. 48

ASSESSMENT
**Music Journal Writing** Describe characteristics of listening selections including tempo and instrumentation

TECHNOLOGY/MEDIA LINK
**Transparency** Use the listening map to help students identify form, melody, and instruments

---

**Connection:** Culture
**Activity:** Discuss the use of music at sporting events in many cultures

CULTURAL CONNECTION *"Tina Singu"* Facts about the song and meaning of lyrics

MEETING INDIVIDUAL NEEDS **Including Everyone** Suggestions for using different mallets as an aid to playing drums

BUILDING SKILLS THROUGH MUSIC **Theatre** Select a song used during sports competitions

**Song** *"Tina Singu"* (Zulu and English)

**More Music Choices**
*"Ochimbo,"* p. 134
*"Hashewie,"* p. 63
*"La copa de la vida,"* p. 414

ASSESSMENT
**Performance/Observation** Differentiate between melodic rhythm and steady beat

TECHNOLOGY/MEDIA LINK
**Web Site** Read more about African music and instruments

| Lesson | Elements | Skills | |
|---|---|---|---|
| LESSON 4 **Music Flows in Mexico** pp. 302-305  | **Element: Form**<br>**Concept:** ABACA<br>**Focus:** Rondo form<br><br>**Secondary Element**<br>Rhythm: meter<br><br>**National Standards**<br>2b 2e 6a 6b 6d 6e 8a | **Skill: Moving**<br>**Objective:** Perform a folk dance from Mexico in rondo form<br><br>**Secondary Skills**<br>• **Singing** Sing in Spanish<br>• **Playing** Play resonator bells; accompany the song on guitar<br>• **:Listening** Identify ABACA (rondo form) aurally; discuss timbre of mariachi instruments | **SKILLS REINFORCEMENT**<br>• **Recorder** Play an accompaniment |
| LESSON 5 **Rowing in Venezuela** pp. 306-307  | **Element: Texture/Harmony**<br>**Concept:** Texture<br>**Focus:** Countermelody<br><br>**Secondary Element**<br>Timbre: Latin instruments<br><br>**National Standards**<br>1c 1d 6b 9b | **Skill: Moving**<br>**Objective:** Create two-part harmony by singing a song with a countermelody<br><br>**Secondary Skills**<br>• **Listening** Identify Latin instruments | **SKILLS REINFORCEMENT**<br>• **Recorder** Play an accompaniment |
| LESSON 6 **Cherry Blossom Time** pp. 308-309  | **Element: Expression**<br>**Concept:** Dynamics<br>**Focus:** Dynamics, phrasing, and mood<br>**Secondary Element**<br>Rhythm: pattern<br><br>**National Standards**<br>1b 1c 2b 6b | **Skill: Singing**<br>**Objective:** Sing a song with dynamics, phrasing, and mood<br><br>**Secondary Skills**<br>• **Listening** Describe expressive singing<br>• **Playing** Play drum ostinato and recorder accompaniment | **SKILLS REINFORCEMENT**<br>• **Keyboard** Play a broken chord accompaniment to reinforce steady beat<br>• **Mallets** Play an accompaniment |

## Connections

## Music and Other Literature

### Connection: Related Arts
**Activity:** Examine the art of Diego Rivera

**ACROSS THE CURRICULUM** **Language Arts** Read and dramatize a folk tale from Mexico

**CULTURAL CONNECTION**
**Folk Dancing** Guests invited to demonstrate traditional folk dances
**Seeing Patterns** Similar characteristics in Mexican music and art

**SPOTLIGHT ON**
**Mariachi Ensembles** Facts about the *mariachi* instruments
**The Artist** Diego Rivera

**TEACHER TO TEACHER** **Teaching *"La raspa"*** Invite proficient student dancers to help others learn steps

**BUILDING SKILLS THROUGH MUSIC** **Writing** Describe artwork in the text using words that could also describe music

**Song** *"La raspa"* (Spanish and English)

**Listening Selection** *El mariachi* (excerpt)

**Poem** "My Song"
**Arts Connection** *Dance in Tehuantepec*

**More Music Choices**
*"Cielito lindo,"* p. 270
*"Corrido de Kansas,"* p. 274
"Heave-Ho!/"Going, Going, Gone"/"The Snow" (speech piece), p. 182
*ABACA Dabble,* p. 184

**ASSESSMENT**
**Performance/Observation** Sing and dance to show rondo form

**TECHNOLOGY/MEDIA LINK**
**MIDI/Sequencing Software** Perform two- and three-notes-per-beat rhythms

### Connection: Social Studies
**Activity:** Sing a song from Venezuela in Spanish

**ACROSS THE CURRICULUM** **Social Studies** Facts on Venezuela

**MEETING INDIVIDUAL NEEDS** **Singing in Parts** Tips for singing in two parts

**BUILDING SKILLS THROUGH MUSIC** **Technology** Using the computer, research Angel Falls in Venezuela

**Song** *"Bogando a la luz del sol"* ("Rowing Toward the Sunlight")

**Listening Selection** *Carnaval Llanero*
**More Music Choices**
"America, the Beautiful," p. 158
"Amazing Grace," p. 160

**ASSESSMENT**
**Performance/Observation** Sing a melody and countermelody

**TECHNOLOGY/MEDIA LINK**
**Web Site** Visit *www.sfsuccessnet*.com to learn more about folk instruments from Latin America

### Connection: Culture
**Activity:** Discuss Japanese *Hana-mi* and folklore

**ACROSS THE CURRICULUM**
**Social Studies** Read a book about Japan and history of the song
**Related Arts** Read a book about Japanese block art

**CULTURAL CONNECTION** ***Hana-mi*** Japanese myth of the maiden who makes the cherry blossoms bloom

**BUILDING SKILLS THROUGH MUSIC** **Writing** Create a Haiku about springtime

**Song** *"Sakura"* (Japanese and English)

**Poem** "House of Spring"

**More Music Choices**
*"Ōsamu kosamu,"* p. 96

**ASSESSMENT**
**Performance/Observation** Perform a song with drum ostinato and recorder, observing appropriate mood, phrasing, and dynamics

**TECHNOLOGY/MEDIA LINK**
**MIDI/Sequencing** Software Improvise on given notes to accompany a song

| Lesson | Elements | Skills | |
|---|---|---|---|
| LESSON 7 **Travel to India** pp. 310-311  | **Element: Timbre**<br>**Concept:** Instrumental tone color<br>**Focus:** Instruments of India<br><br>**Secondary Element**<br>Form: call and response<br><br>**National Standards**<br>1c 2a 6b | **Skill: Listening**<br>**Objective:** Recognize the sound of the *sitar* and *tabla* | **Secondary Skills**<br>• **Singing** Sing call and responses<br>• **Playing** Play a drone on a bell |
| LESSON 8 **Play a Chinese Treasure** pp. 312-315  | **Element: Timbre**<br>**Concept:** Instrumental tone color<br>**Focus:** Instruments of China<br><br>**Secondary Element**<br>Rhythm: meter<br><br>**National Standards**<br>1c 2f 3d 4b 5a 6b 9b 9c | **Skill: Listening**<br>**Objective:** Listen to and describe instruments of China<br><br>**Secondary Skills**<br>• **Reading** Clap and say rhythm syllables<br>• **Singing** Sing in Mandarin<br>• **Playing** Play parts for bells, recorder, and percussion<br>• **Creating** Create rhythm ostinatos | **SKILLS REINFORCEMENT**<br>• **Keyboard** Improvise a four-bar pentatonic introduction and an ostinato bass<br>• **Mallets** Play an accompaniment<br>• **Recorder** Play patterns with D and A |
| LESSON 9 **Israeli Song and Dance** pp. 316-317  | **Element: Rhythm**<br>**Concept:** Beat<br>**Focus:** Steady beat<br><br>**Secondary Element**<br>Melody: tonality<br><br>**National Standards**<br>1d 2f 6e | **Skill: Moving**<br>**Objective:** Maintain a steady beat while performing a dance form Israel<br><br>**Secondary Skills**<br>• **Singing** Sing a two-part round in Hebrew<br>• **Playing** Perform percussion parts<br>• **Creating** Create ostinatos for various instruments | **SKILLS REINFORCEMENT**<br>• **Recorder** Play a duet part to accompany the song<br>• **Mallets** Play an accompaniment |

| Connections | Music and Other Literature | |
|---|---|---|
| **Connection: Social Studies**<br>**Activity:** Discuss India and two famous Indian musicians<br>ACROSS THE CURRICULUM **Social Studies** Locate India on a map and identify features<br>CULTURAL CONNECTION **Indian *Ragas*** Definition of *raga*<br>SPOTLIGHT ON **The Performers** Biographical facts about Ravi and Anoushka Shankar<br>CHARACTER EDUCATION **Respect** Encourage respectful behavior when exposed to something different<br>BUILDING SKILLS THROUGH MUSIC **Language** Outline information in the text | **Song** *"Shri Ram, jai Ram"*<br><br>**Listening Selection** *Charukeshi* (excerpt)<br>M*U*S*I*C M*A*K*E*R*S<br>Anoushka Shankar<br><br>**More Music Choices**<br>*"All Night, All Day,"* p. 180<br>*"Hashewie,"* p. 63 | ASSESSMENT<br>**Music Journal Writing**<br>Describe timbres and other attributes of a listening selection<br><br>TECHNOLOGY/MEDIA LINK<br>**Web Site** Visit the site to learn mor e about Ravi and Anoushka Shankar |
| **Connection: Culture**<br>**Activity:** Explore Chinese culture through its music and art<br>ACROSS THE CURRICULUM<br>**Language Arts** Read book aloud and show pictures of how bamboo grows<br>**Science** Plant shoots and study bamboo growth<br>CULTURAL CONNECTION **China** Facts about Chinese cultures and distinct musical traditions<br>SPOTLIGHT ON<br>***Fen Yang* Songs** History and use of these songs<br>**Brush Painting** Similarity to calligraphy<br>MEETING INDIVIDUAL NEEDS **Coordination** Substitute various fixed instruments for students with coordination difficulties<br>BUILDING SKILLS THROUGH MUSIC **Math** Determine how many times the woodblock accompaniment patterns must be played for one verse of the song | **Songs**<br>*"Feng yang hua gu"* (*"Feng Yang* Song*"*)<br>*"Xiao"* ("Bamboo Flute")<br><br>**Listening Selection** *Birds in the Forest* (excerpt)<br><br>**More Music Choices**<br>*Bumper Harvest Celebration,* p. 337<br>*Wu long,* p. 157 | ASSESSMENT<br>**Music Journal Writing**<br>Identify and describe the timbre of Chinese instruments<br><br>TECHNOLOGY/MEDIA LINK<br>**Web Site** Visit the site to learn more about instruments around the world |
| **Connection: Culture**<br>**Activity:** Explore Israeli culture through its music<br>CULTURAL CONNECTION **Israel** Facts about Zionism and establishment of the Israeli nation<br>MEETING INDIVIDUAL NEEDS **Ostinato Hints** Color code notes as an aid in creating ostinatos<br>BUILDING SKILLS THROUGH MUSIC **Dance/Language** Write dance instructions in your own words | **Songs** *"Yibane amenu"* (Hebrew and English)<br><br>**Listening Selection** *Ve' David y'fey enayiam*<br><br>**More Music Choices**<br>"Ah, Poor Bird," p. 196<br>"Let Music Surround You," p. 236 | ASSESSMENT<br>**Performance/Observation**<br>Perform a dance and maintain a steady beat<br><br>TECHNOLOGY/MEDIA LINK<br>**Sequencing Software**<br>Record rhythm tracks to create a round to accompany the song |

| Lesson | Elements | Skills | |
|---|---|---|---|
|  **A Flight to the Caribbean** pp. 318-319   | **Element: Melody**<br>**Concept:** Pattern<br>**Focus:** Melodic sequences<br><br>**Secondary Element**<br>Form: AB<br><br>**National Standards**<br>2b 2c 5b 6b | **Skill: Listening**<br>**Objective:** Listen to and respond through movement to melodic sequences<br><br>**Secondary Skills**<br>• **Singing** Sing and follow notation to notice sequences<br>• **Playing** Play percussion parts as an accompaniment | **SKILLS REINFORCEMENT**<br>• **Mallets** Play an accompaniment<br>• **Recorder** Play a countermelody |
| LESSON 11 **Reggae Is All Right** pp. 320-321   | **Element: Form**<br>**Concept:** Section Form<br>**Focus:** ABA Form<br><br>**Secondary Element**<br>Rhythm: patterns<br><br>**National Standards**<br>1c 2f 4c | **Skill: Creating**<br>**Objective:** Create a speech piece in ABA form<br><br>**Secondary Skills**<br>• **Analyzing** Identify the ABA form of a song<br>• **Moving** Create and perform body percussion to accompany a song | **SKILLS REINFORCEMENT**<br>• **Mallets** Play an accompaniment |
| | | | |

## Connections

## Music and Other Literature



**Connection: Culture**
**Activity:** Discuss arts and culture from the Caribbean islands

ACROSS THE CURRICULUM **Language Arts/Social Studies** Write and illustrate a "trickster tale" for creation of a class book

CULTURAL CONNECTION **The West Indies** Facts about West Indian cultures and music influences

BUILDING SKILLS THROUGH MUSIC **Social Studies** Research and identify the West Indies

**Song** "Wings of a Dove"

**Listening Selection** *Mwen boyko samba*

**More Music Choices**
*"Thula, thula, ngoana,"* p. 227
*"Tancovačka"* p. 230

ASSESSMENT
**Performance/Observation** Demonstrate understanding of melodic sequence by clapping or tapping its rhythm

TECHNOLOGY/MEDIA LINK
**Web Site Visit** *www.sfsuccessnet*.com for more information on Caribbean music

**Connection: Style**
**Activity:** Discuss the characteristics of reggae style

ACROSS THE CURRICULUM **Social Studies** Discuss the location and climate of Trinidad and Jamaica

CULTURAL CONNECTION **Jamaican Folklore** Learn the tale of the Doctor Bird

BUILDING SKILLS THROUGH MUSIC **Health** Brainstorm ways to relieve worry

**Song** "Three Little Birds"

M*U*S*I*C M*A*K*E*R*S Bob Marley

**More Music Choices**
"Walk in Jerusalem," p. 100
"Dry Bones Come Skipping," p. 218

ASSESSMENT
**Performance/Observation** Identify A and B sections

TECHNOLOGY/MEDIA LINK
**Web Site Visit** *www.sfsuccessnet.com* to learn about reggae music
**MIDI/Sequencing Software** Add a percussion section to students' speech pieces

# Introducing the Unit

In Unit 8, students explore music from many places in the world. They will be interested to hear how American music has been influenced by world music. Students will learn about the elements of music as they relate to world music.

Students will also become familiar with the sounds of non-Western instruments and learn dances from other parts of the world.

For a more detailed unit overview, see Unit at a Glance, pp. 287a–287h.

# Unit Project

Have students create a world music bulletin board. On their bulletin boards, they could include

- Maps of a variety of regions.
- Pictures from magazines.
- Drawings of airplanes, boats, ticket stubs.
- Words in other languages they may know.

Encourage students look through this unit and identify

- Songs in languages other than English.
- The countries from which these songs originated.

Encourage students to share songs in other languages that they may know from home or from class. Have students make a list of all the different styles of music that are represented in this unit. Next to each style, have them write the dominating musical characteristic of the style.

## United We Sing

The United States is made up of people from all over the world. Many American folk songs were influenced by the musical styles of the settlers in the area. **Sing** "Cotton-Eye Joe." Then **listen** to how it is performed in another style.

CD 12-9

### Cotton-Eye Joe

s, l, (d) r m

*Folk Song from Tennessee*

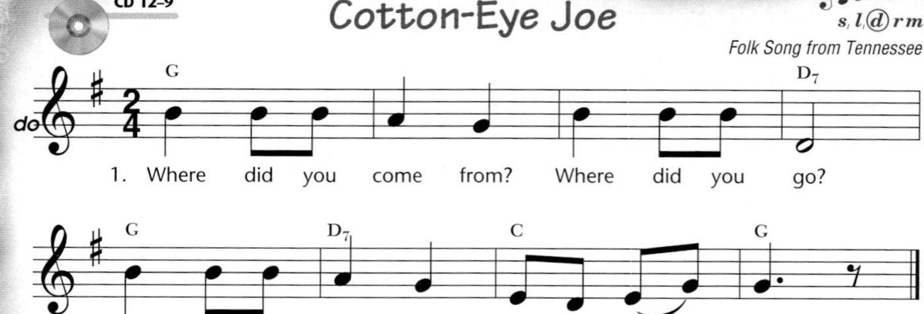


2. I've come for to see you,
I've come for to sing,
I've come for to bring you
A song and a ring.

3. When did you leave here?
Where did you go?
When you coming back here,
Cotton-Eye Joe?

4. Left here last winter,
I've wandered through the year.
Seen people dyin',
Seen them with their fear.

5. I've been to the cities,
Buildings cracking down,
Seen the people calling,
Falling to the ground.

6. I'll come back tomorrow,
If I can find a ride,
Or I'll sail in the breezes,
Blowin' on the tide.

7. Well, when you do come back here,
Look what I have brung,
A meadow to be run in,
A song to be sung.

8. Where did you come from?
Where did you go?
Where did you come from,
Cotton-Eye Joe?

288

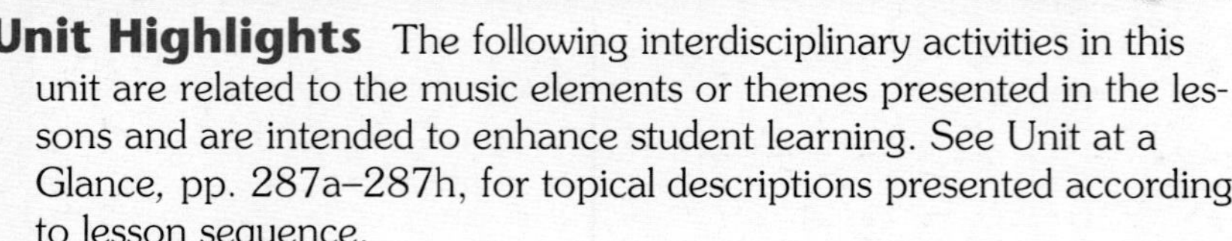


**Unit Highlights** The following interdisciplinary activities in this unit are related to the music elements or themes presented in the lessons and are intended to enhance student learning. See Unit at a Glance, pp. 287a–287h, for topical descriptions presented according to lesson sequence.

**▶ ART/RELATED ARTS**

- Learn more about Russian nesting dolls (p. 292)

**▶ LANGUAGE ARTS**

- Read and dramatize a folk tale from Mexico (p. 302)
- Read a book aloud and show pictures of how bamboo grows (p. 313)
- Write and illustrate a "trickster tale" for creation of a class book (p. 318)

**▶ SCIENCE**

- Plant shoots and study bamboo growth (p. 313)

**▶ SOCIAL STUDIES**

- Research geographical data related to Russia (p. 292)
- Encourage students to locate Ireland on a map (p. 296)
- Discover facts about the geographic characteristics of Venezuela (p. 307)
- Read a book about Japan and history of the song (p. 308)
- Locate India on a map and identify features (p. 310)
- Using a map, locate the places of origin of calypso (p. 320)

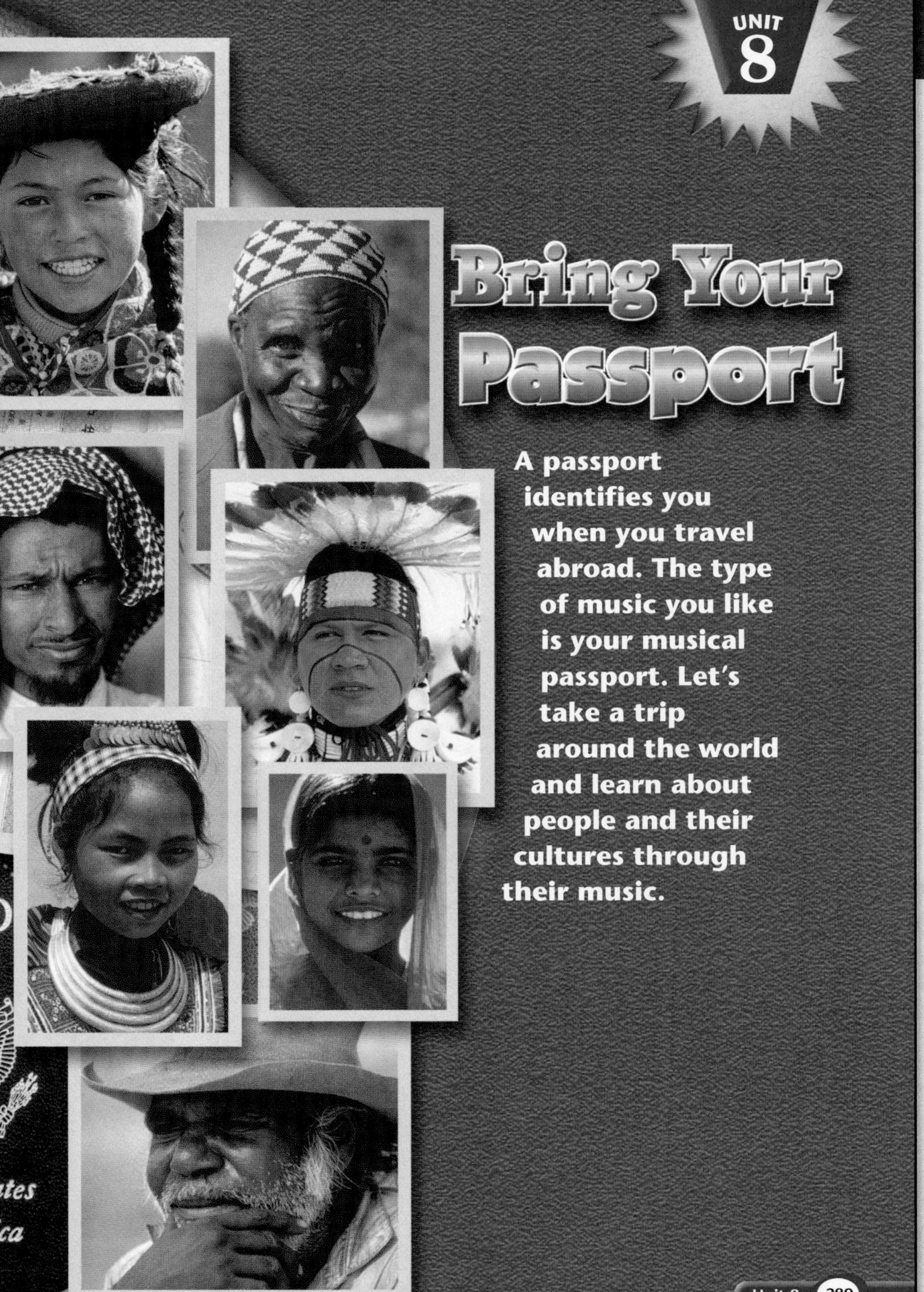
UNIT 8

# Bring Your Passport

A passport identifies you when you travel abroad. The type of music you like is your musical passport. Let's take a trip around the world and learn about people and their cultures through their music.





## Music Skills Assessed in This Unit

### Reading Music: Rhythm

- Differentiate between melodic rhythm and steady beat (p. 301)
- Demonstrate understanding of melodic sequence (p. 319)

### Reading Music: Pitch

- Read pentatonic melodies (p. 299)
- Sing songs with melody and countermelody (p. 307)

### Performing Music: Singing

- Sing and dance to show rondo form (p. 305)
- Perform song while observing appropriate mood, phrasing, and dynamics (p. 309)

### Moving to Music

- Trace melodic contour while listening (p. 295)
- Sing and dance to show rondo form (p. 305)
- Perform a dance and maintain a steady beat (p. 317)

### Performing Music: Playing

- Perform melodic rhythm (p. 301)
- Perform song with drum ostinato and recorder (p. 309)

### Creating Music

- Create two-part harmony by singing a countermelody (p. 307)
- Create a speech piece (p. 321)

### Listening to Music

- Describe characterictics of listening selections including tempo and instrumentation (p. 299)
- Describe timbres and other attributes of a listening selection (p. 311)
- Identify and describe timbre of Chinese instruments (p. 315)

## Cultural Connection

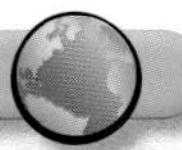

**Unit Highlights** The musical literature in this unit provides many opportunities for students to explore a variety of world cultures. See Unit at a Glance, pp. 287a–287h, for topical descriptions presented according to lesson sequence.

▶ AFRICAN

- "*Tina singu*" (p. 300)

▶ ASIAN; AUSTRALIAN

- "*Sakura*" (p. 308)
- "*Shri Ram, jai Ram*" (p. 311)
- "*Feng yang hua gu*" (p. 313); "*Xiao*" (p. 314)

▶ CARIBBEAN

- "Wings of a Dove" (p. 318)

▶ EUROPEAN

- "*Ai Dunaii moy*" (p. 293); "*Beriozka*" (p. 294)
- "The Bard of Armagh" (p. 296)
- Discover how songs of Irish-American immigrants became transformed in the United States (p. 296)

▶ LATIN AMERICAN

- "*La raspa*" (p. 302)
- Observe performances of traditional folk dances (p. 303)
- Explore patterns in Mexican music and art (p. 305)
- "*Bogando a la luz del sol*" (p. 306)

▶ MIDDLE EASTERN

- "*Yibane amenu*" (p. 316)

# Opening Activities

**MATERIALS**

- "Cotton-Eye Joe" **CD 12-9**
  **Recording Routine:** Intro (8 m.); verses 1–9; instrumental
- *Cotton-Eye Joe* **CD 12-11**
- *Dusty Miller* **CD 12-13**
- **Dance Directions** for *Cotton-Eye Joe* p. 514
- classroom instruments

## Theme Activities

### Singing

Invite students to listen to "Cotton-Eye Joe" **CD 12-9** to become familiar with it. Then, have them speak the words in rhythm. Discuss the meaning of the words. When they are ready, encourage students to sing the song with the recording.

### Listening

Have students listen to the dance version of *Cotton-Eye Joe* **CD 12-11.** DIscuss how this version is different. (tempo and instrumentation)

### Playing

Divide the class into small groups. Ask each group to accompany the song in a different style, using various instruments. Autoharp and guitar would be appropriate to the style of the song.

Help students feel the primary accent of each measure and demonstrate this accent in their playing.

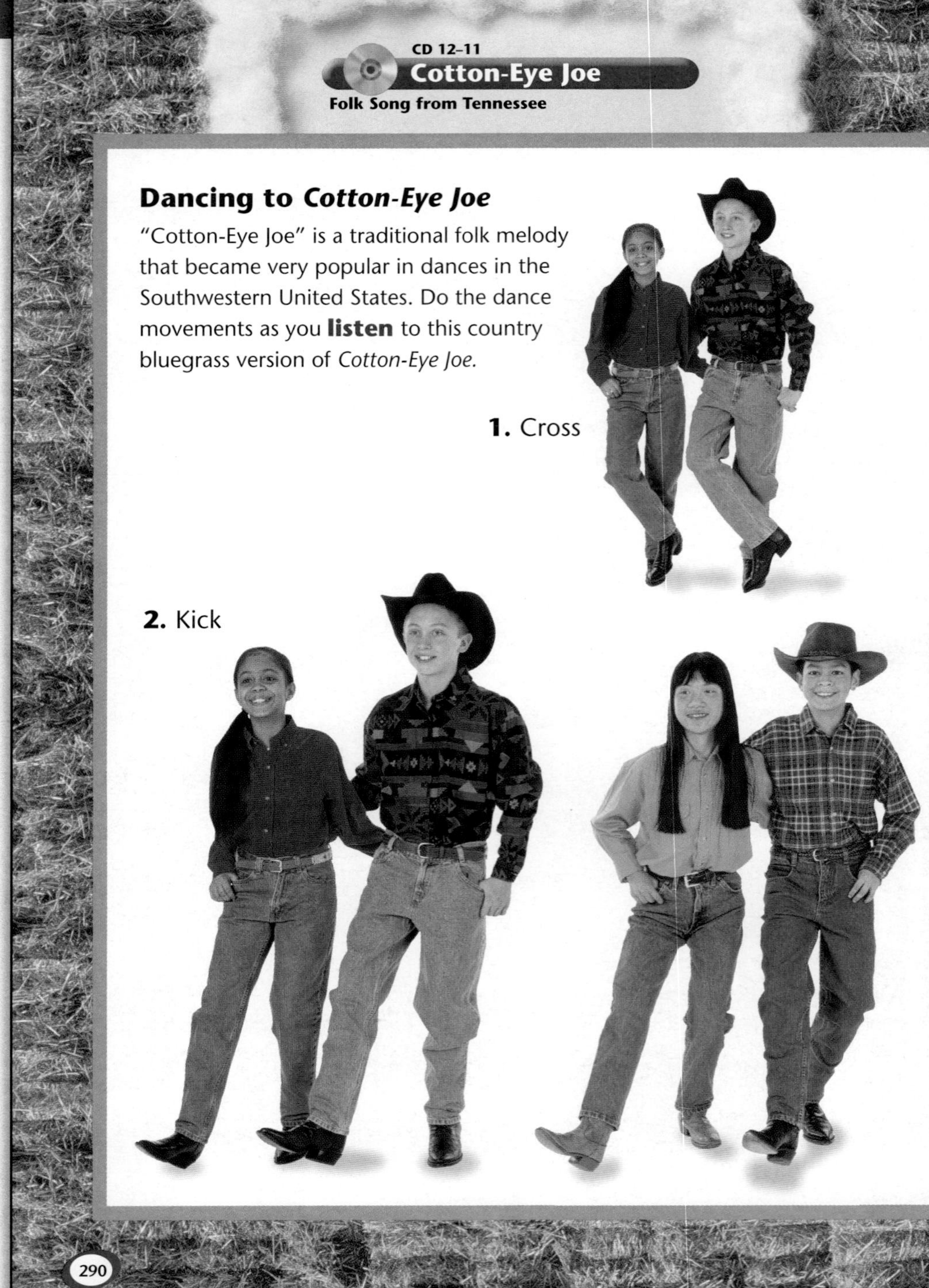

CD 12-11
Cotton-Eye Joe
Folk Song from Tennessee

**Dancing to *Cotton-Eye Joe***

"Cotton-Eye Joe" is a traditional folk melody that became very popular in dances in the Southwestern United States. Do the dance movements as you **listen** to this country bluegrass version of *Cotton-Eye Joe.*

**1.** Cross

**2.** Kick

290


## Assessment

**Unit Highlights** The lessons in this unit were chosen and developed to support the theme "Bring Your Passport." Each lesson, as always, presents a clear element focus, a skill objective, and an end-of-lesson assessment. The overall sequence of lessons, however, is organized according to this theme, rather than concept or skill development. In this context, formal assessment strategies, such as those presented in Units 1–6, are no longer applicable.

**▶ INFORMAL ASSESSMENTS**

At the close of each Teacher's Edition lesson in this unit, one of the following types of assessments is used to evaluate the learning of the key element focus or skill objective.

- Performance/Observation (pp. 295, 301, 305, 307, 309, 317, 319, 321)
- Music Journal Writing (pp. 299, 311, 315)

**▶ RUBRICS**

Visit *www.sfsuccessnet.com* for rubrics to assess students' achievement in music skills.

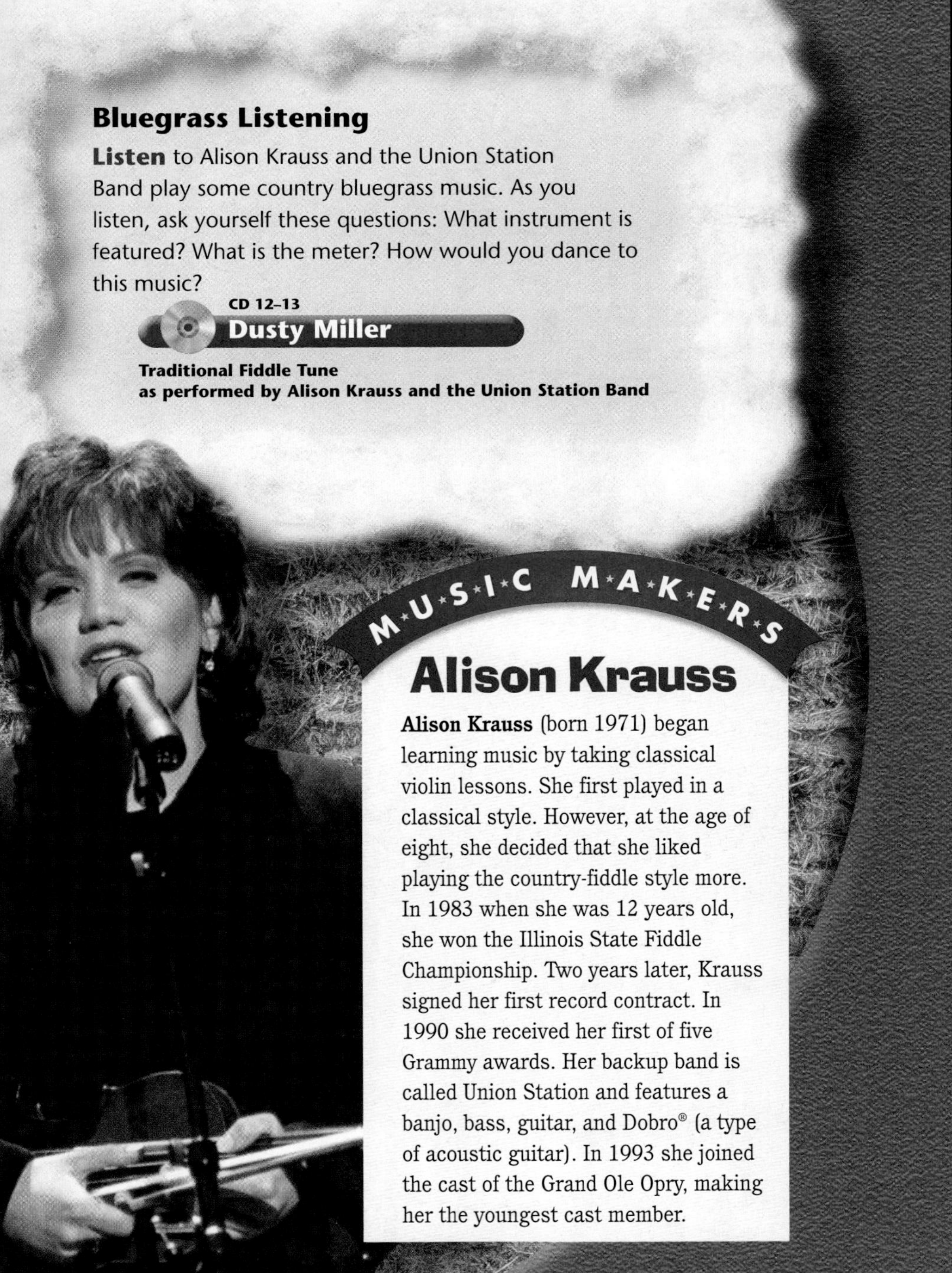

## Bluegrass Listening

**Listen** to Alison Krauss and the Union Station Band play some country bluegrass music. As you listen, ask yourself these questions: What instrument is featured? What is the meter? How would you dance to this music?

CD 12–13
**Dusty Miller**

**Traditional Fiddle Tune**
**as performed by Alison Krauss and the Union Station Band**

M·U·S·I·C M·A·K·E·R·S

## Alison Krauss

**Alison Krauss** (born 1971) began learning music by taking classical violin lessons. She first played in a classical style. However, at the age of eight, she decided that she liked playing the country-fiddle style more. In 1983 when she was 12 years old, she won the Illinois State Fiddle Championship. Two years later, Krauss signed her first record contract. In 1990 she received her first of five Grammy awards. Her backup band is called Union Station and features a banjo, bass, guitar, and Dobro® (a type of acoustic guitar). In 1993 she joined the cast of the Grand Ole Opry, making her the youngest cast member.





### Moving

Refer to the Dance Directions on p. 514 for detailed instructions for *Cotton-Eye Joe.* Allow students to practice the routine using the Dance Practice Track **CD 12-12.**

### Listening

Invite students to read the Music Makers feature on Alison Krauss and listen as she performs *Dusty Miller* **CD 12-13.** Have students discuss the instruments played in this bluegrass selection.

### Innovative Teacher Support for This Unit

- **Making Music DVD, Grade 4** contains video segments that support lessons, including signing and movement.
- **Making Music with Movement and Dance** provides more opportunities for large group activities in music or physical education classes.
- **Making Music with Technology** provides lesson plans for many technology applications; includes MIDI files.
- ***¡A cantar!*** features recorded songs and lessons from around the Spanish-speaking world; includes strategies for bilingual classes and for English-speaking teachers working with Spanish-speaking students.
- **Bridges to Asia** features recorded songs and lessons from Asian and Pacific region cultures.
- ***www.sfsuccessnet.com*** provides an online lesson planner to conveniently create lesson plans at school or at home. Includes rubrics for assessment, lesson modifications to meet the needs of all students, performance musicals based on program content, and more.

## Technology/Media Link

**Unit Highlights** The following components are used in this unit to reinforce and expand students' understanding of music elements and related themes. See Unit at a Glance, pp. 287a–287h, for a descriptive listing according to lesson sequence.

▶ **CD-ROM**

- Use *Making Music* to create an accompaniment (p. 301)

▶ **MIDI/SEQUENCING SOFTWARE**

- Perform two- and three-notes-per-beat rhythms (p. 305)
- Improvise on given notes to accompany a song (p. 309)
- Record rhythm tracks to create a round to accompany the song (p. 317)
- Add a percussion section to student-created speech pieces (p. 321)

▶ **TRANSPARENCY**

- Use the listening map to help students identify form, melody, and instruments (p. 299)

▶ **WEB SITE**

- Read more about Piotr Tchaikovsky at *www.sfsuccessnet.com* (p. 295)
- Learn more about African music and instruments (p. 301)
- Discover more information about folk instruments from Latin America (p. 307)
- Learn more about Ravi and Anoushka Shankar (p. 311)
- Learn more about instruments around the world (p. 315)
- Learn more about Caribbean music and musicians (p. 319)
- Read more about reggae music (p. 321)

LESSON 1

## LESSON AT A GLANCE

**Element Focus** **MELODY** Melodic contour

**Skill Objective** **LISTENING** Listen and show the melodic contour in a Russian folk melody

**Connection Activity** **CULTURE** Explore Russia through its music and related arts

**MATERIALS**

- *"Ai, Dunaiĭ moy"* **CD 12-14**
- "Ah, My Merry Dunaii" **CD 12-15**

  **Recording Routine:** Intro (6 m.); vocal; interlude (6 m.); vocal; coda
- *"Beriozka"* **CD 12-19**
- "The Birch Tree" **CD 12-20**

  **Recording Routine:** Intro (6 m.); v. 1; interlude (6 m.); v. 2; interlude (6 m.); v. 3; interlude (6 m.); v. 4; coda
- **Pronunciation Practice/Translation** p. 486
- *1812 Overture* (excerpt) **CD 12-18**
- *Symphony No. 4,* Movement 4 (excerpt) **CD 12-23**
- **Resource Book** pp. A-29, A-30, F-17
- nonpitched classroom percussion instruments, recorders, Autoharp, xylophones
- world map

**VOCABULARY**

*balalaika* melodic contour

**National Standards**

**1a** Sing independently on pitch
**1c** Sing from memory songs from diverse cultures
**2b** Perform rhythms on appropriate instruments
**2f** Play instruments independently against contrasting parts
**5b** Read notes in treble clef, using letters
**6b** Describe music by answering questions about it
**9a** Listen to identify music from different cultures
**9e** Demonstrate appropriate audience behavior

**MORE MUSIC CHOICES**

For more Slavic songs:
*"Tancovačka,"* p. 230
*"Minka,"* p. 222

LESSON 1 Element: MELODY | Skill: LISTENING | Connection: CULTURE

# Russian Music

## A Tree with Many Branches

Let's take a musical trip to Russia. Russia is located on the continent of Asia. A small part of Russia is located in Europe.

**Listen** to *"Ai, Dunaiĭ moy."* Can you hum the melody of this Russian folk song? Would you recognize the melody if you heard it again?

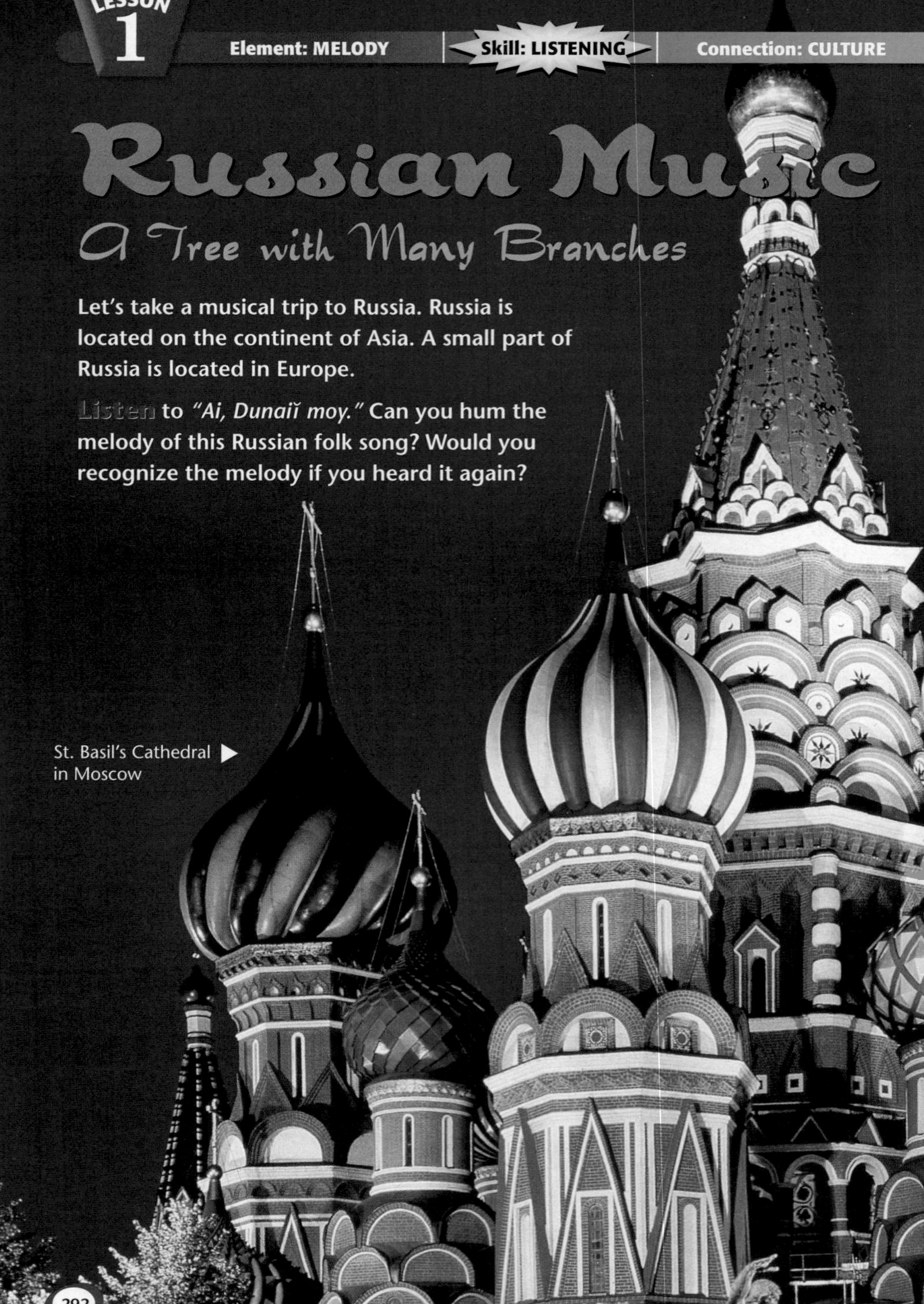

St. Basil's Cathedral in Moscow

292

# Footnotes

## CULTURAL CONNECTION

**Fabergé Eggs** The enameled and jeweled egg pictured on p. 293 is an example of the work of the jewelry studios of Peter Carl Fabergé (1846–1920). During czarist times, decorated eggs were a popular gift at Easter. As jeweler to the Imperial Court, Fabergé had his studios create some eggs out of gold and jewels. Some of them held miniature "surprises," also made of gold and jewels.

## BUILDING SKILLS THROUGH MUSIC

**Art** Share the information on *1812 Overture* from Spotlight On, p. 294. Have students draw or paint a scene to depict the Fourth of July celebration described in the text.

## ACROSS THE CURRICULUM

**Social Studies** Interested students can learn more about Russia and its music by reading *Russia* by Clair Boast (Heinemann Library, 1998).

Invite students to locate Russia on a world map. Which large bodies of water are near Russia? What other countries border Russia? What are some of its rivers?

**Related Arts** Invite students to learn more about Russian nesting dolls, using *Russian Nested Dolls: A Punch-Out Toy* by A.G. Smith (Dover, 1994). A picture of the dolls may be found on p. 224. Also, see Spotlight On, p. 225.

## Folk Melodies in Classical Music

**Listen** to *1812 Overture.* Raise your hand when you hear the melody of *"Ai, Dunaiĭ moy."*

CD 12-18 **1812 Overture**

**by Piotr Tchaikovsky**

Tchaikovsky's [chai-KOF-skee] *1812 Overture* was written to celebrate Russia's victory over France. In some performances, actual cannons are used in the orchestra!

Fabergé egg (1911) ▶ depicting Czar Nicholas II of Russia

CD 12-14
Ai, Dunaiĭ moy

### Ai, Dunaiĭ moy
(Ah, My Merry Dunaii)

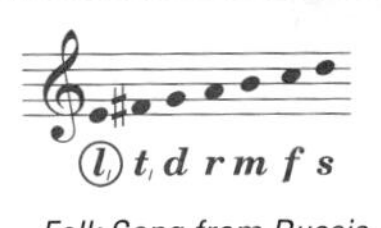

l t d r m f s

*Folk Song from Russia*

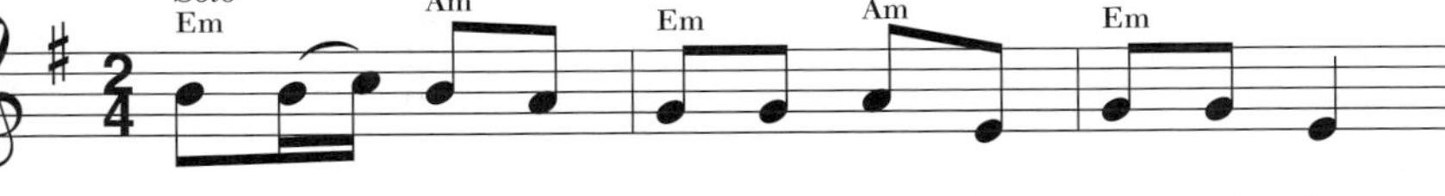

Solo
Em Am Em Am Em
do

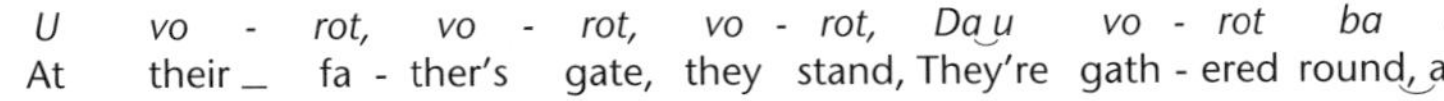

U vo - rot, vo - rot, vo - rot, Da u vo - rot ba -
At their fa - ther's gate, they stand, They're gath - ered round, a

Em Am Tutti Em Am Em
tyush - ki - nykh. Ai, Du - naiĭ moy, Du - naiĭ, Ai, ve - syo -
hap - py band. Oh, My dear Du - naii, Oh, my mer -

Em Am Solo Em D

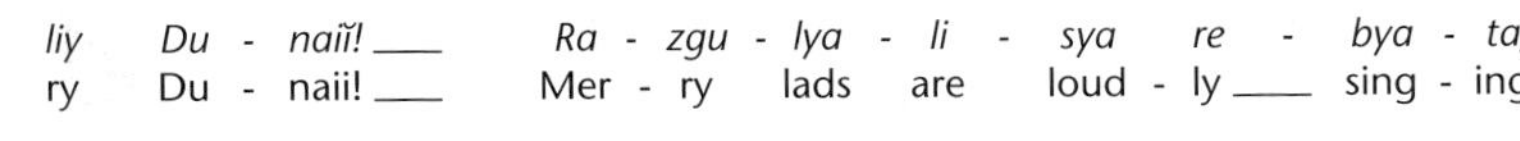

liy Du - naiĭ! Ra - zgu - lya - li - sya re - bya - ta,
ry Du - naii! Mer - ry lads are loud - ly sing - ing,

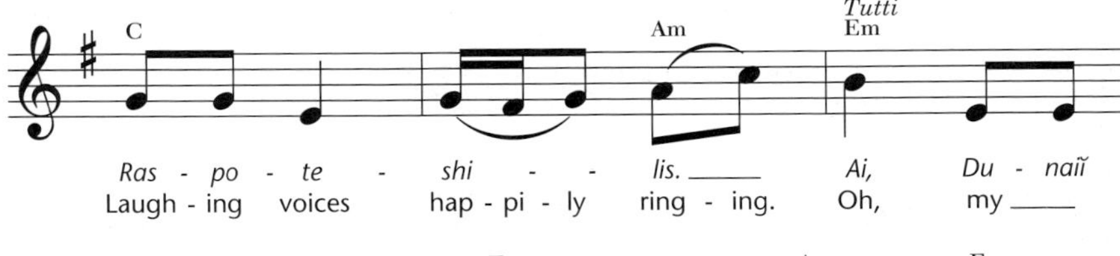

C Am Tutti Em
Ras - po - te - shi - lis. Ai, Du - naiĭ
Laugh - ing voices hap - pi - ly ring - ing. Oh, my

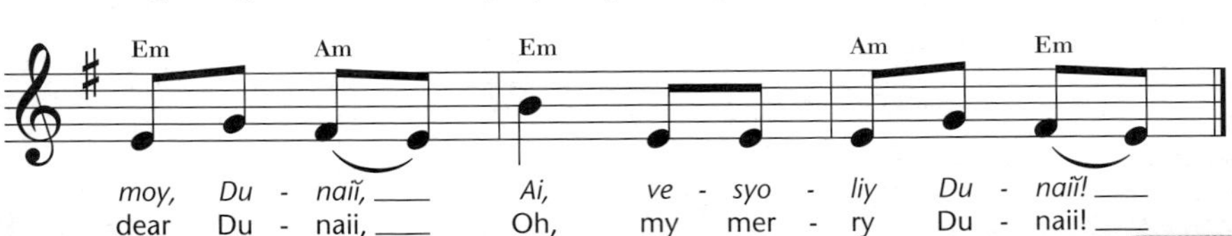

Em Am Em Am Em
moy, Du - naiĭ, Ai, ve - syo - liy Du - naiĭ!
dear Du - naii, Oh, my mer - ry Du - naii!

Bring Your Passport

Unit 8 293

# 1 Introduce

Share and discuss cultural information about Russia with students. Refer to Cultural Connection and Across the Curriculum on p. 292.

Tell students that *"Ai Dunaiĭ moy"* ("Ah, My Merry Dunaii") and *"Beriozka"* ("The Birch Tree") are two well-known folk songs from Russia.

**ASK What is a folk song?** (a song passed from one generation to another through singing, sometimes with slight changes)

**Why would composers incorporate folk songs into their music?** (They might be familiar with the songs, like the songs, or feel patriotism for their country.)

# 2 Develop

### Singing

Play *"Ai Dunaiĭ moy"* **CD 12-14** in Russian and then in English **CD 12-15.** Help students learn to sing the song in English.

Encourage students to notice the melodic skip between E and B that occurs both ascending and descending. Have students look at the notation on p. 293 and count how many times this happens in the song. (eight times)

Encourage students to learn *"Ai Dunaiĭ moy"* in Russian. Invite them to listen to the Pronunciation Practice **CD 12-17** and sing with the students on the recording. Use the Pronunciation Practice Guide on Resource Book p. A-29.

### Playing

2b 2f Have students improvise an accompaniment to *"Ai Dunaiĭ moy"* on nonpitched percussion instruments. Invite them to experiment with different instruments, such as tamborines, finger cymbals, and small drums.

continued on page 294

## Skills Reinforcement

▶ **Mallets** For a mallet accompaniment to *"Beriozka,"* on p. 294, see Resource Book p. F-17.

▶ **Recorder** Students can play a simplified version of *"Beriozka"* on their recorders using A, G, E, and D. When students can play the recorder part, divide the class into four groups. During verse 1, group 1 should play the recorder while the other groups sing. During verse 2, group 2 plays the recorder, and so forth throughout the song.

## Notation

▶ ***"Beriozka"*** Have students learn more Russian words to *"Beriozka."* For a translation, see p. 486.

**Verse 2**
*Nyekamu biryozu zalamati*
*Nyekamu kudryavu zaschipati*
*Lyuli lyuli zalamati*
*Lyuli lyuli zaschipati.*

**Verse 3**
*Kak paydu ya vlyes pagulyayu*
*byeluyu biryozu zalamayu*
*Lyuli lyuli pagulyayu*
*Lyuli lyuli zalamayu.*

**Verse 4**
*Srezhu s beryozu tree prutochka*
*Sdyelayu syebye ya tree gudochka*
*Lyuli lyuli tree prutochka*
*Lyuli lyuli tree gudochka.*

### Listening

Share the information about *1812 Overture* with students. See Spotlight On below.

Play *1812 Overture* (excerpt) **CD 12-18.** Have students raise their hands when they hear the *"Ai Dunaiī moy"* theme.

6b **ASK Is the melody you heard exactly the same as the melody you sang?** (no)

**When the excerpt starts, which section of the orchestra is the most prominent?** (strings)

**When the theme to *"Ai Dunaiī moy"* is heard, which section is featured?** (woodwinds, especially flute, oboe, and bassoon solos)

Have students listen again to confirm their answers.

### Singing

5b 1c Invite students to sing *"Beriozka"* **CD 12-19.** To learn the Russian words, invite students to listen to the Pronunciation Practice **CD 12-22** and sing with the students on the recording. Refer to Resource Book p. A-30, for a Pronunciation Practice Guide, and Notation, p. 293, for Russian words to additional verses. Encourage students to follow the song notation and observe the last four notes of each line.

**ASK What do the last four notes of each line have in common?** (They are the same.)

Invite volunteers to play these notes on xylophones as they occur in the song while the class sings. When students know the song well, ask volunteers to play the entire song on xylophones.

**Russian Tribute to a Tree**

The birch tree is often found in the vast forests of Russia. **Listen** to *"Beriozka,"* a tribute to the tree. As you listen, **move** to show the melodic contour.

CD 12-19
Beriozka
(The Birch Tree)
l t d r m s
Folk Song from Russia
Dm A7 Dm A7 Dm
do
1. Во по - ле бе - рё - зынь - ка сто - я - ла,
1. See the love - ly birch in the mead - ow,
2. Oh, my lit - tle tree, I need branch - es,
3. From an - oth - er branch I will make now,
4. When I play my new bal - a - lai - ka,
Во по - ле куд - ря - ва - я сто - я - ла.
Curl - y leaves all danc - ing when the wind blows.
For three sil - ver flutes I need three branch - es.
I will make a tin - gling bal - a - lai - ka.
I will think of you, my love - ly birch tree.
Лю - ли, лю - ли, сто - я - ла,
Loo - lee - loo, when the wind blows,
Loo - lee - loo, three branch - es,
Loo - lee - loo, bal - a - lai - ka,
Loo - lee - loo, love - ly birch tree,
Лю - ли, лю - ли, сто - я - ла.
Loo - lee - loo, when the wind blows.
Loo - lee - loo, three branch - es.
Loo - lee - loo, bal - a - lai - ka.
Loo - lee - loo, love - ly birch tree.
294


# Footnotes

## SKILLS REINFORCEMENT

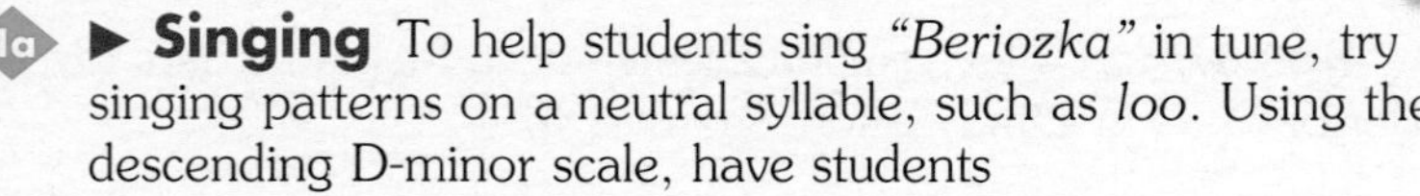

1a ▶ **Singing** To help students sing *"Beriozka"* in tune, try singing patterns on a neutral syllable, such as *loo*. Using the descending D-minor scale, have students

- Echo the melody pattern in the first phrase on *loo*.
- Use A and D tone bars to maintain pitch.
- Show an upward motion with arms while singing the descending pattern.

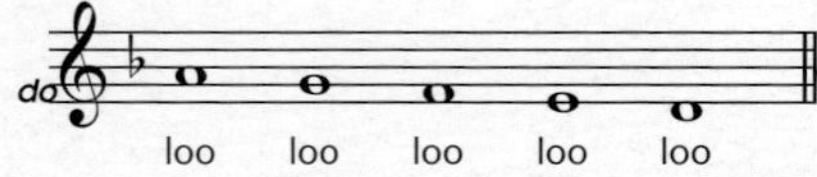


Then have students echo these patterns on *loo*.

## SPOTLIGHT ON

▶ ***1812 Overture*** Although *1812 Overture* is one of Tchaikovsky's most popular pieces, he did not like it that much. He wrote the overture to commemorate the seventieth anniversary of the Russian victory over Napoleon in the War of 1812. When the piece was first performed, it was an immediate success, and it has never lost its appeal with audiences. In 1974, the Boston Pops Orchestra found that its audience was getting smaller. Knowing the popularity of *1812 Overture*, the Pops played this piece to attract the crowd. They performed the piece as a grand finale, complete with cannons firing, church bells ringing, and a spectacular fireworks show at the end. This performance was so successful that it soon became a Fourth of July tradition celebrated across the United States.

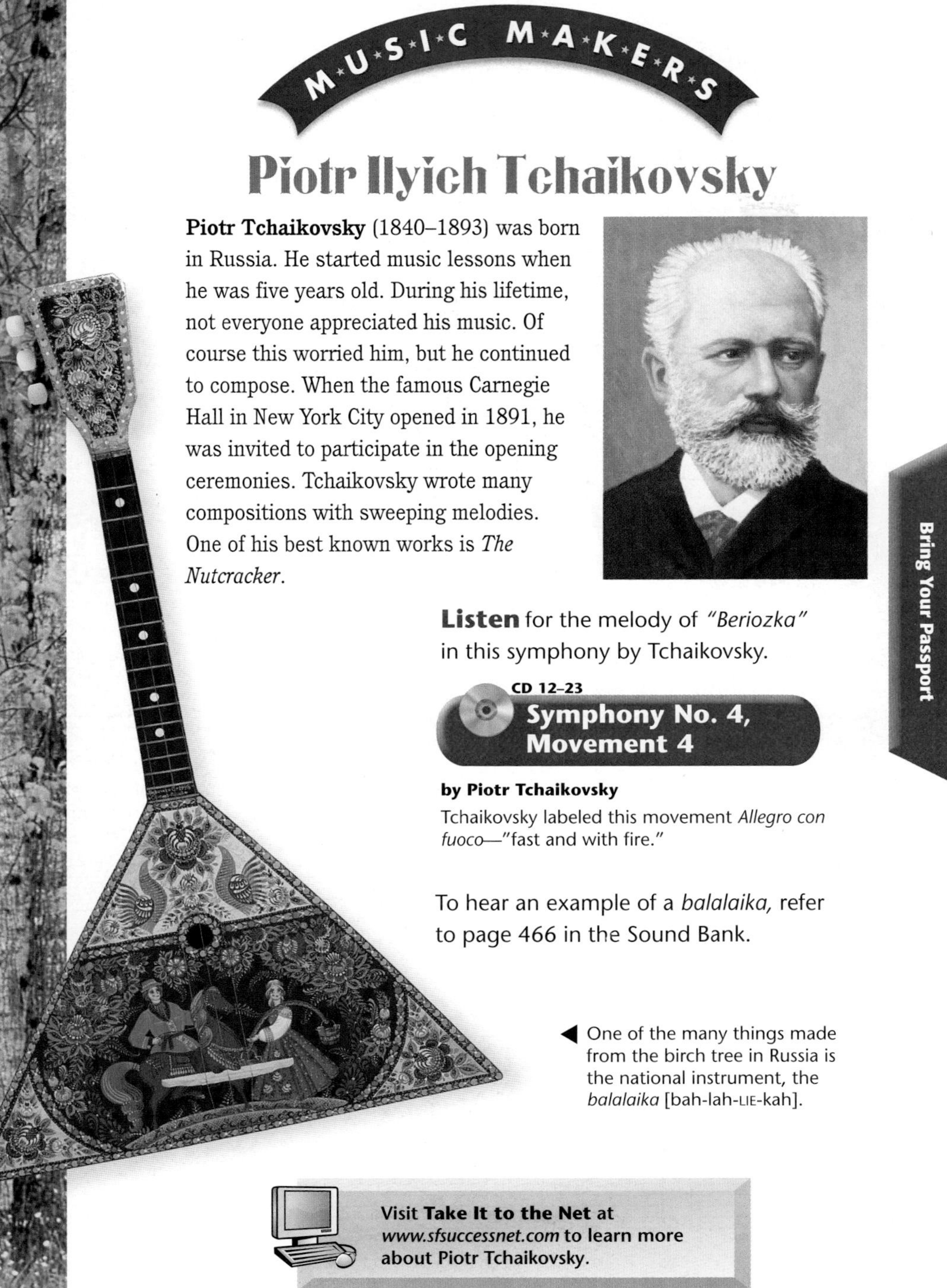


# Piotr Ilyich Tchaikovsky

**Piotr Tchaikovsky** (1840–1893) was born in Russia. He started music lessons when he was five years old. During his lifetime, not everyone appreciated his music. Of course this worried him, but he continued to compose. When the famous Carnegie Hall in New York City opened in 1891, he was invited to participate in the opening ceremonies. Tchaikovsky wrote many compositions with sweeping melodies. One of his best known works is *The Nutcracker*.

**Listen** for the melody of *"Beriozka"* in this symphony by Tchaikovsky.

CD 12–23

**Symphony No. 4, Movement 4**

**by Piotr Tchaikovsky**

Tchaikovsky labeled this movement *Allegro con fuoco*—"fast and with fire."

To hear an example of a *balalaika,* refer to page 466 in the Sound Bank.

◀ One of the many things made from the birch tree in Russia is the national instrument, the *balalaika* [bah-lah-LIE-kah].

Visit **Take It to the Net** at *www.sfsuccessnet.com* to learn more about Piotr Tchaikovsky.

Bring Your Passport



### Listening

Play Movement 4 of Tchaikovsky's *Symphony No. 4* (excerpt) **CD 12-23.** Encourage students to raise their hands when they hear the *"Beriozka"* theme.

ASK **How did Tchaikovsky change the melody to *"Beriozka?"*** (He added two beats of rest to each phrase. He changed the melody in m. 4. He changed the rhythm of the last phrase.)

Have students listen again and snap their fingers in the two extra beats at the end of each phrase of the melody.

Invite students to read about Tchaikovsky on p. 295 of their books. See Cultural Connection, p. 222, for information on the *balalaika.*

## 3 Close

### Listening/Describing

9a Play the recordings associated with this lesson in any order. Ask students to write a sentence or two about each recording that tells something about the music or the culture of Russia. (Example: "This is *1812 Overture,* written by Tchaikovsky. He used a Russian folk song as part of the piece.") Encourage students to refer to their books for spelling and to review the music.

**Skill: LISTENING** — ASSESSMENT

**Performance/Observation** Play the recording of *Symphony No. 4* **CD 12-23** or *"Beriozka"* **CD 12-19** and have students trace the shape of the melodic contour in the air with a hand as they listen. Observe each student's ability to accurately portray the melodic contour.

## Audience Etiquette

9e ▶ **Preparing to Attend a Performance** Encourage students to attend a live performance of Tchaikovsky's *Symphony No. 4* or other symphonic work. To help students prepare, have them

- Research and summarize information about the featured performers and composers.
- Listen to recordings of the music they will hear. (Engage students in the music through movement, listening maps, written responses, or singing/playing themes or rhythms.)
- Read information about the music, including plots or story lines.

## Character Education

▶ **Values** As folk songs are passed down through generations, so beliefs and values are transmitted from generation to generation. What are some character traits and values that have been handed down to your generation? Divide students into groups, assigning one character trait or value to each group. Within each group, discuss how a particular value is transmitted from one generation to another. How were (or are) you taught that this value is important? Talk about one way students can ensure that this value is shared with the next generation.

## Technology/Media Link

**Web Site** For more information about Piotr Tchaikovsky, encourage students to visit *www.sfsuccessnet.com.*

LESSON 2

## LESSON AT A GLANCE

**Element Focus** **TIMBRE** Instruments of Ireland

**Skill Objective** **LISTENING** Identify traditional Irish instruments

**Connection Activity** **CULTURE** Discuss characteristics of music and dance from Ireland

**MATERIALS**

- "The Bard of Armagh" **CD 12-24**
  **Recording Routine:** Intro (4 m.); v. 1; interlude (4 m.); v. 2; coda
- *MacAllistrum's March—Mairseail Alasdroim* **CD 12-26**
- *Crowley's Reel* **CD 12-27**
- *Crowley's/Jackson's* **CD 12-28**
- *Dúlamán* **CD 12-29**
- **Resource Book** p. F-18

**VOCABULARY**

harp flute

**National Standards**

- **1b** Sing expressively with appropriate phrasing
- **2c** Play instruments expressively on a variety of pieces
- **5b** Read notes in treble clef using syllables
- **6a** Listen to identify form
- **6b** Describe music by answering questions about it
- **6c** Use appropriate terms to explain musical instruments
- **6d** Identify the sounds of band and orchestral instruments
- **6e** While listening to music, move to show a prominent feature of the music

**MORE MUSIC CHOICES**

Other songs from Ireland:

"How Can I Keep from Singing?" p. 261

"Oh, Danny Boy," p. 48

LESSON 2 Element: TIMBRE Skill: LISTENING Connection: CULTURE

# The Irish Harper

Welcome to Ireland, its people, and its music! One of the first instruments used in playing the music of Ireland was the harp. When you **listen** to the recording of "The Bard of Armagh," you will hear the harp and another ancient instrument. **Identify** the instrument. Why do you think these instruments were among the first created?

CD 12-24

## The Bard of Armagh

*s, l, t, ⓓ r m f s l*

*Words attributed to Thomas Campbell* *Folk Tune from Ireland*

1. Oh! List to the tale of a poor Ir - ish har - per,
2. At wake or at fair I would twirl my shil - le - lagh,
And scorn not the strings in his old with - er'd ___ hand;
And trip through a jig with my shoes bound with ___ straw;
But re - mem - ber those fin - gers could once move much sharp - er,
And ___ all the ___ pret - ty maid - ens from ___ vil - lage and val - ley,
To wa - ken the ech - oes of his dear na - tive land.
Love the bold Phel - im Bra - dy, the ___ bard of Ar - magh.



296

# Footnotes

## ACROSS THE CURRICULUM

▶ **Social Studies** Encourage students to locate Ireland on a map. Ireland is the second largest island of the British Isles. It is west of the island of Great Britain and separated from it by the North Channel, the Irish Sea, and St. George's Channel. Because it rains so much in Ireland, the island is very fertile. Some regions get as much as 80 inches of rain each year. Ireland is sometimes referred to as the "emerald isle" because of the lush green grass that grows there.

## BUILDING SKILLS THROUGH MUSIC

▶ **Science** Have students look at the picture of the Irish harp on p. 297. Ask, Why is it in that shape? (to hold strings of different lengths) With a shoe box and rubber bands, have students build a harp.

## CULTURAL CONNECTION

▶ **Have Song, Will Travel** In mid-nineteenth century Ireland, most of the people were poor subsistence farmers, relying on potatoes both as food to eat and food to sell. All other crops went to their landlords for sale to wealthier people and for export to foreign countries and to Great Britain. For two consecutive years, the potato crop failed and the people had nothing to eat and no way to make money. During this time, more than a million Irish people emigrated to the United States.

The Irish emigrants brought their songs with them. They altered the songs to suit their new life. In America, "The Bard of Armagh" was transformed into the popular cowboy song "Streets of Laredo."

## The Timbre of Irish Music

**Listen** to the instruments in these musical selections from Ireland. Remember, each instrument has its own timbre.

CD 12-26

**MacAllistrum's March-Mairseail Alasdroim**

**Traditional Irish March as performed by the Chieftains with the Belfast Harp Orchestra**

This music was written to honor Alistar MacAllistrum, a Celtic [KEL-tik] hero.

CD 12-27

**Crowley's Reel**

**Traditional Irish Reel as performed by James Galway**

A reel is a folk dance performed in pairs, with couples facing one another.

▲ Irish harp

MUSIC MAKERS

### James Galway

**James Galway** (born 1939), one of the world's greatest flute players, is from Belfast, Ireland. Galway has played with symphony orchestras, jazz artists, and groups like the Chieftains. He enjoys playing many different styles of music from all over the world. He has many flutes. One is made of gold!

Bring Your Passport



# 1 Introduce

Have students follow the words on p. 296 while listening to the recording of "The Bard of Armagh" **CD 12-24.**

ASK **What do you think the words mean?** (Accept various answers.)

The song is sung from the viewpoint of an aging harpist looking back on his youth. Share the information about the words in Cultural Connection on p. 298.

# 2 Develop

### Listening

Invite students to identify the instruments that accompany "The Bard of Armagh." (flute and harp) Discuss the question on p. 296 regarding the antiquity of these two instruments.

6c ASK **Why do these instruments date back to ancient times?** (They were easy to make from materials people had.)

### Singing

1b Encourage students to sing "The Bard of Armagh." Have students

- Practice singing a smooth octave leap at the beginning of the song.
- Breathe only between the phrases at the end of each line of music.

For those students who are unable to sustain the long phrases, have each breathe in an inconspicuous place or at a different time than the person standing next to them.

continued on page 298

## Spotlight On

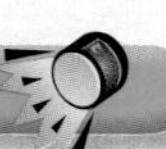

▶ **The Chieftains** The Chieftains were formed in 1963 with an *uilleann* [ILL-uhn] piper (Irish bagpipes), tin whistle, flute, and *bodhran* (drum) players. Later, they would add a harpist. All the players had other jobs, and it was not until 1975, when they gave their first concert at Royal Albert Hall in London, that they decided to become a full-time ensemble. Since then, the Chieftains have been nominated for and have won Grammys in three different categories as well as other prestigious awards. They played for a crowd of over a million people when Pope John Paul II visited Ireland. They toured the world and played with symphony orchestras and artists such as James Galway, Van Morrison, and Marianne Faithfull. The Chieftains have also performed for film and television.

## Skills Reinforcement

2c ▶ **Playing** Students may enjoy playing the Autoharp while singing "The Bard of Armagh" **CD 12-24.** Encourage students to find all the chords necessary to accompany the song before they begin. Then have them accompany the class, changing chords at the appropriate time. Give several students the opportunity to play during the class period.

▶ **Mallets** For a mallet accompaniment to "The Bard of Armagh," refer to Resource Book p. F-18.

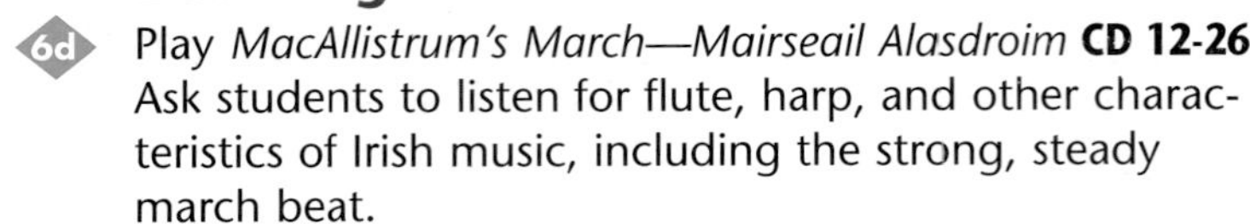

### Listening

6d Play *MacAllistrum's March—Mairseail Alasdroim* **CD 12-26.** Ask students to listen for flute, harp, and other characteristics of Irish music, including the strong, steady march beat.

6b Have students read the information about James Galway, p. 297, and then play *Crowley's Reel* **CD 12-27.**

**ASK What kind of dance would you expect a reel to be from listening to the music? Why?** (lively, energetic dance; music in quick tempo; very rhythmic)

**What instruments do you recognize?** (flute, drum, fiddle, harp, and bones—clappers originally made from ox bones)

**What would you have to do to play as well as James Galway does in *Crowley's Reel?*** (have talent for the instrument, be motivated, and practice)

**What observations can you make about the flute from this solo?** (A flute player can play a wide range and notes can be played very rapidly.)

### Moving

Invite students to read about Irish music on p. 298 and share the information about Riverdance from Spotlight On below. Have students listen to *Crowley's/Jackson's* **CD 12-28** as peformed by Eileen Ivers.

Refer to Movement on p. 299 for a creative movement activity. Encourage students to create movements to perform as they listen to the recording again. Encourage students who have had training in dance to be a partner with those who have not.

## Irish Music in America

Irish melodies have found their way around the world and into the United States. Notice the similarities between "The Bard of Armagh" (page 296) and "Streets of Laredo" (page 272).

**Listen** to another example of Irish dance music and **identify** the instruments.

CD 12-28

**Crowley's/Jackson's**

**Traditional Irish Melody**
**as performed by Eileen Ivers, John Doyle, and Tommy Hayes**

Eileen Ivers is a performer with *Riverdance,* a stage production that showcases traditional Irish dance.

▲ Eileen Ivers

TUNE IN
*Lord of the Dance* has featured a variety of performers, including Irish folk dancers, solo singers, a flute soloist, and a fiddle duet.


▲ *Lord of the Dance* performers

298

## Footnotes

### SPOTLIGHT ON

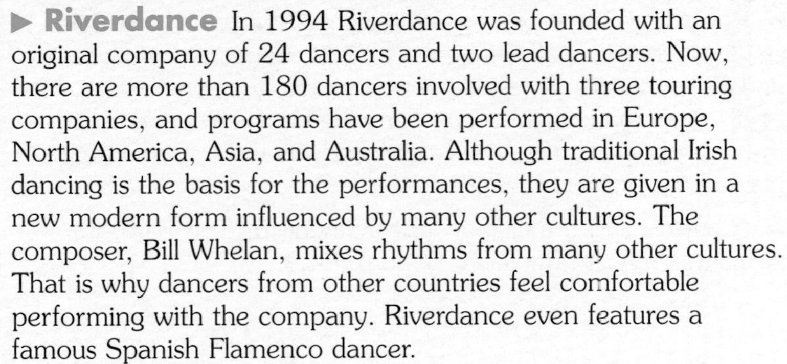

▶ **Riverdance** In 1994 Riverdance was founded with an original company of 24 dancers and two lead dancers. Now, there are more than 180 dancers involved with three touring companies, and programs have been performed in Europe, North America, Asia, and Australia. Although traditional Irish dancing is the basis for the performances, they are given in a new modern form influenced by many other cultures. The composer, Bill Whelan, mixes rhythms from many other cultures. That is why dancers from other countries feel comfortable performing with the company. Riverdance even features a famous Spanish Flamenco dancer.

▶ ***Dúlamán*** *Dúlamán* is a popular children's song from Ireland. The word *Dúlamán* actually means *seaweed.* The seaweed was once gathered and used as a fertilizer for the soil.

### CULTURAL CONNECTION

▶ **Irish Words** Students may be unfamiliar with some of the words in "The Bard of Armagh." Share the meaning of these words with students for greater understanding of the song.

*list*—listen

*Shillelagh*—club/walking stick

*jig*—dance

*bard*—Celtic singer and poet

*Armagh*—area in Northern Ireland

## Listen and Look

**Listen** to the instrumental and vocal timbres used in *Dúlamán*.

CD 12-29
**Dúlamán**

**Traditional Irish Song**
**as performed by Altan**

The word *dúlamán* means seaweed.

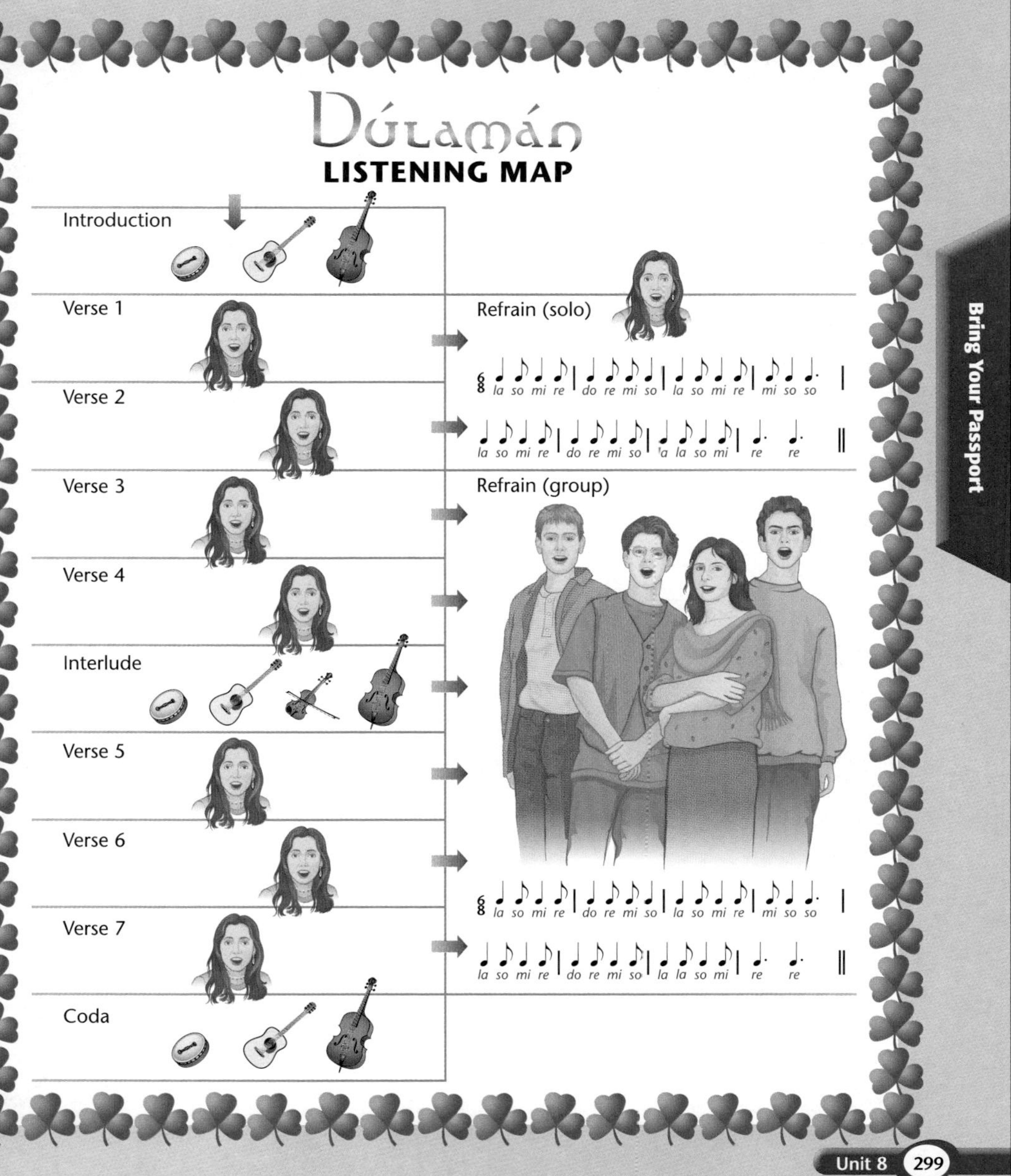


### Reading

5b 6a Refer students to the *Dúlamán* listening map on p. 299. Have them look at the notation for the refrain on the right side of the map. Play a B♭ on the piano and assist students in establishing the B♭-pentatonic tonality in their ears. Then have them read the pitch syllables from the notation in the listening map.

Play the recording of *Dúlamán* **CD 12-29** and encourage students to follow and identify the verse-refrain (AB) form of the piece. Have them sing the refrain each time it occurs, using pitch syllables.

6d **ASK What instruments do you hear in the accompaniment of this piece?** (guitar, *bodhran* [type of drum], fiddle, bass)

Share information about *Dúlamán* from Spotlight On, p. 298.

# 3 Close

**Skill: LISTENING** ASSESSMENT

6c **Music Journal Writing** Have students listen again to various pieces of music they have heard in this lesson. Then, using basic criteria to describe and evaluate each composition, have them write in a music journal about what they have learned about Irish music. Ask them to discuss the tempo and instrumentation of the selections. Evaluate the individual success of each student based upon the accuracy of what has been written about the selections.

## Movement

6e ▶ **Creative Movement** Divide the class into small groups. Ask each group to develop a sequence of movements to go with *Crowley's/Jackson's*. Movements do not necessarily have to involve the whole body. Students can use their arms or pat patterns on their laps. Have one student in each group write down the sequence. Each group can perform for other class members.

## Technology/Media Link

**Transparency** Have students listen for form, melody, and instruments as they follow the listening map for *Dúlamán*. For those students who have difficulty following the map on their own, have them refer to the transparency and guide them through the piece.

## LESSON AT A GLANCE

**Element Focus** **RHYTHM** Melodic rhythm and steady beat

**Skill Objective** **PLAYING** Play melodic rhythms and steady beat to accompany a song

**Connection Activity** **CULTURE** Discuss the use of music at sporting events in many cultures

**MATERIALS**

- *"Tina singu"* (Zulu) **CD 12-30**
- *"Tina singu"* (English) **CD 12-31**

  **Recording Routine:** Intro (4 m.); vocal; coda
- **Pronunciation Practice/Translation** p. 487
- **Resource Book** pp. A-31, F-20
- drums, assorted rhythm instruments
- selected melody instrument

**VOCABULARY**

basic beat melodic rhythm repeat sign

**National Standards**

**1c** Sing songs from diverse cultures

**2f** Play instruments independently against contrasting parts

**5a** Read rhythms in $\frac{4}{4}$ meter

**MORE MUSIC CHOICES**

For more songs from Africa:

*"Hashewie,"* p. 63

*"Ochimbo,"* p. 134

For another sporting event song:

*"La copa de la vida,"* p. 414

# 1 INTRODUCE

Introduce *"Tina singu"* **CD 12-30** as a folk song from South Africa. Share the information about the song in Cultural Connection below. Ask students to name songs from the United States that are played at sporting events to rally the audience and team. Play the recording of *"Tina singu."*



# SONG OF SOUTH AFRICA

Africa has many different peoples and countries. *"Tina singu"* is from South Africa, a country located at the southern tip of the continent. The song is often sung at sporting events. **Sing** *"Tina singu."*

CD 12-30

## Tina Singu

f, s, l, t, (d) r m f s

Folk Song from South Africa

*Introduction (first time only)* *Leader* / *Group*

Ti - na sing - u le - lu - vu - tae - o. Wat-sha, wat-sha, wat-sha,
We burn with the fire of life, oh,

*Leader* / *Group*

Ti - na, Ti - na sing - u le - lu - vu - tae - o.
We burn, we burn with the fire of life, oh,

Wat - sha, wat - sha, wat - sha, wat - sha, la - la - la - la - la -

*Part 2*

1 Wat - sha, wat - sha,

2 la, la - la - la - la - la - la, la - la - la - la - la -



## Footnotes

### CULTURAL CONNECTION

▶ *"Tina singu"* This popular song from South Africa is sung by school children during sports competitions. The words mean "We are the burning fire. Look out and don't get burned."

### BUILDING SKILLS THROUGH MUSIC

▶ **Theatre** Share the information on *"Tina singu"* from Cultural Connection above. Divide the class into groups. Have students

- Select a song used during sports competitions.
- Create movements to dramatize the sports competition they have selected.

### MEETING INDIVIDUAL NEEDS

▶ **Including Everyone** Drums are one of the most desirable instruments for all children to play. Students who lack the strength to strike the drum with their hands can perform the patterns (or a simpler pattern) more easily by striking the drum with a mallet. Wrap the mallet handle with foam and tape to increase the handle grip. The student may need to hold the mallet toward the middle and may need to play a drum with the largest surface. The student should play as independently as possible. Have students with and without disabilities explore different mallets when they play.

### Playing and Singing Parts

**Play** the steady beat of *"Tina singu"* on a drum. Then play the rhythm of the melody. How are they the same? How are they different? Choose one of these rhythm patterns to accompany the song.

**CD-ROM** Use the Melody and Rhythm Maker in *Making Music* to create an accompaniment for *"Tina singu."*

F
C7
F
wat - sha, wat - sha, wat - sha.
la, la - la - la - la - la - la, la - la - la - la - la -

F
B♭
Wat - sha, wat - sha,
la, la - la - la - la - la - la, la - la - la - la - la -

F
C7
F
wat - sha, wat - sha, wat - sha.
la, la - la - la - la - la - la.

Bring Your Passport

## 2 Develop

### Singing

1c Encourage students to learn the song in Zulu by having them practice the words with the Pronunciation Practice **CD 12-33.** Refer to Resource Book p. A-31 for a Pronunciation Practice Guide to the song. Then have students sing the entire song.

This song can be performed in layers. The melody at the beginning and the divided part may be performed simultaneously. When students know the song well, have them divide into three groups and sing all parts at the same time.

### Playing

2f Divide the class into three groups. Have the first group sing *"Tina singu"* **CD 12-30.** Have the second group play the rhythm of the melody on percussion instruments, and have the third group clap or play the steady beat. Switch to let each group perform each part.

5a Ask for a volunteer to play the first line of the song on a melody instrument. The first line can be played as an ostinato throughout the song, if two beats or rests are added at the end of the line.

## 3 Close

**Skill: PLAYING** — **ASSESSMENT**

**Performance/Observation** Invite a small group of students to perform the rhythm of the melody on a nonpitched percussion instrument while the other students sing *"Tina singu"* and tap the steady beat. Observe each student's ability to differentiate between beat and rhythm.

### Skills Reinforcement

▶ **Mallets** For an additional nonpitched percussion playing activity to accompany the singing of *"Tina singu,"* refer to Resource Book p. F-20.

### Technology/Media Link

**Web Site** For more information on African music and instruments, invite students to visit *www.sfsuccessnet.com*.

LESSON 4

## LESSON AT A GLANCE

**Element Focus** **FORM** Rondo form

**Skill Objective** **MOVING** Perform a folk dance from Mexico in rondo form

**Connection Activity** **RELATED ARTS** Examine the art of Diego Rivera

**MATERIALS**

- *"La raspa"* (Spanish) **CD 13-1**
- *"La raspa"* (English) **CD 13-2**

  **Recording Routine:** Intro (2 m.); vocal; interlude (8 m.); vocal; coda
- **Pronunciation Practice/Translation** p. 487
- **Dance Directions** for *"La raspa"* p. 515
- *El mariachi* (excerpt) **CD 13-6**
- "My Song" (poem)
- **Resource Book** pp. A-32, C-8, G-16, I-23
- Autoharp, resonator bells (G, A, B, C), recorders
- keyboard or other melody instrument

**VOCABULARY**

*mariachi* rondo form

**◆ ◆ ◆ ◆ National Standards ◆ ◆ ◆ ◆**

- **2b** Perform chords and melodies on appropriate instruments
- **2e** Play instruments in groups, following a conductor
- **6a** Listen to identify form
- **6b** Describe music by moving to it
- **6d** Identify the sounds of instruments from various cultures
- **6e** While listening to music, move to show a prominent feature of the music
- **8a** Define common terms used with different meanings in the various arts

**MORE MUSIC CHOICES**

Other songs from Mexico:

*"Cielito lindo,"* p. 270

*"Corrido de Kansas,"* p. 274

For more practice with rondo form:

*ABACA Dabble,* p. 184

"Heave-Ho!"/"Going, Going, Gone"/"The Snow" (speech piece) p. 182

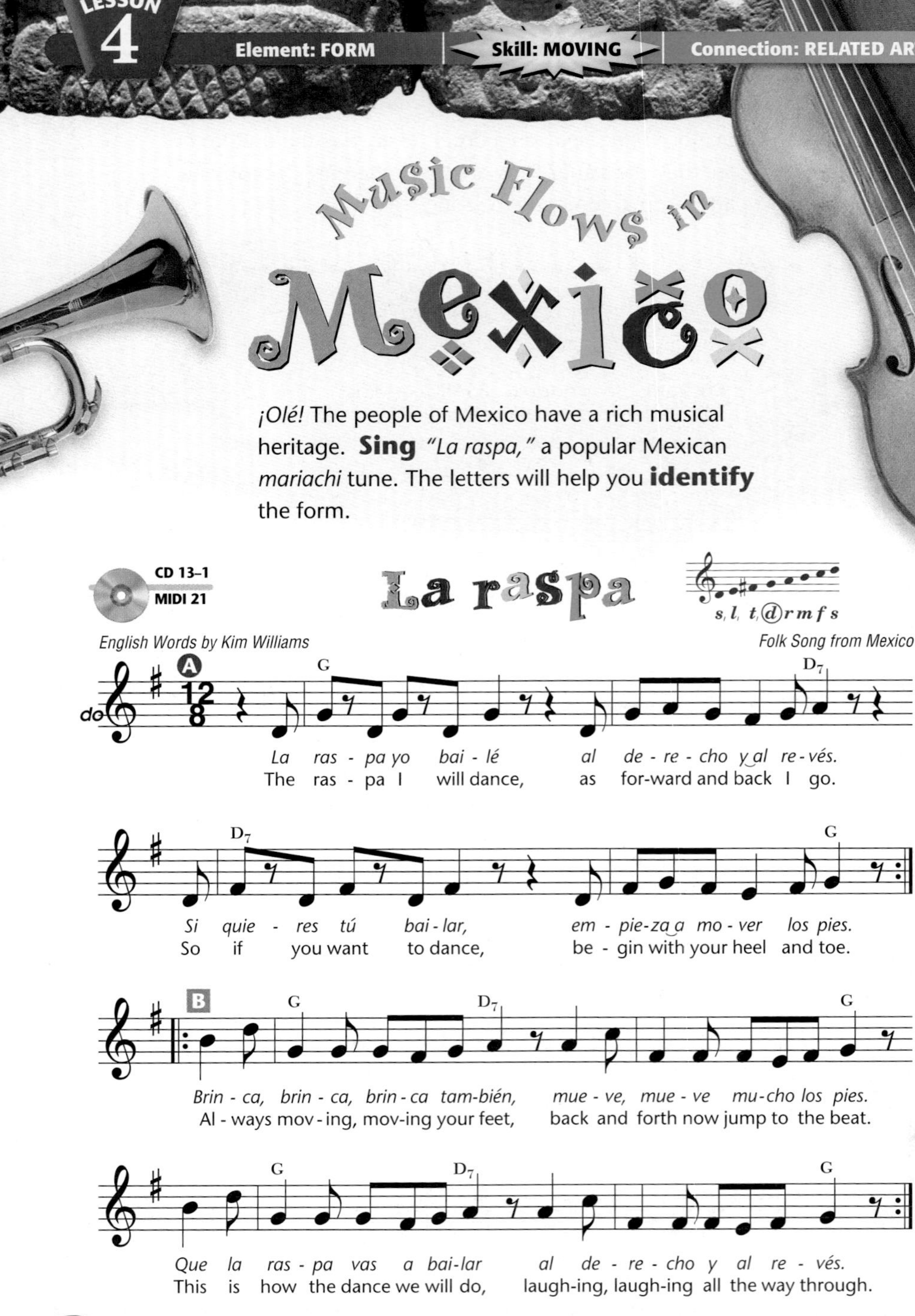
LESSON 4 Element: FORM Skill: MOVING Connection: RELATED ARTS

Music Flows in Mexico

*¡Olé!* The people of Mexico have a rich musical heritage. **Sing** *"La raspa,"* a popular Mexican *mariachi* tune. The letters will help you **identify** the form.

CD 13-1
MIDI 21
La raspa
s, l, t, d r m f s
English Words by Kim Williams
Folk Song from Mexico
A
do
G
D7
La ras - pa yo bai - lé al de - re - cho y al re - vés.
The ras - pa I will dance, as for-ward and back I go.
Si quie - res tú bai - lar, em - pie-za a mo - ver los pies.
So if you want to dance, be - gin with your heel and toe.
B
Brin - ca, brin - ca, brin-ca tam-bién, mue - ve, mue - ve mu-cho los pies.
Al - ways mov-ing, mov-ing your feet, back and forth now jump to the beat.
Que la ras - pa vas a bai-lar al de - re - cho y al re - vés.
This is how the dance we will do, laugh-ing, laugh-ing all the way through.
302

# Footnotes

## SPOTLIGHT ON

▶ ***Mariachi* Ensembles** As they developed in the nineteenth century, *mariachi* ensembles originally had two violins, a *vihuela* (small five-stringed guitar), a guitar, and a harp. In the early twentieth century, a *guitarrón* (a large bass guitar with four strings) was substituted for the harp, which could not be played while the group strolled, as they often do. During the 1930s, two trumpets were added to the standard *mariachi* ensemble. The *guitarrón* and trumpets are still used today, and some ensembles even retain the harp.

## BUILDING SKILLS THROUGH MUSIC

▶ **Writing** Have students write a description of the art work on p. 304. Ask them to include words that could also be used to describe music, such as *repetition, contrast, form, texture, mood, style,* and so on.

## ACROSS THE CURRICULUM

▶ **Language Arts** Students may enjoy the story *The Riddle of the Drum*, translated and retold by Verna Aardema (Four Winds Press, 1979). Remind students that "*La raspa*" is a Mexican folk song and that *The Riddle of the Drum* is a folk tale from the same country. Read the story aloud, inviting students to say together the riddle of the drum with you. Have students retell the story, taking turns playing the characters of the palace guard who chants the riddle, and the prince, runner, archer, hearer, blower, eater, and king. Encourage students to use Mexican names for their characters and as many Spanish words as possible.

**Listen** to this example of a *mariachi* band.

CD 13-6
## El mariachi

**Traditional *Mariachi* from Mexico**

*Mariachi* comes from a Coca Indian word meaning "musician."

A G D7

*Si quie - res tú bai - lar la ras - pa co - mo yo,*
So if you want to dance the ras-pa the way I do,

D7 G

*Me tie - nes que se - guir al de - re - cho y al re - vés.*
Be - gin to move your feet, and you will be danc - ing, too.

C Instrumental C G D7 G

C G D7 G

A G D7

*La ras - pa yo bai - lé al de - re - cho y al re - vés.*
The ras - pa I will dance, as for-ward and back I go.

D7 G

*Si quie - res tú bai - lar, em - pie-za a mo - ver los pies.*
So if you want to dance, be - gin with your heel and toe.

Bring Your Passport



# 1 Introduce

6e Play *"La raspa"* **CD 13-1.** Ask students to pat the steady beat on their knees as they listen to this popular folk song from Mexico.

# 2 Develop

### Singing

Invite students to learn the melody. Have them sing the English version of *"La raspa"* **CD 13-2.** Using Pronunciation Practice **CD 13-4** and the Pronunciation Practice Guide on Resource Book p. A-32, encourage students to listen to and sing each phrase in Spanish and then sing the entire song in Spanish. If you have students who are fluent in Spanish, encourage them to assist other students or model the Pronunciation Practice with the class.

### Playing

2b 2e Using the resonator bells G, A, B, and C, students can play the following pattern during the instrumental in section C:

**continued on page 304**

## Cultural Connection

▶ **Folk Dancing** Ask students if they have any friends or family members who know traditional folk dances from other countries. Invite these guests to informally perform and share traditional dances and music with the students in your class. Ask each student to introduce his or her guest and to say something about the music or dance the guest will share.

## Skills Reinforcement

▶ **Recorder** For a recorder accompaniment to *"La raspa,"* refer to Resource Book p. I-23.

## Listening

Encourage students to listen for the form of *"La raspa."* With student books closed, play mm. 1–4 of *"La raspa,"* using a keyboard or another melody instrument. Label this excerpt the A section. Then play mm. 5–8 and label this excerpt B. Play mm. 9–12.

ASK **What did I just play for you? Was it the A section or the B section?** (A section)

Play mm. 13–16 and ask students the same question. The answer this time will be, "neither A nor B." Identify this section as C. Then play the last four measures. Students should know by now it is the A section.

ASK **If I were to write out the form of this piece, what would it be?** (ABACA)

Explain to students that ABACA is known as rondo form. Have a student go to the board and continue the rondo form. (ABACADAEA, and so on)

Have students listen to the entire recording of *"La raspa"* **CD 13-1.** Help them identify rondo form aurally by asking them to signal each time the A section returns.

## Moving

Have students look at the painting *Dance in Tehuantepec* on p. 304. Share the information about Diego Rivera in Spotlight On below.

ASK **How are the colors in this painting like that music?** (bright, festive)

**What are these dancers celebrating?** (festivals, social gatherings)

Have students refer to the painting by Rivera and the photos of students while they learn the dance to *"La raspa."*

**Arts Connection**

▲ *Dance in Tehuantepec* (1928) by Diego Rivera. Mexican artist Diego Rivera (1866–1957) is sometimes called "the artist of the people." He created large paintings called murals, showing the lives of everyday people.

304

# Footnotes

## Teacher to Teacher

▶ **Teaching *"La raspa"*** Identify any dancers in your class who will learn the dance for *"La raspa"* quickly. Have these students help others who may have trouble learning the proper steps. You may also wish to choose one student to demonstrate the dance with you.

To help students appreciate the rich diversity of folk dance among Latin American and Caribbean cultures, refer them to the Dance Directions for *Sonando* on p. 506.

## Spotlight On

▶ **The Artist** Diego Rivera (1886–1957) was one of the greatest artists of the twentieth century. He was born in Mexico and captured the essence of Mexican life in his paintings. His murals show the relationship of the farmer, the laborer, and folk characters with the earth and each other. Rivera wanted his paintings to be accessible to the public, so he painted his art in public spaces for everyone to enjoy. Rivera's wish was to unite everyone living in North and South America through their common cultural ties.

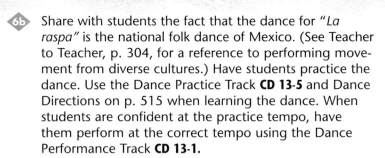

## A Poem of the People

Read this poem. Notice how the words paint a picture. What do you think this poem means?

*Toltec Poem from Ancient Mexico*
*Translated by Toni de Gerez*

Like the feathers
of the quetzal bird
my song is beautiful
Now look!
My song is bending over the earth
My song is born
in the house of butterflies

▲ Mayan pottery with *quetzal* birds

Bring Your Passport

## Doing the Dance

**Move** to show rondo form as you **sing** *"La raspa."*

A ▲ Do the hop step.

B ▲ Take 4 side steps, then reverse.

C ▲ Hook arms with your partner, then spin.

6b Share with students the fact that the dance for *"La raspa"* is the national folk dance of Mexico. (See Teacher to Teacher, p. 304, for a reference to performing movement from diverse cultures.) Have students practice the dance. Use the Dance Practice Track **CD 13-5** and Dance Directions on p. 515 when learning the dance. When students are confident at the practice tempo, have them perform at the correct tempo using the Dance Performance Track **CD 13-1.**

Cultural Connection, below, provides an activity to help students understand the connection between music and art in a culture.

### Listening

Invite students to listen to *El mariachi* **CD 13-6.** As students listen, have them individually write a list of all the instruments they hear in the recording. Discuss the timbre of *mariachi* music with students.

6d ASK **What instruments do the *mariachi* band and the orchestra have in common?** (trumpets and violins)

**Which are not in common?** (guitar, *jarana,* harp, *guitarrón, vihuela*)

For more information on *mariachi* ensembles, see Spotlight On, p. 302.

To help students categorize instruments of various cultures, draw a Venn diagram on the board, showing students the instruments of the *mariachi* band and the orchestra. Have students, as a class, fill in the spaces of the diagram. You may also distribute Venn diagrams to students. See Resource Book p. C-8.

## 3 CLOSE

**Skill: MOVING** ASSESSMENT

**Performance/Observation** Invite students to sing and dance *"La raspa"* with the Dance Performance Track **CD 13-1.** Assess each individual student's understanding of rondo form by observing the correct movements for each section of the song. For students who have difficulty remembering the sequence of the movements, remind them of the rondo form. (ABACA)

## CULTURAL CONNECTION

8a ▶ **Seeing Patterns** An exercise in aesthetic perception and valuing is to identify and explore the connections between music and art in a culture. After singing and dancing *"La raspa"* and viewing a painting by Diego Rivera, find other paintings by him or Frida Kahlo. Make a list of characteristics that you find in Mexican music and song—topical, musical, symbolic, and others. Also make a list of characteristics that are evident in the painting(s). Decide as a class if there are any overlapping characteristics, or if certain characteristics in one medium relate strongly to characteristics in the other medium. Use these identified characteristics to discuss further songs and artwork from Mexico or to construct some pieces of your own in a Mexican style.

## TECHNOLOGY/MEDIA LINK

**MIDI/Sequencing Software** Display the accompaniment tracks for the MIDI song file of *"La raspa."* Zoom in on one measure to show students that some tracks have three notes per beat and some have two notes per beat. Isolate one of the two-notes-per-beat tracks and have students perform the rhythm. Isolate one of the three-notes-per-beat tracks and have them perform that rhythm as well.

LESSON 5

## LESSON AT A GLANCE

**Element Focus** **TEXTURE/HARMONY** Countermelody

**Skill Objective** **SINGING** Create two-part harmony by singing a song with a countermelody

**Connection Activity** **SOCIAL STUDIES** Sing a song from Venezuela in Spanish

**MATERIALS**

- *"Bogando a la luz del sol"* **CD 13-7**
- "Rowing Toward the Sunlight" **CD 13-8**
  **Recording Routine:** Intro (4 m.); vocal (melody); interlude (8 m.); vocal (melody and harmony); coda
- *"Carnaval Llanero"* **CD 13-12**
- **Pronunciation Practice/Translation** p. 488
- **Resource Book** pp. A-33, I-24
- keyboard or guitar
- globe or map of the world

**VOCABULARY**

countermelody *joropo* *cuatro*

**National Standards**

**1c** Sing from memory songs from diverse cultures
**1d** Sing partner songs and rounds
**6b** Describe music by answering questions about it
**9b** Describe how dynamics and texture are used in pieces from various cultures

**MORE MUSIC CHOICES . . .**

For more practice singing countermelodies:
"Amazing Grace," p. 160
"America, the Beautiful," p. 158

# 1 INTRODUCE

Tell students that "*Bogando a la luz del sol*" is a folk song from Venezuela. Have them locate Venezuela on a globe or world map and share Across the Curriculum on p. 307. Play "*Bogando a la luz del sol*" **CD 13-7** and ask students to identify the language. (Spanish)

LESSON 5 Element: TEXTURE/HARMONY Skill: SINGING Connection: SOCIAL STUDI

# Rowing in VENEZUELA

The South American country of Venezuela is a land of many beautiful bodies of water. The largest lake, Lake Maracaibo, is in the northwestern part of the country. "*Bogando a la luz del sol*" describes a calm scene of someone gently rowing across such a lake at sunrise.

**Listen** to the melody of the song.

CD 13-7
Bogando a la luz del sol
(Rowing Toward the Sunlight)
l, t, d r ri m f s l
English Words by David Eddleman
Folk Song from Venezuela
So-plan las bri-sas de la ma-ña-na, Ri-zan-do el la-go mur-mu-ra-dor,
Soft-ly the breez-es of morn-ing are sigh-ing, The whisp'r-ing wa-ters are gent-ly stirred;
Y por o-rien-te su faz a-so-ma Cual ra-ro in-cen-dio la luz del sol.
The sun-light dawn-ing from East is show-ing, Its face a-glow-ing, a rare de-light.
Y por o-rien-te su faz a-so-ma
The sun-light dawn-ing from East is show-ing,
Cual ra-ro in-cen-dio la luz del sol.
Its face a-glow-ing, a rare de-light.
306

Footnotes

## SKILLS REINFORCEMENT

▶ **Recorder** Once students can sing "*Bogando a la luz del sol*" and the countermelody with ease, have them add the recorder part found on p. I-24 of the Resource Book.

## BUILDING SKILLS THROUGH MUSIC

▶ **Technology** Using the classroom computer, assist students in researching Angel Falls in Venezuela.

## MEETING INDIVIDUAL NEEDS

▶ **Singing in Parts** Some students may find singing "*Bogando a la luz del sol*" in two parts very difficult at this age.

**Reinforcement** Encourage students who have difficulty holding a part to sing the melody. Place them between two strong singers who are also performing the melody.

**On Target** Many students will find singing two parts to be challenging and fun. Assign these students to sing the melody the first time through the song. Then let them trade parts and sing the countermelody.

**Challenge** The students who can easily sing the two parts may be given a more difficult task. Place these students in a small group of four or five, and let them sing the countermelody as the rest of the class sings "*Bogando a la luz del sol*."

### Choose a Melody

**Sing** the countermelody below while others sing the melody of "*Bogando a la luz del sol.*" The countermelody adds harmony. **Describe** how this affects the texture of the song.

**Tune In**

Are you familiar with Venice, the city in Italy that is entirely surrounded by water? When the first European explorers came to what is now Venezuela, they chose the name because the country reminded them of Venice. *Venezuela* means "Little Venice."

Countermelody
do
So - plan las bri - sas de la ma - ña - na,
Soft - ly the breez - es of morn - ing are sigh - ing,
Y por o - rien - te su faz a - so - ma.
The sun - light dawn - ing, dawn - ing from East is show - ing.
Y por o - rien - te su faz a - so - ma
The sun - light dawn - ing from East is show - ing,
Cual ra - ro in - cen - dio la luz del sol.
Its face a - glow - ing, a rare de - light.
Bring Your Passport

Rafael Aparicio performing on the Venezuelan harp

**Listen** to this example of a *joropo* [hoh-ROH-poh], a lively dance-song, from the same Llanera plains region as "*Bogando a la luz del sol.*" Both songs feature the Venezuelan harp.

CD 13–12

Carnaval Llanero

**Traditional Joropo from Venezuela as performed by Rafael Angel Aparicio y los Hermanos Aparicios**

The ancestor of the Venezuelan harp was the Spanish harp, an instrument similar to the older Arabic harp. North African Arabic culture was an important influence in Spain, beginning in the Middle Ages.

Unit 8 307

# 2 Develop

### Singing

1c Invite students to sing along with the Pronunciation Practice for "*Bogando a la luz del sol*" **CD 13-10**. See Resource Book p. A-33. Have students sing the song with the recording in Spanish **CD 13-7** and then in English **CD 13-8**.

1d Teach the countermelody on p. 307 to students phrase by phrase. Then divide the class into two groups. Have one group sing the melody of "*Bogando a la luz del sol*" while the other group sings the countermelody.

9b ASK **How does the texture of the song change when we perform the two parts together?** (The addition of the countermelody creates a thicker texture and harmony.)

### Listening

Select a student to read aloud the information about *joropo* and the Venezuelan harp on p. 307. Play the recording of "*Carnaval Llanero*" **CD 13-12**.

6b ASK **How many different instruments do you hear in this piece?** (four: harp, *cuatro* [a small four-string guitar], bass, maracas)

**Is the texture thick or thin?** (moderately thick)

# 3 Close

**Skill: SINGING** — **ASSESSMENT**

**Performance/Observation** Have students sing the melody and countermelody of "*Bogando a la luz del sol*" in two groups as you play the chords on keyboard or guitar. Monitor to determine whether students are successful at singing the two parts together accurately and with good balance between the parts.

## Across the Curriculum

▶ **Social Studies** Venezuela is a country that is located in the northern part of South America. It is home to many bodies of water. To the north, Venezuela borders on the Caribbean Sea and the Atlantic Ocean. This coastline provides many beautiful, white sandy beaches, which are very popular tourist spots. Venezuela is also home to the largest lake in South America, Lake Maracaibo. Probably the most spectacular sight in all of Venezuela, however, is Angel Falls. Angel Falls is the highest waterfall in the world, with a drop of 3,212 feet.

## Technology/Media Link

▶ **Web Site** Invite students to visit *www.sfsuccessnet.com* to learn more about folk instruments from Latin America.

LESSON 6

## LESSON AT A GLANCE

**Element Focus** **EXPRESSION** Dynamics, phrasing, and mood

**Skill Objective** **SINGING** Sing a song with appropriate dynamics, phrasing, and mood

**Connection Activity** **CULTURE** Discuss Japanese *Hana-mi* and folklore

**MATERIALS**

- *"Sakura"* (Japanese) **CD 13-13**
- *"Sakura"* (English) **CD 13-14**

  **Recording Routine:** Intro (4 m.); v. 1; interlude (2 m.); v. 2; coda
- **Pronunciation Practice/Translation** p. 488
- "House of Spring" (poem)
- **Resource Book** pp. A-34, F-21, H-20
- hand drum, recorder

**VOCABULARY**

*koto* ostinato

**◆◆◆◆ National Standards ◆◆◆◆**

**1b** Sing expressively with appropriate interpretation
**1c** Sing from memory songs from diverse cultures
**2b** Perform rhythms and melodies on appropriate instruments
**6b** Describe music by explaining how it sounds

**MORE MUSIC CHOICES**

Another song from Japan:
*"Ōsamu kosamu,"* p. 96

## 1 INTRODUCE

Discuss the *koto* with students and tell them that "*Sakura*" is one of the first songs that children in Japan learn to play on the *koto.* Read the English words of the song, p. 308, aloud. Then share the information about *Hana-mi* from Cultural Connection below.

LESSON 6 Element: EXPRESSION | Skill: SINGING | Connection: CULTURE

# Cherry Blossom Time

In Japan one of the loveliest sights is the cherry blossoms in spring. For more than 1,000 years, the Japanese have been celebrating the cherry blossom ceremony! "*Sakura*" is a song about the beauty of the cherry blossoms.

CD 13-13
MIDI 22

## Sakura

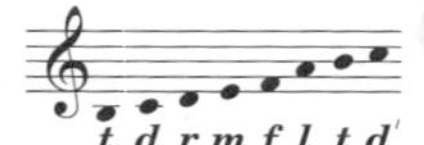
t, d r m f l t d'

*English Words by Lorene Hoyt*

*Folk Song from Japan*
*Modern Arrangement by Henry Burnett*

Sa - ku - ra, Sa - ku - ra, Ya - yo - i no
1. Sa - ku - ra, Sa - ku - ra, Cher - ry blos - soms
2. Sa - ku - ra, Sa - ku - ra, Blos - soms wav - ing

so - ra wa, Mi - wa - ta - su ka - gi - ri,
ev - 'ry - where. Clouds of glo - ry fill the sky,
in the breeze. Yo - shi - no, the cher - ry land,

Ka - su - mi ka ku - mo - ka, Ni - o - i zo i - zu - ru;
Mist of beau - ty in the air, Love - ly col - ors float - ing by,
Tat - su - ta, the ma - ple trees, Ka - ra - sa - ki, pine tree grand,

i - za - ya, i - za - ya Mi ni yu - kan.
Sa - ku - ra, Sa - ku - ra, Let all come sing - ing.
Sa - ku - ra, Sa - ku - ra, Let all come sing - ing.

308

# Footnotes

## ACROSS THE CURRICULUM

▶ **Social Studies** Invite students to locate Japan on a map. What large bodies of water surround Japan? What other countries are near Japan? What are some of the larger cities in Japan? Encourage students to learn more about the history of "*Sakura*" by reading *Japan* by Rebecca Stefoff (Chelsea House, 1998).

## BUILDING SKILLS THROUGH MUSIC

▶ **Writing** Have students read the introductory text on p. 308. Divide the class into small groups. Have them create a *haiku* (a poem with syllabic structure of 5-7-5) that focuses on springtime in their community.

## CULTURAL CONNECTION

▶ ***Hana-mi*** Japanese tradition says that a maiden called The-Princess-Who-Makes-the-Trees-to-Bloom lives high on the slopes of Mount Fuji. Each day in the early spring, children look to see if the princess has come down from her secret palace on the mountain. When at last she comes, she tosses billows of blossoms over the trees, hiding every branch in white and pink clouds of bloom. Since the fifth century, the emperor and his court traveled to a special spot, the Palace of the Young Cherry Trees, in order to view the blossoms. Today, *Hana-mi*, or cherry-blossom viewing, is still a favorite pastime in Japan. From March to May people enjoy the blooms in the parks of large cities and in remote areas where the trees are said to have the loveliest flowers.

### Blossoms in Bloom

**Listen** to the recording of *"Sakura."* The song is accompanied by a Japanese string instrument, the *koto.* **Describe** the dynamics, phrasing, and mood expressed by the performers on the recording. **Sing** *"Sakura"* with expression. **Play** the following ostinato on the drum to accompany *"Sakura."*

**Play** this countermelody for recorder to accompany *"Sakura."*

## House of Spring

*by Muso Soseki*
*Translated by W.S. Merwin and Soiku Shigematsu*

Hundreds of open flowers
all come from
the one branch
Look
all their colors
appear in my garden
I open the clattering gate
and in the wind
I see
the spring sunlight
already it has reached
worlds without number

**MIDI** Play each of the first three *koto* tracks in the MIDI song file for *"Sakura."* Play the patterns on glockenspiel or keyboards.

Bring Your Passport

# 2 Develop

### Listening

Play *"Sakura"* **CD 13-13.** Have students listen carefully to the expression used by the singers.

6b **ASK How would you describe the performance of the singers?** (soft, delicate tone, slow tempo)

### Singing

1c Invite students to listen to the Pronunciation Practice for *"Sakura"* **CD 13-16.** Refer to Resource Book p. A-34 for a Pronunciation Practice Guide. Then have them sing the song in Japanese with the Stereo Performance Track **CD 13-15.** Encourage students to sing the song expressively and with dynamics. Write the symbols and terms for *crescendo* (<) and *decrescendo* (>) on
1b the board and discuss their meanings. Have students interpret these dynamics by placing a slight *crescendo* on the word *sakura* during each statement. Have them place a slight *decrescendo* at the end of each phrase to achieve proper phrasing.

### Playing

2b Direct students' attention to the drum ostinato and recorder accompaniment on p. 309. Have students take turns playing these parts while the rest of the class sings *"Sakura"* **CD 13-13.**

Have students learn the mallet accompaniment for *"Sakura"* on Resource Book p. F-21. Then have some students perform expressive readings of the poem "House of Spring" as the rest of the class plays the accompaniment.

# 3 Close

**Skill: SINGING** — **ASSESSMENT**

**Performance/Observation** Invite students to perform *"Sakura"* **CD 13-13** with the drum ostinato and recorder part. Observe the group in its ability to sing and play with appropriate dynamics, phrasing, and mood.

## Skills Reinforcement

▶ **Mallets** For a mallet accompaniment to "*Sakura,*" refer to Resource Book p. F-21.

▶ **Keyboard** Invite students to play the keyboard accompaniment in the Resource Book p. H–20.

**Reinforcement** To make the transition between A minor and D minor in the left hand, have students use fingers 5 and 2 for A minor, and 3 and 1 for D minor while using minimum hand movement. Teach the right hand part similarly with fingers 1 and 4.

**On Target** Once comfortable with the hands separately, have students practice both hands together, slowly at first.

**Challenge** Select students who perform successfully to accompany the class during the singing of "*Sakura.*"

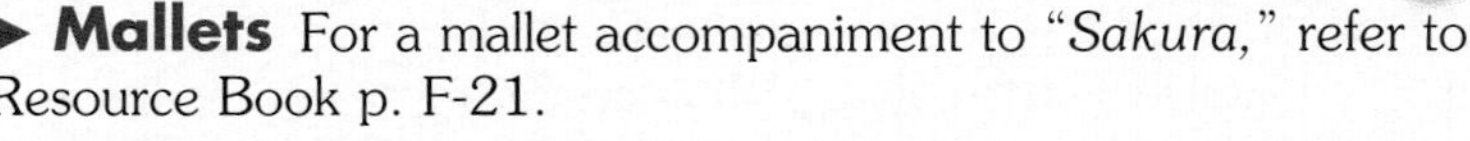

## Technology/Media Link

**MIDI/Sequencing Software** Help students find A, B, C, E, and F on a MIDI keyboard. Have them isolate the *koto* tracks from the MIDI song file *"Sakura"* and play them back. Then encourage students to improvise along with the song on the keyboard, using the notes A, B, C, E, and F while the song is played.

LESSON 7

## LESSON AT A GLANCE

**Element Focus** **TIMBRE** Instruments of India

**Skill Objective** **LISTENING** Recognize the sound of the *sitar* and *tabla*

**Connection Activity** **SOCIAL STUDIES** Discuss India and two famous Indian musicians

**MATERIALS**

- *"Shri Ram, jai Ram"* **CD 13-17**

  **Recording Routine:** Intro (improvisation and 2 m.); vocal; coda
- *Charukeshi* (excerpt) **CD 13-19**
- bass metallophone or xylophone
- map of India

**VOCABULARY**

improvisation *sitar* drone

◆ ◆ ◆ ◆ **National Standards** ◆ ◆ ◆ ◆

**1c** Sing songs from diverse cultures
**2a** Play instruments maintaining a steady tempo
**6b** Describe music by explaining how it sounds

**MORE MUSIC CHOICES**

Other songs in call-and-response style:
"All Night, All Day," p. 180
*"Hashewie,"* p. 63

## 1 INTRODUCE

Show students India on a map and share the information from Across the Curriculum below. Tell students that *"Shri Ram, jai Ram"* is from India.

6b Ask students to follow the notation on p. 311 as they listen to *"Shri Ram, jai Ram"* **CD 13-17.** After listening, have them identify instruments that sound similar to the ones in the recording.

LESSON 7 Element: TIMBRE Skill: LISTENING Connection: SOCIAL STUDIES

# Travel to India

India is a large country with many different geographical regions. India has jungles, forests, large rivers, lakes, oceans, grasslands, and part of the highest mountain range in the world—the Himalayas!

**Listen** to the Hindu chant *"Shri Ram, jai Ram."* The instrument you hear is called the *sitar.* This Indian instrument has a long neck and metal strings.

*"Shri Ram, jai Ram"* is sung by a leader and a group. When you think you know the melody, **sing** along with the group.

To hear another example of the *sitar,* turn to the Sound Bank on page 470.

MUSIC MAKERS

### Anoushka Shankar

**Anoushka Shankar** (born 1981) is one of the world's recognized master sitar players. Like her father, Ravi, she is a master of improvisation and an excellent performer. She studied with her father and made her professional debut at age thirteen.

310

## Footnotes

### CULTURAL CONNECTION

▶ **Indian Ragas** In the classical music of India, melodies are based on *ragas. Raga* literally means "that which colors the mind." A *raga,* somewhat like a scale, is a series of tones and ornaments on which a musical composition is based. There are hundreds of *ragas.* Each one has a particular name, structure, and connection with an emotional state, time of day, season, or other factor beyond the musical.

### BUILDING SKILLS THROUGH MUSIC

▶ **Language** Have students read the introductory information on p. 310 and then make an outline of the information. With partners, have students ask each other questions from their outlines.

### ACROSS THE CURRICULUM

▶ **Social Studies** Have students locate India on a map and identify features of the country. One important feature is the Ganges River, which is considered holy in the Hindu religion. Help students find the Ganges on the map.

Invite students to learn more about the history of India by reading *India* by John Caldwell (Chelsea House, 1998). *Count Your Way Through India* by Jim Haskins (Carolrhoda, 1990) uses the numbers one to ten in Hindi to introduce the land, people, and culture of India.

**Listen** to *Charukeshi* and **identify** the sound of the *sitar* and the *tabla* drums. **Describe** their timbre.

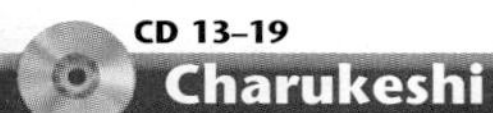

CD 13-19
**Charukeshi**

**Raga from India**
**as performed by Anoushka Shankar**

A *raga* is a special series of notes and patterns. Hundreds of different *ragas* are used in classical Indian music.

Visit **Take It to the Net** at *www.sfsuccessnet.com* to learn more about Ravi and Anoushka Shankar.

Bring Your Passport

Unit 8 311

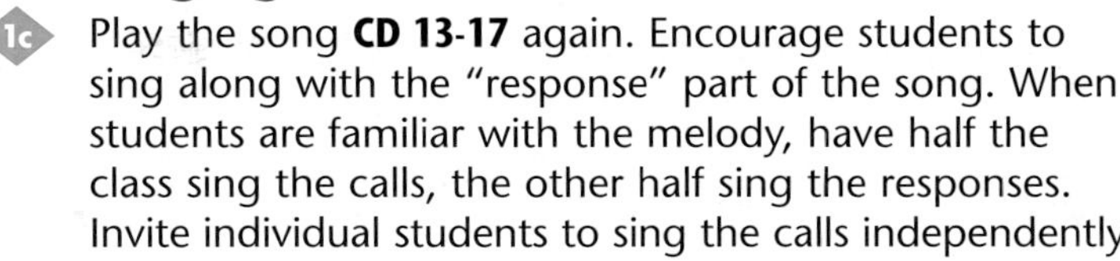

# 2 Develop

## Singing

1c Play the song **CD 13-17** again. Encourage students to sing along with the "response" part of the song. When students are familiar with the melody, have half the class sing the calls, the other half sing the responses. Invite individual students to sing the calls independently.

## Playing

2a Choose a student to continuously play G, D, D, and high G quarter notes on a bass metallophone or a bass xylophone as an accompaniment for "*Shri Ram, jai Ram.*" This continuous unchanging sound is called a *drone,* which is a characteristic of Indian music.

## Listening

Have students read the Music Makers feature on Anoushka Shankar. Invite students to listen to her performance of *Charukeshi* **CD 13-19.**

ASK **What is the instrument being played in the beginning?** *(sitar)*

**At a later time, you hear other instruments playing. What are they?** (*tabla,* a type of drum)

6b Explain that the drumming sounds they hear are *tabla.* Have students describe the sound of *tabla* and how this timbre compares to that of other drums they have heard.

# 3 Close

**Skill: LISTENING** ASSESSMENT

**Music Journal Writing** Have students listen to *Charukeshi* **CD 13-19.** As they listen, have them write descriptions for the tone quality of the *sitar* and *tabla.* Then encourage them to write one sentence descriptions about the tempo, rhythm, form, melody, and texture of the piece. Assess each student's ability to correctly identify and describe the timbre of the instruments.

## Spotlight On

▶ **The Performers** Ravi Shankar (b. 1920) has played Indian classical music on the *sitar* since he was very young. Shankar gave his first concert at age 19 and soon reached stardom in India. He was the first person to bring Indian classical music to the rest of the world. Shankar's daughter, Anoushka (b. 1981), is also a world-renowned musician. She began playing the *sitar* at age nine, and studied with her father for nine years. Today, she tours around the world with her father playing concerts for everyone from the queen of England to local church groups. Together, Ravi and Anoushka Shankar open doors all over the world to classical Indian music.

## Character Education

▶ **Respect** To encourage students to adopt respectful behavior, discuss their reactions when they hear or see something different. What do you do when you see someone who is different from you? What do you do when you hear music that is different from what you usually listen to? Are these respectful behaviors? If not, how could you modify your behavior to make it more respectful? Create a list of behaviors that would show a willingness to treat all people, ideas, and music with dignity and acceptance. (saying thoughtful things, being polite, listening without judging, and so on)

## Technology/Media Link

**Web Site** To learn more about Ravi and Anoushka Shankar, have students visit *www.sfsuccessnet.com.*

## LESSON AT A GLANCE

**Element Focus** **TIMBRE** Instruments of China

**Skill Objective** **LISTENING** Listen to and describe instruments of China

**Connection Activity** **CULTURE** Explore Chinese culture through its music and art

**MATERIALS**

- *"Feng yang hua gu"* **CD 13-20**
- *"Feng Yang* Song" **CD 13-21**
  **Recording Routine:** Intro (4 m.); v. 1; interlude (4 m.); v. 2; coda
- *"Xiao"* **CD 13-24**
- "Bamboo Flute" **CD 13-25**
  **Recording Routine:** Intro (8 m.); vocal; interlude (8 m.); vocal; coda
- **Pronunciation Practice/Translation** pp. 489–490
- *Birds in the Forest* (excerpt) **CD 13-28**
- **Resource Book** pp. A-35, A-36, F-22
- recorders, pitched and nonpitched percussion, bells

**VOCABULARY**

*erhu* *pipa* *sheng* *xiao*

### ◆◆◆◆ National Standards ◆◆◆◆

**1c** Sing songs from diverse cultures
**2f** Play instruments independently against contrasting parts
**3d** Improvise instrumental pieces using traditional sounds
**4b** Compose instrumental pieces within specific guidelines
**5a** Read rhythms in $\frac{2}{4}$ meter
**6b** Describe music by explaining how it sounds
**9b** Describe how dynamics and texture are used in pieces from various cultures
**9c** Identify uses of music in everyday life

**MORE MUSIC CHOICES**

Other examples of Chinese instrumental timbre:
*Bumper Harvest Celebration,* p. 337
*Wu long,* p. 157

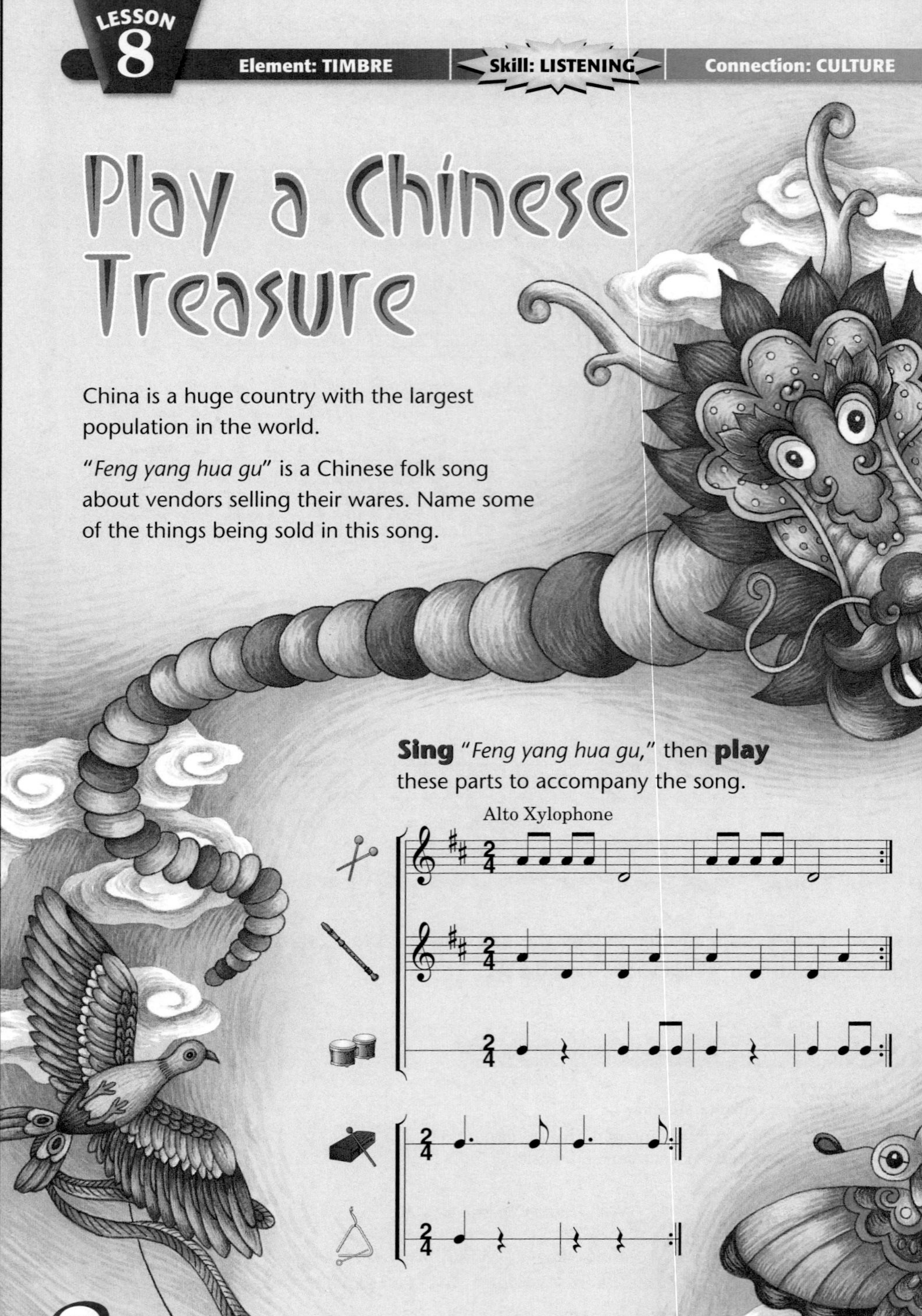

LESSON 8
Element: TIMBRE
Skill: LISTENING
Connection: CULTURE
Play a Chinese Treasure
China is a huge country with the largest population in the world.
*"Feng yang hua gu"* is a Chinese folk song about vendors selling their wares. Name some of the things being sold in this song.
**Sing** *"Feng yang hua gu,"* then **play** these parts to accompany the song.
Alto Xylophone
312

# Footnotes

## MEETING INDIVIDUAL NEEDS

▶ **Coordination** Students with coordination difficulties may find it difficult to play an instrument that moves or is suspended (such as a triangle). Provide substitute instruments for these students, including instruments that can be fixed in place (such as a drum).

## BUILDING SKILLS THROUGH MUSIC

▶ **Math** After students count the number of measures in *"Feng yang hua gu,"* have them determine how many times the woodblock accompaniment patterns on p. 312 should be played for one verse of the song. (15) Is this a division or multiplication problem? (division) Invite students to check the answer as you perform.

## SPOTLIGHT ON

9c ▶ ***Feng Yang* Songs** Long ago, the first Ming emperor of China liberated many Chinese provinces from Mongolian rule. Feng Yang is a farming area in Anhui, one of those liberated provinces. From time to time, famine struck the farmers and they wandered over the countryside, begging and singing their native songs to attract attention. Over time, *Feng Yang* songs were adopted by Chinese street vendors who were advertising wares for sale. The songs are usually sung by a man and a woman who are carrying a musical instrument as well as their wares. This version of a *Feng Yang* song is only one of many. The English lyrics reveal how folk songs can change as they travel from one place to another. Street vendor songs are a part of many diverse cultures. Invite students to perform and compare *"Feng yang hua gu"* and "Chairs to Mend," a street call from England, on p. 149.

# 1 INTRODUCE

Invite students to share what they know about China. Guide their discussion through arts, music, food, clothing, and culture. Then share information about Chinese culture and related arts from Across the Curriculum (below), Cultural Connection (p. 315), and Spotlight On (p. 312).

# 2 DEVELOP

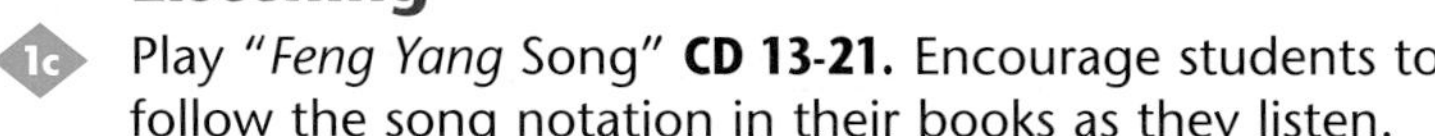

### Listening

1c Play "*Feng Yang* Song" **CD 13-21.** Encourage students to follow the song notation in their books as they listen.

ASK **What are the vendors selling?** (kites, trinkets, toys, gold paper, and bamboo)

**Why are the instruments played?** (to call attention to the vendors and their wares)

Play the song again and invite students to sing along.

### Reading

5a Direct students' attention to the first eight measures of *"Feng yang hua gu."* Invite students to clap the rhythm while saying the rhythm syllables.

**SAY** Name any measures you were unable to perform well as a class. (Accept various appropriate answers.)

If necessary, reinforce any rhythms students missed by repeating the activity or isolating specific measures.

### Singing

Invite students to listen and sing with the Pronunciation Practice for *"Feng yang hua gu"* **CD 13-23.** As they listen, have them follow the Pronunciation Practice Guide on Resource Book p. A-35. Repeat the activity to help students learn the Mandarin words.

### Playing

2f Have students learn the recorder and percussion parts on p. 312 to accompany *"Feng yang hua gu"* **CD 13-20.**

**continued on page 314**

## SKILLS REINFORCEMENT

▶ **Recorder** In addition to the recorder part on p. 312, students can play other patterns using high D, A, and low D to accompany *"Feng yang hua gu."* Remember that patterns with leaps from A down to D may be difficult for some students. First, have students finger the note low D and then lift their bottom four fingers slightly above the holes, so they are in position for A but ready to play D. Now have them play one of the patterns printed here.

2f

## ACROSS THE CURRICULUM

▶ **Language Arts** Read aloud the book *Bamboo Valley: A Story of a Chinese Bamboo Forest* by Ann Whitehead Nagda (Soundprints, 1997). Use pictures from the book to show students how bamboo grows.

▶ **Science** Obtain some bamboo shoots from your local nursery. Invite students to plant these shoots and watch them grow. They can even use larger pieces of bamboo to make musical instruments.

Have students

- Tap and read the rhythm of each part.
- Move in rhythm as though they were playing the part.
- Transfer the rhythm and movement to the appropriate instrument.

### Singing

Invite students to listen to the recording of *"Xiao"* (folk song and lullaby) **CD 13-24.** Then invite students to sing along with the Pronunciation Practice for *"Xiao"* **CD 13-27.** Refer to Resource Book p. A-36 for a Pronunciation Practice Guide. Then sing the entire song together.

### Creating

4b Using the rhythms in *"Xiao"* and the accompaniment on p. 312 for ideas, invite students to create rhythm ostinatos to perform on nonpitched percussion as they sing *"Xiao"* **CD 13-24.** Remind students to create ostinatos that maintain the style of the song and the timbre of Chinese instruments.

### Listening

Have students read the information on p. 315 about the group Music from China. Invite students to listen to an example of the *erhu* as featured in the Sound Bank, p. 466. Encourage students to use standard terminology in describing and explaining the structure and sound of this musical instrument. Then play the recording of *Birds in the Forest* **CD 13-28.**

6b **ASK How would you describe the timbre of this music?** (Accept various answers.)

9b Encourage students to discuss the instruments, tempo, dynamics, and texture of the music.

Chinese Timbres
"Xiao" is another Chinese folk melody. What is this song about?
Listen to "Xiao" and then describe the timbre of the featured instruments.
CD 13-24
MIDI 23
Xiao (Bamboo Flute)
d r m s l d'
Folk Song from China
Yi geng zi zhu zhi miao miao;
From the pur - ple, straight bam - boo;
Sung yu bao bao zuo guan xiao.
I have made a flute for you.
Xiao er dui zheng kou Kou er dui zheng xiao;
Take the bam - boo flute, Put it to your lips,
Xiao zhong chui chu shi xin diao;
Play a new and lilt - ing song.
Xiao bao bao Yi di yi di xue hui liao,
My lit - tle one, Play a new and lilt - ing song,
Xiao bao bao Yi di yi di xue hui liao.
My lit - tle one, Play a new and lilt - ing song.
314


# Footnotes

## Skills Reinforcement

▶ **Keyboard** Have students improvise a four-bar introduction to *"Xiao"* using the pitches of the pentatonic scale and an ostinato bass accompaniment.

3d Pentatonic Scale: Ostinato Bass:

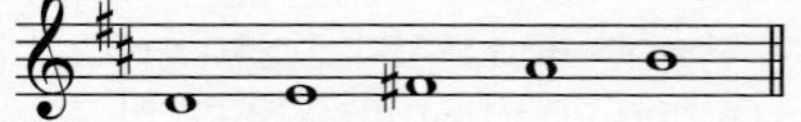

▶ **Mallets** For a mallet accompaniment to *"Feng yang hua gu,"* refer to Resource Book p. F-22.

## Spotlight On

▶ **Brush Painting** Chinese brush painting is closely related to calligraphy and the writing of Chinese characters. The materials are essentially the same for both writing and painting: brush, ink, and paper or silk. The brush that is used is similar to a watercolor brush, but it has a tapered tip that allows the painter to create a variety of shadings. Ink has been used in Chinese calligraphy and painting for over 2000 years. It can be mixed thin or thick in order to achieve various effects. Invite students to make their own brush paintings.

▲ Since 1984, Music from China has been sharing both old and new music with American audiences. The performers in the group play instruments invented hundreds to thousands of years ago.

ipa ▶

▼ *Erhu*

*Sheng* ▶

**Listen** to this musical picture of a bird.

CD 13–28
**Birds in the Forest**

**by Yi Jianquan**
**as performed by Music from China**

This selection features traditional Chinese instruments. The sound of the bird is played on the *gao-hu,* a relative of the *erhu.*

**Video Library** See the video *From Mao to Mozart* for more information on Chinese music.





# 3 Close

**Skill: LISTENING** ASSESSMENT

**Music Journal Writing** Have students listen to *"Xiao"* **CD 13-24** and *Birds in the Forest* **CD 13-28.** As students listen, have them write in their journals the names of Chinese instruments that they hear and describe the timbre of each instrument. Assess each student's ability to use appropriate terminology in writing the responses.

## Cultural Connection

▶ **China** China is the most populous country on earth, with approximately one-fifth of the world's population. Within the boundaries of China, there are hundreds of different groups, many with their own languages, cultures, and distinct musical traditions. The Han is the largest of these groups and the one we traditionally recall when Chinese music is mentioned. Other groups, such as the Hsin, are also quite influential. The dominant musical traditions of China include folk music, art music, popular music, and music for religious rituals.

## Technology/Media Link

**Web Site** Have students visit *www.sfsuccessnet.com* to learn more about instruments from around the world.

LESSON 9

## LESSON AT A GLANCE

**Element Focus** **RHYTHM** Steady beat

**Skill Objective** **MOVING** Maintain a steady beat while performing a dance from Israel

**Connection Activity** **CULTURE** Explore Israeli culture through its music

**MATERIALS**

- *"Yibane amenu"* (Hebrew) **CD 13-29**
- *"Yibane amenu"* (English) **CD 13-30**

  **Recording Routine:** Intro (4 m.); vocal; interlude (4 m.); vocal in canon; coda
- **Pronunciation Practice/Translation** p. 490
- *Ve' David y'fey enayiam* **CD 13-33**
- **Dance Directions** for *Ve' David y'fey enayiam* p. 516
- **Resource Book** pp. A-37, F-23
- recorder, xylophone, drum

**VOCABULARY**

repeat signs round

**National Standards**

**1d** Sing rounds
**2f** Play instruments independently against contrasting parts
**6e** While listening to music, move to show a prominent feature of the music

**MORE MUSIC CHOICES**

Other songs that may be performed as rounds:
"Ah, Poor Bird," p. 196
"Let Music Surround You," p. 236

# 1 INTRODUCE

Share with students the information about music from Israel. Refer to Cultural Connection below. Play *"Yibane amenu"* **CD 13-29** and invite students to listen and sing when they are ready.

LESSON 9 | Element: RHYTHM | Skill: MOVING | Connection: CULTURE

## Israeli Song and Dance

Israel has become one of the most prosperous and modern countries in the Middle East.

*"Yibane amenu"* is an Israeli song sung as a round. **Sing** the song and follow the **repeat signs**.

The **repeat signs** ‖: and :‖ tell the performer to perfo[rm] all the music between the signs twice.

CD 13-29
Yibane amenu
l, t, d m f s l
Round from Israel
I
Dm
Yi - ba - ne a - me - nu b - 'ar - tse - nu;
In our land we shall re - build our na - tion.
II
B - 'ar - tse - nu, yi - ba - ne,
Build our na - tion in our land,
III
1.
2.
Yi - ba - ne, Yi - ba - ne. Yi - ba - ne.
In our land, In our land. In our land.
316

# Footnotes

## MEETING INDIVIDUAL NEEDS

▶ **Ostinato Hints** If students have difficulty remembering notes when creating their own ostinatos, you may wish to have them color code each note. Assign a color to each note students are to use in the ostinato. For example, B is always blue, and G is always green, and so on. It might also be helpful to invite some students to work in pairs to accomplish the tasks of creating and performing.

## BUILDING SKILLS THROUGH MUSIC

▶ **Dance/Language** After learning and performing the dance to *Ve' David y'fey enayiam,* have students write the dance instructions in their own words. Exchange papers with a partner and try out each other's instructions.

## CULTURAL CONNECTION

▶ **Israel** Zionism, the movement to re-establish a Jewish homeland, brought Jewish people from many parts of the world back to the land of Palestine on the eastern shore of the Mediterranean. This area became the country of Israel. Jewish people from many parts of the world joined in a reaffirmation of their shared cultural roots.

With the formation of Israel (1945), music and dance became one of the means by which people from different homelands could share their joy of reunion. The songs were set in Middle Eastern modes, flavored with regional rhythms, and often accompanied by lutes, tambourines, and drums. "*Yibane amenu*" tells of the rebuilding of the first Jewish homeland and of the establishment of the Israeli nation.

## Accompaniment Parts

Choose a rhythm instrument and **play** this part to accompany "*Yibane amenu.*"

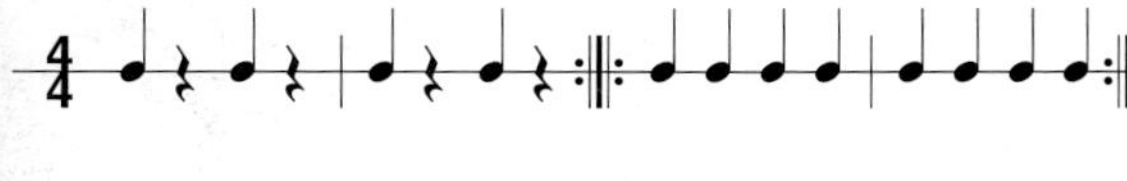

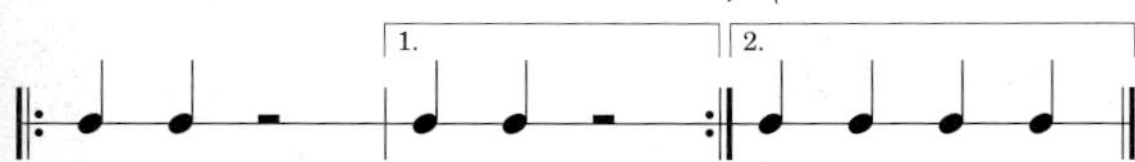

**Create** your own melody ostinato using these notes:

CD 13-33

### Ve' David y'fey enayiam

**by M. Shelem**

*Ve' David y'fey enayiam* is one of the oldest and most popular Israeli dances.

### Move to the Steady Beat

This Israeli dance includes steps that give everyone a chance to dance with a different partner.

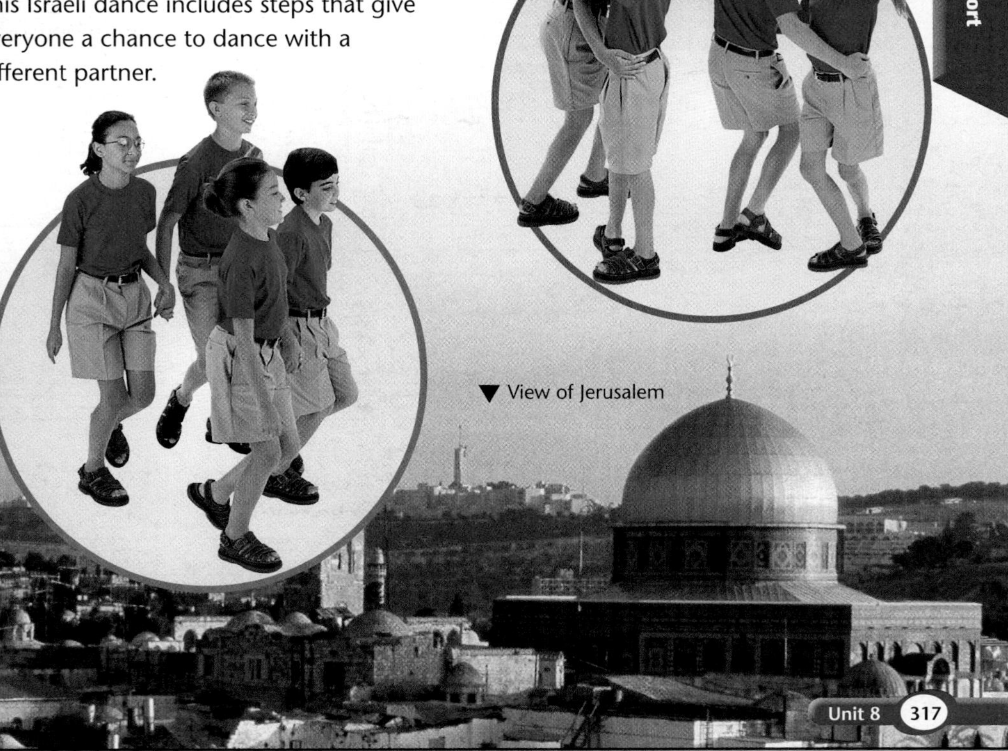

▼ View of Jerusalem

Bring Your Passport



# 2 Develop

### Singing

1d Invite students to learn *"Yibane amenu"* by listening to the Pronunciation Practice **CD 13-32.** Refer to Resource Book p. A-37 for a Pronunciation Practice Guide. When students are confident singing *"Yibane amenu"* in unison, sing it as a two-part round. If students do well with a two-part round, try it in three parts.

### Playing

2f Help students learn to play the percussion parts on p. 317 in their books and maintain a steady beat. Invite volunteers to perform the percussion parts while the class sings.

### Creating

Have students create an ostinato from the pitch set in their books to play with *"Yibane amenu"* **CD 13-29** as they sing the song. Encourage them to use various instruments and to create ostinatos that sound appropriate when played on the instrument.

### Moving

6e Have students first listen to the recording of *Ve' David y'fey enayiam* **CD 13-33.** Then teach them the patterned dance for the recording in their books. Use the Dance Practice Track **CD 13-34** when students are first learning the dance. Then have them perform with the Dance Performance Track **CD 13-33.** Divide the class into small groups to plan performances of *Ve' David y'fey enayiam.* Have each group perform for the rest of the class.

# 3 Close

**Skill: MOVING** — ASSESSMENT

**Performance/Observation** Have students listen to *Ve' David y'fey enayiam* **CD 13-33** and perform the patterned dance. Observe each student's ability to perform the dance and maintain a steady beat.

## Skills Reinforcement

▶ **Recorder** Students can play the recorder part below to accompany the singing of *"Yibane amenu."* A small group of students should play the top note while another small group plays the bottom note. Explain to students that because they are playing two different notes at the same time, their recorders are playing in harmony (drone 5th).

▶ **Mallets** For a mallet and tambourine accompaniment (practice with offbeats) for *"Yibane amenu,"* refer to Resource Book p. F-23.

## Technology/Media Link

**Sequencing Software** Set up a sequencing program to play a click track while recording. Have students set three tracks to channel 10 (GM drum kit). Then record one 12-measure rhythm pattern in $\frac{4}{4}$ time and at the tempo of *"Yibane amenu"* using several drum sounds. Copy the pattern and paste it into another track, starting at measure 5. Paste it into a third track, starting at measure 9. Play the resulting rhythm round as the class sings *"Yibane amenu."*

LESSON 10

## LESSON AT A GLANCE

**Element Focus** **MELODY** Melodic sequences

**Skill Objective** **LISTENING** Listen to and respond through movement to melodic sequences

**Connection Activity** **CULTURE** Discuss arts and culture from the Caribbean Islands

**MATERIALS**

- "Wings of a Dove" **CD 13-35**
  **Recording Routine:** Intro (4 m.); vocal; interlude (20 m.); vocal; coda
- *Mwen boyko samba* **CD 13-37**
- **Resource Book** pp. F-24 through F-26, I-25, J-11
- cowbell, drums, *claves,* maracas, recorders
- map that includes West Indies

**VOCABULARY**

steel drum melodic sequence

**National Standards**

**2b** Perform rhythms on appropriate instruments
**2c** Play instruments expressively on a variety of pieces
**5b** Read notes in treble clef
**6b** Describe music by explaining how it sounds

**MORE MUSIC CHOICES**

Other songs with melodic sequences:
*"Tancovačka,"* p. 230
*"Thula, thula, ngoana,"* p. 227

## 1 INTRODUCE

Tell students that "Wings of a Dove" is a folk song from the West Indies. Help them find the West Indies on a map and share Cultural Connection below. Play "Wings of a Dove" **CD 13-35.** Have students listen to the recording and describe some of the characteristics of the song. (very rhythmic, with a strong offbeat)

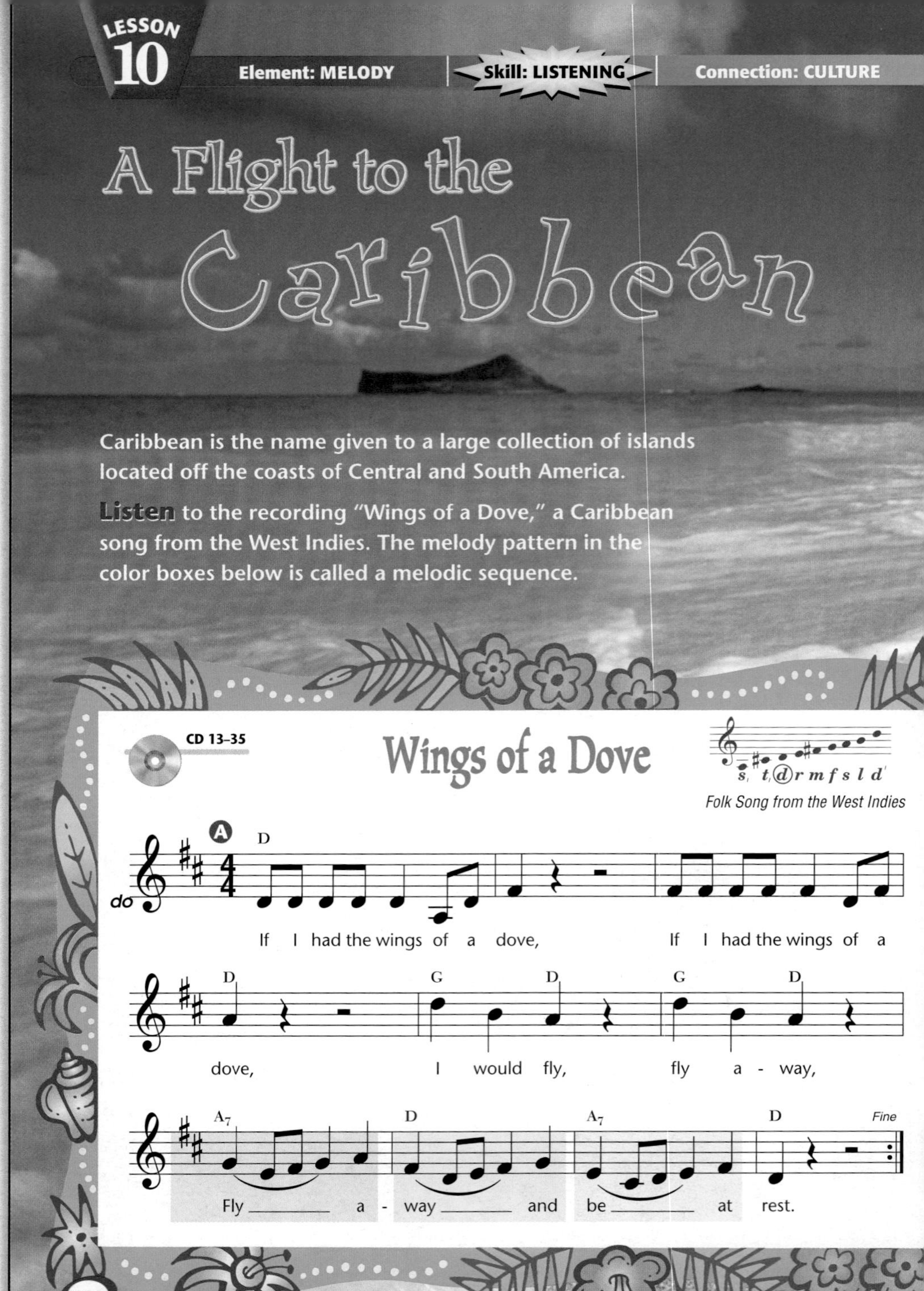

LESSON 10
Element: MELODY
Skill: LISTENING
Connection: CULTURE
A Flight to the Caribbean
Caribbean is the name given to a large collection of islands located off the coasts of Central and South America.
Listen to the recording "Wings of a Dove," a Caribbean song from the West Indies. The melody pattern in the color boxes below is called a melodic sequence.
CD 13-35
Wings of a Dove
Folk Song from the West Indies
s, t, d r m f s l d'
A
do
If I had the wings of a dove, If I had the wings of a dove,
I would fly, fly a - way,
Fly a - way and be at rest.
Fine
318


Footnotes

## ACROSS THE CURRICULUM

▶ **Social Studies/Language Arts** Divide students into small groups. Give each group a tale from the book *A Ring of Tricksters: Animal Tales from America, the West Indies, and Africa* by Virginia Hamilton (Scholastic, 1997). Invite each group to create a dramatic interpretation of the tale and perform it for the class. Have students each write their own "trickster" tale. Have them illustrate their tales, and create a class book.

## BUILDING SKILLS THROUGH MUSIC

▶ **Social Studies** Share the information on the West Indies from Cultural Connection. Have students research and identify the islands and the countries that colonized them.

## CULTURAL CONNECTION

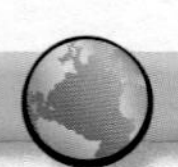

▶ **The West Indies** The West Indies, with about 34 million people, is a large group of islands that stretch from south Florida to the coast of Venezuela. Historically, some of the islands were colonized by the French, others by the Spanish, still others by the Dutch or the English. Yet all of the islands have strong common influences.

The strongest influence is West African culture, brought by slaves in the eighteenth and nineteenth centuries. In music, the West African flavor is created by adding syncopated percussion accompaniments to European-sounding melodies. "Wings of a Dove" has a melody that is very European. The song takes on the flavor of the West Indies when African rhythms and instruments are added.

B
G D A7
Since I have no wings, Since I have no wings, Since I have no wings, how can I
D G D
fly? ________ Since I have no wings, Since I have no wings,
E7 A7 D.C. al Fine
Since I have no wings, I'm gon - na sing, sing, sing, sing.
Bring Your Passport

**Play the Caribbean Way**

**Play** the part below on cowbell, drum, claves, or maracas.

**Listen** to this music from the Caribbean country of Dominica.

CD 13-37

**Mwen boyko samba**

**Traditional *Samba* from Dominica**

**This selection is played on steel drums. Like Trinidad and other Caribbean countries, Dominica has a strong tradition of steel drumming.**

Unit 8 319

## 2 Develop

### Singing

5b Have students listen to "Wings of a Dove" **CD 13-35** again, following the notation on p. 318. Encourage them to follow the contour of the melody with their fingers. Play the recording again and have students sing the song with the recording, following the notation and paying particular attention to the three melodic patterns shown in the color boxes.

ASK **How are the color-box patterns alike and how are they different?** (Help students discover that the three patterns have the same contour, or shape, but that each pattern starts at a different pitch level.)

### Playing

2b 2c Help students learn to play the percussion part in their books. Invite volunteers to accompany the song while the class sings.

### Listening

6b Play *Mwen boyko samba* **CD 13-37.** Ask students how they can recognize that this song is from the West Indies. (steel drums, shakers, strong beat and complex rhythms)

## 3 Close

**Skill: LISTENING** ASSESSMENT

**Performance/Observation** Play the recording of "Wings of a Dove" **CD 13-35** for students. Have them clap or tap the rhythm of the melodic sequences when they are heard in the recording. Observe each student's understanding of melodic sequence as they clap or tap at the appropriate time in the music.

To check for understanding of materials presented in this unit, have students complete Activity Master 9 on Resource Book p. J-11.

### Skills Reinforcement

▶ **Mallets** For a mallet and nonpitched percussion accompaniment for "Wings of a Dove," refer to p. F-24 through F-26 in the Resource Book.

▶ **Recorder** For a recorder countermelody to "Wings of a Dove," refer to p. I-25 in the Resource Book.

### Technology/Media Link

**Web Site** For more information on Caribbean music and musicians, invite students to visit *www.sfsuccessnet.com.*

LESSON 11

## LESSON AT A GLANCE

**Element Focus** **FORM** ABA form

**Skill Objective** **CREATING** Create a speech piece in ABA form

**Connection Activity** **STYLE** Discuss the characteristics of reggae style

**MATERIALS**

- "Three Little Birds" **CD 14-1**
- **Recording Routine:** Intro (4 m.); vocal; interlude (4 m.); vocal; coda

**VOCABULARY**

reggae ABA form

**National Standards**

**1c** Sing from memory songs from diverse cultures
**2f** Play instruments independently against contrasting parts
**4c** Compose music using a variety of sound sources

**MORE MUSIC CHOICES**

For more examples of ABA form:

"Dry Bones Come Skipping," p. 218
"Walk in Jerusalem," p. 100

# 1 INTRODUCE

Have students read the introductory information on p. 320. Play the recording of "Three Little Birds" **CD 14-1** and invite students to tap or clap along with the steady beat. Have the class discuss the meaning of words.

LESSON 11 | Element: FORM | Skill: CREATING | Connection: STYLE

# Reggae Is All Right

Let's continue our tour of the Caribbean with a visit to the island of Jamaica. **Sing** "Three Little Birds," by the Jamaican musician Bob Marley. Using the letters **A** and **B**, **describe** the form of the song. How does the form compare to that of "Wings of a Dove" in the previous lesson?

"Three Little Birds" is an example of reggae [REH-gay] music — a style that combines the sound of American pop music with African-based Jamaican instruments and rhythm patterns. Reggae often uses short ostinatos played on keyboard, electric guitar, bass, and drums.

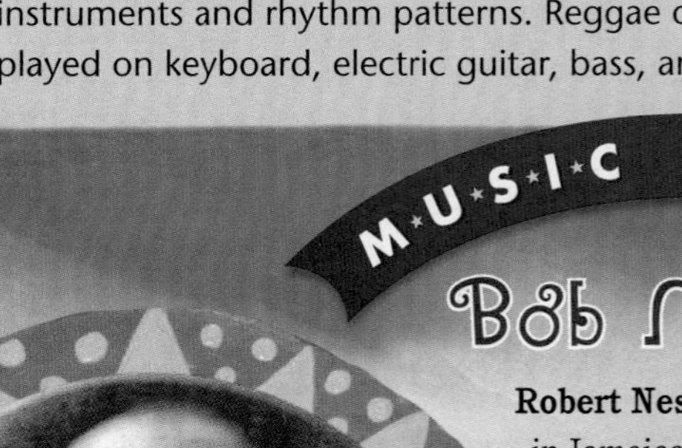

## MUSIC MAKERS
## Bob Marley

**Robert Nesta (Bob) Marley** (1945–1981) was born in Jamaica. He grew up playing music and made his first recording at age 16. Soon after, Marley and several of his musician friends formed a band called the Wailers. It was this group that made reggae music known all over the world.

Much of Bob Marley's music is about social issues, such as unity and peace. In 1978 he was awarded the Peace Medal of the Third World from the United Nations.

320

# Footnotes

## ACROSS THE CURRICULUM

▶ **Social Studies** Using a map of the world, have students find the islands where calypso and reggae are from (Trinidad and Jamaica). Using the distance key, have them measure the approximate distance from their home to a city in Trinidad or Jamaica. Have them name major cities and discuss what they think the climate is like there.

## BUILDING SKILLS THROUGH MUSIC

▶ **Health** Discuss with students the message in the song "Three Little Birds" and the importance of reducing worry in their lives. Have them brainstorm ways to help them not to worry. (talk with a friend, smile, think happy thoughts, and so on)

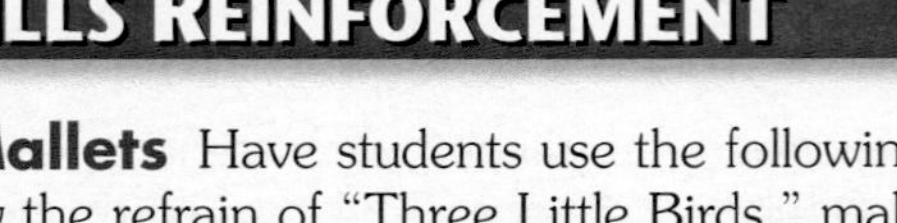

## SKILLS REINFORCEMENT

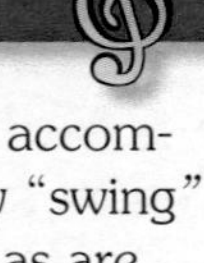

▶ **Mallets** Have students use the following ostinato to accompany the refrain of "Three Little Birds," making sure they "swing" the eighth notes. Utilize as many bass mallet instruments as are available.

2f

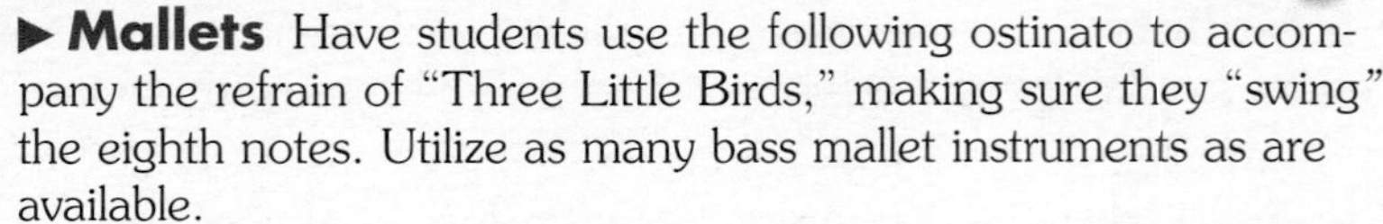

CD 14-1
Three Little Birds
d r m f s l ta d'
Words and Music by Bob Marley
REFRAIN A
Don't wor - ry a - bout a thing,
'cause ev-'ry lit-tle thing gon-na be all right.
Sing-in' don't wor - ry a-bout a thing,
'cause ev-'ry lit-tle thing gon-na be all right.
Fine
VERSE B
Rise up this morn-ing, smile with the ris - ing sun.
Three lit - tle birds sit by my door-step,
Sing-in' sweet songs of mel-o-dies pure and true,
Sing-in': "This is my mes-sage to you - hoo-hoo." Sing-in' don't
D. S. al Fine
Bring Your Passport
Unit 8 321

# 2 Develop

## Analyzing

Play the recording again and ask students to identify the form. (ABA) Have them raise their hands when the B section begins and when the A section returns.

Play an excerpt of the recording and ask students to listen for the rests in the melody. Tell students that the pattern of rests is part of the reggae style.

1c Have the class learn to sing the song along with the recording **CD 14-1**.

To compare a similar form in songs from diverse styles, have students also sing "Cement Mixer" (p. 102).

## Creating

4c On a piece of paper, have students list three things they don't have to worry about. Then divide the class into small groups. Have one student from each group select a nonpitched percussion instrument and play a steady beat in a simple meter. Ask the other members of the group to create a speech piece in ABA form, using their lists and incorporating basic rhythmic patterns.

Ask students to think about tempo, dynamics, and layering their voices for their speech piece.

## Moving

Invite students to create body percussion rhythms to accompany their speech pieces.

Challenge students to use body percussion to accompany "Three Little Birds."

# 3 Close

**Element: FORM** ASSESSMENT

**Performance/Observation** As each group takes a turn performing its newly-created speech piece, have the remainder of the class identify ABA form presented aurally by raising their hands at the beginning of each A and B section.

## Cultural Connection

▶ **Jamaican Folklore** The Swallow-Tail Hummingbird, also known as the Doctor Bird, holds a prominent place in Jamaican folklore stories and songs. This species, which resides only in Jamaica, stands out as one of the most unusual of the 320 species of hummingbirds. It is characterized by iridescent colors and long tail feathers. Invite students to read *Doctor Bird: Three Lookin' up Tales from Jamaica* by Gerald Hausman (Penguin Putnam Books, 1998) for an example of its appearance in Jamaican folklore.

## Technology/Media Link

▶ **Web Site** Students can visit *www.sfsuccessnet.com* to learn more about reggae music.

▶ **MIDI/Sequencing Software** Use sequencing software to add a percussion section to students' speech pieces. Have students work in the same small groups and take turns adding a layer of percussion rhythm.

| Lesson | Elements | Skills | |
|---|---|---|---|
| LESSON 1 **Sing for Freedom** pp. 326-327  | **Element: Rhythm**<br>**Concept:** Pattern<br>**Focus:** Rhythm patterns<br><br>**Secondary Element**<br>Timbre: vocal<br><br>**National Standards**<br>1a 3c 5a 6b 8b | **Skill: Singing**<br>**Objective:** Sing and read rhythm patterns<br><br>**Secondary Skills**<br>• **Reading** Tap and say the rhythm with rhythm syllables and identify note values<br>• **Listening** Identify a performing group and tell what a song is about | **SKILLS REINFORCEMENT**<br>• **Singing** Add harmony to the melody of a song<br>• **Creating** Create new verses for a song<br>• **Signing** Sign a song |
| LESSON 2 **Hope Keeps Dreams Alive** pp. 328-329  | **Element: Rhythm**<br>**Concept:** Meter<br>**Focus:** Meter in 3<br><br>**Secondary Element**<br>Expression: dynamics, tempo<br><br>**National Standards**<br>1b 2b 6a 6b 6e | **Skill: Listening**<br>**Objective:** Listen to identify meter<br><br>**Secondary Skills**<br>• **Singing** Sing a refrain and listen to verses of a song<br>• **Moving** Sing and move in a three-beat pattern | **SKILLS REINFORCEMENT**<br>• **Playing** Play chords on the refrain of a song<br>• **Reading** Identify pitches and sing using pitch syllables |
| LESSON 3 **A Hopeful Refrain** pp. 330-331  | **Element: Form**<br>**Concept:** Form<br>**Focus:** Verse and refrain (AB) form<br><br>**Secondary Element**<br>Rhythm: pattern<br><br>**National Standards**<br>5a 6a 6b 8b | **Skill: Moving**<br>**Objective:** Create contrasting movements to perform during the verse and refrain of a song<br><br>**Secondary Skills**<br>• **Singing** Compare and contrast the verses and refrain of a song<br>• **Reading** Identify identical rhythm patterns in a song | **SKILLS REINFORCEMENT**<br>• **Guitar** Play chords on the refrain of a song<br>• **Recorder** Play the countermelody to a song |

| Connections | Music and Other Literature | |
|---|---|---|
| **Connection:** **Social Studies**<br>**Activity:** Discuss civil rights and freedom<br>SPOTLIGHT ON **Civil Rights and the U.S. Constitution** Information about the Thirteenth and Fourteenth Amendments<br>MEETING INDIVIDUAL NEEDS **Including Everyone** Discuss the importance of civil rights<br>BUILDING SKILLS THROUGH MUSIC **Language** Analyze the lyrics of a song | **Song** "We Shall Overcome"<br>**Listening Selection** *What Kind of Land?* (excerpt)<br>**More Music Choices**<br>"We Shall Not Be Moved," p. 437 | ASSESSMENT<br>**Performance/Observation** Read the rhythm patterns using rhythm syllables in the performance of a song<br>TECHNOLOGY/MEDIA LINK<br>**Web Site** Search for more songs about civil rights |
| **Connection:** **Style**<br>**Activity:** Discuss songs in folk style<br>MOVEMENT **Creative Movement** Create movements to show the verses and refrains of two songs<br>MEETING INDIVIDUAL NEEDS **English Language Learners** Write words from song text with the long i vowel sound<br>CHARACTER EDUCATION **Giving** Emphasize the importance of sharing gifts and talents with one another<br>BUILDING SKILLS THROUGH MUSIC **Physical Education** Create and perform choreography to accompany a song | **Song** "Love Will Guide Us"<br>M*U*S*I*C M*A*K*E*R*S<br>Sally Rogers<br>**More Music Choices**<br>"How Can I Keep from Singing?" p. 261<br>"Waitin' for the Light to Shine," p. 26 | ASSESSMENT<br>**Performance/Observation** Perform a three-beat movement pattern to identify the meter of a song<br>TECHNOLOGY/MEDIA LINK<br>**Web Site** Learn more about musical styles |
| **Connection:** **Social Studies**<br>**Activity:** Discover information about hoboes in American history<br>ACROSS THE CURRICULUM **Language Arts** Share a book in order to inspire composition and improvisation in the classroom<br>CULTURAL CONNECTION **Song Lyrics and History** Analyze the lyrics of a song to determine the time period in which a song was written<br>BUILDING SKILLS THROUGH MUSIC **Social Studies** Identify and classify specific phrases in a song | **Song** "Big Rock Candy Mountain"<br>**More Music Choices**<br>"Oh, Susanna," p. 264<br>"River," p. 58 | ASSESSMENT<br>**Performance/Observation** Create contrasting movements to distinguish between verse and refrain<br>TECHNOLOGY/MEDIA LINK<br>**Notation Software** Create a bass part to a song |

| Lesson | Elements | Skills | |
|---|---|---|---|
| LESSON 4 **Home Is Where the Heart Is** pp. 332-333  | **Element: Melody**<br>**Concept:** Pitch and direction<br>**Focus:** :Letter names<br><br>**Secondary Element**<br>Timbre: instrumental<br><br>**National Standards**<br>2b 2e 3b 5b 8b 9b | **Skill: Playing**<br>**Objective:** Play melody instruments<br><br>**Secondary Skills**<br>• **Singing** Sing a song by Pete Seeger<br>• **Listening** Listen to a song about home | **SKILLS REINFORCEMENT**<br>• **Recorder** Play in two-part harmony |
| LESSON 5 **Pathway to the Stars** pp. 334-337  | **Element: Timbre**<br>**Concept:** Instrumental<br>**Focus:** Chinese instrument timbres<br><br>**Secondary Element**<br>Rhythm: meter<br><br>**National Standards**<br><br>1c 2f 4a 6b 8b 9a 9b | **Skill: Listening**<br>**Objective:** Listen to music played on Chinese instruments<br><br>**Secondary Skills**<br>• **Singing** Sing a song in Mandarin<br>• **Playing** Accompany a song on mallet and percussion instruments<br>• **Creating** Create an instrumental accompaniment to a song | |
| LESSON 6 **Lost and Found** pp. 338-339  | **Element: Rhythm**<br>**Concept:** Duration<br>**Focus:** Tied notes<br><br>**Secondary Element**<br>Melody: phrases<br><br>**National Standards**<br>4b 5a 7a 8b 9e | **Skill: Singing**<br>**Objective:** Sing tied notes in a song<br><br>**Secondary Skills**<br>• **Reading** Identify same rhythm patterns and note values, then say the rhythm of the song | **SKILLS REINFORCEMENT**<br>• **Keyboard** Play an accompaniment to the refrain of a song<br>• **Recorder** Play the refrain of a song |

| Connections | Music and Other Literature | |
|---|---|---|
| **Connection:** Related Arts<br>**Activity:** Identify symbols in artworks<br>ACROSS THE CURRICULUM **Related Arts** Create an artwork related to the word "home"<br>SPOTLIGHT ON **The Seeger Family** Information about the family of musicians<br>BUILDING SKILLS THROUGH MUSIC **Writing** Create phrases about the local community that can be used in a song | **Song** "Sailing Down My Golden River"<br>**Listening Selection** *She'll Be Coming 'Round the Mountain When She Comes*<br>**More Music Choices**<br>"Canoe Song," p. 76<br>"Sailboat in the Sky," p. 374 | ASSESSMENT<br>**Performance/Observation** Play, from notation, recorder and xylophone parts in small groups<br>TECHNOLOGY/MEDIA LINK<br>**Electronic Keyboard** Improvise background music to an original poem |
| **Connection:** Culture<br>**Activity:** Listen to music played on Chinese instruments<br>ACROSS THE CURRICULUM<br>**Science** Discuss facts about stars in two constellations<br>**Language Arts** Read a book of Chinese poems<br>CULTURAL CONNECTION<br>**Mythology** Share the story of a Chinese myth<br>**Chinese Writing** Explanation of pictographs, the Chinese system of writing<br>MOVEMENT **Creative Movement** Create movements to suggest the storyline in the lyrics of a song<br>SPOTLIGHT ON **Chinese Musical Instruments** Association of instruments with geographical directions and the seasons<br>MEETING INDIVIDUAL NEEDS **Working in Groups** Use strategies to help students work together in groups<br>BUILDING SKILLS THROUGH MUSIC **Reading** Compare and contrast the meaning of three poems | **Song** *"Niu lang zhi nü"* ("The Cowherd and the Weaving Maid")<br>**Listening Selection** *Bumper Harvest Celebration*<br>**Listening Map** *Bumper Harvest Celebration*<br>**Poems**<br>"Quiet Night"<br>"News of Home"<br>"Traveler's Song"<br>**More Music Choices**<br>*"Feng yang hua gu,"* p. 313<br>*Wu long,* p. 157 | ASSESSMENT<br>**Music Journal Writing** Summarize the attributes of Chinese music based on two selections<br>TECHNOLOGY/MEDIA LINK<br>**Transparency** Use a listening map to guide students through a selection<br>**MIDI/Sequencing Software** Use the software to change timbre of a melody |
| **Connection:** Language Arts<br>**Activity:** Write a song parody<br>ACROSS THE CURRICULUM **Language Arts** Create and perform parodies of stories or songs<br>MOVEMENT **Patterned Movement** Perform patterned movement to a song at different tempos<br>CHARACTER EDUCATION **Humor** Distinguish between appropriate and inappropriate uses of humor, and the impact each has on us<br>BUILDING SKILLS THROUGH MUSIC **Language** Split into groups to create several parodies of a song | **Song** "My Bonnie Lies Over the Ocean"<br>**Poem** "Cowboy's Dream"<br>**More Music Choices**<br>*"Santa Clara,"* p. 172<br>"Streets of Laredo," p. 272 | ASSESSMENT<br>**Performance/Observation** Perform a song and pay close attention to the full duration of tied notes<br>TECHNOLOGY/MEDIA LINK<br>**Web Site** Learn more about songs of Westward expansion |

| Lesson | Elements | Skills | |
|---|---|---|---|
| LESSON 7 **The Original Forty-Niners** pp. 340-343  | **Element: Texture/Harmony**<br>**Concept:** Harmony<br>**Focus:** Adding accompaniments<br><br>**Secondary Element**<br>Form: AB<br><br>**National Standards**<br>1b 2b 6a 6b 6e 8b | **Skill: Playing**<br>**Objective:** Play Autoharp to accompany a song<br><br>**Secondary Skills**<br>• **Singing** Show understanding of lyrics of a song<br>• **Listening** Describe tempo and recognize A and B sections of a song<br>• **Moving** Create dance steps and do a square dance | **SKILLS REINFORCEMENT**<br>• **Recorder** Play the refrain of a song<br>• **Mallets** Play an Orff orchestration of a song<br>• **Keyboard** Use two basic chord shapes to play an accompaniment<br>• **Playing** Perform an Autoharp accompaniment to a song |
| LESSON 8 **An Appleseed Song** pp. 344-347  | **Element: Form**<br>**Concept:** Form<br>**Focus:** Rondo form<br>**Secondary Element**<br>Expression: tempo<br><br>**National Standards**<br>2f 3b 4b 5a 5c 6a 6e 8b | **Skill: Listening**<br>**Objective:** Listen to identify rondo form<br><br>**Secondary Skills**<br>• **Reading** Identify pitches and rhythms of a song<br>• **Moving** Perform various movements for different sections of a rondo | **SKILLS REINFORCEMENT**<br>• **Improvising** Determine best combined sounds of improvised rhythm ostinatos as an accompaniment to a song<br>• **Recorder** Play a countermelody to a song<br>• **Creating** Create short raps and a refrain and use as a rondo |
|  LESSON 9 **Peace and Harmony** pp. 348-349  | **Element: Texture/Harmony**<br>**Concept:** Harmony<br>**Focus:** Unison/Harmony<br><br>**Secondary Element**<br>Texture: ostinatos<br><br>**National Standards**<br>1d 2f 6e 9d | **Skill: Moving**<br>**Objective:** Move while singing a round<br><br>**Secondary Skills**<br>• **Singing** Sing a round in unison, with vocal ostinatos, then as a two-part round | **SKILLS REINFORCEMENT**<br>• **Playing** Perform an ostinatos to a song using melody instruments<br>• **Recorder** Play an ostinato to accompany singing<br>• **Mallets** Play an Orff orchestration to accompany a song |

# Connections

# Music and Other Literature



**Connection:** Social Studies
**Activity:** Discuss the California Gold Rush and the United States Westward expansion

ACROSS THE CURRICULUM **Social Studies** Discuss the gold rush of 1848

MOVEMENT
**Creative Movement** Create movements that suit the tempos of two different pieces
**Patterned Movement** Create a square dance that closely adheres to the phrasing of a song

SPOTLIGHT ON **Aaron Copland and *Rodeo*** Facts about the composer, his style, and one of his best-known works

TEACHER TO TEACHER **Developing Autoharp Skills** Strategies for developing proficient skills in playing the instrument

BUILDING SKILLS THROUGH MUSIC **Social Studies** Discuss the impact of the gold rush on California

**Song** "Clementine"

**Listening Selections**
"Saturday Night Waltz" from *Rodeo* (excerpt)
*Forked Deer/Fisher's Hornpipe*
*First Night Quadrille*

**Listening Map** "Saturday Night Waltz" from *Rodeo*

**MUSIC MAKERS** Aaron Copland

**More Music Choices**
"The Keel Row," p. 240
*"Ocho kandelikas,"* p. 429

ASSESSMENT
**Performance/Observation** Accompany a classroom song performance, and emphasize the importance of changing chords at the proper time

TECHNOLOGY/MEDIA LINK
**CD-ROM** Create a composition and experiment with various tempos
**Transparency** Use a listening map to help students follow icons of a selection's theme

**Connection:** Language Arts
**Activity:** Gather and summarize facts about Johnny Appleseed

ACROSS THE CURRICULUM
**Science** Read about, sample, and classify different types of apples
**Social Studies** Share a book about Johnny Appleseed; determine states that achieved statehood in his lifetime

CULTURAL CONNECTION **Finding Food** Discuss the role of the apple tree as a food source for settlers

SPOTLIGHT ON **Johnny Appleseed** Information about John Chapman

AUDIENCE ETIQUETTE **Critical Listening** Take notes on what is heard in a listening selection

SCHOOL TO HOME CONNECTION **Meet the Gardener** Interview someone who keeps a garden or orchard

BUILDING SKILLS THROUGH MUSIC **Theatre** Perform a brief action play depicting the journeys of Johnny Appleseed

**Song** "Johnny Appleseed"

**Listening Selection** "Walking Song" from *Acadian Songs*

**Listening Map** "Walking Song" from *Acadian Songs*

**MUSIC MAKERS** Virgil Thomson

**More Music Choices**
"California, Here I Come," p. 287
"Sweet Betsy from Pike," p. 244

ASSESSMENT
**Performance** Identify sections of rondo form aurally

TECHNOLOGY/MEDIA LINK
**Transparency** Use a listening map as a guide to a listening selection

**Connection:** Related Arts
**Activity:** Create personal works of art using peace as the theme

ACROSS THE CURRICULUM **Language Arts/Art** Discuss, create, and display methods of conveying ideas through symbols in art, music, and stories

TEACHER TO TEACHER **Peer Coaching** Incorporate this technique to reinforce various skill levels in everyone

BUILDING SKILLS THROUGH MUSIC **Math** Calculate how many people it would take to reach across the United States

**Song** "Peace Round"

**Listening Selection** *Interview with Jean Richie*

**MUSIC MAKERS** Jean Ritchie

**More Music Choices**
"Ah, Poor Bird," p. 196
"Oh, How Lovely Is the Evening," p. 217

ASSESSMENT
**Performance/Observation** Perform a round with movements to show overlapping phrases and harmony

TECHNOLOGY/MEDIA LINK
**Video Library** Watch a video to learn more about Jean Ritchie

## Introducing the Unit

Hopes and dreams give people purpose or meaning in life. This unit explores the dreams of both our civilization and the individuals in it. Throughout the year, encourage students to set goals and establish a means of reaching them.

See below and pp. 324–325 for unit highlights of related curricular experiences.

## Unit Project

Invite students to read "Revisiting a Dream," on p. 322, and the text on p. 323. Then designate students as "Dream Keepers." Have each student make a list of dreams, hopes, goals, and aspirations. Have students review or add to their lists during the unit. Start a bulletin board with the heading "We Are Dreaming of . . ." Have students write individual, group, or class dreams and hopes on cards and attach them to the bulletin board.

Encourage students to use their "Dream Keepers" information to develop a script for a program based on the material in this unit. Have them think about the dream or hope expressed in the song, listening selection, or literature and then write two sentences that explain the meaning of the work. Have them compare their own hopes and dreams to those expressed in the music they are learning. Help them build a script using their individual dream statements, their group or class dreams and hopes, and their writing about specific examples.

Help students choose songs for their performance and then arrange songs and script into a performance order. Have them set a musical goal for each song they will perform and record their musical goals on their "Dream Keepers" list. Help them choose speakers and rehearse the script and songs. Record or, if allowed, videotape their performance. Then allow students to listen to or watch the results of their performance and assess their work using the goals they established for themselves.

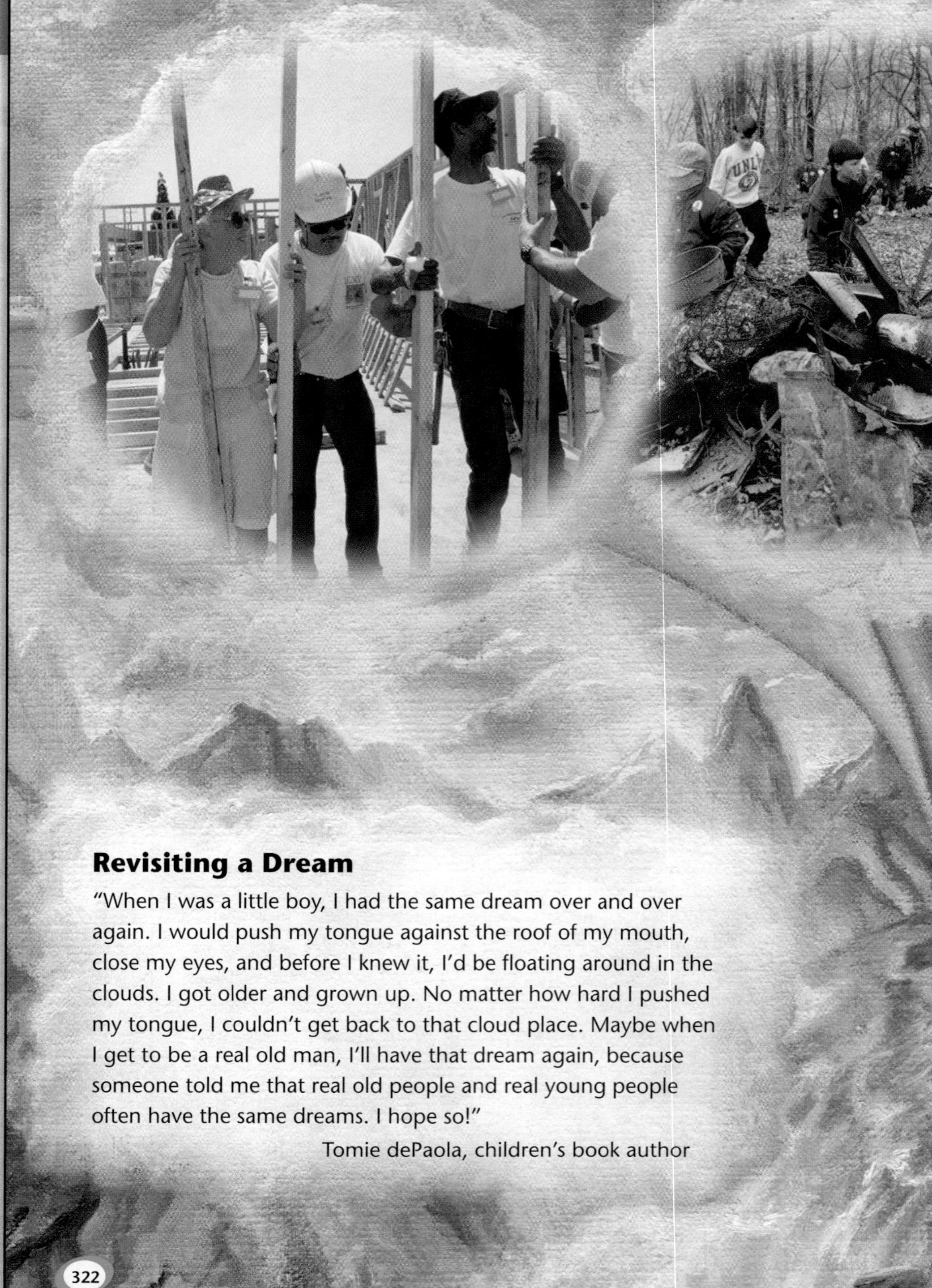

**Revisiting a Dream**

"When I was a little boy, I had the same dream over and over again. I would push my tongue against the roof of my mouth, close my eyes, and before I knew it, I'd be floating around in the clouds. I got older and grown up. No matter how hard I pushed my tongue, I couldn't get back to that cloud place. Maybe when I get to be a real old man, I'll have that dream again, because someone told me that real old people and real young people often have the same dreams. I hope so!"

Tomie dePaola, children's book author

322

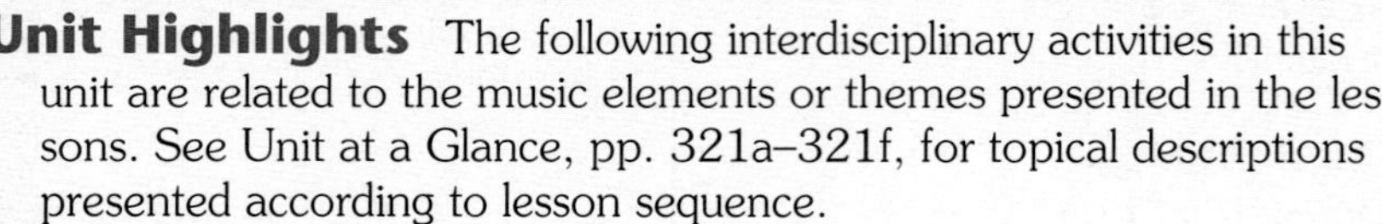

## Across the Curriculum

**Unit Highlights** The following interdisciplinary activities in this unit are related to the music elements or themes presented in the lessons. See Unit at a Glance, pp. 321a–321f, for topical descriptions presented according to lesson sequence.

▶ **ART/RELATED ARTS**

- Create a piece of artwork or other project that relates to the word *home* (p. 332)
- Discuss, create, and display methods of conveying ideas through symbols in art, music, and stories (p. 348)

▶ **LANGUAGE ARTS**

- Share a book about a hobo to motivate improvisation and composition in class (p. 330)
- Read a book of Chinese poetry (p. 336)
- Have students create and perform a parody of one of their favorite stories or songs (p. 338)

▶ **SCIENCE**

- Discuss facts about the stars in two constellations (p. 334)
- Read about, sample, and classify different types of apples (p. 344)

▶ **SOCIAL STUDIES**

- Discuss the gold rush of 1848 (p. 340)
- Read a book about Johnny Appleseed; determine states that achieved statehood in his lifetime (p. 346)

UNIT 9

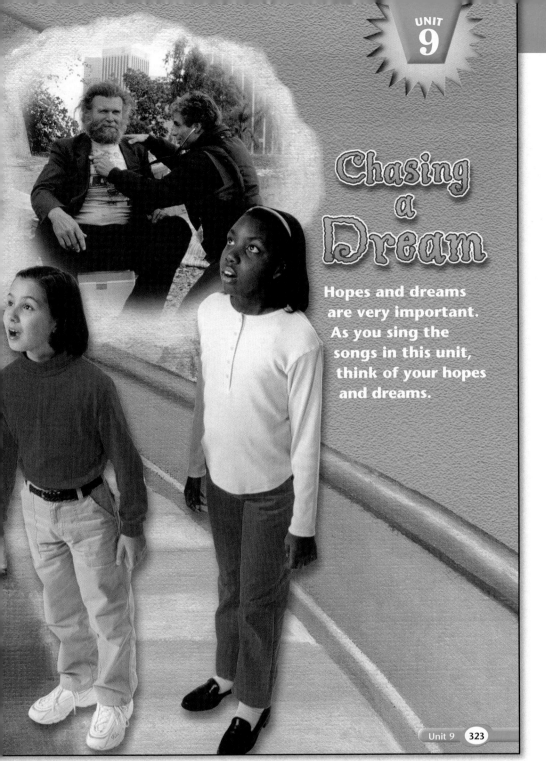

# Chasing a Dream

Hopes and dreams are very important. As you sing the songs in this unit, think of your hopes and dreams.



## MUSIC SKILLS ASSESSED IN THIS UNIT



**Reading Music: Rhythm**

- Read rhythm patterns using rhythm syllables (p. 327)

**Reading Music: Pitch**

- Read notated parts for recorder and xylophone (p. 333)

**Performing Music: Singing**

- Perform a song parody (p. 339)
- Perform a round in unison and in harmony (p. 349)

**Moving to Music**

- Perform a movement pattern to identify meter in 3 (p. 329)

**Performing Music: Playing**

- Accompany a song with recorders and xylophones (p. 333)
- Play Autoharp to accompany a two-chord song (p. 343)

**Creating Music**

- Create movements to illustrate AB form (p. 331)

**Listening to Music**

- Identify and describe timbres of Chinese instruments (p. 337)
- Aurally identify the sections in rondo form (p. 347)

## CULTURAL CONNECTION

**Unit Highlights** The musical literature in this unit provides many opportunities for students to explore a variety of world cultures. See Unit at a Glance, pp. 321a–321f, for topical descriptions presented according to lesson sequence.

▶ AFRICAN AMERICAN

- "We Shall Overcome" (p. 326)

▶ AMERICAN

- "Big Rock Candy Mountain" (p. 330)
- Discuss how the song lyrics of the era would express the lifestyle and experiences of life as a hobo (p. 330)
- "Sailing Down My Golden River" (p. 332)
- "My Bonnie Lies Over the Ocean" (p. 338)
- "Clementine" (p. 341)
- "Johnny Appleseed": Discuss the role of apple trees as a food source for settlers during the Westward movement (p. 345)

▶ ASIAN

- *"Niu lang zhi nü"* (p. 335)
- Explore the Chinese myth about the cowherd and the weaving maid (p. 334)
- Discuss pictographs and their significance in the Chinese writing system (p. 337)

# Opening Activities

| MATERIALS | |
|---|---|
| • "Love Can Build a Bridge" | **CD 14-3** |
| **Recording Routine:** Intro (4 m.); vocal | |

## Listening

Invite students to listen to "Love Can Build a Bridge" **CD 14-3**. Play the recording and ask students to think about the dreams expressed in the lyrics of the song. After listening, have students share their answers.

## Singing

Have students find the word *Refrain* in the music. Play the recording and invite them to sing along during the refrain. Then help them define *refrain* as a section of a song in which both the words and music are repeated.

## Reading

Help students identify the musical symbols in "Love Can Build a Bridge" that show the map or plan of the song. Working in pairs, have students find

- First and second endings.
- Repeat signs.
- *D. S. al Coda.*

As pairs find each symbol, have them explain to each other what the symbol means. Play the recording and have students check their answers and explanations by listening.

## Sharing a Song

Some people dream about living in communities where people care for and help each other. Other people dream about their goals and ambitions. **Sing** "Love Can Build a Bridge." Imagine what we could do by sharing and working together.

## Assessment

**Unit Highlights** The lessons in this unit were chosen and developed to support the theme "Chasing a Dream." Each lesson, as always, presents a clear element focus, a skill objective, and an end-of-lesson assessment. The overall sequence of lessons, however, is organized according to this theme, rather than concept or skill development. In this context, formal assessment strategies, such as those presented in Units 1–6, are no longer applicable.

▶ **INFORMAL ASSESSMENTS**

At the close of each Teacher's Edition lesson in this unit, one of the following types of assessments is used to evaluate the learning of the key element focus or skill objective.

- Music Journal Writing (p. 337)
- Performance/Observation (pp. 329, 331, 333, 339, 343, 347, 349)

▶ **RUBRICS**

Visit *www.sfsuccessnet.com* for rubrics to assess students' achievement in music skills.

## Moving to the Sounds of a Dream

Find the refrain of "Love Can Build a Bridge." Look for repeated words and music. **Create** your own movements to show the meaning of the lyrics of the refrain. **Move** each time the refrain occurs.

Unit 9 325

## Analyzing

Invite students to diagram on the board the form or order of the song: verse 1, refrain, verse 2, refrain, bridge *(when we stand together)*, refrain, coda. Play the recording again **CD 14**–3 and invite students to observe the form as they sing.

## Moving

Invite students to create movements for the refrain of "Love Can Build a Bridge." Working in groups of four or more, have them sing the refrain together and discuss the meaning of the lyrics. Then encourage them to create movements that show the meaning of the music. Have groups demonstrate their movements as the class sings the refrain. Invite students to use movements in a class performance of the song.



### Innovative Teacher Support for This Unit

- **Making Music DVD, Grade 4** contains video segments that support lessons, including signing and movement.
- **Making Music with Movement and Dance** provides more opportunities for large group activities in music or physical education classes.
- **Making Music with Technology** provides lesson plans for many technology applications; includes MIDI files.
- ***¡A cantar!*** features recorded songs and lessons from around the Spanish-speaking world; includes strategies for bilingual classes and for English-speaking teachers working with Spanish-speaking students.
- **Bridges to Asia** features recorded songs and lessons from Asian and Pacific region cultures.
- ***www.sfsuccessnet.com*** provides an online lesson planner to conveniently create lesson plans at school or at home. Includes rubrics for assessment, lesson modifications to meet the needs of all students, performance musicals based on program content, and more.

## Technology/Media Link

**Unit Highlights** The following components are used in this unit to reinforce and expand students' understanding of music elements and related themes. See Unit at a Glance, pp. 321a–321f, for a descriptive listing according to lesson sequence.

▶ **CD-ROM**

- Create a composition and experiment with various tempos (p. 343)

▶ **ELECTRONIC KEYBOARD**

- Improvise background music to an original poem (p. 333)

▶ **MIDI/SEQUENCING SOFTWARE**

- Use the software to change the timbre of a melody (p. 337)

▶ **NOTATION SOFTWARE**

- Create a bass part to a song (p. 331)

▶ **TRANSPARENCY**

- Display a listening map to guide students through a selection (p. 337)
- Use the listening map to help students follow icons of a selection's theme (p. 343)
- Display the listening map to guide students through a selection in rondo form (p. 347)

▶ **VIDEO LIBRARY/DVD**

- Watch a video to learn more about Jean Ritchie (p. 349)

▶ **WEB SITE**

- Go to *www.sfsuccessnet.com* for more information on songs from the Civil Rights movement in the United States (p. 327)
- Explore a variety of musical styles (p. 329)
- Learn more about songs of the Westward movement (p. 339)

LESSON 1

## LESSON AT A GLANCE

**Element Focus** **RHYTHM** Rhythm patterns

**Skill Objective** **SINGING** Sing and read rhythm patterns

**Connection Activity** **SOCIAL STUDIES** Discuss civil rights and freedom

**MATERIALS**

- "We Shall Overcome" **CD 14-5**

  **Recording Routine:** Intro (4 m.); v. 1; v. 2; v. 3; v. 4; modulate to D♭; v. 5; coda
- *What Kind of Land?* (excerpt) **CD 14-7**
- **Resource Book** p. G-19

**VOCABULARY**

dotted-quarter note

**National Standards**

**1a** Sing independently on pitch and in rhythm
**3c** Improvise melodic embellishments on familiar melodies
**5a** Read whole, half, quarter, and eighth notes in $\frac{4}{4}$ meter
**6b** Describe music by answering questions about it
**8b** Identify ways music relates to social studies

**MORE MUSIC CHOICES**

Another song about freedom:
"We Shall Not Be Moved," p. 437

# 1 INTRODUCE

**8b** Invite students to talk about what freedom means to them.

**ASK** **What are civil rights?** (rights to liberties such as freedom of speech, religion, assembly, right to a fair and speedy trial)

Have students look at the photo of a civil rights march on pp. 326–327, and read the information at the top of p. 326. Share the information with students from Spotlight On below.

LESSON 1 | Element: RHYTHM | Skill: SINGING | Connection: SOCIAL STUDIES

# Sing FOR FREEDOM

In the 1960s, "We Shall Overcome" was sung by people seeking civil rights in the United States. **Perform** the last two lines of the song using rhythm syllables. Then **sing** this famous freedom song.

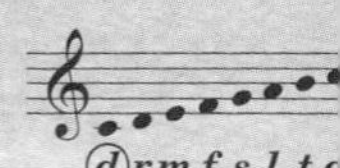

CD 14-5

## WE SHALL OVERCOME

New Words and Arrangement by Zilphia Horton, Frank Hamilton, Guy Carawan, and Pete Seeger

Freedom Song from the United States

1. We shall o - ver - come, ___ We shall o - ver - come, ___
2. We'll walk hand in hand, ___ We'll walk hand in hand, ___
3. We are not a - fraid, ___ We are not a - fraid, ___

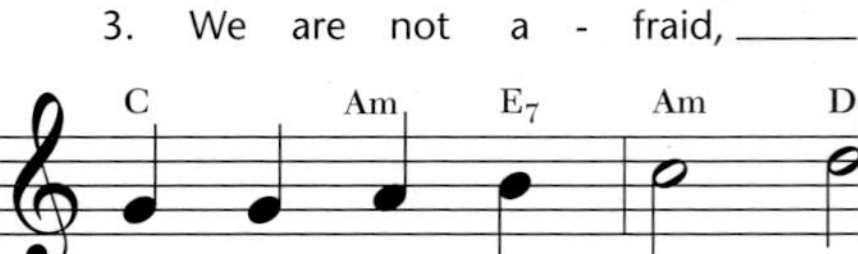


We shall o - ver - come some - day; ___
We'll walk hand in hand some - day; ___
We are not a - fraid to - day; ___

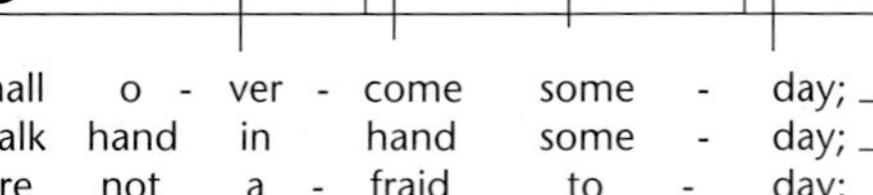


Oh, ___ deep in my heart I do be - lieve,

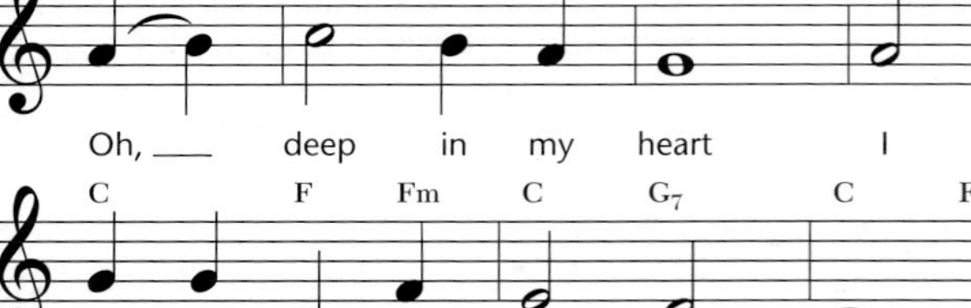


We shall o - ver - come some day. ___

4. We shall broth-ers be, . . .
5. Truth shall make us free, . . .



326

## Footnotes

### SPOTLIGHT ON

▶ **Civil Rights and the U.S. Constitution** The United States Constitution includes 27 amendments. The first ten are called the Bill of Rights. They include freedom of speech and the right to a fair trial. At first, not everyone enjoyed those freedoms. Congress passed the Thirteenth Amendment abolishing slavery and the Fourteenth Amendment guaranteeing everyone the freedoms of the Bill of Rights as well as "equal protection under the law."

### BUILDING SKILLS THROUGH MUSIC

▶ **Language** Have students read the text introducing "We Shall Overcome" on p. 326 of the student text. Then have them read all of the lyrics to the song. Ask students to explain what they believe the phrase *We shall overcome* means. Ask them what the singer is striving to overcome. (adversity, lack of civil rights, discrimination, and so on)

### SKILLS REINFORCEMENT

**3c** ▶ **Singing** Help students add harmony to the end of this song. The last three notes are *mi, re, do.* Add a harmonic ending by having some students sing *so, fa, mi.* Initially, you should choose the tones for the endings. With practice, students will learn to add harmony on their own.

**8b** ▶ **Creating** Point out to students that each verse of "We Shall Overcome" expresses a single idea in a phrase that is repeated. Extend this song to include more verses created by students. During the 1960s, singers routinely took turns improvising additional verses.

▶ **Signing** Students will enjoy performing "We Shall Overcome" with hand signs. See Resource Book p. G-19.

## What Kind of Land?

For most people, freedom means independence, equality, and justice. **Listen** to *What Kind of Land?*, a song that questions the founding of the United States as a free nation while it held some of its people in slavery.

"What kind of land is this gon' be?

Freedom built on slavery.

How will it stand in time?"

CD 14-7

**What Kind of Land?**

**by Bernice Johnson Reagon**

Bernice Johnson Reagon and her daughter Toshi performed *What Kind of Land?* for the PBS television documentary *Africans in America.*

▼Bernice Johnson Reagon





# 2 Develop

### Singing

1a Have students preview "We Shall Overcome."

ASK **How many verses are in this song?** (five)

**What part of the song has the same words for every verse?** (the last two phrases, or lines)

**What can we do to show respect and unity as we sing this important song?** (Answers will vary.)

Play "We Shall Overcome" **CD 14-5** and invite students to sing with the recording.

### Reading

5a Encourage students to tap and say the rhythm using rhythm syllables for the last two lines of "We Shall Overcome." Have them identify each note value. (whole, half, quarter)

Then, have students find the measures in the first line of the song that are the same. (mm. 1–2 and 3–4)

### Listening

6b Play *What Kind of Land?* **CD 14-7.**

ASK **Who is performing?** (a small group of singers)

**What is the song about?** (The song questions how the United States will stand in time.)

# 3 Close

**Skill: SINGING** ASSESSMENT

**Performance/Observation** Invite students to perform the last two lines of "We Shall Overcome" **CD 14-5**, using rhythm syllables. Then have them perform the song with the recording. Encourage small groups and soloists to take turns singing the verse. Observe each student's ability to read the rhythm patterns in the music.

## Meeting Individual Needs

▶ **Including Everyone** By fourth grade, many students develop stability in their friendships and form friendships by admiring the values and strengths of others. "We Shall Overcome" provides an opportunity for students to learn about advocacy and admire those qualities in others. Tell students that many individuals who had the freedom that is expressed in the song were advocates who worked for the civil rights of others, many who were their friends. Students should also know that this song was used to express the values of civil rights by people with and without disabilities as they worked together for passage of the Americans with Disabilities Act (1990) and the Individuals with Disabilities Education Act (1997).

## Technology/Media Link

**Web Site** The listening selection *What Kind of Land?* was composed for the PBS series *Africans in America*. Invite students to go to *www.sfsuccessnet.com* to learn more about songs of the Civil Rights movement in the United States.

## LESSON AT A GLANCE

**Element Focus** **RHYTHM** Meter in 3

**Skill Objective** **LISTENING** Listen to identify meter

**Connection Activity** **STYLE** Discuss songs in folk style

**MATERIALS**

- "Love Will Guide Us" **CD 14-8**

  **Recording Routine:** Intro (6 m.); refrain; interlude (2 m.); v. 1; refrain; interlude (2 m.); v. 2; refrain; interlude (2 m.); v. 3; refrain
- hand drum

**VOCABULARY**

refrain meter in 3 time signature

**National Standards**

**1b** Sing expressively with appropriate phrasing
**2b** Perform chordal patterns on appropriate instruments
**6a** Listen to identify form
**6b** Describe music by answering questions about it
**6e** While listening to music, move to show a prominent feature of the music

**MORE MUSIC CHOICES**

Other songs of hope:

"How Can I Keep from Singing?" p. 261
"Waitin' for the Light to Shine," p. 26

# 1 INTRODUCE

Encourage students to think about their dreams and goals. Tell them that some dreams or goals may be far away, like the kind of work or career they would like to have when they are adults. Others may be closer, like winning a race or finishing a project.

**ASK What are your dreams and goals? What do you hope for?** (Accept a variety of answers.)

Have students read the text at the top of p. 328.

LESSON 2 | Element: RHYTHM | Skill: LISTENING | Connection: STYLE

# Hope Keeps Dreams Alive

Sometimes it takes work and patience to make a dream come true. Hope keeps us focused on our dreams. **Listen** to "Love Will Guide Us," a song of hope.

◀ These workers are building homes with Habitat for Humanit

CD 14-8
Love Will Guide Us
s, l, do r m
Words by Sally Rogers
Traditional Melo
D G C
Refrain Love will guide us, peace has
1. If you can not sing like
G
tried us. Hope in side
an gels, If you can
G D C D
us will lead the way, On the
not speak be - fore thou - sands, You can

## Footnotes

## MOVEMENT

6e ▶ **Creative Movement** Use movement to help students think about the form of the song in this lesson. Have them move (using patterns that show the meter of the song) during the refrain and listen during verses, or sing the refrain and move during the verses. You may also wish to have them use one movement pattern for the refrain and a different pattern for the verses. To extend movement possibilities, have students create choreography for the song.

## BUILDING SKILLS THROUGH MUSIC

▶ **Physical Education** As an extension to the Creative Movement activity above, have students create choreography for "Love Will Guide Us." Divide students into small groups, assigning each group a phrase to choreograph. Then each group can teach their movement to the class. Combine all of the movements for a complete dance and perform the new choreography as a class.

## SKILLS REINFORCEMENT

2b ▶ **Playing** Folk songs or songs in a folk style often have a simple chordal accompaniment. Invite students to play an accompaniment for "Love Will Guide Us." Make a chart of the chords using the notation on pp. 328–329. Use a slash (/) to indicate that students should strum or strike the same chord again. Have students compare the chart to the music and note that there is one chord per measure. The chord is played on the first beat of each measure.

Invite students to play the chords using Autoharps, keyboards, or bells. Have them practice chords alone first, then accompany the song.

### Time Signature Review

**Identify** the time signature at the beginning of "Love Will Guide Us." How many beats are in each measure? Tap the steady beat as you **listen** and **sing** along. **Create** a movement that shows the number of beats in each measure.

MUSIC MAKERS
Sally Rogers

**Sally Rogers,** a folk musician, performs traditional children's songs. She lives in Connecticut and performs throughout the United States. She has sung on radio shows such as *A Prairie Home Companion.* Rogers plays banjo, guitar, and dulcimer. She says, "When we sing together, we can't help but know we are not alone in both our work and our play."

G C G
road ___ from ___ greed __ to giv -
give ___ from ___ deep __ with - in ___
G
ing. Love will ___ guide ___ us ___
you. You can ___ change ___ the ___
D G
through the dark ___ night. (to Verses)
world with your ___ love. (to Refrain)
2. You are like no other being.
What you can give, no other can give,
To the future of our precious children.
To the future of the world where we live.
(to Refrain)
3. Hear the song of peace within you.
Heed the song of peace in your heart.
Spring's new beginning shall lead to the harvest.
Love will guide us on our way.
(to Refrain)

Chasing a Dream

## 2 Develop

### Listening

6a Play "Love Will Guide Us" **CD 14-8** and invite students to follow the words on pp. 328–329 as they listen.

6b ASK **How many times did you hear the refrain?** (four)

**What are the dreams and hopes of the singers?** (Accept a variety of answers.)

### Singing

1b Play "Love Will Guide Us" again. Encourage students to sing the refrain and listen to the verses.

### Moving

6e In the tempo of the song, play a two-beat pattern (strong-weak) on a hand drum. Repeat for three- and four-beat patterns. Then play the recording and ask students to

- Tap the steady beat and choose the pattern that matches the meter of the song. (three-beat pattern)
- Refer to p. 328 and identify the time signature. ($\frac{3}{4}$)
- Create a movement pattern that illustrates a three-beat pattern.
- Sing and perform their movement pattern during the refrains.

## 3 Close

Skill: LISTENING
ASSESSMENT

**Performance/Observation** Have students

- Listen to the recording of "Love Will Guide Us" **CD 14-8.**
- Perform their three-beat movement pattern with the recording to identify the meter.

Observe each student's ability to move appropriately in meter in 3.

## Meeting Individual Needs

▶ **English Language Learners** "Love Will Guide Us" contains a number of spelling patterns that produce the long *i* vowel sound—*guide*, *tried*, *like*, *night*, and so on. You may want to ask students to reread the song text and write down any words they find that have the long *i* vowel sound—"the *i* that says its name."

## Character Education

▶ **Giving** To encourage students to reflect on their unique gifts, discuss the following quotes. "The one thing I know: the only ones among you who will be really happy are those who will have sought and found how to serve" (Albert Schweitzer). "You give but little when you give of your possessions. It is when you give of yourself that you truly give" (Khalil Gibran). Encourage students to identify their individual gifts and how they can share these gifts. Guide students to understand that both the giver and the receiver benefit when gifts are shared.

## Technology/Media Link

**Web Site** Invite students to visit *www.sfsuccessnet.com* to explore other musical styles.

LESSON 3

## LESSON AT A GLANCE

**Element Focus** **FORM** Verse-and-refrain (AB) form

**Skill Objective** **MOVING** Create contrasting movements to perform during the verse and refrain of a song

**Connection Activity** **SOCIAL STUDIES** Discover information about hoboes in American history

**MATERIALS**

- "Big Rock Candy Mountain" **CD 14-10**
  **Recording Routine:** Intro (8 m.); v. 1; interlude (8 m.); v. 2; refrain; coda
- **Resource Book** p. I-26

**VOCABULARY**

verse refrain phrase

**National Standards**

**5a** Read rhythms in $\frac{4}{4}$ meter
**6a** Listen to identify form
**6b** Describe music by moving to it
**8b** Identify ways music relates to social studies

**MORE MUSIC CHOICES**

Other songs with verse-and-refrain form:
"Oh, Susanna," p. 264
"River," p. 58

# 1 INTRODUCE

Explain that an economic depression is a time when there are few jobs and most people have little money. Have students read the text on p. 330 and then follow the words of "Big Rock Candy Mountain" **CD 14-10** as you play the recording. Ask students what they think the hoboes are dreaming about. Help students discuss how the lyrics relate to history, using the Cultural Connection below.

LESSON 3
Element: FORM
Skill: MOVING
Connection: SOCIAL STUDIE
A HOPEFUL REFRAIN
During the Great Depression in the 1930s, many people lost their jobs. Some people became hoboes, travelin from place to place in railroad cars looking for work. "Big Rock Candy Mountain" is a famous hobo song—a song of hope for better times.
CD 14-10
BIG ROCK CANDY MOUNTAIN
Traditior
VERSE
1. In the Big Rock Can-dy Moun-tain, There's a land that's fair and bright,
2. In the Big Rock Can-dy Moun-tain, Where the ho-bo nev-er begs,
Where the hand-outs grow on bush-es, And you sleep out ev-'ry night;
And the bull-dogs all are tooth-less, And the hens lay soft-boiled eggs;
Where the box-cars all are emp-ty, And the sun shines ev-'ry day,
All the trees are full of ap-ples, And the barns are full of hay,
Oh, I'm bound to go where there is-n't an-y snow, Where the rain does-n't fall,
There's a lake of stew and ___ so-da pop, _ too, You can paddle all a-round
330


## Footnotes

### ACROSS THE CURRICULUM

▶ **Language Arts** Share the book *Ty's One Man Band* by Mildred Pitts Walter (Houghton Mifflin, 1992). In this story, a boy named Ty meets a hobo named Andro. Andro uses spoons, a washboard, a comb, and other objects to create music that makes the entire town sing and dance. The book includes text and images that can be used as a springboard for improvisation and composition in the classroom.

### BUILDING SKILLS THROUGH MUSIC

▶ **Social Studies** Once the lesson has been introduced and students have sung "Big Rock Candy Mountain," share with the class the song lyric activity in Cultural Connection. Then have students identify each phrase in the song that can be considered complete fantasy. (*handouts grow on bushes, bulldogs are all toothless, hens lay soft-boiled eggs,* and so on)

### CULTURAL CONNECTION

8b ▶ **Song Lyrics and History** The lyrics of a song often tell about the time in which the song was created. Ask questions about the experiences of hoboes as portrayed in the lyrics of "Big Rock Candy Mountain."

How did hoboes travel the country? (walking or by railroad)

What kind of railroad car did they ride in? (boxcar)

Why would they want a boxcar to be empty? (space for sleeping and moving around)

What is a handout? (something given to a person for free)

What kinds of handouts were hoboes looking for? (food, shelter)

Why would hoboes want dogs to have no teeth? (so the dogs couldn't bite them)

Rock Candy Rhythms
"Big Rock Candy Mountain" has two sections—a verse and a refrain. Find measures with exactly the same rhythm in both verse and refrain. As you sing the song, move in one way during the verse and in a different way during the refrain.
Tune In
Did you know that there is a place called Rock Candy Mountain in Utah, near the town of Marysvale?
F C G7 C
and the wind does-n't blow, In the Big Rock Can - dy Moun-tain.
in a big ca - noe, In the Big Rock Can - dy Moun-tain.
REFRAIN
G7 C
Oh, the buzz - in' of the bees in the syc - a - more trees
F C G7
'Round the so - da wa - ter foun - tain, Where the lem-on-ade springs
C G7 C
and the blue - bird sings in the Big Rock Can - dy Moun-tain.
Chasing a Dream
Unit 9 331

# 2 Develop

## Singing

Play "Big Rock Candy Mountain" **CD 14-10** and invite students to sing along.

ASK **What part of the song is the same each time?** (the refrain)

Have students sing the refrain.

ASK **How many verses are in this song?** (two)

**What is different about verses 1 and 2?** (The words are different; the music is the same.)

## Reading

ASK **Which phrases of the song have exactly the same rhythm?** (1, 2, and 3)

Have students clap and say the rhythm. Then, have them echo clap patterns that include dotted-quarter and eighth notes. Direct students to the words *Big Rock Candy Mountain* and clap the rhythm.

## Moving

Invite students to create movements to perform during the verse and refrain of "Big Rock Candy Mountain" **CD 14-10.** Students may use clues from the words of the song, but the movements should be distinctly different between the verse and refrain.

# 3 Close

Element: FORM

**ASSESSMENT**

6b **Performance/Observation** Divide the class into four groups. Have each group create a movement to go with the verse of "Big Rock Candy Mountain" (A) and a contrasting movement to go with the refrain (B). Have each group identify and illustrate AB form by singing and performing its movements with the recording for the class. Observe each student's ability to distinguish between verse and refrain.

## Skills Reinforcement

▶ **Guitar** On the refrain of "Big Rock Candy Mountain," invite some students to play the guitar. The chords (C, F, and $G_7$) can be played by beginning guitarists as half-chords, which are played by depressing and strumming only three treble strings. Use a simple brush strum with the thumb.

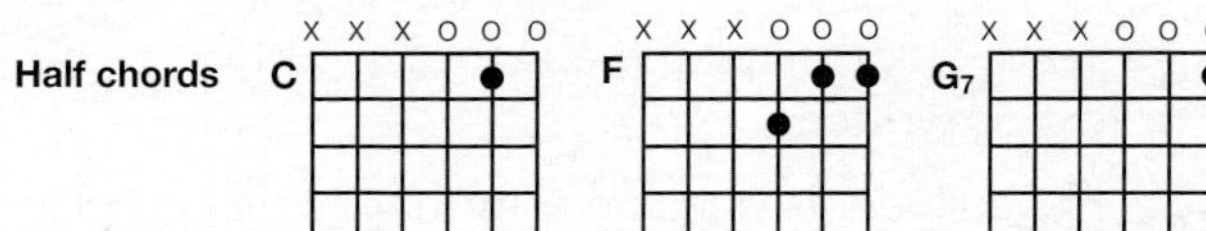
Half chords
C
x x x o o o
F
x x x o o o
G7
x x x o o o

▶ **Recorder** Students can add a recorder countermelody to their performance of "Big Rock Candy Mountain." See Resource Book p. I-26.

## Technology/Media Link

**Notation Software** Organize students into small groups to create a bass part to "Big Rock Candy Mountain" using the classroom computer equipped with notation software. Have students set up treble and bass staffs.

- Choose the time signature $\frac{4}{4}$ and key signature (C).
- Help students set up the pickup measure.
- Enter and play back the melody.
- Use the chord symbols to create a bass part using half notes on the chord roots. (Enter a quarter rest for the pickup beat.)
- Play back the completed work and print a copy of the composition.

LESSON 4

## LESSON AT A GLANCE

**Element Focus** **MELODY** Letter names

**Skill Objective** **PLAYING** Play melody instruments

**Connection Activity** **RELATED ARTS** Identify symbols in artworks

**MATERIALS**

- "Sailing Down My Golden River" **CD 14-12**

  **Recording Routine:** Intro (4 m.); v. 1; interlude (2 m.); v. 2; interlude (2 m.); v. 3; interlude (2 m.); v. 4; coda
- *She'll Be Coming 'Round the Mountain When She Comes* **CD 14-14**
- alto and bass xylophones, recorders, Autoharp

**VOCABULARY**

phrase

**◆◆◆◆ National Standards ◆◆◆◆**

- **2b** Perform melodies on appropriate instruments
- **2e** Play instruments in groups following a conductor
- **3b** Improvise rhythmic and melodic ostinato accompaniments
- **5b** Read notes in treble clef using letters
- **8b** Identify ways music relates to other school subjects
- **9d** Describe roles of musicians in various settings

**MORE MUSIC CHOICES**

Other songs with instrumental accompaniments:

"Canoe Song," p. 76

"Sailboat in the Sky," p. 374

# 1 INTRODUCE

**8b** Invite students to view the art on pp. 332–333 and look for symbols of home or community. Have them create an artwork that represents their home, neighborhood, or community. See Across the Curriculum below.

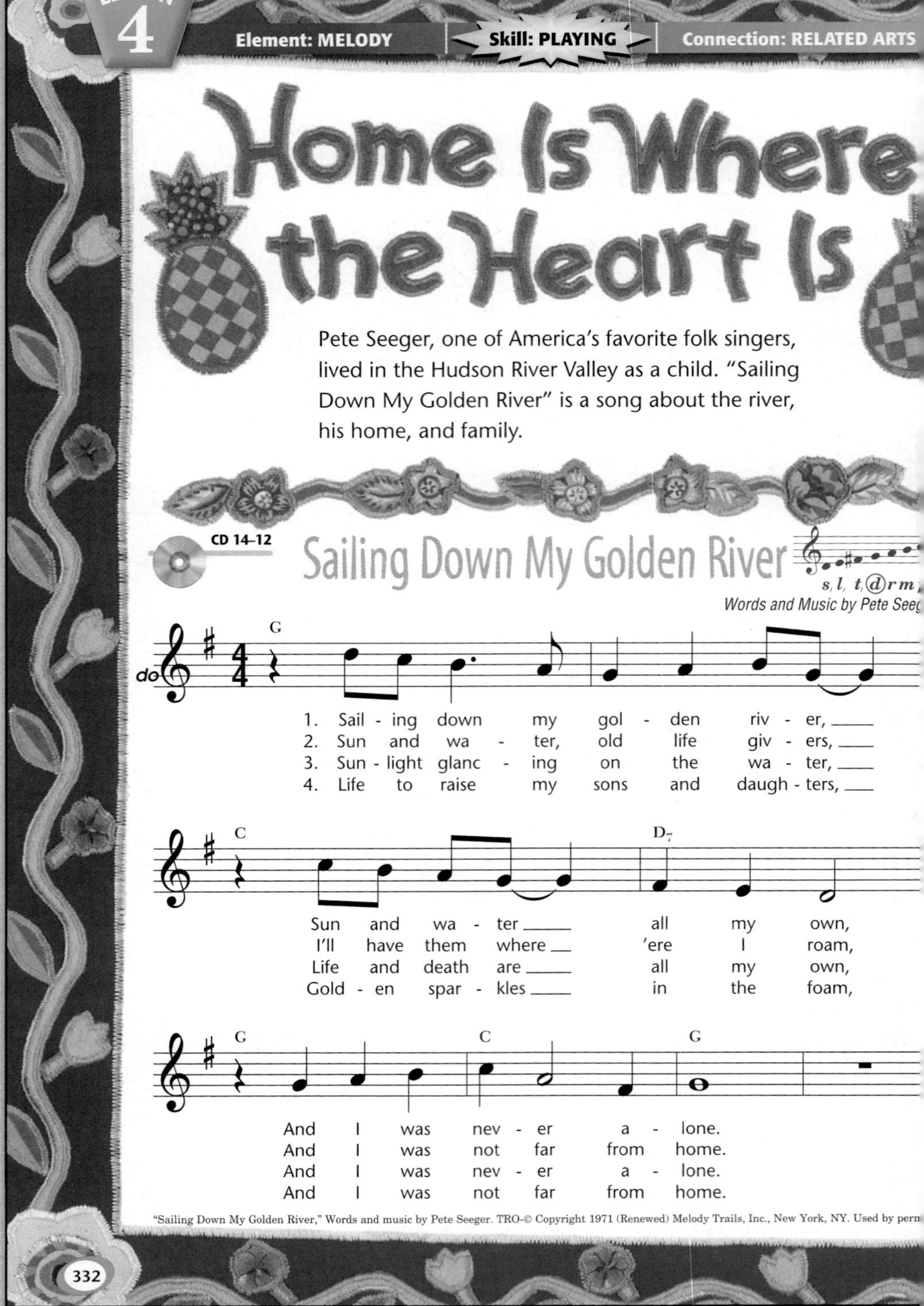

LESSON 4 Element: MELODY | Skill: PLAYING | Connection: RELATED ARTS

# Home Is Where the Heart Is

Pete Seeger, one of America's favorite folk singers, lived in the Hudson River Valley as a child. "Sailing Down My Golden River" is a song about the river, his home, and family.

CD 14-12

## Sailing Down My Golden River

*s, l, t, (d) r m*

*Words and Music by Pete Seeger*

G
C
D7
G
C
G
1. Sail - ing down my gol - den riv - er, Sun and wa - ter all my own, And I was nev - er a - lone.
2. Sun and wa - ter, old life giv - ers, I'll have them where 'ere I roam, And I was not far from home.
3. Sun - light glanc - ing on the wa - ter, Life and death are all my own, And I was nev - er a - lone.
4. Life to raise my sons and daugh - ters, Gold - en spar - kles in the foam, And I was not far from home.





332

## Footnotes

### ACROSS THE CURRICULUM

**8b** ▶ **Related Arts** Help students explore uses of the word *home* in the English language. Discuss words such as *hometown, homemade, home plate, homesick, homeroom, homestead, homestretch,* and so on. Invite students to create an artwork that describes or tells something about their homes. Projects might include stories, poems, drawings, collages, skits, dances, or songs. Arrange for students to share, display, or perform their works in class.

▶ **Writing** Engage students in a brief discussion about characteristics they like about their hometown. As a class, refine these characteristics into a single word or simple phrase. Then, combine these words and phrases to create a spoken ostinato to accompany "Sailing Down My Golden River."

### SKILLS REINFORCEMENT

▶ **Recorder** Students may enjoy playing recorders in harmony. Remind students that when playing leaps, fingers need to move together.

**2b** **Reinforcement** Invite students to play the recorder part on p. 333 of the student text silently, reinforcing accurate fingering.

**On Target** Have students play the recorder part on p. 333 of the student text as written.

**Challenge** Have students needing a further challenge play the recorder part below.

## Dreaming About Home

People share their dreams of home in many ways. Musicians write songs, dancers move, and poets write. Think about what makes your home special. Write a poem or story, **compose** a song, or create a dance that tells something about your home.

## Playing Melody Instruments

**Identify** the notes below by letter name. Then **play** the parts to accompany "Sailing Down My Golden River."

Pete Seeger and other members of the Seeger family have collected and recorded American folk songs. **Listen** to this example.

**CD 14-14**
**She'll Be Coming 'Round the Mountain When She Comes**

**American Folk Song**
**as performed by Peggy and Mike Seeger**
This selection features banjo and guitar.

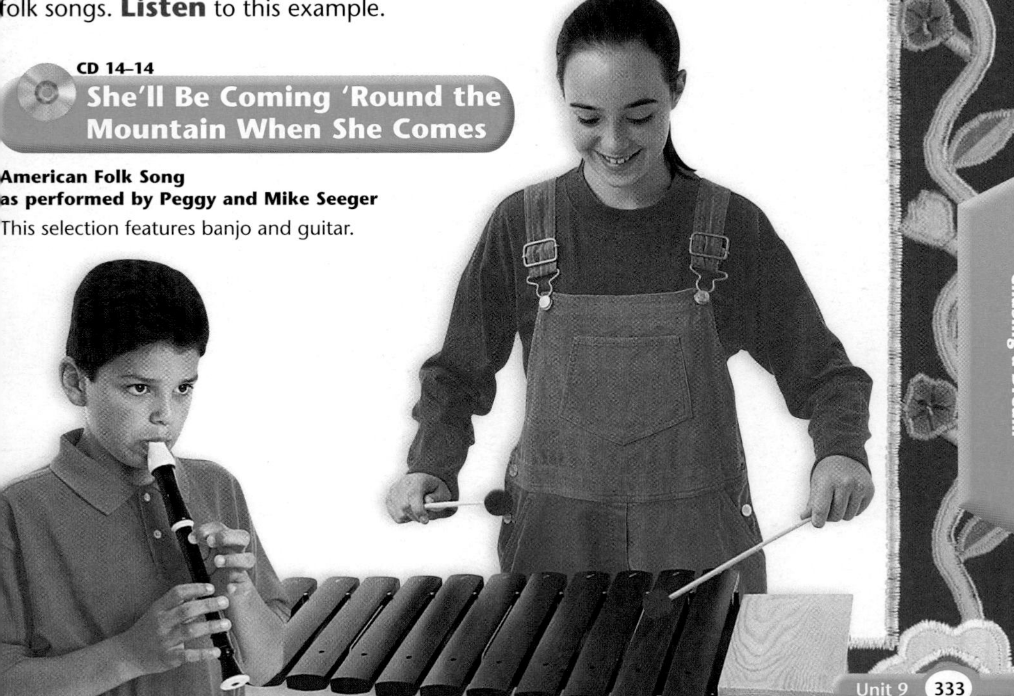

Chasing a Dream

Unit 9 333

# 2 Develop

### Singing

Have students read about Pete Seeger on p. 332. Then play "Sailing Down My Golden River" **CD 14-12.** Discuss with students what the words say Seeger likes about his home. Have students sing with the recording.

### Playing

 Point out the instrumental parts on p. 333. For the xylophone part, have students

- Identify the notes by letter name.
- Practice the part by tapping the right leg for G, left leg for D, and side of the left leg for C. Begin with the right hand and alternate hands throughout.
- Transfer the movements to a xylophone.

For the recorder part, have students

- Sing the notes using hand signs and pitch syllables, then using letter names.
- Move their fingers on recorders as you model the part, then play.

### Listening

Have students listen to and sing with *She'll Be Coming 'Round the Mountain When She Comes* **CD 14-14**—another song about "home." Share information about the Seeger family, in Spotlight On below.

# 3 Close

**Skill: PLAYING** ASSESSMENT

2e **Performance/Observation** Sing "Sailing Down My Golden River" **CD 14-12** together. Then have students play the recorder and xylophone parts in small groups. Observe each student's ability to read and play from notation.

## Spotlight On

 **The Seeger Family** The Seeger family has a prominent place in the history of American music. Charles Seeger (1886–1979), a musicologist, taught some of the first American music and ethnomusicology courses. His oldest son, Pete (b. 1919), is a prominent folk singer and songwriter. His second wife, composer Ruth Crawford Seeger (1901–1953), collected and edited American folk songs. The version of *She'll Be Coming 'Round the Mountain When She Comes* in this lesson is from one of her collections. The recording is sung by her children, Michael (b. 1933) and Peggy (b. 1935), both scholars and folk musicians.

## Technology/Media Link

 **Electronic Keyboard** Have students write a poem and improvise background music to accompany its reading. Have them work in pairs at a keyboard to improvise ostinatos, using the black keys. Students may wish to use drum sounds (or rhythm instruments) to reinforce the meter of the poem. Sound effects selected from the keyboard may further support the mood of the poem.

LESSON 5

## LESSON AT A GLANCE

**Element Focus** **TIMBRE** Chinese instrument timbres

**Skill Objective** **LISTENING** Listen to music played on Chinese instruments

**Connection Activity** **CULTURE** Explore Chinese culture through songs, poetry, legends, and language

**MATERIALS**

- *"Niu lang zhi nü"* **CD 14-15**
- "The Cowherd and the Weaving Maid" **CD 14-16**
  **Recording Routine:** Intro (8 m.); v. 1; interlude (4 m.); v. 2; coda
- **Pronunciation Practice/Translation** p. 491
- *Bumper Harvest Celebration* **CD 14-19**
- "Quiet Night" (poem)
- "News of Home" (poem)
- "Traveler's Song" (poem)
- **Resource Book** p. A-38
- glockenspiel; soprano, alto, bass xylophones; finger cymbal; triangle
- video recording equipment (optional)

**VOCABULARY**

accompaniment *sheng*

**National Standards**

**1c** Sing songs from diverse cultures
**2f** Play instruments independently against contrasting parts
**4a** Compose music to accompany readings
**6b** Describe music by answering questions about it
**8b** Identify ways music relates to social studies
**9a** Listen to identify music from different cultures
**9b** Describe elements in music from various cultures

**MORE MUSIC CHOICES**

Other music from China:
*"Feng yang hua gu,"* p. 313
*Wu long,* p. 157

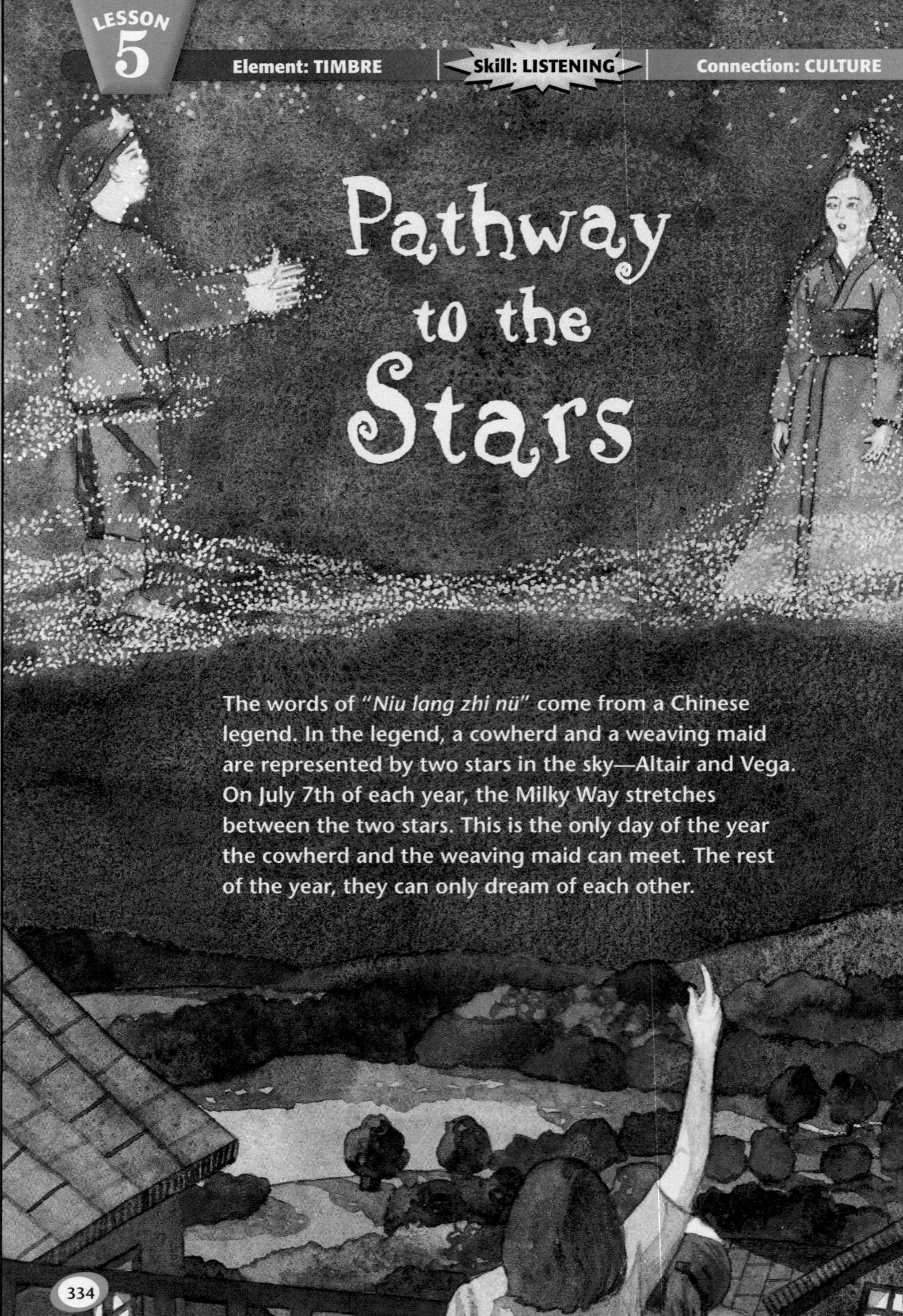

LESSON 5
Element: TIMBRE
Skill: LISTENING
Connection: CULTURE
Pathway to the Stars
The words of "*Niu lang zhi nü*" come from a Chinese legend. In the legend, a cowherd and a weaving maid are represented by two stars in the sky—Altair and Vega. On July 7th of each year, the Milky Way stretches between the two stars. This is the only day of the year the cowherd and the weaving maid can meet. The rest of the year, they can only dream of each other.
334

# Footnotes

## ACROSS THE CURRICULUM

▶ **Science** In a clear night sky, a person can see about 5,000 stars. The stars Vega and Altair are two of three stars that make up a triangle, which is symbolic of summertime in the Northern Hemisphere. Vega is part of the constellation Lyra (a lyre is a type of ancient harp), and Altair is the eye of an eagle-shaped constellation named Aquila.

## BUILDING SKILLS THROUGH MUSIC

▶ **Reading** Share the information from Across the Curriculum on p. 336 with students. Then have them read the three poems on p. 336 of the student text. Engage students in a brief discussion comparing and contrasting the theme of home in each of the three poems.

## CULTURAL CONNECTION

8b ▶ **Mythology** The story of the cowherd and the weaving maid is a legend from Chinese mythology. In the legend, the weaving maid, granddaughter of the Ethereal Emperor, spent all her days weaving cloth in the sky. She noticed the cowherd on Earth, tending an ox. The weaving maid came to Earth. The two fell in love, were married, and became parents of two children. When the Ethereal Emperor discovered them, he ordered the weaving maid back to the sky. The cowherd and weaving maid were very sad, but the Supreme Goddess intervened for them. So the Ethereal Emperor granted them permission to visit once a year as stars—on July 7, when the Milky Way joins Vega and Altair.

## Singing Stars

Vega, the weaving maid in the Chinese legend, is a very bright star in the constellation Lyra. Altair, the cowherd in the Chinese legend, is a star in the constellation Aquila.

**Sing** this folk song from China, *"Niu lang zhi nü."*
**Listen** to the timbres of Chinese instruments in the recording.

CD 14-15
MIDI 24

# Niu lang zhi nü
## (The Cowherd and the Weaving Maid)

s, l, d r f s l

*English Words by Mary Shamrock* *Folk Song from China*

迢 迢 牵 牛 星 皎 皎
1. Tiau tiau chien niu hsing, jiau jiau
1. High a - bove, the cow - herd star, weav - ing maid, so

河 汉 女 织 织 揠 素 手
hĕ han nü hsien hsien ien su shou
bright, so far. Grace - ful hands, soft and white,

扎 扎 弄 机 杼 盈 盈
zha zha nong ji zhu ing ing
weav - ing through each night. Shin - ing

一 水 间 脉 脉 不 得 语
i hsuei jien mu - o mu - o bu de ü
far a - part, weep - ing with a si - lent heart.

2. *Zhong zhru bu cheng zhang,*
*chi ti lei zhru ü*
*ne han ching chie chien*
*hsiang chü fu ji hsü*
*ing ing i hsuei jien*
*muo muo bu de ü*

2. They must wait throughout the day
for the moon to light the way.
Each alone, through the years
freely flow the tears.
Shining far apart,
weeping with a silent heart.

Chasing a Dream

# 1 Introduce

Invite students to share names or information about stars or constellations, such as the North Star or the Big Dipper and Little Dipper. See Across the Curriculum on p. 334.

Tell students that other cultures also name constellations in the night sky. For example, the Chinese have a myth about the constellations Altair and Vega. Share the information about Chinese mythology from the Cultural Connection on p. 334. Invite students to read about the cowherd and weaving maid on p. 334.

# 2 Develop

### Listening

Tell students that many years ago, people looked at the locations and patterns of stars in the sky to help them tell directions, times of night, or times of the year. Sometimes they made up stories about the stars.

Have students listen to the English version of *"Niu lang zhi nü"* **CD 14-16** and follow the words in the song on p. 335.

**ASK How do the cowherd and the weaving maid feel about being apart?** (sad)

**What are they dreaming about?** (being together)

### Singing

1c

Point out the Mandarin characters for *"Niu lang zhi nü"* in the song notation, as well as the transliteration below them. Then, play the Mandarin language recording of *"Niu lang zhi nü"* **CD 14-15** for students.

Use the Pronunciation Practice **CD 14-18** to help students learn the song. Have them listen to and echo each phrase. Refer to Resource Book p. A-38 for a Pronunciation Practice Guide.

Sing *"Niu lang zhi nü"* together.

### Playing

Have students listen to *"Niu lang zhi nü"* **CD 14-15** again.

**continued on page 336**

## Movement

**▶ Creative Movement** Invite students to create movements to perform with *"Niu lang zhi nü."* Encourage them to think about the story of the cowherd and weaving maid as they listen to the music. Then, invite them to use calm and flowing movements to match the mood of the song. Using props such as streamers, scarves, or wands with stars may give support to students who are shy or who have had limited movement experience.

## Spotlight On

**▶ Chinese Musical Instruments** The people of ancient China had an interesting classification system for instruments. Metal instruments, such as bell chimes, were associated with the direction west and the season autumn. Bamboo instruments (flutes) were associated with the east and spring. Instruments made of skins (drums) were associated with north and winter. Instruments with silk (strings on a zither) were associated with south and summer. Some of the instruments heard in *"Niu lang zhi nü"* are the *erhu, pipa,* and *sheng* (string instruments).

6b **ASK What kinds of instrument sounds do you hear?** (strings, winds, drums)

Share the information about Chinese instruments from Spotlight On, p. 335.

2f Help students accompany *"Niu lang zhi nü,"* using the following patterns.

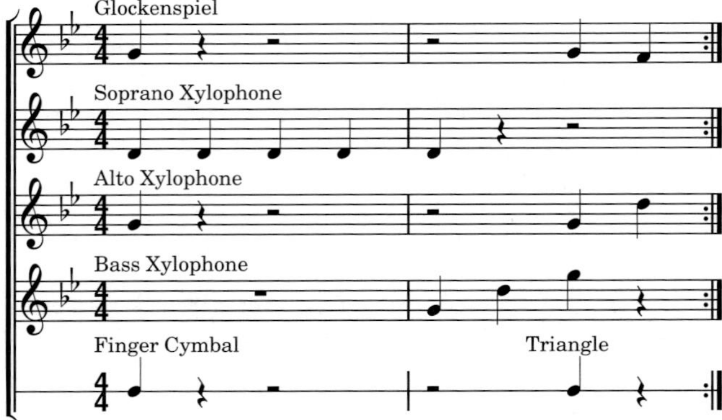


### Creating

Invite students to read the poems on p. 336. Share the information about Chinese poetry from Across the Curriculum below.

Then, divide the class into three or four groups. Have the members of each group

- Select a poem and practice reading it aloud, using their voices expressively.
- Create movements to accompany the poem as it is read aloud.

- 4a Create an instrumental accompaniment (sound effects or ostinatos) to enhance the movement and reading.
- Perform their interpretation of the poem for the other groups.

Request permission to videotape students' performances, then watch the video together. Encourage students to write about their group's interpretation and their role in creating and performing it.

## Guiding Stars

Read aloud these Chinese poems about home, family, and friends. Think of ways to **move** as each poem is read. **Create** an instrumental accompaniment to show the meaning and feeling of the poem.

### Quiet Night

*by Li Bai*

A moonbeam on my bed
Or frost on the ground?
I look up at the full moon,
I look down and think of home.

### News of Home

*by Wang Wei*

You've just come from my old hometown.
You must have some news of home.
The day you left, was the plum tree
By my window in bloom yet?

### Traveler's Song

*by Meng Jai*

My loving mother, thread in hand,
Mended the coat I have on now.
Stitch by stitch, just before I left home,
Thinking that I might be gone a long time.
How can a blade of young grass
Ever repay the warmth of spring sun?

336

## ACROSS THE CURRICULUM

▶ **Language Arts** The poems on p. 336 are from the Tang dynasty (A.D. 618–907), a time when China was at peace and the arts flourished. Li Bai, from the Szechwan province, is considered one of China's best poets. Meng Jai was well known for his poetry, although his life included much suffering and poverty. Wang Wei expressed his love of nature in both poetry and painting.

Poetry is still an important part of Chinese life. Children are taught to read by learning poetry. Adults often write poems for various occasions and special events. For more information about these and other poems, invite students to read *Maples in the Mist,* translated by Minfong Ho (Lothrop, Lee & Shepard, 1996).

## MEETING INDIVIDUAL NEEDS

▶ **Working in Groups** Use these strategies to help students meet the challenge of working in groups during the activity in the Creating section.

- Give each group a printed copy of the instructions.
- Circulate among the groups, asking questions that help students think about and assess their progress.
- Appoint student leaders in each group, including a timekeeper and a manager who keeps everyone on task.

As students work on their creating task, encourage them to match their instrumental accompaniment to the motions they have created.

## Music from China

As you follow the listening map below, **listen** for the timbre of the *sheng.*

CD 14-19

**Bumper Harvest Celebration**

**by Lu Zaiyi and Xu Caoming**
**as performed by the Shanghai National Music Orchestra**

The *sheng*, a native instrument of China, is a type of mouth organ.

Chasing a Dream

Unit 9 337

### Listening

Invite students to listen to *Bumper Harvest Celebration* **CD 14-19** and follow the listening map. Students should listen for the *sheng* (the primary instrument) in the map and for elements of the accompaniment that distinguish the different sections of the map.

## 3 Close

**Skill: LISTENING** ASSESSMENT

**Music Journal Writing** Invite students to sing *"Niu lang zhi nü"* **CD 14-15** or listen to *Bumper Harvest Celebration* **CD 14-19.** Have students review what they have learned about Chinese music and culture. As students work in groups of three, have them

- Make a group list of things they have learned; for example, the timbres produced by such Chinese instruments as the *erhu, pipa,* and *sheng.*
- Ask each other questions to check individual understanding; for example, of how the instruments used in each piece of Chinese music help to give it its special feeling and style.
- Write individual paragraphs to summarize what they have learned and share them with each other.

### Cultural Connection

**Chinese Writing** The Chinese system of writing is essentially pictographic. In instances where words are too abstract to be pictured easily, the pictographs, or characters, indicate their sound. The written language includes basic symbols for words such as man or horse as well as compound pictographs. The earliest examples of Chinese writing date to the early fourteenth century B.C. Until the eighteenth century, China produced more than half the books existing in the world, which reflects the importance of writing to this culture.

When English speakers deal with Chinese characters, the words are usually transliterated according to their phonetic sounds.

### Technology/Media Link

**Transparency** Using the overhead projector and transparency, guide students in listening to *Bumper Harvest Celebration.*

**MIDI/Sequencing Software** After students have performed the song *"Niu lang zhi nü"* with the MIDI song file, discuss the playback timbre of each track. Remind students how General MIDI voices can be changed using the sequencing software. Invite students to come to the computer to change the timbre of the song's melody. Other class members may be invited to stop and start the MIDI playback.

LESSON 6

## LESSON AT A GLANCE

**Element Focus** **RHYTHM** Tied notes

**Skill Objective** **SINGING** Sing tied notes in a song

**Connection Activity** **LANGUAGE ARTS** Write a song parody

**MATERIALS**

- "My Bonnie Lies Over the Ocean" **CD 14-20**

  **Recording Routine:** Intro (4 m.); v. 1; refrain; interlude (4 m.); v. 2; refrain; interlude (4 m.); v. 3; refrain; interlude (4 m.); v. 4; refrain; coda
- "Cowboy's Dream" (poem)
- **Dance Directions** for "My Bonnie Lies Over the Ocean" p. 517
- **Resource Book** p. H-21
- map of the United States

**VOCABULARY**

tied note parody

**National Standards**

**5a** Read rhythms in $\frac{3}{4}$ meter
**7a** Create standards for evaluating performances
**8b** Identify ways music relates to language arts
**9e** Demonstrate appropriate audience behavior

**MORE MUSIC CHOICES**

For more practice reading rhythms in $\frac{3}{4}$:

"Santa Clara," p. 172

"Streets of Laredo," p. 272

# 1 INTRODUCE

**ASK Have you ever missed someone—a friend who moved or someone who lives far away?** (Accept a variety of answers.)



# Lost and Found

As settlers moved across the American frontier, they often sang songs about people and places they left behind. **Sing** "My Bonnie Lies Over the Ocean."

How many ties can you find in this song? Which phrases have exactly the same rhythm?

CD 14-20
My Bonnie Lies Over the Ocean
m s l t d r' m'
Folk Song from the United States
VERSE
do
B♭ E♭ B♭
1. My Bon - nie lies o - ver the o - cean,
2. Last night as I lay on my pil - low,
3. Oh, blow ye winds o - ver the o - cean,
4. The winds have blown o - ver the o - cean,
B♭ C7 F7
My Bon - nie lies o - ver the sea;
Last night as I lay on my bed;
Oh, blow ye winds o - ver the sea;
The winds have blown o - ver the sea;
B♭ E♭ B♭
My Bon - nie lies o - ver the o - cean,
Last night as I lay on my pil - low,
Oh, blow ye winds o - ver the o - cean,
The winds have blown o - ver the o - cean,


338

## Footnotes

### ACROSS THE CURRICULUM

▶ **Language Arts** The lesson above includes an example of a song parody. Show students examples of parodies. For example, *The True Story of the 3 Little Pigs* by Jon Scieszka (Viking Penguin, 1999), is a parody of the *Three Little Pigs* story. *Sneaky Pete and the Wolf* is a parody by Peter Schickele of Prokofiev's *Peter and the Wolf*. Invite students to create parodies of familiar stories or songs. Have a "Parody Party," where students read or perform their creations.

### BUILDING SKILLS THROUGH MUSIC

▶ **Language** Share the information about parodies from Across the Curriculum above and the second singing activity under Develop, on p. 339. Divide the class into groups and have them select a song with which they are all familiar. Have them write a parody of the song and then share their songs with the class.

### MOVEMENT

▶ **Patterned Movement** For a movement activity for "My Bonnie Lies Over the Ocean" that has students moving at different tempos, refer to the Dance Directions on p. 517.

Use the Dance—Practice Tempo Track **CD 14-23** to learn the dance and the Dance—Performance Track **CD 14-22** when ready to perform.

E♭ F7 B♭
Oh, bring back my Bon - nie to me.
I dreamt that my Bon - nie was dead.
And bring back my Bon - nie to me.
And brought back my Bon - nie to me.
REFRAIN
B♭ E♭
Bring back, bring back,
F7 B♭
bring back my Bon - nie to me, to me;
B♭ E♭ C7
Bring back, bring back, oh,
F7 B♭
bring back my Bon - nie to me.

### Almost the Same Song

A parody is a comical imitation of a song or story. Here is a parody of "My Bonnie Lies Over the Ocean." The words are different, but the melody is the same. **Sing** this parody. Then write your own.

## Cowboy's Dream

*Anonymous Parody*

**Last night as I lay on the prairie,**
**And looked at the stars in the sky,**
**I wondered if ever a cowboy,**
**Could drift to that sweet by and by.**

**Roll on, roll on,**
**Roll on, little dogies, roll on, roll on.**
**Roll on, roll on,**
**Roll on, little dogies, roll on.**

Chasing a Dream

# 2 Develop

### Singing

Play "My Bonnie Lies Over the Ocean" **CD 14-20.** Invite students to sing with the recording.

Read the information on p. 338 together. Then, look at a map of the United States. Discuss how people migrated from east to west.

### Reading

5a Invite students to find lines in the song with exactly the same rhythm (verse, lines 1 and 3); identify tied notes, dotted-quarter/eighth patterns, and dotted-half notes; then clap and say the rhythm of the song.

### Singing

8b Tell students that a parody is an imitation of a song or story and that most parodies are comical. Direct students to "Cowboy's Dream" on p. 339. Have them sing the words, using the melody of "My Bonnie Lies Over the Ocean." Invite students to write their own parodies for "My Bonnie Lies Over the Ocean." See Across the Curriculum on p. 338.

# 3 Close

**Skill: SINGING** ASSESSMENT

7a **Performance/Observation** Help students make one list of criteria for singing and another for audience behavior. Divide the class into groups of four or five. Have groups each sing a verse of "My Bonnie Lies Over the Ocean," "Cowboy's Dream," or their own parody. Have group members practice singing together, referring to their list of criteria to help them improve their performance, then perform for the class.

9e Observe that students hold tied notes for the full duration as they sing. You might also have the performers discuss their classmates' success at being a courteous audience, and offer constructive ideas for shaping a healthy performing climate.

## Skills Reinforcement

▶ **Keyboard** Invite students to play a keyboard accompaniment on the refrain of "My Bonnie Lies Over the Ocean." See Resource Book p. H-21.

▶ **Recorder** Have students play the refrain of "My Bonnie Lies Over the Ocean" to expand the right hand range outward from the thumb. Invite students to practice the expansion until it is comfortable and then play the entire refrain.

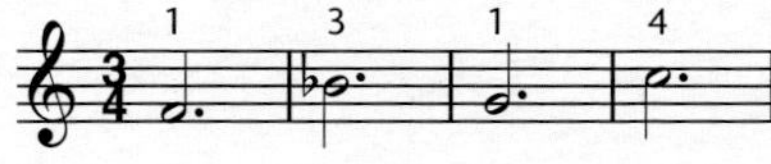
1 3 1 4

## Character Education

▶ **Humor** Discuss the positive impact humor can have in our lives. How does laughing make you feel? How does feeling this way make a difference in the way you treat other people? (When we are happy, we tend to treat others more positively and kindly). Discuss the difference between appropriate and inappropriate uses of humor. How do laughing at someone and laughing with someone differ? What should you do if you see humor being used inappropriately? Discuss ways students can bring more healthy humor into their lives and the lives of those around them.

## Technology/Media Link

**Web Site** Invite students to visit *www.sfsuccessnet.com* to learn more about songs of the Westward movement.

LESSON 7

## LESSON AT A GLANCE

**Element Focus** **TEXTURE/HARMONY** Adding accompaniments

**Skill Objective** **PLAYING** Play Autoharp to accompany a song

**Connection Activity** **SOCIAL STUDIES** Discuss the California gold rush and United States westward expansion

**MATERIALS**

- "Clementine" **CD 15-1**

  **Recording Routine:** Intro (4 m.); v. 1; refrain; v. 2; refrain; v. 3; refrain; interlude (8 m.); v. 4; refrain; coda
- "Saturday Night Waltz" from *Rodeo* (excerpt) **CD 15-3**
- *Forked Deer/Fisher's Hornpipe* **CD 15-4**
- *First Night Quadrille* **CD 15-5**
- **Dance Directions** for *First Night Quadrille* p. 518
- **Resource Book** pp. F-27, H-22
- Autoharps
- map of the United States

**VOCABULARY**

accompaniment chord verse refrain
waltz square dance

**National Standards**

**1b** Sing expressively with appropriate interpretation
**2b** Perform chords on appropriate instruments
**6a** Listen to identify form
**6b** Describe music by moving to it and answering questions about it
**6e** While listening to music, move to show a prominent feature of the music
**8b** Identify ways music relates to social studies

**MORE MUSIC CHOICES**

Other songs with Autoharp accompaniments:
"The Keel Row," p. 240
*"Ocho kandelikas,"* p. 429

LESSON 7 Element: TEXTURE/HARMONY Skill: PLAYING Connection: SOCIAL STUDIES

# The Original Forty-Niners

Gold was discovered in California in 1848. By 1849, thousands of people traveled to this state, dreaming of gold. They were called "forty-niners."

The trip to California was hard and took a long time. The forty-niners had to cross the prairie in wagons. Others sailed from the east coast of the United States around the tip of South America to reach California. They were willing to do all of this to find gold!

▲ Panning for g

**Play** an accompaniment for "Clementine" using an Autoharp. Find the G and $D_7$ chords, then strum as you **sing.** Do the verse and refrain have the same chord pattern?

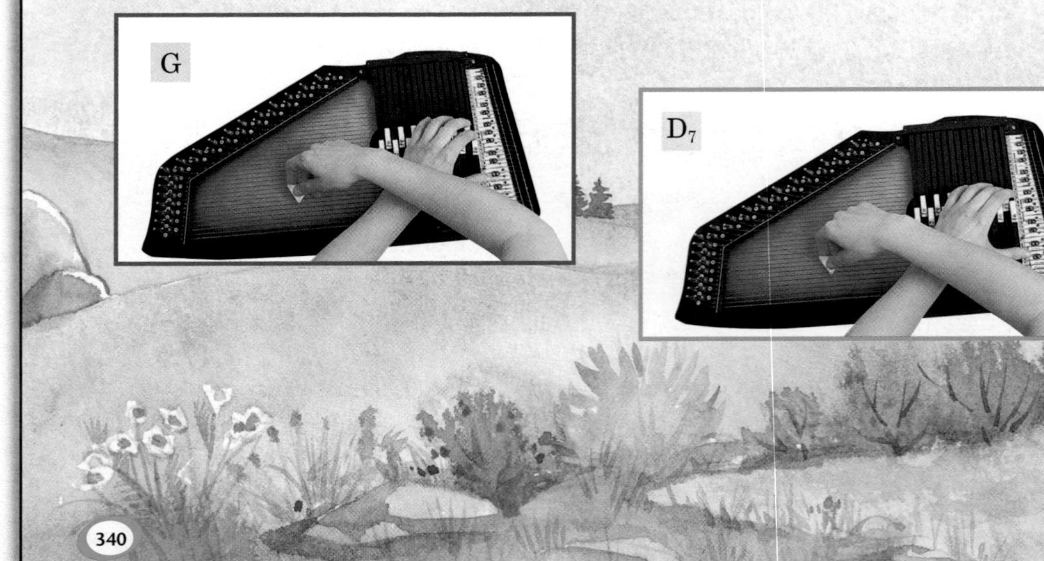


340

# Footnotes

## ACROSS THE CURRICULUM

8b ▶ **Social Studies** In 1848, John Sutter discovered gold in the hills of California near San Francisco. As the news of gold spread, thousands of people from all over the world flocked to that area to find their fortune. The people who went to find their fortune in gold were called forty-niners. Despite the large amounts of gold in California, most of the forty-niners left disappointed, with little to show for their efforts.

## BUILDING SKILLS THROUGH MUSIC

▶ **Social Studies** Share information with students from Across the Curriculum above. Also, ask them to read all of the information about forty-niners on pp. 340–342 of the student text. Then, ask students what impact the gold rush had on California. (It increased the population and expanded the farming and ranching industries.)

## MOVEMENT

6e ▶ **Creative Movement** Invite students to move to show the tempo of the musical examples from this lesson. Play "Clementine" **CD 15-1,** *Saturday Night Waltz* **CD 15-3,** and *Forked Deer/Fisher's Hornpipe* **CD 15-4** in any order. Invite students to

- Move to the music, using motions of their choice.
- Use their own words to describe the tempo of each selection.

## Songs About Life

The forty-niners made up songs about their experiences. Many of their songs were about the hard work of mining and the rough conditions of living in California. **Sing** "Clementine," a song about the gold rush years.

CD 15-1
Clementine
s, t, do r m f s
Folk Song from the United States
VERSE
G
D7
1. In a cav - ern by a can - yon, Ex - ca - vat - ing for a mine,
2. Light she was and like a feath - er, And her shoes were num-ber nine,
Dwelt a min - er, for - ty - nin - er, And his daugh - ter, Clem-en - tine.
Her-ring box - es with-out top - ses, San-dals were for Clem-en - tine.
REFRAIN
Oh, my dar - lin', oh, my dar - lin', Oh, my dar - lin' Clem-en - tine,
You are lost and gone for - ev - er, Dread-ful sor - ry, Clem-en - tine.

3. Drove she ducklings to the water
Every morning just at nine;
Struck her foot against a splinter,
Fell into the foaming brine. *Refrain*

4. Rosy lips above the water
Blowing bubbles mighty fine;
But, alas! I was no swimmer,
So I lost my Clementine. *Refrain*

**Tune In**

The miners seeking their fortunes were called prospectors. When a large deposit of gold was found, it was called the mother lode.

Chasing a Dream

# 1 Introduce

Engage students in the gold rush spirit.

**ASK** **If you heard that someone had found lots of gold in the state next to ours, what would you do?** (Accept a variety of answers.)

**SAY** In 1848, someone discovered gold in California. Let's find out what happened.

Share the information with students about the gold rush in Across the Curriculum on p. 340.

# 2 Develop

### Singing

Invite students to read the information on the California gold rush on p. 340. Display a map of the United States.

**ASK** **Who were the forty-niners?** (people who traveled to California around 1849, looking for gold)

**Where did they come from?** (all across the United States)

**How did they travel to California?** (by wagon, on horseback, or by sailing)

Point out to students that relatively few people lived in California until the gold rush. Thousands of people came to California and stayed there after the gold rush ended.

8b Tell students that the miners and their families sometimes made up songs about their experiences for entertainment. "Clementine" is one of those songs.

1b Play "Clementine" **CD 15-1.** Invite students to

- Follow the verses as they listen.
- Sing the refrain.

Ask students to summarize the story of "Clementine." Then play the recording again and have them sing the entire song.

**continued on page 342**

## Teacher to Teacher

▶ **Developing Autoharp Skills** The Autoharp is usually played by pressing the chord buttons with the left hand and strumming with the right hand over the left, moving from the low strings to high strings. Allow students who have less experience playing the Autoharp to work in pairs. Have one student press the chord buttons while the other strums. To help students feel the chord changes, have them pat the strong beat as they sing. Ask them to pat knees for the G chord and shoulders for the $D_7$ chord. Students can use these motions to lead other class members who are playing the instrument. Making a chart of the chords on the board or on cards placed by the instruments may also help students play with facility.

## Skills Reinforcement

▶ **Recorder** Review the notes D, F♯, G, and A with students. Add the countermelody below during the verse or during the refrain of "Clementine."

▶ **Mallets** For an Orff orchestration to accompany "Clementine," see Resource Book p. F-27.

▶ **Keyboard** For a two-handed keyboard accompaniment for "Clementine," see Resource Book p. H-22.

### Playing

6b Have students show the meter to "Clementine," using a three-beat pattern such as pat-clap-clap. Encourage them to sing as they pat and clap. Tell students that the forty-niners used instruments they could carry with them to accompany their songs.

**ASK What instruments could be carried on horseback or in a wagon?** (Accept a variety of answers, including guitar and banjo.)

2b Invite students to use an Autoharp to accompany "Clementine." Have them

- Identify the G and $D_7$ chords above each line of the song.
- Find G and $D_7$ chords on the Autoharp.
- Strum on the strong beat of each measure; for example, the pat of the pat-clap-clap motion.

See Teacher to Teacher on p. 341 for suggestions on helping students develop Autoharp skills, and Skills Reinforcement on p. 343.

### Listening

Tell students that some forty-niners didn't make it to California. Invite students to read the information on p. 342 to find out what happened. Play *Saturday Night Waltz* **CD 15-3.** Have students

- Follow the listening map of the theme on p. 342.
- Describe the tempo of the music.

6a Play the recording again and have students

- Listen for differences between the A and B sections.
- Stand and step on the strong beat during the A sections.
- Sit in place and sway during the B section.

**ASK What differences did you hear between the A and B sections?** (Accept a variety of answers, including a slower tempo in the B section.)

After students read about Aaron Copland, on p. 343, share with them the information in Spotlight On below.

### Back at the Ranch

Some of the forty-niners found gold in the California hills, while some never reached California at all. Eventually, many became farmers, lumberjacks, or ranchers. Having a successful ranch became a new dream. **Listen** to *Saturday Night Waltz* and follow the map of the melody.

CD 15-3

**Saturday Night Waltz**

**from *Rodeo***
**by Aaron Copland**

In 1942, Aaron Copland wrote music for a ballet called *Rodeo*. The ballet is about life on a ranch. It includes a Saturday night dance scene.

#### SATURDAY NIGHT WALTZ

**LISTENING MAP**

Theme

342

## Footnotes

### Spotlight On

▶ **Aaron Copland and *Rodeo*** American composer Aaron Copland made a conscious decision to write music that would appeal to all kinds of listeners. To do so, he included jazz, folk songs, and folk dances in his music for orchestra. Copland wrote ballet music for the Western story *Billy the Kid* in 1938. In 1942, choreographer Agnes de Mille asked Copland to write a second ballet with a cowboy theme. She even provided the story—a young cowgirl trying to win the affection of the head wrangler on a ranch. The wrangler doesn't notice her tomboyish pranks during a rodeo. But the girl dresses up for the Saturday night dance and gets his attention. This became the ballet *Rodeo*, one of Copland's best-known works.

### Movement

▶ **Patterned Movement** Students can create their own square dance for *Forked Deer/Fisher's Hornpipe*. Before creating their own dances, help students recognize that each phrase has eight beats. Encourage them to organize their movements in eight-beat sections.

Here is a sample dance that has four couples standing in a circle, with boys to the left of their partner.

- Circle right 8; circle left 8.
- Right swing with partner 8; left swing 8.
- Girls right-hand star 16 around the circle, past their partner and to the next boy.
- Right swing new partner 8; left swing 8.

MUSIC MAKERS

## Aaron Copland

American composer **Aaron Copland** (1900–1990) wrote some of the best-loved and most familiar orchestra music of the 20th century. He developed a distinctly American style by using jazz rhythms and folk melodies in his orchestral music. He wrote two ballets about the American West—*Billy the Kid* and *Rodeo*. He also wrote music based on the poems of Emily Dickinson and a composition about Abraham Lincoln called *Lincoln Portrait.*

### Dance with Partners

Learn to do a square dance, one of the kinds of dances done at a hoedown. Choose your partner and get ready to **move**!

CD 15–4

**Forked Deer/Fisher's Hornpipe**

**Traditional Tune**
**as performed by Karen Mueller**

This recording features Autoharp, fiddle, and bass—traditional hoedown instruments.

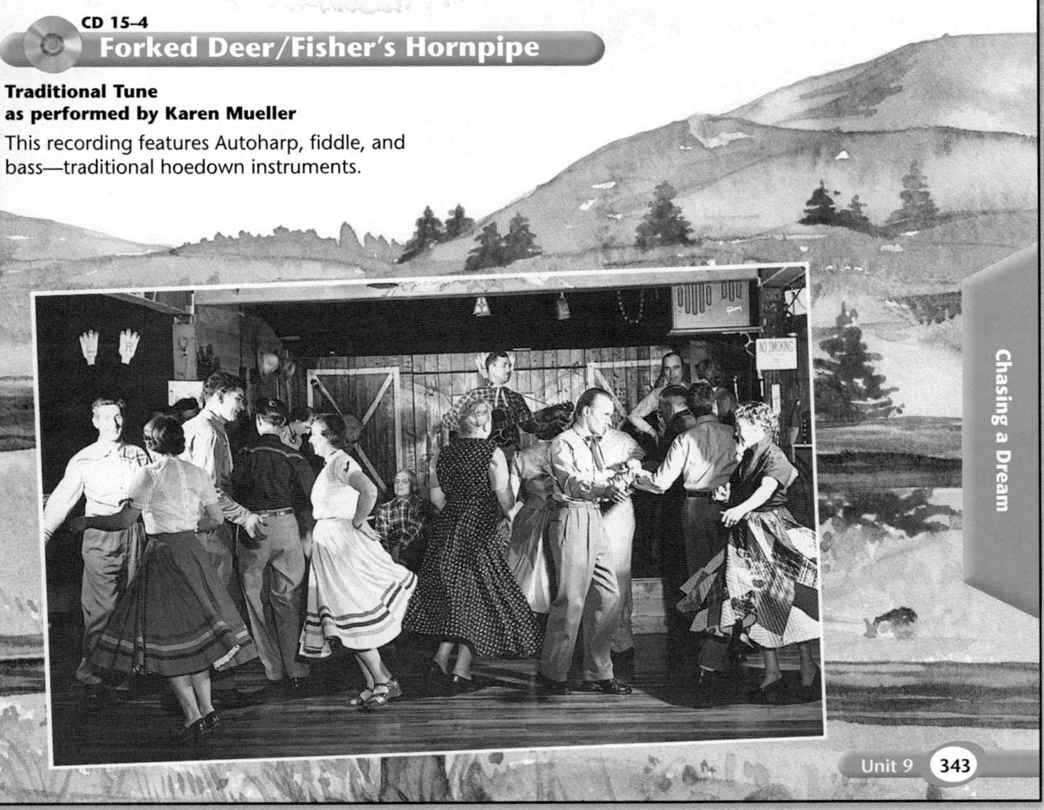

Chasing a Dream



### Moving

Introduce *Forked Deer/Fisher's Hornpipe* as a type of music that might have been played at a hoedown or dance on a ranch.

Play *Forked Deer/Fisher's Hornpipe* **CD 15-4** and have students

- Tap the beat.
- Snap their fingers at the end of each phrase.
- Find the number of beats in each phrase. (eight)

ASK **How does the tempo of this music compare to that of *Saturday Night Waltz?*** (It is faster.)

**What instruments do you hear in this music?** (fiddle, bass, Autoharp plucked and strummed)

Help students review square dance movements, such as circling to the left and right, do-si-do, arm swing, and right-hand and left-hand stars. Invite students to create their own dance for *Forked Deer/Fisher's Hornpipe,* or help them learn the dance in Movement on p. 342.

### Moving

Refer to the Dance Directions on p. 518 and have students perform a square dance to *First Night Quadrille* **CD 15-5.**

## 3 CLOSE

**Element: TEXTURE/HARMONY** ASSESSMENT

**Performance/Observation** Invite students to play the Autoharp and accompany a classroom performance of "Clementine" **CD 15-1.** Assess students' abilities to change chords at the proper time in the music.

### SKILLS REINFORCEMENT

2b ▶ **Playing** The Autoharp is a folk instrument played by musicians today. The recording of *Forked Deer/ Fisher's Hornpipe* features the Autoharp.

**Reinforcement** To prepare students to play the Autoharp accompaniment for "Clementine," have them play the bass notes of the chords on bass xylophones, so they are used to hearing the root of each chord.

**On Target** Have students play the Autoharp accompaniment for "Clementine," as illustrated on p. 340 of the student text.

**Challenge** Have individual students who seek a further challenge play the keyboard accompaniment provided on p. H-22 of the Resource Book, while others play the xylophones and Autoharps.

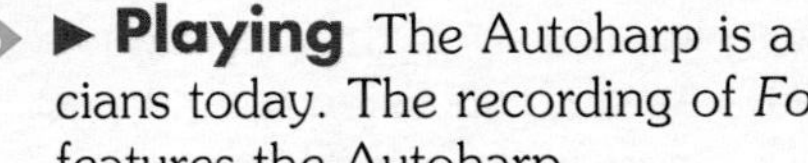

### TECHNOLOGY/MEDIA LINK

**CD-ROM** Invite students to create a short composition, using the *Making Music* software program. Then experiment with tempo by playing the composition at the five different tempos available in the software. Have students select the tempo they like best for their composition and explain their choice verbally or in writing.

**Transparency** Use an overhead projector and the listening map transparency for "Saturday Night Waltz" from *Rodeo* to help students follow the icons of the music's theme.

LESSON 8

## LESSON AT A GLANCE

**Element Focus** **FORM** Rondo form

**Skill Objective** **LISTENING** Listen to identify rondo form

**Connection Activity** **LANGUAGE ARTS** Gather and summarize facts about Johnny Appleseed

**MATERIALS**

- "Johnny Appleseed" **CD 15-7**
  **Recording Routine:** Intro (4 m.); v. 1; interlude (4 m.); v. 2; interlude (4 m.); v. 3; coda
- "Walking Song" from *Acadian Songs* **CD 15-9**
- **Resource Book** p. I-27, J-16
- large map of the United States
- paper and pencils

**VOCABULARY**

rondo

**National Standards**

- **2f** Play instruments independently against contrasting parts
- **3b** Improvise rhythmic ostinato accompaniments
- **4b** Compose songs within specific guidelines
- **5a** Read in $\frac{4}{4}$ meter
- **5c** Identify and use symbols and terms for articulation
- **6a** Listen to identify form
- **6e** While listening to music, move to show changes in the music
- **8b** Identify ways music relates to social studies

**MORE MUSIC CHOICES**

Other songs about American history and culture:

"California, Here I Come," p. 287

"Sweet Betsy from Pike," p. 244

LESSON 8 Element: FORM | Skill: LISTENING | Connection: LANGUAGE ARTS

# An Appleseed Song

Johnny Appleseed was a legendary American figure who had a dream about a world filled with apple trees, where people would never be hungry. **Sing** this song about Johnny Appleseed.

USPS. Displayed with permission.



# Footnotes

## ACROSS THE CURRICULUM

8b ▶ **Science** Engage students in an Apple Discovery project. Have them identify different kinds of apples by reading about them and sampling them in class. Students can make an "Apples" chart and classify different kinds of apples by color, shape, size, and taste. Cut an apple in half lengthwise and another crosswise to look at the core in two different ways. Ask students to find out whether apples are grown locally and what they are used for.

## BUILDING SKILLS THROUGH MUSIC

▶ **Theater** Share information with students about Johnny Appleseed from Spotlight On on p. 345. Then divide students into small groups, inviting them to plan a brief action play (with no dialogue) illustrating an aspect of Johnny Appleseed's unique journeys. Finally, have students perform their plays to the recording of *Walking Song* **CD 15-9.**

## SKILLS REINFORCEMENT

3b ▶ **Improvising** Invite students to improvise rhythm ostinatos to accompany "Johnny Appleseed." As students listen to and sing the song, have them improvise an ostinato using body percussion; for example, pat, clap, snap, or any combination of these. When they can move accurately while listening or singing, invite them to transfer their ostinato to a nonpitched percussion instrument. Try several different ostinatos with the song. Allow students to decide how many ostinatos to add to the musical texture, which ones sound best together, and which instruments make the best combinations. Encourage them to provide reasons for the musical decisions they make.

2f ▶ **Recorder** Students can learn a recorder countermelody to accompany the entire song "Johnny Appleseed." See Resource Book p. I-27.

CD 15-7
Johnny Appleseed
s, l, t,(d) r m f s
From Rosemary and Stephen Vincent Benét
From an American Folk Hymn in the Virginia Sacred Musical Repository
do
G C G C
1. Of Jon - a - than Chap - man two things are known, That
2. For fif - ty years o - ver of har - vest and dew, He
3. Con - sid - er, con - sid - er, and think well up - on, The
G Am7 D7
he loved ap - ples, that he walked a - lone. At
plant - ed his ap - ples where no ap - ples grew. The
mar - vel - ous sto - ry of Ap - ple - seed John. He
G Am7 D7
sev - en - ty - odd he was gnarled as could be, But
winds of the prai - rie might blow through his rags, But he
has no stat - ue, he has no tomb, But he
D7 G
rud - dy and sound as a good ap - ple tree.
car - ried his seeds in the best deer - skin bags. John - ny
has his apple trees still in bloom.
D7 G
Ap - ple - seed! John - ny Ap - ple - seed!
Chasing a Dream
Unit 9 345

# 1 Introduce

Invite students to name all the things they eat that are made out of apples; for example, apple pie, applesauce, apple juice. Have them read the text about Johnny Appleseed on p. 344.

At appropriate times throughout the lesson, share with students the information about Johnny Appleseed in Cultural Connection and Spotlight On, below, and Across the Curriculum on p. 346.

# 2 Develop

## Listening

8b

Play "Johnny Appleseed" **CD 15-7** for students. As they listen to the song, invite them to

- Follow the lyrics on p. 345 and search for facts about Johnny Appleseed.
- Sing along with the last line.

Have students

- Work with a partner and list facts about Johnny Appleseed, based on the song lyrics.
- Find additional facts in the paragraph in their books.
- Listen to the song again.

## Reading

5a

Have students

- Read (tap and say) the rhythm for the first phrase of "Johnny Appleseed" on p. 345.
- Identify the first pitch as low *so*, then identify the remaining pitches in the first phrase.
- Sing the first phrase, using pitch syllables and hand signs.
- Sing the first phrase with the lyrics.

**continued on page 346**

## Cultural Connection

**Finding Food** Johnny Appleseed's dream was for apple trees to provide settlers and people moving westward with food. Help students understand that food was an important resource, and not as easy to obtain as it is today. As people traveled west during the early 1800s, they had to carry their own provisions. There were no grocery stores, and the land had to be cleared for farming. In addition to food carried in their wagons, early settlers relied on hunting, fishing, and food they found along the way. Apple trees were always a welcome sight, for apples could be used in many ways and were relatively easy to store.

## Spotlight On

**Johnny Appleseed** John Chapman was born in Leominster, Massachusetts in 1774. His father was one of the minute men who fought in the Revolutionary War. By 1797, John had an apple tree nursery near Pittsburgh, Pennsylvania. He passed out apple seeds and young trees to neighbors and to settlers moving west. A few years later, he started his own journey west, planting apple seeds and starting apple tree nurseries in many new places. He became known as Johnny Appleseed, and many legends have been told and written about him. He died in Fort Wayne, Indiana in 1845; some of the trees he planted are still alive.

For the remaining phrases, have students

- Read (tap and say) the rhythm. (Note that there is an upbeat note for each phrase.)
-  Identify slurred notes (two notes for one word or syllable).
- Identify steps and skips in the melody.
- Sing the phrases with the lyrics.

Invite students to sing the entire song together, with **CD 15-7.**

## Listening

Have students return to their list of facts about "Johnny Appleseed." Have them

- Identify the states he traveled through on the map on p. 346.
- Find the states on a large classroom map of the United States.

**ASK If Johnny Appleseed had kept walking to other states, where might he have gone next?** (Illinois or Michigan)

Play *Walking Song* **CD 15-9.** To help students identify rondo form presented aurally, have them

- Follow the listening map on p. 347 by tapping the beat. Each long mark indicates the beginning of a measure.
- Identify the form of the music. (ABACA, or rondo)

## Moving

 Play *Walking Song* **CD 15-9** again. Invite students to listen and move to the music, using the listening map on p. 347 as a guide.

- A – walking
- B – resting or slow-motion movements
- A – walking
- C – dancing
- A – walking

## Virgil Thomson

American composer **Virgil Thomson** (1896–1989) was born in Kansas City, Missouri. As a young composer, he traveled to Paris, where he heard the music of Stravinsky, Satie, and other composers. Many of Virgil Thomson's compositions use American folk songs and hymn tunes. He also wrote music for *The River* and *The Plow That Broke the Plains*—documentary films about the United States. In addition to composing, Virgil Thomson was a music critic for the New York *Herald Tribune* newspaper.

# Footnotes

## Across the Curriculum

▶ **Social Studies** Invite students to read more about Johnny Appleseed by sharing the book *Folks Call Me Appleseed John* by Andrew Glass (Bantam Doubleday, 1998).

Johnny Appleseed (John Chapman, 1774–1845) was born as the American Revolution was starting. When he began his travels, most of the states we now know did not exist. Help students locate important places in Johnny Appleseed's life story—Leominster, Massachusetts; Pittsburgh, Pennsylvania; the Allegheny and Ohio rivers; Fort Wayne, Indiana. Then, have students determine which of our current states achieved statehood during his lifetime.

## Skills Reinforcement

4b ▶ **Creating** Using the facts they have collected during the lesson as well as any other information about apples from the Footnotes activities, have students create a rap that is four to six lines long. You may wish to have small groups create raps, then have the class create a refrain that can be spoken at the end of each group's rap or between groups as the A section of a class rondo. Invite students to accompany their raps with nonpitched percussion instruments and body percussion.

Your students might also enjoy creating a rondo, using three body percussion themes with vocal sounds. See Resource Book p. J-16.

## Form and Timbre

Johnny Appleseed walked hundreds of miles to make his dream come true. Follow the listening map below and **identify** the form of *Walking Song.*

CD 15-9

**Walking Song**

**from *Acadian Songs***
**by Virgil Thomson**

This selection features clarinet, flute, violin, trumpet, and oboe.

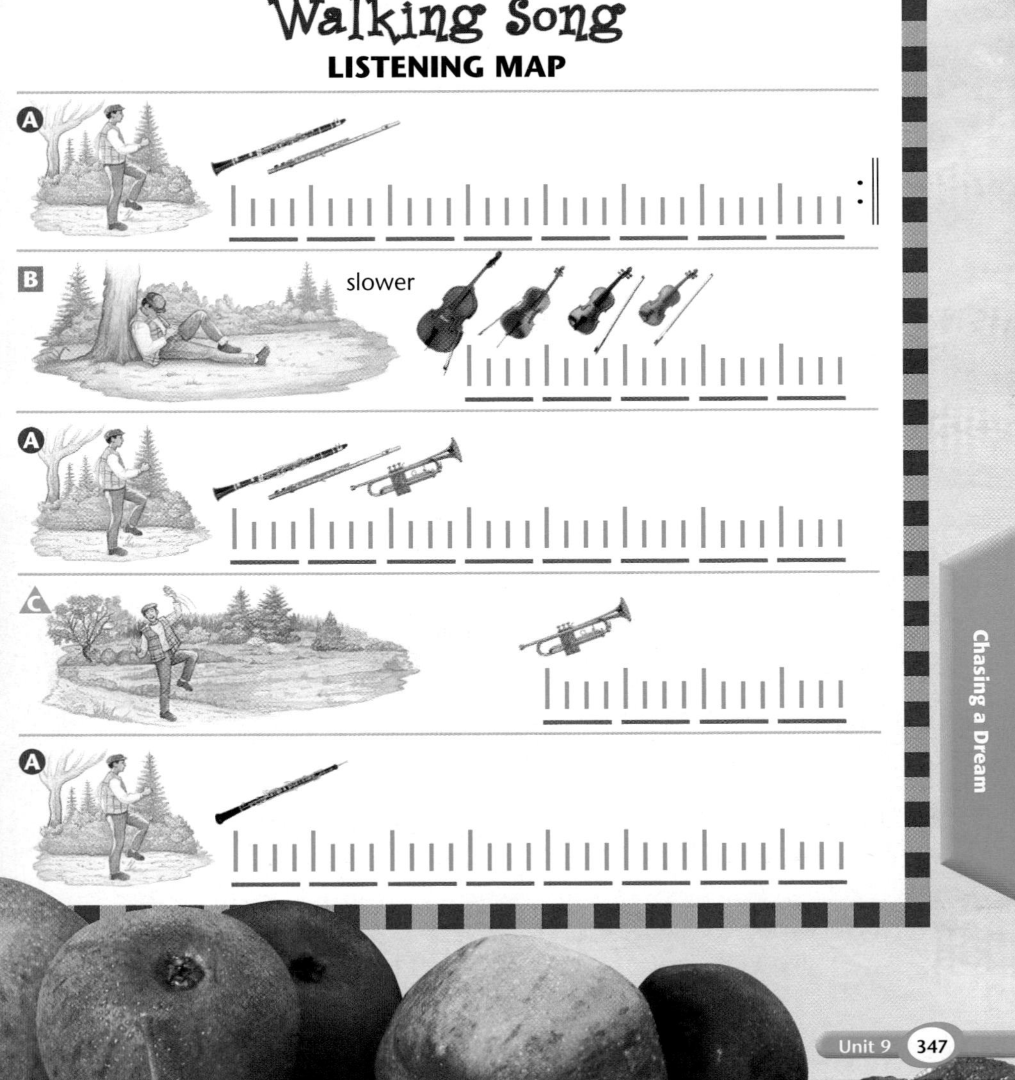


Chasing a Dream



**ASK How does the tempo change in this music?** (B is slower than A; C is faster than A.)

Discuss with the class the information about Virgil Thomson on p. 346. Then, invite students to move with the music again.

# 3 Close

**Skill: LISTENING** ASSESSMENT

**Performance/Observation** Have students listen with their eyes closed to "Walking Song" from *Acadian Songs* **CD 15-9.** Assess students' understanding of form in the following way.

Have them

- Raise one finger when they hear the A section.
- Raise two fingers when they hear the B section.
- Raise three fingers when they hear the C section.

For another activity, invite students to share what they have learned about Johnny Appleseed. Have students

- Compare their list of facts with that of a classmate.
- Summarize their information by writing a paragraph about Johnny Appleseed, using their list of facts.

Review the song "Johnny Appleseed" **CD 15-7.** Invite students to read their paragraphs aloud as an introduction to the song and between verses.

## Audience Etiquette

▶ **Critical Listening** Students who practice active listening skills, such as those called for in the listening map activity above, will be more attentive at live performances. To promote critical listening skills, have students

- Follow visual maps of the music as they listen. (Look for listening maps, such as the example on p. 347, that illustrate or highlight form, dynamics, instrumentation, or other musical elements.)
- Respond to music in class by writing about what they hear in a listening log. (Use effective questioning techniques to encourage students to respond to the music verbally in large groups, small groups, and with partners. Ask questions that invite students to include details in their responses, explain their thinking, and provide support for their answers.)

## School to Home Connection

▶ **Meet the Gardener** Ask students if they know of anyone who grows, plants, or keeps a garden or orchard. Encourage students to interview that person about what they grow and why they devote their time to growing things. If possible, have them bring in a photo of the gardener. Allow students to share what they learned with the class.

## Technology/Media Link

**Transparency** Using an overhead projector and the listening map transparency, guide students as they listen to "Walking Song" from *Acadian Songs.*

## LESSON AT A GLANCE

**Element Focus** **TEXTURE/HARMONY** Unison/harmony

**Skill Objective** **MOVING** Move while singing a round

**Connection Activity** **RELATED ARTS** Create personal works of art using peace as the theme

**MATERIALS**

- "Peace Round" **CD 15-10**

  **Recording Routine:** Intro (8 m.); vocal in unison; interlude (2 m.); vocal in canon; coda
- *Interview with Jean Ritchie* **CD 15-12**
- **Resource Book** p. F-29
- xylophones, metallophones, glockenspiels, recorders

**VOCABULARY**

round ostinato

**◆◆◆◆ National Standards ◆◆◆◆**

**1d** Sing ostinatos and rounds
**2f** Play instruments independently against contrasting parts
**6e** While listening to music, move to show a prominent feature of the music
**9d** Describe roles of musicians in various cultures

**MORE MUSIC CHOICES**

Other rounds:

"Ah, Poor Bird," p. 196

"Oh, How Lovely Is the Evening," p. 217

# 1 INTRODUCE

Discuss with students that some people dream of a world where we can all live together in peace. Invite students to read about Jean Ritchie on p. 349, who wrote the words for "Peace Round," and then listen to an interview with her **CD 15-12.**



# Peace and Harmony

Peace is the dream of people all over the world. Learning to live together with respect and dignity can help make the dream of peace come true. **Sing** "Peace Round" in unison. Then, sing it as a round or with ostinatos to create harmony. How can you be a peacemaker in your school or community?

▲ On May 25, 1986, over five million Americans participated in Hands Across America. At a designated time, participants across sixteen states joined hands to raise money for hungry and homeless people.

348

## Footnotes

### ACROSS THE CURRICULUM

9d ▶ **Language Arts/Art** Talk about how artists, writers, and musicians express important ideas in their works. Have students make a list of peace symbols (a dove, an olive branch, people shaking hands, the '60s peace sign). Encourage students to create poetry, stories, artworks, songs, or dramatizations that express their ideas. Hold a schoolwide Peace Festival during which student works are displayed and performed.

### BUILDING SKILLS THROUGH MUSIC

▶**Math** Have students calculate how many people it would actually take to reach across the United States holding hands. Provide the following information to them to assist their problem solving: Los Angeles, CA to New York, NY is 5,072,320 yards; the average arm span is two yards. (2,536,160 people)

### TEACHER TO TEACHER

▶ **Peer Coaching** Peer coaching is an excellent way for students to work together constructively and to include everyone. Students being coached are reinforcing their skills. Student coaches strengthen their own skills by demonstrating their understanding to someone else. Peer coaching can be used in this lesson as follows.

- Have students practice singing the ostinatos on p. 349 in pairs or threes.
- Have students model or coach playing the ostinatos for others.
- Have students practice the movements for "Peace Round" in small groups.

## Sing for Peace

Below are two ostinatos from "Peace Round." Look up words for peace in different languages and **sing** them as ostinatos. Choose the one you like best, and add the ostinato to your performance of "Peace Round."

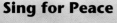

THANKS! for LENDING a HAND!!

## Move for Peace

**Move** to the half-note beat as you **sing** "Peace Round." Then **perform** a movement round.

**Listen** to this interview with Jean Ritchie, who wrote the words of "Peace Round."

CD 15-12
**Interview with Jean Ritchie**

MUSIC MAKERS

### Jean Ritchie

**Jean Ritchie** (born 1922) is one of the most famous folk musicians in the United States. During the 1960s and 1970s, she introduced thousands of people to the folk songs of Kentucky. Some of the music she performed and recorded was passed down from her Irish, English, and Scottish ancestors. Before Jean Ritchie began performing, few people were familiar with the mountain dulcimer. Because of her music, people began to play the instrument again. In 1998, Jean Ritchie won the Folk Alliance Lifetime Achievement Award.

Chasing a Dream

Unit 9 349

# 2 Develop

### Singing

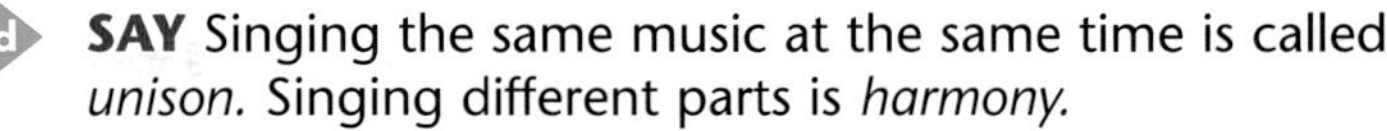

1d **SAY** Singing the same music at the same time is called *unison.* Singing different parts is *harmony.*

Write *unison* and *harmony* on the board. Play "Peace Round" **CD 15-10.** Have students point to each word as they hear the texture in the recording. Have students sing "Peace Round" in unison with and without the recording. Then sing again with the first two measures as an ostinato, then the last two measures as an ostinato. Finally, sing as a two-part round with the class.

### Moving

6e Have students step to the half-note beat as they sing "Peace Round."

Then, have them form a circle, and (phrase 1) sway right, left, right, left; (phrase 2) step right four counts; (phrase 3) turn in place, to the right, four counts; (phrase 4) step to the center, hands up, two counts, then out, lowering hands, two counts.

Have students form an inner and an outer circle and perform the song and movements as a round.

# 3 Close

**Element: TEXTURE/HARMONY** ASSESSMENT

**Performance/Observation** Have students create a performance of "Peace Round" **CD 15-10.** Have them plan ways to perform the round that include movements for each phrase. If school policy permits, videotape their performance.

As students observe the videotape, have them write a review or diagram of their performance and indicate unison and harmony parts.

To check students' understanding of harmony, have them diagram or write a description of their performance, indicating the unison and harmony parts.

## Skills Reinforcement

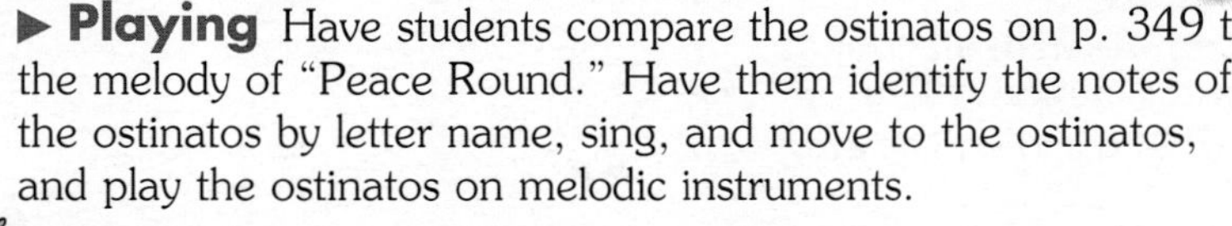

2f ▶ **Playing** Have students compare the ostinatos on p. 349 to the melody of "Peace Round." Have them identify the notes of the ostinatos by letter name, sing, and move to the ostinatos, and play the ostinatos on melodic instruments.

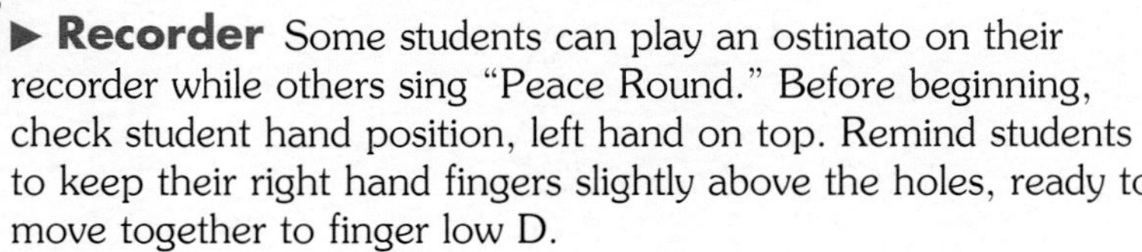

▶ **Recorder** Some students can play an ostinato on their recorder while others sing "Peace Round." Before beginning, check student hand position, left hand on top. Remind students to keep their right hand fingers slightly above the holes, ready to move together to finger low D.

▶ **Mallets** For an Orff orchestration to accompany "Peace Round," see Resource Book p. F-29.

## Technology/Media Link

**Video Library** Show the video sequence featuring a performance by Jean Ritchie. Have students

- Describe the lyrics of the song "Last Old Train's A-Leavin'."
- Identify which part of the song is always sung in harmony.
- Name the different ways the singers perform the harmony.

| Lesson | Elements | Skills | |
|---|---|---|---|
| **LESSON 1** **Our Planet**<br>pp. 354-357 | **Element: Rhythm**<br>**Concept:** Pattern<br>**Focus:** Rhythm patterns<br><br>**Secondary Element**<br>Texture: rounds<br><br>**National Standards**<br>2b 5a 5b 5d 6b | **Skill: Reading**<br>**Objective:** Read known rhythm patterns<br><br>**Secondary Skills**<br>• **Singing** Sing a song in unison and three-part canon using pitch syllables<br>• **Listening** Listen to a song and describe the character of the lyrics<br>• **Performing** Practice a speech canon<br>• **Moving** Perform a body percussion activity | **SKILLS REINFORCEMENT**<br>• **Guitar** Play a three-note melody with a song<br>• **Keyboard** Play a melody with fingering shifts<br>• **Recorder** Play a descant to a song |
| **LESSON 2** **Our Planet—Our Home**<br>pp. 358-359 | **Element: Texture/Harmony**<br>**Concept:** Harmony<br>**Focus:** Vocal harmony<br><br>**Secondary Element**<br>Rhythm: steady beat<br><br>**National Standards** | **Skill: Singing**<br>**Objective:** Sing harmony in parallel fifths<br><br>**Secondary Skills**<br>• **Listening** Listen and describe harmony in a song<br>• **Creating** Create a rhythm ostinato to perform with a poem | **SKILLS REINFORCEMENT**<br>• **Playing** Create an accompaniment for a song using appropriate instruments<br>• **Moving** Move to demonstrate the motion of two melodies of a song |
| **LESSON 3** **Water, Water Everywhere**<br>pp. 360-361 | **Element: Timbre**<br>**Concept:** Instrumental<br>**Focus:** Percussion sounds<br><br>**Secondary Element**<br>Melody: intervals<br><br>**National Standards**<br>4b 5b 6c 6e | **Skill: Creating**<br>**Objective:** Create an introduction and coda for a song, using percussion instruments<br><br>**Secondary Skills**<br>• **Listening** Listen to music and describe the musical setting<br>• **Singing** Sing and sign octaves | |

| Connections | Music and Other Literature | |
|---|---|---|
| **Connection: Social Studies**<br>**Activity:** Discuss with students our responsibility for the environment<br>**Across the Curriculum** **Social Studies** Commit to perform a daily activity that will benefit the environment<br>**Language Arts** Illustrate commitments of preservation in a journal<br>**Movement** **Creative Movement** Perform circle movements while singing a canon<br>**Spotlight On** **The Songwriter** Biographical information about Tom Chapin<br>**Character Education** **Environmental Awareness** Discuss the world's responsibility to preserve the earth for future generations<br>**Building Skills Through Music** **Language** Search for the definition of abstract words in a poem | **Songs**<br>"This Pretty Planet"<br>"For the Beauty of the Earth"<br>**Speech Piece** "The Continents"<br>**Poem** "Written in March"<br>**More Music Choices**<br>"Cumberland Gap," p. 138<br>"America, the Beautiful," p. 158<br>"River," p. 58 | **Assessment**<br>**Performance/Observation** Read and play patterns in a speech canon<br>**Technology/Media Link**<br>**Notation Software** Create and notate a speech piece |
| **Connection: Social Studies**<br>**Activity:** Discuss the Native American understanding of ecological responsibility<br>**Across the Curriculum** **Social Studies** Read and discuss a book narrated by Mother Earth<br>**Spotlight On** **Chief Dan George** Facts about the Native American actor and author<br>**School to Home Connection** **Caring for the Earth** List activities that will conserve the earth's resources<br>**Building Skills Through Music** **Social Studies** Discuss everyday activities that help to conserve the earth's resources | **Song** "The Earth Is Our Mother"<br>**Poem** "And My Heart Soars"<br>**More Music Choices**<br>"Farewell to the Warriors," p. 284<br>"I Walk in Beauty," p. 282 | **Assessment**<br>**Performance/Observation** Sing a song in parallel harmony<br>**Technology/Media Link**<br>**Video Library** Watch a video featuring Native American dancers |
| **Connection: Related Arts**<br>**Activity:** Discuss a famous dancer and movie musicals<br>**Across the Curriculum** **Science/Language Arts** Read and discuss literature about rain<br>**Movement** **Creative Movement** Creative repetitive patterns to perform in two styles<br>**Spotlight On** **Gene Kelly** Facts about the dancer and actor<br>**School to Home Connection** **Movie Memories** Share stories of Gene Kelley movies of the 40s and 50s<br>**Building Skills Through Music** **Science** Create a weather report in imitation of a meteorologist | **Song** "Singin' in the Rain"<br>**More Music Choices**<br>"Heave-Ho!"/"Going, Going, Gone"/"The Snow," p. 182<br>"Rise and Shine," p. 98 | **Assessment**<br>**Performance/Observation** Create a "rainy sounds" introduction and *coda* for a song with percussion instruments<br>**Technology/Media Link**<br>**Electronic Keyboard** Use percussion timbres to create rain sounds |

| Lesson | Elements | Skills |
|---|---|---|

## LESSON 4 When It Rains, It Pours

pp. 362-365

**Element: Texture/Harmony**
**Concept:** Texture
**Focus:** Layers of sound

**Secondary Element**
Rhythm: duple meter

**National Standards**
1d 2b 2f 5a 6b 6e 8b 9a

**Skill: Moving**

**Objective:** Move to show layers of sound

**Secondary Skills**
- **Reading** Read and sign rhythms of a song
- **Singing** Sing a layered song
- **Listening** Listen to a program piece about rain and storms

**SKILLS REINFORCEMENT**
- **Keyboard** Play a piano trio with parts of a song
- **Playing** Play a two-chord accompaniment on the Autoharp

## LESSON 5 Why Is There Day and Night?

pp. 366-369

**Element: Melody**
**Concept:** Pitch and direction
**Focus:** Melodic contour

**Secondary Element**
Rhythm: ♩ and ♫ patterns

**National Standards**
2b 2f 4a 5b 6c 8b

**Skill: Creating**
**Objective:** Create melodies and describe the melodic contour

**Secondary Skills**
- **Listening** Listen to a Hmong folktale
- **Reading/Analyzing** Read and analyze the contour of two melodies
- **Playing** Play melodies on Orff instruments
- **Singing** Sing a song using a mallet tremolo accompaniment
- **Moving** Create movements that reflect the contour of two melodies
- **Dramatizing** Dramatize a Hmong folktale
- **Performing** Present a dramatization of a song

**SKILLS REINFORCEMENT**
- **Listening** Listen to and describe the timbre of wood and metal percussion instruments

## LESSON 6 The Seasons

pp. 370-371

**Element: Texture/Harmony**
**Concept:** Texture
**Focus:** Descant

**Secondary Element**
Form: verse and refrain

**National Standards**
1d 4b 6b 8b

**Skill: Singing**
**Objective:** Sing a descant with a song about nature

**Secondary Skills**
- **Listening/Singing** Describe the lyrics and texture of a song
- **Listening** Listen to a program piece describing spring

**SKILLS REINFORCEMENT**
- **Creating** Ornament the countermelody of a song

| Connections | Music and Other Literature | |
|---|---|---|
| **Connection: Science**<br>**Activity:** Discuss the water cycle<br>MEETING INDIVIDUAL NEEDS **English Language Learners** Illustrate the process of the water cycle<br>ACROSS THE CURRICULUM **Science** Read and discuss books about the water cycle<br>SPOTLIGHT ON<br>**Program Music** Listen to and discuss examples of program music<br>**The Painter** Biographical information on Jean Francois Millet<br>TEACHER TO TEACHER **Working Together** Experiment with student musicians in leadership roles<br>CHARACTER EDUCATION **Cooperation** Discuss the importance of working together during group projects<br>SCHOOL TO HOME CONNECTION **Water Conservation** Experiment with various methods of water conservation<br>BUILDING SKILLS THROUGH MUSIC **Science** Match phrases in a song with terms relating to the water cycle | **Song** "The Wheel of the Water"<br>**Listening Selection** *Symphony No. 6,* Movement 4<br>**Arts Connection**<br>*Wooded Landscape*<br>**More Music Choices**<br>"Little David, Play on Your Harp," p. 394<br>*"Sambalele,"* p. 397 | ASSESSMENT<br>**Performance/Observation** Perform movements to demonstrate understanding of melodic layers<br>TECHNOLOGY/MEDIA LINK<br>**Web Site** Learn more about Ludwig van Beethoven |
| **Connection: Culture**<br>**Activity:** Discuss the Hmong culture and its folklore<br>TEACHER TO TEACHER **Creative Performance** Encourage students to use constructive criticism<br>ACROSS THE CURRICULUM<br>**Language Arts** Read books about opposites and nighttime<br>**Science** Explore facts about daytime, nighttime, and Earth's rotation<br>SPOTLIGHT ON<br>**Folklore** History of stories believed throughout generations<br>***Pa ndau* (Flower Cloth)** History of the Hmong people through quilts<br>CULTURAL CONNECTION **The Hmong People** History, culture, and traditions<br>SCHOOL TO HOME CONNECTION **Folk Tales** Share folk tales of other cultures and family histories<br>BUILDING SKILLS THROUGH MUSIC **Health Education** Discuss the importance of a good night's rest | **Vocal/Orff Parts**<br>"Vocal Part"<br>"Daytime Music"<br>"Nighttime Music"<br>**Listening Selections**<br>*Nruab hnub thiab hmo ntuj*<br>*Why Is There Day and Night?*<br>**Arts Connection**<br>*Paj ntaub* quilt<br>**More Music Choices**<br>"Orfferondo," p. 194<br>"Follow the Drinkin' Gourd," p. 266 | ASSESSMENT<br>**Performance/Observation** Create melodies and describe the contour<br>TECHNOLOGY/MEDIA LINK<br>**Notation Software** Compose original music to accompany a drama using the F-pentatonic scale |
| **Connection: Science**<br>**Activity:** Discuss the seasons<br>ACROSS THE CURRICULUM **Language Arts/Science** Read and discuss a book about seasonal changes<br>SPOTLIGHT ON **Vivaldi and *The Four Seasons*** Information about the composer and the composition<br>BUILDING SKILLS THROUGH MUSIC **Writing** Write a poem describing the season of spring | **Song** "Cycle Song of Life"<br>**Listening Selection** "Spring" from *The Four Seasons*<br>**More Music Choices**<br>"Amazing Grace," p. 160<br>"America, the Beautiful," p. 158 | ASSESSMENT<br>**Performance/Observation** Sing a descant with a song about nature<br>TECHNOLOGY/MEDIA LINK<br>**Notation Software** Improvise and record a descant for the refrain of a song |

| Lesson | Elements | Skills |
|---|---|---|

## LESSON 7 Seeing Stars

pp. 372-373

**Element: Form**
**Concept:** Form
**Focus:** ABABA sectional form

**Secondary Element**
Rhythm: ♩. ♪ patterns

**National Standards**
1a 1b 2d 6a 7a

**Skill: Singing**
**Objective:** Sing a song in ABABA sectional form

**Secondary Skills**
- **Analyzing** Diagram the form of a song (ABABA)

**SKILLS REINFORCEMENT**
- **Recorder** Play a countermelody to a song

## LESSON 8 The Moving Moon

pp. 374-375

**Element: Rhythm**
**Concept:** Beat
**Focus:** Strong/weak beats in duple meter

**Secondary Element**
Melody: extended pentatonic scale

**National Standards**
1c 5c 6e 8b

**Skill: Moving**
**Objective:** Perform strong and weak beat body percussion pattern in duple meter

**Secondary Skills**
- **Singing** Sing a song in Korean, noting the strong and weak beats

**SKILLS REINFORCEMENT**
- **Conducting** Conduct a duple-meter pattern

## LESSON 9 The Planets

pp. 376-377

**Element: Expression**
**Concept:** Tempo
**Focus:** *Accelerando*

**Secondary Element**
Timbre: orchestral instruments

**National Standards**
4b 5c 5d 6e

**Skill: Moving**
**Objective:** Perform a body percussion game with an *accelerando*

**Secondary Skills**
- **Performing/Moving** Perform a speech piece with an *accelerando*
- **Listening** Listen to and discuss a piece in meter in 5

**SKILLS REINFORCEMENT**
- **Creating** Create a speech piece based on a nature theme

## Connections

## Music and Other Literature

**Connection: Science**
**Activity:** Discuss stars and astronomy

ACROSS THE CURRICULUM **Language Arts** Read and discuss a book about constellations

SPOTLIGHT ON **Stars and Astronomy** Facts about star-gazing and constellations

BUILDING SKILLS THROUGH MUSIC **Science** Discuss the constellations, then design an "unknown" constellation

**Song** "Starlight, Star Bright"

M*U*S*I*C M*A*K*E*R*S
James Durst

**More Music Choices**
"Put a Little Love in Your Heart," p. 6

ASSESSMENT
**Performance/Observation** Sing a song accurately, following the form as indicated in the notation

TECHNOLOGY/MEDIA LINK
**Video Library** Watch a video about creating music

---

**Connection: Language Arts**
**Activity:** Share a poem and discuss the phases of the moon

MOVEMENT **Creative Movement** Create movements based upon the lyrics of a song

ACROSS THE CURRICULUM **Language Arts** Read a poem about the phases of the moon

BUILDING SKILLS THROUGH MUSIC **Reading** Analyze the meaning of a poem

**Song** "Sailboat in the Sky" (Korean and English)

**More Music Choices**
*"Tsuki,"* p. 25
*"Ōsamu kosamu,"* p. 96

ASSESSMENT
**Performance/Observation** Perform a body percussion movement to demonstrate strong and weak beats in duple meter

TECHNOLOGY/MEDIA LINK
**Notation Software** Notate a duple-meter melody and add accents

---

**Connection: Language Arts**
**Activity:** Write lyrics based on a nature topic

ACROSS THE CURRICULUM **Science** Read books about the solar system

SPOTLIGHT ON **The Planets** Facts about the planets and the music written by Holst

BUILDING SKILLS THROUGH MUSIC **Science** Create movements that imitate the movement of various objects through space

**Speech Piece** "The Planets Chant"

**Listening Selection** "Mars, the Bringer of War" from *The Planets* (excerpt)

M*U*S*I*C M*A*K*E*R*S
Gustav Holst

**More Music Choices**
"Bundle-Buggy Boogie Woogie," p. 120
"Heave-Ho!"/"Going, Going, Gone"/"The Snow," p. 182

ASSESSMENT
**Performance/Observation** Perform body percussion to accompany a speech piece and demonstrate *accelerando*

TECHNOLOGY/MEDIA LINK
**Web Site** Learn more about Gustav Holst

# Introducing the Unit

Students should learn that their lives are closely intertwined with the health of our planet. This unit features songs and related material that encourage environmental responsibility.

See below and pp. 352–353 for unit highlights of related curricular experiences. For a more detailed unit overview, see Unit at a Glance, pp. 349a–349f.

# Unit Project

Lead a brief discussion on why the words *earth, sea,* and *sky* have been chosen as a title for a unit on the environment—why not include *air, fire, mountains,* and other features? "Earth" can refer to either the entire planet we live on, or land (ground, dirt), as opposed to water. Using the latter meaning, earth, sea, and sky are the *basic* components of our total environment—everything else occurs on them or in them.

Invite students to consider how music and poetry can play a role in preserving our environment. (They can focus our attention on specific issues and, through the special power and attraction that art has, make us aware of how precious the many aspects of our natural environment are to us.)

Ask students in small groups to look briefly at the lessons in the unit (one group per lesson) to find out what environmental feature or issue is addressed in each case.

The songs and activities in the unit can be combined to make a performance musical for presentation to another class or the entire school; special guests and parents could also be invited. It can be a combined effort involving classroom teachers, with development of scripts, props, and staging. Earth Day (April 22) would be an ideal occasion for this presentation.

**Earth Speaks**

Read this poem and think about what you heard Earth say today.

## *Prayer for Earth*

*by Myra Cohn Livingston*

Last night
an owl
called from the hill.
Coyotes howled.
A deer stood still
nibbling at bushes far away.
The moon shone silver.
Let this stay.

Today
two noisy crows
flew by,
their shadows pasted to the sky.
The sun broke out
through the clouds of gray.
An iris opened.
Let this stay.

350

## Across the Curriculum

**Unit Highlights** The following interdisciplinary activities in this unit are related to the music elements or themes presented in the lessons. See Unit at a Glance, pp. 349a–349f, for topical descriptions presented according to lesson sequence.

**▶ LANGUAGE ARTS**

- Create groups for discussion about favorite Earth facts (p. 356)
- Read and discuss literature about rain (p. 360)
- Read books about opposites and nighttime (p. 366)
- Share a poem relating to images of the moon (p. 375)

**▶ SCIENCE**

- Read and discuss books about the water cycle; explore various methods of water conservation (p. 362)
- Explore facts about daytime, nighttime, and the rotation of the Earth (p. 368)
- Read a book about the constellations and have students track the changes they see in the night sky (p. 372)
- Read books about the solar system (p. 376)

**▶ SOCIAL STUDIES**

- Read books about ecology and write about personal commitments to save the Earth (p. 354)
- Read a book about Mother Earth; Write a response to Mother Earth and illustrate it with pictures of modern day events (p. 358)

UNIT
10
Earth, Sea, and Sky
Earth is a home for everyone. It sustains us, providing all that we need to live. Its beauty and wonder inspire our hearts and minds. We are learning that it is also our responsibility to protect our precious Earth.
Unit 10 351

# Music Skills Assessed in This Unit

UNIT 10 INTRODUCTION

### Reading Music: Rhythm

- Read from notation the rhythms of a speech piece (p. 357)

### Reading Music: Pitch

- Read instrumental parts from notation (p. 369)

### Performing Music: Singing

- Sing a Native American song in two-part harmony (p. 359)
- Sing a song with a descant (p. 371)
- Sing a song in ABABA sectional form (p. 373)

### Moving to Music

- Accompany a song with "water cycle" movements (p. 365)
- Perform body percussion to illustrate strong and weak beat (p. 375)
- Perform body percussion to illustrate *accelerando* (p. 377)

### Performing Music: Playing

- Play the rhythms of a speech piece on nonpitched percussion instruments (p. 357)
- Play rain sound effects on percussion instruments (p. 361)
- Perform original eight-measure melodies on mallet instruments (p. 369)

### Creating Music

- Create rain sound effects as an introduction and a *coda* for a song (p. 361)
- Create melodies in F-pentatonic (p. 369)

### Listening to Music

- Listen to examples of program music (p. 371)

## Cultural Connection

**Unit Highlights** The musical literature in this unit provides many opportunities for students to explore a variety of world cultures. See Unit at a Glance, pp. 349a–349f, for topical descriptions presented according to lesson sequence.

▶ AMERICAN

- "Singin' in the Rain" (p. 360)

▶ ASIAN

- Discuss the history, culture, and traditions of the Hmong people (p. 368)
- Perform a traditional Korean hand game to accompany a folk song from Korea (p. 375)

▶ NATIVE AMERICAN

- "The Earth Is Our Mother" (p. 358)

# Opening Activities

**MATERIALS**
- *"Somos el barco"* ("We Are the Boat") **CD 15-13**
  **Recording Routine:**
  Intro (16 m.); refrain; v. 1; refrain; v. 2; refrain; v. 3; refrain; v. 4; refrain; coda
- **Pronunciation Practice/Translation** p. 491
- "Prayer for Earth" (poem)
- **Resource Book** pp. A-39, I-28
- recorders

## Performing

Organize a choral reading of the poem "Prayer for Earth," on p. 350. Divide the reading among individual readers, as follows.

Verse 1: Lines 1–3
Line 4
Lines 5–6
Line 7
Last line: everyone

Verse 2: Lines 1–4
Lines 5–6
Line 7
Last line: everyone

Afterward, discuss the message of this poem (These things are too precious for us to let them disappear.) Ask each person to think for a moment of one or more other things they would not want to see disappear from the natural environment. Then repeat the choral reading, asking students to be particularly thoughtful in their expression.

## Singing

Play *"Somos el barco"* **CD 15-13** through the first refrain to introduce it; then have students sing with the students on the Pronunciation Practice Track **CD 15-15** to learn the Spanish words. For the Pronunciation Practice Guide, refer to Resource Book p. A-39. Play the song again, inviting students to sing along on the refrain portions. Ask them to listen to the verse texts to learn what the message is. (We are all part of one whole and can accomplish much if we all work together.)

### We Sail Together

The song *"Somos el barco"* is about our connection with the world around us. **Sing** this song and think of how you are connected to the world.

## Assessment

**Unit Highlights** The lessons in this unit were chosen and developed to support the theme "Earth, Sea, and Sky." Each lesson, as always, presents a clear element focus, a skill objective, and an end-of-lesson assessment. The overall sequence of lessons, however, is organized according to this theme, rather than concept or skill development. In this context, formal assessment strategies, such as those presented in Units 1–6, are no longer applicable.

▶ **INFORMAL ASSESSMENTS**

At the close of each Teacher's Edition lesson in this unit, the following type of assessment is used to evaluate the learning of the key element focus or skill objective.

- Performance/Observation (pp. 357, 359, 361, 365, 369, 371, 373, 375, 377

▶ **RUBRICS**

Visit *www.sfsuccessnet.com* for rubrics to assess students' achievement in music skills.

## Moving

In a subsequent singing, invite students to improvise movement as they sing the refrain each time; they can also improvise to the verses, responding to the images in the text.

## Reading

Ask students to look at the first four phrases of the refrain in *"Somos el barco"* to discover the similarity and the relationship. (Each phrase consists of four pitches ascending; each phrase is one step lower than the previous, forming a descending sequence.)

Ask students to do the same for phrases 5–8. (Each phrase descends and has exactly the same rhythm; phrases 6 and 8 together form a complete descending scale.)

## Playing

Ask students who are able to play the recorder part to add it to the refrain while others sing. Tell them that to play smoothly, they must be sure to coordinate their fingers with their tongue movements. For another recorder accompaniment, see Resource Book p. I-28.

### Innovative Teacher Support for This Unit

- **Making Music DVD, Grade 4** contains video segments that support lessons, including signing and movement.
- **Making Music with Movement and Dance** provides more opportunities for large group activities in music or physical education classes.
- **Making Music with Technology** provides lesson plans for many technology applications; includes MIDI files.
- ***¡A cantar!*** features recorded songs and lessons from around the Spanish-speaking world; includes strategies for bilingual classes and for English-speaking teachers working with Spanish-speaking students.
- **Bridges to Asia** features recorded songs and lessons from Asian and Pacific region cultures.
- ***www.sfsuccessnet.com*** provides an online lesson planner to conveniently create lesson plans at school or at home. Includes rubrics for assessment, lesson modifications to meet the needs of all students, performance musicals based on program content, and more.

## Technology/Media Link

**Unit Highlights** The following components are used in this unit to reinforce and expand students' understanding of music elements and related themes. See Unit at a Glance, pp. 349a–349f, for a descriptive listing according to lesson sequence.

▶ **ELECTRONIC KEYBOARD**

- Use percussion timbres to create rain sounds (p. 361)

▶ **NOTATION SOFTWARE**

- Create and notate a speech piece with notation software (p. 357)
- Compose original music for *Why Is There Day and Night?*; write several short accompaniments (p. 369)
- Improvise and then notate a descant or countermelody (p. 371)
- Notate a song and invite students to highlight the strong beats of the piece (p. 375)

▶ **VIDEO LIBRARY/DVD**

- Watch a video featuring Native American dancers (p. 359)
- Watch a video on how music is created (p. 373)

▶ **WEB SITE**

- Go to *www.sfsuccessnet.com* for more information on Ludwig van Beethoven and his music (p. 365)
- Go to *www.sfsuccessnet.com* for more information on Gustav Holst (p. 377)

LESSON 1

## LESSON AT A GLANCE

**Element Focus** **RHYTHM** Rhythm patterns

**Skill Objective** **READING** Read known rhythm patterns

**Connection Activity** **SOCIAL STUDIES** Discuss with students our responsibility for the environment

**MATERIALS**

- "This Pretty Planet" **CD 15-16**
  **Recording Routine:** Intro (4 m.); vocal (unison); interlude (4 m.); vocal (twice in 3-part canon); coda
- "For the Beauty of the Earth" **CD 15-18**
  **Recording Routine:** Intro (4 m.); v. 1; interlude (2 m.); v. 2; interlude (2 m.); v. 3; interlude (4 m.); v. 4
- "The Continents" (speech piece) **CD 15-20**
  **Recording Routine:** Intro (2 m.); vocal (unison); interlude (4 m.); vocal (in 3-part canon); coda
- "Written in March" (poem)
- **Resource Book** pp. H-23, I-29, J-17
- large world map
- nonpitched percussion instruments

**VOCABULARY**

rhythm syllables pitch syllables canon

**◆ ◆ ◆ ◆ National Standards ◆ ◆ ◆ ◆**

**2b** Perform rhythms and chords on appropriate instruments
**5a** Read rhythms in duple meter
**5b** Read notes in treble clef using syllables
**5d** Notate rhythms using standard symbols
**6b** Describe music by answering questions about it

**MORE MUSIC CHOICES**

For more practice reading rhythms:
"Cumberland Gap," p. 138
Other songs about the earth:
"America, the Beautiful," p. 158
"River," p. 58



# Our Planet

How would you describe our planet? You could use facts such as "the planet Earth is a sphere and revolves around the sun." You could use feelings like "our planet is very beautiful and exciting." Maybe you would use both.

Read this poem. Does the author use facts, feelings, or both to describe our planet?

### Written in March

*by William Wordsworth*

The cock is crowing,
The stream is flowing,
The small birds twitter,
The green field sleeps in the sun;
The oldest and youngest
Are at work with the strongest;
The cattle are grazing,
Their heads never raising;
There are forty feeding like one!
Like an army defeated
The snow hath retreated,
And now doth fare ill
On the top of the bare hill;
The ploughboy is whooping—anon—anon;
There's joy in the mountains;
There's life in the fountains;
Small clouds are sailing,
Blue sky prevailing;
The rain is over and gone!

Often a composer will use only a few lines from a text to create a song. What lines from this poem would you use?

354

# Footnotes

## ACROSS THE CURRICULUM

▶ **Social Studies** Engage students in a conversation about their responsibility for Earth. Share with them the books *Fifty Simple Things Kids Can Do to Save the Earth* (Andrews McMeel, 1990) and *Fifty Simple Things Kids Can Do to Recycle* (Earthworks, 1994). Invite students to make a commitment to do something for Earth and write it in their journals. Throughout Unit 10, remind them about their commitment to Earth and their chosen activity to save the planet.

## BUILDING SKILLS THROUGH MUSIC

▶ **Language** Invite students to read "Written in March" on p. 354 of the student text. Encourage them to identify words in the poem they may not understand, such as *ploughboy* and *anon.* Then direct students to use a resource in the classroom (dictionary, computer, or experience of fellow student) to determine the meaning of those words.

## MOVEMENT

▶ **Creative Movement** For "This Pretty Planet," divide the class into three groups. Each will form a small, closed circle representing the planet and each will create a circle movement for a part of the song. This could include circling to the right or left, going in and out, raising hands or hand gestures.

Have group 1 create movements for lines 1 and 2, group 2 create movements for lines 3 and 4, and group 3 create movements for lines 5 and 6. Have each group teach their dance to the others and then combine all dances to create a class choreography for the song. Practice this as a class. Finally, divide the groups again and perform the song and dance in canon.

Sing "This Pretty Planet." Is this a song with facts, feelings, or both?
Earth, Sea, and Sky
CD 15-16
This Pretty Planet
s, l, t, d r m f s
Words and Music by John Forster and Tom Chapin
do
I G Am
This pret - ty plan - et spin-ning through space. You're a
D7 G
gar - den. You're a har - bor. You're a ho - ly place.
II G Am
Gold - en sun go - ing down.
D7 G
Gen - tle blue gi - ant. spin us a - round.
III G Am
All through the night
D7 G
Safe till the morn - ing light.
Unit 10 355

# 1 Introduce

Ask students to look at the text of "This Pretty Planet" and decide whether the lyrics express "facts" or "feelings." Invite students to work in pairs to summarize the lyrics of the song in two or three sentences, and think of some of their own feelings about Earth. Have members of each pair share their work with the class.

Then encourage an open discussion with students about personal responsibility to Earth. Refer to Across the Curriculum on p. 354 and share readings from the two books about being custodians of Earth.

# 2 Develop

## Singing

Have students listen to "This Pretty Planet" **CD 15-16**, concentrating on lines 3 and 4. Ask them to sing these lines back. Repeat the procedure with lines 5 and 6; then sing lines 3 through 6. Repeat the process again with lines 1 and 2. Then invite students to sing the entire song.

After the class is comfortable singing the song in unison, divide the class into three groups. Have them perform the song as a three-part canon.

## Listening

Draw students' attention to the lyrics of "For the Beauty of the Earth" **CD 15-18**, on p. 356. Have them listen to the recording.

ASK **How does this text view Earth, compared to "This Pretty Planet"?** (They are both based on "feelings" and focus on positive things about Earth.)

Invite students to read the poem "Written in March" on p. 354.

ASK **Does this poem contain facts or feelings about the planet?** (combinations of both)

continued on page 356

## Spotlight On

▶ **The Songwriter** Tom Chapin (b. 1945), who wrote "This Pretty Planet" along with John Forster, writes, sings, and records songs for children and adults. Chapin was influenced by Pete Seeger and Woody Guthrie. Chapin's home is in Rockland County, New York, but he spends some time each year giving live performances throughout the United States.

## Skills Reinforcement

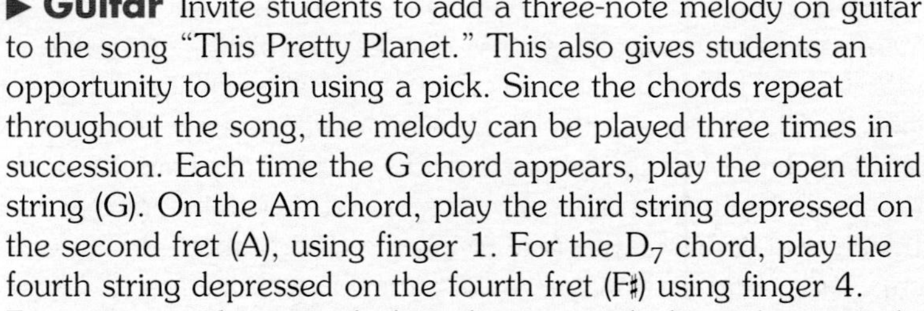

2b ▶ **Guitar** Invite students to add a three-note melody on guitar to the song "This Pretty Planet." This also gives students an opportunity to begin using a pick. Since the chords repeat throughout the song, the melody can be played three times in succession. Each time the G chord appears, play the open third string (G). On the Am chord, play the third string depressed on the second fret (A), using finger 1. For the $D_7$ chord, play the fourth string depressed on the fourth fret (F♯) using finger 4. Encourage students to pluck each string with the pick perpendicular to the strings, held between the thumb and index finger.

Encourage students to choose which lines of the poem would be best suited for being set to music. Have students write their own lyrics or poem based on facts or feelings.

## Reading

Have students listen to "For the Beauty of the Earth" **CD 15-18** again, following the notation on p. 356.

**ASK How many phrases does the song have?** (six)

**Are any of the phrases exactly alike?** (1 and 3; 2 and 4)

5a 6b **ASK How does the rhythm of phrase 2 compare to the rhythm of phrase 1?** (Phrase 2 has only quarter notes; phrase 1 has quarter notes, two eighth notes, and a half note.)

Have students read the first two lines with rhythm syllables.

**What different rhythm pattern occurs in line 3 ?** (♩. ♪)

Invite students to practice reading the measure with the dotted-quarter note.

**ASK Is the rhythm of the last phrase the same as any of the other phrases?** (no)

**Is it almost the same?** (yes, as phrases 2 and 4) **What is the difference?** (The last phrase ends with a half note.)

Play the recording again. Ask students to say the correct rhythm syllables along with the song, paying careful attention to the ♩. ♪ rhythm.

## Singing

5b Have students locate *do* (G) in "For the Beauty of the Earth."

**ASK What are the pitch syllables for measures 9 and 10?** *(mi-re-do-mi-so-fa-mi)*

Have students sing those measures with pitch syllables and hand signs and then sing the entire song **CD 15-18**.

### The Beautiful Earth

What feelings about Earth are expressed in this song?

**Read** this song using rhythm syllables. Now use pitch syllables and hand signs to **read** measures 9 and 10.

CD 15-18
For the Beauty of the Earth
s, l, t, d r m f s
Words by Folliott S. Pierpoint
Music by Conrad Kocher
do
G D7 C G C G D7 G
1. For the beau-ty of the earth, For the beau-ty of the skies,
2. For the beau-ty of each hour Of the day and of the night,
3. For the joy of ear and eye, For the heart and mind's de-light,
4. For the joy of hu-man love, Broth-er, sis-ter, par-ent, child,
For the love which from our birth, O-ver and a-round us lies.
Hill and vale and tree and flower, Sun and moon and stars of light.
For the mys-tic har-mo-ny Link-ing sense to sound and sight.
Friends on earth and friends a-bove, For all gen-tle thoughts and mild.
Lord of all, to Thee we raise This our hymn of grate-ful praise.
356


# Footnotes

## CHARACTER EDUCATION

**▶ Environmental Awareness** To increase students' environmental awareness, discuss our responsibility to preserve the world for future generations. Do you have an obligation to make decisions that positively affect the environment? How do your daily behaviors impact the world's environment now and in the future? Brainstorm specific ways in and out of school that students can contribute to preserving the environment. (recycle items, take shorter showers, reuse paper bags, volunteer to clean up a stream or trail, and so on) For those behaviors that can be instituted at school (for example, turn off lights, use the back of papers as scratch paper, conserve water), create posters reminding others to adopt environmentally friendly actions. Challenge students to list the traits of an environmentally conscious person.

## ACROSS THE CURRICULUM

**▶ Language Arts** You may wish to bring in artifacts, photos, and other material about Earth to share with students. To build vocabulary, divide students in pairs, and invite them to discuss their favorite things about Earth. To check comprehension, ask students to illustrate the commitments to Earth they have written about in their journals.

You might use color-coding to match pictures of the continents with their names to help English language learners recognize and remember the names in English.

## Name the Continents

The largest land masses on Earth are called continents. Here's a great way to remember them!

**Read** "The Continents" using rhythm syllables. Then **perform** it as a **canon.**

A **canon** is a musical form in which the parts imitate each other. One part begins, or leads, and the other parts follow.

Earth, Sea, and Sky

CD 15-20
The Continents
Speech Canon by Grace Nash and 7th Grade Students
I
II
III
A - sia, Af - ri - ca, North A - mer - i - ca, South A - mer - i - ca,
Eu - rope and Ant - arc - ti - ca and Aus - tral - ia!

Unit 10 357

### Performing

Have students look at "The Continents" **CD 15-20.**

Encourage students to practice speaking the speech piece in rhythm until they gain confidence.

ASK **What helps you remember the names of the continents?** (rhythm)

Explain that rhythm can help people memorize things. It is used in television and radio advertising and to help with learning in school.

Show students a large map of the world. Point out all the continents. Divide students into small groups. As each group performs "The Continents," have volunteers point to each continent as it is named.

Divide the class into four groups and perform "The Continents" as a canon.

### Moving

As an additional activity, add this body percussion to students' performance of "The Continents" **CD 15-20.**

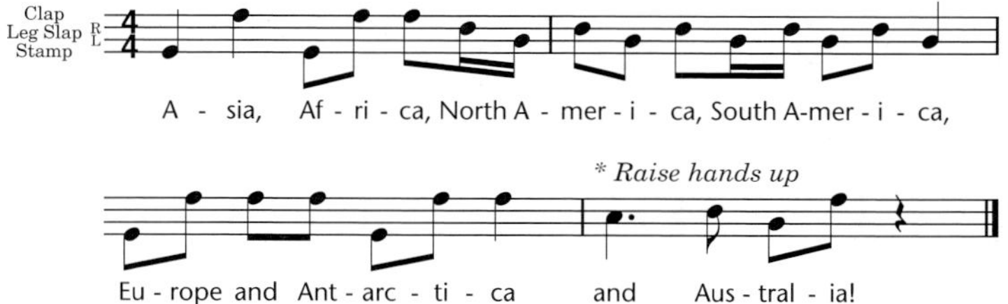

Clap
Leg Slap R L
Stamp
A - sia, Af - ri - ca, North A - mer - i - ca, South A-mer - i - ca,
* Raise hands up
Eu - rope and Ant - arc - ti - ca and Aus - tral - ia!

They might also create sound effects for this piece, using instruments made with recycled items. See Resource Book p. J-17.

## 3 Close

Skill: READING — ASSESSMENT

2b **Performance/Observation** Have students tap and say the rhythms of "The Continents," reading the notation. Then in small groups, have students take turns performing "The Continents" on nonpitched percussion instruments as the rest of the class performs the speech piece in canon.

### Skills Reinforcement

▶ **Keyboard** Invite students to study various phrases from "For the Beauty of the Earth" to see how fingering shifts enable keyboard players to play a melody with a wide range. Refer to Resource Book p. H-23.

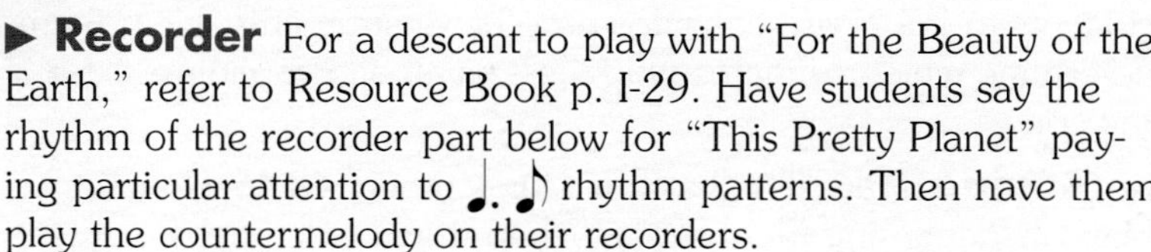

▶ **Recorder** For a descant to play with "For the Beauty of the Earth," refer to Resource Book p. I-29. Have students say the rhythm of the recorder part below for "This Pretty Planet" paying particular attention to ♩. ♪ rhythm patterns. Then have them play the countermelody on their recorders.

### Technology/Media Link

5d **Notation Software** Have students

- Perform "The Continents" as a canon.
- Choose a subject, such as cafeteria food, and create lyrics for a speech canon as a class.
- Write their own speech canon in simple meter on staff paper, incorporating basic rhythmic patterns found in "The Continents."
- Take turns notating their compositions using a notation program or other notation system.
- Print their compositions and perform them in small groups.

LESSON 2

## LESSON AT A GLANCE

**Element Focus** **TEXTURE/HARMONY** Vocal harmony

**Skill Objective** **SINGING** Sing harmony in parallel fifths

**Connection Activity** **SOCIAL STUDIES** Discuss the Native American understanding of ecological responsibility

**MATERIALS**

- "The Earth Is Our Mother" (Traditional) **CD 15-22**
- "The Earth Is Our Mother" (Contemporary) **CD 15-24**

  **Recording Routine:** Intro (5 m.); v. 1; interlude (2 m.); v. 2; interlude (2 m.); v. 3; coda
- "And My Heart Soars" (poem)
- hand drum (one or more)

**VOCABULARY**

parallel harmony

**◆ ◆ ◆ ◆ National Standards ◆ ◆ ◆ ◆**

**2f** Play instruments independently against contrasting parts
**6b** Describe music by answering questions about it
**6e** While listening to music, move to show a prominent feature of the music
**9b** Describe how harmony is used in pieces from various cultures

**MORE MUSIC CHOICES**

Other Native American songs:

"Farewell to the Warriors," p. 284
"I Walk in Beauty," p. 282

## 1 INTRODUCE

**ASK What does ecology mean?** (the relationship of living things and their environment)

Have students listen to "The Earth Is Our Mother" **CD 15-22** and discuss how the song relates to ecology. Share the information from Across the Curriculum below.

LESSON 2 Element: TEXTURE/HARMONY | Skill: SINGING | Connection: SOCIAL STUDIES

# OUR PLANET— Our Home

We are all together on planet Earth, spinning through space. The Earth is our home and our protector, so we all must take care of it. This Cherokee song puts these ideas into music. **Sing** the melody, and then the harmony part. Then, sing both parts together.

CD 15-22

## The Earth Is Our Mother

*Cherokee Song*
*Arranged by Barbara Sletto*

1.,3. The Earth__ is our Moth - er, we must take care of her. The
2. Her sa - cred ground we walk u-pon with ev - ery step we take. Her

Earth__ is our Moth - er, we must take care of her.
sa - cred ground we walk up-on with ev - ery step we take.

Hey__ yan - na, ho__ yan - na, hey__ yan yan.

Hey__ yan - na, ho__ yan - na hey__ yan yan.

358

# Footnotes

## ACROSS THE CURRICULUM

▶ **Social Studies** Invite students to consider what Mother Earth might say to them by reading the book *Dear Children of the Earth: A Letter from Home* by Schim Schimmel (NorthWord Press, 1994). Encourage students to write back to Mother Earth and illustrate their writing with magazine cut-outs. Hang these around the room to remind students that Earth is the focus of the unit.

## BUILDING SKILLS THROUGH MUSIC

▶ **Social Studies** Ask students to read the paragraph titled "Protecting Earth" on p. 359 of the student text. Then, engage students in a brief discussion about initiatives they can take every day to protect the earth. List these initiatives on the board. Finally, create a spoken ostinato from this list to perform with "The Earth Is Our Mother."

## SKILLS REINFORCEMENT

2f ▶ **Playing** Invite students to create a simple rhythm ostinato accompaniment for "The Earth Is Our Mother." Use instruments that would be found in traditional Native American music, such as drums and rattles. Play a steady beat on the largest drum. Ask students to improvise ostinatos on other instruments. Help them determine which ostinatos work best as an accompaniment for the song.

6e ▶ **Moving** Play "The Earth Is Our Mother" **CD 15-22** again. Have students sing the melody. When the parallel melody enters, encourage students to show the motion of the two melodies in the air with their hands.

## Protecting Earth

In the twentieth century, the United States government formed the Environmental Protection Agency (EPA) to protect our planet from damage caused by humans. For centuries, Native American traditions have considered Earth's resources to be precious, to be cared for rather than recklessly consumed. This poem by Chief Dan George expresses this sentiment.



## And My Heart Soars

*by Chief Dan George*

The beauty of the trees,
The softness of the air,
The fragrance of the grass,
  speaks to me.

The summit of the mountain,
The thunder of the sky,
The rhythm of the sea,
  speaks to me.

The faintness of the stars,
The freshness of the morning,
The dew drop on the flower,
  speaks to me.

The strength of fire,
The taste of salmon,
The trail of the sun,

And the life that never goes away,
  They speak to me.

And my heart soars.



# 2 Develop

### Listening

Have students sing "The Earth Is Our Mother" **CD 15-22** with the first (unison) portion of the recording. Encourage them to listen to the rest of the recording.

6b ASK **What happens to the melody?** (A melody that exactly follows the original melody is added at a higher pitch level.)

9b Invite a volunteer to draw lines on the board showing how the melodies relate.

ASK **When two lines are an equal distance apart, what is this relationship called?** (parallel)

### Singing

Give students the starting pitch for the higher melody of "The Earth Is Our Mother" **CD 15-22** and ask them to sing that melody as you play the recording again. Then divide the class into two groups and have one group sing each melody.

### Creating

Have students read the poem "And My Heart Soars" and share the information in Spotlight On below. *Note:* Students need not attempt to read to the drumbeat. This will help preserve the strength of the poem and the spontaneous feeling that their reading creates.

Then have students develop an ostinato on drums as a background to their reading of the poem.

# 3 Close

ASSESSMENT

**Performance/Observation** Ask students, in small groups, to sing "The Earth Is Our Mother" **CD 15-22** in harmony. Assess whether or not each student or group is able to maintain the harmony part while performing.

### Spotlight On

▶ **Chief Dan George** Chief Dan George (1899–1981), who wrote the poem "And My Heart Soars," was an actor, author, and chief of the Salish Band of Native Americans in British Columbia. He was born on a reservation and given the name Geswanouth Slahoot. George was sent to a mission boarding school at age five. His name was changed, and he was forbidden to speak his native language. As an adult, George was a longshoreman and a school bus driver before becoming an actor at age sixty-two. His best-known films were "Little Big Man" (1970), with Dustin Hoffman (for which he received an Academy Award nomination and a New York Film Critics Award), and "The Outlaw Josie Wales" (1976), with Clint Eastwood. George used his fame to call for understanding and acceptance of native people.

### School to Home Connection

▶ **Caring for the Earth** Ask students to create a list of all the things we can do to take care of Earth (recycle, conserve fuel and water, plant trees, protect wildlife, and so on). Write a sentence or two to complete this thought: "We care for our Mother Earth by…." Use student ideas as readings in performances of "The Earth Is Our Mother."

### Technology/Media Link

**Video Library** Students may be interested in learning more about Native American cultures. Invite students to watch the performance by the Alaskan Cape Fox Dancers.

LESSON 3

## LESSON AT A GLANCE

**Element Focus** **TIMBRE** Percussion sounds

**Skill Objective** **CREATING** Create an introduction and coda for a song, using percussion instruments

**Connection Activity** **RELATED ARTS** Discuss a famous dancer and movie musicals

**MATERIALS**

- "Singin' in the Rain" **CD 15-26**

  **Recording Routine:** Intro (4 m.); vocal; interlude (4 m.); vocal; coda
- selected percussion instruments

**VOCABULARY**

introduction coda octave

**◆◆◆◆ National Standards ◆◆◆◆**

**4b** Compose instrumental pieces within specific guidelines
**5b** Read notes in treble clef using letters
**6c** Use appropriate terms to describe music
**6e** While listening to music, move to show a prominent feature of the music

**MORE MUSIC CHOICES**

Other songs about weather:

"Heave-Ho!"/"Going, Going, Gone"/"The Snow" (speech piece) p. 182

"Rise and Shine," p. 98

# 1 INTRODUCE

Talk with students about how people feel about rain.
**ASK** **When would people be happy about rain?** (after a long drought)

**What might make people unhappy about rain?** (when they would like to do things outdoors, or when there has been too much rain)

LESSON 3 Element: TIMBRE | Skill: CREATING | Connection: RELATED ARTS

# Water, Water Everywhere

"Singin' in the Rain" is a song from the movie *Singin' in the Rain*. In this scene, Gene Kelly is singing about being happy and in love, despite the rain and cloudy skies.

As you **sing** the song, think about times you were happy even when skies were gray.

CD 15-26

## Singin' in the Rain

Words by Arthur Freed — Music by Nacio Herb Brown

do

G — I'm sing - in' in the rain, just sing - in' in the

G — rain. What a glo - ri-ous feel - ing, I'm D7 hap - py a -

D7 — gain! I'm laugh - ing at clouds so dark up a -

D7 — bove. The sun's ___ in my heart ___ and I'm G read - y for



# Footnotes

## ACROSS THE CURRICULUM

▶ **Science/Language Arts** Use the book *Acid Rain* by Sally Morgan (Franklin Watts, 1999) to sensitize your students to the dangers of acid rain. Explain that when water droplets in the air absorb chemical pollutants, they produce an acidic rain that is dangerous to plants, animals and human beings.

## BUILDING SKILLS THROUGH MUSIC

▶ **Science** Have students describe different types of weather, as reported by a meteorologist. (rainy, cloudy, snowy, sunny, and so on) Then have students draw a picture of a weather condition and write a weather report to accompany their artwork.

## MOVEMENT

▶ **Creative Movement** The instrumental track for "Singin' in the Rain" **CD 15-27** was recorded in two different styles (traditional theater style and contemporary urban pop style). To help students aurally identify these diverse musical styles, have them listen to the recording and discuss the differences. Then divide the group in half, and have each group create two distinct repetitious patterns of steps that reflect the different styles. Have them consider the use of direction, including forward, backward, sideways, up, and down when inventing their dances. Both groups should work on "dance one" and then "dance two." When the choreography is finished, have the groups perform for each other.

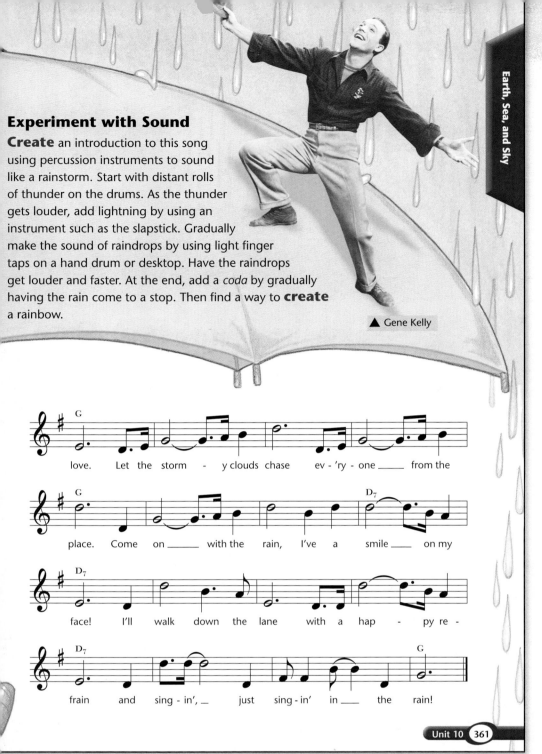

**Experiment with Sound**

**Create** an introduction to this song using percussion instruments to sound like a rainstorm. Start with distant rolls of thunder on the drums. As the thunder gets louder, add lightning by using an instrument such as the slapstick. Gradually make the sound of raindrops by using light finger taps on a hand drum or desktop. Have the raindrops get louder and faster. At the end, add a *coda* by gradually having the rain come to a stop. Then find a way to **create** a rainbow.

▲ Gene Kelly

Earth, Sea, and Sky

G
love. Let the storm - y clouds chase ev - 'ry - one ___ from the

G D7
place. Come on ___ with the rain, I've a smile ___ on my

D7
face! I'll walk down the lane with a hap - py re -

D7 G
frain and sing - in', ___ just sing - in' in ___ the rain!

Unit 10 361

# 2 Develop

### Listening

Invite students to listen to "Singin' in the Rain" **CD 15-26**. Share the information about Gene Kelly in Spotlight On below.

**ASK What is the response to the rain by the person in this song?** (Some will answer that the singer is happy. Actually, in the context of the movie, the singer has just fallen in love and is happy despite the rain.)

### Singing

Have students sing "Singin' in the Rain" with the recording.

5b **ASK What do you see when you look at the first two notes?** (a low note followed by a high note, both D)

6c **What is the word for the space between two notes of the same name?** (an octave)

6e Have students identify other octave leaps and sing the song again using hand motions to show all the octave leaps, both upward and downward.

### Creating

Invite students to experiment with percussion instruments in the classroom. Have them choose instruments that produce sounds similar to what you might hear in a rainstorm. Have them refer to the activity on the student p. 361 and create a storm.

# 3 Close

**Element: TIMBRE** — **ASSESSMENT**

4b **Performance/Observation** Divide the class into small groups. Have each group choose percussion instruments to create a "rainy sounds" introduction and *coda* for "Singin' in the Rain." Assess each student's ability to choose appropriate percussion timbres and independently perform on those instruments to create rainy sounds.

## Spotlight On

▶ **Gene Kelly** Gene Kelly (1912–1996), from Pittsburgh, Pennsylvania, was a famous actor and dancer in many movie musicals. He started dancing lessons as soon as he could walk. Kelly hated the lessons until he found out in high school that his dancing made him very popular. As a young man, Kelly taught dancing while he went to the University of Pittsburgh, where he received a degree in Economics in 1933. This was during the Great Depression, and Kelly worked at many different jobs before landing his first role on Broadway in 1938. Broadway soon led to Hollywood, where Kelly's best-known film musicals were *On the Town, An American in Paris* (for which he won an Oscar), and *Singin' in the Rain,* one of America's all-time favorite musicals.

## School to Home Connection

▶ **Movie Memories** Encourage students to talk with older friends and family members about their memories of Gene Kelly and the movie musicals of the 1940s and 1950s. Invite students to share with the class the stories they collect.

## Technology/Media Link

**Electronic Keyboard** Encourage students to use percussion timbres and other sounds from MIDI keyboards as they create "rain" sounds.

## LESSON AT A GLANCE

**Element Focus** **TEXTURE/HARMONY** Layers of sound

**Skill Objective** **MOVING** Move to show layers of sound

**Connection Activity** **SCIENCE** Discuss the water cycle

**MATERIALS**

- "The Wheel of the Water" **CD 16-1**
  **Recording Routine:** Intro (4 m.); vocal; coda
- *Symphony No. 6,* Movement 4 **CD 16-3**
- **Resource Book** p. H-24
- Autoharp, bells, keyboards, xylophone

**VOCABULARY**

melody layers

**National Standards**

**1d** Sing part songs
**2b** Perform chords on appropriate instruments
**2f** Play instruments independently against contrasting parts
**5a** Read half, quarter, and eighth notes and rests in duple meter
**6b** Describe music by explaining how it sounds
**6e** While listening to music, move to show a prominent feature of the music
**8b** Identify ways music relates to science
**9a** Listen to identify music from different historical periods

**MORE MUSIC CHOICES**

Other songs with independent vocal parts:
"Little David, Play on Your Harp," p. 394
*"Sambalele,"* p. 397

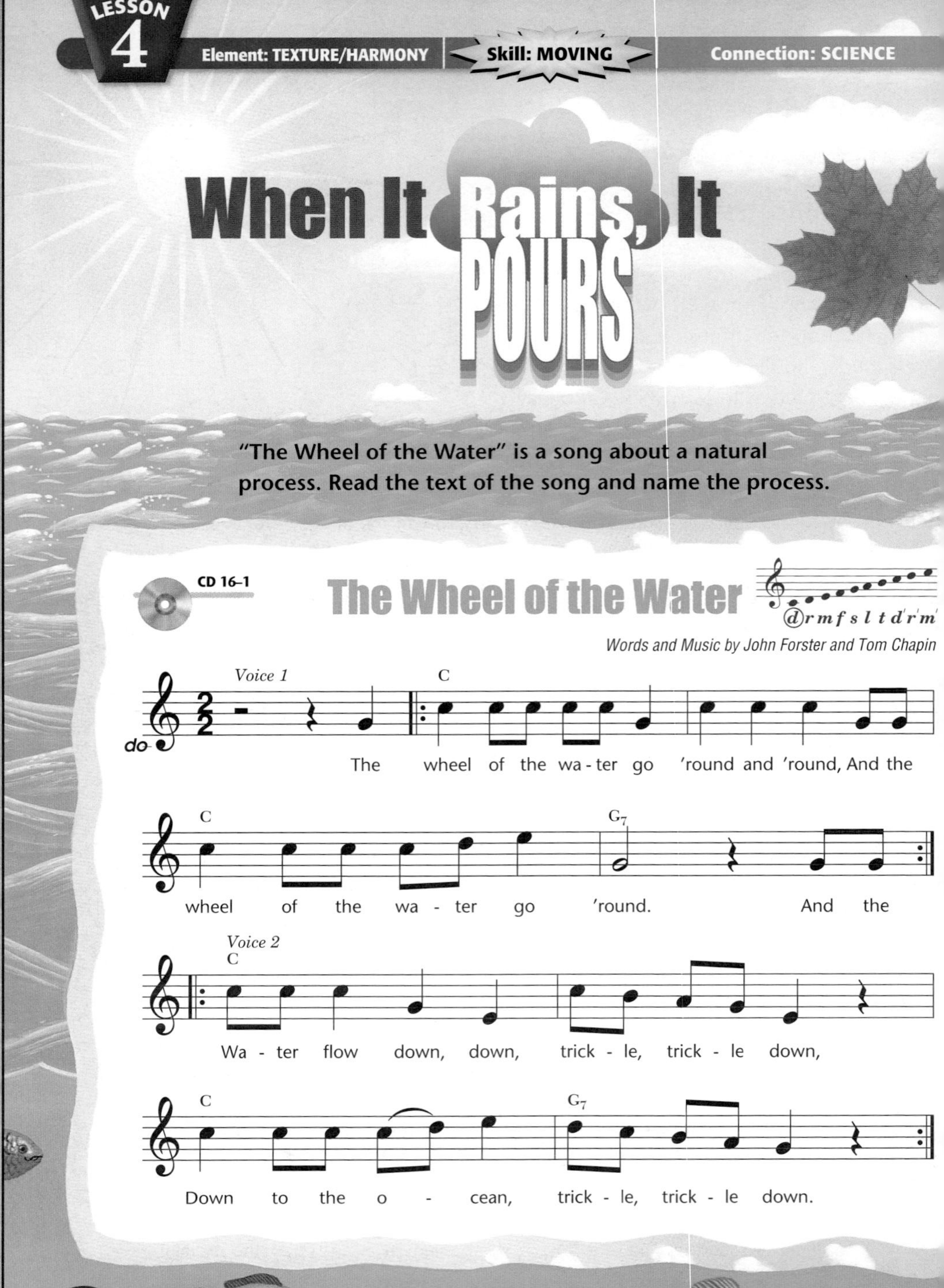

LESSON 4
Element: TEXTURE/HARMONY
Skill: MOVING
Connection: SCIENCE
When It Rains, It POURS
"The Wheel of the Water" is a song about a natural process. Read the text of the song and name the process.
CD 16-1
The Wheel of the Water
d r m f s l t d' r' m'
Words and Music by John Forster and Tom Chapin
Voice 1
The wheel of the wa-ter go 'round and 'round, And the wheel of the wa-ter go 'round. And the
Voice 2
Wa-ter flow down, down, trick-le, trick-le down, Down to the o-cean, trick-le, trick-le down.
362


# Footnotes

## MEETING INDIVIDUAL NEEDS

▶ **English Language Learners** Ask students to divide a piece of paper into four quadrants. Have them write one of the following words or phrases in each of the quadrants: *water flowing, clouds, rain,* and *water bubbling.* Then encourage students to illustrate the idea in each quadrant and to indicate with arrows the process of the water cycle.

## BUILDING SKILLS THROUGH MUSIC

▶ **Science** Write these words involved in the water cycle on the board: evaporation, condensation, precipitation. Ask students to match the appropriate phrases in "The Wheel of the Water" to these words. Then choose classroom instruments to represent each of the three words, having students play the rhythm of the matching phrase on the instrument as they sing the song.

## ACROSS THE CURRICULUM

▶ **Science** Take a trip with a drop of water as it travels around the world. Invite students to read, or read aloud in class, the book *A Drop Around the World* by Barbara Shaw McKinney (Dawn, 1998).

For a more scientific view of the water cycle, encourage students to read *Water, Water Everywhere: A Book About the Water Cycle* by Melvin Berger and Gilda Berger (Ideals Children, 1995). This book focuses on evaporation, condensation, and precipitation, with emphasis on supplying water for humans. The book also provides students with some tips on water conservation.

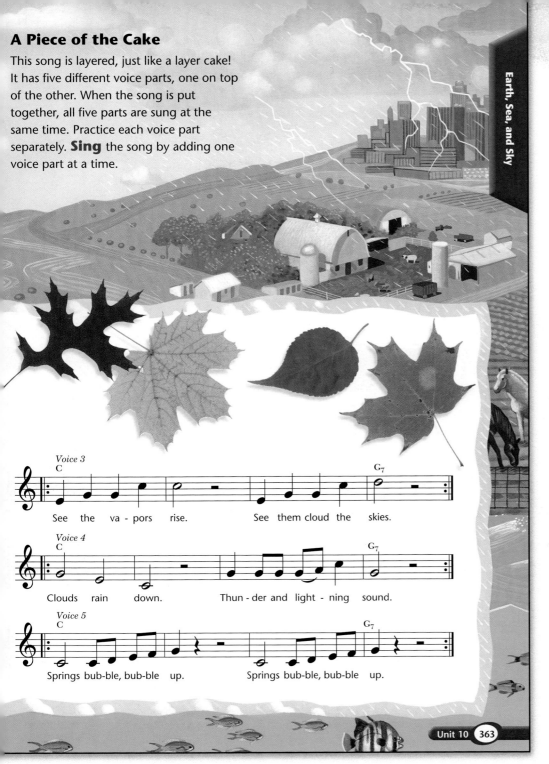

### A Piece of the Cake

This song is layered, just like a layer cake! It has five different voice parts, one on top of the other. When the song is put together, all five parts are sung at the same time. Practice each voice part separately. **Sing** the song by adding one voice part at a time.

Voice 3
C G7
See the va - pors rise. See them cloud the skies.

Voice 4
C G7
Clouds rain down. Thun - der and light - ning sound.

Voice 5
C G7
Springs bub-ble, bub-ble up. Springs bub-ble, bub-ble up.



# 1 Introduce

Discuss "The Wheel of the Water." Invite students to read the text, starting with Voice 2 and then 3, 4 and then 5. Help students understand that the song is talking about how the water cycle constantly repeats in nature.

ASK **What word is used in Voice 1 for "cycle"?** (wheel)

Share with students the science connection in Across the Curriculum on p. 362 and discuss how the water cycle is important in people's lives. To reinforce this concept, have students look at the art around the song on pp. 362–363.

# 2 Develop

### Reading

5a Ask students to silently read the rhythm of Voice 1 (lines 1 and 2) in "The Wheel of the Water." Point out the repeat sign and discuss what it means. Then invite students to read Voice 1 aloud using rhythm syllables. Repeat the activity for each of the other four voice parts. Then play the recording of "The Wheel of the Water" **CD 16-1** and have students follow the rhythm as they listen.

### Singing

Have students listen to "The Wheel of the Water" **CD 16-1**. Ask them to listen carefully to the melody for each voice part.

1d Then have students sing the song in unison, starting with the easier voice parts (4 and 5). When students are confident singing in unison, divide the class into groups and have them combine as many voice parts as they can—starting with two and working up to all five, if possible.

**continued on page 364**

## Spotlight On

9a ▶ **Program Music** Beethoven's *Symphony No. 6* **(CD 16-3)** is a type of music genre called program music. Program music describes a scene or event through music, just as an artist might describe a scene or event in a painting, or an author might describe a scene or event in a story. Beethoven gave *Symphony No. 6* the title *Pastoral* to help listeners understand that the music was about scenes from country life. Beethoven's example influenced later composers like Camille Saint-Saëns, who wrote *Carnival of the Animals* **(CD 4-5)**, in which each movement describes a different animal, and Modest Mussorgsky, whose *Pictures at an Exhibition* **(CD 5-16)** not only describes ten different paintings, but has "walking music" to take listeners from one painting to the next.

## Skills Reinforcement

▶ **Keyboard** Invite students to choose Voice 1, Voice 4, or Voice 5 of "The Wheel of the Water" to play as a trio on a keyboard. One student will play in the written octave, one an octave higher, and one an octave lower. Here are the recommended fingers for Voice 1. Refer to Resource Book p. H-24 for Voices 4 and 5.

2f

### Moving

Divide the class into five groups. Assign each group one of the five parts of "The Wheel of the Water." Ask students to develop a movement pattern for each voice that describes what happens in the text. (See student p. 364.) The movement pattern must be easy to repeat. Encourage each group to share its ideas.

Have each group perform their movement pattern with "The Wheel of the Water" **CD 16-1** as their voice part enters, and drop out accordingly. When students are confident in their movement patterns, you may wish to have them try combining singing and movement.

### Listening

6b Play Beethoven's *Symphony No. 6,* Movement 4 **CD 16-3**. Explain that like other "program" pieces, this music tells a story—of a rainstorm.

Have students listen for

- The beginning drops of rain.
- Flashes of lightning.
- Thunder from a distance and then progressively closer.
- The full-blown storm with lightning, thunder, and heavy rain.
- The tapering off and ending of the storm.

After listening, invite students to comment on how successful they think Beethoven was at describing a rainstorm in music and why. Have them decide what Beethoven might have done differently. For additional information on program music, see Spotlight On, p. 363. Use the given examples to allow students the opportunity to identify aurally-presented excerpts of music representing diverse periods.

Invite students to compare Beethoven's piece with the painting *Wooded Landscape,* shown on p. 365. Guide them in comparing what is the same or different in the subject matter and moods of both artworks and explaining their responses.

### Icing on the Cake

**Create** movements for each layer of "The Wheel of the Water" and make your movements express the text. How many sets of movements do you need? **Listen** to the song and **perform** your movements.

### Our Cake Is Baked

Now it's time to put our piece together. To perform our creation we need five different voice groups and five different movement groups.

Now with all the layers we've created, **perform** the song. Good luck!

# Footnotes

## Teacher to Teacher

▶ **Working Together** For reading activities such as the ones in this lesson, employ the knowledge of students who take music lessons and can read music well already. If possible, make sure one of these capable students is in each group; one could be a "floating helper," answering other students' questions.

## Skills Reinforcement

2b ▶ **Playing** "The Wheel of the Water" has only two chords, C and $G_7$. Invite students to add a chordal accompaniment to the song, using the Autoharp or keyboard. Students may also play the chord roots on bells or xylophones.

## Character Education

**Cooperation** Creating movement and singing different parts together requires cooperation. Discuss with students what behaviors they must demonstrate as they work together to create movement for each voice part. Remind them that both cooperation and independence are important to our society, yet it is cooperation that yields the greatest rewards. Similarly, when they sing the voice parts together, they must listen, perhaps compromise, and accept and respect the efforts of others.

**Arts Connection**

▲ *Wooded Landscape* (1851) by Jean François Millet

### Back to Nature

In the 1700s and early 1800s, many Europeans felt they had moved too far away from nature. As a result, the Pastoral Movement developed in the arts. During this time, many artists created works to express their feelings about nature.

**Listen** for the storm in this music by Ludwig van Beethoven. He composed this music to describe his love of nature.

CD 16-3

**Symphony No. 6, Movement 4**

**by Ludwig van Beethoven**

This symphony, subtitled "Pastorale," was first published in 1809.

Unit 10 365

# 3 Close

**Skill: MOVING** ASSESSMENT

**Performance/Observation** Return to "The Wheel of the Water" **CD 16-1**. Have students review the water cycle movements they developed for each voice of the song.

6e Divide students into groups of five. Have them decide which member of the group will move to each voice part. Give students time to practice their movements, then have each group perform with the recording for the class. Check each student's ability to sustain his or her movement pattern and demonstrate understanding of melody layers.

8b **ASK How is "The Wheel of the Water" like the water cycle found in nature?** (All parts of the song can be sung together. All stages of the water cycle also happen at the same time. It may be in different stages in different places, but it never stops.)

## Spotlight On

▶ **The Painter** Jean François Millet (1814–1875) was the son of a peasant farmer in Normandy, France. From an early age, Millet showed great interest in drawing, and he was a pupil of Paul Delaroche in Paris. Millet moved to Barbizon during the cholera epidemic of 1849, and it was there that he developed his style and subject for his paintings (rural settings). He was also one of the founders of the Barbizon School. Millet influenced many great artists such as Boudin, Monet, Pissarro, Seurat, and van Gogh.

## School to Home Connection

▶ **Water Conservation** Encourage students to research ways they can conserve water at home. Ask them to choose one water conservation idea to try with their family. Invite students to report to the class on the outcome of their project.

## Technology/Media Link

**Web Site** Invite students to visit *www.sfsuccessnet.com* to learn more about Ludwig van Beethoven and his music.

LESSON 5

## LESSON AT A GLANCE

**Element Focus** **MELODY** Melodic contour

**Skill Objective** **CREATING** Create melodies and describe the melodic contour

**Connection Activity** **CULTURE** Discuss the Hmong culture and its folklore

**MATERIALS**

- "Vocal Part"
- "Daytime Music" (Orff part)
- "Nighttime Music" (Orff part)
- *Nruab hnub thiab hmo ntuj* **CD 16-4**
- *Why Is There Day and Night?* **CD 16-5**
- alto and bass xylophones, alto glockenspiel, alto metallophone
- hand props: nine sun drawings, nine moon drawings
- props or costumes for the bull, tiger, rooster, and *lee-nyu* bird (illustration on p. 368 for *lee-nyu* bird)
- world map or globe

**VOCABULARY**

*tremolo* *fermata* melodic contour

**National Standards**

**2b** Perform rhythms and melodies on appropriate instruments
**2f** Play instruments independently against contrasting parts
**4a** Compose music to accompany dramatizations
**5b** Read notes in treble clef, using letters
**6c** Use appropriate terms to explain music
**8b** Identify ways music relates to language arts

**MORE MUSIC CHOICES**

Other pieces using Orff instruments:
"Follow the Drinkin' Gourd," p. 266
"Orfferondo," p. 194



# Why Is There Day and Night?

Long, long ago before people had developed the science of astronomy, the Hmong people had their own system for explaining the stars, the sun, the moon, and other natural events. This is the ancient Hmong story of how day and night might have come to pass.

CD 16-4
**Nruab hnub thiab hmo ntuj**

**"Why Is There Day and Night?"**
**Hmong Folk Tale**

**Listen** to the story. Then using the script, "Vocal Part," "Daytime Music," and "Nighttime Music," **create** a musical play. **Compare** the melodic contour of the musical parts.

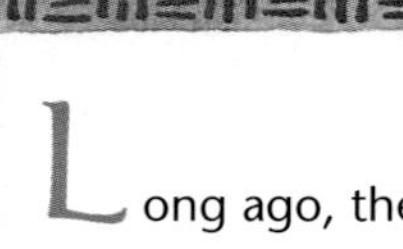

Long ago, there were nine suns and nine moons. When it was night, it was nighttime for a very long time. When it was day, it was daytime for a very long time. However, the people of the world worked very hard and still did not have enough food to eat, and they were angry.



# Footnotes

## TEACHER TO TEACHER

▶ **Creative Performance** Allow students to experiment and explore as they work on *Why Is There Day and Night?* Let the creative experience be foremost. However, let students know that they are expected to do their best. As each part of the play takes shape, allow students to make constructive comments on what is being done well and what can be done better. Ask students guiding questions, such as "How would the rooster stand to emphasize his importance?"

## BUILDING SKILLS THROUGH MUSIC

▶ **Health Education** Share the information about day and night from Across the Curriculum on p. 368. Ask students what they do every night for most of the night. (sleep) Then ask them why it is important to do this every night. (so bodies can regenerate to stay healthy.) Finally, ask them why it is easier to do this at night instead of the day. (because it is dark)

## ACROSS THE CURRICULUM

8b ▶ **Language Arts** Share the book *Night/Day: A Book of Eye-Catching Opposites* by Herve Tullet (Little Brown & Co, 1999). This book is a collection of opposites with illustrations. Invite students to create their own opposites in the format of the book and share them with the class.

Read aloud the poem "Night Comes . . ." by Beatrice Schenk de Regniers or the poem "Night" by Mary Ann Hoberman. Both are from *The Random House Book of Poetry for Children* (Random House, 1983). Each poem paints a picture of nighttime with its own colors—and mood.

Earth, Sea, and Sky

**Arts Connection**

▲ *Paj ntaub* story-telling quilt (1999) by May Chao Lor. The Hmong people use quilts to document folklore and history.

So the people made a crossbow and went to shoot the suns. But the suns and moons would not come out. They were very afraid and were not willing to come out. The people asked what kind of animal could go and call the suns and the moons to come out.

The people asked a bull to call out the suns and moons. A bull came out huffing, puffing, and snorting. "Come out!" he shouted. But the suns and moons would not come out.

Then the people asked a tiger to try. A tiger came out growling and roaring. "Come out!" he shouted. But the suns and moons would not come out.

All instruments

## Vocal Part

But the suns and moons would not come out!

Unit 10 367

# 1 Introduce

Introduce *Why Is There Day and Night?* by posing this situation to students.

**SAY** If you lived very long ago, in a time and place where nothing was known about how the sun, moon, and Earth move, how would you explain the cycle of day and night?

Ask students to "brainstorm" in small groups and come up with the most imaginative and unlikely explanations they can think of. Invite each group to share its explanation with the class.

# 2 Develop

### Listening

Explain to students that they will create a play from a Hmong folk tale that explains why there is day and night. Play *Why Is There Day and Night?* **CD 16-5** for students. After listening, invite students to help list on the board all the characters in the story.

In addition, invite students to listen to a Hmong woman tell the folk tale in her native language. Have students listen to *Nruab hnub thiab hmo ntuj* **CD 16-4.**

### Reading and Analyzing

5b

Ask students to write the pitch names of all the notes in both the "Nighttime" and "Daytime" melodies. (You may wish to have volunteers write on the board.) The notes will include F, G, A, C, and D, creating the F-pentatonic scale. Have students make a quick analysis of melodic direction.

- "Daytime" melody has a long descent, a long ascent, and a long descent, ending in the middle.
- "Nighttime" melody has an ascent, a plateau, an ascent, and a short plateau with a high ending.

continued on page 368

## Spotlight On

▶ **Folklore** There are many words which have similar meanings as folklore, including legend, fairy tale, myth, magic tale, fable, and folktale. *Why Is There Day and Night?* is considered a myth because it is a story about how the world works, and it was believed to be a true story by the ancient Hmong people. Since the beginning of time, humans have created stories to explain their surroundings and allow them to go beyond everyday life. For example, fairy tales make the impossible possible—a magic goose lays golden eggs, a peasant girl marries royalty, and so on. Stories like these are an important part of every culture, so they are passed down, and will continue to be passed down, from generation to generation.

## Skills Reinforcement

▶ **Listening** At an appropriate point in the lesson, have students focus on the timbre of the wood bar instruments (xylophones) that play the "Daytime Music," and the metal bar instruments (metallophones and glockenspiels) that play the "Nighttime Music." Using real instruments or the recordings, invite students to describe the sounds of each group. (Woods: hard, brittle, quick, plunky, staccato; Metals: ringing, bell-like, long sounds) You may then wish to place the instruments where students cannot see them and play a short pattern on each. As students hear each instrument, ask them to write *metal* or *wood* and the name of the instrument. It might be helpful to have instrument names written on the board to assist students with selecting instruments.

Then ask students to compare these with the vocal part on p. 367, which stays on the same note with a step down and back up at the end.

### Playing

2f Select several students to learn the Orff instrument parts for "Daytime Music" on p. 368, and "Nighttime Music" on p. 369. Explain that these pieces are not from the Hmong tradition, but were created especially to be played on Orff instruments for this dramatization.

### Singing

2b Have the entire class learn the "Vocal Part" on p. 367. Use a few mallet percussion instruments to play the tremolo accompaniment.

### Moving

Have students listen to "Daytime Music." Ask them to suggest movements that are appropriate for the sun. Do the same for "Nighttime Music." When the movements are finalized, have all students learn both dances so everyone can participate as needed.

### Dramatizing

Choose students to play the parts of the bull, tiger, *lee-nyu* bird, and rooster. Select a good dramatic reader to be the narrator. Designate nine suns and nine moons, if possible, or have students play more than one sun or moon part.

As students work on creating the dramatization of *Why Is There Day and Night?* share the information from below about the Hmong people of Southeast Asia. Using a globe or map, find the areas that are Hmong homelands.

Discuss with students the illustrations of Hmong life in this lesson. Call attention specifically to the arts connecting Hmong clothing, the style of the houses, the activities, and the animals. Share with students the information from Spotlight On, p. 369.

Next the people asked a lee-nyu bird. The lee-nyu bird came out flapping, hooting, and squawking. "Come out!" she shouted. But the suns and moons would not come out.

Finally, the people asked the rooster to try. The rooster came out puffing up his chest very proudly, and started to crow.

## Daytime Music

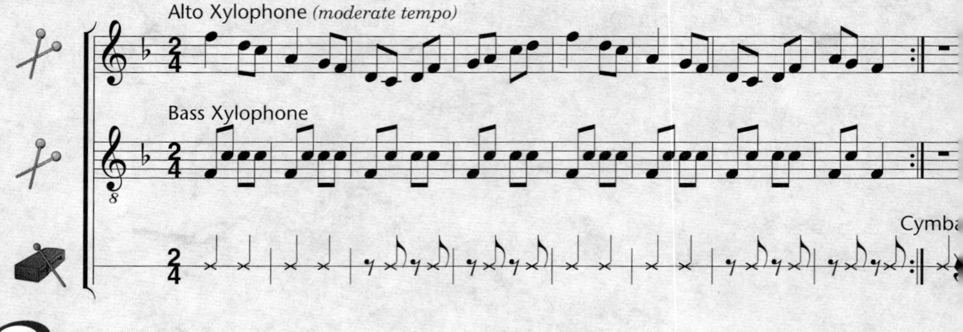


368

# Footnotes

## Cultural Connection

**▶ The Hmong People** Also known as Miao or Meo people, the Hmong people are a tribal group dwelling in the mountains of southern China, Myanmar, Vietnam, Laos, and Thailand, where they live as roving agriculturists. Their culture is believed to have originated about 4,000 years ago in what is now central China. They are called a "tribal group" because their society is organized in clans. Each clan is traditionally known by the color of its costume: White Hmong, Blue Hmong, and so on. Members of a clan must always marry outside their own clan. A woman changes to her husband's clan at marriage, and the children are born as members of the father's clan. Many Hmong left Southeast Asia after the Vietnam War. More than 100,000 now live in the United States and Canada.

## Across the Curriculum

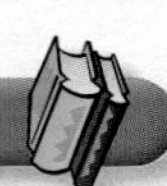

**▶ Science** The scientific explanation for day and night is that Earth spins around its axis. It takes about 24 hours for Earth to spin on its axis once. (The actual rate of rotation varies slightly.) The spinning Earth makes the sun appear to travel from east to west. One half of Earth is facing the sun at any given time. That half is experiencing daytime, while the half facing away from the sun is experiencing nighttime. While most people consider day as the time when the sun shines on their part of the world, night is also part of the cycle of a complete day.

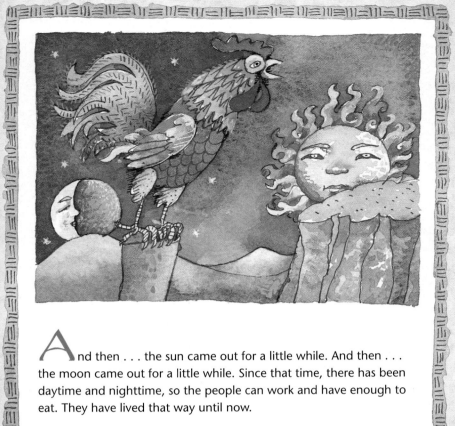

And then . . . the sun came out for a little while. And then . . . the moon came out for a little while. Since that time, there has been daytime and nighttime, so the people can work and have enough to eat. They have lived that way until now.

Earth, Sea, and Sky

## Nighttime Music

# 3 Close

### Performing

Have students present a performance of *Why Is There Day and Night?* Review each part, talk through the connections between them, then perform the entire play.

**Performance/Observation** Have students review the three melodies shown in their books ("Daytime Music," "Nighttime Music," and the vocal part on p. 367).

Ask them to describe the contour, or shape, of each melody. Then have students create their own eight-measure melodies in F- pentatonic and describe the contours. Have them share melodies by playing them on mallet instruments and then posting the notation in a classroom "Composers Corner." Observe students on their ability to use appropriate terminology when describing melodic contour.

## Spotlight On

▶ ***Pa ndau* (Flower Cloth)** The *pa ndau* is a quilt that is a revered art of the Hmong people. The quilts originated during the nineteenth century when Chinese rulers attempted to eliminate the Hmong language. The language and history were preserved by Hmong women in the artwork of the quilts. Since that time, the quilt making has evolved into a form of expression. The *pa ndau* quilts of today trace Hmong history and customs by including panels such as wedding ceremonies, battle in wars (such as Vietnam), and the eventual immigration of many Hmong people to the United States and Canada.

## School to Home Connection

▶ **Folk Tales** Invite students to talk with older friends and family members who might be able to share folk tales from their culture of origin or family history. Students may wish to tape record these stories or write them down. Encourage students to share the folk tales with the class.

## Technology/Media Link

**Notation Software** In small groups, have students compose original music for *Why Is There Day and Night?* Write the F-pentatonic scale used on the board. Using notation software, ask students to use these notes to compose and notate several short musical accompaniments that will highlight their drama.

# LESSON 6

## LESSON AT A GLANCE

**Element Focus** **TEXTURE/HARMONY** Descant

**Skill Objective** **SINGING** Sing a descant with a song about nature

**Connection Activity** **SCIENCE** Discuss the seasons

**MATERIALS**

- "Cycle Song of Life (The River Song)" **CD 16-6**
  **Recording Routine:** Intro (4 m.); v. 1; refrain; interlude (1 m.); v. 2; refrain; interlude (6 m.); v. 3; refrain; refrain with descant; coda
- "Spring" from *The Four Seasons* **CD 16-8**

**VOCABULARY**

descant

**◆◆◆◆ National Standards ◆◆◆◆**

**1d** Sing part songs
**4b** Arrange songs within specific guidelines
**6b** Describe music by explaining how it sounds
**8b** Identify ways music relates to science

**MORE MUSIC CHOICES**

Other songs with descants

"Amazing Grace," p. 160

"America, the Beautiful," p. 158

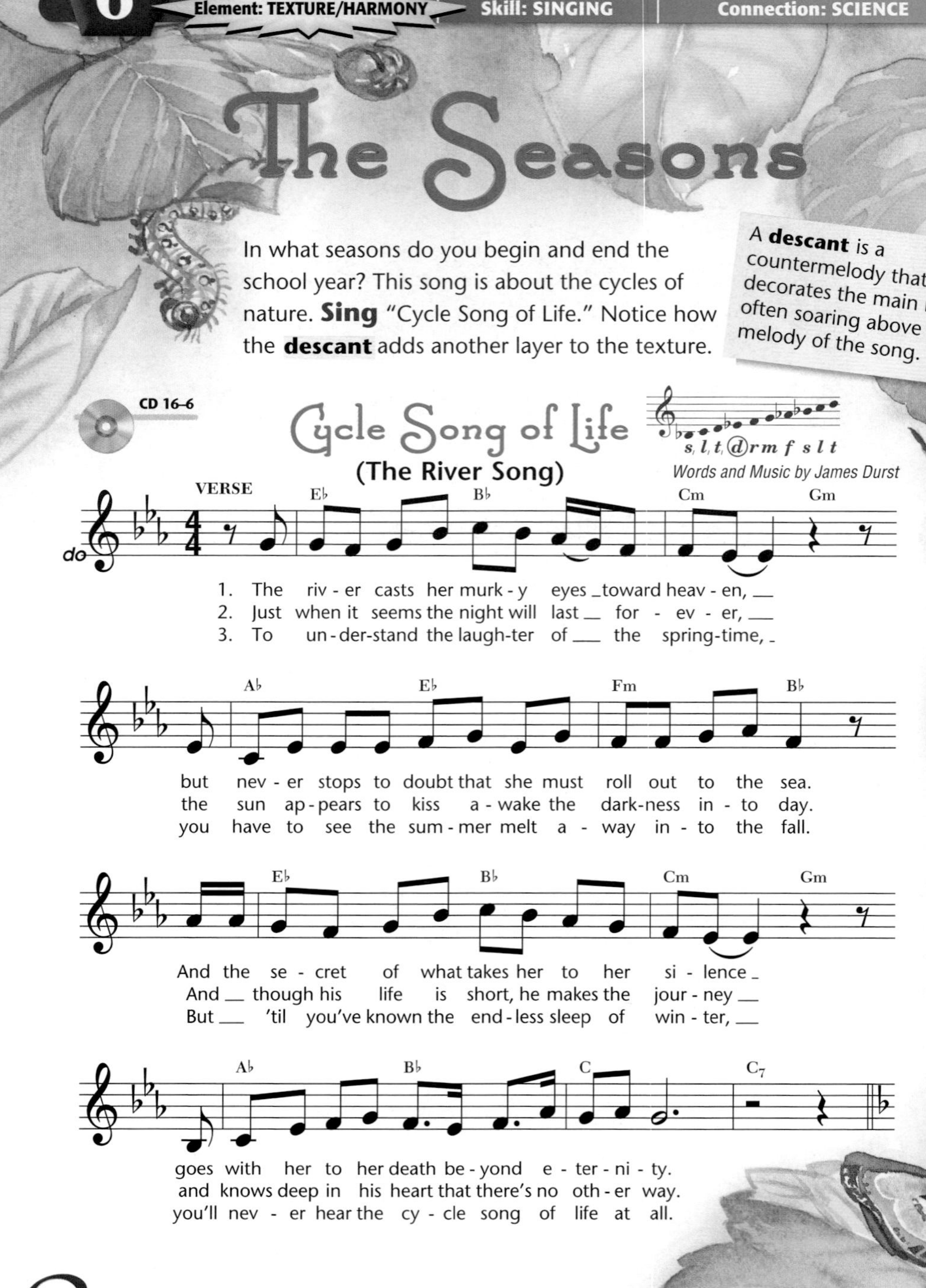
LESSON 6 Element: TEXTURE/HARMONY Skill: SINGING Connection: SCIENCE

The Seasons

In what seasons do you begin and end the school year? This song is about the cycles of nature. **Sing** "Cycle Song of Life." Notice how the **descant** adds another layer to the texture.

A **descant** is a countermelody that decorates the main melody, often soaring above the melody of the song.

CD 16-6

Cycle Song of Life
(The River Song)

Words and Music by James Durst

s, l, t, d r m f s l t
VERSE
do
E♭ B♭ Cm Gm
1. The riv - er casts her murk - y eyes _toward heav - en, __
2. Just when it seems the night will last __ for - ev - er, __
3. To un - der - stand the laugh - ter of __ the spring - time, _
A♭ E♭ Fm B♭
but nev - er stops to doubt that she must roll out to the sea.
the sun ap - pears to kiss a - wake the dark - ness in - to day.
you have to see the sum - mer melt a - way in - to the fall.
E♭ B♭ Cm Gm
And the se - cret of what takes her to her si - lence _
And __ though his life is short, he makes the jour - ney __
But __ 'til you've known the end - less sleep of win - ter, __
A♭ B♭ C C7
goes with her to her death be - yond e - ter - ni - ty.
and knows deep in his heart that there's no oth - er way.
you'll nev - er hear the cy - cle song of life at all.

370

# 1 INTRODUCE

Have students listen to "Cycle Song of Life" **CD 16-6** and follow the song text, p. 370, through the first refrain.

**ASK What cycles of nature have we learned about already?** (water, day/night)

Share information about the seasons along an Alaskan river from the resource referenced in Across the Curriculum below.

# Footnotes

## ACROSS THE CURRICULUM

▶ **Science/Language Arts** Encourage interested students to read *River of Life* by Debbie S. Miller (Clarion Books, 2000), a book that traces seasonal changes along an Alaskan river.

## BUILDING SKILLS THROUGH MUSIC

▶ **Writing** Share with students the information about Vivaldi from Spotlight On, p. 371. Then invite students to listen to *Spring* **CD 16-8.** After listening, write a short poem as a class that describes the season of spring as heard on the recording.

## SKILLS REINFORCEMENT

▶ **Creating** The countermelody to the song "The Cycle Song of Life" is an effective complement to the main melody because it is active when the other melody is not. This countermelody contains many held notes and rests.

**Reinforcement** Have students hum the countermelody with the Stereo Vocal Track for the song **CD 16-6** to reinforce their understanding of the melody and harmony involved in the two parts.

**On Target** Have students sing the countermelody as written.

**Challenge** Students who require a further challenge should be invited to improvise additional notes to the countermelody (ornamentation) so that it is even more entwined with the main melody. They can practice with the Stereo Vocal Track for the song and explore as many different options as possible.

REFRAIN
Descant last time only
C7 F C Dm Am
The riv-er just keeps flow-in' on and
And the riv-er just keeps flow-in' on and on. The
B♭ Gm Csus4 C7
on. The sun keeps go-in' 'round,
sun keeps go-in' 'round to bring the dawn. And
F C Dm Am
life keeps on go-in',
life just keeps on go-in' 'til it looks as though it's gone,
repeat refrain last time
B♭ C Fm Fm7 B♭7
but it real-ly just keeps flow-in' on and on.
Earth, Sea, and Sky

### More of the Seasons

*The Seasons* by Antonio Vivaldi is a set of four concertos describing the seasons. **Listen** to this movement from *Spring.* What "special effects" did the composer use to create a musical image of this season?

CD 16–8
**Spring, Movement 1**

**from *The Four Seasons* by Antonio Vivaldi**

This piece was written for small orchestra and solo violin.

Unit 10 371

## 2 Develop

### Singing

8b Have students listen to the verses of "Cycle Song of Life" **CD 16-6** and sing along with the refrain.

ASK **What cycle is described in verse 2?** (day/night)

**What cycle is described in verse 3?** (seasons)

**What happened near the end that was different?** (There was another melody.)

**Is the new melody higher or lower than the regular melody?** (higher)

1d Explain that the new melody is a descant, a melody above the original melody that makes an interesting addition to the texture. Have students divide into groups to sing "Cycle Song of Life" with both parts.

### Listening

*The Four Seasons* is another piece about cycles in nature. Each section of *The Four Seasons* features a solo violin accompanied by a string orchestra. Share the information about Vivaldi and the music from Spotlight On below.

6b Have students listen to *Spring* **CD 16-8** and help them notice the events of spring's awakening—bird songs, thunder, and water gushing from underground springs. On another day, you might have students compare *Spring* with another piece of program music. Play the excerpt from Beethoven's *Symphony No. 6* **CD 16-3** and have them compare how each composer uses musical events to suggest a story.

## 3 Close

**Element: TEXTURE/HARMONY** ASSESSMENT

**Performance/Observation** Have students sing "Cycle Song of Life" **CD 16-6** and invite different groups of four to sing the descant on each refrain. Observe students' ability to maintain their part as they sing the descant.

### Spotlight On

▶ **Vivaldi and *The Four Seasons*** Antonio Vivaldi (1678–1741) was born in Venice, Italy. He became a priest in 1703, but spent most of his career as the violin teacher at a girls' orphanage. Vivaldi wrote many pieces for the girls at the orphanage, including concertos for almost every orchestral instrument. *The Four Seasons* is a set of four concertos for violin, one for each season. When the printed music for *The Four Seasons* was first published in Amsterdam in 1725, it included a poem by Vivaldi just before each movement that described what the music was supposed to depict.

### Technology/Media Link

**Notation Software** Using a MIDI keyboard and notation software, prepare a file with the refrain of "Cycle Song of Life." Invite students to improvise a descant or countermelody for the refrain, using an F-major scale. With notation software, have them record their performances into a second staff system. Play back their arrangements and encourage students to discuss areas that may need improvement. Make corrections as necessary and print out each student's final arrangement for a portfolio.

LESSON 7

## LESSON AT A GLANCE

**Element Focus** **FORM** ABABA sectional form

**Skill Objective** **SINGING** Sing a song in ABABA sectional form

**Connection Activity** **SCIENCE** Discuss stars and astronomy

**MATERIALS**

- "Starlight, Star Bright" **CD 16-9**

**Recording Routine:** Intro (4 m.); refrain; v. 1; refrain; v. 2; refrain; coda

**VOCABULARY**

theme

**National Standards**

**1a** Sing independently with appropriate posture and diction
**1b** Sing expressively with appropriate dynamics and interpretation
**2d** Play instruments echoing melodic patterns
**6a** Listen to identify form
**7a** Create standards for evaluating performances

**MORE MUSIC CHOICES**

Another song about living in harmony:
"Put a Little Love in Your Heart," p. 6

# 1 INTRODUCE

Ask students if anyone has said or sung the poem "Starlight, Star Bright" in earlier grades. Encourage them to share the wishes they might have made at that time in their lives. Share the information about stars and astronomy from Spotlight On below.

Then invite students to read the Music Makers feature on James Durst, the composer of the song.

LESSON 7 Element: FORM | Skill: SINGING | Connection: SCIENCE

# Seeing Stars

When the first star of the evening appears, make a wish. What did you wish for? In the song "Starlight, Star Bright," what does the composer wish for the world?

Look at the music for "Starlight, Star Bright." Do verses one and two have the same notation? *Identify* the form of the song. Then *sing* "Starlight, Star Bright."

MUSIC MAKERS

## James Durst

**James Durst** is a composer, singer, and guitar player. Durst was born and raised in California. Now he spends his life traveling the world, bringing his music and the message of harmony and understanding to people everywhere. In each country he learns new songs. Recently he has started going into schools to work with students.

372

# Footnotes

## ACROSS THE CURRICULUM

▶ **Science/Language Arts** Interested students may enjoy reading *The Big Dipper and You* by Edwin C. Krupp and Robin Rector Krupp (Mulberry, 1999). Invite students to learn more about the constellations that they can see. Encourage them to keep track of the changes that they see in the night sky.

## BUILDING SKILLS THROUGH MUSIC

▶ **Science** Lead students in a discussion about constellations. Point out that constellations are made up of a pattern of stars. Have students name and describe constellations they may know (for example, Big Dipper, Little Dipper, Orion) and then design an "unknown" constellation and name it. Ask for volunteers to share their constellations.

## SPOTLIGHT ON

▶ **Stars and Astronomy** Ask students what they already know and love about stars. Encourage them to use a simplified star chart to locate constellations. Students may also wish to begin a "star-gazing" journal and sketchbook.

Many of the names attached to constellations go back to the astronomers of ancient Greek civilization. More than 40 were named in that period. European astronomers added some 40 more in the seventeenth and eighteenth centuries. In the twentieth century, astronomers determined the precise boundaries for 88 constellations. Organizing stars into constellations is very useful for astronomers. It is also helpful for ship navigation. Today, people also use constellations to help track satellites and spacecraft.

CD 16-9
Starlight, Star Bright
ⓓ r m f s lo l ta t d'
Words and Music by James Durst
A REFRAIN
do
Star - light, star bright, first star I see to-night. I wish I may, I wish I might. Have the wish I wish to - night.
Fine
B VERSE
1. Shine on peo-ple of the earth; make us wor - thy of our birth. Bright-en paths thru dark of night; that we might walk in truth and light.
Shine on chil-dren ev - 'ry - where; keep them safe and free from care. Feed their bod - ies, souls and minds; that they might bless this world in kind.
2. Shine on an - i - mals and plants; il - lu - mi-nate their life - long dance. Light the land, the sky, and sea; and all that share life's mys - ter - y.
Lit - tle bea-con out in space; shine up - on the hu - man race. Grant this hum - ble, hope - ful prayer; for peace to flour - ish ev - 'ry - where.
D.C. after each verse
Earth, Sea, and Sky
Unit 10 373


# 2 Develop

## Singing

1a Play "Starlight, Star Bright" **CD 16-9**. Have students listen and follow the notation for the entire song on p. 373. Have them sing with all the refrain sections.

ASK **Do verses 1 and 2 have the same notation?** (yes, except for one extra note in verse 2 the first time through)

Invite students to read the text of the song and think about its meaning.

ASK **What are the verses of the song trying to say?** (They ask the stars to shine on the world and its people in ways that will make life better for everyone.)

1b Have individuals or the entire class read the verses aloud, clearly and with expression. Play "Starlight, Star Bright" again, asking students to sing along on all verses and refrains, with appropriate expression.

## Analyzing

6a Have students work in pairs to diagram the form of "Starlight, Star Bright," using the letter A for each refrain and B for each verse. Have students write their answers, and share them with the class. Tell them that the verses are set with repeats to save space. Verses are actually sung only once, making the form ABABA.

# 3 Close

**Skill: SINGING** ASSESSMENT

7a **Performance/Observation** Divide the class into small groups and have students sing "Starlight, Star Bright" with the Stereo Performance Track **CD 16-10.** Observe students' ability to follow the notation and form as they read the song from the page. Help students develop a set of basic criteria to evaluate each musical performance.

## Skills Reinforcement

▶ **Recorder** The part below can be played to accompany the refrain of "Starlight, Star Bright."

2d **Reinforcement** Have students practice patterns on their recorder that begin with a rest on the first beat.

**On Target** Have students play the recorder part below as written.

**Challenge** Invite some students to play the melody of the refrain while the rest of the class plays the recorder part.

## Technology/Media Link

**Video Library** For more information about how music is created, have students watch the *Creating Music* segment on the video.

LESSON 8

## LESSON AT A GLANCE

**Element Focus** **RHYTHM** Strong/weak beats in duple meter

**Skill Objective** **MOVING** Perform a strong and weak beat body percussion pattern in duple meter

**Connection Activity** **LANGUAGE ARTS** Share a poem and discuss the phases of the moon

**MATERIALS**

- "Sailboat in the Sky" (Korean) **CD 16-11**
- "Sailboat in the Sky" (English) **CD 16-12**

  **Recording Routine:** Intro (4 m.); vocal; interlude (2 m.); vocal; coda
- **Pronunciation Practice/Translation** p. 492
- **Resource Book** p. A-39

**VOCABULARY**

strong beat  weak beat

**National Standards**

**1c** Sing from memory songs from diverse cultures
**5c** Identify and use symbols and terms for articulation
**6e** While listening to music, move to show a prominent feature of the music
**8b** Identify ways music relates to language arts

**MORE MUSIC CHOICES**

Other songs from Asia:
*"Tsuki,"* p. 25
*"Osamu kosamu,"* p. 96

# 1 INTRODUCE

8b Ask students if they have ever heard of the "man in the moon." Introduce "Sailboat in the Sky" as a Korean interpretation of what the moon looks like in the night sky. Share the poem from Across the Curriculum on p. 375 and discuss with students the phases of the moon. Then play "Sailboat in the Sky" **CD 16-11**.

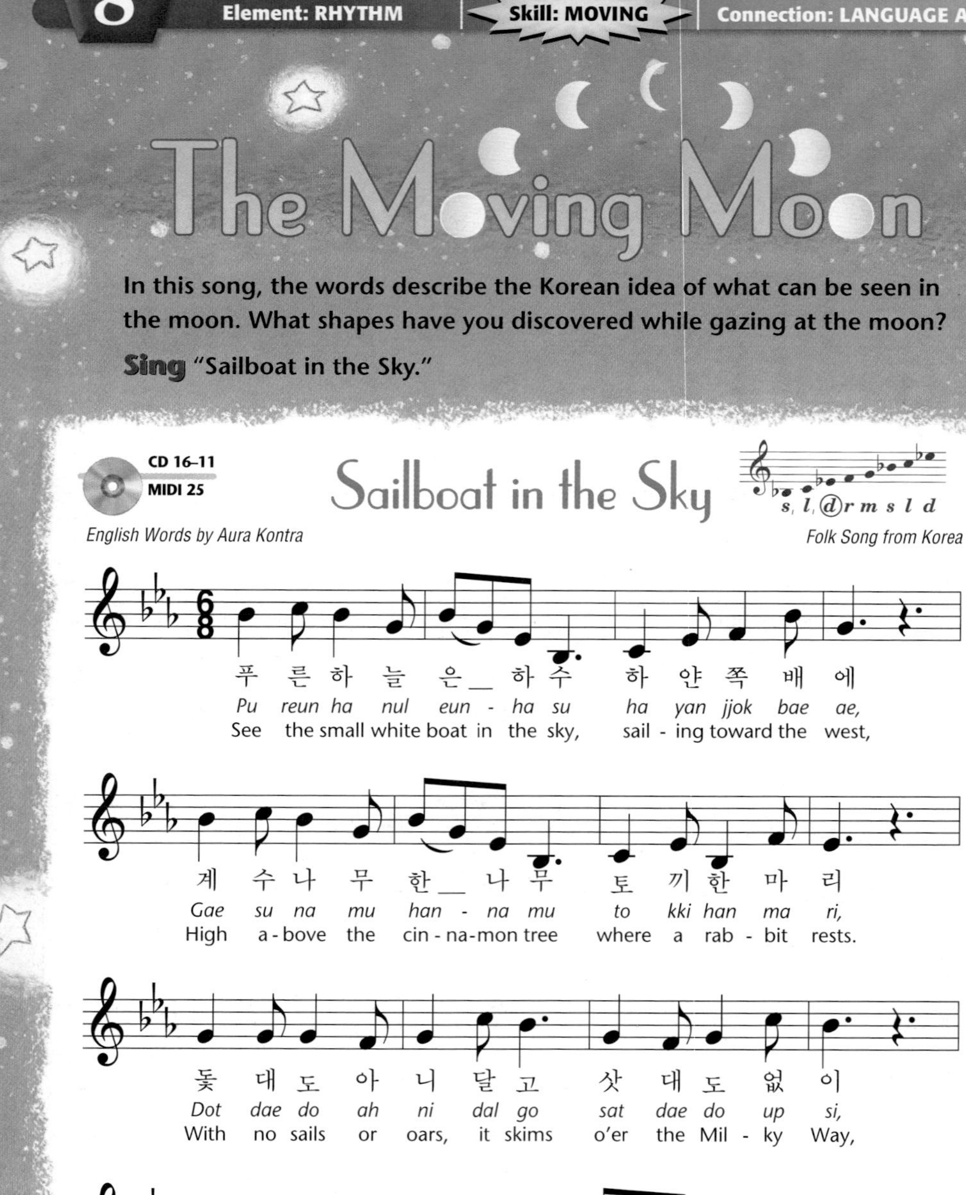

LESSON 8
Element: RHYTHM
Skill: MOVING
Connection: LANGUAGE ART
The Moving Moon
In this song, the words describe the Korean idea of what can be seen in the moon. What shapes have you discovered while gazing at the moon?
Sing "Sailboat in the Sky."
CD 16-11
MIDI 25
Sailboat in the Sky
s, l, d r m s l d
English Words by Aura Kontra
Folk Song from Korea
푸 른 하 늘 은_ 하 수 하 얀 쪽 배 에
Pu reun ha nul eun - ha su ha yan jjok bae ae,
See the small white boat in the sky, sail - ing toward the west,
계 수 나 무 한_ 나 무 토 끼 한 마 리
Gae su na mu han - na mu to kki han ma ri,
High a - bove the cin - na-mon tree where a rab - bit rests.
돛 대 도 아 니 달 고 삿 대 도 없 이
Dot dae do ah ni dal go sat dae do up si,
With no sails or oars, it skims o'er the Mil - ky Way,
가 기 도 잘 도 간 다 서_ 쪽 나 라 로
Ga gi do jal do gahn da so - jjok na ra ro.
Float - ing a - mong the clouds as slow-ly it fades a - way.
374


# Footnotes

## MOVEMENT

▶ **Creative Movement** Discuss the moon movement scenes from the song text of "Sailboat in the Sky." Ask students to create simple scenery and movements to go with this song including a crescent moon, cinnamon tree, rabbit, Milky Way, and clouds. In small groups, invite students to create dramatic movement tableaus to accompany "Sailboat in the Sky." Encourage the groups to perform their ideas for the entire class.

## BUILDING SKILLS THROUGH MUSIC

▶ **Reading** Write "The Moon's the North Wind's Cooky" by Vachel Lindsay from Across the Curriculum on p. 375 on the board. Select a student to read the poem to the class. Then, have students explain the process that the poem is describing, encouraging them to recall specific information in each line and interpret it into common vernacular.

## SKILLS REINFORCEMENT

▶ **Conducting** To reinforce the concept of strong and weak beat in duple meter, have students conduct as they listen to the recording of "Sailboat in the Sky" **CD 16-11.** Encourage students to take turns conducting the class as the rest of the class sings the song and does the movement activity.

**Strong and Weak Beats**

**Sing** the song again. Clap on the first beat of each measure and pat on the fourth beat of each measure.

**Korean Hand Game**

Below is a picture of a traditional Korean hand game often played while singing the song. The game is played quickly. To learn it, **move** slowly and then speed up.



# 2 Develop

## Singing

1c Have students sing "Sailboat in the Sky" **CD 16-12** with English text, and then with the Pronunciation Practice **CD 16-14** to learn the Korean words. Refer to Resource Book p. A-39 for the Pronunciation Practice Guide. Add a slow pat-clap pattern to show the strong and weak beat in each measure. Write a large 1 and 4 on the board. Ask a volunteer to point to the correct number for each beat, as the class sings the song and performs the pattern.

## Moving

Invite students to learn this traditional Korean body percussion game, starting at a slow tempo and speeding up as they gain confidence. Have students stand or sit, facing a partner. There are six motions per measure; 12 in the whole pattern. Ask students to practice motions in sets of 3 and then put them together. Have them

- Clap own hands; touch and roll backs of right hands with partner; clap right palms with partner.
- Clap own hands; touch and roll backs of left hands with partner; clap left palms with partner.
- Clap own hands; clap with partner, right palm down, left palm up; clap both palms straight ahead with partner.
- Clap own hands; clap with partner, one person palms up, the other palms down; clap both palms straight ahead with partner.

# 3 Close

**Skill: MOVING** — **ASSESSMENT**

6e **Performance/Observation** Have students sing "Sailboat in the Sky" **CD 16-11**, performing the body percussion game in pairs. Observe students' ability to perform the strong and weak beat body percussion patterns.

## Across the Curriculum

▶ **Language Arts** Share with students the poem "The Moon's the North Wind's Cooky" by Vachel Lindsay from *The Random House Book of Poetry for Children* (Random House, 1983).

The Moon's the North Wind's cooky.
He bites it, day by day,
Until there's but a rim of scraps
That crumble all away.
The South Wind is a baker.
He kneads clouds in his den,
And bakes a crisp new moon *that...greedy*
*North...Wind...eats...again!*

Remind students of the moon images discussed in the lesson, then have them write their own moon image poem.

## Technology/Media Link

5c **Notation Software** Use a notation program to notate and print the melody of "Sailboat in the Sky." Draw a vertical line above beat 1 and beat 2 of each measure. Give copies to students and play the song for them on the computer.

Show students how to draw an accent. Explain that accents make a note sound stronger. Ask students to draw accents above the strong beats of "Sailboat in the Sky." Invite a volunteer to notate on the computer the accents selected by the class.

Play "Sailboat in the Sky" with the new accents. Ask students how the accents fit the music. Adjust the accents according to students' suggestions and play the song again.

LESSON 9

## LESSON AT A GLANCE

**Element Focus** **EXPRESSION** *Accelerando*

**Skill Objective** **MOVING** Perform a body percussion game with an *accelerando*

**Connection Activity** **LANGUAGE ARTS** Write lyrics based on a nature topic

**MATERIALS**

- "The Planets Chant" (speech piece) **CD 16-16**
  **Recording Routine:** Intro (2m.); vocal; interlude (4 m.); vocal; interlude (4 m.); vocal; interlude (4 m.); vocal; coda
- "Mars, the Bringer of War" from *The Planets* **CD 16-15**
- chart of the planets

**VOCABULARY**

*accelerando*

◆◆◆◆ **National Standards** ◆◆◆◆

**4b** Compose music within specific guidelines
**5c** Identify and use terms for tempo
**5d** Notate rhythms using standard symbols
**6e** Move to show a prominent feature of the music

**MORE MUSIC CHOICES**

Other speech pieces:

"Bundle-Buggy Boogie Woogie," p. 120

"Heave-Ho!"/ "Going, Going, Gone"/ "The Snow," p. 182

LESSON 9
Element: EXPRESSION
Skill: MOVING
Connection: LANGUAGE ARTS
The Planets
The planets in our solar system have long inspired people's imagination. The British composer Gustav Holst wrote an entire suite based on this subject. Listen to "Mars, the Bringer of War" from The Planets.
MUSIC MAKERS
Gustav Holst
Gustavv Holst (1874–1934) was a musician, composer, and teacher. As a child he studied piano. Later, he went to the Royal College of Music in London and studied composition and trombone. As a teacher, Holst was known for encouraging beginners. He was a believer in learning music by "doing" music. Holst composed for both orchestra and wind bands. Perhaps his most famous work is The Planets.
376

# 1 INTRODUCE

Before class, prepare a chart or board presentation of the planets, with their relative distances from the sun. Discuss the chart with students, then have them speak the name of each planet in order. Play "The Planets Chant" **CD 16-16** for students and encourage them to listen carefully.

## Footnotes

### ACROSS THE CURRICULUM

▶ **Science** Invite students to learn more about the planets by sharing *Postcards from Pluto: A Tour of the Solar System* by Loreen Leedy (Holiday House, 1993). This is a humorous, but informative book that tells students about the planets through a series of postcards sent back to Earth. Another informative book for interested students is *Our Solar System* by Jon Kirkwood (Copper Beech, 1998).

### BUILDING SKILLS THROUGH MUSIC

▶ **Science** After completing the lesson, guide students in a more detailed discussion of the planets. Tell students that the planets are part of the solar system. Then ask students to describe other objects in the solar system. (the sun, asteriods, comets, moons) As a class, have students choreograph and perform movement to model how objects in the solar system move through space.

### SKILLS REINFORCEMENT

4b 5d ▶ **Creating** In small groups, encourage students to create their own speech piece. They may wish to use a "nature" topic from this unit. Ideas might include helping the environment; cycles such as day and night, seasons, or the water cycle; or traveling in space. Invite students to experiment with tempo and dynamic changes in their pieces. Help students notate their compositions. Ask each group to perform their speech piece for the class, using a conductor or nonpitched percussion instruments to help keep the steady beat, if the piece has one.

## Moving Through Space

**Perform** this rhythm game several times to learn the names of the planets. Each time, perform it at a slightly faster tempo.

CD 16-16

# The Planets Chant

*Words and Music by Mary Shamrock*

Mer-cu-ry, Ve-nus, Earth, and Mars. Ju-pi-ter, Sat-urn, they're not stars!

U-ra-nus, Nep-tune, Plu-to's last. Now let's hear you say it fast!

Pat thighs

Clap.

Clap right hands.

Clap.

Clap left hands

Clap.

Clap with partner.

Clap.

**Listen** again to Holst's compositon. If you had the chance, which planet would you visit first?

CD 16-15
**Mars, the Bringer of War**

**from *The Planets, Suite for Large Orchestra,* Op. 32**
**by Gustav Holst**

This selection is one of seven pieces in this suite. The other planets included in the entire work are Mercury, Venus, Jupiter, Saturn, Uranus, and Neptune.

# 2 Develop

### Performing/Moving

6e Invite students to speak "The Planet Chant" **CD 16-16** with or without the recording. Have students learn the body percussion pattern on p. 377. Start slowly and progress to a comfortable tempo. Encourage those who feel ready to try the body percussion and chant together. Practice the routine several times.

5c When students are confident, try conducting them in "The Planet Chant." As the speech piece progresses, gradually increase the speed.

ASK **What happened in the music?** (The tempo became faster and faster.)

Explain that the term for this is *accelerando.*

### Listening

Play "Mars, the Bringer of War" from *The Planets* **CD 16-15.** Share the information about the planets from Spotlight On, below, and invite students to read the Music Makers feature about Gustav Holst. Guide students to realize that the meter is in 5. Ask them to tap the meter on their desks, accenting the first and fourth beats—**1** 2 3 **4** 5.

### Creating

Refer to Skills Reinforcement on p. 376 and invite students to create a speech piece based on nature. They may choose to model the piece after "The Planets Chant."

# 3 Close

**Element: EXPRESSION** ASSESSMENT

**Performance/Observation** Divide students into pairs and ask them to perform "The Planets Chant" **CD 16-16** with the body percussion routine. Have them start the chant slowly and *accelerando* to the end. Observe each student's ability to gradually increase the tempo.

## Spotlight On

▶ **The Planets** The ancient Greeks knew about five of the other planets in our solar system—Mercury, Venus, Mars, Jupiter, and Saturn. They named the planets after their gods. The invention of the telescope made it possible to spot other planets. Uranus was discovered in 1781, and Neptune in 1846. Pluto, the outer planet of our solar system, was not discovered until 1930. Gustav Holst wrote *The Planets* from 1914–1916, so he did not know about Pluto. Each movement of *The Planets* has a descriptive subtitle. Besides "Mars, the Bringer of War," there is "Venus, the Bringer of Peace," "Mercury, the Winged Messenger," "Jupiter, the Bringer of Jollity," "Saturn, the Bringer of Old Age," "Uranus, the Magician," and "Neptune, the Mystic."

## Technology/Media Link

**Web Site** Encourage students to visit *www.sfsuccessnet.com* for more information on Gustav Holst, composer of *The Planets.*

| Lesson | Elements | Skills | |
|---|---|---|---|

## A Sequence of Seagulls

pp. 382-383

**Element: Melody**
**Concept:** Pattern
**Focus:** Melodic sequence

**Secondary Element**
Form: *coda*

**National Standards**
1b 1e 5b 6b 7a

**Skill: Singing**
**Objective:** Sing a song with melodic sequence

**Secondary Skills**
- **Reading** Look at the notation of a song, paying close attention to the melodic sequences

**SKILLS REINFORCEMENT**
- **Singing** Sing a song that contains alliteration

LESSON 2

## A Fiddlin' Folk Song

pp. 384–385

**Element: Texture/Harmony**
**Concept:** Harmony
**Focus:** Countermelodies

**Secondary Element**
Timbre: instrumental

**National Standards**
1a 5a 6b 6c 7a

**Skill: Singing**
**Objective:** Sing a song with two countermelodies

**Secondary Skills**
- **Listening** Identify the instruments played in a song

**SKILLS REINFORCEMENT**
- **Mallets** Play an Orff arrangement of a song

## Get It Together

pp. 386–389

**Element: Texture/Harmony**
**Concept:** Harmony
**Focus:** Monophonic, homophonic, and polyphonic singing

**Secondary Element**
Melody: *do-mi-so* patterns

**National Standards**
1a 1b 1c 1d 5a 6b

**Skill: Singing**
**Objective:** Sing and describe how harmony is achieved in the song

**Secondary Skills**
- **Listening** Listen for texture, harmony, style, and instrumentation in a song
- **Reading** Read rhythm patterns of a song
- **Analyzing** Discuss how harmonic textures are achieved in a song
- **Moving** Invent expressive movements for a slow song
- **Creating** Create texture by performing rounds

**SKILLS REINFORCEMENT**
- **Reading** Read syncopated patterns in a song
- **Singing** Review methods for proper enunciation when performing syncopated rhythms

| Connections | Music and Other Literature | |
|---|---|---|
| **Connection:** **Language Arts**<br>**Activity:** Learn about alliteration<br>ACROSS THE CURRICULUM **Language Arts** Discuss the literary device of alliteration<br>MOVEMENT **Creative Movement** Create movements to reflect the contour of each melody<br>BUILDING SKILLS THROUGH MUSIC **Language** Create phrases that use alliteration | **Song** "Seagull, Seagull, Sit on the Shore"<br><br>**More Music Choices**<br>"*Tancovačka*," p. 230<br>"*Thula, thula, ngoana*," p. 227 | ASSESSMENT<br>**Performance/Observation** Consider balance, intelligibility, and pitch accuracy during the performance of a song<br><br>TECHNOLOGY/MEDIA LINK<br>**MIDI/Sequencing Software** Use a MIDI song file to split the two parts of a song onto separate tracks |
| **Connection:** **Social Studies**<br>**Activity:** Discover that dance tunes were an important form of entertainment<br>ACROSS THE CURRICULUM **Social Studies** Discuss the significance of dancing in American history<br>SPOTLIGHT ON **The Performer** Information about Mark O' Connor<br>BUILDING SKILLS THROUGH MUSIC **Physical Education** Perform a folk dance to a song | **Song** "Cindy"<br><br>**Listening Selection** *Bonaparte's Retreat*<br><br>**More Music Choices**<br>"Amazing Grace," p. 160<br>"America, the Beautiful," p. 158 | ASSESSMENT<br>**Performance/Peer Critique** Consider balance, intelligibility, and pitch accuracy during the performance of a song<br><br>TECHNOLOGY/MEDIA LINK<br>**MIDI/Sequencing Software** Use a MIDI song file to compose a bass part |
| **Connection:** **Culture**<br>**Activity:** Discuss some aspects of Cajun culture<br>SPOTLIGHT ON<br>**Lullaby** Uses of lullabies<br>**Play Parties** Information about play parties<br>CULTURAL CONNECTION **Cajun Culture** Cajun life and music<br>ACROSS THE CURRICULUM **Language Arts** Read a book about Cajun culture<br>MOVEMENT **Choreography** Follow specific guidelines to create movements to a song<br>BUILDING SKILLS THROUGH MUSIC **Language** Identify words of a song that contain an apostrophe | **Song** "Lullaby and Dance"<br><br>**Listening Selection** *Jolie Blonde*<br>**Arts Connections**<br>*Fiddling Sailor*<br>*Horse and Rider*<br><br>**More Music Choices**<br>"Ah, Poor Bird," p. 196<br>"*Hey m'tswala*," p. 79<br>"Chairs to Mend," p. 149<br>"Cycle Song of Life," p. 370 | ASSESSMENT<br>**Music Journal Writing** Describe the texture and harmony of a listening selection<br><br>TECHNOLOGY/MEDIA LINK<br>**MIDI/Sequencing Software** Create activities using a MIDI song file |

| Lesson | Elements | Skills |
|---|---|---|

## Lesson 4 Singing Phrases

pp. 390-393

**Element: Rhythm**
**Concept:** Beat
**Focus:** Upbeats

**Secondary Element**
Rhythm: $\frac{3}{4}$ time

**National Standards**
1c 1d 2f 5a 5b 6a 7a

**Skill: Singing**
**Objective:** Sing and read upbeats

**Secondary Skills**
- **Listening** Identify upbeats, harmony, and sequences in a song
- **Reading** Read upbeats in music
- **Performing** Suggestions for performing a song in groups
- **Creating** Create English lyrics for a song
- **Analyzing** Identify the form and range of a song

**SKILLS REINFORCEMENT**
- **Recorder** Perform a countermelody to a song

## Lesson 5 Singing in Layers

pp. 394-395

**Element: Texture/Harmony**
**Concept:** Texture
**Focus:** Melody ostinato

**Secondary Element**
Rhythm: ♪ ♩ ♪

**National Standards**
2a 5a 6a

**Skill: Singing**
**Objective:** Sing melody ostinatos

**Secondary Skills**
- **Analyzing** Discuss how ostinatos affect the texture of a song
- **Reading** Read ostinato patterns in parts

**SKILLS REINFORCEMENT**
- **Guitar** Play an F drone accompaniment to a song
- **Keyboard** Play an ensemble accompaniment to a song
- **Moving** Form shapes and rotate while singing

## Lesson 6 Two Melodies—One Song

pp. 396-401

**Element: Texture/Harmony**
**Concept:** Texture
**Focus:** Partner songs

**Secondary Element**
Rhythm: syncopation

**National Standards**
1a 1d 2a 3b 5a 6e 7a

**Skill: Singing**
**Objective:** Sing two partner songs

**Secondary Skills**
- **Reading** Read syncopated patterns in a song
- **Performing** Improvise syncopated parts using Orff instruments
- **Listening** Listen for syncopated patterns in a song
- **Creating** Improvise syncopated parts for a song

**SKILLS REINFORCEMENT**
- **Creating** Create a partner song
- **Keyboard** Improvise syncopated rhythm patterns for a song

# Connections

# Music and Other Literature



**Connection: Culture**
**Activity:** Explore aspects of Gaelic culture

TEACHER TO TEACHER
**Teaching with MIDI** Use MIDI to teach part singing
**Choral Teaching Tips** Implement choral concepts to develop good singing

SPOTLIGHT ON **Gaelic Language** History of Gaelic language speakers

MOVEMENT **Choreography** Follow specific guidelines to create movements to a song

CULTURAL CONNECTION **Gaelic Culture** Cultural facts about Gaelic culture

ACROSS THE CURRICULUM **Language Arts** Read poems and stories and create performances or illustrations

BUILDING SKILLS THROUGH MUSIC **Math** Compare the number of noteheads to the number of syllables in a song

**Song** "*Einini*"

**More Music Choices**
"Frog Music," p. 200
"Joe Turner Blues," p. 56

ASSESSMENT
**Performance/Observation** Sing upbeat notes of a song accurately with smooth, gentle phrasing

TECHNOLOGY/MEDIA LINK
**Web Site** Learn more about Gaelic music

---

**Connection: Culture**
**Activity:** Discuss African American spirituals

CULTURAL CONNECTION **Spirituals** Discuss history and current performance practices of spirituals

TEACHER TO TEACHER **Singing a Spiritual** Consider suggestions for singing in parts

BUILDING SKILLS THROUGH MUSIC **Physical Education** Create geometric shapes and move them to an ostinato of a song

**Song** "Little David, Play on Your Harp"

**Listening Selections**
*Little David, Play on Your Harp*
*Interview with Moses Hogan*
M*U*S*I*C M*A*K*E*R*S
Moses Hogan

**More Music Choices**
"Gonna Ride Up in the Chariot," p. 20
"I'm Gonna Sing," p. 33

ASSESSMENT
**Performance/Interview** Discuss ostinatos and their effect on the harmony and texture of a song

TECHNOLOGY/MEDIA LINK
**MIDI/Sequencing Software** Use a MIDI song file to layer ostinatos

---

**Connection: Culture**
**Activity:** Explore the music and dance of Brazil

MEETING INDIVIDUAL NEEDS **English Language Learners** Check for comprehension by retelling song texts

SPOTLIGHT ON **Partner Songs**

ACROSS THE CURRICULUM
**Social Studies** Read books about Brazil
**Language Arts** Discuss and research samba bands and instruments

MOVEMENT **Patterned Movement** Follow specific guidelines to perform movements to a song

CULTURAL CONNECTION **Sambas and Carnaval** Historical information about Carnaval and *samba* music

TEACHER TO TEACHER **Part Singing** Suggested sequence

CHARACTER EDUCATION **Friendship** Qualities of a good friendship

AUDIENCE ETIQUETTE **Rehearsal Etiquette for Performers**

BUILDING SKILLS THROUGH MUSIC **Physical Education** Perform movements to a song

**Song** "*Sambalele*" (Portuguese and English)

**Listening Selection** *Bate-papo*

**More Music Choices**
"Turn the World Around," p. 114
"Shake the Papaya Down," p. 378

ASSESSMENT
**Performance/Peer Critique** Two groups perform, and critique each other's performance of a song

TECHNOLOGY/MEDIA LINK
**MIDI/Sequencing Software** Use a MIDI file to sing a song in different ways
**Video Library** Watch a video featuring Brazilian music

| Lesson | Elements | Skills | |
|---|---|---|---|
| LESSON 7 **What's the Score?**<br>pp. 402-409<br> | **Element: Melody**<br>**Concept:** Pattern<br>**Focus:** *Do-mi-so* melodic sequence<br><br>**Secondary Element**<br>Timbre: vocal<br><br>**National Standards**<br>1a 1e 4b 4c 5c 6a 9b | **Skill: Reading**<br>**Objective:** Read *do-mi-so* in different keys<br><br>**Secondary Skills**<br>• **Listening** Identify *do-mi-so* patterns<br>• **Singing** Sing vocalises<br>• **Performing** Sing in semicircles to hear musical effects<br>• **Creating** Create melodies for poem text | **SKILLS REINFORCEMENT**<br>• **Listening** Discuss how accompaniment affects the meaning of a song<br>• **Reading** Read *do-mi-so-mi-do* patterns in songs<br>• **Vocal Development** Develop the modified *r* sound |
| LESSON 8 **Carols in Harmony**<br>pp. 410-413<br> | **Element: Texture/Harmony**<br>**Concept:** Texture and harmony<br>**Focus:** Ostinatos, two-part, and canonic singing<br><br>**Secondary Element**<br>Melody: minor tonality<br><br>**National Standards**<br> | **Skill: Singing**<br>**Objective:** Sing ostinatos, two-part harmony, and canon<br><br>**Secondary Skills**<br>• **Listening** Listen and identify minor tonality in several songs<br>• **Reading** Perform a song using rhythm and pitch syllables<br>• **Playing** Play ostinato accompaniments to a song<br>• **Creating** Create a mini drama for each song | **SKILLS REINFORCEMENT**<br>• **Vocal Development** Distinguish between the singing voice and the speaking voice |

| Connections | Music and Other Literature | |
|---|---|---|
| **Connection: Related Arts**<br>**Activity:** Explore imagery in song lyrics<br>SPOTLIGHT ON<br>**The Performers** The Indianapolis Children's Choir<br>**Word Painting** Information about word painting<br>ACROSS THE CURRICULUM<br>**Language Arts/Related Arts** Discuss imagery in fine arts; create collages of seasonal wonders and images<br>**Art/Language Arts** Practice using imagery in writing<br>TEACHER TO TEACHER<br>**Understand the Story Line** Discuss imagery in the lyrics of the song<br>**Teaching with MIDI** Use song file to practice at various keys and tempos<br>CHARACTER EDUCATION **Adaptation** Discuss the importance of experiencing change<br>MOVEMENT **Choreography** Perform movements to a song<br>BUILDING SKILLS THROUGH MUSIC **Language** Identify common themes in a poem | **Song** "Circle 'Round the Moon"<br><br>**Poem** "Extremes"<br><br>**More Music Choices**<br>"*Tsuki*," p. 25<br>"River," p. 58<br>"The Wheel of the Water," p. 362<br>"Cycle Song of Life," p. 370<br>"Sailboat in the Sky," p. 374 | ASSESSMENT<br>**Interview** Compare and contrast the musical elements of three songs<br><br>TECHNOLOGY/MEDIA LINK<br>**Notation Software** Notate and play melodies for a poem<br>**MIDI/Sequencing Software** Use a MIDI song file and add sound effects |
| **Connection: Culture**<br>**Activity:** Discover the origin of some popular Christmas customs<br>SPOTLIGHT ON<br>**Caroling** Facts about caroling<br>**Modes** History of modes in music<br>TEACHER TO TEACHER<br>**Reinforcing Tonality** Discuss activities to reinforce minor tonality<br>**Teaching with MIDI** Use a MIDI song file to practice at slower tempos<br>ACROSS THE CURRICULUM **Related Arts** Create holiday decorations<br>CULTURAL CONNECTION **Christmas Customs** Information about modern customs<br>MOVEMENT **Choreography** Suggested movements for the song<br>BUILDING SKILLS THROUGH MUSIC **Language** Analyze the meaning of lyrics in a song | **Song** "A Merry Modal Christmas"<br><br>**More Music Choices**<br>"Ah, Poor Bird," p. 196<br>"*Minka*," p. 222 | ASSESSMENT<br>**Performance/Observation** Accurately perform ostinatos, parts, and canonic singing in a song<br><br>TECHNOLOGY/MEDIA LINK<br>**Notation Software** Notate melodies in A minor |
| | | |

# Introducing the Unit

Unit 11 presents a thematic approach to understanding music elements. Singing is an integral part of our society. In this unit, students will learn the fundamentals of good singing. They will also develop good habits in breathing, reading, listening, and learning to sing in harmony. Presented on p. 379 is a brief overview of the skills that are assessed in this unit.

See below and pp. 380–381 for unit highlights of related curricular experiences. For a more detailed unit overview, see Unit at a Glance, pp. 377a–377f.

# Unit Project

Ask students to look through the songs in Unit 11 and determine what they have in common. (All have more than one part to sing.)

Have students plan a performance that will share their choral singing accomplishment with others. Encourage them to prepare 12 to 15 minutes of music. Songs can be selected as work in the unit proceeds. The performance can be done during the class period and other classes, as well as school staff members, parents, and grandparents can be invited.

**Time to Sing**

We'll begin our choral adventure by singing the calypso song "Shake the Papaya Down."

CD 16–18
MIDI 26

## Shake the Papaya Down

s, l, t,(d) r m f

Calypso Song
Arranged by Ruth E. Dwyer and Judith M. Waller
Edited by Henry H. Leck





## Across the Curriculum

**Unit Highlights** The following interdisciplinary activities in this unit are related to the music elements or themes presented in the lessons. See Unit at a Glance, pp. 377a–377f, for topical descriptions presented according to lesson sequence.

▶ **ART/RELATED ARTS**

- Learn about the use of imagery in the fine arts (p. 403)
- Illustrate the moon (p. 405)
- Create a classroom collage or bulletin board with photos and pictures showing the seasons of the year (p. 408)
- Create holiday decorations (p. 412)

▶ **LANGUAGE ARTS**

- Learn about the literary device *alliteration* (p. 382)
- Read a book about Cajun culture (p. 387)
- Read Scottish poems and stories (p. 392)
- Research information about the instruments of a *samba* band (p. 398)
- Read a poem about the moon (p. 405)

▶ **SOCIAL STUDIES**

- Read about the influence of music and dance in the lives of early American settlers (p. 384)
- Read and learn about Brazilian culture (p. 398)

UNIT 11

# Sing Out!

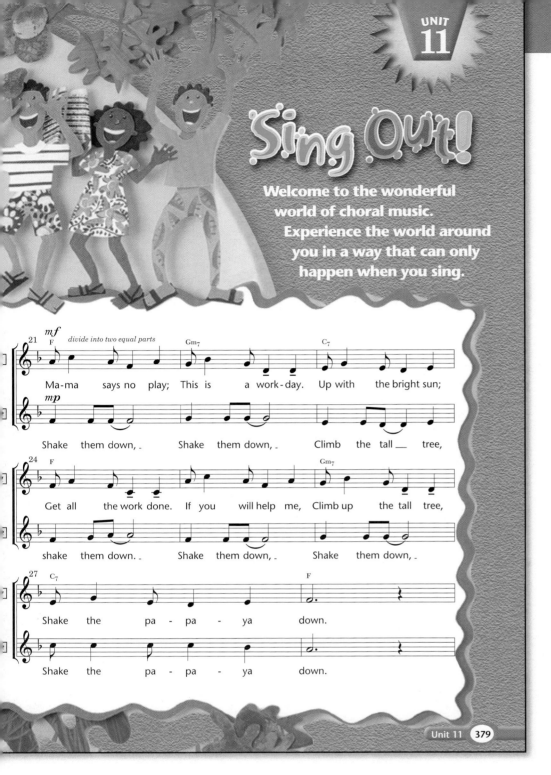

**Welcome to the wonderful world of choral music. Experience the world around you in a way that can only happen when you sing.**

mf — divide into two equal parts

F — Gm7 — C7

Ma-ma says no play; This is a work-day. Up with the bright sun;

mp

Shake them down, Shake them down, Climb the tall tree,

F — Gm7

Get all the work done. If you will help me, Climb up the tall tree,

shake them down. Shake them down, Shake them down,

C7 — F

Shake the pa - pa - ya down.

Shake the pa - pa - ya down.

Unit 11 379



# Music Skills
## Assessed in This Unit

### Reading Music: Rhythm
- Read and tap the rhythm of a song (p. 384)
- Read and clap rhythm patterns (p. 388)

### Reading Music: Pitch
- Read repeated pitch note patterns, sequences, and *do-mi-so* patterns in a choral piece (p. 405)

### Performing Music: Singing
- Perform a partner song in choral form (p. 383)
- Perform a choral piece with countermelodies (p. 385) and vocal ostinatos (p. 395)
- Sing a song with Gaelic lyrics (p. 393)
- Sing a choral song in Portuguese (p. 397)
- Perform a Christmas song with vocal ostinatos (p. 413)

### Moving to Music
- Conduct a choral piece in 3 (p. 393)
- Perform patterned movement with a *samba* song (p. 398)

### Performing Music: Playing
- Perform a recorder part to accompany a Gaelic song (p. 393)
- Perform instrumental music with a Brazilian song (p. 399)

### Creating Music
- Improvise syncopated rhythm patterns to accompany a song (p. 398)
- Create melodies to go with selected text (p. 404)

### Listening to Music
- Listen to and evaluate the performance of a choral piece with a countermelody (p. 385)
- Listen to and evaluate a performance of a song in Portuguese (p. 399)

## Cultural Connection

**Unit Highlights** The musical literature in this unit provides many opportunities for students to explore a variety of world cultures. See Unit at a Glance, pp. 377a–377f, for topical descriptions presented according to lesson sequence.

▶ **AFRICAN AMERICAN**
- Learn about the history and current performance practices of spirituals (p. 394)

▶ **AMERICAN**
- Learn about the Cajun culture of Louisiana (p. 387)

▶ **EUROPEAN**
- Learn facts about Gaelic culture (p. 391)

▶ **LATIN AMERICAN**
- Learn about the South American festival *Carnaval* and *samba* music (p. 397)

# Opening Activities

**MATERIALS**
- "Shake the Papaya Down" **CD 16-18**

  **Recording Routine:**
  Intro ( 4 m.); vocal
- classroom instruments

## Reading

Write the rhythm of the first measure of "Shake the Papaya Down" on the board. Have students

- Clap and say the rhythm.
- Identify the rhythm in the first three lines of music on p. 380.
- Clap and say these lines.

Ask students to look for the same rhythm repeated in the remainder of the song.

## Analyzing

Invite students to sing the first three lines of "Shake the Papaya Down" **CD 16-18.** Then have them look for the same melody in the rest of the song. Play the recording and ask students to sing the first melody whenever they hear it and listen to the rest of the song.

## Singing

Ask students to identify the three separate melodies of "Shake the Papaya Down." (mm. 5, 17, and 29) Have students learn all of the melodies. Then divide the class into three groups. Have each group sing its melody whenever it occurs in the song.

## Assessment

**Unit Highlights** The lessons in this unit were chosen and developed to support the choral theme "Sing Out!" Each lesson, as always, presents a clear element focus, a skill objective, and an end-of-lesson assessment. The overall sequence of lessons, however, is organized according to this theme, rather than concept development. In this context, formal assessment strategies, such as those presented in Units 1–6, are no longer applicable.

**▶ INFORMAL ASSESSMENTS**

At the close of each Teacher's Edition lesson in this unit, one of the following types of assessments is used to evaluate the learning of the key element focus or skill objective.

- Performance/Peer Critique (pp. 385, 399)
- Performance/Observation (pp. 383, 393, 395)
- Music Journal Writing (p. 389)
- Interview (pp. 395, 405)

**▶ RUBRICS**

Visit *www.sfsuccessnet.com* for rubrics to assess students' achievement in music skills.

UNIT 11 INTRODUCTION

### Innovative Teacher Support for This Unit

- **Making Music DVD, Grade 4** contains video segments that support lessons, including signing and movement.
- **Making Music with Movement and Dance** provides more opportunities for large group activities in music or physical education classes.
- **Making Music with Technology** provides lesson plans for many technology applications; includes MIDI files.
- ***¡A cantar!*** features recorded songs and lessons from around the Spanish-speaking world; includes strategies for bilingual classes and for English-speaking teachers working with Spanish-speaking students.
- **Bridges to Asia** features recorded songs and lessons from Asian and Pacific region cultures.
- ***www.sfsuccessnet.com*** provides an online lesson planner to conveniently create lesson plans at school or at home. Includes rubrics for assessment, lesson modifications to meet the needs of all students, performance musicals based on program content, and more.

## Technology/Media Link

**Unit Highlights** The following components are used in this unit to reinforce and expand students' understanding of music elements and related themes. See Unit at a Glance, pp. 377a–377f, for a descriptive listing according to lesson sequence.

**▶ MIDI/SEQUENCING SOFTWARE**

- Sing "Seagull, Seagull, Sit on the Shore" with the MIDI song file (p. 383)
- Create an accompaniment using various timbres to accompany "Cindy" (p. 385)
- Sing "Lullaby and Dance" with the MIDI song file (p. 389)
- Experiment with layering ostinatos using the MIDI song file for "Little David, Play on Your Harp" (p. 395)
- Transpose "*Sambalele*" using the MIDI song file (p. 399)
- Create sound effects using the MIDI file for "Circle 'Round the Moon" (p. 409)

**▶ NOTATION SOFTWARE**

- Notate and play back melodies composed for a poem (p. 405)
- Notate question-answer melodic phrases (p. 413)

**▶ VIDEO LIBRARY/DVD**

- Watch videos about percussion instruments and *samba* ensembles of *Carnaval* (p. 401)

**▶ WEB SITE**

- Go to *www.sfsuccessnet.com* to find more information about Gaelic music and music from Scotland and Ireland (p. 393)

LESSON 1

## LESSON AT A GLANCE

**Element Focus** MELODY Melodic sequence

**Skill Objective** SINGING Sing a song with melodic sequence

**Connection Activity** LANGUAGE ARTS Learn about alliteration

**MATERIALS**

- "Seagull, Seagull, Sit on the Shore" **CD 16-20**
  **Recording Routine:** Intro (8 m.); vocal; coda

**VOCABULARY**

melodic sequence alliteration

**National Standards**

**1b** Sing expressively with appropriate phrasing
**1e** Sing in groups, following a conductor
**5b** Read notes in treble clef using syllables
**6b** Identify ways music relates to language arts
**7a** Create standards for evaluating performances

**MORE MUSIC CHOICES...**

For more practice with melodic sequence:

*"Tancovacka,"* p. 230
*"Thula, thula, ngoana"* p. 227

## 1 INTRODUCE

6b Ask students to read the information in their books on p. 382 about the literary device *alliteration*. Then invite students to cite examples of alliteration they may know from rhymes or poetry and popular songs. Have them write their alliterations on the board.

For more information on alliteration, see Across the Curriculum below.

LESSON 1 Element: MELODY | Skill: SINGING | Connection: LANGUAGE ARTS

# A Sequence of Seagulls

"Seagull, Seagull, Sit on the Shore" is really two songs in one. **Listen** to the recording. You may already know one or both of the partner melodies.

Speak the lyrics of the first two lines of the song. Which beginning letter sound is repeated the most? This device, used by poets and other writers, is called *alliteration* [uh-lih-ter-AY-shun]. (Verse 3 of "Paw-Paw Patch," on page 93, is a good example of alliteration that uses the P sound.)

### Singing Tips

Follow these guidelines when you **sing** "Seagull, Seagull, Sit on the Shore":

- Place a little extra "weight" on beats 1 and 3 to underscore the S consonant and the rhythmic feel of the song.
- Be sure to sing *sit on*, not *si ton*; and *Santy Anna*, not *Santee-yana*.

### Reading Music Tips

In music, a sequence occurs when a melody pattern is repeated, beginning each time on a pitch one step higher or lower. Look at measures 2–4 and measures 14–16 and **identify** whether each sequence moves up or down.

### Knowing the Score

**Listen** to the recording as you follow the score. Then **describe** what happens

- In Voice 2 at measure 13.
- In Voice 1 and Voice 2 in measures 24–32.

The last line of the score (measures 33–36) is a type of *coda*—a short, final ending. **Describe** what happens to the rhythm of the melody in each voice part.

382

## Footnotes

### ACROSS THE CURRICULUM

6b ▶ **Language Arts** *Alliteration* is a literary device in which consonant sounds are repeated. For example, "sweet smell of success," "a dime a dozen," "tinker, tailor, soldier, sailor," and so on. Alliteration is found in many children's rhymes and poetry. It is also featured in the words of popular songs as well as in advertising.

### BUILDING SKILLS THROUGH MUSIC

▶ **Language** Ask students to think of an alliteration that can be substituted for the phrase *Seagull, seagull, sit on the shore* in the song. Stipulate that the new alliterative phrase must be similar to the original.

### MOVEMENT

▶ **Creative Movement** Divide the class into two groups and have them form two concentric circles. Ask group 1 to move left to right and group 2 right to left, using their hands and arms to reflect the shape of the two melodies in "Seagull, Seagull, Sit on the Shore." This will help students observe the distinct characteristics of the contour of each melody.

CD 16-20
MIDI 27
Seagull, Seagull, Sit on the Shore
Arranged by Susan Brumfield
s d r m f s l
Traditional
Sea-gull, sea-gull, sit on the shore, sit on the shore, sit on the shore.
Cap-tain, cap-tain, hoist up the sails, hoist up the sails, hoist up the sails.
Sea-gull, sea-gull, sit on the shore, and sail on, my San-ty An-na.
Cap-tain, cap-tain, hoist up the sails, and sail on, my San-ty An-na.
For my love is far a - way, far a - way, far a - way,
For my love is far a - way, 'cross the o - cean.
Blue hor - i - zon, head-ing for home, head-ing for home, head-ing for home.
'Cross the waves and back a - gain, back a - gain, back a - gain.
Blue hor - i - zon, head-ing for home, oh sail on, my San-ty An - na.
'Cross the waves and back a - gain, San - ty An-na.
Sail on, my San - ty An - na.
San - ty An - na.
Sing Out!
Unit 11 383

# 2 Develop

### Reading

Have students look at the notation for "Seagull, Seagull, Sit on the Shore." Ask them to focus on the melodic sequence in mm. 2–4 and mm. 13–16 and identify whether each sequence moves up or down.

5b Ask students to sing the first and second partner melodies using pitch syllables. Then have students sing the two melodies with text.

### Singing

1b 1e Divide the class into two groups and assign each group one of the partner melodies. Invite students to sing "Seagull, Seagull, Sit on the Shore" **CD 16-20** with the recording.

Monitor students' pronunciation of the words *sit on* and *Santy Anna.*

# 3 Close

**Element: MELODY** — **ASSESSMENT**

7a **Performance/Observation** If school policy permits, videotape a class performance of "Seagull, Seagull, Sit on the Shore." Invite students to view the tape and, applying basic criteria, assess their performance for

- Choral balance.
- Clarity of diction.
- Accuracy of pitches in singing the melodic sequences.

## Skills Reinforcement

▶ **Singing** Use the following suggestions to help students perform "Seagull, Seagull, Sit on the Shore."

**Reinforcement** Some students may have difficulty singing the partner melodies. Have these students form small groups to independently practice each of the partner melodies in isolation.

**On Target** Many students will be able to successfully sing one of the two partner melodies. For additional practice, invite all those wearing blue to sing one melody and those not wearing blue to sing the other. These groupings force students to sometimes sing one of the partner melodies while their neighbors sing the other.

**Challenge** Invite interested students to accompany a class performance of the song by playing one of the partner melodies on recorder or on a mallet instrument.

## Technology/Media Link

**MIDI/Sequencing Software** Record the two parts of "Seagull, Seagull, Sit on the Shore" onto separate tracks using MIDI sequencing software. Remind students how to turn the individual tracks on and off for MIDI playback. Divide the class into small groups and have them

- Listen to the entire MIDI track while following the song notation.
- Listen to their assigned part alone.
- Sing their parts with the appropriate MIDI track.

LESSON 2

## LESSON AT A GLANCE

**Element Focus** **TEXTURE/HARMONY** Countermelody

**Skill Objective** **SINGING** Sing a song with two countermelodies

**Connection Activity** **SOCIAL STUDIES** Discover that dance tunes were an important form of entertainment

**MATERIALS**

- "Cindy" **CD 16-22**

  **Recording Routine:** Intro (8 m.); v. 1; interlude (4 m.); v. 2; refrain; interlude (4 m.); v. 3; refrain; coda
- *Bonaparte's Retreat* **CD 16-25**
- **Dance Directions** for "Cindy" p. 519
- **Resource Book** p. F-30

**VOCABULARY**

countermelody

◆◆◆◆ **National Standards** ◆◆◆◆

**1a** Sing independently on pitch and in rhythm
**5a** Read rhythms in duple meter
**6b** Identify ways music relates to social studies
**6c** Use appropriate terms to explain music
**7a** Create standards for evaluating performances

**MORE MUSIC CHOICES**

For more practice singing countermelodies:
"Amazing Grace," p. 160
"America, the Beautiful," p. 158

LESSON 2 | Element: TEXTURE/HARMONY | Skill: SINGING | Connection: SOCIAL STUDIE

# A Fiddlin' Folk Song

As Americans migrated westward from the original thirteen colonies, they took their music with them. Dancing was a favorite pastime, usually accompanied by fiddles or banjos. **Listen** for these and other instruments as they accompany the fiddle tune "Cindy."

▲ Fiddle and banjo players at Jackson's Ferry, Virginia

### Singing Tips

For a crisp and energetic sound, clearly enunciate the beginning and final consonants of each word. **Sing** words such as *wish, hangin', sweet,* and *fine* with added emphasis and expression.

### Reading Music Tips

Each phrase in section Ⓐ begins with an eighth-note pick-up. Say "1 and 2 **and 1**" to emphasize the pick-up and the downbeat that follows. Next, say the words of each phrase in rhythm. Then **sing** the entire section.

### Knowing the Score

"Cindy" has two sections—a verse and a refrain. Learn one of the countermelodies in the refrain and then **perform** it with the other voice parts. **Describe** how this affects the texture of the song.

CD 16-22
MIDI 28

## Cindy

m, s, l, ⓓ r m f s l

*Folk Song from the Southern United State*

Ⓐ VERSE
F
C7
do
1. I wish I was an ap - ple, A - hang - in' on a tree;
2. She took me to her par - lor, She cooled me with her fan,
3. Now Cin - dy is a pretty girl, Cin - dy is a peach;
5 F Bb F Bb F
And ev - 'ry time my Cin - dy passed She'd take a bite of me.
She swore I was the pur - tiest thing in the shape of mor - tal man.
She threw her arms a - round my neck and hung on like a leech.

384

# 1 INTRODUCE

6b Point out to students that as Americans moved westward, dancing was a highly valued pastime. Share the information in Across the Curriculum below. Then invite students to suggest reasons why dance and its music were important forms of entertainment.

## Footnotes

### SKILLS REINFORCEMENT

▶ **Mallets** An Orff arrangement of "Cindy" can be found on p. F-30 of the Resource Book.

### BUILDING SKILLS THROUGH MUSIC

▶ **Physical Education** Invite students to perform a folk dance with "Cindy" **CD 16-22.** See Dance Directions p. 519.

### ACROSS THE CURRICULUM

6b ▶ **Social Studies** Early American settlers enjoyed dancing as a means of entertainment. They attended community events such as country frolics, husking bees, hoedowns, barn raisings, weddings, and square dances where tunes like "Cindy" were played and danced to.

The fiddle (violin) came to America with English, Scottish, and Irish settlers. The fiddle was ideally suited for playing dances because it could be heard above almost any other sound, including voices. In addition, fiddlers could call the dance movements as they played. The banjo came from African prototypes and gradually evolved into the five-string version we know today.

9 F C7

You ought to see my Cin - dy, She lives a - way down South;
I wish I had a nee - dle, As fine as I could sew,
Well, Cin - dy had one blue eye, She al - so had one brown;

13 F B♭ F B♭ F

She is so sweet the hon - ey bees All swarm a - round her mouth.
I'd sew that gal to my coat - tail, And down the road I'd go.
One eye looked in the coun - try, 𝄎 The other one looked in town.

**B** REFRAIN

*Countermelody 1*

17 B♭ F

1 Get a-long home, Get a-long home,

*Countermelody 2*

2 Get a-long home, dear Cin - dy, Home, sweet Cin - dy,

*Melody*

3 Get a-long home, Cin - dy, Cin - dy, Get a-long home, Cin - dy, Cin - dy,

21 B♭ F C7 F

1 Get a-long home. I'll mar - ry you some day!

2 Get a-long home, my dear lit - tle girl, I'll mar - ry you some day!

3 Get a-long home, Cin - dy, Cin - dy, I'll mar - ry you some day!

**Listen** to another American country fiddle tune.

CD 16-25

**Bonaparte's Retreat**

**Traditional Dance Tune**
**arranged and performed by Mark O'Connor**

Mark O'Connor is a U.S. National Fiddle Champion.

◀ Mark O'Connor

Sing Out!



# 2 Develop

## Reading

5a Have students look at the notation for "Cindy." Ask them to tap the rhythm of the verse, followed by the rhythm of the refrain and the two countermelodies.

## Singing

1a Have students

- Sing the melody of "Cindy" **CD 16-22.** with the recording.
- Learn Countermelody 1; then combine it with the refrain.
- Do the same with Countermelody 2, and note how the texture becomes thicker as each counter-melody is added.

## Listening

6c Play the recording of *Bonaparte's Retreat* **CD 16-25.**

ASK **What instrument do you hear on this recording?** (violin, or "fiddle")

# 3 Close

7a **Performance/Peer Critique** Ask half of the class to sing "Cindy" **CD 16-22** while the other half listens and evaluates the performance for

- Balance of parts.
- Clarity of diction.
- Correct rhythms and pitches.

## Spotlight On

▶ **The Performer** Mark O'Connor (b. 1962) is an internationally recognized composer and performer. He began his violin studies with Texas fiddler Benny Thomason and jazz violinist Stephane Grappelli. Since then, he has branched out by composing music for films and various symphony orchestras, including the Academy of St. Martin in the Fields. O'Connor has performed at the White House and the ceremonies of the Atlanta Centennial Olympic Games. In addition to guest teaching at music schools across the country, he hosts the Mark O'Connor Fiddle Camp and String Conference every year.

## Technology/Media Link

**MIDI/Sequencing Software** Have students compose a bass part for a dance tune. They can

- Choose a banjo or fiddle timbre and record the melody of "Cindy" in step-time on one track.
- Choose a string bass timbre and record a bass part using quarter-note roots and fifths, according to the chord symbols.
- Select a guitar or accordion patch for a harmony track and record the chords in any rhythm pattern they choose.
- Play back the sequence to accompany class singing.

LESSON 3

## LESSON AT A GLANCE

**Element Focus** **TEXTURE/HARMONY** Monophonic, homophonic, and polyphonic singing

**Skill Objective** **SINGING** Sing and describe how harmony is achieved in the song

**Connection Activity** **CULTURE** Discuss some aspects of Cajun culture

**MATERIALS**

- "Lullaby and Dance" **CD 16-26**
  **Recording Routine:** Intro (2 m.); vocal; coda
- *Jolie Blonde* **CD 16-28**

**VOCABULARY**

texture harmony

**National Standards**

**1a** Sing independently with appropriate diction
**1b** Sing expressively with appropriate phrasing
**1c** Sing from memory songs from diverse cultures
**1d** Sing part songs
**5a** Read rhythms in duple meter
**6b** Describe music by answering questions about it

**MORE MUSIC CHOICES**

For more practice in texture and harmony:
"Ah, Poor Bird," p. 196
*"Hey, m'tswala,"* p. 79
"Chairs to Mend," p. 149
"Cycle Song of Life," p. 370

# Get It Together

"Lullaby and Dance" is a song with two very different sections. "Lullaby" is Cajun. The Cajun are descendants of early French settlers in Nova Scotia and New Brunswick in Canada and later in Louisiana and Texas. "Dance" is based on a traditional American play-party song.

**Arts Connection**

◀ *Fiddling Sailor* by Christian Pierre, a contemporary Cajun American artist

### Singing Tips

**Sing** the vowel *e* in words such as *sweep, dreams,* and *seems* with slightly rounded lips to avoid a wide vowel quality. When singing the word *away,* prolong the *a* vowel sound in *way* for four beats.

### Reading Music Tips

**Identify** and **sing** the *do, mi,* and *so* pattern in measures 4–5. Find and sing all the other *do, mi,* and *so* patterns in "Lullaby and Dance."

### Knowing the Score

Which voice part has the melody in measures 11–14 and in measures 22–25? Where do Voice 1 and Voice 2 sing the same rhythms and pitches together? To discover when the texture and harmony of this composition change, find the measures where Voice 1 has different rhythms and pitches from those found in Voice 2.

The proper *e* vowel mouth position ▶

386

## Footnotes

▶ **Lullaby** The word *lull* means "the action of soothing or calming." A lullaby is used to put children to sleep (a cradle song) and, therefore, should be soothing and calming. Pitches in a lullaby may have very little variety. A lullaby can also mean farewell or goodbye, which explains the *by* in *lullaby*. In "Coventry Carol" ("A Merry Modal Christmas," p. 411), the lulling words are *by, by, lully, lullay*.

### BUILDING SKILLS THROUGH MUSIC

▶ **Language** Ask students to look at the lyrics for "Lullaby and Dance," on p. 388. Have them identify words that contain an apostrophe. *(won't, high'r, kickin', 'round)* Then ask them how these words would be written in standard usage. *(will not, higher, kicking, around)*

5a ▶ **Reading** Syncopation is the rhythmic interplay caused by having accented sounds begin between beats and frequently sustain through them. In "Alabama Gal," the words *come out tonight* are examples of syncopation. Have students clap and say the rhythm of measures 30–37 and then find other examples of syncopation in the music. For more practice, have students examine "Little David, Play on Your Harp," p. 394; *"Sambalele,"* p. 397; and "A Merry Modal Christmas," p. 411, to see how the syncopated patterns appear.

CD 16–26
MIDI 29
Lullaby and Dance
Traditional
Arranged by Ruth E. Dwyer
mp
unison
Sweep, sweep, sweep a - way. Sweep the road of dreams. Peo-ple say that in the
night, The tur-tle will talk it seems. The tur-tle will talk it seems.
Sweep, sweep a - way. Sweep the road of
Sweep, sweep, sweep a - way. Sweep the road of
dreams. Peo-ple say that in the night, The tur-tle will talk it
dreams. Peo-ple say that in the night, The tur-tle will
seems. The tur - tle will talk it seems.
talk it seems. Will talk it seems.
Sing Out!
Unit 11 387

# 1 Introduce

Share with students the information about Cajun culture in Cultural Connection below and lullabies in Spotlight On, p. 386. Then invite students to identify the dynamic level at which a performer should sing a lullaby and a dance song. (Consider the words, mood, tempo, and purpose.)

# 2 Develop

## Listening

Invite students to listen to "Lullaby and Dance" **CD 16-26** to hear unison singing, two-part singing, and rhythmic imitation.

Select students to expressively read the words of part 1 and part 2 of the song.

6b ASK **How do the performers create a sense of rocking in the "Lullaby" (first section of the song)?** (Part 1 begins on beat 2 while part 2 begins on beat 1 on the word *sweep.*)

**How do the rhythm patterns in "Dance" (the second section of the song) affect the music or mood?** (The faster rhythm patterns produce a lighter dance-like quality.)

Have students explain how the interlude between the two songs leads to the second song. (The interlude contains words and rhythm patterns found in "Dance.")

ASK **How do the details in the pieces of art on pp. 386 and 388 help suggest each song?** (The soft colors and night setting used on p. 386 recall the subject and matter of "Lullaby"; on p. 388, the motion of the galloping horse and of the repeated details in the border art evoke the more spirited feeling of "Dance.")

**continued on page 388**

## Cultural Connection

▶ **Cajun Culture** Acadians migrated from Nova Scotia to Louisiana in 1754. *Cajun* is an Americanization of the word *Acadian*. Cajun farmers settled on the prairie, and the trappers and fishers built their houses in the *bayous* [BI-yoos] (A Native American word for *creeks* or *small rivers*). Cajun music is about the lives, strengths, sorrows, and joys of the people. The voice and the fiddle were the instruments of choice in early Cajun country. When two fiddlers played together, one played the tune and the other played the harmony. A typical Cajun band includes a fiddle, an accordion, a guitar, and a triangle for rhythm. Sometimes mandolins, banjos, and even a washboard are included.

## Across the Curriculum

▶ **Language Arts** For interested students, share the book *Cajun Through and Through* by Tynia Thomassie (Little, Brown & Co., 2000), about a city boy who visits his cousins in "Cajun country" and begins to understand the Cajun ways of life.

### Reading

Have students clap the rhythms in measures 1 and 2 of the "Lullaby" section. Then have them find and clap those same rhythms wherever the rhythms appear in the song. (m. 11, parts 1 and 2)

5a Invite students to find how many times the syncopated rhythmic pattern in measure 31 is repeated in the "Dance," not including the interlude. (eight times—measures 31, 32, 33, 35, 47, 48, 49, and 51) Have students sing the harmonized rhythms of both songs and discuss how they differ in sound and rhythmic character.

### Analyzing

6b Ask students how changes in texture are achieved in "Lullaby and Dance." (Through the use of monophonic [unison singing], homophonic [two parts singing the same rhythms], and polyphonic singing [two parts singing different rhythms].)

### Moving

1b Invite students to expressively sing "Lullaby and Dance" **CD 16-26** with the recording. Have them invent rocking movements for the "Lullaby" section and dance movements for the "Dance" section. To help students get the special feeling of the song "Alabama Gal," which is a play party, see Spotlight On below.

Students may also be interested in creating movements for the various sections of the "Dance." For more choral movement activities, refer to Movement on p. 389.

### Creating

1d For additional practice with texture and harmony, have the class sing two- and three-part rounds. Have students form three concentric circles that move in opposite directions. (This can be shown by drawing three concentric circles of stick figures with each circle going in a different direction.)

22 F C+ F
Come out to-night, Come out to-night, Come out to - night.
Come out to-night, Come out to-night, Come out to - night.
26 4 unison F
Al - a - bam - a Gal, won't you come out to - night,
32 C F F
Come out to-night, Come out to-night. Al - a - bam - a Gal, won't you
35 C F
come out to-night and dance by the light of the moon. The
38 B♭ F C7 F
moon shines bright the wind blows cool, I set my wag-on and un-hitched my mule.
42 B♭ F G7 C7
Fid - dles tune a might bit high'r, Set your heels kick-in' 'round the fire.
Arts Connection
Horse and Rider weather vane (1870). This is a classic example of 19th-century American folk ar
388

## Footnotes

### Skills Reinforcement

1a ▶ **Singing** Singing words set to syncopated rhythms can be challenging. Making syncopation clear is related to good diction and how the consonants are accented. In the words *come out tonight*, the letter *c* in *come* must have a hard "kuh" sound and the *t* in *tonight* requires that the tip of the tongue make hard contact with the upper teeth. Have students study other songs that have syncopated rhythms, and then practice enunciating consonants in the words.

### Spotlight On

▶ **Play Parties** Play parties are songs, such as "Alabama Gal," that can be sung and danced to at the same time. The type of dance can be circle, line, or square. Dancers usually dance in pairs and in groups. Each dance has specific steps for each part of the song. Even though "Alabama Gal" has four beats per measure, when it is danced and sung, it should feel and move as if it were two beats to the measure.

46 F C
Al - a - bam - a Gal, won't you come out to - night, Come out to - night,
Al - a - bam - a Gal, Come out to - night, Come out to - night,
49 F
Come out to - night. Al - a - bam - a Gal, won't you
Come out to - night. Al - a - bam - a Gal,
51 F C F div.
come out to - night and dance by the light of the moon. And
Come out to - night and dance by the light of the moon.
dance by the light
54 F/ C C7 F
dance by the light of the moon.
dance by the light of the moon.

Sing Out!

## Listen to an American Folk Tune

Here is another example of a folk tune from the southern United States.

**Listen** to *Jolie Blonde.*

CD 16-28
Jolie Blonde

**Cajun Folk Melody**
**as performed by the Hackberry Ramblers**
This song is a favorite at Cajun dances.

Unit 11 389

### Listening

Invite students to listen to *Jolie Blonde* **CD 16-28,** as performed by the Hackberry Ramblers. Have them identify the style of music as well as the instrumentation.

# 3 Close

**Element: TEXTURE/HARMONY** ASSESSMENT

1c **Music Journal Writing** Have the class form two concentric circles. Have circle 1 sing the unison parts in "Lullaby and Dance" **CD 16-26** and have circle 2 join in on the harmonized parts.

Have students describe in their music journals how texture and harmony are achieved in "Lullaby and Dance." Have them explain the difference between monophonic, homophonic, and polyphonic singing. Review students' responses to assess their understanding of different textures.

## Movement

▶ **Choreography** Encourage students to move in these ways as they sing "Lullaby and Dance." Sway by lines in opposite directions, one measure in each direction for the lullaby. For the introduction to the dance, continue swaying lines in opposite directions, and have students gesture and look to the side with one hand as if to say "Come over here" on the words *come out tonight.* Reverse sides the second time it is sung. Then face front and use both hands during the third time. While they sing the verse of the dance, have students put their hands on their hips and continue to sway in a bouncy style. On the word *moon,* have students stop swaying and raise both hands. For the ending, have students in each line lean to one side with hands on their hips.

## Technology/Media Link

**MIDI/Sequencing Software** Using the MIDI song file for "Lullaby and Dance," have small groups of students

- Review how to turn off and on the individual tracks for playback.
- Listen to all of the MIDI tracks together as they use the book to follow their part.
- Listen to only their assigned part.
- Sing their part with the MIDI track.
- Sing their part with all of the MIDI tracks together.

The MIDI song file can be used also to transpose the song to a new key or change the tempo.

# LESSON 4

## LESSON AT A GLANCE

**Element Focus** RHYTHM Upbeats
**Skill Objective** SINGING Sing and read upbeats
**Connection Activity** CULTURE Explore aspects of Gaelic culture

**MATERIALS**
- *"Einini"* CD 17-1
  **Recording Routine:** Intro (4 m.); vocal; coda
- **Pronunciation Practice/Translation** p. 492
- **Resource Book** p. A-40
- recorders

**VOCABULARY**
upbeat *(anacrucis)* *legato*

**National Standards**
**1c** Sing from memory songs from diverse cultures
**1d** Sing part songs
**2f** Play instruments independently against contrasting parts
**5a** Read rhythms in $\frac{3}{4}$ meter
**5b** Read notes in treble clef, using syllables
**6a** Listen to identify form
**7a** Create standards for evaluating performances

**MORE MUSIC CHOICES**
For more songs with upbeats:
"Frog Music," p. 200
"Joe Turner Blues," p. 56

# Singing Phrases

*"Einini"* is a Gaelic lullaby. Feel the rocking movement as you **sing** the song. Give the first note of each measure a little extra weight to create a swinging motion.

## Singing Tips

This song uses many *e* and *a* vowels. They are similar and should be sung in almost the same way. Place the tip of your tongue against your lower teeth inside your mouth.

## Reading Music Tips

Find *do* in the song and **identify** the key. Notice *mi, re,* and *do* are highlighted in the music. What is the first pitch syllable of the song? The composer suggests the song be sung *andante,* which means "walking tempo." The dynamic marking indicated is *mf*. Why were these expressions chosen?

## Knowing the Score

On what beat of the measure does each phrase start? You already know the name for this. It is called an upbeat. How many upbeats are there in this song? Each upbeat in the song is the same note. Name the pitch.

View of Skellig and Puffin Island off the coast of Ireland

390

# Footnotes

## TEACHER TO TEACHER

▶ **Teaching with MIDI** Students may find singing in two-part harmony to be challenging. When they use the MIDI song file for *"Einini,"* have students turn off the part they are not learning to sing and practice with the one they are learning. Once they have adequately learned their part, have them add in the part they are not singing.

## BUILDING SKILLS THROUGH MUSIC

▶ **Math** Have students look at the notation for *"Einini"* on p. 391. Ask them to count the number of noteheads on the first two lines. (24) Then have them count the number of syllables sung. (22) Ask students why there are fewer syllables than notes. (because of the use of slurs)

## SPOTLIGHT ON

▶ **Gaelic Language** *Gaelic* comes from the word *Gael,* an English word for any of three languages which form one half of the Celtic language family group: Irish Gaelic, Manx Gaelic, and Scottish Gaelic. These languages are spoken in Ireland, the Isle of Man, and Scotland. The Gaels are the people who speak this language. Today, 80,000 individuals speak Gaelic in the north of Scotland and the Western Isles. *"Einini"* is an example of a Gaelic folk song.

CD 17-1
MIDI 30
Einini
t, d r m f s l d'
Gaelic Folk Song
Arranged by Cyndee Giebler
Andante
unison
mf
Ein - in - i, ein - in - i, cod - al -
ai - gi, cod - al - ai - gi, ein - in - i, ein - in - i, cod - al -
ai - gi, cod - al - ai - gi. Cod - al - ai - gi, cod - al - ai - gi, cois an
chlai amuigh, cois an chlai amuigh, cod - al - ai - gi, cod - al -
ai - gi, cois an chlai amuigh, cois an chlai amuigh.
Sing Out!
Unit 11 391

# 1 Introduce

7a Share with students the information in Spotlight On, p. 390, and Cultural Connection below. Then ask students to explain the purpose of a lullaby. Have them determine how fast a lullaby would be sung (*andante,* a walking tempo) and explain why.

# 2 Develop

### Listening

Play the recording of *"Einini"* **CD 17-1.** Have students use p. 390 to help them

- Identify the ♩ and ♫ upbeats.

- Identify phrase endings when a breath can be taken.
- Identify the measures when the melody is harmonized.
- Identify how often the word *einini* in the first phrase (mm. 1–12) repeats itself. (four times)
- Identify how often the words *codal aigi* in the second phrase (mm. 12–20) repeat themselves. (six times)

### Singing

As a warm-up exercise, write phrase I and phrase 2 on the board staff without the text. Invite students to perform both phrases using hand signs and pitch syllables. Have students

- Sing the same phrases on the neutral syllable *lee* and then *lay.* Sing the A section of the song on *lee* and the B section of the song on *lay.*
- Listen to the Pronunciation Practice for *"Einini"* **CD 17-3** and then sing the Gaelic text. (For the Pronunciation Practice Guide, refer to Resource Book p. A-40.)
- Sing *legato* and stress the upbeats to create a rocking motion.

**continued on page 392**

## Movement

**Choreography** Students can add these movements to their performance of *"Einini."* For the unison verse, sway, with the body facing front, for two measures to the right and two measures to the left. Repeat this pattern four times, for a total of 16 measures. For the verse sung in harmony, turn the body to the left and keep the head to the audience. Create smooth right arm movements from side to side, one measure in each direction. Reverse the body position to face right and repeat the arm movements with the left arm. Again, repeat this pattern four times. Turn to the front again for the *coda,* and do symmetrical up-and-down arm movements, two measures in each direction, for a total of four measures.

## Cultural Connection

**Gaelic Culture** For a better appreciation of Gaelic culture, you may wish to share the following cultural facts with students.

- Gaelic is one of the languages of the Scottish highlands and is one of the few surviving Celtic languages.
- Family groupings such as the MacGregors are called *clans.*
- Bagpipe music, highland dancing, and traditional songs have enriched the music of the world.
- Scottish history has been the source for great poetry, novels, and movies such as *Braveheart,* which portrayed the life of William Wallace.

### Reading

Direct students to clap the rhythms in measures 4–11 plus beats 1 and 2 of measure 12. Invite students to sing the pitch syllables in the same measures. Repeat these procedures for measures 13–20. Beginning on beat 3 of measure 12, have students

- Identify the beat note as the quarter note.

- Identify that each phrase begins on an upbeat. *(anacrusis)*
- Identify that the *anacrusis* is *so* for the beginning of every phrase.
- Identify the A and B sections and the close of the song. (Discuss the use of the *fermata* signs and tempo change in the last line of the song.)

### Performing

Divide the class into two groups. Have half the class sing the A section (mm. 4–12) and the other half sing the B section (mm. 12–20) of *"Einini"* **CD 17-1.**

Another option is to have group 1 sing part 1 and group 2 sing part 2 (mm. 24–40) and then reverse voice parts.

Then encourage students to sing the song as written, and sway from left to right.

### Creating

Review with students what the Gaelic words to *"Einini"* mean.

Little birdies sleep.

Sleep beside the fence over there.

Ask students to create a list of words that would be appropriate for a lullaby. *(sleep baby, sleep little one, close your eyes, go to sleep)* Write the words on the board, putting all one-, two-, and three-syllable words in separate columns. Have students create an English text for *"Einini,"* drawing from the words on the board, to fit the rhythm of the song.

24 D A7 D/F♯ Em7 A
Ein - in - i, ein - in - i, cod-al - ai - gi, cod-al - ai - gi, ein -
Ein - in - i, ein - in - i, cod-al - ai - gi, cod-al - ai - gi, ein -
29 D A7 D Em7 A7 D
in - i, ein - in - i, cod - al - ai - gi, cod - al - ai - gi. Cod - al -
in - i, ein - in - i, cod - al - ai - gi, cod - al - ai - gi. Cod - al -
33 G D Em7 A D/F♯
ai - gi, cod - al - ai - gi, cois an chlai amuigh, cois an chlai amuigh, cod - al -
ai - gi, cod - al - ai - gi, cois an chlai amuigh, cois an chlai amuigh, cod - al -
392

# Footnotes

## ACROSS THE CURRICULUM

▶ **Language Arts** Share the book *The Wee Scot Book: Scottish Poems and Stories* by Linda Greenburg (Pelican, 1994). Divide the class into groups and invite each group to create a performance for one of the poems or stories in the book. Students can also create illustrations for the poems and stories that they perform.

Invite students to create their own poems based on the formats presented in the book.

## TEACHER TO TEACHER

▶ **Choral Teaching Tips** Some of the choral concepts to consider in this song include breathing, phrase shape, vowel placement, and production. Have students

- Count to three slowly four times in one breath to match the phrase lengths of the song and then speak the phrase text the same way.
- Shape the text of the phrase by emphasizing *EINini.*
- Sing *i* and *e* vowels and maintain the concept of a tall *i* and *e* inside the mouth.
- Produce a warm, resonant sound from syllable to syllable in each word.

37
G D Em7 A7 D
ai - gi, cod-al - ai - gi, cois an chlai amuigh, cois an chlai amuigh.
ai - gi, cod-al - ai - gi, cois an chlai amuigh, cois an chlai amuigh.
44
slower
p
G D Em7 A7 D
Cod-al - ai - gi, cod-al - ai - gi, cois an chlai amuigh, cois an chlai amuigh.
Cod-al - ai - gi, cod-al - ai - gi, cois an chlai amuigh, cois an chlai amuigh.
Sing Out!
Unit 11 393

# 3 Close

## Analyzing

Have students

- Identify how many measures are in each phrase of *"Einini."*
- Identify how many phrases are in the A section and B section of the song.
- Identify the highest and lowest notes in the A and B sections.

**Element: RHYTHM** **ASSESSMENT**

5b **Performance/Observation** Have students sing *"Einini"* **CD 17-1** in Gaelic and then with their newly created English verse. As they sing, invite students to conduct in 3. Observe whether they accurately perform the upbeat note and sing each phrase of the melody smoothly and gently.

## Skills Reinforcement

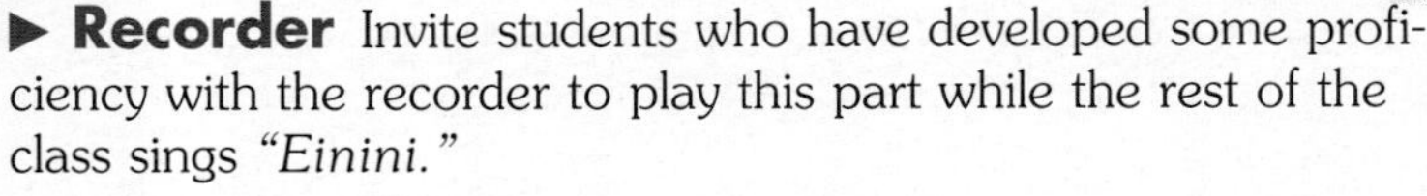

2f ▶ **Recorder** Invite students who have developed some proficiency with the recorder to play this part while the rest of the class sings *"Einini."*

4
Fine
3
last time
D.S. al Fine

## Technology/Media Link

**Web Site** Encourage students to visit *www.sfsuccessnet.com* to learn more about Gaelic music and music from Scotland and Ireland.

LESSON 5

## LESSON AT A GLANCE

**Element Focus** **TEXTURE/HARMONY** Melody ostinato

**Skill Objective** **SINGING** Sing melody ostinatos

**Connection Activity** **CULTURE** Discuss African American spirituals

**MATERIALS**

- "Little David, Play on Your Harp" **CD 17-4**

  **Recording Routine:** Intro (7 m.); refrain; v. 1; refrain; v. 2; refrain with ostinato 1; v. 3; refrain with ostinatos 1 and 2; v. 4 (same as v. 1); refrain with ostinatos 1, 2, and 3; coda
- *Little David, Play on Your Harp* **CD 17-6**
- *Interview with Moses Hogan* **CD 17-7**
- **Resource Book** p. H-25

**VOCABULARY**

ostinato syncopation
refrain verse

**◆◆◆◆ National Standards ◆◆◆◆**

**2a** Play instruments in rhythm maintaining steady tempo
**5a** Read rhythms in $\frac{2}{4}$ meter
**6a** Listen to identify form

**MORE MUSIC CHOICES**

For more African American spirituals:
"Gonna Ride Up in the Chariot," p. 20
"I'm Gonna Sing," p. 33

# 1 INTRODUCE

Share with students the information in Cultural Connection below. Then have students identify how a performer would sing an African American spiritual. (Consider the words, mood, tempo, and style.) Introduce "Little David, Play on Your Harp" **CD 17-4.**

# Singing in Layers

"Little David, Play on Your Harp" is an African American spiritual.

### Singing Tips

As you **sing** the words *play on your harp, hallelu,* make certain the *p* in the word *harp* is not connected to the *h* in *hallelu.*

### Reading Music Tips

Practice speaking the syncopated rhythm pattern in the words *play on your.* Then practice the word *hallelu* with an accent on the *h.*

### Knowing the Score

Find the words *Refrain, Verse,* and *ostinato.* What do these words mean? Is the melody ostinato sung with the verse or refrain?

CD 17-4
MIDI 31
Little David, Play on Your Harp
s, l, d r m f s l d
African American Spiritual
Arranged by Shirley McRae
REFRAIN
F Bb F Bb
Lit - tle Da - vid, play on your harp, hal - le - lu, hal - le -
F Bb F C7 F Fine
lu, Lit - tle Da - vid, play on your harp, hal - le - lu.
VERSE F Bb F
1., 4. Lit - tle Da - vid was a shep - herd boy, he
2. Old Dan - iel in the li - on's den, but
3. Lit - tle Da - vid was a might - y king, and
Bb F C7 F D.C. al Fine
slew Go - li - ath and sang for joy.
he came out all whole a - gain.
all the peo - ple came to sing.
394

## Footnotes

## CULTURAL CONNECTION

▶ **Spirituals** Many spirituals express the sorrow of daily life as well as the desire for freedom. "Little David, Play on Your Harp" is a lively, up-tempo spiritual that celebrates the biblical triumphs of David and Daniel. The hope of eventual triumph against slavery is implied.

## BUILDING SKILLS THROUGH MUSIC

▶ **Physical Education** Divide the class into four equal groups. Have the three groups that sing the ostinatos on p. 395 form a triangle. Have the group that sings the refrain form a circle inside the triangle, facing the triangle. As they sing the ostinatos, students in the circle should rotate counterclockwise.

## TEACHER TO TEACHER

▶ **Singing a Spiritual** The singing style for "Little David, Play on Your Harp" should be rhythmically alive and full of vocal energy. Have students

- Enunciate initial consonants crisply.
- Accent syncopated notes.
- Separately and distinctly sing consonants in the middle of words such as *little* and *hallelu.*
- Sing ostinatos 1 and 2 as two-measure phrases with a quick breath between phrases.
- Sing ostinato 3 with a slight vocal break between the words *harp* and *sing* (measures 25–26).

The listening version of *Little David, Play on Your Harp* features the Moses Hogan Chorale. Share the *Interview with Moses Hogan* **CD 17-7** with students.

14 Refrain ostinato 1
Play on your harp, sing hal - le - lu.
19 Refrain ostinato 2
Play, play, sing hal - le - lu.
24 Refrain ostinato 3
Play on your harp, sing hal - le - lu - jah.

**Listen** for the melody as the Moses Hogan Chorale performs its version of *Little David, Play on Your Harp.* Then listen to Moses Hogan talk about his experiences in music. (In the photo below, he is in the first row, fourth from left.)

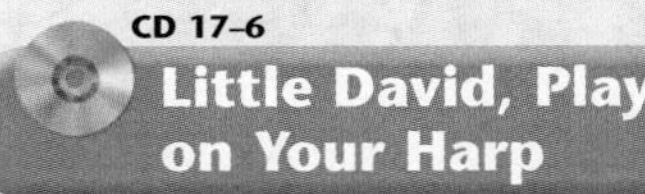

CD 17-6
**Little David, Play on Your Harp**

**African American Spiritual as performed by the Moses Hogan Chorale**

This version is performed *a cappella.*

Sing Out!

MUSIC MAKERS

# Moses Hogan

**Moses Hogan** (1957–2003) was an accomplished pianist, conductor, and arranger. His awards included winning the Kosciuszko Foundation Chopin Competition. He was also the founder of the Moses Hogan Chorale, a group famous for its high quality choral performances.

CD 17-7 **Interview with Moses Hogan**

# 2 Develop

### Analyzing

6a Invite students to discuss how the ostinato patterns on p. 395 change the texture of the song. Play "Little David, Play on Your Harp" **CD 17-4** and have them listen for the syncopated characteristics of this spiritual. Have students identify the refrain, verse, and ostinatos.

### Reading

5a Invite students to tap the rhythms of the ostinato patterns. Divide the class into three equal groups. Have groups learn to sing their ostinato and then combine them. Divide the class into four equal groups: Have group 1 sing verse and refrain, group 2 sing refrain ostinato 1, group 3 sing refrain ostinato 2, and group 4 sing refrain ostinato 3. Have them all speak their part simultaneously.

### Singing

Invite students to sing the song with crisp enunciation. Have them sing accented ♪ ♩ ♪ patterns *(play on your harp)* and sing the *h* in *harp* and *hallelu* with an accent. Students singing ostinatos 1 and 2 should sing the rhythms in an accented manner. Students should sing ostinato 2 in *legato* style.

# 3 Close

**Skill: SINGING** ASSESSMENT

**Performance/Interview** Have some students sing the ostinatos on p. 395, while other students sing the verse and refrain. Allow groups to switch. Assess students' ability to sing the ostinatos accurately. Have them explain how the ostinatos affect the harmony and texture. Then have them listen to *Little David, Play on Your Harp* **CD 17-6** and explain how they would sing the song to create a style similar to that of the Moses Hogan Chorale.

## Skills Reinforcement

▶ **Guitar** The song "Little David, Play on Your Harp" has easy guitar chords but some very quick chord changes. This 2a problem can be solved by tuning the guitar to an open F chord and playing it as a drone accompaniment to the song. Play two down-strums for every measure throughout the song including the refrain ostinatos.

▶ **Keyboard** Invite students to play an ensemble keyboard accompaniment for "Little David, Play on Your Harp." See Resource Book p. H-25.

▶ **Singing** To compare songs from diverse styles that incorporate vocal ostinatos, have students sing "Peace Round" (p. 348) in addition to "Little David, Play on Your Harp."

## Technology/Media Link

**MIDI/Sequencing Software** Using the MIDI song file for "Little David, Play on Your Harp," encourage students to experiment with layering the three ostinatos. Students will develop an understanding of how texture and harmony are created in music.

The MIDI song file can also be used to change the tempo or transpose to another key.

LESSON 6

## LESSON AT A GLANCE

**Element Focus** **TEXTURE/HARMONY** Partner songs

**Skill Objective** **SINGING** Sing two partner songs

**Connection Activity** **CULTURE** Explore the music and dance of Brazil

**MATERIALS**

- *"Sambalele"* (Portuguese) **CD 17-8**
- *"Sambalele"* (English) **CD 17-9**

  **Recording Routine:** Intro (5 m.); vocal; coda
- *Bate-papo* **CD 17-12**
- **Pronunciation Practice/Translation** p. 493
- **Resource Book** pp. A-41, H-27
- *guiro*, drums, claves, maracas, whistle, conga

**VOCABULARY**

syncopation

**National Standards**

- **1a** Sing independently on pitch and in rhythm
- **1d** Sing part songs
- **2a** Play instruments in rhythm
- **3b** Improvise rhythmic ostinato accompaniments
- **5a** Read rhythms in $\frac{2}{4}$ meter
- **6e** While listening to music, move to show a prominent feature of the music
- **7a** Create standards for evaluating performances

**MORE MUSIC CHOICES**

For more partner songs:

"Turn the World Around," p. 114

"Shake the Papaya Down," p. 378

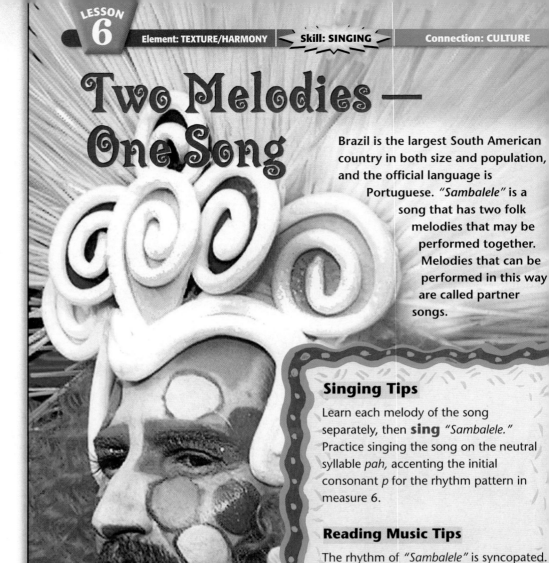

# Two Melodies — One Song

Brazil is the largest South American country in both size and population, and the official language is Portuguese. *"Sambalele"* is a song that has two folk melodies that may be performed together. Melodies that can be performed in this way are called partner songs.

### Singing Tips

Learn each melody of the song separately, then **sing** *"Sambalele."* Practice singing the song on the neutral syllable *pah,* accenting the initial consonant *p* for the rhythm pattern in measure 6.

### Reading Music Tips

The rhythm of *"Sambalele"* is syncopated. Find this pattern in the song.

Practice this pattern before you **sing** the song. How many other rhythm patterns can you find in the song?

*Carnaval* celebration in Brazil ▶

396

## Footnotes

### MEETING INDIVIDUAL NEEDS

▶ **English Language Learners** Invite students to read and sing the English lyrics for *"Sambalele."* Sometimes comprehension is challenging for students learning English. Oral retellings are one effective way to monitor comprehension. Ask students to tell a partner what the song text is about. You may want to ask students specific questions about the meanings or intents of lines of song text such as "forgot how to park it" or "rarely gets to his pillow."

### BUILDING SKILLS THROUGH MUSIC

▶ **Physical Education** Students may enjoy performing movements with *"Sambalele"* that indicate when each partner song is sung and when the songs are sung together. For more detailed instructions, see Movement on p. 399.

### SPOTLIGHT ON

▶ **Partner Songs** Harmony may be created when two different songs are sung at the same time. It is only possible to combine two songs when the chord structures for each song are compatible. Partner songs are often sung around a campfire, at family gatherings, at school, and as entertainment after social banquets. The fun in singing partner songs is hearing the harmony and words sounding at the same time. Some examples of partner songs include "Hang Down Your Head Tom Dooley" and "Polly-Wolly Doodle," or "Three Blind Mice" and "Row, Row, Row Your Boat."

**Knowing the Score**

What is the purpose of the five-measure rest at the beginning of the song? In which part of the song does the arranger create texture and harmony? Explain your answer.

CD 17-8
MIDI 32

**Sambalele**

English Words by Henry Leck

Folk Song from Brazil
Arranged by Henry Leck

f, s, l, t, (d) r m f s
Unison
5
F Gm C7
Sam-ba - le - le ta do - en - te, tac - oa ca - be - ça que
Sam-ba - le - le is a fel - low, Who rare - ly gets to his
9
bra - da Sam-ba - le - le pre - ci - sa - va de u-mas de zoi - to lam-
pil - low, He spends his time loud - ly play - ing. No one can tell where he's
13
ba - das, Sam - ba - le - le ta do - en - te, tac - oa ca - be - ça, que
stay - ing, Sam - ba - le - le went out danc - ing, With his new cart he went
17
bra - da Sam - ba - le - le pre - ci - sa - va
pran - cing, then he ar - rived at the mar - ket,
20
de u-mas de zoi - to lam - ba - das, Sam - ba sam - ba
but he for - got how to park it. Sam - ba sam - ba
23
sam - ba - le - le Pi - sa - na ba - ra da sa - ia le - le!
sam - ba - le - le We wish your neigh-bors could tell where you stay.
Sing Out!
Unit 11 397

# 1 Introduce

Share with students the information and activities in Cultural Connection below and Across the Curriculum, p. 398. Point out that this arrangement of *"Sambalele"* has two Brazilian folk songs combined to create harmony. When two songs are sung at the same time, they are called partner songs. Both melodies use the *samba* rhythm and the *so-mi-do* pattern.

# 2 Develop

## Reading

5a Have students look at the notation for *"Sambalele"* on p. 397. Help them discover that measures 6–7 are imitated rhythmically and melodically in measures 8–9. Then have them determine how often syncopation is used in measure 6. (twice) Ask students how often parts 1 and 2 sing the syncopated pattern together. (There are 17 exact repetitions.)

**ASK How many measures are in each phrase?** (two measures)

## Singing

1a Divide the class into two groups. Have group 1 tap the rhythm of measures 6–7 (Part 1) while group 2 speaks the rhythm on the neutral syllable *pah.* Then reverse the process. Have students use the same technique for part 2. Have group 1 learn to sing part 1 while group 2 learns part 2. When the two melodies are learned, have students sing the parts together. Have students listen to the Pronunciation Practice **CD 17-11** for *"Sambalele"* and sing the Portuguese words. Refer to Resource Book p. A-41 for the Pronunciation Practice Guide.

continued on page 398

## Cultural Connection

▶ **Sambas and Carnaval** Brazil is the land of *Carnaval*, the pre-Lenten celebration during which people sing and dance in the streets. It is also the land of Brazil's most popular music and dance, the *samba. Samba* was the first Brazilian style to become popular worldwide through the voice of Carmen Miranda. The *samba* is a mix of the strong beats of African music and expressive Brazilian tunes.

The music and dance styles of *Carnaval* are becoming popular throughout the world. *Samba* schools for both children and adults now thrive in various locations in Japan, the United States, and Europe.

## Skills Reinforcement

▶ **Creating** Ask students to create a partner song of their own. First, provide them with a known song that has a straightforward chord progression, using only "I" and "V" chords. Some examples may include "He's Got the Whole World in His Hands," or "Skip to My Lou." Draw students' attention to the chord progression by writing it on the board in such a way that they can see "when" the chords change. Then ask them to compose another song of their own, or find one with the identical meter and chord pattern, that can be sung at the same time. Have students perform the two songs together. Invite them to revise or refine their work, or have students describe, either verbally or in writing, how effective their partner songs are.

If you have time to do combined chorus singing, another option for singing this piece is to teach the *"Sambalele"* melody to one class, and teach the *"Balaio"* melody to another class. Then put the entire piece together during a rehearsal.

### Performing

2a Invite students to perform the syncopated rhythms in the song, using rhythm sticks or a drum. Then have the class sing the song all the way through in Portuguese **CD 17-8** and then in English **CD 17-9**.

### Listening

Review the information in Cultural Connection on p. 397 about *samba* and *Carnaval* with students. Have them listen for syncopated *samba* rhythms in *Bate-papo* **CD 17-12.**

### Creating

Hand out available Latin rhythm instruments and encourage students to improvise syncopated rhythms and play along with the recording of *Bate-papo* **CD 17-12** or the Stereo Performance Track of *"Sambalele"* **CD 17-10.**

Another option is to establish a steady beat with one drum. Then model an improvised *samba* pattern for a student. Have the student echo the pattern and join in the ensemble. Gradually model and add in more instruments. Have students create a small *samba* ensemble to play as the rest of the class sings *"Sambalele"* **CD 17-8.** Students may rotate between being part of the *samba* ensemble and singing.

### Moving

Refer to Movement on p. 399 and encourage students to move as they perform *"Sambalele."*

▼ Dancers at *Carnava*

*Sam - ba sam - ba sam-ba - le - le! Pi - sa - na bar - ra da*
Sam - ba sam - ba sam-ba - le - le! Of - ten we just can - not

*sa - ia Ba - la - io meu bem, Ba - la - io sin-ha ba -*
find you. Ba - la - io the brave, Ba - la - io the fair ba -

*la-io do co - ra - ção Mo - ça - que não tem ba - la - io sin - ha bo-taa*
la-io whom we a - dore. I know your dark hair and pret-ty dark eyes are the

*cos - tu - ra no chão. Ba - la - io meu bem, ba -*
en - vy of us all. Ba - la - io so sweet ba -

*la - io sin - ha ba - la - io do co - ra - ção Mo -*
la - io so kind ba - la - io we can't ig - nore. The

*ça - que não tem ba - la - io sin - ha bo - taa cos - tu - ra no*
beau-ty you bring how hap - py you sing we all want to see you

398

## Footnotes

### ACROSS THE CURRICULUM

▶ **Social Studies** Share the book *Brazil: Many Voices, Many Faces* by Irene Flum Galvin (Benchmark, 1996) and explore the Brazilian culture. Invite students to learn about one special feature of Brazil—the rain forest—*Discovering the Amazon Rainforest* by J. Bradley Cruxton (Oxford, 1999).

▶ **Language Arts** At *Carnaval* time in Brazil, thousands of musicians perform and parade through the streets. Groups of musicians from local *samba* schools rehearse for months and compete for prizes during *Carnaval.* Invite students to do research at home and report back to class about the instruments used in *samba* bands or about how members of these bands learn their music.

### SKILLS REINFORCEMENT

▶ **Keyboard** Use the following teaching suggestions to help all students improvise using the rhythm pattern ♪ ♩ ♪ on the pitches of the F-pentatonic scale.

**Reinforcement** Some students may not be able to accurately perform the ♪ ♩ ♪ rhythm and improvise a melody. Allow these students to gain confidence by performing the rhythm pattern on F only.

**On Target** Most students will be able to improvise using ♪ ♩ ♪. For additional help, see Resource Book p. H-27.

**Challenge** Invite interested students to create a countermelody for "*Sambalele*" using ♪ ♩ ♪.

46 F *div.* Gm

1: *chão! Ba - la - io meu bem, ba - la - io sin - ha, ba -*
more. Ba - la - io so nice, ba - la - io pre-cise ba -

2: *chão! Sam-ba - le - le ta do - en - te,*
more. Sam-ba - le - le is a fel - low,

49 $C_7$ F

1: *la - io do co - ra - ção Mo - ça - que não tem ba -*
la - io you live next door. We hope that you stay, so

2: *tac - ao ca - be - ça que bra - da! Sam - ba - le - le pre - ci -*
who rare - ly gets to his pil - low, He spends his time loud - ly

# 3 Close

**ASSESSMENT**

1d **Performance/Peer Critique** Divide the class into two choruses. Have choir 1 sing *"Sambalele"* **CD 17-8** in Portuguese. Have choir 2 evaluate the diction and rhythmic clarity of choir 1's performance. Have groups reverse roles and repeat the evaluation process. Students should consider the following areas in their evaluations.

- Did the parts stay together for the duration of the performance?
- Were melodies dynamically balanced when performed together?
- Did each phrase have dynamic shape?
- Was the vocal energy strong throughout each phrase?
- Were the strong syllables of the Portuguese language emphasized?

continued on page 400

## Movement

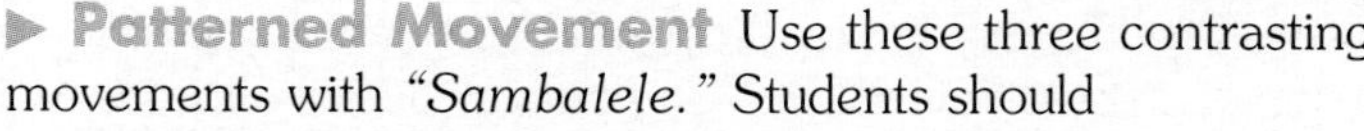

6e ▶ **Patterned Movement** Use these three contrasting movements with *"Sambalele."* Students should

- Step-touch left and right on the quarter note for the first melody.
- Hold the right hand out with the elbow bent at a right angle; then shake the right hand in time and place the left hand over the stomach for the second melody.
- Bend both arms at the elbow with the palms of the hands just below the collarbone; then bounce the shoulders up and down in the time to the music when the melodies are sung together.

At the end of the song, invite students to create a gesture as if they are trying to find someone and freeze in that position.

## Technology/Media Link

**MIDI/Sequencing Software** If you wish to have students sing *"Sambalele"* in a different key to accompany the song with instruments in a different key, use the MIDI song file to transpose the song.

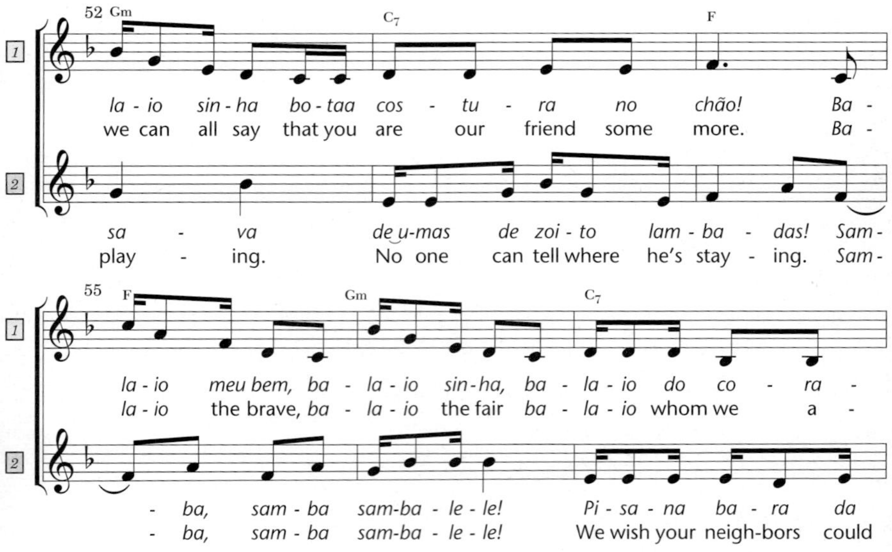

52 Gm C7 F

1 la - io sin - ha bo - taa cos - tu - ra no chão! Ba -
we can all say that you are our friend some more. Ba -

2 sa - va de u-mas de zoi - to lam - ba - das! Sam -
play - ing. No one can tell where he's stay - ing. Sam -

55 F Gm C7

1 la - io meu bem, ba - la - io sin-ha, ba - la - io do co - ra -
la - io the brave, ba - la - io the fair ba - la - io whom we a -

2 - ba, sam - ba sam-ba - le - le! Pi - sa - na ba - ra da
- ba, sam - ba sam-ba - le - le! We wish your neigh-bors could

400

# Footnotes

## TEACHER TO TEACHER

▶ **Part Singing** Singing in parts can be a challenging experience for most young singers. In order to prepare them for higher level part singing, try the following sequence of activities over the course of the year. Have students first sing ostinatos. Follow that with partner songs and countermelodies. Present rounds as layers of ostinatos (each group singing one part). Then have students sing rounds as written. Finally, students may begin singing two and three-part arrangements.

## CHARACTER EDUCATION

▶ **Friendship** To help students consider qualities of good friendships, discuss what words in *"Sambalele"* describe the object of the song. *(sweet, kind, beauty you bring, happy you sing, want to see you more, and so on)* From the text, it is obvious that the object of the song is a friend to many. Help students make a list of the characteristics of a good friend. Ask, When you are looking for a friend, what characteristics do you consider? Of these qualities, which are the most important? How does someone show you that he/she possesses these traits? For example, if kindness is important to you, what specific behaviors show you that someone is kind? Do people just naturally have these characteristics, or is it necessary to develop traits of a good friend? Is it all right to have more than one friend? Why or why not?

Sing Out!

## Sound of the *Samba*

**One of the most beloved kinds of music in Brazil is the *samba*. Every year a big celebration called *Carnaval* takes place. Many people parade through the streets singing and dancing to *samba* music.**

**Listen for the *samba* rhythms in this recording of *Bate-papo*.**

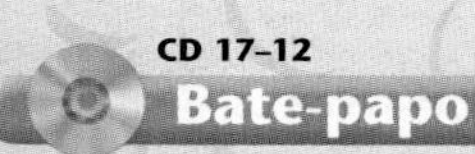

**CD 17–12**

**Bate-papo**

***Batucada Street Samba* from Brazil**
**as performed by *Bateria Nota 10***

The *batucada samba* is the rhythmic foundation for *Carnaval*.



## AUDIENCE ETIQUETTE

**▶ Rehearsal Etiquette for Performers** Productive choral rehearsals prepare musicians for the best performance possible. Help students develop a set of "rehearsal etiquette" guidelines, such as

- Be on time and converse with friends only after the rehearsal is finished.
- Come prepared for rehearsal with a pencil and your music.
- Listen to others in your section and to other sections. Listen to all instructions.
- Be attentive to your personal space, and respect the space of others.
- Say "thank you" to the leaders of the group at the end of rehearsal.

## TECHNOLOGY/MEDIA LINK

**Video Library** Invite students to watch the *Batukara: samba* performance to learn more about the *samba* ensembles of *Carnaval*.

LESSON 7

## LESSON AT A GLANCE

**Element Focus** **MELODY** *Do-mi-so* melodic sequences

**Skills Objective** **READING** Read *do-mi-so* in different keys

**Connection Activity** **RELATED ARTS** Explore imagery in song lyrics

**MATERIALS**

- "Circle 'Round the Moon" **CD 17-13**
  **Recording Routine:** Intro (4 m.); vocal; coda
- "Extremes" (poem)

**VOCABULARY**

| | |
|---|---|
| word painting | tempo |
| call and response | dynamics |

**◆ ◆ ◆ ◆ National Standards ◆ ◆ ◆ ◆**

- **1a** Sing independently on pitch with appropriate diction
- **1e** Sing in groups, following a conductor
- **4b** Compose songs within specific guidelines
- **4c** Compose music using a variety of sound sources
- **5c** Identify and use terms and symbols
- **6a** Listen to identify form
- **9b** Describe how musical elements are used in pieces from various cultures

**MORE MUSIC CHOICES**

For more songs about nature:

*"Tsuki,"* p. 25
"River," p. 58
"The Wheel of the Water," p. 362
"Cycle Song of Life," p. 370
"Sailboat in the Sky," p. 374



# What's the Score?

The beauty of nature is all around us. Read the words to "Circle 'Round the Moon." What do they mean? One challenge in reading music is to follow your part in a complete score. As you **listen** to "Circle 'Round the Moon," trace your part in the score.

### Singing Tips

Learn the first phrase of "Circle 'Round the Moon." **Sing** this phrase wherever it appears in the song. Next, learn measures 13–15 and **sing** this phrase wherever it appears in the song. Now **sing** each phrase without taking a breath in the middle.

### Reading Music Tips

**Read** measures 5–8 using pitch syllables. The melody often uses pitch syllables *do, mi,* and *so.* The melody also uses a ♫ ♫ rhythm pattern. Why does this rhythm pattern change to larger note values? How does this make the music feel?

### Knowing the Score

The composer of "Circle 'Round the Moon" uses **word painting** to help create mood. An example of word painting appears in measure 13. Notice in the words *high above the trees,* the note for the word *high* is the highest note in the measure and the lowest note is for *trees.* How many other examples of word painting can you find?

**Word painting** is the positioning of pitch and rhythm patterns to resemble the meaning of words.

402

## Footnotes

## SKILLS REINFORCEMENT

9b ▶ **Listening** Accompaniments add interest and additional musical information to a composition. Encourage students to listen to "Circle 'Round the Moon" and other songs and determine how accompaniment contributes to the meaning of the song.

## BUILDING SKILLS THROUGH MUSIC

▶ **Language** Ask students to look at the poem "Extremes" on p. 409. Have them

- Identify common elements or themes in the two verses. (The rhyme scheme is the same; both verses involve children; nature is speaking in both verses.)
- Determine why the poem was titled "Extremes."

## SPOTLIGHT ON

▶ **The Performers** One of the most successful children's choirs in the country, the Indianapolis Children's Choir consists of 1,200 singers who reflect many religions, races, cultures, and economic backgrounds. Their repertoire includes such works as "Come, Come, Ye Sons of Art," *"Non nobis Domine,"* and "Can't Buy Me Love." Founded by Henry Leck and housed at Butler University, the chorus enjoys an educational program in which singers are taught music theory, vocal technique, music history, sight-reading, and foreign language skills. The ICC has toured extensively. It has visited England, Scotland, Hawaii, New York, Norway, Italy, and Germany. It has even recorded with the Canadian Brass. The Indianapolis Children's Choir recorded "Circle 'Round the Moon" and other songs in MAKING MUSIC.

CD 17-13
MIDI 33
Circle 'Round the Moon
(From "Reflections of Youth")
Words and Music by
Mark Hierholzer
Piano
p unison
Cir-cle 'round the moon in-vites me to stay out in the win-ter - time.
Crys-tals in the air sug-gest that I pre-pare for the cold night air.
High a-bove the trees you will make me see that with such a sight
Sing Out!
Unit 11 403

# 1 Introduce

Share with students the information in Across the Curriculum below and Spotlight On, p. 404. Invite them to think of different types of word images.

9b "Circle 'Round the Moon" uses descriptive phrases to create pictures. The words *circle 'round the moon* and *crystals in the air* are examples. Have students find other word pictures in the song and discuss possible interpretations.

# 2 Develop

### Listening

6a Play "Circle 'Round the Moon" **CD 17-13** and have students

- Identify the *do-mi-so* patterns when heard. (mm. 5–6, 9–10, 14–15, 21–22, and 25–26)
- Identify the call-and-response sections when heard. (mm. 29–33 and mm. 46–47)
- Raise their hands every time they hear word pictures.

### Reading

5c Have students

- Identify and sing *so-mi-do* and *do-mi-so* patterns.
- Sing the sequence in mm. 13 and 29.
- Clap the textual call and response (mm. 29, 30, 46, and 47).
- Sing the melody for mm. 5–12 with hand signs and pitch syllables.

continued on page 404

## Across the Curriculum

**▶ Language Arts/Related Arts** Imagery in the fine arts is a common occurrence. Poetry, novels, plays, songs of all types, movies, and television shows all use imagery. Metaphor ("screaming headlines"), simile ("cunning as a fox"), alliteration ("'round the rock the ragged rascal ran"), onomatopoeia ("*tinkling* of the bells"), and descriptive adjectives are poetic devices used by poets, authors, and lyricists.

*Icicles of stone* in "Circle 'Round the Moon" is a metaphoric image for stalactites that hang from the ceiling of a cave or cavern. Have students look at lyrics in the songs listed in More Music Choices and locate other examples of word images.

## Teacher to Teacher

**▶ Understanding the Story Line** The words in "Circle 'Round the Moon" are very descriptive. To help students gain a good understanding of the lyrics and how to express them in their singing, have them

- Read each phrase and discuss its meaning.
- Identify the type of imagery in each phrase.
- Practice expressing each phrase.
- Describe how the composer captured the meaning of the words in the music.

### Singing

1e Have students

- Warm up singing *do-mi-so-mi-do* in the keys of C, D, and F.
- Speak the text of the first phrase of "Circle 'Round the Moon" on a single pitch in one breath at different tempos to develop breath support.
- Sing the song with tall vowels inside the mouth for all words.

### Moving

Invite students to add choreography to their performance of "Circle 'Round the Moon." See Movement on p. 407.

### Performing

1a Have students stand in two semicircles facing each other. When the call-and-response and the harmony parts are performed, students will be able to see and hear the musical effect.

Have students turn and face away from each other, sing, and observe the musical effect.

### Creating

For additional practice with interpreting poetic imagery, have the class use the poem "Extremes" or find other poems with imagery and read the descriptions aloud. Have them pick two or three examples and compose brief melodies for the text. Have students try word painting in their compositions. (See Spotlight On below for examples of word painting.)

## Footnotes

### Skills Reinforcement

▶ **Reading** The pitch syllable pattern *do-mi-so-mi-do* can be found in many songs. Encourage students to look at other songs in the book and find examples of this ascending and descending pattern. Help them observe the rhythmic characteristics of each pattern. ("Soldier, Soldier," p. 11 [ascending]; *"Tsuki,"* p. 25 [descending]; and *"Eh, cumpari!,"* p. 68 [descending])

### Spotlight On

▶ **Word Painting** Word painting is a technique used by composers since the sixteenth century. When the pitch placement and rhythmic characteristics of tones, together with tempo and dynamics, seek to capture the meaning of words in vocal music, word painting is occurring. Natural sounds, such as birds, thunder, sighing, and sobbing are typical candidates for word painting. Music that is high, low, ascending, descending, loud, soft, fast, or slow may be associated with the meaning of a particular word. Good examples of word painting are

- When the word *heaven* is associated with music that is high or ascending in pitch.
- When slow moving low notes are intended to depict a lumbering elephant.

# 3 Close

**Element: MELODY** ASSESSMENT

**Interview** Have students verbally compare "Circle 'Round the Moon" with "Wings of a Dove," p. 318, for melodic similarities. In "Wings of a Dove," have students find and read

- Repetition of repeated pitch note patterns. (mm. 1, 3, 12, 13, 14, 15, and 17)
- Sequences. (mm. 7–8, 11–12, and 15–16)
- Word painting. (mm. 7 and 14, the word *fly*)
- *do-mi-so* patterns. (mm. 3–4, beat 4 through beat 1)

continued on page 406

## Across the Curriculum

▶ **Art/Language Arts** Ask students to draw the moon on the night before they learn this song. During class, they should look at their illustrations and try to remember what they were thinking when they were drawing. They should write in their journals with the prompt "Last night, the moon made me think of . . ."

Share the poem "The Night Is a Big Black Cat" by G. Orr Clark (Random House Book of Poetry, 1983). With its images of the night as a big black cat, the moon's topaz eyes, and the stars as hunted mice, Clark's poem will set up rich possibilities for setting text to music.

## Technology/Media Link

**Notation Software** Use software to notate and play back melodies composed for a poem. Have students

- Create a notation file and set the meter signature.
- Use mouse entry to select and place notes of a melody they compose.
- Type lyrics (poem text) under the melody.
- Add the title of the poem, the poet's name, and the composer's name.

Have students play their compositions and edit as needed. Then display printed melodies in the classroom.

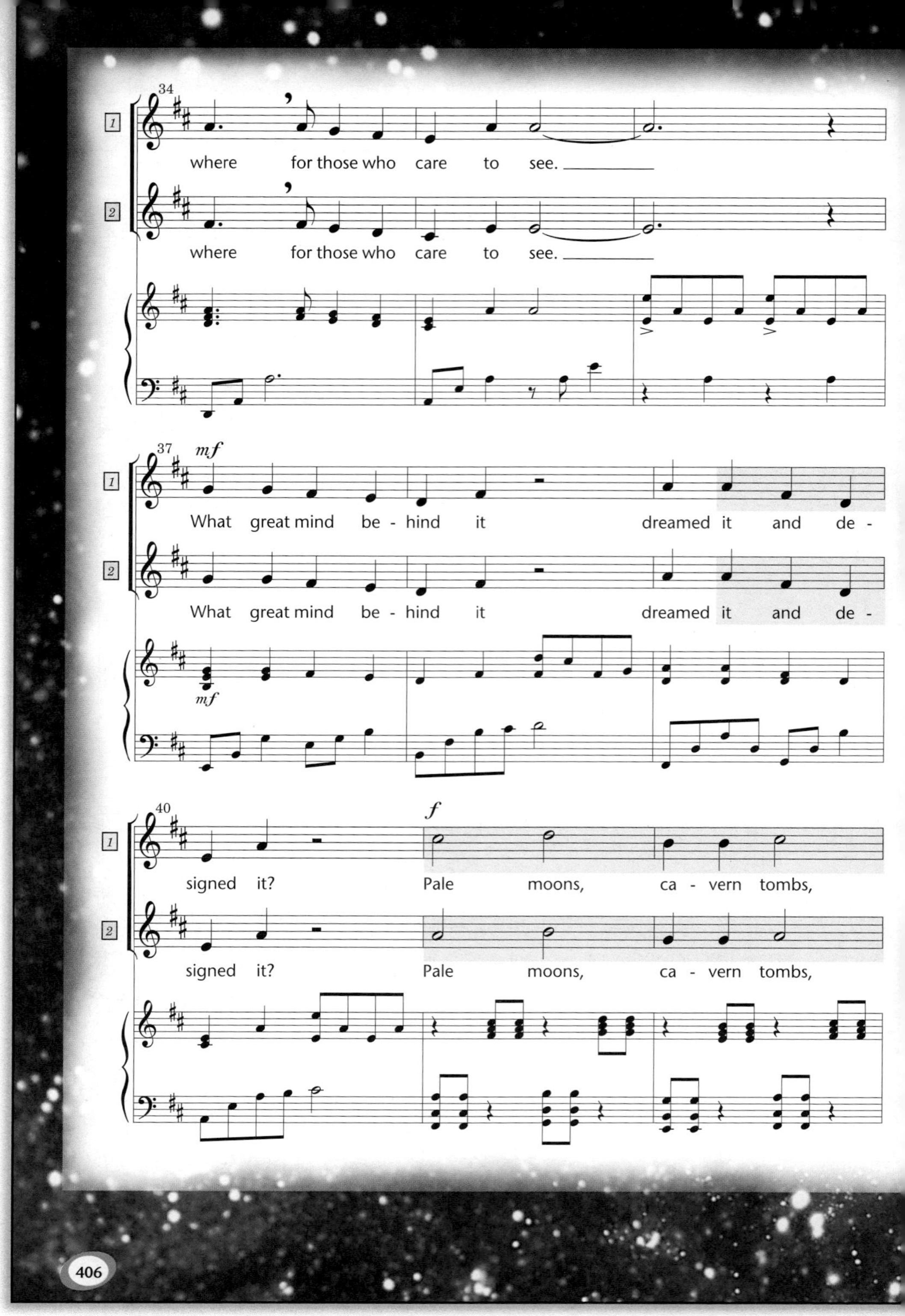

34
where for those who care to see.

37
What great mind be - hind it dreamed it and de -

40
signed it? Pale moons, ca - vern tombs,



# Footnotes

## SKILLS REINFORCEMENT

1a ▶ **Vocal Development** Help students pay special attention to the *r* consonant while singing. To sing a gentle *r*, maintain the preceding vowel sound and include a slight *r* or *uh* sound. The gentle *r* is used at the end of a word (father [FAH-thuh], remember [reh-MEM-buh]) and when followed by a consonant (lord [lawd], mercy [MUH-see]). It is also used when followed by a pause or breath.

When singing a gentle *r*, have students listen for clarity and appropriate style. Ask these questions.

- Can the listener understand the word?
- Does the word's pronunciation fit the style of the song?

## CHARACTER EDUCATION

▶ **Adaptation** Use the text of "Circle 'Round the Moon" (changing seasons) as a springboard for discussion about change. What are some changes evident in the natural world? (seasons, weather, moon phases) What are some changes in our lives? (going to a new school, moving to a new place, playing a new sport, growing physically) Discuss any changes individual students might have experienced recently that they feel comfortable sharing. How did these changes make you feel? Do you feel you adapted well to this change? Why or why not? If you were going to give advice to someone who is experiencing change, what would you say to him/her? (be flexible, look for the positive aspects) Why might change be difficult for people? (It makes us feel insecure, makes things different, makes us unsure how we are to act.) Why is change important? (It helps us grow, mature, and have new experiences.)

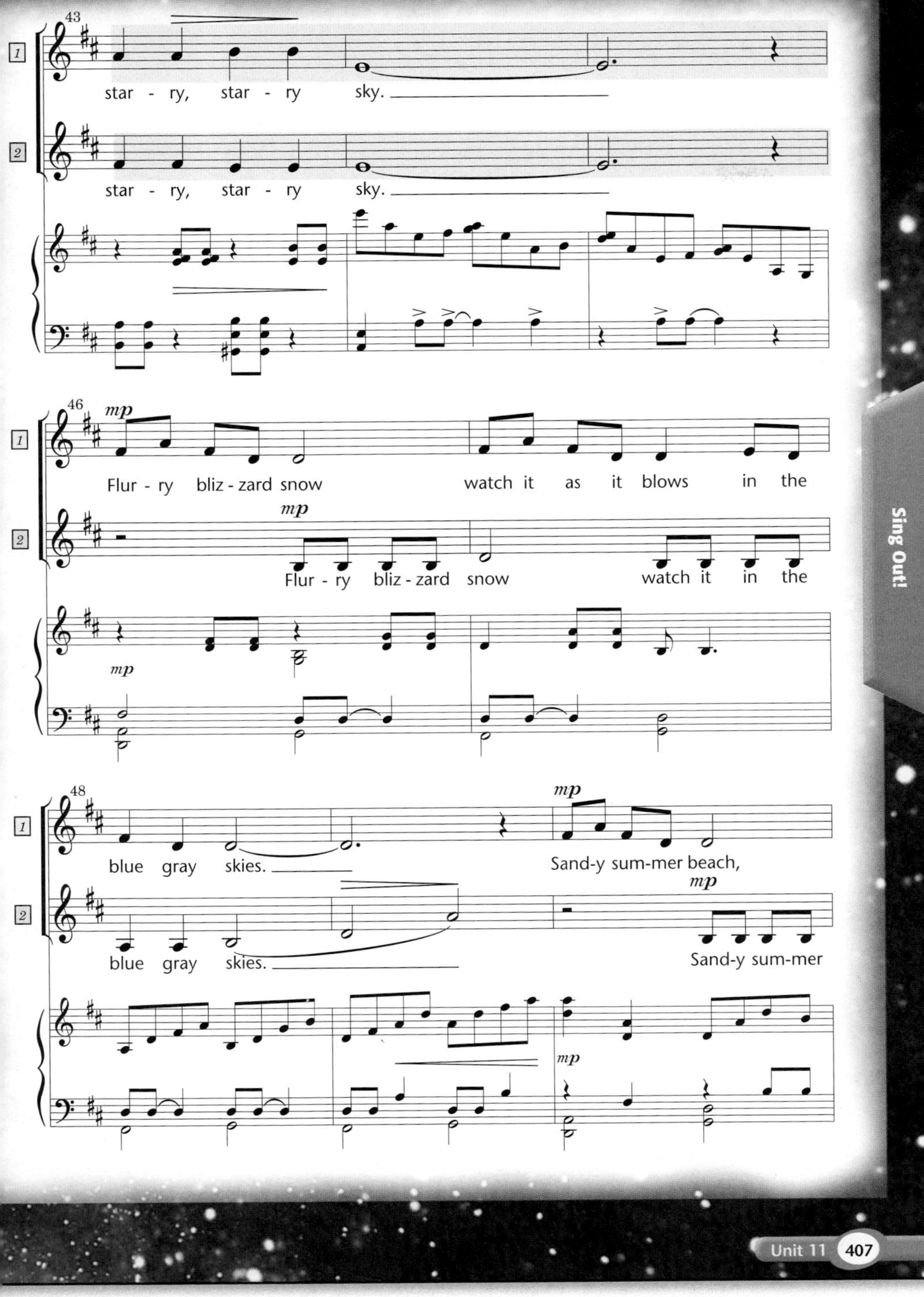


continued on page 408

## Movement

**▶ Choreography** Have students use the following four basic gestures in a very natural style to "tell the story" suggested by "Circle 'Round the Moon."

- Hands are clasped behind the back.
- Arms crossed in front of the body and the head is tilted a bit to one side.
- Left hand is on the hip, and the right hand is out front, palm up.
- The left hand with the palm up moves up and down every four beats.

Ask students to find words in the song that could be punctuated by individual moves. Have them do each move only once and then return to doing the basic movements outlined above.

## Teacher to Teacher

**▶ Teaching with MIDI** Use the "Circle 'Round the Moon" MIDI song file if you need an accompaniment in a different key or to perform the song at a different tempo.

# Footnotes

## ACROSS THE CURRICULUM

▶ **Related Arts** Ask students about their favorite sights and scenery within each of the seasons of the year. Ask them to find and clip pictures from magazines or photo albums to use in making collages or classroom bulletin boards about seasonal wonders of the natural world.

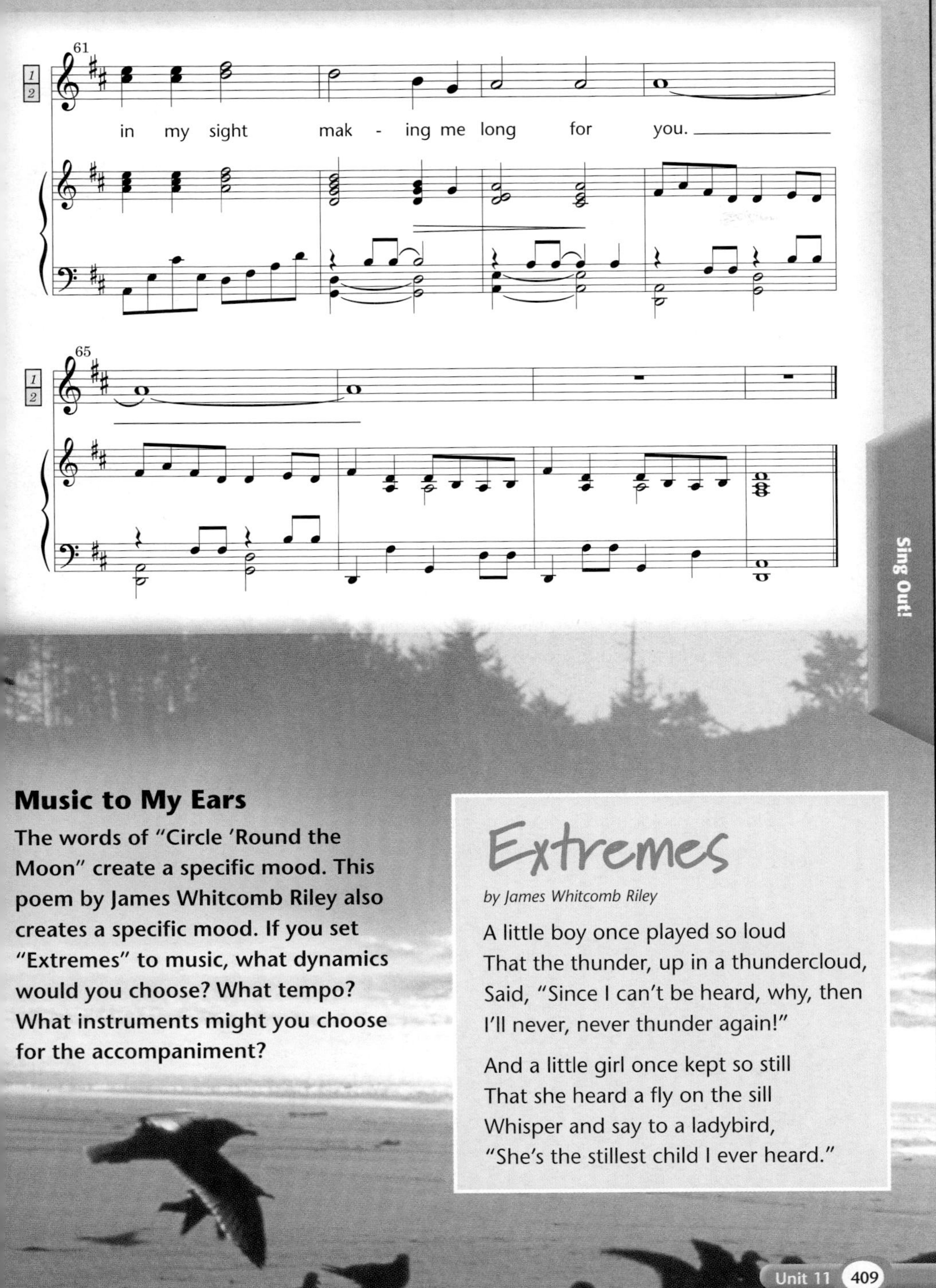


## Music to My Ears

**The words of "Circle 'Round the Moon" create a specific mood. This poem by James Whitcomb Riley also creates a specific mood. If you set "Extremes" to music, what dynamics would you choose? What tempo? What instruments might you choose for the accompaniment?**

## Extremes

*by James Whitcomb Riley*

A little boy once played so loud
That the thunder, up in a thundercloud,
Said, "Since I can't be heard, why, then
I'll never, never thunder again!"

And a little girl once kept so still
That she heard a fly on the sill
Whisper and say to a ladybird,
"She's the stillest child I ever heard."

Unit 11 409

## TECHNOLOGY/MEDIA LINK

**MIDI/Sequencing Software** Have students open the MIDI song file for "Circle 'Round the Moon" in a sequencing program. Have them work in pairs to add sound effects in separate tracks that augment the word painting. After the class has learned the song, mute the melody tracks and have the class sing along with the MIDI song file and the sound effects.

LESSON 8

## LESSON AT A GLANCE

**Element Focus** **TEXTURE/HARMONY** Ostinatos, two-part, and canonic singing

**Skill Objective** **SINGING** Sing ostinatos, two-part harmony, and canon

**Connection Activity** **CULTURE** Discover the origin of some popular Christmas customs

**MATERIALS**

- "A Merry Modal Christmas" **CD 17-15**
  **Recording Routine:** Intro (1 m.); vocal; coda
- **Pronunciation Practice/Translation** pp. 494–495
- **Resource Book** p. A-43
- finger cymbals, drum

**VOCABULARY**

*legato* major/minor mode

### ◆◆◆◆ National Standards ◆◆◆◆

**1a** Sing with appropriate diction
**1b** Sing expressively with appropriate interpretation
**1c** Sing from memory songs from diverse cultures
**1d** Sing ostinatos, part songs, and rounds (canons)
**2a** Play instruments in rhythm
**5a** Read rhythms in $\frac{2}{2}$, $\frac{3}{4}$, and $\frac{4}{4}$ meters
**6b** Describe music by answering questions about it

**MORE MUSIC CHOICES**

For more songs in minor modes:
"Ah, Poor Bird," p. 196
*"Minka,"* p. 222

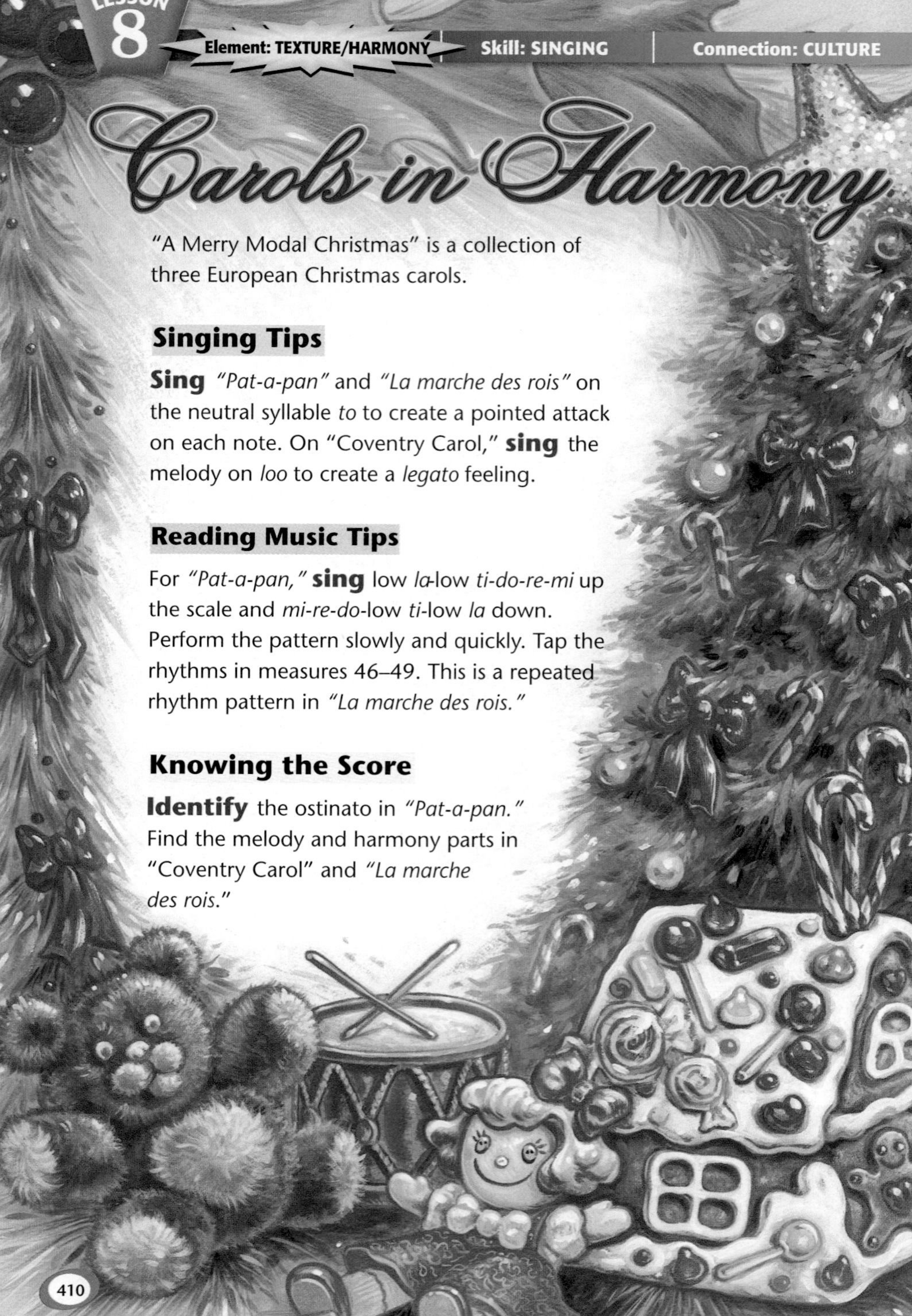
LESSON 8 Element: TEXTURE/HARMONY | Skill: SINGING | Connection: CULTURE

# Carols in Harmony

"A Merry Modal Christmas" is a collection of three European Christmas carols.

**Singing Tips**

**Sing** *"Pat-a-pan"* and *"La marche des rois"* on the neutral syllable *to* to create a pointed attack on each note. On "Coventry Carol," **sing** the melody on *loo* to create a *legato* feeling.

**Reading Music Tips**

For *"Pat-a-pan,"* **sing** low *la*-low *ti-do-re-mi* up the scale and *mi-re-do*-low *ti*-low *la* down. Perform the pattern slowly and quickly. Tap the rhythms in measures 46–49. This is a repeated rhythm pattern in *"La marche des rois."*

**Knowing the Score**

**Identify** the ostinato in *"Pat-a-pan."* Find the melody and harmony parts in "Coventry Carol" and *"La marche des rois."*

410

## Footnotes

### SPOTLIGHT ON

▶ **Caroling** A carol is a Christmas song dating primarily from the fourteenth and fifteenth centuries in England, but carols date back earlier elsewhere in Europe. Oftentimes the words are about the birth of Christ. In many carols, the refrain can be secular in character. The Medieval carol began with a bordun (refrain) followed by verses (stanzas). "Waits" or carolers would go through the streets at Christmas time and sing carols for small gifts of money. They walked and danced as they sang.

### BUILDING SKILLS THROUGH MUSIC

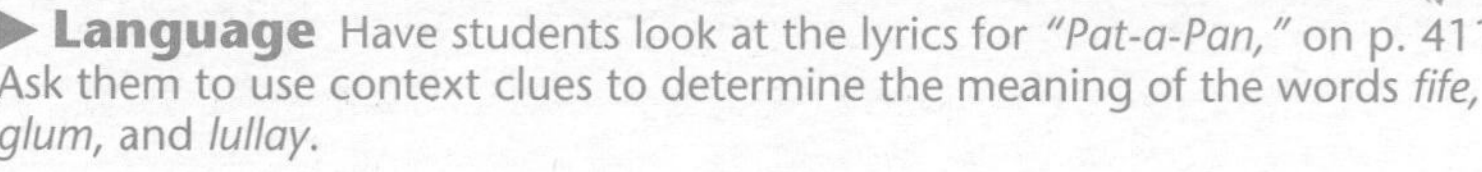
▶ **Language** Have students look at the lyrics for *"Pat-a-Pan,"* on p. 411. Ask them to use context clues to determine the meaning of the words *fife, glum,* and *lullay.*

### TEACHER TO TEACHER

▶ **Reinforcing Tonality** Each song in "A Merry Modal Christmas" is in a minor mode. Invite students to

- Listen to each song to hear the minor quality (tonality).
- Practice listening to and singing *do-re-mi-fa-so* and *la$_{|}$-ti-do-re-mi.*
- Listen to other carols in minor keys and aurally identify the diverse periods and styles that are represented.
- Do a listening competition of several songs to challenge students to determine if the song has a major or minor quality.

▶ **Teaching with MIDI** For students who are having difficulty singing the French words at tempo, practice with the MIDI song file for "A Merry Modal Christmas" at a slower tempo.

# 1 Introduce

Invite students to look at the art on p. 410. Students will immediately recognize the Christmas setting. Encourage students to share some of the customs they practice with their families during special holidays. Share the information from Spotlight On, p. 410, and Cultural Connection below about Christmas customs and caroling. Tell students that "A Merry Modal Christmas" is based on two French carols and an English carol.

# 2 Develop

## Listening

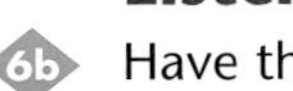

6b Have the students listen to the recording of "A Merry Modal Christmas" **CD 17-15.**

ASK **How many different songs did you hear?** (3)

**Were the songs in major or minor modes?** (minor)

**Which song (1, 2, or 3) began with unison singing?** (song 3)

## Reading

5a Have students

- Tap the rhythms of *"Pat-a-pan."*
- Speak the rhythm syllables.
- Speak the text in the rhythm of the song.
- Sing pitch syllables and perform hand signs for selected phrases in *"Pat-a-pan."*

Have students follow the same steps for "Coventry Carol" and *"La marche des rois."*

**continued on page 412**

## Skills Reinforcement

1a ▶ **Vocal Development** The pronunciation we use in daily speech and correct diction for singing usually are not the same. Words are modified in singing to make lyrics clearer and to produce better vocal tone. Here is a list of words that are commonly mispronounced in singing. Work with students to correctly pronounce the words.

| | **Incorrect** | **Correct** |
|---|---|---|
| I am | I yam | ah(e) am |
| Christmas | Chris-mis | CHRIH-smuhs |
| heaven | hea-vun | HEH-vehn |
| better | bed-der | BEH-tuh |
| bless you | bleh-shoo | bless-yoo |
| alleluia | a-leh-loo-yuh | ah-leh-LOO-yah |

## Cultural Connection

▶ **Christmas Customs** Students might be interested to know the history of some modern Christmas customs.

- Christmas was not celebrated as a holiday until the fourth century. It was made to coincide with the Roman feast of the "Invincible Sun."
- Santa Claus was modeled after the Germanic "hearth spirits" who would visit homes in a pointed red cap and red jacket to give favors.
- Decorating the Christmas tree comes from Martin Luther who brought a tree into the house and placed candles on it to show children what the forest looks like on a starry night.
- Exchanging gifts is based on the gifts the three wise men brought to Jesus.

### Singing

Have students

- Perform warm-up singing on *too* and then *loo*, using the pitch syllables *la*$_{|}$-*ti*$_{|}$-*do-re-mi* and *mi-re-do-ti*$_{|}$-*la*$_{|}$.
- Sing *"Pat-a-pan"* and "Coventry Carol," using the neutral syllable *too,* and focusing on expressive phrasing.

- Listen to the Pronunciation Practice for *"Pat-a-pan"* **CD 17-18** and *"La marche des rois"* **CD 17-19.** Then sing the French text. (For the Pronunciation Practice Guide, refer to Resource Book p. A-43.)

### Playing

Have individuals and small groups of students

- Accompany the ostinato *(Prum, pum, pum!)* with a drum for *"Pat-a-pan."*
- Play finger cymbals at the phrase endings of "Coventry Carol."

### Creating

Divide the class into three groups. Assign one song to each group. Have students in each group create a mini drama for their song. Students should consider props, costumes, and makeup. Also, they should decide how each group would come forward during the singing of the song. For choreography suggestions, see Movement on p. 413.

By, by, lul - ly, lul - lay, lul - lay.
By, by lul - ly, lul - lay; Lul -
Lul - lay, Thou ti - ny Child,
lay, Thou lit - tle ti - ny Child,
By, by, lul - ly, lul - lay.
By, by, lul - ly, lul - lay.
m, si, l, t d r m f
La marche des rois
Ce ma - tin, Ce ma - tin, Ce ma - tin, J'ai
This great day, This great day, This great day, I
ren - con - tré le train, De trois grands rois qui al - laient en - voy - a - ge
met up - on the way, The Kings of East as they came rid - ing proud - ly,
Ce ma - tin, j'ai ren - con - tré le train, De trois grands rois des - sus le
This great day, I met up - on the way, The Kings of East with all their
grand che - min. Tout char - gés d'or les sui - vant d'a - bord, De
fine ar - ray. The gifts of gold, frank - in - cense, and myrrh, Were
412

## Footnotes

## SPOTLIGHT ON

▶ **Modes** Modes in music began with the Greeks and influenced the early Christian Church. Modal music can be found in the monophonic and polyphonic church music of the Middle Ages and Renaissance era. The use of modes in music can also be found in the music of many composers including Palestrina, Bach, Handel, and Beethoven. It is also found in the folk songs of many lands. Today, we think about modes in terms of a major or minor quality in sound. Each song in "A Merry Modal Christmas" is in the minor mode.

## ACROSS THE CURRICULUM

▶ **Related Arts** During the holiday season, invite students to create their own decorations. Garlands can be made easily by stringing popcorn or cranberries on a thread. Paper garlands can be made by cutting strips of paper, linking them into a chain, and pasting them closed one at a time.

Pretty (and tasty) ornaments can be made of gingerbread cookie dough. Using any standard gingerbread recipe, roll out the dough and cut it with a "gingerbread man" (or "gingerbread woman") cookie cutter. Make a hole at the top with a straw. Decorate your cookie with raisins. Hard bake it in a cool oven. When cool, thread a ribbon through the hole, tie it, and hang the cookie on a tree.

56
grands guer-riers et les gar - des du tré - sor, Tout char - gés d'or les sui -
guard - ed close by a band of sturd-y war - riors, Their swords, their shields, and their
59
vant d'a - bord De grands guer - riers a - vec leurs bou - cli - eres.
buck - lers bright, a - gleam and spark-ling in the morn - ing light.
62
Ce ma - tin, j'ai ren-con-tré le train, De trois grands rois qui al - laient
This great day, I met up-on the way, The Kings of East as they came
62
Ce ma - tin, j'ai ren-con-tré le train, De trois grands
This great day, I met up-on the way, The Kings of
65
en - voy - a - ge, Ce ma - tin, j'ai ren-con-tré le train, De
rid - ing proud-ly, This great day, I met up-on the way, The
65
rois qui al - laient en - voy - a - ge, Ce ma - tin, j'ai ren-con-tré le
East as they came rid - ing proud-ly, This great day, I met up-on the
68
trois grands rois des-sus le grand che - min. Ce ma - tin,
Kings of East with all their fine ar - ray. This great day,
68
train, De trois grands rois des-sus le grand che - min. Ce ma -
way, The Kings of East with all their fine ar - ray. This great
71
Ce ma - tin, Ce ma - tin, ma - tin!
This great day, This great day, great day!
71
tin, Ce ma - tin, Ce ma - tin!
day, This great day, This great day!
Sing Out!
Unit 11 413

# 3 Close

**Element: TEXTURE/HARMONY** ASSESSMENT

**Performance/Observation** Have students

- Sing the *"Pat-a-pan"* ostinato and discuss its musical purpose.
- Sing the first phrase of each song and discuss how they are melodically different.
- Sing measures 62–73 and analyze how the canonic technique makes the song joyful. (Hint: Look at the words and rhythmic shape of the phrases.)

Have students perform "A Merry Modal Christmas" **CD 17-15** with groups assigned to sing ostinatos, parts, and in canon. Observe how successful students are in performing the three methods of creating harmony.

## Movement

▶ **Choreography** Here are suggestions for adding movement to performances of "A Merry Modal Christmas."

- For *"Pat-a-pan,"* have students stand tall and sing, moving their arms as if playing a drum to the continued rhythm of the ostinato.
- For "Coventry Carol," have students sway from side to side. Students should strive to sway in unison.
- For *"La marche des rois,"* have students stand still and gently tap the chest in a kingly fashion on the beat. During mm. 54–61, have students bend one leg at a time as if marching. During mm. 62–72, have them return to gently striking the chest.

## Technology/Media Link

**Notation Software** Have students use *la*$_{|}$, *ti*$_{|}$, *do, re,* and *mi* to write answer phrases to teacher-created question phrases. Before class begins, use a notation program to notate several four-measure question phrases in the key of A minor, followed by four blank measures. Print the file as a handout for each class member. Have students

- Listen to each phrase and learn to play it on classroom mallet or keyboard instruments.
- Explore answer phrases and notate them on the handout.
- Take turns using the computer learning center to enter their answer phrases in the blank measures of a notation file.
- Play back and print their work.

| Lesson | Elements | Skills | |
|---|---|---|---|
|  LESSON 1<br>**Sing in Peace**<br>pp. 418-421<br> | **Element: Rhythm**<br>**Concept:** Patterns<br>**Focus:** Repeated rhythm patterns<br><br>**Secondary Element**<br>Melody: melodic contour<br><br>**National Standards**<br>1a 1b 2b 2d 3b 5a | **Skill: Singing**<br>**Objective:** Sing repeated rhythm patterns in a song about peace<br><br>**Secondary Skills**<br>• **Analyzing/Reading** Read the melodic rhythm in a song<br>• **Playing** Create ostinatos to play on appropriate percussion instruments<br>• **Listening/Playing** Play a rhythm echo game with percussion instruments | **SKILLS REINFORCEMENT**<br>• **Vocal Development** Develop techniques for better singing |
| LESSON 2<br>**Movin' and Groovin' Is a "Boo"tiful Thing**<br>pp. 422-423<br> | **Element: Melody**<br>**Concept:** Pitch and direction<br>**Focus:** Limited-range melody<br><br>**Secondary Element**<br>Rhythm: ties<br><br>**National Standards**<br><br>2b 3d 6e 9e | **Skill: Playing**<br>**Objective:** Play a melody with a limited range<br><br>**Secondary Skills**<br>• **Singing** Sing a song, observing the pitch names<br>• **Moving** Create a backup singer routine | **SKILLS REINFORCEMENT**<br>• **Recorder** Play a seven-note accompaniment to a song |
| LESSON 3<br>**Holiday Harmony**<br>pp. 424-427<br> | **Element: Texture/Harmony**<br>**Concept:** Texture<br>**Focus:** Partner songs<br><br>**Secondary Element**<br>Form: verse and refrain<br><br>**National Standards**<br>1a 1d 2b 4b 6b 6e 7a | **Skill: Singing**<br>**Objective:** Sing two partner songs<br><br>**Secondary Skills**<br>• **Listening** Describe the texture and style of several songs<br>• **Creating** Create and notate nonpitched percussion accompaniments for a song<br>• **Performing** Perform songs in a winter holiday program | **SKILLS REINFORCEMENT**<br>• **Recorder** Play a countermelody to a song<br>• **Singing** Encourage self evaluation of performances |

Holidays and Celebrations

| Connections | Music and Other Literature | |
|---|---|---|
| **Connection:** Culture<br>**Activity:** Discuss important peacemakers from different cultures<br>**ACROSS THE CURRICULUM**<br>**Social Studies** Locate Jerusalem on a world map and discuss<br>**Language Arts** Collect poems, stories, and art about peace<br>**CULTURAL CONNECTION** **Israel** Geographical and historical facts<br>**SPOTLIGHT ON** **Peacemakers** Facts regarding Noble Peace Prize winners<br>**MOVEMENT** **Creative Movement** Create different ways to hold hands and link arms<br>**CHARACTER EDUCATION** **Peace** Discuss the importance of maintaining a peaceful environment<br>**BUILDING SKILLS THROUGH MUSIC** **Social Studies** Associate countries of the world with their nation's flag | **Song** *"Shir l'shalom"* ("Hand in Hand – A Song for Peace")<br><br>**More Music Choices**<br>"Put a Little Love in Your Heart," p. 6<br>"Limbo Like Me," p. 18<br>"All Night, All Day," p. 180"<br>"Love Can Build a Bridge," p. 324 | **ASSESSMENT**<br>**Performance/Observation** Accurately sing rhythm patterns in a song<br><br>**TECHNOLOGY/MEDIA LINK**<br>**Web Site** Learn more about Middle Eastern music<br>**Sequencing Software** Record a performance using a separate audio track |
| **Connection:** Related Arts<br>**Activity:** Research careers in musical theater<br>**SPOTLIGHT ON** **Little Shop of Horrors** History of the movie from screen to stage to screen<br>**ACROSS THE CURRICULUM**<br>**Related Arts** Explore different careers in theater<br>**Language Arts** Read and discuss a Halloween book<br>**BUILDING SKILLS THROUGH MUSIC** **Visual Arts** Create costumes for the character of a song | **Song** "Little Shop of Horrors"<br><br>**More Music Choices**<br>"We Go Together" from *Grease*, p. 44<br>"Over the Rainbow" from *The Wizard of Oz*, p. 140 | **ASSESSMENT**<br>**Performance/Observation** Play a limited-range melody on percussion instruments<br><br>**TECHNOLOGY/MEDIA LINK**<br>**Electronic Keyboard** Improvise a percussion accompaniment to a song |
| **Connection:** Science<br>**Activity:** Explore Winter in various climates<br>**MEETING INDIVIDUAL NEEDS** **English Language Learners** Monitor comprehension through oral retellings<br>**ACROSS THE CURRICULUM**<br>**Science/Language Arts** Read books about contrasting views of winter<br>**Art** Create paper program covers for a winter holiday concert<br>**TEACHER TO TEACHER** **Singing Partner Songs** Discuss strategies for successful partner song singing<br>**MOVEMENT** **Creative Movement** Play a mirror movement game using gestures one would do in the snow<br>**BUILDING SKILLS THROUGH MUSIC** **Language** Write a journal entry about favorite seasons | **Songs**<br>"Winter Fantasy"<br>"Let It Snow! Let It Snow! Let It Snow!"<br><br>**Listening Selection** *Let It Snow! Let It Snow! Let It Snow!*<br>**M*U*S*I*C M*A*K*E*R*S** Harry Connick, Jr.<br><br>**More Music Choices**<br>*"Ōsamu kosamu,"* p. 96<br>"Turn the World Around," p. 114<br>*"Sambalele,"* p. 397 | **ASSESSMENT**<br>**Performance/Observation** Perform two partner songs<br><br>**TECHNOLOGY/MEDIA LINK**<br>**Notation Software** Compose a harmony part for a song |

| Lesson | Elements | Skills | |
|---|---|---|---|
| LESSON 4 **Harmony in Chanukah** pp. 428-429   | **Element: Texture/Harmony**<br>**Concept:** Harmony<br>**Focus:** Two-chord song<br><br>**Secondary Element**<br>Melody: minor tonality<br><br>**National Standards**<br>1a 2b 8b | **Skill: Playing**<br>**Objective:** Play a two-chord accompaniment on mallet instruments<br><br>**Secondary Skills**<br>• **Singing** Sing a Ladino song using neutral syllables | **SKILLS REINFORCEMENT**<br>• **Signing** Perform a signing activity for a song |
| LESSON 5 **Christmas Rhythms** pp. 430-433   | **Element: Rhythm**<br>**Concept:** Meter<br>**Focus:** Meter changes<br><br>**Secondary Element**<br>Form: cumulative song<br><br>**National Standards**<br>1a 2b 4b 6b 6e | **Skill: Creating**<br>**Objective:** Create ostinatos to perform with a song that has meter changes<br><br>**Secondary Skills**<br>• **Singing** Sing a song about Christmas<br>• **Analyzing** Identify meter changes in a song<br>• **Playing** Create an instrumental accompaniment for a song<br>• **Listening** Listen to a choral recording to reinforce good singing<br>• **Reading** Read lyrics to practice a song in Spanish | **SKILLS REINFORCEMENT**<br>• **Recorder** Play a countermelody to a song<br>• **Keyboard** Play a two-handed accompaniment to a song<br>• **Creating** Create music with mixed meters |
| LESSON 6 **Kwanzaa—Hello and Goodbye** pp. 434-435    | **Element: Melody**<br>**Concept:** Pattern<br>**Focus:** Phrases<br><br>**Secondary Element**<br>Rhythm: upbeat<br><br>**National Standards**<br>1b 2f 4b | **Skill: Singing**<br>**Objective:** Sing a song with appropriate phrasing<br><br>**Secondary Skills**<br>• **Playing/Creating** Create and play two-measure rhythm patterns to accompany a song | **SKILLS REINFORCEMENT**<br>• **Creating** Create percussion ostinatos to accompany a song |

| Connections | Music and Other Literature | |
|---|---|---|
| **Connection: Culture**<br>**Activity:** Discuss the celebration of Chanukah<br>CULTURAL CONNECTION **Chanukah** Information about the origin and customs of Chanukah<br>SPOTLIGHT ON **The Song** Historical information about *"Ocho kandelikas"*<br>BUILDING SKILLS THROUGH MUSIC **Social Studies** Share stories of family culture and traditions | **Song** *"Ocho kandelikas"* ("Eight Little Candles")<br>**More Music Choices**<br>"I'm Gonna Sing," p. 33<br>"Over My Head," p. 118 | ASSESSMENT<br>**Performance/Observation**<br>Accompany a song using a guitar or mallet instruments<br>TECHNOLOGY/MEDIA LINK<br>**Electronic Keyboard**<br>Incorporate ideas for playing an accompaniment to a song |
| **Connection: Culture**<br>**Activity:** Discuss how Christmas is celebrated in Mexico<br>MEETING INDIVIDUAL NEEDS **English Language Learners** Use notecards to reinforce lyrical understanding<br>ACROSS THE CURRICULUM<br>**Language Arts/Writing** Read and discuss a book about Christmas<br>**Art** Create a *piñata* using *papier-maché*<br>CULTURAL CONNECTION<br>**Christmas in Mexico** History of the two-week *Las posadas* celebration<br>**Legend of the Poinsettia** Basic story of the legend<br>BUILDING SKILLS THROUGH MUSIC **Math** Calculate the total number of gifts given in a song | **Songs**<br>"The Twelve Days of Christmas"<br>*"Al quebrar la piñata"* ("*Piñata* Song")<br>**Listening Selections**<br>*Good King Wenceslas*<br>*Feliz Navidad*<br>**More Music Choices**<br>*"Cantando mentiras,"* p. 146<br>*"Los niños en España canton,"* p. 197 | ASSESSMENT<br>**Performance/Observation**<br>Create ostinatos in $\frac{2}{2}$ and $\frac{3}{4}$ time and perform them with a song<br>TECHNOLOGY/MEDIA LINK<br>**Electronic Keyboard**<br>Create sound effects for a song |
| **Connection: Culture**<br>**Activity:** Discuss Kwanzaa, an African American celebration<br>ACROSS THE CURRICULUM **Language Arts/Writing** Read and discuss a book about Kwanzaa<br>CULTURAL CONNECTION **Seven Principles of Kwanzaa** Discuss the significance of Kwanzaa in America<br>TEACHER TO TEACHER **Singing Holiday Songs** Present holidays in an educational context<br>BUILDING SKILLS THROUGH MUSIC **Social Studies** Compare and contrast two songs using a Venn diagram | **Song** *"Harambee"*<br>**More Music Choices**<br>"Somebody's Knockin' at Your Door," p. 53<br>"Over My Head," p. 118 | ASSESSMENT<br>**Performance/Observation**<br>Sing the song with appropriate phrasing and check against a list of criteria<br>TECHNOLOGY/MEDIA LINK<br>**Notation Software**<br>Create and notate ostinatos for a song |

| Lesson | Elements | Skills |
|---|---|---|

## LESSON 7 Guide Our Hope

pp. 436-437

**Element: Melody**
**Concept:** Tonality
**Focus:** Major scale

**Secondary Element**
Form: verse and refrain

**National Standards**
2b 5a 5b 5d 8b

**Skill: Playing**
**Objective:** Play the melody of a song in a major tonality

**Secondary Skills**
- **Analyzing** Determine the scale of a song
- **Reading** Read a song with pitch and rhythm syllables

**SKILLS REINFORCEMENT**
- **Listening/Playing** Review suggestions for teaching students to play by ear

## LESSON 8 Creating Living Traditions

pp. 438-439

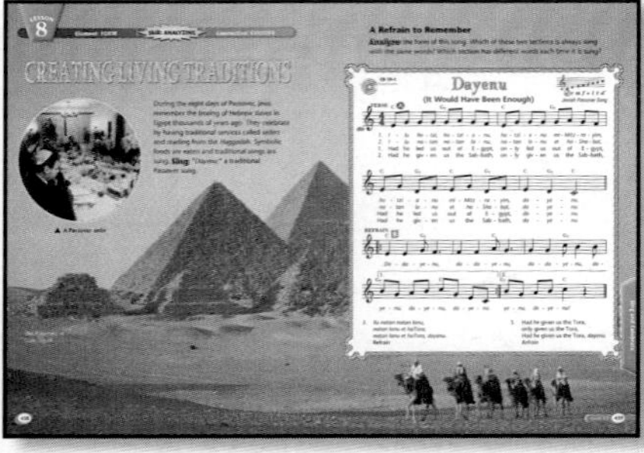


**Element: Form**
**Concept:** Form
**Focus:** Verse-and-refrain form

**Secondary Element**
Expression: tempo

**National Standards**
2b 4b 6b 6c

**Skill: Analyzing**
**Objective:** Analyze a song to discover its form

**Secondary Skills**
- **Playing** Play a recorder accompaniment for a song
- **Creating** Create different ways to perform a song

**SKILLS REINFORCEMENT**
- **Playing** Play the melody of a song on a pitched instrument
- **Mallets** Play an Orff accompaniment to a song

## LESSON 9 Heartbeat of a Nation

pp. 440-441

**Element: Rhythm**
**Concept:** Meter
**Focus:** Meter in 3

**Secondary Element**
Melody: melodic contour

**National Standards**
1c 1e 6b 6e

**Skill: Moving**
**Objective:** Move to show meter in 3

**Secondary Skills**
- **Listening** Determine the meter of a song
- **Singing** Sing a song using proper breath support

**SKILLS REINFORCEMENT**
- **Singing** Review suggestions for teaching students to memorize the national anthem

| Connections | Music and Other Literature | |
|---|---|---|
| **Connection: Social Studies**<br>**Activity:** Discuss the American Civil Rights movement<br>ACROSS THE CURRICULUM **Social Studies** Read and discuss a book about Martin Luther King. Jr.<br>CULTURAL CONNECTION **Civil Rights Movement** Discuss the treatment of African Americans during the 1960s<br>CHARACTER EDUCATION **Character Traits** Discuss the traits shared by people who were active in the Civil Rights movement<br>BUILDING SKILLS THROUGH MUSIC **Social Studies** Identify the teaching of Dr. King in a song | **Song** "We Shall Not Be Moved"<br>**More Music Choices**<br>"Gonna Ride up in the Chariot," p. 20<br>"America," p. 206 | ASSESSMENT<br>**Performance/Observation** Play a melody in major tonality on mallet instruments<br>TECHNOLOGY/MEDIA LINK<br>**Notation Software** Create six-note melodies |
| **Connection: Culture**<br>**Activity:** Discuss the Jewish holiday of Passover<br>ACROSS THE CURRICULUM **Social Studies** Read and discuss books about Passover<br>CULTURAL CONNECTION **Passover** Facts about the traditional Passover meal<br>BUILDING SKILLS THROUGH MUSIC **Language** Discuss the meaning of the lyrics of a song | **Song** *"Dayenu"* ("It Would Have Been Enough")<br>**More Music Choices**<br>*"La Tarara,"* p. 176<br>"All Night, All day," p. 180 | ASSESSMENT<br>**Interview** Find other songs in the book in verse-and-refrain form<br>TECHNOLOGY/MEDIA LINK<br>**Electronic Keyboard** Accompany a song using I and $V_7$ chords |
| **Connection: Social Studies**<br>**Activity:** Discuss the history of the writing of the national anthem<br>ACROSS THE CURRICULUM **Social Studies/Art** Read and discuss a book concerning the history of the United States of America<br>SPOTLIGHT ON **The National Anthem** Historical information about the lyrical inspiration for "The Star-Spangled Banner"<br>BUILDING SKILLS THROUGH MUSIC **Language** Rewrite the lyrics of a song | **Songs**<br>"America"<br>"The Star-Spangled Banner"<br>**More Music Choices**<br>*"Santa Clara,"* p. 172<br>*"Doraji,"* p. 174<br>"America, the Beautiful," p. 158 | ASSESSMENT<br>**Performance/Observation** Conduct songs in $\frac{3}{4}$ time<br>TECHNOLOGY/MEDIA LINK<br>**Web Site** Learn more about Francis Scott Key and Samuel Francis Smith<br>**Electronic Keyboard** Use the "drum set" to accompany several songs |

# Introducing the Unit

Unit 12 presents a thematic approach to understanding music elements. Everyone enjoys a celebration and this unit adds to the festivities by providing the music. Students will enjoy singing these songs during special occasions. Presented on p. 415 is a brief overview of the skills that are assessed in this unit.

See below and pp. 416–417 for unit highlights of related curricular experiences. For a more detailed unit overview, see Unit at a Glance, pp. 413a–413f.

# Unit Project

Have students create a chart entitled "Events to Celebrate." Construct the chart in three columns. Write the name of the event in the first column, when the celebration occurs in the second column (*note:* "when" does not mean a specific date), and music used for the celebration in the third column. (Multiple entries may be included in the third column.)

Encourage students to plan a "Celebrations!" performance using songs and dances they learn in this unit or have them plan the music for a school or community celebration. Help students determine a musical goal for each song included in their program. Ask them to assess their performance using their own goals.

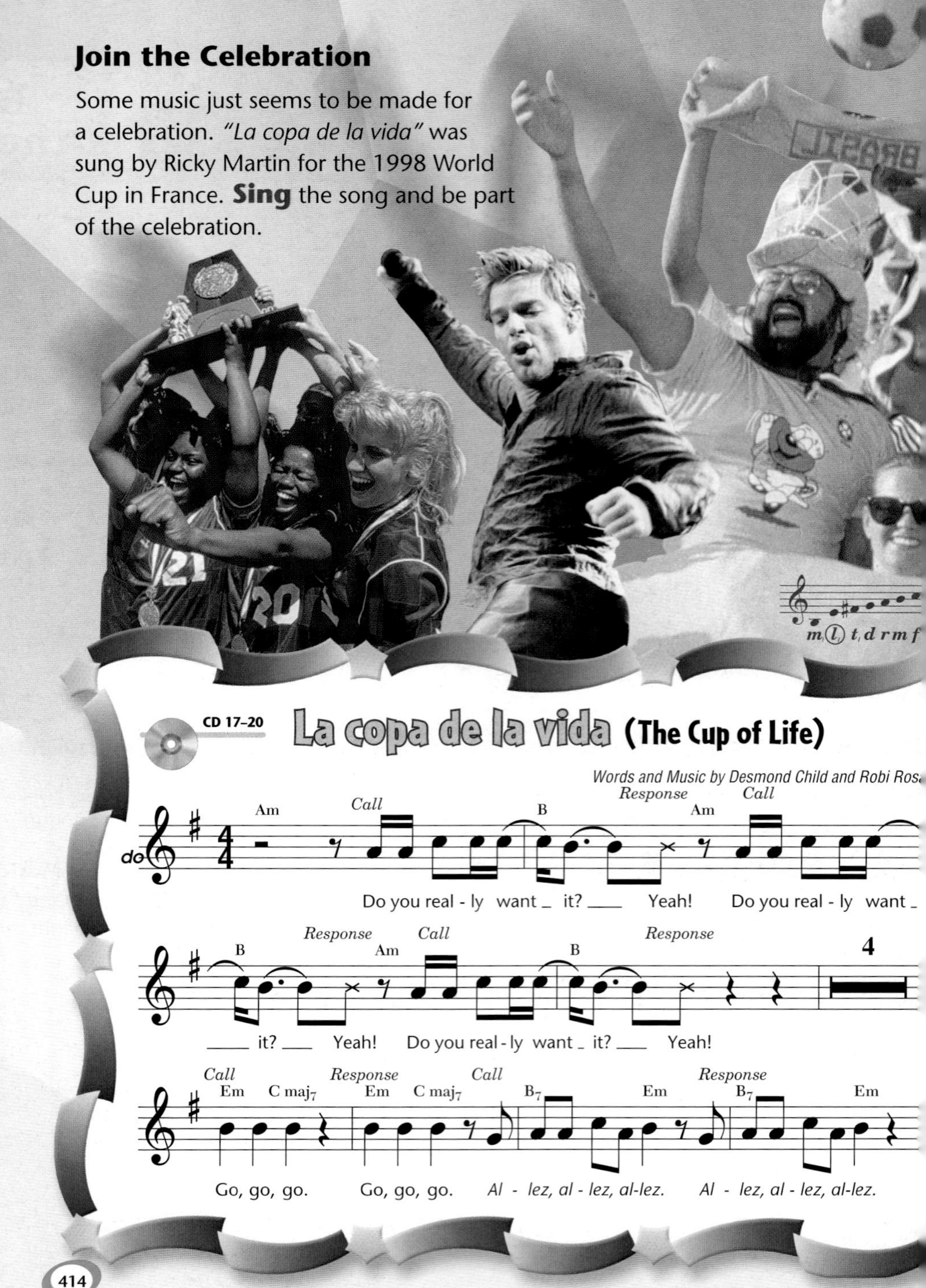

**Join the Celebration**

Some music just seems to be made for a celebration. *"La copa de la vida"* was sung by Ricky Martin for the 1998 World Cup in France. **Sing** the song and be part of the celebration.

m l t, d r m f
CD 17-20
La copa de la vida (The Cup of Life)
Words and Music by Desmond Child and Robi Rosa
Call Response Call
Am B Am
do
Do you real - ly want _ it? ___ Yeah! Do you real - ly want _
Response Call Response
B Am B
4
___ it? ___ Yeah! Do you real - ly want _ it? ___ Yeah!
Call Response Call Response
Em C maj7 Em C maj7 B7 Em B7 Em
Go, go, go. Go, go, go. Al - lez, al - lez, al-lez. Al - lez, al - lez, al-lez.
414

## Across the Curriculum

**Unit Highlights** The following interdisciplinary activities in this unit are related to the music elements or themes presented in the lessons. See Unit at a Glance, pp. 413a-413f, for topical descriptions presented according to lesson sequence.

**▶ ART/RELATED ARTS**

- Research different professions involved with creating musicals (p. 422)
- Create a program cover for a holiday concert (p. 427)
- Make a *piñata* out of *papier-mâché* (p. 432)
- Create holiday decorations (p. 412)
- Create illustrations for the national anthem (p. 440)

**▶ LANGUAGE ARTS**

- Collect songs, poems, stories, and art about peace for a class project (p. 420)
- Read a Halloween book (p. 422)
- Read various books about winter (p. 424)
- Read a humorous book about Christmas thank-you letters; write a thank-you letter (p. 430)
- Read a book about Kwanzaa; write about a special family member (p. 434)

**▶ SOCIAL STUDIES**

- Locate Jerusalem on a world map and read about its origins (p. 418)
- Read books about Dr. Martin Luther King, Jr (p. 436)
- Read books about the history and customs of Passover (p. 438)
- Read a book about the history of the United States flag (p. 440)

**▶ SCIENCE**

- Compare perspectives on winter in various books (p. 424)

UNIT 12

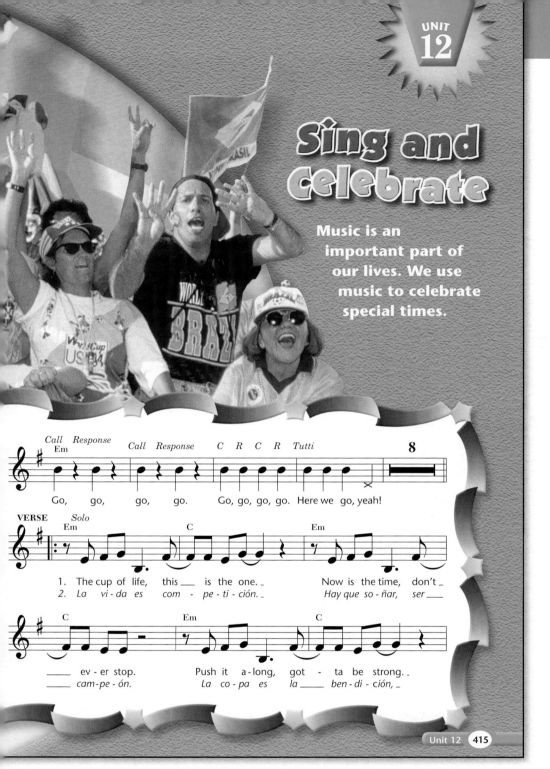

# Sing and Celebrate

**Music is an important part of our lives. We use music to celebrate special times.**

Unit 12 415

## Music Skills Assessed in This Unit

### Reading Music: Rhythm

- Read and identify repeated rhythms (p. 419)
- Read the rhythm of a song using rhythm syllables (p. 437)

### Reading Music: Pitch

- Read the melody of a song using pitch syllables and hand signs (p. 437)

### Performing Music: Singing

- Sing using good vocal technique (p. 421)
- Sing partner songs about Christmas (p. 427)

### Moving to Music

- Create backup singer movements (p. 423)
- Conduct meter in 3 while singing (p. 441)

### Performing Music: Playing

- Play a section of a song on mallet instruments (p. 423)
- Perform two-measure ostinatos to accompany a Christmas song (p. 427)
- Accompany a Chanukah song on guitars and mallet instruments (p. 429)
- Perform an ostinato (p. 435)
- Accurately play a song melody on mallet instruments (p. 437)

### Creating Music

- Compose nonpitched percussion accompaniments (p. 427)
- Create two-measure ostinatos (p. 433)
- Create two-measure percussion ostinatos for a Kwanzaa song (p. 435)

### Listening to Music

- Listen to a popular Christmas song recorded in a jazz style (p. 426)
- Listen to a choral piece (p. 432)

## Cultural Connection

**Unit Highlights** The musical literature in this unit provides many opportunities for students to explore a variety of world cultures. See Unit at a Glance, pp. 413a–413f, for topical descriptions presented according to lesson sequence.

▶ **AFRICAN AMERICAN**

- Learn about the seven principles of Kwanzaa (p. 434)
- Read about the American Civil Rights movement (p. 436)

▶ **AMERICAN**

- "America" (p. 440); "The Star-Spangled Banner" (p. 441)

▶ **EUROPEAN**

- "The Twelve Days of Christmas" (p. 430)

▶ **LATIN AMERICAN**

- Learn about Christmas in Mexico (p. 431)
- Read the legend of the poinsettia (p. 433)

▶ **MIDDLE EASTERN**

- Learn about Israel (p. 418)
- Learn about the origins of Chanukah (p. 428)
- Read about the Jewish holiday Passover (p. 438)

# Opening Activities

**MATERIALS**

- *"La copa de la vida"* ("The Cup of Life") **CD 17-20**
  **Recording Routine:**
  Intro ( 4 m.); vocal
- **Pronunciation Practice/Translation** p. 495
- **Resource Book** p. A-45
- classroom instruments

## Analyzing

Ask students to look at *"La copa de la vida."* Explain that there is an introduction, a verse section with two verses, and a refrain. Point out that the verse section is a solo, which was sung by singer Ricky Martin for the soccer 1998 World Cup in France.

Ask students to look at the introduction section (the part before the verse). Point out the call-and-response style. Ask students to find other places in the song that are in call-and-response style. (refrain)

## Singing

Invite students to listen to the Pronunciation Practice for *"La copa de la vida"* **CD 17-22** and sing with the students on the recording. For the Pronunciation Practice Guide, refer to Resource Book p. A-45.

Have students speak the words of the introduction and the refrain in rhythm. Then divide the class into two groups. Along with the recording **CD 17-20**, have one group sing the calls and the other group sing the responses. Invite everyone to sing the *tutti* sections. Those that feel comfortable singing the verse should be invited to do so.

# Assessment

**Unit Highlights** The lessons in this unit were chosen and developed to support the theme "Sing and Celebrate." Each lesson, as always, presents a clear element focus, a skill objective, and an end-of-lesson assessment. The overall sequence of lessons, however, is organized according to this theme, rather than concept development. In this context, formal assessment strategies, such as those presented in Units 1–6, are no longer applicable.

**▶ INFORMAL ASSESSMENTS**

At the close of each Teacher's Edition lesson in this unit, one of the following types of assessments is used to evaluate the learning of the key element focus or skill objective.

- Interviews (p. 439)
- Performance/Observation (pp. 421, 423, 427, 429, 433, 435, 437, 441)

**▶ RUBRICS**

Visit *www.sfsuccessnet.com* for rubrics to assess students' achievement in music skills.

## Tune In

Every four years, the best soccer teams from around the world play in a month-long tournament called the World Cup. The first World Cup took place in 1930 and was won by Uruguay.

Coda Em Call B Response Call Response Call

Al - lez, al-lez, al-lez, al-lez. Al - lez, al-lez, al-lez, al-lez. Al -

B Response Tutti 1. Em Call

lez, al - lez, al - lez, al - lez. Al - lez, al - lez, al - lez. Al -

2. B Em Call Am B Response

lez, al-lez, al-lez. Yeah! Do you real-ly want it? Yeah!

Unit 12 417

### Moving

Have students create movements that show contrast between the sections of the song.

### Improvising

Invite students to create ostinatos to accompany *"La copa de la vida"* **CD 17-20.** Have them tap or clap the ostinato as they listen to the recording, then transfer to a nonpitched percussion instrument. Encourage students to balance the volume of the ostinatos and their singing as they perform.

### Innovative Teacher Support for This Unit

- **Making Music DVD, Grade 4** contains video segments that support lessons, including signing and movement.
- **Making Music with Movement and Dance** provides more opportunities for large group activities in music or physical education classes.
- **Making Music with Technology** provides lesson plans for many technology applications; includes MIDI files.
- ***¡A cantar!*** features recorded songs and lessons from around the Spanish-speaking world; includes strategies for bilingual classes and for English-speaking teachers working with Spanish-speaking students.
- **Bridges to Asia** features recorded songs and lessons from Asian and Pacific region cultures.
- ***www.sfsuccessnet.com*** provides an online lesson planner to conveniently create lesson plans at school or at home. Includes rubrics for assessment, lesson modifications to meet the needs of all students, performance musicals based on program content, and more.

## Technology/Media Link

**Unit Highlights** The following components are used in this unit to reinforce and expand students' understanding of music elements and related themes. See Unit at a Glance, pp. 413a–413f, for a descriptive listing according to lesson sequence.

▶ **ELECTRONIC KEYBOARD**

- Improvise a percussion accompaniment using the drum kits (p. 423)
- Accompany a Chanukah song on electronic keyboard (p. 429)
- Enhance a Christmas song with song effects (p. 433)
- Use electronic keyboard to accompany a Passover song (p. 439)
- Play "drum set" with two patriotic songs (p. 441)

▶ **MIDI/SEQUENCING SOFTWARE**

- Use digital audio tracks to record group performances (p. 421)

▶ **NOTATION SOFTWARE**

- Compose and notate a harmony part for "Let It Snow! Let It Snow! Let It Snow!" (p. 427)
- Notate ostinatos (p. 435)
- Create and notate six-note melodies (p. 437)

▶ **WEB SITE**

- Go to *www.sfsuccessnet.com* to find more information about music from Israel and the Middle East (p. 421) and more about "The Star-Spangled Banner," "America," and the composers (p. 441)

LESSON 1

## LESSON AT A GLANCE

**Element Focus** **RHYTHM** Repeated rhythm patterns

**Skill Objective** **SINGING** Sing repeated rhythm patterns in a song about peace

**Connection Activity** **CULTURE** Discuss important peacemakers from different cultures

**MATERIALS**

- *"Shir l'shalom"* **CD 17-23**
- "Hand in Hand—A Song for Peace" **CD 17-24**
  **Recording Routine:** Intro (4 m.); vocal
- **Pronunciation Practice/Translation** p. 496
- **Resource Book** p. A-46
- selected nonpitched percussion instruments

**VOCABULARY**

rhythm pattern

**◆◆◆◆ National Standards ◆◆◆◆**

**1a** Sing independently with appropriate posture and diction
**1b** Sing expressively with appropriate interpretation
**2b** Perform rhythms on appropriate instruments
**2d** Play instruments, echoing rhythms
**3b** Improvise rhythmic ostinato accompaniments
**5a** Read rhythms in $\frac{4}{4}$ meter

**MORE MUSIC CHOICES**

Other songs with repeating rhythm patterns:
"Put a Little Love in Your Heart," p. 6
"Limbo Like Me," p. 18
"All Night, All Day," p. 180
"Love Can Build a Bridge," p. 324

LESSON 1 Element: RHYTHM Skill: SINGING Connection: CULTURE

# SING in Peace

Yitzhak Rabin
▼ Nobel Peace Pr

This song from Israel could be from any country. The message is universal—peace in our world. Israel's Prime Minister, Yitzhak Rabin, was working for peace when he was assassinated. A copy of this song was found in his pocket.

Look at the song *"Shir l'shalom."* Notice the melodic rhythm is repeated many times. Clap the rhythm of the first phrase.

Now we're ready to **sing** the song.

▲ Jane Addams
Nobel Peace Prize, 1931

418

# Footnotes

## ACROSS THE CURRICULUM

▶ **Social Studies** Invite students to locate Jerusalem on a world map. Where is it? What countries border Israel?

Read aloud *The Two Brothers: A Legend of Jerusalem* by Neil Waldman (Atheneum, 1997), and invite students to learn more about the tale of sibling love that accounts for the origins of Jerusalem.

## BUILDING SKILLS THROUGH MUSIC

▶ **Social Studies** Have students look at the flags that border pp. 419–421. Provide students with resources to research and identify each flag's country. Then ask them to locate the various countries on a world map or globe.

## CULTURAL CONNECTION

▶ **Israel** Israel is situated at the eastern edge of the Mediterranean Sea. It was established in 1948 as a homeland for Jewish people. It is bordered by Egypt, Jordan, Syria, and Lebanon. Israel has fought many wars with its Arab neighbors. Peace in the Middle East seems to be a difficult prospect. Yitzhak Rabin served twice as Prime Minister of Israel. He worked hard to try to make peace with Israel's neighboring countries. Rabin was shot on November 4, 1995, by a man who did not agree with his views.

CD 17-23
Shir l'shalom
(Hand in Hand–A Song for Peace)
s, l, t, d r m f fi s l
Hebrew Words by Jacob Rotblitt
English Adaptation by Stanley Ralph Ross and Michael Isaacson
Music by Yair Rosenblum
Arranged by Michael Isaacson
Cm Fm B♭7
do
1. Tnu la - she - mesh la - a - lot, la - bo - ker l' - ha -
2. Tnu la - she - mesh la - cha - dor mi - ba - 'ad la - pra -
1. Ev - 'ry day, the sun will rise and shine u - pon our
2. As we gath - er side by side to plead for what we
E♭ Cm Fm
ir. Ha - za - kah she - ba - tfi - lot o -
chim. Al ta - bi - tu l' - a - chor, ha -
land, Urg - ing us to re - a - lize we
need, Throw a - way mis - ta - ken pride and
G Cm
ta - nu lo tach zir. Mi a - sher ka -
ni - chu la - hol - chim. Su ey - na - yim
must walk hand - in - hand. Peo - ple who were
peace will then suc - ceed. Broth - ers will em -
Fm B♭7 E♭
va ne - ro u - v' - a - far nit - man,
b' - tik - vah, lo de - rech ka - va - not.
once at war at last will un - der - stand,
brace a - gain and sis - ters will u - nite,
Cm Fm
Be - chi mar lo ya - i - ro lo
Shi - ru shir la - a - ha - vah, v' -
It's a sign we can't ig - nore, we
Ev - 'ry day we live in peace will
Sing and Celebrate
Unit 12 419

# 1 Introduce

Talk with students about peace. Ask if they can think of any symbols of peace. (dove, peace sign, and so on) Discuss what it would mean if everyone in the world could live peacefully together. Invite students to identify the national flags that border the pages of this lesson.

Then share the information about several famous Nobel Peace Prize recipients. Refer to Spotlight On below and on p. 420. Have students reference the pictures in their books as you discuss the peacemakers.

**SAY** This song of peace is from Israel, but the words could be from any country in the world. The message of peace is universal. We all want to have peace in our world.

Play *"Shir l'shalom"* **CD 17-23.** After listening, discuss with students the meaning of the words.

# 2 Develop

### Analyzing/Reading

5a Help students identify the melodic rhythm that is repeated many times in this song. Invite students to clap and say the rhythm of the first four measures of *"Shir l'shalom."*

Have students find another phrase in the song that has the same rhythm as the first line. (mm. 9–12)

Then encourage students to look at measures 5–8, and find another phrase with the same rhythm. (mm. 13–16)

continued on page 420

## Spotlight On

▶ **Peacemakers** Yitzhak Rabin (1922–1995), born in Jerusalem, was prime minister of Israel from 1974 to 1977, then again from 1992 until his death in 1995. In 1994, he shared the Nobel Peace Prize with Israeli foreign minister Shimon Peres and Palestinian leader Yasir Arafat.

Jane Addams (1860–1935) was a social worker and human rights activist who won the Nobel Peace Prize in 1931. She founded a settlement house, with programs ranging from day care to college courses for the people of Chicago.

Mother Teresa (1910–1997) was a Catholic nun who spent her adult life caring for the poor and dying. She received the Nobel Peace Prize in 1979.

## Movement

▶ **Creative Movement** To highlight the image of friendship and peace, have students work with a partner and invent two different ways to hold hands. Next, have the partners invent two different ways to link arms. Have the partners change and teach each other their hand holds and arm links. Finally, have students form a circle and connect to the person next to them sequentially, in an inventive and friendly way.

### Singing

Before singing, discuss elements of good-quality, expressive singing. To help students sing more expressively, encourage them to

- Take deep breaths before each phrase of music to help produce a good tone.
- Pronounce each word clearly.
- Hold whole notes for their full value.

Remind students to think about these hints as they sing.

1b Invite students to listen to the Pronunciation Practice for *"Shir l'shalom"* **CD 17-26** and then have them sing with the students on the recording. Refer to Resource Book p. A-46 for the Pronunciation Practice Guide. After students are comfortable with the Hebrew words, have them sing with the Stereo Performance Track **CD 17-25.**

### Playing

2b 3b Form small groups and ask students to create ostinatos to perform on nonpitched percussion instruments to accompany *"Shir l'shalom"* **CD 17-23.** If possible, offer a variety of instruments from which to choose. Help students decide on appropriate rhythms for each instrument. When groups are confident with their accompaniments, invite each group to perform for the class.

## Footnotes

### Across the Curriculum

▶ **Language Arts** Start a class project of collecting songs, poems, stories, and art about peace. Students should be able to discuss the content of each selection. Encourage students to write their own poems about peace.

### Character Education

▶ **Peace** Ask students to describe behaviors that disrupt peace. (arguing, complaining, disobeying rules) Discuss why these behaviors are detrimental to peace and brainstorm alternative, peaceful responses. (forgiveness, kindness, respect) Question students about peacemakers in their lives. What characteristics make them peacemakers? How would you rate yourself as a peacemaker? How would your friends, parents, and teachers rate you as a peacemaker? Encourage students to discuss and defend their responses.

### Spotlight On

▶ **More Peacemakers** Nelson Mandela (b. 1918) served as South Africa's first black president. He spent much of his life working against *apartheid,* or racial segregation. For his efforts, he was imprisoned for 27 years. Mandela was released from prison February 11, 1990. Eventually the *apartheid* laws were overturned in the early 1990s, and Mandela shared the Nobel Peace Prize in 1993 with another South African, F. W. de Klerck.

Aung San Suu Kyi (b. 1945) is a Burmese pro-democracy and pro-human rights activist. She went to college in England, married a British professor, and had two children. In 1998 Suu Kyi returned to Burma to care for her mother and became involved in politics. The Burmese government kept her under house arrest from 1989 to 1995. In 1991 Suu Kyi won the Nobel Peace Prize.

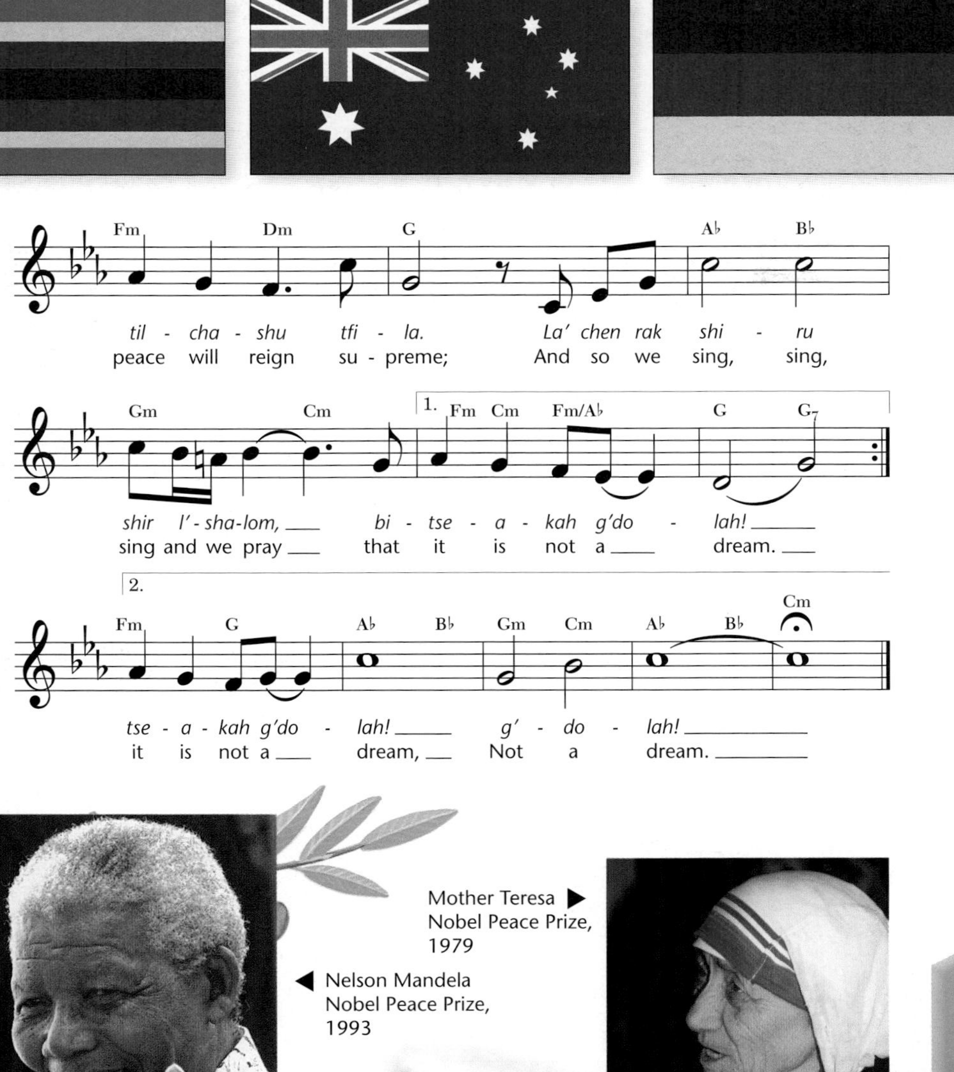


Mother Teresa ▶
Nobel Peace Prize, 1979

◀ Nelson Mandela
Nobel Peace Prize, 1993

Aung San Suu Kyi ▶
Nobel Peace Prize, 1991

Sing and Celebrate

Unit 12 421

### Listening/Playing

 Invite students to play this rhythm game.

- Have each student choose a percussion instrument. Be sure that at least four or five students choose drums.
- Play the rhythm of mm. 1–4 of *"Shir l'shalom"* for the class.
-  Ask them to echo it on their instruments.
- Play and have students echo play other rhythm patterns not necessarily in the song.
- Insert the song rhythm every few examples.
- Whenever the rhythm of *"Shir l'shalom"* mm. 1–4 is played, only the drum players should respond.
- All students should listen carefully and play only at the appropriate time.

## 3 Close

Skill: SINGING — ASSESSMENT

**Performance/Observation** Have students form small groups and sing *"Shir l'shalom"* **CD 17-23,** using the proper singing techniques discussed earlier in the lesson. Observe each group's ability to accurately sing the repeated rhythm patterns in the song.

### Skills Reinforcement

1a ▶ **Vocal Development** This is a good time to remind students to use good posture, breathing, and support techniques while singing. Encourage students to sit upright in their chairs, away from the back of the chair, with both feet on the floor. Ask them to raise their music to eye level so that they can keep their heads upright and to relax their shoulders. If students are standing, have them keep their feet about a shoulder width apart. Remind them not to lock their knees. Invite students to breathe as if they were sipping a milkshake through a straw, or slurping a long strand of spaghetti. Breathing like this allows them to take in a great deal of air while keeping the throat open. Encourage students to push their navel toward their backbone to support their singing—not to push from the throat.

### Technology/Media Link

**Web Site** Students may be interested in learning more about music from Israel and the Middle East. Have them visit *www.sfsuccessnet.com.*

**Sequencing Software** After students are able to play the percussion parts they created in the lesson, use digital audio tracks on sequencing software to record each group's performance in a separate audio track.

LESSON 2

## LESSON AT A GLANCE

**Element Focus** **MELODY** Limited-range melody

**Skill Objective** **PLAYING** Play a melody with a limited range

**Connection Activity** **RELATED ARTS** Research careers in musical theater

**MATERIALS**

- "Little Shop of Horrors" **CD 18-1**
  **Recording Routine:** Intro (4 m.); vocal; coda
- **Resource Book** p. I-30
- xylophones

**VOCABULARY**

range

**National Standards**

**2b** Perform melodies on appropriate instruments
**3d** Improvise instrumental pieces, using electronic sounds
**6e** While listening to music, move to show a prominent feature of the music
**9e** Demonstrate appropriate audience behavior

**MORE MUSIC CHOICES**

Other songs from musicals or movies:
"We Go Together" from *Grease*, p. 44
"Over the Rainbow" from *The Wizard of Oz*, p. 140

# 1 INTRODUCE

Talk about Halloween—a scary, fun-filled celebration. Then introduce "Little Shop of Horrors," a song from a scary show, using the information in Spotlight On below. Play the song **CD 18-1** and ask students to listen for the limited range of the melody.

Invite volunteers to research careers in musical theater and report to the class. See Across the Curriculum below.

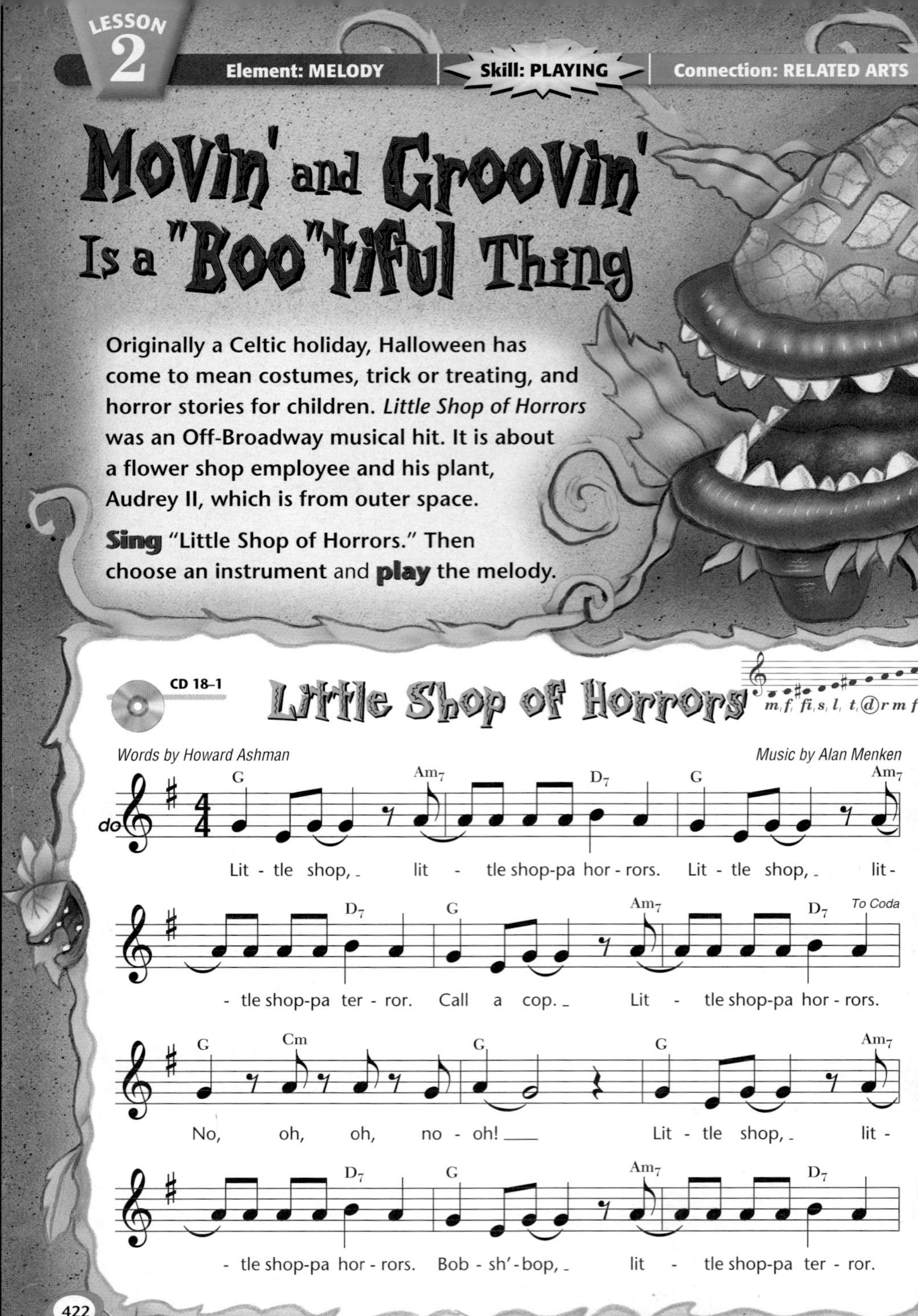

LESSON 2
Element: MELODY
Skill: PLAYING
Connection: RELATED ARTS
Movin' and Groovin' Is a "Boo"tiful Thing
Originally a Celtic holiday, Halloween has come to mean costumes, trick or treating, and horror stories for children. Little Shop of Horrors was an Off-Broadway musical hit. It is about a flower shop employee and his plant, Audrey II, which is from outer space.
Sing "Little Shop of Horrors." Then choose an instrument and play the melody.
CD 18-1
Little Shop of Horrors
Words by Howard Ashman
Music by Alan Menken
Lit - tle shop, lit - tle shop-pa hor - rors. Lit - tle shop, lit - tle shop-pa ter - ror. Call a cop. Lit - tle shop-pa hor - rors.
To Coda
No, oh, oh, no - oh! Lit - tle shop, lit - tle shop-pa hor - rors. Bob - sh'-bop, lit - tle shop-pa ter - ror.
422


# Footnotes

## SPOTLIGHT ON

▶ ***Little Shop of Horrors*** *Little Shop of Horrors* was originally a 1960 movie. Alan Menken and Howard Ashman took the story and made it into a musical, which opened Off-Broadway in 1982. The musical was made into another movie starring Rick Moranis, Steve Martin, and Ellen Greene in 1986. The story tells about Seymour, a flower-shop employee, his man-eating plant, named Audrey II, and his love for a girl named Audrey.

## BUILDING SKILLS THROUGH MUSIC

▶ **Visual Arts** Invite students to sing "Little Shop of Horrors" **CD 18-1.** Ask them to imagine how costumes for Audrey II might look. Provide students with paper, crayons, markers, and any other necessary supplies to design costumes for Audrey II.

## ACROSS THE CURRICULUM

▶ **Related Arts** Staging a musical show involves many people with different talents. Encourage students to research the different professions involved in creating a musical. They include scene designer, set builder, actor, dancer, producer, director, conductor, musician, choreographer, costume designer, and costume maker.

▶ **Language Arts** Share the book *13 Monsters Who Should Be Avoided* by Kevin Shortsleeve (Peachtree, 1998). This is a great read-aloud book for Halloween. Students will love these 13 newly invented monsters!

Watch 'em drop. Lit - tle shop-pa hor-rors. No, oh, oh, no - oh!
Shing-a - ling, what a creep-y thing to be hap - pen-ing! (Look
out, look out, look out, look out!) Shang-a-lang, feel the *Sturm* and *Drang* in the
air. (Yeah, yeah, yeah.) Sha - la - la,
stop right where you are. Don't move a thing. You bet - ter,
you bet - ter, tell - in' you, you bet - ter tell your ma-ma
some-thin's gon - na get her. She bet - ter,
ev-'ry-bod-y bet-ter be-ware. (Come-a come-a come-a.)
D. C. al Coda
Coda
No, oh, oh, no, oh, oh, no, oh, oh, no!
Sing and Celebrate
Unit 12 423

# 2 Develop

## Singing

After students have listened to "Little Shop of Horrors" **CD 18-1,** ask volunteers to sing any parts of the song they can remember. Point out that most of the song is centered around four different pitches (E, G, A, B). Help students learn to sing the entire song.

## Playing

2b Using pitched mallet instruments such as xylophones, encourage students to play as much of "Little Shop of Horrors" as they can by ear. Give them the starting pitch (G), as well as opportunities to hear, sing, and play the song "in the air" before playing it on instruments.

## Moving

6e Ask students to think of times when they have seen backup singers performing with a soloist. Have them share their answers. Divide the class into groups of three or four, and have students

- Choose solo phrases from p. 423 for each person to sing.
- Create backup singer movements to perform while singing "Little Shop of Horrors" **CD 18-1.**
- Practice doing their movements and solos in small groups.
- 9e Take turns performing their group's version of "Little Shop of Horrors" for the rest of the class.

# 3 Close

**Skill: PLAYING** — **ASSESSMENT**

**Performance/Observation** Have students sing "Little Shop of Horrors" **CD 18-1** while playing mm. 1–16 on a mallet instrument. Observe each student's ability to accurately perform the limited-range melody.

## Skills Reinforcement

▶ **Recorder** For practice playing low D, low E, G, A, B, C, and D on the recorder, invite students to play the accompaniment for "Little Shop of Horrors" on Resource Book p. I-30.

## Technology/Media Link

3d **Electronic Keyboard** Use electronic keyboards to help students improvise a percussion accompaniment for "Little Shop of Horrors." Have them

- Use the drum kits on electronic keyboards and classroom percussion to improvise a rock 'n' roll drum beat.
- Select a bass drum voice to play a ♩. ♪ ♩ ♩ pattern.
- Select a ride cymbal to play repeated eighths.
- Select a snare sound to play on beats two and four.
- Add other percussion sounds and patterns.

Other students may play a bass line or chordal pattern.

LESSON 3

## LESSON AT A GLANCE

**Element Focus** **TEXTURE/HARMONY** Partner songs

**Skill Objective** **SINGING** Sing two partner songs

**Connection Activity** **SCIENCE** Explore winter in various climates

**MATERIALS**

- "Winter Fantasy" **CD 18-3**
  **Recording Routine:** Intro (4 m.); vocal
- "Let It Snow! Let It Snow! Let It Snow!" **CD 18-5**
  **Recording Routine:** Intro (4 m.); vocal; interlude (8 m.); bridge; coda
- *Let It Snow! Let It Snow! Let It Snow!* **CD 18-7**
- nonpitched percussion instruments, sleighbells

**VOCABULARY**

partner songs

### ◆◆◆◆ National Standards ◆◆◆◆

**1a** Sing independently on pitch and in rhythm
**1d** Sing part songs
**2b** Perform melodies on appropriate instruments
**4b** Compose instrumental pieces within specific guidelines
**6b** Describe music by answering questions about it
**6e** While listening to music, move to show a prominent feature of the music
**7a** Create standards for evaluating performances

**MORE MUSIC CHOICES**

Another cold-weather song:
*"Ōsamu kosamu,"* p. 96
Other partner songs:
"Turn the World Around," p. 114
*"Sambalele,"* p. 397

LESSON 3 Element: TEXTURE/HARMONY | Skill: SINGING | Connection: SCIENCE

# Holiday Harmony

The shortest day of the year occurs on the winter solstice, December 21 or 22. In the northern parts of the world, snow, ice, and cold are associated with winter. This song paints a picture of a cold winter day. **Sing** the partner song "Winter Fantasy" and imagine the picture the song creates.

CD 18-3

## Winter Fantasy

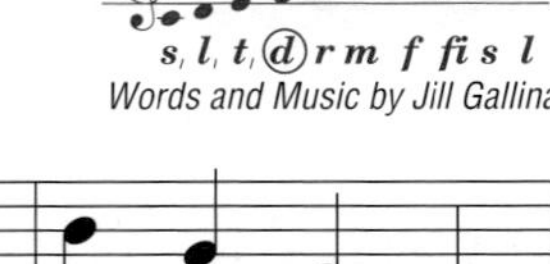


Words and Music by Jill Gallina

Part I

Snow-flakes fall - ing all o - ver town, slip - ping slid - ing
There's an i - cy chill in the air, tell - ing us that

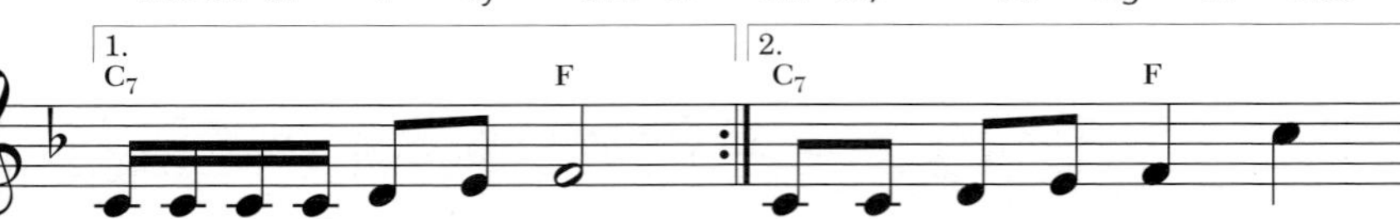

ev - 'ry - bod - y rush - in' 'round. win - ter's real - ly here. Oh!

I'm so glad that win - ter is here. Grab your sled and

let out a hap-py cheer be-cause it's snow-ing, blow-ing, all through the day.

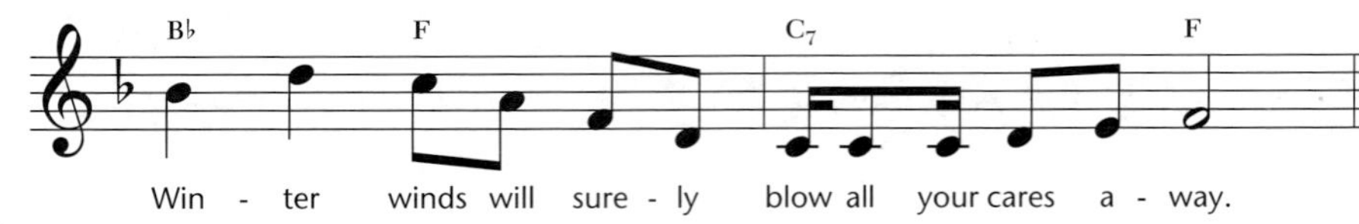

Win - ter winds will sure - ly blow all your cares a - way.

424

# Footnotes

## MEETING INDIVIDUAL NEEDS

▶ **English Language Learners** Sometimes comprehension is challenging for students learning English. Oral retellings are one effective way to monitor comprehension. Ask students to tell a partner what the song text is about. You may want to ask students specific questions about the meanings or intents of phrases in "Winter Fantasy," such as *rushin' round* or *blow all your cares away.*

## BUILDING SKILLS THROUGH MUSIC

▶ **Language** After students are familiar with the songs in this lesson, have them discuss the winter season in their location. Then have them discuss spring, summer, and fall. Ask them to write a brief paragraph about their favorite season. Invite volunteers to share their paragraphs.

## ACROSS THE CURRICULUM

▶ **Science/Language Arts** Invite students to compare the perspectives on winter in the following books.

*Alfie's Long Winter* by Greg McEvoy (Stoddart Kids, 1996)

*Beaver Stream* by Marilyn F. Holmer (Soundprints, 1996)

*Dear Rebecca, Winter Is Here* by Jean Craighead George (HarperCollins, 1993)

*Is That You, Winter? A Story* by Stephen Gammell (Harcourt Brace, 1997)

Part II
do
F Bb C7
Dash-ing thru the snow in a one-horse o-pen sleigh. O'er the fields we go
laugh-ing all the way. Bells on bob-tails ring, mak-ing spir-its bright. What
fun it is to laugh and sing a sleigh-ing song to-night. Oh!
Jin-gle bells, jin-gle bells, jin-gle all the way.
Oh, what fun it is to ride in a one-horse o-pen sleigh.
Jin-gle bells, jin-gle bells, jin-gle all the way.
Oh, what fun it is to ride in a one-horse o-pen sleigh.
Sing and Celebrate
Unit 12 425

# 1 Introduce

Ask students to share experiences they have had in the wintertime. Discuss what it might be like to experience winter in another part of the country. For example, a person who lives in a northern climate experiences much more snow than a person living in a southern climate.

Using the books recommended in Across the Curriculum, p. 424, or similar books, invite interested students to read them and then share winter-related information with the class.

# 2 Develop

### Listening

Invite students to listen to "Winter Fantasy" **CD 18-3.**

6b **ASK What winter song do you recognize in this piece?** ("Jingle Bells")

Play "Let It Snow! Let It Snow! Let It Snow!" **CD 18-5.**

**ASK How are these songs different?** ("Winter Fantasy" is in two parts, and the other song is in one part; accept other comparisons, as well.)

### Singing

Have students sing "Jingle Bells," then "Winter Fantasy" **CD 18-3**, in unison.

Ask students to sing each song again in unison, while the other song plays on the recording.

1d When students are comfortable singing as "partners" with the recording, divide the class into two groups and invite one group to sing "Jingle Bells" while the other sings "Winter Fantasy." Switch parts so that each group gets a chance to sing both songs.

7a Have students assess their performance. Refer to Skills Reinforcement on p. 426 for a list of assessment criteria.

continued on page 426

## Skills Reinforcement

▶ **Recorder** Review the fingering for G, A, high C, and high D with students before having them play this countermelody with "Winter Fantasy." Some students should sing the song while others play. Encourage students to blend their recorder sounds with the vocal sounds.

2b

1.
2.

## Teacher to Teacher

▶ **Singing Partner Songs** Use the following teaching suggestions to help all students sing "Winter Fantasy."

**Reinforcement** Allow weaker singers to sing "Jingle Bells" (Part II). Ask a few stronger singers to sing this part to provide extra support.

**On Target** Most students will be able to sing "Winter Fantasy" and "Jingle Bells" with ease. Monitor these students to make sure they are not blocking out the other part by singing too loudly.

**Challenge** Invite interested students to perform one of the partners songs on a melody instrument as an accompaniment.

**ASK When we sing just one melody together, what word describes our singing?** (unison)

**When we sing two melodies at the same time, what word describes our singing?** (harmony)

**What are two different songs that can be sung together called?** (partner songs)

Have students sing "Winter Fantasy" **CD 18-3** as a partner song again.

## Listening

Play the Harry Connick, Jr. recording of *Let It Snow! Let It Snow! Let It Snow!* **CD 18-7.**

**ASK What words would you use to describe this recording?** (jazz style, exciting)

Play the other recording of "Let It Snow! Let It Snow! Let It Snow!" **CD 18-5.**

**ASK How are these two recordings different?** (One recording is sung by a children's chorus, the other by an adult male soloist.)

Help students categorize the children's voices and the adult male voice by comparing the two timbres.

## Singing

The melody to "Let It Snow! Let It Snow! Let It Snow!" has several large vocal leaps to perform. Prepare students for singing the song by having them perform vocalises with large leaps. Insist that students stand or sit properly and take deep breaths from the bottom of the abdomen. Have students

- Sing a *do-so-mi-do* pattern beginning on F. Repeat the pattern five times (moving up by half steps) until the students are vocalizing up to high E.
- Repeat this activity, using a *do-do*ˡ*-so-mi-do* pattern.

Check for a clean and supported leap in each vocalise. (Avoid sliding.) Once students are able to manage the large leaps, invite them to sing "Let It Snow! Let It Snow! Let It Snow!" **CD 18-5.**

### A Cool Holiday Song

Many popular performers enjoy recording holiday music. **Listen** to this version of *Let It Snow! Let It Snow! Let It Snow!* by Harry Connick, Jr. Then **sing** your own version of the song.

s, l, t, d r m f fi s l t
CD 18-5
Let It Snow! Let It Snow! Let It Snow!
Words by Sammy Cahn
Music by Jule Styne
VERSE
do
The snow-man in the yard is fro-zen hard; He's a sor-ry sight to see,
If he had a brain he'd com-plain, Bet he wish-es he were me.
REFRAIN
Oh! the weath-er out-side is fright-ful, but the fire is so de-light-ful. And since we've no place to go, Let it snow! Let it snow! Let it snow!
It ___ does-n't show signs of stop-ping, and I brought some corn for pop-ping; The lights are turned way down low. Let it snow! Let it snow! Let it snow!

426

# Footnotes

## Movement

**▶ Creative Movement** Have students work with a partner. Have the partners face each other and play a mirror game. Suggest concentrating on activities and gestures one would do in the snow, but while staying in one place. One person is the leader and the other is the mirror or follower. Have students perform their winter gestures in slow motion.

Discuss whether leading the movements or following them is easier and why.

## Skills Reinforcement

7a **▶ Singing** Ask students to think about how successful they were in singing their assigned part in "Winter Fantasy." Have students ask themselves the following questions:

- Did you listen to those singers around you?
- Did you listen to the accompaniment?
- Did you listen to the recording?
- Were you able to listen to the other vocal part?
- How would you rate your ability to sing in parts? (excellent, good, fair, needs work)
- Has your ability to sing independently improved?

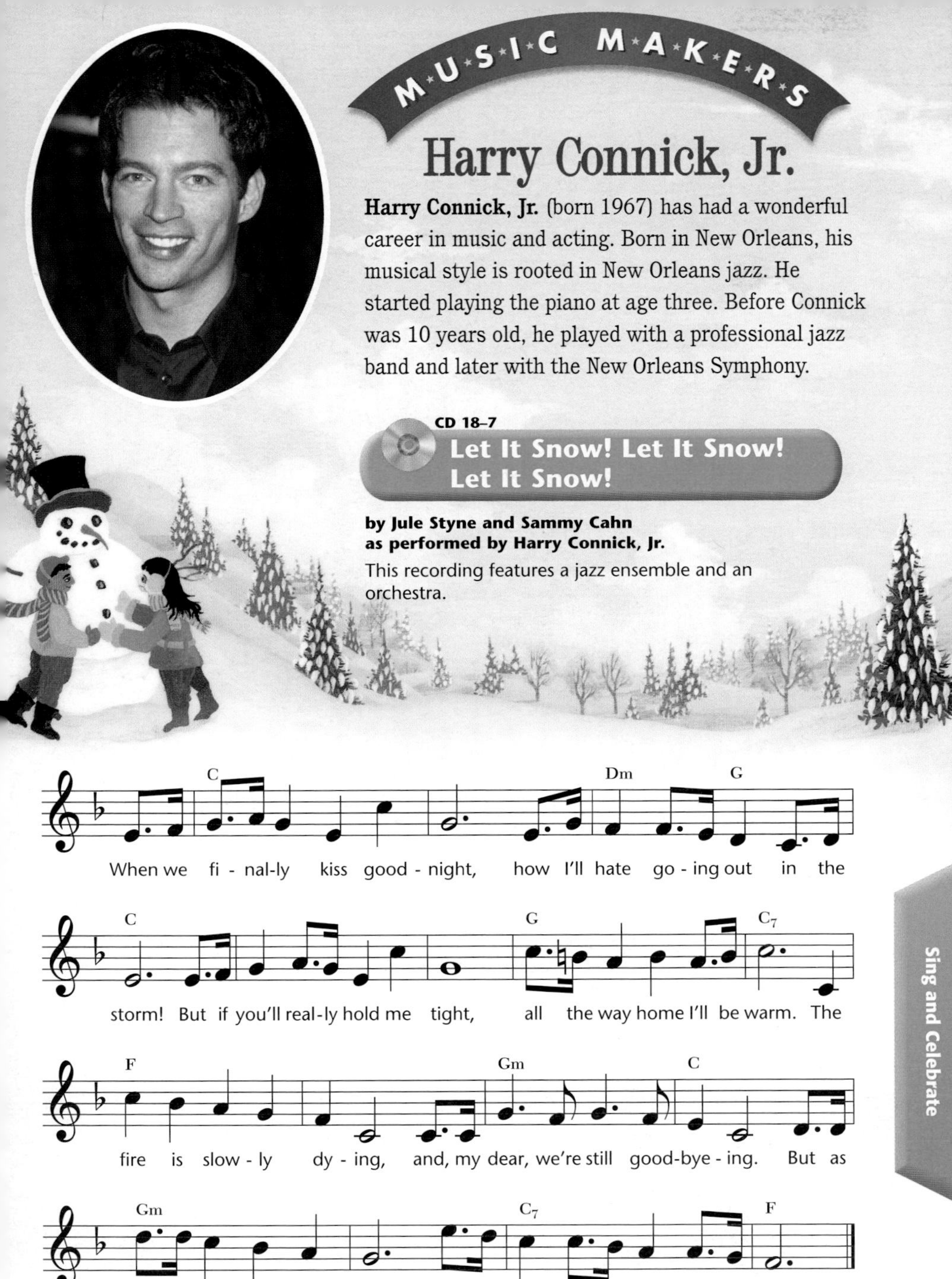

MUSIC MAKERS

## Harry Connick, Jr.

**Harry Connick, Jr.** (born 1967) has had a wonderful career in music and acting. Born in New Orleans, his musical style is rooted in New Orleans jazz. He started playing the piano at age three. Before Connick was 10 years old, he played with a professional jazz band and later with the New Orleans Symphony.

CD 18-7

**Let It Snow! Let It Snow! Let It Snow!**

**by Jule Styne and Sammy Cahn as performed by Harry Connick, Jr.**

This recording features a jazz ensemble and an orchestra.

C Dm G
When we fi - nal-ly kiss good - night, how I'll hate go - ing out in the
C G C7
storm! But if you'll real-ly hold me tight, all the way home I'll be warm. The
F Gm C
fire is slow - ly dy - ing, and, my dear, we're still good-bye - ing. But as
Gm C7 F
long as you love me so, Let it snow! Let it snow! Let it snow!

Sing and Celebrate

Unit 12 427

### Creating

4b Invite students to compose nonpitched percussion accompaniments to perform with the songs in this lesson. Divide the class into three groups. Assign each group one of the three songs. Allow groups time to experiment with their accompaniments. Then have them notate their compositions on staff paper. Have each group play its accompaniment as the rest of the class sings the song.

### Performing

6e Use "Let It Snow! Let It Snow! Let It Snow!" as a feature in a winter holiday program. Invite students to add a quarter-note sleighbell accompaniment and create simple swaying movements to perform as they sing the song with the Stereo Performance Track **CD 18-6.**

## 3 CLOSE

**Element: TEXTURE/HARMONY** ASSESSMENT

1a **Performance/Observation** Divide the class into two groups. Have students sing "Jingle Bells" and "Winter Fantasy" **CD 18-3** in unison, then as partner songs.

Observe whether students are able to simultaneously perform the two melodies.

## ACROSS THE CURRICULUM

▶ **Art** Invite students to illustrate a program cover for a holiday concert on a half-sheet of folded white paper. Encourage students to illustrate winter scenes, holidays, or ideas from the song texts and cultures of holiday music. Be sure students sign and date their artwork with their name, grade, and teacher.

Use this student art as covers for your concert's printed programs. The students may give their artwork program to family members a day before the concert and ask family members to bring the program to the performance. These programs make great reminder invitations and holiday keepsakes.

## TECHNOLOGY/MEDIA LINK

**Notation Software** Use a notation software program to help students compose a harmony part for "Let It Snow! Let It Snow! Let It Snow!"

- Create a notation file and notate the melody of the refrain on p. 426 for "Let It Snow! Let It Snow! Let It Snow!"
- Have students work in pairs to add an alto harmony part in thirds below the melody. In some places, a third does not work. Have students experiment until they find the correct note.
- Ask students to play back their composition and find any notes that need to be changed.
- Have them change the identified notes and print their projects.

## LESSON AT A GLANCE

**Element Focus** **TEXTURE/HARMONY** Two-chord song

**Skill Objective** **PLAYING** Play a two-chord accompaniment on mallet instruments

**Connection Activity** **CULTURE** Discuss the celebration of Chanukah

**MATERIALS**

- *"Ocho kandelikas"* **CD 18-8**
- "Eight Little Candles" **CD 18-9**

**Recording Routine:** Intro (9 m.); v. 1; refrain; v. 2; refrain; v. 3; refrain; coda

- **Pronunciation Practice/Translation** p. 497
- **Resource Book** pp. A-49, G-21
- guitar(s), bass marimba/metallophone

**VOCABULARY**

chord

**National Standards**

**1a** Sing independently with appropriate diction
**2b** Perform chords on appropriate instruments
**8b** Identify ways music relates to social studies

**MORE MUSIC CHOICES**

Other songs with easy chordal accompaniment:
"I'm Gonna Sing," p. 31
"Over My Head," p. 118

# 1 INTRODUCE

8b Share with students the information about the Jewish holiday Chanukah, using the Cultural Connection below. Then discuss the information about *"Ocho kandelikas"* from Spotlight On below. Point out that when people emigrate from one place to another, their language and music travel with them. Allow students to share examples of this from their cultures.



# Harmony in Chanukah

Chanukah is a holiday observed by Jewish people. It is also called "The Festival of Lights." The eight days of Chanukah are celebrated by lighting candles on a *menorah*, exchanging gifts, and eating traditional foods such as *latkes* (potato pancakes). Families and friends also play games using a top called a *dreidel.*

Accompany the Chanukah song *"Ocho kandelikas"* on the guitar. Practice playing the E string and the B string on the guitar. Then follow the music on page 429 and **play** E or B as you sing the song.

▼ *Dreidel*

428

## Footnotes

### CULTURAL CONNECTION

▶ **Chanukah** Long ago, Syrian King Antiochus IV Epiphanes, in an attempt to destroy the Jewish faith, destroyed the Second Temple of Jerusalem. When the Jewish people, led by Judas Maccabeus, reclaimed the Temple in 164 B.C., they found enough holy oil for one day. That tiny amount of oil burned instead for eight days. To commemorate both the military victory and the miracle of the oil, Jewish people light candles in a *menorah* for eight days and eat foods cooked in oil, such as potato pancakes *(latkes)* and donuts.

### BUILDING SKILLS THROUGH MUSIC

▶ **Social Studies** Invite students to share their heritage and traditions. Ask them to name their culture or that of their ancestors. As a class project, develop a pictograph using students' responses.

### SPOTLIGHT ON

▶ **The Song** *"Ocho kandelikas"* is a song from Sarajevo, Bosnia, a city that once had a large Sephardic Jewish population. Flory Jagoda, who wrote the song, used Ladino, or the Judeo-Spanish language, because her ancestors came from Spain. Even when they lived in other places, Jagoda's family continued to speak the Ladino language. In Jagoda's home, her family and friends sang *"Ocho kandelikas"* during the eight-night celebration of Chanukah. They also held matchmaking parties during this time. There was a different party every night, where young people could meet and maybe fall in love. The parties had singing, dancing, and lots of good food, including honey-and-almond cakes, which were supposed to bring happiness to those who ate them.

## Singing in Ladino

When the Jews left Spain in 1492, they took with them a local Spanish language. It is called Judeo-Spanish or Ladino. This language is still known in many countries of the world where Jews have settled. **Sing** this Ladino song.

CD 18-8
Ocho kandelikas
(Eight Little Candles)
Words and Music by Flory Jagoda
VERSE
Em B7 Em
do
1. Ha - nu - ka lin - da sta a - ki o - cho kan - de - las pa - ra mi.
2. Mu-chas fi - e - stas vo fa - zer kon a - le - gri - as i pla - zer.
1. O love-ly Cha-nu-kah is here, eight can-dles' light to bring me cheer.
2. Cha-nu-kah par-ties ev-'ry day, drei-del games for all to play.
Ha - nu - ka lin - da sta a - ki o - cho kan - de - las pa - ra mi.
Mu-chas fi - e - stas vo fa - zer kon a - le - gri - as i pla - zer.
O love-ly Cha-nu-kah is here, eight can-dles' light to bring me cheer.
Cha-nu-kah par-ties ev-'ry day, drei-del games for all to play.
REFRAIN
O u - na kan-de - li - ka, dos kan-de - li - kas, tres kan-de - li - kas,
O one lit - tle can - dle, two lit - tle can-dles, three lit - tle can-dles,
kuat - ro kan - de - li - kas, sin - ko kan - de - li - kas, sej kan - de - li - kas,
four lit - tle can - dles, five lit - tle can - dles, six lit - tle can - dles,
sie - te kan - de - li - kas, o - cho kan - de - las pa - ra mi.
sev - en lit - tle can - dles, eight lit - tle can-dles all for me.
3. Los pastelikos vo komer
kon almendrikas i la myel.
Los pastelikos vo komer
kon almendrikas i la myel.
Refrain
3. Sweet little pastries we will eat,
filled with almonds and honey.
Sweet little pastries we will eat,
filled with almonds and honey.
Refrain
Sing and Celebrate
Unit 12 429

# 2 Develop

### Singing

**1a** Play *"Ocho kandelikas"* **CD 18-8.** Encourage students to sing along on a neutral syllable. Then use the Pronunciation Practice **CD 18-11** to help students learn the Ladino (Judeo-Spanish) words. For the Pronunciation Practice Guide, refer to Resource Book p. A-49. Encourage students to practice the song phrase by phrase, until they are comfortable with the words.

### Playing

**2b** Students can accompany *"Ocho kandelikas"* on guitar. First have students practice playing E and B (the 6th string and the 2nd string). Encourage them to practice each note individually until they are confident and then practice going back and forth between the two notes. Then have students follow the song notation on p. 429 as they play E and B—the roots of the chords. As students sing the song, they should follow the chords in the music and only play when it is appropriate to do so.

Invite students to also play a mallet accompaniment to *"Ocho kandelikas."* Have students play the chord root on a bass marimba with a simple dotted-quarter eighth pattern. As with the guitar playing activity, they should follow the chords in the music and alternate between E and B at the appropriate time.

# 3 Close

**Skill: PLAYING** — **ASSESSMENT**

**2b** **Performance/Observation** Have students accompany *"Ocho kandelikas"* **CD 18-8** on guitars or mallet instruments. Use the following criteria for evaluating performances: Can students change notes fluently, play with a steady beat, and change notes at the correct time?

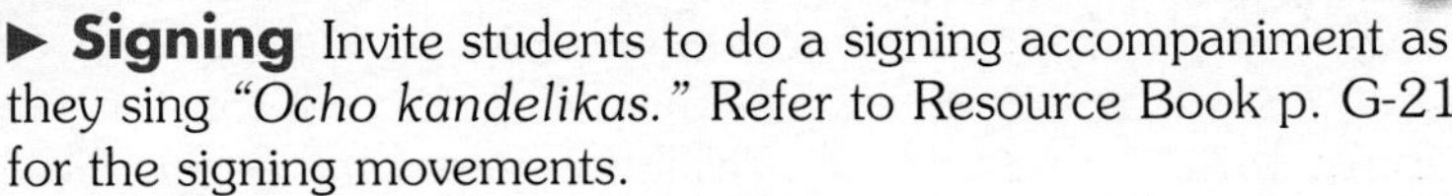

## Skills Reinforcement

▶ **Signing** Invite students to do a signing accompaniment as they sing *"Ocho kandelikas."* Refer to Resource Book p. G-21 for the signing movements.

## Technology/Media Link

**Electronic Keyboard** Invite students to accompany *"Ocho kandelikas"* on electronic keyboards. Have students

- Play chord roots.
- Improvise percussion layers.
- Play simple *arpeggios*.
- Choose sound effects from the keyboard's built-in sounds.

LESSON 5

## LESSON AT A GLANCE

**Element Focus** **RHYTHM** Meter changes

**Skill Objective** **CREATING** Create ostinatos to perform with a song that has meter changes

**Connection Activity** **CULTURE** Discuss how Christmas is celebrated in Mexico

**MATERIALS**

- "The Twelve Days of Christmas" **CD 18-12**
  **Recording Routine:** Intro (6 m.); verses 1–12; ritard on last phrase
- *"Al quebrar la piñata"* **CD 18-15**
- "*Piñata* Song" **CD 18-16**
  **Recording Routine:** Intro (7 m.); vocal; interlude (3 m.); vocal; coda
- **Pronunciation Practice/Translation** p. 498
- *Good King Wenceslas* **CD 18-14**
- *Feliz Navidad* **CD 18-19**
- **Resource Book** pp. A-51, F-32, H-28, J-18
- xylophones, recorders, keyboards
- selected nonpitched percussion instruments

**VOCABULARY**

meter

**National Standards**

**1a** Sing independently on pitch and in rhythm
**2b** Perform melodies and chords on appropriate instruments
**4b** Compose instrumental pieces within specific guidelines
**6b** Describe music by answering questions about it
**6e** While listening to music, move to show a prominent feature of the music

**MORE MUSIC CHOICES**

Other Spanish-language songs:
*"Cantando mentíras,"* p. 146
*"Los niños en España cantan,"* p. 197

LESSON 5 | Element: RHYTHM | Skill: CREATING | Connection: CULTURE

# CHRISTMAS RHYTHMS

Christmas is a holiday celebrated by Christians all over the world. Christmas traditions differ from country to country. Although only one day is celebrated as Christmas Day, the Christmas season is actually twelve days.

**Sing** the song and notice the changes in meter. s, l, t, ⓓ r

CD 18-12

## THE TWELVE DAYS OF CHRISTMAS

*Christmas Song from England*

F Dm B♭ C7 F
On the se - cond day of Christ - mas my true love gave to me,
third
fourth

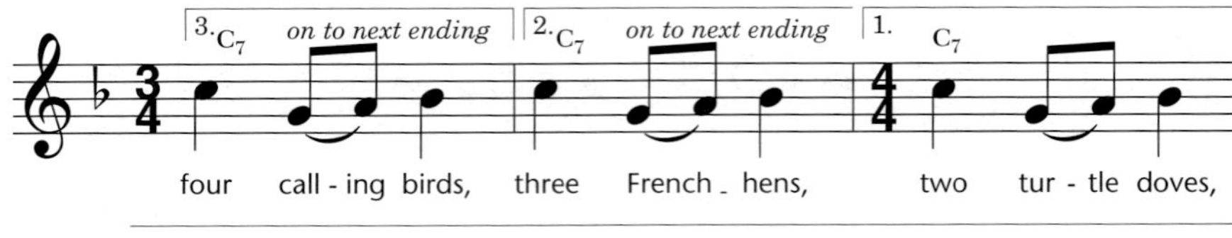


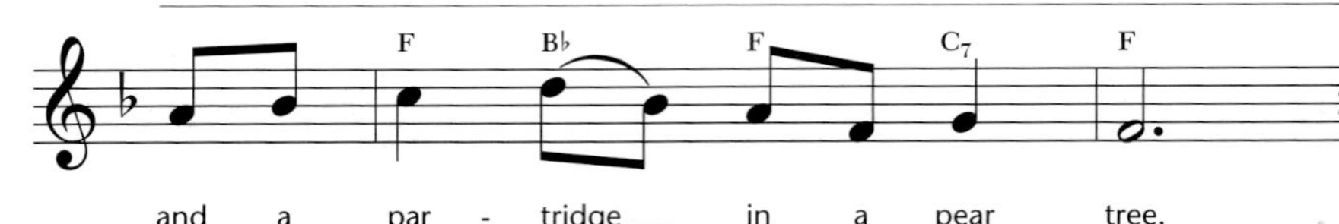




# Footnotes

## MEETING INDIVIDUAL NEEDS

**▶ English Language Learners** On 5 × 7 cards, write the numbers 1 through 12. On another set of cards, paste illustrations of each item in "The Twelve Days of Christmas" (for example, partridge, turtle doves, and so on). As students sing this song, they should match the number with the item as a way of demonstrating their comprehension of the song.

## BUILDING SKILLS THROUGH MUSIC

**▶ Math** Have students read the lyrics of "The Twelve Days of Christmas." Ask them to calculate the total number of gifts given in the song. (For example, one partridge plus two turtle doves plus three French hens, and so on.)

## ACROSS THE CURRICULUM

**▶ Language Arts** Read aloud the book *The Twelve Days of Christmas: Correspondence* by John Julius Norwich (St. Martins, 1999), a hilarious and delightful spoof on thank-you letters a young woman might send to her unseen admirer for each of the items in the song.

Invite students to write a thank-you letter for something that they have received during the year. Remind them to emphasize the things they really appreciate about the gift.

F Dm B♭ C7 F
On the fifth day of Christ-mas my true love gave to me,
sixth
seventh
eighth
ninth
tenth
eleventh
twelfth
8. C7 on to next ending 7. C7 on to next ending 6. C7 on to next ending
twelve drum-mers drum-ming, eleven pip-ers pip-ing, ten lords a leap-ing,
5. C7 on to next ending 4. C7 on to next ending 3. C7 on to next ending
nine la-dies danc-ing, eight maids a milk-ing, seven swans a swim-ming,
2. C7 on to next ending 1. F G C7 F Dm
six geese a lay-ing, five gold-en rings, four _ call-ing birds,
Gm C7 F B♭ F C7 F
three French hens, two _ tur-tle doves, and a par-tridge _ in a pear tree.
Sing and Celebrate
**Listen** to *Good King Wenceslas* [WEN-ses-lahs].
What story does this Christmas song tell?
CD 18–14
Good King Wenceslas
Traditional Carol
as performed by the Westminster Choir
This traditional carol may have come from Bohemia, a section of the former Czechoslovakia.
Unit 12 431

# 1 Introduce

Discuss with students that "The Twelve Days of Christmas" and *"Al quebrar la piñata"* both tell of Christmas celebrations from different cultures. Invite students to examine the music and art for the lesson to determine which cultures are represented. Play the recording of "The Twelve Days of Christmas" **CD 18-12** and then share the humorous book mentioned in Across the Curriculum on p. 430.

# 2 Develop

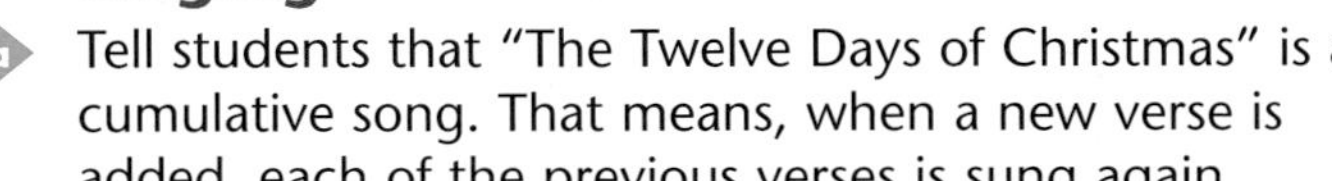

## Singing

1a Tell students that "The Twelve Days of Christmas" is a cumulative song. That means, when a new verse is added, each of the previous verses is sung again.

Select twelve soloists, one for each gift in "The Twelve Days of Christmas." Have the entire class sing *On the first day of Christmas, my true love gave to me* and the soloist sing *a partridge in a pear tree.* Repeat for the other verses. Remind soloists that once their "day" is sung, they must be ready to sing on each successive verse.

On another day, invite students to create their own lyrics to "The Twelve Days of Christmas," using Resource Book p. J-18.

## Analyzing

Have students identify the measures in "The Twelve Days of Christmas" in which the meter changes. Have them look through their books and identify the time signatures in the printed notation.

## Playing

Divide the class into 12 groups. Assign each group to one of the "days of Christmas." Invite each group to create an appropriate instrumental accompaniment for its "day." Have the entire class sing "The Twelve Days of Christmas" **CD 18-12**, as each small group performs its accompaniment.

**continued on page 432**

## Skills Reinforcement

▶ **Recorder** Students can play a recorder countermelody during the refrain of *"Al quebrar la piñata."* Remind them to 2b breathe at the end of each two-measure phrase and to be sure their fingers move simultaneously when playing leaps.

▶ **Keyboard** Invite students to play a two-handed accompaniment with *"Al quebrar la piñata,"* using the I, IV, and $V_7$ chords in closest position. Remind students that the song changes meter for the refrain. Refer to Resource Book p. H-28.

## Cultural Connection

▶ **Christmas in Mexico** Christmas in Mexico is called *Fiesta Navidad.* Everyone who is able takes the last two weeks of December off to celebrate. The nine-day *Las posadas* celebration begins on December 16th. Children gather in the evening to re-enact Mary and Joseph's quest for lodging in Bethlehem. Two children play Mary and Joseph, three play the Wise Men, and any number play angels and shepherds. After careful planning amongst the villagers, the pilgrims depart—and are turned away at the first two houses they go to. At the third house, they are recognized as the holy family and are allowed inside the house. Then the whole group is invited inside for a party that includes breaking a *piñata* filled with treats.

### Listening

To reinforce good singing habits, invite students to listen to *Good King Wenceslas* **CD 18-14,** as performed by the Westminster Choir. Encourage students to listen for phrasing and tall vowels.

Play *"Al quebrar la piñata"* **CD 18-15.**

**ASK What words suggest the joys of the celebration?** *(happy days, gladness fill the air, excitement, treasure, pleasure)*

Share with students information about the nine-day Christmas celebration in Mexico. Refer to Cultural Connection on pp. 431 and 433. Play the recording of *Feliz Navidad* **CD 18-19,** as performed by Jose Feliciano, as part of the discussion.

### Reading

Have students

- Learn to sing *"Al quebrar la piñata"* **CD 18-16** in English.
- Listen to the Pronunciation Practice for *"Al quebrar la piñata"* **CD 18-18** and sing with the students on the recording. (For the Pronunciation Practice Guide, refer to Resource Book p. A-51.) Then sing the song in Spanish **CD 18-15.**
- Pat the basic beat of the song.
- Point to the measures in the song where the meter changes.

### Creating

Divide students into small groups and ask them to create a rhythm accompaniment for *"Al quebrar la piñata."* Encourage them to practice the accompaniment on nonpitched percussion instruments. Give each group an opportunity to perform its accompaniment as the rest of the class sings the song with the Stereo Performance Track **CD 18-17.**

Nine-Day Celebration
In Mexico, Christmas is celebrated for nine days and is called Las Posadas. Create ostinatos in meter in 3 and meter in 2. Perform them while you sing "Al quebrar la piñata."
CD 18-15
AL QUEBRAR LA PIÑATA
(Piñata Song)
t ⓓ r m f s l ta t d'
English Words by Verne Muñoz
Christmas Song from Mexico
A
do
C F G7 C C7 F G7 C
En las no - ches de po - sa - das,
In the hap - py days of Christ - mas,
La pi - ña - ta es lo me - jor;
Sounds of glad - ness fill the air;
La ni - ña más re - mil - ga - da
When it's time for the pi - ña - ta,
Se al - bo - ro - ta con ar - dor.
There's ex - cite - ment ev - 'ry - where.
432


# Footnotes

## SKILLS REINFORCEMENT

▶ **Creating** The alternation of simple and compound meters is common in Latin American music (called "*sesquialtera*"). Help students look for other listening examples of mixed meter. As an extension of the performance activity, ask students to create a piece that mixes simple and compound meters to create a "Latin sound." As in the Creating activity above, students can use xylophones and percussion. One easy way to create contrasting sections is to have one of the meters differ in texture (for example, have singers drop out, add more low percussion). Allow students to generate their own ideas before making suggestions.

## ACROSS THE CURRICULUM

▶ **Art** Work with students to make a *piñata* out of *papier-mâché*. You will need balloons, newspaper cut into strips, *papier-mâché* glue or flour and water, paints for decorating, trinkets, and/or candy for filling the *piñata*. Blow up a balloon and secure it. Dip newspaper in *papier-mâché* glue and lay strip over strip in various directions until the balloon is completely covered. Be sure to make a wire loop at the top of the *piñata* to hang it by when it is complete. Leave a small uncovered area at the bottom of the balloon. Let it dry overnight. Paint the dry *papier-mâché* with appropriate designs. Pop the balloon through the opening in the bottom and remove. Fill the *piñata* with candy and/or trinkets. Use more newspaper and glue to secure the bottom. Let dry and decorate.

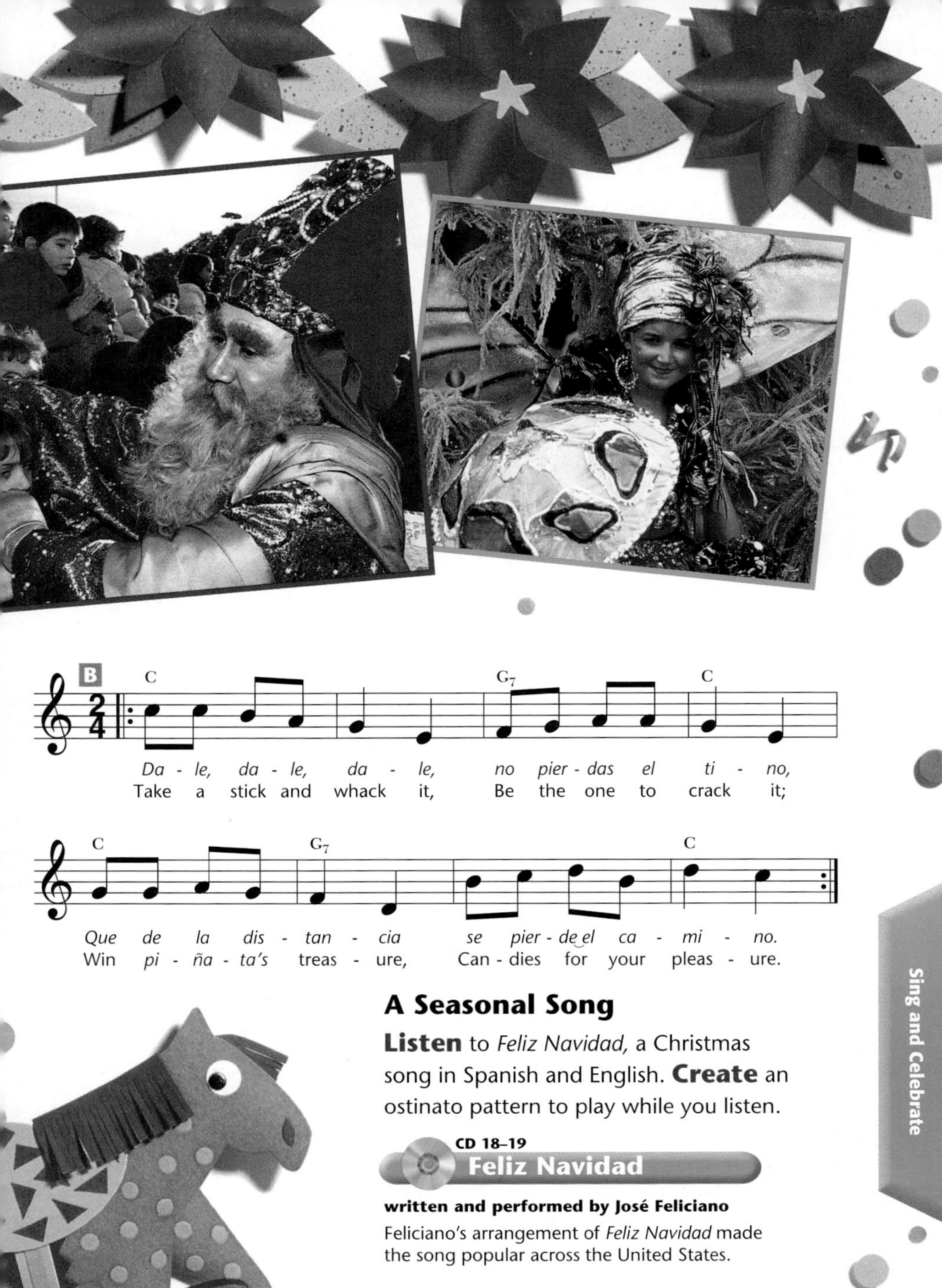

B
C G7 C
Da - le, da - le, da - le, no pier - das el ti - no,
Take a stick and whack it, Be the one to crack it;
C G7 C
Que de la dis - tan - cia se pier - de el ca - mi - no.
Win pi - ña - ta's treas - ure, Can - dies for your pleas - ure.

### A Seasonal Song

**Listen** to *Feliz Navidad,* a Christmas song in Spanish and English. **Create** an ostinato pattern to play while you listen.

**CD 18–19**
**Feliz Navidad**

**written and performed by José Feliciano**

Feliciano's arrangement of *Feliz Navidad* made the song popular across the United States.

Sing and Celebrate

# 3 Close

**Element: RHYTHM** — **ASSESSMENT**

4b **Performance/Observation** Have students work in small groups and create two-measure ostinatos in $\frac{3}{4}$ time and $\frac{2}{4}$ time to perform as they sing *"Al quebrar la piñata"* **CD 18-15.** Observe that students play the ostinatos accurately and at the correct time as they sing the song.

## Cultural Connection

▶ **Legend of the Poinsettia** Although there are variations on the legend, the basic story has stayed the same. In a small village in Mexico, children gathered at the church to give gifts to Jesus on Christmas Eve. One little girl had nothing to offer because she was quite poor. In desperation, she grabbed some weeds outside the church and covered them with her shawl. As the children came in giving their beautiful gifts, the little girl became nervous, but she remembered that she had been told, "even the most humble gift is acceptable if it is given with love." The little girl approached the altar and uncovered the weeds which had changed into bright red flowers. The people were amazed, and since that time, the poinsettia has been a part of the Christmas celebration.

## Technology/Media Link

**Electronic Keyboard** Use electronic keyboards to enhance a song with sound effects.

- Assign each "day" of "The Twelve Days of Christmas" to a different group of students.
- Ask each group to imagine sound effects and fills that would fit their section.
- Have the groups use electronic keyboards and other classroom instruments to choose sounds and improvise fills for their section.
- Have the groups rehearse their sound effects and perform them as the class sings the song.

## LESSON AT A GLANCE

**Element Focus** **MELODY** Phrases

**Skill Objective** **SINGING** Sing a song with appropriate phrasing

**Connection Activity** **CULTURE** Discuss Kwanzaa, an African American celebration

**MATERIALS**

- *"Harambee"* **CD 18-20**
  **Recording Routine:** Intro (4 m.); vocal; coda
- selected nonpitched percussion instruments

**VOCABULARY**

ostinato

**National Standards**

**1b** Sing expressively, with appropriate interpretation
**2f** Play instruments independently against contrasting parts
**4b** Compose instrumental pieces within specific guidelines

**MORE MUSIC CHOICES**

Other African American songs:

"Somebody's Knockin' at Your Door," p. 53

"Over My Head," p. 118

# 1 INTRODUCE

Share with students the information about Kwanzaa on p. 434 of their student text, as well as in Cultural Connection and Across the Curriculum below. Play *"Harambee"* **CD 18-20.** Ask students to listen carefully to the words to find out more about the celebration of Kwanzaa.

# KWANZAA
## Hello and Goodbye

*Kwanzaa* is a Swahili word that means "first." The holiday, *Kwanzaa,* was created by Dr. Maulana Karenga to remind African Americans of their heritage. It is celebrated from December 26 through January 1.

**Identify** the phrases as you **listen** to *"Harambee."* **Sing** the song, and **perform** a slight *crescendo* at the beginning and a slight *decrescendo* at the end of each phrase.

32
USA
KWANZAA
1997

©1997—USPS. Displayed with permission.

CD 18-20
MIDI 35

Harambee

l, t, d r m f s

Words and Music by James McBr

VERSE
E♭
A♭
E♭
do
1. We gath - er for the Kwan -zaa hol - i - day this time each year_ With
2. Sev - en dif-f'rent prin - ci - ples that help us learn to grow_ We
3. Build-ing as a na - tion with our hon-or and our pride,_ We

A♭
B♭
rel - a - tives and friends from far and wide,__
cel - e - brate our faith and u - ni - ty,__
learn to hon - or truth and show our love,__

E♭ A♭ E♭

Shar - ing in a peace - ful time of trust and love and song,_ With
Hop - ing that the best_ of all your wish - es do come true,_ We
Car - ing is a part_ of our re - spon - si - bil - i - ty.__ We

## Footnotes

### ACROSS THE CURRICULUM

▶ **Language Arts** Read aloud the book *Together for Kwanzaa* by Juwanda Ford and Shelly Hokenberger (Random House, 2000). This book will teach students about the traditions and practices that make Kwanzaa special.

Ask students to write in their journals about a special family member and why that family member is important to them.

### BUILDING SKILLS THROUGH MUSIC

▶ **Social Studies** Distribute copies of the Venn diagram from Resource Book p. C-8. Have students compare and contrast *"Harambee"* and *"Ocho kandelikas."* Some characteristics that might be mentioned include subject matter, time signature, timbre, form, and so on.

### CULTURAL CONNECTION

▶ **Seven Principles of Kwanzaa** The seven principles of Kwanzaa, called *nguzo saba,* are explained on each of the seven nights of Kwanzaa. They are

- *Umoja*—staying together.
- *Kujichagulia*—self-determination.
- *Ujima*—working together but taking individual responsibility.
- *Ujamaa*—cooperative economics.
- *Nia*—fulfilling potential for greatness.
- *Kuumba*—creativity.
- *Imani*—faith in one's self and one's people.

Kwanzaa was created in 1966. It gives African Americans a special time to remember their ancestors and culture.

Fm7
Bb
joy e - nough to last the whole year long.
wish a hap - py Kwan - zaa to you.
want the world to live in har - mo - ny.
REFRAIN
Fm7
Eb
A Kwan-zaa hol - i - day is a spe-cial hol - i - day, A
Ha - ram - bee means hel - lo and good-bye, too, A
1.
Fm7
Bb
time to cel - e - brate our his - to - ry.
2.
Ab
Bb
Eb
way of show - ing that I care for you.
Sing and Celebrate
Unit 12 435

Celebrating *Kwanzaa* ▶

# 2 Develop

### Singing

 To help students sing *"Harambee"* **CD 18-20** with appropriate style and technique, have them

- Point to the end of each two-measure phrase in the music.
- Sing and shape each phrase of the song with a slight *crescendo* at the beginning and a slight *decrescendo* at the end.
- Continue to sing the entire song with appropriate phrasing and breaths. (Make sure students are beginning and ending each phrase together.)

### Playing/Creating

 Have students work in small groups and create two-measure percussion ostinatos for *"Harambee,"* using these guidelines:

- Choose appropriate percussion instruments.
- Create a two-measure rhythm pattern.
- Experiment by playing each group's ostinato with the song; then try combining two or more ostinatos with the song.

# 3 Close

**Skill: SINGING** **ASSESSMENT**

 **Performance/Observation** Have each group perform its ostinato for *"Harambee"* **CD 18-20** while the rest of the class sings the song with appropriate phrasing. Observe and assess students' performances using the following criteria. Did students

- Begin each phrase together?
- Breathe together?
- Sing with a pleasant tone?
- Shape each phrase?

## Skills Reinforcement

▶ **Creating** Use the following teaching suggestions to help students create percussion ostinatos to perform with *"Harambee."*

**Reinforcement** Some students may not feel comfortable creating percussion ostinatos. Allow these students to handclap on beats 2 and 4 of the song.

**On Target** Most students will be able to create percussion ostinatos. If they are still having difficulty, have them use the suggestion given above.

**Challenge** Students who can easily create percussion ostinatos may be invited to create two different ostinatos to highlight the verse and refrain of the song.

## Technology/Media Link

**Notation Software** Invite students to notate the ostinatos they created in the lesson in separate staves of a notation program file. Have them add a repeat sign and play back the file as others sing *"Harambee."*

## LESSON AT A GLANCE

**Element Focus** **MELODY** Major scale

**Skill Objective** **PLAYING** Play the melody of a song in a major tonality

**Connection Activity** **SOCIAL STUDIES** Discuss the American Civil Rights movement

**MATERIALS**

- "We Shall Not Be Moved" **CD 18-22**
  **Recording Routine:** Intro (4 m.); v. 1; interlude (1 m.); v. 2; interlude (1 m.); v. 3; coda
- mallet instruments

**VOCABULARY**

whole note half note quarter note dotted-half note

**National Standards**

- **2b** Perform melodies on appropriate instruments
- **5a** Read rhythms in quadruple meter
- **5b** Read notes in treble clef, using letters
- **5d** Notate pitch and rhythm, using standard symbols
- **8b** Identify ways music relates to social studies

**MORE MUSIC CHOICES**

Other freedom songs:

"Gonna Ride Up in the Chariot," p. 20

"America," p. 206

# 1 INTRODUCE

8b Share with students information about the American Civil Rights movement from Cultural Connection below. Then play "We Shall Not Be Moved" **CD 18-22** and lead a discussion about the meaning of the lyrics.



# Guide Our Hope

Singing brings people together during times of struggle. "We Shall Not Be Moved" is associated with the Civil Rights Movement in this country. This song reminds us of Dr. Martin Luther King's fight for the rights of African Americans.

**Sing** the song and then **play** it on a melody instrument.

▲ Martin Luther King, Jr. and his wife, Coretta, lead marchers in Selma, Alabama, in 1965.

## Footnotes

### ACROSS THE CURRICULUM

▶ **Social Studies** Read aloud the book *If You Lived at the Time of Martin Luther King* by Ellen Levine (Demco, 1994), and ask students to compare the world today to the times in which Dr. King lived. What is different now? What do we have that they didn't have?

For readers who would like to learn more, suggest *America in the Time of Martin Luther King, Jr: 1948 to 1976* by Sally Senzell Isaacs (Heinemann, 1999).

### BUILDING SKILLS THROUGH MUSIC

▶ **Social Studies** Invite students to read the lyrics of "We Shall Not Be Moved." Ask them to identify ideas and teachings of Dr. Martin Luther King, Jr. within the song.

### CULTURAL CONNECTION

▶ **Civil Rights Movement** After the Civil War and the Thirteenth Amendment ended slavery in the United States in 1865, African American people were still discriminated against. In many cases, they could not go to the same schools, restaurants, hotels, or even restrooms that were open to Caucasian Americans. This situation lasted for many years until African Americans and other people who believed discrimination was wrong began to protest and demonstrate against injustice. The United States government responded with the Civil Rights Act of 1964, which made it illegal for businesses that serve the public, as well as employers, to discriminate against people on the basis of their race, color, religion, or national origin. In 1969, the Supreme Court ordered integration of all school systems in the United States.

CD 18-22

# We Shall Not Be Moved

s, l, t,(d)r m f

Traditional Freedom Song

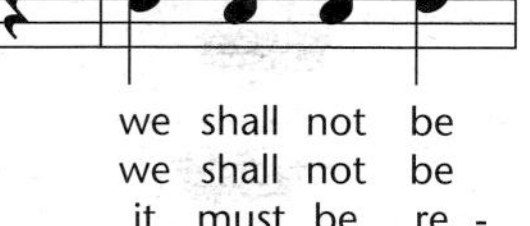

do
G C D7
1. We shall not, we shall not be
2. We're on our way to vic-tor - y, we shall not be
3. Segre - ga-tion is our en - e - my, it must be re -

D7 G G7
moved. We shall not, we shall not be moved.
moved. We're on our way to vic-tor - y, we shall not be moved.
moved. Segre - ga - tion is our en - e - my, it must be re-moved.

C
Just like a tree, that's plant - ed by the

G B7 Em G D7 G
wa - ter. We shall not be moved.

In 1963 Dr. King gave his famous "I Have a Dream" speech to a huge gathering in Washington, D.C. This event is called the March on Washington. ▶

Sing and Celebrate

Unit 12 437

# 2 Develop

## Analyzing

5b Have students look at the notation for "We Shall Not Be Moved."

**ASK How many different pitches are in this song?** (seven)

Tell students that the melody of the song contains all the notes of the major scale. Review with students the notes of the G-major scale by writing it on the board. Extend the major scale down to low D.

**ASK How do low D, low E, and low F♯ fit into our G-major scale?** (They are a descending extension of the scale.)

## Reading

Have students

- Look at the notation for "We Shall Not Be Moved."
- Name each different note value found in the song.
- Sing "We Shall Not Be Moved" with rhythm syllables.
- Sing "We Shall Not Be Moved" with pitch syllables and hand signs.

## Playing

Encourage students to play "We Shall Not Be Moved" on mallet instruments by ear or by reading the notation.

Divide the class into two groups. Have the groups take turns singing and playing.

# 3 Close

**Element: MELODY** ASSESSMENT

**Performance/Observation** Have students play the melody of "We Shall Not Be Moved" **CD 18-22** on mallet instruments. Assess each student's ability to play the correct notes and rhythms.

## Skills Reinforcement

▶ **Listening/Playing** Students may need practice learning to play music by ear. For "We Shall Not Be Moved," have students

- Echo sing a two-measure phrase.
- Work out the two-measure phrase on the instrument.
- Repeat the activity for the next two-measure phrase.
- String together multiple phrases into longer memorized sections.

## Character Education

▶ **Character Traits** Discuss character traits shared by people who were active in the Civil Rights movement (for example, perseverance, courage, integrity, respect). Divide the class into small groups and assign each group one of the character traits identified by the class. Within each group, students should define the trait, list the characteristics of a person who possesses this trait, and delineate three specific examples of how they could demonstrate that trait in their daily lives.

## Technology/Media Link

**Notation Software** Invite students to create their own six-note melodies, using the same pitches as "We Shall Not Be Moved." Use notation software to help students notate their melodies. Encourage students to play their melodies for the class.

LESSON 8

## LESSON AT A GLANCE

**Element Focus** **FORM** Verse-and-refrain form

**Skill Objective** **ANALYZING** Analyze a song to discover its form

**Connection** **CULTURE** Discuss the Jewish holiday of Passover

**Activity**

**MATERIALS**

- *"Dayenu"* **CD 19-1**
- "It Would Have Been Enough" **CD 19-2**

  **Recording Routine:** Intro (9 m.); v. 1; refrain; interlude (2 beats); v. 2; refrain; interlude (2 beats); v. 3; refrain; coda
- **Pronunciation Practice/Translation** p. 499
- **Resource Book** pp. A-52, F-34, I-31
- selected classroom instruments, recorders

**VOCABULARY**

verse refrain

**National Standards**

**2b** Perform chords on appropriate instruments
**4b** Arrange songs within specific guidelines
**6b** Describe music by answering questions about it
**6c** Use appropriate terms to explain music notation

**MORE MUSIC CHOICES**

Other songs in verse-and-refrain form:

*"La Tarara,"* p. 176

"All Night, All Day," p. 180

# 1 INTRODUCE

Share with students the information about Passover in Cultural Connection below. Point out that the Hebrew word *dayenu* means "it would have been enough." Play *"Dayenu"* **CD 19-1** as students follow the notation.

LESSON 8 Element: FORM Skill: ANALYZING Connection: CULTURE

# CREATING LIVING TRADITIONS

During the eight days of Passover, Jews remember the freeing of Hebrew slaves in Egypt thousands of years ago. They celebrate by having traditional services called *seders* and reading from the *Haggadah.* Symbolic foods are eaten and traditional songs are sung. **Sing** *"Dayenu,"* a traditional Passover song.

▲ A Passover *seder*

The Pyramids at Giza, Egypt

438

# Footnotes

## ACROSS THE CURRICULUM

▶ **Social Studies** Read aloud the book *All About Passover* by Judyth Saypol Groner and Madeline Wikler (Kar-Ben, 2000), and invite students to learn more about the history and customs of Passover.

Share the book *Festival of Freedom: The Story of Passover* by Maida Silverman (Simon and Schuster Books, 1988), which includes instructions for a traditional holiday *Seder.*

## BUILDING SKILLS THROUGH MUSIC

▶ **Language** Share the information from Cultural Connection and then have students sing *"Dayenu"* **CD 19-1.** Afterward, lead students in a discussion of the meaning of the lyrics.

## CULTURAL CONNECTION

▶ **Passover** Passover is a solemn, yet joyous, holiday celebrated by Jewish people all over the world. It is celebrated every spring for eight days. Families gather together to have the Passover meal, or *Seder,* where they say prayers from a book called the *Haggadah*, sing songs, and narrate the events that led to their deliverance from slavery in Egypt. It is a holiday that celebrates freedom. All the foods eaten at the Passover meal are symbolic. Matzo, an unleavened bread, is eaten for the whole week because the Israelites, in their haste to leave Egypt, did not have time for their bread dough to rise. Other symbolic foods served at the Passover *Seder* are bitter herbs, a roasted lamb bone, and a mixture of apples, nuts, honey, and wine.

## A Refrain to Remember

**Analyze** the form of this song. Which of these two sections is always sung with the same words? Which section has different words each time it is sung?

CD 19-1
Dayenu
(It Would Have Been Enough)
d r m f s l t d'
Jewish Passover Song
VERSE A
do
1. I - lu ho - tzi, ho - tzi - a - nu, ho - tzi - a - nu mi - Mitz - ra - yim,
2. I - lu na - tan na - tan la - nu, na - tan la - nu et ha - Sha - bat,
1. Had he led us out of E - gypt, on - ly led us out of E - gypt,
2. Had he giv - en us the Sab-bath, on - ly giv - en us the Sab-bath,
ho - tzi - a - nu mi - Mitz - ra - yim, da - ye - nu.
na - tan la - nu et ha - Sha - bat, da - ye - nu.
Had he led us out of E - gypt, da - ye - nu.
Had he giv - en us the Sab - bath, da - ye - nu.
REFRAIN B
Da - da - ye - nu, da - da - ye - nu, da - da - ye - nu, da -
ye - nu, da - ye - nu, da - ye - nu. ye - nu, da - ye - nu!
3. Ilu natan natan lanu,
natan lanu et haTora,
natan lanu et haTora, dayenu.
Refrain
3. Had he given us the Tora,
only given us the Tora,
Had he given us the Tora, dayenu.
Refrain
Sing and Celebrate
Unit 12 439

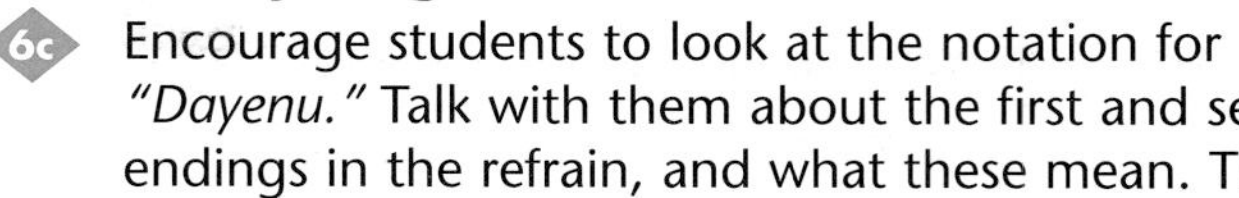

# 2 Develop

### Analyzing

6c Encourage students to look at the notation for *"Dayenu."* Talk with them about the first and second endings in the refrain, and what these mean. Then have students

- Learn *"Dayenu"* **CD 19-2** in English.
- Use the Pronunciation Practice **CD 19-4** to learn *"Dayenu"* in Hebrew. (For the Pronunciation Practice Guide, refer to Resource Book p. A-52.)

6b **ASK Which part of the song has words that are always the same?** (the refrain)

**Which part has words that change?** (the verse)

**What is the best name for the form of *"Dayenu"*?** (verse-and-refrain form)

### Playing

Invite a group of students to play a recorder accompaniment for *"Dayenu"* **CD 19-1** as the rest of the class sings the song. This particular accompaniment reinforces agility with the right hand by playing the notes low D and low E. Refer to Resource Book p. I-31.

### Creating

4b Divide the class into small groups. Ask each group to perform the refrain of *"Dayenu"* in a different way each time to accompany the song. For example, students might use percussion instruments or selected voices.

# 3 Close

**Skill: ANALYZING** — **ASSESSMENT**

**Interviews** Have students search their textbooks to find at least one other example of a song in verse-and-refrain form. Assess students' ability to identify the verse and the refrain in each of their selections.

## Skills Reinforcement

▶ **Playing** Invite students who need a challenge to play the six-note melody for the verse of *"Dayenu"* on a pitched instrument. To start, have students find the six notes of the verse, starting with C, then locate E, the starting note of the song. For an extra challenge, have students play the refrain, as well.

▶ **Mallets** Invite students to play an Orff accompaniment as they sing *"Dayenu."* Refer to Resource Book p. F-34, and have students pat each part before transferring over to the instruments.

## Technology/Media Link

2b **Electronic Keyboard** Have students use electronic keyboards to accompany *"Dayenu"* by playing I and $V_7$ chords.

- Show students how to play the C chord in root position and the $G_7$ chord in first inversion.
- Select students to play the chords as the class sings *"Dayenu."*
- Two students may play at one keyboard.
- Students may play only one of the chords instead of both.
- Students may play only the chord roots.

LESSON 9

## LESSON AT A GLANCE

**Element Focus** **RHYTHM** Meter in 3

**Skill Objective** **MOVING** Move to show meter in 3

**Connection Activity** **SOCIAL STUDIES** Discuss the history of the writing of the national anthem

**MATERIALS**

- "America" **CD 19-5**
  **Recording Routine:** Intro (5 m.); 4 verses with 1 m. interludes; coda
- "The Star-Spangled Banner" **CD 19-7**
  **Recording Routine:** Intro (4 m.); 3 verses

**VOCABULARY**

meter

**◆◆◆◆ National Standards ◆◆◆◆**

**1c** Sing from memory songs from diverse cultures
**1e** Sing in groups, following a conductor
**6b** Describe music by answering questions about it
**6e** While listening to music, move to show a prominent feature of the music

**MORE MUSIC CHOICES**

Other songs in $\frac{3}{4}$ time:
*"Santa Clara,"* p. 172
*"Doraji,"* p. 174
Another patriotic selection:
"America, the Beautiful," p. 158

## 1 INTRODUCE

Discuss with students information about "The Star-Spangled Banner" from Spotlight On, p. 441.

**6b** **ASK On what occasions have you heard this song sung?** (sporting events, school assemblies, and so on)

LESSON 9 | Element: RHYTHM | Skill: MOVING | Connection: SOCIAL STUDIES

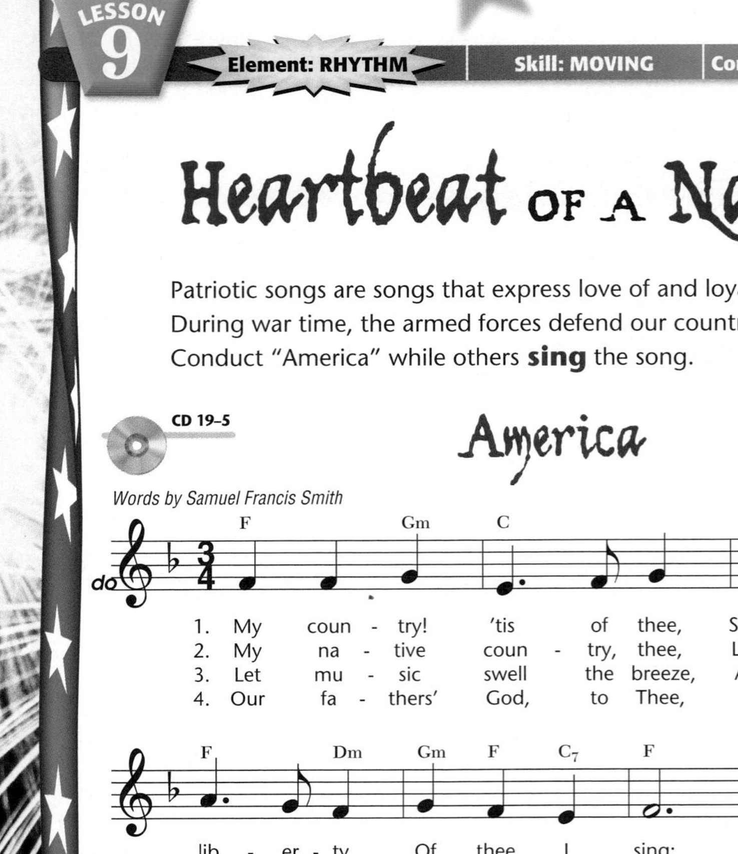

# Heartbeat OF A Nation

Patriotic songs are songs that express love of and loyalty to one's country. During war time, the armed forces defend our country and our freedom. Conduct "America" while others **sing** the song.

CD 19-5

## America

t,ⓓr m f s l

Words by Samuel Francis Smith — Traditional Melody

1. My country 'tis of thee, Sweet land of liberty, Of thee I sing; Land where my fathers died, Land of the pilgrims' pride, From ev'ry mountainside Let freedom ring!
2. My native country, thee, Land of the noble free, Thy name I love; I love thy rocks and rills, Thy woods and templed hills; My heart with rapture thrills Like that above.
3. Let music swell the breeze, And ring from all the trees Sweet freedom's song; Let mortal tongues awake, Let all that breathe partake; Let rocks their silence break, The sound prolong.
4. Our fathers' God, to Thee, Author of liberty, To Thee we sing; Long may our land be bright With Freedom's holy light; Protect us by Thy might, Great God, our King!

440

# Footnotes

## ACROSS THE CURRICULUM

▶ **Social Studies/Art** Share the book *The Star-Spangled Banner* by Peter Spier (Bantam Doubleday Dell, 1992). This book contains the music, background history, and pictures of United States flags, past and present. Students will enjoy learning more about this important song. Invite small groups of students to create their own illustrations for the song. Use the illustrations for a bulletin board display.

## BUILDING SKILLS THROUGH MUSIC

▶ **Language** Ask students to rewrite the first verse of "America" in standard usage. Students may substitute a modern word for *thee,* write out *tis* as *it is,* and replace *fathers* with *ancestors.* Invite students to update any other words that would be more clear in modern or nonpoetic language.

## SKILLS REINFORCEMENT

**1c** ▶ **Singing** The songs "America" and "The Star-Spangled Banner" are a permanent part of our American musical heritage and will be heard, played, and sung many times in different contexts throughout the students' lives. They should enjoy singing these songs beautifully and from memory. Have students sing these songs frequently throughout the school year. Begin classes with one or both songs as an "opening." Students may sing while looking at word cues on the board or visuals. As they become more successful singing from memory, gradually erase the cues. Students will enjoy their achievement as they see words "disappear." Although all verses for "America" and "The Star-Spangled Banner" are worthy, focus on the first verse, which is sung more often at national and community events.

## Our National Anthem

**Sing** "The Star-Spangled Banner" with pride. People stand to show respect for our country while they sing the National Anthem.

d m fi s l t d r' m' f' s'
CD 19-7
The Star-Spangled Banner
Words by Francis Scott Key
Music by John Stafford Smith
do
A♭ E♭ Fm C7 Fm B♭7 E♭
Oh, __ say! can you see, by the dawn's ear - ly light, What so
stripes and bright stars, through the per - il - ous fight, O'er the
A♭ E♭ A♭ 1.
proud - ly we hailed at the twi - light's last gleam-ing, Whose broad
ram - parts we watched were so gal - lant - ly

2. A♭ E♭7
stream-ing? And the rock - ets' red glare, the bombs burst - ing in

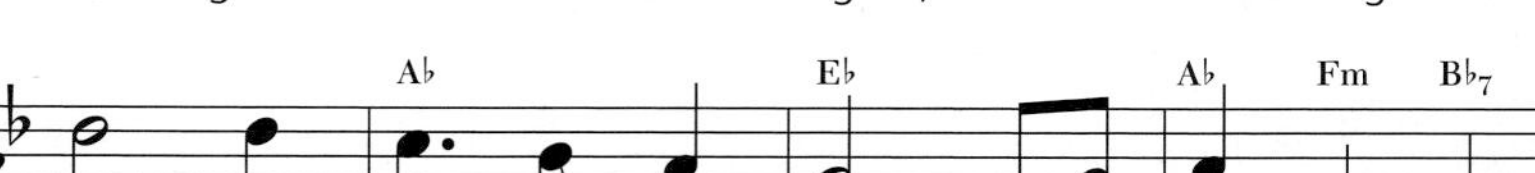

A♭ E♭ A♭ Fm B♭7
air, Gave proof through the night that our flag was still

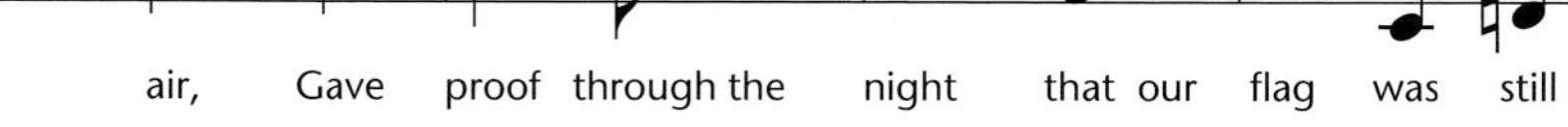

E♭ E♭7 A♭ D♭ F7 B♭m
there. Oh, say, does that __ Star - Span - gled Ban - ner __ yet __

A♭ E♭ E♭7 A♭ E♭7 A♭
wave __ O'er the land __ of the free and the home of the brave?

Sing and Celebrate

Unit 12 441

# 2 Develop

### Listening

Play "America" **CD 19-5.** Encourage students to pat the steady beat as they listen to the song. Remind them to make the first beat of each measure the strongest.

6b **ASK What is the meter of this song?** ($\frac{3}{4}$ time)

### Moving

1e Show students the conducting pattern for $\frac{3}{4}$ time. Play "The Star-Spangled Banner" **CD 19-7.** Have students stand and practice conducting. Point out the upbeat that begins the song, and tell students this means they will start conducting on beat 3. As students become confident with conducting, have them take turns leading as the rest of the class sings.

### Singing

Remind students to breathe deeply and use proper breath support when singing "The Star-Spangled Banner." A deep breath is especially important before singing *and the rockets' red glare.*

# 3 Close

**Element: RHYTHM** — **ASSESSMENT**

6e **Performance/Observation** Have students conduct in $\frac{3}{4}$ time as they sing "America" **CD 19-5.** Observe that students are able to conduct a steady three-beat pattern with a slight emphasis on the first beat.

## Spotlight On

▶ **The National Anthem** On August 23 through 25, 1814, British troops set fire to the Capitol and other buildings in Washington, D.C. When the British returned to their ships, they took a friend of Francis Scott Key prisoner. Key, a lawyer, and John Skinner, an American agent for prisoner exchange, boarded a British ship near Baltimore to get Key's friend released. The British agreed to release the friend but would not let Key's ship leave until their attack on Fort McHenry. During daylight, Key could see the American flag flying over the fort. At night, he saw "bombs bursting in air." When daylight came again, the flag was still flying. Key was inspired to write the text of "The Star-Spangled Banner." In 1931, "The Star-Spangled Banner" became the national anthem of the United States.

## Technology/Media Link

**Web Site** Students will be interested in finding out more about the writers of "The Star-Spangled Banner" and "America." Have them visit *www.sfsuccessnet.com* to learn more about Francis Scott Key and Samuel Francis Smith.

**Electronic Keyboard** Invite students to play "drum set" on an electronic keyboard, using the drum kit settings. Have them find the bass drum sound to play on beat one and a snare drum or cymbal sound to play on beats two and three while they sing "America" or "The Star-Spangled Banner."

Music Reading Practice
Playing the Recorder
Mallet Instruments
Playing the Guitar
Playing the Keyboard
Sound Bank

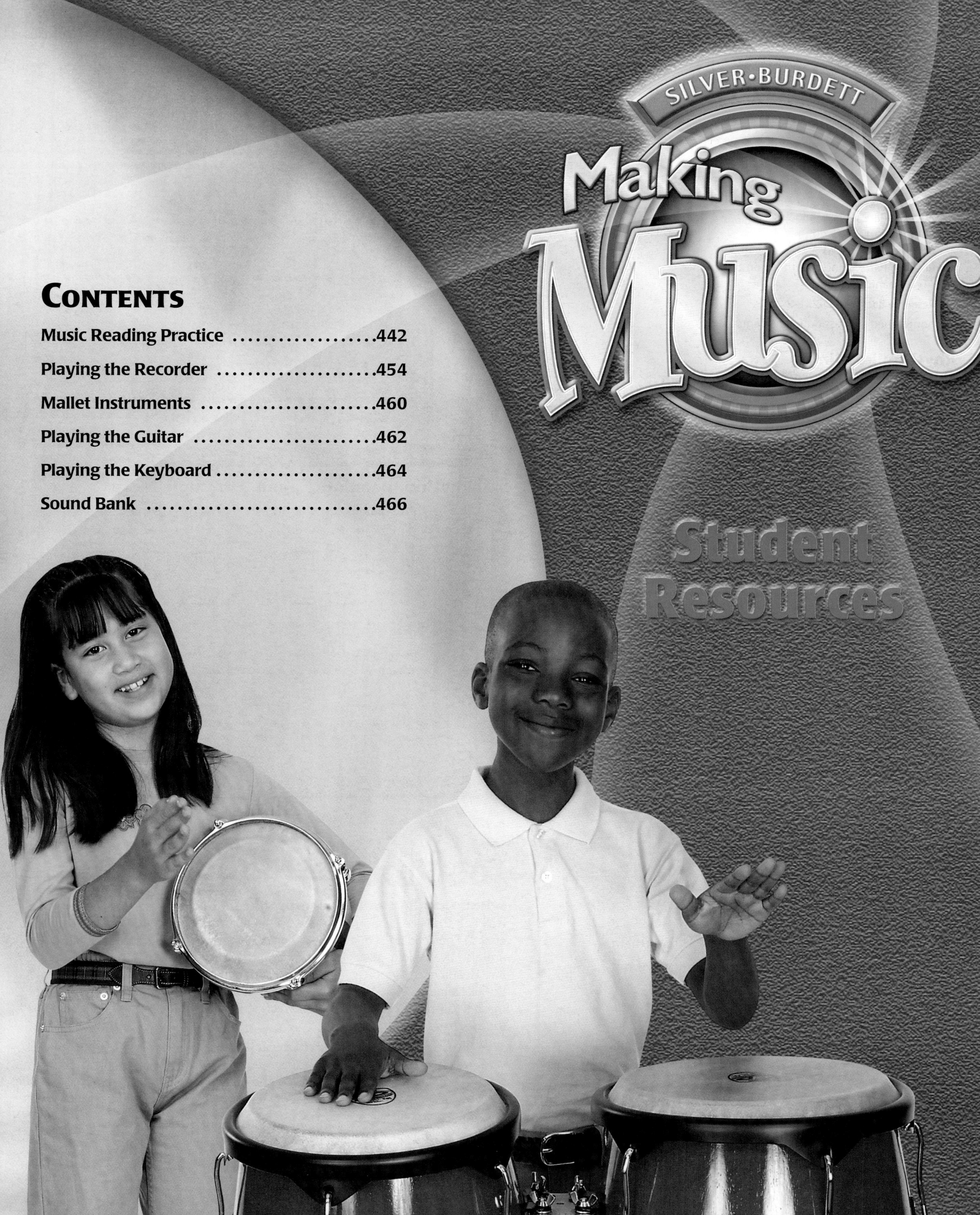
SILVER•BURDETT
Making
Music
Student
Resources

## Contents

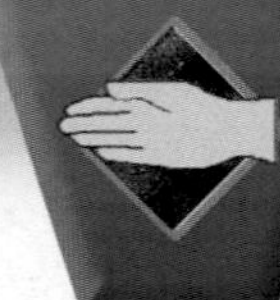

# Unit 1 Music Reading Practice

## Reading Sequence 1, page 10

**MATERIALS**

- "Soldier, Soldier," p. 11 **CD 1-7**
- Reading Sequence 1
  Rhythm Part 1 (woodblock) **CD 1-9**
  Rhythm Part 2 (triangle) **CD 1-10**
  Rhythm Parts 1 and 2 **CD 1-11**
  Rhythm Parts 1 and 2 with accompaniment **CD 1-12**
  Accompaniment only **CD 1-13**
- **Resource Book** pp. D-2, E-2
- nonpitched percussion instruments

### Rhythm: Reading ♫., ♩., 𝅗𝅥

Review meter in 4 and ask students to perform the conducting pattern in a moderate, steady tempo. Direct students to Reading Sequence 1 and have them

- Read, clap, and count Part 1 using rhythm syllables.
- Read, clap, and count Part 2 using rhythm syllables.
- Choose a nonpitched percussion instrument for each part, then play each part.
- Perform the parts separately and then together with the accompaniment track **CD 1-13** or the song **CD 1-7**.

*Note:* See "Using the MIDI Files" in the Footnotes on p. 445 for suggestions on implementing this feature.

## Reading Sequence 2, page 14

**MATERIALS**

- *"Gakavik,"* p. 14 **CD 1-17**
- "The Partridge," p. 14 **CD 1-18**
- Reading Sequence 2
  Rhythm part (drum) **CD 1-21**
  Rhythm part with accompaniment **CD 1-22**
  Accompaniment only **CD 1-23**
- **Resource Book** p. E-3
- nonpitched percussion instruments

### Rhythm: Reading ♫ and ♩ in Duple Meter

Play *"Gakavik"* **CD 1-17** and ask students to

- Clap on each beat (two claps per measure).
- Accent the first beat of each two-beat pattern.
- Clap on the first beat of each measure.

Direct students to Reading Sequence 2 and have them

- Read, clap, and count the exercise using rhythm syllables.
- Choose a nonpitched percussion instrument and perform the exercise.
- Perform the exercise with the accompaniment track **CD 1-23** or the song **CD 1-17**.

UNIT 1 *Music Reading Practice*

## Reading Sequence 1, page 10

### Rhythm: Reading ♫., ♩., 𝅗𝅥

Use rhythm syllables to **read** and **perform** this two-part rhythm accompaniment for "Soldier, Soldier."

## Reading Sequence 2, page 14

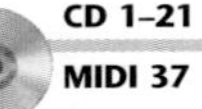


### Rhythm: Reading ♫ and ♩ in Duple Meter

Use rhythm syllables to **read** and **perform** this rhythm accompaniment for *"Gakavik."*

442

## Footnotes

▶ **Reading Sequence Formats** The 24 Reading Sequences of the Music Reading Practice section reinforce and extend students' music reading experiences. The reading sequences appear as student pages within the pupil book and are also available as blackline masters in the Resource Book. You may complete any Reading Sequence as a class project by creating an overhead transparency of the blackline master. You might also use the same Reading Sequence blackline master to prepare worksheets on which students can make individual responses for assessment.

▶ **Introducing Rhythm Patterns (Reading Sequences 1 and 2)** For those students new to music reading in this grade, the rhythms in "Soldier, Soldier" and *"Gakavik"* may be introduced in one or two lessons. Spreading the activities over several lessons will allow students to practice rhythm reading while reinforcing other musical skills.

## Reading Sequence 3, page 20

CD 1–30
MIDI 38

### Melody: Reading Steps, Skips, Repeated Pitches

For inner-hearing practice, **read** and **sing** this countermelody for "Gonna Ride Up in the Chariot." Use pitch syllables and hand signs.

## Reading Sequence 4, page 24

CD 1–40
MIDI 39

### Melody: Reading Pentatonic Patterns

Use pitch syllables and hand signs to **read** and **sing** this countermelody for *"Tsuki."*

443

▶ **Aural Preparation (Reading Sequence 3)** "Gonna Ride Up in the Chariot" contains rhythmic and melodic elements that students will encounter consciously in later lessons. Singing the song provides aural preparation for those elements. Teachers following the reading sequence may wish to have students read the exercise (which contains only known elements) instead of the full staff version. Once the new elements have been learned, students can revisit the song and read the actual notation.

▶ **Pentatonic Patterns (Reading Sequence 4)** For those students new to music reading, the pentatonic patterns and hand signs used in *"Tsuki"* may be quickly introduced in one or two lessons. Start with *mi-re-do, so-mi,* and *so-mi-re-do.* Then add *so-la-so* and other pentatonic patterns. Give students opportunities for aural practice with short patterns by using echo singing, memory games, and vocal and instrumental improvisation.



## Reading Sequence 3, page 20

**MATERIALS**

- "Gonna Ride Up in the Chariot," p. 20 **CD 1-28**
- Reading Sequence 3
  Melody part **CD 1-30**
  Melody part with accompaniment **CD 1-31**
  Accompaniment only **CD 1-32**
- **Resource Book** p. E-4

### Melody: Reading Steps, Skips, Repeated Pitches

Review the definition and examples of intervals on p. 21. Direct students to Reading Sequence 3 and have them

- Read the pitch syllables and identify measures where the melody contains steps, skips, and repeated notes.
- Describe the direction (up, down, same) of specific intervals.
- Read, clap, and count the rhythm of the exercise.
- Sing the exercise, using hand signs and pitch syllables.

Notate the exercise on the board in C-*do* and then ask students to read it from staff notation.

## Reading Sequence 4, page 24

**MATERIALS**

- *"Tsuki,"* p. 25 **CD 1-36**
- "The Moon," p. 25 **CD 1-37**
- Reading Sequence 4
  Melody part **CD 1-40**
  Melody part with accompaniment **CD 1-41**
  Accompaniment only **CD 1-42**
- **Resource Book** pp. D-3, E-5
- melody instruments

### Melody: Reading Pentatonic Patterns

Review "Reading Pentatonic Scales" on p. 25. Direct students to Reading Sequence 4 and have them

- Sing the exercise using pitch syllables and hand signs.
- Sing the exercise using pitch letter names.
- Perform the exercise on melody instruments while others sing the song **CD 1-36.**

Use the Reading Music Worksheet on p. D-3 in the Resource Book to help students create and perform their own pentatonic patterns.

# Unit 2
# Music Reading Practice

## Reading Sequence 5, page 52

**MATERIALS**

| | |
|---|---|
| • "Somebody's Knockin' at Your Door," p. 53 | **CD 3-3** |
| • Reading Sequence 5 | |
| Rhythm Part 1 (drum) | **CD 3-4** |
| Rhythm Part 2 (tambourine) | **CD 3-5** |
| Rhythm Parts 1 and 2 | **CD 3-6** |
| Rhythm Parts 1 and 2 with accompaniment | **CD 3-7** |
| Accompaniment only | **CD 3-8** |
| • **Resource Book** pp. D-5, E-6 | |
| • nonpitched percussion instruments | |

### Rhythm: Reading with Ties

Review how ties create syncopated rhythms in music. Direct students to Reading Sequence 5 and have them

- Read, clap, and count Part 1 using rhythm syllables.
- Analyze Part 2 and identify how it differs from Part 1. (Part 2 uses syncopated rhythms, Part 1 uses ties to show syncopation; Part 2 imitates Part 1, until the last two measures.)
- Read, clap, and count Part 2 using rhythm syllables.

Divide the class into three groups and have

- Group 1 perform Part 1 **CD 3-4.**
- Group 2 perform Part 2 **CD 3-5.**
- Group 3 sing the song **CD 3-3.**
- All groups perform the parts on nonpitched percussion instruments to accompany the song.

## Reading Sequence 6, page 54

**MATERIALS**

| | |
|---|---|
| • "Rock Island Line," p. 54 | **CD 3-9** |
| • Reading Sequence 6 | |
| Rhythm part (claves) | **CD 3-11** |
| Rhythm part with accompaniment | **CD 3-12** |
| Accompaniment only | **CD 3-13** |
| • **Resource Book** pp. D-6, E-7 | |
| • nonpitched percussion instruments | |

### Rhythm: Reading ♪ ♩ ♪

Have students sing "Rock Island Line" **CD 3-9** and

- Keep a steady beat.
- Identify the recurring short-long-short rhythm pattern.

Review the rhythm syllables in Reading Sequence 6 and have students

- Describe the form of the exercise. (refrain-verse-refrain)
- Clap and count the exercise using rhythm syllables.
- Perform the exercise as an accompaniment while they sing "Rock Island Line" **CD 3-9.**



UNIT 2

## Reading Sequence 5, page 52

CD 3-4
MIDI 40

### Rhythm: Reading with Ties

Use rhythm syllables to **read** and **perform** this two-part rhythm accompaniment for "Somebody's Knockin' at Your Door."

## Reading Sequence 6, page 54

CD 3-11
MIDI 41

### Rhythm: Reading ♪♩ ♪

Use rhythm syllables to **read** and **perform** this rhythm accompaniment for "Rock Island Line."

444

## Footnotes

▶ **Aural Preparation (Reading Sequences 5 and 8)** "Somebody's Knockin' at Your Door" and "Sourwood Mountain" contain rhythmic and melodic elements that students will encounter consciously in later lessons. Singing the songs provides aural preparation for those elements. Teachers following the reading sequence may wish to have students read the exercises on those pages (which contain only known elements) instead of the full staff version. Once the new elements have been learned, students can revisit the songs and read the actual notation.

▶ ♪ ♩ ♪ **(Reading Sequence 6)** This is the first syncopated pattern that most students learn to read. Once students learn to recognize the short-long-short arrangement of three sounds over two beats, they can recognize hidden syncopation caused by rests and tied notes. Have students compare the exercises above to the notation of the songs. Later they can use rests and tied notes to create and notate more complex syncopated patterns.

## Reading Sequence 7, page 62

CD 3–25
MIDI 42

### Melody: Reading $la_{|}$ and $so_{|}$

Use pitch syllables and hand signs to **read** and **sing** this melody accompaniment for *"Hashewie."*

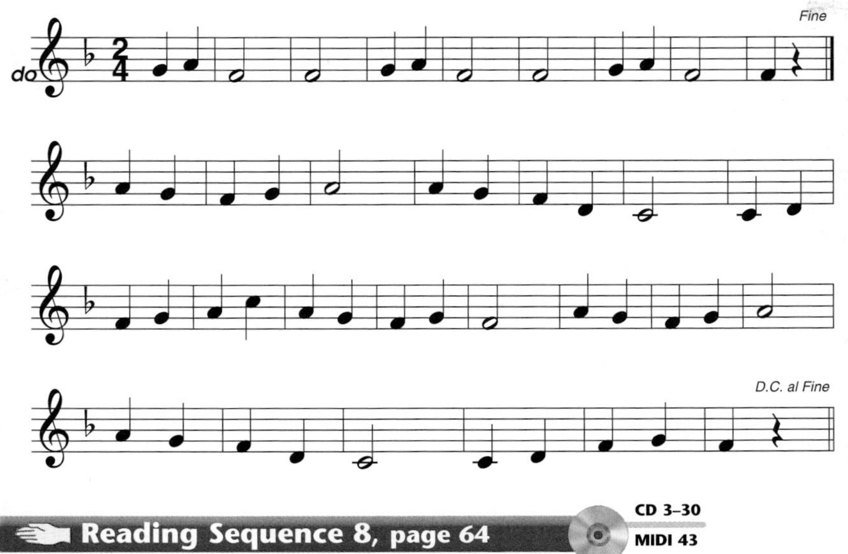


## Reading Sequence 8, page 64

CD 3–30
MIDI 43

### Melody: Reading $do^{|}$

For inner-hearing practice, **read** and **sing** this countermelody for "Sourwood Mountain." Use pitch syllables and hand signs.

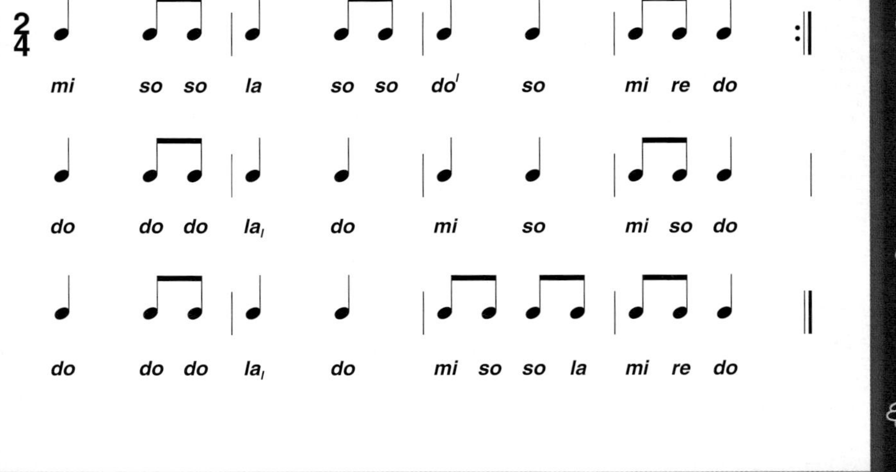




▶ **Skeleton Rhythms (Reading Sequence 7)** Reading Sequence 7 contains only the basic, or skeleton, rhythm patterns of *"Hashewie."* This permits students to focus on melody reading from staff notation. The phrase structure of the exercise and the corresponding song is the same. Have students begin the exercise after the introduction.

▶ **Using the MIDI Files** MIDI files are provided for all Reading Sequence exercises. Each file contains individual tracks for specific melody or rhythm parts, as notated in the corresponding exercise on the pupil page, and a full accompaniment for the song on which the exercise is based. As an instructional tool, the files can be used to isolate individual parts, accompany any combination of parts, and transpose the pitches or change the tempo of the exercise and accompaniment.



## Reading Sequence 7, page 62

**MATERIALS**

- *"Hashewie,"* p. 63 — **CD 3-21**
- "Going 'Round," p. 63 — **CD 3-22**
- Reading Sequence 7
  - Melody part — **CD 3-25**
  - Melody part with accompaniment — **CD 3-26**
  - Accompaniment only — **CD 3-27**
- **Resource Book** pp. D-8, E-8

### Melody: Reading $la_{|}$ and $so_{|}$

Have students sing the extended pentatonic scale. Invite them to refer to the hand signs along the side of the page and practice the hand placement for low *la* and low *so.* Have students

- Review $\frac{2}{4}$ meter and its conducting pattern.
- Read, clap, and count the rhythms in Reading Sequence 7.
- Find *do* on the staff and then identify low *la* and low *so.*
- Sing the exercise using pitch syllables and hand signs.

Invite students to sing this exercise as an accompaniment to *"Hashewie"* **CD 3-21.** Divide the class into two groups. Have one group sing the song while the other group sings the exercise. Invite students to switch parts and sing again.

## Reading Sequence 8, page 64

**MATERIALS**

- "Sourwood Mountain," p. 65 — **CD 3-28**
- Reading Sequence 8
  - Melody part — **CD 3-30**
  - Melody part with accompaniment — **CD 3-31**
  - Accompaniment only — **CD 3-32**
- **Resource Book** pp. D-9, E-9

### Melody: Reading $do^{|}$

Refer students to the hand signs along the side of the page and have them practice low *la,* low *so,* and high *do.* Then have students

- Clap and count the rhythm of Reading Sequence 8.
- Sing the exercise using pitch syllables and hand signs.
- Perform the exercise as a countermelody to "Sourwood Mountain" **CD 3-28.**

Notate the exercise on the board in F-*do* and then ask students to read it from staff notation.

# Unit 3 Music Reading Practice

## Reading Sequence 9, page 92

**MATERIALS**

- "Paw-Paw Patch," p. 93 — **CD 4-36**
- Reading Sequence 9
  - Rhythm Part 1 (woodblock) — **CD 4-38**
  - Rhythm Part 2 (cowbell) — **CD 4-39**
  - Rhythm Parts 1 and 2 — **CD 4-40**
  - Rhythm Parts 1 and 2 with accompaniment — **CD 4-41**
  - Accompaniment only — **CD 4-42**
- **Resource Book** pp. D-10, E-10
- nonpitched percussion instruments

### Rhythm: Reading ♩, ♫♩, ♬♬

Play the recording of "Paw-Paw Patch" **CD 4-36** and ask students to pat or clap a steady beat. Direct students to Reading Sequence 9 and have them

- Clap and count Parts 1 and 2 using rhythm syllables.
- Find measures in "Paw-Paw Patch," p. 92, and Reading Sequence 9 that use the same rhythm pattern.
- Play the parts separately and together on nonpitched percussion instruments.
- Perform the exercise with the song **CD 4-36.**

## Reading Sequence 10, page 98

**MATERIALS**

- "Rise and Shine," p. 98 — **CD 5-7**
- Reading Sequence 10
  - Rhythm part (tambourine) — **CD 5-9**
  - Rhythm part with accompaniment — **CD 5-10**
  - Accompaniment only — **CD 5-11**
- **Resource Book** p. E-11
- nonpitched percussion instruments

### Rhythm: Reading ♩, 𝄽, ♫♩, ♪♩ ♪ in Meter in 4

Play the recording of the exercise **CD 5-9** and ask students to

- Pat their knees on beat 1 and choose different body percussion for beats 2, 3, and 4.
- Identify examples of ♩, 𝄽, ♫♩, ♪♩ ♪ in Reading Sequence 10.
- Clap and count the exercise using rhythm syllables.
- Play the exercise on nonpitched percussion instruments.
- Perform the exercise with the accompaniment track **CD 5-11** or the song **CD 5-7.**



## Reading Sequence 9, page 92

CD 4-38
MIDI 44

### Rhythm: Reading ♩, ♫♩, ♬♬

Use rhythm syllables to **read** and **perform** this two-part rhythm accompaniment for "Paw-Paw Patch."

## Reading Sequence 10, page 98

CD 5-9
MIDI 45

### Rhythm: Reading ♩, 𝄽, ♫♩, ♪♩ ♪ in Meter in 4

Use rhythm syllables to **read** and **perform** this rhythm accompaniment for "Rise and Shine."

## Footnotes

▶ **Performance Options (Reading Sequences 9 and 10)** Ask students to suggest different ways to perform the exercises above as accompaniment for "Paw-Paw Patch" and "Rise and Shine." For example, organize available nonpitched percussion instruments into two groups according to timbre. Then, perform Reading Sequence 9 in a call-and-response format of two-measure phrases.

▶ **Aural Preparation (Reading Sequence 10)** "Rise and Shine" contains rhythmic elements that students will encounter consciously in later lessons. Singing the song provides aural preparation for those elements. Teachers following the reading sequence may wish to have students read the exercise (which contains only known elements) instead of the full staff version. Once the new elements have been learned, students can revisit the song and read the actual notation.

## Reading Sequence 11, page 104

### Melody: Reading $la_{|}$ and $so_{|}$

**Read** and **sing** both written versions of this melody accompaniment for "Weevily Wheat." Use pitch syllables and hand signs.

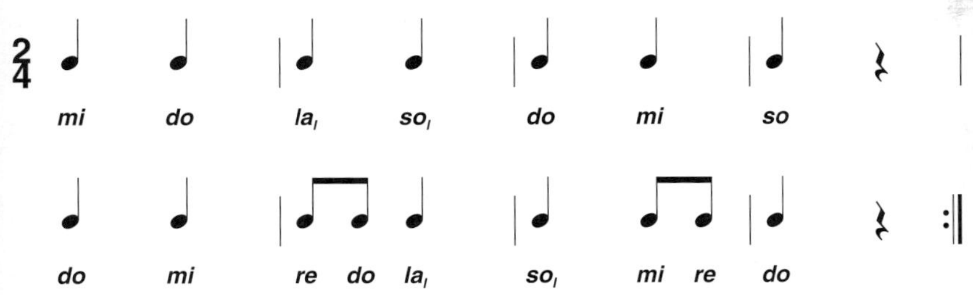

## Reading Sequence 12, page 106

### Melody: Reading *la* Pentatonic Patterns

Use pitch syllables and hand signs to **read** and **sing** this countermelody for "See the Children Playin'."

## Reading Sequence 11, page 104

**MATERIALS**

- "Weevily Wheat," p. 105 **CD 5-17**
- Reading Sequence 11
  Melody part **CD 5-19**
  Melody part with accompaniment **CD 5-20**
  Accompaniment only **CD 5-21**
- **Resource Book** pp. D-12, E-12
- melody instruments

### Melody: Reading $la_{|}$ and $so_{|}$

Refer students to the extended pentatonic scale on p. 104 and the hand signs along the side of this page. Ask students to use pitch syllables and hand signs to read $la_{|}$- $so_{|}$-*do* and then the entire pentatonic scale.

Direct students to the stick notation for Reading Sequence 11 and have them

- Sing the exercise using pitch syllables and hand signs.
- Play the exercise on a melody instrument.
- Repeat the activity, reading from the printed staff notation.
- Sing or play the exercise alone or with the accompaniment track **CD 5-21** or the song **CD 5-17.**

## Reading Sequence 12, page 106

**MATERIALS**

- "See the Children Playin'," p. 107 **CD 5-22**
- Reading Sequence 12
  Melody part **CD 5-24**
  Melody part with accompaniment **CD 5-25**
  Accompaniment only **CD 5-26**
- **Resource Book** pp. D-13, E-13

### Melody: Reading *la* Pentatonic Patterns

Ask students to identify *do* on the staff of Reading Sequence 12 (line 2). Then have students

- Point to examples of *low la* (the tonic note) throughout the score.
- Sing the exercise using pitch syllables and hand signs.
- Sing the exercise using note letter names.
- Sing the exercise as a countermelody with "See the Children Playin'" **CD 5-22.**

▶ **Aural Preparation (Reading Sequences 11 and 12)** "Weevily Wheat" and "See the Children Playin'" contain rhythmic elements that students will encounter consciously in later lessons. Singing the songs provides aural preparation for those elements. Teachers following the reading sequence may wish to have students read the exercises (which contain only known elements) instead of the full staff versions. Once the new elements, including eighth notes tied across the barline, have been learned, students can revisit the songs and read the actual notation.

# Unit 4 Music Reading Practice

##  Reading Sequence 13, page 134

**MATERIALS**

- *"Ochimbo,"* p. 134 — **CD 6-11**
- Reading Sequence 13
  Rhythm part (drum) — **CD 6-13**
  Rhythm part with accompaniment — **CD 6-14**
  Accompaniment only — **CD 6-15**
- **Resource Book** pp. D-16, E-14
- nonpitched percussion instruments

### Rhythm: Reading Upbeats

Ask students to identify the meter of Reading Sequence 13. (4/4) Review meter in 4 and ask students to perform the conducting pattern. Then have students

- Read, clap, and count the exercise using rhythm syllables.
- Perform the exercise using body percussion or nonpitched percussion instruments.
- Perform the exercise with the accompaniment track **CD 6-15** or the song **CD 6-11.**

##  Reading Sequence 14, page 138

**MATERIALS**

- "Cumberland Gap," p. 138 — **CD 6-22**
- Reading Sequence 14
  Rhythm part (woodblock) — **CD 6-24**
  Rhythm part with accompaniment — **CD 6-25**
  Accompaniment only — **CD 6-26**
- **Resource Book** pp. D-18, E-15
- nonpitched percussion instruments

### Rhythm: Reading ♩♫, ♫♩

Have students use the Reading Music Worksheet on p. D-18 in the Resource Book to review the rhythm patterns used in Reading Sequence 14. Then ask students to

- Identify the measures in the exercise in which the meter changes from 2/4 to 3/4. (mm. 9 and 14)
- Clap and count the exercise using rhythm syllables.
- Perform the exercise using body percussion or nonpitched percussion instruments.
- Perform the exercise while others sing the song **CD 6-22.**



UNIT 4

### Reading Sequence 13, page 134

CD 6-13
MIDI 48

**Rhythm: Reading Upbeats**

Use rhythm syllables to **read** and **perform** this rhythm accompaniment for *"Ochimbo."*

### Reading Sequence 14, page 138

CD 6-24
MIDI 49

**Rhythm: Reading ♩♫, ♫♩**

Use rhythm syllables to **read** and **perform** this rhythm accompaniment for "Cumberland Gap."

## Footnotes

**▸ Improving Conducting Skills (Reading Sequences 13 and 14)**
*"Ochimbo"* and "Cumberland Gap" provide good opportunities for practice in conducting. Use the conducting pattern for meter in 4 to draw attention to the "upbeats" at the beginning of each phrase in *"Ochimbo."* Use the conducting patterns for meter in 2 and meter in 3 to demonstrate the asymmetrical phrasing of the refrain in "Cumberland Gap." Experiment with various changes in meter; discuss word stress and its effect on the meter.

CD 6–35
MIDI 50

## Melody: Reading *do, re, mi, fa, so*

Jse pitch syllables and hand signs to **read** and **sing** this
nelody accompaniment for *"Canción de cuna."*

Reading Sequence 16, page 148

CD 7–3
MIDI 51

## Melody: Reading *fa* in a New Key

Jse pitch syllables and hand signs to **read** and **sing** this
countermelody for "Chairs to Mend."

449

## Reading Sequence 15, page 144

**MATERIALS**

- *"Canción de cuna,"* p. 144 **CD 6-31**
- "Cradle Song," p. 144 **CD 6-32**
- Reading Sequence 15
  Melody part **CD 6-35**
  Melody part with accompaniment **CD 6-36**
  Accompaniment only **CD 6-37**
- **Resource Book** pp. D-19, E-16

### Melody: Reading *do, re, mi, fa, so*

Have students sing the pentatonic scale on p. 145. Direct students to Reading Sequence 15 and ask them to

- Identify *do* (G) on the staff and then point to the example of *fa* in the score. (m. 4)
- Identify the note letter name of *fa.* (C)
- Read the exercise in unison, using pitch syllables and hand signs.
- Read the exercise using note letter names.
- Perform the exercise with *"Canción de cuna"* **CD 6-31.**

Notate the exercise on the board in C-*do* and ask students to repeat the first four activity sequences above.

## Reading Sequence 16, page 148

**MATERIALS**

- "Chairs to Mend," p. 149 **CD 7-1**
- Reading Sequence 16
  Melody part **CD 7-3**
  Melody part with accompaniment **CD 7-4**
  Accompaniment only **CD 7-5**
- **Resource Book** pp. D-21, E-17

### Melody: Reading *fa* in a New Key

Ask students to identify the meter of Reading Sequence 16 ($\frac{4}{4}$) and perform the conducting pattern. Direct students to the exercise and ask them to

- Identify *do* (F) on the staff, noting that B♭ is *fa.*
- Read the exercise in unison, using pitch syllables, hand signs, and letter names.
- Perform the exercise in canon.
- Divide into two groups and perform the exercise in canon with "Chairs to Mend" **CD 7-1.**

▶ **Including Recorder (Reading Sequence 15)** The five pitches used in the exercise for *"Canción de cuna"* (G-A-B-C-D) are easy to play on the recorder. Help students use the accompaniment track to create their own instrumental arrangement. For example, have students play the melody, then the exercise, and then combine both parts. Or, have students play the exercise on recorder as others sing.

▶ **Aural Preparation (Reading Sequence 16)** "Chairs to Mend" contains a rhythm element that students will encounter consciously in later lessons. Singing the song provides aural preparation for that element. Teachers following the reading sequence may wish to have students read the exercise (which contains only known elements) instead of the full staff version. Once the new rhythm element has been learned, students can revisit the song and read the actual notation.

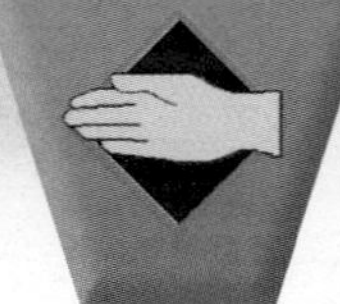

# Unit 5 Music Reading Practice

## Reading Sequence 17, page 176

**MATERIALS**

- *"La Tarara"* (Spanish), p. 176 — **CD 8-1**
- *"La Tarara"* (English), p. 176 — **CD 8-2**
- Reading Sequence 17
  Rhythm part (tambourine) — **CD 8-5**
  Rhythm part with accompaniment — **CD 8-6**
  Accompaniment only — **CD 8-7**
- **Resource Book** pp. D-22, E-18
- nonpitched percussion instruments

### Rhythm: Reading ♩. and ♪

Ask students to describe the form of Reading Sequence 17. (refrain-verse-refrain) Play the recording **CD 8-5** and have students pat or clap the steady beat while following the music. Review meter in 2 and then have students

- Clap and count the exercise using rhythm syllables.
- Point to each example of ♩. ♪
- Perform the exercise using nonpitched percussion instruments.
- Perform the exercise to accompany the song **CD 8-1**.

## Reading Sequence 18, page 178

**MATERIALS**

- "Old House, Tear It Down!" p. 178 — **CD 8-8**
- Reading Sequence 18
  Rhythm part (cowbell) — **CD 8-10**
  Rhythm part with accompaniment — **CD 8-11**
  Accompaniment only — **CD 8-12**
- **Resource Book** pp. D-23, E-19
- nonpitched percussion instruments

### Rhythm: Reading ♪ and ♩.

Have students locate the rhythm ♪ ♩. in Reading Sequence 18. Then ask them

- How is this rhythm similar to ♩. ♪ ?
- How is it different?

Review meter in 4 and ask students to

- Clap and count Reading Sequence 18 using rhythm syllables.
- Clap the rhythm of the exercise again but choose a different body percussion for the ♪ ♩. rhythm.
- Perform the exercise to accompany the song **CD 8-8**, using nonpitched percussion instruments.

UNIT 5

## Music Reading Practice

### Reading Sequence 17, page 176

CD 8–5
MIDI 52

### Rhythm: Reading ♩. and ♪

Use rhythm syllables to **read** and **perform** this rhythm accompaniment for *"La Tarara."*

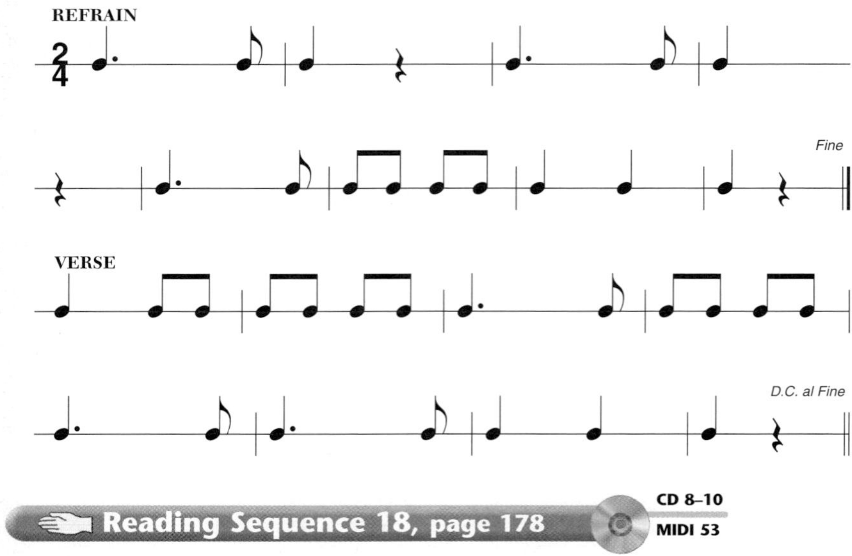


### Reading Sequence 18, page 178

CD 8–10
MIDI 53

### Rhythm: Reading ♪ and ♩.

Use rhythm syllables to **read** and **perform** this rhythm accompaniment for "Old House, Tear It Down!"

450

## Footnotes

▶ **Creating New Patterns (Reading Sequences 17 and 18)** Help students create their own rhythm patterns in $\frac{2}{4}$ and $\frac{4}{4}$ using both ♩. and ♪. Students can begin by choosing four-beat motives from each exercise and combining them into new patterns or phrases to accompany either song.

CD 8-21
MIDI 54

## Reading Sequence 19, page 186

### Melody: Reading *ti*

**Read** and **sing** both written versions of this countermelody for "Kookaburra." Use pitch syllables and hand signs.

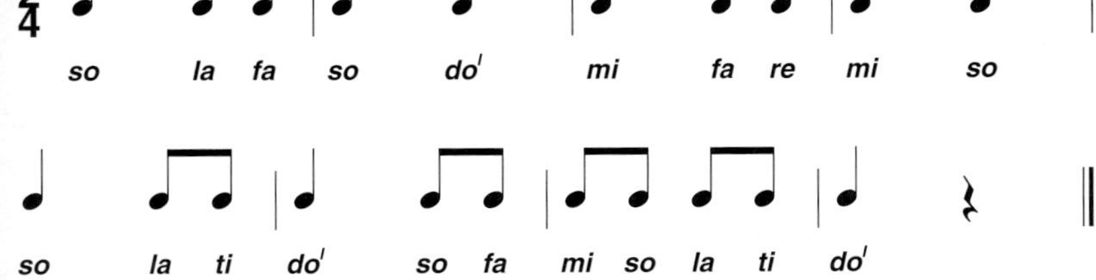

do

CD 8-27
MIDI 55

## Reading Sequence 20, page 188

### Melody: Reading *ti* and the Major Scale

Use pitch syllables and hand signs to **read** and **sing** this melody accompaniment for "Missy-La, Massa-La."

## Reading Sequence 19, page 186

**MATERIALS**

- "Kookaburra," p. 186 **CD 8-19**
- Reading Sequence 19
  - Melody part **CD 8-21**
  - Melody part with accompaniment **CD 8-22**
  - Accompaniment only **CD 8-23**
- **Resource Book** pp. D-24, E-20

### Melody: Reading *ti*

Have students identify and conduct the meter of Reading Sequence 19. Have them identify and demonstrate the two note values used in the exercise. (♩ and ♫) Then ask students to

- Sing from stick notation using pitch syllables and hand signs.
- Identify C-*do* on the staff and re-read the exercise from staff notation using pitch letter names.
- Identify the measures in which *ti* appears. (m. 5 and m. 7)
- Perform the exercise as a round, with parts entering at two-measure intervals.

## Reading Sequence 20, page 188

**MATERIALS**

- "Missy-La, Massa-La," p. 188 **CD 8-25**
- Reading Sequence 20
  - Melody part **CD 8-27**
  - Melody part with accompaniment **CD 8-28**
  - Accompaniment only **CD 8-29**
- **Resource Book** pp. D-25, E-21

### Melody: Reading *ti* and the Major Scale

Direct students to Reading Sequence 20 and ask them to

- Clap and count the rhythm. (See "A New Time Signature" below.)
- Identify C-*do* on the staff and sing the exercise using pitch syllables and hand signs.
- Identify phrases that are the same or similar.
- Sing the exercise using pitch letter names.
- Perform the exercise with the accompaniment track **CD 8-29** or the song **CD 8-25**.

▶ **Syllables/Letter Names (Reading Sequence 19)** As students learn new pitches, it is important that they continue to practice reading and singing using both pitch syllables and pitch letter names. Because the countermelody for "Kookaburra" contains easy rhythms and is in C-*do*, it works well for this sort of practice. Students can also practice singing pitch letter names as they play the countermelody on appropriate mallet instruments.

▶ **A New Time Signature (Reading Sequence 20)** "Missy-La, Massa-La" contains a new new time signature, $\frac{2}{2}$, which students will encounter consciously in later lessons. Teachers may wish to have students read and say the rhythm of the exercise in $\frac{4}{4}$ first. Then have students conduct in 2 to the half-note beat as they read the exercise again.

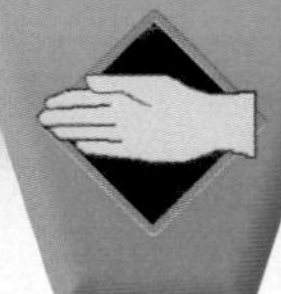

# Unit 6 Music Reading Practice

##  Reading Sequence 21, page 216

**MATERIALS**

- "Oh, How Lovely Is the Evening," p. 217 — **CD 9-10**
- Reading Sequence 21
  - Rhythm part (triangle) — **CD 9-12**
  - Rhythm part with accompaniment — **CD 9-13**
  - Accompaniment only — **CD 9-14**
- **Resource Book** pp. D-26, E-22
- nonpitched percussion instruments

### Rhythm: Reading in Meter in 3

Play Reading Sequence 21 **CD 9-12** and ask students to pat beat 1 and clap beats 2 and 3 of each measure. Refer students to the exercise and have them

- Clap and count the exercise using rhythm syllables.
- Perform the exercise on nonpitched percussion instruments.
- Perform the exercise in canon. (The parts may enter at either six-measure or one-measure intervals.)

Encourage students to create a new accompaniment, using the same rhythm patterns in Reading Sequence 21, and perform it with the song **CD 9-10.**

##  Reading Sequence 22, page 218

**MATERIALS**

- "Dry Bones Come Skipping," p. 218 — **CD 9-15**
- Reading Sequence 22
  - Rhythm part (woodblock) — **CD 9-17**
  - Rhythm part with accompaniment — **CD 9-18**
  - Accompaniment only — **CD 9-19**
- **Resource Book** p. E-23
- nonpitched percussion instruments

### Rhythm: Reading in Meter in 4

Have students compare the rhythm of Reading Sequence 22 with that of Reading Sequence 9, p. 446. Ask them to describe

- At least one similarity. (Both use ♩, ♪♪, ♬♬)
- The meter of each exercise.

Then have students

- Clap and count Reading Sequence 22 using rhythm syllables.
- Perform the exercise on nonpitched percussion instruments.
- Perform the exercise with the accompaniment track **CD 9-19** or the song **CD 9-15.**



UNIT 6 **Music Reading Practice**

## Reading Sequence 21, page 216

CD 9–12
MIDI 56

### Rhythm: Reading in Meter in 3

Use rhythm syllables to **read** and **perform** this counter-rhythm for "Oh, How Lovely Is the Evening."

## Reading Sequence 22, page 218

CD 9–17
MIDI 57

### Rhythm: Reading in Meter in 4

Use rhythm syllables to **read** and **perform** this counter-rhythm for "Dry Bones Come Skipping."

452

## Footnotes

▶ **Fun with Phrases** **(Reading Sequence 21)** "Oh, How Lovely Is the Evening" is a unique "meter in 3" song because it is organized into three six-measure phrases. Encourage students to

- Experiment with shaping the phrases, using word stress and dynamics.
- Show the legato style of the phrasing with their conducting gestures.

▶ **Musical Term Review** **(Reading Sequence 22)** The counter-rhythm for "Dry Bones Come Skipping" provides an opportunity for review of two musical terms: *D.C. al Fine* and *Fine.* Perform the rhythm of the exercise for students as they point to each measure. Stop at the last measure and ask them to describe what should happen next. (Return to the first measure and continue until the word *Fine.*) Allow students to suggest possible meanings for the each term. Then review the definitions.

## Reading Sequence 23, page 226

CD 9-31
MIDI 58

### Melody: Reading a Melodic Sequence

Use pitch syllables and hand signs to **read** and **sing** this melody accompaniment for *"Thula, thula, ngoana."*

## Reading Sequence 24, page 230

CD 9-43
MIDI 59

### Melody: Reading a Melodic Sequence

Use pitch syllables and hand signs to **read** and **sing** this melody accompaniment for *"Tancovačka."*

453

**▶ Comparing Sequences (Reading Sequences 23 and 24)** Have students compare the melody of *"Thula, thula, ngoana"* **CD 9-27** to the melody of the first section (verse) of *"Tancovačka"* **CD 9-39**. Ask students to describe

- How they are similar. (Both are in F-*do*; both contain the same basic melodic sequence of *mi-so-fa, re-fa-mi, do-mi-re.*)
- How they are different. (The rhythm is different; the fourth phrase of *"Tancovačka"* does not follow the sequence.)

As an additional activity, present the exercises for Reading Sequences 23 and 24 interchangeably.

Music Reading Practice

## Reading Sequence 23, page 226

**MATERIALS**

- *"Thula, thula, ngoana,"* p. 227 — **CD 9-27**
- "Sleep, Sleep, Baby," p. 227 — **CD 9-28**
- Reading Sequence 23
  - Melody part — **CD 9-31**
  - Melody part with accompaniment — **CD 9-32**
  - Accompaniment only — **CD 9-33**
- **Resource Book** p. E-24

### Melody: Reading a Melodic Sequence

Review melodic sequence with students by having them trace the melodic contour of *"Thula, thula, ngoana"* **CD 9-27** as they listen to the recording. Repeat the activity with Reading Sequence 23 **CD 9-31**. Direct students to the exercise and ask them to

- Identify measures where the melodic sequence occurs, and describe its pattern in steps and skips.
- Read, clap, and count the rhythm.
- Identify F-*do* on the staff and read the exercise using pitch syllables and hand signs.
- Sing the exercise using pitch letter names.

Notate the exercise on the board in C-*do* and G-*do* and ask students to repeat the activity sequence above.

## Reading Sequence 24, page 230

**MATERIALS**

- *"Tancovačka,"* p. 230 — **CD 9-39**
- "Dancing," p. 230 — **CD 9-40**
- Reading Sequence 24
  - Melody part — **CD 9-43**
  - Melody part with accompaniment — **CD 9-44**
  - Accompaniment only — **CD 9-45**
- **Resource Book** p. E-25

### Melody: Reading a Melodic Sequence

Direct students to the first line of Reading Sequence 24 and ask them to

- Identify F-*do* on the staff and sing the notes using pitch syllables and hand signs.
- Describe the pattern of steps and skips.

Refer students to the complete exercise and ask them to

- Sing lines 2 and 3 using pitch syllables and hand signs.
- Describe how these lines are a melodic sequence of line 1.
- Sing the entire exercise using pitch syllables and hand signs.
- Sing the exercise, using pitch letter names, with the song **CD 9-39.**

# Playing the Recorder

**MATERIALS**
- *Pipes Around the World* **CD 19-9**
- **Resource Book** pp. I-1 through I-31
- recorders

**VOCABULARY**
countermelody aerophones

## ACTIVITIES

### Getting Ready

Ask students if they have ever seen or played a soprano recorder. In order for students to understand that the recorder has a long history, share some of the historical information about the recorder from the History footnote, p. 456.

Explain to students that when playing the recorder only a slight amount of air is needed. Have students read the directions under Getting Ready on p. 454 and try the feather trick. If small feathers are available, students can use real feathers to experiment with blowing the feathers so they move but do not fall off their palms.

Have students hold their recorders without covering any holes and blow into the instruments while thinking about the amount of air they used with the feather trick. Students should produce a pleasing tone.

Repeat the activity and have students play individually. Ask students who use too little or too much air to adjust accordingly.

### Covering the Holes

Help students learn how to hold the recorder with their left hand on top. Students should use the illustration on p. 455 as a guide to fingering the note G.

After students read the text on p. 454, have them try the Covering the Holes test for the notes G and A. They should see the outline of a circle or a small "doughnut" on each finger.

# Playing the Recorder

This section of your book will help you learn to **play** the soprano recorder, a small wind instrument.

### Getting Ready

Extend your hand forward with palm upward. Pretend you have a small feather on your palm. Blow the "feather" gently so it moves across your palm without falling. This is all the air you need to produce a good sound.

### Covering the Holes

Using your left hand, cover the holes shown in the picture. Be sure to press just hard enough so that the holes make a light mark on your fingers. Remove your hand to check that there is an outline of a circle on each finger.

## Footnotes

▶ **Recorder Playing Position** Here are some general guidelines for proper recorder technique.

- Hold the recorder at about a 45 degree angle with the holes facing out and the single thumb hole closer to the body.
- Place the left thumb on the hole in the back and curve the left fingers over the first, second, and third holes.
- Place the right thumb on the back of the recorder between the fourth and fifth holes.
- When covering holes, use the cushions (pads) of the fingers. Fingers should be slightly curved.
- Each hole is covered by a specific finger.
- Rest the mouthpiece lightly on the lower lip.
- Press the upper lip against the mouthpiece with a slight amount of pressure.

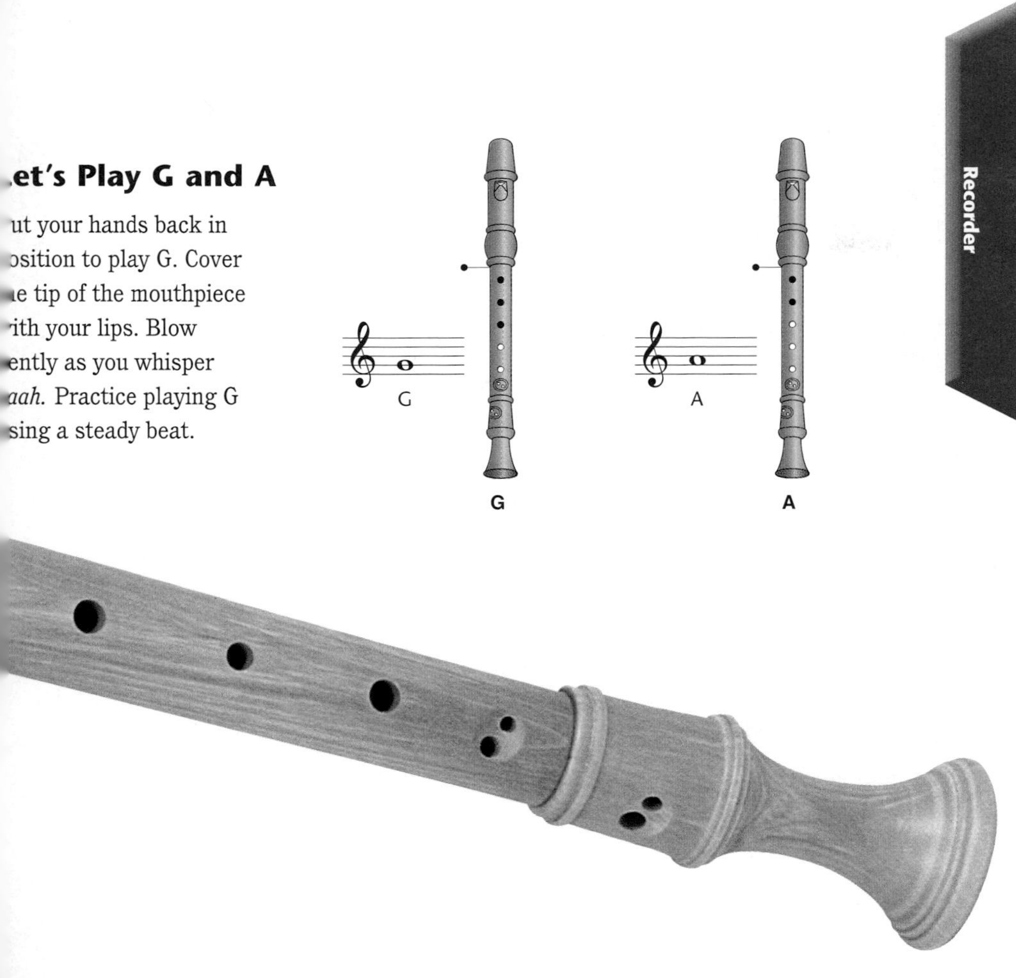

.et's Play G and A
ut your hands back in
osition to play G. Cover
e tip of the mouthpiece
ith your lips. Blow
ently as you whisper
aah. Practice playing G
sing a steady beat.
G
A
G
A
Recorder

:ounter this Melody

lay this countermelody throughout the first section of "Oh, Susanna" page 264). **Create** a hand jive to perform as you **sing** the refrain.

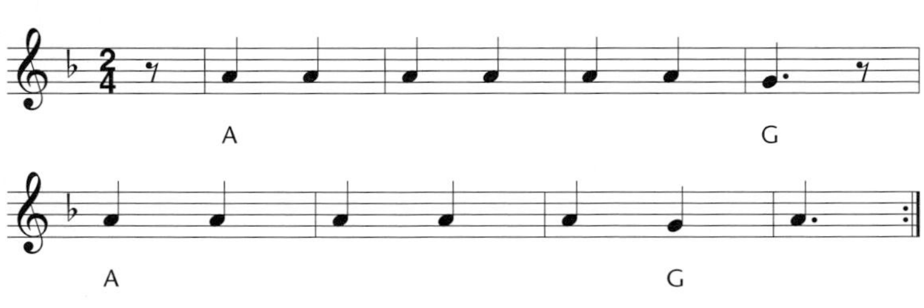

▶ **Care of Plastic Recorders** After playing, dry the interior with a swab such as a large feather or small cloth attached to a cleaning rod. If the mouthpiece becomes clogged, blow into the recorder while covering the top hole or window of the mouthpiece. Plastic recorders can be washed in the top shelf of most dishwashers or by hand with warm soapy water. Be sure to rinse and dry the recorder after washing.

▶ **Care of Wood Recorders** Warm up the instrument before playing. Each time you play, take the recorder apart and dry the inside with a swab. Do not expose the wood recorder to extreme temperature changes or water. Use cork grease sparingly for easier assembly of the instrument and to prevent the cork from drying. Wood recorders will require a "break in" period.

▶ **Inclusion** A soprano recorder is available for students with finger disabilities. Sections are put together and the holes are rotated and plugged according to the needs of the player.

## Let's Play G and A

When students understand how to cover the holes for G, have them whisper *daah* into their recorders to play G.

Have a successful student play the note G so others can hear its sound produced correctly. Do the same for A.

Be aware that beginning recorder players often forget to keep their thumb hole or the first hole covered. If students are squeaking they may be using too much air or they may not be covering the holes securely. Have students

- Look at the fingering illustrations on p. 455 for the notes G and A.
- Practice the fingering for each of these notes.
- Whisper *daah* on each note.
- Remember to blow gently.
- Play four-beat patterns on each of these notes.

## Counter This Melody

Have students look at the countermelody on p. 455. They should notice that it uses only G and A. Have
students

- Sing the letter names of the notes in rhythm.
- Sing the letter names of the notes while fingering their recorders.
- Play the recorder countermelody.

To help students remember to use their left hand on top, have them play Section A and do a hand jive during Section B of "Oh, Susanna," p. 264.

Students could create their own hand jives to perform, or try the following hand jive: pat, pat, clap, clap

Have students play the recorder with the recording of "Oh, Susanna" **CD 11-3,** Remember to have them play Section A and sing and perform a hand jive during Section B. Students should put their recorders under the arm, on the desk, or on the floor while they do the hand jive. The interlude between verses should be enough time for them to pick up their recorders and be ready to play G when the verse begins.

**continued on page 456**

Playing the Recorder

## Adding B

Once students can play G and A, have them look at the fingering chart on p. 456 to learn to play B.

ASK **Do you think B will sound higher or lower than G or A?** (Higher. Have students explain their answers.)

Have students experiment with playing B, A, and G in order to confirm their responses. Invite students to sing the song "Missy-La, Massa-La" **CD 8-25** on p. 188. As they sing, they should feel the half-note pulse.

Now have students look at the recorder countermelody on p. 456. They should see that the recorder part uses all half notes. Point out that the time signature indicates that the half note gets the beat. To help students feel phrases, encourage them to take a breath only when they come to a rest.

For other materials using G, G-A, A-B, and G-A-B, see the Recorder Index on p. 574. Encourage students to practice playing their recorder at home. Provide them with copies of recorder activities from the Resource Book. Each Resource Book page contains the fingerings needed to perform the activity.

## Three New Notes

In order to build right hand strength, introduce students to D, E, and F♯. Have students refer to the fingering illustrations on p. 456. Explain to students that they need very little air when playing notes in the low register. When first playing notes that use the right hand, students may forget to completely cover the left hand holes. Remind students to use the Cover the Hole test to check for proper hand placement and coverage.

## Adding B

Now you are ready to learn to play B. Cover the holes shown in the diagram. Before playing, predict if B will sound higher or lower than G or A. Here is a recorder part that you can **play** while others **sing** "Missy-La, Massa-La" on page 188. Make sure you observe the repeat signs at the end of each phrase.

B

## Three New Notes

Here are three new notes. Cover the holes securely with your fingers arched and whisper *daah.*

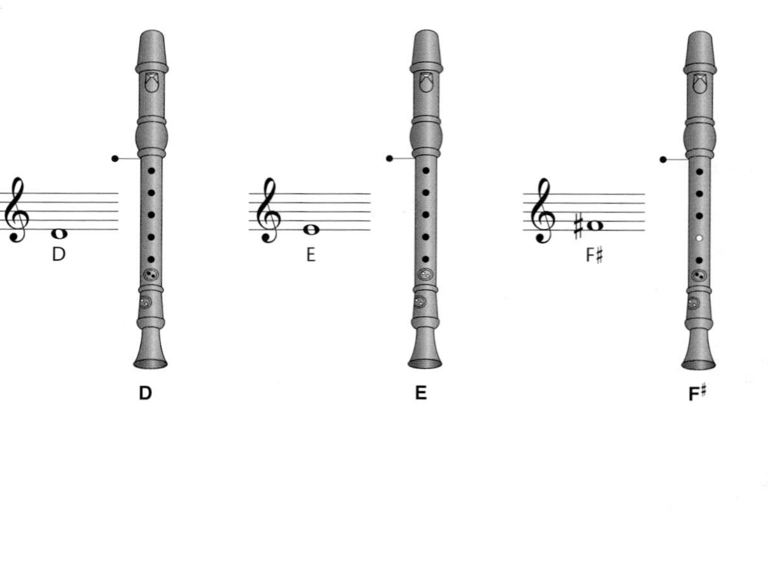


456

**▶ History** A recorder is a simple wood flute that dates back to medieval times. Henry VIII, king of England, was a skilled musician who played the recorder. When he died, it is said that he owned 76 different recorders. The recorder comes in many sizes—the larger ones sounding lower, the smaller ones sounding higher. During the Renaissance, recorders were primarily played in consorts or ensembles rather than as a solo instrument.

**▶ Geography** Using a world map, have students locate the places where the aerophones found in their books originated. They should notice that only one continent is not represented (Antarctica). Have students record in music journals why they think there are no known aerophones from Antarctica.

**▶ Listening** Provide students with opportunities to listen to music that includes a recorder or other similar aerophone. Some examples are:

- "How Do You Doo-Tee" **CD 8-24**, didgeridoo
- "Little David, Play on Your Harp" **CD 17-4**, recorder

ow you are ready to **play** a countermelody to accompany the singing of "The eel Row" on page 240. Does the countermelody have mostly leaps or steps?

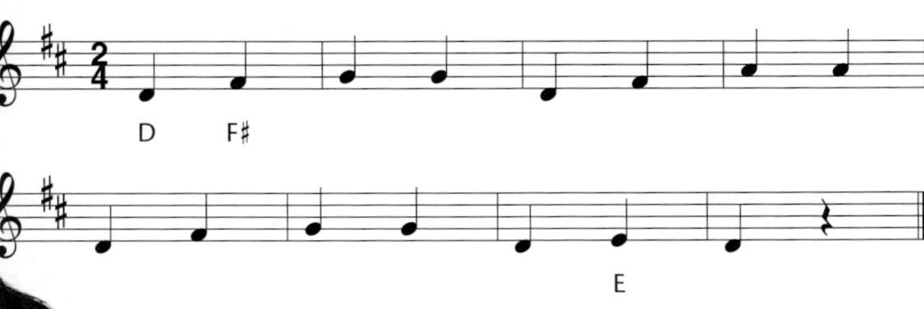


Recorder

## "B-A-G" Songs Plus

Now that you can play G, A, B, D, and E, you will be able to **play** some of the songs in your book. Look at "See the Children Playin'," page 107; "Old House, Tear It Down," page 178; and "Love Will Guide Us," page 328. Practice individual phrases before playing the entire song.

## Ready for High C and High D

Practice playing two new notes. Move your thumb slightly away from the hole when playing D.

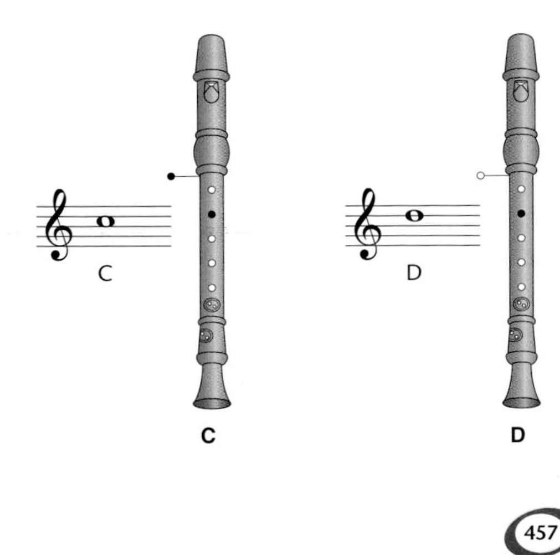


457

- "I Walk in Beauty" **CD 12-1**, Native American flute
- "Missy-La, Massa-La" **CD 8-25**, penny whistle
- *"Tsuki"* **CD 1-36**, shinobue wood flute

▶ **Music Notation Software** To reinforce note playing, encourage students to use music notation software to compose their own melodies for recorder. For their first experience, give students a simple rhythm pattern to use as the foundation for their pieces. Once they have composed and printed their melodies, have them perform the melodies on recorder.

## "B-A-G" Songs Plus

Before they play the countermelody for "The Keel Row," have students play four-beat patterns on D, E, and F♯.

**SAY** I will play a four-beat pattern on my recorder. After I play the pattern, echo the pattern on your recorder.

Play patterns for students to echo that use the notes from "The Keel Row" countermelody. Always begin a new pattern on the same note on which the previous pattern ended. Have students look at the countermelody on p. 457 to identify the steps, leaps, and repeats.

**ASK** **Which leap requires you to move only one finger?** (D to F♯)

Have students read the countermelody for "The Keel Row" in their books. They should play during the verse of the song and sing during the refrain **CD 10-10**, p. 240.

When students can play G, A, B, D, and E, have them try to play some of the song melodies found in their books.

- "See the Children Playin'," p. 107
- "Old House, Tear It Down!" p. 178
- "Love Will Guide Us," p. 328

For more activities, see the Resource Book.

- *"Ōsamu kosamu,"* p. I-9
- "Rise and Shine," p. I-10
- "Weevily Wheat," p. I-11
- *"Dayenu,"* p. I-31

## Ready for High C and High D

Have students look at the fingering chart on p. 457 to learn to play high C and high D. Remind students to move their thumb only slightly away from the hole when playing high D.

Playing the Recorder

continued on page 458

### Going Up the Scale

**ASK What is the melody pattern in the countermelody for "Frog Music"?** (a scale)

Have students play the countermelody. When they are comfortable, have them try the same melody using different rhythm patterns.

### Pipes Around the World

Have students discuss the instruments pictured on pp. 458–459.

**ASK Have you ever heard or seen any of these instruments? How do you think they will sound?** (Accept a variety of answers, but encourage students to give reasons for their answers based on the size of the instruments, the number of holes or tubes, how the instruments are played, and the origin of the instruments.)

Play the sound montage *Pipes Around the World* **CD 19-9**. As students listen, have them point to the picture of the instrument they hear in the recording.

(The instruments occur in the following order: *didgeridoo*, panpipes, *shakuhachi*, Native American flute, recorder, *kudu* horn.)

## Going Up the Scale

The recorder part below for "Frog Music," on page 200, uses the first five notes of the G scale. Can you name these notes? After playing the recorder melody as written, **create** a new one. Keep the same melody but change the rhythm patterns. Before beginning, think of some patterns that can be used in place of quarter notes.

## Pipes Around the World

**Listen** to these musical examples. Point to each instrument as you hear it being played.

**Aerophones** are instruments that produce sound by vibrating air.

CD 19-9
**Pipes Around the World**
**Sound Montage**

As you read the captions, study the pictures of these **aerophones** from around the world. Then **describe** how the size and shape of each instrument influences its sound.

***Didgeridoo***, a five-foot-long wooden instrument from Australia, is played by Aboriginals during various ceremonies and rituals. ▶

▲ ***Shakuhachi***, an end-blown bamboo flute from Japan, can be found in various lengths, but most only have four finger holes and one thumb hole.

458

## Footnotes

▶ **Literature/Social Studies** Students may enjoy reading the Australian Aboriginal tale "Didgeridoo Magic" and other multicultural tales about musical instruments found in *Play Me a Story: Nine Tales About Musical Instruments* by Naomi Adler (Millbrook Press, 1998). To obtain historical information on aerophones, students may enjoy reading the interactive book, *Musical Instruments: From Flutes Carved of Bone, to Lutes, to Modern Electric Guitars* (Scholastic, Inc., 1994).

▶ **Music at Home** Students can search at home for more information and recordings of woodwind instruments like the ones heard in the sound montage *Pipes Around the World*. Have them search through family recordings and find pictures of instruments in books or magazines for a bulletin board display in the classroom. Sound files of these instruments can be recorded on cassette or CD and students can develop their own What Do You Hear? listening games.

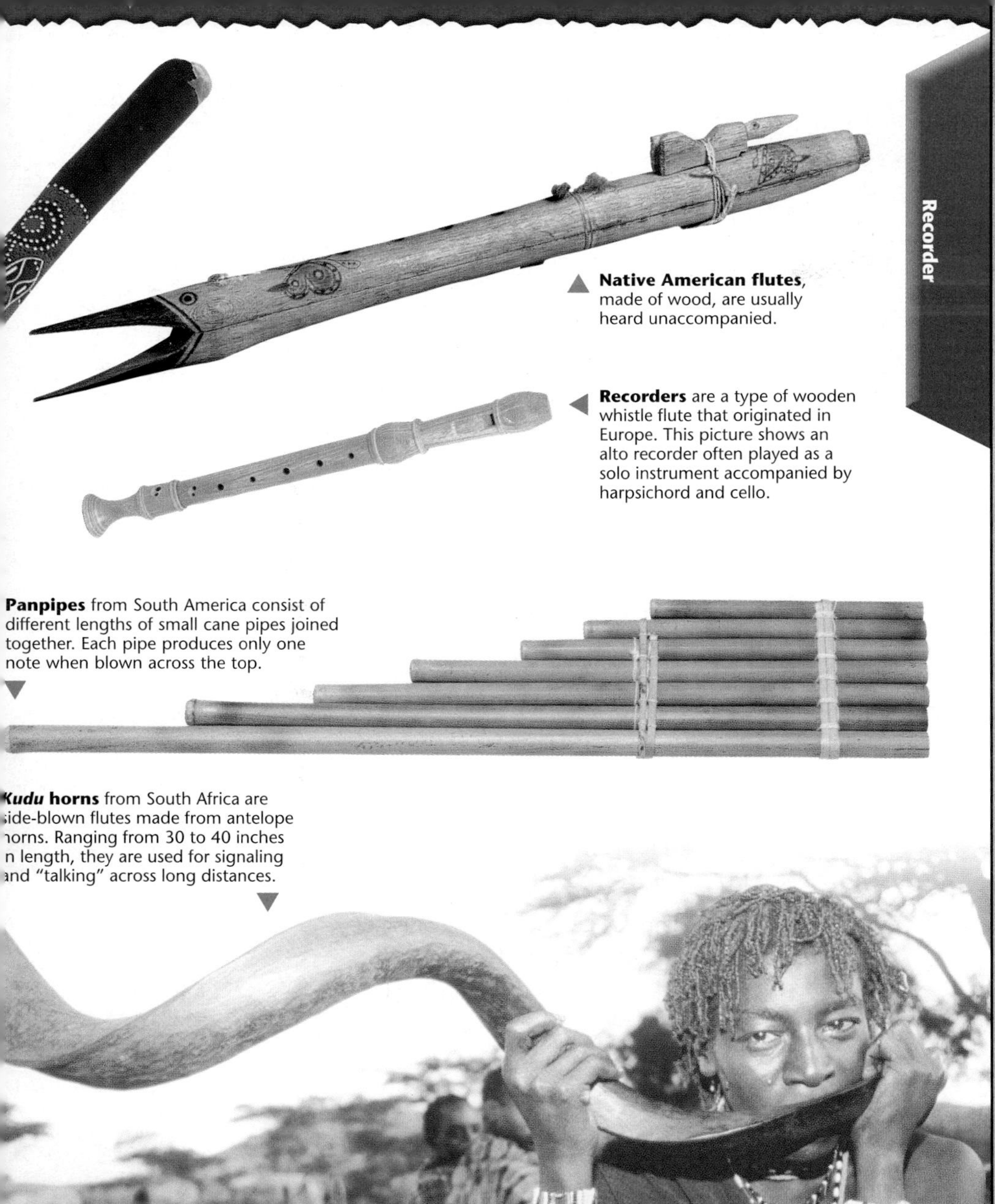


**Native American flutes**, made of wood, are usually heard unaccompanied.

**Recorders** are a type of wooden whistle flute that originated in Europe. This picture shows an alto recorder often played as a solo instrument accompanied by harpsichord and cello.

**Panpipes** from South America consist of different lengths of small cane pipes joined together. Each pipe produces only one note when blown across the top.

***Kudu* horns** from South Africa are side-blown flutes made from antelope horns. Ranging from 30 to 40 inches in length, they are used for signaling and "talking" across long distances.

459

Playing the Recorder

▶ **Playing** Students should be encouraged to play in ensembles with other recorders, keyboards, guitars, Autoharps, and percussion instruments. Remind students to listen to the other instruments and blend the sound of their recorders. Ensembles can provide accompaniment for singing in the classroom or for special programs.

▶ **Working in Small Groups** As students get older, they enjoy working in groups rather than as an entire class. Try structuring part of the music class for small group work with the teacher as a facilitator.

# Mallet Instruments

**MATERIALS**

- "Ah, Poor Bird," p. 196
- "Follow the Drinkin' Gourd," p. 266
- "Orfferondo," p. 194 **CD 8-35**
- "Enjoy the Earth" (proverb), p. 81
- **Resource Book** pp. F-1 through F-37
- soprano and alto glockenspiels; soprano, alto, and bass xylophones; soprano, alto, and bass metallophones; a variety of mallets

**VOCABULARY**

bordun

## ACTIVITIES

### Moving and Playing

Prepare students for coordinated playing of Orff mallet instruments with movement, body percussion, and small percussion practice. Have students pat a steady beat with both hands on their legs, then have them pat with alternating hands. When students show proficiency, have them pat with a crossover movement left, right, then left-over-right. These movement activities help prepare students to play simple, alternating, and crossover borduns on xylophones, metallophones, and glockenspiels. It is also beneficial to pat tricky rhythm patterns before playing them on instruments.

### Listening

**Choosing Mallets** Have students read about mallets on p. 460 of the student text. Then demonstrate the various timbres that can be produced when different mallets are used on the instruments. For example, play a metallophone with a soft yarn-headed mallet. Then play with a hard rubber-headed mallet. Have students compare the timbres.

### Improvising

Mallet instruments can be used creatively and to reinforce music reading skills. Set up the instruments in the following scales.

- C-*do* pentatonic: C-D-E-G-A
- F-*do* pentatonic: F-G-A-C-D
- G-*do* pentatonic: G-A-B-D-E
- e-*la* pentatonic: e-g-a-b-d
- d-*la* pentatonic: d-f-g-a-c

Have students improvise with specific rhythms on unspecified pitches. The rhythms used can be derived from words in poetry, song lyrics, or other sources.

The instruments can also be used to play sound effects to enhance meaning in poetry. Have students read the Yoruba proverb "Enjoy the Earth Gently" on p. 81. Invite them to explore timbres on glockenspiels, metallophones, and xylophones, using various mallet types, and to create random textures to accompany the proverb.

# Mallet Instruments

## Playing Mallets

When using mallets to play instruments, follow these simple suggestions.

### Holding the Mallets

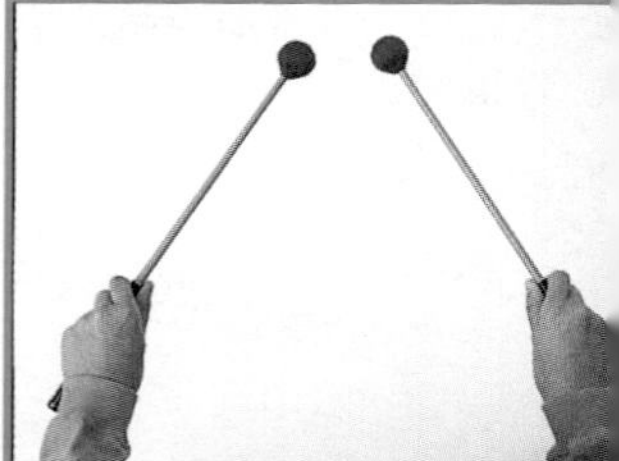

Fold your fingers and thumbs around the mallet handle—the thumb should lie alongside the handle, but the pointer finger should not sit on top of the mallet. The backs of your hands should face the ceiling. Grip the handles on the hand grips, but not at the very end. (Smaller hands may need to grip further up toward the mallet head.) Elbows should hang easily at your sides. Avoid elbows that stick out to the side or hug the body.

### Striking the Bars

Strike each bar at its center, not at either end. Let your mallet strike quickly and then bounce away. If you let the mallet stay on the bar, the sound is stopped.

### Matching Mallets to Instruments

It is important to choose the appropriate mallet for each instrument to make its best sound.

For special effects, use hard wood mallets or mallet handles. Avoid anything that would damage the surface of the bars.

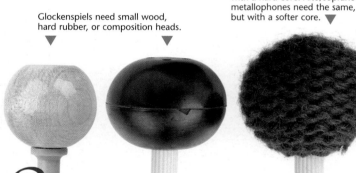

Glockenspiels need small wood, hard rubber, or composition heads.

Alto/soprano xylophones need medium-sized felt or yarn heads with a hard core. Alto/soprano metallophones need the same, but with a softer core.

Bass instruments need large felt or yarn heads. Choose softer mallets for metallophones, and harde[r] mallets for xylophones.

460

## Footnotes

**▶ Care of Mallet Instruments** Show students how to set up the instruments in specific scales. Have them lift the bars up carefully with two hands, one hand at each end of the bar. Caution them to make sure the nails that hold the bars in place do not get bent. Explain to students that the bars are being removed so that they can make "good" sounding music together. Have students practice walking to the instruments by "moon-walking" slowly around them. They should not step over the instruments because their toes can easily get hooked on them and cause injury to the student and damage to the instrument.

**▶ Position and Technique** Students should kneel, stand, or sit in front of an instrument. Have them hold the mallets by wrapping their fingers in a relaxed way over and around the grip of the mallet, arms slightly away from their sides. Have students strike the bars at the center and "pull" the sound from the instrument with a light, upward, and buoyant stroke. If students push downward into the bars, the vibration of the bars will be muted, making a dull sound.

ʟaying Position
ou may sit or stand while playing
nallet instruments. This depends
n the distance of the top of the
nstrument from the floor. Your
ody should stay straight with
our arms placed easily in front
f you to strike the bars.
Sit on the floor.
Sit in a chair to play bass instruments.
Stand
Sit in a chair.
Mallet Instruments
461


## Playing Borduns

A simple bordun is the first and fifth pitches of a scale played together or alternated. In *do* pentatonic on C, the bordun would be C and G. In d *la* pentatonic, the bordun would be d and a. Students should always use two hands when playing.

Have students play the bass xylophone crossover bordun on p. 197 as the class sings "Ah, Poor Bird" **CD 8-36** on p. 196. Invite them to experiment with playing with various types of mallets.

A simple moving bordun involves one hand changing pitches while the other hand remains on the same pitch. A double moving bordun involves both hands changing pitches. The accompaniment for "Follow the Drinkin' Gourd" **CD 11-5** on p. 266 has a simple moving bordun in the bass xylophone part at the beginning, which changes to a double moving bordun after the second measure.

## Ensemble Playing

Have students set up the instruments in C-*do* pentatonic by removing the Fs and Bs. Play the recording of "Orfferondo" **CD 8-35** on p. 194. Assign mallet parts to the students and have them pat the rhythms of their parts as they listen, emulating the gestures necessary for playing the instruments. Point out that the soprano and alto xylophone parts in the A section are not borduns, but stepwise passages. Allow students to experiment with ways of malleting these parts, such as left-right-left-right-left, or left-left-right-left-right. Then transfer all parts to the instruments and play "Orfferondo."



▶ **Orff Instrumentarium** See Resource Book p. F-36 for a key to instrument abbreviations on a score. Set up the instruments in the classroom as an ensemble, grouping the families together in the following manner. Place a bass xylophone for you to play in the center, facing the group. On the left, set up the soprano and alto glockenspiels in two rows. Similarly, to the right, set up the soprano and alto metallophones, with a bass metallophone in a third row. Set up the xylophones in similar formation to the metallophones. Then set up other percussion and drums to the right and behind the xylophones.

▶ **Malleting** When there is an instrument part that involves repeated pitches, encourage students to explore malleting patterns to make the part easier to play. For example, in the arrangement for "Frog Music" on p. 201, the alto xylophone part may be easier to play with this malleting pattern: left-right-left-right-right. This way the rhythm pattern always starts on the left hand.

# Playing the Guitar

**MATERIALS**
- Guitars
- Sound Bank **CD 19-10**
- "Johnny Appleseed" **CD 15-7**
- "The Earth Is Our Mother" (contemporary) **CD 15-24**
- "Cycle Song of Life" **CD 16-6**

This section introduces three types of guitars and their parts, some applications, and proper playing position.

## Playing the Guitar

Ask students to remove guitars from their cases. Point out the major parts of the instrument as captioned in the student text. Ask students to locate them on their guitars.

Write out a list of acoustic guitar parts on the board or distribute to help students remember the parts of the guitar and their purpose.

- Soundhole: Allows the string vibrations amplified in the resonator to project outward.
- Bridge: Allows vibrations to enter the resonator.
- Tuning Pegs: Tighten and loosen the strings to change pitch.
- Nut: Keeps strings spaced properly on the finger-board above the frets, and takes some of the string tension off the tuning pegs.

Add the following list for electric guitar.

- Pick-ups: Pick up, or amplify, the vibrations, since there is no resonance on a solid body guitar.
- Tone/volume controls: Change the sensitivity of the pickups.
- Tremelo arm: Allows string tension to be con-trolled by the right hand.

Use the listening selections listed in the Materials section above to explore the sound of the different instruments.

## Tuning the Guitar

Explain string numbers to students, using p. 462 as a guide. Refer to strings by size or thickness, not "high" or "low," until the students learn their numbers. Have the class play and count each string as a group, then have each student strum separately with the right thumb.

Explain the general rules for using tuning pegs: Tightening the string *raises* the pitch. The player turns the tuning peg away from him or her. Loosening the string *lowers* the pitch. The player turns the tuning peg toward him or her.

Then have students practice tuning with a keyboard. This is a new skill that may take some time. Ask stu-dents to listen for whether strings need to sound higher or lower to match the target pitch, and therefore if the strings should be tightened or loosened.

Consider using an electronic tuner for those students who are visual learners.



# Playing the Guitar

## Types of Guitars

There are three types of guitars—nylon-string classical, steel-string acoustic, and electric. Look at these photographs and learn the names of their parts.

▲ Nylon-String Classical Guitar
▲ Steel-String Acoustic Guitar
▲ Electric Guitar

## Tuning the Guitar

The strings on a guitar need to be tuned to certain pitches. It is also necessary to fine-tune and re-tune during long periods of performance. Follow these steps to tune the guitar.

- To get started quickly, you may ask your teacher to tune the guitar for you.
- Guitar strings are numbered 1, 2, 3, 4, 5, and 6, with string number 6 being the lowest (or largest).
- You can tune the guitar using the keys of the piano. The illustration at right shows what keys to use for tuning each guitar string.

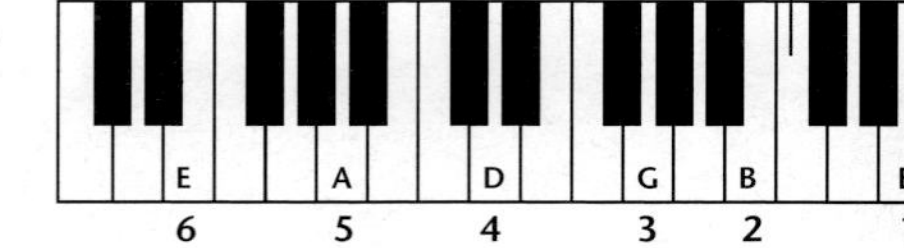

# Footnotes

▶ **Proper Playing Position** It is important for students to use a proper playing position from the very beginning. Point out that students should slightly angle the neck of the guitar, which aligns the left hand for chording.

The inside of the right elbow should straddle the widest part of the guitar body, and the right hand should be placed directly over the sound hole.

The body should be upright and relaxed to maximize the students' dexterity and reduce muscle fatigue. You may find this difficult to communicate, since many students will assume a "casual" stance, which is often seen in the popular media, but which is not healthy for developing technique. A good way to demonstrate proper posture is to have each student stand with the back straight, shoulders relaxed, and arms down at sides. Then have the student sit, keeping back straight, and hand him or her the instrument. Students will need to be reminded of proper posture often throughout the lesson.

## etting Ready to Play

ollow these directions to learn how to **play** the guitar.

The left-hand fingers press the strings on the frets to produce chords.

The right-hand thumb brushes the strings in order to make the sound.

Use the left-hand finger numbers when you read guitar chords.

Always relax your body. The guitar neck should be slanted slightly upward.

## laying Your First Chords

hords are indicated in most songs in this book. The hord names tell you which chords to play, and when play them.

play chords on the guitar

Place the thumb of your left hand behind the neck.

Keep your fingers arched as you reach around the neck to press the strings.

Press the strings down onto the fingerboard.

Keep your palm away from the neck.

## uitar Chords

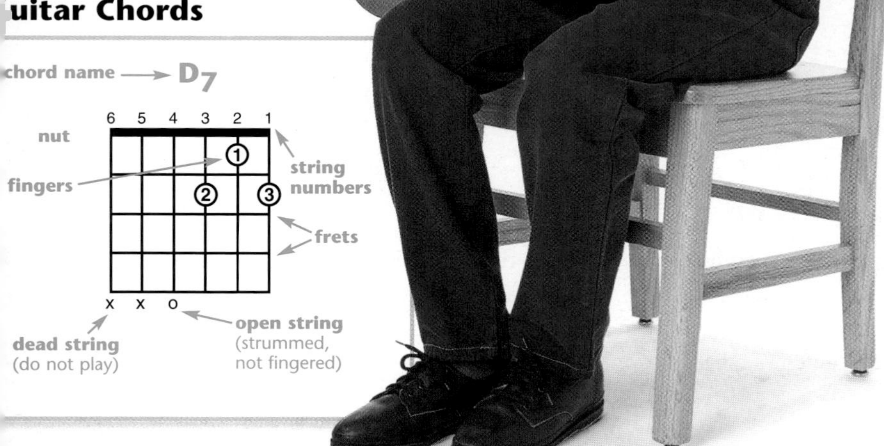




## Getting Ready to Play

Have students wrap the thumb of the left hand around the neck of the guitar as they practice the thumb strum described on p. 462. Then teach a strum, which uses the thumb and index finger. Explain that the thumb plays the bass note on string 6, and the rest of the strings are brushed with the nail of the index finger in a smooth downward motion. Teach these patterns.

Thumb-Strum-Thumb-Strum ($\frac{2}{4}$, $\frac{4}{4}$, and $\frac{6}{8}$ meter)

Thumb-Strum-Strum ($\frac{3}{4}$ meter)

As before, practice playing as a group first. Then ask each student to play the strum individually. It is important that each student hears himself or herself individually to build confidence and a discriminating ear.

## Playing Your First Chords

To begin developing left-hand technique, have students observe and then repeat the numbering of the left-hand fingers, as illustrated on p. 463.

Start with the $D_7$ chord shown on p. 463 of the student book. Ask students to locate the fingers on the neck, keeping the fingers of the left hand relaxed and "round," with space between the guitar neck and the hand. The palm does not touch the guitar.

Direct students to press the strings down only before actually playing to reduce finger fatigue. When not playing, the fingertips are rested on the strings.

## Strum Diagrams

Teach these strum patterns to students as part of their chord mastery. Draw these diagrams on the board, or duplicate them and distribute.

### Tango Strum

First, play "down strums" on these counts:

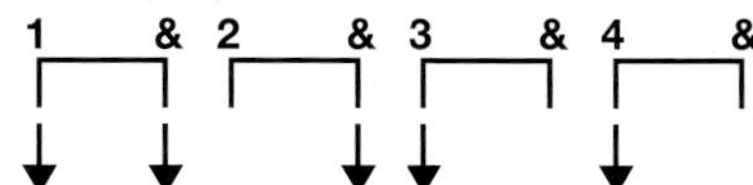


Now fill in "up strums" on the remaining counts:

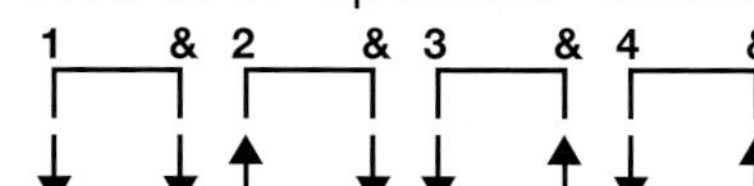

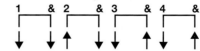

The "down strums" are stronger than the "up strums."

Aural learners may have more success if you or a partner teaches the strum by saying the pattern: "down-down-up-down-down-up-down-up."

### Charleston Rhythm Strum

The first down-strum of each measure should be "dampered" with the heel of the palm on the strings. The second should ring free.

**▶ Developing a Repertoire** The following list of songs can be played by students in grade 4. Allow students to "ease into" guitar accompaniment by playing with other classroom instruments in small groups.

**Songs in C** (a capo can be placed on the third fret and play in A)

Big Rock Candy Mountain, p. 330
The Wheel of the Water, p. 362
We Shall Overcome, p. 326
Sweet Betsy from Pike, p. 244

**Songs in D**

Somebody's Knockin' at Your Door, p. 53
Gonna Ride up in the Chariot, p. 20
Pay Me My Money Down, p. 38
Sourwood Mountain, p. 65

**Songs in G**

Clementine, p. 341
Love Will Guide Us, p. 328
Sailing Down My Golden River, p. 332
All Night, All Day, p. 180

# Playing the Keyboard

**MATERIALS**
- Textbook
- Keyboards

This section is designed to assist you in class keyboard instruction, in addition to or in place of private instruction.

## Sitting Position

Have each student (or as many as you have keyboards) sit facing the keyboard, as far forward on the bench as is necessary for the student's feet to reach the floor. The edge of the bench should touch just below the top of the leg. If a student's feet do not comfortably reach the floor when he or she is properly seated, provide a large telephone book or other support under the feet. It is important that the upper body be high enough for the forearms to be on the same level as the keyboard, with wrists parallel to the keyboard.

## Hand Position

Ask students to stand with arms down at the side. Have them look down and observe the shape of the hand in a relaxed position. Then, ask students to sit at the keyboard and put their hands above the keys, holding their hands loosely in that same position. You can ask them to lightly swing their elbows to check flexibility. Point out that the curved fingers need to rest far enough in on the keys so that the thumb touches a white key.

If necessary, have students switch places so that all have a chance to find their playing position.

## Finger Numbers

Ask students to hold up their hands and count off 1, 2, 3, 4 and 5, while wiggling that finger. You may wish to have students count off each hand separately first, and then together.

## Fingering for Melodies

Ask students to look at the diagrams at the top of p. 465. Then, after checking students for proper playing position, ask them to locate the illustrated keys on their keyboards. Using first the right and then the left hand, ask students to play the patterns first individually, then as a group. Have students switch places if necessary so that all have a turn.

# Playing the Keyboard

In this section of your book, we will learn to **play** keyboard instruments.

## Sitting Position

For maximum support from your arms, shoulders, and back, sit slightly forward on the bench with your feet resting on the floor at all times. Your knees should be just under the front edge of the keyboard. You should feel a center of gravity, which will allow you to lean from side to side if necessary.

## Hand Position

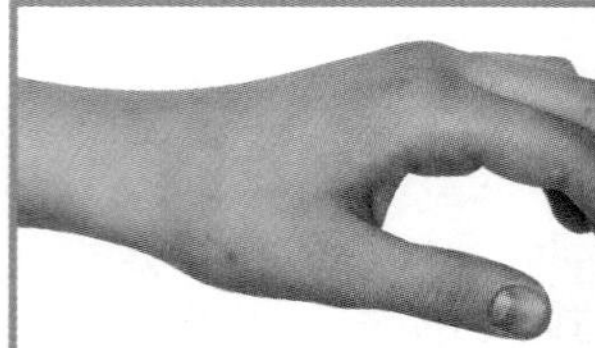

The best hand position is the shape of your hand as it hangs at your side. When you bring your hand up to the keyboard, curve your fingers at the middle joint and make your wrist parallel to the keyboard. You should feel "flexibility" in your elbows as they hang near your side. The elbow should follow through with the natural movement of your wrist.

## Finger Numbers

The fingers are numbered as pictured here.

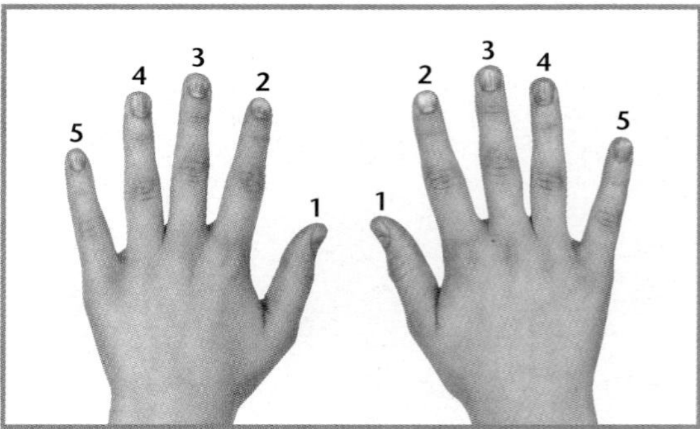


## Fingerings for Melodies

How a melody moves determines the fingering on the keyboard. Look at the diagrams at the top of page 465. By translating the keyboard examples to one- and two-line staves, it is easy to see how right/left movement on the keyboard relates to up/down movement on the staff.

# Footnotes

▶ **Meeting Individual Needs** Create transparencies of each keyboard example on p. 465 and display for the class. Invite students to play each example. Some students may be more successful if the class works in pairs. Sitting side by side, have the more skilled partner demonstrate the keys to be played and the other student imitate. Consider having each pair play the patterns as if in duet.

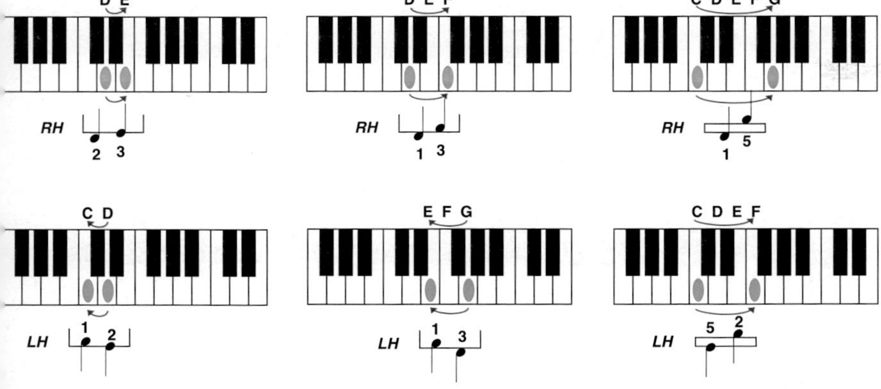


## Three- and Five-Line Reading

**Play** these examples. Determine the fingering before you begin each one.

RH Begin on G:

LH Begin on C:

## Playing from Treble and Bass Clefs

When playing keyboard music, read the music by following the upward and downward direction of the melody to determine if it moves by step, by leap, or if it stays on a repeated tone. You must also determine where to play the notes on the keyboard. Each note in printed music indicates one place, and only one place, where it can be played. **Play** the following examples in the treble and bass clefs.

## Three-Line Reading

Ask students to look at the three-line examples on p. 465. Point out the last measure in the right-hand line. Note that the last pitch and the first pitch of the pattern are the same.

ASK **What is the distance between the highest and lowest note?** (a fifth)

Have them place the thumb and fifth finger of the right hand on these keys. Check each student for proper playing position, then ask them to play each pattern as a group.

Repeat the question and positioning for the left hand pattern and have students play again as a group.

## Playing from Treble and Bass Clefs

Ask students to look at the examples at the bottom of p. 465 and find the lowest and highest notes in the example. Point out that those pitches will use the outer fingers of the hand. Check each student for proper playing position, then ask students to play each line separately, then together.

ASK **What do you notice about the melody patterns?** (They are the same for each hand.)

As a review, consider duplicating the pattern at the bottom of the page and asking students to mark the fingering numbers above each pitch. Remind them to pay attention to which clef and hand they are working with in making their determination.

▶ **Integrating the Curriculum** Students may be interested in maintaining a bulletin board filled with images of famous keyboard players past and present. Performers may be grouped according to time period, style, or specific instrument. The bulletin board may be updated as the year progresses. Encourage students to bring in photographs or articles of performers to include in the class bulletin board.

# Sound Bank

**MATERIALS**
- Sound Bank — **CD 19**, tracks 10–45

**VOCABULARY**

percussion, vibration, pitch, resonance, timbre, tension, bow, reed, valve

## USING THE SOUND BANK

**Sound Bank** is a glossary of the principal instruments discussed in this book. Text, pictures, and recordings are designed to be used together to help students integrate the definitions, illustrations, and sounds.

**Ready Reference** When an instrument is studied in the book, reinforce the learning by having students

- Look at the illustration.
- Listen to the sound.
- Read the definition.

**Evaluation** Test students' comprehension by playing the recorded examples in random order and having students respond orally or on paper.

**Instrument Families** The instruments shown in the student text are listed alphabetically but are divided into families—strings (orange), percussion (blue), woodwinds (purple), brass (green) and keyboard (red). The color codes will help students immediately identify the family to which an instrument belongs.

## ACTIVITIES

### Vibrations and Sound

**SAY** All sound sources make vibrations. Vibrations are back-and-forth movements that come to our ears through the air. Our ears "hear" the vibrations as sound.

To demonstrate vibration, hit a cymbal or pluck the free end of a ruler that is braced on a desk.

Use the following instruments for additional demonstrations of vibration and sound. Allow students to touch the instruments lightly, in order to feel as well as see the vibrations.

- drumhead
- Autoharp strings
- guitar strings
- piano strings

Guide students in experimenting with other classroom percussion instruments to feel vibrations. Point out that

- On some instruments, the vibrations may be obvious.
- On others, such as the guiro, the vibrations may be very delicate and difficult to feel. (On the sand blocks, they cannot be felt at all.)



# Sound Bank

**Bagpipes** Drone pipes and an air reservoir contained in an animal skin bag are the main characteristics of this reed instrument. The bagpipe is common in Arabic and European countries. *Uillean* [ILL-uhn] refers to Irish bagpipes. CD 19–10 p. 260

**Balalaika** [bah-lah-LIE-kah] A flat, triangular, long-necked instrument with a small sound hole on the front. It produces sound when any of the three metal strings are plucked. The *balalaika* is popular in Russian folk music and is a member of the lute family. CD 19–11 p. 295

**Bassoon** A large, tube-shaped, woodwind instrument with a double-reed. Lower notes on the bassoon can be gruff or comical. Higher notes are softer, sweeter, and gentler sounding. CD 19–12 p. 70

**Cello** A large, wooden string instrument. The player sits with the cello between his or her knees and reaches around the front to pluck or bow the strings. The cello has a low, rich-sounding voice. CD 19–13 p. 95

**Clarinet** A wind instrument shaped like a cylinder. It is usually made of wood and has a reed in the mouthpiece. Low notes on the clarinet are soft and hollow. The middle and highest notes are open and bright. CD 19–14 p. 70

Instrument Key: strings | percussion | woodwind | brass | keyboard

## Footnotes

**▶ Playing Percussion Instruments** Almost anything that makes noise can be used as a percussion instrument. Percussion instruments can be struck, shaken, or scraped.

- Struck: most percussion instruments; struck with hands, mallets, sticks
- Shaken: maracas (seeds or pebbles strike the inside)
- Scraped: sand blocks, guiro

The percussion section of a concert band or a symphony orchestra is usually placed toward the rear, since it can be heard easily. In addition to adding specific effects and colors to the ensemble, percussion instruments help provide a rhythmic foundation.

Percussion instruments can also be grouped according to those that make a definite pitch (timpani, mallet percussion) and those that produce a sound of indefinite pitch (drums, maracas, triangle).

◀ **Conga** An Afro-Cuban drum with a long, barrel-shaped body. It comes in two sizes, the small *quinto* and the large *tumbador*. The conga is struck with the fingers and the palm of the hand. CD 19–15 p. 320

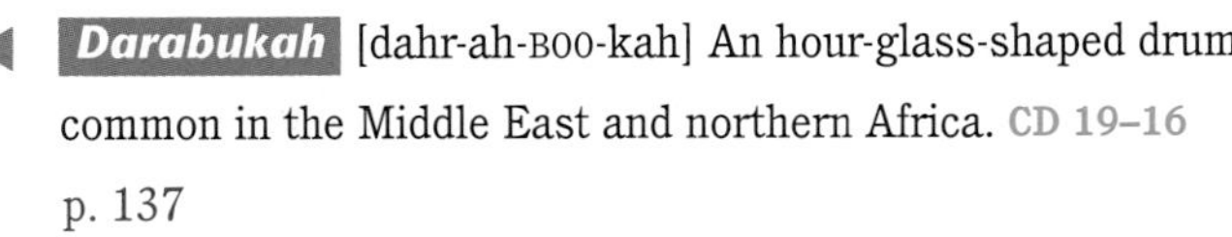

◀ ***Darabukah*** [dahr-ah-BOO-kah] An hour-glass-shaped drum common in the Middle East and northern Africa. CD 19–16 p. 137

◀ ***Didgeridoo*** [DIJ-er-ee-doo] This instrument from northern Australia is made from a termite-hollowed eucalyptus branch after its outer bark is removed. It is a straight natural trumpet that is end-blown. CD 19–17 p. 36



◀ **Dulcimer** A sound box made of wood, with strings across it. The strings are usually plucked. CD 19–18 p. 349

◀ **Dundun Drums** [DOON-doon] Most of these double-headed drums from West Africa have an hour-glass shape with the ends covered with goatskin drumheads that are fastened together with cords stretched down the length of the drum. Pressing the cords tightens the drumheads, producing sharp, high sounds. Relaxing the pressure on the cords lowers the pitch of the sound produced. CD 19–19 p. 154

◀ ***Erhu*** [EHR-hoo] A Chinese string instrument played with a bow. CD 19–20 p. 315



▶ **Playing String Instruments** String instruments make sounds when the strings vibrate. The strings are stretched over sound boxes of various shapes. Most string instruments are held between chin and shoulder or rested on the floor. Some, such as the guitar and harp, are plucked or strummed with the fingers or a pick. The orchestral strings (violin, viola, cello, and string bass) may also be plucked or even strummed, but they are usually bowed.

String players press the strings with their left hand to make different pitches. The right hand draws the bow across the strings or plucks the strings, creating sound. String players (including guitarists) must do two very different things—one with each hand—to make music.

During the eighteenth century, the string family became the foundation of the orchestra. A symphony orchestra today might have 20 to 30 violins (divided between "first" and "second"), 8 to 12 violas, 8 to 12 cellos, and 6 to 10 string basses.

## Resonance

**SAY** Resonance can make sounds louder and fuller. Let's try this experiment to hear resonance.

Have students

- Say something—"hello," or their names—into the air.
- Say the same thing into a resonating chamber—an empty cardboard box or an empty wastebasket.

**ASK What happened to the sound?** (It got louder and fuller.)

## Timbre

**SAY** Every instrument—and every voice—has its own timbre. Usually, we can tell who is speaking or what is being played just by the sound—we don't even have to look. Let's listen to the timbres of our voices.

Divide the class into two parts. Face the "listeners" away from the "speakers." Have the

- Speakers take turns saying the same sentence or phrase at about the same dynamic level.
- Listeners try to identify the speaker from the timbre.
- Groups switch roles.

Turn this activity into a game by keeping score.

Repeat this activity, using instruments featured in the Sound Bank. Use the recordings to review, if necessary.

## Making a Pitch

**ASK Some of the percussion instruments pictured in your book have a definite pitch. Can you tell which they are?** (glockenspiel, marimba, steel drum, timpani)

**SAY** Other percussion instruments have an indefinite pitch, although some can make high or low sounds. The conga, for instance, is larger than the *darabukah* and makes a lower sound.

**SAY** Pitches can be made higher or lower in three ways: size, tension, and thickness. If the sound sources are equal in two of the ways, the third will determine the pitch.

**continued on page 468**

### Size

**SAY** A large drum makes a lower sound than a small drum. A large dog barks at a lower pitch than a small dog. You might also be able to see how size determines pitch in your own family: A man's voice will sound lower than your own voice or a woman's voice.

Demonstrate the effect of size on pitch with a piano or an Autoharp. Larger (longer) strings make lower sounds. That is why a grown person's voice is generally lower than a child's—the vocal cords (in the voice box) are larger and longer.

### Tension

**SAY** Tension means tightness; the tighter you make the string or the drumhead, for instance, the higher the pitch.

**ASK** **On some instruments, like the triangle, the player can't change the tension. How can the player get different pitches?** (by using larger or smaller triangles)

Guide students in experimenting with tension using rubber bands.

**ASK** **What happens to the sound of a rubber band when you pull it to make it longer—increase the tension?** (The pitch gets higher.)

**Is the sound loud?** (no) **Is it attractive?** (no) **How can it be made louder and more attractive?** (Add resonance.)

Have students work in pairs to demonstrate tension, pitch, and resonance. One student stretches a rubber band across the open end of a glass, cup, or box. Another student plucks the rubber band.

**SAY** When resonance is added, it is easier to hear the sound of the rubber band.

**ASK** **How can you raise the pitch?** (Stretch the rubber band more.)

**What happens to the sound when the rubber band is stretched?** (It gets higher.) **When it is relaxed?** (It gets lower.)

### Thickness

Experiment by playing individual strings of an Autoharp or a guitar.

**ASK** **What happens when you pluck a string that is thicker?** (It makes a lower sound.) **Thinner?** (It makes a higher sound.)

◀ **Flute** A metal instrument shaped like a pipe. The player holds the flute sideways and blows across an open mouthpiece. The flute's voice is pure, clear, and sweet. Its low notes are the same ones children sing, but it can also play very high. CD 19–21 p. 70

◀ **French Horn** A medium-sized instrument made of coiled brass tubing. At one end is a large bell. The player holds the horn on his or her lap and keeps one hand inside the bell. The sound of the horn is very mellow. CD 19–22 p. 71

◀ **Glockenspiel** [GLAHK-ehn-shpeel] A row of metal bars mounted on a wooden frame and struck with mallets. It produces high-pitched bell-like sounds. CD 19–23 p. 154

◀ **Guitar** A six- or 12-string instrument that is a member of the lute family. It has a modified hour-glass shape with a flat back. The strings are strummed or plucked. CD 19–24 p. 214

◀ **Harpsichord** A keyboard instrument similar to a piano. However, unlike the piano, the strings are plucked by a quill, not struck by a hammer. CD 19–25 p. 232

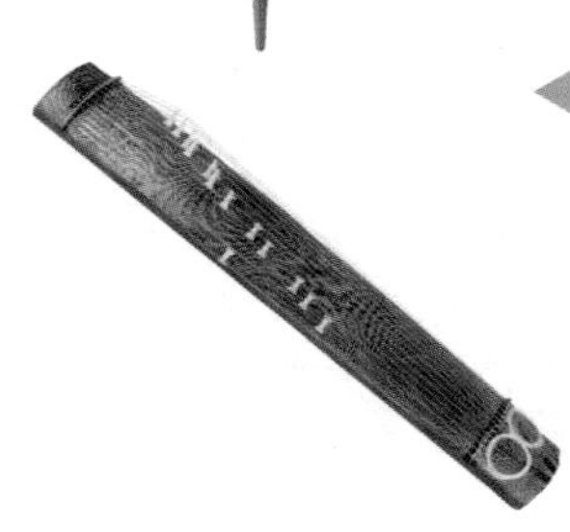

◀ ***Koto*** [KOH-toh) An instrument with movable frets and 7 to 17 strings. It is a member of the zither family and is known as the national instrument of Japan. The player sits on the floor, either cross-legged or in a kneeling position. Sound is produced when the player plucks the silk strings with a bamboo, bone, or ivory pick. The sound is similar to that of a harp. CD 19–26 p. 110

**Instrument Key:** strings percussion woodwind brass keyboard

## Footnotes

▶ **Playing Woodwind Instruments** All wind instruments make sound when the air inside them vibrates. The tubes and bells of wind instruments contain the vibrating air and give the sound resonance. Woodwind players make sounds by blowing across a hole (flute), by vibrating a reed (clarinet, saxophone), or by vibrating two reeds against each other (oboe, bassoon). The player changes the size of the instrument, making it longer or shorter by opening or closing holes along the instrument's length.

Flutes, oboes, and bassoons can be traced back to the 1400s. Composers since the 1700s have incorporated them in the orchestra because each woodwind is easily capable of playing melodies and because each brings a unique timbre to the orchestra. Clarinets are relatively new and were not added to the orchestra until the late eighteenth century (the time of Mozart and Haydn). Although the recorder is a woodwind instrument, it was replaced by the more popular and more powerful flute in the 1700s. The saxophone is used mostly in stage bands, jazz ensembles, and concert bands.

**Lute** This string instrument usually has a bowl-shaped back and is played by strumming or plucking the strings. CD 19–27 p. 110

**Maracas** Dried seeds or pebbles fill this pair of rattles. They are rhythm instruments. CD 19–28 p. 154

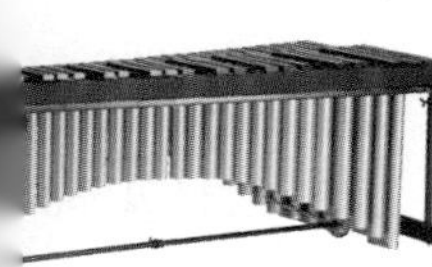

**Marimba** A large barred instrument. The bars are made of rosewood and are struck with yarn mallets. Below the bars are resonating tubes that help carry the sound. CD 19–29 p. 155

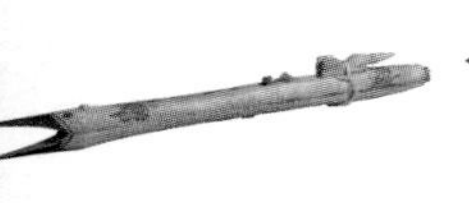

**Native American Flute** A handcrafted wind instrument made from wood, cane, clay, bone, or hollowed-out stalk of a plant. The sound of a Native American flute is similar to that of a recorder. Traditionally a solo instrument used for courtship, healing, and ceremonial gatherings, it has become popular in ensemble performances. CD 19–30 p. 459

**Oboe** A slender, woodwind instrument with a double-reed. In its low voice, the oboe may sound mysterious. These are the notes children sing. When it goes higher, the sound is light and sweet. CD 19–31 p. 70

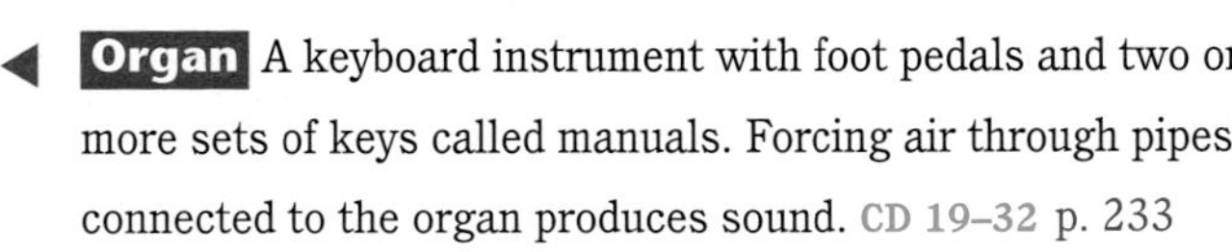

**Organ** A keyboard instrument with foot pedals and two or more sets of keys called manuals. Forcing air through pipes connected to the organ produces sound. CD 19–32 p. 233

**Saxophone** A metal-bodied reed instrument with 18 to 20 holes controlled by keys. The saxophone family consists of baritone, tenor, alto, and soprano saxophones. CD 19–33 p. 75

Sound Bank

## Playing Keyboard Instruments

The piano, organ, and synthesizer are keyboard instruments. All keyboard instruments are played the same way, but the sound is made in different ways.

**SAY** When the piano keys are pushed down, padded hammers strike the strings inside the instrument, in much the same way that the bars are struck on the glockenspiel and marimba.

Demonstrate, if possible, by exposing the inside mechanism of a piano, allowing students to see the hammers strike the strings.

**SAY** When electronic keyboard or electronic organ keys are pushed down, circuits in the machine are turned on in a way that makes sound. Both instruments are really synthesizers, since these circuits can be made to produce many different sounds, even some not available in nature.

## Playing Longer and Shorter Sounds

**ASK Which percussion instruments make sounds that last for a short time?** (conga, *darabukah*, *dundun* drums, maracas, snare drum, *timbales*)

**How can you make the sound of a drum longer?** (by hitting it repeatedly, as in a roll on the snare drum)

## Experimenting with Sound

Some instruments can be played in more than one way. For instance, an Autoharp can be played by

- Strumming in the usual way, using a pick or, for comfort, a door stop.
- Striking the strings with a mallet.
- Scraping with a guitar pick or other object.
- Plucking individual strings.

**ASK Can you use an instrument to make a sound like corn popping, or trees rustling, or a sound of your choice?** (Allow students to experiment with different ways to play the instruments as well as different volumes.)

When students have discovered how to create sounds in new ways or to imitate another sound, encourage them to create sound effects to accompany a poem in the book.

For another sound experiment, have students try to make a bottle "play." They should use a bottle with a small neck and blow across the top toward the other side, trying to aim the air so that it is split in half.

**ASK Are there any instruments in the Sound Bank that make sound in this way?** (Yes; the modern flute. The Native American flute uses the same principle, but is end-blown. The whistle mouthpiece divides the air.)

continued on page 470

▶ **Playing Brass Instruments** Brass players make the air inside the instrument vibrate by buzzing their lips against the mouthpiece. The lips must be tight and the air forced through them.

Brass players change pitches by tightening their lips even more or by pressing one valve or a combination of valves (except the trombone, although valve trombones can sometimes be found). Each time a valve is pressed, another length of tubing is added, changing the instrument's size by making it longer.

Although brass instruments existed from the 1400s, they are the last instrumental family to become full-fledged members of the orchestra. Prior to the early 1800s, brass instruments were used only for special effects or on special occasions. As the orchestra became larger, however, more brass instruments were included. Now, it is common to see two to four of each member of the family. Due to its mellow sound and ease of blending, the French horn, derived from the hunting horn, won acceptance before the others.

Sound Bank

# Instruments Featured in the Recordings

Many of the listening selections, songs, and illustrations in this book may be used to supplement the lessons on timbre. See the specific references below for selected instruments in the Sound Bank.

- BALALAIKA: *"Dayenu"* **CD 19-1**
  Illustration: p. 295
- BASSOON: *Sonata in F Minor for Bassoon, "Vivace"* **CD 4-4**
  Illustration: p. 70
- CELLO (with violin, piano): *Piano Trio No. 2 in E-flat Major, Op. 100, Scherzo* **CD 8-31**
  Illustration: p. 192
- CLARINET: *The Bee (L'Abeille)* **CD 4-2**
  Illustration: p. 70
- CONGA: *"Sonando"* **CD 2-9**
- DIDGERIDOO: *Brolga One* **CD 2-17**
  Illustration: p. 36
- DULCIMER: *Lazy John* **CD 1-14**
  Illustration: p. 349
- ERHU: *Birds in the Forest* **CD 13-28**
  Illustration: p. 315
- FLUTE: *Carnival of the Animals*, "Aviary" **CD 4-5**
  Illustration: p. 70
- FRENCH HORN: *Concerto in E-flat for Horn and Orchestra, K. 417, Rondo* **CD 4-8**
  Illustration: p. 71
- GLOCKENSPIEL (with percussion ensemble): *Toccata for Percussion*, Movement 3 **CD 7-11**
  Illustration: p. 154
- GUITAR: "River" **CD 3-18**
  Illustration: p. 214
- HARPSICHORD: *French Suite No. 5*, "Gigue" **CD 10-1**
  Illustration: p. 232
- KOTO: *"Sakura"* **CD 13-13**
  Illustration: p. 110
- LUTE (with harmonium): "Chairs to Mend" **CD 7-1**
  Illustration: p. 110
- MARACAS: *"Sonando"* **CD 2-9**
  Illustration: p. 34
- NATIVE AMERICAN FLUTE: "Farewell to the Warriors" **CD 12-3**
  Illustration: p. 459
- OBOE: *Pulcinella Suite, "Serenata"* **CD 4-3**
  Illustration: p. 70
- ORGAN: *Toccata in D Minor* **CD 10-2**
  Illustration: p. 233
- SAXOPHONE: *B.B.'s Blues* **CD 4-1**
  Illustration: p. 70
- SITAR: *Charukeshi* **CD 13-19**
  Illustration: p. 310

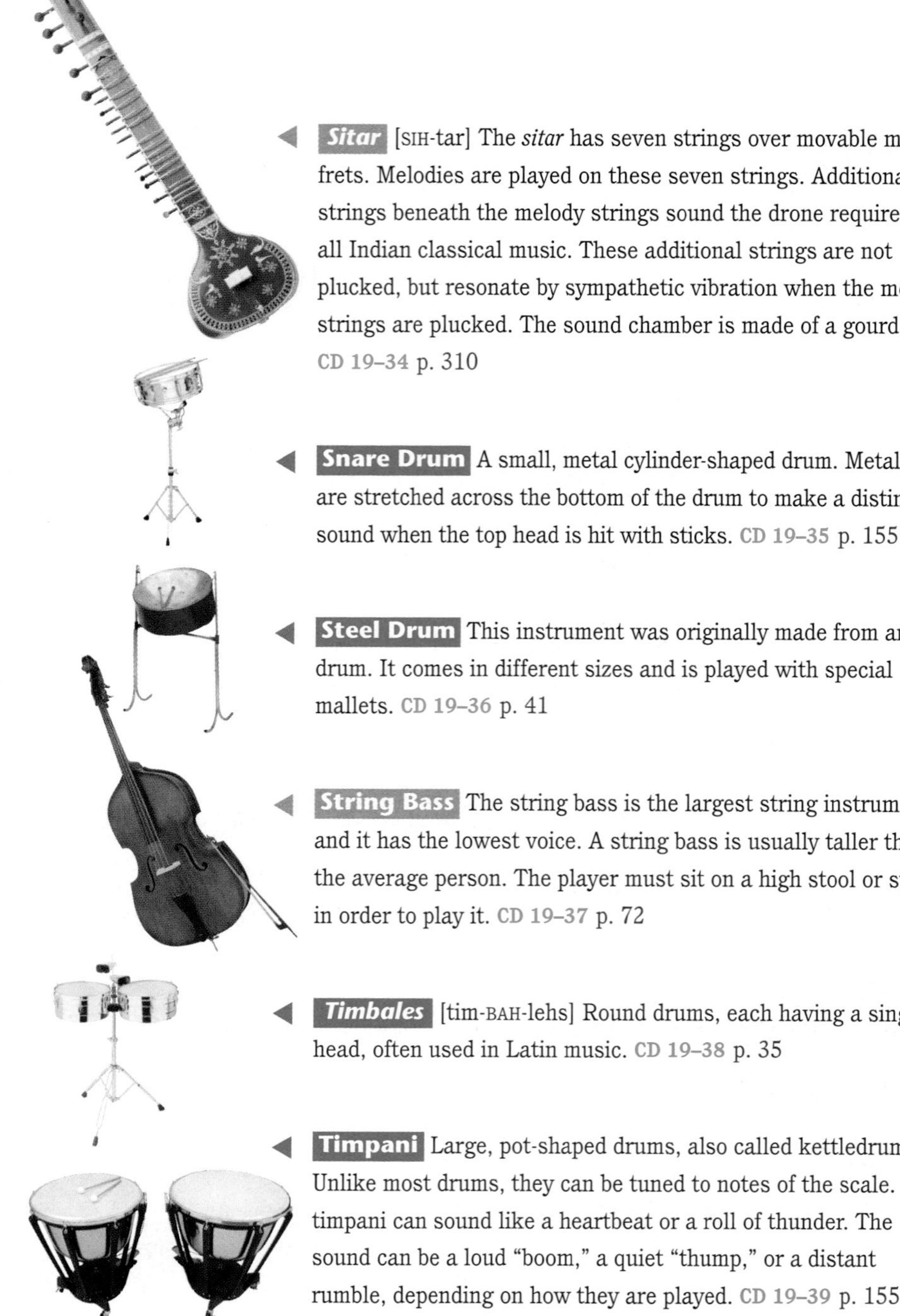

**Sitar** [SIH-tar] The *sitar* has seven strings over movable metal frets. Melodies are played on these seven strings. Additional strings beneath the melody strings sound the drone required of all Indian classical music. These additional strings are not plucked, but resonate by sympathetic vibration when the melody strings are plucked. The sound chamber is made of a gourd. CD 19–34 p. 310

**Snare Drum** A small, metal cylinder-shaped drum. Metal coils are stretched across the bottom of the drum to make a distinctive sound when the top head is hit with sticks. CD 19–35 p. 155

**Steel Drum** This instrument was originally made from an oil drum. It comes in different sizes and is played with special mallets. CD 19–36 p. 41

**String Bass** The string bass is the largest string instrument, and it has the lowest voice. A string bass is usually taller than the average person. The player must sit on a high stool or stand in order to play it. CD 19–37 p. 72

**Timbales** [tim-BAH-lehs] Round drums, each having a single head, often used in Latin music. CD 19–38 p. 35

**Timpani** Large, pot-shaped drums, also called kettledrums. Unlike most drums, they can be tuned to notes of the scale. The timpani can sound like a heartbeat or a roll of thunder. The sound can be a loud "boom," a quiet "thump," or a distant rumble, depending on how they are played. CD 19–39 p. 155

470 **Instrument Key:** strings percussion woodwind brass keyboard

**▶ Active Listening** At the same time that they are listening to the recorded Sound Bank or supplementary examples, students should also look at the illustration of the instrument either in the Sound Bank or on the cited page. This will help them to remember the sound of the instrument when they see it, and vice versa. Reinforcing this association will help students' future listening.

Begin with two examples. Test students' ability to differentiate the instruments. Use dissimilar sounds at first, then gradually make them more similar.

When several instruments are learned in this way, divide the class into teams and have students challenge each other. Keep score of correct answers.

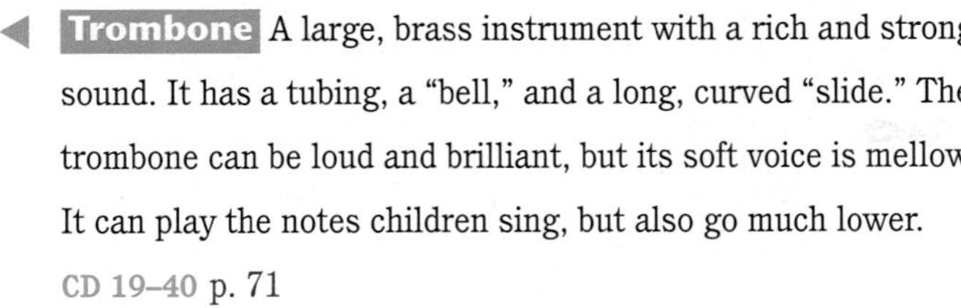

**Trombone** A large, brass instrument with a rich and strong sound. It has a tubing, a "bell," and a long, curved "slide." The trombone can be loud and brilliant, but its soft voice is mellow. It can play the notes children sing, but also go much lower. CD 19–40 p. 71

**Trumpet** The smallest brass instrument, but one with a big sound. The trumpet's voice can be loud and bright but can also sound warm and sweet. Most of its notes are the same as children sing. CD 19–41 p. 71

Sound Bank

**Tuba** The largest brass instrument, the one with the lowest voice. The tuba's low notes are deep and dark sounding. The higher ones are hearty and warm. CD 19–42 p. 71

***Vihuela*** [vee-WHEH-lah] A Spanish string instrument shaped like a guitar and tuned like a lute. It usually has six courses of paired strings. CD 19–43 p. 177

**Viola** A wooden string instrument played like a violin. It is slightly larger than the violin. The viola's voice is similar to the violin's, but deeper, richer, and darker. CD 19–44 p. 113

**Violin** A wooden string instrument held under the player's chin. The strings can be plucked or bowed. The violin plays the notes children sing, but can also go much higher. CD 19–45 p. 113

- Snare Drum (with percussion ensemble): *Toccata for Percussion*, Movement 3 **CD 7-11**
  Illustration: p. 155
- Steel Drum: *Somebody* (excerpt) **CD 2-22**
  Illustration: p. 41
- String Bass (with violin, cello): *College Hornpipe* **CD 5-1**
  Illustration: p. 73
- Timbales: *A Night in Tunisia* **CD 2-14**
  Illustration: p. 35
- Timpani (with percussion ensemble): *Toccata for Percussion*, Movement 3 **CD 7-11**
  Illustration: p. 155
- Trombone: *Pulcinella Suite, "Vivo (Duetto)* **CD 4-9**
  Illustration: p. 71
- Trumpet: *Concerto for Two Trumpets in C Major, RV 537,* Movement 1, *"Allegro"* **CD 4-7**
  Illustration: p. 71
- Tuba: *Sweet Georgia Brown* **CD 4-10**
  Illustration: p. 71
- Vihuela: *"La Tarara"* **CD 8-1**
  Illustration: p. 177
- Viola (with chamber ensemble): "Ah, Poor Bird" **CD 8-36**
  Illustration: p. 73
- Violin: *Partita in E Major*, "Gigue" **CD 5-31**
  Illustration: p. 113

Pronunciation Practice and Translations
Movement Glossary
Dance Directions
Helps for the Teacher

Pronunciation Practice and Translations

Movement Glossary

Dance Directions

Helps for the Teacher

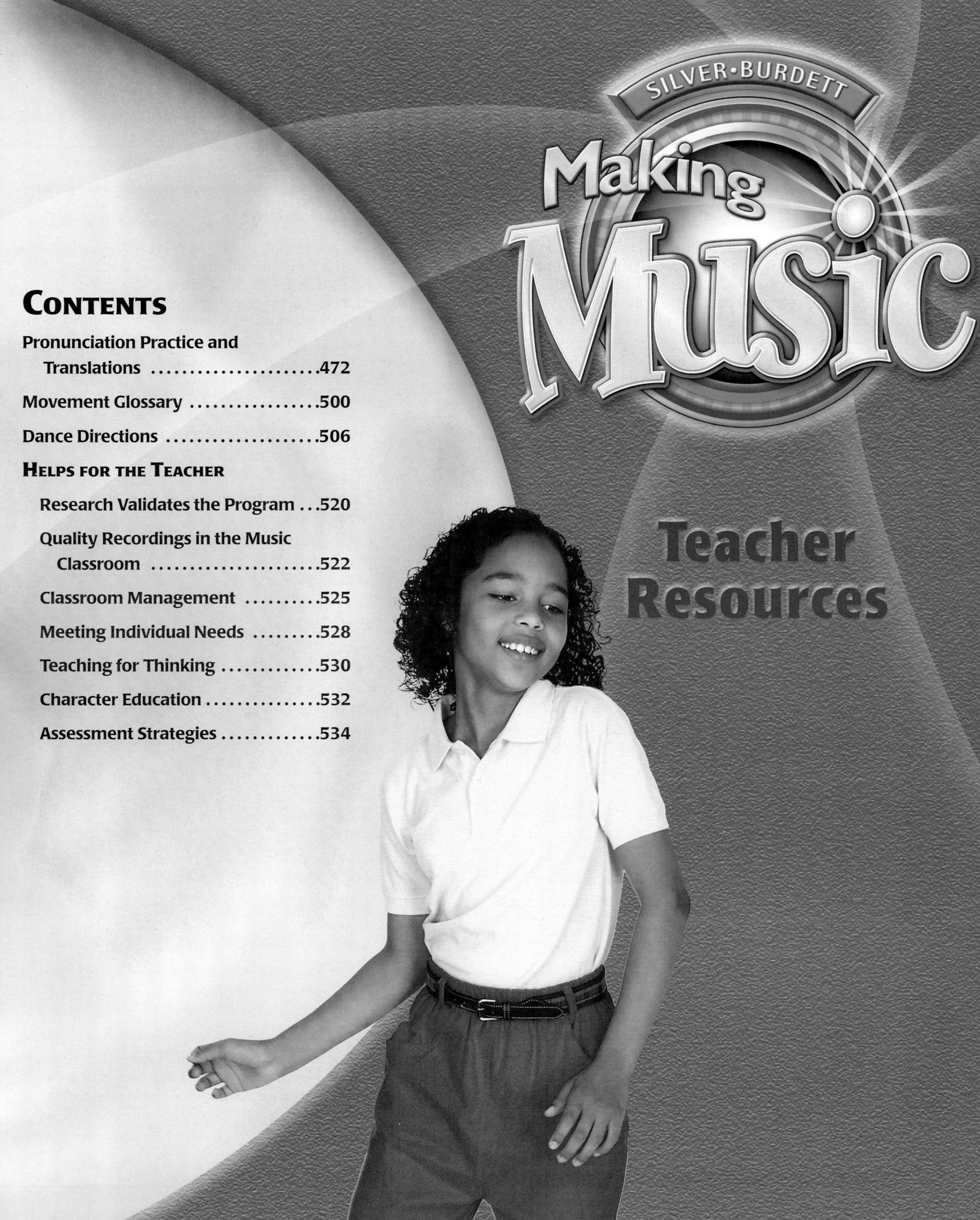
SILVER•BURDETT
Making Music
Teacher Resources

# Contents

# Pronunciation Practice

## *Phonetic Respellings for Pronunciation of Non-English Songs*

These simplified phonetic guides will assist you and your students in pronouncing non-English words. All pronunciation phonetics are matched to those of the native singer on the Pronunciation Practice Track and have been verified by the CP Language Institute. The Pronunciation Practice Guide provides a phonetic respelling in syllabic form, based on sounds in the English language that most nearly approximate the non-English sounds. When words do not have an English equivalent, we have provided the nearest approximation or instructions for making the sound. The Key to Pronunciation below refers to the system used in the Pronunciation Practice Guides.

Where possible, vowel sounds have been written with beautiful vocal tones in mind. For example, it is difficult to sing a sustained long *i* sound. Instead students are taught to sustain an *ah* sound, adding a small touch of *ee* to the release of the vowel.

**Key to Pronunciation**

| | |
|---|---|
| ah | as in father |
| ah‿ee | as in light (diphthong; a long *ah* sound with a hint of *ee* at close) |
| aw | as in awe |
| eh‿ee | as in day (diphthong; a long *eh* sound with a hint of *ee* at close) |
| b | as in button |
| ch | as in church |
| d | as in dad |
| dj | as in judge |
| ee | as in seed |
| eh | as in let |
| ew | used for French u (pronounce a bright *ee* and round the lips as if to whistle) |
| f | as in face |
| g | as in goat |
| h | as in hat |
| hkh | guttural, aspirant h of German, Hebrew ch, and Spanish j |
| ih | as in fit |
| I | as in light (a harsh *i* sound; where possible an *ah‿ee* has been suggested for singing the I sound) |
| k | as in kite |
| l | as in let |
| ll | prolonged l sound |
| m | as in man |
| (m) | French nasal m; not articulated as a distinct letter but as an open nasal sound |
| n | as in note |
| (n) | French nasal n; not articulated as a distinct letter, but as an open nasal sound |
| (ng) | as in sang (sometimes sounded as a prolonged nasal tone) |
| oh | as in tone |
| oo | as in spoon |
| ow | as in powder |
| p | as in pat |
| r | as in ran |
| (r) | as in turn (combined with another vowel sound in German) |
| rr | rolled r |
| rrrr | extended trilled r |
| s | as in song |
| t | as in tell |
| th | as in that |
| thh | as in feather |
| uh | as in up |
| v | as in van |
| w | as in way |
| wh | as in what |
| y | as in yes (not a vowel sound) |
| z | as in zone |
| zh | as in azure |

## *English Translations by CP Language Institute*

The English translations for these songs were provided by CP Language Institute. For over two decades, the Institute has been one of the leading language consultants for clients in the New York City area and in other locations. The Institute specializes in translation, interpretation, typesetting, graphic design, language instruction, and voice overs. Its highly qualified staff of native translators guided and monitored the pronunciation and recording of each Pronunciation Track for Silver Burdett MAKING MUSIC.

## *Gakavik* (The Partridge), p. 14 CD 1–20

*Folk Song From Armenia*

### Pronunciation Practice

Phrase
1. *A-rev paats-vedz*
   ah-rehv pahts-vehdz
2. *tugh am be-ren,*
   toohkh ahm beh-rehn,
3. *ga-kav te-rav*
   gah-kahv teh-rahv
4. *ga-nach sa-ren.*
   gah-nahkh tsah-rehn.
5. *Ga-nach sa-ren*
   gah-nahkh tsah-rehn
6. *sa-ri dze-ren,*
   sah-ree tzeh-rehn,
7. *pa-rev pe-rav*
   pah-rehv peh-rahv
8. *dza-ghik-ne-ren:*
   tzah-gihkh-neh-rehn:
9. *Si-rov-nig si-rov-nig,*
   see-roo-nihgh see-roo-nihgh,
10. *si-rov-nig, nakh-shoun*
    see-roo-nihgh, nahkh-shoon
11. *ga-ka-vik.*
    gah-kah-veek.

### Translation

The sun rose from the dark clouds.
A partridge flew from the green mountain.
From the green mountain, from the end of the mountain,
He brought greetings from the flowers.
Beautiful, beautiful, Beautiful cute little partridge.
Your face so cute and pretty,
Small beak, red little feet.
With red, red little feet
You wander with your chicks.
Beautiful, beautiful, Beautiful cute little partridge
Your face so cute and pretty.

## *Tsuki* (The Moon), p. 25 CD 1–39

*School Song from Japan*

### Pronunciation Practice

**Verse 1**

Phrase
1. *De-ta, de-ta, tsu-ki ga*
   deh-tah, deh-tah, tsoo-kee gah
2. *Ma-ru-i ma-ru-i ma-n-ma-ru-i,*
   mah-roo-ee mah-roo-ee mah-(n)-mah-roo-ee,
3. *Bo-n-no yo-na tsu-ki ga.*
   boh-(n)-noh yoh-nah, tsoo-kee gah.

**Verse 2**

Phrase
1. *Ka-ku, re-ta ku-mo-ni,*
   kah-koo, reh-tah koo-moh-nyee,
2. *ku-roi, ku-roi ma-ku-roi,*
   koo-roh‿ee, koo-roh‿ee mah-koo-roh‿ee,
3. *Su-mi-no yo-na ku-mo-ni.*
   soo-mee-noh yoh-nah, koo-moh-nyee.

### Translation

**Verse 1** Out, out came the moon
Round, round, very round
The moon that is like a round tray.

**Verse 2** Gone is the moon
Black, black, jet black
It hid behind an ink-like dark cloud.

## *Sonando,* p. 34 CD 2–12

*Words and Music by Peter Terrace*

### Pronunciation Practice

Phrase 1. *So-nan-do*
soh-nahn-doh

2. *pa-ra bai-lar,*
pah-rah bI-lahr,

3. *Go-za*
goh-tsah

4. *mi cha-cha-cha.*
mee chah-chah-chah.

5. *Lle-ga-ré Ma-rí-a, lle-ga-ré.*
djeh-gah-reh mah-ree-ah, djeh-gah-reh.

### Translation

[Music is] playing for dancing.
Enjoy my cha-cha-cha.
I will arrive, Maria, here I am.

## *Hashewie* (Going 'Round), p. 63 CD 3–24

*Folk Song from Eritrea, Africa*

### Pronunciation Practice

Phrase 1. *Ha-shew-i-e Shew-i-e*
hah-sheh-wee-eh sheh-wee-eh

2. *Ha-shew-i-e Shew-i-e*
hah-sheh-wee-eh sheh-wee-eh

3. *Ha-shew-i-e Shew-i-e*
hah-sheh-wee-eh sheh-wee-eh

4. *Bi-ha-de ha-bir-na Shew-i-e*
bee-hah-deh hah-beerr-nah sheh-wee-eh

5. *Ha-shew-ie‿e-na-bel-na Shew-i-e*
hah-sheh-wee‿eh-nah-behl-nah sheh-wee-eh

6. *A-lem kit-fel-to Shew-i-e*
ah-lehm kiht-fehl-toh sheh-wee-eh

7. *Ku-lu-me-nin-et-na Shew-i-e*
koo-loo-meh-nihn-eht-nah sheh-wee-eh

8. *Ha-shew-i-e ni-bel Shew-i-e*
hah-sheh-wee-eh nee-behl sheh-wee-eh

9. *Nef́-lit-a-di-na Shew-i-e*
nehf-lih-tah-dih-nah sheh-wee-eh

10. *Bi-ha-de ha-bir-na Shew-i-e.*
bee-hah-deh hah-beerr-nah sheh-wee-eh.

### Translation

Going round and round, round (three times),
All together, round,
Saying round, round;
So the world would know, round
Who we are, round,
Let's say, round,
All together, round,
Going round and round, round (three times).

## ***Riqui rán,*** **p. 66** CD 3–36

*Folk Song from Latin America*

### Pronunciation Practice

**Verse 1**

Phrase 1. *A-se-rrín, a-se-rrán. Los ma-de-ros de San Juan*
ah-seh-rreen, ah-seh-rrahn. lohs mah-deh-rohs deh sahn hwahn

2. *co-men que-so, co-men pan.*
koh-mehn keh-soh, koh-mehn pahn.

3. *Los de Ri-que, al-fe-ñi-que;*
lohs deh ree-keh, ahl-feh-nyee-keh;

4. *los de Ro-que, al-fon-do-que,*
lohs deh roh-keh, ahl-fohn-doh-keh,

5. *Ri-qui, ri-que, ri-qui rán.*
ree-kee, ree-keh, ree-kee rahn.

**Verse 2**

Phrase 1. *A-se-rrín, a-se-rrán. Los a-be-jas vie-nen, van;*
ah-seh-rreen, ah-seh-rrahn. lohs ah-beh-has vyeh-nehn, vahn;

2. *Miel la-bo-ran pa-ra‿el pan.*
myehl lah-boh-rahn pah-rah‿ehl pahn.

3. *Li-ban flo-res las de Ri-que*
lee-bahn floh-rehs lahs deh ree-keh

4. *cual al-mi-bar de‿al-fe-ñi-que,*
kwahl ahl-mee-bahr deh‿ahl-feh-nyee-keh,

5. *Y‿el pa-nal de los de Ro-que*
yehl pah-nahl deh lohs deh roh-keh

6. *se pa-re-ce‿a‿un al-fon-do-que.*
seh pah-reh-seh‿ah‿oon ahl-fohn-doh-keh.

7. *Ri-qui, ri-que, ri-qui rán.*
ree-kee, ree-keh, ree-kee rahn.

**Verse 3**

Phrase 1. *A-se-rrín, a-se-rrán. Los chi-qui-llos. ¿Dón-de‿es-tán?*
ah-seh-rreen, ah-seh-rrahn. lohs chee-kee-djohs. dawn-dehs-tahn?

2. *To-dos a dor-mir se van.*
toh-dohs ah dohr-meer seh vahn.

3. *So-ña-rán con al-fe-ñi-que*
so-nyah-rrahn kohn ahl-feh-nyee-keh

4. *co-mo sue-ñan los de Ri-que,*
koh-moh sweh-nyahn lohs deh ree-keh,

5. *Y ma-ña-na‿un al-fon-do-que*
ee mah-nyah-nah‿oon ahl-fohn-doh-keh

6. *co-me-rán con los de Ro-que.*
koh-meh-rahn kohn lohs deh roh-keh.

7. *Ri-qui, ri-que, ri-qui rán.*
ree-kee, ree-keh, ree-kee rahn.

### Translation

Aserrin, aserran. The lumberjacks from San Juan
They eat cheese, they eat bread.
Those from Rique *alfenique;**
Those from Roque *alfondoque;**
Riqui, riqui, riqui, rán.

**Alfenique* and *alfondoque* are types of caramel sweets made from sugar cane extract.

## *Eh, cumpari!* (Hey, Buddy!), p. 68 CD 3–40

*Words and Music by Julius La Rosa and Archie Bleyer*

### Pronunciation Practice

Phrase
1. *Eh, cum-pa-ri!*
   eh, koom-pah-ree!
2. *Ci vo´ su-na-ri.*
   chee voh soo-nah-ree.
3. *Chi si so-na*
   kee see soh-nah
4. *´U fris-ca-le-ttu?*
   oo frees-kah-leh-too?
5. *´U sax-o-fo-na?*
   oo sahks-oh-foh-nah?
6. *´u man-du-li-nu?*
   oo mahn-doo-lee-noo?
7. *´U vi-u-li-nu?*
   oo vee-oo-lee-noo?
8. *A la trum-bet-ta?*
   ah lah troom-beht-tah?
9. *A la trom-bo-na?*
   ah lah trohm-boh-nah?
10. *E co-mu si so-na*
    eh koh-moo see soh-nah
11. *´u fris-ca-let-tu?*
    oo frees-kah-leh-too?
12. *´U sax-o-fo-na?*
    oo sahks-oh-foh-nah?
13. *´u man-du-li-nu?*
    oo mahn-doo-lee-noo?
14. *´U vi-u-li-nu?*
    oo vee-oo-lee-noo?
15. *A la trum-bet-ta?*
    ah lah troom-beht-tah?
16. *A la trom-bo-na?*
    ah lah trohm-boh-nah?

**Last ending**

Phrase
1. *´u fris-ca-le-tt´e ti-pi-ti ti-pi-ti-ta.*
   oo frees-kah-leh-teh tih-pih-tih tih-pih-tih-tah.

### Translation

Hey good buddy!
It's time to play!
Who's gonna play on...the slide trombone?
And how do you play on...the slide trombone?
A foom-a-foom on the trombone!
Pa-pa-pa-pap-ah on the trumpet!
A dzing-a-dzing the violin!
Ah pling-a-pling the mandolin!
Too-too-ta-toot the saxophone!
... whistle...the piccolo
and tippity tippity tah!

## *Hey, m'tswala,* p. 79 CD 4–21

*Folk Song from Africa*

### Pronunciation Practice

Phrase 1. *Hey, m'tswa-la,*
heh, mtswah-lah,

2. *ne-ye ti-pa sa-me tswa-la.*
neh-yeh tee-peh sah-meh tswah-lah.

### Translation

Hey cousin, give me my knife.

*Note:* This is an African hunting song. It was sung during the skinning process in which the men would take turns.

## *Ōsamu kosamu* (Biting Wind), p. 96 CD 5–5, 6

*Folk Song from Japan*

### Pronunciation Practice

**Part 1**

Phrase 1. *Ō-sa-mu, ko-sa-mu*
oh-sah-moo, koh-sah-moo

2. *na-n to it-te*
nah-(n) toh eet-teh

3. *na-i-te-ki-ta?*
nah-ee-teh-kee-tah?

4. *Ō-sa-mu ko-sa-mu.*
oh-sah-moo, koh-sah-moo.

**Part 2**

Phrase 1. *Ya-ma-ka-ra ko-zoo ga*
yah-mah-kah-rah koh-tzoh gah

2. *na-i-te-ki-ta;*
nah-ee-teh-kee-tah;

3. *"Sa-mu-i to it-te*
sah-moo-ee toh eet-teh

4. *na-i-te-ki-ta!"*
na-ee-teh-kee-tah!

5. *Ko-sa-mu.*
koh-sah-moo.

### Translation

**Part 1** Biting wind, biting cold;
Why are they crying, crying from the cold?
Biting wind, biting cold.

**Part 2** Children of the mountains are crying from the cold;
We are in the wind; it's bitter, bitter cold!
Biting cold.

## *T'hola, t'hola* (Softly, Softly), p. 132 CD 6–10

*Folk Song from South Africa*

### Pronunciation Practice

Phrase 1. *T'ho-la, t'ho-la ngoa-na-me;*
too-lah, too-lahn gwah-nah-meh;

2. *T'ho-la, t'ho-la ngoa-na-me,*
too-lah, too-lahn gwah-nah-meh,

3. *Li pe-re se-ra peng.*
dee peh-reh see-rah pehng.

4. *Ra-peng sa-ma ha-pu.*
rah-pehng sah-mah hah-poo.

5. *Ei-tsa li lo tse-la*
eh‿ee-tsah dee loh tseh-lah

6. *tsa ea-ngoa-na-me,*
tsah ee‿ahn-gwah-nah-meh,

7. *E pu-tsoa ea khoa-ha mo*
eh poo-tswoh‿ah eh‿ah hkhwoh‿ah-hah moh

8. *ko-ko Hon-goa-na-me*
koh-koh hohn-gwah-nah-meh

9. *E-i, e-i-ngoa-na-me,*
eh-yee, eh-yeen-gwah-nah-meh,

10. *E-i, e-i-ngoa-na-me.*
eh-yee, eh-yeen-gwah-nah-meh.

11. *Ha le so bone kon-ko-ti,*
hah lee see bohn kohn-koh-tee,

12. *Ha le so bone kon-ko-ti,*
hah lee see bohn kohn-koh-tee,

13. *T'ho-la, t'ho-la ngoa-na-me,*
too-lah, too-lahn gwah-nah-meh,

14. *T'ho-la, t'ho-la ngoa-na-me.*
too-lah, too-lahn gwah-nah-meh.

### Translation

Softly, softly, my baby;
Softly, softly, my baby.
Hush, it is just the wind.
Blowing through the branches.
Once on a time was a young lion baby.
Took him to the doctor to make him mind his manners.
Ei, softly, my baby,
Ei, softly, my baby.
There was a little white dove,
Yes, there was a little dove,
"T'hola, t'hola," he sang me,
"T'hola, t'hola," he sang me.

## *Ala Da'lona,* p. 136 CD 6–21

*Arabic Folk Song*

### Pronunciation Practice

Phrase 1. *A-la Da´-lo-na,*
ah-lah dah-loh-nah,
2. *A-la Da´-lo-na,*
ah-lah dah-loh-nah,
3. *Hi-war shi-ma-li*
how-wahr shee-mah-lee
4. *gha-yar ih-lo-na.*
gwah-ee‿yahr ee loo nah.
5. *Ma-ba-di i-mi*
mah-bah-dee ee-mee
6. *ma-ba-di ba-yi;*
mah-bah-dee bah-yee;
7. *Ba-di ha-bi-bi*
bah-dee hah-bee-bee
8. *as-mar ih-lo-na.*
hahs-mahr ih-loo-nah.

### Translation

Ala Da´lona, Ala Da´lona,
Through the night the voice of the desert winds blow crazily.
Tell me where my love has gone, my gorgeous Delona.
Dark and lovely braids, my gorgeous Delona.
She is sweet and kind and brings such gladness.
Has she gone forever? Oh, what sadness.

## *Canción de cuna* (Cradle Song), p. 144 CD 6–34

*Folk Song from Latin America*

### Pronunciation Practice

Phrase 1. *Duer-me pron-to, ni-ño mí-o,*
dwehr-meh prohn-toh, nee-nyoh mee-oh,
2. *Duer-me pron-to‿y sin llo-rar.*
dwehr-meh prohn-toh‿ee seen yoh-rahr.
3. *Que‿es-tás en los bra-zos de tu*
keh‿ehs-tahs ehn lohs brah-zohs deh too
4. *ma-dre, que te va a can-tar.*
mah-dreh, keh teh vah kahn-tahr.

### Translation

Go to sleep soon, my child,
Go to sleep soon without crying;
You who are in your mother's arms,
She who will sing to you.

## *Cantando mentíras* (Singing Tall Tales), p. 146 CD 6–41

*Folk Song from Latin America*

### Pronunciation Practice

**Verse 1**

Phrase 1. *A-ho-ra que‿es-ta-mos des-pa-cio,*
ah-oh-rah kehs-tah-mohs dehs-pah-see-oh,
2. *Va-mos a can-tar men-tí-ras.*
vah-mohs ah kahn-tahr mehn-tee-rahs.
3. *Por el rí-o van las lie-bres,*
pohr ehl rree-oh vahn lahs lee‿eh-brehs,
4. *Por el mon-te las an-gui-las.*
pohr ehl mohn-teh lahs ahn-gee-lahs.

**Verse 2**

Phrase 1. *Los pe-rru-cos po-nen hue-vos,*
lohs peh-rroo-kohs poh-nehn hweh-vohs,
2. *Las ga-lli-nas a la-drar,*
lahs gah-yee-nahs ah lah-drahr,
3. *Y‿a los sa-pos cre-cen co-las,*
ee‿ah los sah-pohs kreh-sehn koh-lahs,
4. *Por-que no sa-ben na-dar.*
pohr-keh noh sah-behn nah-dahr.

### Translation

**Verse 1** Now that things are slow, let's sing tall tales!
The hares swim down the river;
the eels cross the mountains!

**Verse 2** The dogs lay eggs, the hens bark,
And the frogs grow tails
Because they don't know how to swim!

## *Ode to Joy,* p. 152 CD 7–10

*Words by Friedrich Schiller, Music by Ludwig van Beethoven*

### Pronunciation Practice

Phrase 1. *Freu-de, schön-*er Göt-ter-fun-ken,*
fraw‿ee-deh, shuh(r)n-ehr guh(r)t-tehr-foon-kehn,

2. *Toch-ter aus E-ly-si-um,*
tohk-tehr ows** eh-lee-see-oom,

3. *wir be-tre-ten feu-er-trunk-en,*
veer beh-treh-tehn faw‿ee-ehr-troonk-ehn,

4. *Himm-li-sche, dein Hei-lig-tum!*
heem-lih-sheh, dIn hI-lihg-toom!

5. *Dei-ne Zau-ber bin-den wie-der,*
dI-neh tsow-behr bihn-dehn vee-dehr,

6. *was die Mo-de streng ge-teilt;*
vahs dee moh-deh shtreng geh-tIlt,

7. *al-le Men-schen wer-den Brü-der,*
ahl-leh mehn-shehm vehr-dehn broo(r)-dehr,

8. *wo dein sanf-ter Flü-gel weilt.*
voh dIn sahnf-tehr floo(r)-gehl vIlt.

* Sing the preceding vowel while shaping the mouth as if to sing an (r).
**ow: as in "pow"

### Translation

Joy, fair divine spark,
Daughter of Elysium,
Intoxicated with fire, we enter,
O Heavenly One, your sacred shrine.
Your magic once again unites
All that fashion had sternly divided.
All men become brothers
Where your gentle wings abide.

## *Santa Clara,* p. 172 CD 7–35

*Folk Song from the Philippines*

### Pronunciation Practice

**Verse**

Phrase 1. *San-ta Cla-ra,*
sahn-tah klah-rahng,

2. *pi-nung pi-no*
pee-nuhng pee-noh

3. *Ang pa-nga-ko*
ahng pah-nah-koh

4. *ko ay ga-ni-to.*
koh ah‿ee gah-nee-toh.

5. *Pag-da-ting ko po*
pahg-dah-teeng koh poh

6. *sa U-ban-do.*
sah oo-bahn-doh.

7. *Ay mag-sa-sa-yaw*
ah‿ee mahg-sah-sah-yah‿ow

8. *ng pan-dang-go.*
nuhng pahn-dahng-goh.

**Refrain**

Phrase 1. *A-ru-ray, a-ra-ru-ray,*
ah-roo-rah‿ee, ah-rah-ruh-rah‿ee,

2. *Ang pa-nga-ko'y tu-tu-pa-rin.*
ahng pah-ngah-koh‿ee too-too-pah-reen.

3. *A-ru-ray, a-ra-ru-ray,*
ah-roo-rah‿ee, ah-rah-ruh-rah‿ee,

4. *Ang pa-nga-ko'y tu-tu-pa-rin.*
ahng pah-ngah-koh‿ee too-too-pah-reen.

### Translation

**Verse** Santa Clara, so very fine, this is my promise.
When I get to Ubando, I will dance the Pandango.

**Refrain** *Aruray**, my promise will be fulfilled. (Repeat.)

**Aruray*—nonsense syllables

## *Doraji* (Bluebells), p. 174 CD 7–39

*Folk Song from Korea*

### Pronunciation Practice

Phrase 1. *Do-ra-ji, do-ra-ji,*
doh-rah-djee, doh-rah-djee,

2. *pek do-ra-ji,*
pehk doh-rah-djee,

3. *Sim-sim san-chuh neh*
sheem-sheem sahn-choo neh

4. *pek do-ra-ji.*
pehk doh-rah-djee,

5. *Hahn du bu-ri-man*
hahn doo boo-ree-mahn

6. *keh-yuh-do*
keh-yuh-doh

7. *Teh kwang-chu-ri su-ri-sal sal*
teh kwahng-choo-ree shoo-ree-tsahl tsahl

8. *num-num-goo-na.*
nuhm-noom-goo-nah.

### Translation

Bellflower, bellflower, white bellflower,
White bellflower in deep, deep mountains and streams.
Only with one or two dug-up root(s),
A bamboo basket overflows.

## *La Tarara,* p. 176 CD 8–4

*Folk Song from Spain*

### Pronunciation Practice

**Refrain**

Phrase 1. *La Ta-ra-ra, sí, la Ta-ra-ra, no,*
lah tah-rah-rah, see, lah tah-rah-rah, noh,

2. *La Ta-ra-ra, ma-dre, que la bai-lo yo.*
lah tah-rah-rah, mah-dreh, keh lah bah‿ee-loh yoh.

**Verse 1**

Phrase 1. *Tie-ne la Ta-ra-ra un jar-dín*
tyeh-neh lah tah-rah-rah oon hahr-deen

2. *de flo-res y me da, si quie-ro, siem-pre las me-jor-es.*
deh floh-rehs ee meh dah, see kyeh-roh, syehm-preh lahs meh-hohr-ehs.

**Verse 2**

Phrase 1. *Tie-ne la Ta-ra-ra un ces-to*
tyeh-neh lah tah-rah-rah oon sehs-toh

2. *de fru-tas y me da, si quie-ro, siem-pre las ma-du-ras.*
deh froo-tahs ee meh dah, see kyeh-roh, syehm-preh lahs mah-doo-rahs.

### Translation

**Refrain** The Tarara, yes, the Tarara, no,
The Tarara, mother, because I dance it.

**Verse 1** La Tarara has a garden of flowers and, if I want, she always gives me the best ones.

**Verse 2** La Tarara has a basket of fruit and, if I want, she always gives me the ripe ones.

*Note: La Tarara* is both the name of a Spanish dance and a name that can be given to a woman or girl.

## *Los niños en España cantan* (In Spain, the Children Sing), p. 197 CD 8–41

*Folk Song from Mexico.*

### Pronunciation Practice

Phrase 1. *Los ni-ños en Es-pa-ña can-tan,*
lohs nee-nyohs ehn ehs-pah-nyah kahn-tahn,
2. *can-tan en Ja-pón.*
kahn-tahn ehn hah-pohn.
3. *Los pa-ja-ri-tos can-tan,*
lohs pah-hah-ree-tohs kahn-tahn,
4. *can-tan to-dos su can-ción.*
kahn-tahn toh-dohs soo kahn-see‿ohn.

### Translation

The children in Spain sing; they sing in Japan.
The little birds sing, they all sing their song.

## *El rancho grande* (The Big Ranch), p. 215 CD 9–9

*Music by Silvano R. Ramos*

### Pronunciation Practice

**Verse**

Phrase 1. *A-llá‿en el ran-cho gran-de,*
ah-yah‿ehn ehl rahn-choh grrahn-deh,
2. *A-llá don-de vi-ví-a,*
ah-yah dohn-deh vee-vee-ah,
3. *Ha-bía‿u-na ran-che-ri-ta,*
ah-bee‿ah‿oo-nah rahn-cheh-rree-tah,
4. *Que‿a-le-gre me de-cí-a,*
keh‿ah-leh-greh meh deh-see-ah,
5. *Que‿a-le-gre me de-cí-a,*
keh‿ah-leh-greh meh deh-see-ah,

**Refrain**

Phrase 1. *Te voy ha-cer tus cal-zo-nes,*
teh voh‿ee ah-sehr toos kahl-soh-nehs,
2. *Co-mo los u-sa‿el ran-che-ro;*
koh-moh lohs oo-sah‿ehl rrahn-che-roh;
3. *Te los co-mien-zo de la-na,*
teh lohs koh-myehn-soh deh lah-nah,
4. *Te los a-ca-bo de cue-ro.*
teh lohs ah-kah-boh deh kweh-roh.

### Translation

Over there on the big ranch,
There where I used to live,
There was a little cowgirl
Who would happily tell me,
Who would happily tell me,
I'm going to make you a pair of pants
Like the ones the rancher wears.
I'll start them out of wool,
I'll finish them out of leather.

## *Minka,* p. 222 CD 9–24

*Folk Song from Ukraine*

### Pronunciation Practice

Phrase 1. *Tizh men-ye pid-ma-nu-la,*
tee‿zhuh mehn-eh peed-mah-noo-lah,
2. *tizh men-ye pid-ve-la.*
tee‿zhuh mehn-eh peed-veh-lah.
3. *Tizh men-ye mo-lo-do-va,*
tee‿zhuh mehn-eh moh-loh-doh-vah,
4. *zu-ma, ra-zu-ma zve-la.*
tzoo-mah, ehz‿roh-zoo-moo zhveh-lah.
5. *Tizh men-ye pid-ma-nu-la,*
tee‿zhuh mehn-eh peed-mah-noo-lah,
6. *tizh men-ye pid-ve-la.*
tee‿zhuh mehn-eh peed-veh-lah.
7. *Tizh men-ye mo-lo-do-va,*
tee‿zhuh mehn-eh moh-loh-doh-vah,
8. *zu-ma, ra-zu-ma zve-la.*
tzoo-mah, ehz‿roh-zoo-moo zhveh-lah.

### Translation

You're the one who's let me down.
You're the one who has betrayed me.
I so young and innocent and
You drove me insane.

## *Thula, thula, ngoana* (Sleep, Sleep, Baby), p. 227 CD 9–30

*Folk Song from the Lesotho Region of South Africa*

### Pronunciation Practice

Phrase 1. *Thula, thula, ngoa-na,*
too-lah, too-lah, ngwah-nah,
2. *thula, thula, ngoa-na,*
too-lah, too-lah, ngwah-nah,
3. *thula, thula, ngoa-na,*
too-lah, too-lah, ngwah-nah,
4. *thula, thula, ngoa-na.*
too-lah, too-lah, ngwah-nah.

### Translation

Hush, hush, baby.

## *Tengo, tengo, tengo* (I Have Three Sheep), p. 228 CD 9–38

*Folk Song from New Mexico*

### Pronunciation Practice

**Verse 1**

Phrase 1. *Ten-go, ten-go, ten-go,*
tehn-goh, tehn-goh, tehn-goh,
2. *y tú no tie-nes na-da;*
ee too noh tee‿eh-nehs nah-thah;
3. *Ten-go tres o-ve-jas,*
tehn-goh trehs oh-veh-hahs,
4. *a-llá en la ca-ña-da.*
ah-djah ehn lah kah-nyah-dah.

**Verse 2**

Phrase 1. *U-na me da le-che,*
oo-nah meh dah leh-cheh,
2. *y o-tra me da la-na;*
ee oh-trah meh dah lah-nah;
3. *Y‿o-tra man-te-qui-lla,*
ee‿oh-trah mahn-teh-kee-djah,
4. *¡Ay! Pa-ra la se-ma-na.*
ah‿ee! pah-rah lah seh-mah-nah.

### Translation

I have, I have, I have,
I have, I have, I have, and you don't have anything;
I have three sheep, there in the ravine.

One gives me milk, another gives me wool;
another gives me butter. Oh! enough for the week.

## *Tancovačka* (Dancing), p. 230 CD 9–42

*Slovak Folk Song*

### Pronunciation Practice

Phrase 1. *Tan-cuj, tan-cuj,*
tahn-tsoo‿ee, tahn-tsoo‿ee,
2. *vy-krú-caj, vy-krú-caj,*
vee-kroo-tsah‿ee, vee-kroo-tsah‿ee,
3. *Len mi pie-cku*
lehn mee pyeh-tskoo
4. *ne-zrú-caj, ne-zrú-caj.*
nyeh-tzroo-tsah‿ee, nyeh-tzroo-tsah‿ee.
5. *Do-brá pie-cka*
doh-brah pyeh-tskah
6. *na zi-mu, na zi-mu,*
nah zee-moo, nah zee-moo,
7. *Ked' ne-má-me*
kehdj nyeh-mah-meh
8. *pe-ri-nu, pe-ri-nu.*
peh-ree-noo, peh-ree-noo.

### Translation

Come, let's dance 'round and 'round
But leave the hot stove on the ground, on the ground.
The good old hot stove [is] for the cold, for the cold,
Since a warm down we can't afford, can't afford.

## *El borrego* (The Lamb), p. 242 CD 10–15

*Folk Song from Mexico*

### Pronunciation Practice

Phrase 1. *Se-ño-ra, su bo-rre-gui-to,*
seh-nyohr-ah, soo boh-rreh-ghee-toh,
2. *me quie-re lle-var al rí-o,*
meh kee‿eh-reh djeh-vahr ahl ree-oh,
3. *y yo le di-go que no,*
ee djoh leh dee-goh keh noh,
4. *por-que me mue-ro de frí-o.*
pohr-keh meh mweh-roh deh free-oh.
5. *Sa-le la lin-da,*
sah-leh lah leen-dah,
6. *sa-le la fe-a,*
sah-leh lah feh-ah,
7. *y‿el bo-rre-gui-to*
ee‿yehl boh-rreh-ghee-toh
8. *con su za-le-a.*
kohn soo sah-leh-ah.
9. *To-pe que to-pe,*
toh-peh keh toh-peh,
10. *to-pe con e-lla.*
toh-peh kohn eh-djah.
11. *To-pe que to-pe,*
toh-peh keh toh-peh,
12. *to-pe con él.*
toh-peh kohn ehl.

### Translation

Miss, your lamb wants to take me to the river,
And I tell it no, because I'm too cold.
The pretty one goes out; the ugly one goes out,
And the little lamb with its sheepskin goes out.
Bump, bump, bump into her.
Bump, bump, bump into him.

## *Cielito lindo,* p. 270 CD 11–13

*Folk Song from Mexico*

### Pronunciation Practice

**Verse 1**

Phrase 1. *De la sie-rra mo-re-na,*
deh lah syeh-rah moh-reh-nah,
2. *Cie-li-to lin-do,*
syeh-lee-toh leen-doh,
3. *vie-nen ba-jan-do,*
vyeh-nehn bah-hahn-doh,
4. *Un par de‿o ji-tos ne-gros,*
oon pahr deh‿oh-hee-tohs neh-grohs,
5. *Cie-li-to lin-do,*
syeh-lee-toh leen-doh,
6. *de con-tra-ban-do.*
deh kohn-trah-bahn-doh.

**Refrain**

Phrase 1. *Ay, ay, ay ay!*
I, yI, yI, yI!
2. *Can-ta‿y no llo-res.*
kahn-tah‿ee noh yoh-rehs.
3. *Por-que can-tan-do se‿a-le-gran,*
pohr-keh kahn-tahn-doh seh‿ah-leh-grahn,
4. *Cie-li-to lin-do,*
syeh-lee-toh leen-doh,
5. *los co-ra-zo-nes.*
lohs koh-rah-soh-nehs.

**Verse 2**

Phrase 1. *E-se lu-nar que tie-nes,*
eh-seh loo-nahr keh tyeh-nehs,
2. *Cie-li-to lindo,*
syeh-lee-toh leen-doh,
3. *jun-to a la bo-ca,*
hoon-twah lah boh-kah,
4. *No se lo des a na-die,*
noh seh loh des ah nah-dyeh,
5. *Cie-li-to lin-do,*
syeh-lee-toh leen-doh,
6. *que‿a mí me to-ca.*
keh‿ah mee meh toh-kah.

**Refrain**

### Translation

**Verse 1** From the dark mountain, Cielito lindo,
Are going down, a couple of little black eyes,
Cielito lindo, Illegally.

**Refrain** Ay, ay, ay, ay! Sing and don't cry
Because singing gladdens, Cielito lindo,
Hearts gladden.

**Verse 2** That mole you have, Cielito lindo, next to your mouth—Don't give it to anybody, Cielito lindo.

## *Corrido de Kansas* (Kansas *Corrido*), p. 274 CD 11–20

*Folk Song from Mexico*

### Pronunciation Practice

**Verse 1**

Phrase 1. *Cuan-do sa-li-mos pa' Kan-sas*
kwahn-doh sah-lee-mohs pah kahn-sahs
2. *Con u-na gran-de par-ti-da,*
kohn oo-nah grahn-deh pahr-tee-dah,
3. *Nos de-cí-a‿el ca-po-ral:*
nohs deh-see-ah‿ehl kah-poh-rahl:
4. *"No cuen-to ni con mi vi-da."*
noh kwehn-toh nee kohn mee vee-dah.

**Verse 2**

Phrase 1. *Quin-ien-tos no-vi-llos er-an*
kee-nee‿ehn-tohs noh-vee-djohs eh-rahn
2. *Pe-ro to-dos muy li-via-nos,*
peh-roh toh-dohs moo‿ee lee-vee‿ah-nohs,
3. *No los po-día-mos re-par-ar*
noh lohs poh-dee‿ah-mohs reh-pah-rahrr
4. *Sien-do trein-ta mex-i-ca-nos.*
see-ehn-doh trehn-tah meh-hee-kah-nohs.

**Verse 3**

Phrase 1. *Cuan-do di-mos vis-ta‿a Kan-sas*
kwahn-doh dee-mohs vee-stah‿ah kahn-sahs
2. *Er-a pu-ri-ti-to co-rrer,*
eh-rah poo-ree-tee-toh koh-rrehr,
3. *Er-an los ca-mi-nos lar-gos,*
eh-rahn lohs kah-mee-nohs lahr-gohs,
4. *Y pen-sa-ba yo en vol-ver.*
ee pehn-sah-bah djoh ehn vohl-vehr.

### Translation

When we left for Kansas
With a big party,
The chief said to us,
"Even my life is in danger."

### Translation (continued)

There were five hundred steers,
But they were all very fickle,
We couldn't keep an eye on all of them all,
Being just thirty Mexicans.

When we first saw Kansas,
We just ran and ran.
The roads were long,
And I thought about going back.

When we got to Kansas,
A little bull starting thrashing.
A young boy went to stop it
And his horse turned over.

The mother of an adventurer
Asked the chief,
"Listen, tell me why
I have not seen my son arrive."

"Miss, I will tell you,
But do not cry.
A bull killed your son
At the door of a corral."

He had only thirty pesos.
That was all he had.
And I put in three hundred
To have him buried.

All the adventurers
Went to accompany him,
With their hats in their hands,
To see him buried.

## *Farewell to the Warriors,* p. 284 CD 12–5

*Native American Song of the Chippewa*

### Pronunciation Practice

Phrase 1. *Um-be a-ni-ma-djag*
oom-beh ah-nee-mah-dyagh
2. *wa-su-gi-di-zha-min,*
wah-soo-djee-dee-zhah-meen,
3. *ya wi a ya wi a*
yah wee ah yah wee ah
4. *ya ya wi a ya wi a*
yah yah wee ah yah wee ah

### Translation

Come. It is time for you to depart.
We are going on a long journey.

## *Ai Dunaiĭ moy* (Ah, My Merry Dunaii), p. 293 CD 12–17

*Folk Song from Russia*

### Pronunciation Practice

Phrase 1. *U vo-rot, vo-rot, vo-rot,*
oh vah-roht, vah-roht, vah-roht,
2. *Da a vo-rot ba-tyush-ki-nykh,*
dah ah vah-roht bah-tyoosh-kee-nyeekh,
3. *Ai, Du-naiĭ moy, Du-naiĭ,*
ah‿ee, doo-na‿hee mo‿hee, doo-na‿hee,
4. *Ai, ves-yo-lyi Du-naiĭ.*
ah‿ee, vee-syoh-lyee doo-na‿hee.
5. *Ra-zy-gra-il-sya re-bya-ta,*
rah-zgew-lyah-lee-syah reh-bee‿yah-tuh,
6. *ras-po-te-shi-lis,*
rahs-poh-teh-shee-lees,
7. *Ai, Du-naiĭ moy, Du-naiĭ,*
ah‿ee, doo-na‿hee mo‿hee, doo-na‿hee,
8. *Ai, ve-syo-lyi Du-naiĭ.*
ah‿ee, vee-syoh-lyee doo-na‿hee.

### Translation

Near the gates, the gates, near the gates of his father,
Oh, my dear Dunai, oh, my merry Dunai.
The fellows revelled and the fellows made merry,
Oh, my dear Dunai, oh, my merry Dunai.

## *Beriozka* (The Birch Tree), p. 294 CD 12–22

*Folk Song from Russia*

### Pronunciation Practice

**Verse 1**

Phrase 1. *Va pa-lye bi-ryo ziny-ka sto-ya-la*
vah pah-leh bih-rryoh zihn‿yuh-kah stah-yah-lah
2. *Vo pa-lye kud-rya-va-ya sto-ya-la*
vah pah-leh kood-ryah-vah-yah stah-yah-lah
3. *Lyu-li lyu-li sta-ya-la*
loo-lee-loo-lee stah-yah-lah
4. *Lyu-li lyu-li sta-ya-la.*
loo-lee-loo-lee stah-yah-lah.

**Verse 2**

Phrase 1. *Nye-ka-mu bi-ryo-zu za-la-ma-ti*
nyeh-kah-moo bee-ryoh-zoo zah-lah-mah-tee
2. *Nye-ka-mu kud-rya-vu za-chi-pa-ti*
nyeh-kah-moo kood-ryah-voo zah-chee-pah-tee
3. *Lyu-li lyu-li za-la-ma-ti*
loo-lee-loo-lee zah-lah-mah-tee
4. *Lyu-li lyu-li za-chi-pa-ti.*
loo-lee-loo-lee zah-chee-pah-tee.

**Verse 3**

Phrase 1. *Kak pay-du ya vlyes pa-gu-lya yu*
kahk pah‿ee-doo yah vlyehs pah-goo-lyah yoo
2. *bye-lu-yu bi-ryo-zu za-la-ma-yu*
byeh-loo-yoo bee-ryoh-zoo zah-lah-mah-yoo
3. *Lyu-li lyu-li pa-gu-lya-yu*
loo-lee-loo-lee pah-goo-lyah-yoo
4. *Lyu-li lyu-li za-la-ma-yu.*
loo-lee loo-lee zah-lah-mah-yoo.

**Verse 4**

Phrase 1. *Srez-hu s be-ryo-zu tree pru-toch-ka*
sreez-yoo ihs beh-rryoh-zoo tree proo-tohch-kah
2. *Sdye-la-yu sye-bye ya tree gu-doch-ka*
sdee-luh-yoo syeh-byeh yeh tree goo-dohch-kah
3. *Lyu-li lyu-li tree pru-toch-ka*
loo-lee-loo-lee tree proo-tohch-kah
4. *Lyu-li lyu-li tree gu-doch-ka.*
loo-lee-loo-lee tree goo-dohch-kah.

### Translation

**Verse 1**

In the meadow stood a little birch tree.
In the meadow stood a leafy birch tree.
Liuli, liuli, a birch tree.
Liuli, liuli, a birch tree.

**Verse 2**

No one put an axe to the birch tree.
No one harmed the little leafy birch tree.
Liuli, liuli, a birch tree.
Liuli, liuli, a birch tree.

**Verse 3**

In the woods today I am going
All to end the silver birch tree's growing.
Liuli, liuli, I'm going.
Liuli, liuli, end its growing.

**Verse 4**

I will cut from the birch tree three branches.
I will make myself three wood flutes.
Liuli, liuli, three branches.
Liuli, liuli, three wood flutes.

## *Tina singu,* p. 300 CD 12–33

*Folk Song from South Africa*

### Pronunciation Practice

Phrase

1. *Ti-na sing-u la-lu-vu tae-a*
   tee-nah seeng-oom leh-loh-voh tah‿ee-yoh
2. *Wat-sha, wat-sha, wat-sha,*
   waht-chah, waht-chah, waht-chah,
3. *Ti-na, Ti-na sing-u le-lu-vu‿tae-o,*
   tee-nah, tee-nah seeng-oom leh-loh-voh‿tah‿ee-yoh,
4. *wat-sha, wat-sha, wat-sha.*
   waht-chah, waht-chah, waht-chah.

### Translation

We are a burning fire. Look out! Don't get burnt.

## *La raspa,* p. 302 CD 13–4

*Folk Song from Mexico*

### Pronunciation Practice

Phrase

1. *La ras-pa yo bai-lé*
   lah rahs-pah yoh bah‿ee-leh
2. *al de-re-cho y‿al re-vés.*
   ahl deh-reh-choh yahl reh-vehs.
3. *Si quie-res tú bai-lar,*
   see kyeh-rehs too bah‿ee-lahr,
4. *em-pie-za‿a mo-ver los pies.*
   ehm-pyeh-sah moo-vehr lohs pyehs.
5. *Brin-ca, brin-ca, brin-ca tam-bién,*
   brin-kah, brin-kah, brin-kah tahm-byehn,
6. *mue-ve, mue-ve mu-cho los pies.*
   mweh-veh, mweh-veh moo-choh lohs pyehs.
7. *Que la ras-pa vas a bai-lar*
   keh lah rahs-pah vahs ah bah‿ee-lahr
8. *al de-re-cho y al re-vés.*
   ahl deh-reh-choh yahl reh-vehs.
9. *Si quie-res tú bai-lar*
   see kyeh-rehs too bah‿ee-lahr
10. *la ras-pa co-mo yo,*
    lah rahs-pah koh-moh yoh,
11. *Me tie-nes que se-guir*
    meh tyeh-nehs keh sah-gheer
12. *al de-re-cho y‿al re-vés.*
    ahl deh-reh-choh yahl reh-vehs.
13. *La ras-pa yo bai-lé*
    lah rahs-pah yoh bah‿ee-leh
14. *al de-re-cho-y‿al re-vés.*
    ahl deh-reh-choh yahl reh-vehs.
15. *Si quie-res tú bai-lar,*
    see kyeh-rehs too bah‿ee-lahr,
16. *em-pie-za‿a amo-ver los pies.*
    ehm-pyeh-sah moo-vehr lohs pyehs.

### Translation

I danced the raspa back and forth.
If you want to dance begin to move your feet.
Also, jump, jump, jump.
Move, move your feet a lot.
For the raspa you are going to dance
Back and forth.
If you want to dance the raspa the way I do,
You have to follow me back and forth.

## *Bogando a la luz del sol* (Rowing Toward the Sunlight), p. 306 CD 13–10, 11

*Folk Song from Venezuela*

### Pronunciation Practice

**Melody**

Phrase
1. *So-plan las bri-sas*
   soh-plahn lahs bree-sahs
2. *de la ma-ña-na,*
   deh lah mah-nyah-nah,
3. *Ri-zan-do‿el la-go*
   ree-sahn-doh‿ehl lah-goh
4. *mur-mu-ra-dor,*
   moorr-moo-rah-dohrr,
5. *Y por o-rien-te*
   ee pohr oh-ryehn-teh
6. *su faz a-so-ma*
   soo fahs ah-soh-mah
7. *Cual ra-ro‿in-cen-dio*
   kwahl rrah-roh‿een-sehn-dyoh
8. *la luz del sol.*
   lah loos dehl sohl.
9. *Y por o-rien-te*
   ee pohr oh-ryehn-teh
10. *su faz a-so-ma*
    soo fahs ah-soh-mah
11. *Cual ra-ro‿in-cen-dio*
    kwahl rrah-roh‿een-sehn-dyoh
12. *la luz del sol.*
    lah loos dehl sohl.

**Countermelody**

Phrase
1. *So-plan las bri-sas*
   soh-plahn lahs bree-sahs
2. *de la ma-ña-na,*
   deh lah mah-nyah-nah,
3. *Y por o-rien-te*
   ee pohr oh-ryehn-teh
4. *su faz a-so-ma.*
   soo fahs ah-soh-mah.
5. *Y por o-rien-te*
   ee pohr oh-ryehn-teh
6. *su faz a-so-ma*
   soo fahs ah-soh-mah
7. *Cual ra-ro‿in-cen-dio*
   kwahl rah-roh‿een-sehn-dyoh
8. *la luz del sol.*
   lah loos dehl sohl.

### Translation

Rowing to the light of the sun,
Morning breezes blow,
Rippling the murmuring lake.
And in the east the remarkable fire of the sunlight shows its face.
And in the east the remarkable fire of the sunlight shows its face.

## *Sakura*, p. 308 CD 13–16

*Folk Song from Japan*

### Pronunciation Practice

Phrase
1. *Sa-ku-ra, sa-ku-ra,*
   sah-koo-rah, sah-koo-rah,
2. *Ya-yo i no so-ra wa*
   yah-yoh ee noh soh-rah wah
3. *Me-wa-ta-su ka-gi-ri*
   mee-wah-tah-soo kah-gee-rree
4. *Ka-su-me ka ku-mo-ka,*
   kah-soo-mee kah koo-moh-kah,
5. *Ni-o-i zo i-zu-ru;*
   nee-hoh-ee tzoh ee-tzoo-roo;
6. *i-za-ya, i-za-ya,*
   ee-tzah-yah, ee-tzah-yah,
7. *Mi ni yu-kan.*
   mee nee yoo-kah(n).

### Translation

Cherry blossoms, cherry blossoms,
The March sky, as far as one can see.
(is filled with cherry blossoms.)
Is it mist or clouds?
Fragrance wafts through.
Now, now,
Let's go and see them.

## *Feng yang hua gu* (*Feng Yang* Song), p. 313 CD 13–23

*Folk Song from China*

### Pronunciation Practice

Phrase
1. *Zuo shou luo,*
   tzwoh show loo‿wow,
2. *you shou gu,*
   yoh show goo,
3. *Shou na zhe luo gu*
   show nah juh loo‿wow goo
4. *lai chang ge!*
   lah‿ee chahng guh!
5. *Bie di ge er*
   bee‿yeh dee guh uhr
6. *wo ye bu hui chang,*
   wow yeh boo hweh‿ee chahng,
7. *Zhi hui chang ge Feng Yang ge.*
   jihr hweh‿ee chahng guh fuhng yahng guh.
8. *Feng la, feng yang*
   fuhng lah, fuhng yahng
9. *ge er lai,*
   guh uhr lah‿ee,
10. *Der lang dang piao yi piao,*
    d'rrrr luhng-duhng pyow yee pyow,
11. *Der lang dang piao yi piao,*
    d'rrrr luhng-duhng pyow yee pyow,
12. *Der piao! Der piao!*
    d'rrrr pyow! d'rrrr pyow!
13. *Der piao der piao piao ye der piao piao piao yi piao!*
    d'rrrr pyow d'rrrr pyow pyow yee d'rrrr pyow pyow pyow yee pyow!

### Translation

Left hand plays the gong.
Right hand plays the drum.
Holding the instrument and singing,
I don't know how to sing any other songs.
I only know how to sing the Feng Yang song.

## *Xiao* (Bamboo Flute), p. 314 CD 13–27

*Folk Song from China*

### Pronunciation Practice

Phrase 1. *Yi geng zi zhu*
yee gawng dzuh joo
2. *zhi miao miao;*
juh mee‿ow mee‿ow;
3. *Sung yu bao bao zuo guan xiao.*
sohng yuh bow bow tshoo‿oh gwahn shee‿ow.
4. *Xiao er dui zheng kou*
shee‿ow ehr dweh jehng koh
5. *Kou er dui zheng xiao;*
koh ehr dweh jehng shee‿ow;
6. *Xiao zhong chui chu*
shee‿ow juhng chweh choo
7. *shi xin diao;*
shee sheen dee‿ow;
8. *Xiao bao bao*
shee‿ow bow bow
9. *yi di yi di xue hui liao,*
yee dee yee dee shau wheh lee‿ow,
10. *Xiao bao bao*
shee‿ow bow bow
11. *Yi di yi di xue hui liao.*
yee dee yee dee shau wheh lee‿ow.

### Translation

From the purple straight bamboo
I have made a flute for you.
Take the bamboo flute. Put it to your lips.
Play a new and lilting song
My little one. Play a new and lilting song,
My little one. Play a new and lilting song.

## *Yibane amenu,* p. 316 CD 13–32

*Round from Israel*

### Pronunciation Practice

Phrase 1. *Yi-ba-ne a-me-nu*
yee-bah-neh ah-meh-noo
2. *b-´ar-tse-nu;*
buh-ahr-tzeh-noo;
3. *Yi-ba-ne a-me-nu*
yee-bah-neh ah-meh-noo
4. *b-´ar-tse-nu;*
buh-ahr-tzeh-noo;
5. *B-´ar-tse-nu, yi-ba-ne,*
buh-ahr-tzeh-noo, yee-bah-neh,
6. *B-´ar-tse-nu, yi-ba-ne,*
buh-ahr-tzeh-noo, yee-bah-neh,
7. *Yi-ba-ne, Yi-ba-ne.*
yee-bah-neh, yee-bah-neh.
8. *Yi-ba-ne, Yi-ba-ne.*
yee-bah-neh, yee-bah-neh.

### Translation

Our nation will be rebuilt in our land.

## *Niu lang zhi nü* (The Cowherd and the Weaving Maid), p. 335 CD 14–18

*Folk Song from China*

### Pronunciation Practice

**Verse 1**

Phrase 1. *Tiau tiau chien niu hsing,*
dzah-oh dzah-oh chee‿ehn nyow sheeng,
2. *jiau jiau hĕ han nü*
jee-ow jee-ow suh hahn new
3. *hsien hsien ien su shou*
shyeh-ehn shyehn yehn shoo shoh
4. *zha zha nong ji zhu*
dzah dzah nuhng jee dzhoo
5. *ing ing i hsuei jien*
eeng eeng ee shweh djee‿ehn
6. *mu-o mu-o bu de ü.*
mwah-oh mwah-oh boo dah ew.

**Verse 2**

Phrase 1. *Zhong zhru bu cheng zhang,*
tzhawng zhroo boo chehng dzahng,
2. *chi ti lei zhru ü*
chee tee leh zhroo ew
3. *ne han ching chie chien*
nuh hahn cheeng chee-eh chee-ehn
4. *hsiang chü fu ji hsü*
shee‿ahng chew foo jee shew
5. *ing ing i hsuei jien*
eeng eeng ee shweh djee‿ehn
6. *mu-o mu-o bu de ü.*
mwah-oh mwah-oh boo dah ew.

### Translation

**Verse 1**

Far away is the cowherd star,
Beautiful is the Milky Way maid,
Lifting up her whited hands to weave,
Moving the shuttle back and forth.
With a river in between,
Full of feelings but cannot talk.

**Verse 2**

The days are in havoc,
Tears are flowing like rain.
The river of stars is clear and shallow,
The distance is not far away,
With a clear river in between,
Full of love but cannot talk.

## *Somos el barco* (We Are the Boat), p. 352 CD 15–15

*Words and Music by Lorre Wyatt*

### Pronunciation Practice

Phrase 1. *So-mos el bar-co,*
soh-mohs ehl bahr-koh,
2. *So-mos el mar.*
soh-mohs ehl mahr.
3. *Yo na-ve-go en ti,*
yoh nah-veh-goh ehn tee,
4. *Tu na-ve-gas en mí.*
too nah-veh-gahs ehn mee.

### Translation

We are the boat, we are the sea.
I sail in you, you sail in me.

## ***Sailboat in the Sky,* p. 374 CD 16–14**

*Folk Song from Korea*

### Pronunciation Practice

Phrase 1. *Pu reun ha nul eun-ha su ha yan jjok bae ae,*
poo roon hah nuhl oon-hah soo hah yahn johk beh eh,

2. *Gae su na mu han-na mu to kki han ma ri,*
geh soo nah moo hahn-nah moo toh kee hahn mah ree,

3. *Dot dae do ah ni dal go sat dae do up si,*
doht deh doh ah nee dahl goh sah deh doh oop see,

4. *Ga gi do jal do gahn da so-jjok na ra ro.*
gah ghee doh jahl doh gahn dah soh-johk nah rah roh.

### Translation

In the small white boat in the sky of the Milky Way (half moon)
There is a cinnamon tree (the greta laurel tree in the moon) where a rabbit lives.
With no sails or oars
It floats away smoothly, sailing toward the west.

## ***Einini,* p. 391 CD 17–3**

*Gaelic Folk Song*

### Pronunciation Practice

**Part 1**

Phrase 1. *Ein-in-i, ein-in-i,*
eh‿ee-nee-nee, eh‿ee-nee-nee,

2. *cod-al-ai-gi, cod-al-ai-gi,*
kohd-ahl-ee-gee, kohd-ahl-ee-gee,

3. *ein-in-i, ein-in-i,*
eh‿ee-nee-nee, eh‿ee-nee-nee,

4. *cod-al-ai-gi, cod-al-ai-gi.*
kohd-ahl-ee-gee, kohd-ahl-ee-gee.

5. *Cod-al-ai-gi, cod-al-ai-gi,*
kohd-ahl-ee-gee, kohd-ahl-ee-gee,

6. *cois an chlai am-uigh, cois an chlai am-uigh,*
kohsh uhn klee uhm-wee, kohsh uhn klee uhm-wee,

7. *cod-al-ai-gi, cod-al-ai-gi,*
kohd-ahl-ee-gee, kohd-ahl-ee-gee,

8. *cois an chlai am-uigh, cois an chlai am-uigh.*
kohsh uhn klee uhm-wee, kohsh uhn klee uhm-wee.

9. *Cod-al-ai-gi, cod-al-ai-gi,*
kohd-ahl-ee-gee, kohd-ahl-ee-gee,

10. *cois an chlai amuigh, cois an chlai amuigh.*
kohsh uhn klee uhm‿wee, kohsh uhn klee uhm‿wee.

**Part 2**

(Same as above)

### Translation

Little birdies sleep.
Sleep,
Beside the fence over there.

## *Sambalele,* p. 397 CD 17-11

*Folk Song from Brazil*

### Pronunciation Practice

Phrase 1. *Sam-ba-le-le ta do-en-te,*
sahm-bah-lah-leh tah doh‿ehn-chee,
2. *tac-oa ca-be-ça que bra-da*
tah-kwah kah-beh-sah keh brah-dah
3. *Sam-ba-le-le pre-ci-sa-va*
sahm-bah-lah-leh preh-see-sah-vah
4. *de‿u-mas de zoi-to lam-ba-das,*
djoo-mahsh dee zoh‿ee-too lahm-bah-dahsh,
5. *Sam-ba-le-le ta do-en-te,*
sahm-bah-lah-leh tah doh‿ehn-chee,
6. *ta coa ca-be-ça, que bra-da*
tah-kwah kah-beh-sah keh brah-dah
7. *Sam-ba-le-le pre-ci-sa-va*
sahm-bah-lah-leh preh-see-sah-vah
8. *de‿u-mas de zoi-to lam-ba-das,*
djoo-mahsh dee zoh‿ee-too lahm-bah-dahsh,
9. *Sam-ba sam-ba sam-ba-le-le*
sahm-bah sahm-bah sahm-bah-leh-leh
10. *Pi-sa-na ba-ra da sa-ia le-le!*
pee-sah-nah bah-hah dah sah-yoh leh-leh!
11. *Sam-ba sam-ba sam-ba-le-le!*
sahm-bah sahm-bah sahm-bah-leh-leh!
12. *Pi-sa-na bar-ra da sa-ia*
pee-sah-nah bah-hah dah sah-yah
13. *Ba-la-io meu bem, Ba-la-io sin-ha*
bah-lah-yoh meh‿oh behm, bah-lah-yoh seen-yah
14. *ba-la-io do co-ra-ção*
bah-lah-yoh doo koh-rah-sow(n)*
15. *Mo-ça-que não tem ba-la-io sin-ha*
mah-sah-keh now tehn bah-lah-yoh see-yah
16. *bo-taa cos-tu-ra no chão.*
boh-tah kohs-too-rah noo show.*
17. *Ba-la-io meu bem, ba la-io sin-ha*
bah-lah-yoh meh‿oh behm, bah-lah-yoh seen-yah
18. *ba-la-io do co-ra-ção*
bah-lah-yoh doo koh-rah-sow(n)*
19. *Mo-ça-que não tem ba-la-io sin-ha*
mah-sah-keh now tehn bah-lah-yoh seen-yah
20. *bo-taa cos-tu-ra no chão!*
boh-tah kohs-too-rah noo show!*

*ow: as in "cow"

### Translation

Sambalele is ailing, he has a broken head.
Sambalele he deserves eighteen lashes. (Repeat)
Samba, samba, sambao-le-le, step on the hem of the skirt. (Repeat)
Dance the balaio, my love, Missy, the balaio of my heart.
If a girl has no basket, she puts her sewing on the floor. (Repeat)

## *A Merry Modal Christmas, Pat-a-pan,* p. 411 CD 17–18

*Words and Music by Bernard de la Monnoye*

### Pronunciation Practice

**Verse 1**

Phrase 1. *Guil-lo, prends ton tam-bou-rin,*
gee-yoh, prahn tohn tahm-boh-rah(n),
2. *Toi prends tai flü-te, Ro-bin;*
twah, prah(n) tah floo-tuh, roh-beh(n);
3 *Au son de cés in-stru-ments,*
oh soh(n) duh sehs een-stroo-mah(n),
4. *Tu-re-lu-re-lu, pat-a-pat-a-pan;*
too-ruh-loo-ruh-loo, pah-tah-pah-tah-pah(n),
5. *Au son de cés in-stru-ments,*
oh soh(n) duh sehs een-stroo-mah(n),
6. *Je di-rai No-ël gaie-ment.*
zhuh dee-reh noh-ehl geh-mah(n).

### Translation

Willie take your little drum. You take your flute and come.

At the sound of these instruments, tu-re-lu-re-lu, pat-a-pat-a Pan.

At the sound of these instruments, I will say Christmas happily.

## *A Merry Modal Christmas, La marche des rois,* p. 411 CD 17–19

*Carol from France*

### Pronunciation Practice

Phrase 1. *Ce ma-tin,*
suh mah-tah(n),
2. *J'ai ren-con-tré le train,*
zheh rah(n)-kohn-treh luh trah(n),
3. *De trois grands Rois*
duh twah grah(n) rwah
4. *qui al-laient en-voy-a-ge,*
kee ahl-leht ah(n)-voh-ah-zhuh,
5. *Ce ma-tin,*
suh mah-tah(n),
6. *J'ai ren-con-tré le train,*
zheh rah(n)-kohn-treh luh trah(n),
7. *De trois grands Rois*
duh twah grah(n) rwah
8. *des-sus le grand che-min.*
deh-soo luh grah(n)d shuh-mah(n).
9. *Tout char-gés d'or les sui-vant d'a-bord,*
too shahr-zheh dohr leh swee-vahnt dah-bohr,
10. *De grands guer-riers*
duh grah(n) geh-reeyehr
11. *et les gar-des du tré-sor,*
eh leh gahr-deh doo treh-sohr,
12. *Tout char-gés d'or les sui-vant d'a-bord*
too shahr-zheh dohr leh swee-vahnt dah-bohr
13. *De grands guer-riers*
duh grah(n) geh-reeyehr
14. *a-vec leurs bou-cli-ers.*
ah-vehk luhr boo-klee-ehr.

### Translation

This morning, I met the train,
Three great kings who went to travel.
This morning I met the train, three great kings over the great way, all full with gold following them first.
Great warriors and the treasure guards, all full with gold
Following them first. Great warriors with their shield. (Repeat)

## *La copa de la vida* (The Cup of Life), p. 414 CD 17–22

*Words and Music by Desmond Child and Robi Rosa*

### Pronunciation Practice

**Verse 1**

Phrase
1. *Co-mo Cain y A-bel*
   koh-moh kah‿een ee ah-behl
2. *es un par-ti-do cruel.*
   ehs oon pahr-tee-thoh kroo‿ehl.
3. *Tie-nes que pe-le-ar por un-a es-tre-lla*
   tyeh-nehs keh peh-leh-ahrr pohr oo-nah ehs-treh-yah
4. *Con-si-gue con hon-or*
   kohn-see-geh kohn oh-nohr
5. *la co-pa del a-mor.*
   lah koh-pah dehl ah-mohrr.
6. *Pa-ra so-bre vi-vir y lu-char por e-lla*
   pah-rah soh-breh vee-veer ee loo-chahr pohr eh-yah
7. *Lu-char por e-lla.*
   loo-chahr pohr eh-yah.

**Verse 2**

Phrase
1. *La vi-da es com-pe-ti-ción.*
   lah vee-thah ehs kohm-peh-tee-syohn.
2. *Hay que so-ñar, ser cam-pe-ón.*
   ah‿ee keh soh-nyahr, sehr kahm-peh-ohn.
3. *La co-pa es la ben-di-ción,*
   lah koh-pah ehs lah behn-dee-syohn,
4. *la ga-na-rás, go, go, go.*
   lah gah-nah-rahs, goh, goh, goh.

**Refrain**

Phrase
1. *Uno, dos, tres, o-lé, o-lé, o-lé.*
   oo‿noh, dohs, trehs, oh-leh, oh-leh, oh-leh.
2. *Un, deux, trois, Al-lez, al-lez, al-lez.*
   uh(n) duh, twah, ah-leh, ah-leh, ah-leh.

### Translation

**Verse 1** Like Cain and Abel it is a cruel game.
You have to fight for a star.
Obtain the Cup of love with honor.
In order to survive and fight for it, fight for it.

**Verse 2** Life is a competition.
You have to dream, be a champion.
The cup is a blessing, you will win it.

**Refrain** One, two, three.

## *Shir l'shalom* (Hand in Hand—A Song for Peace), p. 419 CD 17–26

*Words by Jacob Rotblitt, Music by Yair Rosenblum*

### Pronunciation Practice

**Verse 1**

Phrase 1. *Tnu la-she-mesh la-a-lot,*
tnoo lah-sheh-mehsh lah-ah-loht,
2. *la-bo-ker l'-ha-ir.*
luh-boh-kehr leh-hah-eer.
3. *Ha-za-kah she-ba-tfi-lot*
hah-zah-kah sheh-bah-t'fee-loht
4. *o-ta-nu lo tach zir.*
oh-tah-noo loh tah-khzihr.
5. *Mi a-sher ka-va ne-ro*
mee ah-sheer kah-vah neh-roh
6. *u-v'-a-far nit-man,*
oo-vuh-ah-fahr neet-mahn,
7. *Be-chi mar lo ya-i-ro*
beh-hkhee mahr loh yah-ee‿raw
8. *lo yach-zi-ro l'-chan.*
loh-yakh-zee-roh luh-hkhahn.
9. *Ish o-ta-nu lo ya-shiv*
eesh oh-tah-noo lah yah-sheev
10. *mi-bor tach-teet a-fel.*
mee-bohr tahkh-teet ah-fehl.
11. *Kan lo yo-i-lu lo shi-rey*
kahn loh yoh-ee-loo loh shee-reh
12. *ha-ni-tsa-chon*
hah-nee-tzah-hkhohn
13. *v'-lo shi-rey ha-lel.*
vuh-loh shee-reh hah-lehl.
14. *La´ chen rak shi-ru shir l'-sha-lom,*
lah hkhehn rahk shee-roo shihr lah-shah-lohm,
15. *al til-cha-shu tfi-la.*
ahl tee-lkha-shoo tfee-lah.
16. *La´ chen rak shi-ru shir l'-sha-lom*
lah hkhehn rahk shee-roo shihr lah-sha-lohm
17. *bi-tse-a-kah g'do-lah!*
buh-tzah-ah-kah guh-doh-lah!

**Verse 2**

Phrase 1. *Tnu la-she-mesh la-cha-dor*
tnoo lah-sheh-mehsh lah-hkhah-dohrr
2. *mi-ba-'ad la-pra-chim.*
mee-bah-ahd lah-prah-hkheem.
3. *al ta-bi-tu l'-a-chor,*
ahl tah-bee-too leh-ah‿hkhohrr,
4. *ha-ni-chu la-hol-chim.*
hah-nee-hkhoo lah-hkhohl-hkheem.
5. *Su ey-na-yim b'-tik-vah,*
suh-oo eh-nah-yeem buh-teek-vah,
6. *lo de-rech ka-va-not.*
loh deh-rehkh kah-vah-noht.
7. *Shi-ru shir la-a-ha-vah,*
shee-roo shihr lah-ah-hah-vah,
8. *v'-lo la-mil-cha-mot.*
vuh-loh lah-mihl-hkhah-moht.
9. *Al ta-gi-du yom ya-vo,*
ahl tah-gee-doo yohm yah-vaw,
10. *ha viy-u et ha-yom!*
hah-vee-oo eht hah-yohm!
11. *Ki lo-cha-lom hu. U-v'-chol*
kee lah-hkhah-lohm hoo. oo-vuh-hkhohl
12. *ha-ki-ka-rot ha-ri-u l'-sha-lom!*
hah-kee-kah-rawt hah-ree-oo lah-shah-lohm!
13. *La´ chen rak shi-ru shir l'-sha-lom,*
lah hkhehn rahk shee-roo shihr lah-shah-lohm,
14. *al til-cha-shu tfi-la.*
ahl tee-lkha-shoo tfee-lah
15. *La´ chen rak shi ru shir l'-sha-lom*
lah hkhehn rahk shee-roo shihr lah-sha-lohm
16. *bi-tse-a-kah g'do-lah!*
buh-tzeh-ah-kah guh-doh-lah!
17. *g'do-lah!*
guh-doh-lah!

### Translation

**Verse Traditionally Sung**

1. Sing a song of peace for those who have fallen.
   Tears, prayers and words of praise will not return them to life.
   But peace will sanctify their deaths.

**Original Lyrics of Jacob Rotblitt**

2. Let the sun penetrate [come] through the petals of the flowers.
   Don't look backward;
   Let go of those who "passed on" [went].
   Raise your eyes in hope,
   Not "through" [the way of] arms.
   Sing a song for love,
   And not for war.
   Don't tell me the day will come;
   Bring the day! (Implied: "Make the day happen!")
   Because it isn't a dream.
   And in all the town squares
   Cheer for peace!

## *Ocho kandelikas* (Eight Little Candles), p. 429 CD 18–11

*Words and Music by Flory Jagoda*

### Pronunciation Practice

**Verse 1**

Phrase 1. *Ha-nu-ka lin-da sta a-ki*
hah-noo-kah lihn-dah stah ah-kee

2. *o-cho kan-de-las pa-ra mi.*
oh-choh kahn-deh-lahs pah-rah mee.

3. *Ha-nu-ka lin-da sta a-ki*
hah-noo-kah lihn-dah stah ah-kee

4. *o-cho kan-de-las pa-ra mi.*
oh-choh kahn-deh-lahs pah-rah mee.

**Refrain**

Phrase 1. *u-na kan-de-li-ka, dos kan-de-li-kas,*
oo-nah kahn-deh-lee-kah, dohs kahn-deh-lee-kahs,

2. *tres kan-de-li-kas, kuat-ro kan-de-li-kas,*
trrehs kahn-deh-lee-kahs, kwaht-rro kahn-deh-lee-kahs,

3. *sin-ko kan-de-li-kas, sej kan-de-li-kas,*
seen-koh kahn-deh-lee-kahs, sehdj kahn-deh-lee-kahs,

4. *sie-te kan-de-li-kas,*
see‿eh-teh kahn-deh-lee-kahs,

5. *o-cho kan-de-las pa-ra mi.*
oh-choh kahn-deh-lahs pah-rah mee.

**Verse 2**

Phrase 1. *Mu-chas fi-e-stas vo fa-zer*
moo-chahs fee-eh-stahs voh fah-zehrr

2. *kan a-le-gri-as i pla-zer.*
kahn ah-leh-gree-ahs ee plah-zehrr.

3. *Mu-chas fi-e-stas vo fa-zer*
moo-chahs fee-eh-stahs voh fah-zehrr

4. *kon a-le-gri-as i pla-zer.*
kahn ah-leh-gree-ahs ee plah-zehrr.

**Verse 3**

Phrase 1. *Los pas-te-li-kos vo ko-mer*
lahs pahs-teh-lee-kohs voh koh-mehrr

2. *kon al-men-dri-kas i la myel.*
kohn ahl-mehn-drree-kahs ee lah myehl.

3. *Los pas-te-li-kos vo ko-mer*
lahs pahs-teh-lee-kohs voh koh-mehrr

4. *kon al-men-dri-kas i la myel.*
kohn ahl-mehn-drree-kahs ee lah myehl.

### Translation

**Verse 1**

Beautiful Chanukah is here.
Eight candles for me. (Repeat)

**Refrain**

Oh…
One candle,
Two candles,
Three candles,
Four candles,
Five candles,
Six candles,
Seven candles,
Eight candles for me.

**Verse 2**

Many parties I will have
With happiness and pleasure. (Repeat.)

**Verse 3**

The little pastries we will eat,
Filled with almonds and honey. (Repeat.)

## *Al quebrar la piñata* (*Piñata* Song), p. 432 CD 18–18

*Christmas Song from Mexico*

### Pronunciation Practice

Phrase 1. *En las no-ches de po-sa-das,*
ehn lahs noh-chehs deh poh-sah-dah,

2. *La pi-ña-ta‿es lo me-jor;*
lah peen-yah-tah‿ehs loh meh-hohr;

3. *La ni-ña mas re-mil-ga-da*
lah neen-yah mahs reh-meel-gah-dah

4. *Se‿al-bo-ro-ta con ar-dor.*
seh‿ahl-boh-roh-tah kohn ahr-dohr.

5. *Da-le, da-le, da-le*
dah-leh, dah-leh, dah-leh

6. *no pier-das el ti-no.*
noh p'yehr-dahs ehl tee-noh.

7. *Que de la dis-tan-cia*
keh deh lah dee-stahn-s'yah

8. *se pier-de‿el ca-mi-no.*
seh p'yehr-deh‿ehl kah-mee-noh.

### Translation

On the nights of (Christmas) parties
the piñata is the best;
the little girl most shy
Becomes excited with ardor.

Hit it, hit it, hit it,
don't lose (your) aim,
for from the distance,
one loses the way.

## *Dayenu* (It Would Have Been Enough), p. 439 CD 19–4

*Jewish Passover Song*

### Pronunciation Practice

**Verse 1**

Phrase 1. *I-lu ho-tzi, ho-tzi-a-nu,*
ee-loo hoh-tzee, hoh-tzee-yah-noo,

2. *ho-tzi-a-nu mi-Mitz-ra-yim,*
hoh-tzee-yah-noo mee-mihtz-rah-yihm,

3. *hoh-tzi-a-nu mi-Mitz-ra-yim, da-ye-nu.*
hoh-tzee-yah-noo mee-mihtz-rah-yeem,
dah‿ih-yehy-noo.

**Refrain**

Phrase 1. *Da-da-ye-nu, da-da-ye-nu,*
dah‿ih-dah‿ih -yehy-noo,
dah‿ih-dah‿ih -yehy-noo,

2. *da-da-ye-nu, da-ye-nu, da-ye-nu, da-ye-nu*
dah‿ih-dah‿ih-yehy-noo,
dah‿ih-yehy-noo, dah‿ih-yehy-noo,
dah‿ih-yehy-noo

3. *Da-da-ye-nu, da-da-ye-nu,*
dah‿ih-dah‿ih-yehy-noo,
dah‿ih-dah‿ih-yehy-noo,

4. *da-da-ye-nu, da-ye-nu, da-ye-nu.*
dah‿ih-dah‿ih-yehy-noo,
dah‿ih-yehy-noo, dah‿ih-yehy-noo.

**Verse 2**

Phrase 1. *I-lu na-tan na-tan lo-nu,*
ee-loo nah-tahn nah-tahn lah-noo,

2. *na-tan lo-nu et ha-Sha-bat*
nah-tahn lah-noo eht hah-shah-baht

3. *na-tan lo-nu et ha-Sha-bat, da-ye-nu.*
nah-tahn lah-noo eht hah-shah-baht,
dah‿ih-yehy-noo.

**Verse 3**

Phrase 1. *I-lu na-tan na-tan lo-nu,*
ee-loo nah-tahn nah-tahn lah-noo,

2. *na-tan lo-nu et ha-To-ra,*
nah-tahn lah-noo eht hah-toh-rah,

3. *na-tan lo-nu et ha-To-ra, da-ye-nu.*
nah-tahn lah-noo eht hah-toh-rah,
dah‿ih-yehy-noo.

### Translation

1. Had he done nothing more than take us out of Egypt, dayenu (for that alone we should be grateful).
2. Had he given us the Sabbath and nothing more, dayenu.
3. Had he given us the Torah and nothing more, dayenu.

# Movement Glossary

## A

**action words** Words (verbs) that readily evoke movement. Examples include *freeze, flutter, melt, pop, crumple, swivel, creep, ripple, dart,* and *explode*.

**allemande left** In square or contra dances, corners grasp left forearms, wrists, hands, or elbows and walk around clockwise back to place. They bend left elbows and pull away a bit.

**allemande right** The same movement using right forearms, etc.

**arch** Two people raise one or two joined hands for others to duck under.

## B

**ballroom** A partner hold in which the man's right arm is around the woman with his right hand firmly in the middle of her back. (See **hand holds**.)

**basket** (or basket hold) Dancers join hands with second person on one side, as well as a person beside them. Baskets can be formed in front of the body or in back. Longer arms may be on top, or arms may weave with left arm under and right over, or vice versa. (See **hand holds**.)

**bend** A basic stationary movement, bend brings two body parts closer together. The opposite of stretch, bend is done in the joints of the body.

**body percussion** Sounds produced by the contact of two or more body parts.

- **clap** body percussion in which hands strike.
- **pat** body percussion in which both hands tap the thighs simultaneously or alternately.
- **snap** body percussion in which the sound is produced by friction between the thumb and third finger.
- **stamp** body percussion in which the foot strikes the floor.

**bow** In classroom dances, an acknowledgment of the partner with a dip of the head or a quick bend at the waist. Although in traditional dances the man may bow more dramatically while the woman acknowledges with a bend of knees or curtsy, the simple bow described here is appropriate for both genders.

**buzz step** (or buzz turn) A movement with a down-up motion in an uneven rhythm (slow-quick). When turning clockwise, dancers step on right foot with slightly bent knee and then push with ball of left foot as though on a scooter. Use opposite footwork for counterclockwise. Movement is smooth with feet close to the floor and no leaps. Partners keep the outsides of their right feet close.

## C

**CW, CCW** Movement directions clockwise and counterclockwise. (See individual listings.)

**cast off** Dancers at head of longways set turn away from each other and lead their lines around the outside to the foot of the set.

CAST OFF

**circle formation** A dance in a ring with hands joined or not. Examples of circles include single, double, concentric, closed, and open. (See individual listings.)

**classroom choreography** A dance pattern arranged for successful teaching in school settings. It may be based on traditional movements but made more appropriate for schoolchildren. (See **traditional dances**.)

**clockwise** A movement direction that progresses as do the hands of the clock, or around the circle to the left. Referred to in most dance notes as CW.

**close** A movement when the free foot comes up next to the supporting foot and takes weight. Also referred to as "together," as in step-together.

**closed circle** A circular formation that has no beginning or end. Hands may be joined or not.

**collapse** A basic stationary movement, collapse is the complete release of the body or body part into gravity.

**concentric-circle formation** Closed circles within circles, sometimes each moving to a different pattern or in opposite directions. Hands may be joined or not.

CONCENTRIC-CIRCLE FORMATION

**contra dance** A traditional dance form, originally from the U.S. New England region. It is called "contra" because it is usually performed in longways sets with partners opposite (from the French *contre*).

**contrast** The diversity or variety between adjacent movements or patterns.

**corner** In contra dance or square dance, the person next to you who is not your partner.

**counterclockwise** A movement direction that progresses opposite to the hands of the clock, or around the circle to the right. Referred to in most dance notes as CCW.

**crawl** A basic locomotor movement, crawl is a weight transfer on a low level in space, using hands and knees or hands and feet.

**creative dance** Within the context of music education, a form of dance that develops skills related to the elements and concepts of movement while exploring possibilities for kinesthetic self-expression.

## D

**direction** The spatial orientation of the line of motion. Directions include forward, backward, sideways, up, and down.

**do-si-do** Dancers face and pass right or left shoulders, then go around each other back-to-back and return backwards, with no turns, to place. Originally, and sometimes still, called in square dancing do-sa-do (named for the French *dos-á-dos* or *back-to-back*).

**double circle** A couples formation in which partners stand side by side facing the same direction, or front-to-front with one person's back to the center and the other facing into the center.

DOUBLE CIRCLE

DOUBLE CIRCLE

## E

**effort actions** The twentieth century movement theorist Rudolf van Laban's terms referring to basic qualities of movement. The eight effort actions are slash, press, thrust (punch), glide, wring, flick, float, and tap (dab). (See individual listings.)

**elbow swing** (or elbow turn) Two dancers link right or left elbows and move in a circle.

ELBOW SWING

**energy** One of the basic elements of dance, energy provides the "texture" or "color" of movement. Although variously described through the terms *force, dynamics, weight,* and *movement qualities,* energy refers to the way muscular power is used to produce qualities of motion.

**entrance/exit** The range of possibilities for entering and leaving the performing space.

## F

**flick** A light, quick movement that is scattered or curved; one of the Laban effort actions. An example is the quick movement of butterfly wings.

**float** A light, slow, drifting movement; one of the Laban effort actions. An example is the movement of astronauts in outer space.

**focus** The direction of attention in movement. Focus most commonly refers to the gaze of the eyes.

**formation** Arrangement of dancers in the space. Examples include scattered, line, circle, Sicilian circle, concentric circle, double circle, longways set, and square set.

## G

**gallop** A basic locomotor movement with a forward step and a closing step in an uneven rhythm (slow-quick or quick-slow). Either of the steps can be leaps. The leading foot does not alternate. It is also possible to gallop backward.

**general space** (also shared-space) The larger space in which movement can occur.

**gesture** A movement of a single part of the body usually on the periphery. Examples include a nod of the head, a tap of the foot, and a wave. Gestures can have predetermined meanings, many of these translate worldwide.

**glide** A smooth, sustained, linear movement; one of the Laban effort actions. An example is the movement of skating or sledding.

**grand right and left** (also right and left grand or grand chain) A movement sequence in which partners progress around the circle in opposite directions by joining right hands and pulling past each other's right shoulder, then giving left hands to next person and passing left shoulders. They continue to alternate rights and lefts until they meet their partner, or the seventh or eighth person, as designated in the dance pattern.

**grapevine pattern or step** An intertwining 4-step movement pattern that can have several combinations and move clockwise or counterclockwise: step to side/cross in front/step to side/cross in back, or cross in front/step to side/cross in back/step to side, or other weaving patterns. In country-western "line" dances, grapevine means a 3-step pattern: side/back/side/touch.

**group shape (group design)** The sculptural grouping of more than one body in space, also known as "tableau," "portrait," or "stage picture."

## H

**hand holds** Different ways to connect hands for dancing. Examples include ballroom, basket, pinkie, skater's, T, V, and W. (See individual listings.)

**HAND HOLDS**

Ballroom | Basket | Pinkie | Skater's

T | V | W

**hand jive** A nonlocomotor movement activity in which hand motions are performed to the musical beats.

**head couple** (or top couple) In a longways set, the couple closest to the band and caller or CD player and teacher.

**hop** A basic locomotor movement in even beat that has a takeoff and landing from one foot to the same foot.

## I

**improvise** Movement that is created spontaneously, ranging from free-form to highly structured form. Improvisation always has an element of chance.

**in place** Movements performed without traveling.

## J

**jig** A musical meter in $\frac{6}{8}$ as well as a set dance or solo exhibition dance, traditionally from the British Isles, in $\frac{6}{8}$ meter.

**jump** A basic locomotor movement in even beat that has a takeoff and landing from one or both feet to both feet.

## L

**leader/follower** In this versatile relationship, the follower imitates or copies the movement of a leader. The imitation can be sequential or simultaneous. Simultaneous leader/follower exercises can be done as mirrors where the leaders and followers are face-to-face, or as shadows where the followers are behind the leader. (See individual listings.)

**leap** A basic locomotor movement in even beat that has a takeoff from one foot with a landing on the other, usually higher than that of a walk or run.

**levels** High, medium, and low areas of space.

**line** A formation in which dancers are side by side, facing the same direction. Hands are joined, using a variety of handholds. Lines can be short and straight or long and curved (sometimes called **open circles**).

**locomotor movement** (or traveling movement) Movement that carries the body from place to place using a transfer of weight. Examples include run, walk, skip, hop, jump, gallop, turn, crawl, and leap. (See individual listings.)

**longways/contra set** A dance formation that consists of partners facing in two parallel lines. The part closest to the caller and the music is the top or head, farthest away is the bottom or foot. Dancers travel up toward the top, or down toward the bottom.

**LONGWAYS / CONTRA SET**

## M

**march** To walk with a rhythmic stride to the steady beat.

**mirroring** To follow in unison the movements of a partner or leader as if looking in a mirror.

**mixer** A group dance or singing game in which participants change partners each time the pattern repeats.

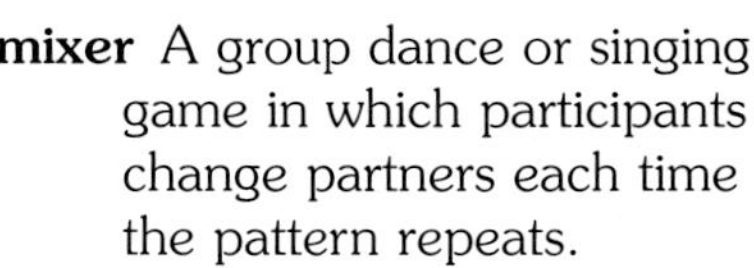

MIRRORING

**movement echo** Echoing repeats or copies a movement after the movement is done by a leader.

**movement exploration** To experiment with movements using variations on time, space, and energy.

**movement phrase** Similar to a grammatical phrase, a movement phrase is a natural grouping of movements with a sense of completion.

**movement qualities** Styles of movement created by the way force is used to begin and continue the actions.

- **percussive** characterized by sharp, forceful, explosive attack.
- **suspended** movement characterized by a momentary hanging of the body or a body part in space, followed by a collapse to gravity.
- **sustained** movement begun and continued with smooth, even force.
- **vibratory** movement in which the body or body part(s) shivers and shakes as a result of rapid contractions and releases of muscles.

**movement rondo** Like the musical form, a movement rondo alternates contrasting movements or patterns with a recurring movement or pattern. For example, ABACAD.

## N

**nonlocomotor movement** (or **stationary movement**) Movements that do not involve traveling from place to place. Some examples are bend, drop, swing, and twist.

## O

**open circle** A nonclosed circular formation that has a leader at one or both ends.

OPEN CIRCLE

## P

**pathway** The line or trajectory created by movement in the air or on the floor. Spatial (air) pathways or floor pathways may be straight or curved.

**pattern** The smallest unit of form. Pattern usually involves several movements and makes use of repetition.

**patterned dances** Dances with a prescribed sequence of steps and/or movements.

**peel off** The movement enacted when individuals in a single file or column reach a designated spot and turn back down the line alternately to the right or left.

**personal space (**or **self-space)** The sphere or "bubble" of space that immediately surrounds the body in stillness or motion.

**pinkie hold** A hand hold, usually in the W position, in which little fingers are joined. Generally it is right under and left over ("right under the leftovers"). (See **hand holds**.)

**pivot** A turn clockwise or counterclockwise on the ball of one or both feet.

**play-party** A music game, originating in nineteenth-century U.S. in response to religious prohibitions against dancing. Traditionally, the accompaniment was only singing and foot stomping, as the fiddle was "the devil's instrument."

**press** A strong, slow, sustained linear movement where the force is focused in direction; one of the Laban effort actions. An example is the movement of rowing a boat.

**progression** Mostly in contra dances and those of the British Isles, the movement of each couple is to the next position in the set.

**promenade** A figure in which partners join hands and walk together around the circle.

**promenade position** (or **skater's position**) A partner position in which individuals stand side by side, facing the same direction, with right hands joined over left hands in front of the body. There are also other promenade positions; this is best for school-age students.

**pull** A basic stationary movement that moves toward the center of the body. Beginning with a stretch, pull moves into a bend with the use of force.

**push** A basic stationary movement that moves away from the center of the body. Beginning with a bend, push extends into a stretch with the use of force.

## R

**reel** A musical meter in $\frac{4}{4}$ as well as a set dance from the British Isles and the U.S. in $\frac{4}{4}$ meter. A reel is also a way to join arms in traditional longways dances, sometimes called "strip the willow."

**right-hand star** A figure in which four or more dancers join right hands and circle clockwise. A left-hand star goes counterclockwise. Also called a wheel, a mill, or right-hands-across, hands may be joined by piling them in the middle, grasping the one opposite, or holding the wrist ahead.

RIGHT-HAND STAR

**ring** Another way to refer to circle formations, especially in historic dances.

**run** A basic locomotor movement in even rhythm that transfers weight from one foot to the other with a moment when both feet are off the ground.

## S

**sashay (or chassé, side gallop, slide, slip)** A sideways locomotor movement in uneven rhythm (slow-quick, slow-quick) in a side-close, side-close pattern.

**scattered formation** A random arrangement of dancers within the assigned space.

**set** An arrangement of dancers in square, longways, or groups-of-three formations. Also refers to the setting step, or balance step, in English country dances.

**shadow** To imitate the movements of a person from behind him or her.

SHADOW

**shape** The sculptural line or design of one or more bodies in space. (See **group shape**.)

**Sicilian circle** A dance formation in which couples face other couples around the circle, with one pair facing and progressing counterclockwise, the other facing and progressing clockwise.

SICILIAN CIRCLE

**single circle** A ring formation with dancers usually facing the center of the circle; hands may be joined or not.

**skater's hold** A partner hold in which right hands join over left hands in front of or behind the body. (See **hand holds**.)

**skater's position (or promenade position)** A partner position where individuals stand side by side, facing same direction, with right hands joined over left hands in front of or behind the body.

**skip** A basic locomotor movement that combines a step and a hop with alternating feet in an uneven rhythm (slow-quick, slow-quick).

**slash** A sharp, strong, curved movement; one of the Laban effort actions. An example is the movement of whirling helicopter blades.

**slide** See **sashay**.

**space** A basic dance element, referring to the area through which one moves.

**square dance** A traditional U.S. form performed by four couples in a four-sided or box formation.

**square set** An arrangement of four couples in an imaginary box formation, each couple standing on a different side of the box, all facing center. In U.S. and British Isles squares, couple 1 has its back to the music, then count counterclockwise for couples 2, 3, and 4. Couples 1 and 3 are head couples, 2 and 4 are side couples.

**stage directions:**

- **down stage** portion of the performance area closest to the audience.
- **stage left** portion of stage area to left of performer.
- **stage right** portion of the performance area to right of performer.
- **up stage** portion of the performance area most distant from the audience.

**stamp** As used in patterned dances, placing the foot firmly on the floor and lifting it slightly so as not to take weight (see also **stomp**); the next movement is done on the same foot. As body percussion, a stamp takes weight.

**stationary movement** (or **nonlocomotor movement**) Movement done in place. Stationary movement does not travel. Examples include bend, stretch, twist, swing, sway, push/pull, and collapse. (See individual entries.)

**step-close** A step pattern in which the dancer steps on one foot and brings the other foot beside the first foot (step-together), taking the weight also on the second foot.

**step-hop** A basic step pattern that includes a step and a hop in an even rhythm.

**step-in-place** Walking without traveling through space.

**step-together** See **step-close**.

**step-touch** A step pattern where the dancer steps on one foot and brings the other foot beside the first foot, touching it to the floor but not putting weight on it.

**stomp** As used in patterned dances, placing the foot firmly on the floor and taking weight on it. (See also **stamp**.) The next movement will be on the other foot.

**stretch** A basic stationary movement in which there is full extension of a body part or the whole body.

**sway** A stationary movement that moves side to side, or front and back. Sway is a gentle, rocking movement of one body part or the whole body shifting weight in place.

**swing** A basic stationary movement that occurs when the body or a body part moves in an arc or circle. Swinging includes several phases: the release of the body/body part into gravity, and the lift and suspension of the body/body part on the other side of the arc.

**swing** As used in patterned dances, turning with various hand or arm holds such as a two-hand swing or elbow swing. Also, swing is a nonlocomotor movement in which one knee lifts as its foot lightly swings across the other leg. (Also, swing is, of course, the popular couple dance that used to be called the jitterbug.)

## T

**T hold** The shoulder hold in which dancers, usually in a circle formation, place their hands on their neighbors' nearest shoulders. Arms are somewhat extended to form a "T". (See **hand holds**.)

**tap** A quick, light, staccato movement that moves to one point; one of the Laban effort actions. An example is the movement of knocking on the door.

**thrust** A fast, strong, linear movement that moves to one point; one of the Laban effort actions. An example is the movement of a karate blow.

**top-of-the-set** The end of the set closest to the band and caller or the music source.

**traditional dances** Dances that have roots in a culture, or have been passed down through generations mostly unchanged, or have some claim to historical accuracy.

**turn** A locomotor movement that indicates the body revolving around its vertical axis while traveling through space. Turning can be done while walking, skipping, hopping, galloping, or leaping.

**twist** A nonlocomotor movement in which the body or body part rotates on its axis.

**two-step** A movement pattern in which the dancer steps forward on the first foot, closes with the second foot, steps forward again on the first foot, and holds for a beat. It may also be done in other directions.

## U

**unison movement** Two or more dancers performing the same movement at the same time.

## V

**V hold** A partner or group position in which individuals stand side by side with hands joined and held down, making "Vs" between them. (See **hand holds**.)

## W

**W hold** A partner or group position in which individuals stand side by side with hands joined at shoulder level and elbows down, making "Ws" between them. (See **hand holds**.)

**walk** A basic locomotor movement in even rhythm in which weight is transferred from one foot to the other, keeping continual contact with the floor. There is a wide range of possibilities for varying the walk. Examples include character walks, inventive walks, walks of varying tempos and directions, and walks expressing various emotions.

**weaving (or winding)** A movement pattern in which some dancers go around other dancers who are standing still, often with arms raised in arches or windows.

**weight** The concept of weight includes several different meanings. In the context of transferring weight, it refers to the downward force of the vertical axis of the body as it moves in space. Laban's use of the term refers to weight as the intensity of force used in the muscles as in light or heavy. Weight can also refer to the quality of the body giving in to gravity or allowing gravity to work on it.

**wring** A strong, sustained, twisting movement; one of the Laban effort actions. An example is the movement of squeezing water from a towel.

**wring the dishrag** Partners face, joining two hands and swinging them overhead in the same direction to complete a circle while turning the bodies back-to-back and ending up face-to-face.

## *Sonando,* p. 34 CD 2-9, 13

*Choreography by Maggie Hoffee and Sanna Longden*

**Routine:** Intro (10 m.); vocal; interlude (16 m.); vocal; coda

This movement pattern is based on a Cuban dance called the *Guajira,* a slow, easy dance in a *samba* rhythm. *"Sonando"* is only one of many songs in the *Guajira* rhythm. The dance style is relaxed with small steps, soft knees, and bent arms moving to the beat.

**Formation:** Divide the class into partners, and have them stand scattered around the dance space, starting side by side, all facing counterclockwise.

**Basic step:** The rhythm is slow quick-quick, or ♩ ♫ pattern. First, have students practice moving their feet to this rhythm.

- Beat 1—step a bit forward on right foot
- Beat 2—hold
- Beat 3—step in place on left foot
- Beat 4—step back into place on right foot

  Have students repeat this basic step, starting with the left foot. The basic step may begin on either the right or left foot.

**Introduction**
- Have students perform 6 basic steps in place, beginning when they hear the *guiro* part (24 beats).

**Vocal**

**Measures 1–4** ***Sonando para bailar . . .***
- Have students perform 4 basic steps moving forward counterclockwise: right, left-right; left, right-left; right, left-right; left, right-left (16 beats).
- Have students perform 4 basic steps moving backward clockwise, repeating the left and right-foot pattern above (16 beats).

**Measures 5–6** (Instrumental)
- Have students perform 8 basic steps in place (32 beats).

**Measures 7–8** ***Llegaré, María, llegaré.***
- Have partners face each other. Partner 1, starting on right foot, takes 2 basic steps forward, while Partner 2, starting on left foot, takes 2 basic steps backward.
- Then Partner 1, starting on right foot, takes 2 basic steps backward as Partner 2, starting on left foot, takes 2 basic steps forward.
- Have students repeat the pattern (32 beats).

**Measures 9–10** (Instrumental)
- Repeat pattern in m. 5–6 (16 beats).

**Measures 11–14** ***Sonando para bailar . . .***
- Repeat pattern in m. 1–4 (32 beats).

**Interlude**
- Using the basic step as a starting point, invite partners to create their own pattern. They may use any of the patterns above or others, making new combinations (64 beats).

**Vocal**
- Have students repeat above patterns.

**Coda**
- Invite students to create a flashy finale, using 2 basic steps (8 beats).

## *The Chicken Dance,* p. 51 CD 3-1, 2

*Notated by Sanna Longden*

**Routine:** Intro (4 m.); instrumental 5 times; coda

This dance started in Germany in the late 1970s, and almost immediately swept around the western world. The song has been translated into many languages.

**Formation:** Individuals, partners, or groups can do this dance. Part 1 is done alone. Part 2 is usually done with others. Have students choose a single partner, or form small circular groups of 4–8. Ask students to start by standing in place with hands in front of their faces and elbows out to the side.

### Part 1

**Chirp with your hands**
- Have students open and close their fingers to their thumbs four times.

**Flap your wings**
- Have students flap elbows by bringing them down and up four times.

**Waddle downward**
- Have students bend knees and shake hips to one side and the other four times.

**Clap four times**
- Have students clap hands together four times.

Students will perform Part 1 four times, and end by facing their partner, or small group.

### Part 2

**Performing as partners**
- Have students do a right-elbow turn for 16 steps or 8 skips, then repeat with a left-elbow turn. They might also try doing a right-elbow turn for 8, a left-elbow turn for 8, then repeat the figures. Partners could also try other movements.

**Performing in small circular groups**
- Have students join hands in a circle and do 8 skips or 16 steps to the left, then to the right. Another idea is to form a right-hand star (see Movement Glossary, p. 500) and walk clockwise 16 steps, then form a left-hand star and walk counterclockwise 16 steps. Groups may also wish to try other movements.

Repeat the dance from the beginning, using different partners and groups for Part 2.

## Joe Turner Blues, p. 56 CD 3–14, 16

*Notated by Sanna Longden*

**Routine:** Intro (4 m.); v. 1; v. 2; v. 3

This dance pattern was popular in the United States during the 1920s and 1930s, according to Sister Lorna Zemke, a well-known Kodály music educator and expert in jazz, blues, and boogie. The pattern may be danced to any 12-bar blues tune, but it goes particularly well with "Joe Turner Blues."

**Formation:** Help students choose partners. Each set of partners stand anywhere in the dance space, facing each other. Partners join hands and hold arms out at the sides from the shoulders, like airplane wings.

**Verses**

Measures 1–4 ***They tell me Joe Turner's come and gone.***

- Partners move slowly counterclockwise around the dance space: step, side & close & side & close & side & close & side & touch. Students rock outstretched arms up and down with each beat.

Measures 5–8 ***They tell me Joe Turner's come and gone.***

- Students repeat the pattern for Measures 1–4, moving clockwise this time.

Measures 9–12 ***He left me here to sing this song.***

- Partners turn away from each other, slowly walking around in a full circle as follows: Step 1& 2 & 3 & 4 & 5 & 6 & 7 & 8. Students raise arms and waggle hands in the air in the 1920s "Charleston" style.

Students repeat the pattern for each verse.

## Paw-Paw Patch, p. 93 CD 4–43, 44

*Traditional Dance*

**Routine:** Intro (2 m.); verses 1–3 (3 times); coda

"Paw-Paw Patch" has been a favorite play-party song for almost 100 years. A paw-paw is a United States fruit that grows on trees. It tastes a little like a banana, pear, or mango. Four cities are named for it: Paw Paw, Illinois; Paw Paw, Kentucky; Paw Paw, Michigan; and Paw Paw, West Virginia. Like most dances that have been done for a long time, there are different ways to perform "Paw-Paw Patch." Here is one popular way.

**Formation:** Have students make a longways set (see Movement Glossary, p. 500), facing each other, about fingertips apart. According to tradition, and as indicated in the song, boys and girls should be partners. However, students may be partnered in any manner. If girls and boys are in separate lines, have the girls turn their right shoulders toward the source of the music and boys turn their left shoulders.

**Verse 1**

- The first person in the girls' line skips or walks alone all around the set, going down the outside of her line and continuing around the outside of the boys' line back to her own place. Her name can be inserted in the song (16 beats).

**Verse 2**

- The same girl now leads the entire line of boys around the set on the same pathway. They beckon one another onward with a sweep of their left arms on the words *Come on, boys* (boys can be changed to all, kids, or another non-gender specific word if needed). This verse can also be done without the girl leading. The boys' line can go around the set independently (16 beats).

**Verse 3**

- Partners join inside hands and skip or walk the same pathway as boys walked in Verse 2. They use their free hands for pickin' up paw-paws, then patting pockets. When the first pair reaches the bottom of the set, they join two hands in an arch. The others go under and follow one another up to the top to start the pattern again with a new "Susie." This verse may also be done with the top couple leading the others all the way back to place, then sashaying (see Movement Glossary, p. 500) down the center or outside of their own lines to end at the foot of the set (16 beats).

When repeating the dance, it is also fun to let the first person in the boys' line begin the action, with the girls' line going to find him.

## *Bongo (Jin-go-lo-ba),* p. 134 CD 6–16, 17

*Adapted by Sanna Longden*

**Routine:** Free form

Bongo is a competitive, follow-the-leader dance game that may be performed to *Jin-go-lo-ba*. It was originally done only by men to ward off evil spirits. This version is adapted from the traditional improvised form for classroom enjoyment. It offers students a structure within which to be creative.

**Formation:** Students stand in one or several circles with a leader in the center of each. Their hands are not joined.

**Game**

- Before starting the game, everyone should practice some special movements of their own to the musical beat. For a structure on which to base creativity, the movement can be some form of a hop, jump, shuffle, or all three. Suggested variations include moving in different directions, at different levels, adding heads or hands or other body parts, swinging, swaying, bouncing, and so on. After students are comfortable with being creative, they may choose something besides the hop, jump, and shuffle. The only rule is that movements must be with the beat of the music.
- The game begins when the center person leads a movement, and everyone else copies. Then the leader points at or shuffles over to someone in the circle who becomes the next leader. It is a good idea to require that girls choose boys and boys choose girls. Another way to decide the next person is to go around the circle, one after another. Encourage students to see when their turn is coming and to be prepared. When all have taken a turn, perform a finale with everyone doing "his/her own thing."

## *Cumberland Gap,* p. 138 CD 6–22

*Arranged by Jill Trinka*

**Routine:** Intro (4 m.); verses 1–4 with refrains and 1 m. interludes; coda

**Formation:** Have students make a single circle of partners. In each set of partners, the girl stands to the right of the boy (or "red" to the right of "blue," if you are using non-gender specific roles). Before beginning, have everyone identify their partner and their "corner" (person on the other side of them). All have hands joined down in V position.

**Verses**
- Everyone takes 4 steps into center and 4 steps back. Repeat.

**Refrains**
- Partners face and do a right-elbow turn in 4 beats, going halfway round to end facing their corner. On measures 2 and 3 of the refrain, all pause dramatically, then nod goodbye to partners (on *Ooo*) and hello to corners (on *Hoo*). Students do a left-elbow turn with their corner for 4 beats, to end facing partner.

**Interludes**
- In 4 beats, partners exchange places by boys walking in back of partners to the right (counterclockwise) and girls walking in front of partners to the left. The original partners are now the corners, and the new partners are on boys' right and girls' left, as above.

## *How Do You Doo-Tee?* p. 186 CD 8–24

*Greeting Activity from Australia*

**Routine:** Intro (4 m.); vocal; interlude (2 m.); instrumental with 2 m. interludes (5 times); coda

Many schools in Australia do not have music teachers. However, there is an active national family music association called "Parents for Music." Often their programs begin with "How Do You Doo-Tee?" a well-known, humorous music game.

**Formation:** Students stand in a closed circle with arms crossed over those of the people on either side and hands joined. They will start with a "left under/right over" arm position, unless relative heights require something more comfortable.

**Speech Piece** Invite students to learn the speech piece and say the last word of each line in the Australian way, as in the well-known greeting, "G'day, Mate" [geh-DIE, mIt].

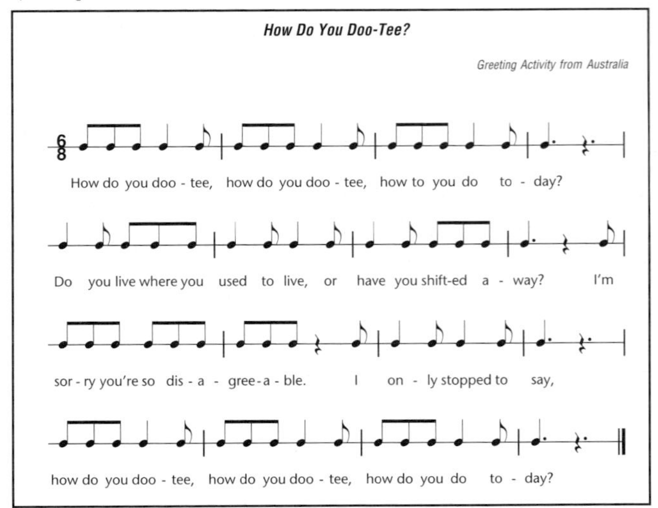

How Do You Doo-Tee?
Greeting Activity from Australia
How do you doo - tee, how do you doo - tee, how to you do to - day?
Do you live where you used to live, or have you shift-ed a - way? I'm
sor - ry you're so dis - a - gree-a - ble. I on - ly stopped to say,
how do you doo - tee, how do you doo - tee, how do you do to - day?

### Game

**Measures 1–4** ***How do you doo-tee, how do you doo-tee . . .***
- All students turn their head to the person on one side of them (they may or may not be looking back) and say the first phrase.

**Measures 5–8** ***Do you live where you used to live, . . .***
- Next, students will switch crossed arms so the other arm is on top, turn their head the other way, and say the second phrase.

**Measures 9–12** ***I'm sorry you're so disagreeable, . . .***
- Students will switch crossed arms again, turn their head to the first person, and say the third phrase.

**Measures 13–16** ***How do you doo-tee, how do you doo-tee . . .***
- Finally, students will drop arms and move quickly to another place in the circle as they say the last phrase.

Students reform the circle, cross arms, and begin the game again. It is fun to increase the tempo of the speech piece with each repetition.

## *Minka,* p. 222 CD 9–21, 25

*Traditional Ukrainian Dance*

**Routine:** Intro (4 m.); vocal; instrumental with variations; interlude (1 m.); vocal; instrumental

Ukraine is the second largest country in Europe. It was formerly part of the Soviet Union, which broke up in 1991. In Ukrainian dancing, men enjoy competing with strong, flashy steps. Women are also strong athletic dancers.

**Formations:** Here are two possible formations.

**Circles**
- Form circles if genders are about even in number, or if there are more girls, have students form two concentric circles. The boys create the inner circle, facing center with straight backs and arms folded in front of their chests. The girls are in a circle behind the boys, facing counterclockwise, hands joined down in V position.

**Lines**
- Form lines if genders are about even in number, or if there are more boys than girls, make straight lines of boys and girls, far enough apart so boys' kicks will not land on girls. Boys face girls with arms folded in front. Girls join hands down in V position and prepare to move to right.

**Boys' Pattern** Experiment with formations and numbers of boys and girls so that boys get back in time to first position.

**Measures 1–4** ***Said the Cossack to the maiden, . . .***
- Boys take 4 kick-steps forward, then 4 kick-steps backward, and repeat (16 beats).

**Measures 5–7** ***I beseech you fairest Minka, . . .***
- With arms folded, one boy leads others in a squat-walk under girls' raised arms (12 beats).

**Measure 8** ***with your faithful heart!"***
- Boys continue squat-walk back to original formation in circle or line (4 beats).

When the song repeats, if anyone can do other Ukrainian showoff steps, this should be encouraged. This might include *cazatsky* (squatting while alternating legs), big leaps with or without partner, and so on. Add more fancy steps for each repeat.

**Girls' Pattern**

*Measures 1–4* ***Said the Cossack to the maiden, . . .***
- In circle formation, girls move counterclockwise with either 8 two-steps, 8 step-hops, or 16 little running steps (16 beats).
- In line formation, girls move to the right with either 4 two-steps, 4 step-hops, or 8 running steps. Then repeat those movements to the left, to end directly across from the boys (16 beats).

Measures 5–8 ***I beseech you fairest Minka, . . .***
- Girls stand with joined hands raised in "windows" for boys to go under (14 beats).
- Lower hands on last two beats.

On repeats of the verse, girls may bend knees down and up to the beat, or clap raised hands on alternate beats (clasp, clap, clasp, clap), or sway, turn in place, and stamp to challenge the boys.

## *Tancovǎcka,* p. 230 CD 9–39, 46

*Traditional Slovak Dance*

**Routine:** Intro (8 m.); verse; interlude (4 m.); verse; coda

A characteristic figure in Slovak dance is the *cárdás* [CHAR-dahsh]. This is also a common figure in Hungarian dance.

**Formation:** Students begin with a closed circle, all facing center, with hands joined down in V position. Choose one person to be the first leader for the refrain, with the person to her or his right being the second leader.

**Verse** (*čárdás* step)

Measures 1–4 ***Tancuj, tancuj, vykrúcaj, vykrúcaj,***
- Students step side right, close left, side right, close left, side right, close left, side right, touch left. Have them try to bend knees slightly on each beat.

Measures 5–8 ***Len mi piecku nezrúcaj, nezrúcaj,***
- Have students repeat *čárdás* step to the left, ending with a touch on the right foot.

Measures 9–16 ***Dobrá piecka na zimu, na zimu, . . .***
- Have students repeat *čárdás* step to right and left, as above.

**Refrain** (snails and snakes)

Measures 17–24 ***Tra la la la, Tra la la la . . .***
- Dropping hands with the person on the right, the first leader winds the whole group in a snail formation, in 16 steps.

**Measures 25–32** ***Tra la la la, Tra la la la . . .***

- The second leader on the other end of the snail unwinds the group back into a circle.

  On the repeats of the refrain, the leaders could guide the group in snakes or other formations. Always end back in the closed circle to begin again with the *čárdás* step.

**Interlude**

- Reform the circle and choose two new leaders for the refrain (8 beats).

## *Theme from New York, New York,* p. 250 CD 10–22, 24

*Arranged by Sanna Longden*

**Routine:** Intro (3 m.); vocal; coda

**Formation:** Face audience in one or two lines.

**Introduction**

- Students step on right foot (beat 1), touch left foot (no weight) while snapping fingers to right (beat 2), step on left foot (beat 3), touch right foot (no weight) while snapping fingers to left (beat 4). Have students repeat this measure as often as needed. They could vary the steps by beginning to the left, or could have two lines with one starting to the left and the other to the right.

### Part I

**Measure 1** ***Start spreadin' the***

- Students start with hands on side of mouth, like shouting into a megaphone, then perform 3 knee-bounces, one for each word.

**Measures 2–43** ***news, I'm leaving today, . . .to find I'm*** **(2nd time)**

- Students step on right foot, touch left heel in front, with raised arms and wiggling fingers, then step on left foot, touch right heel in front (4 beats). Repeat.
- Students step in with right foot, step in place with left foot, step out with right foot, step in place with left foot (4 beats). Repeat.

Have students repeat the routine to the end of Part I.

### Part 2

**Measures 44–48** ***king of the hill, . . . My little town***

- Students strike poses in each measure that imitate the words of the song. Encourage student creativity.

### Part 3

**Measures 49–63** ***blues are melting away, . . .***

- Students move right foot to right side, left foot steps in back, move right foot to right side, touch left foot and clap (4 beats).
- Repeat the movement to the left (4 beats).
- Students move forward toward audience, stepping right, left, right, then kicking with the left foot (4 beats).
- Students move backward, stepping left, right, left, then touching right (4 beats).

Have students repeat the routine, or variations on it, to the end of the song.

Dance Directions

## *Blow, Ye Winds,* p. 255 CD 10–25, 27

*Arranged by Sanna Longden*

**Routine:** Intro (4 m.); verses 1–2 with refrains; interlude (6 m.); verses 3–5 with refrains; interlude (6 m.); verses 6–7 with refrains; coda

This dance pattern combines some traditional figures and some creative movement and encourages community by starting each verse with a new partner.

**Formation:** Students stand in a single circle with partners facing each other.

**Introduction**
- Students shake right hands for two beats, shake left hands for two beats, bend in a bow for two beats, come up and face each other on last beats.

**Verses**
- Begin with the structured pattern, then encourage students to create their own patterns.

**Structured Pattern**
- Partners perform a right-shoulder *do-si-do* (see Movement Glossary, p. 500) for 8 beats, then repeat with left shoulders.

**Creative Ideas**
- Have students use the story in each verse to create a 16-beat movement sequence.

**Refrains**

*(Right-and-left-grand to 7th person)*
- Alternating right and left hands and shoulders, students perform a grand right and left to the 7th person (see Movement Glossary, p. 500). Make sure students pull past the 7th person with right hands, and pat both hands with the 8th person, who becomes their next partner.
- Be sure students have a new partner each time through. If dancers keep meeting the same people, rearrange students so they will have new partners.

**Interludes**
- Students pat thighs, clap own hands, pat partner's right hand, clap own hands, pat partner's left hand, clap own hands, pat knees, hold and prepare for verse (8 beats).

On the coda, students add a final, emphatic pat on partner's hands.

## *Cotton-Eye Joe,* p. 290 CD 12–11, 12

*Notated by Sanna Longden*

**Routine:** Intro (12 m.); instrumental (8 times); coda

This song has been around a long time, so there are different ways to sing it, play it, and dance it. Although it came from Tennessee, "Cotton-Eye Joe" is now one of the best-known country dances in the southwestern United States. There are several different dance patterns for this popular traditional song. One of the original country-western dances, it is sometimes called the Texas Two-Step. While most of the dance patterns require partners, this version is useful for young dancers because it does not.

**Formation:** Students are in small lines of four to six people standing side by side, arms crossed behind backs and holding on to the neighbor's waist or belt loop. All lines are in a circular pattern around a center pivot point. Each line is facing counterclockwise around the dance space.

**Introduction** • Bounce to the beat during the instrumental and vocal lead-in.

**Part 1** • Use a vocal reminder to teach these movements. Invite students to say "Cross, Kick, Right-Left-Right," and "Cross, Kick, Left-Right-Left."

**Measures 1–2** ***"Cross, Kick, Right-Left-Right."***
- Standing on the left foot, cross right foot in front, touching right toe to the floor. Kick right foot forward. Step right-left-right, traveling backward.

**Measures 3–4** ***"Cross, Kick, Left-Right-Left."***
- Standing on the right foot, cross left foot in front, touching left toe to the floor. Kick left foot forward. Step left-right-left traveling backward.

Repeat.

**Part 2** • Invite students to say "Right-Left-Right," and "Left-Right-Left."

**Measures 9–16** ***"Right-Left-Right, Left-Right-Left"***
- Leaning the hip towards the leading foot, step right-left right, left-right-left, and so on.

Repeat the entire sequence for additional verses. Once students are comfortable with the steps, they may stop saying the vocal reminders. It is also fun to do variations on the two-step part. Try wheeling the whole line around one way and the other, turning inside out, changing places, or other creative movements. This is a happy, noisy dance, so Texas-style "whooping" is encouraged.

## *La raspa,* p. 302 CD 13–1, 5

*Traditional Dance*

**Routine:** Intro (2 m.); v. A twice; v. B twice; v. A twice; interlude (8 m.) twice; v. A twice; coda

This version of *La raspa* has been around long enough to be considered a traditional dance. It is similar to some European dances and may have actually originated in Germany. There is also an Italian version of *La raspa*. Other arrangements have been created for this popular song as well. This pattern includes a third figure for the B Section, typical of many traditional Mexican dances.

**Formation:** Divide students into pairs. Have partners stand facing each other in a double circle. They can also stand scattered around the dance space. Their hands are on their own waists.

**Basic step:** The basic step takes four beats. Students begin by standing on one foot and placing the other heel on the floor in front. They switch feet positions (beat 1), switch again (beat 2), switch once more (beat 3), then hold and clap twice (beat 4).

This figure is known as the "bleking step" in European dances. In Mexico people perform the step by scraping their feet on the floor. This imitates the sound of the rasp (a metal sandpaper-like tool) for which the dance is named.

### Dance

A Section — ***La raspa yo bailé . . .***
- Students perform 8 basic steps, and repeat.

B Section — ***Brinca, brinca, brinca también . . .***
- Partners still face each other, with hands clasped behind their own backs. Each person moves to right as follows: side-close-side-close-side-close-side-touch. Students perform the same moves to the left.
- Repeat the entire sequence to the right and left.

A Section — ***Si quieres tú bailar . . .***
- Students perform 8 basic steps, and repeat.

**Interlude** — (Instrumental)
- Walking or skipping, partners do a right-elbow turn in 8 beats, then a left-elbow turn in 8 beats.
- Students repeat both the right- and left-elbow turns.

A Section — ***La raspa yo bailé . . .***
- Students perform 8 basic steps, and repeat.

**Coda**
- Students place left hand on hip and raise right arm high while taking 3 firm steps in place.

## *Ve' David y'fey enayiam,* p. 317 CD 13–33, 34

*Choreography by Rivka Sturman*

*Notated by Sanna Longden*

**Routine:** Intro (2 m.); vocal (10 m.) and instrumental (10 m.) 3 times; vocal

During and after World War II, people emigrated from many countries to the new nation of Israel. One of the most poignant groups was the children who were orphaned by the Holocaust. They arrived in boatloads, traumatized and bereft. The Israeli people gathered them into the community in every way possible. One important way was through songs and dances, such as circle dances in which each person holds hands with the person on either side, and mixer dances, like *Ve' David y'fey enayiam,* where everyone meets a new partner during each repeat of the dance.

**Formation:** Divide students into pairs. Have them stand in a double circle of partners, facing counterclockwise with inside hands joined down at sides. Girls stand on right of boys (in outer circle), although it is not necessary to have boy/girl pairs.

### Vocals and Instrumentals

**Measures 1–2**
- Everyone walks 4 steps forward (counterclockwise). Then all join hands and form a single circle by taking 4 steps to turn inward and face the center.

**Measures 3–4**
- Everyone walks into the center 4 steps, then backward out of the center 4 steps.

**Measures 5–6**
- Girls (or right-hand partners) walk into the center in 4 steps, then backward out in 4 steps. Left-hand partners clap to the beat. Girls with skirts can swish them.

**Measures 7–8**
- Boys (or left-hand partners) walk into the center of the circle in 3 steps, turning to right on the 4th step to face out. In 4 more steps, they walk diagonally to meet a new partner (person on the right of their original partner). Girls clap as boys do these figures. Boys may also clap, or fold arms in front of their chests as they walk. New partners along the circle don't wait but go to meet the person coming toward them.

**Measures 9–10**
- Partners swing (or right-elbow turn) for 6 beats and open up in last 2 beats to face counterclockwise to begin the dance again. Students may wish to try the "Israeli swing." Partners stand facing each other with right shoulders and hips adjacent. Their right arms cross in front of their partner, and hold at the waist. Their left arms are raised high with hands open. Students can pivot on right foot in buzz steps (see Movement Glossary, p. 500) or simply walk around the partner. If this is too complicated, simplify to a right-elbow turn.

## *My Bonnie Lies Over the Ocean,* p. 338 CD 14–22, 23

*From "Step Lively 2: Canadian Dance Favourites" by Marian Rose*

**Routine:** Intro (4 m.); 4 verses and refrains with interludes (4 m.); coda

The Butterfly, a simple old-time trio dance, is popular in Canadian, Scandinavian, and many European cultures. "My Bonnie Lies Over the Ocean" is a favorite tune for this dance, but many others can be used. The focus is on tempo changes. On the recording, the tempo changes with each repeat.

**Formation:** Students stand in groups of 3, with hands joined or arms linked, all facing counterclockwise around the dance space.

**Music:** Practice the dance pattern in a slow tempo. Then, in the traditional spirit of the Butterfly, vary the tempo as well as the number of measures in both the A and B parts. Accompany these humorous variations by singing, or playing on keyboard, barred, or other instruments.

### Verses

**Measures 1–16** ***My Bonnie lies over the ocean . . .***
- Each group moves slowly forward to the music (note that it is in triple meter) with a step-swing: step with right foot (beat 1), swing left foot gently across right (beats 2 and 3). Repeat, starting on left foot.
- Students will do 16 step-swings in all.

### Refrains

**Measures 17–32** ***Bring back, bring, back . . .***
- Center person does a right-elbow turn with the right-hand person in 4 measures, then a left-elbow turn with the left-hand person in 4 measures.
- Students repeat the elbow turns.

Dancers may do many wild elbow turns, then slow down for some stately step-swings. They may also do fast step-swings and slow elbow turns, or more measures of elbow turns than they expected.

## *First Night Quadrille,* p. 343 CD 15–5, 6

*From "Listen to the Mockingbird" by the New England Dancing Masters*

**Routine:** Square dance with calls

**Formation:** Students stand in sets of 4, couples facing couples. The couple with their backs to the caller or music source and the couple facing the caller or music source are the head couples. The couples standing sideways to the caller or music source are the side couples.

### Opening

**A1**
- Students honor their partner (bow or curtsy) (8 beats).
- Students honor the corner and wave to opposite (8 beats).

**A2**
- All join hands and circle left (8 beats).
- Everyone circles to the right (8 beats).

**B1**
- All perform an *allemande* left with corner (see Movement Glossary, p. 500) (8 beats).
- Each person gives their right hand to their partner and begins a grand right and left (see Movement Glossary, p. 500) (8 beats).

**B2**
- All meet partners and *do-si-do* (see Movement Glossary, p. 500) (8 beats).
- Everyone promenades home (see Movement Glossary, p. 500) (8 beats).

### Main Figure

**A1**
- Head couples go forward and back (8 beats) and circle left (8 beats).

**A2**
- The same four circle right (8 beats).
- The same four make a right hand star (see Movement Glossary, p. 500) (8 beats).

**B1**
- All perform an *allemande* left with the corner (8 beats).
- All give right hand to partner and begin a grand right and left (8 beats).

**B2**
- All meet partner and do-si-do (8 beats).
- Everyone promenades home (8 beats).
- Repeat the main figure for side couples.

### Middle break

**A1**
- Everyone circles left (8 beats).
- Everyone circles right (8 beats).

**A2**
- All move into the center with a shout and back out (8 beats).
- All move into the center again and back out (8 beats).

**B1**
- All perform an *allemande* left with the corner (8 beats).
- All give right hand to partner and begin a grand right and left (8 beats).

**B2**
- All meet partner and do-si-do (8 beats).
- Everyone promenades home (8 beats).
- Students repeat main figure for four gents, then for four ladies.

### Closing

| | |
|---|---|
| **A1** | • Everyone circles left (8 beats). |
| | • Everyone circles right (8 beats). |
| **A2** | • All move into the center with a shout and back out (8 beats). |
| | • All move into the center again and back out (8 beats). |
| **B1** | • All perform an *allemande* left with the corner (8 beats). |
| | • All give right hand to partner and begin a grand right and left, all the way around (8 beats). |
| **B2** | • All continue the grand right and left back to place (8 beats). |
| | • Everyone swings their partner (8 beats). |

Have students practice the individual figures before trying to perform the whole dance. Be sure to have them practice the grand right and left going part of the way and all the way around. Begin teaching the dance with the grand right and left. After dancers have walked through the grand right and left, add the *allemande* left that precedes it. During the right-hand star in A2, the four dancers who are waiting in place should get their left hands ready for the *allemande* left that begins B1.

## *Cindy,* p. 384 CD 16–22, 24

*Dance based on traditional figures, notated by Sanna Longden*

**Routine:** Intro (8 m.); v. 1; refrain; interlude (4 m.); v. 2; refrain; coda

This is the kind of community dance people have performed for many years with songs like *Cindy* and still do today at Appalachian dance parties.

**Formation:** Assign partners then have students stand in a single circle, facing counterclockwise, with one partner in front of the other through the introduction to the song. Their hands are not joined.

| | |
|---|---|
| **Verse 1** | • All walk forward 30 steps. On counts 31-32, back partners move forward to stand beside front partners on the inside, to form a double circle. |
| **Refrain** | • Partners "git along home" as they promenade (see Movement Glossary, p. 500) counterclockwise. As music is ending, outside partner gets in front to form a single circle again, and all face center. |
| **Interlude** | • All go into the center in four steps and back out in four steps. |
| **Verse 2** | • Partners perform a grand right and left (see Movement Glossary, p. 500) to the fifteenth person. Students take two steps to pass each person, and finish with a new partner in promenade position, facing counterclockwise. If there are fifteen to seventeen pairs, everyone goes back to their original partner. Otherwise, they continue around the circle until stopping with the fifteenth hand clasp (a R hand), and stay with this new partner. |
| **Interlude** | • All go into the center and back out as above. |
| **Verse 3** | • Partners turn with R elbows in eight counts, then with L elbows in eight counts. Repeat the elbow turns; finish facing center. |
| **Coda** | • All go into the center and back, as above. Go into the center in four more steps, take three stomps in place, raise arms and cheer! |

Dance Directions

# RESEARCH Validates the Program

## MAKING MUSIC Research Base

Silver Burdett MAKING MUSIC incorporates the rich tradition and history of a company that has served the music education profession for almost 120 years. Because this experience has been merged with applications of the most recent research on learning in music, teachers may safely rely on the curriculum, instructional models, and methods that comprise the program. The strong, empirical base of the program is strengthened by the considerable number of authors who are themselves researchers in music teaching and learning and have published works in their specific fields. Many of the authors have specialized in and researched areas such as curriculum design, perception, acquisition of music skills, and repertoire for music learning. Authors for Orff Process, Listening Maps, Signing, Child Voice, Adolescent Voice, and other specific areas, a Multicultural Advisory Panel, and a Teacher Advisory Panel also helped to shape MAKING MUSIC.

Research documents the ways in which children perceive and respond to music, how individuals approach the task of learning, and how they gain insights through involvement with music materials. MAKING MUSIC takes into account that every child is inherently musical and has the potential for musical growth. It also reflects the research in how that growth occurs. For example, MAKING MUSIC recognizes that children go through several stages in their ability to sing accurately and expressively. Therefore the program provides effective strategies and materials for nurturing vocal growth at every stage of development.

Research in music learning shows that students often understand a concept before they can accurately perform the related skill. For example, the concept of beat is often attained at a fairly young age, but the ability to maintain a steady beat at a variety of speeds or tempos does not occur until around the age of nine. MAKING MUSIC was created to distinguish between skills development and conceptual understandings. Skills strands are introduced, developed slowly, and practiced over time. Analogous concepts are introduced and interwoven as appropriate so that meaning is not separated from practice.

According to Howard Gardner, children come to school already knowing a great deal about music. Children are usually able to apply to music the concepts of loud/soft, high/low, fast/slow, and long/short. They respond readily to style and can often name different styles. They know the names and sounds of many instruments and are eager to manipulate sounds to create interesting effects and patterns. Students are open to a wide range of music. They have a strong sense of the syntax of music from their own cultures. Most importantly, they do not question whether they are musical but naturally employ the human language of music.

**MAKING MUSIC takes into account that every student is inherently musical and has the potential for musical growth.**

When children begin formal schooling, the challenge for the music educator is to ensure that children grow musically from their intuitive knowledge to discipline-specific knowledge. The National Standards for Arts Education provide guidelines for this process. These standards, issued by MENC: National Association for Music Education, identify the music elements and skills that should be covered at each grade level, and these same elements and skills form the foundation of MAKING MUSIC.

Activities for skills development, written by many excellent teachers who understand the development of music skills, are woven through the series. Complementing the skills strand is an in-depth focus on concept development. MAKING MUSIC has dedicated an entire section of each grade to the development of music elements and skills, using an appropriate and pedagogically sound sequence. Elements are introduced through discovery, expanded, assessed, reviewed, and applied, using new materials that demand increasingly sophisticated listening and perception.

### Skills Acquisition

- Many research studies related to music skills acquisition have agreed that students learn more about music when they use keyboards. This has proven to be true for both elementary and middle school students. Therefore, a keyboard skills strand has been incorporated into grades K-8 of MAKING MUSIC.
- In another skills area, the Listening Map Transparencies included in this program are visuals designed to represent musical sounds. By using simplified scores students are provided a greater awareness of specific elements of music. Listening map transparencies in MAKING MUSIC are of this type, and while they illustrate the sound, they are careful not to apply any subjective meanings to the listening selections.
- Common sense tells us that reading notation, or in the case of songs, reading notation with lyrics simultaneously, can be a difficult skill to acquire. MAKING MUSIC always prints songs (with lyrics and notation) against a white background. Also, color-coded identification of vocal parts is placed before the music staff begins instead of surprinting the actual vocal part.

### Assessment Practices

- Recent research also suggests that assessment practices reflect and document the range of behaviors specific to the discipline being studied. Studies on the value of written assessment as a self-teaching tool have encouraged the addition of writing projects to lessons. Ideas for reflective thinking and self-assessment through maintenance are particularly appropriate to music instruction. Ideas for use of video, audio, and written entries that may comprise portfolios are given throughout the series.

### Contemporary/Popular Music

- One aspect of student motivation and involvement in music learning is subjective task value, which includes attraction as a source of enjoyment for its own sake. Music preference and attitude studies show that students prefer music styles that are popular and regarded as their own. The shift to preference for popular music may begin as early as age five or six. MAKING MUSIC offers students contemporary and popular music that speaks to students' interests outside the classroom, while it also offers more traditional, multicultural, and "classical" selections than any other program. Interviews with popular musicians of proven ability and appeal further relate students' daily music with music learning and help them recognize the commitment necessary to become a "pro."

### Culturally Diverse Music

- MAKING MUSIC also recognizes that music literature representing a diversity of cultures and countries is an important contributor to multicultural education, now mandated in many schools.

**The inclusion of music literature from a student's own culture increases his or her sense of self-esteem.**

With the advancement of cultural pluralism, there is increased necessity for students to understand and appreciate music of cultures different from their own. Also, the inclusion of music literature from a student's own culture increases his or her sense of self-esteem. Research shows that students learn more and have a greater appreciation for diversity in music when they are actively involved. MAKING MUSIC actively involves students in music literature from many different cultures and countries.

### Teaching Style Concepts

- Studies have confirmed the effectiveness of teaching style concepts by comparing pieces and excerpts of the style being studied as well as pieces of a contrasting style. This practice is incorporated into all levels of MAKING MUSIC.

### Music Literacy

- MAKING MUSIC is a program that sustains students' interest as it brings them to music literacy and proficiency. Research on these different factors has been integrated into MAKING MUSIC by authors who were selected for their strong credentials in the various fields of music learning. This outstanding group of music professionals has created a program with which teachers can accomplish the goal of all music instruction—enthusiastic, musically literate students capable of a lifetime of active involvement in music.

# QUALITY RECORDINGS in the Classroom

**_True To The Music_**
*—A Commentary by Buryl Red*

***Few musicians are as well known in nearly every niche of the music industry as Buryl Red. He has an international reputation as a composer, arranger, conductor, and producer. Not surprisingly, he is also a staunch advocate of music education, serving most recently as Executive Producer of recordings for Silver Burdett MAKING MUSIC. The following article contains his beliefs regarding the role and purpose of recordings in music education, both past and present.***

## Today's Children and the Contemporary Sound

Since first becoming aware of its power, people throughout the ages have listened to music through "mental earphones." These earphones have always delivered music to us with sound that originates from the technological, environmental, and social conditions of the era. Whether a log drum in the jungles of Africa or a harpsichord in an eighteenth-century French drawing room, the sound of an instrument is fashioned by the available material from which it was made, the shape to which that material was transformed, the way in which the performer plays, and the site of the performance. The social context in which the music takes place also influences our way of listening. In church, at a high tea, in a salon, at a sporting event—each of these situations influences how we hear and respond to music.

Though we may not like to think of music as a product of technology, it nevertheless is colored by technology in critical and profound ways. The electronic organ, for example, has changed the sound of African American music so much that its special "electric" tone color has become a natural part of our perception of the gospel sound.

Electronics has had a deep and lasting impact on the ways we listen to music. Whether we listen through sound speakers or a headset, in an arena or in a Broadway theater, music is often heard through electronic reproduction. Even symphony concerts and opera performances, once the haven for unamplified performances, are sometimes assisted through subtle electronic enhancement. This "electronicization" of contemporary music has produced a generation of children steeped in the electronically amplified sound. Such children have difficulty as they first encounter the traditional venues of the concert hall and opera house when amplification is not being employed. The sound, to these children, sounds somehow distant and without presence. The common complaint is, "It isn't loud enough!" Some of these children grow up to become recording engineers who have never heard the sound of a real acoustic violin or flute or piano. Having never been to a concert, they are unacquainted with the pure sound of those instruments unembellished by electronic wizardry. Even some adult concertgoers are beginning to complain that the Mahler symphony they hear in the concert hall is not as compelling sonically as what they hear on their CD players at home.

These, then, are our children—reared in a new tradition and accustomed to a sound that their elders did not experience as they grew up. So in presenting recordings to today's children, especially in a classroom series, it is of greatest importance that those recordings have the intensity and energy that young contemporary ears want to experience and have come to expect. In MAKING MUSIC, the full weight of modern recording technology has been brought to bear on the wonderful songs that are the backbone and strength of this program. Instrumental tracks have been created that favorably compare to the sound of recordings children hear at home and on the street.

## Recording for Authenticity in All Cultures and Styles

In MAKING MUSIC, concern and sensitivity have gone into the recordings to ensure that they provide authenticity in the program's multicultural songs and listening selections. Care has been taken to create recorded performances that reflect the style and conditions of each culture. Recording an ethnic selection involves making subtle choices. In recording a blues song, for example, I must ask myself a number of questions: Is the song a blues from the old folk tradition? Is it a modern blues composed for a Broadway show? Is it a hybrid of the two, or perhaps something in-between? Once that has been decided, an arrangement must be written to create that exact sound and flavor, and the performance and recording must represent the subtleties of the particular tradition. The days are now past when that traditional blues song can be recorded with flute, harp, and vibraphone and sung by young children who do not represent and cannot produce the sound of the singers who would sing that blues song. We might record it, but our children wouldn't "buy" it.

I believe, too, that as we recognize and respect the styles of various non-Western cultures and ethnic groups, we must be equally zealous in maintaining the stylistic integrity of the varied musical expressions of Western cultures. Presenting a song from a Broadway musical would mean that we have recorded the tune as it sounds on Broadway rather than as it would sound were it recorded in some concocted manner that suits "children's music." We have made a very special effort to represent the traditions of all types of music in their proper context.

## The Myth of Children's Music

The recordings of contemporary popular music in MAKING MUSIC sound like contemporary popular music rather than watered-down imitations. In the not-so-distant past, such imitations served to make this style of music more suitable as "children's music" or, worse, "textbook music." We have too long subscribed to the idea that music for children must be "dumbed down" to ensure that they grasp it easily. That may be one of the most damaging of myths about children and their ability to hear and perceive music aesthetically. Children are eager to demonstrate that they can handle almost any music that excites them; textbook recordings have, in the past, often failed to do this.

I don't believe there is such a thing as "children's music." There is only music that reaches out and touches people, both young and old. A friend once pointed out to me that children's music is any music that children enjoy singing or hearing. Children need not be talked down to musically. They are capable of listening to and enjoying pieces that may strike adults as technically complex, because they listen with open ears and no preconceived notions. These pieces need to be recorded for them with full attention to their expressive content, authenticity, and validity. Even if the purpose of the arrangement is to place emphasis on a particular musical concept, we do not want to say that the performance of the music itself doesn't really matter, or that it doesn't need to be artistically or emotionally convincing. Even with those pieces that have been composed with a pedagogical point in mind, we want to communicate to our young audience the emotional impact of the music. After all, isn't that what it's all about?

**...children's music is any music that children enjoy singing or hearing.**

Most children already have some skill in perceiving stylistic differences in music by the time they arrive at school. They know the difference between a pop song and a rap, for example. It is equally important to present music that is not so familiar to them, such as concert (or "serious") music, folk music from diverse cultures, and music from distant historical periods. To do that properly, these styles must be presented with equal intensity, as well as emotional and artistic integrity. If this is not done, children will gain the impression that music recorded offhandedly or with obvious lack of care has no feeling and is not worthy of attention. That would do a great deal of harm. For this reason, all genres of music must be presented within their broadest definitions. For example, African American music is so rich in its varied styles that even a spiritual can be presented in many different ways, all of which are valid from historical viewpoints. That spiritual might have been performed as a church or field song, or an Underground Railroad song in the nineteenth century. Today it might be performed as a gospel song.

## Recording Performances

Recordings in MAKING MUSIC contain performances that capture this integrity and intensity. We asked our instrumentalists and singers to perform with the same attention to artistic detail that they would bring to any concert, recording date, or theatrical performance. The music dominated and the musicians played more than dots on paper. They paid attention to the stylistic and dynamic nuances of any professional performance. There were *rubatos* and *ritardandos*, shades of loud and soft, and the artists lent their own deeply felt interpretations. In short, the performers came to the studio to make *real* music. Best of all, thanks to the superb quality of the arrangements and original compositions, we were freed from the "jingle" sound that has for too many years dominated the educational music recording field.

Communication is what good musical performance is, and we tried never to forget it. Often this effort to communicate the style and feeling of the music determined the choice of vocalists. In the majority of cases we featured children's choruses on the song selections, but at times we realized that children's voices could not always communicate the energy and the intensity of the music—in a gospel song, for instance. In such situations it was clear that adult voices could more adequately acquaint children with the goal we were aiming for—to demonstrate what the music is really supposed to sound like. Appropriately, both children and adults have often been used together, a very felicitous combination.

In using adult voices, only the very best from their stylistic fields were chosen to perform for these recordings. A song from India called for singers who were associated with a Hindu temple, who knew the song from personal experience, and who knew how it was supposed to be sung. An African song brought in singers from the African continent— singers such as South African stars Thuli Dumakude and Blondie Chaplin, who brought true authenticity and feeling to the music.

Folk songs from South America were beautifully recreated by the group Andes Mata, who arrived at the studio with panpipes and *charangos*. When we wanted a more contemporary South American sound, we found the best in Gustavo Moretto, whose studies in this country have led to his recognition as a serious concert composer in the United States but who is considered a pop and jazz performer in South America.

For an African American gospel song, we chose performers who could represent that style impeccably— Carol Woods, for example, one of our finest African American singing stars of Broadway and film.

Other world-class musicians whom we involved in these recordings were Yomo Toro, the great guitarist well known in the Latino community; Joseph Joubert, who has been musical director for Judy Collins and accompanist for Wynton Marsalis, Kathleen Battle, and Ben Vereen; and Linda Twine, who has conducted such hit musicals as *Jelly's Last Jam*, *Big River*, and *The Wiz*.

## Notation—A Matter of Interpretation

In many ways we are just beginning to be comfortable with other ways of producing sound. This is an issue, especially in vocal music, for those of us who have been schooled in the purest Western choral tradition, which includes jazz and pop styles as well as the Western "classical" tradition. The multicultural movement has shown us that there are other equally valid ways of producing vocal sound, although some of these styles may make us uncomfortable because of our lack of experience with them. Our first impulse is to try to notate the songs and melodies of these non-Western cultures. Notation was conceived and developed specifically to record on paper the music of Western Europe. Unfortunately, most non-Western music cannot be contained, rhythmically or tonally, within the Western notational system.

It's a dilemma. But I feel we have been too much a slave to notation in past music series. After all, even within the context of Western music of all eras and styles—especially in jazz and popular music—music is rarely performed exactly as it is printed on the page. Music is dependent on an interpretation by a performer, unless the composer has written for a computer and has been in control of every nuance. This is why we have chosen the very best performers to make these recordings. We know that their interpretations will be valid ones, even though there might be elements that another musician might have done a little differently. I think we have addressed very well that dilemma between notation and interpretation and provided an example for every student of the ways in which notation becomes a "blueprint" for performance without being a dictator.

## Pick-A-Track™ vs. Stereo Performance Track

The Pick-A-Track technique, introduced over two decades ago by Silver Burdett, was handy for teaching songs using the recorded voices and then "dialing them out" so that children in the classroom could sing the song with the instrumental track only. Teachers loved this recording feature. The problem with Pick-A-Track is that it is unnatural. Music is not naturally heard the way it is presented in Pick-A-Track. When you attend a live performance, the sound from the singers and the instrumentalists is heard from roughly the same source. No one hears the singers' sound coming from one sole spot and the instrumentalists from another.

A better way of dealing with the "voices versus instrumentalists" question is provided by the stereo vocal and the stereo performance tracks. In the stereo vocal, the sound is recorded and mixed just as it is in commercial recordings, providing a rich, full stereo sound that has depth, balance, and clarity. Songs in MAKING MUSIC are recorded as full stereo vocals with techniques used in the best commercial recordings.

## A Philosophy of Recording

We have approached the recording process of MAKING MUSIC with a definite philosophy in mind: to create recordings that are true to the music—recordings that will stimulate a child's interest and create an exciting response in a way that the old textbook recording philosophy, with its super-simple accompaniments, basic harmonic structure, unmusical interpretations, and babyish singers, did not. We know now that children need to be able to hear "classroom" music in the same aurally exciting way they hear their favorite recording artists.

# Classroom Management

*As we know, unresolved classroom discipline and management issues can often be at the heart of teacher stress and dissatisfaction. How can we begin to improve our own music classroom discipline and management strategies in order to increase student learning and also increase our own happiness and satisfaction in our classrooms?*

## Creating Positive Environments for Musical Learning

The rewards of teaching music to young students are obvious, but may deserve focus here as we balance a discussion of the ever-present discipline and management concerns in many of our music classrooms. We music teachers enjoy frequent reminders of the success of our hard work in the classroom. Among these joys are the treasured moments when we actually see and hear evidence of our students' musical development—the satisfying sounds of their active music making; their faces reflecting their hard work and accompanying sense of personal and group accomplishment; the pride of increasing music skills and knowledge; and, of course, our group performance goals well met and received. However, we also know that these and other rewarding moments don't come easily. They are often accompanied by recurring challenges involving music classroom discipline and management.

As music teachers, we are aware of the need for constructive suggestions and direct action toward improving our music classroom environments. Evidence of successful hard work in this area often includes the following teacher-centered events:

- careful pre-thought and classroom organizational planning
- the establishment and practice of positive and effective discipline and management techniques
- consistent expectations and appropriate reinforcement of students' efforts
- reflection with other teachers resulting in classroom experimentation, growth, and development of discipline and management skills throughout one's career.

Simply put, many music teachers seek some guidance about their discipline and management practices including the enhancement of communication skills and relationships with students. Furthermore, they need to talk and listen to one another, especially those closest to the problems at hand.

The following sections of this article will offer a variety of practical suggestions and strategies for planning/organizing, implementing, evaluating, and reflecting upon discipline and management techniques in the classroom.

## Organizing for a Successful Year (Pre-planning)

Try some of the following ideas for increased organization and communication at your school site.

- **Plan ahead for less performance stress.**
  Meet with your appropriate school-site administrator before the school year begins. Outline your needs for rehearsal space, dates, and times, as well as tentative dates and times for actual performances and assemblies. Once you have these agreed dates, be sure they actually appear on the school's master calendar. Create a brief flyer with this information to share with classroom teachers, administrators, and parents. Make it known that all is scheduled.

- **Toot your own horn.**
  Share a one-page description that highlights selected activities and learning which will take place in your classroom. Be sure to list performance dates. Share this information at faculty meetings. The more opportunities you have in which you can share your teaching with others, the better. Invite peers and administrators to your classroom to witness what the students can do in music class.

- **Open the door to communication about music's solid role within the entire school curriculum.**
  Invite administrators, school board members, parents, and classroom teachers to join in your performance efforts. Administrators might be willing to greet parents. Other teachers might be willing to narrate or join your efforts by displaying at actual performances student artwork, poetry, and other projects related to your performance themes and song texts.

## Music Classroom Tips: Selected Strategies for Positive Environments

One overriding goal within a well-managed, positive learning environment is the development of individual student self-discipline and self-control. The following suggestions are also meant to increase your positive interactions with the students, and students with each other.

- **Avoid chaos upon entry to the music classroom.**
  Many teachers experience problems with misbehavior right at the start of the music lesson. What may be needed is a non-verbal focus activity. Try posting a chart with interesting, different ways for students to enter your classroom each day. For example, "Walk in very slow motion, no talking… and be seated by the end of the metallophone music." Greet your class outside the door, point to the sign, and start the entry. Be sure to reward students who follow the suggestion. You might ask students to think of interesting ways to enter. For example, "Tip-toe to the table, get your music books, open to page 53, and wave." Write these suggestions on cards and start a collection of ideas!
- **Every good meal has a tempting menu!**
  Create a very brief outline "menu" of your lesson. Write key words (make them interesting) on the board and go over the plan with the students. Let them know where the lesson is going. For example, "New partner dance from a surprise desert country" or "New note on the recorder=?" Menus provide a way to keep the class moving forward time-wise and, at the same time, involve students in looking forward to what will happen next.
- **Use your classroom space to increase student focus.**
  Consider using different areas of your classroom for different general music activities. These areas can be very close together. For example, students may learn that musical listening is near the AV equipment, recorder practice and reading/notation drill is near a chart area, movement is in an open space, related children's literature and dramatization is in a reading/visuals corner, and Orff instruments is in another corner. If you do not have your own music room, consider how this idea can be adapted to other classroom spaces, usually within more confined spaces. Simply changing direction and focus may be a way of increasing interest in your lesson activities.

**Aim for increasingly positive feedback!**

## Specific Activity Tips

- **Singing**
  Behavior problems often occur when students do not know what to do next, particularly when beginning new song material using printed music. Try asking students to work with a partner to survey a new song by saying to them, "Point to the first ending and show your partner where we are" or "Point to the words of the song text as we listen to the CD recording" or "Point to the words as we say them together in rhythm," and so on. You might also say, "I may stop the recording. If I do, please silently show your partner where we are in the music. Then we will go on." Also, ask students to take turns with a partner and read song texts aloud, or sing phrases back and forth for extra practice. Reward pairs who can do this well.

- **Movement**
  Many teachers desire to teach movement on a frequent basis but may dread the possible chaos. You may wish to try the following.

  **Bus Stop** Designate a known area in the front of your room (for example, in front of the piano or table) as the "bus stop." During movement activities where students must find a partner, there are two simple rules— no one can say no if asked, and if you cannot find a partner, simply go to the "bus stop" and wait. The first person you meet there is your partner, as the person can't say no.

  **Specific Commands** Students can misuse a lot of valuable class time to form one or more dance circles. Try saying to them, "We need a standing-up single circle in the middle of our space by the time I finish counting to 10. Please go there without talking. Let's see if you can do it. Let me know when you are ready." Then count to "10" slowly. Look away and let the students tell you the circle is ready. Lavish them with praise. If unsuccessful, have the class do it again. They will want to please you.

- **Listening**
  Try structuring your music listening episode into three parts by using simple non-verbal cues and known responses (depending on the type of listening you are doing). For example, if students are listening to a recorded instrument featured within pictures in the student books, tell them, "We will have a signal for three things. When you see one finger up, listen quietly. Two fingers up means you are to point to the picture of the

instrument you hear. Three fingers up means you are to write the name of the instrument and some words describing its sound." Observe how closely students pay attention to your non-verbal signals!

- **Instrument Buddies**
  Most of us must have our students share Orff and other classroom percussion instruments. Pair up students (including those with special needs) with another before instruments are assigned. One student plays while the other watches and sings. When it is time to change instrument players, take a moment of class time for the first buddy to "teach" their part to the next. Buddies can also help the new players by conducting the actual playing motion, steady beat, and so on. Students can then repeat the same routine by going to different instruments, always with the former "player" teaching the new player.

**Remember you are not alone!**

## When things go wrong, consider. . .

- **Are you as positive as you think you are?**
  Research points to the fact that effective teachers make positive comments approximately three out of four times to their students. Video tape yourself on a typical day and tally your comments to your students (negative, positive, neutral). You may be surprised!
- **Aim for increasingly positive feedback.**
  Provide positive comments for student behavior that are actually appropriate for the task at hand. These positive re-enforcements do not need to be artificial or forced in nature and can include a nod of the head, a "thumbs-up," and a smile. Verbal comments can include "That recorder descant is really coming along," or "Way to go! I didn't have to ask you to put away the instruments." Aim to increase your positive comments in class, and your students will in turn desire to behave in order to hear your praise. Remember to reserve praise for true growth and effort.

## Try the following.

- **Younger children**
  Choose an indestructible item such as a beanbag, stuffed animal, plastic cup, and so on. Keep this colorful item in the same place, visible to all students to the front and side of the classroom. Teach your students that the object will be handed to anyone who is talking, off-task, and so on. If given the item, they must hold it silently until they stop what they are doing and are willing to join the group again. They simply must put the object back in its regular place. Then, when and if a student misbehaves, simply hand the student the object (saying nothing) and let them determine when to physically put it back. Follow up with a discussion with that student (after class) about what behavior they changed.
- **Older children**
  Sometimes a student must be isolated from the group. Make this isolation time productive by putting that student to work. Provide a piece of paper with two columns. One is "What went wrong today," the other is "What I will do next time instead." After class, discuss the student's responses, tear up the "wrong" side, and have the student keep (or send to the parent with return signature and/or phone call home) the "What I will do next time instead" side.

## Invite discussion and reflection about discipline and management.

Remember, you are not alone. Many teachers report that some of their best solutions to discipline and management problems come from other teachers—music teachers, classroom teachers, and specialists. Try the following suggestions.

- Don't depend on others to start a dialogue on this subject! Invite a peer to listen to your situation and give you feedback and suggestions. Let them know how it went when you implemented suggestions. Keep track of things that work well. Offer the same help to them and others in person, over the phone, via e-mail, and so on. We often can help others more than we can help ourselves, and, in doing so, end up solving some of our own challenges along the way.
- Ask your school-site administrator and music/arts coordinators for professional time to observe others teach and exchange discipline strategies.
- Request that decision-makers create opportunities at professional growth days and meetings for teachers to talk to other teachers about discipline and management ideas. Encourage teachers to share their strengths in this area.
- Reach out to student teachers and new teachers who many times are in great need of your experience with discipline and management. Offer to mentor others.

# MEETING INDIVIDUAL NEEDS

## INCLUSION

Legislative mandates have resulted in hundreds of thousands of children with disabilities receiving a free, appropriate education—a free, appropriate music education—that had previously been denied to them. Children with disabilities are now singing, playing instruments, listening to music, dancing, and making friends in inclusive music classrooms.

Since the passage of *The Individuals with Disabilities Education Act* (formerly *The Education for All Handicapped Children Act of 1975*), concerned parents, guardians, teachers, administrators, and other professionals have continuously worked to provide in inclusive settings the highest quality education for children with and without disabilities. These efforts are documented by a wealth of printed literature, clinics, and in-service programs that focus on educational opportunities that will result in children with disabilities living maximally independent, happy, and productive lives in their homes, schools, and communities.

**A challenge of inclusive classrooms is to maintain the highest expectations for each student.**

Music can enrich the quality of life of all children, and children with disabilities can participate, or partially participate, in the same meaningful music activities as their peers. The inclusive music classroom may be the only opportunity for children with disabilities to learn music skills and apply knowledge that will enhance the quality of their musical lives. In some cases, children with disabilities may be gifted or musically talented. Because of the high emphasis on verbal and motor skills in school, these children are not easily identified.

A challenge of inclusive classrooms is to maintain the highest expectations for each student and to carefully observe, assess, and nurture a wide range of music responses, from the simple to the more complex. Children may be different in many ways, but what remains constant are the long-term values that we hold for their well-being, happiness, and musical development.

### Collaboration, Communication, and Support

The long-term effectiveness of any music program for a child with disabilities requires communication and collaboration with others who are knowledgeable about the individual. Time spent at the beginning of the school year, and ongoing contact, can build an important support group for the student as well as the music teacher. The particular type of disability category is relatively unimportant compared to knowing pertinent information about the student's safety. Information that will specifically affect instructional decisions includes the nature of any physical disabilities or health impairments, medications, or medical procedures.

Children with disabilities are important resources because they can communicate ways in which the teacher can structure activities for inclusion. In conversations with others, no matter how brief, teachers should inform parents (and others, including the child) about the child's successes in the music classroom—no matter how small they may seem at the time.

Teachers should communicate music and social goals to classroom aides and define the ways in which they can help the child progress socially and musically. Likewise, it is important that tolerance and social problem solving are taught to classrooms of students throughout the year. Students without disabilities should be taught when and how to help their disabled peers, although each student with a disability should be given every opportunity to participate successfully and as independently as possible.

### Planning and Implementing Lessons

Children with and without disabilities are exposed to essentially the same music curriculum for each grade level, and expectations should be high for each child. A flexible curriculum that provides multiple ways of expressing competency and achievement will not lower standards. Specific adaptations for any child should be minimal and in keeping with the intent of the lesson and the lesson's activities. In some cases, adaptations that are necessary to meet the individual needs of a child may be appropriate for all students and can be incorporated easily into the lesson.

Well-established teaching principles apply to teaching all children in every situation, and yet the success of each child's learning is dependent upon individualizing those principles. Some examples of these principles are:

- knowing what is important to teach and when

- knowing what will motivate a child
- knowing when and what kind of questions or tasks to ask of a child
- knowing when and how to give a child feedback
- knowing how to teach skills, knowledge, and confidence.

Individualizing instruction remains at the core of excellence in teaching and learning. Planning individually focused accommodations facilitates instruction that is aligned with the music curriculum and relevant to individual needs.

### Strategies

Here are several principles and specific strategies to consider in planning and implementing lessons.

- Encourage children to perform music, even simple choral accompaniments or improvisation, at home when they are alone or for family and friends.
- Provide opportunities to make choices and decisions about music and music making that are similar to those that are given to non-disabled peers.
- Provide frequent opportunities for social interactions with peers in small groups and with a kind partner.
- Communicate and greet the child in the same manner as you would other children of the same age from the same class. Monitor your proximity and interactions with the child and make adjustments when needed.
- Use small groups and partners early in the school year. Place no more than one child with a disability in any group, along with kind, sensitive children who are good musical models.
- Analyze sequences and implement relevant steps that move from simple tasks to more complex ones. Even the simplest task should be experienced in an age-appropriate context.
- Provide an adequate range of examples to exemplify a concept.
- Provide adequate practice across activities that are interesting and engaging. When children perform a rhythm or sing a phrase correctly, have them repeat that experience as a class, in small groups, individually, and in a variety of related activities.
- Although some children may have specific behavioral programs that require individual procedures, develop a set of classroom rules, routines, and management techniques that are consistently applied with all children.
- Teach children what to do when they lose their place or make a mistake. Good musicians develop skills for recovering from errors.
- Give individual specific praise and corrective feedback as a matter of routine.
- If a child cannot participate fully, develop minimal adaptations to allow him or her to participate as completely and independently as possible.
- Some children may have difficulty with tasks involving printed materials (such as tracing musical phrases or locating music symbols). Single word cues at the beginning of lines may help organize the search. Have children work in pairs on some occasions, tracing and locating symbols and words together.
- Have children with physical disabilities play a variety of instruments and instrumental parts for accompaniments and in ensembles. First, observe physical movements as children perform simple and more complex patterns on different "silent instruments." Then provide choices of instruments that you know the children will be able to play, and give them choices of rhythms they have performed successfully during "silent practice."
- In many cases, assessment can be the same as for non-disabled students. In other cases, children simply may need more time or a change in the assessment context or modality. Alternative forms of assessment might include providing a cassette tape recorder, an enlarged version of printed material, an extended time, a separate room, a scribe, a reader, a computer, or a sign-language interpreter. In all cases, assessment should be consistent with the individual goals that are set for the child and should include both effort and individual achievement.
- If peer tutors are used, help them understand the importance of showing sensitivity about how and when to help their peers with disabilities.
- In some cases, teacher aides may provide support for students with more severe disabilities. Instruct aides as to how and when to help. The aide should allow the child to participate as independently as possible. Children who come with aides from special education classrooms should arrive for class and leave class at the same time as their non-disabled peers.

**Individualizing instruction remains at the core of excellence in teaching and learning.**

# Teaching for Thinking

***Graphic organizers are overt strategies that can help make students' thinking visible and concrete by organizing information visually. They employ various levels of thinking skills and effectively advance vocabulary and concept development.***

The main objective of teaching for thinking is to help children understand how they know what they know. Critical thinking can be taught, practiced, learned, and assessed. There is much to think about in music, and teaching for thinking should be an integral part of the music program.

Teaching for thinking can happen simply and in a few minutes through modeling the thinking process. Think aloud about the content of a lesson or problem and how you would solve it. For example, "I'm not sure which of these instruments I want to use for the accompaniment. Let me think about their sounds as I try them out to see how each would fit the style of the song." Structure brief, but frequent opportunities for students to practice thinking and to talk about their decisions with partners or in small groups.

Before students can think creatively and critically, however, they must have a solid knowledge base of meaningful concepts and ideas and a basic understanding of their connections and relationships. As you work with the strategies listed below, carefully choose activity material, concepts, and ideas that students have thoroughly learned. Remember that thinking critically can involve active music making as well as verbal activities.

## GRAPHIC ORGANIZERS

Graphic organizers are overt strategies that can help make students' thinking visible and concrete by organizing information visually. They employ various levels of thinking skills and effectively advance vocabulary and concept development. They can be used by individuals, pairs, and small groups or with the whole class as an instructional tool, extension activity, or evaluation.

It is important to model the process for using the graphic organizers before asking the children to use them on their own. Adapt materials to meet your specific purpose. It is not necessary to fill in all the spaces each time. If necessary, add lines or boxes to accommodate the needed information.

The graphic organizers found in the Resource Book can be made into transparencies for use on the overhead projector or reproduced. They may include any of the following: Story Map, Semantic Map, Comparison Chart, Venn Diagram, KWHL Chart, and Semantic Feature Analysis Chart.

## STORY MAP

Story maps are simple vertical flow charts that identify the main story elements. They are usually a post-reading or post-listening activity, but can also be used as a formula for creating a story. They can also be used with ballads, such as "Don Gato," and program music, such as Peter and the Wolf.

### Key Elements of Story Maps

**WHEN (time)**

**WHERE (place)**

**WHO (characters)**

**WHAT (the dilemma that the main characters try to solve)**

**HOW (the series of steps taken to solve the problem)**

**ENDING (the resolution of the story's problem and new understandings created by it)**

### Teaching Sequence

1. Using a transparency of the story map, explain to the students that using a story map will help them see how the parts of a story or ballad fit together and help them remember the story line. Discuss the map headings to make sure the students understand them.
2. Listen to a ballad, stopping at the end of each verse to discuss the story map headings and fill in any information. Ask students, "Were the WHO, WHAT, WHERE, and WHEN introduced? Was the problem introduced? Could you infer any information?" Sometimes the information isn't available in the lyrics.
3. It is important to have the students predict and summarize each time. Have students give reasons for their predictions. Ask questions sequentially and logically so that the students can identify the most important information in the story.

4. Now listen to the selection all the way through and discuss their responses.

5. After they have worked through several story maps with your help, have students work in pairs or small groups to map another ballad or to create one of their own. Always discuss the completed map with them, leading them to think about how all the parts of the story are related.

## SEMANTIC MAP

A semantic map graphically illustrates the relationships among a group of words or concepts. Surrounding the central concept are categories related to it.

### Teaching Sequence

1. Select a central word or concept related to the lesson and write it in the center circle; for example, classroom instruments.
2. Ask the children to think of words related to the central word and write them down on a sheet of paper.
3. Select children to share orally some of the words they have written. List these on the chalkboard. Assist the children in categorizing the words and naming the categories. To reinforce or assess concepts previously taught, provide the category headings and ask the children to list related words under the appropriate headings.
4. Discuss the map and, most importantly, help children understand how they arrived at their choices. Help them think about their thinking (meta-cognition).

## COMPARISON CHART

A comparison chart simply lists how two things are alike and how they are different by writing similarities in the left-hand column and differences in the right-hand column.

## VENN DIAGRAM

With two overlapping circles, Venn diagrams illustrate the relationships among categories of items as students examine unique characteristics and common characteristics.

### Teaching Sequence

1. Select two categories that share common characteristics familiar to your children, such as two songs.
2. Label each circle with its category or composition title.
3. Ask the children to suggest items or words that belong in at least one of the categories. If the word belongs in only one category, place it in the outer area of that circle. If it is common to more than one category, write it in the overlapping area of the circles.

## KWHL CHART

A KWHL chart is used for gathering and organizing information. It is helpful as a pre- and post-reading or pre- and post-listening activity for the recorded interviews.

### Teaching Sequence

1. **K** stands for **what I already know**. In the first box list what is already known about the subject being studied or the person to be interviewed.

2. **W** stands for **what I want to know**. Help the students generate questions about the subject matter or develop interview questions for the individual to be interviewed and list them in the second box.

3. **H** stands for **how am I going to learn this**. Help students brainstorm and list ways to learn; for example, read books or magazines, watch videos, interview someone, and listen to recorded interviews. In the third box, write the method(s) they are going to use.

4. **L** stands for **what I learned**. In the last column list the information gathered from reading, listening, and so on. Review the questions listed in the second box to see if they were answered sufficiently.

## SEMANTIC FEATURE ANALYSIS CHART

Semantic maps show how items or words are alike. Semantic feature analysis shows how they are alike and different by using a grid design to graphically display the common features. In this way, items can be compared and contrasted by specific features or characteristics.

### Teaching Sequence

1. Begin with a list of known words that share several common features. Write these in the left-hand column; for example, musical instruments.

2. Ask students to suggest features common to several of the words. Write the features in a row across the top of the grid; for example, metal, wood, strings.

3. Complete the grid by putting plus (+) or yes, or minus (–) or no, beside each word beneath each feature to indicate if a word does or does not incorporate a listed feature. Students may find a feature that may not apply precisely to one or more words in the category. Use this discovery as a spark for lively discussion.

4. Encourage students to discuss the unique meaning of each word. Point out that no two words share exactly the same pattern of features.

# Character Education in Our Music Classroom

*"What does it mean to teach children lifelong skills to develop positive character traits? Are we now responsible to teach this, too?*

## Toward Lifelong Skill Development

Among the many terms currently used around the nation to describe lifelong skill goals toward positive character development are the following: trustworthiness, truthfulness, listening to others, achieving your personal best, responsibility, effort, perseverance, friendship, controlling anger, fairness, cooperation, conflict management and resolution, and citizenship.

Most of us are in agreement that our students need repeated opportunities in continuing to develop these and other positive character traits. We recognize that our students may naturally exercise these lifelong skills as members of their families, as participants in their class and school communities, and as future adult members and citizens of their surrounding community, state, and nation. But what responsibility do we have as teachers to make sure these concepts and skills are taught? Why does this responsibility have to be added to our list of things to accomplish in the music classroom?

As music teachers, we may naturally feel overwhelmed in tackling such skill development because of the multiple requirements and accountability systems we already must meet and document. Furthermore, we may be frustrated by what we believe to be powerfully negative influences of the media, popular culture, and trends in youth social behavior on any efforts toward the development of a child's good character— character that was once primarily developed and shaped at home and within many forms of religious education and community life. At the same time, we also know that we already provide many opportunities toward character skill development through activities in our daily music classroom. We may simply need to highlight ways to communicate what is innate in our music classroom learning environments in order to point out the natural connections to the character development of our students.

***When you build character, you must address. . . the head, the heart, and the hand.***

Toward this goal, it may be helpful to understand what it means to educate character in others. It has been said that teaching good character involves teaching toward knowing the good, loving the good, and doing the good. These are powerfully motivating concepts which move many educators, administrators, parents, community and religious leaders, and other child advocates toward educative action designed to benefit the common good of not only the child, but of our entire society.

Of course, there are many approaches to action in meeting these goals. One truth may be that there is more involved than just saying and reminding children of good character words and traits. When you build character, you must address the cognitive, the emotional, and the behavioral—the head, the heart, and the hand. Music learning activity, as we know, involves all three realms. In so doing, it provides daily opportunities for our students to develop good character traits and skills.

The remainder of this article will offer you specific connections between selected character or lifelong skills concepts and concrete examples found in music classroom activities. What is important here are not the specific terms themselves, but rather the overall concepts and connections. We hope these connections may serve to help you in your communications with others about how music education is vitally linked to and an active reinforcement of character education for children.

## Connections Involving Self

**Responsibility** We require students to arrive on time, put away their supplies, follow directions, be well-behaved, and and prepared musically. Successful musical rehearsal and performance requires and rewards personal responsibility toward a group effort.

**Curiosity** Students are exercising this trait when they are asked to find the new note and its fingering on the recorder, figure out what beats are missing in a particular measure, guess the cultural origin of a recorded listening segment, and so on. When we ask older students to explore and find out information about instruments, composers, styles of music, or have them ask new probing questions about what they play, sing, or hear, students are exercising their curiosity in an active, productive manner.

**Effort and Perseverance** The act of practicing music alone or in a group requires continual effort and the exercise of perseverance. Students cannot give up on practicing and must "try again and again" if they are to improve the musical sound. Music teachers motivate by modeling these traits for their students, as music making itself is a natural composite of both perseverance and effort.

**Courage** When we praise and reward students for their ability to overcome being self-conscious and nervous in performance, we are helping them develop this trait of courage. The need for courage never ends. In reviewing how far a student or group has come, we are pointing out that courage is what this effort demanded in order to succeed. Also, many music teachers teach about famous composers and performing artists who overcame impossible odds to develop their skills and performance talents. Determination and resolve are companion traits with courage.

## Connections Involving Others

**Listening to Others** The ability to listen is at the heart of all musicianship. Cooperative group projects and partner work in music class involve shared decision-making and compromise. Students must listen to the teacher for direction and criticism, as well as to one another in order to complete a specific group project or task. Also, we listen to others making music to learn how to make music for others and with others.

**Friendship** One of the best motivators for student participation in music and music performance groups is reported simply as, "We get to make friends." Research indicates that many at-risk students value school because of their participation in music. Friendships in the music classroom often naturally evolve from working together toward a rewarding common goal. A community of friends is established because our students enjoy working with others who enjoy the same things they do.

**Caring** Students help other students to learn music, critique and support others' efforts, and take care of one another within the larger group. Students are actively caring for one another when they offer to help, lend a hand to and include students with special needs, and understand when others need their assistance.

***The ability to listen is at the heart of all musicianship.***

**Cooperation** All music making requires active cooperation with the leader and other performers. Students are exercising this skill continually in the music classroom by making sound together, moving, trading instruments, picking partners, setting up and cleaning up, and countless other activities.

We ask our students to share and work together in the music classroom. We model and expect students to be fair to others as we give everyone a turn. We ask students to work out their different points of view in making decisions for a group project. We say to younger children, "Show me that you and your partner know how to share and put away the instruments." Many music teachers ask older students to work out a class problem and lead others to do the same.

**Truthfulness** We encourage our students to critique one another with the goal of helping others improve their music making. We ask students to tell us the truth about what they think of a performance. "Which part needs to be louder?" "What needs to be done for this to sound better?" "Where's the hard part and what do we need to do to be able to play or sing it?"

**Flexibility and Sense of Humor** We can teach our students to be flexible by modeling this trait ourselves, especially in our ability to laugh at our mistakes and the world around us. We model flexibility by accepting human error, being accommodating, and adapting to the needs of individuals and the group. Many teachers and students learn to exercise this important skill when working with students with special needs. We learn to adapt and not be inflexible in demanding that all students do musical tasks in the same way. We are open to students who often think of alternative ways to make music as they compose and experiment with musical sounds.

**Controlling Anger** Students are asked to exercise individual control over their physical and emotional reactions to others and less-than-perfect events in the music classroom. We ask and reward students for controlling themselves and being patient with others during music making.

**Building Community and Citizenship** A well-managed music classroom is a model for future adult citizenship in the larger community. In this classroom, individuals have a role to add to the composite community effort by learning their part through hard work and self-discipline, directly participating in constructive and creative action with others, electing and supporting leaders, respecting the rights of the majority, and caring about the overall goal and effort of the many. Simply put, students work toward projects and performance in community, every member offering an important and valued addition to the whole.

## Evaluation Criteria and Procedures Built Into MAKING MUSIC

At every grade level of MAKING MUSIC, evaluation criteria (referred to as assessments throughout the program) are provided within lessons and at the ends of units. Assessments incorporated into each lesson affect perceptions of students, teachers, administrators, and all who care about what is accomplished by studying music, and they serve to provide essential information about what students achieve from taking a music course based on MAKING MUSIC.

Because individual teachers seldom have the time or resources to develop truly comprehensive assessments, and because effective assessments must include a rich diversity of methods and strategies that encourage all students to be successful, the authors and editors of MAKING MUSIC have incorporated the following types of assessment into the program.

- **Observations**
  Teachers observe individuals, small groups, or the entire class during an activity to assess some aspect of student learning. Students may also observe one another for peer assessment. Possibilities for observations include checklists of elements or skills, anecdotal comments, and student performances.

- **Performances**
  Teachers assess progress on or attainment of skills and behaviors through individual or group performances, including composition, movement activities, sound pieces, projects, demonstrations, cooperative learning, and, of course, all performing skills.

- **Self-Assessments**
  Students are asked to think about themselves as musicians. These self-assessments may include descriptions of things they have learned to do well, are continuing to work on, are planning to do, or would like to learn. Self-assessments may be reflections, checklists, journal writing, interest inventories, attitudinal surveys, or descriptions of students' feelings and values.

- **Interviews**
  Teachers formally or informally talk with students individually or in groups in order to better understand students' thinking processes and attitudes. Interviews may be conferences or discussions that demonstrate processing, problem solving, critical thinking, and so on.

- **Music Journals/Journal Writing**
  Opportunities are provided for students to write as they formulate, organize, internalize, and evaluate concepts. Writing provides a good record of the student's thinking, an indicator of what the student is learning and how the student feels. Writing may be a separate activity or may be part of a larger project. Journals may include students' written evaluations of music, specific assignments, or actual compositions. Musical compositions may be in the form of notated compositions, compositional sketches, or graphic notations.

- **Audio Journals and Video Journals**
  Opportunities are provided for students to make recordings of their performances, interviews, and so on. A student's audio or video journal may be a record of his or her "critical incidents" in music making or listening.

- **Portfolios**
A music portfolio will include examples of a student's musical work. Examples may include representative work, "best" work, mandatory assignments, and so on. Examples often reflect the variety of contexts in which the learning occurs. Portfolios in music might include audio recordings, video recordings, photos, graphic notation leading to actual notation, examples of tests or "What Do You Hear?" exercises, graphic organizers, and so on. Teachers may have students develop individual portfolios or may create group portfolios for the whole class.

> ***Assessments demonstrate what is accomplished by studying music and show what students learn from a course using MAKING MUSIC.***

- **What Do You Hear?**
Cognitive assessments provide an objective way to measure students' understanding of music concepts. "What Do You Hear?" exercises are provided at every grade level. They include blackline masters for student answer sheets and recorded excerpts that the student must listen to and analyze.

- **Reaction Letters or Reaction Memos**
Students might be asked to write letters to "Old Dan Tucker" or to the Boys Choir of Harlem or to Mozart. In setting up the activity, the Teacher's Edition provides the "stem" to get the student started, such as "I wish I could be part of your group because...." Also, students might write reaction letters or memos to each other regarding their work in class.

- **Peer Critiques**
Students might provide, either by discussion or in writing, critiques of interviews, in-process work, final work, or performances.

- **Written Assessments**
Written assessments include quizzes and tests, activity sheets, and graphic organizers. Opportunities for assessment using written language are found at the ends of units and within each lesson of MAKING MUSIC, where they help to focus the entire lesson and help teachers and students to conceptualize the learning that is taking place.

- **Attitude Inventory**
Students respond to a checklist or provide written responses to music. Attitude inventories may be used as pretests and posttests to learning. In this way, teachers learn the attitudes students had before studying a particular selection and compare it to how students' attitudes might have changed.

Correlation to the National Standards
Elements Scope and Sequence
Skills Scope and Sequence
Pitch and Rhythm Syllable Systems
Glossary

Correlation to the National Standards
Elements Scope and Sequence
Skills Scope and Sequence
Pitch and Rhythm Syllable Systems
Glossary

## Contents

# CORRELATION OF Silver Burdett Making Music

## to the National Standards for Music Education

"Because music is a basic expression of human culture, every student should have access to a balanced, comprehensive, and sequential program of study in music." This goal, as expressed by the authors of the National Standards for Arts Education, is the driving force behind MAKING MUSIC and the correlation chart below. The chart, and the corresponding on-page National Standards references in this Teacher's Edition (shown with the icon 1a), will provide valuable assistance in tracking your students' progress and making this goal a reality.

### Organization

The National Standards have been developed and organized according to two specific grade-level clusters: Grades K–4 and Grades 5–8. Within each cluster, students may work towards a degree of competency in the skills described in any of the Standards. Full competency, however, is not expected until students have exited the last grade of each cluster. The process of meeting each Standard, then, is a cumulative one in which some Standards may not be fully applicable until the last grade of the cluster.

The page references in the chart below reflect this understanding. The musical activities presented in the earlier grades of MAKING MUSIC engage students in developmentally appropriate learning experiences, which are designed to prepare students to achieve specific Standards by the end of Grades 4 and 8.

| Content Standard | Achievement Standard | Teacher's Edition Page |
|---|---|---|
| **1** **Singing, alone and with others, a varied repertoire of music** | 1a Students sing independently, on pitch and in rhythm, with appropriate timbre, diction, and posture, and maintain a steady tempo | 7, 15, 107, 146, 181, 187, 191, 216, 244, 256, 257, 267, 268, 284, 294, 327, 373, 385, 388, 397, 404, 406, 411, 420, 421, 427, 429, 431 |
| | 1b Students sing expressively, with appropriate dynamics, phrasing, and interpretation | 8, 27, 33, 49, 89, 131, 143, 160, 181, 212, 219, 255, 256, 261, 276, 277, 287, 297, 309, 329, 341, 373, 383, 388, 412, 420, 435 |
| | 1c Students sing from memory a varied repertoire of songs representing genres and styles from diverse cultures | 15, 19, 21, 23, 25, 35, 39, 40, 55, 63, 79, 97, 151, 174, 228, 229, 241, 242, 259, 261, 275, 285, 294, 301, 307, 309, 311, 313, 321, 335, 375, 389, 391, 412, 440 |
| | 1d Students sing ostinatos, partner songs, and rounds | 77, 80, 115, 119, 149, 159, 161, 187, 197, 199, 201, 212, 217, 237, 245, 307, 317, 349, 363, 371, 388, 392, 399, 413, 425 |
| | 1e Students sing in groups, blending vocal timbres, matching dynamic levels, and responding to the cues of a conductor of 3, on a scale of 1 to 6, including some songs performed from memory | 9, 159, 163, 179, 181, 217, 264, 383, 404, 441 |

| Content Standard | Achievement Standard | Teacher's Edition Page |
|---|---|---|
| **2** **Performing on instruments, alone and with others, a varied repertoire of music** | 2a Students perform on pitch, in rhythm, with appropriate dynamics and timbre, and maintain a steady tempo | 12, 16, 239, 256, 270, 271, 272, 273, 284, 311, 395, 398, 412 |
| | 2b Students perform easy rhythmic, melodic, and chordal patterns accurately and independently on rhythmic, melodic, and harmonic classroom instruments | 29, 35, 37, 52, 67, 77, 97, 116, 119, 121, 132, 135, 137, 145, 152, 156, 162, 163, 177, 178, 181, 189, 195, 198, 199, 201, 203, 212, 214, 227, 237, 243, 245, 251, 261, 265, 268, 274, 275, 278, 281, 285, 293, 303, 309, 319, 328, 332, 333, 342, 343, 355, 357, 364, 368, 420, 421, 423, 425, 429, 431, 437, 439 |
| | 2c Students perform expressively a varied repertoire of music representing diverse genres and styles | 229, 243, 297, 319 |
| | 2d Students echo short rhythms and melodic patterns | 54, 118, 264, 281, 421 |
| | 2e Students perform in groups, blending instrumental timbres, matching dynamic levels, and responding to the cues of a conductor | 272, 278, 303, 333 |
| | 2f Students perform independent instrumental parts[1] while other students sing or play contrasting parts | 35, 37, 67, 77, 80, 92, 97, 99, 107, 108, 115, 132, 135, 148, 155, 157, 163, 171, 184, 194, 197, 201, 203, 218, 223, 236, 243, 259, 264, 293, 301, 313, 317, 320, 336, 344, 349, 358, 363, 368, 393, 435 |
| **3** **Improvising melodies, variations, and accompaniments** | 3a Students improvise "answers" in the same style to given rhythmic and melodic phrases | 102, 234 |
| | 3b Students improvise simple rhythmic and melodic ostinato accompaniments | 25, 40, 50, 56, 57, 62, 64, 80, 105, 107, 108, 212, 238, 333, 344, 398, 420 |
| | 3c Students improvise simple rhythmic variations and simple melodic embellishments on familiar melodies | 19, 20, 326 |
| | 3d Students improvise short songs and instrumental pieces, using a variety of sound sources, including traditional sounds, nontraditional sounds available in the classroom, body sounds, and sounds produced by electronic means[2] | 38, 180, 182, 314, 423 |

| Content Standard | Achievement Standard | Teacher's Edition Page |
|---|---|---|
| **4** **Composing and arranging music within specified guidelines** | 4a Students create and arrange music to accompany readings or dramatizations | 61, 80, 132, 143, 203, 212, 336, 369 |
| | 4b Students create and arrange short songs and instrumental pieces within specified guidelines[3] | 25, 70, 90, 121, 133, 134, 149, 157, 161, 185, 187, 212, 215, 220, 221, 224, 225, 229, 237, 240, 256, 261, 264, 265, 314, 346, 361, 371, 376, 404, 427, 432, 433, 435, 439 |
| | 4c Students use a variety of sound sources when composing | 90, 233, 273, 321, 405 |
| **5** **Reading and notating music** | 5a Students read whole, half, dotted half, quarter, and eighth notes and rests in $\frac{2}{4}$, $\frac{3}{4}$, and $\frac{4}{4}$ meter signatures | 11, 22, 37, 53, 55, 93, 97, 99, 122, 137, 139, 177, 180, 181, 197, 211, 215, 219, 223, 224, 231, 261, 263, 264, 283, 301, 313, 327, 331, 339, 345, 356, 363, 385, 386, 388, 391, 395, 397, 411, 419, 437 |
| | 5b Students use a system (that is, syllables, numbers, or letters) to read simple pitch notation in the treble clef in major keys | 25, 63, 64, 65, 67, 95, 105,109, 145, 149, 189, 217, 220, 227, 231, 255, 281, 294, 299, 319, 333, 356, 361, 367, 383, 392, 437 |
| | 5c Students identify symbols and traditional terms referring to dynamics, tempo, and articulation and interpret them correctly when performing | 49, 89, 171, 213, 346, 375, 377, 403, 405 |
| | 5d Students use standard symbols to notate meter, rhythm, pitch, and dynamics in simple patterns presented by the teacher | 94, 95, 99, 103, 107, 138, 146, 149, 180, 185, 199, 357, 376, 437 |
| **6** **Listening to, analyzing, and describing music** | 6a Students identify simple music forms when presented aurally | 19, 59, 103, 141, 184, 185, 219, 259, 263, 283, 299, 304, 329, 331, 342, 346, 391, 395, 403 |
| | 6b Students demonstrate perceptual skills by moving, by answering questions about, and by describing aural examples of music of various styles representing diverse cultures | 10, 13, 16, 17, 27, 33, 51, 57, 59, 60, 63, 65, 69, 74, 116, 139, 142, 151, 155, 156, 159, 161, 163, 171, 172, 173, 184, 187, 190, 215, 219, 225, 228, 231, 234, 237, 242, 245, 272, 287, 294, 298, 305, 307, 309, 310, 311, 314, 319, 327, 329, 331, 336, 337, 342, 356, 359, 364, 371, 382, 384, 387, 388, 411, 425, 426, 432, 439, 440, 441 |
| | 6c Students use appropriate terminology in explaining music, music notation, music instruments and voices, and music performances | 7, 8, 31, 33, 57, 59, 63, 65, 69, 71, 93, 101, 102, 105, 107, 111, 135, 141, 146, 155, 177, 183, 190, 193, 211, 213, 267, 277, 297, 299, 361, 369, 385, 439 |

| Content Standard | Achievement Standard | Teacher's Edition Page |
|---|---|---|
| | 6d Students identify the sounds of a variety of instruments, including many orchestra and band instruments, and instruments from various cultures, as well as children's voices and male and female adult voices | 33, 37, 71, 74, 113, 136, 155, 175, 177, 193, 213, 223, 235, 267, 298, 299, 305 |
| | 6e Students respond through purposeful movement[4] to selected prominent music characteristics[5] or to specific music events[6] while listening to music | 11, 12, 13, 29, 39, 52, 55, 99, 101, 102, 121, 131, 139, 141, 152, 159, 163, 174, 175, 177, 179, 183, 215, 217, 219, 224, 233, 239, 257, 275, 278, 287, 299, 303, 317, 328, 329, 340, 347, 349, 358, 361, 365, 375, 377, 399, 423, 427, 432, 441 |
| 7 Evaluating music and music performances | 7a Students devise criteria for evaluating performances and compositions | 339, 373, 383, 385, 391, 399, 425, 426 |
| | 7b Students explain, using appropriate music terminology, their personal preferences for specific musical works and styles | 141, 199, 277 |
| 8 Understanding relationships between music, the other arts, and disciplines outside the arts | 8a Students identify similarities and differences in the meanings of common terms[7] used in various arts | 77, 212, 305 |
| | 8b Students identify ways in which the principles and subject matter of other disciplines taught in the school are interrelated with those of music[8] | 20, 21, 60, 67, 68, 69, 71, 92, 119, 158, 160, 224, 258, 267, 326, 330, 332, 334, 339, 340, 341, 344, 345, 365, 366, 371, 374, 428, 436 |
| 9 Understanding music in relation to history and culture | 9a Students identify by genre or style aural examples of music from various historical periods and cultures | 10, 11, 31, 33, 111, 235, 239, 264, 266, 267, 277, 295, 337, 363 |
| | 9b Students describe in simple terms how elements of music are used in music examples from various cultures of the world[9] | 34, 282, 284, 307, 314, 337, 359, 402, 403 |
| | 9c Students identify various uses of music in their daily experiences[10] and describe characteristics that make certain music suitable for each use | 20, 52, 75, 151, 255, 312 |
| | 9d Students identify and describe roles of musicians[11] in various music settings and cultures | 69, 74, 152, 175, 226, 333, 348 |
| | 9e Students demonstrate audience behavior appropriate for the context and style of music performed | 74, 111, 185, 194, 295, 339, 423 |

# ELEMENTS Scope and Sequence

| | K | 1 | 2 |
|---|---|---|---|
| **Expression** | | | |
| **Dynamics** | Loud/soft<br>Getting louder/getting softer<br>Soft dynamics | Loud/soft<br>Getting louder/getting softer | Loud/soft<br>Dynamics and dynamic markings including ***p***, ***f***, *crescendo/ decrescendo*<br>Getting louder/getting softer<br>Sudden changes |
| **Tempo** | Fast/slow<br>Getting faster/getting slower<br>Changes in tempo | Fast/slow<br>Getting faster/getting slower<br>Changes in tempo | Getting faster/getting slower<br>Tempo markings: *fermata* 𝄐<br>Changes in tempo |
| **Articulation** | Smooth and connected<br>Short and detached<br>*Legato/staccato* | Smooth and connected<br>Short and detached<br>*Legato/staccato* | Smooth and connected<br>Short and detached<br>*Legato/staccato*<br>Accents |
| **Mood** | Variety of moods | Variety of moods | Variety of moods |
| **Rhythm** | | | |
| **Beat** | Steady beat<br>Steady beat/no beat<br>Beat/rhythm<br>Beat/silent beat (rest) | Steady beat<br>Steady beat/no beat<br>Beat/rhythm<br>Sound/silence<br>Beat/silent beat (rest) | Steady beat<br>Steady beat/no beat<br>Beat/rhythm<br>Beat/offbeat |
| **Duration** | Long and short sounds<br>Longer/shorter<br>One sound per beat = ♩<br>Two sounds per beat = ♫ | Longer/shorter<br>One sound per beat = ♩<br>Two sounds per beat = ♫<br>No sound on a beat = 𝄽 | Longer/shorter<br>Tie<br>One sound per beat = ♩<br>Two sounds per beat = ♫<br>No sound on a beat = 𝄽<br>Four sounds on a beat = ♬♬<br>𝅗𝅥 |
| **Meter** | Strong beat/weak beat | Strong beat/weak beat<br>Meter in 2<br>Meter in 3 | Strong beat/weak beat<br>Meter in 2<br>$\frac{2}{4}$ meter<br>Meter in 3<br>$\frac{3}{4}$ meter |

| 3 | 4 | 5 | 6 |
|---|---|---|---|
| Dynamics and dynamic markings including ***p***, ***f***, *crescendo/ decrescendo*, sudden changes (*subito*, ***p***, ***f***), *mezzo* (***mp***, ***mf***), ***pp***, ***ff***<br>Dynamic contrasts<br>Dynamics as an expressive choice | Dynamics and dynamic markings including *crescendo/decrescendo*, *subito*, ***p***, ***f***, *mezzo* (***mp***, ***mf***), ***pp***, ***ff***<br>Changes in dynamics<br>Appropriateness of dynamic choices<br>Dynamics as an expressive choice | Dynamics and dynamic markings including *crescendo/decrescendo*, *subito*, ***p***, ***f***, *mezzo* (***mp***, ***mf***), ***pp***, ***ff***<br>Changes in dynamics<br>Appropriateness of dynamic choices<br>Dynamics as an expressive choice | Dynamics and dynamic markings including *crescendo/decrescendo*, *subito*, ***p***, ***f***, *mezzo* (***mp***, ***mf***), ***pp***, ***ff***<br>Balancing dynamics<br>Changes in dynamics<br>Appropriateness of dynamic choices<br>Dynamics as an expressive choice |
| Tempos and tempo markings including *accelerando*, *ritardando*, *allegro*, *moderato*, *adagio*<br>Changes in tempo<br>Tempo as an expressive choice | Tempos and tempo markings including *accelerando*, *presto*, *andante*, *subito*<br>Changes in tempo<br>Sudden changes in tempo<br>Appropriateness of tempo choices<br>Tempo as an expressive choice | Tempos and tempo markings including *allegretto*, *lento*<br>Changes in tempo<br>Appropriateness of tempo choices<br>Tempo as an expressive choice | Tempos and tempo markings including *rubato*, *fermata* 𝄐<br>Changes in tempo<br>Appropriateness of tempo choices<br>Tempo as an expressive choice |
| Articulations and articulation markings including *legato/ staccato*, accents, *pizzicato/arco*<br>Articulation as an expressive choice | Articulations and articulation markings including *legato/ staccato*, accents, *pizzicato/arco*, various slurs, *marcato*<br>Phrasing<br>Articulation as an expressive choice | Articulations and articulation markings including *legato/ staccato*, accents, *pizzicato/arco*, various slurs, *marcato*<br>Articulation as an expressive choice | Articulations and articulation markings including *legato/ staccato*, accents, *pizzicato/arco*, various slurs, *marcato*<br>Vocal/instrumental methods<br>Articulation as an expressive choice |
| Variety of moods | Variety of moods | Variety of moods | Variety of moods |
| Beat/rhythm<br>Beat/offbeat<br>Upbeat | Beat/offbeat<br>Upbeat | Beat/offbeat<br>Upbeat<br>Backbeat | Backbeat<br>Anacrusis |
| Tie | Tie | Tie<br>Augmentation<br>Diminution | Tie<br>Augmentation<br>Diminution<br>Relative duration |
| 2/4, 3/4, 4/4 meters | 2/4, 3/4, 4/4, 6/8 meters<br>Changes in meter | 2/4, 3/4, 4/4, 6/8 meters<br>Meter in 5<br>Meter in 7<br>Mixed meter | 2/4, 3/4, 4/4, 6/8, 3/8, 2/2 meters<br>Mixed meter<br>Compound meters<br>Changing meters |

| Rhythm (continued) | K | 1 | 2 |
|---|---|---|---|
| **Pattern** | Sound/silence<br>Same/different<br>Combinations including: ♩ , ♫ , 𝄽<br>Repeated patterns | Sound/silence<br>Same/different<br>Ostinato<br>Combinations including: ♩ , ♫ , 𝄽<br>Repeated patterns | Ostinato<br>Combinations including:<br>♩ , ♫ , 𝄽 , 𝅗𝅥 , 𝅘𝅥𝅯𝅘𝅥𝅯𝅘𝅥𝅯𝅘𝅥𝅯 |
| **Form**<br>**Phrase Form** | Same/different phrases<br>Echo (imitation)<br>Call and response<br>Introduction | Same/different phrases<br>Question/answer phrase<br>Long and short phrases<br>Echo (imitation)<br>Call and response<br>Repetition/contrast<br>Phrase forms including: ab, aba<br>Introduction and coda<br>Cumulative song | Same/different phrases<br>Question/answer phrase<br>Long and short phrases<br>Repetition/contrast<br>Phrase forms including: ab, aba, aaba, aabb<br>Solo/chorus<br>Call and response<br>Introduction and coda<br>Cumulative song |
| **Section Form** | Same/different sections | Same/different sections<br>Introduction and coda<br>Verse/refrain (AB)<br>Section forms including: AB (binary), ABA | Same/different sections<br>Introduction and coda<br>Verse/refrain (AB)<br>*D.C. al fine* (ABA)<br>Section forms including: AB, ABA, AABA, ABACA (rondo) |
| **Composite Form** | | | |
| **Melody**<br>**Pitch & Direction** | High/low<br>Higher/lower<br>Upward/downward<br>Low to high<br>High to low | High/low<br>Higher/lower<br>Upward/downward<br>Low to high<br>High to low<br>Steps, skips, and repeated pitches | Melodic direction<br>Higher/lower<br>Upward/downward<br>Steps, leaps, and repeated pitches |

| 3 | 4 | 5 | 6 |
|---|---|---|---|
| Ostinato<br>Even and uneven rhythm patterns (dotted rhythms)<br>Syncopation/no syncopation<br>Combinations including | Even and uneven rhythm patterns (dotted rhythms)<br>Syncopation/no syncopation<br>Combinations including<br>Swing eighths | Even and uneven rhythm patterns (dotted rhythms)<br>Syncopation/no syncopation<br>Motive<br>Combinations in simple meter:<br>Combinations in compound meter:<br>Combinations of 2 and 3 in mixed meter: and | Syncopation<br>Motive<br>Combinations in duple meter:<br>Combinations in compound meter:<br>Combinations of 2 and 3 in mixed meter: and<br>Layered patterns<br>Rock 'n' roll shuffle<br>Even rock rhythms |
| Question/answer phrase<br>Long and short phrases<br>Repetition/contrast<br>Phrase forms including ab, aba, aaba, aabb<br>Solo/chorus<br>Call and response<br>Introduction, interlude, and coda<br>Cumulative song | Question/answer phrase<br>Long and short phrases<br>Repetition/contrast<br>Motive<br>Phrase forms including ab, aba, aaba, aabb<br>Solo/chorus<br>Call and response<br>Introduction, interlude, and coda<br>Cumulative song<br>Ballad | Question/answer phrase<br>Long and short phrases<br>Repetition/contrast<br>Motive<br>Phrase forms including ab, aba, aaba, aabb, abac<br>Solo/chorus<br>Call and response<br>Introduction, interlude, and coda<br>Ballad<br>12-bar blues | Motive<br>Phrase forms including ab, aba, aaba, abbb, aabb, abac<br>Solo/chorus<br>Call and response<br>Introduction, interlude, and coda<br>Ballad<br>12-bar blues<br>Canons and rounds<br>Fugue |
| Same/different sections<br>Introduction and coda<br>Interlude<br>Verse/refrain (AB)<br>*D.C. al fine* (ABA)<br>First and second endings<br>*D.S. al fine*<br>Section forms including AB, ABA, AABA, ABACA (rondo) | Introduction and coda<br>Interlude<br>Verse/refrain (AB)<br>*D.C. al fine* (ABA)<br>First and second endings<br>*D.S. al fine*<br>Section forms including AB, ABA, AABA, ABACA (rondo)<br>Theme/variations | Section forms including AB, ABA, AABA, ABACA<br>Theme/variations<br>March<br>Overture<br>Finale<br>Movement | Section forms including AB, ABA, AABA, ABACA, ABCA, AABAA<br>Theme/variations<br>Overture<br>Finale<br>Movement<br>Through-composed<br>Fugue<br>Minuet and Trio<br>Bridge |
| | Opera, operetta, musical theater, piano prelude, symphony | Opera, operetta, musical theater, piano prelude, symphony, sonata-allegro, concerto | Opera, operetta, musical theater, piano prelude, symphony, sonata-allegro, concerto |
| Melodic sequence<br>Melodic direction<br>Steps, skips, and repeated pitches<br>Intervals: unison, octave<br>Pitch letter names | Melodic imitation<br>Melodic sequence<br>Melodic contour<br>Steps, skips, and repeated pitches<br>Intervals: unison, octave, third<br>Pitch letter names<br>Range and register<br>Definite and indefinite pitch | Melodic imitation<br>Melodic sequence<br>Melodic contour<br>Intervals: unison, second, third, fourth, fifth, sixth, seventh, octave<br>Pitch letter names<br>Range and register<br>Definite and indefinite pitch<br>Ornamentation<br>Whole and half steps | Intervals: unison, second, third, fourth, fifth, sixth, seventh, octave<br>Pitch letter names<br>Range and register<br>Definite and indefinite pitch<br>Ornamentation<br>Whole and half steps<br>Accidentals<br>Blues notes<br>Manipulation of pitches as compositional devices: sequence, repetition, contrast; melodic ideas and development; theme, motive, melodic ostinato |

| Melody (continued) | K | 1 | 2 |
|---|---|---|---|
| **Tonality** | | Tonal center<br>*do*-pentatonic | Tonal center<br>*do*-pentatonic<br>*la*-pentatonic |
| **Pattern** | Same/different | Same/different<br>Combinations including *so-mi, la, so-mi-la, do, so-mi-la-do* | Same/different<br>Motive<br>Pentatonic pitch patterns, including *so-mi, so-mi-la, do, so-mi-la-do, mi-re-do, re, la-so-mi-re-do* |
| **Timbre**<br>**Environmental** | Nature sounds<br>Found sounds<br>Machine sounds | Nature sounds<br>Found sounds<br>Machine sounds | Nature sounds<br>Found sounds<br>Machine sounds |
| **Vocal** | Various tone qualities produced by individuals and groups<br>Individual: sing, speak, shout, whisper | Various tone qualities produced by individuals and groups<br>Individual: sing, speak, shout, whisper; adult, child | Various tone qualities produced by individuals and groups<br>Individual: male, female, child<br>Group: duet, trio, quartet, chorus |

| 3 | 4 | 5 | 6 |
|---|---|---|---|
| Tonal center<br>*do*-pentatonic<br>*la*-pentatonic<br>*so*-pentatonic<br>Major/minor | Tonal center<br>Key signature<br>*do*-pentatonic<br>*la*-pentatonic<br>*so*-pentatonic<br>Major/minor<br>Whole and half steps<br>Scales: pentatonic, major, minor<br>Changes of key (modulation) | Tonal center<br>Key signature<br>*do*-pentatonic<br>*la*-pentatonic<br>*so*-pentatonic<br>Major/minor<br>Whole and half steps<br>Scales: pentatonic, major, natural minor, harmonic minor<br>Modes: aeolian, dorian, mixolydian<br>Changes of key (modulation)<br>Cadence | Major/minor<br>Whole and half steps<br>Scales: pentatonic, chromatic, major, natural minor, harmonic minor, whole-tone, blues<br>Modes: aeolian, dorian, mixolydian<br>Atonality (chance music)<br>Changes of key (modulation) |
| Motive<br>Melodic ostinato<br>Pentatonic pitch patterns, including *mi-re-do, so-mi-re-do, la-so-mi-re-do, so,-la,-do-re-mi-so-la-do'* | Motive<br>Melodic ostinato<br>Melodic sequence<br>Diatonic pitch patterns including *la-so-mi-re-do, la,, so,, do', so-do', fa', so,-la,-do-re-mi-fa-so-la-do', ti* | Motive<br>Melodic ostinato<br>Melodic sequence<br>Diatonic pitch patterns including *la-so-mi-re-do, la,, so,, do', so-do', fa', so,-la,-do-re-mi-fa-so-la-do', ti*<br>*la* diatonic (natural minor)<br>*si* in melodic minor<br>*ti* in dorian mode<br>*te* in mixolydian mode | Motive<br>Melodic ostinato<br>Melodic sequence<br>Melodic repetition<br>Motive manipulation<br>Diatonic pitch patterns including *so,-la,-do-re-mi-fa-so-la-ti-do'*<br>*la* diatonic (natural minor)<br>*si* in melodic minor<br>*ti* in dorian mode<br>*te* in mixolydian mode<br>Pitches in compositional devices: sequence, retrograde, imitation, inversion, repetition, transposition, modulation |
| Nature sounds<br>Found sounds<br>Machine sounds | Nature sounds<br>Found sounds<br>Machine sounds | Nature sounds<br>Found sounds<br>Machine sounds | Nature sounds<br>Found sounds<br>Machine sounds<br>Elemental acoustics<br>Sound quality determined by the sound source<br>Sound quality affected by the material, shape, and size of the source<br>Sound quality affected by the way the sound is produced |
| Various tone qualities produced by individuals and groups<br>Individual: male, female, child<br>Group: duet, trio, quartet, chorus | Various tone qualities produced by individuals and groups<br>Individual: soprano, alto, tenor, bass<br>Group: large and small ensembles<br>Vocal blending<br>*A capella* singing<br>Variety of vocal styles including: opera, operetta, musical theater, and popular singers | Various tone qualities produced by individuals and groups<br>Individual: soprano, alto, tenor, bass<br>Group: large and small ensembles<br>Vocal blending<br>*A capella* singing<br>Variety of vocal styles including: opera, operetta, musical theater, and popular singers<br>Vocal production | Various tone qualities produced by individuals and groups<br>Individual: soprano, alto, tenor, bass<br>Group: large and small ensembles<br>Vocal blending<br>*A capella* singing<br>Variety of vocal styles including: opera, operetta, musical theater, and popular singers<br>Vocal production<br>Vocal production and style of diverse cultures |

| Timbre (continued) | K | 1 | 2 |
|---|---|---|---|
| **Instrumental** | Body percussion<br>Classroom percussion<br>Various tone qualities produced by individual instruments and groups of instruments<br>Individual instruments including flute, trumpet, snare drum, piano, guitar<br>Group: large and small ensembles | Body percussion<br>Classroom percussion<br>Various tone qualities produced by individual instruments and groups of instruments<br>Tuned percussion<br>Individual instruments including trombone, violin, timpani, trumpet, clarinet, flute<br>Group: large and small ensembles | Various tone qualities produced by individual instruments and groups of instruments<br>Individual instruments including timpani, clarinet, African percussion, trumpet<br>Group: large and small ensembles<br>Families: strings, percussion, winds<br>Instrumentation from diverse cultures |
| **Electronic** | | | Synthesized sounds |

## Texture & Harmony

| | K | 1 | 2 |
|---|---|---|---|
| **Texture** | One sound/more than one sound<br>Accompaniment/no accompaniment<br>Layers of sound<br>Thick/thin | One sound/more than one sound<br>Accompaniment/no accompaniment<br>Layers of sound<br>Thick/thin<br>Ostinato<br>Bordun | Accompaniment/no accompaniment<br>Layers of sound<br>Thick/thin<br>Ostinato<br>Bordun |
| **Harmony** | | | |

| 3 | 4 | 5 | 6 |
|---|---|---|---|
| Various tone qualities produced by individual instruments and groups of instruments<br>Individual instruments<br>Group: large and small ensembles<br>Families: strings, percussion, winds, keyboards<br>Instrumentation from diverse cultures including:<br>Cambodian pinpeat orchestra, Irish instruments, Japanese instruments | Various tone qualities produced by individual instruments and groups of instruments<br>Individual instruments<br>Group: large and small ensembles including orchestra, concert band, *jarocho, gamelan,* symphony orchestra<br>Families: strings, percussion, winds, keyboards<br>Instruments from diverse cultures including: Irish instruments, Indian instruments, Chinese instruments | Various tone qualities produced by individual instruments and groups of instruments<br>Individual instruments<br>Group: large and small ensembles including orchestra, symphony orchestra, *jarocho, gamelan,* bands (marching, symphonic, dance, military, rock)<br>Families: strings (chordophones), percussion (idiophones and membranophones), winds (aerophones) | Various tone qualities produced by individual instruments and groups of instruments<br>Individual instruments<br>Group: large and small ensembles including orchestra, symphony orchestra, concert band, *jarocho, gamelan,* bands (marching, symphonic, dance, military, rock), jug band<br>Families: strings (chordophones), percussion (idiophones and membranophones), winds (aerophones)<br>Folk instruments<br>Instrument making: student-made instruments<br>Instruments from diverse cultures including: West African percussion, Middle Eastern percussion, Caribbean percussion, drums from around the world |
| Synthesized sounds | Synthesized sounds<br>Electric guitar | Synthesized sounds<br>Electric guitar | Synthesized sounds<br>Electric guitar<br>Sampling |
| Layers of sound<br>Thick/thin<br>Ostinato<br>Partner songs<br>Echo songs<br>Countermelodies and descants | Layers of sound<br>Thick/thin<br>Ostinato<br>Partner songs<br>Echo songs<br>Countermelodies and descants<br>Rounds and canons<br>Monophonic, homophonic, polyphonic textures | Ostinato<br>Partner songs<br>Countermelodies and descants<br>Rounds and canons<br>Monophonic, homophonic, polyphonic textures | Ostinato<br>Partner songs<br>Countermelodies and descants<br>Rounds and canons<br>Change in texture density<br>Combining independent melodies<br>Monophonic, homophonic, polyphonic textures |
| Harmony/no harmony<br>Unison/chordal harmony<br>Major/minor<br>Chord changes including:<br>$I–V_7$<br>2-part singing | Harmony/no harmony<br>Unison/chordal harmony<br>Major/minor<br>Chord changes including:<br>$I–V_7$<br>I–IV<br>$I–IV–V_7$<br>Chord roots<br>2-part singing<br>Harmony in thirds and sixths<br>Harmonic styles including: parallel and contrary motion | Major/minor<br>Chord changes including:<br>$I–V_7$<br>I–IV<br>$I–IV–I–V_7$<br>$I–IV– V_7$<br>Construction of triads and other chords<br>Chord intervals: root, third, fifth, seventh<br>Chord progressions<br>Cadence<br>2-part singing<br>Harmony in thirds and sixths<br>3-part singing<br>Harmonic styles including: organum, parallel motion, contrary motion, countermelodies | Major/minor triads and inversions<br>Chord changes including:<br>$I–V_7$<br>I–IV<br>$I–IV–I–V_7$<br>$I–IV–V_7$<br>Construction of triads and other chords<br>Chord intervals: root, third, fifth, seventh<br>Chord progressions<br>Cadence<br>2-part harmony<br>Harmony in thirds and sixths<br>3-part harmony<br>SATB<br>Harmonic styles including: organum, parallel motion, contrary motion, countermelodies |

# Skills Scope and Sequence

| | K | 1 | 2 |
|---|---|---|---|
| **Singing**<br>**Vocal Development** | Vocal range C4–A4; *tessitura* D4–A4<br>Engage in vocal exploration using speaking, singing, calling, and whispering<br>Engage in vocal exploration using high, middle, and low registers<br>Explore producing head voice sounds and sustaining tones<br>Engage in vocal exploration using descending and ascending *glissandi* on vowel *oo*<br>Expand vocal range upward<br>Sing a variety of simple songs in various keys and meters, alone and with a group<br>Practice good vocal health | Vocal range D4–D5; *tessitura* D4–B4<br>Engage in vocal exploration using speaking, singing, calling, and whispering and descending and ascending *glissandi*<br>Engage in vocal exploration using high, middle, and low registers<br>Develop head voice sounds in the upper register and sustain tones<br>Expand vocal range upward<br>Develop good singing posture<br>Sing a variety of simple songs in various keys and meters, alone and with a group<br>Practice good vocal health | Vocal range C4–D5; *tessitura* D4–B4<br>Engage in vocal exploration, blending chest and head voice throughout the vocal range to produce uniform tonal quality in each register<br>Practice producing head voice sounds in the upper register and sustaining tones<br>Expand vocal range upward<br>Practice good singing posture<br>Sing a variety of simple songs in various keys and meters, alone and with a group, responding to cues from a conductor<br>Practice good vocal health |
| **Intonation** | Develop aural perception of different tones, patterns, and/or sounds<br>Develop inner hearing of rhythms, tones, patterns, and melodies<br>Develop pitch matching skills | Develop aural perception and inner hearing of different tones, patterns, rhythms, melodies, and/or sounds<br>Develop pitch matching skills for *so-mi*, *so-la-so-mi*, and *do*<br>Develop aural perception of melodic steps and skips | Develop aural perception and inner hearing skills<br>Develop resonance singing on a neutral syllable (*oo*)<br>Practice pitch matching for *mi-so-la* and expand to include *do-re-mi*<br>Develop aural perception of home tone or tonal center<br>Develop correct intonation singing *do*-pentatonic songs |
| **Expression** | Sing songs using dynamics of *mp* | Sing songs using dynamics of *mp* | Expand dynamics range *mp–mf*, maintaining appropriate vocal quality<br>Develop articulation skills of singing with connected and separated notes (legato and staccato)<br>Develop singing in complete phrases with energy and direction<br>Practice singing ritardando following a conductor |
| **Part Singing** | Sing melodic echoes and dialogue songs | Sing melodic patterns in echo and call-and-response forms | Sing melodic patterns in echo and call-and-response forms<br>Perform speech pieces in canon<br>Sing simple drones and melodic ostinatos |
| **Diction** | Develop good diction through modeling | Develop good diction through modeling<br>Sing on a neutral syllable (*oo*) to develop resonant singing | Improve good diction through modeling<br>Sing on a neutral syllable (*oo*) to develop resonant singing |
| **Song Repertoire** | Sing songs representing genres and styles from diverse cultures<br>Memorize a repertoire of songs | Sing songs representing genres and styles from diverse cultures<br>Memorize a repertoire of songs | Sing songs representing genres and styles from diverse cultures<br>Memorize a repertoire of songs |

| 3 | 4 | 5 | 6 |
|---|---|---|---|
| Vocal range B3–E5; *tessitura* D4–D5<br>Engage in vocal exploration, blending chest and head voice throughout the vocal range to produce uniform tonal quality in each register<br>Expand vocal range upward<br>Develop correct breathing techniques<br>Practice good singing posture<br>Sing a variety of songs in various keys and meters, alone and with a group, responding to cues from a conductor<br>Practice good vocal health | Vocal range A3–G5; *tessitura* C4–D5<br>Expand core vocal range<br>Practice blending chest and head voice throughout the vocal range to produce uniform tonal quality in each register<br>Develop deep breathing skills and breath control<br>Practice good sitting and standing postures for singing<br>Build confidence in solo singing<br>Sing with sensitivity to blend in a group or choral ensemble, responding to cues from a conductor<br>Practice good vocal health | Vocal range A3–G5; *tessitura* C4–D5<br>Sing vocalises using basic arpeggios to expand core vocal range<br>Perform warm-up exercises and sing vocalises to prepare for singing<br>Practice blending chest and head voice throughout the vocal range to produce uniform tonal quality in each register<br>Improve deep breathing skills and breath control<br>Build confidence in solo singing<br>Refine good sitting and standing postures for singing<br>Sing with sensitivity to blend in a group or choral ensemble, responding to cues from a conductor<br>Practice good vocal health | Average vocal range G3–G5; *tessitura* D4–D5<br>Understand and adapt vocal range to accommodate changing voices<br>Perform warm-up exercises and sing *mi-re-do* and *do-re-mi-fa-so* vocalises in varied keys<br>Practice blending chest and head voice throughout the vocal range<br>Refine deep breathing skills, breath control, and staggered breathing techniques for long notes or phrases<br>Refine good sitting and standing postures for singing<br>Build confidence in solo singing<br>Sing with sensitivity to blend in a choral ensemble, responding to cues from a conductor<br>Practice good vocal health |
| Develop aural perception and inner hearing skills<br>Develop resonance singing on a neutral syllable (*oo*)<br>Develop pitch matching skills<br>Develop correct intonation singing *do*-, *la*-, and *so*- pentatonic songs<br>Develop octave singing | Develop aural perception and inner hearing skills<br>Develop correct intonation, singing extended pentatonic patterns and scales<br>Develop singing half steps in tune using *do*-pentatonic scale<br>Identify and sing *do*-pentatonic intervals | Develop aural perception and inner hearing skills<br>Perform vocalises to improve resonance and placement<br>Sing with correct intonation<br>Identify and sing intervals in *do*-pentatonic and major scales | Develop aural perception and inner hearing skills<br>Perform vocalises to improve resonance and placement<br>Sing with correct intonation<br>Recognize change of mode<br>Sing dorian and mixolydian modes and harmonic minor scales<br>Identify natural and harmonic minor scales |
| Expand dynamics range ***p*–*mp*–*mf*–*f***, maintaining appropriate vocal quality<br>Practice singing complete phrases on neutral syllables | Expand dynamics range, maintaining appropriate vocal quality<br>Develop *legato* singing | Develop techniques for incorporating *crescendo* and *diminuendo* into singing expressively while maintaining the appropriate tempo<br>Practice *legato* singing<br>Develop *staccato* singing using proper breath support<br>Sing songs using appropriate phrasing | Expand dynamics range, incorporating *crescendo* and *diminuendo* into singing expressively while maintaining the appropriate tempo<br>Practice *legato* and *staccato* singing<br>Sing with *rubato* while maintaining the appropriate dynamic level<br>Sing using appropriate phrasing<br>Sing major scales, arpeggios, and chords |
| Sing echo songs, melodic ostinatos, partner songs, rounds, countermelodies, descants, and easy 2-part canons<br>Add harmony to songs by singing chord roots | Sing melodic ostinatos, partner songs, rounds, canons, descants, countermelodies, and 2-part songs<br>Add harmony to songs by singing chord roots<br>Add harmonic endings to songs in preparation for singing parallel harmonies<br>Experience 3-part singing | Sing melodic ostinatos, partner songs, rounds, canons, countermelodies, descants, and 2- and 3-part songs<br>Add harmony to songs by singing chord roots and 2- and 3-part chordal accompaniments using the following chords: I, IV, $V_7$, I<br>Sing in parallel thirds | Sing melodic ostinatos, partner songs, rounds, canons, countermelodies, descants, and 2- and 3-part songs<br>Add harmony to songs by singing chord roots and 2- and 3-part chordal accompaniments in major and minor modes using the following chords: I, IV, $V_7$, I; i, $V_7$<br>Sing in parallel thirds and sixths |
| Develop correct production of uniform vowel sounds and well-articulated consonants<br>Sing on a neutral syllable (*oo*) to develop resonant singing | Sing vocalises of pure vowels: *a(ah)*, *e(eh)*, *i(ee)*, *o(oh)*, and *u(oo)* to develop resonant singing<br>Practice correct production of uniform vowel sounds<br>Develop correct articulation of consonant *r*<br>Develop correct articulation of voiced and unvoiced consonants | Refine correct production of uniform vowel sounds<br>Practice correct articulation of consonant *r* and voiced and unvoiced consonants<br>Develop correct articulation of diphthongs<br>Learn and apply basic rules for correct English diction | Refine correct production of uniform vowel sounds<br>Refine correct articulation of consonant *r* and voiced and unvoiced consonants<br>Practice correct articulation of diphthongs<br>Develop techniques for singing sustained words correctly |
| Sing songs representing genres and styles from diverse cultures<br>Memorize a repertoire of songs | Sing songs representing genres and styles from diverse cultures<br>Memorize a repertoire of songs | Sing music from diverse genres and cultures, with appropriate expression and tone quality<br>Memorize a repertoire of songs | Sing music from diverse genres and cultures, with appropriate expression and tone quality<br>Memorize a repertoire of songs |

| | K | 1 | 2 |
|---|---|---|---|
| **Playing**<br>**Percussion (Mallets, unpitched, drumming)** | Explore timbre possibilities using body percussion and nonpitched instruments<br>Learn correct playing techniques for pitched and nonpitched percussion<br>Use instruments as "sound effects" for stories, poems, and dramatizations<br>Play a steady beat using bilateral motions<br>Play rhythm patterns on nonpitched percussion instruments, individually and in unison with others<br>Play melodic patterns on mallet instruments<br>Play and invent simple rhythm patterns<br>Use patterns as introductions, interludes, and codas for songs and speech pieces | Expand instrumental sound resources, playing each with appropriate technique<br>Explore techniques for playing mallet instruments and nonpitched percussion<br>Use body percussion in different levels<br>Play a steady beat using bilateral and alternating motions<br>Imitate and invent rhythmic and melodic patterns, individually and in unison with others<br>Play melodic patterns (ostinatos, melodic fragments)<br>Play elemental harmonies (simple bordun)<br>Repeat simple rhythmic and melodic patterns to accompany songs<br>Play instruments in combination with each other (ensemble)<br>Incorporate expressive elements into playing<br>Develop awareness of timbre categories: woods, metals, shakers, scrapers, and so on | Play a steady beat and strong beat using bilateral and alternating lateral motions<br>Play rhythmic patterns and ostinatos from notation<br>Imitate and invent rhythmic and melodic patterns both in isolation and to accompany songs, speech pieces, and movement<br>Develop basic mallet techniques<br>Play melodic patterns to accompany songs (ostinatos, melodic fragments)<br>Play simple melodies by rote on mallet instruments<br>Play elemental harmonies (simple bordun, moving bordun, crossover bordun)<br>Play instruments in groups (ensemble) |
| **String Instruments (Autoharp, Guitar)** | | | Play one-chord and two-chord strums on the Autoharp |

| 3 | 4 | 5 | 6 |
|---|---|---|---|
| Develop "crossover" mallet technique for playing borduns and ostinatos<br>Play accompaniments for songs and speech pieces using body percussion, nonpitched percussion, and/or mallet instruments.<br>Play combined patterns in ensemble to accompany songs, speech pieces, and movement, including borduns, melodic ostinatos, rhythmic ostinatos, and melodic/rhythmic fragments<br>Develop a knowledge base for selecting accompaniment instruments appropriate to the style and culture of a song<br>Develop original accompaniments as a group | Refine mallet techniques<br>Include syncopation in rhythmic and melodic patterns<br>Use body percussion and/or non-pitched percussion instruments to perform rhythm rounds, and create question/answer rhythmic phrases<br>Use mallet instruments, keyboard, and/or recorder to create question/answer rhythmic phrases<br>Play accompaniments on mallet instruments involving two chords—I–V, I–VI, I–VII<br>Develop familiarity with chromatic structure of the keyboard<br>Play melodies on mallet instruments by rote and by reading<br>Develop simple instrumental pieces | Include offbeat rhythms in rhythmic and melodic patterns<br>Play accompaniments on mallet instruments involving the I–IV–$V_7$ harmonic progression<br>Develop more extended instrumental pieces. Include opportunities for rhythmic and/or melodic solos (composed or improvised)<br>Provide opportunities for individuals to play small pieces alone, demonstrating good technique and style<br>Develop ability to play culture-specific instruments and styles; e.g., various African drumming genres | Incorporate harmonization into the development of accompaniments using mallet instruments<br>Play accompaniments on mallet instruments involving the I–IV–$V_7$ harmonic progression<br>Expand familiarity and capability with culture-specific styles and instruments<br>Provide opportunities for individuals to play small pieces alone, demonstrating good technique and style<br>Develop ability to play culture-specific instruments and styles; e.g., various African drumming genres<br>Play basic rock rhythm patterns with popular songs |
| Play two-chord Autoharp accompaniments for songs using simple strums | Play Autoharp accompaniments, both major and minor, using three chords and simple strums<br>Identify types of guitars (nylon-string classical, steel-string acoustic, electric)<br>Identify parts of the guitar<br>Tune the guitar from a piano<br>Develop proper guitar playing posture<br>Use finger numbers for the left-hand<br>Learn how to form chords<br>Learn fundamental right-hand techniques (basic strumming patterns, picking)<br>Learn fundamental left-hand techniques (chords A, D, $E_7$, G, C, $D_7$)<br>Learn half chords<br>Learn techniques for smooth transitions between chords<br>Learn open tuning<br>Begin use of the capo<br>Create simple accompaniments to songs including short introductions, refrains, and ostinatos<br>Play songs in the keys of C, D, and G | Play Autoharp accompaniments, both major and minor, using three or more chords<br>Review types of guitars (nylon-string classical, steel-string acoustic, electric)<br>Review parts of the guitar<br>Tune the guitar using relative tuning<br>Reinforce proper guitar playing posture (three different approaches)<br>Learn to read chord diagrams<br>Review and reinforce techniques for smooth transitions between chords<br>Continue using the capo<br>Play common chord progressions<br>Learn alternative playing techniques<br>Continue to learn and use open tuning<br>Learn classic songs from guitar repertoire<br>Continue left-hand techniques (review chords and learn $A_7$, $E_7$, $G_7$, Em, Am, Dm)<br>Create accompaniments to songs including introductions, verses, refrains, and ostinatos<br>Play songs in the keys C, D, G, F, Em, and Dm<br>Discuss guidelines for improving practice time<br>Discuss guidelines of self-assessment of skill progress | Use Autoharp accompaniments in conjunction with other string band instruments such as guitar<br>Review parts of the guitar<br>Tune the guitar from a piano<br>Tune the guitar using relative tuning<br>Reinforce proper guitar playing posture (three different approaches)<br>Review and learn to read chord diagrams<br>Review and reinforce techniques for smooth transitions between chords<br>Continue using the capo<br>Learn right-hand techniques (strumming patterns, picking)<br>Continue to learn and use open tuning<br>Learn alternating bass string technique<br>Play music from the classical, pop, and folk genres<br>Begin playing the electric guitar<br>Learn to use mallet chords<br>Continue left-hand techniques (review chords and learn Bm, $B_7$, B♭, Gm)<br>Create accompaniments to songs including introductions, verses, refrains, and ostinatos<br>Play songs in the keys C, D, G, F, and several minor keys |

| | K | 1 | 2 |
|---|---|---|---|
| **Keyboard and MIDI** | Identify black and white keys<br>Maintain a steady beat<br>Locate high and low sounds<br>Play with supported index fingers<br>Identify and play basic pulse<br>Use timbre to identify range<br>Play a two-handed accompaniment<br>Discover and play pitches that move up and pitches that repeat<br>Play strong beats<br>Play an ostinato<br>Play repeated phrases | Play with supported fingers<br>Discover and play rhythm patterns<br>Identify and play high and low sounds<br>Accompany reinforcing a steady beat<br>Play an ostinato<br>Play call-and-response melodies<br>Play a melodic phrase with ascending and descending skips<br>Play a two-handed accompaniment<br>Play a refrain | Play a two-handed accompaniment using supported index fingers<br>Identify and play specific pitches<br>Play duet accompaniments<br>Read prestaff notation<br>Discover and play *mi-re-do* patterns<br>Determine melodic direction and play steps, skips, and repeats<br>Determine appropriate finger numbers<br>Play phrases using *do-re-mi-so*<br>Play an ostinato<br>Play melodies<br>Accompany in various styles<br>Read note values |
| **Recorder** | | | |

| 3 | 4 | 5 | 6 |
|---|---|---|---|
| Read prestaff notation<br>Read finger numbers and note values<br>Play rhythm patterns to show high and low sounds on specific pitches<br>Read a five-line staff<br>Show timbre by playing a duet accompaniment<br>Play sixteenth notes<br>Play accompaniments using harmonic intervals<br>Play extended range with melodies divided between hands<br>Identify and accompany songs in different meters<br>Play broken chord accompaniments<br>Play melodies with an octave range<br>Play I and $V_7$ chords | Review prestaff notation<br>Review five-line reading and fingering<br>Identify and play same and different phrases<br>Play triads<br>Expand five-finger position to achieve "closest position"<br>Play ensembles<br>Play walking bass lines<br>Play broken chord accompaniments<br>Improvise using pentatonic scales<br>Play fingering shifts<br>Play melodies with a large stretch<br>Play ♩. ♪ rhythm patterns<br>Play using thumb crossing<br>Improvise on a given pentascale and rhythmic pattern<br>Play I, IV, and $V_7$ chords | Review five-line reading and fingering<br>Play syncopated rhythm patterns<br>Play two-handed broken chords<br>Play a strumming accompaniment<br>Play a descant<br>Play a tritone accompaniment for blues<br>Play a two-handed accompaniment with crush notes<br>Play a three-part round<br>"Comp" a blues accompaniment<br>Improvise on a blues pentascale and scat syllables<br>Play an accompaniment using triplets<br>Play an introduction and an interlude | Review five-line reading and fingering<br>Play a rhythmic ostinato<br>Play a harmonic ostinato<br>Play a broken-chord accompaniment<br>Play a tritone blues accompaniment<br>Determine and play different dynamic levels<br>Play a strumming accompaniment<br>Determine and play multiple fingering positions<br>Play a countermelody using finger crossing<br>Play closest position chords<br>Play a trio<br>Play I, IV, and $V_7$ chords<br>Play a piano piece |
| Read notes B, A, G, E, D<br>Play with holes properly covered<br>Use proper hand position with left hand on top<br>Play with the pads of slightly curved fingers<br>Move fingers together<br>Play one-, two-, and three-note tonal patterns, ostinatos, and countermelodies<br>Show phrases by breathing<br>Blend sound with other recorder players<br>Blend sound with singers and/or other instruments | Read new notes C', D', and F♯<br>Play with holes properly covered<br>Use proper hand position with left hand on top<br>Play with the pads of slightly curved fingers<br>Move fingers together<br>Build right-hand strength<br>Play two-, three-, four-, and five-note tonal patterns, ostinatos, melodies, and countermelodies<br>Play syncopated rhythm patterns<br>Play melodic phrases using steps, skips, and repeats<br>Accompany 2-chord songs in keys G, D<br>Create ostinatos<br>Create introductions and interludes<br>Improvise using notes E, G, A, B<br>Show phrases by breathing<br>Blend sound with other recorder players<br>Blend sound with singers and/or other instruments<br>Blend harmony with melody | Read new notes G♯, C, F, and B♭<br>Improve playing and breathing techniques and hand dexterity<br>Develop right-hand strength<br>Play melodic phrases using steps, skips, and repeats<br>Play ostinatos, abbreviated melodies, melodies, and countermelodies<br>Play syncopated rhythm patterns<br>Play contrasting sections<br>Play a phrase of a round as an ostinato<br>Play partner songs<br>Create introductions, interludes, and codas<br>Improvise in major and *la*-pentatonic (G and e)<br>Create ostinatos<br>Create melodies based upon a rhythm<br>Practice proper articulation<br>Blend sound with other performers<br>Practice proper breathing and phrasing<br>Blend harmony with melody<br>Learn to read ahead<br>Listen to recorder music played in different styles | Read the new note E'<br>Introduce alto recorder<br>Read C, D, E, F, and G for alto recorder<br>Improve playing and breathing techniques and hand dexterity<br>Play ostinatos, abbreviated melodies, melodies, and countermelodies<br>Blend sound with other performers<br>Blend harmony with melody<br>Play enharmonic tones<br>Play a phrase of a round as an ostinato<br>Play ensemble recorder music<br>Play vocal scores for recorder consort<br>Play partner songs<br>Create ostinatos<br>Improvise in phrases as contrasting sections to melodies<br>Improvise 12-bar blues in A using pentatonic scale tones A, C, D, E, and G<br>Improvise recorder parts following chord progressions<br>Create melodies based upon a rhythm<br>Practice proper articulation<br>Refine playing in the low register<br>Add breath marks at phrase endings and practice proper breathing and phrasing<br>Learn to read ahead<br>Listen to recorder music played in different styles |

| | K | 1 | 2 |
|---|---|---|---|
| **Creating**<br>**Improvising** | Improvise patterns, using sound and movement<br>Improvise rhythmic ostinato accompaniments<br>Improvise introductions to songs, stories, poems, and dramatizations, using patterns of sound and movement<br>Explore a range of sound possibilities with voices, body percussion, instruments, and environmental and electronic sound sources<br>Improvise sound pieces to describe moods or images<br>Improvise sound pieces and/or sound effects to accompany stories, poems, and songs | Improvise simple rhythms, using sound and movement, in call-and-response form<br>Improvise a contrasting or B section in an AB or ABA form, using sound and/or movement<br>Improvise rhythmic, melodic, and movement patterns and use as accompaniments to songs and speech pieces<br>Improvise, using sound and movement, backgrounds or settings for poems, stories, songs, and speech pieces<br>Use tempo and dynamic changes and contrasts in improvisations<br>Improvise simple sound pieces for voices, body percussion, instruments, and environmental and electronic sounds | Improvise the b phrase in an aaba form<br>Improvise body percussion patterns to accompany songs or speech pieces<br>Invent strumming patterns for one-chord Autoharp accompaniments<br>Improvise melodic phrases using the pentatonic scale<br>Improvise sound pieces and music to accompany movement, poetry, and storytelling, using a variety of media, including technology sources |
| **Composing** | Create movements and dramatizations for songs and poems<br>Create new words and movements for familiar songs<br>Compose soundscapes for voices, body percussion, instruments, and environmental sounds | Compose, using sound and movement, backgrounds or settings for poems, stories, songs, and speech pieces<br>Create introductions for songs and speech pieces, using sound and movement<br>Invent systems for notating musical ideas<br>Compose original verses to familiar songs<br>Use tempo and dynamic changes and contrasts in compositions<br>Compose simple sound pieces for voices, body percussion, instruments, and environmental and electronic sounds | Create settings, sound effects, or accompaniments for songs, poems, dances, and speech and creative movement pieces, using a variety of sound sources and movement ideas<br>Compose simple AB and ABA pieces, using sound and movement<br>Compose introductions and codas for songs and speech pieces, using sound and movement<br>Compose B and C sections to create an ABACA piece<br>Compose and notate rhythmic and melodic ostinato accompaniments to pentatonic melodies, using classroom percussion or technology sources |
| **Reading/Notating**<br>**Rhythm** | Beat icons<br>Long/short icons | Interpret icons representing beat/strong beat, long/short, and tempo and dynamic changes<br>Durations including:<br>♩, 𝄽, ♫<br>Follow and create listening charts | Iconic notation<br>Durations including:<br>♩, 𝄽, ♫, ♬♬, 𝅗𝅥<br>Meters including: $\frac{2}{4}$, $\frac{3}{4}$<br>Tie |

| 3 | 4 | 5 | 6 |
|---|---|---|---|
| Improvise contrasting B and C sections in a rondo (ABACA) form, using sound and movement<br>Improvise rhythmic, melodic, and movement ostinatos in accompaniments for songs or speech pieces<br>Improvise simple pieces that show thick and thin texture contrasts; use movement to show texture<br>Improvise simple melodies based on the pentatonic scale<br>Use variation in dynamics, tempo, and articulation in improvisations<br>Experiment with various electronic and environmental sound sources and alternative ways to play instruments | Use melodic sequences in improvisations<br>Improvise music to accompany movement or dance<br>Improvise introductions, codas, and interludes<br>Improvise melodies in major and minor<br>Improvise simple sound and movement variations on a theme<br>Improvise pieces in rondo (ABACA) form, using a variety of sound sources, including technology and movement<br>Invent playing techniques (strumming, mallet) for I-V and I-IV accompaniments | Improvise extended phrases in question/answer form, using movement, rhythms, and melody<br>Improvise melodies over accompaniments, using the I, IV, and V chords<br>Improvise melodies, using various scales<br>Experiment with strumming or other playing techniques to create rhythmic variety in chordal accompaniments | Use melodic sequences in improvisations<br>Improvise answer phrases when given question phrases<br>Improvise music to accompany movement and movement to accompany music<br>Improvise chordal accompaniments for familiar songs<br>Use given and original motives and themes as the basis for improvising with sound and movement<br>Use acoustic and electronic instruments to improvise melodies over given chord patterns including rock and blues |
| Compose accompaniments and dramatizations for songs and readings, using a variety of sound sources and movements<br>Compose rhythmic, melodic, and movement ostinatos in accompaniments for songs or speech pieces<br>Compose simple melodies based on the pentatonic scale<br>Create AB, ABA, and ABACA pieces, using speech, instruments, voices, and movement<br>Compose and notate two short rhythm pieces that can be performed together as partners<br>Compose simple pieces that show thick and thin texture contrasts; use movement to show texture<br>Use variation in dynamics, tempo, and articulation in compositions<br>Compose simple percussion and wind instrument pieces to explore sound sources and timbres | Compose music to accompany movement or dance<br>Compose accompaniments of or backgrounds and dramatizations for songs, poems, and stories, using music and movement<br>Create, notate, and perform a pentatonic melody<br>Create and perform speech, rhythm, and movement canons<br>Compose introductions, codas, and interludes<br>Use melodic sequences in compositions<br>Create, notate, and perform rhythmic, speech, or movement variations on a theme<br>Compose pieces in rondo (ABACA) form, using a variety of movement and sound sources, including technology options | Compose and arrange accompaniments for songs, poems, stories, and dramas, using music and movement<br>Compose, notate, and perform compositions in AB, ABA, and ABACA forms<br>Compose a music or movement theme and variations on the theme<br>Compose, notate, and perform melodies in major and minor mode, using various media, including technology<br>Invent a scale, using classroom instruments and technology options, and compose a melody using that scale | Compose, notate, and perform original songs, instrumental works, speech pieces, and dramatizations<br>Compose music to accompany dance or dramatic presentations<br>Use given and original motives and themes as the basis for composing with sound and movement<br>Compose chordal accompaniments for familiar songs<br>Create new verses for a song<br>Invent new arrangements of simple pieces, using voices, acoustic instruments, or electronic instruments other than those for which the music was originally written<br>Compose and notate short arrangements, using computer software<br>Experiment with found sounds and new sound sources to create music<br>Compose accompaniments in different musical styles using auto-accompaniment on MIDI keyboards |
| Durations including:<br>Meters including: 2/4, 3/4, 4/4 | Upbeat<br>Durations including:<br>Meters including: 2/4, 3/4, 4/4 | Upbeat<br>Durations including:<br>Meters including: 2/4, 3/4, 4/4, 6/8 | Steady beat/back beat<br>Durations including:<br>tied notes<br>Meters including: 2/4, 3/4, 4/4, 2/2, 6/8<br>Compound, changing, and asymmetrical meters<br>Syncopation |

| | K | 1 | 2 |
|---|---|---|---|
| **Melody** | Upward/downward melodic motion icons<br>Preparation for *so-mi* patterns | Interpret icons representing melodic motion<br>Patterns including: *so-mi*, *so-mi-la*, *so-mi-la-do*<br>*do*-pentatonic in C, F, G for playing on mallet instruments | Patterns including: *so-mi*, *so-mi-la*, *so-mi-la-do*, *mi-re-do*, *so-mi-re-do*, *la-so-mi-re-do*<br>*do*-pentatonic in C, F, and G<br>*la*-pentatonic in *e* |
| **Listening/Analyzing/Describing** | Respond to characteristics of phrase form: same and different<br>Respond to characteristics of rhythm: steady beats, strong beats, silent beats, long/short sounds, repeated rhythm patterns<br>Respond to characteristics of melodies: high/low pitches; upward/downward melodic direction; repeated melodic patterns<br>Identify accompaniment/no accompaniment<br>Identify environmental sounds: animals, machines, and weather<br>Identify instrumental sounds of classroom percussion instruments, keyboards, flute, and trumpet<br>Identify differences between vocal sounds: speaking, singing, shouting, whispering, humming<br>Respond to expressive qualities in music: fast/slow and loud/soft<br>Listen to music of diverse cultures and styles<br>Demonstrate appropriate audience behavior while observing classroom performances<br>Discuss appropriate audience behaviors | Respond to characteristics of phrase form: same/different, call and response, and solo/chorus<br>Respond to characteristics of sectional form: verse and refrain<br>Respond to characteristics of rhythm: steady beats, strong beats, silent beats, absence of beats, long and short sounds, rhythm patterns<br>Respond to characteristics of melody: high/low pitches, upward/downward direction, melodic patterns<br>Identify and describe various accompaniments<br>Identify various found sounds<br>Identify sounds of nonpitched and pitched percussion instruments; trombone, violin, flute, clarinet, and trumpet<br>Identify vocal timbres: male, female, child<br>Identify qualities of speech, singing, shouting, whispering<br>Respond to expressive qualities in music: fast, slow, and changing tempos; loud, soft, and changing dynamics<br>Describe mood and style in a variety of music<br>Identify music of diverse cultures and styles<br>Listen to music that suggests a story or subject<br>Demonstrate appropriate audience behavior while observing classroom performances<br>Discuss appropriate audience behaviors | Identify characteristics of phrase form: same and different, call and response, aab, and aaba<br>Identify characteristics of sectional form: verse and refrain, AB, ABA, and ABACA<br>Identify rhythmic elements: steady beat, long and short sounds, repeated rhythm patterns, $\frac{2}{4}$, $\frac{3}{4}$ meters<br>Identify high/low pitches, steps/skips, melodic direction, and melodic patterns<br>Contrast styles of two pieces<br>Identify melodic and rhythmic ostinatos<br>Identify vocal timbres of individuals and groups: male, female, child<br>Identify various instrumental timbres, including nonpitched and pitched percussion, strings, woodwinds, brass, and electronic instruments<br>Respond to expressive qualities in music: fast, slow, and changing tempos; loud, soft, and changing dynamics<br>Perceive and respond to articulation changes (*legato* and *staccato*)<br>Identify and respond to section changes<br>Describe mood and style in a variety of music<br>Identify music of diverse cultures and styles<br>Listen to music that suggests a story or subject<br>Demonstrate appropriate audience behavior while observing classroom performances<br>Discuss appropriate audience behaviors |

| 3 | 4 | 5 | 6 |
|---|---|---|---|
| Patterns including: *mi-re-do*, *so-mi-re-do*, *la-so-mi-re-do*, *la*$_{\mid}$, *so*$_{\mid}$, *do*$^{\mid}$, *so*$_{\mid}$-*la*$_{\mid}$-*do-re-mi-so-la-do*$^{\mid}$<br>*do*-pentatonic scale<br>*la*-pentatonic scale<br>*so*-pentatonic scale<br>Letter names for pitches | *do*-pentachordal<br>Patterns including: *la-so-mi-re-do*, *la*$_{\mid}$, *so*$_{\mid}$, *so-do*$^{\mid}$, *fa*, *ti*, *so*$_{\mid}$-*la*$_{\mid}$-*do-re-mi-fa-so-la-ti-do*$^{\mid}$<br>*do*-pentatonic scale<br>*la*-pentatonic scale<br>*so*-pentatonic scale<br>Letter names for pitches | Major/minor diatonic<br>Dorian<br>Mixolydian<br>*do*-pentachordal<br>Patterns including: *la-so-mi-re-do*, *fa*, *so*$_{\mid}$-*la*$_{\mid}$-*do-re-mi-fa-so-la-ti-do*$^{\mid}$<br>*do*-pentatonic scale<br>*la*-pentatonic scale<br>*so*-pentatonic scale<br>Letter names for pitches | Half/whole steps<br>Accidentals; intervals<br>Ornamentation<br>Major/minor scales<br>Pitch sets (12-tone, whole-tone)<br>Motive<br>Repetition and contrast<br>*do*-pentatonic scale<br>*la*-pentatonic scale<br>*so*-pentatonic scale<br>Letter names for pitches |
| Identify AB, ABA, AABB, and ABACA forms<br>Identify rhythmic elements: steady beat, $\frac{2}{4}$ and $\frac{3}{4}$ meters, patterns<br>Identify same/different, longer/shorter, higher/lower, upward/downward, louder/softer, faster/slower<br>Identify patterns and themes<br>Identify chord changes in two-chord songs<br>Distinguish between major and minor tonality<br>Analyze and describe how tempo, dynamics, and timbre affect the mood of a piece<br>Identify various vocal timbres of individual performers and groups<br>Identify instrument families in the orchestra: strings, woodwinds, brass, percussion<br>Respond to expressive qualities in music: fast, slow, and changing tempos; loud, soft, and changing dynamics<br>Identify music of diverse cultures and styles<br>Listen to program and nonprogram music<br>Listen to standard orchestral and chamber music<br>Demonstrate appropriate audience behavior while observing classroom performances<br>Discuss appropriate audience behaviors | Identify form in instrumental pieces<br>Identify rhythmic elements in $\frac{2}{4}$, $\frac{3}{4}$, and $\frac{4}{4}$ meters<br>Identify same/different, longer/shorter, higher/lower, upward/downward, louder/softer<br>Distinguish between major and minor tonality<br>Analyze and describe how tempo, dynamics, and timbre affect the mood of a piece<br>Identify vocal timbres of groups<br>Identify individual instruments<br>Identify families of instruments from diverse cultures: strings, woodwinds, brass, percussion<br>Analyze and describe differences between orchestra and band sound<br>Respond to expressive qualities in music: fast, slow, and changing tempos; loud, soft, and changing dynamics<br>Compare and describe the elements of style in two contrasting pieces<br>Analyze music of diverse cultures and styles<br>Analyze standard orchestral and chamber music<br>Listen to choral works<br>Demonstrate appropriate audience behavior while observing classroom performances<br>Discuss appropriate audience behaviors | Identify and analyze sectional, theme and variations, and ABACA/rondo form<br>Identify rhythmic elements of meter in $\frac{2}{4}$, $\frac{3}{4}$, $\frac{4}{4}$, and $\frac{6}{8}$<br>Identify chords<br>Distinguish between major, minor, and other modes<br>Analyze and compare rhythmic elements in terms of steady beat, meter, rhythm patterns, and relative duration<br>Analyze and compare melodic structure in terms of movement, contour, sequence, phrase, cadence, and mode<br>Analyze and compare pieces in terms of texture and chordal and linear harmony<br>Identify timbres of individual singing voices and vocal ensembles<br>Identify timbres of individual instruments and ensembles<br>Respond to expressive qualities in music: fast, slow, and changing tempos; loud, soft, and changing dynamics<br>Respond to show form in music<br>Respond to show interpretation of lyrics in music<br>Analyze and compare elements of style in several contrasting pieces<br>Analyze music of diverse cultures and styles<br>Identify complete sections from longer musical forms<br>Compare program and absolute music<br>Listen to chamber groups<br>Demonstrate appropriate audience behavior while observing classroom performances<br>Discuss appropriate audience behaviors | Identify repetition and contrast<br>Identify sectional forms: AB, ABA, ABACA/rondo, and theme and variations<br>Identify chords<br>Distinguish between major, minor, and other modes<br>Identify intervals: thirds and sixths<br>Identify cadence<br>Identify and describe how the words of a song affect the form and expressive qualities<br>Identify *rubato*<br>Recognize appropriateness of tempo choices<br>Identify tempo category for selection: *largo*, *adagio*, *andante*, *moderato*, *allegro*, *vivace*, *presto*, *prestissimo*<br>Discern individual and group timbres<br>Discern vocal timbres from a variety of cultures<br>Identify similarities and differences among string instruments from different cultures<br>Move to show form, melodic contour, tempo changes, and changes in dynamics<br>Respond to expressive qualities in music: fast, slow, and changing tempos; loud, soft, and changing dynamics<br>Identify and describe style differences determined by rhythm, melody, and timbre<br>Analyze music of diverse cultures and styles<br>Recognize composite forms: opera, cantata, mass, and others<br>Identify dance styles<br>Recognize and describe a variety of vocal styles<br>Identify various styles of drumming<br>Demonstrate appropriate audience behavior while observing classroom performances<br>Discuss appropriate audience behavior while listening to peers and guest musicians perform for the class |

| | K | 1 | 2 |
|---|---|---|---|
| **Moving**<br>**Nonlocomotor** | Acquire a repertoire of nonlocomotor movements: pat, clap, stamp, bend, stretch, twist, shake<br>Perform nonlocomotor motions in finger plays and action songs | Practice basic repertoire of nonlocomotor movements in finger plays and action songs<br>Develop these alternating patterns: pat-clap, pat-tap, pat-stamp | Practice nonlocomotor movements<br>Practice alternating patterns<br>Develop repertoire of bilateral movements: snap and hand jive motions |
| **Locomotor** | Develop a repertoire of locomotor movements: walk, run, hop, jump, twirl<br>Coordinate locomotor movements during singing games and circle dances | Practice basic locomotor movements: walk, run, hop, jump, twirl<br>Practice coordinating locomotor movements during singing games and circle dances<br>Develop these locomotor movements: skip, slide, leap, gallop | Practice basic locomotor movements during singing games and circle dances<br>Develop facility with basic patterned locomotor movements: line and folk dances |
| **Time** | Perform creative movements while exploring concepts of time: rhythm (pulse, beat, speed-time or tempo); accent (light or strong); and duration (length) | Perform creative movements while exploring concepts of time: rhythm, accent, tempo, and duration | Perform creative movements while exploring concepts of time: rhythm, accent, tempo, and duration |
| **Space** | Perform creative movements while exploring concepts of space: level (low, middle, high); direction (forward, backward, sideways, up, down); size (large or small); place-pathways (on the floor, in the air); focus | Perform creative movements while exploring concepts of space: level, direction, size, place-pathways, focus | Perform creative movements while exploring concepts of space: level, direction; size, place-pathways, focus |
| **Energy** | Perform creative movements while exploring concepts of energy: attack (smooth, sharp); weight (heavy, light); strength/tension (tight, loose); flow (sudden or sustained, bound or free)<br>Experiment with qualities of movement including effort actions such as flick, tap, thrust, slash, float, glide | Perform creative movements while exploring concepts of energy: attack, weight, strength/tension, and flow<br>Experiment with qualities of movement including effort actions such as flick, tap, thrust, slash, float, glide | Perform creative movements while exploring concepts of energy: attack, weight, strength/tension, and flow<br>Experiment with qualities of movement including effort actions such as thrust, slash, float, glide, wring, press |
| | | | |

| 3 | 4 | 5 | 6 |
|---|---|---|---|
| Refine nonlocomotor movements<br>Practice alternating patterns<br>Develop these alternating patterns: clap-snap, stamp-snap, pat-clap-snap<br>Practice bilateral movements | Refine nonlocomotor movements<br>Refine alternating patterns<br>Develop these alternating patterns: alternating snap, stamp-pat-clap, stamp-pat-clap<br>Refine bilateral movements | Refine nonlocomotor movements<br>Refine alternating patterns<br>Develop these alternating patterns: alternating pat-snap, clap-snap, stamp-snap, pat-clap-snap, stamp-pat-clap-snap<br>Refine bilateral movements | Refine nonlocomotor movements<br>Refine alternating patterns<br>Refine bilateral movements |
| Practice basic locomotor movements<br>Practice patterned locomotor movements in singing games; circle, line, and folk dances<br>Develop this pattern of locomotor movement: square dance | Refine basic locomotor movements<br>Practice patterned locomotor movements<br>Develop these patterns of locomotor movements: social and popular (or contemporary) dances | Refine basic locomotor movements<br>Refine patterned locomotor movements<br>Develop these patterns of locomotor movements: social and popular (or contemporary) dances | Refine locomotor movements<br>Refine patterned locomotor movements<br>Develop these patterns of locomotor movements: social and popular (or contemporary) dances |
| Perform creative movements while exploring concepts of time: rhythm, accent, tempo, and duration | Perform creative movements while exploring concepts of time: rhythm, accent, tempo, and duration | Perform creative movements while exploring concepts of time: rhythm, accent, tempo, and duration | Perform creative movements while exploring concepts of time: rhythm, accent, tempo, and duration |
| Perform creative movements while exploring concepts of space: level, direction; size, place-pathways, focus | Perform creative movements while exploring concepts of space: level, direction; size, place-pathways, focus | Perform creative movements while exploring concepts of space: level, direction; size, place-pathways, focus | Perform creative movements while exploring concepts of space: level, direction; size, place-pathways, focus |
| Perform creative movements while exploring concepts of energy: attack, weight, strength/tension, and flow<br>Experiment with qualities of movement including effort actions such as thrust, slash, float, glide, wring, press | Perform creative movements while exploring concepts of energy: attack, weight, strength/tension, and flow<br>Experiment with qualities of movement including effort actions such as thrust, slash, float, glide, wring, press | Perform creative movements while exploring concepts of energy: attack, weight, strength/tension, and flow<br>Experiment with qualities of movement including effort actions such as thrust, slash, float, glide, wring, press | Perform creative movements while exploring concepts of energy: attack, weight, strength/tension, and flow<br>Experiment with qualities of movement including effort actions such as thrust, slash, float, glide, wring, press |
| | | | |

# Pitch Syllable Systems

Several systems of both pitch and rhythm syllables are available for use in the music classroom. The purpose of using syllables is to ensure that students develop the ability to associate musical notation with a corresponding sound. When choosing a system, consider the developmental level of the students and the ease with which they can achieve success. Also, take into account consistency between grade levels and performance-based music programs.

### *Solfeggio* or *solfa*

There are two types of *solfége* systems. Both systems use the following syllables and their chromatic alterations.

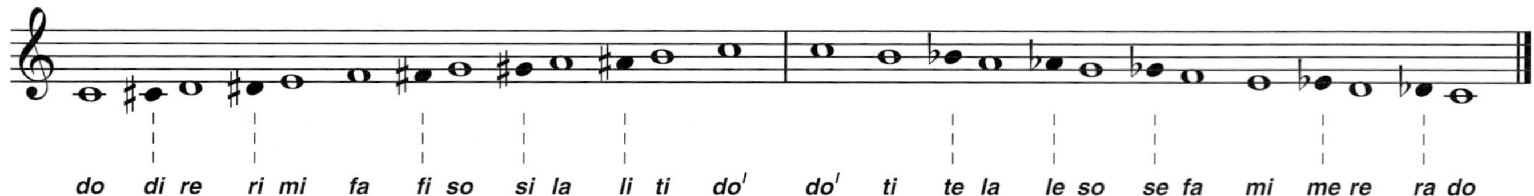


### Moveable *do*

The syllable *do* is the tonic pitch in any major key. Minor keys are based on *la.* The advantage to this system is that it establishes patterns that can easily be adapted to any key (for example, a minor third always exists between *so* and *mi,* and there is always a half-step between *mi* and *fa*). This method tends to favor early success particularly for younger students, since the introduction of letter names and key signatures can be postponed until a more age-appropriate time.

**Moveable Major Scale**

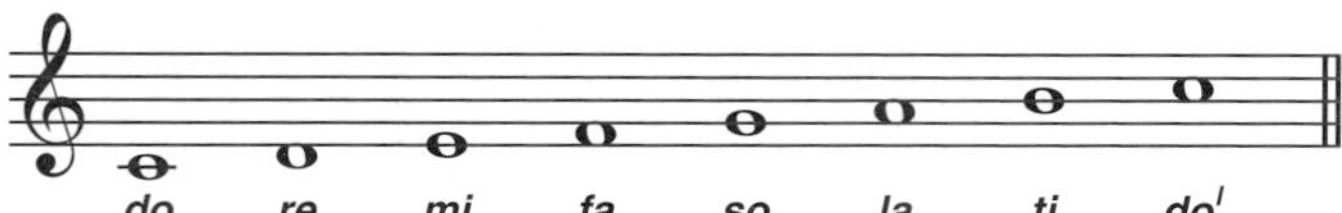


**Relative Harmonic Minor Scale**

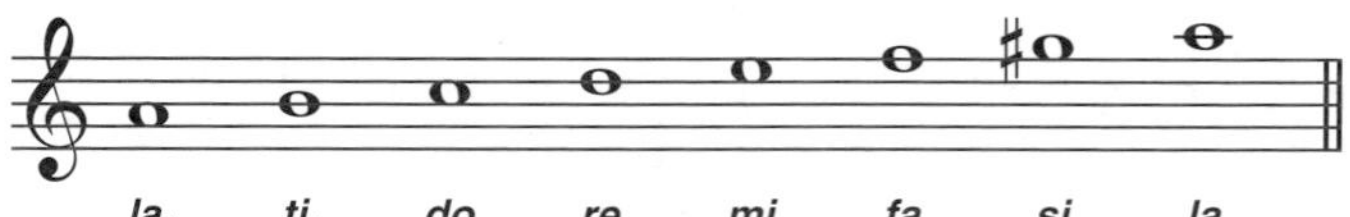


### Fixed *do*

The pitch C is always *do,* regardless of key. Proponents of this system argue that it more accurately represents true music reading, since the lines and spaces of the staff are always associated with the same sound. Knowledge of key signatures is required for success with this system.

**Fixed Major Scale**

**Fixed Harmonic Minor Scale**

### Moveable Numbers

Similar to moveable *do,* this system uses numbers (usually 1–7) with 1 functioning as the tonic. Students can often achieve success early on because of their familiarity with numbers, although the numbers themselves can be less musical to sing than *solfa* syllables. This system does not allow for half step alteration, and rhythmic accuracy can be a factor when using 7.

**Moveable Major Scale – Numbers**

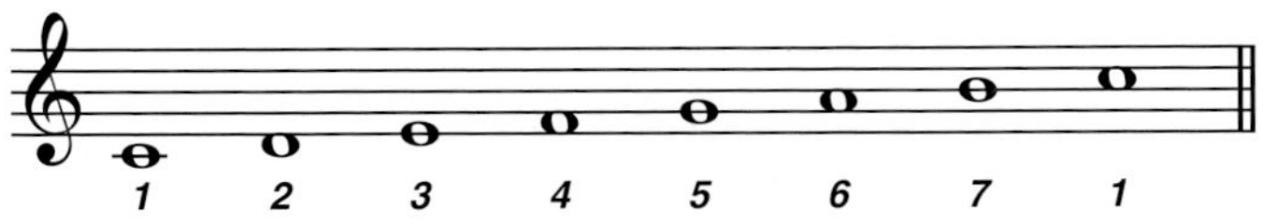


**Moveable Harmonic Minor Scale – Numbers**

### Fixed Numbers

Similar to fixed *do,* the numbers correspond to a specific pitch class. C is usually 0 and this advanced system is often reserved for twelve-tone music.

**Fixed Major Scale – Numbers**

### Neutral Syllable

This system uses a neutral syllable such as *la, lu, du,* etc. It is most beneficial for students who are already proficient readers and possess a strong aural sense of intervallic relationships. These students appreciate the lack of need to transfer pitches to any type of syllable.

| | Traditional | Kodály-based | Gordon |
|---|---|---|---|
| | This numbers-based method reinforces meter by starting each measure with *1*. Each beat is numbered and subdivisions of the beat are represented by the use of syllables *&* and *e*. A variation of this system uses *ta, te, la,* and *lee*. The most widely used system in instrumental music programs, this method is less singable because it incorporates multi-syllable numbers. | Although Zoltán Kodály used these syllables, they were developed by Emil Chevé in nineteenth-century France. Rather than using numbers, each beat is represented by *ta*. Subdivision of the beat is based on *ti* and each rhythmic pattern is assigned a distinct syllable. This method lends itself to singing and/or playing patterns without having to distort melodies by using numbers. | Gordon's syllables are designed to promote audiation, or the ability to hear a musical sound when looking at notation. Like the Kodály-based syllables, the use of *du, da,* and *de* are easily singable. |
| **Simple Meter** | | | |
| ♩ | 1 | ta | du |
| ♫ | 1-& OR 1-te | ti-ti | du-da |
| ♬♬ | 1-e-&-a OR 1-ta-te-ta | ti-ri-ti-ri OR ti-ka-ti-ka | du-ta-de-ta |
| ♪♬ | 1-&-a OR 1-te-ta | ti-ti-ri OR ti-ti-ka | du-de-ta |
| ♬♪ | 1-e-& OR 1-ta-te | ti-ri-ti OR ti-ka-ti | du-da-de |
| 𝅘𝅥𝅯♪𝅘𝅥𝅯 | 1-e-a OR 1-ta-ta | ti-ri-ti OR ti-ka-ti | du-ta-ta |
| ♪.𝅘𝅥𝅯 | 1-a OR 1-ta | teem-ri OR teem-ka | du-ta |
| 𝅘𝅥𝅯♪. | 1-e OR 1-ta | ti-reem OR tik-um | du-ta |
| 𝅗𝅥 | 1-2 | ta-am OR to-o | du- |
| ♩.♪ | 1-2 OR 1-2 te | tam ti | du de |
| ♪ ♩. | 1 &-2 OR 1 te-2 | ti tam | du da |
| ♪ ♩ ♪ | 1 &-2 & OR 1 te-2 te | syn-co-pa OR ti ta ti | du-du de |
| 𝅗𝅥. | 1-2-3 | ta-a-am OR to-o-om | du-u-u |
| 𝅝 | 1-2-3-4 | ta-a-a-am OR toe | du-u-u-u |

| Compound Meter | | | |
|---|---|---|---|
| | 1 | ta | du |
| | 1-&-a OR 1-la-lee | ti-ti-ti | du-da-di |
| | 1-e-&-a-&-a OR 1-ta-la-ta-lee-ta | ti-ri-ti-ri-ti-ri OR ti-ka-ti-ka-ti-ka | du-ta-da-ta-di-ta |
| | 1-e-&-& OR 1-ta-la-lee | ti-ri-ti-ti OR ti-ka-ti-ti | du-ta-da-di |
| | 1-&-a-& OR 1-la-ta-lee | ti-ti-ri-ti OR ti-ti-ka-ti | du-da-ta-di |
| | 1-e-& OR 1 -ta-lee | teem-ri-ti OR teem-ka-ti | du-ta-di |

## Breath Impulse

A variation of the traditional method, the breath impulse system uses numbers to represent each beat in a measure. When performing longer durations or sustained notes, the numbers are extended *(Wu-un, Two-oo,* and so on) with pulses of air that correspond to the underlying rhythmic pulse. The pulses vary to achieve the correct subdivision *(Wu-uh-uh-un* for sixteenth notes; *Wu-uh-un* for compound meter). Supporters of this method maintain that it emphasizes rhythmic subdivision, promotes good breath control, and contributes to success in vibrato development. This method is more widely used by instrumental teachers, since it does not lend itself to singing melodies expressively.

# Glossary

**Highlighted terms appear as vocabulary words in the Student Text.**

## A

**AB form** A musical plan that has two different sections.

**ABA form** A musical plan that has three sections. The first and last sections are the same. The middle section is different.

**absolute music** Music that has no suggestion of any nonmusical thing, idea, story, or event (see program music).

***accelerando*** Making the tempo, or speed of music, get gradually faster.

**accent** Indicates to play or sing a note with more emphasis than the other notes.

**accidental** A sign in music notation used to designate a chromatically altered note. The most common accidentals are sharps, flats, and naturals.

**accompaniment** Music that supports the sound of the featured performer(s).

**aerophones** Instruments that produce sound by vibrating air.

## B

**ballad** A song that tells a story.

**band** A group of instruments consisting mainly of woodwinds, brass, and percussion.

**bar line** The vertical line drawn through a staff to separate measures.

**beat** A repeating pulse that can be felt in some music.

**blues** A twentieth-century African American vocal jazz style, characterized by melancholy lyrics, flattened third and seventh notes, slow, syncopated rhythms, and the 12-bar blues harmonic structure.

**brass** A group of wind instruments, including trumpets, French horns, trombones, and tubas, used in bands and orchestras.

## C

**call and response** A musical device in which a portion of a melody (call) is followed by an answering portion (response).

**canon** A musical form in which the parts imitate each other. One part begins, or leads, and the other parts follow.

**chamber music** Music written for small groups, often having only one voice or instrument for each part, as in a string quartet.

**choir** Commonly used to mean a group of singers performing together. Also, a group of instruments, as in a brass choir.

**chord** Three or more notes arranged in intervals of a third, sounded at the same time.

**chord progression** The order of chords in a piece of music.

**chorus** A large group of singers.

***coda*** A "tail" or short section, added at the end of a piece of music.

**composer** A person who makes up pieces of music by putting sounds together in his or her own way.

**concerto** A composition written for solo instrument(s) with orchestra.

**contour** The "shape" of a melody made by the way it moves upward and downward in steps, leaps, and repeated tones.

**contrast** Two or more things that are different. In music, for example, slow is a contrast to fast; Section A is a contrast to Section B.

**countermelody** A contrasting melody that is played or sung at the same time as the main melody.

## D

**density** The thickness or thinness of sound.

**descant** A countermelody that decorates the main melody, often soaring above the melody of the song.

**duet** A composition written for two performers.

**duple meter** A basic pattern in which a measure has one strong and one weak beat.

**dynamics** The different levels of loudness and softness of sound.

## E

**ensemble** A group of musicians who perform together.

## F

***fermata*** A sign 𝄐 indicating that a note is held longer than its written note value, stopping or "holding" the beat.

**form** The overall plan of a piece of music.

## H

**half step** On a keyboard, the distance between one key and the next black or white key.

**harmony** Two or more different tones sounding at the same time.

## I

**improvise** To make up music as it is being performed.

**interlude** A short musical connection between sections of a piece of music.

**interval** The distance between two pitches.

**introduction** Music played before the main part of a composition begins.

## J

**jazz** An American musical style made of traditional Western music combined with African rhythms and melodic contours.

## K

**key signature** Tells which notes are to be performed with a flat or sharp throughout a piece of music.

## L

**ledger lines** Extra lines for pitches above and below the staff.

***legato*** A term that describes music performed in a smooth and connected style.

**lullaby** A quiet song, often sung when rocking a child to sleep.

**lyrics** The words of a song.

## M

**major scale** An arrangement of eight tones according to the following pattern of steps or intervals: whole, whole, half, whole, whole, whole, half.

**measure** A grouping of beats set off by bar lines.

**melodic rhythm** The rhythm of a melody.

**melodic seuqence** A melody pattern that begins on a different pitch each time it is repeated.

**melody** A line of single tones that move upward, downward, or repeat.

**melody pattern** An arrangement of pitches into a small grouping, usually occurring often in a piece.

**meter** The way the beats of music are grouped, often in sets of two or in sets of three.

**mood** The feeling that a piece of music gives.

**movement** Each of the smaller, self-contained sections (usually three or four) that together make up a symphony, concerto, string quartet, and so on.

## N

**notes** Symbols for sound in music.

## O

**opera** A theatrical production combining drama, vocal and orchestral music, costumes, scenery, and sometimes, dance.

**orchestra** A group of instruments usually consisting of strings, woodwinds, brass, and percussion.

**ornamentation** In the arts, the addition of decorations, or embellishments, to the basic structure of the work.

**ostinato** A repeated rhythm or melody pattern played throughout a piece or a section of a piece.

## P

**parody** A humorous imitation.

**partner songs** Two or more different songs that can be sung at the same time to create a thicker texture.

**pentatonic scale** A scale of five notes.

**percussion** A group of pitched or nonpitched instruments that are played by striking, or scraping them.

**phrase** A musical "sentence." Each phrase expresses one thought.

**phrase mark** A symbol above the staff in the shape of an arc, similar to a slur, that shows the length of a phrase.

**pitch** The location of a tone with respect to highness or lowness.

***pizzicato*** A term that refers to plucking the strings instead of bowing.

**program music** Music that suggests or describes some nonmusical idea, story, or event. (See **absolute music**).

## Q

**quartet** A composition for four voices or instruments, each having a separate part; a group of four singers or instrumentalists, each playing or singing a different part.

# Glossary

## R

**range** In a melody, the span from the lowest tone to the highest tone.

**refrain** A section of a song that is sung the same way every time it repeats.

**reggae** A Caribbean style of rock music.

**register** The pitch location of a group of tones. If a group of tones are all high sounds, they are in a high register. If a group of tones are all low sounds, they are in a low register.

**repeat signs** Tell the performer to perform all the music between the signs twice.

**repeated tones** Two or more tones in a row that have the same sound.

**rests** Symbols for the length of silences.

**rhythm** The way duration is organized in a piece of music using beat, no beat, long and short sounds, meter, accents, no accents, tempo, syncopation, and so on.

**rhythm pattern** A grouping of long and short sounds. Some rhythm patterns have even sounds. Others have uneven sounds.

**rondo** A musical form in which the first section always returns. A common rondo form is ABACA.

**root** The tone on which a chord is built.

**round** A follow-the-leader process in which all perform the same melody but start at different times.

## S

**scale** An arrangement of pitches from lower to higher according to a specific pattern of intervals or steps.

**score** The musical notation of a composition with each of the instrumental (or vocal) parts shown in a vertical alignment.

**sequence** The repetition of a melody pattern at a higher or lower pitch level. (See **melodic sequence**).

**shanty** Sailors' work song.

**skip** To move from one tone to another, skipping over the tones in between.

**slur** A curved line connecting two or more notes of different pitch that tells the performer to play or sing the notes *legato*.

**solo** Music for a single singer or player, often with an accompaniment.

***staccato*** A term that describes music performed in a short and detached style.

**staff** A set of five horizontal lines on which music notes are written.

**steady beat** A regular pulse.

**step** To move from one tone to another without skipping tones in between.

**strings** A term used to refer to string instruments that are played by bowing, plucking, or strumming.

**strong beat** Usually, the first beat in a measure.

**style** The special sound that is created when music elements such as rhythm and timbre are combined.

**suite** An instrumental work of several movements, often programmatic or descriptive.

**syncopation** An arrangement of rhythm in which important tones begin on weak beats or weak parts of beats, giving an off-balance movement to the music.

## T

**tempo** The speed of the beat.

**texture** The layering of sounds to create a thick or thin quality in music.

**theme** An important melody that occurs several times in a piece of music.

**theme and variations** A musical form in which each section is a variation of the original theme.

**tie** A musical symbol that connects two notes of the same pitch.

**timbre** The unique difference or tone color of sounds.

**time signature** Tells how many beats are in each measure (top number) and the kind of note that gets one beat (bottom number).

**tonal center** A pitch that acts as a resting place or "home" for all of the other pitches that happen around it.

**tonic** The key or home tone in a scale.

**trio** Any composition for three voices or instruments, each having a separate part.

## U

**unison** The same pitch.

**upbeat** One or more notes that occur before the first bar line of a phrase.

## V

**variation** Music that is repeated, but changed in some important way.

**verse** A section of a song where the melody stays the same when it repeats, but the words change.

**vocal style** The manner in which a person sings a song.

## W

**weak beat** Usually, the second or last beat in a measure.

**whole step** On a keyboard, the distance between any two keys with a single key between.

**woodwinds** A term used to refer to wind instruments, now or originally made of wood.

**word painting** The positioning of pitch and rhythm patterns to resemble the meaning of words.

Themes Index
Pitch and Rhythm Index
Recorder Index
Classified Index
Listening Index
Song and Speech Piece Index

## Contents

# THEMES INDEX

The content of MAKING MUSIC can be used to support teaching thematically in an integrated curriculum. This list shows many of the topical ideas teachers might use from this program. We urge teachers to consider this list as a starting point only, a framework that can be enlarged easily. As you use the material in this way, you help children to create meaning for the music literature as well as other disciplines.

# Pitch and Rhythm Index

The Pitch and Rhythm Index provides a listing of songs for teaching specific pitches and rhythms. Specific measure numbers are indicated in parentheses when the rhythms or pitches apply to only a portion of a song. The letter *a* indicates that the anacrusis to the measure is included.

The Pitch Index is organized by the teaching sequence used in MAKING MUSIC. Pitch categories are listed in the order in which they are presented in the series.

The Rhythm Index is also organized by the teaching sequence used in MAKING MUSIC. The songs or portions of songs that are listed contain only rhythms that have been taught up to that point in the sequence.

An asterisk (*) next to a song title indicates that the song is used to present the pitch or rhythm in this grade level.

## Pitch Index

# Pitch and Rhythm Index

# Rhythm Index



Pitch and Rhythm Index

# Recorder Index

# Classified Index

# C



Classified Index

# E



# F

# G



Classified Index

# H



# I



# L



# M

Classified Index

# N

# O



# P

# R

# S

## SCHOOL TO HOME CONNECTION

# T

Classified Index

# V



Classified Index

# Acknowledgments and Credits

**Design and Electronic Production:** Kirchoff/Wohlberg, Inc.

**Listening Maps and Music Reading Practice:** MediaLynx Design Group

**Photo Research:** Feldman & Associates, Inc., Kirchoff/Wohlberg, Inc., and Scott Foresman. Every effort has been made to obtain permission for all photographs found in this book and to make full acknowledgment for their use. Omissions brought to our attention will be corrected in subsequent editions.

## Photograph Credits

8 Photofest 9 Laura Farr/TimePix 12 George Lepp/Corbis 12 David Stover/Stock South/PictureQuest 15 Dean Conger/Corbis 17 Bettmann/Corbis 22 (TL) Tim Thompson/Getty Images 24 © Orion Press 24 Hiroshige/The Granger Collection, New York 25 © Orion Press 26 Paul Natkin/Photo Reserve 28 Rudi Von Briel/PhotoEdit 28 The Granger Collection, New York 29 Bettmann/Corbis 30 Odile Noel/Lebrecht Collection 31 Adele Starr/Corbis 31 Christopher Berkey/AP/Wide World 32 Deborah Davis/PhotoEdit 32 Nubar Alexanian/Corbis 32 Melodie Gimple/Warner Bros. Records/Photofest 35 © Dorling Kindersley 36 Torsten Blackwood/© AFP 44 Abigail Hadeed/Visuals Concepts 41 Abigail Hadeed/Visuals Concepts 47 Photofest 48 Alain Le Garsmeur/Stone 50 Corbis 54 Lowell Georgia/Corbis 57 The Granger Collection, New York 58 David Muench/Stone 60 Chad Ehlers/Stone 62 Scott Daniel Peterson/Gamma Liaison 63 Scott Daniel Peterson/Gamma Liaison 71 © Jonathan Blair/Corbis 72 Oliver Theil/San Francisco Symphony 73 Archivo Iconografico, S.A./Corbis 74 © Danny Lehman/Corbis 74 Arnaldo Magnani 74 Tim Wright/Corbis 74 Odile Noel/Lebrecht Collection 75 © 2000 Scott Saltzman/Barefoot Photography 75 Arnaldo Magnani 77 Gerrit Greve/Corbis 78 Bruno De Hogues/Stone 79 Jack Vartoogian 80 Jack Vartoogian 80 Leslye Borden/PhotoEdit 81 SuperStock 81 Art Wolfe/Stone 84 The Purcell Team/Corbis 86 Patrick Bennett/Corbis 86 AP/Wide World 88 John P. Kelley/Image Bank 90 Karl Weatherly/Corbis 91 Archivo Iconografico/Corbis 91 PhotoDisc 92 Gerry Schneiders/Unicorn Stock Photos 97 Kenneth Hamm 104 Richard T. Nowitz/Corbis 106 Robert Gwathmey, "Children Dancing" 107 © Bob Krist/Corbis 107 Corbis 110 Dave King/© Dorling Kindersley 110 Wolfgang Kaehler/Corbis 110 Getty Images 112 Francis G. Mayer/Corbis 112 PhotoDisc 113 Paul Natkin/Photo Reserve 117 Ebet Roberts Photography 122 Grosset Simon/Spooner/Liaison Agency 123 Ousama Ayoub/© AFP 130 Daryl Balfour/Stone 132 Reuters/Fred Prouser/Archive Photos 134 Duncan Willetts 135 Jagdish Agarwal/Unicorn Stock Photos 137 SuperStock 139 SuperStock 139 David Muench/Corbis 142 SuperStock 143 Norman Parkinson Limited/Fiona Cowen/Corbis 144 Robert Freck/Odyssey Productions 145 Danny Lehman/Corbis 145 Kevin Schafer/Corbis 147 Dan Polin/Lights, Words, and Music 147 Stephanie Maze/Corbis 150 AP/Wide World 152 Iwao Kataoka/Panoramic Images 154 Chris Stock/Lebrecht Collection 156 Leo de Wys Photo Agency 156 Christopher Liu/ChinaStock 159 Michelle Wood 160 © David Muench/Corbis 166 Popperfoto/Archive Photos 166 Culver Pictures Inc. 166 Universal Studios/Photofest 167 ©/Hulton/Archive by Getty Images 168 Bettmann/Corbis 168 Dagmar Fabricius/Stock Boston/PictureQuest 169 Burke/Triolo Productions/FoodPix 169 Hulton Getty Picture Archive/Stone 169 Phil Banko/Stone 169 Joseph Sohm/Visions of America, LLC/PictureQuest 170 PhotoDisc 171 The Granger Collection, New York 172 ©Victor Englebert 173 Bonnie Kamin/PhotoEdit 174 Jane Gifford/Stone 177 Robert Freck/Odyssey Productions 177 Photo courtesy of John J. van Gool from his website http://www.lutherie-van-gool.nl 177 Kenwood House, Hampstead, London/Bridgeman Art Library, London/SuperStock 181 American David David Gallery, Philadelphia/SuperStock 188 Robert Evans/Stone 190 © Cary Wolinsky/Stock Boston/PictureQuest 190 Bob Krist/Stone 191 Tony Arrzua/Corbis 192 Kate Mount/Lebrecht Collection 193 (TL) Roger Berg, Creative Photo, Inc. Columbia, MO/Canadian Brass 193 Michael Ochs Archives, Venice, CA 193 AP/Wide World 196 Joe McDonald/Corbis 197 (CL) Jennifer Coppersmith/Index Stock Imagery 197 (TR) Joe McDonald/Corbis 198 Stephen Johnson/Stone 198 Stephen Johnson/Stone 199 Teri Bloom Photography, Inc 204 Michael Ochs Archives, Venice, CA 206 (Bkgd) Corbis 207 (L) ©Joseph McNally/The Image Bank/Getty Images 208 (TL) © David McNew/Online USA/Liaison/Getty Images 209 (TC) Diana Ong, America/SuperStock 212 Philadelphia Museum of Art, Pennsylvania/Giraudon,Paris/SuperStock. © 2002 Estate of Pablo Picasso/Artists Rights Society (ARS), New York 213 Richard Hamilton Smith/Corbis 216 © Mark Segal/Index Stock Imagery/PictureQuest 216 James L. Amos/Corbis 220 Paul A. Souders/Corbis 220 Hulton-Deutsche Collection/Corbis 222 Kent Gavin/Archive Photos 222 © Richard T. Nowitz/Corbis 223 © Dorling Kindersley 223 © Dorling Kindersley 224 © Kevin R. Morris/Corbis 225 Lebrecht Collection 226 Odd Andersen/© AFP 226 Letraset Creative Opportunities 228 (Bkgd) Donovan Reese/PhotoDisc/Getty Images 230 Barry Lewis/Corbis 231 Barry Lewis/Corbis 232 Getty Images 233 Bettman/Corbis 233 G Salter/Lebrecht Collection 234 Mary Robert/Lebrecht Collection 234 © Archivo Iconografico, S.A./Corbis 235 Astrid & Hanns-Frieder Michler/Photo Researchers, Inc. 236 (CR) Mauritius/Index Stock Imagery 237 (BR) Mike Timo/Stone 238 © Hulton-Deutsch Collection/Bettmann/Corbis 239 © Bettmann/Corbis 243 (TC) Max Alexander/©Dorling Kindersley 259 (TC) Courtesy of the Rosenberg Library, Galveston, Texas 260 David Drew/Corbis 260 Michael St. Maur Sheil/Corbis 269 The Granger Collection, New York 274 Kansas Pacific Railway Cattle Trail Map/Kansas State Historical Society 275 (CL) James Walker, California Vaqueros/The Anschutz Collection 275 (BR) 278 (Getty Images) 279 Underwood & Underwood/Corbis 280 UPI/Bettmann/Corbis 281 AP/Wide World 282 SuperStock 282 SuperStock 283 North Wind Picture Archives 283 @2000 John Running 285 J. Bryan Burton 285 John Oldenkamp/San Diego Museum of Man 286 Hulton-Deutsch Collection/Corbis 288 Joe Viesti/Viesti Collection, Inc. 288 SuperStock 289 F Good 289 B Vikander 289 SuperStock 290 ChromoSohm/Sohm/Image Works 291 AP/Wide World 292 SuperStock 293 Forbes Collection, New York City/Bridgeman Art/SuperStock 294 Michael Busselle/Stone 297 Hulton Getty/Stone 298 Susan Sterner/AP/Wide World 298 Kyndell Harkness/AP/Wide World 298 Jack Vartoogian 302 Corbis 304 Corbis 305 Corbis 307 (BL) Courtesy, Northwest Folklife and University of Washington Ethnomusicology Archives 309 David Samuel Robbins/Corbis 310 Seth Kushner/Corbis Sygma 315 Michael Damas/Music From China, Inc. 316 Sarah Stone/Stone 318 Randy Faris/Corbis 322 A. Ramey/Unicorn Stock Photos 322 Aneal Vohra/Unicorn Stock Photos 326 AP/Wide World 327 Jack Vartoogian 328 Steve Gates/AP/Wide World 328 PhotoDisc 337 PhotoDisc 340 SuperStock 343 SuperStock 343 Nancy R. Schiff/Archive Photos 344 Blank Archives/Archive Photos 344 Gary Holscher/Stone 346 Bernard Gotfryd/Archive Photos 346 Gary Holscher/Stone 348 A. Tannenbaum/Corbis Sygma 349 Michael Ochs Archives, Venice CA 349 Joseph Sohm/ChromoSohm Inc./Corbis 350 Chip and Rosa Maria de la Cueva Peterson 351 Courtesy of Henry A. Waxman; President, Earth Flag, Ltd. 352 Corbis 354 World Perspectives/Stone 354 Nigel Press/Stone 356 ©John Fortunato 356 Nigel Press/Stone 358 Bill Bachmann/PhotoEdi 358 Kim Westerkov/Stone 359 James Randklev/Stone 361 MGM/Kobal Collection 365 SuperStock 366 Dave G. Houser/Corbis 367 The Green Bay Chronicle/H. Marc Larson/AP/Wide World 372 Photo by Greg Braun, Courtesy of James Durst, www.james durst.com 372 John Warden/Stone 374 Photri, Inc. 375 Photri, Inc. 375 World Perspectives/Stone 378 Lebrecht Collection 382 (Bkgd) © Cindy Kassab/Corbis 384 (TCL) © Underwood & Underwood/Corbis 385 (BL) Jack Vartoogian for the New York Times ALL RIGHTS RESERVED/Jack Vartoogian/Photographer 388 Chritsian Pierre/SuperStock 390 Peter Harholdt/SuperStock 390 Liam Blake/Panoramic Images 392 SuperStock 398 AFP/Corbis 399 SuperStoc 400 Stephanie Maze/Corbis 400 SuperStock 401 Aldo Torelli/Stone 402 Jim Zuckerman/Corbis 402 Donald Nausbaum/Stone 404 Sorensen/Bohmer Olse/Stone 404 Trip/TH-FOTO Werbung 406 Tom Till/Stone 406 Bonnie Kamin/PhotoEdit 408 PhotoDisc 408 Myrleen Ferguson/PhotoEdit 414 (CC) Getty Images 418 SuperStock 418 Miki Kratsman/Corbis 418 Archive Photos 419 Reuters NewMedia Inc./Corbis 419 Bob Daemmrich/Image Works 419 David Young Wolff/Stone 421 Odd Andersen/AP/Wide World 421 Gavin Wickham; Eye Ubiquitous/Corbis 421 Richard Vogel/AP/Wide World 421 SuperStock 427 Victor Malafronte/Archive Photos 427 Mitchell Gerber/Corbis 428 FoodPix 432 A. Ramey/PhotoEdit 432 AP/Wide World 433 Doug Armand/Stone 434 © United States Postal Service. Displayed with permission. All rights reserved. Written authorization from the Postal Service is required to use, reproduce, post, transmit, distribute, or publicly display these images. 435 David Young-Wolff/PhotoEdit 436 William Lovelace/Hulton Getty Picture Collection/Stone 436 Hulton Getty Picture Collection/Stone 438 David Sutherland/Stone 438 Leland Bobbe/Stone 440 Brian Stablyk/Stone 468 Chris Stock/Lebrecht Collection

(A) TAB1 ©Mary Kate Denny/PhotoEdit (B) TAB 2 ©Dannielle Hayes/©Fotopic/Omni-Photo.Com (C) TAB 3 ©David Young-Wolff/PhotoEdit (D) TAB 4 ©John Garrett/Getty Images

## Illustration Credits

6 Steve Barbaria 8 Steve Barbaria 8 Michael Di Giorgio 9 Estelle Carol 9 Steve Barbaria 10 Ron Himler 12 Andrew Wheatcroft 12 Andrew Wheatcroft 14 Annoushka Galouchko 16 Annoushka Galouchko 16 Tony Nuccio 18 Eunice Moyle 20 Antonio Cangemi 22 Antonio Cangemi 24 Jane Dill 25 Jane Dill 34 Donna Perrone 36 Eileen Hine 37 Eileen Hine 38 Stacey Schuett 40 Stacey Schuett 44 Shawn Finley 46 Shawn Finley 50 Michael Di Giorgio 51 Fian Arroyo 53 Esther Baran 56 Elizabeth Rosen 64 David McCall Johnston 66 David Diaz 68 John Hovell 70 John Hovell 71 John Hovell 76 Rae Ecklund 92 Tom Leonard 94 Deborah White 94 Tom Barrett 96 Jean & Mou-Sien Tseng 98 Krystyna Stasiak 100 John Hovell 102 John Hovell 114 Carlos Ochagavia 116 Carlos Ochagavia 120 Gerald Bustamante 123 Gerald Bustamante 126 Carmelo Blandino 128 Carmelo Blandino 129 Carmelo Blandino 148 John Hovell 153 Michael Di Giorgio 158 Linda Wingerter 162 Nancy Freeman 172 Tom Leonard 174 Tom Leonard 178 Esther Baran 180 Esther Baran 186 Rosiland Solomon 190 Michael Di Giorgio 200 David Galchutt 202 George Baquero 210 Steve Barbaria 212 Steve Barbaria 218 Tom Leonard 219 Joe Boddy 220 Tom Leonard 222 Krystyna Stasiak 225 Krystyna Stasiak 232 John Hovell 235 Michael Di Giorgio 244 Lane Yerkes 254 Arvis Stewart 258 Ron Himler 261 Vilma Ortiz-Dillon 262 Ralph Canaday 264 Ralph Canaday 266 Larry Johnson 268 Larry Johnson 269 Tom Leonard 270 Craig Spearing 272 Craig Spearing 276 T. L. Ary 278 T. L. Ary 286 Mike Tofanelli 293 Tom Leonard 296 John Hovell 297 John Hovell 299 John Hovell 299 Vilma Ortiz-Dillon 299 Tony Nuccio 300 Donna Perrone 308 Jean & Mou-Sien Tseng 310 Fahimeh Amiri 312 Chi Chung 314 Chi Chung 318 Eileen Hine 319 Eileen Hine 322 Jerry Tiritilli 324 Jerry Tiritilli 330 Roger Roth 332 Nancy Freeman 334 Oki Han 336 Oki Han 337 Vilma Ortiz-Dillon 338 Ron Himler 340 Bradley Clark 342 Bradley Clark 342 Deborah White 346 Craig Spearing 347 Vilma Ortiz-Dillon 360 Lane Gregory 362 Tom Leonard 364 Tom Leonard 366 Alexi Natchev 367 Alexi Natchev 368 Alexi Natchev 369 Alexi Natchev 370 Bradley Clark 376 Donna Perrone 378 Dave Jonason 379 Dave Jonason 380 Susan Swan 386 Susan Swan 388 Alexandra Wallner 390 Alexandra Wallner 391 Tom Leonard 392 Tom Leonard 393 Tom Leonard 398 Jennifer Bolten 399 Jennifer Bolten 400 Jennifer Bolten 402 Jennifer Bolten 412 Nora Koerber 418 Tom Leonard 420 Tom Leonard 422 Cameron Eagle 424 Robert LoGrippo 426 Robert LoGrippo 430 Sally Jo Vitsky 432 Sally Jo Vitsky 434 Patti Green 440 Michael Di Giorgio

## Acknowledgments

Credits and appreciation are due publishers and copyright owners for use of the following:

2: "Turn the Beat Around" from the Motion Picture *The Specialist*, Words and Music by Peter Jackson, Jr. and Gerald Jackson. Copyright © 1975 by Unichappell Music Inc. This arrangement Copyright © 2001 by Unichappell Music Inc. International Copyright Secured. All Rights Reserved. 6: "Put a Little Love in Your Heart" by Jimmy Holiday, Randy Myers and Jackie DeShannon. © 1969 (Renewed) EMI Unart Catalog Inc. All Rights Reserved. Used by Permission. WARNER BROS. PUBLICATIONS U.S. INC., Miami, FL 33014. 13: "Haul Away, Joe" © 2002 Pearson Education, Inc. 13: "Until I Saw the Sea" by Lilian Moore from *Sing a Song of Popcorn*, Scholastic, 1988. 14: "Gakavik" (The Partridge) an Armenian Folk Song. Courtesy of Pomegranate Music. www.PomegranateMusic.com. English version by Pearson Education, Inc. 18: "Limbo Like Me" New Words and new Music adapted by Massie Patterson and Sammy Heyward. (Based on a traditional song) TRO-© 1963 (Renewed) Ludlow Music, Inc., New York, NY. Used by Permission. 22: "Deep In The Heart Of Texas," Words by June Hershey, Music by Don Swander. Copyright 1941 by Melody Lane Publications, Inc. Copyright Renewed. This arrangement Copyright © by 2003 Melody Lane Publications, Inc. International Copyright Secured. All Rights Reserved. Used by Permission. 23: Orchestral Suite No. 3, BWV 1068, *"Air in D,"* Movement 2, Listening Map by Kay Greenhaw. 25: "Tsuki" (The Moon) from *Children's Songs from Japan* written by Florence White and Kazuo Akiyama. © 1960 Edward B. Marks Music Company. Copyright renewed. Used by Permission. All Rights Reserved. 26: "Waitin' for the Light to Shine" from *Big River*. Words and Music by Roger Miller. Copyright © 1985 Sony/ATV Songs LLC and Roger Miller Music. This arrangement copyright © 2001 Sony/ATV Songs LLC and Roger Miller Music. All Rights Administered by Sony/ATV Music Publishing, 8 Music Square West, Nashville, TN 37203. International Copyright Secured. All Rights Reserved. Used by Permission. 34: "Sonando" Words and Music by Peter Terrace. Reprinted by permission of Peter Terrace. English version by Pearson Education, Inc. 37: "Tie Me Kangaroo Down, Sport" Words and Music by Rolf Harris. © 1960, 1961 (Renewed 1988, 1989) Castle Music Pty. Ltd. This arrangement © 2001 Castle Music Pty. Ltd. All Rights for the U.S. and Canada Controlled and Administered by Beechwood Music Corp. All Rights Reserved. International Copyright Secured. Used by Permission. 38: "Pay Me My Money Down" from *Hootenanny Song Book* collected and adapted by Lydia Parish. Copyright © 1963 (Renewed) Consolidated Music Publishers. International Copyright Secured. All Rights Reserved. Reprinted by permission. 44: "We Go Together" from *Grease*. Words and Music by Warren Casey and Jim Jacobs. © 1971, 1972 WARREN CASEY and JIM JACOBS. This arrangement © 2001 WARREN CASEY and JIM JACOBS. Copyright Renewed. All Rights Reserved. Used by Permission. 54: "Rock Island Line" New Words and new Music arrangement by Huddie Ledbetter. Edited with new additional material by Alan Lomax. TRO - © Copyright 1959 (Renewed) Folkways Music Publishers, Inc., New York, New York. Used by Permission. 58: "River" Words and Music by Bill Staines. © 1988 Mineral River Music (BMI) Administered by Bug Music. All Rights Reserved. Used by Permission. 60: "River Winding" from *River Winding* by Charlotte Zolotow. Copyright © 1970 by Charlotte Zolotow. Reprinted by permission of Scott Treimel NY. 63: "Hashewie" (Going Round) from *Roots and Branches*. Courtesy World Music Press. 66: "Riqui Ran" folk song from Latin America, translated by J. Olcutt Sanders. Copyright © 1948 CRS, transferred 1978 World Around Songs, 120 Colberts Creek Rd., Burnsville, NC 28714. Reprinted by permission. 68: "Eh, cumpari!" (Hey, Buddy!) Words and Music by Julius LaRosa and Archie Bleyer. Memory Lane Music Corporation, 1990. Used by Permission. 79: "Hey, m'tswala" from *The Melody Book* by Patricia Hackett, © 1991. Reprinted by permission of Prentice-Hall, Inc., Upper Saddle River, NJ. 81: "Enjoy the Earth" Yoruba Poem by Anonymous, from *Earthways Earthwise*. Selected by Judith Nicholls, p. 78. Copyright © 1993 by Judith Nicholls. Reprinted by permission of Oxford University Press. 89: "The Happy Wanderer" Music by Friedrich W. Möller and Words by Antonia Ridge, 1954. Sam Fox Publishing Company Inc. Used with permission. 96: "Osamu kosamu" (Biting Wind) Japanese Folk Song. Translation © 1993 Gloria J. Kiester. Used by Permission. 102: "Cement Mixer " (Put-ti, Put-ti) Words and Music by Slim Gaillard and Lee Ricks. Copyright 1946 (Renewed) EMI Mills Music, Inc. All Rights Reserved. Used by Permission of WARNER BROS. PUBLICATIONS U. S. INC., Miami, FL 33014. 107: "See the Children Playin'" Words by Reginald Royal © 2000 Reijiro Music, ASCAP. 114: "Turn the World Around" Words and Music by Harry Belafonte and Robert Freedman. Published by Clara Music Publishing Corp. (ASCAP) Administered by Next Decade Entertainment, Inc. All Rights Reserved. Used by Permission. 115: "So Is Life" Words and Music by Harry Belafonte and Robert Freedman. Published by Clara Music Publishing Corp. (ASCAP) Administered by Next Decade Entertainment, Inc. All Rights Reserved. Used by Permission. 120: "Bundle Buggy Boogie Woogie" from *Jelly Belly* (Macmillan of Canada, 1983) Copyright © 1983 Dennis Lee. With permission of the author. Rhythmic setting © 2002 Pearson Education, Inc. 128: "Straighten Up and Fly Right," Words and Music by Nat King Cole and Irving Mills. Copyright 1944 (renewed) by EMI Mills Music, Inc. All Rights Reserved. Reprinted by permission of WARNER BROS. PUBLICATIONS U.S. INC., Miami, FL 33014 131: "The Lion Sleeps Tonight," New lyrics and revised Music by George David Weiss, Hugo Peretti, and Luigi Creatore. © 1961 Folkways Music Publishers, Inc. © Renewed by George David Weiss, Luigi Creatore, and June Peretti. © Assigned to Abilene Music, Inc. All Rights Reserved. Used by Permission. WARNER BROS. PUBLICATIONS U.S. INC., Miami, FL 33014. 132: "T'hola t'hola" (Softly, Softly) from *African*

*Roots* by Jerry Silverman New York: Chelsea House Publishers. 134: "Ochimbo" English Words © 1964 Silver Burdett Company 136: "Ala Da'lona" English Words © 1995 Silver Burdett Ginn 138: "Cumberland Gap" adapted by Jill Trinka © 1996 Jill Trinka. All Rights Reserved. Used by Permission. 140: "Over the Rainbow" Words by E.Y. Harburg and Music by Harold Arlen. 1938 (Renewed © 1966) Metro-Goldwyn-Mayer Inc. 1939 (Renewed © 1967) EMI Feist Catalog Inc. All Rights Reserved. Used by Permission. WARNER BROS. PUBLICATIONS U.S. INC., Miami, FL 33014. 142: "Prism in the Window" from *Who Shrank my Grandmother's House?* Music by Barbara Juster Esbensen, pp. 24-25. Text copyright © 1992 by Barbara Juster Esbensen. Reprinted by permission of HarperCollins Publishers. 144: "Cancion de Cuna" (Cradle Song) English Words © 2002 Pearson Education, Inc. 146: "Cantando mentiras" (Singing Tall Tales) from *Cantemos en Espanol* by The Krones. © 1961 Beatrice and Max Krone, Neil A. Kjos Music Co., Publisher. Used by Permission of the publisher. English Words © 2002 Pearson Education, Inc. 152: "Ode to Joy" (Come and Sing), Words by Georgette LeNorth. Used by Permission of the author. 168: "At The Hop" Words and Music by David White, John Madara and Arthur Singer. Copyright © 1957 (Renewed) Arc Music Corporation (BMI) and Six Continents Music Publishing, Inc. (BMI). All Rights Reserved. Used by Permission. International Copyright Secured. 170: "Can You Canoe?" from *Jelly Belly* (Macmillan of Canada, 1983) Copyright © 1983 Dennis Lee. With permission of the author. Rhythmic setting © 2002 Pearson Education, Inc. 172: "Santa Clara" English Words © 1998 Silver Burdett Ginn. 174: "Doraji" (Bluebells) Arrangement © 1988 Silver, Burdett & Ginn. 176: "La Tarara" English Words © 2002 Pearson Education, Inc. 185: *Piano Sonata No. 8 in C Minor ("Pathéthique")*, Op. 13, No. 8, Movement 3, Rondo: Allegro, Listening Map by Kay Greenhaw. 186: "Kookaburra Sits In The Old Gum Tree" Words and Music by Marion Sinclair. Copyright © 1934 (Renewed) Larrikin Music Pub. Pty. Ltd. All Rights Administered by Music Sales Corporation for the Western Hemisphere. International Rights Secured. All Rights Reserved. Reprinted by Permission. 188: "Missy-La, Massa-La" from *Brown Girl in the Ring* by Alan Lomax. Copyright © 1997 by Alan Lomax. Reprinted by permission of Pantheon Books, a division of Random House, Inc. 199: "Computer" from *I Wish I Had a Computer That Makes Waffles*, Words by Fitzhugh Dodson, 1978. Reprinted by permission of Sterling Lord Literistics, Inc. Copyright by Fitzhugh Dodson. Music © 2002 Pearson Education, Inc. 200: "Advice for a Frog (Concerning a Crane)" from *Advice for a Frog* by Alice Schertle. Text copyright © 1995 by Alice Schertle. Reprinted by permission of HarperCollins Publishers. 203: "Do Wah Diddy Diddy" by Jeff Barry and Ellie Greenwich, © 1963, 1964 (Copyrights Renewed) Trio Music Co. Inc. and Universal-Songs of Polygram International, Inc. This arrangement © 2001 Trio Music Co. Inc. and Universal-Songs of Polygram International, Inc. All Rights Reserved. Used by Permission. WARNER BROS. PUBLICATIONS U. S. INC., Miami, FL 33014, and Hal Leonard Corporation. 206: "America" Words and Music by Neil Diamond. © Bicycle Music Co. 210: "America, the Free" Words and Music by Phyllis Wolfe-White (adapted). © 2000 Heritage Music Press, a division of The Lorenz Corporation. Reprinted by Permission. 215: "El rancho grande" (The Big Ranch) Words and Music by Silvano Ramos. © 1927 - Edward B. Marks Music Company, Copyright renewed. Used by Permission. All Rights Reserved. English version by Pearson Education, Inc. 219: "Bones" excerpted from *Bone Poems*. Text copyright © 1997 by Jeff Moss. Used by Permission of Workman Publishing Co., Inc., New York. All Rights Reserved. 219: "Poem to Help Figure Out What the Patella Is" excerpted from *Bone Poems*. Text copyright © 1997 by Jeff Moss. Used by Permission of Workman Publishing Co., Inc., New York. All Rights Reserved. 221: "Gotta Find a Footprint" excerpted from *Bone Poems*. Text copyright © 1997 by Jeff Moss. Used by Permission of Workman Publishing Co., Inc., New York. All Rights Reserved. 222: "Minka" English Words © 1971 Silver Burdett. 228: "Tengo, Tengo, Tengo" (I Have Three Sheep) from the J.D. Robb Collection of Folk Music Recordings at the University of New Mexico Center for Southwest Research. Used by Permission. English version by Pearson Education, Inc. 230: "Tancovačka" (Dancing) Slovak Words © 2002 Pearson Education, Inc. 236: "Let Music Surround You" Words and Music by Fran Smartt Addicott, 1986. Used by Permission. 242: "El Borrego" (The Lamb) from *They Came Singing: Songs From California's History*, Arlen, Batt, Benson, Kester, 1995, © Calicanto Associates, 6067 Aspinwall Rd, Oakland, CA 94611. Used by Permission. English version by Pearson Education, Inc. 250: "Theme from New York, New York" by John Kander and Fred Ebo. © 1977 United Artists Corporation. All Rights Controlled by EMI Unart Catalog Inc. All Rights Reserved. Used by Permission. WARNER BROS. PUBLICATIONS U.S. INC., Miami, FL 33014. 255: "Blow, Ye Winds" from *Songs of Sailormen* by Joanna C. Colcord. Copyright 1938 by W.W. Norton & Co. Used by Permission of W.W. Norton & Company, Inc. 257: "The Sea Wolf" from Wandering Fires by Mary and Violet McDougal. 258: "Round the Bay of Mexico". from *Shanties of the Seven Seas*, collected by Stan Hugill © 1996 Mystic Seaport Museum, Inc. Reprinted by permission. 266: "Follow the Drinkin' Gourd" © 1995 Silver Burdett Ginn. 268: "The Little Black Train", Collected and adapted by John A. Lomax. TRO-© Copyright 1941 (Renewed) Ludlow Music, Inc., New York, NY. Used by Permission. 269: "Harriet Tubman" HarperCollins Publishers, New York, NY. 270: "Cielito lindo" English Words © 1995 Silver Burdett Ginn. 273: "The Cow" from *Zoo Doings* by Jack Prelutsky. Text copyright © 1983 by Jack Prelutsky. Reprinted by permission of HarperCollins Publishers. 274: "Corrido de Kansas" (Kansas Corrido) from *Immigrant Songbook* by Jerry Silverman, 1992. Reprinted by permission of Saw Mill Music Corp. English version by Pearson Education, Inc. 276: "Route 66" Words and Music by Bobby Troup. Copyright © 1946, Renewed © 1973, Assigned 1974 to Londontown Music. This arrangement copyright © 2001 Londontown Music. All Rights outside the U.S.A. controlled by E.H. Morris & Company. International Copyright Secured. All Rights Reserved. Used by Permission. 280: "Pastures of Plenty" Words and Music by Woody Guthrie. TRO © Copyright 1960 (Renewed) 1963 (Renewed) Ludlow Music, Inc., New York, New York. Used by Permission. 282: "I Walk in Beauty" Words and Music by Arliene Nofchissey Williams. Courtesy World Music Press. 284: "Farewell to the Warriors" from *A Cry from the Earth: Music of the North American Indians* by John Bierhorst, Ancient City Press, 1992. Used with permission of the author. 287: "California, Here I Come" Words and Music by Al Jolson, B. G. Desylva, and Joseph Meyer. © 1924 (Renewed) Warner Bros. Inc. Rights for Extended Renewal Term in U. S. controlled by Warner Bros. Inc., Stephen Ballentine Music and Meyer-JoRo Music. All Rights Reserved. Used by Permission. WARNER BROS. PUBLICATIONS U.S. INC., Miami, FL 33014. 293: "Ai Dunaii moy" (Ah, My Belov'd Dunaii) Folk song from Russia. English Words © 2002 Pearson Education, Inc. 300: "Tina singu" Copyright © 1957 CRS, 1976 transferred to World Around Songs, Inc., 20 Colberts Creek Rd., Burnsville, NC 28714. Reprinted by permission. 302: "La raspa" English Words © 1995 Silver Burdett Ginn. 305: "My Song" from *My Song Is a Piece of Jade*, adapted by Toni deGerez. Copyright © 1981 by Organizacion Editorial Novaro, S.A. English translation copyright © 1984 by Organizacion Editorial Novaro. Reprinted by permission of Little, Brown and Company (Inc.). 306: "Bogando a la luz del sol" from *Folk Songs of the World* edited by Charles Haywood. Copyright © 1966 by Charles Haywood. Reprinted by permission of HarperCollins Publishers Inc. English version by Pearson Education, Inc. 309: "House of Spring" from *Sun at Midnight* by Muso Soseki, translated by W. S. Merwin and Soiku Shigematsu. Copyright © W. S. Merwin. Reprinted with the permission of The Wylie Agency, Inc. 311: "Shri Ram, jai Ram" © 1958, CRS Transferred to World Around Songs 1976, 20 Colberts Crk. Burnsville, NC 28714. Used with permission. 314: "Xiao" (Bamboo Flute) English Words © 1995 Silver Burdett Ginn. 318: "Wings of a Dove" © Berandol Music Publishers. Reprinted by permission. 320: "Three Little Birds" Words and Music by Bob Marley. Copyright © 1977 Fifty Six Hope Road Music Ltd./Odnil Music Ltd./Blue Mountain Music Ltd. (PRS). All rights for United States and Canada controlled and administered by RykoMusic (ASCAP). All Rights Reserved. Used by Permission. 322: "When I Was a Little Boy..." by Tomie dePaola. Text copyright © 1991 by Tomie dePaola. Reprinted by permission of Whitebird, Inc. 324: "Love Can Build a Bridge" Words and Music by Paul Overstreet, Naomi Judd, and John Jarvis. Copyright © 1990 Scarlet Moon Music, Inc. (administered by Copyright Management International), Kentucky Sweetheart Music, and Inspector Barlow Music. All Rights Reserved. International Copyright Secured. Used by Permission. 326: "We Shall Overcome" Musical and lyrical adaptation by Zilphia Horton, Frank Hamilton, Guy Carawan and Pete Seeger. Inspired by African American Gospel Singing, members of the Food & Tobacco Workers Union, Charleston, SC and the southern Civil Rights

Movement. TRO - © 1960 (Renewed) and 1963 (Renewed) Ludlow Music, Inc., New York, International Copyright Secured. Made in U.S.A. All Rights Reserved including Public Performance for Profit. Royalties derived from this composition are being contributed to the We Shall Overcome Fund and The Freedom Movement under the Trusteeship of the writers. Used by Permission. 328: "Love Will Guide Us" Lyrics © 1985 Sally Rogers, (p) Thrushwood Press Pub., BMI. Tune: "I Will Guide Thee" (PD). Reprinted by permission. 330: "Big Rock Candy Mountain" © 2002 Pearson Education, Inc. 332: "Sailing Down My Golden River" Words and Music by Pete Seeger. TRO-© Copyright 1971 (Renewed) Melody Trails, Inc., New York, NY. Used by Permission. 335: "Niu lang zhi nü" (The Cowherd and the Weaving Maid) English Words © 1998 Silver Burdett Ginn. 336: "Traveler's Song" by Meng Jai from *Maples in the Mist*, translated by Minfong Ho. Text copyright © 1966 by Minfong Ho. Lothrop, Lee and Shepard Books. Used by Permission of Harper Collins publishers. 336: "News of Home" by Wang Wei from *Maples in the Mist*, translated by Minfong Ho. Text copyright © 1996 by Minfong Ho. Lothrop. Lee and Shepard Books. Used by Permission of Harper Collins Publishers. 345: "Johnny Appleseed" Words by Stephen Vincent Benet, from A Book of Americans by Rosemary and Stephen Vincent Benet. Copyright © 1933 by Rosemary and Stephen Vincent Benet. Copyright renewed © 1961 by Rosemary Carr Benet. Reprinted by permission of Brandt and Brandt Literary Agents, Inc. 348: "Peace Round" Words by Jean Ritchie. © 1964, 1977 Jean Ritchie, Geordie Music Publishing Co. Reprinted with permission. 350: "Prayer for Earth" from *Flights of Fancy and Other Poems* by Myra Cohn Livingston. Copyright © 1993, 1994 by Myra Cohn Livingston. Used by Permission of Marian Reiner. 355: "This Pretty Planet" Words and Music by John Forster and Tom Chapin. Copyright © 1988 The Last Music Company (ASCAP) /Limousine Music Co. (ASCAP) This arrangement © 1989 The Last Music Company/Limousine Music Co. Reprinted by permission. 357: "The Continents" from *Music with Children* by Grace Nash and 7th Grade Students. Used by Permission of Grace Nash, author, Nash Publications. 358: "The Earth Is Our Mother," arranged by Barbara Sletto, edited by Henry H. Leck. Copyright Transferred 2000, Colla Voce Music, Inc., 4600 Sunset Avenue, #83, Indianapolis, IN 46208. Reprinted by permission of Colla Voce Music, Inc. 359: "And My Heart Soars" from *My Heart Soars* by Chief Dan George. Used by Permission of Hancock House Publishers. 360: "Singin' in the Rain" Words and Music by Nacio Herb Brown and Arthur Freed. © 1929 (Renewed) Metro-Goldwyn-Mayer Inc. All Rights controlled by EMI Robbins Catalog Inc. All Rights Reserved. Used by Permission. WARNER BROS. PUBLICATIONS U.S. INC., Miami, FL 33014. 362: "The Wheel of Water" Words and Music by John Forster and Tom Chapin. © 1990 Limousine Music Co. & The Last Music Co. (ASCAP) Reprinted by permission. 366: "Nruab Hnub Thiab Hmo Ntuj" ("Why Is There Day and Night?") by Nhia Lor Vang from *Grandmother's Path, Grandfather's Way*, 2nd Edition by Lue Vang & Judy Lewis. Copyright © 1990 by Lue Vang & Judy Lewis. Reprinted by permission of Vang & Lewis. 370: "Cycle Song of Life (The River Song)" Words and Music by James Durst. Copyright © 1974, 1997, PhoeniXongs ASCAP. Reprinted with permission. 373: "Starlight, Star Bright" Words and Music by James Durst. Copyright © 1993 PhoeniXongs ASCAP. Reprinted with permission. 374: "Sailboat in the Sky" English Words © 1995 Silver Burdett Ginn. 377: "The Planets Chant" © 2002 Pearson Education, Inc. 378: "Shake the Papaya Down" Calypso Song arranged by Ruth E. Dwyer and Judith M. Waller, edited by Henry H. Leck. Copyright Transferred 2000, Colla Voce Music, Inc. 4600 Sunset Avenue, #83, Indianapolis, IN 46208. Reprinted by permission of Colla Voce Music, Inc. 383: "Seagull, Seagull, Sit on the Shore" Arranged by Susan Brumfield. © 2000 Colla Voce Music, Inc. All Rights Reserved. Printed in U.S.A. 384: "Cindy" Arrangement © 2002 Pearson Education, Inc. 387: "Lullaby and Dance" arranged by Ruth E. Dwyer. Copyright transferred 2000, Colla Voce Music, Inc. Used by Permission. 391: "Einini" (Gaelic Folk Song) arranged by Cyndee Geibler. Used by Permission of Colla Voce Music, Inc. 394: "Little David, Play on Your Harp" Arrangement © 2002 Pearson Education, Inc. 397: "Sambalele" © 2002 Pearson Education, Inc. 403: "Circle 'Round the Moon" Words and Music by Mark Hierholzer. Used by Permission of Colla Voce Music, Inc. 411: "A Merry Modal Christmas" Arrangement © 2002 Pearson Education, Inc. 414: "La copa de la vida" (The Cup of Life) English lyrics by Robi Rosa and Desmond Child. Spanish lyrics by Luis Gomez Escolar. © 1998, 1999 A Phantom Vox Publishing, Universal-Polygram International Publishing, Inc., Desmophobis and Musica Calaca, S.L. All Rights for A Phantom Vox Publishing administered by Warner-Tamerlane Publishing Corp. All Rights Reserved. Used by Permission. WARNER BROS. PUBLICATIONS U.S. INC., Miami, FL 33014. 419: "Shir L'Shalom" (Hand in Hand-A Song for Peace) Last Song of Yitzchak Rabin. Music and Words by Yair Rosenblum, arranged by Michael Isaacson. Used by Permission Transcontinental Music Publications. 633 Third Avenue. NY, NY 10017. 422: "Little Shop of Horrors" Words by Howard Ashman, Music by Alan Menken. © 1982 Trunksong Music, Ltd. (BMI) Menken Music (BMI), & MCA-Geffen Music (ASCAP). All Rights o/b/o Trunksong Music Ltd. administered by Warner-Tamerlane Publishing Corp. (BMI). All Rights Reserved. Used by Permission. WARNER BROS. PUBLICATIONS U.S. INC., Miami, FL 33014. 424: "Winter Fantasy" Words and Music by Jill Gallina. Copyright © 1982 by Shawnee Press, Inc. (ASCAP) International Copyright Secured. All Rights Reserved. Reprinted by Permission. 426: "Let It Snow, Let It Snow, Let It Snow," by Sammy Cahn and Jule Styne. © 1945 Cahn Music Company. © Renewed, assigned to Cahn Music Company & Producers Music Pub. Co., Inc. All Rights o/b/o Cahn Music Company administered by WB Music Corp. All rights c/b/o Producers Music Pub. Co., Inc. administered by Chappell & Co. All Rights Reserved. Used by Permission. WARNER BROS. PUBLICATIONS U.S. INC., Miami, FL 33014 429: "Ocho kandelikas" (Eight Little Candles) Words and Music by Flory Jagoda from *The Flory Jagoda Songbook*, 1993. Reprinted with permission of the author. 432: "Al quebrar la piñata" (Piñata Song) English Words © 1988 Silver Burdett Ginn. 434: "Harambee" © 1995 Silver Burdett Ginn.

The editors of Scott Foresman have made every attempt to verify the source of "River" (p. 61), "The Snow", (p. 183), "Dry Bones Come Skipping" (p. 218), "Somos el barco" (We Are the Boat) (p. 353), "How Do You Doo-tee?" (p. 510), but were unable to do so. Every effort has been made to locate all copyright holders of material used in this book. If any errors or omissions have occurred, corrections will be made.

# Teacher Notes

# Teacher Notes

# Teacher Notes

# Teacher Notes

# Teacher Notes

# Listening Index

## Listening Selections by Composer

## Listening Selections by Title

# SONG AND SPEECH

# PIECE INDEX

## W



## X



## Y